한 권으로 끝내는

Jump Up
TOEIC

Jump Up TOEIC
Intermediate

발행인	권오찬
발행처	

편집	윤경림
디자인	이미화, 김혜경
마케팅	정연철, 박천산, 고영노, 박찬경, 김동진, 김윤하

초판발행	2013년 11월 22일
3쇄발행	2016년 2월 19일
개정판 6쇄발행	2022년 2월 10일

신고일자	1964년 3월 28일
신고번호	제 300-1964-3호
주소	서울시 종로구 종로 104
전화	(02) 2000-0515[구입문의] / (02) 2000-0345[내용문의]
팩스	(02) 2285-1523
홈페이지	www.ybmbooks.com

ISBN 978-89-17-22595-2

TOEIC is a registered trademark of Educational Testing Service in the United States of America and other countries throughout the world. This product is not approved or endorsed by ETS.

저작권자 ⓒ 2016 임지완, 임정섭

이 책의 저작권은 저자에게 있으며, 책의 제호 및 디자인에 대한 모든 권리는 출판사인 YBM에게 있습니다.
서면에 의한 저자와 출판사의 허락 없이 내용의 일부 혹은 전부를 인용 및 복제하거나 발췌하는 것을 금합니다.

낙장 및 파본은 교환해 드립니다.
구입철회는 구매처 규정에 따라 교환 및 환불처리 됩니다.

Preface

> ## 토익 시험을 준비하는 모든 분들께

매월 많은 분들이 토익 시험을 치르고 있습니다. 취업을 위해, 졸업을 위해, 승진을 위해, 기타 시험 응시 자격을 위해 등등, 어떤 이유로 토익 시험을 준비하건 한 가지 공통 관심사는 '어떻게 하면 빨리 목표 점수를 달성할 수 있을까'일 것입니다.

미국의 유명한 언어 학자인 스티븐 크라센(Steven Krashen)은 아주 흥미로운 이론을 제시하고 있습니다. 바로 'i+1'이론입니다. 여기서 i는 학습자의 현재 수준이고, 1은 이해 가능한 학습 자료(comprehensive input)입니다. 본인의 수준에 맞게 이해 가능한 자료를 투입할 때, 학습 효과가 가장 좋다는 것입니다. 자신에게 이해 가능한 자료를 투입하면 i가 커지게 되고, 다시 1을 투입해 i를 계속 키워가는 학습 방식을 말합니다. 시중에 나와 있는 많은 책들과는 달리, 본 교재는 크라센의 이론을 근거로 단계별 학습에 초점을 두고 제작되었습니다. 무엇보다 학습자들이 흥미를 느끼고 다음 페이지로 술술 넘어갈 수 있는 교재를 만들고자 노력했습니다.

이 책의 LC 구성은 이런 점을 염두에 두고 단계별로 난이도를 조절했습니다. 처음에는 받아 쓰기와 짧은 문장으로 정답을 찾는 연습을 한 다음, 점차 난이도를 높여 실전 수준의 문제까지 다룰 수 있게 구성하였습니다. 또한 모든 문장들은 시험에 가장 자주 등장하는 어휘와 표현들로 이루어졌기 때문에 가장 정확하고도 확실한 시험 준비가 될 것입니다.

RC의 구성은 문법과 회화는 별개가 아니라 같은 것이라는 생각에 기초하여 집필하였습니다. 영어회화 책을 2~3권을 통째로 외우고 나도, 막상 회화 책대로 상황이 펼쳐지는 순간은 거의 없기 때문에, 새로운 상황에 대비해서 영작을 하려면 문법과 어휘 공부는 필수입니다. 시중의 거의 모든 토익책들과 인터넷 정보들이 파트별 요령을 소개하고 있지만, 이러한 '요령'들을 실제에 적용하지 못하면 소용이 없습니다. 그것은 바로 '기본 실력'의 차이라는 것입니다. 이 책은 토익의 '기본 실력'을 확립시켜 줌과 동시에 실제 시험장에서도 쉽게 적용되는 '요령'도 겸비할 수 있도록 구성하였습니다.

10권의 책을 한 번씩 보는 것보다 한 권의 책을 10번 보는 게 더 효과적이라는 점을 명심하세요. 이 책의 내용은 10번을 봐도 질리지 않도록 모든 문제와 내용이 토익 시험과 직결되는 사항들입니다. 토익 점수에 대한 '절실함'을 에너지로 삼아 공부한다면, 모든 것을 이룰 수 있습니다. 이 책을 가지고 공부하는 모든 분들의 건투를 빕니다!

2016년 임지완, 임정섭 드림

Contents

LISTENING COMPREHENSION
청해 기초 다지기 10

PART 1

Unit 1	1인 등장 사진	16
Unit 2	2인 이상 다수 등장 사진	22
Unit 3	사물 / 배경 사진	30
Part 1 Review Test		38

PART 2

Unit 4	Who / When / Where 의문문	44
Unit 5	Why / How / What 의문문	52
Unit 6	일반의문문 / 선택의문문	60
Unit 7	간접의문문 / 부정의문문 / 부가의문문	68
Unit 8	평서문	76
Part 2 Review Test		82

PART 3

Unit 9	업무	84
Unit 10	사무기기 / 주문 / 구매 / 계약	92
Unit 11	여행 / 여가 / 교통 / 쇼핑	100
Unit 12	부동산 / 은행 / 병원 / 호텔 / 식당 (기타 일상 생활)	108
Part 3 Review Test		116

PART 4

Unit 13	광고 / 방송	120
Unit 14	안내 방송 / 소개	128
Unit 15	녹음 메시지 / 설명문	136
Part 4 Review Test		144

READING COMPREHENSION

문법 기초 다지기 — 146

PART 5&6

Unit 1	명사와 대명사	152
Unit 2	형용사와 부사	164
Unit 3	부정사와 동명사	176
Unit 4	분사	188
Unit 5	동사의 종류	200
Unit 6	시제	212
Unit 7	수동태	224
Unit 8	전치사 (1)	236
Unit 9	전치사 (2)	248
Unit 10	접속사 (1)	260
Unit 11	접속사 (2)	272
Unit 12	관계사	284
Part 5&6 Review Test		296

PART 7

Unit 13	편지 / 이메일 / 광고	302
Unit 14	문자 메시지 및 온라인 채팅 / 기사 / 정보문 / 회람	314
Unit 15	이중지문 / 삼중지문	332

Final Test — 358

Features

Listening comprehension

1 청해 기초 다지기
각 파트를 본격적으로 학습하기 전에 살펴보는 선행 학습 코너로, 발음 관련 학습 내용을 수록하고 있다. 미국식/영국식 발음 비교, 혼동하기 쉬운 유사발음, 전반적인 발음 규칙 등을 배우며 청취력 향상을 도모한다.

2 콕콕 찍어주는 출제 포인트
실전 시험에서 가장 많이 출제되는 주제들을 선별하여 포인트별로 어떤 내용이 시험에 출제되는지, 꼭 알고 넘어가야 하는 출제 포인트를 제시하는 코너이다.

3 파트별 문제 분석 및 문법/어휘 정리

1단계 ➡ 기본 문제 유형 파악
실제 시험 대비를 위해 파트별로 문제 유형을 세분화하여, 실전 형식으로 예제를 수록하고 있다. 모든 예제는 미국식/영국식으로 들려주며, 듣고 따라할 수 있도록 구성하였다.

2단계 ➡ 파트별 필수 문법/어휘 숙지
파트별 특성에 맞게 파트 1은 시제에 관한 문법을, 파트 2는 유사발음 어휘 및 다의어, 파트 3, 4는 주제별 단어 및 표현을 수록하였다. 모든 예문과 어휘는 무료 음원을 제공하고 있으며, 미국식/영국식으로 읽어주고 있다. 또한 배운 내용을 점검할 수 있도록 페이지 하단에 간단한 연습문제가 수록되어 있다.

3단계 ➡ 단계별로 심화되는 청취 집중 훈련
파트별로 2~3단계로 나눠지는 약식 문제 유형으로, 실전으로 넘어가기 전 도움닫기를 위해 구성한 연습문제이다. 이 훈련을 통해 실전에 대한 자신감을 북돋울 수 있다.

4 실전 감각 익히기
실제 시험에 출제되는 문제와 동일한 난이도의 문제들을 풀어봄으로써 문제 풀이 기술 및 문제 해결력을 기르는 코너이다. ETS 기출문제를 분석하여 최신 경향의 문제를 수록하고 있다.

5 파트별 Review Test
각 파트가 끝날 때마다 파트별로 실제 시험 문제와 같은 형태의 문제를 풀어본다. 주제별 세부 학습을 한 후 출제 포인트가 총망라된 문제를 풀어봄으로써 파트별 복습 및 실제 시험에 대한 자신감을 가질 수 있다.

Reading comprehension

1 문법 기초 다지기

문장의 기본 구성 요소인 주어, 동사, 목적어, 보어, 수식어에 대한 설명과 8품사, 구와 절의 비교 등 영어 문장을 보는 눈을 열어줄 핵심적인 부분이다. 문장의 구조가 눈에 들어오면, 문법뿐만 아니라 독해의 속도도 빨라진다.

2 토익 필수 문법 및 Check-up

이전 단계인 〈Jump Up TOEIC (Basic)〉에서 공부했던 기초적인 내용을 확인하고 보다 심화해 나가는 과정이다. 가장 기본적인 내용에 덧붙여 새롭게 배우는 내용으로 토익 점수를 한 단계 더 높일 수 있다.

3 토익 필수 어휘 및 Check-up

토익 문법과 어휘는 파트 5, 6을 구성하는 양대산맥이다. 시험에 나오는 필수 어휘를 품사별로 정리하여 각 유닛마다 수록했으며, 배운 어휘를 복습할 수 있도록 5문항씩 Check-up을 수록하였다.

4 파트 5, 6 실전 연습

핵심 문법 포인트와 어휘를 익혔으니, 이제 문제를 통해 적용해 보아야 한다. 틀린 문제는 다시 공부해서 실전에서는 틀리지 않도록 오답 유형을 정리하도록 한다.

5 파트 5, 6 Review Test

문법 12개 유닛 전체 내용을 묶어서 복습할 수 있도록 Review Test를 구성하였다. 주제별로 나누어진 문법 학습과 테스트는 유형 및 출제 포인트 정리에 도움이 되지만, 실전에서는 문제유형이 모두 혼합되어 출제되므로 Review Test를 통해서 실제 시험을 치르듯 문제를 풀어보고 실전에 대비하도록 한다.

6 파트 7의 대표 지문 유형을 다룬 독해 섹션

3개 유닛에 걸쳐 토익에 출제되는 대표적인 지문 유형 7개와 이중·삼중지문을 다루고 있다. 각 유닛 후반에는 표현 및 패러프레이징, 실전형 연습문제가 수록되어 있다.

Final Test

실제 토익에서 본인의 성적을 예상해 볼 수 있는 코너이다. 가장 최근의 시험 문제를 100% 반영하여 실전 문제와 가장 유사한 문제들을 풀어봄으로써 본인의 현재 실력과 취약점을 파악하여 보완할 수 있다.

What is TOEIC?

TOEIC은 Test of English for International Communication의 약자로 영어가 모국어가 아닌 사람들을 대상으로 의사소통 능력에 중점을 두고 일상생활 또는 국제업무 등에 필요한 실용영어 능력을 평가하는 시험입니다.

토익의 시험 구성

구성	파트	파트별 내용		문항 수	시간	배점
Listening Test	1	사진 묘사		6	45분	495점
	2	질의 응답		25		
	3	짧은 대화		39	100	
	4	짧은 담화		30		
Reading Test	5	단문 빈칸 채우기(문법/어휘)		30	75분	495점
	6	장문 빈칸 채우기		16		
	7	독해	단일 지문	29	100	
			이중 지문	10		
			삼중 지문	15		
Total		7개 파트		200문항	120분	990점

시험 진행 일정

시 간	내 용
09:30 ~ 09:45 (15분)	OMR 답안지 배부 및 답안지 작성에 관한 Orientation
09:45 ~ 09:50 (5분)	수험자 휴식시간
09:50 ~ 10:05 (5분)	1차 신분증 검사 (감독교사)
10:05 ~ 10:10 (15분)	문제지 배부 및 파본 확인
10:10 ~ 10:55 (45분)	듣기 평가 (Listening Test)
10:55 ~ 12:10 (75분)	독해 평가 (Reading Test) *정확한 신분확인 및 대리응시 등 부정행위 방지를 위해 2차 신분확인 실시

※ 위 일정은 고사장에 따라 약간의 차이가 있을 수 있습니다.

접수

접수 방법		상세 내용
정기접수	방문	- 해당 회차 접수 기간에 지정된 접수처(서울, 부산, 대전, 대구, 광주)에서 신청서 작성하고 접수 - 응시료: 44,500원 - 준비물: 반명함 사진
	인터넷	- 미리 공지된 시험 일정에 따라 토익 홈페이지(www.toeic.co.kr)에서 진행. 원하는 고사장 선택하고 신용카드, 실시간 계좌이체, 인터넷 뱅킹 등으로 결제 후 접수 - 응시료: 44,500원
특별 추가접수	방문	불가능
	인터넷	특별 추가 접수기간 확인 후 토익 홈페이지에서 접수

※ **시험 취소**: 인터넷 취소는 인터넷 접수일부터 시험 시행 직전 수요일 또는 목요일 오전 8시까지, 방문 취소는 방문 접수일부터 시험 시행 1일 전(토요일) 낮 12시까지, 우편 취소는 방문 접수일부터 시험 시행 1일 전 소인까지 유효하며, 환불 금액은 기간 경과에 따라 차등 적용합니다.

시험 준비

시험 당일 준비물 정해진 신분증(주민등록증, 운전면허증, 기간 만료 전의 여권, 공무원증), 필기구(연필, 지우개), 수험표

입실 시간 9시 20분까지 입실 (9시 50분 이후에는 입실 절대 불가)

입실 안내 시험 당일 해당 고사장 중앙현관에 성명순(가나다순) 명단이 부착되어 있으며 본인의 이름에 해당하는 고사실 확인 후 입실

성적표 확인 및 수령

성적발표 시험 시행일로부터 19일째 되는 날 오후 3시

성적조회 TOEIC 홈페이지(www.toeic.co.kr)나 ARS 060-800-0515에서 조회 가능
성적표 수령 우편 수령 – 성적 발표 후 약 7~10일 소요
온라인 발급 – 인터넷 출력을 통해 성적 유효 기간 내 최초 1회 무료로 발급

청해 기초다지기

미국식 발음 vs. 영국식 발음 비교 체험

토익 Listening은 미국, 캐나다, 영국, 호주 네 나라의 성우가 녹음하게 되는데, 캐나다는 미국식 발음과, 호주는 영국식 발음과 크게 차이가 없습니다. 따라서 미국식과 영국식의 두 가지 발음만 신경 써서 학습하면 됩니다.

1 모음 a
미국식 발음에서는 모음 a가 들어간 음절에 강세가 있는 경우, [애]로 발음하는 반면, 영국식 발음에서는 [아]로 발음할 때가 많습니다.

발음	branch	class	path
미국식	[브랜취]	[클래ㅆ]	[패ㅆ]
영국식	[브란-취]	[클라-ㅆ]	[파-ㅆ]

2 모음 o
미국식 발음에서는 o를 [아]로 발음하는 반면, 영국식 영어에서는 [오]로 발음합니다.

발음	box	office	copy
미국식	[박ㅆ]	[아피ㅅ]	[카피]
영국식	[복ㅆ]	[오피ㅅ]	[코피]

3 자음 r
일반적으로 미국식 발음에서는 r을 항상 발음하는 반면, 영국식 발음에서는 r/re로 단어가 끝나거나 r/re 다음에 자음이 오는 경우에는 발음을 하지 않습니다.

발음	enter	there	bird
미국식	[엔터r]	[데어r]	[버-rㄷ]
영국식	[엔터]	[데어]	[버-ㄷ]

4 자음 t / d
미국식 발음에서는 모음과 모음 사이에 오는 t나 d를 우리말의 [ㄷ]나 [ㄹ]로 발음하는 경우가 많은 반면, 영국식 영어에서는 t/d를 그대로 발음합니다. 모음과 자음 l 사이에 t/d가 올 때도 동일한 현상이 자주 발생합니다.

발음	computer	ladder	little
미국식	[컴퓨-러r]	[래더r] [래러r]	[리들] [리를]
영국식	[컴퓨-터]	[래더]	[리틀]

혼동하기 쉬운 유사발음

영어에는 우리말에 없거나 구분이 명확하지 않은 유사발음이 많은데, 토익 Part 1에서는 이러한 발음들을 이용한 오답들이 자주 출제됩니다.

1 [l] vs. [r]

[l]은 혀를 뻗어서 윗니 뒤에 대면서 발음합니다. [r]은 혀를 안쪽으로 살짝 말되 입 천장에 닿지 않게 해서 발음합니다.

[l]	lead [liːd] 인솔하다	light [lait] 전등	glass [glæs] 유리잔
[r]	read [riːd] 읽다	right [rait] 바로, 우측으로	grass [græs] 잔디

2 [p] vs. [f]

[p]는 우리말의 'ㅍ'소리에 해당하며, 입술을 붙였다가 공기를 터뜨려서 발음합니다. [f]는 우리말에 없는 소리로, 입술을 약간 벌린 채, 윗니를 아랫입술에 살짝 대고 그 사이로 공기를 내보내면서 발음합니다.

[p]	pile [pail] 더미; 쌓다	pull [pul] 당기다	copy [kápi] 사본; 복사하다
[f]	file [fail] 파일; 철하다	full [ful] 가득한	coffee [kɔ́ːfi] 커피

3 [b] vs. [v]

[b]는 우리말의 'ㅂ' 소리에 해당하며, 입술을 붙였다가 터뜨리면서 발음합니다. [v]는 우리말에 없는 소리로, 윗니를 아랫입술에 살짝 대고 그 사이로 공기를 내보내면서 발음하되, 목이 떨리는 소리여야 합니다.

[b]	globe [gloub] 지구본	base [beis] 기초	curb [kəːrb] 연석
[v]	glove [glʌv] 장갑	vase [veis] 꽃병	curve [kəːrv] 곡선; 휘다

4 [s] vs. [θ]

[s]는 우리말의 'ㅅ'소리에 해당하는 소리로, 혀가 윗니 뒤쪽에 닿지 않게 하면서 발음하되, 강하게 숨이 새나오도록 합니다. [θ]는 우리말에 없는 둔탁한 소리로, 입술을 약간 벌린 상태로 윗니와 아랫니 사이로 혀를 살짝 내밀어 발음하되, 가볍게 숨이 새나오도록 합니다.

[s]	sink [siŋk] (부엌의) 싱크대	pass [pæs] 통과하다, 건네다	sought [sɔːt] 찾았다
[θ]	think [θiŋk] 생각하다	path [pæθ] 길	thought [θɔːt] 생각했다

아는 만큼 들리는 발음 규칙

영어에는 다양한 소리 규칙들이 있습니다. 이를 이해하고 들으면 어렵게만 느껴지던 토익 LC가 한결 쉬워집니다.

1 끝 자음과 첫 모음이 만났을 때
앞 단어가 자음으로 끝나고 뒤에 오는 단어가 모음으로 시작하면, 끝 자음과 첫 모음이 연결되어 한 단어처럼 발음됩니다.

take off	테이크 어프 → 테이꺼프
half an hour	해프 언 아워 → 해퍼나워
a lot of	어 랏 오브 → 얼라럽

2 동일하거나 유사한 발음의 자음끼리 만났을 때
동일하거나 유사한 발음의 자음이 연달아 오면 앞의 자음을 발음하지 않고 뒤의 자음만 한 번 발음합니다.

dark color	다크 컬러 → 다컬러
last Tuesday	래스트 튜즈데이 → 래슷튜즈데이
convenience store	컨비니언스 스토어 → 컨비니언스또어

3 자음 세 개가 연속으로 나올 때
우리말에도 발음하기 힘든 단어가 있듯, 영어에도 발음하기 힘든 소리가 있게 마련입니다. 한 단어 내에 자음 세 개가 연속으로 나오는 경우, 자음들을 하나하나 분명히 발음하기 어렵습니다. 따라서 발음 편의상 중간 자음이 탈락되거나 약화됩니다.

department	디파트먼트 → 디팔먼트
appointment	어포인트먼트 → 어포인먼트
empty	엠프티 → 엠티

4 d나 t가 모음과 모음 사이에 올 때
t나 d가 모음과 모음 사이에 올 때는 [트]나 [드]로 발음하지 않고 [ㄹ]처럼 발음합니다.

automatic	오토매틱 → 오로매릭
medical	메디컬 → 메리컬
get on	게ㄷ온 → 게런

5 t가 단어의 끝에 올 때

t가 단어의 끝에 올 경우에는 주로 [ㅌ]를 발음하지 않고 생략합니다.

don't know	돈ㅌ 노우 → 돈노우
next month	넥스ㅌ 먼ㅆ → 넥스먼ㅆ
must not	머스ㅌ 낫 → 머스낫

6 n과 t가 만났을 때

n과 t가 만나면 t발음을 생략합니다.

center	센터 → 쎄너
Internet	인터r넷 → 이너r넷
in front of	인 프런트 어브 → 인 프러너브

7 끝자음 d/t가 y를 만났을 때

앞 단어와 뒤에 오는 단어의 소리가 서로에게 영향을 주어 바뀌어 발음하는 경우가 있는데, 끝자음 d가 y 앞에 올 경우에는 [쥬]처럼, 끝자음 t가 y 앞에 올 경우에는 [츄]처럼 발음됩니다.

would you	우ㄷ 유 → 우쥬
told you	토울ㄷ 유 → 토울쥬
meet you	미ㅌ 유 → 미츄

8 and의 다양한 발음

and는 [앤드]로 또박또박 들리는 경우보다는 바로 앞 단어의 끝자음과 연음이 되거나 약화되어 발음되는 경우가 많습니다.

read and write	리ㄷ 앤 라이ㅌ → 리댄 라이ㅌ
go and get	고우 앤 겟 → 고은겟
wait and see	웨잇 앤 씨 → 웨이랜씨

PART 1

Unit 1 1인 등장 사진
Unit 2 2인 이상 다수 등장 사진
Unit 3 사물 / 배경 사진

Part 1 Review Test

UNIT 1　1인 등장 사진

★ 콕콕 찍어주는 출제 포인트

Part 1에서 사진 속 인물이 한 명인 경우는 먼저 인물의 동작이나 자세를 잘 살펴보아야 합니다. 그리고 각 문장을 들을 때는 동사에 집중하는 것이 좋습니다. 왜냐하면 1인 사진의 경우 주어는 대체로 동일하지만 동사가 서로 다르게 제시되는 경우가 많기 때문입니다. 그리고 간혹 인물 주변의 배경이나 주변 사물도 언급될 수 있으므로 주의해야 합니다.

사진 및 보기 분석　🎧 P1-U01-1

다음 보기들을 미국식과 영국식으로 듣고 따라 읽어 보세요.

(A) He is looking out the window.
　　그는 창 밖을 내다보고 있다.

(B) He is talking to a waiter.
　　그는 웨이터에게 말을 하고 있다.

(C) He is ordering some food.
　　그는 음식을 주문하고 있다.

(D) He is reading some notes.
　　그는 메모를 읽고 있다.

해설 및 어휘

1인 등장 사진 유형에서는 주로 한 사람의 동작이나 상태를 묘사하게 되므로, 동사를 잘 들어야 한다. 여기서도 각각의 보기에 서로 다른 동작을 묘사하는 is looking out, talking to, is ordering, is reading이 쓰였는데, 사진 내용과 부합하는 것은 is reading 단 하나뿐이므로 쉽게 답이 (D)임을 알 수 있다.

look out ~ 밖을 내다보다　　order 주문하다　　note 기록, 문서, 메모

Possible Answers

- He is sitting at a table.　　남자는 탁자에 앉아 있다.
- He is wearing glasses.　　남자는 안경을 끼고 있다.
- He is holding a pen.　　남자는 펜을 쥐고 있다.

🔍 알면 잘 들리는 청취 문법 1_ 현재진행시제 🎧 P1-U01-2

현재진행시제는 진행되고 있는 현재의 동작을 나타낼 때 쓰입니다. 현재진행형의 형태는 〈am/are/is + ~ing〉이며 '~하고 있다, ~하는 중이다'라는 뜻입니다. 현재진행형은 동작뿐만 아니라 '상태'를 나타낼 때에도 쓸 수 있는데요. 예문과 연습을 통해서 현재진행시제의 쓰임을 살펴보겠습니다.

💬 동작의 진행을 나타내는 현재진행시제
다음 예문들을 미국식과 영국식으로 듣고 따라 읽어 보세요.

1 She **is using** a desktop computer.   그녀는 탁상용 컴퓨터를 쓰고 있다.
2 They **are crossing** the street.   그들은 길을 건너고 있다.
3 They **are shaking** hands.   그들은 악수를 하고 있다.
4 The woman **is reaching for** an item.   여자는 물건을 집으려고 손을 뻗치고 있다.
5 They **are unloading** the truck.   그들은 트럭에서 물건을 내리고 있다.

💬 인물/사물의 상태를 나타내는 현재진행시제
다음 예문들을 미국식과 영국식으로 듣고 따라 읽어 보세요.

6 The woman **is resting** her chin on her hand.   여자가 손으로 턱을 괴고 있다.
7 They **are looking at** some pictures.   그들은 그림 몇 점을 보고 있다.
8 The picture frame **is hanging** on the wall.   그림 액자가 벽에 걸려 있다.
9 People **are resting** on the grass.   사람들이 잔디 위에서 쉬고 있다.
10 She **is wearing** a hat.   그녀는 모자를 쓰고 있다. (상태 묘사)

cf) wear는 (모자·옷·안경 등의) 착용 상태를 나타내는 반면, put on은 착용을 하고 있는 동작을 나타낼 때 쓴다.

✏️ 받아쓰기 연습   해설 p.3
다음은 한 사람의 동작이나 상태를 나타내는 문장입니다. 음원을 듣고 해석을 참고하여 빈칸을 채워보세요.

1 He _____ the wall.   그는 벽에 페인트칠을 하고 있다.
2 He _____ a vehicle.   그는 차를 수리하고 있다.
3 She _____ on the phone.   그녀는 전화 통화를 하고 있다.
4 He _____ on his stomach.   그는 엎드려 있다.
5 They _____ across from each other.   그들은 마주보고 앉아 있다.

청취 집중 훈련 1 P1-U01-3 / 해설 p.3

사진마다 들려주는 각 문장의 빈칸을 채운 후, 사진 내용과 맞으면 T, 틀리면 F에 표시하세요.

1.

(A) He's _____ a pamphlet. (T / F)
그는 팸플릿을 읽고 있다.

(B) He's writing in a _____. (T / F)
그는 달력에 글씨를 쓰고 있다.

(C) He's _____ postcards. (T / F)
그는 엽서 몇 장을 사고 있다.

(D) He's standing _____ a store. (T / F)
그는 가게 앞에 서 있다.

2.

(A) She's _____. (T / F)
그녀는 팩스를 보내고 있다.

(B) She's greeting a _____. (T / F)
그녀는 고객을 맞이하고 있다.

(C) She's talking _____. (T / F)
그녀는 전화 통화를 하고 있다.

(D) She's _____ in an office. (T / F)
그녀는 사무실에서 일하고 있다.

3.

(A) He's going for a walk _____. (T / F)
그는 공원으로 산책을 가고 있다.

(B) He's _____ a uniform. (T / F)
그는 유니폼을 입고 있다.

(C) He's pushing a _____ down the _____. (T / F)
그는 인도에서 카트를 밀고 있다.

(D) He's _____ some utensils. (T / F)
그는 몇 개의 주방도구를 나르고 있다.

4.

(A) He's sitting _____. (T / F)
그는 로비에 앉아 있다.

(B) He's _____ the bag. (T / F)
그는 가방 안을 보고 있다.

(C) He's _____ a fire. (T / F)
그는 불을 지피고 있다.

(D) He's _____ the plants. (T / F)
그는 화초에 물을 주고 있다.

청취 집중 훈련 2   🎧 P1-U01-4 / 해설 p.3-4

사진을 보고, 들려주는 두 개의 보기 중 사진 내용에 맞는 것을 고르세요.

1.

(A)   (B)

2.

(A)   (B)

3.

(A)   (B)

4.

(A)   (B)

UNIT 1

실전 감각 익히기 🎧 P1-U01-5 / 해설 p.4-6

사진을 보고, 들려주는 네 개의 보기 중 사진 내용에 맞는 것을 고르세요.

1.

(A)　(B)　(C)　(D)

2.

(A)　(B)　(C)　(D)

3.

(A)　(B)　(C)　(D)

4.

(A)　(B)　(C)　(D)

5.

(A) (B) (C) (D)

6.

(A) (B) (C) (D)

7.

(A) (B) (C) (D)

8.

(A) (B) (C) (D)

UNIT 2 2인 이상 다수 등장 사진

★ 콕콕 찍어주는 출제 포인트

사진에 2명 이상이 등장할 경우, 사람들이 동일한 행동을 하는지, 각자 개별적인 동작을 하는지 살펴봐야 합니다. 실제 시험에서는 사람들의 공통적인 모습을 묘사한 것이 답이 될 수도 있고, 한 두 명의 부각되는 동작이나 상태 묘사가 답이 될 수도 있기 때문입니다. 주의할 것은 인물의 복장 상태나 주변 사물에 대한 묘사가 보기 중 하나로 제시될 수 있다는 점입니다.

사진 및 보기 분석 1_ 공통적인 동작 🎧 P1-U02-1

사진 속 인물들의 공통점에 초점을 맞춘 유형으로, 4개 보기의 주어가 모두 동일한 경향이 있습니다.
다음 보기들을 미국식과 영국식으로 듣고 따라 읽어 보세요.

(A) They're boarding the bus.
그들은 버스에 오르고 있다.

(B) **They're getting into the car.**
그들은 차에 타고 있는 중이다.

(C) They're searching for a parking space.
그들은 주차할 곳을 찾고 있다.

(D) They're riding in a taxi cab.
그들은 택시를 타고 있다.

해설 및 어휘

사진 중앙에 있는 차를 중심으로 주변 사람들의 행동을 살펴보면, 자동차에 타려고 하거나 내리려는 공통점을 파악할 수 있다. (A)의 bus, (D)의 taxi cab은 사진 속 자동차와 거리가 멀고, (C) 주차 공간을 찾는다는 것도 사진에서 이미 차를 주차시킨 상황과 맞지 않다. 보기 중 (B) getting into the car만이 사진을 올바르게 묘사하고 있으므로 (B)가 정답이다.

board ~에 타다 (= get into, ride in)   search for ~을 찾다   parking space 주차 공간   taxi (cab) 택시

Possible Answers

- They are about to get into the car.   그들은 막 차를 타려 한다.
- The car doors are open.   차 문이 열려 있다.
- The car is parked near the curb.   차가 도로변 가까이에 주차되어 있다.

사진 및 보기 분석 2_개별적인 동작 🎧 P1-U02-2

서로 다른 주어를 사용해 개별적인 동작이나 사물의 상태에 초점을 맞춘 유형입니다.
다음 보기들을 미국식과 영국식으로 듣고 따라 읽어 보세요.

(A) A child is drinking from a fountain.
   한 아이가 분수대 물을 마시고 있다.

(B) The parasol is open.
   파라솔이 펴져 있다.

(C) A woman is reading a book in a restaurant.
   한 여자가 식당 안에서 책을 읽고 있다.

(D) Some people are having a conversation.
   일부 사람들이 대화를 하고 있다.

해설 및 어휘

사진에 여러 사람과 사물이 등장하므로 다양한 보기 내용이 나올 수 있다. 어떤 대상을 어떻게 묘사하는지 주어와 동사에 귀를 기울여야 한다. (A)는 아이(a child)가 보이고 분수대(fountain)도 있지만 물을 마시고 있지(drinking) 않으므로 동사 오류, (B)는 파라솔이 펴져 있지(the parasol is open) 않으므로 서술부 오류, (C)는 사진에 한 여성(woman)이 책(book)을 들고 있는 것을 이용한 함정이다. 계단 밑에서 두 사람이 탁자에 앉아 대화를 나누고 있는(having a conversation) 모습을 묘사한 (D)가 정답이다.

fountain 분수대   have a conversation 대화를 나누다

Possible Answers

- The parasol is folded up. 파라솔이 접혀 있다.
- A child is putting his hand on the fountain. 아이가 손으로 분수대를 짚고 있다.
- A woman is holding some books in her arms. 한 여자가 책을 품에 안고 있다.

알면 잘 들리는 청취 문법 2_ (단순) 현재시제 / 현재완료시제

1. (단순) 현재시제   🎧 P1-U02-3

인물이나 사물의 현재 상태를 나타낼 때, 〈주어 + is/are + 형용사〉나 〈주어 + 일반동사의 현재형〉 구문을 씁니다. 또한 인물이나 사물이 '~에 있다'라는 위치 관계를 나타낼 때는 〈주어 + is/are + 위치/장소 전치사구〉 또는 〈There is/are + 주어 + 위치/장소 전치사구〉 구조를 흔히 사용합니다. 다음 예문을 통해서 현재시제의 쓰임을 살펴보겠습니다.

💬 주어 + is/are + 형용사
다음 예문들을 미국식과 영국식으로 듣고 따라 읽어 보세요.

1. The water is calm. — 물결이 잔잔하다.
2. All the items are identical. — 모든 상품이 똑같이 생겼다.
3. All the people are in their uniforms. — 모든 사람들이 유니폼을 입고 있다.

💬 주어 + 일반동사의 현재형
다음 예문들을 미국식과 영국식으로 듣고 따라 읽어 보세요.

4. The trail curves to the left. — 산길이 왼쪽으로 굽어져 있다.
5. A path goes[winds] through the park. — 공원에 오솔길이 나 있다[굽어져 있다].
6. The man has a beard. — 남자는 턱수염이 있다.

💬 주어 + is/are + 위치/장소 전치사구
다음 예문들을 미국식과 영국식으로 듣고 따라 읽어 보세요.

7. The desks are against the wall. — 책상들이 벽에 붙어 있다.
8. Lampposts are along the road. — 가로등이 도로를 따라 있다.
9. They are across from each other. — 그들은 서로 맞은편에 있다.

💬 There is/are + 주어 + 위치/장소 전치사구
다음 예문들을 미국식과 영국식으로 듣고 따라 읽어 보세요.

10. There are framed pictures on the wall. — 벽에 액자에 든 그림들이 붙어 있다.
11. There are cars parked on both sides of the road. — 도로 양쪽에 주차된 차들이 있다.
12. There are a lot of people in the auditorium. — 강당 안에 많은 사람들이 있다.

2. 현재완료시제 🎧 P1-U02-4

현재완료란 과거의 한 시점에 시작한 동작이나 상태가 현재 완료되었거나 계속되고 있음을 나타내는 시제입니다. 현재완료시제는 〈주어 + have/has + 과거분사〉의 형태로 '주어가 ~했다'라는 뜻이 되는데요. 참고로, 현재완료시제와 과거시제의 차이점은, 과거에 일어난 일의 결과가 현재까지 계속될 경우 현재완료시제를, 과거에 일어난 일을 단순히 설명하기만 할 뿐 현재 어떻게 되었는지 알 수 없는 경우 과거시제를 사용해야 합니다.

다음 예문들을 미국식과 영국식으로 듣고 따라 읽어 보세요.

1. All the leaves have fallen off the trees. — 모든 나뭇잎이 나무에서 떨어졌다.
2. A plane has landed on the runway. — 비행기가 활주로에 착륙했다.
3. They have set the tables. — 그들은 식탁을 차려 놓았다.
4. A crowd has gathered in front of a store. — 많은 사람들이 상점 앞에 모여 있다.
5. They have loaded the boxes into a truck. — 그들은 트럭에 상자들을 실었다.
6. A tree has fallen across the street. — 나무 한 그루가 길에 가로질러 쓰러졌다.
7. People have formed a line. — 사람들이 한 줄로 서 있다.
8. The man has opened a car door. — 남자가 차 문을 열어 놓았다.

✏️ 받아쓰기 연습 🎧 P1-U02-4 / 해설 p.6

다음은 현재시제와 현재완료시제를 사용하는 문장입니다. 음원을 듣고 해석을 참고하여 빈칸을 채워보세요.

1. The top shelf _____. — 맨 위의 선반이 비어 있다.
2. The curtains _____. — 커튼이 열려 있다.
3. A railing _____ along the bridge. — 난간이 다리를 따라 나 있다.
4. Skyscrapers _____ the water. — 고층건물들이 물을 내려다보고 있다.
5. A potted plant _____. — 화분이 창문 옆에 있다.
6. Some performers _____ stage. — 무대 위에 몇몇 공연자들이 있다.
7. There are buildings _____ the shore. — 해변을 따라 건물들이 있다.
8. There is a bridge _____. — 강 위로 다리가 있다.
9. Some vehicles _____ at the traffic light. — 몇몇 차량들이 신호등 앞에서 멈췄다.
10. The train _____ at the platform. — 기차가 승강장에 도착했다.

청취 집중 훈련 1 P1-U02-5 / 해설 p.6

사진마다 들려주는 각 문장의 빈칸을 채운 후, 사진 내용과 맞으면 T, 틀리면 F에 표시하세요.

1.

(A) They're _____ a conference. (T / F)
그들은 회의를 열고 있다.

(B) They're _____ to each other. (T / F)
그들은 서로에게 손을 흔들고 있다.

(C) They're _____. (T / F)
그들은 악수를 하고 있다.

(D) They're facing _____. (T / F)
그들은 서로 마주보고 있다.

2.

(A) The floor in the lobby _____. (T / F)
로비 바닥에 카펫이 깔려 있다.

(B) The bookshelf _____. (T / F)
책장이 비어 있다.

(C) One woman is _____ a movie. (T / F)
여자 한 명이 영화를 보고 있다.

(D) One of the women is _____. (T / F)
여자들 중 한 명은 컴퓨터를 쓰고 있다.

3.

(A) The people _____ the intersection. (T / F)
사람들이 교차로를 건너고 있다.

(B) Some people _____ on the corner of the street. (T / F)
몇몇 사람들이 길 모퉁이에 모여 있다.

(C) The equipment is placed _____. (T / F)
장비가 건물 앞에 놓여 있다.

(D) The furniture is being _____ a truck. (T / F)
가구가 트럭에 실리고 있다.

4.

(A) One woman is _____. (T / F)
한 여자가 수화물의 무게를 재고 있다.

(B) There is a monitor _____. (T / F)
각각의 카운터에 모니터가 있다.

(C) The women _____ the plane. (T / F)
여자들은 비행기에 탑승하고 있다.

(D) They are _____ their meals. (T / F)
그들은 식사를 주문하고 있다.

청취 집중 훈련 2 🎧 P1-U02-6 / 해설 p.7

사진을 보고, 들려주는 보기 중 사진 내용에 맞는 것을 고르세요.

1.

(A)   (B)

2.

(A)   (B)

3.

(A)   (B)

4.

(A)   (B)

실전 감각 익히기   🎧 P1-U02-7 / 해설 p.7-9

사진을 보고, 들려주는 네 개의 보기 중 사진 내용에 맞는 것을 고르세요.

1.

(A)　(B)　(C)　(D)

2.

(A)　(B)　(C)　(D)

3.

(A)　(B)　(C)　(D)

4.

(A)　(B)　(C)　(D)

5.

(A)　(B)　(C)　(D)

6.

(A)　(B)　(C)　(D)

7.

(A)　(B)　(C)　(D)

8.

(A)　(B)　(C)　(D)

UNIT 2 **29**

UNIT 3 사물/배경 사진

★ **콕콕 찍어주는 출제 포인트**

사진 속에 사람이 없고 사물과 배경만 보일 때는 먼저 부각되는 사물의 위치나 상태, 또는 전체적인 배경을 살펴봐야 합니다. 그 다음에는 주변 사물의 모양이나 위치 또는 상태를 빠르게 확인합니다. 사물/배경 사진의 경우 사물이 문장의 주어가 되어 〈사물 주어 + be + 과거분사〉 또는 〈사물 주어 + have/has been + 과거분사〉와 같은 수동태 문장으로 묘사될 가능성이 높다는 것을 알아두세요.

사진 및 보기 분석 1_ 사물 중심 P1-U03-1

다음 보기들을 미국식과 영국식으로 듣고 따라 읽어 보세요.

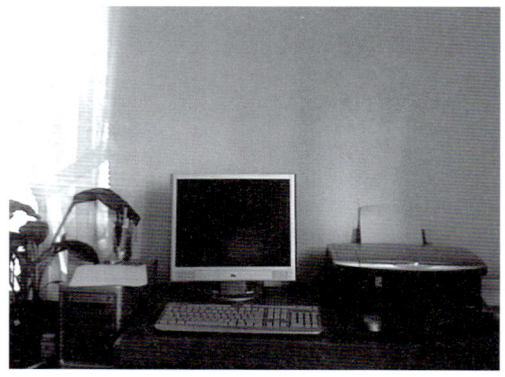

(A) The printer is under the desk.
프린터가 탁자 밑에 있다.

(B) The computer has been placed on the desk.
컴퓨터가 탁자 위에 놓여 있다.

(C) A woman is typing on a keyboard.
한 여성이 자판을 치고 있다.

(D) The computer is being used.
컴퓨터가 사용되고 있는 중이다.

해설 및 어휘

사물 중심 사진의 묘사는 보기에 언급되는 사물의 위치나 상태를 알맞게 묘사했는지를 파악해야 한다. (A)는 사진에 등장하는 프린터(printer), 책상(desk)은 맞지만 위치 묘사(is under)가 틀리다. (C)는 사진에 등장하지 않는 사람을 언급한 오답이고, (D)는 〈by + 사람 주체〉가 문장 뒤에 생략된 진행형 수동태로, 역시 오답이다. 정답은 사물과 위치 묘사가 올바른 (B)이다.

be placed 놓여 있다   type 타자를 치다

Possible Answers

· The computer is not in use.   컴퓨터를 사용하고 있지 않다.
· The monitor[printer] is turned off.   모니터[프린터]가 꺼져 있다.
· There is a printer next to the computer.   컴퓨터 옆에 프린터가 있다.

사진 및 보기 분석 2_ 배경 중심 🎧 P1-U03-2

다음 보기들을 미국식과 영국식으로 듣고 따라 읽어 보세요.

(A) The people are crossing the bridge.
  사람들이 다리를 건너고 있다.
(B) The water is very rough.
  물살이 매우 거칠다.
(C) Boats are floating in the river.
  배들이 강에 떠 있다.
(D) The river flows through the town.
  강이 도시를 통과해 흐르고 있다.

해설 및 어휘

배경 사진의 경우, 뚜렷한 특징을 찾기보다는 전체적인 배경을 두루 살펴야 한다. 사진에 보이지 않는 사물이 언급된 보기들은 바로 오답으로 처리한다. (A)는 사진에 등장하지 않는 사람(people)을 언급한 오답, (B)는 서술부(rough) 오류, (C)는 사진에서 보이지 않는 사물(Boats)을 언급한 오답이다. 강 양쪽에 건물들이 있고, 강이 도시를 통과해 흐르고(flow through) 있으므로, 이를 적절히 묘사한 (D)가 정답이다.

cross 건너다   rough 거친   float 떠 있다   flow 흐르다

Possible Answers

- The water is calm.   물이 잔잔하다.
- There is a bridge over the river.   강 위에 다리가 있다.
- There are buildings on both sides of the river.   강 양쪽에 건물들이 있다.

🔍 알면 잘 들리는 청취 문법 3_ 수동태 🎧 P1-U03-3

사람이 없는 사물이나 배경 묘사는 대개 사물을 주어로 쓰게 됩니다. 그런데 사물이나 배경은 행위를 직접 할 수 없고 행위를 '당하는' 대상이 되기 때문에 이를 묘사하는 문장에서는 수동태 동사를 주로 사용하게 됩니다. Part 1에서 수동태는 〈is/are + 과거분사〉, 〈have/has been + 과거분사〉, 또는 〈is/are being + 과거분사〉 중 하나의 형태로 제시됩니다.

💬 단순 수동태 – is/are + 과거분사

사물이 '~되다', 또는 '~되어 있다'라는 의미로 현재의 수동적 상태를 나타냅니다.
다음 예문들을 미국식과 영국식으로 듣고 따라읽어 보며 수동태 시제를 익혀보세요.

1	Some bottles **are arranged** on the shelf.	몇몇 병들이 선반 위에 정리되어 있다.
2	The dishes **are stacked** in the cupboard.	접시들이 찬장에 쌓여 있다.
3	The house **is reflected** in the lake.	그 집은 호수에 비쳐지고 있다.
4	Passengers **are seated** on the bus.	승객들이 버스에 앉아 있다.
5	The clothes **are folded** in the closet.	옷들이 옷장에 개어져 있다.
6	The tools **are stored** in a box.	공구들이 상자에 보관되어 있다.
7	The tables **are lined up** against the wall.	탁자들이 벽에 맞대어 일렬로 놓여 있다.
8	Bicycles **are chained** to the rack.	자전거들이 보관대에 묶여 있다.
9	The benches **are covered** with snow.	의자들이 눈으로 덮여 있다.

💬 현재완료 수동태 – have/has been + 과거분사

과거의 수동적 상태가 현재에도 유지되어 있음을 나타내며 '~이 되었다', '~해졌다'라는 의미를 갖습니다.
다음 예문들을 미국식과 영국식으로 듣고 따라읽어 보면서 현재완료 수동태 구문을 익혀두세요.

1	The items **have been separated**.	물건들이 분리되었다.
2	The street **has been cleared** of snow.	거리에 눈이 치워져 있다.
3	The windows **have been closed**.	창문들이 닫혀 있다.
4	The sink **has been filled** with dishes.	싱크대가 접시들로 가득 찼다.
5	The trees **have been planted** in rows.	나무들이 여러 줄로 심어져 있다.
6	The road **has been paved**.	도로는 포장되었다.
7	The tables **have been set**.	식탁이 차려져 있다.
8	A sheet **has been covered** over the vehicle.	얇은 천이 차량 위에 덮여 있다.
9	The road **has been blocked off** for construction.	도로가 공사 때문에 막혔다.

현재진행 수동태 – is/are being + 과거분사

사람이 어떤 사물을 대상으로 특정 행위를 한창 하고 있을 때, 사물의 입장에서는 '~되는 중이다'라는 의미가 성립되며, 이를 현재진행 수동태(is/are being + 과거분사) 동사로 표현합니다. 따라서 현재진행 수동태 동사가 들리면 사진에 사람이 등장해서 동사에 해당되는 행위를 사물에 가하고 있어야 하는데요. 사진 속 상황이 그와 다르다면, 현재진행 수동태 문장은 오답으로 처리해야 합니다.

다음 예문들을 미국식과 영국식으로 따라읽으며 익혀보세요.

1 Some food **is being served** to the customers.   음식이 손님들에게 제공되고 있는 중이다.
2 The vehicle **is being repaired**.   차량이 수리되고 있는 중이다.
3 The floor **is being cleaned**.   바닥이 청소되고 있는 중이다.
4 A car **is being towed**.   차가 견인되는 중이다.
5 The shelf **is being stocked**.   선반에 물건이 채워지고 있다.
6 A tent **is being put up**.   텐트가 쳐지고 있다.
7 Some flowers **are being watered**.   몇몇 꽃에 물을 주고 있다.
8 The pants **are being ironed**.   바지가 다림질되고 있다.
9 The machine **is being adjusted**.   기계가 조정되고 있다.

받아쓰기 연습   해설 p.9

다음은 사물의 상태를 나타내는 수동태 문장입니다. 음원을 듣고 해석을 참고하여 빈칸을 채워보세요.

1 Some electronics _____ in a store.   몇몇 전자제품들이 상점에 진열되어 있다.
2 The ship _____ at the terminal.   배가 터미널에 정박해 있다.
3 Vehicles _____ in a parking garage.   차량이 주차장에 주차되어 있다.
4 The construction _____.   공사가 완료되었다.
5 The boxes _____ onto the truck.   상자들이 트럭 위에 실려 있다.
6 The potted plant _____ by the window.   화분에 든 식물이 창가에 놓여 있다.
7 The wall _____.   벽에 페인트가 칠해지는 중이다.
8 The car _____.   차가 세차되는 중이다.
9 A bridge _____.   다리가 지어지고 있다.

청취 집중 훈련 1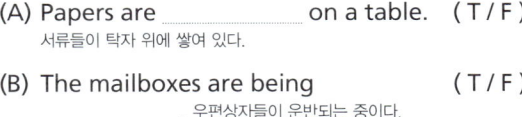

사진마다 들려주는 각 문장의 빈칸을 채운 후, 사진 내용과 맞으면 T, 틀리면 F에 표시하세요.

1.

(A) Papers are _____ on a table. (T / F)
서류들이 탁자 위에 쌓여 있다.

(B) The mailboxes are being _____. (T / F)
우편상자들이 운반되는 중이다.

(C) _____ are on the floor. (T / F)
복사기가 바닥 위에 있다.

(D) The _____ is empty. (T / F)
선반이 비어 있다.

2.

(A) Cars are being _____. (T / F)
차들이 세차되는 중이다.

(B) A parking garage is being _____. (T / F)
주차장이 지어지고 있는 중이다.

(C) Cars are parked _____. (T / F)
차들이 주차장에 주차되어 있다.

(D) Pillars _____ in the garage. (T / F)
기둥이 주차장에 일렬로 늘어서 있다.

3.

(A) The platform _____ equipment. (T / F)
승강장이 장비로 가득 채워져 있다.

(B) The ship has many _____. (T / F)
배에 창문이 많다.

(C) The passengers are _____ the boat. (T / F)
승객들이 배에 탑승 중이다.

(D) The cruise ship _____ at the terminal. (T / F)
유람선이 터미널에 정박해 있다.

4.

(A) The road _____ rocks. (T / F)
길이 바위로 덮여 있다.

(B) A road has been made _____. (T / F)
공사장에 길이 하나 만들어져 있다.

(C) The _____ winds through the park. (T / F)
오솔길이 공원을 가로질러 굽어져 있다.

(D) There is heavy _____ on both sides of the road. (T / F)
길 양쪽에 중장비가 있다.

청취 집중 훈련 2 P1-U03-5 / 해설 p.10

사진을 보고, 들려주는 보기 중 사진 내용에 맞는 것을 고르세요.

1.

(A)   (B)

2.
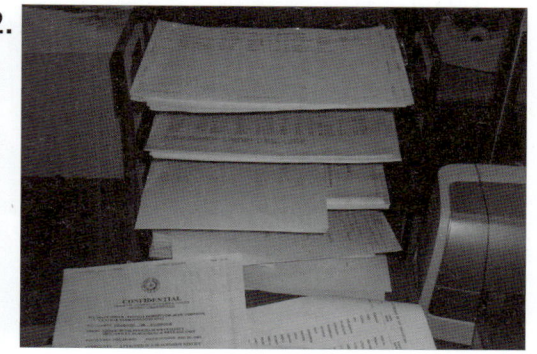
(A)   (B)

3.

(A)   (B)

4.

(A)   (B)

실전 감각 익히기 🎧 P1-U03-6 / 해설 p.10-12

사진을 보고, 들려주는 네 개의 보기 중 사진 내용에 맞는 것을 고르세요.

1.

(A) (B) (C) (D)

2.

(A) (B) (C) (D)

3.

(A) (B) (C) (D)

4.

(A) (B) (C) (D)

5.

(A) (B) (C) (D)

6.

(A) (B) (C) (D)

7.

(A) (B) (C) (D)

8.

(A) (B) (C) (D)

PART 1 Review Test RT 1 / 해설 p.13–15

사진을 보고, 들려주는 네 개의 보기 중 사진 내용에 맞는 것을 고르세요.

1.

(A)　(B)　(C)　(D)

2.

(A)　(B)　(C)　(D)

3.

(A)　(B)　(C)　(D)

4.

(A)　(B)　(C)　(D)

PART 1 Review Test **39**

5.

(A)   (B)   (C)   (D)

6.

(A)   (B)   (C)   (D)

7.

(A)   (B)   (C)   (D)

8.

(A)   (B)   (C)   (D)

9.

(A)　(B)　(C)　(D)

10.

(A)　(B)　(C)　(D)

Unit 4 Who / When / Where 의문문
Unit 5 Why / How / What 의문문
Unit 6 일반의문문 / 선택의문문
Unit 7 간접의문문 / 부정의문문 / 부가의문문
Unit 8 평서문

Part 2 Review Test

UNIT 4 Who / When / Where 의문문

★ 콕콕 찍어주는 출제 포인트

Part 2에서는 who나 when과 같은 의문사로 시작하는 의문문과 yes/no로 대답할 수 있는 일반의문문이 출제되는데, 의문사의문문은 매회 평균 10문제 정도 출제되고 있습니다. yes/no로 대답할 수 없는 의문사의문문은 의문사만 들어도 쉽게 정답을 찾을 수 있는데요. 여기서는 매월 각각 2~3문제씩 출제되는 who, when, where 의문문을 살펴보겠습니다.

Who 의문문의 질문과 응답 분석 🎧 P2-U04-1

아래 질문과 응답을 미국식과 영국식으로 듣고 따라읽으며 응답 유형을 익혀보세요.

정답 유형 1. 사람 이름

Q: Who is going to manage the branch office? — 누가 지점을 관리할 예정입니까?
A1: Becky will take over the position. — 베키가 그 자리를 맡을 겁니다.
A2: I think Ms. Bailey is. — 베일리 씨라고 생각합니다.

정답 유형 2. 직책, 부서명

Q1: Who are they waiting for? — 그들이 누구를 기다리는 거죠?
A1: Their manager. — 그들의 관리자요.

Q2: Who arranged this event? — 누가 이 행사를 준비했나요?
A2: The marketing department. — 마케팅 부서요.

정답 유형 3. 회피성 또는 우회적 답변

Q: Who will we hire to decorate the shop? — 우리는 상점을 장식하기 위해 누구를 고용하죠?
A1: It hasn't been decided yet. — 아직 결정되지 않았습니다.
A2: I have no idea. — 잘 모르겠어요.

어휘
1. manage 관리하다   branch office 지점   take over 맡다, 인계하다
2. wait for ~을 기다리다   arrange 준비하다   event 행사
3. hire 고용하다   decorate 장식하다   decide 결정하다   yet (부정문) 아직

When 의문문의 질문과 응답 분석 🎧 P2-U04-2

아래 질문과 응답을 미국식과 영국식으로 듣고 따라읽으며 응답 유형을 익혀보세요.

정답 유형 1. **시간 전치사구(시간 전치사 + 시점)**	
Q: When will the construction be finished?	공사는 언제 끝날까요?
A1: It'll be done in November.	11월에 끝납니다.
A2: In two weeks.	2주 후에요.

정답 유형 2. **시간 부사절(시간 접속사 + 주어 + 동사 ~)**	
Q: When are you going to visit the construction site?	언제 공사 현장을 방문할 거죠?
A: Right after I finish the meeting.	회의를 마친 직후에요.

정답 유형 3. **회피성 또는 우회적 답변**	
Q: When is the fundraiser?	기금 조성 행사가 언제죠?
A: Ask Mr. Harper.	하퍼 씨에게 물어보세요.

 1. construction 공사   be finished 끝나다(= be done)
2. construction site 공사 현장[부지]   right after ~ 직후에   meeting 회의
3. fundraiser 기금 모금 행사; 기금 모금을 하는 사람

잠깐!

'제3자에게 확인하라 / 확인해보겠다'는 의미의 회피성 답변

· Let me check with someone. / Let me ask someone.
· Why don't you check it with someone?
· Someone is a better person to ask about it.
· Someone knows it better than me.
· Someone will be able to answer it for you.

Where 의문문의 질문과 응답 분석 🎧 P2-U04-3

아래 질문과 응답을 미국식과 영국식으로 듣고 따라읽으며 응답 유형을 익혀보세요.

정답 유형 1. 장소, 방향 표현

Q: Where can I get a train ticket? | 어디서 기차표를 살 수 있습니까?
A: You have to go to the east wing. | 동쪽 부속 건물로 가야 합니다.

정답 유형 2. 출처를 나타내는 사람 제시

Q: Where did you put the contract? | 계약서를 어디에 두셨죠?
A1: The vice president is reviewing it now. | 부사장이 지금 검토 중입니다.
A2: The receptionist in the lobby. | 로비에 있는 접수원에게요.

정답 유형 3. 회피성 또는 우회적 답변

Q: Where is the nearest bank? | 가장 가까운 은행이 어디에 있죠?
A1: Sorry, but I'm new here. | 죄송하지만 저는 이곳이 처음입니다.
A2: Sorry, but I'm not sure. | 죄송하지만 모르겠습니다.

어휘
1. wing 부속 건물, 별관
2. contract 계약서   vice president 부사장   review 검토하다   receptionist 접수원   lobby 로비

유사발음 및 다의어 1 P2-U04-4

유사발음				다의어	
coffee	커피	copy	복사	park	공원
expensive	비싼	extensive	광범위한		주차하다
plan	계획 (하다)	plant	식물; 공장	meet	만나다
leave	떠나다, 두다	live	살다		응하다, 충족시키다
read	읽다	lead	이끌다	hold	열다, 개최하다
walk	걷다	work	일하다		쥐다, 잡다
run	달리다	learn	배우다	store	상점
do	하다	due	~가 기한인		보관하다
contact	연락하다	contract	계약 (서)	book	책
close	닫다	clothes	옷		예약하다

예제

Q: When can I **contact** you? — 제가 언제 연락 드릴까요?
A: I am available after 3. (O) — 저는 3시 이후에 시간이 됩니다.
   You should sign the **contract** with them. (X) — 당신은 그들과 계약을 체결해야 합니다.

Q: Where should we **hold** the awards ceremony? — 시상식을 어디에서 개최할 겁니까?
A: The Royal Hotel has a grand ballroom. (O) — 로열 호텔이 대연회장을 갖고 있습니다.
   You should **hold** the handle tight. (X) — 당신은 손잡이를 꽉 잡아야 합니다.

받아쓰기 연습 해설 p.16

다의어 및 유사발음 어휘를 활용한 다음 질문과 보기의 음원을 듣고, 빈칸을 채워보세요.

1. _____ should I _____? — 어디에 주차를 해야 합니까?
   (A) Behind the _____. — 건물 뒤쪽에요.
   (B) The _____ is closed now. — 그 공원은 지금 닫혀 있습니다.

2. _____ can repair the _____ machine? — 누가 복사기를 수리할 수 있죠?
   (A) _____ the maintenance department. — 관리부서에 전화해 보세요.
   (B) There is a _____ shop on the corner. — 모퉁이에 커피숍이 있어요.

3. _____ is the sales report _____? — 매출 보고서 기한이 언제입니까?
   (A) _____. — 다음주 금요일입니다.
   (B) I have a lot of things to _____ today. — 저는 오늘 할 일이 많습니다.

청취 집중 훈련 1

의문사와 핵심 동사에 유의하며 음원을 듣고 빈칸을 채운 후 정답을 고르세요.

1. _____ can we _____ for the seminar?
   (A) _____ before the 25th.
   (B) The _____ was great.
   (C) Thank you for _____.

2. _____ do I have to _____ the report to?
   (A) To the accounting _____.
   (B) The least expensive one _____.
   (C) By the _____ of every month.

3. _____ do you think you'll _____ for lunch?
   (A) _____ the meeting.
   (B) Maybe that new seafood _____.
   (C) It was _____.

4. _____ will you _____ a customer survey?
   (A) Participants have to _____ the form.
   (B) To our _____ customers.
   (C) As _____ as I get the manager's approval.

5. _____ did you _____ yesterday?
   (A) I'm too _____ today.
   (B) I need to _____ a client.
   (C) I had a doctor's _____.

6. _____ is _____ the contest?
   (A) Oh, is he _____ to attend?
   (B) _____ on the sales team.
   (C) No, it was _____.

7. _____ the folders on my desk?
   (A) _____ dropped them off for you.
   (B) His _____ is in the corner.
   (C) Yes, they just need to be _____.

8. _____ can I get my shoes _____?
   (A) They are very _____.
   (B) I _____ all my clothes online.
   (C) There's a good _____ on Main Street.

청취 집중 훈련 2

보기만 제시되어 있는 다음 문제들을 듣고 질문에 알맞은 응답을 고르세요.

1. _____?

(A) No, I'd rather not.
(B) I haven't finished it yet.
(C) Before I leave the office.

2. _____?

(A) In the supply cabinet.
(B) The store is closed.
(C) Five or six pages.

3. _____?

(A) In Room C.
(B) Tomorrow at 2 P.M.
(C) Everybody attended.

4. _____?

(A) Yes, we charged the batteries.
(B) Just pay in cash this time.
(C) Janet handles it, I think.

5. _____?

(A) In the conference room.
(B) Thursday at 3, I think.
(C) To discuss the sales figures.

6. _____?

(A) I have no idea.
(B) No, it's in the same location.
(C) He stepped out a few minutes ago.

7. _____?

(A) I think Anna will.
(B) It has been postponed until next week.
(C) I really enjoy reading.

8. _____?

(A) About 250 pages long.
(B) I'll file it now.
(C) Ask the accounting manager.

청취 집중 훈련 3   P2-U04-7 / 해설 p.18

질문만 제시되어 있는 다음 문제들을 듣고 질문에 알맞은 응답을 고르세요.

1. When will the company announce staff promotions?
   (A)   (B)   (C)

2. Who is the new desk for?
   (A)   (B)   (C)

3. Where's Ms. Finchley?
   (A)   (B)   (C)

4. When is your doctor's appointment?
   (A)   (B)   (C)

5. Where can I exchange Japanese yen for U.S. dollars?
   (A)   (B)   (C)

6. Who's overseeing the Hamilton construction project?
   (A)   (B)   (C)

7. When is your job interview?
   (A)   (B)   (C)

8. Where is the nearest convenience store?
   (A)   (B)   (C)

실전 감각 익히기 🎧 P2-U04-8 / 해설 p.19-21

질문과 그에 따른 보기 세 개를 듣고 질문에 알맞은 응답을 고르세요.

1. (A) (B) (C)

2. (A) (B) (C)

3. (A) (B) (C)

4. (A) (B) (C)

5. (A) (B) (C)

6. (A) (B) (C)

7. (A) (B) (C)

8. (A) (B) (C)

9. (A) (B) (C)

10. (A) (B) (C)

UNIT 5 Why / How / What 의문문

★ 콕콕 찍어주는 출제 포인트

이번에는 이유나 목적을 묻는 의문사 why, 수단이나 방법 또는 진행 상황을 물어보는 how, 그리고 다양한 정보나 내용에 대해 물어보는 what을 학습해보겠습니다. 각각의 의문문은 매회 2~3문제 정도 출제되고 있습니다.

Why 의문문의 질문과 응답 분석 🎧 P2-U05-1

의문사 why가 이유나 목적을 물어보기 위해 사용될 때는 yes/no로 응답할 수 없습니다. 하지만 Why don't you/we ~?로 물어보면, '(당신이/우리가) ~하는 게 어때요?'라는 뜻의 제안 의문문이 되는데, 이 경우 yes/no로 응답할 수 있습니다. 다음에 제시된 why 의문문과 그 응답들을 미국식과 영국식으로 듣고 따라읽으며 응답 유형을 익혀보세요.

정답 유형 1. 이유나 목적을 묻는 질문에 to부정사로 응답

Q: **Why** did the company open a branch office?	회사는 왜 지점을 열었죠?
A: **To attract** more customers.	더 많은 고객들을 끌어들이기 위해서요.

정답 유형 2. 제안 의문문에 대한 수락/거절의 응답

Q: **Why don't you** take a subway?	지하철을 타는 게 어때요?
A: **Okay**, that sounds good.	네, 좋아요.

정답 유형 3. '모른다' 식의 답변

Q: **Why** did Greg resign last month?	그렉이 왜 지난달 사직했죠?
A: **No one has told me** about that.	아무도 그것에 대해 제게 얘기해주지 않았어요.

 1. branch office 지사, 지점　attract 끌어들이다, 유치하다　customer 고객
2. take a subway 지하철을 타다　sound ~하게 들리다
3. resign 사직하다

How 의문문의 질문과 응답 분석 🎧 P2-U05-2

의문사 how는 일반적으로 수단/방법(How), 수량(How many), 가격(How much), 기간(How long), 빈도(How often), 그리고 진행 상황(How is ~ing?) 및 의견(How about)을 물어볼 때 사용합니다. 아래 제시된 질문과 응답들을 미국식과 영국식으로 듣고 따라읽으며 응답 유형을 익혀보세요.

정답 유형 1. 수단이나 방법

Q: **How** would you like to pay for your purchase?	구입품에 대해 어떻게 지불하시겠어요?
A: **By** credit card.	신용카드로요.

정답 유형 2. 수량/가격/기간/빈도

Q1: **How many** computers did they order?	그들은 얼마나 많은 컴퓨터를 주문했나요?
A1: They wanted 10.	그들은 10대를 원했어요.
Q2: **How often** does the manager visit our plant?	부장이 얼마나 자주 우리 공장을 방문하죠?
A2: Normally once a month.	보통 한 달에 한 번입니다.

정답 유형 3. 진행 상황 및 의견

Q1: **How is** your advertising campaign *going*?	광고 캠페인은 어떻게 진행되고 있습니까?
A1: We are getting good reviews.	우리는 좋은 평가를 받고 있어요.
Q2: **How do you like** the product design?	제품 디자인이 어떻습니까?
A2: It's very impressive.	매우 인상적이에요.

어휘
1. pay for ~에 대해 지불하다   purchase 구매(품)
2. order 주문하다   manager 부장, 관리자   plant 공장   normally 보통
3. advertising 광고   review 평가   product design 제품 디자인   impressive 인상적인, 훌륭한

 잠깐!

빈도를 묻는 의문문에 대한 답변 유형

- once a week/month/year — 일주일/한 달/일 년에 한 번
- every week/month/year — 매주/매월/매년
- every (two, three…) weeks/months/years — 매 …주/달/해마다

UNIT 5

What 의문문의 질문과 응답 분석 P2-U05-3

What 의문문은 시간, 이름, 날씨, 방법, 이유, 종류 등 질문의 범위가 매우 다양해서, 다른 의문사의문문과 달리 특정 유형의 답변이 있지 않기 때문에 난이도가 꽤 높습니다. 다음 질문과 응답들을 미국식과 영국식으로 두 번씩 듣고 따라읽으며 다양한 응답을 익혀보세요.

정답 유형 1. 사실이나 정보

Q1: What is the fastest way to the head office? 본사에 가는 가장 빠른 방법은 뭐죠?
A1: Take the Amsterdam Highway. 암스테르담 고속도로를 이용하세요.

Q2: What are you working on these days? 요즘 무엇에 관한 일을 하고 계시나요?
A2: It's a new marketing strategy. 새로운 마케팅 전략에 관한 겁니다.

Q3: What time does the shopping mall close? 그 쇼핑몰은 몇 시에 문을 닫죠?
A3: They're open until 12. 그들은 12시까지 문을 열어요.

정답 유형 2. 회피성 또는 우회적 답변

Q: What is your delivery charge for online orders? 온라인 주문에 대한 배송비는 얼마입니까?
A: It depends on the destination. 그건 목적지가 어딘지에 달려 있습니다.

어휘
1. head office 본사 highway 고속도로 these days 요즘 strategy 전략 shopping mall 쇼핑몰 close (문을) 닫다, (영업을) 마치다
2. delivery 배달, 배송 charge 비용 online 온라인의 order 주문 depend on ~에 달려 있다, ~에 따라 다르다 destination 목적지

유사발음 및 다의어 2 🎧 P2-U05-4

유사발음

prepare	준비하다	repair	수리 (하다)
call	전화하다	cold	추운
ladder	사다리	letter	편지
replace	교체하다	place	장소; 두다
form	형식, 서식	firm	회사
lunch	점심	launch	출시 (하다)
low	낮은	law	법
apartment	아파트	department	부서
quite	꽤	quiet	조용한
inspect	점검하다	expect	예상하다

다의어

charge	청구하다
	담당, 책임
last	지난
	지속되다
show	공연
	보여주다
present	선물; 현재의
	제시하다
break	깨다
	휴식

예제

Q: How much did they **charge** you? 그들이 당신에게 얼마를 청구했습니까?
A: Almost 50 dollars. (O) 거의 50달러요.
    I am in **charge** of that. (X) 제가 그 일을 맡고 있습니다.

Q: How often do you **inspect** the equipment? 그 장비를 얼마나 자주 점검하나요?
A: On a monthly basis. (O) 매달 합니다.
    I don't **expect** that to happen. (X) 그런 일이 발생하리라고는 예상하지 않습니다.

✏️ 받아쓰기 연습 해설 p.21

다의어 및 유사발음 어휘를 활용한 다음 질문과 보기의 음원을 듣고, 빈칸을 채워보세요.

1 Why is Tim _____ customers? 팀은 왜 고객들에게 전화를 하고 있죠?
   (A) _____ inform them _____ clearance sale. 그들에게 재고정리 할인에 대해 알려주려고요.
   (B) It is very _____ today. 오늘 매우 춥습니다.

2 _____ did you replace the copier? 왜 복사기를 교체했죠?
   (A) It made a loud _____. 심한 잡음이 났어요.
   (B) I moved to a new _____. 저는 새로운 곳으로 옮겼어요.

3 What did she do _____ weekend? 그녀는 지난 주말에 무엇을 했나요?
   (A) She _____. 그녀는 하이킹을 갔어요.
   (B) The lecture _____ two hours. 그 강의는 두 시간 동안 진행됩니다.

청취 집중 훈련 1

의문사와 핵심 동사에 유의하며 음원을 듣고 빈칸을 채운 후 정답을 고르세요.

1. _____ was the training session _____?
   (A) The _____ already left.
   (B) The instructor had a scheduling _____.
   (C) I _____ a lot.

2. _____ is the Web site _____?
   (A) Usually every _____.
   (B) Yes, it _____ very new.
   (C) It'll _____ on January 7.

3. _____ of software does the accounting team _____?
   (A) They have to _____ formal clothing.
   (B) By the time the _____ is arrived.
   (C) _____ me check for you.

4. _____ were our _____ during the holiday period?
   (A) _____ two weeks.
   (B) Ten percent off _____.
   (C) Better _____ expected.

5. _____ will it take to _____ the items?
   (A) _____ the client.
   (B) _____ sea and air.
   (C) About 3 to 5 _____.

6. _____ we go out for _____ now?
   (A) I will _____ today's lunch special.
   (B) The restaurant is too _____.
   (C) Sure, _____ do you want to go?

7. _____ people _____ the competition?
   (A) I _____ first place.
   (B) There were about _____ hundred.
   (C) The _____ is through those doors.

8. _____ are you going to do at the convention?
   (A) No, I don't _____.
   (B) I'm giving a _____.
   (C) Yes, they often _____ it.

청취 집중 훈련 2   P2-U05-6 / 해설 p.22-23

보기만 제시되어 있는 다음 문제들을 듣고 질문에 알맞은 응답을 고르세요.

1. _____?
   (A) Good idea, I think I will.
   (B) We met yesterday.
   (C) No, it's before the meeting.

2. _____?
   (A) It's the smallest size.
   (B) It's $80.
   (C) It's leather.

3. _____?
   (A) Four more people.
   (B) They usually serve chicken.
   (C) They're for 6 o'clock.

4. _____?
   (A) About 9 A.M. at the latest.
   (B) Maybe the subway was delayed.
   (C) Sure, I'll call you if I'm late.

5. _____?
   (A) It was very informative.
   (B) No, I won't attend.
   (C) By shuttle bus.

6. _____?
   (A) It's still under development.
   (B) Antivirus program.
   (C) I need to type this report.

7. _____?
   (A) No, dinner's at 6 o'clock.
   (B) Right next to the dry cleaner's.
   (C) Okay, I heard their food is good.

8. _____?
   (A) It's very interesting.
   (B) Your signature is required.
   (C) I will ask and let you know soon.

UNIT 5

청취 집중 훈련 3   P2-U05-7 / 해설 p.23-25

질문만 제시되어 있는 다음 문제들을 듣고 질문에 알맞은 응답을 고르세요.

1. Why don't you give me a hand with this box?
   (A)   (B)   (C)

2. How do you usually come to work?
   (A)   (B)   (C)

3. What does Andy do at his firm?
   (A)   (B)   (C)

4. What time are you supposed to meet with your client?
   (A)   (B)   (C)

5. Why did Ms. Lee leave so suddenly?
   (A)   (B)   (C)

6. How did you like the concert?
   (A)   (B)   (C)

7. How much time should we allow to get to the airport?
   (A)   (B)   (C)

8. Why did Jack postpone his presentation?
   (A)   (B)   (C)

실전 감각 익히기   P2-U05-8 / 해설 p.25-26

질문과 그에 따른 보기 세 개를 듣고 질문에 알맞은 응답을 고르세요.

1. (A)   (B)   (C)

2. (A)   (B)   (C)

3. (A)   (B)   (C)

4. (A)   (B)   (C)

5. (A)   (B)   (C)

6. (A)   (B)   (C)

7. (A)   (B)   (C)

8. (A)   (B)   (C)

9. (A)   (B)   (C)

10. (A)   (B)   (C)

UNIT 6 일반의문문 / 선택의문문

★ 콕콕 찍어주는 출제 포인트
의문사를 사용하지 않는 의문문을 일반의문문이라고 하는데, 일반의문문에는 be동사의문문과 조동사 can, do, have 등을 사용하는 조동사의문문이 있으며, 의문사의문문과 달리 yes/no로 대답할 수 있습니다. 선택의문문은 or를 사용해서 두 가지 선택 사항을 제시하는 의문문을 말하는데, 둘 중 하나를 선택해야 하므로 yes/no로 응답할 수 없습니다.

Be동사의문문의 질문과 응답 분석 🎧 P2-U06-1

be동사로 시작하는 be동사의문문은 주로 주어의 신분, 성질이나 상태, 존재 여부 등을 물어볼 때 사용하며 yes나 no로 대답이 가능합니다. 아래 제시된 질문과 응답들을 미국식과 영국식으로 듣고 따라읽으며 다양한 응답을 익혀보세요.

정답 유형 1. 직업, 신분

Q: Was Katherine promoted last month? — 캐서린이 지난달 승진했나요?
A: Yes, she is vice president now. — 네, 그녀는 이제 부사장이에요.

정답 유형 2. 성질, 상태, 진행

Q: Are you finished preparing for the presentation? — 발표 준비는 끝났습니까?
A: Yes, I think I am ready. — 네, 준비가 되었다고 생각합니다.

정답 유형 3. 존재 유무

Q: Is there a copy machine on this floor? — 이 층에 복사기가 있습니까?
A: Yes, it's at the end of the hallway. — 네, 복도 끝에 있습니다.

어휘
1. be promoted 승진되다   vice president 부사장
2. finish ~ing ~하는 것을 마치다   prepare for ~을 준비하다   presentation 발표   ready 준비된
3. copy machine 복사기   hallway 복도

조동사의문문의 질문과 응답 분석 🎧 P2-U06-2

조동사의문문은 be동사를 제외한 do, have, can, will 등의 조동사로 시작하는 의문문으로, yes/no 응답이 가능합니다. 조동사의문문에서는 주어 뒤에 나오는 본동사가 의미의 중심이므로 본동사를 놓치지 말아야 하는데요. 아래 제시된 조동사의문문과 그 응답들을 미국식과 영국식으로 듣고 따라읽으며 다양한 응답을 연습해보세요.

정답 유형 1. 행위 중심(do의문문에 대한 응답)

Q: Did you send an application?	당신은 지원서를 보냈나요?
A: Yes, I emailed it yesterday.	네, 저는 어제 이메일로 보냈습니다.

정답 유형 2. 완료, 경험 중심(완료의 have동사로 시작하는 의문문에 대한 응답)

Q: Have you submitted the sales report?	매출 보고서를 제출했나요?
A: No, it's not due until 5 this afternoon.	아니요, 오늘 오후 5시가 마감 기한이에요.

정답 유형 3. 의지(will), 가능(can, may), 당위(should), 공손함(would, could)

Q1: Can you take a message now?	지금 메시지를 받아 적으실 수 있나요?
A1: Sure, just let me get a pen.	물론이죠. 제가 펜을 갖고 올게요.
Q2: Would you mind turning off the air conditioner?	에어컨을 꺼주시겠습니까?
A2: No, not at all.	네, 물론입니다.

어휘
1. application 지원서   email 이메일로 보내다
2. submit 제출하다   sales report 매출 보고서   due 만기가 된, 기한이 된
3. take a message 메시지를 받아 적다   Would you mind ~ing? ~해주시겠어요?   turn off (전원을) 끄다
   air conditioner 에어컨   not at all 전혀 ~ 아니다; 천만에요

선택의문문의 질문과 응답 분석 🎧 P2-U06-3

선택의문문은 중간에 or를 사용하여 A, B 두 가지 선택 사항을 제시하는 의문문입니다. 정답으로는 선택 사항 두 가지 중 하나를 고르거나, 둘 다 선택, 둘 다 거부, 또는 어떤 것이든 상관 없음으로 대답하는 경우가 많습니다. 아래 제시된 질문과 응답들을 미국식과 영국식으로 듣고 따라읽으며 다양한 응답을 익혀보세요.

정답 유형 1. **둘 중 하나 선택**	
Q: Do you want a laptop or desktop computer?	휴대용 컴퓨터를 원하세요, 탁상용 컴퓨터를 원하세요?
A: I'll have a laptop.	휴대용 컴퓨터로 하겠습니다.

정답 유형 2. **둘 다 선택 또는 둘 다 거부**	
Q: Are you going to bring a driver's license or passport?	운전면허증을 갖고 올 겁니까, 아니면 여권을 갖고 올 겁니까?
A: Both of them.	둘 다요.

정답 유형 3. **상관 없음 또는 제3의 선택**	
Q: Do you prefer a window seat or aisle seat?	창가 좌석을 원하세요, 통로 좌석을 원하세요?
A: Any seat is okay with me.	아무 좌석이라도 좋습니다.

어휘
1. laptop (computer) 휴대용 컴퓨터　desktop (computer) 탁상용 컴퓨터
2. driver's license 운전면허증　passport 여권
3. prefer 선호하다　aisle 복도, 통로

선택의문문에서 자주 정답으로 출제되는 표현

- Either is OK.   어느 쪽이든 괜찮아요. (= Either one is fine.)
- It doesn't matter.   상관 없어요.
- It makes no difference.   별 차이 없어요.
- It's up to you.   당신 뜻대로 하세요.
- Neither, thanks.   둘 다 별로네요, 어쨌든 고마워요.
- Whichever is 비교급.   더 ~한 쪽이 좋아요.

유사발음 및 다의어 3 P2-U06-4

유사발음				다의어	
colleague	직장 동료	college	대학	work	직장, 일; 작품
account	계정	count	세다		일하다; 작동되다
long	긴	wrong	잘못된	board	이사회
correct	올바른	collect	수집하다		탑승하다
hold	잡다; 개최하다	fold	접다	room	방
find	발견하다	fine	좋은; 벌금		공간; 가능성
closet	옷장	closed	닫힌	hand	손; 도움
personnel	인사과, 직원	personal	개인적인		건네다
resign	사직하다	design	설계하다	run	달리다
old	오래된	all	모든		경영하다

예제

Q: Did you draw the picture by **hand**? — 손으로 그린 그림입니까?
A: No, I used a graphic program. (O) — 아니요, 저는 그래픽 프로그램을 사용했습니다.
   I will give you a **hand**. (X) — 제가 당신을 도와드릴게요.

Q: Has Mr. Miller **resigned**? — 밀러 씨가 사직했나요?
A: No, he has moved to the Sydney office. (O) — 아니요, 그는 시드니 사무실로 옮겼습니다.
   He **designed** a variety of cars. (X) — 그는 다양한 자동차를 디자인했습니다.

받아쓰기 연습 해설 p.27

다의어 및 유사발음 어휘를 활용한 다음 질문과 보기의 음원을 듣고, 빈칸을 채워보세요.

1 Do you _____ coins or bills? — 동전을 수집합니까, 아니면 지폐를 수집합니까?
   (A) Neither of _____. — 둘 다 모으지 않습니다.
   (B) _____ are correct. — 당신이 옳습니다.

2 Is this a new model or _____ one? — 이것이 신형입니까, 아니면 구형입니까?
   (A) _____ released _____ yesterday. — 그것은 어제 막 출시되었습니다.
   (B) I will take _____ of them. — 저는 모두 다 선택하겠습니다.

3 _____ Ms. Crawford _____ her own business? — 크로포드 씨는 자신의 사업체를 운영합니까?
   (A) _____ she does. — 저는 그렇다고 생각합니다.
   (B) She _____ it from her parents. — 그녀는 부모님께 그것을 배웠습니다.

청취 집중 훈련 1   P2-U06-5 / 해설 p.27

조동사와 핵심 동사/명사에 유의하며 음원을 듣고 빈칸을 채운 후 정답을 고르세요.

1. _____ you _____ the extension for Mr. Ken's office?
   (A) Yes, it's 902.
   (B) His _____ is on the third floor.
   (C) Go down the _____ and to your left.

2. _____ I _____ a moving company?
   (A) Actually, he's _____ to a new city.
   (B) No, my friends are going to _____ me.
   (C) Call me at your convenience.

3. _____ you like to _____ in the center or on the side?
   (A) I _____ the center.
   (B) She's _____ inside.
   (C) It has a great _____.

4. _____ you _____ that Carol is leaving next week?
   (A) She _____ in Westchester.
   (B) No, I didn't _____ that.
   (C) No, but I can _____ you.

5. _____ there any salad _____?
   (A) It _____ with soup.
   (B) It's _____.
   (C) No, but more is being _____.

6. _____ you _____ helping me with these bags?
   (A) Sure, I'll _____ you later.
   (B) No, _____ at all.
   (C) Yes, I was _____ for them.

7. _____ you _____ a brochure?
   (A) To a _____.
   (B) It was _____.
   (C) Sure, I'll _____ you one.

8. _____ you like to _____ by cash or credit card?
   (A) We _____ major credit cards.
   (B) Sure, here's my _____ card.
   (C) I'll pay by _____.

청취 집중 훈련 2 🎧 P2-U06-6 / 해설 p.28-29

보기만 제시되어 있는 다음 문제들을 듣고 질문에 알맞은 응답을 고르세요.

1. _____ ?

(A) Please, put them on the table.
(B) Oh, I forgot to do it.
(C) I will treat you to dinner tonight.

2. _____ ?

(A) Sorry, I'm working on something urgent.
(B) No, I don't have any.
(C) They're usually busy on Saturdays.

3. _____ ?

(A) I couldn't catch what he said.
(B) The fare was less than $10.
(C) Yes, there's a cab stand up the street.

4. _____ ?

(A) It's five cents per copy.
(B) I saw the advertisement in the paper.
(C) How many pieces do you want?

5. _____ ?

(A) No, it's too far to walk.
(B) The train departed on time.
(C) They will build a new station.

6. _____ ?

(A) It's very important.
(B) Yes, it's from Italy.
(C) No, I'm not going to purchase it.

7. _____ ?

(A) Here you go.
(B) I plan to go later.
(C) The plants are growing well.

8. _____ ?

(A) Thank you for the invitation.
(B) I think that we should.
(C) I am honored to receive this award.

청취 집중 훈련 3

질문만 제시되어 있는 다음 문제들을 듣고 질문에 알맞은 응답을 고르세요.

1. Are there any samples left?
   (A) (B) (C)

2. Would you rather walk to the office or take a subway?
   (A) (B) (C)

3. Does the store have a delivery service?
   (A) (B) (C)

4. Did you hear taxi fares are going up?
   (A) (B) (C)

5. Can you join us for a quick meeting?
   (A) (B) (C)

6. Does this bus go to Central Plaza?
   (A) (B) (C)

7. Should we have our office party this weekend or next?
   (A) (B) (C)

8. Is there anything you want to find?
   (A) (B) (C)

실전 감각 익히기 🎧 P2-U06-8 / 해설 p.31–32

질문과 그에 따른 보기 세 개를 듣고 질문에 알맞은 응답을 고르세요.

1. (A)　(B)　(C)

2. (A)　(B)　(C)

3. (A)　(B)　(C)

4. (A)　(B)　(C)

5. (A)　(B)　(C)

6. (A)　(B)　(C)

7. (A)　(B)　(C)

8. (A)　(B)　(C)

9. (A)　(B)　(C)

10. (A)　(B)　(C)

UNIT 7 간접의문문 / 부정의문문 / 부가의문문

★ **콕콕 찍어주는 출제 포인트**

간접의문문은 점차 출제 빈도가 줄어 매회 1문항 내외 등장하지만 의외로 많은 수험자가 틀리는 유형이므로 잘 알아두어야 합니다. 부정의문문과 부가의문문은 파트 후반부에 등장하며 매회 2~3문항씩 출제되고 난이도가 있는 편이어서 고득점을 확보하기 위해 반드시 숙지해야 할 문제 유형입니다.

간접의문문의 질문과 응답 분석 🎧 P2-U07-1

간접의문문은 Do you know what ~?, Can you tell me why ~? 등과 같이 일반의문문 뒤에 의문사의문문이 결합된 형태로서, yes / no 응답이 가능하지만 문장 중간에 나오는 의문사에 초점을 맞춰 응답해야 합니다. 아래 질문과 응답을 미국식과 영국식으로 듣고 따라읽으며 응답 유형을 익혀보세요.

정답 유형 1. 시간 / 장소 중심 응답 (When / Where 관련 응답)

Q: Do you know when our next meeting will be held?   다음 회의가 언제 열리는지 아세요?
A: It won't take place until next month.   다음 달에나 열릴 겁니다.

정답 유형 2. 대상 / 사물 중심 응답 (Who / What 관련 응답)

Q: Can you tell me who was chosen as the winner?   누가 우승자로 뽑혔는지 말씀해주실래요?
A: Yes, Ms. Kim in accounting.   네, 경리부서의 김 씨입니다.

정답 유형 3. 이유 / 방법 중심 응답 (Why / How 관련 응답)

Q: May I ask why you were absent from the workshop?   연수에 왜 불참했는지 여쭤봐도 될까요?
A: I wasn't feeling well.   제가 몸이 좋지 않았어요.

---

 1. meeting 회의   be held (회의·행사 등이) 열리다   take place (행사 등이) 일어나다, 개최되다
2. choose 선택하다, 뽑다(choose-chose-chosen)   winner 우승자   accounting (department) 경리부서
3. absent from ~에 불참한   workshop 연수, 워크숍

부정의문문의 질문과 응답 분석 🎧 P2-U07-2

부정의문문은 be동사, do동사, 또는 조동사(can, will 등)에 not을 결합시켜 Isn't she ~, Don't they ~, Can't you ~와 같이 시작하는 의문문을 말하는데요, 응답은 긍정의문문과 마찬가지로 응답자의 입장에서 긍정이면 yes, 부정이면 no로 대답합니다. 아래 질문과 응답을 미국식과 영국식으로 듣고 따라읽으며 응답 유형을 익혀보세요.

정답 유형 1. 긍정 응답

Q: **Aren't you** coming to the party tonight?	오늘밤 파티에 오지 않을 건가요?
A: **Yes, I'm** looking forward to it.	물론 가죠. 저는 매우 기대하고 있어요.

정답 유형 2. 부정 응답

Q: **Don't** you want to work the night shift?	야간 근무를 원하지 않으세요?
A: **No**, I have to take an evening class.	네, 저는 저녁 수업을 들어야 해서요.

정답 유형 3. 조동사 반복 응답

Q: **Hasn't Clara** asked for a transfer to New York?	클라라가 뉴욕 전근을 요청하지 않았나요?
A1: **Yes, she has.**	네, 그녀는 요청을 했습니다.
A2: **No, she hasn't.**	아니요, 그녀는 요청을 하지 않았습니다.

정답 유형 4. 긍정/부정 생략 답변

Q: **Won't** the shipment be here by noon?	선적물이 정오까지 이곳에 오지 않을까요?
A: **Actually**, it already arrived this morning.	사실 오늘 아침에 벌써 도착했습니다.

어휘
1. tonight 오늘밤　look forward to ~을 고대하다
2. shift 근무조, 교대조　take a class 수업을 듣다
3. ask for ~을 요청하다　transfer 전근, 이동
4. shipment 선적물　actually 사실, 실은

 잠깐!

부정의 의미를 내포하는 전환어구
· well 글쎄요.　· in fact 사실　· actually 실제로　· I think 제 생각에

부가의문문의 질문과 응답 분석 🎧 P2-U07-3

부가의문문은 상대방의 동의를 구하거나 내용을 확인하기 위해 평서문 끝에 〈동사 + 주어?〉 형태로 덧붙이는 의문문인데요. 부가의문문의 동사는 앞에 제시된 평서문의 동사와 긍정/부정 관계가 역전됩니다. 부가의문문이 부정인지 긍정인지에 상관 없이, 부가의문문 앞에 나오는 평서문의 주어와 동사에 초점을 맞추어 응답해야 합니다. 아래 질문과 응답을 미국식과 영국식으로 듣고 따라읽으며 응답 유형을 익혀보세요.

정답 유형 1. 현재시제 응답

Q: You are an architect, aren't you?	당신은 건축가죠, 그렇죠?
A1: Yes, I am.	네, 맞습니다.
A2: No, I'm not.	아니요, 아닙니다.

정답 유형 2. 과거시제 응답

Q: The employees worked late last night, didn't they?	직원들이 어젯밤 야근을 했죠, 그렇죠?
A1: Yes, they did.	네, 그랬어요.
A2: No, they didn't.	아니요, 안 했습니다.

정답 유형 3. 조동사 응답

Q: Bolton and Martin will return tomorrow, won't they?	볼튼과 마틴이 내일 돌아오죠, 그렇죠?
A1: Yes, they will.	네, 그럴 겁니다.
A2: No, they won't be back until next Monday.	아니요, 다음주 월요일에나 돌아올 겁니다.

어휘
1. architect 건축가
2. employee 직원

잠깐!

부가의문문에서 정답으로 자주 출제되는 표현

- That's true. — 그건 사실이에요.
- That's what I heard, too. — 저도 그렇게 들었어요.
- I don't know. — 모르겠어요.
- It is still uncertain. — 아직 불확실해요.

유사발음 및 다의어 4 P2-U07-4

유사발음				다의어	
car	차	card	카드	house	집
kitchen	주방	chicken	닭		보관[수용]하다
sample	견본	example	예	order	순서, 명령
concert	콘서트	concern	염려		주문 (하다)
fix	고치다	fax	팩스 (로 보내다)	outstanding	뛰어난
think	생각하다	sink	싱크대		미납의
late	늦은	rate	요금, 비율	return	돌아가다
except	~을 제외하고	accept	받아들이다		반납하다
alone	혼자	along	~을 따라	decline	거절하다
ready	준비된	already	이미		하락하다

예제

Q: You traveled **alone**, didn't you? — 당신은 혼자 여행을 갔죠, 그렇죠?
A: No, I went with my friends. (O) — 아니요, 저는 친구와 함께 갔습니다.
　Yes, we walked **along** the beach. (X) — 네, 우리는 해변을 따라 걸었습니다.

Q: Don't you want to **order** any dessert? — 어떤 후식도 주문하고 싶지 않으세요?
A: No, thank you. (O) — 아니요, 괜찮습니다.
　The meals are listed in **order** of price. (X) — 음식들은 가격 순서로 나열되어 있습니다.

받아쓰기 연습 해설 p.33

다의어 및 유사발음 어휘를 활용한 다음 질문과 보기의 음원을 듣고, 빈칸을 채워보세요.

1 Do you know _____ our sales _____ last month? — 왜 지난달 매출이 하락했는지 아세요?
　(A) _____ a lot of people went on vacation. — 많은 사람들이 휴가를 갔기 때문입니다.
　(B) You shouldn't have _____ the offer. — 당신은 그 제안을 거절하지 말았어야 했어요.

2 _____ the documents _____ for the meeting? — 회의를 위해 서류들이 준비되지 않았나요?
　(A) Yes, they are _____ on each desk. — 네, 각각의 책상 위에 올려져 있습니다.
　(B) It _____ began 10 minutes ago. — 10분 전에 이미 시작되었습니다.

3 May I ask _____ the _____ was postponed? — 콘서트가 왜 연기되었는지 여쭤봐도 될까요?
　(A) There were some problems with the _____. — 장비에 몇 가지 문제가 있었어요.
　(B) I am _____ about it. — 저는 그것에 대해 걱정됩니다.

UNIT 7

청취 집중 훈련 1   P2-U07-5 / 해설 p.33

질문 앞 부분과 핵심 표현에 유의하며 음원을 듣고 빈칸을 채운 후 정답을 고르세요.

1. Can you tell us _____ we _____ the museum?
   (A) It's out of my _____.
   (B) No, you _____.
   (C) Okay, don't _____.

2. _____ you going to the _____ this afternoon?
   (A) No, I _____ this morning.
   (B) I deposited the _____.
   (C) No, I _____.

3. The _____ is on Friday, _____ it?
   (A) We are behind _____.
   (B) Yes, at _____ sharp.
   (C) _____ is Wednesday.

4. You _____ tickets for the movie, _____ you?
   (A) It's a _____.
   (B) I've never _____ it before.
   (C) Sorry, I haven't had a _____.

5. _____ this John's latest _____?
   (A) He was 30 minutes _____.
   (B) Yes, it _____ out last Friday.
   (C) He is a good _____.

6. Do you know _____ the next train will _____?
   (A) Not for _____ 10 minutes.
   (B) It'll _____ tomorrow morning.
   (C) The _____ to Centerville.

7. _____ we _____ for Mr. Harrington?
   (A) He's _____ there.
   (B) He's the one in the brown _____.
   (C) I can _____ you for 3 o'clock.

8. Smith is _____ a speech in Oakland, _____ he?
   (A) I haven't _____ yet.
   (B) No, he _____.
   (C) Yes, at the Devlin _____.

청취 집중 훈련 2

보기만 제시되어 있는 다음 문제들을 듣고 질문에 알맞은 응답을 고르세요.

1. _____?
- (A) It will be fun.
- (B) No, I didn't have time to.
- (C) Yes, I want to see it.

2. _____?
- (A) It was exciting.
- (B) Yes, at 6:30.
- (C) In the main stadium.

3. _____?
- (A) No, Francis did.
- (B) I didn't realize that.
- (C) I pressed the button.

4. _____?
- (A) No, when did he send it?
- (B) I'll send it before I leave for the day.
- (C) Mr. Jack is in his office.

5. _____?
- (A) That's not my pencil.
- (B) Could you close it, please?
- (C) No, we're all out.

6. _____?
- (A) They always provide good service.
- (B) Yes, it stopped working earlier.
- (C) Yes, you can take the elevator.

7. _____?
- (A) Yes, the store is open now.
- (B) Yes, but there is no room.
- (C) It's on the first floor.

8. _____?
- (A) Yes, before lunch.
- (B) No employee has come yet.
- (C) No, he was five minutes late.

청취 집중 훈련 3 P2-U07-7 / 해설 p.35-36

질문만 제시되어 있는 다음 문제들을 듣고 질문에 알맞은 응답을 고르세요.

1. Don't you want to try the new restaurant?
   (A)   (B)   (C)

2. May I ask why you work from home?
   (A)   (B)   (C)

3. Do you know where the nearest convenience store is?
   (A)   (B)   (C)

4. Aren't we supposed to finish this report today?
   (A)   (B)   (C)

5. The new interns start working today, don't they?
   (A)   (B)   (C)

6. We can reserve train tickets by phone, can't we?
   (A)   (B)   (C)

7. The discussion ends at 3, doesn't it?
   (A)   (B)   (C)

8. Do you know where the staff lounge is?
   (A)   (B)   (C)

실전 감각 익히기 🎧 P2 - U07 - 8 / 해설 p.37–38

질문과 그에 따른 보기 세 개를 듣고 질문에 알맞은 응답을 고르세요.

1. (A) (B) (C)

2. (A) (B) (C)

3. (A) (B) (C)

4. (A) (B) (C)

5. (A) (B) (C)

6. (A) (B) (C)

7. (A) (B) (C)

8. (A) (B) (C)

9. (A) (B) (C)

10. (A) (B) (C)

UNIT 8　평서문

★ 콕콕 찍어주는 출제 포인트

의문사나 조동사 없이 바로 〈주어 + 동사〉로 시작하며 문장 끝에 마침표가 있는 문장이 평서문입니다. 평서문은 난이도가 높은 편으로, 매회 3~5문제 정도 출제되고 있는데요. 주어, 동사, 목적어와 같은 핵심어에 초점을 맞추어 들어야 합니다.

 평서문의 질문과 응답 분석　🎧 P2-U08-1

평서문의 내용은 날씨 상황, 회의 일정, 주문 내역, 주말 계획, 회사 업무 등 매우 다양합니다. 평서문에는 긍정/부정 또는 동의/반대의 응답이 가능하지만, yes/no를 생략한 채 역질문이나 우회적 답변으로 응답하는 경우가 많으니 주의해야 합니다.

정답 유형 1. 긍정적인 답변

A: I need to renew my license.　저는 면허증을 갱신해야 합니다.
B: OK, just fill out this form.　좋아요. 이 양식을 작성해주세요.

정답 유형 2. 부정이나 반대되는 답변

A: The deadline for the application is tomorrow.　신청 마감일은 내일입니다.
B: No, it has been extended until next Monday.　아니에요. 다음 주 월요일까지 연장되었어요.

정답 유형 3. 역질문 또는 우회적 답변

A: I'd like to check on my order.　제 주문을 확인하고 싶습니다.
B: What's your order number?　주문번호가 어떻게 되시죠?

평서문에 대한 〈긍정적 답변〉
- yes 네
- great 좋아요
- I think so 그렇습니다
- no problem 그럼요
- sure 물론입니다
- of course 당연하죠
- thank you 감사합니다
- all right 그렇습니다

평서문에 대한 〈부정적 답변〉
- sorry 죄송합니다
- I don't think so 그렇지 않습니다
- well 글쎄요
- in fact 사실
- actually 사실은

유사발음 및 다의어 5 🎧 P2-U08-2

유사발음				다의어	
road	길	load	~에 (짐을) 싣다	leave	휴가
world	세상	word	단어		~에 두다; 떠나다
grass	풀	glass	유리	free	자유로운
cross	건너다	across	~을 가로질러		무료의
won't	will not의 축약형	want	원하다	carry	나르다, 운반하다
bedroom	침실	bathroom	욕실		(상점에서 상품을) 취급하다
view	보다	review	검토 (하다)	bill	지폐; 법안
day	하루; 요일	date	날짜		청구서
tire	(자동차) 타이어	tired	피곤한	address	주소 (를 쓰다); 연설
very	아주	vary	다르다; 변하다		다루다

예제

A: Let me help you **load** the truck with boxes. 제가 트럭에 상자를 싣는 것을 도와줄게요.
B: I'd appreciate that. (O) 그렇게 해주시면 고맙겠습니다.
   You have to look at the **road** signs. (X) 당신은 도로 표지판을 봐야 합니다.

A: We **carry** a variety of household appliances. 우리는 다양한 가전제품을 취급합니다.
B: OK, can you show me some washing machines? (O) 좋아요, 세탁기 좀 보여주실래요?
   They are too heavy to **carry**. (X) 그것들은 너무 무거워서 나를 수가 없어요.

받아쓰기 연습 해설 p.38

다의어 및 유사발음 어휘를 활용한 다음 질문과 보기의 음원을 듣고, 빈칸을 채워보세요.

1 You should ＿＿＿＿ books by the due ＿＿＿＿. 마감날짜까지 책을 반납해야 합니다.
   (A) OK, I ＿＿＿＿. 좋아요. 그렇게 할게요.
   (B) I ＿＿＿＿ books all ＿＿＿＿ yesterday. 저는 어제 하루 종일 책을 읽었습니다.

2 I'm supposed to ＿＿＿＿ an ＿＿＿＿ tomorrow. 제가 내일 연설을 하기로 되어 있습니다.
   (A) You will do a ＿＿＿＿ job. 잘 해낼 겁니다.
   (B) It was ＿＿＿＿ to the wrong ＿＿＿＿. 그것은 엉뚱한 주소로 배달되었습니다.

3 I'd like you to ＿＿＿＿ the manuscript. 원고를 검토해주시면 좋겠어요.
   (A) Actually, I ＿＿＿＿ did it. 사실 벌써 다 했습니다.
   (B) You can ＿＿＿＿ our creations ＿＿＿＿. 온라인으로 우리의 창작품을 볼 수 있습니다.

청취 집중 훈련 1

주어, 동사, 목적어 등 문장의 핵심어에 유의하며 음원을 듣고 빈칸을 채운 후 정답을 고르세요.

1. I need to _____ a new _____.
   (A) I haven't _____ him.
   (B) I'll put out an _____.
   (C) You _____ me a lot.

2. _____ go _____.
   (A) Sure, at _____ time?
   (B) No, it _____.
   (C) No, I _____ been there yet.

3. I'm not _____ very _____.
   (A) She said she _____ it.
   (B) _____ don't you go home early?
   (C) No, it was _____.

4. I'd like to _____ my _____.
   (A) I've _____ for the seminar.
   (B) All right, your ticket _____, please.
   (C) I'll be _____ tomorrow at two.

5. These _____ need to be _____.
   (A) I _____ the files by e-mail.
   (B) No, _____ are they?
   (C) Sure, I'll _____ care of that.

6. I'm thinking of _____ the _____.
   (A) He _____ he would.
   (B) Where do you want to _____ it?
   (C) That's a good _____.

7. I need a _____ to _____ some things.
   (A) What _____ do you need?
   (B) There's _____ in the drawer.
   (C) You can _____ tickets at the box office.

8. I _____ this _____ would stop.
   (A) It's the next _____.
   (B) Just let me _____ when.
   (C) It's supposed to _____ the entire week.

청취 집중 훈련 2   P2-U08-4 / 해설 p.39-41

보기만 제시되어 있는 다음 문제들을 듣고 질문에 알맞은 응답을 고르세요.

1. _____?

(A) Yes, he saw it yesterday.
(B) Okay, I'll let him know.
(C) We didn't hear the news.

2. _____?

(A) Admission for children under 12 is free.
(B) You can visit me anytime.
(C) Sure, let's go on Saturday.

3. _____?

(A) I'm sorry, we only take cash.
(B) You will be paid by the hour.
(C) It only takes a minute to apply.

4. _____?

(A) I looked at it on the Web site.
(B) I lost them.
(C) Is there a particular one you'd like?

5. _____?

(A) Oh no, please find out how long.
(B) No, she put them on the table.
(C) Please make double-sided copies.

6. _____?

(A) Okay, let me get a pen.
(B) I'll give you a massage.
(C) Tom called you this morning.

7. _____?

(A) No, I remember to close them.
(B) Thank you for reminding me.
(C) I still need to pack for the trip.

8. _____?

(A) Where should I sign it?
(B) No, I haven't contacted them yet.
(C) Congratulations.

UNIT 8

청취 집중 훈련 3 P2-U08-5 / 해설 p.41-42

질문만 제시되어 있는 다음 문제들을 듣고 질문에 알맞은 응답을 고르세요.

1. I'll pick you up at seven sharp this evening.
   (A)   (B)   (C)

2. The bathroom sink is leaking.
   (A)   (B)   (C)

3. I'm going to be late for work tomorrow.
   (A)   (B)   (C)

4. If the radio is too loud, I can turn it down.
   (A)   (B)   (C)

5. I think I'm catching a cold.
   (A)   (B)   (C)

6. I have ten copies of the report for the presentation.
   (A)   (B)   (C)

7. Let's invite George to our grand opening.
   (A)   (B)   (C)

8. It's raining really hard outside.
   (A)   (B)   (C)

실전 감각 익히기   🎧 P2-U08-6 / 해설 p.42-44

질문과 그에 따른 보기 세 개를 듣고 질문에 알맞은 응답을 고르세요.

1. (A)   (B)   (C)

2. (A)   (B)   (C)

3. (A)   (B)   (C)

4. (A)   (B)   (C)

5. (A)   (B)   (C)

6. (A)   (B)   (C)

7. (A)   (B)   (C)

8. (A)   (B)   (C)

9. (A)   (B)   (C)

10. (A)   (B)   (C)

PART 2　Review Test

질문과 그에 따른 보기 듣고 질문에 알맞은 응답을 고르세요.

1.	(A)	(B)	(C)	16. (A)	(B)	(C)
2.	(A)	(B)	(C)	17. (A)	(B)	(C)
3.	(A)	(B)	(C)	18. (A)	(B)	(C)
4.	(A)	(B)	(C)	19. (A)	(B)	(C)
5.	(A)	(B)	(C)	20. (A)	(B)	(C)
6.	(A)	(B)	(C)	21. (A)	(B)	(C)
7.	(A)	(B)	(C)	22. (A)	(B)	(C)
8.	(A)	(B)	(C)	23. (A)	(B)	(C)
9.	(A)	(B)	(C)	24. (A)	(B)	(C)
10.	(A)	(B)	(C)	25. (A)	(B)	(C)
11.	(A)	(B)	(C)	26. (A)	(B)	(C)
12.	(A)	(B)	(C)	27. (A)	(B)	(C)
13.	(A)	(B)	(C)	28. (A)	(B)	(C)
14.	(A)	(B)	(C)	29. (A)	(B)	(C)
15.	(A)	(B)	(C)	30. (A)	(B)	(C)

PART 3

- **Unit 9** 업무
- **Unit 10** 사무기기 / 주문 / 구매 / 계약
- **Unit 11** 여행 / 여가 / 교통 / 쇼핑
- **Unit 12** 부동산 / 은행 / 병원 / 호텔 / 식당 (기타 일상 생활)
- **Part 3** Review Test

UNIT 9 업무

★ 콕콕 찍어주는 출제 포인트

Part 3 대화 문제에서 가장 자주 등장하는 주제가 회사 업무인데, 보다 세부적으로 주제를 나누면 회의 참석, 출장, 승진, 은퇴, 시상식, 일정 변경, 주문 및 배달, 사무기기 고장 등이 있습니다. Part 3는 먼저 문제와 보기를 빠르게 읽어서 사전 지식을 갖고 대화 내용을 듣는 것이 훨씬 유리하므로, 평상시 문제와 보기를 미리 읽고 푸는 연습을 많이 해둘 필요가 있습니다.

빈출 질문 익히기

- Where does this conversation most likely take place? — 이 대화는 어디에서 일어나겠는가?
- When is the meeting scheduled to begin? — 회의는 언제 시작할 예정인가?
- What is the woman asked to do? — 여자는 무엇을 하라고 요청 받았는가?
- When will the man be at the office? — 남자는 언제 사무실에 있을 것인가?
- Why does the man plan to call his clients? — 남자는 왜 고객들에게 전화 걸 계획인가?

문제 보기

1. What is the man doing?
   (A) Filing a complaint
   (B) Delivering a package
   (C) Making an appointment
   (D) Discussing a project

2. In what department does Mr. Dunwoody work?
   (A) Sales
   (B) Design
   (C) Marketing
   (D) Customer service

3. What will the man most likely do next?
   (A) Fill out a form
   (B) Write his name
   (C) Go to another floor
   (D) Open a package

1. 남자는 무엇을 하고 있는가?
   (A) 불만 제기
   (B) 소포 배달
   (C) 약속 잡기
   (D) 프로젝트에 대한 논의

2. 던우디 씨는 어느 부서에서 일하는가?
   (A) 영업
   (B) 디자인
   (C) 마케팅
   (D) 고객 서비스

3. 남자가 아마도 무엇을 하겠는가?
   (A) 양식을 작성한다.
   (B) 그의 이름을 쓴다.
   (C) 다른 층으로 간다.
   (D) 소포를 열어본다.

대화 보기 🎧 P3-U09-1

다음 대화를 미국식과 영국식으로 들어보세요.

M: Hello, I **have a delivery**[1] here for Mr. Felix Dunwoody. Where is his office?

W: I'm sorry, but who is the package for? I'm not familiar with that name.

M: Felix Dunwoody? It says here that **he's in the design department**[2] on the 15th floor.

W: Hold on a moment, sir. Let me look up his name. Oh yes, I see. **He's actually on the 14th floor.**[3]

 delivery 배달, 배달물   package 소포   be familiar with ~에 익숙하다   it says that ~ 그것에 ~라고 써 있다   floor 층
hold on a moment 잠깐만 기다리다   look up 찾아보다   actually 사실, 실제

문제 해설

1. 질문의 키워드: 무엇(What), 남자(man)
→ 남자의 대사에 초점을 맞춰 들어야 한다. 문제 중 첫 번째 문제의 정답은 대개 대화 초반부에 등장한다.

2. 질문의 키워드: 어느 부서(what department), 던우디 씨(Mr. Dunwoody)
→ 근무 부서를 묻는 질문으로, 남자의 후반 대사에서 유일하게 부서명(design department)이 언급되고 있다.

3. 질문의 키워드: 무엇(What), 남자(man), 다음에 하다(do next)
→ 미래 행동에 대한 단서는 대화 후반부를 주목해야 한다.

업무 관련 어휘 및 관용 표현 🎧 P3-U09-2

업무 관련 어휘

agenda 안건
participant 참석자
schedule 일정; 일정을 잡다
conference call 전화 회의
office supplies 사무용품
copier 복사기 (=copy machine)
laptop 노트북
refrigerator 냉장고
cartridge 카트리지
applicant 지원자
candidate 후보자
résumé 이력서
job opening 공석
qualified 자격이 있는
contract 계약
temporary worker 임시 직원
hire 고용하다
hold (회의 따위를) 열다, 개최하다
review 검토하다
revise 수정하다

업무 관련 관용 표현

make/give/deliver a presentation 발표하다
go/look over 검토하다
hand/turn in 제출하다
fill out/complete a form 양식을 작성하다
place an order for ~을 주문하다
meet the deadline 마감일을 맞추다
get a promotion 승진하다
take a business trip 출장 가다
put off 연기하다 (=postpone)
call off 취소하다 (=cancel)
commute to work 통근하다
ahead of[behind] schedule 일정보다 빠른[늦은]
launch a product 제품을 출시하다
lay off 해고하다 (=fire, dismiss)
resign from ~를 사직하다
apply for a job 일자리에 지원하다
call in sick 아파서 결근하겠다고 전화하다
take a day off 하루 휴가를 내다
 (*cf.* be on vacation 휴가 중이다)

✏️ 어휘 및 표현 점검 해설 p.50

우리말 뜻을 보고 빈칸에 알맞은 단어를 넣으세요.

1 We had to work overtime to meet the _____. 우리는 마감을 맞추기 위해 야근을 해야 했습니다.
2 Can you _____ this report, please? 이 보고서 좀 검토해 주시겠어요?
3 I need to _____ to attend my sister's wedding. 여동생 결혼식에 참석하기 위해 하루 휴가를 내야 합니다.
4 There are too many _____ for the job. 그 일자리에 지원한 사람이 너무 많습니다.
5 I often _____ abroad. 저는 해외로 출장을 자주 갑니다.

청취 집중 훈련 1

아래 제시된 대화의 음원을 듣고 빈칸을 채워보세요.

1. 한 단어 받아쓰기 연습

W: Where do you _____ we should take Ms. Pritchard for the lunch _____?

M: Well, why _____ we take her to O'Charley's? We know they have good _____.

W: Yes, but I'm tired of _____ there. I think we should try _____ a little different, with a _____ menu.

M: Oh, then we should go to Dovington Gardens. They have a wide _____ of salads and healthy food. It'll be a good place for a meeting, too, because it's _____.

여: 우리가 점심 회의를 위해 프리챠드 씨를 어디로 데리고 가야 할까요?

남: 음, 오찰리스로 데려가는 게 어떨까요? 우리가 알기에 그들의 음식은 훌륭하잖아요.

여: 네, 하지만 저는 그곳에서 먹는 게 싫증이 나요. 건강에 좋은 메뉴가 있는 좀 다른 곳을 가볼까 하는데요.

남: 아, 그럼 도빙튼 가든스로 가죠. 그곳엔 다양한 샐러드와 건강에 좋은 음식이 있잖아요. 또한 조용하기 때문에 회의 장소로도 좋을 겁니다.

2. 두 단어 이상 받아쓰기 연습

M: Good morning, Ms. Rothkowitz. Today you _____ with Mr. Greer at 11:00 A.M. Also, a Ms. James from Spark Systems _____. What would you like me to say?

W: I'm not _____ Spark Systems. Do you know what it is about?

M: Spark Systems is a technology review organization. Ms. James wants to _____ about our _____ of the Air Draw software.

W: Oh, that would be good publicity. Sure, _____ with her.

남: 안녕하세요, 로스코비츠 씨. 오늘 오전 11시에 그리어 씨와 회의가 있습니다. 그리고 스파크 시스템의 제임스라는 사람이 인터뷰를 요청했습니다. 제가 어떻게 전할까요?

여: 저는 스파크 시스템스가 생소하군요. 어떤 회사인지 아세요?

남: 스파크 시스템스는 기술 평가 기관입니다. 제임스 씨는 우리의 에어 드로 소프트웨어 제품 출시에 관해 인터뷰를 하고자 합니다.

여: 오, 좋은 홍보 기회군요. 좋아요, 그녀와의 미팅 일정을 잡아주세요.

UNIT 9 **87**

청취 집중 훈련 2

제시된 두 문제를 재빨리 훑어본 후, 핵심 내용을 빈칸 처리한 채 제시된 대화의 음원을 들으며 정답을 고르세요.

1. What does the man ask the woman about?
   (A) A price quote   (B) A guest list

2. What is the problem?
   (A) A number is not certain.   (B) A price was raised.

M: Pamela, did you print out _____ for the _____ banquet?
W: No, I didn't. Not everyone has confirmed _____ yet.
M: OK, let me know _____ of participants as soon as possible.

3. What is the woman doing?
   (A) Making copies   (B) Making spreadsheets

4. What event will be held next week?
   (A) A conference   (B) An awards ceremony

M: Olivia, _____ or do you have time to help me now?
W: Well, I have to _____ first, but I should be free after that.
M: Can you book a hotel for _____ on organic farming next weekend?

5. Why is the man calling?
   (A) To postpone an appointment   (B) To make an appointment

6. What does Mr. Lawrence want to review?
   (A) Blue prints   (B) Construction costs

M: Hello, Ms. West. I'm calling to _____ with you for some time next week.
W: Sure, Mr. Lawrence. What is the appointment about?
M: It's about the _____. I just want to _____ with you.

청취 집중 훈련 3   🎧 P3-U09-5 / 해설 p.51~52

각 대화를 듣고 그에 관련된 두 문제를 풀어보세요.

1. What is the problem with the man's computer?

   (A) It is very slow.
   (B) It will not turn on.
   (C) It will arrive late.
   (D) It is not connected to the printer.

2. What does the woman suggest the man do?

   (A) Request a new computer
   (B) Use her computer
   (C) Scan his computer for viruses
   (D) Borrow a software for the printer

3. What does the woman ask the man about?

   (A) His business trip
   (B) His job application
   (C) His weekend plans
   (D) His presentation

4. Why does the man say he is worried?

   (A) He cannot find his receipt.
   (B) He does not have marketing experience.
   (C) He didn't reserve a ticket.
   (D) He didn't apply for a job.

5. Why will Mr. Shields leave the company?

   (A) He will retire.
   (B) He will go back to school.
   (C) He will start a new career.
   (D) He will open his own store.

6. What does the man say about Ms. Adams?

   (A) She should attend a trade fair.
   (B) She will hire additional staff.
   (C) She will transfer to another office.
   (D) She should replace Mr. Shields.

실전 감각 익히기

각 대화를 잘 듣고 그에 관련된 세 문제를 풀어보세요.

1. What are the speakers asked to do?

   (A) Create an energy conservation plan
   (B) Give a customer a tour of the facilities
   (C) Purchase office supplies
   (D) Design a product

2. When will the department meeting take place?

   (A) On Wednesday
   (B) On Thursday
   (C) On Friday
   (D) On Monday

3. What will the woman probably do next?

   (A) Send a product to a client
   (B) Go to another floor
   (C) Unpack some items
   (D) Submit a proposal

4. What is the man doing?

   (A) Preparing an advertisement
   (B) Applying for a position
   (C) Conducting an interview
   (D) Meeting a new employee

5. When is the man's deadline?

   (A) 3:00 P.M.
   (B) 4:00 P.M.
   (C) 5:00 P.M.
   (D) 6:00 P.M.

6. What is indicated about the position?

   (A) The salary is a fixed amount.
   (B) Three years of experience is required.
   (C) It is a part-time position.
   (D) It must be filled by the next day.

7. What kind of business is opening on Saturday?

   (A) A computer store
   (B) A clothing shop
   (C) A coffee shop
   (D) A furniture store

8. Who is Jeff?

   (A) A clothing designer
   (B) A store owner
   (C) A musician
   (D) A chef

9. What will the woman bring on Saturday?

   (A) T-shirts
   (B) Beverages
   (C) Flyers
   (D) Cups

10. What is the speakers' company asked to make?

    (A) Hats
    (B) T-shirts
    (C) Picnic baskets
    (D) Training manuals

11. When does the speakers' company plan to ship the items?

    (A) On Wednesday
    (B) On Thursday
    (C) On Friday
    (D) On Monday

12. What will the client send the speaker?

    (A) Some shirt samples
    (B) Some design software
    (C) A payment
    (D) A logo

UNIT 10 사무기기 / 주문 / 구매 / 계약

★ 콕콕 찍어주는 출제 포인트

사무실 업무 상황의 연장선상으로, 각종 사무기기/장비 등의 설치, 고장 및 수리, 또는 비품의 주문, 구매 및 배송 관련 상황, 그리고 계약 체결 등이 시험에 자주 출제됩니다. 화자들은 주로 구매자-판매자 관계이거나 직장 동료 관계가 대부분입니다. 또한 질문에 있어서 "What does the man[woman] mean when he[she] says ~?"의 형태로 화자의 의도 파악 문제가 출제되기도 합니다. 이와 같은 의도 파악 문제는 대화 문맥을 잘 이해한 후 정답을 선택해야 합니다.

 빈출 질문 익히기

- What item does the woman want to return? — 여자가 반품하고 싶어하는 물건은 무엇인가?
- When will the man most likely arrive at the store? — 남자는 언제 가게에 도착할 것 같은가?
- What does the woman want to purchase? — 여자가 구매하려 하는 것은 무엇인가?
- When will Mi-Jung review the contract? — 미정은 언제 계약서를 검토할 것인가?
- What does the man request? — 남자는 무엇을 요청하는가?

 문제 보기

1. (Where) most likely are the (speakers)?
   (A) In a business office
   (B) At a recording studio
   (C) At a construction site
   (D) At an appliance store

1. 화자들이 있는 곳은 어디이겠는가?
   (A) 회사 사무실
   (B) 녹음 스튜디오
   (C) 공사 현장
   (D) 가전제품 상점

2. (What) does the (woman) (ask) the man to do?
   (A) Lead her to a product
   (B) Install a device
   (C) Give a refund
   (D) Speak in a low voice

2. 여자가 남자에게 요청하는 것은?
   (A) 그녀를 제품이 있는 곳으로 안내한다.
   (B) 장치를 설치한다.
   (C) 환불을 해 준다.
   (D) 조용한 목소리로 말한다.

3. (What) does the (woman) (mean) when she says, "The ones we have now are just too loud"?
   (A) She purchased defective products.
   (B) She cannot concentrate in her office.
   (C) She wants to buy items that are quiet.
   (D) She thinks some colors are too bright.

3. 여자가 "저희가 지금 쓰고 있는 것들은 소음이 너무 심하거든요"라고 말할 때 의미하는 바는 무엇인가?
   (A) 그녀는 결함이 있는 상품을 구입했다.
   (B) 그녀는 자신이 일하는 사무실에서 집중을 할 수가 없다.
   (C) 그녀는 조용한 물건을 구입하고 싶다.
   (D) 그녀는 일부 색상이 너무 밝다고 생각한다.

대화 보기 🎧 P3-U10-1

다음 대화를 미국식과 영국식으로 들어보세요.

M: Welcome to Richard's Surplus. Can I help you find anything? W: Yes, **I need to buy a couple of floor fans for my office.**[1] M: OK. Our fans are in aisle twelve, beside the computer desks and chairs. W: **Would you mind showing me?**[2] I've never been here before. M: Sure, right this way. So what kind of features are you looking for in a floor fan? W: Well, the ones we have now are just too loud. That's the main reason we're replacing them. M: **I think you'll like the Smooth Air XL model, then. I've heard several customers say they forget that theirs is even turned on.**[3] W: Sounds promising. Please show me one of those.	남: 리처드 서플러스에 오신 것을 환영합니다. 찾는 걸 도와드릴까요? 여: 네, 사무실에 쓸 스탠드형 선풍기를 두 대 정도 사야 하거든요. 남: 알겠습니다. 저희 선풍기는 12번 통로의 컴퓨터용 책상과 의자 옆에 위치해 있습니다. 여: 보여 주실 수 있나요? 제가 이곳에 와 본 적이 없어서요. 남: 물론입니다. 이쪽으로요. 어떤 기능이 있는 스탠드형 선풍기를 찾고 계십니까? 여: 음, 저희가 지금 쓰고 있는 것들은 소음이 너무 심하거든요. 그게 그것들을 교체하려고 하는 주된 이유예요. 남: 그렇다면 스무드 에어 XL 모델이 마음에 드실 겁니다. 몇몇 고객들이 선풍기를 켜 놓은 줄도 모르겠더라고 하는 걸 들었거든요. 여: 좋을 것 같은데요. 그것으로 하나 보여주세요.

 **floor fan** 플로어 팬: 바닥에 세워 사용하는 일반적인 선풍기   **aisle** 통로   **feature** 특징, 특색   **replace** 대체하다   **turn on** 켜다
promising 유망한, 조짐이 좋은

📢 문제 해설

1. 질문의 키워드: 어디(Where), 화자들(speakers)
   → 앞부분을 들으면 금방 알 수 있는 질문이다. 여자가 사무실에 쓸 선풍기를 사러 왔다고 말하고, 남자가 안내해주는 것으로 보아 대화 장소가 가전제품 상점임을 알 수 있다.

2. 질문의 키워드: 무엇(What), 여자(woman), 요청하다(ask)
   → 요청할 때 많이 사용하는 문장이 나오는 부분(Would you mind showing me?)에 유의해 듣는다. 남자가 선풍기가 있는 위치를 말해 주자, 선풍기가 있는 곳을 직접 보여 달라고 요청하고 있다.

3. 질문의 키워드: 무엇(What), 여자(woman), 의미하다(mean), "The ones we have now are just too loud"
   → 이 말의 뒷부분을 특히 유의해 듣도록 한다. 여자의 이 말에 이어, 남자는 틀어도 소리가 나는 줄도 모를 정도로 조용하다는 모델을 소개하고 있다. 따라서 여자는 소리가 시끄럽지 않은 선풍기를 사고 싶어하는 것임을 알 수 있다.

UNIT 10   93

주문/구매/계약 관련 어휘 및 관용 표현 🎧 P3-U10-2

주문 / 구매 / 계약 관련 어휘

- **order** 주문(하다); 주문품
- **arrive** (물건이) 도착하다
- **delivery** 배달, 배송
- **stock** 재고; 비축하다
- **delay** 지연(시키다)
- **shipment** 선적(물)
- **supplier** 공급업체
- **product/goods/item** 상품
- **purchase** 구매(하다); 구매품
- **guarantee** 보증하다
- **refund** 환불
- **defective** 하자가 있는
- **contract** 계약
- **invoice** 송장
- **agreement** 합의
- **expire** 만기가 되다
- **negotiation** 협상
- **merger** 합병
- **acquisition/takeover** 인수
- **estimate** 견적서
- **office supplies** 사무용품

주문 / 구매 / 계약 관련 관용 표현

- **within three business days** 영업일 기준 3일 이내에
- **take three days** 3일이 걸리다
- **in[out of] stock** 재고가 있는[없는]
- **by courier** 택배로
- **make a purchase** 구매하다
- **replace A with B** A를 B로 교체하다
- **exchange A for B** A를 B로 교환하다
- **get a refund** 환불받다 (*cf.* give A(사람) a refund A에게 환불을 해주다)
- **give A(사람) a discount** A에게 할인해주다
- **pay in cash** 현금으로 내다
- **at an additional/extra cost** 추가 비용으로
- **upon receipt of** ~을 수령하자마자
- **sold out** 매진된, 다 팔린
- **cooperate with** ~와 협력하다
- **sign a contract** 계약을 체결하다
- **win a contract** 계약을 따내다
- **reach an agreement** 합의에 이르다
- **look/go over** 검토하다
- **buy insurance** 보험을 들다
- **do business with** ~와 거래하다

어휘 및 표현 점검 해설 p.55

우리말 뜻을 보고 빈칸에 알맞은 단어를 넣으세요.

1. I will pick up my order personally rather than wait for the _____.
   배송을 기다리기보다 제가 직접 주문품을 가져오겠습니다.

2. I would like to _____.
   저는 환불을 받고 싶습니다.

3. I am sorry but you can only _____ it another item.
   죄송합니다만 손님께서는 그것을 다른 상품으로 교환하는 것만 가능합니다.

4. Didn't you say your car insurance _____ next month?
   다음 달에 당신 자동차 보험이 만기가 된다고 하지 않았어요?

5. Who is responsible for ordering _____?
   누가 사무용품 주문하는 걸 담당하나요?

청취 집중 훈련 1 🎧 P3-U10-3 / 해설 p.55

아래 제시된 대화의 음원을 듣고 빈칸을 채워보세요.

1. 한 단어 받아쓰기 연습

M: Betty, you _____ a local cleaning company yesterday, right? _____ was your meeting with them?

W: It went well. I _____ a contract with them. Actually, they are coming in tomorrow to _____ the floors. Before you _____ the office, please put all your _____ on top of your desk.

M: Tomorrow? OK, can I leave my chair on the _____?

W: Please, put it on your desk. Otherwise, it might get _____ or damaged during the cleaning.

남: 베티, 어제 지역 청소업체 방문했었죠? 그들과 회의는 어땠습니까?

여: 잘 진행됐어요. 그들과 계약 체결했구요. 실은 그들이 바닥 청소를 하러 내일 올 겁니다. 퇴근하기 전에 당신 소지품 전부를 책상 위에 놓아두세요.

남: 내일요? 좋아요. 의자는 바닥에 두어도 될까요?

여: 그것도 책상 위에 올려주세요. 그렇지 않으면 청소하다가 젖거나 파손될 수 있거든요.

2. 두 단어 이상 받아쓰기 연습

W: Hello, this is Sheila speaking. _____ help you?

M: Hi, Sheila. It's Bill. I was _____ to edit some photos. But just a moment ago, the computer froze and _____.

W: Oh, hi, Bill. It _____ you need a system reset. I could explain the steps _____, but it would be easier to e-mail the directions. Can you _____ on your desktop computer?

M: Sure, my desktop is running well. _____.

여: 안녕하세요, 저는 쉴라입니다. 어떻게 도와드릴까요?

남: 안녕하세요, 쉴라. 저 빌이에요. 제가 사진 몇 장을 편집하려고 제 노트북을 사용하고 있었어요. 그런데 조금 전에 컴퓨터가 갑자기 다운되더니 작동이 안 돼요.

여: 오, 안녕하세요, 빌. (컴퓨터) 시스템을 리셋해야 할 것처럼 들리는데요. 제가 전화상으로 절차를 설명해줄 수도 있지만, 이메일로 지시사항을 보내는 것이 더 쉬울 것 같아요. 당신 데스크톱으로 메시지를 수신할 수 있나요?

남: 물론이죠, 제 데스크톱은 작동이 잘 됩니다. 정말 고마워요.

UNIT 10 **95**

청취 집중 훈련 2 🎧 P3-U10-4 / 해설 p.55

제시된 두 문제를 재빨리 훑어본 후, 핵심 내용을 빈칸 처리한 채 제시된 대화의 음원을 들으며 정답을 고르세요.

1. What does the man want to borrow?
   (A) A car   (B) A pen

2. What does the man request?
   (A) A contract   (B) A receipt

> M: Hi, I'd like to _____ for July and August. Do you have any available?
> W: Yes, this car is one of our most _____ and available for the two months.
> M: OK, it looks good. Could you show me a _____ that I have to _____?

3. Why has the man come to the woman's office?
   (A) To have a meeting (B) To deliver a package

4. What is the woman asked to do?
   (A) Call her coworker (B) Sign her name

> M: Good afternoon, I _____ here for Ms. Green.
> W: She just _____ the office. Could I receive the package for her?
> M: Sure. Would you _____, please?

5. What does the woman want to purchase?
   (A) Books   (B) Cabinets

6. How will the woman pay?
   (A) In cash   (B) By credit card

> W: Excuse me, I want to _____. How much are they?
> M: Each one is 30 dollars. You can pay for them with your store _____.
> W: I know but I'll _____ this time. I'm going to use it for my next purchase.

청취 집중 훈련 3 🎧 P3-U10-5 / 해설 p.56–57

각 대화를 듣고 그에 관련된 두 문제를 풀어보세요.

1. What is the woman's problem?
   (A) A document is missing.
   (B) She doesn't know how to use a machine.
   (C) An article will be submitted late.
   (D) She cannot find a client's telephone number.

2. When will Mi-Jung review the contract?
   (A) During the weekend
   (B) Next Monday
   (C) Next Tuesday
   (D) Next Wednesday

3. What does the man want to do?
   (A) Hold a seminar
   (B) Use a computer
   (C) Borrow a book
   (D) Attend a class

4. What will the woman give the man?
   (A) A password
   (B) A Web site address
   (C) An e-mail address
   (D) A parking permit

5. What does the man request from the woman?
   (A) A training schedule
   (B) Some invoices
   (C) A finance report
   (D) Some office supplies

6. What does the woman mean when she says, "I'll send a text message to his mobile phone"?
   (A) The manager cannot talk on the phone now.
   (B) The manager is waiting for a message.
   (C) She will check with the manager about the order.
   (D) She wants to leave the office early today.

실전 감각 익히기

각 대화를 잘 듣고 그에 관련된 세 문제를 풀어보세요.

1. Why is the man calling?

   (A) To check the cost of a repair
   (B) To know when a repair will be done
   (C) To order some equipment
   (D) To cancel an order

2. What is Mr. Farmer doing now?

   (A) Checking an Internet connection
   (B) Installing a software program
   (C) Repairing a car
   (D) Cleaning a device

3. When will the man most likely arrive at the store?

   (A) At 4 P.M.
   (B) At 5 P.M.
   (C) At 6 P.M.
   (D) At 7 P.M.

4. What does the man have now?

   (A) An air purifier
   (B) A laptop
   (C) A camera
   (D) A fan

5. Where is Ms. Neilson's office?

   (A) On the 2nd floor
   (B) On the 4th floor
   (C) On the 6th floor
   (D) On the 10th floor

6. What is the man asked to do?

   (A) Call back in an hour
   (B) Review a report
   (C) Work overtime
   (D) Return to the second floor

7. What is the purpose of this phone call?

   (A) To complain about service
   (B) To request a refund
   (C) To arrange a rental
   (D) To inquire about a job opening

8. What product are the speakers discussing?

   (A) A coffee maker
   (B) A vending machine
   (C) A photocopier
   (D) Computer software

9. When does the man want to have a meeting?

   (A) This afternoon
   (B) This evening
   (C) Tomorrow morning
   (D) Tomorrow afternoon

10. What problem does the man mention?

    (A) He received a broken item.
    (B) He misplaced his order number.
    (C) He gave the wrong shipping address.
    (D) He was overcharged for a product.

11. What does the man mean when he says, "I ordered that sauce for a dinner party that was on Wednesday"?

    (A) He thinks a certain sauce brand is the best.
    (B) He no longer needs the sauce.
    (C) He received the wrong product.
    (D) He would like to order more sauce.

12. What will the woman most likely give the man?

    (A) A replacement product
    (B) A shipping voucher
    (C) A cash refund
    (D) A store credit

UNIT 11 여행 / 여가 / 교통 / 쇼핑

★ 콕콕 찍어주는 출제 포인트

업무상 출장, 퇴근 후나 주말의 계획, 휴가 기간과 장소 등에 대한 내용이 주로 다루어집니다. 교통과 관련해서는 교통편 문의나 예약, 길 찾기, 공사로 인한 도로 폐쇄 등에 대한 대화를 들을 수 있습니다. 또한 질문으로 시간표, 표지판, 리스트 등 다양한 시각 정보를 참고해서 정답을 찾아야 하는 문제가 출제될 수 있습니다. 시각 정보는 대화를 듣기 전에 미리 읽어 두어야 대화를 이해하기 쉽습니다.

빈출 질문 익히기

- How many indirect flights are available per day? — 하루에 얼마나 많은 연결 항공편이 있나?
- Why is the man concerned about the play? — 남자는 연극에 대해 왜 걱정하는가?
- Where is the woman's final destination? — 여자의 최종 목적지는 어디인가?
- What is the problem with the clothes? — 옷은 무엇이 문제인가?
- When are the speakers scheduled to arrive? — 화자들은 언제 도착할 예정인가?

문제 보기

Exit 1	Waterfront
Exit 2	Business District
Exit 3	Downtown
Exit 4	Arts Center

출구 1	바닷가
출구 2	상업 지구
출구 3	시내
출구 4	아트 센터

1. Look at the graphic. What exit will the speakers most likely take?
   (A) 1
   (B) 2
   (C) 3
   (D) 4

1. 도표를 보세요. 화자들은 어떤 출구로 나가겠는가?
   (A) 1 (B) 2
   (C) 3 (D) 4

2. Who most likely is Hugo Greer?
   (A) A critic
   (B) An actor
   (C) A painter
   (D) A taxi driver

2. 휴고 그리어는 누구겠는가?
   (A) 비평가 (B) 배우
   (C) 화가   (D) 택시 기사

3. What does the man mention about tickets?
   (A) They are sold out.
   (B) They were discounted.
   (C) They need to be picked up.
   (D) They were purchased online.

3. 남자가 티켓에 대해 언급하고 있는 것은?
   (A) 모두 매진되었다.
   (B) 할인되었다.
   (C) 직접 받으러 가야 한다.
   (D) 온라인으로 구입했다.

대화 보기 🎧 P3-U11-1

다음 대화를 미국식과 영국식으로 들어보세요.

W: Richard, would you mind looking at the directions again? Which exit should I take?

M: **Well, the theater is in the Arts Center, so take that exit.**[1]

W: OK, thanks. I'm excited about this play.

M: Me too. I read on a critic's Web site that **this is Hugo Greer's best performance of his life.**[2]

W: Wow!

M: Um, we better hurry, though. The play starts in thirty minutes, and **we still have to get our tickets in person from the box office window.**[3]

W: Don't worry. There's not too much traffic, so we'll be there soon.

여: 리처드, 방향 좀 다시 한 번 봐 줄래요? 어떤 출구로 나가야 하는 거죠?

남: 음, 극장이 아트 센터에 있으니까 그 출구로 나가요.

여: 네, 고마워요. 이번 연극은 정말 흥분이 되는데요.

남: 나도 그래요. 어떤 비평가가 웹 사이트에 올린 글을 읽었는데, 이 연극은 휴고 그리어 인생의 최고 공연이라고 하네요.

여: 와!

남: 음, 어쨌든 서두르는 게 좋겠어요. 30분 후면 연극이 시작되는데, 매표소 창구에서 직접 표를 구입해야 하니까요.

여: 걱정하지 마세요. 교통이 혼잡하지 않으니 금방 그곳에 도착할 거예요.

어휘 directions 길 안내, 방향 | exit 출구 | critic 평론가, 비평가 | performance (개인의) 연기, 연주 | in person 본인이 직접

문제 해설

1. 질문의 키워드: 보다(Look), 도표(graphic), 어떤 출구(What exit), 화자들(speakers), 택하다(take)
   → 도표를 보면서 대화를 들어야 한다. 대화 앞부분에서 남자가 극장이 아트 센터에 있으니 그쪽 방향으로 가자는 말이 나온다. 도표에서 Arts Center 방향은 Exit 4로 나와 있음을 알 수 있다.

2. 질문의 키워드: 누구(Who), 휴고 그리어(Hugo Greer)
   → 휴고 그리어라는 이름이 나오는지 유의하며 듣는다. 대화 중반에 남자가 이 연극은 휴고 그리어가 그의 일생 최고의 공연(this is Hugo Greer's best performance of his life)이라고 말하는 부분이 나온다. 따라서 그가 배우라는 것을 알 수 있다.

3. 질문의 키워드: 무엇(What), 남자(man), 언급하다(mention), 티켓(tickets)
   → tickets이라는 표현이 나오는지 유의하며 듣는다. 대화 후반부에서 남자가 표를 매표소 창구에서 직접 구입해야 한다고 했다. 대화의 get our tickets in person을 정답에서는 need to be picked up으로 바꾸어 표현했다.

여행/여가/교통/쇼핑 관련 어휘 및 관용 표현 🎧 P3-U11-2

여행 / 여가 / 교통 / 쇼핑 관련 어휘

- travel agency 여행사
- itinerary 여행 일정(표)
- tourist attraction 관광지
- accommodations 숙박시설
- book/reserve 예약하다
- window[aisle] seat 창가[통로]쪽 좌석
- one-way[round-trip] ticket 편도[왕복] 티켓
- destination 목적지
- closed (도로 등이) 폐쇄된
- delay 지연(시키다)
- parking lot 주차장
- parking garage 주차 건물, 차고
- grocery 식료품
- gift certificate 상품권
- brand-new 새로 출시된
- state-of-the-art 최첨단의
- browse 천천히 구경하다
- checkout counter 계산대
- proof of purchase 구매 확인증, 영수증

여행 / 여가 / 교통 / 쇼핑 관련 관용 표현

- take a tour of ~을 견학하다[둘러보다]
- go on vacation[a business trip] 휴가를[출장을] 가다
- take a trip to ~로 여행을 가다
- take A(기간) off A 동안 휴가를 내다
- take a train[bus] 기차[버스]를 타다
- by train[bus, subway] 기차[버스, 지하철]로
- check in (공항에서) 짐을 부치다; (호텔) 투숙 절차를 밟다
- bound for ~로 향하는
- get on[off] the car 차에(서) 타다[내리다]
- give A(사람) a ride A를 태워주다
- due to heavy traffic 교통 체증 때문에
- free of charge/cost 무료로
- go/do shopping 쇼핑을 가다/하다
- try on ~을 착용해보다
- take inventory 재고 조사를 하다
- in stock 재고가 있는
- on sale 할인 중인 (cf. have a sale 할인을 하다)
- sold out 다 팔린, 매진된
- be released/launched 출시되다
- during business hours 영업시간 동안
- on display 진열된

어휘 및 표현 점검 해설 p.60

우리말 뜻을 보고 빈칸에 알맞은 단어를 넣으세요.

1. Let me check if we have these shoes in size 4 _____.
   이 구두의 치수 4의 재고가 있는지 확인해보겠습니다.
2. I'm afraid that the newest model has been _____.
   죄송하지만 최신 모델은 다 팔렸습니다.
3. Do you want an _____ or a window seat?
   복도쪽 좌석에 앉으시겠습니까, 창가쪽 좌석에 앉으시겠습니까?
4. I haven't decided the _____ for my vacation yet.
   저는 아직 휴가 목적지를 정하지 못했습니다.
5. To give you a refund, I must get the _____ _____ from you.
   환불해 드리려면, 고객님의 영수증이 있어야 합니다.

청취 집중 훈련 1

아래 제시된 대화의 음원을 듣고 빈칸을 채워보세요.

1. 한 단어 받아쓰기 연습

M: If it's all right, I'd like to _____ some of my _____ days next month.

W: Sure, no problem. You'll just need to fill out a vacation _____ form and _____ it to Ms. Swenson's office. What days are you thinking about _____ off?

M: Only June 11 to 15. I'm _____ on going to Boracay for a few days. Have you ever _____ there?

W: Yes, the _____ are amazing. You're really going to enjoy yourself.

남: 괜찮으시다면 저는 다음 달에 휴가를 좀 쓰고 싶습니다.

여: 물론이죠, 좋습니다. 휴가 요청 양식 작성하시고 스웬슨 씨 사무실에 제출하기만 하시면 돼요. 언제 휴가를 갈 생각이세요?

남: 6월 11일에서 15일까지만요. 저는 며칠간 보라카이에 갈 계획입니다. 거기 가본 적 있으세요?

여: 네, 해변이 아주 멋집니다. 정말 좋은 시간을 보내실 거예요.

2. 두 단어 이상 받아쓰기 연습

M: Hi, I'm going to Bangkok this weekend. _____ a good travel guidebook?

W: Sure. The *Visit Bangkok* book is very good. It's _____ as well – 20% off.

M: Well, it has _____, but there are too many of them. I'd rather get a book with a lot of _____ and lists of things to do.

W: OK, then, _____ you the *Travel Smart* books. They come with computer CDs _____ interactive maps and must-see places.

남: 안녕하세요, 저는 이번 주말에 방콕에 가는데요. 좋은 여행 안내서를 추천해 주시겠어요?

여: 물론입니다. 〈방콕 방문하기〉라는 책이 꽤 괜찮아요. 20% 할인 중이기도 하고요.

남: 음, 사진이 좋기는 한데 너무 많군요. 저는 세부 지도가 많고 할 수 있는 활동 목록이 있는 책이 좋겠어요.

여: 좋아요, 그럼 제가 〈똑똑한 여행〉이라는 책을 보여 드릴게요. 그 책에는 대화식 지도와 꼭 가봐야 할 장소를 담은 컴퓨터 CD가 들어 있습니다.

UNIT 11

청취 집중 훈련 2 🎧 P3-U11-4 / 해설 p.60

제시된 두 문제를 재빨리 훑어본 후, 핵심 내용을 빈칸 처리한 채 제시된 대화의 음원을 들으며 정답을 고르세요.

1. What does the woman want to do?
   (A) Park her car   (B) Do some shopping

2. What does the man say is in the building's basement?
   (A) A supermarket   (B) A gift shop

> W: Excuse me, where can I do some _____?
> M: There is a _____ in the basement of the building.
> W: Thank you. I will be back at least 30 minutes _____.

3. Where most likely are the speakers?
   (A) On a train   (B) At a restaurant

4. When are the speakers scheduled to arrive?
   (A) At 8:00   (B) At 10:00

> M: Helen, we _____ at 4, and it's 8 now. How much longer do we have to go?
> W: Well, we're scheduled to _____, so about two more hours. Aren't you hungry?
> M: Yes, I haven't eaten anything since lunch. I think _____ has a dining car.

5. What does the woman want to buy?
   (A) A bicycle   (B) A dress

6. What is indicated about the item?
   (A) It has a modern design.   (B) It comes with a three-year warranty.

> W: Hello, I'm _____ for my 10-year-old daughter.
> M: OK, this BX-10 bike is designed for children and comes with _____.
> W: It looks like it's too big. Is this _____?

청취 집중 훈련 3 P3-U11-5 / 해설 p.61–62

각 대화를 듣고 그에 관련된 두 문제를 풀어보세요.

International Food Festival at Applebee Park	
June 1 (Thursday)	French Food
June 2 (Friday)	Italian Food
June 3 (Saturday)	Korean Food
June 4 (Sunday)	Japanese Food

1. What prevented the woman from going to an event?
   (A) Her business trip
   (B) Her busy work schedule
   (C) Traffic congestion
   (D) Bad weather

2. Look at the graphic. What kind of food will the speakers most likely try?
   (A) French food
   (B) Italian food
   (C) Korean food
   (D) Japanese food

3. What is the woman looking for?
   (A) A bus
   (B) A schedule
   (C) A train station
   (D) A ticket window

4. What does the man mention about the express bus?
   (A) It leaves in ten minutes.
   (B) It does not stop in Berkeley.
   (C) It does not have any seats left.
   (D) It is more expensive than the local bus.

5. Where most likely are the speakers?
   (A) At a university
   (B) At a restaurant
   (C) At a store
   (D) At a company orientation

6. What is indicated about the advertised item?
   (A) It is very expensive.
   (B) It only comes in one color.
   (C) It is currently sold out.
   (D) It is very popular.

실전 감각 익히기

각 대화를 잘 듣고 그에 관련된 세 문제를 풀어보세요.

1. What did the man send the woman?
   (A) An itinerary
   (B) An e-mail address
   (C) Ticket information
   (D) A reservation confirmation

2. Where does the woman want to go?
   (A) To Asia
   (B) To Africa
   (C) To Australia
   (D) To South America

3. What is suggested about the woman's trip?
   (A) She frequently visits the area.
   (B) She will travel for six months.
   (C) It will be her first trip overseas.
   (D) She will visit her cousin.

4. What does the woman want to buy?
   (A) A desk
   (B) A chair
   (C) A pair of shoes
   (D) A bookcase

5. What does the man say about the item?
   (A) It's expensive.
   (B) It's comfortable.
   (C) It's durable.
   (D) It's popular.

6. How many colors are available?
   (A) Three
   (B) Four
   (C) Five
   (D) Six

7. What problem does the woman mention?

   (A) She didn't bring her ticket.
   (B) She could not find her baggage.
   (C) The shuttle bus arrived late.
   (D) The Web site is not working properly.

8. From where did the flight leave?

   (A) Dubai
   (B) London
   (C) Denver
   (D) Lisbon

9. What is stated about the flight?

   (A) It was delayed.
   (B) It is fully booked.
   (C) It is now boarding passengers.
   (D) It can accept standby passengers.

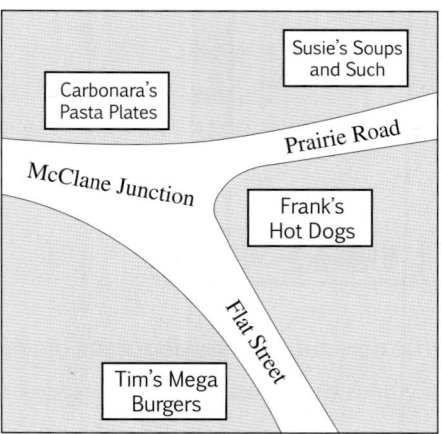

10. What does the man mention about Rexton?

    (A) It gets busy on weekends.
    (B) A festival there is postponed.
    (C) It has many tourist attractions.
    (D) He does not like its restaurants.

11. Look at the graphic. Where will the woman most likely eat lunch?

    (A) At Susie's
    (B) At Frank's
    (C) At Tim's
    (D) At Carbonara's

12. What does the man give the woman?

    (A) A festival map
    (B) A city brochure
    (C) An attraction ticket
    (D) A restaurant coupon

UNIT 12 부동산/은행/병원/호텔/식당(기타 일상생활)

★ 콕콕 찍어주는 출제 포인트

부동산에 관한 대화는 주거지 이전, 지점으로의 전근, 새 건물의 위치 및 특징, 건물이나 부동산을 보기 위한 약속 잡기 등에 대한 내용이 주로 등장합니다. 회사 외의 일상생활 관련 대화는 특정 상황이나 장소에 국한되지 않고 식당, 병원, 은행, 호텔, 우체국, 세탁소 또는 가정집 등에서 일어나는 다양한 내용을 다루게 됩니다. 또한 대화자 수에 있어서 2인 대화뿐만 아니라 3인 대화가 제시될 수도 있음을 유의해야 합니다.

빈출 질문 익히기

- What does the man say about the dining area? — 남자가 식사 장소에 관해 이야기 한 것은 무엇인가?
- Why does the woman want insurance? — 여자는 왜 보험을 원하는가?
- What housing option is offered? — 어떤 주거 옵션이 제공되는가?
- What is indicated about the indoor room? — 내부 방에 대하여 언급된 것은 무엇인가?
- Where does the conversation most likely take place? — 대화는 어디에서 이루어질 것 같은가?

문제 보기

1. Who most likely are the women?
   (A) Real estate agents
   (B) Photographers
   (C) Interior designers
   (D) Apartment landlords

   1. 여자들은 누구일 것 같은가?
   (A) 부동산 중개인
   (B) 사진 작가
   (C) 인테리어 디자이너
   (D) 아파트 주인

2. What is indicated about the apartment?
   (A) It is under renovation
   (B) It has two bedrooms.
   (C) It is on the fourth floor.
   (D) It has three bathrooms.

   2. 아파트에 대해 무엇이 언급되고 있는가?
   (A) 보수공사 중이다.
   (B) 침실이 두 개다.
   (C) 4층에 있다.
   (D) 욕실이 세 개다.

3. What will the man most likely do next?
   (A) Move into an apartment
   (B) Take pictures of an apartment
   (C) Visit a real estate agency
   (D) Meet her new roommate

   3. 남자는 다음에 무엇을 할 것 같은가?
   (A) 아파트로 입주한다.
   (B) 아파트 사진을 찍는다.
   (C) 부동산 중개소를 방문한다.
   (D) 새로운 룸메이트를 만난다.

대화 보기 🎧 P3-U12-1

다음 3인 대화를 들어보세요.

W1:	Good afternoon, Mr. Boyd. Please have a seat. **I'm happy to say that I think I've found an apartment you will like.**[1]	여:	안녕하세요, 보이드 씨. 앉으시죠. 기쁘게도 보이드 씨가 마음에 들어할 만한 아파트를 찾은 거 같습니다.
M:	That's wonderful news to hear. My current lease ends next Saturday.	남:	좋은 소식이군요. 저의 현재 임대 계약이 다음 주 토요일에 끝나거든요.
W1:	**It's a two-bedroom apartment**[2] that covers about 100 square meters. It's on the fifth floor of the building. If you want to take a look at it, **Emily, my coworker, can show it to you.**[1]	여1:	대략 100제곱 미터 크기의 침실 두 개짜리 아파트입니다. 건물의 5층에 있고요. 만약 아파트를 보고 싶으시면 제 동료 에밀리가 보여줄 수 있습니다.
M:	That sounds great. Can we go look at it now? **I'd like to take some pictures**[3] to show to my roommate.	남:	좋습니다. 지금 가서 볼 수 있을까요? 제 룸메이트에게 보여줄 사진을 좀 찍고 싶어요.
W2:	Sure, but it's a little far from here. It will take about 40 minutes by car. Is it okay?	여2:	물론입니다만 여기서 좀 멀어요. 차로 대략 40분 정도 걸립니다. 괜찮을까요?

어휘 have[take] a seat 앉다   I'm happy to say that ~ 기쁘게도 ~이다   find 발견하다   current 현재의   lease 임대차 계약
end 끝나다   cover + 면적 (면적)에 걸치다   take a look at ~을 보다   sound like ~처럼 들리다   go look at 가서 ~을 보다
take a picture 사진을 찍다

1. 질문의 키워드: 누구(Who), 여자들(women)
→ 여자들의 신분/직책을 묻는 질문으로, 화자들 중 여자들의 대사를 잘 들어야 한다. 여자1의 첫 대사와 동료 Emily가 집을 보여준다는 대사를 통해 이들이 누구인지 알 수 있다.

2. 질문의 키워드: 무엇(What), 언급되다(indicated), 아파트(apartment)
→ What is indicated[mentioned, stated, suggested] about+명사?는 질문에 쓰인 명사를 신속하게 확인한 후 대화 속에서 그 명사가 언급된 부분에서 정답을 찾아야 한다. 이 문제에서는 아파트(apartment)가 언급되는 부분을 노려 들어야 한다.

3. 질문의 키워드: 무엇(What), 남자(man), 다음에 하다(do next)
→ 미래 행동에 대한 단서는 대화 후반부를 주목해야 하며, 남자가 할 일을 묻고 있으므로 남자의 말에 집중해야 한다.

부동산/은행/병원/호텔/식당 관련 어휘 및 관용 표현 🎧 P3-U12-2

부동산 / 은행 / 병원 / 호텔 / 식당 관련 어휘

- **rent** 임대하다; 임대료
- **lease** 임대하다; 임대차 계약
- **property** 부동산 (=real estate)
- **real estate agent** 부동산 중개인 (=realtor)
- **move into** 입주하다
- **tenant** 세입자
- **landlord** 집주인
- **bank account** 은행 계좌
- **transfer** 송금하다 (=remit)
- **investment** 투자
- **interest (rate)** 이자(율), 금리
- **bank statement** 은행 거래 내역서
- **balance** 잔액
- **regular checkup** 정기 검진
- **symptom** 증상
- **medical record** 의료 기록
- **prescription** 처방전
- **ingredient** 음식 재료
- **dining room** 식당
- **catering service** 출장 뷔페 서비스
- **server** 서빙 담당자

부동산 / 은행 / 병원 / 호텔 / 식당 관련 관용 표현

- **be conveniently located** 편리한 곳에 위치해 있다
- **within walking distance of** ~에서 걸어갈 수 있는
- **fully furnished** 가구가 모두 갖추어진
- **be under renovation** 보수공사 중이다
- **a room with an ocean view** 바다가 보이는 방
- **be transferred to** ~로 전근 보내지다
- **make a deposit[withdrawal, transfer]** 예금[출금, 송금]을 하다
- **open an account** 계좌를 개설하다
- **issue a credit card** 신용카드를 발급하다
- **apply for a loan** 대출을 신청하다
- **credit one's account** ~의 계좌에 입금하다
- **get a(n) shot/injection** 주사를 맞다
- **make/schedule an appointment** (진료 등) 예약을 하다
- **take medicine** 약을 먹다
- **have a reservation** 예약이 되어 있다
- **hold a meeting[party]** 회의를[파티를] 열다
- **take an order** 주문을 받다
- **a table for four** 4인용 테이블
- **hold a table** 테이블을 잡아 놓다
- **look forward to** ~을 고대하다

어휘 및 표현 점검 해설 p.65

우리말 뜻을 보고 빈칸에 알맞은 단어를 넣으세요.

1. What do I need to open a _____ here?
   이곳에 은행 계좌를 개설하려면 무엇이 필요한가요?
2. I have an appointment with a _____ this afternoon.
   오늘 오후에 부동산 중개업자와 약속이 있습니다.
3. My _____ is going to raise the rent from September.
   집주인이 9월부터 집세를 올릴 겁니다.
4. Harry went to see a doctor for his _____.
   해리는 정기 검진을 받으러 의사에게 갔습니다.
5. Good evening. I'm your _____ tonight.
   안녕하세요. 제가 오늘 손님의 서빙 담당입니다.

청취 집중 훈련 1 🎧 P3-U12-3 / 해설 p.65

아래 제시된 대화의 음원을 듣고 빈칸을 채워보세요.

1. 한 단어 받아쓰기 연습

M: Hi, I have a 6 o'clock _____ for five people under the name Kim, but I _____ to go back to my office now. I probably _____ be back until a little after 6.

W: That's OK. We'll _____ your table for your other guests and _____ them know that you'll be a little late.

M: Thank you. Also, I don't want them to _____ for me, so can I _____ my meal now?

W: Yes, of course. Let me _____ you a menu.

남: 안녕하세요, 저는 김이라는 이름으로 5명이 6시에 예약되어 있습니다만 제가 지금 사무실로 돌아가야 합니다. 아마도 6시 조금 넘어 돌아올 겁니다.

여: 괜찮습니다. 저희가 고객님의 일행을 위해 테이블을 잡아놓고 고객님이 조금 늦을 거라고 그분들께 알려드리겠습니다.

남: 고맙습니다. 그리고 그들이 저를 기다리는 걸 원치 않기 때문에 지금 제가 식사를 주문할 수 있을까요?

여: 네, 물론입니다. 메뉴를 갖다 드릴게요.

2. 두 단어 이상 받아쓰기 연습

W: Hi, Mr. Anderson. This is Wendy calling from the Stone Health Center. I just _____ you about your appointment tomorrow afternoon for a _____. Is 5:30 still a good time for you?

M: Oh, I have a meeting tomorrow afternoon, and it _____ until after 5. _____ possible for me to come in at 6?

W: Six o'clock is fine. The building's main entrance _____ 5:30, so you'll need to use _____ by the staff parking lot.

여: 안녕하세요, 엔더슨 씨. 저는 스톤 건강센터의 웬디입니다. 내일 오후에 정기 검진이 있다는 것을 다시 알려드리려고요. 5시 30분이 여전히 괜찮으십니까?

남: 아, 제가 내일 오후에 회의가 있는데 5시가 넘어서야 끝날 것 같아요. 제가 6시에 가도 괜찮을까요?

여: 6시면 괜찮습니다. 건물 정문이 5시 30분에 문을 닫으니까 직원 주차장 옆쪽에 있는 옆문을 이용해야 할 겁니다.

UNIT 12

청취 집중 훈련 2 🎧 P3-U12-4 / 해설 p.65-66

제시된 두 문제를 재빨리 훑어본 후, 핵심 내용을 빈칸 처리한 채 제시된 대화의 음원을 들으며 정답을 고르세요.

1. Where does the conversation most likely take place?
   (A) In a hotel   (B) In a restaurant

2. What does the man order?
   (A) Pizza   (B) Chicken

> M: Hello, I'd like to order _____ for room 1309.
> W: Of course, what would you _____?
> M: I'd like the honey-glazed _____ with green beans. When will it be delivered?

3. What does the woman want to get made?
   (A) A suit   (B) A dress

4. What type of fabric does the woman want?
   (A) Wool   (B) Silk

> W: I'm interested in getting a _____ made. What are your rates?
> M: It _____ the fabric and some other factors.
> W: I would like a _____ appropriate for winter.

5. Where are the speakers?
   (A) In a bank   (B) In a real estate office

6. Where does the woman want to live?
   (A) Near her office   (B) Near the subway station

> W: Excuse me, I'd like to lease a house. My company is _____ here next fall.
> M: OK, let me help you. _____ do you have in mind?
> W: Well, I'd just prefer an apartment _____ of my office.

청취 집중 훈련 3

각 대화를 듣고 그에 관련된 두 문제를 풀어보세요.

1. Where might this conversation be heard?
   (A) At a post office
   (B) At a dry cleaner's
   (C) At a hotel
   (D) At an airport

2. When is the package expected to arrive?
   (A) This Saturday
   (B) Next Monday
   (C) Next Tuesday
   (D) Next Wednesday

3. Why most likely is the man calling?
   (A) To cancel a reservation
   (B) To change the location of an event
   (C) To change the time of a reservation
   (D) To ask about the restaurant's menu items

4. What will Pam send to the man?
   (A) An updated menu
   (B) A credit card application
   (C) A new confirmation number
   (D) A service invoice

5. Why most likely is the man visiting the office?
   (A) To pay a rental deposit
   (B) To view an apartment
   (C) To negotiate a rental contract
   (D) To inquire about a training program

6. What does the woman suggest the man do?
   (A) Meet with her at another time
   (B) Look at a different apartment
   (C) Provide some contact information
   (D) Visit another real estate office

실전 감각 익히기

각 대화를 잘 듣고 그에 관련된 세 문제를 풀어보세요.

1. What are the speakers doing?
   (A) Repairing a truck
   (B) Cleaning a swimming pool
   (C) Working on a fence
   (D) Planting a garden

2. What does the woman say is missing?
   (A) Pieces of wood
   (B) Truck parts
   (C) Batteries
   (D) Paint

3. When does the woman say the work will be completed?
   (A) This morning
   (B) This afternoon
   (C) Tomorrow morning
   (D) Tomorrow afternoon

4. What does the woman want to do?
   (A) Reserve a hotel room
   (B) Attend a meeting
   (C) Look at some apartments
   (D) Apply for a job

5. What housing option is offered?
   (A) Studios
   (B) Two bedrooms
   (C) Three bedrooms
   (D) Four bedrooms

6. When will the speakers most likely meet?
   (A) In the afternoon
   (B) In the evening
   (C) The following morning
   (D) The following evening

7. How many people are in the woman's group?

   (A) Two
   (B) Three
   (C) Four
   (D) Five

8. What does the man suggest the woman's group do?

   (A) Visit the restaurant's other location
   (B) Make a reservation online
   (C) Come at a later time
   (D) Eat at a counter

9. What does the woman request from the man?

   (A) A seat in a different section
   (B) A reservation for dinner
   (C) A lunch menu
   (D) A club registration form

10. Why most likely is the man calling Ms. Jackson?

    (A) To apologize for a banking error
    (B) To explain a personnel change
    (C) To suggest opening a new account
    (D) To discuss an upcoming business trip

11. What does Ms. Jackson indicate about Albany Bank?

    (A) She makes weekly trips there.
    (B) She used to work there.
    (C) She has an online account there.
    (D) She hired their finance manager.

12. What does the man offer to do for Ms. Jackson?

    (A) Hire additional staff
    (B) Make some photocopies
    (C) Issue a new credit card
    (D) E-mail a document

PART 3 Review Test

각 대화를 잘 듣고 그에 관련된 세 문제를 풀어보세요.

1. What kind of event are the speakers organizing?
   (A) A film festival
   (B) A seminar
   (C) A press conference
   (D) An interview

2. How do the speakers plan to advertise the event?
   (A) On the radio
   (B) In the newspaper
   (C) On television
   (D) Through the Internet

3. Who will the man ask for help?
   (A) His coworker
   (B) His friend
   (C) His brother
   (D) His manager

4. Why do the speakers want to have a sale?
   (A) To promote the store's anniversary
   (B) To make room for new inventory
   (C) To celebrate an opening of a new store
   (D) To advertise a new line of products

5. What season most likely is it now?
   (A) Spring
   (B) Summer
   (C) Autumn
   (D) Winter

6. What is indicated about the sale?
   (A) It will last for one week.
   (B) It will start on Wednesday.
   (C) Store members will get an e-mail about it.
   (D) There will be savings of up to 50%.

7. What does the woman say about the traffic?
   (A) It can be avoided.
   (B) It is from a celebration.
   (C) It will not cause a delay.
   (D) It will be over soon.

8. What does the woman imply when she says, "The dentist is running behind schedule, too"?
   (A) The dentist missed an appointment.
   (B) The man should visit a different dentist.
   (C) There are several problems at the office.
   (D) The man arriving late will not cause problems.

9. What does the man say he will do?
   (A) Take a shortcut
   (B) Participate in a parade
   (C) Call again later
   (D) Speak to the dentist

10. Where most likely does the conversation take place?
    (A) At a train station
    (B) At a bus stop
    (C) At an airport
    (D) At a convention center

11. What does the man do for the woman?
    (A) Provides her with a meal voucher
    (B) Shows her a new computer
    (C) Gives her some information
    (D) Offers her a refund

12. What will the woman probably do next?
    (A) Go to a waiting area
    (B) Purchase a ticket
    (C) Pay for a meal
    (D) Board a vehicle

13. Where most likely do the speakers work?
    (A) At a television network
    (B) At a photo studio
    (C) At a security firm
    (D) At a news publication

14. What problem is discussed?
    (A) A security guard cannot be reached.
    (B) A newspaper was not delivered.
    (C) An image was misused.
    (D) A farm is not open.

15. What will most likely happen tomorrow?
    (A) A company will apologize.
    (B) Customers will receive a refund.
    (C) An appointment will be missed.
    (D) Products will be recalled.

16. Where most likely does the conversation take place?
    (A) In a hotel
    (B) In a library
    (C) In a publishing company
    (D) In a clothing store

17. What has the man lost?
    (A) A cell phone
    (B) A wallet
    (C) A battery charger
    (D) A map

18. What will the woman probably do next?
    (A) Show the man a map
    (B) Make a phone call
    (C) Go to a cafeteria
    (D) Enter information on a computer

Employee Directory	
Evelyn Pierce	+521
Chuck Whitley	+522
Beth Parrent	+523
Tyler Wong	+524

19. What will the man most likely send the woman?
    (A) A healthy recipe
    (B) A doctor's name
    (C) A clinic's address
    (D) An allergy medicine

20. What does the man say about a doctor's office?
    (A) It closes at five.
    (B) It is next to his office.
    (C) It is opening next week.
    (D) It is reasonably priced.

21. Look at the graphic. What number will the woman most likely call?
    (A) 521
    (B) 522
    (C) 523
    (D) 524

PART 4

Unit 13   광고 / 방송
Unit 14   안내 방송 / 소개
Unit 15   녹음 메시지 / 설명문

Part 4   Review Test

UNIT 13 광고/방송

★ 콕콕 찍어주는 출제 포인트

Part 4의 출제 내용 중 먼저 광고와 방송을 살펴볼까요. 광고는 신제품 소개나 할인 행사 등이 주로 소개되고, 방송은 교통 상황이나 일기예보 등이 출제됩니다. 광고와 방송에 자주 등장하는 어휘를 알고 있으면 청취가 한결 쉬워지므로 관련 어휘도 철저히 공부해두세요.

빈출 질문 익히기

- Where most likely could this advertisement be heard? — 어디에서 이 광고를 들을 수 있겠는가?
- Who is the advertisement aimed at? — 이 광고는 누구를 대상으로 하는가?
- What item does the speaker mention? — 화자는 어떤 품목을 언급하고 있는가?
- What will the transportation department do? — 교통부는 무엇을 할 것인가?
- When is the rain expected to end? — 비는 언제 그칠 것으로 예상되는가?

문제 보기

1. What is the Let's Go 100?
   (A) An operating system
   (B) A suitcase
   (C) A navigation system
   (D) An electronic dictionary

   1. 렛츠 고 100은 무엇인가?
   (A) 운영 시스템
   (B) 여행 가방
   (C) 네비게이션 시스템
   (D) 전자 사전

2. Who most likely is the advertisement for?
   (A) Drivers
   (B) Teachers
   (C) Students
   (D) Internet users

   2. 광고는 누구를 위한 것이겠는가?
   (A) 운전자
   (B) 교사
   (C) 학생
   (D) 인터넷 사용자

3. What information does the Web site offer about the Let's Go 100?
   (A) Prices
   (B) Designs
   (C) Maps
   (D) Sizes

   3. 웹사이트는 렛츠 고 100에 대한 어떤 정보를 제공하는가?
   (A) 가격
   (B) 디자인
   (C) 지도
   (D) 크기

지문 보기 🎧 P4-U13-1

다음 지문을 미국식과 영국식으로 들어보세요.

Tired of using maps? Are you bad with directions? **Try the Let's Go 100 Navigator. This new GPS navigation system**[1] is small enough to fit in your pocket and easily mountable in your car. It includes maps for every city in North America including Canada and Mexico. The Let's Go 100 is **the perfect gift for anyone who drives**[2] or travels frequently. Traveling abroad? You can download **maps**[3] from Europe, South America, and even Asia **from our Web site, wayfinder.com.**[3] Stop getting lost and start traveling smart with the Let's Go 100.

지도를 이용하는 데 싫증이 납니까? 길눈이 어둡습니까? 렛츠 고 100 네비게이터를 써보세요. 이 새로운 GPS 네비게이션 시스템은 당신의 주머니에 쏙 들어갈 정도로 작고 자동차에 쉽게 설치할 수 있습니다. 이것은 캐나다와 멕시코를 포함한 북미의 모든 도시의 지도를 담고 있습니다. 렛츠 고 100은 운전이나 여행을 많이 하는 사람들에게 완벽한 선물입니다. 해외 여행을 하신다고요? 저희 웹사이트 wayfinder.com에서 유럽, 남미, 심지어 아시아 지도도 다운받을 수 있습니다. 렛츠 고 100으로 이제 길을 잃지 마시고 현명하게 여행하시기 바랍니다.

어휘 be tired of ~에 싫증이 나다   be bad with directions 길눈이 어둡다   try 써보다
navigation system (자동차의) 운행 유도 시스템   fit in ~에 들어가다, ~에 맞다   mountable 설치 가능한   get lost 길을 잃다
travel smart 똑똑하게 여행하다

문제 해설

1. 질문의 키워드: 무엇(What), 렛츠 고 100(Let's Go 100)
→ 광고에서 제품명이나 회사명은 이야기 초반부에 나오는 경우가 많다. 사람 이름이나 제품명과 같은 고유명사가 있을 경우 그 단어를 속으로 미리 읽어둔다.

2. 질문의 키워드: 누구를(Who), 대상(for)
→ 제품의 이용자를 묻는 질문이다.

3. 질문의 키워드: 어떤 정보(What information), 웹사이트(Web site), 제공하다(offer)
→ 웹사이트가 제공하는 정보를 묻는 질문으로, Part 4 지문에서 웹사이트에 대한 정보는 후반부에 언급하는 경우가 많다.

UNIT 13 **121**

광고/방송 관련 어휘 및 관용 표현 🎧 P4-U13-2

광고 / 방송 관련 어휘

discount 할인
save 절약하다
advertisement 광고
available 이용 가능한
replacement 교체(품)
clearance sale 재고 정리 세일
special offer 특별 할인가
complimentary 무료의
traffic jam/congestion/delay 교통 체증
northbound[southbound] lane 북쪽[남쪽]행 차선
commuter 통근자
inconvenience 불편
closed 폐쇄된 (=blocked off)
alternative/alternate route 대체 도로
weather forecast 일기예보
temperature 기온
foggy 안개가 낀
the high[low] 최고[최저] 기온
a cold[warm] front 한랭[온난] 전선
inclement weather 악천후

광고 / 방송 관련 관용 표현

Attention, shoppers. 손님 여러분 주목해주세요.
a wide selection of 매우 다양한 ~
30% off the regular price 정가에서 30% 할인
stop/drop/come by ~에 들르다
buy one, get one free 하나 사면 하나가 공짜
on a first-come, first-served basis 선착순으로
under warranty 보증기간 중
a new line of 새로운 종류의 ~
affordable/reasonable prices 저렴한 가격
weather update 최신 날씨 정보
be stuck in traffic 교통체증에 걸리다
Two lanes are closed. 두 개 차선이 폐쇄되었다.
take a detour 우회하다
Traffic will not be permitted. 교통이 통제될 것이다.
clear up (날씨가) 개다
chance of rain 비 올 확률
stay tuned 채널을 고정하다
I'll be back after ~. ~ 후에 다시 오겠습니다.

✏️ 어휘 및 표현 점검 해설 p.75

우리말 뜻을 보고 빈칸에 알맞은 단어를 넣으세요.

1. We sincerely apologize for the _____ caused by this. 이로 인해 발생한 불편에 대해 진심으로 사과 드립니다.
2. Please _____ we also offer catering services. 저희가 출장 요리 서비스도 제공해드린다는 점을 잊지 마십시오.
3. This _____ is available only for this month. 이 특별 할인가는 이달에만 적용됩니다.
4. We have a 10% _____ if you present your student ID card. 학생증을 제시하시면 10퍼센트를 할인해드립니다.
5. Please _____ for further updates on the weather. 일기예보를 계속 업데이트해 드리니 채널을 고정해주세요.

청취 집중 훈련 1

아래 제시된 지문의 음원을 듣고 빈칸을 채워보세요.

1. 한 단어 받아쓰기 연습

Discount Tires is having a _____ sale! Save up to _____ % off all of our _____ items. _____ you're shopping for snow tires for the upcoming winter or _____ tires for now, they're on sale now. You can also _____ on other car _____ during our sale. Discount Tires is on First Street, and we're _____ every day from nine to seven. Hurry, our sale is for this _____ only.

디스카운트 타이어스는 파격 세일을 하고 있습니다. 우리의 모든 인기 상품에 대해 최대 60%를 절약해 보세요. 다가오는 겨울용 스노우 타이어를 찾으시든지, 지금 쓸 교체 타이어를 찾으시든지 간에, 타이어가 현재 할인 중입니다. 세일 동안 기타 자동차 보조용품에 대해서도 할인을 받을 수 있습니다. 디스카운트 타이어스는 1번 가에 있으며 9시부터 7시까지 매일 문을 엽니다. 서두르세요, 할인은 단지 이번 주말에만 합니다.

2. 두 단어 이상 받아쓰기 연습

Good morning. I'm Laura Lee with a _____ for tomorrow. The _____ is 8 degrees Celsius with _____. On Tuesday, the winds will be calm but the _____ in the Dover County region will be just 2 degrees Celsius. _____ or rain is predicted, but if you have _____, you'll want to _____ or bring them inside. _____ next, we'll have Dave Nelson with a traffic _____ your morning commute. _____.

좋은 아침입니다. 저는 내일의 날씨 정보를 전하는 로라 리입니다. 약한 바람이 부는 가운데 현재 기온은 섭씨 8도입니다. 화요일엔 바람은 잠잠하겠지만 도버 카운티 지역의 최고 기온이 단지 섭씨 2도 정도가 되겠습니다. 눈이나 비가 예상되지는 않지만 옥외 식물을 가지고 있으면 단단히 덮어 씌우거나 실내로 옮겨 놓으세요. 이어서 여러분의 아침 통근을 위해 데이브 넬슨이 교통 정보를 전해드립니다. 채널 고정해주세요.

UNIT 13

청취 집중 훈련 2   P4-U13-4 / 해설 p.75-76

제시된 두 문제를 재빨리 훑어본 후, 핵심 내용을 빈칸 처리한 채 제시된 지문의 음원을 들으며 정답을 고르세요.

1. Who can use SunProtect?
   (A) All people   (B) Only adults

2. Where can SunProtect be purchased?
   (A) Online   (B) At most supermarkets

It's important that you _____ every day. SunProtect sun lotions can be used for _____ from young children to adults. SunProtect sun lotions are set at $10.99, so you _____ shop around for cheaper lotions. SunProtect is _____ supermarkets.

3. What type of program is being announced?
   (A) A travel show   (B) A cooking show

4. When will the program air?
   (A) On Thursday   (B) On Friday

This week on PLN _____, we will cover Bulgaria. We'll show you all that Bulgaria _____. Boasting nine UNESCO heritage sites, Bulgaria is becoming a _____ these days. _____ more about this beautiful country, at 7 P.M. only on PLN.

5. What does Ms. Matthews suggest people do on Saturday?
   (A) Bring an umbrella   (B) Enjoy the outdoors

6. What will happen Sunday night?
   (A) It will rain.   (B) It will get warmer.

I'm Sarah Matthews with the _____ for this weekend. Saturday is the perfect day to _____. However, there's an _____ on Sunday. The rain will _____ Monday morning and start to _____ Monday afternoon.

124

청취 집중 훈련 3

각 지문을 듣고 그에 관련된 두 문제를 풀어보세요.

1. What insurance is being advertised?
   (A) Car
   (B) House
   (C) Life
   (D) Travel

2. What is mentioned about Wright Insurance?
   (A) It is looking for new employees.
   (B) It offers a free estimate.
   (C) It has branch offices across the nation.
   (D) It recently opened a new office in Europe.

3. What will the transportation department do?
   (A) Pave the roads
   (B) Repair guardrails
   (C) Build a sidewalk
   (D) Install traffic lights

4. What does the speaker advise commuters to do?
   (A) Leave earlier than usual
   (B) Stay in the right lane
   (C) Take an alternate route
   (D) Use public transportation

5. When is the rain expected to end?
   (A) In the morning
   (B) In the evening
   (C) The next morning
   (D) The next evening

6. What most likely will be heard next?
   (A) Health news
   (B) Cooking advice
   (C) A traffic update
   (D) Business advice

실전 감각 익히기

각 지문을 잘 듣고 그에 관련된 세 문제를 풀어보세요.

1. Where might this advertisement be heard?
   (A) At a shoe store
   (B) At a book store
   (C) At an electronics store
   (D) At a department store

2. When will the sale end?
   (A) On Friday
   (B) On Saturday
   (C) On Sunday
   (D) On Monday

3. What is the most customers can save?
   (A) 15 percent
   (B) 35 percent
   (C) 55 percent
   (D) 75 percent

4. Who does Ms. Kim most likely work for?
   (A) The transportation system
   (B) A radio news program
   (C) A local newspaper
   (D) The city subway

5. How low are temperatures predicted to get?
   (A) -10 Celsius
   (B) -15 Celsius
   (C) -20 Celsius
   (D) -25 Celsius

6. What are listeners advised to do?
   (A) Put their pets outside
   (B) Turn off their heaters
   (C) Leave earlier for work
   (D) Put snow tires on their cars

7. What is the reason for the delays?

   (A) A car accident
   (B) A marathon race
   (C) Road construction
   (D) Inclement weather

8. What does the speaker advise those who plan to leave the city to do?

   (A) Take the Parkway
   (B) Use public transportation
   (C) Take an alternative route
   (D) Leave early in the morning

9. What can be expected to happen in the next few hours?

   (A) Delays will be even longer.
   (B) Traffic will clear up.
   (C) It will take a long time to get into the city.
   (D) An event will take place.

10. What is on sale?

    (A) Shoes
    (B) Accessories
    (C) Electronics
    (D) Sporting goods

11. What item does the speaker mention?

    (A) Jackets
    (B) Notebooks
    (C) Sunglasses
    (D) Dress shoes

12. When does the sale end?

    (A) In March
    (B) In April
    (C) In May
    (D) In June

UNIT 14 안내 방송 / 소개

★ 콕콕 찍어주는 출제 포인트

안내 방송은 회사 관련 상황에서는 사내 회의나 행사, 새로운 장비/시설의 설치 및 공사 등에 대한 내용이 주로 나오고, 일상과 관련해서는 상점이나 공공시설의 개·폐점 시간, 항공편 지연, 또는 시설 이용 안내가 나오기도 합니다. 안내 방송이나 소개 지문은 〈인사말 → 공지의 목적 → 세부 사항 → 권고나 요청〉의 순서로 이야기가 전개된다는 것을 알아두세요. 또한 질문에서 화자의 의도를 묻는 문제가 있을 경우 문맥에 맞게 해당 문장의 의미를 파악한 후 정답을 선택해야 합니다.

빈출 질문 익히기

- Where most likely would this announcement be heard? 이 안내 방송은 어디에서 들을 수 있겠는가?
- What is indicated about the museum? 박물관에 대해 무엇이 언급되었는가?
- How long has Ms. Cheng worked at the company? 쳉 씨는 얼마나 오랫동안 근무했는가?
- What department does Ms. Park work in? 박 씨는 어느 부서에서 근무하는가?
- What will probably happen after this talk? 이 이야기 다음에 무슨 일이 일어날 것 같은가?

문제 보기

1. Where do the listeners most likely work?
   (A) At a magazine
   (B) At a restaurant
   (C) At a design firm
   (D) At a furniture store

2. What does the speaker imply when he says, "there is no need"?
   (A) A news article is unnecessary.
   (B) He has finished preparations.
   (C) The listeners should be confident.
   (D) New jobs are not available.

3. What will the listeners most likely do next?
   (A) Set up work areas
   (B) Contact a journalist
   (C) Buy a newspaper
   (D) Apply for a job

1. 청자들은 어디에서 일하는 사람들이겠는가?
   (A) 잡지사
   (B) 레스토랑
   (C) 디자인 회사
   (D) 가구점

2. 화자가 "그럴 필요가 없습니다"라고 말할 때 의미하는 바는 무엇인가?
   (A) 신문 기사는 필요치 않다.
   (B) 그가 준비 작업을 다 끝냈다.
   (C) 청자들은 자신감을 가져야 한다.
   (D) 새로운 일자리가 없다

3. 청자들은 다음에 무엇을 하겠는가?
   (A) 작업 공간을 준비한다.
   (B) 기자에게 연락한다.
   (C) 새 신문을 산다.
   (D) 일자리에 지원한다.

지문 보기 🎧 P4-U14-1

다음 지문을 미국식과 영국식으로 들어보세요.

As you all know, the food critic for the *Melbourne Tribune* is eating here tonight[1]. Now, since he's reviewing us, I'm sure everyone is a little bit nervous, but really, there is no need[2]. We make delicious food, and our waitstaff is superb. All we need to do is provide our usual, excellent service and everything else will take care of itself. Also, remember that we'll have a lot more regular customers than food critics, so pay attention to all of the tables tonight, OK? All right, let's go ahead and start preparing the kitchen and dining room[3].

여러분 모두 알고 있는 것처럼, 〈멜버른 트리뷴〉의 음식 비평가가 오늘밤 이곳에서 식사를 합니다. 자, 그가 우리를 평가할 것이므로 모두들 어느 정도 긴장을 하고 있을 거라고 생각하는데요, 하지만 그럴 필요는 없습니다. 우리는 맛있는 음식을 만들며, 우리 직원들은 아주 훌륭합니다. 단지 우리가 할 일은 평소에 하던 그대로 뛰어난 서비스를 제공하는 것뿐이며 그러면 나머지 일들은 알아서 해결이 될 것입니다. 그리고 우리는 음식 비평가들보다 훨씬 많은 수의 단골 손님들을 받는다는 사실을 잊지 말아야 하며, 따라서 오늘밤 모든 테이블에 신경을 써 주셔야 하겠습니다. 아시겠죠? 좋습니다. 이제 각자 주방과 식당으로 가서 작업을 시작하시기 바랍니다.

어휘 food critic 음식 비평가 review ~을 비평하다, 검토하다, 조사하다 delicious 맛있는 waitstaff 웨이터들, 종업원들 superb 매우 훌륭한, 아주 뛰어난 provide 제공하다 regular customer 단골 손님[고객]

문제 해설

1. 질문의 키워드: 어디(Where), 청자들(listeners), 일하다(work)
→ 안내 방송이 나오는 장소는 대체로 담화 앞부분에서 알 수 있다. '음식 비평가가 오늘밤 여기서 식사를 할 것이다'라는 말은 여기가 음식점임을 알게 해준다.

2. 질문의 키워드: 무엇(What), 화자(speaker), 암시하다(imply), "there is no need"
→ 화자는 직원들 모두 긴장을 하고 있을 것(I'm sure everyone is a little bit nervous)이라는 말에 이어 "그럴 필요가 없다(there is no need)"라고 말하고 있다. 즉 직원들은 위축될 필요 없이 자신감을 가지라는 뜻이다.

3. 질문의 키워드: 무엇(What), 청자들(listeners), 다음에 하다(do next)
→ 이런 질문에 대한 답은 주로 담화 끝부분에 나온다. 담화 마지막에 화자는 직원들에게 각자 주방과 식당으로 가서 작업을 시작하라(let's go ahead and start preparing the kitchen and dining room.)고 말하고 있다.

안내 방송/소개 관련 어휘 및 관용 표현 🎧 P4-U14-2

안내 방송 / 소개 관련 어휘

- **hold** 열다, 개최하다
- **inspect** 점검하다
- **inform** 알리다 (=notify)
- **release** 출시하다 (=launch)
- **expand** 확장하다
- **install** 설치하다
- **board** 탑승하다
- **flight attendant** 승무원
- **captain** 기장, 선장
- **ticket counter** 매표소
- **exhibit** 전시회; 전시하다
- **prohibit** 금지하다
- **introduce** 소개하다
- **cooperation** 협조
- **outstanding** 뛰어난
- **eligible** 자격이 있는
- **dedicated** 헌신적인
- **expert** 전문가
- **guest speaker** 초청 연사
- **retire** 은퇴하다

안내 방송 / 소개 관련 관용 표현

- **I'd like to remind that ~** ~을 다시 알려드립니다
- **due to/because of the bad weather** 날씨가 안 좋기 때문에
- **comply with the regulations** 규정을 준수하다
- **sign up for** ~에 등록하다 (=register for, enroll in)
- **Please make your way to** ~로 가주시기 바랍니다
- **encourage A(사람) to**부정사 A에게 ~하길 권하다
- **be required to**부정사 ~해야 하다
- **be asked to**부정사 ~해달라고 요청 받다
- **apologize for** ~에 대해 사과하다
- **be pleased to**부정사 ~을 하게 되어 기쁘다
- **The award goes to** 수상자는 ~입니다
- **specialize in** ~을 전문으로 하다
- **It's a great honor to**부정사 ~하게 되어 큰 영광입니다
- **give a round of applause** 박수를 보내다
- **give a warm welcome to** ~를 반갑게 맞이하다
- **be known for** ~로 유명하다

어휘 및 표현 점검 해설 p.80

우리말 뜻을 보고 빈칸에 알맞은 단어를 넣으세요.

1. This ceremony is being _____ in appreciation of your hard work.
   이 기념식은 여러분의 노고에 감사하는 뜻에서 진행되고 있습니다.

2. Smoking is _____ in airplanes.
   기내에서 흡연은 금지되어 있습니다.

3. You can _____ the seminar at the Admission Desk.
   접수석에서 세미나 등록을 하실 수 있습니다.

4. It's _____ to receive this award for my film.
   제 영화로 이 상을 받게 되어 영광입니다.

5. It is my pleasure to _____ Mr. Mendel Awori as our keynote speaker.
   멘델 아워리 씨를 우리의 기조 연설자로 소개하게 되어 기쁩니다.

청취 집중 훈련 1

아래 제시된 지문의 음원을 듣고 빈칸을 채워보세요.

1. 한 단어 받아쓰기 연습

_____ all employees. On Friday, June 1, Brockford Middleton from Point Consulting will be here to _____ a _____ on Building Customer Relations. Since many of you are _____ to the company, employee _____ at the event is strongly _____. _____ the seminar, Mr. Middleton will take questions from you. Sign-up is not _____ but _____. You can _____ by calling Annie at extension 100. The seminar will begin at 2 in the auditorium.

모든 직원 여러분, 주목해 주세요. 6월 1일 금요일에 포인트 컨설팅의 브록포드 미들튼이 고객 관계 형성에 대한 세미나를 진행하기 위해 이곳에 올 겁니다. 여러분 중 많은 분들이 회사에 새로 들어오셨기 때문에 이번 행사에 대한 직원 여러분의 참석을 적극 권장합니다. 세미나 이후에 미들튼 씨가 여러분들로부터 질문을 받을 겁니다. 신청이 필수적인 것은 아니지만 추천해 드리는 바입니다. 내선번호 100으로 애니에게 전화해서 신청하시면 됩니다. 세미나는 강당에서 2시에 시작됩니다.

2. 두 단어 이상 받아쓰기 연습

Today, I am very pleased to introduce _____, Mr. Harry Gibbons to you. He is _____ an expert on _____ in workplace culture. He _____ lecturing on creating excitement and productivity _____. Mr. Gibbons _____ and _____, *How to Be Happy at Work*, which is currently at the top of _____ list. He is here to _____ on workplace innovation today. Please give a _____ to Mr. Harry Gibbons.

저는 오늘 여러분들에게 초청 연사이신 해리 기븐스 씨를 소개해드리게 되어 무척 기쁩니다. 그는 직장 문화에서의 혁신적인 변화에 대한 전문가로 매우 유명합니다. 그는 전국을 순회하며 직장에서의 즐거움과 생산성 창출에 대한 강의를 합니다. 기븐스 씨는 최근에 〈행복한 직장 생활의 비법〉이라는 책을 저술 출판했으며 현재 그 책은 비즈니스 베스트셀러 중에서 가장 잘 팔리고 있습니다. 그는 오늘 직장 혁신에 대한 연설을 하기 위해 이곳에 오셨습니다. 해리 기븐스 씨를 반갑게 맞이해주십시오.

청취 집중 훈련 2

제시된 두 문제를 재빨리 훑어본 후, 핵심 내용을 빈칸 처리한 채 제시된 지문의 음원을 들으며 정답을 고르세요.

1. What is indicated about the festival?

   (A) It is held every year.　　(B) It takes place for a week.

2. Who most likely is Mr. Nelson?

   (A) A film producer　　(B) An event planner

> _____ Andover Culture Festival. We have lots of great events planned over the _____, including this week's independent film festival. Our first film screening tonight is the documentary film *A Photographer's Life*, produced by _____ Ray Nelson.

3. What is being announced?

   (A) Two firms will merge.　　(B) A company CEO will retire.

4. What type of company is Prime Solutions?

   (A) A consulting firm　　(B) An insurance company

> I _____ to make. Our founder and CEO of Prime Solutions Justin Yoon will formally retire in December. Mr. Yoon _____ 28 years ago. Under Mr. Yoon's leadership, Prime Solutions became the _____. Vice president Dale Montvale _____ Mr. Yoon.

5. Where might this announcement be heard?

   (A) At an exhibition　　(B) At an opening ceremony

6. Who is John Darcy?

   (A) The mayor　　(B) An entrepreneur

> Welcome to the _____ of the Buckley Center. First, I'd like to take the time to thank Pitney and Sommers for their _____. The City of Greenville was also instrumental in _____. With that in mind, please give a warm welcome to _____, John Darcy.

청취 집중 훈련 3   P4-U14-5 / 해설 p.81-82

각 지문을 듣고 그에 관련된 두 문제를 풀어보세요.

1. What is the purpose of the announcement?
   (A) To review upcoming events
   (B) To announce a schedule change
   (C) To introduce a guest speaker
   (D) To announce the opening of a museum

2. What does the speaker mean when he says, "we must be sure to maintain a strict guest list"?
   (A) We must submit a guest list on time.
   (B) Only those with an invitation have to be admitted to the gallery.
   (C) We have to accept new guests.
   (D) A guest list has be made before June 8

3. What has Ms. Logan recently done?
   (A) She received an award.
   (B) She wrote a book.
   (C) She designed a new product.
   (D) She started a radio talk show.

4. What are listeners encouraged to do after the lecture?
   (A) Shop at an online store
   (B) Attend workshops
   (C) Meet with a company CEO
   (D) Fill out a form

5. What is the purpose of the speech?
   (A) To explain a new sales contest
   (B) To discuss yearly sales figures
   (C) To recognize an employee
   (D) To mention new job openings

6. How long has Ms. Cheng worked at the company?
   (A) For 2 years
   (B) For 5 years
   (C) For 10 years
   (D) For 20 years

실전 감각 익히기

각 지문을 잘 듣고 그에 관련된 세 문제를 풀어보세요.

1. What is the main purpose of the talk?
   - (A) To praise top salespeople
   - (B) To discuss survey results
   - (C) To schedule a staff social event
   - (D) To prepare for a software release

2. Who most likely is the audience?
   - (A) Photographers
   - (B) Sales managers
   - (C) Product designers
   - (D) Computer programmers

3. What are the listeners asked to do?
   - (A) Design a Web site
   - (B) Meet with their teams
   - (C) Attend a training seminar
   - (D) Finish work early

4. Where most likely would this announcement be heard?
   - (A) In an office
   - (B) In a school
   - (C) In a library
   - (D) In a bookstore

5. Who is Ms. Cohen?
   - (A) An author
   - (B) A customer
   - (C) A librarian
   - (D) A teacher

6. When will the event begin?
   - (A) At 10 A.M.
   - (B) At 11 A.M.
   - (C) At 1 P.M.
   - (D) At 2 P.M.

7. What does the speaker mention about regional farmers?

   (A) They use Mr. Ray's farming technique.
   (B) They are pioneers of sustainable farming.
   (C) They work together to harvest crops.
   (D) They recently appeared on television.

8. What does the speaker mean when she says, "Banks turned him down"?

   (A) Banks declined Mr. Ray.
   (B) Banks confused Mr. Ray.
   (C) Banks redirected Mr. Ray.
   (D) Banks assisted Mr. Ray.

9. What will the speaker most likely do next?

   (A) Visit a farm
   (B) Play an interview clip
   (C) Speak to a university student
   (D) Give a weather forecast

10. When will the museum close?

    (A) At 9:00 P.M.
    (B) At 9:30 P.M.
    (C) At 10:00 P.M.
    (D) At 10:30 P.M.

11. What is indicated about the museum?

    (A) It will be closed tomorrow.
    (B) Admission is free for children this month.
    (C) Members may enter for free.
    (D) It will move to a new location this month.

12. What will be displayed next month?

    (A) Paintings
    (B) Pottery
    (C) Sculptures
    (D) Photographs

UNIT 15 녹음 메시지/설명문

★ 콕콕 찍어주는 출제 포인트

녹음 메시지에서는 예약 확인이나 변경, 요청 받은 사항에 대한 답변, 제품이나 서비스에 대한 문의, 회사의 영업 시간 안내 등이 주로 제시됩니다. 설명문은 사내에서의 제품 홍보 계획, 신입 사원에 대한 공지 사항 등이 나옵니다. 녹음 메시지와 설명문은 대체로 〈인사/소개 → 구체적인 용건/일정 → 요청 사항/계획〉의 순서대로 전개된다는 것을 알아두세요. 아울러 질문에 시각 정보가 포함되어 있을 경우 미리 읽어 두면 지문을 이해하는 데 도움이 됩니다.

 빈출 질문 익히기

- Who is this message intended for? 이 메시지는 누구를 대상으로 하는 것인가?
- What is the purpose of this message? 이 메시지의 목적은 무엇인가?
- What will the listeners probably do next? 청자들은 다음에 무엇을 하겠는가?
- What is mentioned about the program? 프로그램에 대해 무엇이 언급되었는가?
- What will happen after the introduction session? 소개 시간 후에 무엇이 있겠는가?

 문제 보기

Fresh'Ns Catering

Customer: Sam Zakaria   Order Number: B01752

Item	Quantity
Lemonade	20 glasses
Spring Salad	3 bowls
Fried Chicken	3 trays
Chocolate Cake	12 pieces

후레쉬앤스 케이터링

고객: 샘 자카리아   주문번호 #: B01752

품목	수량
레모네이드	20병
스프링 샐러드	3그릇
후라이드 치킨	3쟁반
초콜릿 케이크	12조각

1. What does the speaker say about Crescent Data?
   (A) It is a good place to work.
   (B) Its picnic schedule changed.
   (C) It is participating in a contest.
   (D) It has a government contract.

2. Look at the graphic. What item will be removed from the order?
   (A) Lemonade   (B) Spring Salad
   (C) Fried Chicken   (D) Chocolate Cake

1. 화자가 크레센트 데이터에 대해 말하는 것은?
   (A) 일하기 좋은 곳이다.
   (B) 야유회 일정이 변경되었다.
   (C) 대회에 참가하고 있다.
   (D) 정부와 계약을 맺고 있다.

2. 도표를 보세요. 어떤 품목이 주문에서 제거될 것인가?
   (A) 레모네이드   (B) 스프링 샐러드
   (C) 후라이드 치킨   (D) 초콜릿 케이크

3. Where does the speaker say the food should be delivered?
   (A) To a park
   (B) To a fitness center
   (C) To City Hall
   (D) To an office building

3. 화자는 음식이 어디로 배달되어야 한다고 말하는가?
   (A) 공원으로
   (B) 헬스 클럽으로
   (C) 시청으로
   (D) 사무실 빌딩으로

지문 보기

다음 지문을 미국식과 영국식으로 들어보세요.

Hello. This is Sam Zakaria from Crescent Data. I placed a catering order for my company's annual picnic, but I need to make a slight change to the order. Actually, our office is taking part in the Glenndale City fitness challenge,[1] and we decided that to help us reach our fitness goal, we should all skip desserts for this month. So, please remove the last item on our order.[2] Oh, and just to confirm, the rest of the order needs to be delivered to the west picnic area at Red Belt Park[3]. Give me a call if there are any problems. Thanks again.

안녕하세요. 크레센트 데이터의 샘 자카리아입니다. 저희 회사의 연례 야유회를 위해 제가 출장 요리 주문을 했습니다만 주문을 약간 변경할 필요가 생겼습니다. 실은, 저희 회사가 글렌데일 시의 건강 챌린지에 참가하고 있습니다. 그래서 저희가 세운 건강 목표를 달성하는 데 도움이 되기 위해서는 이달의 디저트를 모두 건너뛰어야 한다는 결정을 내렸습니다. 그러니 저희 주문에서 마지막 품목을 지워 주십시오. 아, 그리고 확인을 위해, 나머지 주문 품목들 모두는 레드 벨트 공원의 서쪽 야유회 공간으로 배달되어야 합니다. 혹시 무슨 문제가 있으면 전화 주십시오. 다시 한 번 감사드립니다.

어휘 catering 음식 조달 annual 연례의, 해마다의 take part in ~에 참가하다 fitness 건강 challenge 도전 skip 거르다, 건너뛰다 remove 제거하다 quantity 수량, 양 jug 저그, 물병 tray 쟁반

문제 해설

1. 질문의 키워드: 무엇(What), 화자(speaker), 말하다(say), 크레센트 데이터(Crescent Data)
   → Crescent Data가 무엇인지부터 듣고 알아내야 한다. 이런 키워드는 주로 앞부분에 나오니 주의 깊게 듣고 이 키워드에 대해 어떤 이야기가 나오는지 준비하도록 한다.

2. 질문의 키워드: 보다(Look), 도표(graphic), 어떤 품목(What item), 삭제되다(be removed), 주문(order)
   → 도표를 보며 들어야 하는 문제이다. 담화 중반 이후 주문에서 마지막 품목을 지워 달라(please remove the last item on our order)는 말이 나오고 있다.

3. 질문의 키워드: 어디(Where), 화자(speaker), 말하다(say), 음식(food), 배달되다(be delievered)
   → 장소가 나오길 기다리며 들으면 되는 질문이다. 담화 후반부에 나머지 주문 품목을 Red Belt Park으로 배달하라는 말이 나오고 있다.

녹음 메시지/설명문 관련 어휘 및 관용 표현 🎧 P4-U15-2

녹음 메시지 / 설명문 관련 어휘

respond to ~에 응답하다
inquire about ~에 대해 문의하다
regarding ~에 관한 (=concerning)
pick up ~을 찾아가다
extension 내선번호
inconvenience 불편함
implement 실행하다 (=carry out)
approve 승인하다
process 처리하다
collaborate 협력하다
compensate 보상하다
procedure 절차
immediately 즉시, 바로
reschedule 일정을 변경하다
postpone 연기하다 (=put off)
cancel 취소하다 (=call off)
remind 상기시키다
ensure ~을 확실히 하다
arrange 준비하다, 마련하다
follow 따르다, 지키다

녹음 메시지 / 설명문 관련 관용 표현

be busy 통화 중이다
hold the line 전화를 끊지 않고 기다리다
leave a message 메시지를 남기다
be scheduled to부정사 ~할 예정이다
set up ~를 마련하다 (=arrange, schedule)
let A(사람) know A에게 알려주다
inform/notify A(사람) of B A에게 B를 알리다
wonder if ~ ~인지 궁금하다
get back to ~에게 다시 연락하다
call A (사람) back A에게 다시 전화를 하다 (=return one's call)
according to the procedures 절차에 따라
be allowed/permitted to부정사 ~이 허락되다
take a tour of ~를 견학하다
take the time to부정사 ~할 시간을 내다
should you have any questions 어떤 질문이 있으시면
as soon as possible 가능한 한 빨리

✏️ 어휘 및 표현 점검 해설 p.85

우리말 뜻을 보고 빈칸에 알맞은 단어를 넣으세요.

1 This tour will take place _____ after our meeting. 이 관람은 우리가 회의를 끝내자마자 이루어질 것입니다.
2 I was _____ I have to pay a fine. 제가 벌금을 내야 하는지 궁금했습니다.
3 Please call me by pressing _____ #151. 내선번호 151번을 눌러 제게 전화해주십시오.
4 Please call me back _____ about this matter. 이 문제와 관련하여 가능한 한 빨리 전화해주십시오.
5 I asked if I could _____ my newspaper subscription. 저는 신문 구독을 해지할 수 있는지를 문의했습니다.

청취 집중 훈련 1

아래 제시된 지문의 음원을 듣고 빈칸을 채워보세요.

1. 한 단어 받아쓰기 연습

In this position, you'll have various day-to-day _____. Generally, you'll be required to do things to make sure projects are completed _____ to client _____. It's very important that you make sure our clients are _____ their business goals with our agency. So, this post _____ a high degree of professionalism. You were _____ for this _____ because you have some _____ and _____ in public relations. OK, let's look at the job _____ now.

이 직책에서 당신은 다양한 일일 책무를 맡게 될 겁니다. 일반적으로 고객 지침에 따라 프로젝트들을 완료하기 위한 여러 가지 일들을 해야 합니다. 고객들이 우리 회사와 함께 그들의 사업 목표를 달성할 수 있도록 하는 것은 매우 중요합니다. 그래서 이 자리는 높은 수준의 전문성을 필요로 합니다. 당신은 홍보 분야에서의 배경과 경험을 어느 정도 갖고 있기 때문에 이 자리에 뽑힌 겁니다. 좋습니다. 이제 직무 기술서를 같이 봅시다.

2. 두 단어 이상 받아쓰기 연습

Hi, this _____ Ms. Donna Kim. It's Mike at Smart Shuttle Service. I just want to _____ you know the _____ using the airport-downtown _____ you've _____. First, we have your flight listed as _____ at 8:40. Once you arrive, please _____ your cell phone and our driver will call to confirm the pick-up. We're _____ pick you up at 9:15. Please go out Exit Number 2 and _____ your driver at Arrivals Area Number 1. Thanks, and have a _____.

안녕하세요. 이 메시지는 도나 김 씨를 위한 것입니다. 저는 스마트 셔틀 서비스의 마이크입니다. 고객님께서 저희에게 예약하신 공항-시내 간의 셔틀 버스 이용에 대한 절차를 알려드리고자 합니다. 먼저, 8시 40분에 고객님 비행편이 들어오는 걸로 되어 있습니다. 도착하시자마자 휴대폰을 켜주시면 저희 기사가 픽업 확인 전화를 할 겁니다. 저희가 9시 15분에 모시러 가겠습니다. 2번 출구로 나오시면 1번 도착 구역에서 기사를 만나게 될 겁니다. 감사 드리며 안전한 비행을 하시기 바랍니다.

청취 집중 훈련 2

제시된 두 문제를 재빨리 훑어본 후, 핵심 내용을 빈칸 처리한 채 제시된 지문의 음원을 들으며 정답을 고르세요.

1. What kind of business is the speaker most likely calling?
   (A) A moving company   (B) An apartment rental agency

2. What does the speaker request that Ms. Nelson do?
   (A) Cancel an appointment   (B) Meet him at an earlier time

> Hello, this is Henry Dodson calling. This message is for one of your _____, Liz Nelson. I have a 3 o'clock _____ to view an apartment on Irving Street. I'm actually in the Irving Street area now and _____ if I can see her _____ if possible. Please _____ on my mobile as soon as possible. Thank you.

3. Where does the talk most likely take place?
   (A) At a trade show   (B) At a photo studio

4. What is mentioned about the program?
   (A) It is easy to use.   (B) It is very cheap.

> Greetings, everyone. I hope you're all enjoying our _____ today. Now, I'll show the features of the Photo-Maker software program. It's been a big success since it _____ last month. While it's _____ editing software on the market, it has the _____. Even beginners can use it.

5. When did the speaker begin designing the building?
   (A) Five years ago   (B) Seven years ago

6. Who does the speaker thank?
   (A) The building owners   (B) The design staff

> When I started the design for the Lincoln Building _____, I had no idea it would be successful. I'd like to _____ of the Lincoln Building for approaching me to work on the project and for _____ me in designing something that was both _____.

청취 집중 훈련 3 P4-U15-5 / 해설 p.86-88

각 지문을 듣고 그에 관련된 두 문제를 풀어보세요.

This week's bestseller (3/10-3/16)

Title	Author	Publisher
1. *The Mystery of Nature*	Mitchem Thoreau	Suntree Circle
2. *Delights of Cooking*	Emily Rivera	Orion Publishing
3. *How to be Different*	Ryan Howard	Alpha Human
4. *A Final Choice*	Allen Tyler	Greenlove

1. Who most likely is speaking?
   (A) An author
   (B) A customer
   (C) An art professor
   (D) A bookstore owner

2. Look at the graphic. What book will the speaker most likely recommend?
   (A) *The Mystery of Nature*
   (B) *Delights of Cooking*
   (C) *How to be Different*
   (D) *A Final Choice*

3. Who most likely is the talk intended for?
   (A) New employees
   (B) Visiting students
   (C) Prospective interns
   (D) Senior executives

4. What will happen after the introduction session?
   (A) Individual interviews
   (B) A product demonstration
   (C) A question and answer session
   (D) A tour of different departments

5. Where most likely can this talk be heard?
   (A) At a bus station
   (B) On a tour bus
   (C) At a restaurant
   (D) On the beach

6. What does the speaker ask listeners NOT to do?
   (A) Fishing
   (B) Swimming
   (C) Taking pictures
   (D) Leaving the bus

실전 감각 익히기 P4-U15-6 / 해설 p.88-90

각 지문을 잘 듣고 그에 관련된 세 문제를 풀어보세요.

1. Who most likely is Mr. Yu?
   (A) A Web site developer
   (B) A restaurant chef
   (C) A property manager
   (D) A clothing designer

2. What is Mr. Yu being offered?
   (A) A photography course
   (B) An upgraded software package
   (C) An employment contract
   (D) A piece of artwork

3. At what time does the caller suggest meeting on Friday?
   (A) 12 P.M.
   (B) 1 P.M.
   (C) 2 P.M.
   (D) 3 P.M.

4. What does Profex most likely sell?
   (A) Computers
   (B) Printers
   (C) Televisions
   (D) Copy machines

5. What are callers asked to have available?
   (A) A phone number
   (B) A serial number
   (C) A receipt number
   (D) A credit card number

6. What does the speaker ask international callers to do?
   (A) Purchase software
   (B) Visit the Web site
   (C) Provide an address
   (D) Call another number

7. What should listeners do before reserving a conference room?

   (A) Confirm the size of the room
   (B) Log onto an e-mail program
   (C) Make a list of participants' names
   (D) Review the meeting's agenda

8. How many conference rooms does the company have?

   (A) One
   (B) Two
   (C) Three
   (D) Four

9. What are listeners requested to include in their reservation request?

   (A) The type of refreshments served in the meeting
   (B) The number of participants in the meeting
   (C) The purpose of the meeting
   (D) The equipment needed for the meeting

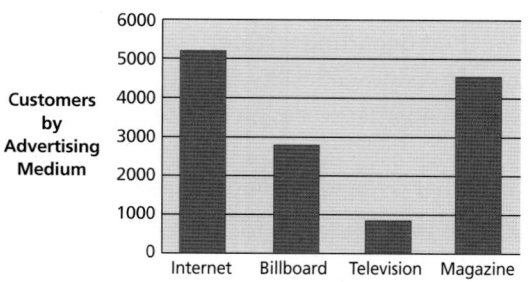

10. What type of product is the speaker discussing?

    (A) A sports drink
    (B) A computer program
    (C) A financial service
    (D) A television model

11. Look at the graphic. What type of advertising does the speaker want to invest more in?

    (A) Television
    (B) Magazine
    (C) Billboard
    (D) Internet

12. According to the speaker, what will happen next year?

    (A) An advertisement will be recorded.
    (B) A sports competition will begin.
    (C) A new product line will launch.
    (D) A logo will be redesigned.

PART 4 Review Test

각 지문을 잘 듣고 그에 관련된 세 문제를 풀어보세요.

1. What is being advertised?
   (A) A furniture store
   (B) A department store
   (C) A storage facility
   (D) An interior design service

2. What is mentioned about prices?
   (A) They are lower for store members only.
   (B) They are cheaper than at other stores.
   (C) They are up to 30 percent off the original price.
   (D) They are discounted for two weeks only.

3. What service is introduced in the advertisement?
   (A) A three-year warranty
   (B) Regular e-mail updates
   (C) 24-hour security monitoring
   (D) Free delivery and installation

4. What will the temperature be tonight?
   (A) 58 degrees Fahrenheit
   (B) 62 degrees Fahrenheit
   (C) 70 degrees Fahrenheit
   (D) 80 degrees Fahrenheit

5. What does Ms. Matthews suggest people do on Saturday?
   (A) Wear a jacket
   (B) Stay inside
   (C) Bring an umbrella
   (D) Enjoy the outdoors

6. What will happen on Sunday?
   (A) It will rain.
   (B) It will get warmer.
   (C) There will be strong winds.
   (D) The temperatures will be high.

7. What department does the speaker most likely work in?
   (A) Accounting
   (B) Customer service
   (C) Human resources
   (D) Market research

8. What are listeners instructed to do?
   (A) Complete paperwork
   (B) Pick up paychecks
   (C) Go to the lunchroom
   (D) Register for a workshop

9. What most likely will happen in 20 minutes?
   (A) A procedure will be explained.
   (B) A meal break will begin.
   (C) A research study will begin.
   (D) A workshop will conclude.

10. What is the main purpose of the announcement?
    (A) To explain a registration process
    (B) To announce a delayed starting time
    (C) To promote the benefits of a new product
    (D) To give directions to an exhibit area

11. What is indicated about the Smarter Lighting Expo?
    (A) It is designed for photographers.
    (B) It requires an admission fee.
    (C) It is unique in the area.
    (D) It will be held over two days.

12. When does the product demonstration begin?
    (A) At 8 A.M.
    (B) At 10 A.M.
    (C) At 11 A.M.
    (D) At 12 P.M.

13. According to the speaker, who should visit the company's Web site?
    (A) Rapid Reserve staff members
    (B) Customers looking for flight times
    (C) People looking for staff members
    (D) Customers in need of special reservations

14. What does the speaker mean when she says, "please hold for the next available customer service representative"?
    (A) Hang up and try again
    (B) Call at another time
    (C) Leave a callback number
    (D) Wait for the next operator

15. What does the speaker remind callers about?
    (A) Discount tickets
    (B) A cancellation policy
    (C) Changes to flight times
    (D) Weekend service

16. What is Ms. Medford's new position?
    (A) Marketing manager
    (B) Human resources manager
    (C) Sales director
    (D) Vice president

17. What will happen in the afternoon?
    (A) A new procedure will be demonstrated.
    (B) A training program will begin.
    (C) A staff survey will be distributed.
    (D) An award ceremony will be held.

18. What does the speaker request that listeners do?
    (A) Get new employee ID cards
    (B) Nominate colleagues for awards
    (C) Provide updated contact information
    (D) Hold small group meetings

List of Suppliers	
Supplier	Item
Top's Silverware Co.	Cutlery and Plates
Cleanall Store	Napkins and Wet Towels
Dailydairy Farm	Butter and Cheese
Wholnutri Store	Fruits and Vegetables

19. Look at the graphic. Which supplier failed to bring its items?
    (A) Top's Silverware Co.
    (B) Cleanall Store
    (C) Dailydairy Farm
    (D) Wholnutri Store

20. What does the speaker tell the listeners to do during lunchtime?
    (A) Take a break from work
    (B) Get supplies from a local store
    (C) Recommend items from a special menu
    (D) Promote an online ordering system

21. What will the speaker do next?
    (A) Go to the restaurant's kitchen
    (B) Distribute a list
    (C) Visit a warehouse
    (D) Confirm the time of a delivery

문법 기초다지기

8품사
문장 속에서 어떤 역할을 하는지에 상관없이, 어휘 자체만을 놓고서 부를 때 사용하는 용어입니다.

1 명사
사람이나 사물 등 우리 주변의 모든 것들에 대한 '이름'을 명사라고 합니다. 이름뿐 아니라 shoes(신발), bag(가방)과 같은 사물과 love(사랑), dream(꿈)과 같은 추상적인 것들을 모두 통틀어 일컫는 용어가 명사입니다. 명사는 크게 셀 수 있는 가산명사와 셀 수 없는 불가산명사로 나눌 수 있습니다.

명사 예: **company** 회사   **product** 제품   **customers** 고객들   **money** 돈

2 대명사
대명사란 말 그대로 명사를 '대신해서 쓰는 명사'를 말하며, 앞이나 뒤에 나오는 명사를 대신해서 지칭하는 기능을 합니다. 대명사는 그 나름대로 단수와 복수, 인칭, 격이 존재합니다.

대명사 예: **I** 나   **you** 너   **it** 그것   **they** 그들   **he** 그   **she** 그녀

3 동사
다른 품사와는 다르게 동사는 문장 요소로서도 동사라는 명칭을 그대로 사용합니다. 누군가가 또는 무엇이 '~하다/~되다' 라는 뜻으로, 사람이나 사물의 동작이나 상태를 나타내는 단어입니다. 동사는 크게 뒤에 목적어가 필요 없는 자동사와 목적어를 필요로 하는 타동사로 구분합니다.

자동사 예: **go** 가다   **come** 오다   **rise** 상승하다   **arrive** 도착하다
타동사 예: **have** ~를 가지고 있다   **make** ~를 만들다   **say** ~를 말하다   **discuss** ~를 논의하다

4 형용사
사람이나 사물의 성질이나 상태를 나타내는 단어를 형용사라고 칭합니다. 우리말로 'ㄴ'으로 끝나는 대부분의 말은 형용사로 볼 수 있습니다. '예쁜, 사랑스러운, 멋진, 아름다운' 등이 모두 형용사입니다.

형용사 예: **beautiful** 아름다운   **big** 큰   **interesting** 재미있는   **new** 새로운   **old** 오래된

5 관사

a, an, the를 통틀어서 관사라 하는데, 반드시 명사를 꾸미기 위해서 존재하는 어휘입니다. 부정관사인 a나 an은 셀 수 있는 단수 가산명사 앞에만 붙을 수 있지만, 정관사 the는 명사의 종류에 상관없이 모든 명사 앞에서 사용할 수 있습니다. 우리말에서는 관사의 개념이 존재하지 않기 때문에 정확하게 우리말로 딱 맞는 해석이 없지만, 보통 a와 an은 '하나의'이라고 해석하고, the는 '그'라는 해석을 붙이는 경우가 많습니다.

6 부사

부사는 동사뿐만 아니라 형용사, 부사, 문장 전체도 수식하면서 의미를 풍부하게 만들어 주는 품사입니다. 수식어 역할을 하는 대표적 품사이며, 대체로 문장에서 빠져도 구조적으로 큰 영향을 주지 않는 품사이기도 합니다.

부사 예: **normally** 보통 **really** 정말 **very** 매우 **dramatically** 급격하게

7 전치사

전치사란 우리말의 조사와 같이 '~에, ~부터' 등으로 해석되는 단어들이며 명사를 연결할 때 사용합니다. 예를 들어 the book on the desk(책상 위의 그 책)처럼 the book(책)과 the desk(책상)이라는 두 개의 명사를 the book the desk(그 책 그 책상)이라고 쓸 수 없으므로 중간에 전치사를 사용하여 연결하는 것입니다.

전치사 예: **in** ~안에 **on** ~위에 **at** ~에 **from** ~로부터 **between** ~사이에서

8 전치사

접속사는 한 문장이 끝나고 나서 또 다른 문장을 연결하여 말할 때 쓰는 어휘들입니다. 전치사와는 다르게 뒤에 〈주어+동사〉로 구성되는 문장을 수반하며, 어떤 기능을 하느냐에 따라서 몇 가지 종류로 세분화 할 수 있습니다.

접속사 예: **and** 그리고 **or** 또는 **but** 그러나 **because** ~때문에

문장 요소

1 주어(S)

문장 전체의 주체로서, 우리말로 '~은/는/이/가'를 붙여서 해석하며, 주로 문장 맨 앞에 위치합니다.

He has two cars. 그는 두 대의 차를 가지고 있다.
The company sells various products. 그 회사는 다양한 제품들을 판매한다.

2 동사(V)

주어의 동작이나 상태를 나타내는 서술어(~하다/~되다)를 말하며, 주어와 더불어 문장의 핵심 요소입니다.

We **built** the house last year. 우리는 그 집을 작년에 지었다.

3 목적어(O)

주어가 하는 동작의 대상이 되는 어휘로서, 영어에서는 주로 동사 다음에 위치합니다. 예를 들어 '나는 신문을 읽는다'에서 우리말로 '~을/~를'을 붙여서 해석하는 '신문을'이 목적어에 해당됩니다.

They discussed **the topic**. 그들은 그 주제를 논의했다.

4 보어(C)

보어는 말 그대로 보충하는 말로서, 주어나 목적어를 더 명확하게 묘사할 때 사용합니다. 주어를 보충 설명하는 것을 주격보어, 목적어를 보충 설명하는 것을 목적격보어라 합니다.

Their presentation was **excellent**. (주격보어) 그들의 발표는 훌륭했다.
Many people consider credit cards **convenient**. (목적격보어) 많은 사람들이 신용카드를 편리하게 생각한다.

5 수식어

문장을 구성하는 필수 요소는 아니지만, 그러한 필수 요소들을 꾸며주는 역할을 담당하는 것을 수식어라고 합니다. 예를 들어 '구름이 높이 떠 있다.'라고 한다면 구름이 떠 있는 모습에 '높이'라는 의미를 추가한 것입니다. 이러한 수식어가 들어감으로써 문장의 의미를 좀 더 풍부하게 만들어줄 수 있습니다.

The train arrived **late**. 기차가 늦게 도착했다.
Employees in the sales department work **rapidly**. 영업부서의 직원들은 일을 빨리 한다.

구와 절

단어 하나가 문장 내에서 명사, 동사 등의 품사로 쓰이듯이 구와 절도 문장 내에서 품사와 같은 역할을 할 수 있습니다.

구 [단어+단어]

구는 단어와 단어가 합쳐 쓰이는 것을 말합니다. 문장이나 절의 일부분으로 쓰여요.

예: **on the stage** 그 무대에서 = **on** ~에서 + **the** 그 + **stage** 무대

절 [주어+동사]

절은 구보다 큰 개념으로 〈주어+동사〉 형태가 문장의 일부분으로 쓰이는 것을 뜻해요.

예: This is the laptop **that I bought yesterday**. 이게 내가 어제 산 휴대용 컴퓨터야.

1. 명사구/명사절: 명사처럼 주어, 목적어, 보어로 쓰입니다.

명사구	명사절
To make new friends is exciting. 　　　　주어 새로운 친구를 사귀는 것은 흥미롭다.	I hope that everything goes well for you. 　　　　　　　hope의 목적어 모든 일이 잘 될 바래.
I want to buy a new mobile phone. 　　　　want의 목적어 새 휴대폰을 사고 싶어.	My hope is that we can win the game. 　　　　　　　보어 제 소망은 우리가 그 경기에서 이기는 것입니다.

2. 형용사구/형용사절: 명사를 수식합니다.

형용사구	형용사절
I ate the cookies on the table. 　　　　명사 cookies를 수식 내가 탁자 위의 쿠키를 먹었어.	I will try the restaurant that Amy recommended. 　　　　　　　restaurant를 수식 에이미가 권한 식당에 가볼 거야.

3. 부사구/부사절: 동사, 형용사, 또는 문장 전체를 수식합니다.

부사구	부사절
He usually studies in the library. 　　　　동사 studies를 수식 그는 대개 도서관에서 공부해.	Because the price is low, I will buy that dress. 　　　　앞에서 콤마 뒤 문장 전체를 수식 가격이 저렴하니까 저 드레스를 살거야.
I'm happy to hear the news. 　　　　동사 happy를 수식 그 소식을 들으니 기쁘군요.	I was watching TV when Tim got home. 　　　　뒤에서 앞 문장 전체를 수식 팀이 집에 왔을 때 나는 TV를 보고 있었어.

PART 5 & 6

Unit 1	명사와 대명사	**Unit 8**	전치사 (1)
Unit 2	형용사와 부사	**Unit 9**	전치사 (2)
Unit 3	부정사와 동명사	**Unit 10**	접속사 (1)
Unit 4	분사	**Unit 11**	접속사 (2)
Unit 5	동사의 종류	**Unit 12**	관계사
Unit 6	시제		
Unit 7	수동태	**Part 5&6**	Review Test

UNIT 1 명사와 대명사

★ 콕콕 찍어주는 출제 포인트

명사란 사람이나 사물의 이름을 붙여서 부르는 모든 것을 말하고, 대명사는 문장 속에서 앞에 나온 명사를 대신 부르기 위해서 만든 것이다. 명사와 대명사 모두 문장의 주어나 목적어 역할을 한다는 점이 같다.

1 가산명사와 불가산명사

가산명사 (사람/구체적인 사물)	단수명사	관사(a, an, the) 중의 하나를 반드시 붙인다.
	복수명사	부정관사(a, an)가 붙지 않고, 명사 뒤에 -(e)s를 붙인다.
불가산명사 (추상적인 개념)		부정관사(a, an)가 붙지 않고 복수형 없이 단수형으로만 쓴다.

1 수식어 + 단수명사

단수명사 수식어

a/an (하나의)   one (하나의)   another (다른 하나의)   every (모든)   each (각각의)

We need **another computer**. (O) 우리는 다른 컴퓨터 하나가 필요하다.
We need **another computers**. (X)
We need **another information**. (X) 우리는 다른 정보가 필요하다.

→ another 다음에는 단수명사가 와야 하며 복수명사(computers)와 불가산명사(information)는 올 수 없다.

2 수식어 + 복수명사

복수명사 수식어

many (많은)   two, three... (둘, 셋...)   several (몇 개의)   few (별로 없는)/a few (약간의)   a number of (많은 수의)

Three people came from Asia. 세 사람이 아시아에서 왔습니다.

→ 숫자를 나타내는 표현 중에서 one(하나)은 단수명사를 수식하지만 two부터 나머지 모든 수 뒤에는 복수명사가 와야 한다.

> **잠깐!**
>
> a number of / the number of
>
> - A number of 복수명사 + 복수동사 (많은 수의 ~)
>   **A number of visitors are** enjoying the show. 많은 수의 사람들이 쇼를 즐기고 있다.
> - The number of 복수명사 + 단수동사 (~의 숫자)
>   **The number of visitors is** increasing. 방문객들의 숫자가 증가하고 있습니다.

3 수식어 + 불가산명사

다음의 수식어가 앞에 있으면 그 다음은 반드시 불가산명사만 와야 하며, 가산명사를 붙일 수 없다.

불가산명사 수식어	토익에 나오는 대표적인 불가산명사	
much (많은)	information (정보)	furniture (가구)
little (적은, 별로 없는)/a little (약간의)	mail (우편)	advice (충고, 자문)
less (더 적은)	equipment (장비)	luggage = baggage (짐, 수하물)

He gave me **a little advice**. 그는 내게 약간의 충고를 해주었다.
→ a little은 '약간의'라는 의미의 긍정적 느낌이다.

He gave me **little advice**. 그는 내게 충고를 별로 주지 않았다.
→ little은 '별로 없는'이라는 의미의 부정적 느낌이다.

Check-up

해설 p.96

STEP 1

1. Every _____ should register for the seminar.
   (A) member   (B) members

2. We recently had a few _____ with the new system.
   (A) problem   (B) problems

3. We need _____ information to find and fix the problem.
   (A) many   (B) much

STEP 2

4. Our new personnel manager will contact each _____ to schedule an interview.
   (A) apply   (B) applicant   (C) applicants   (D) applying

5. We would like to share _____ basic considerations with you before the meeting.
   (A) little   (B) much   (C) a few   (D) less

UNIT 1 153

2 혼동되는 명사

1 의미가 비슷한 가산명사와 불가산명사

가산명사 (단수/복수)		불가산명사
an employee (직원)	employees (직원들)	employment (직장, 채용)
a competitor (경쟁자, 경쟁업체)	competitors (경쟁자들, 경쟁업체들)	competition (경쟁)
an attendee (참석자)	attendees (참석자들)	attendance (참석, 출석)
a permit (허가증)	permits (허가증들)	permission (허가)

They are seeking **employees**. (O) 그들은 직원들을 구하고 있다.
They are seeking **employee**. (X)
→ employee(직원)은 가산명사이므로 앞에 관사가 없으면 복수로 써야 한다.

They are seeking **employment**. (O) 그들은 직장을 구하고 있다
→ employment(직장)는 불가산명사이므로 관사 없이 사용할 수 있다.

2 명사와 형용사가 다 되는 어휘

영어에서는 품사가 두 개 이상인 단어들이 종종 있다. 토익에 나오는 대표적인 명사/형용사는 다음과 같다.

명사		형용사	
an individual (개인)	a professional (전문가)	individual (개인적인)	professional (전문적인)
an objective (목적, 목표)	potential (잠재력)	objective (객관적인)	potential (잠재적인)
normal (정상, 표준)	quality (품질)	normal (정상적인, 평균적인)	quality (질 좋은)

The company has **the potential** for growth. 그 회사는 성장 잠재력이 있다.
→ potential 앞에 정관사 the가 있으므로 여기서 potential(잠재력)은 명사이다.

They are **potential customers**. 그들은 잠재적인 고객들이다.
→ potential(잠재적인)이 customers(고객들)를 앞에서 수식하고 있으므로 여기서는 형용사이다.

3 명사와 동사가 다 되는 어휘

토익에 자주 나오는 명사/동사는 다음과 같다. 문장에서 주어/목적어 역할인지, 동사 역할인지를 보고 품사를 판단할 수 있다.

명사		동사	
an increase (증가, 상승)	a decrease (하락, 감소)	increase (증가하다, 증가시키다)	decrease (감소하다, 감소시키다)
a rise (증가, 상승)	a raise (인상)	rise (상승하다, 올라가다)	raise (~를 인상시키다)
damage (손상)	demand (요구, 수요)	damage (~를 손상시키다)	demand (~를 요구하다)
experience (경험, 경력)		experience (~를 경험하다)	

You will see **an increase** in sales. 당신은 판매 증가를 볼 것입니다.
→ 앞에 부정관사 an이 있으므로 여기서 increase(증가)는 명사이다.

Sales **have increased** steadily. 판매가 꾸준하게 증가해 왔습니다.
→ 여기서 increase는 주어를 설명하는 동사이다.

잠깐!

복수형태의 단수명사/불가산명사

어미 형태가 -s로 끝났더라도 복수명사가 아닌 어휘들이 있는데, a means (방법, 수단), a series (일련, 연속), news (뉴스)는 시험에 자주 나오므로 꼭 알아두어야 한다. means와 series는 가산명사이고, news는 불가산명사이다.

This is **an effective means** of communication. 이것은 효과적인 의사소통 수단입니다.

Check-up

해설 p.96

STEP 1

1. _____ in the car industry will increase.
   (A) Competition　　　　　(B) Competitor

2. The board consists of health _____.
   (A) professional　　　　　(B) professionals

3. A dramatic _____ in the fuel cost surprised many people.
   (A) rise　　　　　(B) risen

STEP 2

4. In most companies, salary _____ are decided by performance reviews.
   (A) increase　(B) increasing　(C) increases　(D) increased

5. The _____ of the program is to provide participants with new information.
   (A) effective　(B) creative　(C) objective　(D) protective

UNIT 1 **155**

3 대명사

대명사는 앞에서 언급된 명사를 똑같이 반복하는 것을 피하기 위해서 쓰는 '대신하는 명사'라는 의미이다. 이는 문장의 간결함을 위해서 사용되는데, 항상 똑같은 형태가 아니라 문장에서의 역할에 따라 격(주격, 목적격, 소유격 등)이 달라진다.

1 인칭대명사

인칭대명사는 주어나 목적어 역할 등 그 역할에 따라서 다음과 같이 나누어진다.

주 격	소유격	목적격	소유대명사
I (나)	my (나의)	me (나를)	mine (나의 것)
You (너)	your (너의)	you (너를)	yours (너의 것)
He (그)	his (그의)	him (그를)	his (그의 것)
She (그녀)	her (그녀의)	her (그녀를)	hers (그녀의 것)
It (그것)	its (그것의)	it (그것을)	its (그것)
We (우리)	our (우리의)	us (우리를)	ours (우리의 것)
They (그들)	their (그들의)	them (그들을)	theirs (그들의 것)

I attended the meeting yesterday. (O) 나는 어제 회의에 참석했다.
Me attended the meeting yesterday. (X)
→ 문장의 맨 앞부분에는 주어가 들어갈 자리이므로 주격 대명사를 써야 한다.

We **informed him** of the change in the schedule. (O) 우리는 그에게 스케줄상의 변경에 대해서 통보했다.
We **informed he** of the change in the schedule. (X)
→ 동사 inform의 목적어 자리에는 목적격 대명사를 써야 한다.

Her presentation was so impressive. 그녀의 발표는 매우 인상적이었다.
→ 소유격 her는 명사 presentation(발표)을 수식한다. her는 목적격과 형태가 동일하다는 점에 주의한다.

Her presentation was so impressive, but **mine** was better. 그녀의 발표는 매우 인상적이었으나, 내 것이 더 좋았다.
→ my presentation(나의 발표)을 줄여서 쓴 mine은 '내 것'이라는 소유대명사이다.

2 재귀대명사

'재귀'라는 말은 '원래 자리로 돌아오다'는 의미로, 재귀대명사란 주어가 주어 자신을 가리킬 때 사용되는 대명사이다. 인칭대명사 뒤에 –self나 –selves를 붙인 형태를 말한다.

myself (나 자신)	yourself (너 자신)	himself (그 자신)	herself (그녀 자신)
ourselves (우리 자신)	yourselves (너희들 자신)	themselves (그들 자신)	itself (그것 자체)

❶ 재귀적 용법

주어와 목적어가 동일할 때 사용하는 용법으로 이 경우는 반드시 재귀대명사를 써야 한다. 이 때 재귀대명사는 '자신'이라고 해석하고 문장의 목적어이므로 생략할 수 없다.

I will introduce **myself**. (O) 제 자신을 소개하겠습니다.
I will introduce **me**. (X)

→ 주어인 I와 목적어가 동일하므로, 이 경우는 반드시 me 대신 myself(내 자신)를 사용해야 한다.

❷ 강조 용법

문장에서 주어나 목적어의 행위나 상태를 강조하기 위해 재귀대명사를 쓰기도 하는데, 이 때는 강조하기 위해 쓴 것이므로 생략해도 문장이 성립되고, '직접'이라고 해석한다.

I **myself** drove the car. = I drove the car **myself**. 내가 직접 그 차를 운전했다.

❸ 관용적 표현

- **by oneself = on one's own** ① 홀로 ② 스스로
  They moved the furniture **by themselves**. = They moved the furniture **on their own**.
  그들은 가구를 스스로 옮겼다.

- **for oneself** 자신을 위해서
  You should choose the password **for yourself**. 당신은 당신 자신을 위한 패스워드를 선택해야 한다.
  → for oneself는 '스스로'가 아니라 '자신을 위한'이라는 의미이다.

Check-up

해설 p.97

STEP 1

1. During _____ vacation, Fedor traveled to France and Italy.
   (A) he   (B) his

2. If you have a question, please contact _____.
   (A) our   (B) us

3. After she introduced _____, she talked about several topics.
   (A) myself   (B) herself

STEP 2

4. If the item doesn't operate properly, you can repair it by _____.
   (A) your   (B) your own   (C) yourself   (D) yours

5. Instead of inviting a specialist, the director _____ decided to train the staff members.
   (A) he   (B) him   (C) himself   (D) his

4 혼동되는 대명사

1 지시대명사

지시대명사는 사물/사람이나 이전에 언급된 내용을 가리킬 때 쓰인다. 거리나 시간상 가까운 것을 가리킬 때 this(이것)를 쓰고, 먼 것을 가리킬 때 that(저것)을 쓰며, 복수형은 각각 these(이것들)와 those(저것들)를 쓴다.

단수	복수
• this (이것, 이 사람) **This** is a car. 이것은 차이다. **This** is my student. 이 사람은 내 학생이다.	• these (이것들, 이 사람들) **These** are cars. 이것들은 차이다. **These** are my students. 이 사람들은 내 학생이다.
• that (저것, 저 사람/그것, 그 사람) **That** is a car. 저것은 차이다. **That** is my student. 저 사람은 내 학생이다.	• those (저것들, 저 사람들/그것들, 그 사람들) **Those** are cars. 저것들은 차이다. **Those** are my students. 저/그 사람들은 내 학생들이다.
• that (저것, 저 사람/그것, 그 사람) + 단수명사 **This car** is mine. 이 차는 내 것이다. **That car** is mine. 저/그 차는 내 것이다.	• these/those (이/저, 그) + 복수명사 **These cars** are theirs. 이 차들은 그들의 것이다. **Those cars** are theirs. 저/그 차들은 그들의 것이다.

2 부정대명사

부정대명사란 부정적(negative)이라는 뜻이 아니라, 구체적이고 정확한 숫자가 언급되지 않고, 수나 양이 정해지지 않은 것들을 일컫는 대명사를 말한다. 즉, 불특정한 대명사라는 뜻이다.

❶ one and the other (하나와 나머지 하나)

두 개의 범위에서 하나를 말할 때는 one 이라 하고, 나머지 하나를 말할 때는 the other라 한다.

one   the other

I have two computers. **One** is a desktop, and **the other** is a laptop.
나는 두 대의 컴퓨터가 있습니다. 하나는 데스크톱이고, 나머지 하나는 노트북입니다.

❷ one and another (하나와 다른 하나)

세 개 이상의 범위에서 하나를 말할 때는 one이라 하고, 또 다른 하나를 말할 때는 another라 한다.

one   another

One of the team members is from Korea, and **another** is from Japan.
팀원들 중에 한 명은 한국에서 왔고, 또 다른 한 명은 일본에서 왔습니다.

❸ one and the others (하나와 나머지들)

세 개 이상의 범위에서 하나를 말할 때는 one이라 하고, 나머지 전부를 말할 때는 the others라 한다.

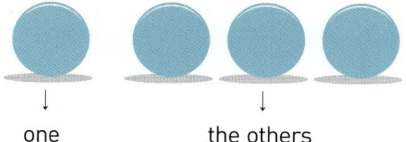

I have four brothers. **One** lives in Baltimore, and **the others** live in Atlanta.
나는 네 명의 남자형제들이 있습니다. 하나는 볼티모어에 살고, 나머지 형제들은 전부 애틀랜타에 삽니다.

❹ some and others (몇몇 그리고 다른 것[이]들)

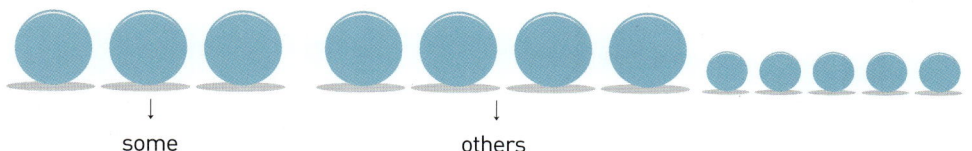

I bought a lot of used books. **Some** are very interesting, but **others** are not.
나는 많은 중고책들을 샀다. 몇몇은 매우 재밌는데, 다른 것들은 그렇지 않다.

Check-up

해설 p.98

STEP 1

1. Please respond to this _____.
   (A) message (B) messages

2. Our products are more durable than _____ of competitors.
   (A) that (B) those

3. One of the two plans is possible to implement, but _____ is not.
   (A) another (B) the other

STEP 2

4. If the scanner is out of order, we will replace it with _____ or refund your money.
   (A) other (B) the others (C) another (D) each other

5. Wages are consistently higher for nighttime workers than _____ on the daytime.
   (A) this (B) that (C) another (D) those

토익 필수 어휘 1_ 명사 (1)

1. employee	*n.* 직원 full-time **employees** 정규직 직원들 **employee** participation 직원 참여
2. value	*n.* 가치, 중요성, 가치관 *a.* 유용한, 가치 있는 *v.* ~를 중요시하다, (가치, 가격을) 평가하다 land **values** 부동산 가격, 지가 **value** of the nation's currency 국가 통화가치
3. attendant	*n.* 수행원, 간병인, 승무원 flight **attendants** 항공기 승무원 **attendants** at the health care center 건강보호센터 간병인
4. strategy	*n.* 전략, 계획 production **strategy** 생산 전략 company's new marketing **strategy** 기업의 새로운 마케팅 전략
5. choice	*n.* 선택, 선택권, 선택한 것, 선택 범위, 선택된 사람 the final **choice** 최종선택 ※ have no choice but to ~할 수 밖에 없다 have no choice but to charge higher fees 높은 수수료를 매길 수밖에 없다
6. support	*n.* 지지, 지원 *v.* ~를 지원하다 financial **support** 재정 지원 technical **support** representatives 기술 지원 직원들
7. comparison	*n.* 비교, 유사성 in **comparison** with ~와 비교하여 **comparison** with competitor companies 경쟁업체들과의 비교
8. material	*n.* 물질, 재료, 자료 necessary **materials** for the project 프로젝트를 위한 필수적인 자료들 raw **materials** 원자재

9. development	*n.* 발달, 성장, 개발 reduce **development** costs 개발 원가를 절감하다 the product **development** team 제품개발팀
10. reference	*n.* 참고, 참조, 조회, 추천서, 참고문헌 a letter of **reference** 추천서 a valuable **reference** for researchers 연구자에게 귀중한 참고문헌
11. study	*n.* 연구 *v.* 연구하다 major area of **study** 전공 연구 분야 **Study** shows that ~ 연구에 따르면 ~이라고 한다
12. use	*n.* 사용 *v.* 사용하다 be in **use** 사용 중이다 make the best **use** of ~을 최대한 활용하다
13. convenience	*n.* 편리함, 편의 at your earliest **convenience** 형편 닿는 대로 조속히 **convenience** facilities 편의 시설

Check-up

해설 p.98

1. There are some (employment / **employees**) working outside.   야외에서 일하고 있는 몇몇 직원들이 있습니다.

2. They should hire more flight (attend / **attendants**).   그들은 더 많은 비행기 승무원들을 고용해야 한다.

3. The company's new sales (**strategy** / appearance) was very effective.   회사의 새로운 판매 전략은 매우 효과적이었다.

4. He made the final (choose / **choice**).   그는 최종 선택을 했다.

5. The project is under (develop / **development**).   그 프로젝트는 개발 중이다.

PART 5&6_ 실전연습 1

1. LKH chemical company will first hire _____ that want to work in an assembly from next week.

   (A) employers
   (B) employment
   (C) employees
   (D) employ

2. The manager instructed _____ to organize our desks because clients are expected to visit the office today.

   (A) we
   (B) us
   (C) our
   (D) ours

3. According to the report, the _____ of the nation's currency fell sharply during the recession.

   (A) cost
   (B) expense
   (C) value
   (D) fare

4. Our couple thanks the _____ for great care on a plane in spite of repeated requests.

   (A) attendant
   (B) attendance
   (C) attendee
   (D) attends

5. Customers were asked to complete a satisfaction survey by _____ before leaving the store.

   (A) they
   (B) their
   (C) them
   (D) themselves

6. The innovative promotional _____ proposed by the marketing department will draw consumers' attention.

   (A) goal
   (B) strategy
   (C) responsibility
   (D) number

7. We allow our employees to schedule their working hours themselves as long as they receive the manager's _____.

   (A) approve
   (B) approval
   (C) approved
   (D) approves

8. If you want to attend the workshops scheduled next month, please indicate your _____ on the space.

   (A) option
   (B) suggestion
   (C) choice
   (D) idea

9. The city committee decided to provide financial _____ for building a library equipped with rare books.

   (A) supported
   (B) supportive
   (C) supportively
   (D) support

10. In _____ with other companies, the performance of our products are far superior.

    (A) compared
    (B) compare
    (C) comparison
    (D) comparable

11. According to a recent survey, brick is one of the most widely used _____ in construction today.

    (A) ingredients
    (B) parts
    (C) materials
    (D) portions

12. Mr. Bruno will receive a _____ mostly due to his outstanding performance last quarter.

    (A) promotion
    (B) promotes
    (C) promote
    (D) promoted

13. Now that winter is over, work will resume on the final phase of the housing _____ project.

    (A) development
    (B) refreshment
    (C) supplement
    (D) requirement

14. Please confirm your hotel _____ before departure, in case unexpected problems occur.

    (A) reservation
    (B) reserving
    (C) reserves
    (D) reserve

Questions 15-18 refer to the following e-mail.

From: samnorth@kmobile.net
To: rachelk@bradley.nz.edu
Title: Questions about advertised apartment
Date: June 1

Dear Ms. Koontz,

I am writing to inquire about the apartment you listed on the Lofty Goals Web site. ------- **15.** Before I sign a lease, I have a few questions I hope you can clear up for me. The listing mentions that the apartment is ------- **16.** furnished. Can you be more specific? ------- **17.** exactly does it include? Also, what kind of ------- **18.** does the building offer? Generally, apartments at the price you are asking include fitness centers and parking garage access. Thank you in advance.

Kindly,
Samuel North

15. (A) I am interested in renting the unit.
    (B) I would like to recommend my apartment.
    (C) I recently rented a room next door.
    (D) I heard that listing is no longer available.

16. (A) full
    (B) fully
    (C) fuller
    (D) fullest

17. (A) What
    (B) Where
    (C) Which
    (D) When

18. (A) amenities
    (B) discount
    (C) utilities
    (D) view

UNIT 2 형용사와 부사

★ **콕콕 찍어주는 출제 포인트**
형용사는 명사를 수식하거나 동사의 보어 역할로 사용되지만, 부사는 명사를 제외한 모든 품사를 꾸미는 데 사용된다. 둘 다 수식어이므로 무언가를 수식한다는 공통점이 있지만, 문장에서 위치하는 자리가 다르므로 그 차이를 알아두어야 한다.

1 형용사와 부사의 차이

1 명사 수식은 형용사, 동사 수식은 부사

형용사 역할	① 명사 수식 ② be동사(류)의 보어 역할
부사 역할	① 동사 수식 ② 명사를 제외한 모든 품사 수식

The company designed **a new car**. (O) 그 회사는 새로운 차를 고안했다.
The company designed **a newly car**. (X)
→ 부정관사(a)와 명사(car) 사이에 들어가는 것은 형용사(new)이다.

The price **has recently risen**. (O) 가격은 최근에 상승했다.
The price **has recent risen**. (X)
→ 현재완료시제 동사(has risen)사이에 들어가는 것은 부사(recently)이다.

잠깐!
부사 중에서도 명사를 수식하는 어휘가 있는데, 바로 only와 just로 이들을 초점부사라 한다.
It was **only / just** a joke. 그것은 단지 농담이었어.
Only / Just boys can participate in the contest. 단지 남자 아이들만 이 대회에 참가할 수 있습니다.

2 be동사의 보어는 형용사, be동사와 형용사 사이는 부사 자리

대표 형용사 자리	대표 부사 자리
be/become + _____	be/become + _____ + 형용사

The project **was / became successful**. (O) 그 프로젝트는 성공했다. / 성공하게 되었다.
The project **was / became successfully**. (X)
→ be/become의 보어 역할은 형용사가 한다.

The project **was / became successfully complete**. (O) 그 프로젝트는 성공적으로 마무리 되었다.
The project **was / became successful complete**. (X)
→ be/become과 형용사 complete(완성된, 마무리 된) 사이에는 형용사를 수식할 수 있는 부사가 들어가야 한다.

3 조심해야 할 품사의 자리싸움

형용사가 명사를 수식하고, 부사는 형용사를 수식하기 때문에 다음의 문젯거리가 생길 때가 있다.

- 부사 + 형용사 + 명사
- 형용사 + 형용사 + 명사

→ 형용사 두 개 이상이 명사 앞에 있어도 괜찮다. 모두 다 명사를 수식하기만 하면 가능하다.

It is a **financially stable job**. (O) 그 것은 재정적으로 안정적인 직업이다.
It is a **financial stable job**. (X)

→ 부사(financially)가 형용사(stable)를 수식하고 형용사가 명사(job)를 꾸며준다.

We have **international direct flights**. (O) 우리는 국제적인 직항편을 갖추고 있습니다.
We have **internationally direct flights**. (X)

→ 이 경우 internationally(국제적으로)가 direct(직항의)를 꾸미지 못하며, 형용사 international(국제적인)이 명사 flights(항공편)를 수식하는 구조의 표현이다.

Check-up

STEP 1

1. We should update the _____ report.
   (A) annual   (B) annually

2. Her advice was _____ helpful.
   (A) real   (B) really

3. We would like to work with _____ new companies.
   (A) innovation   (B) innovative

STEP 2

4. The factory will not be _____ until all the safety equipment has been tested.
   (A) operate   (B) operator   (C) operationally   (D) operational

5. The hotel is _____ located between the international airport and the shopping district.
   (A) convenient   (B) convenience   (C) conveniently   (D) conveniences

2 주의해야 할 형용사

1 a + 명사 + of = 형용사(구)

영어에서는 a lot of와 같이 'a + 명사 + of'로 이루어진 형용사구가 많이 존재하는데, 이러한 표현들은 '관사 + 명사 + 전치사'로 조각내지 않고 하나의 형용사로 봐야 한다.

a + 명사 + of	의미	a + 명사 + of	의미
a lot of	많은	a series of	일련의
a number of	많은 (수의)	a selection of	선택된
a variety of	다양한	a collection of	한 모음의, 모아진

A lot of people will participate in the game. 많은 사람들이 게임에 참가할 것입니다.
→ a lot of(많은)를 lots of로 바꾸어도 같은 표현이다.

We have **a variety of** plans. 우리는 다양한 계획들을 가지고 있다.
→ a variety of(다양한)는 형용사 various와 같다.

This book features **a selection of** recipes. 이 책은 일련의 선택된 요리법들을 특징으로 한다.
→ a selection of(선택된)는 형용사 selected와 같다.

2 토익에 자주 출제되는 숙어

❶ be + 형용사 + to부정사

be able to부정사	~할 수 있다	be reluctant to부정사	~하기를 꺼려하다
be likely to부정사	~할 것 같다	be pleased to부정사	~하는 것을 기뻐하다
be willing to부정사	기꺼이 ~하다	be ready to부정사	~할 준비가 되어 있다

I'm **willing to accept** your offer. 나는 기꺼이 당신의 제안을 받겠습니다.

The Central Bank **is ready to** raise interest rates. 중앙은행은 금리를 올릴 준비가 되어 있습니다.

❷ be + 형용사 + 전치사

be eligible for/to부정사	~에 자격 있다/~할 자격 있다	be skilled at/in	~에 능하다
be dependent on	~에 의존하다	be familiar with	~에 정통하다
be aware of	~를 알다	be capable of	~를 할 수 있다

He **is eligible for the prize**. 그는 그 상에 대한 자격이 있다.

He **is eligible to receive** the prize. 그는 그 상을 받을 자격이 있다.

be eligible과 be entitled의 차이점과 공통점

be eligible과 be entitled는 둘 다 '자격 있다'는 의미의 표현이다. 하지만 뒤에 붙는 구문에 약간 차이가 난다. be eligible 다음에는 전치사 for가 붙거나 to부정사가 붙지만 be entitled 다음에는 전치사 to와 to부정사가 수반된다.

She **is eligible for** the position. 그녀는 그 직책에 자격이 있다.
She **is entitled to** the position.

→ 뒤에 붙는 전치사는 다르다.

She **is eligible to get** the position. 그녀는 그 직책을 얻을 자격이 있다.
She **is entitled to get** the position.

→ to부정사를 수반하는 것은 차이가 없다.

Check-up

STEP 1

1. They offer a _____ of salads.
   (A) variety   (B) various

2. Many people are reluctant _____ about their personal information.
   (A) talk   (B) to talk

3. The manager should be _____ with all the company policies.
   (A) familiar   (B) accustomed

STEP 2

4. To be _____ for the position, candidates must have a university degree in economics.
   (A) entitled   (B) eligible   (C) capable   (D) able

5. The success of our company is _____ on maintaining dedicated staff members.
   (A) aware   (B) able   (C) ready   (D) dependent

3 주의해야 할 부사 (1)

1 같은 형태의 형용사와 부사

영어에는 형용사와 형태가 같은 부사들이 꽤 많이 있는데, 무엇을 수식하는지에 따라서 품사가 달라지므로 주의해야 한다.

단어	형용사 의미	부사 의미	단어	형용사 의미	부사 의미
early	이른	일찍	enough	충분한	충분히
fast	빠른	빨리	high	높은	높이
hard	어려운, 단단한	열심히, 심하게	late	늦은	늦게
hourly	매시간의	매시간마다	much	많은	많이
daily	매일의	매일마다	quarterly	분기별의	매분기마다
monthly	매월의	매월마다	yearly	연간의	매년마다

He requested the **quarterly** budget report. 그는 분기별 예산보고서를 요청했다.
→ 여기서 quarterly(분기별의)는 명사 budget report(예산 보고서)를 수식하는 형용사이다.

The newsletter is distributed **quarterly**. 그 뉴스레터는 분기별로 배포된다.
→ 여기서 quarterly(분기별로)는 동사 is distributed(배포되다)를 수식하는 부사이다.

잠깐!

형용사 enough와 부사 enough의 차이

① enough + 명사(충분한: 형용사)
We don't have **enough time**. 우리는 충분한 시간이 없다.

② 동사/형용사/부사 + enough(충분히: 부사)
He hasn't **practiced enough**. 그는 충분히 연습하지 않았다.
The meeting room is **large enough**. 회의실은 충분히 크다.
→ 부사 enough는 동사(practiced), 형용사(large), 부사를 반드시 뒤에서 수식한다.

2 no는 형용사, not, never는 부사

I had **no chance** to interview him. 나는 그를 인터뷰할 기회가 전혀 없었다.
→ no는 형용사로 명사(chance)를 수식한다.

We **will not return** within three days. 우리는 3일 이내에 돌아오지 않을 것이다.
→ not은 부사로 동사(return)를 수식한다.

They **have never participated** in the seminar before. 그들은 전에 그 세미나에 한 번도 참석해 본적이 없었다.
→ never는 부사로 동사(have participated)를 수식한다. not보다 의미가 더 강하다.

None of the managers were happy with the result. 관리자들 중 아무도 그 결과에 기뻐하지 않았다.
→ none은 대명사로 주어 자리에 사용된다.

3 already / still / yet

	already	still	yet
의미	이미, 벌써	아직도, 여전히	아직
쓰이는 문장의 종류	긍정문	긍정문, 부정문	부정문, 의문문

❶ already (이미, 벌써)

예상보다 빨리 발생한 상황이나 이전에 일어났던 일/말에 대해서 강조하는 의미이다.

The performance **had already started**. 그 공연은 이미 시작했다.

❷ still (여전히)

어떤 일이 '여전히' 이루어지지 않았거나 '여전히' 계속되고 있을 때 사용한다.

We **still** have **not** received our orders. 우리는 주문품을 여전히 받지 못하고 있다.

→ still은 not을 기준으로 보았을 때 앞에 쓴다. (not 바로 앞에 써도 된다.)

❸ yet (아직)

예상했던 일이 '아직' 이루어지지 않았을 때 사용하는 표현이며, '앞으로 할 것'이라는 의미도 포함된다.

We have **not yet** received our orders. 우리는 주문품을 아직 못 받았다.

→ yet은 not을 기준으로 볼 때 뒤에 쓴다. (문장 맨 뒤에 써도 된다.)

Check-up

해설 p.102–103

STEP 1

1. They will _____ be able to join us.
   (A) no   (B) not

2. The performance _____ started when we arrived.
   (A) already   (B) yet

3. I _____ have not made a decision.
   (A) still   (B) yet

STEP 2

4. _____ notices should be posted on the doors without the approval of the custodian.
   (A) No   (B) None   (C) Not   (D) Never

5. Despite several months of study, Dr. Grenville has not _____ finished the project.
   (A) still   (B) already   (C) yet   (D) never

UNIT 2 **169**

4 주의해야 할 부사 (2)

1 very와 so, too의 차이

very (매우)	so (매우)	too (너무)
동사 수식 못함	기본적으로 very와 같음	부정의 의미
비교급 수식 못함	비교급 수식 못함	비교급 수식 못함
that절 수반 못함	that절 수반 가능	that절 수반 못함

Their new product is **very expensive**. = Their new product is **so expensive**. 그들의 신제품은 매우 비싸다.

Their new product is **so expensive that** I can't buy it. (O) 그들의 새로운 제품은 매우 비싸서 나는 그것을 살 수 없다.
Their new product is **very expensive that** I can't buy it. (X)
→ very와 so가 의미적으로는 동일하지만 뒤에 that절이 있을 경우는 so만 사용해야 한다.

Their new product is **too expensive**. 그들의 새로운 제품은 너무 비싸다.
→ too는 부정의 의미로 해석한다.

2 ever (여태껏 ~중에)

❶ 부정부사 + ever (거의 ~ 않다)
부정부사(hardly, rarely, seldom 등)를 뒤에서 강조할 때 쓰는데, 이 때 ever는 해석을 하는 것이 아니고 강조의 의미만 갖게 된다.

We hardly **ever** went out. 우리는 거의 밖에 나가지 않았다.

❷ 최상급 + ever (여태껏 ~중에 가장)
최상급 표현 뒤에 ever를 쓰면 '여태껏 ~중에 가장'이라는 의미로 최상급이 강조될 수 있다.

It was **the largest** trade show **ever**. 그것은 여태껏 중 가장 큰 무역박람회였다.

❸ ever since (~이래로 줄곧)
since(~이래로) 앞에 ever를 쓰면 since가 강조되어서 '~이래로 줄곧, 여태껏'이라는 의미가 된다.

The building has been vacant **ever since** 2001. 그 빌딩은 2001년 이래로 줄곧 비어 있었다.

❹ than ever (이전보다)
비교 대상을 나타내는 than(~보다)에 ever를 붙이면 '이전보다, 여태껏보다'라는 관용구가 된다.

Last night's show was better **than ever**. 어제 저녁 쇼는 여태껏 보던 것보다 훨씬 더 좋았다.

3 숫자 수식 부사

영어에서 숫자는 명사도 되고 형용사도 되는 어휘이다. 숫자를 수식하는 품사는 부사이며, 이러한 부사들은 다음과 같이 정해져 있다.

거의	almost = nearly	이상	more than = over
대략	approximately = around = about = roughly	최소한	at least
~까지	up to	단지	only = just

Almost / Nearly 10,000 commuters will benefit from the new system.
거의 1만 명의 통근자들이 새로운 시스템으로부터 혜택을 볼 것이다.

At least 40 passengers had to transfer to another flight. 최소한 40명의 승객들은 다른 비행편으로 환승해야만 했다.

4 동사 수식을 못하는 부사

동사를 수식하는 대표적인 품사는 부사인데, 형용사나 부사만 수식하는 부사로 very(매우)와 extremely(대단히, 극도로)가 있다.

Sales will **increase very rapidly**. (O) 판매가 매우 급속하게 증가할 것이다.
Sales will **increase very**. (X)
→ 여기서 very는 그 다음 부사 rapidly(급속하게)를 수식한다. 동사 increase를 수식하는 것은 rapidly이다.

The project was **extremely successful**. (O) 그 프로젝트는 대단히 성공적이었다.
The project **succeeded extremely**. (X)
→ 부사 extremely(대단히)는 동사를 수식하지 못하므로, 형용사(successful)를 수식하는 문장구조가 되어야 한다.

Check-up

STEP 1

1. He hardly _____ washes the dishes.
   (A) before   (B) ever

2. _____ 1,000 people are likely to attend the event.
   (A) Near   (B) Nearly

3. The new smart-phone sales have increased _____.
   (A) extremely   (B) dramatically

STEP 2

4. The report is _____ confidential that only three people have access to it.
   (A) very   (B) too   (C) really   (D) so

5. _____ 20,000 commuters will benefit from the addition of two new subway lines.
   (A) More   (B) Approximate   (C) Over   (D) Near

UNIT 2

토익 필수 어휘 2_ 명사 (2)

1. care
n. 돌봄, 관리, 관심   *v.* 돌보다

take special **care** 특별히 주의를 기울이다
be handled with **care** 조심해서 다루어지다

2. response
n. 응답, 반응

a written **response** 서면 응답
in **response** to ~에 응답하여

3. exception
n. 예외

with few **exceptions** 거의 예외 없이
make an **exception** 예외로 하다

4. critic
n. 비평가, 평론가

a harsh **critic** 혹평가
an art **critic** 예술평론가

5. cost
n. 값, 비용, (사업상) 경비

at no **cost** 무료로
reduce operating **costs** 운영비용을 절감하다

6. addition
n. 추가, 추가된 것

in **addition** to ~에 더하여, ~일 뿐 아니라
the **addition** of a new ingredient 새로운 재료의 첨가

7. relationship
n. 관계, 관련성

build new **relationships** 새로운 관계를 형성하다
a mutually beneficial **relationship** 상호 혜택적인 관계

8. refund
n. 반환, 환불   *v.* 반환하다, 환불하다

issue a **refund** check to you 당신에게 환급수표를 발행해 주다
provide a replacement or a full **refund** 교환 또는 전액환불을 제공하다

9. request	*n.* 요청　*v.* ~를 요청하다, ~를 요구하다 upon **request** 요청하자마자 submit a **request** 요청서를 제출하다
10. capacity	*n.* 수용력, 용량, 능력 an advisory **capacity** 조언자 역할, 자문 역할 seating **capacity** of the outdoor theater 노천극장의 수용 능력(좌석 수)
11. claim	*n.* 요구, (배상) 청구　*v.* 주장[요구]하다 a **claim** for damages 손해 배상 청구 make an insurance **claim** for any goods lost 분실된 모든 상품에 대해 보험(료) 청구를 하다
12. combination	*n.* 결합, 조합 in **combination** with ~와 결합하여[연합하여] make a good **combination** 좋은 콤비가 되다
13. variety	*n.* 다양성, 여러 가지 a wide **variety** of 다양하고 폭넓은 ~ for a **variety** of reasons 여러 가지 이유로

Check-up

해설 p. 103-104

1. You should handle it with (care / careful).　　당신은 그것을 조심해서 다루어야 합니다.

2. The law was passed in (respond / response) to public pressure.　　그 법규는 대중의 압력에 응해서 통과되었다.

3. Everyone must attend the meeting without (except / exception).　　모든 사람은 예외 없이 회의에 참석해야 한다.

4. The (addition / additional) of the new software will improve the system.　　새로운 소프트웨어의 추가는 시스템을 향상시킬 것이다.

5. He made an urgent (request / requested).　　그는 긴급한 요청을 했다.

PART 5&6_ 실전연습 2

1. Please review the letter _____ before sending it, because it contains sensitive information.
   (A) careful
   (B) carefully
   (C) care
   (D) careless

2. Marco will be _____ for ensuring that safety procedures are followed by Rio Construction employees.
   (A) response
   (B) responsibly
   (C) responsible
   (D) responsibility

3. Job candidates are advised to dress _____ for job interviews.
   (A) approximately
   (B) extremely
   (C) appropriately
   (D) very

4. If Ms. Ahmad is out of the office, please leave a message with her _____ all the time.
   (A) secretary
   (B) attendant
   (C) professional
   (D) husband

5. The director is well-known for being _____ of work performance when it does not meet his standards.
   (A) criticized
   (B) critic
   (C) critical
   (D) criticizing

6. Some employees who exceed this year's sales goal will be awarded substantial pay _____ starting next year.
   (A) costs
   (B) freezes
   (C) budgets
   (D) raises

7. Passengers should note that luggage exceeding the 20kg limit is subject to _____ fees.
   (A) additional
   (B) addition
   (C) additionally
   (D) more addition

8. Maintaining good relationships with your colleagues is _____ important while you are on duty.
   (A) extreme
   (B) extremes
   (C) extremely
   (D) extremity

9. Customers need to present their receipt in order to receive a full _____ on their purchase.
   (A) profit
   (B) refund
   (C) receipt
   (D) purchase

10. Failure to submit complete and accurate information in a _____ manner can result in the cancellation of the application.
    (A) timing
    (B) timed
    (C) timely
    (D) time

11. The owner politely refused the customer's _____ to cater a private event next month.
    (A) interest
    (B) request
    (C) reference
    (D) complaint

12. Customers of our company can pay online without _____ charges or transaction fees at all times.
    (A) any
    (B) few
    (C) some
    (D) every

13. _____ half of the employees at HNC volunteer to attend the benefit show at the nearby theater.

(A) Rarely
(B) Roughly
(C) Considerably
(D) Urgently

14. Please remember to fill out the _____ documents in blue or black ink and mail them in the enclosed envelope.

(A) office
(B) officially
(C) official
(D) officialdom

Questions 15-18 refer to the following information on a Web site.

Pullman Printing and Stationery Inc. is a ---**15.**--- name in the area of custom greeting card printing and design. We have the know-how that is needed to manufacture a ---**16.**--- range of printed materials, including calendars, notebooks, diaries, and envelopes. Our expert staff can help you with every ---**17.**--- of your next printing job, from the graphic design to the choice of paper. Whatever the requirements of your project might be, we can offer you a printing solution. ---**18.**---.

Call us today to discuss your next project.
Contact us: (010) 555-1999 (phone) / (010) 555-2120 (fax)
e-mail: pullman@mail.com

---

15. (A) lead
    (B) leading
    (C) leader
    (D) led

16. (A) full
    (B) fully
    (C) fulfill
    (D) fulfilling

17. (A) conduct
    (B) outlook
    (C) bearing
    (D) aspect

18. (A) The printer offered to you can be returned for free.
    (B) You are asked to complete your project on schedule.
    (C) Our company grarantees quality results at an affordable price.
    (D) Some of the papers you chose are out of stock.

UNIT 3 부정사와 동명사

★ **콕콕 찍어주는 출제 포인트**

우리말 '하다'를 '하는 것', '하기 위해서' 등으로 바꿔 표현할 수 있듯이 영어에서도 동사 앞에 to를 붙이거나 또는 뒤에 ~ing를 붙여서 여러 가지 의미 변화를 줄 수 있다. 동사 앞에 to를 붙여서 쓰는 것을 'to부정사'라 하고 동사 뒤에 ~ing를 붙이는 것을 '동명사'라 한다.

1 부정사와 동명사

1 공통점

❶ 둘 다 동사가 아니다.

I will **meet** the clients tomorrow. (O) 나는 내일 고객들을 만날 것이다.
I will **to meet** the clients tomorrow. (X)
I will **meeting** the clients tomorrow. (X)

→ to meet(to부정사)와 meeting(동명사)은 동사가 아니므로 동사 자리에 사용할 수 없다.

❷ 둘 다 준동사이다.

준동사란 동사와 비슷하게 생겨서 동사처럼 목적어나 보어를 갖지만, 결국 문장에서는 다른 품사로 쓰이는 것들을 말한다.

부정사	① 명사 역할(~하는 것, ~하기) ② 형용사 역할(~할, ~할 수 있는) ③ 부사 역할(~하기 위해서, ~해서)
동명사	명사 역할(~하는 것, ~하기)

I want **to buy** a car. 나는 차 사는 것을 원한다.

→ to buy(~를 사는 것)가 타동사 want의 목적어가 되는 명사 역할

I had an opportunity **to meet** him. 나는 그를 만날 수 있는 기회를 가졌다.

→ to meet(~를 만날 수 있는)가 명사 opportunity(기회)를 뒤에서 수식하는 형용사 역할

We left early **to catch** the train. 우리는 기차를 잡기 위해서 일찍 떠났다.

→ to catch(~를 잡기 위해서)가 동사 left(떠났다)를 수식하는 부사 역할

We enjoy **making** wooden toys. 우리는 나무로 된 장난감을 만드는 것을 즐긴다.

→ making(~를 만드는 것)이 타동사 enjoy의 목적어인 명사 역할

2 차이점

	기본 형태	차이점
부정사	to + 동사원형	① 주어 자리에서 가급적 피함 ② be동사 보어 자리에 사용 가능 ③ 전치사의 목적어로 불가능
동명사	동사원형 + ~ing	① 주어 자리에 사용 ② be동사 보어 자리에서 가급적 피함 ③ 전치사의 목적어로 사용 가능

❶ 주어 자리

To make a good decision is not easy. = **It** is not easy **to make a good decision**. 좋은 결정을 내리는 것은 쉽지 않다.
Making a good decision is not easy. 좋은 결정을 내리는 것은 쉽지 않다.

→ 현대 영어에서는 주어를 강조할 경우 외에는 부정사를 주어로 사용하지 않고 가주어(it)를 이용한 문장으로 대부분 사용한다. 동명사는 주어로 사용하는 데 전혀 문제가 없으므로 부정사처럼 뒤로 보내지 않는다.

❷ be동사의 보어 자리

My goal **is to become** a leader. / My goal **is becoming** a leader. 나의 목표는 리더가 되는 것이다.

→ be동사 다음에 보어로 동명사가 올 경우 현재진행형 동사(be ~ing)로 오해될 수 있으므로 보통 부정사를 더 잘 사용한다.

❸ 전치사의 목적어 자리

Before buying a computer, think carefully. 컴퓨터를 사기 전에 주의 깊게 생각하세요.

→ 전치사 다음에는 원래 명사나 명사상당어구가 온다. 부정사와 동명사 중 전치사 다음에 올 수 있는 것은 동명사이다.

Check-up

STEP 1

1. We _____ at the meeting last week.
   (A) to meet (B) met

2. A clean work environment will _____ productivity.
   (A) increase (B) to increase

3. We create value by _____ with local vendors.
   (A) to work (B) working

STEP 2

4. Because of _____ three languages, he will definitely be hired by the international company.
   (A) speak (B) spoke (C) to speak (D) speaking

5. We cannot continue to proceed with the project without _____ more information.
   (A) receive (B) to receive (C) receiving (D) receives

2 부정사와 동명사의 용법 차이

부정사는 동사를 여러 가지 품사(명사, 형용사, 부사)로 사용하려고 만든 준동사이지만, 실제 문장에서 많이 사용되는 용법은 몇 개로 정해져 있다. 그리고 동명사는 동사를 명사로 사용하려고 만든 것이므로 명사 자리에만 들어간다.

1 부정사의 보편적 용법

❶ 타동사의 목적어 (~하는 것)

The company expects **to finish** the work by today. 그 회사는 작업을 오늘까지 끝낼 것으로 예상한다.

→ 부정사(to finish)가 타동사 expect(~를 예상하다)의 목적어 역할을 한다.

❷ 불완전 타동사의 목적격 보어 (목적어가 ~하는 것)

I want **you to go** there. 나는 네가 거기에 가기를 원한다.

→ to go는 목적어 you를 설명하는 목적격 보어이다. 목적어 you와 to go가 마치 '주어 + 동사'의 의미 관계를 형성한다.

❸ 부사 역할 (~하기 위해서)

They use a lot of information **to find** a good product. 그들은 좋은 제품을 찾기 위해서 많은 정보를 이용합니다.

→ 부정사(to find)가 동사 use(~를 이용하다)를 뒤에서 수식하고 있다. '~하기 위해서'로 해석하면 된다.

잠깐!

부사적 용법 중에서 '목적'을 나타내는 부정사는 그 앞에 in order나 so as를 붙여서 목적을 강조하거나 조금 더 격식 있는 표현을 만든다.

We had a meeting **to discuss** the matter. 우리는 그 문제를 논의하기 위해서 회의를 했다.
= We had a meeting **in order to discuss** the matter. (목적 강조)
= We had a meeting **so as to discuss** the matter. (격식 있는 표현)

2 동명사의 용법

동명사는 동사를 명사로 사용하기 위해서 만든 것이므로 전적으로 명사 자리에서 사용된다. 하지만 다음과 같은 차이가 있다.

	관사	목적어	수식어	해석
명사	O	X	형용사가 수식	사람이나 사물의 이름
동명사	X	O	부사가 수식	'~하는 것, 하기'

❶ 관사의 유무 – 관사는 명사 앞에 붙고, 동명사 앞에는 붙지 않는다.

You should make **a request** in writing. (O) 당신은 서면으로 요청할 수 있다.
You should make **a requesting** in writing. (X)

→ 부정관사(a)가 있으면 동명사를 쓸 수 없고 반드시 명사만을 써야 한다.

❷ **목적어의 유무** – 동명사는 뒤에 목적어를 수반할 수 있고, 명사는 할 수 없다.

It is used for **producing computer chips**. (O) 그것은 컴퓨터 칩을 생산하는 데 사용된다.
It is used for **production computer chips**. (X)
→ 명사 production(생산)은 목적어를 수반할 수 없지만, 동명사 introducing(~를 생산하는 것)은 뒤에 목적어 computer chips(컴퓨터 칩)를 수반할 수 있다.

❸ **수식어의 차이** – 명사 수식은 형용사가 하고 동명사 수식은 부사가 한다.

We can upgrade by **constant introduction** of technological innovations.
우리는 기술적 혁신들의 끊임없는 도입으로 업그레이드 할 수 있다.
→ 형용사 constant(끊임없는)가 명사 introduction(도입)을 수식한다.

We can upgrade by **constantly introducing** technological innovations.
우리는 기술적인 혁신들을 끊임없이 도입함으로써 업그레이드 할 수 있다.
→ 부사 constantly(끊임없이)가 동명사 introducing(~를 도입하는 것)을 수식한다.

❹ **해석의 차이** – 명사는 자체 이름이 따로 있지만 동명사는 동사에 '~하기'를 붙여 해석한다.

We had **a meeting** yesterday in the main conference room. 우리는 어제 중앙 회의실에서 회의를 했다.
→ 여기서 a meeting은 관사가 있으므로 명사이며, '회의'라는 자체 이름이 있다.

Meeting our president was a good experience. 우리 회장을 만난 것은 좋은 경험이었다.
→ 여기서 meeting은 뒤에 our president라는 자체 목적어가 있으므로 동명사이고, '만난 것'이라고 해석한다.

Check-up

STEP 1

1. I want you _____ with the new employees tomorrow.
   (A) to meet (B) meet

2. We recently conducted an _____.
   (A) investigation (B) investigating

3. After _____ considering her work experience, they hired her.
   (A) careful (B) carefully

STEP 2

4. _____ deleted files is not too difficult because many powerful tools are available on the Internet.
   (A) Recover (B) Recovered (C) Recovery (D) Recovering

5. In order to _____ on writing a book, Ms. Flores resigned from her position.
   (A) concentrate (B) concentration (C) concentrating (D) concentrates

3 동사 + 부정사/동명사

1 부정사를 목적어로 취하는 동사

다음은 명사는 물론이고 부정사를 목적어로 취하는 동사들을 정리해 놓은 것이다.

want to부정사	~하기를 원하다	intend to부정사	~할 의도이다
hope to부정사	~하기를 희망하다	need to부정사	~할 필요가 있다
plan to부정사	~할 계획이다	refuse to부정사	~하기를 거부하다
decide to부정사	~하기로 결정하다	propose to부정사	~하기를 제안하다
would like to부정사	~하고 싶다	wish to부정사	~하고 싶어하다

I **want the report**. (O) 나는 그 보고서를 원한다. / I **want to see** the report. (O) 나는 보고서 보기를 원한다.
I **want seeing** the report. (X)

→ 타동사 want는 목적어로 명사와 부정사를 취할 수는 있지만, 동명사를 목적어로 취하진 않는다.

2 동명사를 목적어로 취하는 동사

다음은 명사와 동명사가 모두 목적어로 올 수 있는 동사들이다. 단, 부정사는 목적어로 취하지 않는다.

enjoy ~ing	~하는 것을 즐기다	include ~ing	~하는 것을 포함하다
consider ~ing	~하는 것을 고려하다	mind ~ing	~하는 것을 꺼려하다
finish ~ing	~하는 것을 끝내다	stop ~ing	~하는 것을 멈추다
quit ~ing	~하는 것을 그만두다	postpone ~ing	~하는 것을 연기하다
avoid ~ing	~하는 것을 피하다	discontinue ~ing	~하는 것을 중단하다

Alan narrowly **avoided the accident**. (O) 앨런은 가까스로 그 사고를 피했다.

Drivers should **avoid using** mobile phones while driving. (O) 운전자들은 운전하는 동안에 휴대폰 사용하는 것을 피해야 한다.
Drivers should **avoid to use** mobile phones while driving. (X)

3 부정사와 동명사 둘 다 목적어로 취하는 동사

❶ 의미 차이가 생기는 동사들

동명사 목적어(과거의 일을 ~하다)	부정사 목적어(미래의 일을 ~하다)
remember ~ing ((과거에) ~한 것을 기억하다)	remember to부정사 (~할 것을 기억하다)
forget ~ing ((과거에) ~한 것을 잊어버리다)	forget to부정사 (~할 것을 잊어버리다)

Employees should **remember to turn off** all the office lights.
직원들은 모든 사무실 전등불을 꺼야 하는 것을 기억해야 한다.

The employee **remembers turning off** all the office lights last night.
그 직원은 어제 저녁 모든 사무실 전등불을 끈 것을 기억한다.

❷ 의미 차이가 없는 동사들

시작, 계속의 의미를 갖는 동사들		좋아하거나 싫어하는 의미를 갖는 동사들	
start to부정사/~ing	~하기를 시작하다	like to부정사/~ing	~하기를 좋아하다
begin to부정사/~ing	~하기를 시작하다	hate to부정사/~ing	~하기를 싫어하다
continue to부정사/~ing	~하기를 계속하다	prefer to부정사/~ing	~하기를 선호하다

He always **likes to sleep** late on Sundays. = He always **likes sleeping** late on Sundays.
그는 항상 일요일에 늦게까지 자는 것을 좋아한다.

목적어에는 부정사가 안 오지만 목적격 보어에 부정사가 오는 동사들

다음은 목적어가 아니고 '목적격 보어'로 부정사를 취하는 동사들이다.

- request A(목적어) to부정사 (A가 ~하도록 요청하다)
- require A(목적어) to부정사 (A가 ~하도록 요구하다)
- recommend A(목적어) to부정사 (A가 ~하도록 추천하다)

We **recommend you to make** reservations early. (O) 우리는 당신이 일찍 예약하기를 추천합니다.
We **recommend to make** reservations early. (X)
→ 동사 recommend 다음에 목적어로 부정사가 올 수는 없지만 목적격 보어로 수반되는 것은 가능하다.

Check-up

STEP 1

1. We hope _____ your group soon.
   (A) to join   (B) joining

2. The company will discontinue _____ this camera model.
   (A) to produce   (B) producing

3. I don't mind _____ for a long time.
   (A) to drive   (B) driving

STEP 2

4. We would like _____ the cancellation of your reservation at our hotel.
   (A) confirm   (B) to confirm   (C) confirming   (D) confirms

5. We recommend _____ some additional office equipment for the next seminars.
   (A) purchase   (B) to purchase   (C) purchasing   (D) purchases

4 주의해야 할 부정사와 동명사 구문

1 의문사 + to부정사 = 명사 역할

원래 의문사는 뒤에 '주어 + 동사'로 이루어진 절을 수반하지만, 주어가 겹치는 번거로움을 피하기 위해서 '주어 + 동사'를 부정사로 축약할 수 있다.

what to부정사 무엇을 ~할지	where to부정사 어디서 ~할지	when to부정사 언제 ~할지
how to부정사 어떻게 ~할지	whether to부정사 ~할지 안 할지	whom to부정사 누구를 ~할지

I don't know **what I should do** tonight. = I don't know **what to do** tonight.
나는 오늘 저녁에 무엇을 해야 할지 모르겠다.

They are learning **how they should deal with** children. 그들은 어린아이들을 어떻게 다룰지 배우고 있다.
= They are learning **how to deal with** children.

2 전치사 to가 들어가는 관용구

영어에는 두 종류의 to가 있는데, 부정사 to와 전치사 to이다. 부정사 to 다음에는 동사원형, 전치사 to 다음에는 명사나 동명사가 오므로 주의해야 한다.

전치사 to가 들어 있는 관용구	의미	동의 표현
object to 명사/~ing	~하는 데 반대하다	= be opposed to 명사/~ing
be used to 명사/~ing	~하는 데 익숙하다	= be accustomed to 명사/~ing
look forward to 명사/~ing	~하기를 고대하다	
be dedicated to 명사/~ing	~하는 데 전념[헌신]하다	= be devoted to 명사/~ing = be committed to 명사/~ing
be subject to 명사/~ing	~에 영향 받다/~하기 쉽다	

I **am used to working** at night now. 나는 이제 저녁에 일하는 것에 익숙해졌다.

→ be used to 명사/~ing를 관용구로 기억해 두지 않으면 부정사와 혼동될 수 있다.

The director says that she's **looking forward to meeting** you. 이사가 당신 만나기를 고대한다고 합니다.

→ look forward to 구문에 있는 to는 전치사이므로 그 다음에는 명사나 동명사가 나온다.

3 to가 없는 부정사 (원형부정사)

부정사는 대체로 'to + 동사원형'의 꼴을 취하지만, 때로는 to 없이 동사원형으로만 나오는 경우가 있는데 그것을 '원형부정사'라 한다.

❶ 목적격 보어로 원형부정사를 취하는 사역동사와 지각동사

- 사역동사(make, have, let) + 목적어 + 목적격 보어(원형부정사)
- 지각동사(hear, see) + 목적어 + 목적격 보어(원형부정사)

➡ 사역동사나 지각동사는 목적어 다음에 to부정사를 쓰면 안 되고, to가 없는 동사원형을 써야 한다.

I will **have** my secretary **take** your message. (O) 나는 내 비서에게 당신의 메시지를 받도록 시킬 것입니다.
I will **have** my secretary **to take** your message. (X)

She **heard** Tom **go** upstairs. (O) 그녀는 톰이 위층으로 올라가는 소리를 들었다.
She **heard** Tom **to go** upstairs. (X)

❷ 목적격 보어로 to부정사와 원형부정사를 모두 취할 수 있는 준 사역동사 help

We will **help** your company **(to) reduce** employee absences. 우리는 귀사가 직원 결근을 감소시키도록 도울 것입니다.

※ help는 목적격 보어뿐만 아니라, 목적어로도 to부정사와 원형부정사 둘 다 취할 수 있다.

We will **help (to) reduce** employee absences. 우리는 직원 결근을 감소시키도록 도울 것이다.

➡ help 다음에 목적어로 to부정사나 원형부정사가 바로 나올 수 있다.

Check-up

해설 p. 108-109

STEP 1

1. You should know how _____ the photocopier.
    (A) operate   (B) to operate

2. The store is dedicated to _____ good products.
    (A) provide   (B) providing

3. The teacher will let students _____ their scores.
    (A) know   (B) to know

STEP 2

4. Passengers should note that some flights are subject to _____ due to bad weather.
    (A) cancels   (B) be cancelled   (C) cancellation   (D) have cancelled

5. The personnel department will help us _____ the most effective rotation schedule.
    (A) determine   (B) determining   (C) determines   (D) determined

토익 필수 어휘 3_ 명사 (3) 해설 p.98-101

1. license
n. 허가증, 면허증   *v.* ~를 허가하다

a valid driver's **license** 유효한 운전면허증
applying for a **license** 허가증을 신청하다

2. effort
n. 노력, 작품, 행사

in an **effort** to부정사 ~하려는 노력으로
make every **effort** to부정사 ~하려고 최선의 노력을 다하다

3. charge
n. 요금; 담당, 책임

at no extra **charge** 추가 요금 없이
in **charge** of ~을 맡아서, ~을 담당하여

4. schedule
n. 일정표, 스케줄   *v.* ~의 일정을 잡다

on **schedule** 정시에, 예정대로, 일정표대로
behind **schedule** 예정보다 늦게

5. process
n. 과정, 공정   *v.* ~를 처리하다, ~를 가공처리하다

interdepartmental communication **process** 각 부처의 의사소통 과정
assembly and shipping **processes** 조립 및 배송 과정

6. commitment
n. 전념, 헌신; 약속

the **commitment** of the staff 직원들의 전념[헌신]
show **commitment** 헌신적인 태도를 보이다

7. transaction
n. 거래, 매매

improper **transaction** 부적절한 거래
bank **transactions** 은행 거래

8. discussion
n. 논의, 토의

a **discussion** of the company's new strategies 기업의 새로운 전략에 관한 토론
panel **discussion** participants 패널 토론 참석자

9. profit	*n.* 이익, 수익, 이윤 net **profit** 순수익 a decline in **profits** 수익 감소
10. reimbursement	*n.* 보상, 환급 **reimbursement** for moving expenses 이사 비용에 대한 보상 **reimbursement** for the cost of tuition and fees 수업료와 수수료에 대한 환급
11. delay	*n.* 지연, 지체 *v.* 지연시키다 without **delay** 지체 없이 shipping **delay** 배송 지연
12. exposure	*n.* 노출, 직면 **exposure** to danger 위험에 노출됨[직면함] long **exposure** to computer screens 컴퓨터 화면에 장시간 노출됨(=컴퓨터의 장시간 사용)
13. notice	*n.* 통지, 공지 *v.* 알아차리다 until further **notice** 추후 통지가 있을 때까지 short **notice** 촉박한 통보

Check-up

해설 p.109

1. He is in (charge / responsible) of the project. 그가 그 프로젝트를 담당하고 있다.

2. We are now behind (scheduled / schedule). 우리는 지금 예정보다 뒤쳐져 있다.

3. He will report any improper (transact / transaction). 그는 어떠한 부적절한 거래라도 보고할 것이다.

4. We had a (discuss / discussion) about the matter. 우리는 그 문제에 대한 논의를 했다.

5. Our company offers (reimburse / reimbursement) for moving expenses. 우리 회사는 이사 비용에 대한 보상을 제공한다.

PART 5&6_ 실전연습 3

1. Any contractor who fails to _____ with building regulations may be subject to a license suspension.

    (A) comply
    (B) complied
    (C) complying
    (D) complies

2. Northern Auto decided to inspect all finished cars in every _____ to satisfy clients.

    (A) influence
    (B) effort
    (C) strength
    (D) interest

3. _____ customers satisfied is the duty of everyone that works in the store.

    (A) Keep
    (B) Keeping
    (C) Kept
    (D) Have kept

4. Members and their families are free to use the club's facilities at no extra _____.

    (A) concern
    (B) right
    (C) guideline
    (D) charge

5. If you want _____ quickly, you have to endure a lot of unexpected trouble with you.

    (A) to succeeding
    (B) succeed
    (C) to succeed
    (D) to being succeeded

6. Atlantic Industries is presently in the _____ of installing new anti-virus software to strengthen security.

    (A) process
    (B) resource
    (C) reflection
    (D) assembly

7. Customers could be offered reimbursements upon _____ related documents required.

    (A) receive
    (B) receiving
    (C) receives
    (D) receipt

8. Dr. Patel held a _____ in order to reduce risks of heart surgery along with some physicians.

    (A) contribution
    (B) survey
    (C) discussion
    (D) agreement

9. Atlantic Airlines considered _____ its advertising budget due to falling profits from next year.

    (A) to reduce
    (B) reducing
    (C) reduce
    (D) be reduced

10. Even though he was on a tight _____, Brian finally managed to finish the book.

    (A) position
    (B) appointment
    (C) schedule
    (D) consideration

11. Angela's explanation helped executives _____ new tax laws taking effect next year.

    (A) understand
    (B) understands
    (C) understanding
    (D) to understanding

12. Spectators were impressed by the energy and _____ shown by the players in the field.

    (A) warranty
    (B) extension
    (C) commitment
    (D) reference

13. _____ sales goals of 8 million dollars, we are dedicated to meeting customers' need.

(A) By achieving
(B) To achieve
(C) As achieved
(D) By achievement

14. In order to have clients' faith, all the _____ of business should be open to the public.

(A) alternatives
(B) invitations
(C) transactions
(D) measurements

Questions 15-18 refer to the following notice.

Award Claims Center
9302 Primary Drive
Arlington, TX 76013

Dear Ms. Renee Thompson,

This is to ------- **15.** you that you are an official prizewinner in our new car promotion. We are giving away a new Percedes, VMW, Audis, or your choice of $40,000. Other prizes include two round-trip tickets to Hawaii, a luxury 4-night Caribbean cruise for four, and a $2,000 shopping spree. To avoid ------- **16.** your status as a prizewinner, you must contact our office before July 1. You can call us toll free at 1-800-392-9583 from 8 A.M. to 6 P.M. on weekdays and on Saturday from 9 A.M. to 4 P.M. -------. **17.** You are ------- **18.** to receive a prize.

Sincerely,

Michael Evans

15. (A) notify
    (B) notifies
    (C) notified
    (D) notifying

16. (A) forfeit
    (B) forfeited
    (C) forfeiting
    (D) to forfeit

17. (A) For example, you can meet the office manager in person.
    (B) However, the deadline is approaching quickly.
    (C) There is no obligation to make a purchase.
    (D) All employees are off-duty on Saturday.

18. (A) guaranteed
    (B) sought
    (C) advanced
    (D) remained

UNIT 4 분사

> ★ 콕콕 찍어주는 출제 포인트
>
> 분사는 부정사나 동명사와 마찬가지로 동사의 형태를 조금 변형해서 형용사로 쓰려고 만든 것이다. 그러므로 분사 또한 단독적으로 동사 역할을 할 수 없고 명사를 수식하는 역할로 주로 사용된다.

1 분사의 기본 개념

1 분사의 형태

분사는 현재분사와 과거분사로 나누어진다. 현재분사는 동사원형 뒤에 ~ing를 붙이는 한 가지 형태지만, 과거분사는 동사원형에 ~ed를 붙이는 규칙 동사와 일괄적인 규칙 없이 형태가 변하는 불규칙 동사 두 가지가 있다.

	동사(원형)	현재분사(동사원형 + ~ing)	과거분사(p.p.)
어휘 예	make	making	made (불규칙 동사)
	start	starting	started (규칙 동사)
	do	doing	done (불규칙 동사)

2 분사의 역할

분사는 애초에 동사를 형용사로 사용하기 위해 만들어졌지만, 동사의 진행형이나 완료시제, 수동태로도 사용된다.

	현재분사	과거분사(p.p.)
형용사적 용법	**falling** leaves (떨어지는 나뭇잎) → 명사 수식	**fallen** leaves (떨어진 나뭇잎) → 명사 수식
동사의 일부분	be + ~ing → 동사의 진행형	have + p.p. / be + p.p. → 완료시제/수동태

The **falling / fallen leaves** are red and gold. 떨어지는/떨어진 나뭇잎들은 붉은색과 금색이다.
→ 분사가 명사 leaves(나뭇잎)를 수식하는 형용사 역할을 한다.

We are **accepting** proposals. 우리는 제안서를 받고 있습니다.
→ 현재분사 accepting이 be동사와 함께 동사의 진행형을 만들고 있다.

I have **lived** here since I was five. 나는 다섯 살 때부터 여기서 살았다.
→ 과거분사 lived가 have동사와 결합해서 현재완료시제 동사를 만들고 있다.

The letter was **sent** yesterday. 편지는 어제 보내졌다.
→ 과거분사 sent가 be동사와 결합해서 수동태를 만들고 있다.

3 동명사와 현재분사의 차이

	문장에서의 역할	해석 차이
동명사(동사원형 + ~ing)	명사 역할(주어, 목적어, 보어 자리)	~하는 것, ~하기
현재분사(동사원형 + ~ing)	① 동사의 진행형 구성 ② 형용사 역할(명사 수식)	① ~하는 중이다 ② ~하는, ~한

❶ be + ~ing

His hobby is **collecting coins**. 그의 취미는 동전을 수집하는 것이다. → His hobby = collecting의 동격 관계 성립
　　　　　　　동명사 보어

He is **collecting** coins. 그는 동전을 모으는 중이다. → 현재진행형 동사를 구성하는 현재분사
　　　　동사

❷ 명사/형용사 역할

Staying here is really relaxing. 여기서 머무르는 것은 정말 편안하다.
→ staying(머무르는 것)은 주어 자리에서 명사 역할을 하는 동명사이다.

The only people **staying** are students and film critics. 머무르는 사람들은 학생들과 영화 비평가들뿐이다.
→ staying(머무르는)은 앞에 있는 people(사람들)을 수식한다. 즉, 형용사 역할을 하는 현재분사이다.

Check-up

해설 p. 111–112

STEP 1

1. I was _____ a restaurant at that time.
   (A) find (B) finding

2. Car sales have recently _____ .
   (A) increasing (B) increased

3. Everyone was surprised to know that the city hall was _____ in 1880.
   (A) build (B) built

STEP 2

4. Recently _____ vehicles from SM Motors will be repaired free of charge for the first 20,000 km.
   (A) purchased (B) purchases (C) purchase (D) have purchased

5. The convention organizers have _____ special group rates from the Merrion Hotel.
   (A) obtain (B) obtaining (C) obtained (D) obtains

2 분사가 명사를 앞에서 수식할 때

1 현재분사와 과거분사

	분사와 명사의 관계	의미/예
현재분사(~ing) + 명사	능동 관계	~하는/예: surprising (놀라게 하는)
과거분사(p.p.) + 명사	수동 관계	~된/예: surprised (놀라는, 놀란)

2 감정동사의 분사

동사의 의미가 감정을 나타낼 때 '현재분사는 사물명사를 수식'하고, '과거분사는 사람명사를 수식'한다는 규칙을 적용하자.

감정동사	현재분사(~ing) + 사물명사	과거분사(p.p.) + 사람명사
excite (타) (~를 흥미롭게 하다)	exciting story (흥미로운 이야기)	excited audience (신이 난 청중들)
satisfy (타) (~를 만족시키다)	satisfying product (만족스러운 제품)	satisfied customers (만족한 고객들)
interest (타) (~를 재밌게 하다)	interesting book (재미있는 책)	interested readers (재미를 느낀 독자들)
disappoint (타) (~를 실망시키다)	disappointing results (실망스러운 결과)	disappointed students (실망한 학생들)
bore (타) (~를 따분하게 하다)	boring game (따분한 경기)	bored spectators (따분해진 관객들)
tire (타) (~를 피곤하게 하다)	tiring trip (피곤한 여행)	tired travelers (피곤해진 여행객들)
surprise (타) (~를 놀라게 하다)	surprising score (놀라운 점수)	surprised participants (놀란 참가자들)

3 일반동사의 분사

감정동사가 아닌 일반동사의 분사는 뒤에 나오는 명사가 사람이든 사물이든 구분 없이 능동/수동 관계의 해석으로 접근해야 한다.

❶ 타동사의 분사

뿌리가 타동사인 어휘들은 능동과 수동의 의미를 모두 갖기 때문에 현재분사와 과거분사형 형용사 모두가 가능하다. 분사의 수식을 받는 명사가 능동적으로 '~할' 때는 현재분사로 수식, 수동적으로 '~당할' 때는 과거분사로 수식한다.

뿌리가 되는 동사	현재분사(~ing) + 명사	과거분사(p.p.) + 명사
damage (타) (~를 손상시키다)	damaging effects (손상을 주는 영향)	damaged goods (손상된 제품)
finish (타) (~를 끝내다)	finishing touch (마무리 손질)	finished product (완성된 제품)
pollute (타) (~를 오염시키다)	polluting gas (오염시키는 가스)	polluted air (오염된 공기)
request (타) (~를 요청하다)	requesting letter (요청하는 편지)	requested information (요청된 정보)
confuse (타) (~를 혼동시키다)	confusing figures (혼동을 주는 수치)	confused scientists (혼동스러운 과학자들)
propose (타) (~를 제안하다)	proposing message (제안하는 메시지)	proposed project (제안된 계획)

❷ 자동사의 분사

자동사는 수동의 의미가 없으므로 일반적으로 능동의 의미가 있는 현재분사(~ing)형 형용사만 사용한다.

뿌리가 되는 동사	현재분사형 형용사 + 명사	의미
remain (자) (남다)	**remaining** guests	남아 있는 손님들
exist (자) (존재하다)	**existing** equipment	기존의 장비
last (자) (지속하다)	**lasting** impression	지속적인 인상
rise (자) (상승하다)	**rising** price	상승하는 가격

Remaining guests will be asked to leave here. (O) 남아 있는 손님들은 이곳을 떠나도록 요청받을 것이다.
Remained guests will be asked to leave here. (X)

→ 자동사 remain은 수동의 의미가 없으므로 과거분사를 쓰지 않고 현재분사 형태로만 쓴다.

Check-up

STEP 1

1. It was a _____ speech.
   (A) boring   (B) bored

2. Last night's performance was so _____.
   (A) exciting   (B) excited

3. Travellers should be careful not to drink _____ water.
   (A) polluting   (B) polluted

STEP 2

4. This special service from AFI Creative Design is available to all _____ customers.
   (A) exist   (B) existing   (C) existed   (D) exists

5. Mr. Ramos was so kind and gentle that he made a _____ impression on all of his clients.
   (A) lasted   (B) lasting   (C) lasts   (D) lastly

3 분사가 명사를 뒤에서 수식할 때

분사가 형용사 역할로 명사를 앞에서 수식할 때는 분사와 명사의 관계에 따른 해석이 중요했지만 뒤에서 수식할 때는 약간의 문법적 규칙이 있다.

1 분사가 명사를 뒤에서 수식하는 이유

분사가 명사를 앞이 아니라 뒤에서 수식하는 이유는 분사 뒤에 또 다른 수식어가 있기 때문이다.

I saw the station **built in 1950**. (O) 나는 1950년에 지어진 역을 보았다.
I saw the **built** station in 1950. (X)

→ 위 문장에서 과거분사 built(지어진)는 앞에 나온 the station(역)을 뒤에서 수식하고 있다. 이 때 built 또한 뒤에 자체 수식어 in 1950(1950년에)이 있기 때문에 built만 단독으로 station 앞으로 갈 수 없다.

People **staying here** enjoy various activities. 여기서 머무르는 사람들은 다양한 활동을 즐긴다.

→ 이 경우 역시 staying이 뒤에 here라는 자체 수식어가 있기 때문에 people(사람들)을 뒤에서 수식할 수밖에 없다.

2 명사 + (주격 관계대명사 + be동사) + 분사

분사가 명사를 뒤에서 수식할 때 그 명사와 분사 사이에는 〈주격 관계대명사 + be동사〉가 생략된 개념으로 이해할 수 있다.

I received **a letter written** in English. = I received **a letter which was written** in English.
나는 영어로 쓰인 편지 하나를 받았다.

The man looking at the picture is Mr. Kim. = **The man who is looking** at the picture is Mr. Kim.
그 그림을 보고 있는 남자는 김 씨이다.

3 타동사의 현재분사는 뒤에 목적어(명사)를 수반한다.

타동사의 현재분사 뒤에는 명사 형태의 목적어가 올 수 있지만 과거분사 뒤에는 명사가 바로 나올 수 없다.

Anyone **ordering supplies** should tell the manager. (O) 물품을 주문하는 사람은 누구든지 매니저에게 말해야 한다.
Anyone **ordered supplies** should tell the manager. (X)

→ 현재분사 ordering(주문하는)은 뒤에 목적어 supplies(물품)를 수반할 수 있지만 과거분사는 목적어를 가질 수 없다.

A survey **conducted by the company** will be released. (O) 그 회사에 의해 실시된 설문조사가 공개될 것이다.

→ 과거분사 conducted(실시된)는 뒤에 목적어 없이 '전치사 + 명사(by the company)'로 이어지는 것은 가능하다.

4 자동사의 분사는 과거분사가 없으며, 현재분사만 있다.

자동사의 분사는 수동의 의미가 없으므로 현재분사만 있다. 또한 자동사에서 비롯되었기 때문에 뒤에 목적어가 수반되지 않고 전치사구가 이어질 수 있다.

명사 +	working (at) ~에서 일하는 (명사)	staying (at) ~에 머무르는 (명사)
	agreeing (to) ~에 동의하는 (명사)	remaining (on/at) ~에 남아 있는 (명사)

Staff members working at the supermarket should use the rear door.
슈퍼마켓에서 일하는 직원들은 뒷문을 이용해야 한다.
Employees remaining at the facility will receive compensation. 그 시설에 남아 있는 직원들은 보상을 받을 것이다.

대명사 those와 anyone은 관용적으로 분사가 뒤에서 수식을 한다.

Those killed were innumerable. = **Those who were killed** were innumerable.
죽은 사람들은 셀 수 없었다.
Anyone interested in the position should contact me. = **Anyone who is interested** in the position should contact me. 그 직위에 관심 있는 사람은 누구든지 나에게 연락해야 한다.

Check-up

STEP 1

1. I will send you a letter _____ proof of residence.
   (A) show (B) showing

2. The meeting _____ for today has been cancelled.
   (A) scheduling (B) scheduled

3. People _____ for an interview will be called soon.
   (A) waiting (B) waited

STEP 2

4. The engineers _____ in the assembly area must always wear safety gear.
   (A) working (B) worked (C) have worked (D) are working

5. According to the notice, anyone _____ in the project must attend the meeting tomorrow.
   (A) involve (B) involving (C) involved (D) involves

4 분사구문

분사구문은 아주 쉽게 얘기하면 분사로 시작하는 구문이라는 뜻으로서, 부사절(접속사 + 주어 + 동사)이 축약된 형태로 주절을 다시 한 번 설명해 주는 역할을 한다.

1 분사구문의 개념과 형태

부사절 접속사 다음에 나오는 '주어 + 동사'를 현재분사나 과거분사로 축약해서 표현하는 것이다.

부사절 접속사 + 주어 + 동사 ┬ 접속사 + 현재분사(~ing)
　　　　　　　　　　　　　　└ 접속사 + 과거분사(p.p.)

While I was waiting for a bus, I met him. = **While waiting** for a bus, I met him.
버스를 기다리는 동안에 나는 그를 만났다.

➡ 접속사 다음에 주어와 be동사(I was)를 생략하고 waiting이라는 분사만 남았기 때문에 이를 '분사구문'이라 하고, waiting은 현재분사이므로 이를 '현재분사구문'이라 한다.

While they are parked here, cars must have a permit.
= **While parked** here, cars must have a permit. 여기에 주차된 동안에, 차들은 반드시 허가증을 가지고 있어야 한다.

➡ 접속사 다음에 주어와 be동사(they are)를 생략하고 parked라는 분사만 남았기 때문에 이를 '분사구문'이라 하고, parked는 과거분사이므로 이를 '과거분사구문'이라 한다.

2 현재분사구문을 만드는 방법 (1)

접속사 다음에 주어를 빼고 동사를 ~ing 형태로 바꾼다.

접속사 + 주어 + 동사 + ~, 주절의 주어 + 동사 + ~
　　　　 ↓　　 ↓
(접속사) + 현재분사(~ing) + ~, 주절의 주어 + 동사 + ~

When you purchase a product here, you will get a discount. 여기서 제품을 구매할 때, 당신은 할인을 받게 될 것이다.
= **When purchasing** a product here, you will get a discount.

➡ 접속사 when 다음에 주어(you)를 빼고 동사 purchase를 분사 purchasing으로 바꾼 것이다.

3 현재분사구문을 만드는 방법 (2)

부사절에서 주어 다음에 동사가 진행형이라면, 주어와 be동사를 한꺼번에 생략한다.

접속사 + 주어 + be + 현재분사(~ing) + ~, 주절의 주어 + 동사 + ~
　　　　 ↓　　　↓
(접속사) + 현재분사(~ing) + ~, 주절의 주어 + 동사 + ~

While I was driving, I got a phone call. = **While driving**, I got a phone call. 운전하는 동안 전화를 받았다.

➡ 부사절이 진행형 시제인 경우 주어와 be동사를 한꺼번에 생략한다.

4 과거분사구문을 만드는 방법

과거분사구문은 원래 접속사가 이끄는 부사절 안에서의 동사가 수동태일 때 축약해서 만든 구문이다. 부사절의 동사가 수동태인지 확인하고, 주어와 be동사를 생략해 버리면 과거분사만 남게 되면서 과거분사구문이 된다.

접속사 + 주어 + be + 과거분사(p.p.) + ~, 주절의 주어 + 동사 + ~
         ↓   ↓
(접속사) + 과거분사(p.p.) + ~, 주절의 주어 + 동사 + ~

When they are purchased in bulk, products will be discounted.
= **When purchased** in bulk, products will be discounted.

→ 접속사 when 다음에 주어와 be동사(they are)를 한꺼번에 생략한다.

잠깐!

분사구문에서 접속사를 살릴 것인가 뺄 것인가?

부사절을 축약해서 분사구문을 만들 때, 접속사를 남기는 경우도 있고 빼는 경우도 있는데, 문맥을 통해서 어떤 접속사가 빠졌는지 충분히 예측할 수 없을 경우에는 접속사를 남기는 편이 좋다. 토익에는 접속사가 함께 나오는 분사구문이 대부분이다.

While I was waiting for a bus, I met him. 버스를 기다리는 동안에 나는 그를 만났다.
= **While waiting** for a bus, I met him. / **Waiting** for a bus, I met him.

Check-up

STEP 1

1. If _____ in transit, the products can be exchanged.
   (A) damaging   (B) damaged

2. While _____ a speech, speak clearly and loudly.
   (A) making   (B) made

3. Although _____ on Monday, the computer was not shipped until Friday.
   (A) buying   (B) bought

STEP 2

4. Travelers should read all service contracts carefully when _____ cars.
   (A) rent   (B) rented   (C) renting   (D) rents

5. Children under 14 are not allowed to enter this area unless _____ by an adult.
   (A) accompany   (B) accompanied
   (C) accompanying   (D) accompanies

토익 필수 어휘 4_ 명사 (4)

1. procedure

n. 절차, 규제

approved **procedures** 승인된 절차
waste removal **procedures** 폐기물 처리 절차

2. presence

n. 인지도, 위상, 존재, 참석

have a strong **presence** 강한 존재감을 갖고 있다
in the **presence** of ~의 면전에서, ~에 직면하여

3. remainder

n. 나머지

throughout the **remainder** of the week 그 주의 나머지 내내
for the **remainder** of the month 그 달의 남은 기간 동안

4. morale

n. 사기, 의욕

improve **morale** among staff members 직원들의 사기를 향상시키다
raise workplace **morale** 작업장의 사기를 고취시키다

5. interest

n. 관심, 흥미; 이자   *v.* ~의 관심을 끌다

interest in this position 이 직책에 대한 관심
raise **interest** rates 이자율을 올리다

6. concern

n. 걱정, 관심사, 관심, 책임   *v.* ~를 걱정시키다, ~에 영향을 미치다

address students' **concerns** 학생들의 걱정을 다루다
contact us with further **concerns** 추가적인 관심이 있으면 우리에게 연락 주세요

7. agreement

n. 합의, 약속, 동의, 협정서

a purchasing **agreement** 구매 동의
reach an **agreement** carefully 신중히 합의에 도달하다

8. advance

n. 전진, 진보, 발전

advances in medical technology 의학기술의 발전
in **advance** 사전에, 미리

9. representative	*n.* 대표, 대표자 a union **representative** 노조 대표 customer service **representatives** 고객 서비스 상담원
10. effect	*n.* 결과, 효과, 영향 *v.* ~을 야기하다 secondary **effects** of environmental pollution 환경오염의 부차적인 효과 come into **effect** 효력을 발휘하다, 시행되다
11. advantage	*n.* 이점 take **advantage** of (기회 따위를) 이용하다, (남을) 이용하다 many **advantages** of the new technology 신기술의 많은 이점들
12. expertise	*n.* 전문 지식, 전문가적인 기술 **expertise** in healthcare 건강 관리에 대한 전문 지식 technical **expertise** 기술에 관한 전문 지식
13. management	*n.* 관리, 운영; 경영진 time **management** 시간 관리 **management** and labor 노사

Check-up

해설 p.114

1. This is the (procedure / proceed) for applying for a visa.   이것은 비자를 신청하는 절차이다.

2. It will be on display for the (remain / remainder) of the month.   그것은 이 달 나머지 기간 동안에 전시될 것이다.

3. We should improve (moral / morale) among employees.   우리는 직원들 사이에서 사기를 향상시켜야 한다.

4. The director will address recent (concerns / concerned).   이사는 최근의 걱정들을 다룰 것이다.

5. They reached an (agree / agreement).   그들은 합의에 도달했다.

PART 5&6_ 실전연습 4 해설 p.114–117

1. Haney Chemicals announced that it would open a factory, _____ more than a thousand jobs.

    (A) create
    (B) creates
    (C) creating
    (D) created

2. ATT along with national Internet providers, will increase rates against government's _____.

    (A) quality
    (B) quantity
    (C) development
    (D) procedure

3. Fashion Square is a large shopping mall _____ with inexpensive clothing and accessory shops.

    (A) filling
    (B) filled
    (C) fills
    (D) fill

4. While _____ economics in China, Jane enrolled in language courses.

    (A) study
    (B) studied
    (C) studying
    (D) to study

5. To increase brand presence, products _____ in the warehouse will be distributed to passers-by for free.

    (A) remain
    (B) remains
    (C) remaining
    (D) remainder

6. The head of the department came up with an effective way to boost _____ among employees.

    (A) morale
    (B) behavior
    (C) rumor
    (D) workplace

7. Anyone _____ in this year's awards ceremony should contact Monica at extension 523 by Thursday.

    (A) interest
    (B) interested
    (C) interesting
    (D) interests

8. The government plans to address people's _____ about shortage of job opportunities.

    (A) effort
    (B) caution
    (C) agreement
    (D) concern

9. Novartis is _____ to the security of its employees and all measures are regularly reviewed to ensure safety.

    (A) committed
    (B) committment
    (C) commits
    (D) commit

10. _____ in chemical technology has enabled our company to increase economic presence in the world.

    (A) Approach
    (B) Advantage
    (C) Opening
    (D) Advances

11. The board of directors has not yet _____ new products because of a problem with the manufacturing operations.

    (A) announce
    (B) announcing
    (C) announced
    (D) announcement

12. The _____ of every dairy were gathered in order to take steps against government's rules.

    (A) opponents
    (B) presenters
    (C) announcers
    (D) representatives

13. Students who registered for fall classes _____ next Monday, August 26 should take history courses beforehand.
    (A) begin
    (B) begins
    (C) beginner
    (D) beginning

14. Once the law to protect customers comes into _____, it will reduce their serious damage.
    (A) progress
    (B) result
    (C) effect
    (D) order

Questions 15-18 refer to the following e-mail.

From: Jack Pierce [jackpierce@solisco.com]
To: Haley Brown [haleybrown@solisco.com]
Subject: Travel Arrangements
Date: November 7

Haley,

This message is to remind you that you will be ------- a client from Danbury and Davila at
                                                  15.
their offices on Wednesday, December 2 at 3 P.M. -------. He will pick you up and drive you to
                                                   16.
the meeting. After the meeting, the company car and driver will again be

------- available to you to return to your home. You also have prior authorization to use the
17.
company car to take the client out to lunch during the course of your meeting. For any

questions ------- your transportation to, from, and during the meeting, please contact me at
          18.
extension 1172.

Jack

15. (A) meet
    (B) met
    (C) meeting
    (D) meets

16. (A) The company's driver will be in front of our building at 2:15.
    (B) However, you will take a tour of the offices with a guide.
    (C) Some paperwork for submission has been assigned to you.
    (D) In other words, the client will make a apology for his mistake.

17. (A) making
    (B) made
    (C) make
    (D) to make

18. (A) without
    (B) despite
    (C) until
    (D) concerning

UNIT 5 동사의 종류

★ **콕콕 찍어주는 출제 포인트**

동사란 사람이나 사물의 동작이나 상태를 설명하는 말이며, 주어가 '~하다/~되다'라고 하는 서술어이다. 영어에서 동사를 구분하는 방법은 여러 가지가 있을 수 있는데 토익 공부를 위해서 가장 필요한 것은 자동사와 타동사의 분류법이다.

1 자동사와 타동사

영어에서는 동사를 크게 자동사와 타동사로 분류한다. 자동사는 혼자서도 의미가 완전해서 뒤에 목적어를 수반하지 않지만, 타동사는 그 동작의 대상이 되는 목적어(명사)를 꼭 뒤에 붙여야 한다.

1 자동사와 타동사 구분

동사	자동사 → 목적어(명사) 없음	자동사 + 전치사 + 목적어
	타동사 → 목적어(명사) 있음	타동사 + ~~전치사~~ + 목적어

He **talked to** me. (O) / He **talked** me. (X) 그는 내게 말했다.
→ 동사 talk(말하다)는 자동사이므로 그 다음에 목적어(me)가 곧바로 나올 수 없고 전치사(to)가 있어야 한다.

The report **emphasizes it**. (O) / The report **emphasizes on it**. (X) 그 보고서는 그 점을 강조한다.
→ 동사 emphasize(~를 강조하다)는 타동사이므로 그 다음에 전치사가 나오면 틀린다.

2 자동사 + 전치사 = 타동사 역할

❶ 빈출 자동사 + 전치사

자동사 + 전치사	의미	자동사 + 전치사	의미
respond to	~에 응답하다	deal with	~를 다루다
listen to	~를 듣다	comply with	~를 따르다[지키다]
object to	~에 반대하다	interfere with	~를 방해하다
refrain from	~를 삼가다	depend on	~에 의존하다
account for	~를 설명하다/차지하다	enroll in	~에 등록하다

Cosmetic products **account for** 70% of the total sales. 화장품 판매가 총 매출의 70%를 차지한다.

Please **refrain from** speaking loudly while in the museum. 박물관에 있는 동안, 시끄럽게 떠드는 것을 삼가주십시오.

❷ 전치사에 따라 의미가 달라지는 자동사

apologize	to + 사람	~에게 사과하다
	for + 이유	~에 대해 사과하다
result	in + 결과	~(결과)를 초래하다
	from + 원인	~(원인)으로부터 초래되다
talk = speak	to/with + 사람	~에게 말하다
	about + 내용	~에 대해 말하다

I sincerely **apologize to** you. 나는 진심으로 당신에게 사과드립니다.

We would like to **apologize for** the error. 우리는 그 실수에 대해 사과드리고 싶습니다.

3 토익에 자주 출제되는 타동사

타동사	의미	자동사 + 전치사	타동사	의미	자동사 + 전치사
discuss	~에 대해서 논의하다	= talk about	answer	~에 응답하다	= respond to
attend	~에 참석하다	= participate in	await	~를 기다리다	= wait for
handle	~를 다루다	= deal with	reach	~에 도착하다	= arrive at

Check-up

해설 p. 117–118

STEP 1

1. You should _____ the rule.
   (A) comply   (B) comply with

2. We would like to apologize _____ the inconvenience.
   (A) to   (B) for

3. He is excited to _____ in the volleyball game.
   (A) attend   (B) participate

STEP 2

4. We guarantee that Southampton House _____ the finest goods on the market.
   (A) deal   (B) speak   (C) handle   (D) respond

5. Due to its many features, the new museum is expected to _____ tourists to the city.
   (A) appeal   (B) arrive   (C) appear   (D) attract

2 자동사

자동사는 원래 목적어가 필요 없는 동사를 통칭하는 것인데, 그 안에서도 완전 자동사와 불완전 자동사로 구분된다.

1 완전 자동사

완전 자동사란 그 자체 혼자만으로도 의미가 완벽한 동사를 말한다.

❶ 완전 자동사 공식: 완전 자동사 + 아무것도 없음/부사/전치사 + 명사

He **arrived**. 그는 도착했다.
→ 완전 자동사는 그 자체만으로 의미가 완전하기 때문에 뒤에 아무것도 없어도 된다.

He **arrived** early. 그는 일찍 도착했다.
→ 완전 자동사를 수식하는 것은 부사이며, 여기서 early는 '일찍'이라는 의미이다.

He **arrived** at the hotel. 그는 호텔에 도착했다.
→ at the hotel(전치사 + 명사)도 수식어이므로 부가적인 표현일 뿐 필수 요소는 아니다.

❷ 토익에 잘 나오는 완전 자동사

come 오다	go 가다	work 일하다	live 살다	speak 말하다
happen 발생하다	grow 성장하다	arrive 도착하다	exist 존재하다	appear 나타나다
disappear 사라지다	function 작동하다	vary 다양하다	rise 상승하다	emerge 떠오르다

They **spoke** quietly. 그들은 조용히 말했다.

Gold prices will steadily **rise**. 금 가격은 꾸준히 상승할 것이다.

2 불완전 자동사

자동사 중에서 그 의미가 불완전하여 뒤에 보충하는 어휘를 붙여주어야 하는 것들을 불완전 자동사라 한다. 불완전 자동사를 보충하는 어휘를 '보어'라 하며, 이는 명사나 형용사이다.

❶ 불완전 자동사 공식: 불완전 자동사 + 명사 보어(주어와 동격)/형용사 보어(주어의 상태 설명)

She **is** a student. (O) 그녀는 학생이다.
→ 주어인 she(그녀)와 명사 보어인 student(학생)는 동격이므로 올바른 표현이다.

She **is** happy. (O) 그녀는 행복하다.
→ 형용사 보어 happy(행복한)가 주어(she)의 상태를 설명하므로 올바른 표현이다.

She **is** happiness. (X) 그녀는 행복이다.
→ 주어인 she와 명사 보어인 happiness(행복)가 동격이 아니므로 틀린 표현이다.

❷ 토익에 잘 나오는 불완전 자동사

불완전 자동사	+ 명사 보어일 때 의미	불완전 자동사	+ 형용사 보어일 때 의미
be	~(명사)이다	be	~(형용사)하다
become	~(명사)가 되다	become	~(형용사)해지다
seem + like	~(명사)처럼 보이다	seem	~(형용사)인 듯 보이다
remain	~(명사)로 남다	remain	~(형용사)한 상태로 남다

※ 위 동사들 중에서 seem만 뒤에 명사보어를 붙일 때 전치사 like(처럼)을 동반해서 명사를 연결하고 나머지는 동일하다.

She **became** a **doctor**. 그녀는 의사가 되었다.
The weather **became warm**. 날씨가 따뜻해졌다.

→ become 다음에 명사가 나오면 '~가 되다'로 해석하고, 형용사가 나오면 '~해지다'로 해석한다. 참고로 become은 불규칙 동사로서 과거형은 became, 과거분사는 become이다.

He **seems nice**. 그는 친절한 듯 보인다.
He **seems like** a nice guy. 그는 친절한 사람처럼 보인다.

→ seem 다음에 형용사는 그대로 붙이지만, 명사를 붙일 때는 전치사 like를 이용해서 연결한다.

Check-up

해설 p.118

STEP 1

1. They _____ Detroit now.
   (A) live   (B) live in

2. Mr. Kim is very _____ to us.
   (A) importance   (B) important

3. The proposed royalty rates seem _____.
   (A) high   (B) highly

STEP 2

4. Chinese tea was exported to Europe and soon became _____ in many Western countries.
   (A) popular   (B) popularity   (C) popularly   (D) popularities

5. All of the candidates seem _____, so it is not easy to select one to fill the position.
   (A) know   (B) knowledge   (C) knowledgeable   (D) knowledgeably

3 타동사와 수여동사

타동사 뒤의 목적어 다음에는 의미를 보충해주는 〈전치사 + 명사〉가 붙는 경우가 많다. 이 때 해당 동사에 따라 특정 전치사가 사용된다.

1 타동사

They **replaced** the old computer (**with** a new one). 그들은 오래된 컴퓨터를 (새것으로) 교체했다.

→ replace(교체하다)는 타동사이므로 뒤에 목적어 the old computer(오래된 컴퓨터)까지만 있어도 틀린 문장이 아니다. 어떤 것과 교체했는지 부연 설명이 필요할 때 뒤에 전치사 with를 붙여서 설명한다.

❶ 타동사 A with B

타동사 A with B	의미	타동사 A with B	의미
replace A with B	A를 B로 교체하다	share A with B	A를 B와 공유하다
reward A with B	A에게 B로 보상하다	compare A with B	A를 B와 비교하다
provide A with B	A에게 B를 제공하다	confuse A with B	A를 B와 혼동하다

He **provided** me **with** a job. = He **provided** a job **to** me. 그는 나에게 일자리를 제공했다.

→ provide는 목적어로 A(사람)보다 B(사물)가 먼저 나오게 되면 provide B to A로 바뀔 수 있으니 주의해야 한다.

❷ 타동사 A to B

타동사 A to B	의미	타동사 A to B	의미
attribute A to B	A를 B의 탓으로 돌리다	prefer A to B	A를 B보다 선호하다
add A to B	A를 B에 첨가하다	expose A to B	A를 B에게 노출하다
attach A to B	A를 B에 첨부하다	deliver A to B	A를 B에게 전달하다

You must **attach** a recent photograph **to** your application form. 당신은 지원서에 최근 사진을 붙여야 합니다.

❸ 타동사 A of B

타동사 A of B	의미	타동사 A of B	의미
inform/notify A of B	A에게 B를 알리다/통지하다	convince A of B	A에게 B를 확신시키다
remind A of B	A에게 B를 상기시키다	assure A of B	A에게 B를 보장하다

The manager **informed/notified** us **of** the plan. 부장은 우리들에게 계획에 대해서 통보해주었다.

❹ 타동사 A from B

타동사 A from B	의미	타동사 A from B	의미
prevent A from B	A가 B하는 것을 막다	obtain A from B	A를 B로부터 얻다
distinguish A from B	A를 B로부터 구별하다	collect A from B	A를 B로부터 징수하다

The security guard **prevented** us **from** entering the building. 그 경비원은 우리가 빌딩에 들어가는 것을 막았다.

2 수여동사

타동사 중에서 목적어가 두 개인 동사들을 수여동사라 하는데, 보통 '주다'라는 의미를 갖는 어휘들이다.

❶ 토익에 잘 나오는 수여동사

수여동사 + A(사람) + B(사물) → 타동사 B(사물) to A(사람)	
give A B → give B to A A에게 B를 주다	lend A B → lend B to A A에게 B를 빌려주다
offer A B → offer B to A A에게 B를 제공하다	send A B → send B to A A에게 B를 보내다
grant A B → grant B to A A에게 B를 주다	

※ 수여동사 다음에 나온 목적어 두 개를 A와 B라고 할 때 이들의 순서를 바꾸게 되면 목적어를 하나만 갖는 일반적인 타동사가 된다.

He **offered me a job**. = He **offered a job** to me. 그는 나에게 일자리를 제공해주었다.

❷ 수여동사로 착각하면 안 되는 타동사

suggest A B (X)	→ suggest B to A (O)	A에게 B를 제안하다
recommend A B (X)	→ recommend B to A (O)	A에게 B를 추천하다
provide A B (X)	→ provide A with B (O)	A에게 B를 제공하다

※ 특히 provide는 수여동사 offer와 의미가 같으므로 혼동하지 않도록 주의해야 한다.

I **recommend** this book **to** you. 나는 네게 이 책을 추천한다.

Check-up

해설 p. 118–119

STEP 1

1. We don't _____ information with other teams.
   (A) lend   (B) share

2. The company will notify us _____ its final decision.
   (A) to   (B) of

3. Our company will be able to _____ customers better service.
   (A) recommend   (B) offer

STEP 2

4. If your bike has been stolen, the store will _____ you a bike for free for one week.
   (A) recommend   (B) suggest   (C) inform   (D) lend

5. The directors _____ the company's high levels of productivity to its devoted employees.
   (A) shared   (B) obtained   (C) attributed   (D) replaced

4 불완전 타동사

목적어 다음에 목적어의 의미를 보충 설명해 주는 어휘 즉, 목적격 보어를 수반하는 동사들을 말한다. 목적격 보어로 명사, 형용사, 부정사, 분사가 가능하다.

1 목적어와 목적격 보어의 관계

목적어만 있는 문장 (완전 타동사)	목적격 보어가 있는 문장 (불완전 타동사)
I want to read this book. (나는 이 책을 읽고 싶다.) 주어 동사　목적어	I want you to read this book. (나는 네가 이 책을 읽기를 원한다.) 주어 동사 목적어 목적격 보어

❶ 목적격 보어의 정의

I want **you to read** this book. 나는 네가 이 책을 읽기를 원한다.

→ 목적어 다음에 있는 보어는 주어를 설명하는 게 아니라 '목적어가 무엇을 ~하는지' 설명하는 역할로 목적어를 보충하는 어휘라는 개념이다.

❷ 목적격 보어의 분류

명사/대명사	목적어와 목적격 보어가 동격일 때	I call **him Bob**. (나는 그를 밥이라 부른다.)
부정사	목적어를 동사처럼 설명해주고자 할 때	I want **you to read** this book. (나는 네가 이 책을 읽기를 원한다.)
원형부정사	본동사가 사역동사/지각동사일 때	I'll let **you know**. (내가 너에게 알려줄게.)
형용사	목적어의 상태를 표현할 때	He made **me angry**. (그는 나를 화나게 만들었어.)

※ 원형부정사란 to 없이 동사의 원형을 그대로 사용하는 것을 말한다.
※ 대명사를 목적격 보어로 많이 쓰는 동사로 call과 consider가 있다. 이들 동사가 쓰이면 〈목적어=목적격 보어〉라는 공식이 성립되어 목적어를 두 개 취하는 수여동사와 구분된다.

2 부정사를 목적격보어로 많이 쓰는 동사

한 문장에서는 동사를 두 번 쓸 수 없다는 규칙이 있다. 때문에 목적어의 동작이나 행동을 동사처럼 설명할 때는 동사 앞에 to를 붙여서 만든 부정사를 쓴다.

동사 + A(목적어) + to부정사		동사 + A(목적어) + to부정사	
allow A to부정사	(A가 ~할 수 있게 하다)	persuade A to부정사	(A가 ~하도록 설득하다)
enable A to부정사	(A가 ~할 수 있게 하다)	ask A to부정사	(A가 ~하도록 요청하다)
permit A to부정사	(A가 ~하도록 허락하다)	request A to부정사	(A가 ~하도록 요청하다)
instruct A to부정사	(A가 ~하도록 지시하다)	require A to부정사	(A가 ~하도록 요구하다)

The loan **enabled Jan to buy** the house. 대출은 잰으로 하여금 그 집을 구입할 수 있게 했다. (잰은 대출로 그 집을 구입할 수 있었다.)

3 원형부정사를 목적격 보어로 쓰는 동사

❶ 사역동사의 공식

목적어 A가 사람일 때 + 원형부정사 (A가 ~하도록 시키다)	목적어 A가 사물일 때 + 과거분사 (A가 ~되도록 /~해지도록 하다)
make/have/let + A (사람) + 원형부정사	make/have/let + A (사물) + 과거분사/형용사

I will **have** my secretary **take** your message. 나는 내 비서에게 당신의 메시지를 받아적도록 시킬 것이다.
→ 목적어인 secretary가 능동적으로 메시지를 받도록 시키는 것이므로 원형부정사인 take를 쓴다.

I will **have** your message **taken** (by my secretary). 나는 당신의 메시지를 받아두도록 할 것이다.
→ 목적어인 message는 '받아지는 대상'이므로 수동의 의미를 갖는 taken을 뒤에 수반한다.

❷ 지각동사의 공식

지각동사 + A(목적어) + 원형부정사	의미	다른 용법
hear/see + A + 원형부정사	A가 ~하는 것을 듣다/보다	hear/see + A + ~ing

She **heard** Tom **go** upstairs. 그녀는 톰이 위층으로 올라가는 소리를 들었다.
→ 처음부터 끝까지 올라가는 소리를 다 들었다는 의미이다.

She **heard** Tom **going** upstairs. 그녀는 톰이 위층으로 올라가고 있는 소리를 들었다.
→ 위로 올라가는 도중에 그 소리를 들었다는 의미이다.

Check-up

STEP 1

1. I will have my children _____ hard for their upcoming tests.
   (A) study (B) to study

2. I saw him _____ a few minutes ago.
   (A) leave (B) to leave

3. The manager requested staff members _____ over the weekend.
   (A) work (B) to work

STEP 2

4. This coupon _____ customers to get a discount of 20% of the total amount of the first order.
   (A) allows (B) promotes (C) lets (D) gives

5. Please let Wanda _____ if you have any questions about how to operate the new machine.
   (A) know (B) to know (C) knows (D) knowing

토익 필수 어휘 5_ 동사 (1)

1. face
v. (어려운 상황) ~에 직면하다 *n.* 얼굴, 표정

face A with B A를 B와 마주치게 하다
face hardships 어려움에 직면하다

2. hold
v. (행사 등을) 열다; (어떤 위치·상태를) 유지하다, 취하다; 잡다, 쥐다

hold a banquet 연회를 열다
hold one's judgement 판단을 유보하다

3. prohibit
v. ~를 금지하다

prohibit candidates from revealing details
지원자들이 세부사항을 누설하는 것을 금지하다.
prohibit the use of mobile phones 휴대폰 사용을 금지하다

4. avoid
v. ~를 피하다

avoid further inconvenience 다른 불편을 피하다
avoid any damage 손상을 피하다

5. enroll in
v. ~에 등록하다, 신청하다

enroll in the courses 강의를 신청하다
enroll in a certification program 인증 프로그램을 신청하다

6. raise
v. ~를 증가시키다; ~를 모금하다; ~를 제기하다 *n.* 증가, 상승

raise the rent 임대료를 올리다
raise next year's production 내년 생산량을 증가시키다

7. talk
v. 이야기하다, 말하다 *n.* 이야기, 회담, 논의, 강연, 연설, 대화

talk to colleagues 동료와 이야기하다
talk about the new project 새로운 프로젝트에 관하여 이야기하다

8. depend on
v. ~에 의존하다

depend on regular contributions 정기적인 기부금에 의존하다
depend on the participation of each member 각 멤버의 참여에 의존하다

9. demonstrate

v. ~을 증명하다, 입증하다, 보여주다

demonstrate the ability to work 일할 수 있는 능력을 증명하다
demonstrate performance of new equipment 새로운 장비의 성능을 시연하다

10. submit

v. ~를 제출하다, ~를 제안하다; 굴복하다

submit original receipts 영수증 원본을 제출하다
submit to violence and threat 폭력과 협박에 굴복하다

11. acknowledge

v. 인정하다; (수령을) 알리다; 사의를 표하다; 답례하다

acknowledge receipt of the letter 편지 수신을 알리다
acknowledge the donation 기부에 감사하다
※ **as an acknowledgement for/of** ~의 답례로[감사 표시로]

12. attract

v. ~끌어들이다, 유치하다; (주의 따위를) 끌다

attract new customers 신규 고객을 끌어들이다[유치하다]
attract one's attention to ~에 주의를 끌다

13. consider

v. 고려하다, 곰곰히 생각하다

consider the offer 제안을 생각해보다
consider all their options 그들의 모든 옵션을 고려해보다

Check-up

1. We will (make / hold) a meeting.   우리는 회의를 열 것이다.

2. They (prohibit / allow) visitors from taking pictures.   그들은 방문객들이 사진 찍는 것을 금지한다.

3. Students should (enroll / apply) in the program.   학생들은 그 프로그램에 등록해야 한다.

4. The landlord will (rise / raise) the rent.   집주인이 월세를 올릴 것이다.

5. The plan (depends / participates) on funding.   그 계획은 자금 지원에 의존한다.

PART 5&6_ 실전연습 5   해설 p.120-122

1. The law would force companies to reduce their carbon emissions or _____ heavy fines.

    (A) look   (B) face
    (C) feature   (D) express

2. Automobile Company _____ its annual dinner concert tonight to raise money for the poor.

    (A) held   (B) will be held
    (C) is holding   (D) had been holding

3. The institute has decided to _____ non-members from using the parking garage because of its fast-growing membership.

    (A) prohibit   (B) refuse
    (C) check   (D) shield

4. Honey Entertainment _____ to install the state-of-the-art operations systems to improve productivity.

    (A) plan   (B) planning
    (C) is planning (D) have been planned

5. The flight reservations must be canceled at least 24 hours in advance to _____ additional fees.

    (A) avoid   (B) except
    (C) permit   (D) withdraw

6. All equipment at the conference hall must _____ at least 20 minutes before the event.

    (A) be prepared (B) preparing
    (C) prepared   (D) being prepared

7. It is the duty of the personnel manager to _____ with each new employee about company rules and regulations.

    (A) say   (B) tell
    (C) speak   (D) express

8. All new electronics will _____ at discounts of up to 40% during our winter sales event.

    (A) offers   (B) be offered
    (C) offering   (D) has offered

9. The orgnization would _____ money for the poor people and help them to stand on their own feet.

    (A) happen   (B) take place
    (C) raise   (D) arise

10. Reports in *Autos Today Magazine* _____ consumers choose a car that they want exactly.

    (A) helps   (B) is helping
    (C) has helped   (D) help

11. If you have any questions about products, _____ a sales representative at the information desk.

    (A) speak   (B) contact
    (C) depend   (D) talk

12. As you know, the speed of a car is _____ on the size of the engine and regular maintenance.

    (A) dependent   (B) depends
    (C) depend   (D) dependence

13. Air Travel instructed the marketing director to _____ a presentation to the clients concerning its recent work.

    (A) talk
    (B) demonstrate
    (C) make
    (D) elect

14. Bros Film Company _____ all employees who have worked for over 5 years permanent jobs.

    (A) rewards
    (B) provides
    (C) says
    (D) offers

Questions 15-18 refer to the following advertisement.

For amateur gardeners that struggle to keep plants alive, the A-Pot makes growing flowers, herbs, and vegetables a ---15.--- task. With an array of sensors, A-Pot detects when soil is too dry or when ---16.--- current location is not receiving enough light. ---17.---. Additionally, A-Pot can connect wirelessly to the Internet so it can be monitored remotely. This also permits users to ---18.--- settings for growing different types of plants. Look for A-Pot today wherever you buy gardening supplies.

15. (A) manager
    (B) managerially
    (C) manageable
    (D) manages

16. (A) it
    (B) its
    (C) their
    (D) theirs

17. (A) The pot then notifies the user via a built-in display.
    (B) A good fertilizer is essential for healthy plants.
    (C) Only professionals use this type of technology.
    (D) A-Pot will be available early next summer.

18. (A) distribute
    (B) download
    (C) diminish
    (D) devote

UNIT 6 시제

★ **콕콕 찍어주는 출제 포인트**
영어에 있어서 시제는 한 마디로 말하면 시간에 따른 동사의 변화를 말한다. 우리말로 '먹는다'를 '먹을 것이다' 또는 '먹었다'로 표현할 수 있듯이 영어에서도 여러 가지 형태로 시간을 나타낼 수 있다.

1 시제의 형태

현재	① (단순) 현재	② 현재진행	③ 현재완료
과거	① (단순) 과거	② 과거진행	③ 과거완료
미래	① (단순) 미래	② 미래진행	③ 미래완료

1 현재 (현재 일어나고 있는 상황이나 동작의 묘사)

❶ (단순) 현재 (동사의 원형/3인칭 단수형)

I **drink** coffee every day. 나는 매일 커피를 마신다. / He **eats** bread every morning. 그는 매일 아침에 빵을 먹는다.

→ 현재시제는 동사의 원형을 쓰거나 3인칭 단수형(동사원형 + s/-es)을 쓴다.

❷ 현재진행 (is/am/are + ~ing)

I'm **drinking** coffee now. 나는 지금 커피를 마시는 중이다.

→ 현재진행시제는 be동사 다음에 동사의 현재분사형(~ing)을 붙여서 만든다.

❸ 현재완료 (have/has + p.p.)

They **have** already **started** the plan. 그들은 이미 계획을 시작했다.

→ 현재완료시제는 have나 has 다음에 동사의 과거분사형(p.p.)을 붙여서 만든다.

2 과거 (과거에 있었던 일이나 동작·상태의 묘사)

❶ (단순) 과거 (규칙 변화/불규칙 변화)

The company **announced** its decision yesterday. 그 회사는 어제 결정을 발표했다.
I **drank** coffee last night. 나는 어젯밤에 커피를 마셨다.

→ 과거시제는 동사의 과거형을 사용해야 하는데, 규칙 변화 동사는 '동사원형 + -d/-ed'의 형태이고 불규칙 변화 동사는 규칙성이 없으므로 암기해야 한다. announce는 규칙 동사, drink는 불규칙 동사이다.

❷ 과거진행 (was/were + ~ing)

I **was drinking** coffee when you called. 네가 전화했을 때 나는 커피 마시고 있었어.

→ 과거진행시제는 was나 were 다음에 현재분사형(~ing)을 붙여서 만든다.

❸ 과거완료 (had + p.p.)

The plane **had left** before they reached the airport. 그들이 공항에 도착하기 전에 비행기는 떠나버렸다.
→ 과거완료시제는 had 다음에 과거분사형(p.p.)을 붙여서 만든다.

3 미래 (미래에 있을 일이나 동작·상태의 묘사)

❶ (단순) 미래 (will + 동사원형)

I **will go** swimming tomorrow. 나는 내일 수영하러 갈 거야.
→ 미래시제는 조동사 will 다음에 동사원형을 붙여서 만든다.

❷ 미래진행 (will + be ~ing)

We **will be closing** at 9:00 P.M. 우리는 저녁 9시에 문을 닫을 것이다.
→ 미래진행시제는 조동사 will 다음에 be ~ing를 붙여서 만든다.

❸ 미래완료 (will + have p.p.)

I **will have finished** the work by next week. 나는 다음 주까지는 그 작업을 끝낼 것이다.
→ 미래완료시제는 조동사 will 다음에 have p.p.를 붙여서 만든다.

Check-up

해설 p.122-123

STEP 1

1. I _____ the report yesterday.
   (A) read   (B) reading

2. They were _____ a conversation about sales.
   (A) have   (B) having

3. She has _____ surveys across the country.
   (A) conducting   (B) conducted

STEP 2

4. Bon China Appliance _____ the newest kitchen products at the trade fair last week.
   (A) shows   (B) showed   (C) will show   (D) is showing

5. Passengers complain that delays at Vancouver Airport have _____ frequent.
   (A) become   (B) became   (C) becomes   (D) becoming

2 현재시제(단순, 진행, 완료)

1 (단순) 현재시제 (~한다/~할 것이다)

❶ 현재의 사실/반복적 사실

He **is** a teacher. 그는 선생님이다.
→ '그가 선생님이다'라는 현재의 사실을 묘사하고 있다.

We **go** to the park every Sunday. 우리는 매주 일요일마다 공원에 간다.
→ 매주 공원에 '간다'는 반복적 사실/습관을 묘사하고 있다.

> **잠깐!**
>
> **(단순) 현재시제와 같이 잘 쓰이는 부사 – 빈도부사**
>
> 반복적인 일을 나타내는 현재시제와 같이 잘 쓰이는 부사들은 다음과 같으며 이런 부사들을 '빈도부사'라 한다.
> - always (항상)   · usually (보통)   · frequently (자주)   · often (자주)   · every day (매일)

❷ 계획된 일정

현재시제가 tomorrow, next, soon 등과 같은 미래시간 표현과 같이 사용되면 '~할 것이다'라는 계획된 일정을 의미할 수도 있다.

The bus **leaves** at 9 A.M. 버스는 오전 9시에 떠난다.
→ 버스가 늘 '오전 9시에 떠난다'는 계획된 일정을 뜻한다.

The bus **leaves** at 9 A.M. tomorrow. 버스는 내일 오전 9시에 떠날 것이다.
→ 뒤에 tomorrow(내일)가 있으므로 오전 9시에 '떠날 것이다'는 의미이다.

2 현재진행시제 (~하고 있다/~할 것이다)

❶ 지금 순간의 일

We **are seeking** professional designers. 우리는 전문적인 디자이너들을 찾고 있는 중이다.
→ 지금 이 순간 '찾고 있다'는 진행의 의미이다.

❷ 가까운 미래

현재진행시제는 미래시간 표현이 없어도 가까운 미래를 의미할 수 있다. 하지만 보통은 (단순) 현재시제처럼 미래시간 표현을 동반하는 편이다.

I'm **participating** in the game. 나는 게임에 참가할 것이다.
→ 특별한 미래시간 표시가 없어도 가까운 미래를 의미할 수 있다.

I'm **participating** in the game tomorrow. 나는 내일 게임에 참가할 것이다.
→ 뒤에 tomorrow(내일)가 있으므로 더욱 확실하게 미래를 의미하게 된다.

3 현재완료시제 (~했다, 했던 적이 있다 / ~해 왔다, 해오고 있다)

현재완료시제를 크게 둘로 나누면, 이미 끝난 일(완료, 경험)을 표현하거나 과거부터 지금까지 해오고 있는 일(계속)을 의미한다.

❶ 이미 끝난 일

We **have selected** five candidates. 우리는 5명의 후보자를 선택했다.
→ '선택을 끝냈다'는 완료의 의미이다.

I **have spoken** with her before. 나는 전에 그녀와 얘기 나눈 적이 있다.
→ 이전에 '~했던 적 있다'는 경험을 의미한다.

❷ 계속되는 일

I **have lived** here since last year. 나는 작년부터 쭉 여기서 살고 있다.
→ 여기서 have lived는 과거부터 지금까지 '살아오고 있다'는 계속의 의미이다.

Check-up

STEP 1

1. He usually _____ the newspaper in the morning.
   (A) reads   (B) is reading

2. They _____ a new branch next week.
   (A) opened   (B) are opening

3. He _____ at the company since 2009.
   (A) works   (B) has worked

STEP 2

4. The growth of the company over the past two quarters _____ shareholder's expectations.
   (A) exceeds   (B) will exceed   (C) has exceeded   (D) is exceeding

5. The executive committee meeting is _____ held on the first Monday of each month.
   (A) recently   (B) usually   (C) lately   (D) yesterday

3 과거시제(단순, 진행, 완료)

1 (단순) 과거시제 (~했다)

과거시제는 과거의 일이나 동작, 상태를 나타내며 과거에만 한정되고 현재와는 관련이 없다. 과거 시점을 의미하는 표현을 잘 알아두어야 한다.

He **delivered** the catalog to the wrong office **last week**. 그는 지난주에 카탈로그를 다른 사무실로 잘못 배송했다.
→ last week(지난주에)는 확실한 과거시간 표현이므로 동사를 과거시제로 써야 한다.

She **told** me about it **yesterday**. 그녀는 어제 나에게 그 점에 대해서 말했다.
→ yesterday(어제)도 확실한 과거시간 표현이므로 동사를 과거시제로 써야 한다.

잠깐!

과거시제를 결정짓는 단서 4총사!

문장에서 다음의 어휘들이 보이면 확실한 과거시간을 말하는 표현들이므로 동사를 과거시제로 써야 한다.

- yesterday (어제)
- last + 시간표현 (지난 ~)
- 시간표현 + ago (~ 전에)
- in + 과거년도 (~년도에)

2 과거진행시제 (~하고 있었다)

과거의 어느 시점에서 동작이 진행되고 있었음을 묘사하며, was/were 다음에 현재분사형(~ing)을 붙여서 만든다.

I **was discussing** the matter with my coworker. 나는 그 문제를 동료와 논의하던 중이었다.
→ '논의하던 도중'이라는 의미고, '끝냈다'는 의미는 아니다.

I **discussed** the matter with my coworker. 나는 그 문제를 동료와 논의했다.
→ (단순) 과거시제를 쓰면 '논의를 끝냈다'는 의미가 내포된다.

3 과거완료시제 (~했었다)

과거의 두 사건 중 먼저 일어난 사건을 나타낼 때 사용하며 had 다음에 과거분사형(p.p.)을 붙여서 사용한다.

주어 + <u>had p.p.</u> + before 주어 + <u>과거 동사</u>   ②하기 전에 ①했다
　　　　①　　　　　　　　　　　②

주어 + <u>과거 동사</u> + after 주어 + <u>had p.p.</u>   ②한 후에 ①했다
　　　　①　　　　　　　　　　　②

※ 토익에서 과거완료시제가 나올 때는 시간의 전후를 명확하게 구분하도록 보통 before(~전에)나 after(~후에)와 함께 쓰인다.

The meeting **had begun** before we **arrived**. 우리가 도착하기 전에 회의는 시작했었다.
→ 우리가 도착한 것보다 회의가 시작한 시점이 먼저이다.

They **remodeled** the old building after they **had bought** it. 그들은 그 오래된 빌딩을 구매한 후에 리모델링했다.
→ 빌딩을 리모델링한 것보다 구매한 시점이 먼저이다.

(단순) 과거와 과거완료시제가 같다!

현재 시점으로 보면 (단순) 과거시제와 과거완료시제는 둘 다 과거에 일어난 사건이므로 무엇이 먼저 일어났는지 구분해서 말할 필요가 없는 경우가 많다. 때문에 현대 영어에서는 (단순) 과거시제가 과거완료시제를 대신하는 경우가 많고, 토익에서는 둘 중 하나만 보기에 제시된다.

Before they **talked about** the problem, members **had suggested** many ideas.
= **Before** they **talked about** the problem, members **suggested** many ideas.
그들이 그 문제점에 대해서 이야기 나누기 전에, 멤버들은 많은 아이디어를 제안했다.

→ 이야기를 나눈 시점이나 아이디어를 제안한 시점이나 어차피 현재를 기준으로 보면 둘 다 과거의 일이므로 둘 다 올바른 표현이다.

Check-up

STEP 1

1. They _____ to Japan two months ago.
   (A) go   (B) went

2. The employees _____ on a sales report last night.
   (A) have worked   (B) worked

3. The local government _____ the tax plan last year.
   (A) revised   (B) revises

STEP 2

4. The tour group had _____ for Paris before they received their complete itinerary.
   (A) leave   (B) left   (C) leaving   (D) leaves

5. Although they _____ a lot of money on the project, it was not successful.
   (A) has invested   (B) investing   (C) to invest   (D) had invested

4 미래시제(단순, 진행, 완료)

1 (단순) 미래시제 (~할 것이다)

미래의 일, 상태, 동작을 나타낼 때 쓰며, 조동사 will에 동사원형을 붙여서 사용한다.

They **will provide** you with detailed information. 그들은 당신에게 상세한 정보를 제공할 것이다.
= They**'ll provide** you with detailed information.

→ 조동사 will은 종종 'll 형태로 축약해서 사용된다.

잠깐!

be going to와 will의 차이

미래의 일을 말할 때 구어체에서 be going to로 말하는 경우가 많은데, will과의 차이는 다음과 같다.

- be going to/will be ~ing (이전부터 계획된 일을 말할 때)

  We **will be introducing** the new product at the trade fair. 우리는 신상품을 무역 박람회에서 소개할 겁니다.
  = We **are going to introduce** the new product at the trade fair.
  → 이전부터 계획했거나 예정된 일이라는 의미이다.

- will + 동사원형 (지금 막 생각한 일을 말할 때)

  We **will introduce** the new product at the trade fair. 우리는 신상품을 무역 박람회에서 소개할 겁니다.
  → 지금이나 조금 전에 그렇게 생각했다는 느낌이다.

2 미래진행시제 (~하고 있을 것이다/~할 것이다)

미래의 어느 한 시점에서 진행되고 있는 사건을 말하기도 하지만, 보통은 예정된 일을 표현할 때 더 많이 사용한다. 토익에서 미래진행 시제(will be ~ing)가 나오면 대부분 두 번째 용법이다.

❶ 미래의 순간

At 9 o'clock tomorrow she **will be watching** the game. 내일 9시에 그녀는 게임을 시청하고 있을 것이다.
→ 미래의 특정 시점을 의미하므로 '~하고 있을 것이다'로 해석한다.

❷ 예정된 일

We will **be conducting** a survey soon. 우리는 곧 설문조사를 실시할 것이다.
→ 여기서 will be conducting을 '실시하고 있을 것이다'가 아니라 '실시할 것이다'로 해석한다.

3 미래완료시제 (~했을 것이다/하게 될 것이다)

미래완료시제는 어떤 사건이나 동작이 미래의 특정한 시점에 완료될 때 사용하는 시제로 (단순) 미래시제와의 차이점을 알아두어야 한다.

(단순) 미래 (will + 동사원형)	① 미래에 시작하는 일	② 미래의 한 순간
미래완료 (will have p.p.)	① 미래에 완료되는 일	② 과거(또는 현재)부터 미래까지의 기간 표현

The train **will leave** at 11 o'clock. 기차는 11시에 떠날 것이다.
→ '떠나는 것이 11시에 시작된다'는 의미로, 미래에 '시작되는' 일을 나타낸다.

The train **will have left** at 11 o'clock. 기차는 11시에 떠났을 것이다. (떠나고 없을 것이다.)
→ '떠나는 것이 11시까지 끝날 것이다'라는 의미로, 미래에 '완료되는' 일을 나타낸다.

My father **will have worked for 30 years** by the time he retires. (O)
아버지가 은퇴할 때까지 그는 30년 동안 일하게 될 것이다.
My father **will work for 30 years** by the time he retires. (X)
→ 문장에서 'for + 기간 (~동안)'이 있으면 단순미래시제로 그 기간을 표현하긴 어렵다. 과거부터 미래까지 '30년 동안'을 표현하기 위해서는 미래완료시제를 쓴다.

Check-up

STEP 1

1. She will _____ the report for the meeting.
   (A) bring   (B) brings

2. We will be _____ a new copy machine tomorrow.
   (A) install   (B) installing

3. I think the movie _____ when we get to the theater.
   (A) started   (B) will have started

STEP 2

4. At the press conference tomorrow, Mr. Sekizaki will _____ the company's new plan.
   (A) reveal   (B) to reveal   (C) revealing   (D) reveals

5. It is reported that the company _____ with Jansen Production by the end of next year.
   (A) merge   (B) has merged
   (C) will have merged   (D) had merged

토익 필수 어휘 6_ 동사 (2)

1. plan
v. 계획하다   *n.* 계획, 예정
plan the upcoming meeting 다가오는 회의를 계획하다
plan to attend training sessions 훈련 연수회에 참석할 계획이다

2. help
v. 돕다, 도움이 되다   *n.* 도움, 원조
help you choose computer options 당신이 컴퓨터 옵션을 선택하는 데 도움이 되다
help each other 서로 돕다

3. accommodate
v. 공간을 제공하다, 수용하다
accommodate everyone's preferences 모든 사람들의 선호를 수용하다
accommodate a welcoming party 환영파티 공간을 제공하다

4. affect
v. ~에 영향을 미치다, 유발하다
affect the taste 맛에 영향을 미치다
affect the company's stock price 회사의 주가에 영향을 미치다

5. complain
v. 불평하다, 항의하다
complain about the publicity campaign 광고 캠페인에 대해 불평하다
complain bitterly 심하게 항의하다

6. recommend
v. 추천하다, 권고하다, 권장하다
recommended by her employer 그녀의 고용주에 의해 추천되는
recommend reading the book 책을 읽어보라고 권장하다

7. increase
v. 증가하다, 인상되다   *n.* 증가, 증진; 이익, 이자
increase dramatically 극적으로 증가하다
increase costs 가격을 인상하다

8. compare
v. 비교하다, 필적하다
compare products and prices 제품과 가격을 비교하다
compared to others in its field 그 분야에서 다른 사람들과 필적하는

9. inspect	v. 점검하다, 검사하다 **inspect** every item 모든 품목을 검사하다 be **inspected** by a safety technician 안전 기술자에 의해 점검되다
10. accept	v. 받아들이다, 수락하다 **accept** the discount coupon 할인쿠폰을 받다 **accept** our offer 우리의 제안을 수락하다
11. contact	v. 연락하다 n. 연락(처), 접촉; 지인 Feel free to **contact** us. 편하게 연락하세요. be in/out of **contact** with ~와 연락하고 있다 / 있지 않다
12. notify	v. 통지하다 **notify** the customer in advance 고객에게 미리 통지하다 **notify** someone immediately about the shipment 선적에 대해 즉시 알리다
13. utilize	v. 활용하다, 이용하다 **utilize** alternative energy sources 대체 에너지원을 활용하다 **utilize** a variety of measures 여러 가지 방법[방안]을 이용하다

Check-up

해설 p.125

1. They can (accomodate / **accommodation**) 100 people.   그들은 100명을 수용할 수 있다.

2. It will (**affect** / effect) the result.   그것은 결과에 영향을 끼칠 것이다.

3. I will (**complain** / complaint) about the service.   나는 서비스에 대해서 불평을 할 것이다.

4. He (**recommended** / recommendation) the hotel.   그가 그 호텔을 추천했다.

5. Consumers often (comparison / **compare**) prices and products.   소비자들은 종종 가격과 제품들을 비교한다.

PART 5&6_ 실전연습 6

1. The board of directors announced that our company _____ other competing firms next month.
   (A) has acquired (B) acquired
   (C) acquires (D) will acquire

2. Herbal products that Bio-technology newly releases _____ you relax and sleep.
   (A) help (B) enable
   (C) allow (D) raise

3. Located outside the city, the stadium is designed to _____ approximately 30,000 people.
   (A) prohibit (B) face
   (C) accommodate (D) talk

4. After strike, it was reported that many of the employees _____ in the near future.
   (A) has been fired (B) are fired
   (C) had been fired (D) will be fired

5. Customs officers will _____ the contents of luggage carefully before illegal goods are out of the airport.
   (A) inspect (B) affect
   (C) plan (D) conduct

6. In the last five years, the housing expense _____ an average of 5% per year.
   (A) has increased (B) had increased
   (C) was increasing (D) will have increased

7. The recycling company will _____ all used cellphones and then repair them for resale.
   (A) enable (B) accept
   (C) access (D) appear

8. Daniel _____ an ad agency specializing in sports marketing eight years ago.
   (A) joined (B) joins
   (C) has joined (D) will have joined

9. Tourists using the new airport _____ that there is uncomfortable facilities and poor service.
   (A) notify (B) complain
   (C) satisfy (D) tell

10. Mr. Douglas _____ for nearly 25 years at Ridgewood Air by the time he retires.
    (A) works (B) worked
    (C) has worked (D) will have worked

11. Our shipping company usually _____ all products within three days regardless of customers' location.
    (A) has delivered (B) delivered
    (C) delivers (D) will deliver

12. Customers will _____ from the growing competition among Internet providers.
    (A) receive (B) provide
    (C) benefit (D) offer

13. The musical performance _____ when Jeremy and his girl friend arrived at the theater.

    (A) started
    (B) has started
    (C) starts
    (D) had started

14. We _____ that you make a reservation for the hotel in advance before leaving.

    (A) specialize
    (B) consider
    (C) compare
    (D) recommend

Questions 15-18 refer to the following letter.

May 31
Embassy of Japan
Visa Section
299 Park Avenue 18th Floor
New York, New York 10171

Glaxton-Jenner Company would like to introduce our head of licensing and contracts Ms. Pei Xi who ---15.--- to Tokyo from June 13 to 22 to obtain a manufacturing license. While in Tokyo, Ms. Xi will meet with executives at Matsumoto Corp. to discuss and ---16.--- a manufacturing license agreement of electronic products including computer parts and accessories.

Glaxton-Jenner Company will provide Ms. Xi with the financial means to sustain herself during her visit to Japan. ---17.---. We greatly ---18.--- your help in issuing Ms. Xi a visa on behalf of Glaxton-Jenner Company.

Sincerely,

Jin Li Zhang
Manager, Glaxton-Jenner Company

---

15. (A) will be traveling
    (B) had traveled
    (C) has traveled
    (D) was traveling

16. (A) depend
    (B) proceed
    (C) disregard
    (D) negotiate

17. (A) New electronic products are scheduled to be released.
    (B) Obtaining a license is so difficult in New York.
    (C) Also, it will offer her a return ticket to New York.
    (D) The visit to Tokyo will be rescheduled upon her request.

18. (A) appreciated
    (B) appreciate
    (C) was appreciate
    (D) had appreciated

UNIT 7 수동태

> ★ 콕콕 찍어주는 출제 포인트
> 수동태란 〈be동사 + 과거분사(p.p.)〉의 동사의 형태를 말하며, 주어가 능동적으로 행위를 하는 주체가 되면 '능동태'를 쓰고 주어가 동사의 행위를 당하는 대상이 되면 '수동태'를 쓴다. 토익에서 능동태와 수동태를 구분하는 단서들을 파악해 보자.

1 수동태의 특징

1 능동태를 수동태로 바꾸기

수동태는 행위를 당하는 대상이 주어가 되므로 능동태의 목적어가 수동태의 주어가 된다.

능동태   I repaired the car. 나는 차를 수리했다.
          주어   동사   목적어

수동태   The car was repaired by me. 차는 나에 의해서 수리되었다.
          주어   수동태 동사   행위자 (~에 의해서)

→ 능동태의 목적어인 the car가 수동태의 주어로 가고, 능동태의 주어인 I가 수동태에서는 by me라는 행위자로 표시된다.

2 자동사는 수동태 불가능

능동태 문장을 수동태로 바꾸기 위해서는 목적어가 있어야 한다. 따라서 목적어가 없는 자동사는 수동태로 변형시킬 수 없다.

수동태를 만들 수 없는 대표적인 자동사		
work 일하다	happen 일어나다, 발생하다	rise 상승하다
arrive 도착하다	seem ~인 듯 보이다	remain ~로 남다
stay ~로 유지하다	look 보다	become ~이 되다

Mr. Kim **has worked** at the company for seven years. (O) 김 씨는 회사에서 7년 동안 일해왔다.
Mr. Kim **was worked** at the company for seven years. (X)

→ work는 자동사이므로 수동태(was worked)로 표현할 수 없다. has worked는 능동태(현재완료시제)이므로 옳은 표현이다.

> **잠깐!**
> 자동사가 수동태가 되는 경우도 있는데, 〈동사 + 전치사〉 구문이 목적어를 취할 때이다.
>
> I **dealt with** the problem. 나는 그 문제를 처리했다.
> → The problem **was dealt with** (by me). 그 문제는 (나에 의해서) 처리되었다.

3 수동태는 목적어가 없다.

능동태의 목적어가 수동태의 주어가 되므로 수동태는 목적어가 없게 된다.

능동태 The government approved **the construction plan**. 정부는 그 건축 계획을 승인했다.

수동태 **The construction plan** was approved (by the government). 그 건축 계획은 (정부에 의해서) 승인되었다.

→ 능동태의 목적어인 the construction plan(그 건축 계획)이 수동태의 주어가 되면서 목적어가 사라졌다. by the government(정부에 의해서)는 '전치사 + 명사'의 행위자 표시이므로 목적어가 아니다.

Check-up

해설 p.128

STEP 1

1. Conference participants _____ in the designated hotel.
   (A) stay   (B) are stayed

2. I have been _____ the tax document for about three hours now.
   (A) reviewed   (B) reviewing

3. The economic researchers _____ that the data must be interpreted accurately.
   (A) emphasized   (B) were emphasized

STEP 2

4. The traffic signs in the city can sometimes _____ confusing to people unfamiliar with the area.
   (A) seem   (B) are seemed   (C) seems   (D) to seem

5. Even though the company will renovate its electrical system tomorrow, all offices will _____ open.
   (A) remain   (B) remains   (C) remaining   (D) be remained

2 시제에 따른 수동태

수동태도 동사의 한 형태이므로 시제에 따라 다양하게 변형된다. 능동형 시제의 변형된 형태에 따라서 be + p.p.개념을 추가한다고 보면 된다.

시제 명칭		능동태 문장	수동태 문장
현재	단순	He **writes** it. (그는 그것을 쓴다.)	It **is written**. (그것은 쓰여진다.)
	진행	He **is writing** it. (그는 그것을 쓰는 중이다.)	It **is being written**. (그것은 쓰여지는 중이다.)
	완료	He **has written** it. (그는 그것을 썼다/써 왔다.)	It **has been written**. (그것은 쓰여졌다/쓰여 왔다.)

능동태 She **is signing** the paper. 그녀는 문서에 서명하고 있다.

수동태 The paper **is being signed** by her. 문서는 그녀에 의해서 서명되고 있다.

시제 명칭		능동태 문장	수동태 문장
과거	단순	He **wrote** it. (그는 그것을 썼다.)	It **was written**. (그것은 쓰여졌다.)
	진행	He **was writing** it. (그는 그것을 쓰는 중이었다.)	It **was being written**. (그것은 쓰여지던 중이었다.)
	완료	He **had written** it. (그는 그것을 썼었다.)	It **had been written**. (그것은 쓰여졌었다.)

능동태 We **were repairing** the car. 우리는 차를 수리하고 있었다.

수동태 The car **was being repaired** by us. 차는 우리들에 의해서 수리되고 있었다.

시제 명칭		능동태 문장	수동태 문장
미래	단순	He **will write** it. (그는 그것을 쓸 것이다.)	It **will be written**. (그것은 쓰일 것이다.)
	진행	He **will be writing** it. (그는 그것을 쓰는 중일 것이다.)	It **will be being written**. (그것은 쓰여지는 중일 것이다.)
	완료	He **will have written** it. (그는 그것을 쓰고 있을 것이다.)	It **will have been written**. (그것은 쓰이게 될 것이다.)

능동태 We **will take** quick action. 우리는 빠른 조치를 취할 것이다.

수동태 Quick action **will be taken** by us. 빠른 조치가 우리에 의해서 취해질 것이다.

조동사가 있을 때의 수동태

will, can, may, should 등의 조동사가 붙어 있는 능동태 동사를 수동태로 바꿀 때에는, 조동사는 그대로 살리고 수동태의 기본구조인 〈be + p.p.〉가 이어져야 한다. 조동사 다음에는 동사원형이 와야 하므로 〈be + 동사의 과거분사형〉을 붙여주면 된다.

능동태 You **can find** a hotel easily. 당신은 호텔을 쉽게 발견할 수 있습니다.

수동태 A hotel **can be found** easily (by you). 호텔은 (당신에 의해) 쉽게 발견될 수 있습니다.
→ find는 불규칙 동사로, 과거분사는 found이다.

Check-up

STEP 1

1. The company has been _____ its employees to work over the weekend.
   (A) encouraging (B) encouraged

2. When the firm _____ its divisions, several managers were laid off.
   (A) was restructured (B) was restructuring

3. Although a great deal of money _____ in the project, it was a failure.
   (A) had invested (B) had been invested

STEP 2

4. Many items in the store _____ at discounted prices on the Web site.
   (A) offered (B) is offered (C) have offered (D) are being offered

5. Tickets can _____ at the main box office before the film festival begins.
   (A) buy (B) bought (C) be bought (D) buying

3 by 외에 다른 구문과 함께 쓰이는 수동태

수동태 (be + p.p.)뒤에는 무조건 'by + 행위자(~에 의해서)'만 수반되는 것이 아니라 다른 구문으로 연결되기도 한다.

1 by 외의 다른 전치사와 연결되는 수동태

be satisfied with	~에 만족하다	be replaced with	~로 교체되다
be pleased with	~에 기뻐하다	be filled with	~로 가득차다
be surprised at	~에 놀라다	be composed of	~로 구성되다
be interested in	~에 관심 있다	be known for	~때문에 알려지다[유명하다]
be involved in	~에 연루되다	be prohibited from	~를 금지당하다

능동태 The test results **satisfied** the teacher. 시험 결과가 선생님을 만족시켰다.

수동태 The teacher **was satisfied with** the test results. 선생님은 시험 결과에 만족하셨다.
→ 동사 satisfy는 수동태로 쓰일 때 뒤에 전치사 with를 수반한다.

능동태 We **replaced** several computers **with** new ones. 우리는 몇몇 컴퓨터들을 새 것들로 교체했다.

수동태 Several computers **were replaced with** new ones. 몇몇 컴퓨터들이 새 것들로 교체되었다.
→ replace A with B(A를 B로 교체하다)가 수동태가 되면서 be replaced with(~로 교체되다)가 되었다.

2 to부정사와 연결되는 수동태

be asked to부정사	~할 것을 요청받다	be permitted to부정사	~하도록 허락되다
be requested to부정사	~하도록 요청받다	be allowed to부정사	~하도록 허락되다
be required to부정사	~하도록 요구받다	be instructed to부정사	~하도록 지시받다
be advised to부정사	~하도록 충고받다	be reminded to부정사	~하라고 상기되다
be encouraged to부정사	~하도록 장려되다	be expected to부정사	~할 것이 예상되다

능동태 We **ask** you **to speak** quietly. 우리는 여러분에게 조용하게 말하기를 요청 드립니다.

수동태 You **are asked to speak** quietly. 여러분은 조용히 말하도록 요청받습니다. (조용히 말해주십시오.)

능동태 The doctor **advised** him **to quit** smoking. 의사는 그에게 금연하라고 충고했다.

수동태 He **was advised to quit** smoking. 그는 금연하라고 충고 받았다.

잠깐!

수동태는 뒤에 나오는 구문을 뺐을 때 완전한 문장이 남아야 한다.

수동태는 그 자체로 완전한 동사 형태이므로 뒤에 아무것도 없어도 완전한 문장이 성립되어야 한다.

The old computer was replaced. 그 오래된 컴퓨터는 교체되었다.
→ was replaced 다음에 아무것도 없이 문장이 끝나도 괜찮다.

The old computer was replaced with a new one. 그 오래된 컴퓨터는 새것으로 교체되었다.
→ with a new one(전치사 + 명사구)은 문장에서 없어도 되는 수식구이다.

The old computer was replaced recently. 그 오래된 컴퓨터는 최근에 교체되었다.
→ 부사 recently(최근에)는 문장에서 없어도 되는 품사이다.

The old computer was replaced to improve security. 그 오래된 컴퓨터는 보안을 향상시키기 위해서 교체되었다.
→ 부정사 to improve(향상시키기 위해서)는 수식구에 불과하므로 없어도 된다.

Check-up

STEP 1

1. The team is composed _____ seven people.
   (A) at   (B) of

2. If you are interested _____ the position, submit your application by tomorrow.
   (A) to   (B) in

3. Conference participants are encouraged _____ before 9:00 A.M.
   (A) arriving   (B) to arrive

STEP 2

4. Motorists _____ to drive very carefully when they cross the bridge.
   (A) is advised   (B) have advised   (C) are advised   (D) advised

5. Visitors to the museum are prohibited _____ taking photographs of all our exhibits.
   (A) by   (B) to   (C) from   (D) about

4 예외적인 수동태

동사의 수동태(be + p.p.)는 뒤에 목적어나 보어가 없어야 정상이지만, 때로는 목적어나 보어가 붙기도 한다.

1 수여동사의 수동태

수여동사는 목적어가 두 개이므로 두 가지 종류의 수동태가 만들어진다.

직접목적어를 주어로 한 수동태		간접목적어를 주어로 한 수동태	
be given to 명사	~에게 주어지다	be given 명사	~를 받다
be offered to 명사	~에게 제공되다	be offered 명사	~를 제공받다
be awarded to 명사	~에게 수여되다	be awarded 명사	~를 수여받다
be sent to 명사	~에게 보내지다	be sent 명사	~를 받다
be granted to 명사	~에게 수여되다	be granted 명사	~를 수여받다

❶ 능동태 문장 (주어 + 동사 + 간접목적어 + 직접목적어)

He **gave me money**. 그는 나에게 돈을 주었다.
　　동사　간접목적어　직접목적어

❷ 직접목적어를 주어로 수동태를 만들 경우

능동태　He **gave me money**.

수동태　**Money was given to me** (by him). 돈은 (그에 의해서) 나에게 주어졌다.

→ 이 경우 수동태(was given) 다음에 to me라는 〈전치사 + 명사〉 구조가 수반되었으므로 일반적 수동태의 꼴이다.

❸ 간접목적어를 주어로 수동태를 만들 경우

능동태　He **gave me money**.

수동태　**I was given money** (by him). 나는 (그에 의해서) 돈을 받았다.

→ 능동태에서 앞에 나온 간접목적어인 me를 주어로 수동태를 만들면, 뒤에 나온 직접목적어(money)가 수동태에 그대로 사용된다.

2 5형식 동사의 수동태

5형식 동사들은 목적어 다음에 목적격보어가 있으므로, 수동태가 되어도 목적격보어는 그대로 남게 된다.

- call + A(목적어) + B(목적격보어) A를 B라고 부르다 → A be called + B A가 B라고 불리다
- appoint + A(목적어) + B(목적격보어) A를 B로 지명하다 → A be appointed + B A가 B에 지명되다
- consider + A(목적어) + B(목적격보어) A를 B로 고려하다 → A be considered + B A가 B로 고려되다

능동태   We **called him Bob**. 우리는 그를 밥이라 부른다.

수동태   He **is called Bob** (by us). 그는 밥이라 불린다.

→ is called 다음에 수반되는 Bob은 원래 목적격보어로 있던 Bob이 수동태가 되어도 그대로 남아 있다.

잠깐!

be동사 다음에 과거분사(p.p.)를 쓰면 동사의 수동태가 되고, 형용사를 쓰면 보어가 된다. 문법적으로 둘 다 가능하기 때문에 무조건 수동태를 선택해선 안 된다. 수동태를 쓸지 형용사를 쓸지는 해석으로 접근하거나 뒤의 전치사를 보고 판단한다.

- be doubted for (~ 때문에 의심되다)
- be criticized for (~ 때문에 비판받다)
- be doubtful about (~에 대해 의심하다)
- be critical of (~를 비판하다)

The plan will **be criticized for** its increased costs. 그 계획은 인상된 비용 때문에 비판받을 것이다.
Some educators **are critical of** the plan. 몇몇 교육자들은 그 계획을 비판한다.

Check-up

STEP 1

1. He was _____ a job yesterday.
   (A) offered   (B) offers

2. Passengers will _____ an option of booking an upgraded seat.
   (A) given   (B) be given

3. Mr. Chen _____ the expert when it comes to dealing with customers.
   (A) consider   (B) is considered

STEP 2

4. The workshop presenters _____ the schedule last week and should follow each item.
   (A) were sent   (B) was sending   (C) will be sent   (D) have sent

5. Customer service personnel should not be _____ of customers who call with complaints.
   (A) criticize   (B) critical   (C) critically   (D) criticized

토익 필수 어휘 7_ 형용사 (1)

1. costly
a. 비싼, 비용이 많이 드는
the **costly** investments 비싼 투자
too **costly** 너무 비싼

2. likely
a. ~할 것 같은, 그럴듯한
the **likely** cause of the problem 그 문제의 그럴듯한 이유
be **likely** to increase overall productivity 전반적인 생산력이 증가할 것 같다

3. friendly
a. 친절한, 친숙한, 우호적인
environmentally-**friendly** fuel 환경 친화적인 연료
family-**friendly** entertainment 가족 친화적인 오락

4. valid
a. 유효한, 효력 있는
a **valid** passport 유효한 여권
a **valid** driver's license 유효한 운전 면허증

5. affordable
a. 이용할 수 있는, 구입 가능한, 저렴한, 합리적인
offer **affordable** goods and services 합리적인 상품과 서비스를 제공하다
at a most **affordable** price 가장 저렴한 가격에

6. timely
a. 빠른, 시기적절한
in a **timely** fashion 시기적절하게, 빠른 시일 내에
in a **timely** manner 시기적절하게

7. poor
a. 형편없는; (날씨가) 나쁜, 불순한
the firm's **poor** performance 회사의 형편없는 실적
due to **poor** weather 악천후 때문에

8. frequent
a. 빈번한, 자주 있는
join a **frequent** shoppers club 단골 고객 클럽에 가입하다
in response to **frequent** requests 빈번한 요청에 응하여

9. eager	*a.* 열렬한, 간절히 바라는, 열심인 be **eager** to reach agreement 합의에 이르기를 간절히 바라다 be **eager** to become a teacher 선생님이 되기를 간절히 바라다
10. comparable	*a.* 비슷한, 필적할 만한 be **comparable** in terms of the quality 질적인 측면에서 비슷하다 **comparable** to the market share of last year 지난해와 견줄만한 시장 점유율
11. annual	*a.* 매년의, 연례의 the **annual** awards ceremony 연례 시상식 an **annual** income[salary] 연 소득[연봉]
12. upcoming	*a.* 곧 있을, 다음의 **upcoming** price hike 곧 있을 가격 인상 register for the **upcoming** seminar 곧 있을 세미나에 등록하다
13. effective	*a.* 효과적인 take an **effective** measure 효과적인 조치를 취하다 **effective** way to increase employee productivity 직원 생산성을 향상시킬 효과적인 방법

Check-up

해설 p.131

1. The new system is very (costly / price). 새로운 시스템은 매우 비싸다.

2. You need a (valid / validate) passport. 당신은 유효한 여권이 필요합니다.

3. They offer (affordable / afford) prices. 그들은 적당한 가격을 제공한다.

4. She is a (frequent / frequently) visitor to the club. 그녀는 그 클럽에 자주 오는 방문객이다.

5. We are (eagerness / eager) to open a new branch. 우리는 새로운 지점을 오픈하기를 열망한다.

PART 5&6_ 실전연습 7

1. Today's baseball game will _____ until next Monday because of heavy rain.
   (A) be postponing
   (B) postpone
   (C) be postponed
   (D) have postponed

2. In order to ensure _____ delivery, you should write your address and phone number clearly.
   (A) tentative
   (B) timely
   (C) aware
   (D) limited

3. The construction materials are expected to _____ late in the afternoon.
   (A) have delivered
   (B) delivering
   (C) be delivered
   (D) be delivering

4. Increasing market share and profits is less _____ than establishing brand images.
   (A) wealthy
   (B) friendly
   (C) costly
   (D) doubtful

5. A wooden desk and chairs need special treatment before they _____ in the living room.
   (A) have used
   (B) are using
   (C) are used
   (D) has been using

6. Novartis is _____ to develop new drugs regarding lung cancer resulting from fine dusts.
   (A) likely
   (B) potential
   (C) appropriate
   (D) skillful

7. All students are asked to _____ a survey after the lecture in order to evaluate their instructors.
   (A) completing
   (B) be completed
   (C) complete
   (D) have been completed

8. You must have a _____ photo identification in order to apply for a credit card.
   (A) costly
   (B) frequent
   (C) poor
   (D) valid

9. Travelers who _____ in the Wesker Hotel can go to Sanoi International Airport by subway.
   (A) staying
   (B) are stayed
   (C) stay
   (D) have been stayed

10. Due to _____ performances, Donna will not be promoted at the end of the year.
    (A) timely
    (B) eager
    (C) poor
    (D) steady

11. Mr. Stevens, who has worked for the past 10 years, _____ the director of the marketing department.
    (A) considered
    (B) is considered
    (C) is considering
    (D) have been considering

12. Our store is open from 10:00 A.M. to 7:00 P.M. Mondays to Saturdays and _____ on Sundays.
    (A) closing
    (B) is closed
    (C) have closed
    (D) is closing

13. HMK Inc. is seeking alternative tiles which is _____ in quality to the brand that is no longer available.
    (A) balanced
    (B) affordable
    (C) common
    (D) comparable

14. Once visiting the concert, people _____ an opportunity to listen to the new music.
    (A) have given
    (B) will be giving
    (C) is giving
    (D) will be given

Questions 15-18 refer to the following memo.

From: Alan Mossberg
To: All department staff
Subject: New computers

Dear all,

The new computers for the market research department ------- on Friday, June 9 between
                                                          15.
4 P.M. and 6 P.M. during this time period, the IT staff will also remove the computers you currently use and ship them out of the office. The company plans to donate the old computer equipment to schools and other organizations that need it. The new computers ------- memories and faster processors, so they should be ------- to handle all of your
  16.   17.
computing needs. However, if you ever notice your computer gradually slowing down, please contact the IT department (extension 1582). -------.
                                                                                18.
Should you have any other questions about the replacement process, please let me know.

Alan Mossberg,
Office Manager

15. (A) has been installed
    (B) will be installed
    (C) are installing
    (D) will install

16. (A) have been expanded
    (B) expand
    (C) have expanded
    (D) has expanded

17. (A) able
    (B) unlikely
    (C) capable
    (D) responsible

18. (A) However, the system could get a lot worse.
    (B) Afterwards, you can find the new computers less stable than ever.
    (C) The research department will implement a new system.
    (D) Then, their staff will service and upgrade the system.

UNIT 8 전치사 (1)

★ 콕콕 찍어주는 출제 포인트

전치사는 명사를 연결하면서 시간, 장소, 방향, 이유, 목적 등을 나타내는 말이다. 우리말에서는 명사 뒤에서 '~에, ~로, 안에, 밑에, 위에' 등과 같은 의미로 쓰이는 것들과 유사하다. 단, 이러한 어휘들이 한국말에서는 명사 뒤에 붙지만 영어에서는 명사 앞에 쓰이는 게 차이점이다.

1 전치사의 개념과 접속사와의 차이

1 전치사의 기본 개념

at the airport 공항에서 **to** the airport 공항으로 **from** the airport 공항으로부터	이들 표현에서 명사 the airport(공항)는 동일하지만 그 앞의 어휘 at, to, from에 따라서 의미가 달라진다. 이런 어휘들을 전치사라 하고, 그 뒤의 명사 the airport를 '전치사의 목적어(명사)'라 한다.

2 전치사의 특징과 역할

전치사는 명사를 연결하는 어휘이므로 반드시 뒤에 명사나 동명사가 오고, 이를 〈전치사 + 명사〉의 합성어로 '전명구' 또는 '전치사구'라 한다. '전명구'는 문장에서는 형용사나 부사처럼 수식어로 사용된다. 전치사와 명사 사이에는 관사나 형용사가 들어갈 수도 있다.

The pen **under the desk** is mine. 그 책상 밑의 펜은 내 것이다.
→ 전명구 under the desk(책상 밑의)가 명사 the pen을 뒤에서 수식하는 형용사 역할을 한다.

He left here **with disappointment**. 그는 실망감을 가지고 여기를 떠났다.
→ 전명구 with disappointment(실망감을 가지고)가 그 앞의 동사 left(떠났다)를 뒤에서 수식하는 부사 역할을 한다.

He left here **with great disappointment**. 그는 대단한 실망감을 가지고 여기를 떠났다.
→ 전치사 with와 명사 disappointment(실망감) 사이에 형용사 great(대단한)이 있다. great은 disappointment를 수식한다.

3 전치사와 접속사 구별

전치사와 접속사는 동일한 의미의 어휘들이 많기 때문에 뒤에 명사/동명사가 오는지 〈주어 + 동사〉가 오는지에 따라 품사 판단을 해야 한다.

Upon arrival, you must show your ID card. 도착하자마자, 당신은 신분증을 보여주어야 합니다.

Although she is young, Janet is very smart. 재닛은 어리지만, 매우 영리하다.

구분	전치사(+ 명사/동명사)	접속사(+ 주어 + 동사)	의미
양보	despite/in spite of	although/though/even though	~에도 불구하고
시간	during	while	~동안에
	upon	when, as soon as	~할 때, ~하자마자
	after	after	~후에
	before/prior to	before	~전에
조건	in case of	in case (that)	~할 경우에
이유	because of/due to	because/since/as	~때문에
예외	except (for)/excluding	except that	~를 제외하고
	without	unless	~가 없다면, ~하지 않으면

잠깐!

전치사 다음에 간혹 〈주어 + 동사〉로 이루어진 절이 나오는 경우도 있는데, 이는 의문사(what, when, where, why, how, whether)가 이끄는 명사절일 경우에 가능하다.

Everything depends on whether we will pass the exam. 모든 것은 우리가 시험에 합격하느냐 마느냐에 달려있다.

Check-up

해설 p. 134

STEP 1

1. You should handle it with _____.
   (A) care (B) carefully

2. Before _____ an official proposal, review it several times.
   (A) write (B) writing

3. We went out _____ the rain.
   (A) although (B) in spite of

STEP 2

4. The new road project is likely to improve the traffic flow in the city _____ peak hours.
   (A) while (B) during (C) when (D) as soon as

5. The company's final decision depends on _____ the proposal is within the budget or not.
   (A) with (B) to (C) whether (D) for

UNIT 8 237

2 주로 시점 표현과 같이 쓰는 전치사

1 시점과 기간의 차이

❶ 시점 표현 vs. 기간 표현

시점 표현		기간 표현	
6 o'clock (6시)	last night (어젯밤에)	two hours (두 시간)	three days (3일)
Monday (월요일)	March 11 (3월 11일)	four years (4년)	30 seconds (30초)

- 시점 I will meet him **at 6 o'clock**. 나는 그를 6시에 만날 것이다.
- 기간 She has worked here **for four years**. 그녀는 여기서 4년 동안 일을 해왔다.

❷ 시점 표현 전치사 vs. 기간 표현 전치사

시점 표현을 수반하는 대표 전치사	at, on, by, until, before, since
기간 표현을 수반하는 대표 전치사	for, in, within, throughout

They have to finish it **by the required date**. (O) 그들은 요구되는 날짜까지 그 일을 끝내야 합니다.
They have to finish it **within the required date**. (X)

→ the required date(요구되는 날짜)는 시점 표현이므로 기간 표현 전치사 within을 사용할 수 없다.

He cannot come **within three days**. (O) 그는 3일 이내에 돌아올 수 없다.
He cannot come **before three days**. (X)

→ three days는 기간 표현이므로 시점 표현 전치사 before를 사용할 수 없다.

2 at / on / in

기본적으로 at은 시각, on은 날짜나 요일, in은 월이나 연도 앞에서 사용되지만, 각각 다른 명사를 수반하는 경우도 많다.

at + 시각, 시점 (~에)	at 6 o'clock (6시에), at noon (정오에), at first (우선)
on + 날짜, 요일 (~에)	on March 11 (3월 11일에), on Friday (금요일에), on my birthday (내 생일에)
in + 월, 년도 (~에)	in October (10월에), in 2014 (2014년도에), in spring (봄에)

We had a meeting **at 6 o'clock / on Friday / in October**. 우리는 6시에 / 금요일에 / 10월에 회의를 했다.

3 by / until + 시점

by와 until은 둘 다 '~까지'라는 의미로 뒤에 붙는 명사를 가지고 구분하긴 어렵다. 문장에 쓰인 동사의 종류에 따라서 용도가 결정된다.

❶ 완료성 동사 + by

We will have to **submit** the report **by tomorrow**. (O) 우리는 내일까지 보고서를 제출해야 한다.
We will have to **submit** the report **until tomorrow**. (X)

→ 동사 submit(제출하다)는 한 번 제출하면 동작이 완료된다는 의미이므로 by와 함께 사용한다.

❷ 지속성 동사 + until

wait (기다리다)	stay (머무르다)	last (지속되다)	
remain (남다)	continue (계속하다)	postpone (연기하다)	+ until

I **stayed** there **until 10 P.M.** 나는 저녁 10시까지 거기에서 머물렀다.
→ 동사 stay(머무르다)는 지속성의 의미를 가진 동사이므로 by가 아닌 until과 같이 사용한다.

4 before / after / since

before + 시점 (~전에)	before 8 A.M. (오전 8시 전에), before May (5월 전에), before ~ing (~하기 전에)
after + 시점/기간 (~후에)	after the meeting (회의 후에), after two weeks (2주 후에), after ~ing (~하고 난 후에)
since + 과거시점 (~이래로)	since February (2월 이후로), since 4 o'clock (4시 이후로), since ~ing (~한 이래로)

He will come back **before 8 A.M. / after the meeting / after two weeks**.
그는 8시 전에 / 회의 후에 / 2주 후에 돌아올 것이다.
→ before는 뒤에 시점만 오지만 after는 시점과 기간이 모두 올 수 있다는 점에 주의한다.

He has been here **since June**. (O) 그는 여기에 6월부터 쭉 있어 왔다.
→ since는 원래 '과거 시점 이래로 지금까지'라는 의미이므로 뒤에 과거 시점이나 사건만 수반할 수 있다.

Check-up

해설 p. 134-135

STEP 1

1. The store will close _____ 9 P.M.
   (A) at   (B) on

2. They should complete the task _____ tomorrow.
   (A) by   (B) until

3. Some employees have worked at the company since _____.
   (A) last year   (B) next year

STEP 2

4. A few public hospitals throughout the province remain open _____ 8 o'clock on Saturdays.
   (A) until   (B) by   (C) on   (D) between

5. The sales of the new software have increased by six percent _____ last April.
   (A) on   (B) at   (C) since   (D) when

3 주로 기간 표현과 같이 쓰는 전치사

1 for / during

for는 뒤에 기간 표현이 있을 때만 '~ 동안에'라는 의미이고, 그 밖에는 '~를 위해서'나 '~에 대해서' 등 다른 의미로도 사용이 되지만, during은 무조건 '~ 동안에'라는 뜻이다.

for + 사건 (~를 위해서, ~에 대해서)	during + 사건/기간 (~동안에)
for + 기간 (~동안에)	

He was unable to show his slides **during the meeting**. 그는 회의 동안에 슬라이드를 보여줄 수 없었다.
He was unable to show his slides **for the meeting**. 그는 회의를 위한 슬라이드를 보여줄 수 없었다.

For the three months in Korea, I stayed at the same hotel. 한국에서의 3개월 동안 나는 같은 호텔에 머물렀다.
= **During the three months** in Korea, I stayed at the same hotel.

→ for와 during은 뒤에 특정 기간을 수반할 때는 '~동안'이라는 같은 뜻이 된다.

for / during / in / over	+ the past[last] + 기간 표현 (지난 ~동안에)
	+ the next + 기간 표현 (다음 ~동안에)

※ 기간 표현 앞에 the past[last] 또는 the next를 붙이게 되면 기간 전치사 for, during, in, over의 의미가 모두 동일해진다.

I haven't done any traveling **for the last two years**. 나는 지난 2년 동안 어떠한 여행도 하지 못했다.
= I haven't done any traveling **during the last two years**.
= I haven't done any traveling **in the last two years**.
= I haven't done any traveling **over the last two years**.

2 in / over

in + 기간 (~ 안에/~ 후에)	in two hours (두 시간 안에/후에), in four weeks (4주 안에/후에)
over + 사건/기간 (~ 동안에)	over the last few days (지난 며칠간에 걸쳐서), over the weekend (주말 동안에)

※ 전치사 in은 동사의 시제에 따라 '~안에'가 되기도 하고 '~후에'가 되기도 한다.

They finished the project **in two hours**. 그들은 두 시간 안에 그 프로젝트를 끝냈다.
→ 문장의 동사가 finished(끝냈다)라는 과거시제이므로 이 경우 in은 '~ 안에'나 '~ 만에'라고 해석한다.

She will leave here **in two hours**. 그녀는 두 시간 후에 여기를 떠날 것이다.
→ 문장의 동사가 will leave(떠날 것이다)는 미래시제이므로 이 경우 in은 '후에'라고 해석한다.

Some employees have to work **over the weekend**. 몇몇 직원들은 주말 동안에 일을 해야 한다.
→ 전치사 over가 시간적 의미로 사용되면 during(동안에)과 흡사하다고 보면 된다.

3 within / throughout

within + 기간 (~이내에)	within ten minutes (10분 이내에), within 24 hours (24시간 이내에)
throughout + 기간 (~내내)	throughout the day (하루 종일), throughout the month (한 달 내내)

The weather will be sunny **throughout the day**. 날씨는 하루 종일 맑을 것이다.

Mr. Kim will not return **within three hours**. (O) 김 씨는 3시간 이내에는 돌아오지 않을 것이다.
Mr. Kim will not return **before three hours**. (X)
→ within은 뒤에 시점 표현이 아니라 기간 표현이 수반되는 전치사이다.

Check-up

STEP 1
1. She has lived here _____ six years.
   (A) since   (B) for

2. The results will be announced _____ two weeks.
   (A) until   (B) in

3. They are expected to arrive at the airport _____ three hours.
   (A) before   (B) within

STEP 2
4. To attract more customers, some stores are open every weekend _____ the year.
   (A) among   (B) throughout   (C) between   (D) about

5. New employees have been trained at the headquarters _____ the past six months.
   (A) over   (B) between   (C) by   (D) until

4 장소를 나타내는 전치사

1 at / on / in / within

at + 지점 (~에)	at the airport (공항에), at the company (회사에서), at the meeting (회의에서)
in (~안에서)	in + 도시/국가 (도시/국가에서), in the company (회사 안에서), in the sales division (영업부에서)
within (~내부에서)	within the company (회사 내부에서), within short/walking distance (짧은 거리 이내에/도보 거리 이내에)
on (~표면 위에)	on the table (테이블 위에), on the fourth floor (4층에), on the wall (벽에)

He has worked **at / in / within the company** for five years. 그는 5년 동안 그 회사에서/안에서/내부에서 일해왔다.

→ 같은 건물이나 장소 앞에 at, in, within을 사용할 수 있다. 그 장소를 '지점'의 개념으로 보면 at을 쓰고, 그 장소의 안이나 내부를 표현할 때는 in과 within을 쓰면 된다. within이 in보다 '내부'를 강조하는 느낌이다.

There is a book **on the table**. 테이블 위에 책이 하나 있다.

→ 전치사 on은 반드시 무언가의 표면에 접촉해서 '위에'라는 의미이므로, 접촉면과 분리되어 공중에 떠 있으면 사용할 수 없다.

2 throughout / into / out of

throughout (~전역에)	throughout the country (전국적으로), throughout the area (전 지역에 걸쳐서)
into (~안으로)	into the river (강물 속으로), insert A into B (A를 B에 주입하다)
out of (~밖으로)	out of stock (재고가 없는), out of service (서비스 중지의), out of print (절판된)

The disease spread rapidly **throughout Europe**. 그 병은 유럽 전역에 급속하게 퍼졌다.

Don't dump anything **into the river**. 강물 속으로 어떤 것도 버리지 마시오.

→ into는 전치사 in(~안에)과 to(~로)의 합성어로 이해하면 된다.

We regret to tell you that the items are **out of stock**. 그 물건 재고가 없다는 점을 말하게 되어 유감입니다.

→ out of는 주로 장소나 방향의 의미보다는 다른 관용구로 많이 쓴다.

onto라는 전치사도 있다?

전치사 into가 〈in + to〉의 합성어이듯이 onto는 〈on(~위에) + to(~로)〉의 합성어라 이해하면 된다. 즉, 무언가 '밑에서 위로' 움직이면서 점프하듯이 올라갈 때 사용하는 전치사이다. 사용 빈도가 매우 낮으며 토익에서는 거의 오답용 보기 어휘라 생각할 수 있다.

Don't **jump onto the bus** while it's moving. 버스가 움직이는 동안 뛰어 올라타지 마시오.

3 between / among

❶ between A and B / between ~ two + 복수명사

The ship sails **between** Stockholm **and** Copenhagen. 그 배는 스톡홀름과 코펜하겐 사이를 운행한다.

Charlotte sat **between her two sons** at the reception. 샬롯은 환영식에서 그녀의 두 아들 사이에 앉았다.

→ between은 기본적으로 두 가지 명사를 나타내는 표현 앞에서 사용한다.

❷ among + (3개 이상) 복수명사

He is standing **among a crowd of children**. 그는 한 무리의 어린이들 사이에 서 있다.

Check-up
해설 p.136

STEP 1

1. The meeting room is _____ the third floor.
   (A) among   (B) on

2. The elevator is _____ service.
   (A) into   (B) out of

3. We will hire new managers _____ the company.
   (A) between   (B) within

STEP 2

4. The new changes in the industry will result in 2,000 job losses _____ railway workers.
   (A) among   (B) into   (C) on   (D) at

5. New laws to protect consumers against false advertising will come _____ effect next year.
   (A) for   (B) by   (C) with   (D) into

토익 필수 어휘 8_ 형용사 (2)

1. considerable

a. 상당한

receive **considerable** bonuses 상당한 보너스를 받다
undergo **considerable** downsizing 상당한 인원축소를 겪다

2. common

a. 흔한, 일반적인, 공통의

the most **common** request 가장 일반적인 질문
the most **common** ways 가장 흔한 방법들

3. creative

a. 창의적인, 창조적인

search for **creative** ways 창의적인 방법들을 찾다
a **creative** idea 창의적인 생각

4. useful

a. 유용한, 쓸모 있는

the most **useful** function 가장 유용한 기능
a convenient and **useful** Web site 편리하고 유용한 웹사이트

5. current

a. 현재의, 현행의, 통용되는

current market share 현재 시장 점유율
the **current** shortage of labor 현재 노동력의 부족

6. close

a. 가까운, 친밀한

the **close** relation between demand and supply
수요와 공급 사이의 밀접한 관계
location **close** to the subway station 지하철역에서 가까운 위치

7. informative

a. 정보를 주는, 유익한

informative articles 정보를 주는 기사들
an **informative** meeting 유익한 회의

8. partial

a. 부분적인, 불완전한

offer **partial** subsidies 보조금 일부를 제공하다
a **partial** listing of the products 품목들의 일부 목록

9. experienced	*a.* 경험이 많은, 능숙한 **experienced** salespeople 경험이 많은 판매원들 an **experienced** air traffic controller 능숙한 항공교통 관제사
10. expanded	*a.* 넓어진, 확대된, 확장된 **expanded** product line 확장된 제품군 an **expanded** selection of vehicles 광범위한 차량 선택권
11. impressive	*a.* 인상적인, 감동적인 **impressive** background in business operations 사업 운영에 있어서 인상적인 경력 an **impressive** performance 인상적인[감동적인] 공연
12. innovative	*a.* 혁신적인 an **innovative** design 혁신적인 디자인 the **innovative** promotional approach 혁신적인 홍보 전략
13. prospective	*a.* 잠재적인, 장래의 a **prospective** employer 잠재적인 고용주(= 취업 가능성이 있는 회사) the **prospective** customer's credit record 잠재 고객의 신용 기록

Check-up

해설 p.136

1. He anticipates a (consider / considerable) bonus. 그는 상당한 보너스를 기대한다.

2. They are working toward a (common / differ) goal. 그들은 공통의 목표를 향해서 일을 하고 있다.

3. The book is full of (usefully / useful) information. 이 책은 유용한 정보로 가득 차 있다.

4. He gave a very (inform / informative) speech. 그는 매우 유익한 정보를 주는 연설을 했다.

5. The exhibition was only a (partial / partially) success. 그 전시회는 단지 부분적인 성공이었다.

PART 5&6_ 실전연습 8 해설 p.136-139

1. Our employees worked _____ 4 A.M. to finish the project work faster than expected.
   (A) until
   (B) during
   (C) for
   (D) within

2. All new employees will be given _____ brochures on company's rules and procedures.
   (A) experienced
   (B) informative
   (C) comparable
   (D) positive

3. Please call us _____ May 23rd since we calculate the exact number of people attending the meeting.
   (A) for
   (B) until
   (C) by
   (D) during

4. We are seeking _____ professionals dealing with customer complaints in a friendly manner.
   (A) considerable
   (B) competitive
   (C) experienced
   (D) valid

5. Samuel has been with the company _____ nearly 25 years and will retire at the end of this month.
   (A) until
   (B) by
   (C) for
   (D) since

6. Deloitte Inc. has developed a(n) _____ version of the accounting software to resolve the trivial errors.
   (A) responsible
   (B) common
   (C) creative
   (D) expanded

7. Blue Consulting will give workers, who have the lack of service mind, training programs _____ the year.
   (A) among
   (B) throughout
   (C) by
   (D) between

8. Online shopping is a(n) _____ way to buy products wherever customers are.
   (A) useful
   (B) leading
   (C) temporary
   (D) existing

9. To reduce the high rent, we are scheduled to move into the new office _____ two months.
   (A) by
   (B) until
   (C) before
   (D) within

10. Universities spend a(n) _____ amount of time developing marketing strategies to attract outstanding students.
    (A) available
    (B) considerable
    (C) detailed
    (D) understanding

11. The speaker is expected to deliver a presentation _____ 10:00 and 12:00 this morning.
    (A) between
    (B) among
    (C) by
    (D) until

12. Royal Hansen Hotel, where the conference is being held, is located _____ to Pine Creek Stadium.
    (A) permanent
    (B) proper
    (C) close
    (D) timely

13. _____ financial incentives and health benefits, all employee will be given paid vacation.

   (A) Due to
   (B) Because of
   (C) Despite
   (D) In addition to

14. We need some workers _____ and enthusiastic to take on this project forward.

   (A) poor
   (B) partial
   (C) current
   (D) creative

Questions 15-18 refer to the following article.

Osaka—If you ever visit Soshi's Pie, don't bother looking for the menu. It only offers one item that is baked on premises daily—lemon pie. Soshi Harada has been serving customers this special dessert ------- over fifteen years. -------. But will he ever consider ------- his menu?
15.   **16.**   **17.**
Harada says people have been asking him this question for years. And his ------- has always
                                                                                     18.
been the same. "Maybe," he says with a wink. Soshi's Pie is open daily from 11 A.M. to 8 P.M.

15. (A) since
    (B) to
    (C) for
    (D) on

16. (A) The baker plans on moving to this place next month.
    (B) In one day, he sells as many as 500 pies.
    (C) It includes strawberry, vanilla, and chocolate.
    (D) Then, the baked goods are shipped all over the country.

17. (A) expands
    (B) expanding
    (C) expansion
    (D) expandable

18. (A) recipe
    (B) location
    (C) success
    (D) answer

UNIT 9 전치사 (2)

★ 콕콕 찍어주는 출제 포인트
전치사는 어휘 싸움이라는 말이 있다. 즉 문법적으로는 뒤에 명사나 동명사를 연결하는 간단한 규칙만 알고 있으면 된다는 뜻이고, 나머지는 말 그대로 전치사 어휘를 많이 아느냐가 문제이다.

1 to / from / under

1 to (~로, 에게, 까지)

❶ 동사 + to

respond to (~에게 응답[반응]하다)	reply to (~에게 응답하다)	object to (~에 반대하다)
attribute A to B (A를 B탓으로 돌리다)	attach A to B (A를 B에 첨부하다)	prefer A to B (A를 B보다 선호하다; 비교의 to)

The company **attributed** its recent profits **to** price cutting. 그 회사는 최근의 수익을 가격 삭감 탓으로 돌렸다.

We **prefer** this proposal **to** the old one. 우리는 이전 것보다 이 제안서를 선호한다.

❷ be + 형용사 + to

be equal to (~와 똑같다[동일하다])	be available to (~에게 이용[구입] 가능하다)	be accustomed[used] to (~에 익숙하다)
be accessible to (~에게 이용될 수 있다)	be committed to (~에 헌신[약속]하다)	be dedicated to (~에 전념[헌신]하다)

The products **are equal to** those of our global competitors. 이 제품들은 우리의 전 세계 경쟁사들의 제품들과 똑같습니다.

2 from + 명사 (~로부터)

❶ from + 장소, 시간

from Boston (보스턴으로부터)	from 2 o'clock (2시부터)	from 20 to 30 people (20명에서 30명까지)

❷ 동사 + from

benefit from (~로부터 혜택을 받다)	refrain from (~를 삼가다)	differ from (~와 다르다)
borrow A from B (A를 B로부터 빌리다)	prevent A from B (A를 B로부터 막다[예방하다])	remove A from B (A를 B로부터 제거하다)

City residents will **benefit from** a better transportation system.
도시 거주민들이 더 좋은 교통 시스템으로부터 혜택을 받을 것이다.

❸ be + 형용사 + from

| be absent from (~에 결석[결근]하다) | be different from (~와 다르다) | be prohibited from (~가 금지되다) |

He **has been absent from** work for three days. 그는 직장에 3일 동안 결근했다.

3 under (~밑에, ~하는 중, ~하에)

| under the bridge
(다리 밑에) | under construction
(공사 중) | under consideration
(고려 중, 숙고 중) |
| under development
(개발 중) | under warranty
(보증 기간 중인) | under the new management
(새로운 경영진 하에서) |

You can place your bag **under the seat**. 당신은 의자 밑에 가방을 둘 수 있습니다.

The building is currently **under construction**. 그 빌딩은 현재 공사 중이다.

Check-up

해설 p.139-140

STEP 1

1. They will respond _____ the request soon.
   (A) to   (B) for

2. Patrons can borrow books _____ the library for three days.
   (A) to   (B) from

3. Several new products are currently _____ development.
   (A) from   (B) under

STEP 2

4. We believe that many of the city residents will benefit _____ a better transportation system.
   (A) to   (B) for   (C) from   (D) under

5. The terms and conditions regarding the merger of the two companies are _____ consideration.
   (A) into   (B) from   (C) under   (D) outside

2 이유와 목적, 소유

1 because of (~때문에)

because of, due to, owing to, on account of는 모두 같은 의미의 표현으로서 뒤에 좋은 내용이 오든 나쁜 내용이 오든 상관없지만 thanks to는 긍정적인 내용을 수반하여 '~덕분에'라고 해석한다.

The restaurant's success was **due to** its new manager. 그 식당의 성공은 새로운 매니저 때문이었다.

Thanks to this treatment, her condition has improved. 이 치료 덕분에 그녀의 상태는 호전되었다.

2 for (~로, 위해서, 대해서)

for 관용구	
for sale (팔기 위한, 판매용의)	for your convenience (당신의 편의를 위해서)
for more information (더 많은 정보를 위해)	for pleasure (재미로)

That particular item is **not for sale**. 그 특정한 품목은 판매를 위한 게 아닙니다.

→ sale은 판매 행위를 의미할 경우 불가산명사로 사용하며, for sale은 '팔기 위한'이라는 뜻이다. 추가로, on sale이라는 표현은 '할인 판매 중'이라는 뜻으로 우리가 흔히 말하는 '세일 중'으로 이해할 수 있다.

be + 형용사 + for	
be famous for (~때문에 유명하다)	be prepared for (~를 위해 준비해두다)
be eligible for (~에 자격 있다)	be responsible for (~에 책임 있다)

He **is responsible for** recruiting and training new staff. 그는 새로운 직원들을 채용하고 교육시키는 데 대한 책임이 있다.

→ be responsible for(~에 대해 책임 있다)는 be in charge of(~을 책임지다[담당하다])로 바꾸어 써도 된다.

동사 (A) for B	
thank A for B (A에게 B에 대해 감사하다)	apply for (~에 지원하다)
reimburse A for B (A에게 B에 대해 보상하다)	apologize for (~에 대해 사과하다)
praise A for B (A에게 B에 대해 칭찬하다)	exchange A for B (A를 B와 교환하다)

We **thank** you **for** your interest in our product. 저희 제품에 대한 당신의 관심에 대해 감사드립니다.

I **apologize for** the inconvenience. 불편을 드린 점에 대해서 사과드립니다.

3 of (~의, ~에 대해)

명사 + of + 명사	be + 형용사 + of	동사 + of
as a result of (~의 결과로서)	be critical of (~에 대해 비판적이다)	consist of (~로 구성되다)
this area of the city (도시의 이 지역)	be indicative of (~를 나타내다)	dispose of (~를 버리다)
the example of (~의 예)	be appreciative of (~에 대해 감사하다)	be made of + 소재, 재료 (~로 만들어지다)

As a result of the pilots' strike, all flights had to be cancelled. 조종사들의 파업의 결과로, 모든 비행편들이 취소되었다.

Financial experts **are critical of** the government's new policy. 재정 전문가들은 정부의 새로운 정책에 대해 비판적이다.

These figures **are indicative of** a slowing economy. 이러한 수치들은 둔화된 경기를 나타낸다.

The team **consists of** software engineers and designers. 그 팀은 소프트웨어 엔지니어와 디자이너들로 구성되어 있다.

The product **is made of** glass. 그 제품은 유리로 만들어져 있다.

잠깐!

자동사 apologize(사과하다) 다음에는 전치사 to, for 모두 올 수 있는데, 그 뒤에 목적어로 오는 명사가 무엇이냐에 따라 선택해야 한다.

- **apologize to** 사람 (~에게 사과하다)   I would like to **apologize to** you. 당신에게 사과하고 싶습니다.
- **apologize for** 이유 (~에 대해 사과하다)   I would like to **apologize for** the delay. 그 지연에 대해서 사과하고 싶습니다.

Check-up

해설 p. 140

STEP 1

1. _____ bad weather, the outdoor concert was cancelled.
   (A) Because   (B) Due to

2. She is responsible _____ ordering office equipment.
   (A) from   (B) for

3. We are appreciative _____ your interest in our product.
   (A) to   (B) of

STEP 2

4. _____ your convenience, we are open 24 hours a day including national holidays.
   (A) To   (B) By   (C) For   (D) Of

5. All employees should dispose _____ all the confidential documents in a proper manner.
   (A) by   (B) with   (C) of   (D) on

UNIT 9 **251**

3 첨가, 제외, 참조의 전치사

1 in addition to = besides = on top of (~이외에도)

In addition to making money, the company donates money to cancer research.
돈 버는 것 이외에도 그 회사는 암 연구에 돈을 기부한다.

He will make stops in five Midwestern cities, **including** Chicago and Detroit.
그는 시카고와 디트로이트를 포함한 5개의 중서부 도시들을 방문할 것이다.

→ 전치사 including(~을 포함한, 포함해서)을 쓸 때는 앞의 명사(cities)가 뒤의 명사(Chicago, Detroit)를 포괄하는 개념이어야 한다.

잠깐!

besides와 beside의 차이점?

전치사 besides와 beside는 생긴 것은 비슷해도 다른 어휘이다. besides는 '~이외에도'라는 첨가의 의미이지만, beside는 '~옆에'라는 장소를 연결하는 전치사이다.

People choose jobs for other reasons **besides** money. 사람들은 돈 이외에 다른 이유들 때문에 직업을 선택한다.
We found a picnic area right **beside** the river. 우리는 강 바로 옆의 피크닉 장소를 찾았다.

2 except (for) = excluding = but (~를 제외하고)

I can come any day **except (for) / excluding / but Thursday**. 나는 목요일을 제외하곤 어떤 날이든 올 수 있습니다.

→ but은 접속사로 쓰이면 '그러나'이지만 전치사가 되면 '~를 제외하고'라는 의미이다.

잠깐!

except와 except for의 차이는?

전치사 except와 except for의 차이는 거의 없다고 봐도 된다. 하지만 except 하나만 있을 경우는 문장 맨 앞에서 사용할 수 없으며, except for는 문장 앞머리에서 사용할 수 있다.

The store is open every day **except / except for** Sundays. (O) 그 상점은 일요일을 제외하고는 매일 문을 연다.
Except for Sundays, the store is open every day. (O) 일요일을 제외하고는 그 상점은 매일 문을 연다.
Except Sundays, the store is open every day. (X)

3 about (~에 대해서)

전치사 about의 동의어/동의 표현		
regarding	concerning	as to
in[with] regard to	in[with] reference to	

※ in[with] regard to 와 in[with] reference to는 매우 격식 있는 표현으로 비즈니스 편지나 이메일에서 주로 사용한다.

We have several questions **about / regarding / concerning** it. 우리는 그것에 대해서 몇 가지 질문이 있습니다.

I am writing to you **in reference to** the job opening in your department.
나는 귀 부서의 공석에 대해서 편지를 쓰고 있습니다.

4 regardless of = irrespective of (~에 상관없이)

regardless of (~에 상관없이)	= irrespective of 명사 (~에 상관없이)

You can participate in the event **regardless[irrespective] of** experience.
당신은 경험에 상관없이 그 행사에 참여할 수 있습니다.

Check-up

해설 p. 140-141

STEP 1

1. _____ a high salary, you can get a lot of bonuses.
   (A) Due to   (B) In addition to

2. Everyone will be attending the seminar _____ for me.
   (A) exception   (B) except

3. The shop often sends letters to customers _____ special discounts.
   (A) concern   (B) concerning

STEP 2

4. Please note that we consider all qualified job applicants _____ of age or nationality.
   (A) regard   (B) regarding   (C) regardless   (D) regards

5. The agents earn a five-percent commission on the total amount _____ local sales taxes.
   (A) included   (B) excluding   (C) regardless   (D) unless

4 양보, 방법, 자격, 동반의 전치사

1 despite = in spite of (~에도 불구하고)

Despite a few flaws, his proposal will probably be adopted. 약간의 결점에도 불구하고, 그의 제안서는 아마 채택될 것이다.

> **잠깐!**
>
> 전치사 despite 다음에도 〈주어 + 동사〉로 이루어진 절이 붙을 수 있는데, the fact that(~라는 사실)이라는 표현을 이용해서 절을 연결해야 한다.
>
> She went to Spain **despite the fact that** she was very sick. 그녀는 매우 아팠음에도 불구하고 스페인으로 갔다.
> = She went to Spain **although** she was very sick.
>
> → despite 하나만 있으면 전치사이지만, despite the fact that이 되면 마치 접속사처럼 역할을 하므로 하나의 접속사 although(~에도 불구하고)와 바꾸어 쓸 수도 있다.

2 by (~에 의해서)

by라는 전치사는 워낙 다양한 의미와 용법으로 사용되기 때문에, '~에 의해서'라는 방법이나 수단을 확실하게 의미하고자 할 경우는 by means of(~라는 방법[수단]에 의해서)라는 표현을 쓴다. through 역시 '~에 의해서, ~를 통해서'라는 의미가 있으나, 가장 첫 번째 의미는 '~을 관통해서' 지나간다는 의미이다.

We will go to London **by** car/train/bus/airplane. 우리는 차/기차/버스/비행기로 런던에 갈 것이다.
→ 전치사 by 다음에는 교통, 통신, 지불 수단을 나타내는 표현이 잘 나온다.

They succeeded **by means of** patience and sacrifice. 그들은 참을성과 희생에 의해서 성공했다.
→ by means of 다음에는 특별한 방법이나 수단을 의미하는 표현이 잘 나온다.

The company went **through** difficult times financially. 그 회사는 재정적으로 어려운 시기를 겪었습니다.
→ through는 '~를 관통해서' 지나간다는 의미가 우선적으로 쓰인다.

I heard about it **through** a friend. 나는 친구를 통해서 그 얘기를 들었다.
→ 여기서 through는 '~을 통해서'라고 해석하지만 의미는 '~에 의해서'와 같은 맥락이다.

3 as (~로서)

❶ as (~로서) / such as (~와 같은)

She is now working **as** a physician in a private clinic. 그녀는 지금 개인 병원에서 의사로 일하고 있다.
→ as는 '~로서'라는 의미로 신분이나 직책을 말할 때 쓴다.

We don't use personal information **such as** e-mail addresses. 우리는 이메일 주소와 같은 개인 정보를 이용하지 않습니다.
→ such as(~와 같은)는 as와 달리 무언가 예를 들어 말할 때 쓴다.

❷ like (~처럼) / unlike (~와 달리)

Like / Unlike other companies, we offer travel expenses. 다른 회사처럼/다른 회사와 달리, 우리는 교통비를 제공합니다.

4 with (~와 함께; ~를 가진) / without (~가 없이[없는])

❶ with = together with = along with (~와 함께[같이])

Dennis attended the conference **with** eleven other designers. 데니스는 11명의 다른 디자이너들과 함께 컨퍼런스에 참석했다.
Dennis attended the conference **together with** eleven other designers.
Dennis attended the conference **along with** eleven other designers.

❷ with = having

We have employees **with[having]** special skills. 우리는 특별한 기술을 가진 직원들이 있다.

❸ without

We cannot complete the project **without** your assistance. (O) 우리는 당신의 도움이 없이는 그 프로젝트를 완성할 수 없다.
We cannot complete the project **unless** your assistance. (X)

→ 보통 토익에서는 전치사 without이 보기에 나올 때 접속사 unless(~하지 않으면)가 오답 보기로 자주 나온다.

Check-up

해설 p.141-142

STEP 1

1. _____ severe competition, the company was very successful.
   (A) In spite   (B) Despite

2. You can reserve the tickets _____ phone.
   (A) in   (B) by

3. _____ sales manager, he has a lot of responsibilities.
   (A) On   (B) As

STEP 2

4. Companies must not disclose their customers' personal information to anyone _____ their consent.
   (A) unless   (B) without   (C) if   (D) although

5. The orientation will include topics _____ benefits and company safety procedures.
   (A) such as   (B) same   (C) so   (D) when

UNIT 9

토익 필수 어휘 9_ 부사 (1)

1. finally
ad. 마침내, 드디어, 결국, 최종적으로

be **finally** approved 최종적으로 승인받다
finally go on sale 드디어 세일을 시작하다

2. specially
ad. 특별히, 특히

specially designed 특별히 고안되다
the **specially** marked items 특별히 표시된 물품들

3. shortly
ad. 곧, 금방, 얼마 안 되어, 간단히

be finished **shortly** 곧 끝나다
be expected to improve **shortly** 곧 개선될 것으로 예상되다

4. significantly
ad. 상당히, 중요하게, 현저하게

significantly increase the rate of production 생산율이 상당히 증가하다
significantly improve the traffic flow 교통흐름을 현저하게 개선하다

5. initially
ad. 처음에, 당초에, 원래

be hired **initially** for 6 months 처음 6개월 동안 고용되다
initially remove it 초기에 제거하다

6. lately
ad. 최근에, 요즘, 근래

received **lately** 최근에 받았다
was hired **lately** 최근에 채용되었다

7. increasingly
ad. 점점, 더욱 더, 갈수록, 점차적으로

increasingly draw attention 점점 관심을 끌다
become **increasingly** important 점차적으로 중요해지다

8. dramatically
ad. 극적으로, 급격하게

increase **dramatically** 극적으로 증가하다
the **dramatically** improved performance 급격하게 향상된 성과

9. accordingly	*ad*. 그에 따라, 따라서, 적절히 be prescribed a prescription **accordingly** 처방전에 따라서 처방되다 need to be updated **accordingly** 적절하게 갱신될 필요가 있다
10. strongly	*ad*. 강력히, 강하게, 적극적으로 be **strongly** encouraged to read the safety guide 안전가이드 읽기가 강력하게 장려되다 respond **strongly** to criticism 비판에 적극적으로 반응하다
11. currently	*ad*. 현재, 지금 **currently** under construction 현재 공사 중인 be **currently** exploring our options 우리가 선택할 수 있는 옵션들을 현재 검토 중이다
12. promptly	*ad*. 정확히, 정각에; 즉시 **promptly** at 10 o'clock 정각 10시에 process all credit card applications **promptly** 모든 신용카드 신청서를 즉시 처리하다
13. steadily	*ad*. 꾸준히, 지속적으로 **steadily** narrow its gap 꾸준히 격차를 좁히다 Labor costs have **steadily** increased. 인건비가 꾸준히 상승했다.

Check-up

해설 p. 142

1. The problem was (final / finally) solved.   그 문제점은 마침내 해결되었다.

2. The cost of oil has increased (significant / significantly).   기름 가격이 상당히 상승했다.

3. They were (specify / specially) trained for the task.   그들은 그 임무를 위해서 특별히 교육을 받았다.

4. Marketing techniques are becoming (increase / increasingly) important.   마케팅 기술은 점점 중요해지고 있다.

5. I (strong / strongly) recommend him for the position.   나는 그를 그 직책에 강력하게 추천합니다.

PART 5&6_ 실전연습 9   해설 p.142-145

1. Businesses should react immediately _____ consumers' complaints caused by employees.

   (A) of
   (B) to
   (C) for
   (D) despite

2. Shuttle service at the Mondale Hotel operates _____ the city center to the airport at no extra cost.

   (A) with
   (B) on
   (C) from
   (D) of

3. A plan to construct child-care facilities in the workstation is currently _____ consideration.

   (A) along
   (B) among
   (C) toward
   (D) under

4. The housing construction has been temporarily postponed _____ the inclement weather.

   (A) in spite of
   (B) as to
   (C) because of
   (D) besides

5. After the survey results are analyzed, please dispose _____ documents containing personal information.

   (A) out
   (B) of
   (C) for
   (D) by

6. _____ extraordinary performance of the vehicle MD-300, most of the customers were reluctant to buy it.

   (A) Despite
   (B) Although
   (C) In spite
   (D) Thanks to

7. Emily selected by personnel committee last month, will work _____ an intern in the Miami Airline.

   (A) at
   (B) toward
   (C) as
   (D) on

8. Workers are not allowed to leave for work early _____ prior permission of department head.

   (A) into
   (B) beyond
   (C) besides
   (D) without

9. After Mario had retired at the company, he joined another competing one _____.

   (A) nearly
   (B) significantly
   (C) shortly
   (D) previously

10. Employees creating innovative marketing strategies contributed _____ to company's growth.

    (A) currently
    (B) significantly
    (C) easily
    (D) immediately

11. Before management implements the plan to build another plant, they must consider it profitable _____.

    (A) initially
    (B) easily
    (C) already
    (D) dramatically

12. Inspectors have _____ found out the problems that equipment didn't work properly.

    (A) severely
    (B) lately
    (C) closely
    (D) extremely

13. Because the price of apartments rose _____, potential clients are reluctant to buy them.
    (A) willingly
    (B) efficiently
    (C) dramatically
    (D) productively

14. Personnel committee gathers related information and then will revise employment standards _____.
    (A) initially
    (B) lately
    (C) easily
    (D) accordingly

Questions 15-18 refer to the following notice.

NOTICE : To all residents of Melbourne Apartments

From October 23 to December 7, the apartment parking area will be closed and ------- **15.** construction in order to install a new parking system.

The new parking lot will be a space-saving and adjustable two-level system which can be ------- operated. With this new equipment, we will have enough space to hold up to 250 **16.** automobiles.

So, starting October 23, when the construction work starts, please be sure to use the temporary parking area ------- our apartments. **17.**

-------. We hope that the new parking system will provide everyone with a parking space. **18.**

Your cooperation is appreciated.
Thank you.

Terry John
Manager of Melbourne Apartments

---

15. (A) toward
    (B) among
    (C) under
    (D) into

16. (A) closely
    (B) nearly
    (C) nearly
    (D) manually

17. (A) as to
    (B) in front of
    (C) besides
    (D) in spite of

18. (A) We are sorry for the inconvenience.
    (B) Therefore, the area will be busy with residents.
    (C) I hope you can join us in Melbourne.
    (D) We look forward to working with you.

UNIT 10 접속사 (1)

★ 콕콕 찍어주는 출제 포인트

'접속사'란 말 그대로 두 문장을 접속시켜주는 품사이다. 즉, 〈주어 + 동사〉로 이루어진 한 문장과 다른 문장을 이어주는 품사인데, 그 역할에 따라서 몇 가지 종류로 나누어진다.

1 접속사의 종류

1 등위 접속사

등위 접속사는 문법적으로 서로 같은 성격의 단어, 구, 절을 대등하게 연결한다. 즉 뒤에 꼭 문장이 나오지 않아도 된다.

❶ 등위 접속사 and, but, or, nor

She is **cute and smart**. 그녀는 귀엽고 영리하다.
→ 등위 접속사 and를 두고 앞뒤에 형용사 두 개(cute, smart)가 병치되고 있다.

잠깐!

등위 접속사는 다른 접속사와 달리 접속사 뒤에 이어지는 문장에서 주어만 생략할 수 있는 특징이 있다.

He joined the company last year, **and** is now the sales manager. 그는 작년에 회사에 입사했고, 지금은 영업부장이다.

❷ (등위) 상관 접속사

both A and B (A와 B 둘 다)	either A or B (A 또는 B)
neither A nor B (A와 B 둘 다 ~아니다)	not only A but (also) B (A 뿐만 아니라 B 또한)

She can **both** speak **and** write Japanese. 그녀는 일본어를 말할 수도 있고 쓸 수도 있다.

He was **not only** a writer **but also** an actor. 그는 작가였을 뿐 아니라 또한 배우였다.

2 명사절 접속사

명사절은 '명사 역할을 하는 절'이므로, 기본 형태는 〈접속사 + 주어 + 동사〉이지만 문장에서 주어, 보어, 목적어 등으로 쓰인다.

❶ 완전한 문장을 취하는 that vs. 불완전한 문장을 취하는 what

둘 다 우리말로 '~하다는 것, ~것'으로 해석되는 접속사이므로, 이 두 개의 차이를 물어보는 문제가 종종 시험에 나온다.

Vendors know **what** they must reach. 상인들은 그들이 달성해야 하는 것을 알고 있다. = 무엇을 달성해야 하는지 알고 있다.
→ 이 문장에서는 reach(~에 도달하다, 달성하다)의 목적어가 없는 불완전한 문장이므로 what 자리에 that을 쓸 수 없다.

Vendors know **that** they must reach sales targets. 상인들은 그들이 반드시 판매 목표를 달성해야 한다는 것을 알고 있다.
→ 타동사 reach의 목적어 sales targets(판매 목표)까지 있으므로 이 경우 that 자리에 what을 쓸 수 없다.

❷ whether = if

명사절 접속사 whether는 if와 같은 의미인데 주로 의구심을 나타내는 표현과 함께 잘 사용된다.

don't know whether[if] 주어 + 동사 (~인지를 잘 모르겠다)	doubt whether[if] 주어 + 동사 (~인지를 의심하다)	wonder whether[if] 주어 + 동사 (~인지 궁금하다)
ask A whether[if] 주어 + 동사 (A에게 ~할지를 물어보다)	decide whether[if] 주어 + 동사 (~할지를 결정하다)	inquire whether[if] 주어 + 동사 (~할지를 문의하다)

I wonder **whether[if] you can come tonight**. 나는 당신이 오늘 저녁에 올 수 있을지 궁금합니다.
→ if나 whether절이 타동사 wonder(~를 궁금해 하다)의 목적어 역할을 하고 있다.

❸ whether ≠ if

명사절 접속사 whether와 if 중 whether만 되는 경우는, whether절이 주어일 경우, 전치사 다음, 그리고 to부정사가 이어질 때이다.

Whether we win or lose makes no difference. 우리가 이기든 지든 중요하지 않다.
→ 주어 역할을 하는 명사절의 경우 whether를 if로 바꿀 수 없다.

Everything depends **upon whether** we have enough money. 모든 것은 우리가 충분한 돈을 가지고 있는지에 달려 있다.
→ 전치사 다음에 명사절을 쓸 때 whether는 가능하지만 if는 쓰지 않는다.

I can't decide **whether to** postpone it or cancel it. 나는 그것을 연기할 것인지 취소할 것인지 결정할 수가 없다.
→ whether는 접속사이면서 의문사이므로 그 다음에 to부정사를 연결할 수 있지만 if는 그 다음에 부정사를 수반할 수 없다.

Check-up

해설 p.145

STEP 1
1. Their food is not only cheap, _____ delicious.
   (A) or   (B) but also

2. Please remember _____ you should finish it by tomorrow.
   (A) what   (B) that

3. _____ we have a chance to meet him is not sure.
   (A) Whether   (B) If

STEP 2
4. As the leading tire manufacturer, we always try to know _____ competitors are doing.
   (A) what   (B) about   (C) that   (D) regarding

5. This brochure will help you make a decision on _____ to purchase the new software.
   (A) if   (B) both   (C) whether   (D) either

2 부사절 접속사

부사절은 말 그대로 〈접속사 + 주어 + 동사〉가 하나의 부사 역할을 한다는 의미이다. 부사가 원래 문장에서 빠져도 지장이 없듯이 부사절 또한 문장에서 빼도 주절만으로 문장이 성립된다.

분류	부사절 접속사의 종류
시간	when, while, as soon as, before, after, until, since
이유	because = since = as
목적	so that = in order that
조건	if, unless, in case (that), as long as = provided that
양보	although = though = even though = even if, while = whereas

1 부사절의 위치

부사절은 말 그대로 부사처럼 자유롭게 이동할 수 있다. 즉, 주절 앞 뒤 상관없이 사용할 수 있다.

Because I was sick, I couldn't attend the meeting. 나는 아팠기 때문에 회의에 참석할 수 없었다.
  부사절   주절

I couldn't attend the meeting **because I was sick**. 나는 회의에 참석할 수 없었다 / 아팠기 때문에.
        주절   부사절

Because I was sick. (X) 나는 아팠기 때문에 / I couldn't attend the meeting. (O) 나는 회의에 참석할 수 없었다.

→ 부사절은 주절 없이 독립적으로 존재할 수 없고, 주절은 독립적으로 존재할 수 있다.

2 부사절의 축약

❶ 주어만 생략할 수 없다.

부사절에서는 등위접속사절과 달리 주어를 생략해서 동사 하나만 쓸 수 없다. 접속사 다음에 주어와 동사를 모두 쓰든지 분사구문으로 바꾸어서 표현을 해야 한다.

Please use the rear exit **when you leave / when leaving**. 떠날 때 뒷문을 이용해주십시오.

❷ 시간, 조건, 양보 부사절에서 〈주어 + be동사〉 생략 가능

시간	when / while / until
조건	if / unless
양보	although / though

You should wear a hat **while (you are) working** here. 당신은 여기서 일하는 동안에 모자를 써야 합니다.
→ while 다음에 '주어와 be동사'를 생략하고 while working으로 쓸 수 있다.

Although (I was) tired, I had to work overtime. 비록 피곤했지만, 나는 초과 근무를 해야 했다.
→ Although 다음에 '주어와 be동사'를 생략하고 Although tired로 쓸 수 있다.

3 부사절 접속사 vs. 전치사

❶ 접속사와 전치사 형태가 동일한 before, after, since, until

He rarely changes his mind **after he makes** a decision. 그는 결정을 내린 후에는 거의 마음을 바꾸지 않는다.
→ after 다음에 〈주어 + 동사〉가 있으므로 여기서 after는 접속사이다.

He rarely changes his mind **after making** a decision. 그는 결정을 내린 후에는 거의 마음을 바꾸지 않는다.
He rarely changes his mind **after his decision**. 그는 결정 후에는 거의 마음을 바꾸지 않는다.
→ after는 접속사뿐 아니라 전치사도 되므로 뒤에 동명사(making)든 명사(decision)든 둘 다 올 수 있다.

❷ 전치사와 의미가 같은 접속사들

접속사	전치사	의미
although/though/even though	= despite/in spite of	~에도 불구하고
while	= during	~동안에
when/as soon as	= upon	~할 때, ~하자마자
in case (that)	= in case of	~할 경우에
because/since/as	= because of/due to	~때문에
except that	= except (for)/excluding	~를 제외하고
unless	= without	~가 없다면, ~하지 않으면

((During) / While) the summer, she worked as a lifeguard. 여름 동안에 그녀는 구조원으로 일했다.

Check-up

해설 p. 145–146

STEP 1

1. _____ he was young, he was not admitted.
   (A) That   (B) Because

2. _____ it was expensive, we decided to buy it.
   (A) Although   (B) Despite

3. _____ it rains, you should take an umbrella.
   (A) In case   (B) In case of

STEP 2

4. All employees must attend the meeting _____ they have their manager's written permission.
   (A) except   (B) without   (C) unless   (D) during

5. _____ the building was completed several years ago, some of the offices are still vacant.
   (A) But   (B) And   (C) Although   (D) Despite

UNIT 10 263

3 시간 부사절

시간의 의미를 나타내는 접속사는 그 개수가 많으므로 각 어휘의 특징과 의미를 잘 정리해야 한다.

접속사	의미	접속사	의미	접속사	의미
when	~할 때	after	~후에	since	~이래로
while	~동안에	until	~까지	whenever	~할 때마다
before	~전에	by the time	~할 때쯤	as soon as	~하자마자

1 현재시제가 미래 대신

시간 부사절에서는 현재시제가 미래를 의미하므로 그 안에서는 will을 쓰지 않는다. 하지만 그 뒤나 앞에 있는 주절에서 미래를 나타내는 will을 써서 두 문장의 시간 관계를 일치시킨다.

As soon as he comes back, I **will** call you. (O) 그가 돌아오자마자 내가 전화해 줄게요.
As soon as he will come back, I **will** call you. (X)
→ 시간 접속사 as soon as가 이끄는 절에서는 will을 쓰면 틀린다.

After I finish home work, I **will** play the computer game. 숙제를 끝낸 후에, 나는 컴퓨터 게임을 할 것이다.
→ 시간 접속사 after 다음에도 역시 will을 쓰지 않는다.

2 when / while

시간 접속사 when(~할 때)은 시간의 순간을 말하는 '시점'의 개념이고 while은 어느 시점과 시점 사이의 '기간'을 의미한다.

❶ when은 while이 들어가는 자리에 다 쓸 수 있다.

They arrived **while[when]** we were having dinner. 우리가 저녁을 먹고 있는 동안에/먹고 있을 때 그들이 도착했다.
→ while을 쓰면 '저녁을 먹는 동안'이라는 기간을 의미하고 when을 쓰면 '저녁을 먹고 있던 순간'을 의미한다. 때문에 while이 들어가는 문장은 when도 들어갈 수 있는 경우가 대부분이다.

❷ while은 when이 들어갈 자리에 못 쓰는 경우가 대부분이다.

His parents died **when** he was twelve. (O) 그가 12살이었을 때 아버지가 돌아가셨다.
His parents died **while** he was twelve. (X)
→ while을 쓰면 12살이었던 1년 동안을 의미하게 되므로 앞 문장과 연결될 수 없다.

3 since

❶ ~ 이래로

since는 '과거 이래로 지금까지'라는 의미로, since절의 동사는 과거를, 주절에는 현재완료/현재완료진행을 써야 한다.

I have lived[have been living] here **since I was** five. 나는 다섯 살 이래로 여기서 살고 있다.

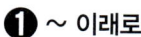

❷ ~ 때문에

접속사 since가 '~이래로'의 의미가 아니라 '~ 때문에'라는 의미일 경우는 시제와 상관없이 사용한다.

Since they are young, they have several options. 그들은 어리기 때문에 몇 가지 옵션들이 있다.

4 by the time

주어 + will + 동사 (~할 것이다)	+ by the time + 주어 + 현재동사 (~할 때쯤)
주어 + will + have p.p. + for 기간명사 (~하게 될 것이다)	
주어 + had p.p. (~했었다)	+ by the time + 주어 + 과거동사 (~했을 때)

My father **will be** 62 years old **by the time he retires**. 나의 아버지는 은퇴할 때쯤 62세가 될 것이다.

My father **will have served** for 33 years **by the time he retires**.
나의 아버지가 은퇴할 때까지 그는 33년 동안을 근무하게 될 것이다.

Carol **had left** the office **by the time I visited** her yesterday.
캐롤은 내가 어제 그녀를 방문했을 때 사무실을 나가고 없었다.

Check-up

해설 p.146-147

STEP 1

1. Before you _____ the office, turn off the lights.
   (A) leave   (B) will leave

2. He has been promoted three times _____ he joined the company.
   (A) when   (B) since

3. He waited _____ she had finished speaking.
   (A) until   (B) by

STEP 2

4. Dr. Roberto Lionello _____ for the airport by the time we took the group photo.
   (A) leaves   (B) will leave   (C) had left   (D) is leaving

5. All the employees have been more productive _____ the new software was installed.
   (A) since   (B) due to   (C) when   (D) before

UNIT 10 **265**

4 이유/양보/비유 부사절

1 이유를 나타내는 접속사

❶ because / since / as

because (~ 때문에) 〈 since ① ~ 때문에 ② ~ 이래로 〈 as ① ~하듯이 ② ~ 때문에 ③ ~할 때

We went by bus **because / since / as** it was cheaper. 우리는 버스가 더 저렴했기 때문에 버스를 타고 갔다.

❷ for (~때문에)

for는 기본적으로 전치사로 대부분 쓰이는 어휘인데 때로는 접속사로도 사용된다. 이 경우 반드시 앞에 콤마가 있어야 하며, 주절 뒤에만 사용해야 하는 규칙이 있다.

I couldn't attend the seminar, **for I was sick**. (O) 나는 아팠기 때문에 세미나에 참석할 수 없었다.
For I was sick, I couldn't attend the seminar. (X)
→ because/since/as 와 달리 for가 이끄는 부사절은 주절 뒤에만 위치해야 한다.

❸ now that (지금은 ~이기 때문에)

Now that the item is out of stock, we cannot accept more orders.
지금은 그 품목이 재고가 없기 때문에, 우리는 주문을 더 받을 수 없습니다.

2 양보를 나타내는 접속사

토익이 비즈니스 영어 기반 시험이므로 보통 무엇인가를 설명하거나 말할 때 정중한 표현을 많이 쓰게 된다. 때문에 문장을 정중하게 만들어주는 양보의 접속사들이 토익에서는 자주 나오게 된다.

❶ though = although = even though (비록 ~하지만)

셋 다 똑같은 의미지만 though 〈 although 〈 even though 순으로 의미가 강해진다. 즉, though가 가장 부드럽고 even though가 가장 강조하는 느낌이다. 때문에 중간인 although가 무난하게 가장 많이 쓰인다.

Though / Although / Even though there is a budget cut, the project will be successful.
비록 예산 삭감이 있지만, 그 프로젝트는 성공할 것이다.

❷ even if (비록 ~일지라도)

though/although/even though와 달리 even if는 앞으로의 상황을 가정해서 쓰는 말이다.

Even though I was tired, I had to finish the job. 피곤했음에도 불구하고 나는 그 일을 끝내야 했다.
→ though/although/even though는 사실적 상황에서 쓴다.

Even if you are tired, you will have to finish the job. 피곤할지라도 당신은 그 일을 끝내야 할 것이다.
→ even if는 사실이 아니라 상황을 가정해서 하는 말이다.

❸ while = whereas (반면에)

접속사 while은 '동안에'라는 뜻도 있지만, '반면에, 하지만'이라는 뜻도 있다. 이 경우 whereas가 동의어가 된다.

While you are using the facility, please wear protective clothing. 시설을 이용하는 동안에는 보호복을 입어주세요.
→ 이 경우 while은 '~ 동안에'라는 의미로 whereas로 바꿀 수 없다.

The old system was complicated **while[whereas]** the new one is very simple.
오래된 시스템은 복잡하지만, 반면에 새로운 것은 매우 간단하다.
→ 이 경우 while은 '반면에'라는 의미로 whereas가 동의어가 된다.

3 비유를 의미하는 as if / as though

그동안 토익에서 주로 오답으로 출제빈도가 높았던 어휘인 as if와 as though가 최근 시험에서는 정답으로 나오고 있다.

She spoke **as if[though]** she has been really sick. 그녀는 정말로 아팠던 것처럼 말했다.

Gary was behaving **as if[though]** nothing happened. 개리는 마치 아무 일도 없었던 것처럼 행동하고 있었다.

Check-up

해설 p.147

STEP 1

1. _____ the weather was so bad, we couldn't enjoy the picnic.
   (A) For　　　　　　　　　(B) Because

2. _____ that she has been promoted, she has more responsibilities.
   (A) Now　　　　　　　　　(B) Due to

3. It looks _____ the building has been vacant for a long time.
   (A) except　　　　　　　　(B) as if

STEP 2

4. _____ workers will perform regular maintenance work tomorrow, all offices will be open.
   (A) As though　　(B) In spite of　　(C) According to　　(D) Even though

5. Our new software processes data very fast, _____ the old program took much more time.
   (A) whereas　　(B) through　　(C) such as　　(D) despite

토익 필수 어휘 10_ 부사 (2)

1. highly
ad. 매우, 고도로
the **highly** advanced digital camera 최첨단 디지털 카메라
highly qualified candidates 아주 적격인 후보자들

2. nearly
ad. 거의, 가까이
nearly two hundred million dollars 거의 200만 달러
a **nearly** impossible task 거의 불가능한 업무

3. immediately
ad. 즉시, 바로, 곧
immediately after a job interview 직무 면접 직후에
immediately past the water tower 분수 타워를 지난 직후에

4. extremely
ad. 매우, 극도로, 굉장히
examine **extremely** carefully 매우 신중하게 조사하다
extremely disappointed 매우 실망한

5. easily
ad. 쉽게, 용이하게, 수월하게
easily accessible 쉽게 접근할 수 있는
clear and **easily** understandable 간결하고 쉽게 이해되는

6. carefully
ad. 신중하게, 주의하여, 조심스럽게, 세심하게
read the instructions **carefully** 지시사항을 주의 깊게 읽다
review the contract **carefully** 계약서를 신중하게 검토하다

7. hardly
ad. 거의 ~가 아니다, 거의 ~하지 않다
hardly recognize the place 그 장소를 거의 알아볼 수 없다
hardly ever see 거의 보지 못하다

8. clearly
ad. 분명히, 명확히, 알기 쉽게
clearly indicate a response 응답을 명확하게 나타내다
clearly mark the number 분명하게 숫자를 표시하다

9. closely	*ad.* 긴밀히, 면밀하게, 유심히, 가까이 work **closely** with their mentor 그들의 멘토와 함께 긴밀히 작업하다 **closely** investigate the incident 그 사건을 면밀히 조사하다
10. frequently	*ad.* 자주, 종종, 빈번히 **frequently** stand in for his colleagues 종종 그의 동료들을 대신하다 meet **frequently** with the marketing team 마케팅팀과 자주 만나다
11. thoroughly	*ad.* 철저하게 **thoroughly** investigate 철저히 조사하다 wash all utensils **thoroughly** before using them 모든 주방기구를 사용 전에 철저히 씻다
12. completely	*ad.* 완전히, 전적으로 be **completely** cured with a single dose of the medicine 그 약을 단 한 번 복용한 것으로 완전히 치료되다 available **completely** free of charge 완전히 무료로 이용 가능한
13. directly	*ad.* 바로, 곧장, 직접 report **directly** to the vice president 부사장에게 직접 보고하다 send the document **directly** to the accountant 그 서류를 회계사에게 바로 보내다

Check-up

해설 p. 147

1. It will take (near / **nearly**) two days to complete.   마무리하는 데 거의 이틀 걸릴 겁니다.

2. The telephone rang, and he answered (immediate / **immediately**).   전화가 울렸고, 그는 즉시 받았다.

3. Please read the instructions (care / **carefully**).   지시사항을 주의 깊게 읽어 주십시오.

4. You should speak (clear / **clearly**) during the presentation.   당신은 발표 동안에 명확하게 말을 해야 합니다.

5. Famous people (frequent / **frequently**) visit the café.   유명한 사람들이 그 카페에 자주 방문한다.

PART 5&6_ 실전연습 10

1. Justin would like to expand the facility, _____ he is concerned about the cost.
   (A) as
   (B) nor
   (C) but
   (D) because

2. The tour guide recommends that we bring _____ a raincoat or umbrella in case of rain.
   (A) neither
   (B) between
   (C) both
   (D) either

3. _____ the company is relatively small, their average salary tends to be fairly high.
   (A) But
   (B) While
   (C) That
   (D) So that

4. _____ network doesn't function properly, you should contact a service center promptly.
   (A) In case
   (B) Unless
   (C) Due to
   (D) Yet

5. The new membership card will be issued to you immediately _____ you join the club.
   (A) until
   (B) as soon as
   (C) unless
   (D) whereas

6. _____ interest rates are highly low, fewer people are applying for home loans.
   (A) That
   (B) Whether
   (C) Even though
   (D) In spite of

7. _____ the price is fully refunded is our policy, if they are not satisfied with the goods.
   (A) That
   (B) What
   (C) Once
   (D) Although

8. Erica must determine _____ or not to assume the project to construct the highway.
   (A) while
   (B) whether
   (C) that
   (D) what

9. The orientation handbook describes _____ freshmen need to know regarding university policies and regulations.
   (A) if
   (B) what
   (C) that
   (D) whether

10. If over 30,000 people withdraw all deposits _____, the financial company will go bankrupt soon.
    (A) especially
    (B) immediately
    (C) recently
    (D) easily

11. Polaroid films are _____ ever used now and there are no camera within our store that can use them.
    (A) mainly
    (B) largely
    (C) hardly
    (D) closely

12. His development as a successful entrepreneur is _____ connected with efforts and expertise.
    (A) softly
    (B) properly
    (C) soon
    (D) closely

13. The service training is _____ effective in ensuring that employees improve their performances.

(A) extremely
(B) carefully
(C) previously
(D) approximately

14. The advertisement for the new product should be examined _____ before it is broadcast nationally.

(A) lately
(B) carefully
(C) possibly
(D) extremely

Questions 15-18 refer to the following notice.

Bicycle Rider magazine - providing expert cycling advice every month

Dear Reader,

To better serve our readers, we are conducting a brief survey ------- **15.** the magazine's content and layout. Those readers completing the survey will not be placed on any mailing lists, ------- **16.** *Bicycle Rider* does not share its reader information with any outside companies. To participate in the survey, please go to www.bicycle-rider.com/survey and answer the eight questions. -------. **17.** The winner of the drawing will receive a free one-year ------- **18.** to the magazine along with our annual special issue, *Great Bicycle Trips*.

15.
(A) regarding
(B) that
(C) despite
(D) as though

16.
(A) while
(B) as
(C) nor
(D) although

17.
(A) We will deliver a bicycle to all riders free of charge.
(B) Increasingly, overseas companies are interested in lists.
(C) All completed surveys will automatically go into our drawing.
(D) On the other hand, you cannot notice any mistakes in our survey.

18.
(A) agreement
(B) duration
(C) subscription
(D) discussion

UNIT 11 접속사 (2)

> ★ 콕콕 찍어주는 출제 포인트
> 접속사의 대부분은 부사절 접속사가 차지한다. 등위 접속사와 명사절 접속사는 그 개수가 적지만 부사절 접속사는 수십 개에 이르기 때문이다. 결국 접속사도 전치사처럼 어휘 싸움인 것이다.

1 조건을 나타내는 접속사

접속사	의미	특징
if	~하면, ~할 경우에	가장 대표적인 조건 접속사
in case (that) / in the event (that)	~하면 / ~할 경우에 대비해서	전치사로 변할 때 in case of / in the event of
only if / provided (that)	~할 경우에만, ~하는 한	if보다는 조건이 더 강한 느낌
unless	~하지 않으면	if의 반대

1 if

❶ 명사절 if (~할지, ~인지 아닌지)

타동사 know, wonder, decide, ask 등 다음에 곧바로 if가 붙으면 이는 그 타동사의 목적어 역할을 하는 명사절의 if이다.

I **wonder if** you can participate in the conference. 나는 당신이 회담에 참석할 수 있을지 궁금합니다.

→ 이 경우 if를 부사절의 if처럼 '~하면'이라고 해석하지 않도록 한다.

❷ 부사절 if (~하면)

타동사의 목적어가 아니라 주절과 완전히 분리된 부사절에서 if는 '~하면'이라는 조건의 의미이다.

We will stay at the hotel **if it rains** tomorrow. 내일 비가 오면 우리는 호텔에 머무를 것입니다.

→ 접속사 if가 이끄는 절(if it rains tomorrow)은 앞 문장에서 완전히 분리시킬 수 있는 부사절이다.

2 in case / in the event

❶ ~하면

In case / In the event (that) you can't come, give me a call. 네가 올 수 없으면 내게 전화 좀 줘.

→ 이 경우 in case는 if의 의미로 사용되어 '~하면'이라는 조건의 의미이다.

❷ ~할 경우에 대비해서

Take an umbrella in case / in the event (that) it rains. 비가 올 경우에 대비해서 우산을 가져가라.

→ 이 경우 in case는 '앞으로 일어날 일에 대비해서 무언가 준비해서'라는 의미로 사용되었다.

3 only if / provided (that)

only if(~할 경우에만)는 접속사 if를 부사 only가 수식하는 것이므로 if보다 좀더 강한 느낌이 된다. 동의어로 provided (that)을 쓸 수 있는데, that은 써도 되고 생략해도 된다.

We offer refunds **if / only if** customers present the original receipt.
우리는 고객들이 영수증 원본을 제시할 경우에/경우에만 돈을 환불해드립니다.

You can borrow the car, **provided (that)** you can give it back by 6 o'clock.
당신은 6시까지 차를 돌려줄 수 있는 경우에만 차를 빌릴 수 있습니다.

4 unless

접속사 unless는 그 자체가 '~하지 않으면'이라는 부정어이므로 not과 함께 쓸 수 없다.

Unless you **have** two ID cards, you can't enter the building.
당신이 두 개의 신분증을 가지고 있지 않다면, 그 건물에 들어갈 수 없습니다.

Check-up

해설 p.150–151

STEP 1

1. _____ you have any question, please tell me immediately.
   (A) And
   (B) If

2. _____ it doesn't work properly, you should bring it to us.
   (A) In case that
   (B) In the event of

3. Employees can't get a reimbursement _____ they submit the expense report.
   (A) without
   (B) unless

STEP 2

4. Regional managers can receive considerable bonuses _____ they reach their sales goals.
   (A) due to   (B) as if   (C) in order to   (D) provided that

5. We will issue refunds for damaged computer software _____ it is returned within 30 days.
   (A) except   (B) in case of   (C) despite   (D) only if

UNIT 11

2 목적과 결과를 나타내는 접속사

1 목적

접속사	의미	같은 의미 부정사
so that	~하기 위해서	so as to부정사
in order that		= in order to부정사 = to부정사

❶ so that / in order that (~하기 위해서)

so that과 in order that은 접속사이므로 뒤에 〈주어 + 동사〉가 반드시 와야 한다.

I'm studying hard **so that** I can pass that exam. 나는 시험에 합격하기 위해서 열심히 공부하고 있다.
= I'm studying hard **in order that** I can pass that exam.

❷ so as to부정사 / in order to부정사 / to부정사 (~하기 위해서)

so as to부정사와 in order to부정사/to부정사는 부정사이므로 당연히 그 다음에 〈주어 + 동사〉가 아닌 동사원형이 온다.

He is working hard **so as to / in order to / to** succeed. 그는 성공하기 위해서 열심히 일하고 있다.

2 결과를 나타내는 접속사

❶ so (그래서, 그러므로)

접속사 so는 so that(~하기 위해서)과 달리 '결과'를 의미하여 '그래서'나 '그러므로'라고 해석한다. so가 이끄는 부사절은 다른 부사절과는 달리 주절 앞에서는 쓸 수 없고 반드시 뒤에서만 써야 한다.

There are no buses, **so** you'll have to walk. (O) 버스가 없어서 당신은 걸어가야만 할 것이다.
      주절   부사절
So you'll have to walk, there are no buses. (X)

❷ so + 형용사[부사] + that (매우 ~해서 that 이하 하다)

so는 부사이고 that이 접속사인데 두 개가 이어지면서 '매우 ~해서 that 이하 하다'라는 구문이 된다.

The road surface became **so hot that** it melted. 도로의 표면이 매우 뜨거워져서 녹아버렸다.
→ so가 형용사 hot을 수식하면서 결과의 의미인 that절을 수반했으므로 올바른 문장이다.

Everything happened **so quickly that** I didn't have time to think.
모든 일이 너무나 빨리 발생해서 나는 생각할 시간이 없었다.
→ so가 형용사 quickly를 수식하면서 결과의 의미인 that절을 수반했으므로 올바른 문장이다.

She is **so** nice a **manager that** all staff members like her.
그녀는 매우 친절한 매니저이므로 모든 직원들이 그녀를 좋아한다.
→ 〈so + 형용사 + 관사 + 명사〉의 형태로는 쓸 수 있다.

❸ such + (관사) + 형용사 + 명사 + that (매우/그처럼 ~해서 that 이하 하다)

such는 명사를 꾸며주는 어휘 중에서 가장 앞에 온다. 가산이냐 불가산이냐에 따라서 such 다음에 관사가 있을 수도, 없을 수도 있다.

She is **such a nice manager that** all staff members like her. 그녀는 매우 친절한 매니저이므로 모든 직원들이 그녀를 좋아한다.
→ such 다음에 〈관사 + 형용사 + 명사〉 순으로 연결되어 올바른 문장이다.

This is **such important information that** everyone should read it.
이것은 매우 중요한 정보여서 모든 사람이 읽어보아야 한다.
→ information(정보)이 불가산명사이므로 such 다음에 부정관사 a가 없는 게 맞는 표현이다.

잠깐!

such와 such as는 다르다.

such는 '매우, 그처럼'이라는 의미로 보통 'such + (관사) + 형용사 + 명사'의 형태로 쓰이지만 such as(~와 같은)는 전치사이며 무언가 예를 들 때 쓰는 표현이다.

We would like to interview successful CEOs **such as you**. (O)
우리는 당신과 같은 성공적인 CEO들을 인터뷰 하고 싶습니다.
We would like to interview successful CEOs **such you**. (X)

Check-up

해설 p.151–152

STEP 1

1. He worked overtime _____ he could meet the deadline.
   (A) so that   (B) in order to

2. We were unable to get enough funding, _____ we had to give up the project.
   (A) so   (B) because of

3. Thank you _____ much that I would like to give you something.
   (A) such   (B) so

STEP 2

4. This is _____ a big car that it can accommodate eight adults quite comfortably.
   (A) so   (B) very   (C) such   (D) really

5. We will hold a meeting soon in order _____ we can discuss the most recent problems.
   (A) that   (B) to   (C) for   (D) with

3 접속부사

접속부사는 앞 문장과 뒷 문장의 내용을 연결하는 어휘이므로 의미상으로는 접속사의 역할을 하지만 문법적으로는 부사이다. 때문에 일반 접속사와 차이가 있고 파트 6에서 자주 출제되는 편이다.

1 접속부사의 자리

주어 + 동사 ~. 접속부사, 주어 + 동사 ~
주어 + 동사 ~; 접속부사, 주어 + 동사 ~

Anna is highly intelligent. **However**, she is very lazy. 애나는 매우 똑똑하다. 하지만 그녀는 매우 게으르다.
　　　　　　　　　　　　　　접속부사

Anna is highly intelligent; **however**, she is very lazy. ※ 세미콜론이 나오면 뒤에 접속사가 아닌 접속부사만 올 수 있다.
　　　　　　　　　　　　　　접속부사

➡ however는 접속사가 아니라 접속부사이므로 but과 같이 앞 문장 다음에 콤마(,)를 찍고 소문자(however)로 쓰고 곧바로 뒷 문장을 연결하지 못한다. 앞 문장을 마침표(.)로 마무리 짓고 뒷 문장 앞에서 대문자로 쓰거나 또는 세미콜론과 더불어 소문자로 사용한다.

2 접속부사의 종류

결과	그러므로	therefore, consequently, accordingly, thus
반대	그러나, 하지만	however, nonetheless, nevertheless
추가	더욱이, 게다가	moreover, furthermore, in addition, besides
조건	그렇지 않으면	otherwise

❶ 결과를 의미하는 접속부사

I was nervous. **Therefore**, I could not do my best. 나는 긴장했었다. 그러므로 나는 최선을 다할 수 없었다.

No complaint was made. **Accordingly**, the police took no action.
어떠한 불평도 제기되지 않았다. 따라서 경찰도 행동을 취하지 않았다.

❷ 반대를 의미하는 접속부사

We wanted to arrive on time; **however**, we were delayed by traffic.
우리는 정시에 도착하고 싶었다. 하지만 차가 막혀 지연되었다.

It's a difficult race. **Nevertheless**, thousands of runners participate every year.
그것은 어려운 경주이다. 하지만 수천 명의 경주자들이 매년 참가한다.

❸ 추가를 의미하는 접속부사

She is very intelligent; **moreover**, she is very ambitious. 그녀는 매우 똑똑하다. 게다가 매우 야망적이다.

I enjoy my job. **In addition**, I really like my new coworkers. 나는 내 일이 즐겁다. 게다가 새로운 동료들이 정말 좋다.

> **잠깐!**
>
> **in addition과 in addition to는 다르다.**
>
> in addition은 두 단어로 이루어진 부사이지만 in addition to는 세 단어로 이루어진 하나의 전치사이다. 때문에 뒤에 명사나 동명사를 꼭 붙여야 한다.
>
> I have sales experience. **In addition**, I have excellent communication skills.
> 나는 영업 경험이 있습니다. 게다가 뛰어난 의사소통 기술도 있습니다.
> **In addition to** sales experience, I have excellent communication skills.
> 영업 경험이외에도, 나는 뛰어난 의사소통 기술이 있습니다.

❹ 조건을 의미하는 접속부사

We should consult them; **otherwise**, they may be upset.
우리는 그들과 상의해 봐야 한다. 그렇지 않으면 그들은 화가 날지도 모른다.

Check-up

해설 p.152

STEP 1

1. The company offered me a position. _____, I didn't accept it.
   (A) However (B) Moreover

2. The product is damaged; _____ I just want a refund.
   (A) therefore (B) so that

3. You should quit smoking. _____, you will lose your health.
   (A) Before (B) Otherwise

STEP 2

4. Magnacore Ltd. gives a very competitive salary; _____, it offers comprehensive benefits.
   (A) however (B) nevertheless (C) in addition (D) nonetheless

5. Progress has been very good so far; _____ we hope that the work will be completed on time.
   (A) but (B) although (C) therefore (D) according

4 비교구문

1 비교급의 분류

원급 비교	A = B	A와 B가 ~만큼 같다
비교급 비교	A > B or A < B	A가 B보다 더/덜 하다
최상급 비교	A가 최고	A가 ~중에서 가장 ~하다

❶ 원급 비교   as A (형용사/부사) as B (B만큼 똑같이 A하다)

He is **as tall as** his brother. 그는 그의 동생만큼 키가 크다. (둘의 키가 같다.)

→ as ~ as 사이에 들어가는 단어는 어휘의 변형 없이 써주면 된다.

❷ 비교급 비교

- A + -er / more A than B (**B보다 더 A하다**)

She is **older than** you. 그녀는 너보다 나이가 많다.

→ 2음절 이하인 짧은 어휘는 뒤에 er를 붙이고, 긴 어휘는 앞에 more를 붙여서 만든다.

- less A than B (**B보다 덜 A하다**)

This is **less expensive than** your car. 이것은 네 차보다 덜 비싸다.

→ less를 붙이면 '더 ~하다'가 아니라 '덜 ~하다'라는 반대의 의미이다.

❸ 최상급 비교   the A + -est / the most A (가장 A하다)

He is **the youngest** student in the class. 그가 학급에서 가장 나이가 어린 학생이다.

→ 최상급은 3개 이상 중에서 최고를 말하는데 여기서는 in the class(학급에서)가 힌트이다.

2 비교구문의 특징

❶ as ~ as 사이의 품사 결정

as ~ as 사이에는 형용사나 부사가 들어가는데 이것은 as ~ as 앞의 동사에 달려 있다.

This machine will be **as good as** the old one. 이 기계는 예전 것만큼 좋을 것이다.

→ as ~ as 앞의 동사가 be동사이므로 그 사이에는 형용사가 들어간다.

You should finish it **as quickly as** possible. 당신은 그 일을 가능한 한 빨리 끝내야 한다.

→ as ~ as 앞의 동사가 일반동사 finish(~를 끝내다)이므로 부사가 뒤에서 수식한다.

❷ ~er/more ~ than 구문에서 than이 없는 경우

문맥상 무엇과 비교하는지 유추할 수 있을 때는 than(~보다) 이하의 구문이 아예 나오지 않는 경우가 아주 많다.

The plan would require more time (than the old plan). 이 계획은 (예전 계획보다) 더 많은 시간을 필요로 할 것이다.

→ ~er이나 more 비교급 구문에서는 뒤에 than(~보다) 이하가 없이 사용되는 경우도 많다. 하지만 거꾸로 than이 있으면 앞에는 비교급 표현 ~er/more가 반드시 있어야 한다.

❸ 비교급 수식부사 much, even, far, still

이 어휘들은 각각 기본적으로 다른 의미를 가지고 있는 부사들이지만 비교급을 앞에서 강조할 때 모두 '훨씬'이라고 해석된다.

This is **much bigger than** that. 이것은 저것보다 훨씬 크다.

The new project is **far more important than** any other project.
새로운 프로젝트는 다른 어떠한 프로젝트보다 훨씬 더 중요하다.

❹ 최상급의 단서

of all (the) 복수명사 (모든 ~중에서)	in the 범위 (~안에서)	ever (여태껏 ~중에서)

He is **the most** intelligent **of all the** students. 모든 학생들 중에서 그가 가장 똑똑하다.

This is **the newest** building **in the city**. 이것은 그 도시에서 가장 새로운 빌딩이다.

It is **the largest** restaurant **ever**. 그것은 여태껏 있었던 것 중에 가장 큰 레스토랑이다.

잠깐!

토익에서 잘 나오는 비교급과 최상급 관용구

① no later than/by (~보다 늦지 않게, ~까지)
　We must receive all invoices **no later than/by** tomorrow. 우리는 내일까지 모든 송장을 받아야 한다.

② than ever (예전보다)
　The information is more reliable **than ever**. 그 정보는 예전보다도 더욱 믿을만하다.

③ at least (최소한)
　They need **at least** two days to complete it. 그들은 그 일을 마무리하는 데 최소한 2일이 필요하다.

Check-up

해설 p. 152–153

STEP 1

1. The new system is as _____ as the old one.
   (A) reliable　　(B) reliably

2. He will get a higher salary _____ now.
   (A) than　　(B) that

3. Of all the applicants, he is _____ qualified.
   (A) more　　(B) the most

STEP 2

4. We guarantee that our new heater is the most efficient model _____.
   (A) ago　　(B) before　　(C) ever　　(D) previously

5. In order to complete the project on time, we will need _____ more administrative support.
   (A) very　　(B) so　　(C) even　　(D) great

UNIT 11

토익 필수 어휘 11_ 어구

1. put in for
~을 신청하다
put in for a transfer 전근 신청하다
put in for the competition 대회 신청하다

2. on behalf of
~을 대신하여
on behalf of the entire staff 전체 직원을 대신하여
on behalf of the Junior Editors Association
주니어 편집자 협회를 대신하여

3. in observance of
~을 준수하여, ~을 기념하여
in observance of a trade agreement 무역협정을 준수하여
in observance of the public holiday 공휴일을 준수하여

4. put A into practice
A를 실행에 옮기다
put them **into practice** shortly 빠른 시간 안에 그것들을 실천으로 옮기다
put the opportunity **into practice** 그 기회를 실행에 옮기다

5. take A into consideration
A를 고려하다
take into consideration each member's strengths and weaknesses 각 멤버의 강점과 약점을 고려하다
take candidates' career **into consideration** 후보자들의 경력을 고려하다

6. at least
적어도, 최소한
at least two weeks in advance 최소 2주 전에
at least three years of relevant experience 최소 3년의 관련 경력

7. due to
~ 때문에 (= because of)
due to unfavorable weather conditions 악천후 때문에
due to the lack of qualified applicants
자격을 갖춘 지원자들이 부족하기 때문에

8. be comparable to
~와 유사하다, ~에 필적할 만하다, ~와 견줄 만하다
be comparable to buying used machinery
중고기계를 구매하는 것과 비슷하다
be comparable to the market share last quater
지난 분기 시장 점유율과 비슷하다

	~에 관계 없이
9. regardless of	**regardless of** the reason for the termination 종료 사유에 관계 없이 **regardless of** previous experience 과거 경력에 관계 없이
10. be available to/ for	~에게 이용 가능하다 **be available to/for** attendees 참석자들에게 이용 가능하다 **be available to/for** customers 소비자들에게 이용 가능하다
11. in accordance with	~에 따라, ~대로 **in accordance with** the manufacturer's instructions 제조사의 사용 설명대로 **in accordance with** the new regulations 새로운 규정에 따라
12. at no charge	무료로 be offered to you **at** absolutely **no charge** 완전히 무료로 여러분에게 제공되다 can be downloaded from our Web site **at no charge** 우리 웹사이트에서 무료로 다운 받을 수 있다
13. instead of	~ 대신에 **instead of** Boarding Gate 5 5번 탑승구 대신에 using plastic parts **instead of** metal 금속 대신 플라스틱 부품을 사용하는 것

Check-up

해설 p. 153

1. On (half / behalf) of the entire staff, I would like to thank you.   전체 직원들을 대신해서 나는 당신에게 감사드리고 싶습니다.

2. In (observe / observance) of the national holiday, we will close tomorrow.   국경일을 준수해서, 우리는 내일 문을 닫습니다.

3. We should take our budget into (consider / consideration).   우리는 우리의 예산을 고려해야 합니다.

4. The results are (consistent / consistently) with earlier research.   그 결과들은 이전의 조사와 일치합니다.

5. The organization is (dedication / dedicated) to helping poor people.   그 단체는 가난한 사람들을 돕는 데 전념한다.

PART 5&6 _ 실전연습 11

1. _____ unexpected accidents occur, please obtain at least one of the medical insurances.

   (A) Unless (B) In case
   (C) But (D) In the event of

2. Kara Corporation makes the _____ apartments used by innovative technologies in the construction industry.

   (A) strong (B) stronger
   (C) strongest (D) strongly

3. _____ all employees, I sincerely appreciate special service that you extended to us last month.

   (A) Despite (B) Except
   (C) In addition to (D) On behalf of

4. First-quarter profits fell; _____, the board of directors decided to reduce operational costs.

   (A) in addition (B) so that
   (C) however (D) therefore

5. There are additional fees _____ you are not notified otherwise about our insurance.

   (A) what (B) in case of
   (C) provided that (D) pending

6. Before making a final decision, we should take into _____ the quality and price of various products.

   (A) care (B) consideration
   (C) custody (D) confidence

7. Everyone knows that the quality is _____ important than the price to buy products.

   (A) most (B) the most
   (C) as (D) more

8. Brandon did not participate in the conference; he did, _____, deliver an impressive presentation.

   (A) moreover (B) however
   (C) additionally (D) accordingly

9. The customer service department is _____ to providing prompt and friendly service.

   (A) used (B) about
   (C) dedicated (D) willing

10. Employees should keep the jewellery shop tightly locked _____ they get off work there.

    (A) except (B) while
    (C) when (D) unless

11. Ronald has worked as _____ as any other team member in our accounting division.

    (A) hardest (B) hard
    (C) more hard (D) harder

12. All buildings should be _____ with specifications and quality standards of the construction laws.

    (A) consistent (B) conscious
    (C) accessible (D) different

13. The rock concert attracted _____ many people that we focused on their safety particularly.

    (A) such
    (B) very
    (C) as
    (D) too

14. Please have your passport and ticket ready at all times _____ we speed up boarding procedures.

    (A) in order to
    (B) so that
    (C) if
    (D) provided that

Questions 15-18 refer to the following advertisement.

Excellent Transportation Company

We move to almost all airports and train stations. ---15--- we offer convenient and comfortable transportation services from morning to night. Our luxury vehicles are available for a range of services, such as wedding ceremonies, retirement and farewell parties, and reception events.

All cars are ---16--- with air conditioning and a up-to-date surrounding sound system. ---17---. ---18--- you mention this advertisement, you can ride to the airport at a $15 discount!

Call now: 342-5885 or fax or e-mail your request at: 342-5886 or reservation@etc.com.

---

15. (A) In addition to
    (B) Also
    (C) Additional
    (D) Beside

16. (A) capable
    (B) equipped
    (C) composed
    (D) consisted

17. (A) Sometimes, the system is told to be obsolete.
    (B) It is likely that the vehicles would cause heavy traffic.
    (C) You can use all of them absolutely at no cost.
    (D) Make a reservation 24 hours in advance.

18. (A) If
    (B) Unless
    (C) Except
    (D) During

UNIT 12 관계사

★ 콕콕 찍어주는 출제 포인트

관계사에는 관계대명사와 관계부사 두 종류가 있다. 두 문장을 한 문장으로 합치는 과정에서 '접속사 + 대명사' 기능을 하면 관계대명사이고, '접속사 + 부사' 기능을 하면 관계부사라 부른다. 관계사는 겹치는 정보를 줄이고 문장을 경제적이고 효과적으로 만들 때 주로 사용된다. 접속사의 기능을 가지고 있으므로 접속사가 없는 문장에서 사용해야 한다.

1 관계대명사 특징 및 종류

1 관계대명사의 생성 과정

❶ 원래의 두 문장에서 접속사와 대명사 빼기

I have a friend **and he** lives in L.A. 나는 친구 하나가 있는데, 그는 L.A에 산다.
↓
I have a friend (**and he**) lives in L.A.
       　　　　　접속사 대명사

❷ 대명사 자리 확인하고 관계대명사 집어넣기

I have a friend ＿＿＿＿＿＿ lives in L.A.

➡ 위의 예문에서 he가 차지하고 있었던 자리는 주어 자리이다.

I have a **friend who** lives in L.A. 나는 L.A에 사는 친구 하나가 있다.
　　　　　선행사　관계대명사

➡ 최초의 문장에서 he가 차지하던 자리가 주어 자리이며, friend가 사람이므로 접속사와 대명사가 빠진 자리에는 사람을 나타내는 주격 관계대명사 who를 쓴다. 관계대명사 앞에 있는 명사는 '선행사'라 부른다.

2 관계대명사와 의문사의 차이

관계대명사는 새롭게 만든 어휘가 아니고 기존에 있던 의문사를 재활용한 것이므로 생김새는 동일하지만 다음의 차이가 있다.

의문사	선행사가 없고, 자체 의미를 갖는다
관계대명사	선행사가 있고, 자체 의미가 없다

I don't know **who will come** to the meeting. 나는 회의에 누가 올지 모르겠다.

➡ 여기서 who는 앞에 명사(선행사)가 없으므로 의문사이고, '누가'라고 해석할 수 있다.

I don't know **the man who will come** to the meeting. 나는 회의에 오게 될 그 남자를 모른다.

➡ 여기서 who는 앞에 명사 the man이 있으므로 관계대명사이고 해석하지 않는다.

3 관계대명사의 종류

관계대명사는 선행사가 사람인지 사물인지에 따라 달라진다. 하지만 선행사의 구분이 모호한 경우가 많으므로 편하게 that을 사용하는 경우가 많다.

선행사	주격	목적격	소유격
사람	who	whom	whose
동물, 사물	which	which	whose
사람, 동물, 사물	that	that	

He is a college student **who[that]** is studying math. 그는 수학을 공부하고 있는 대학생이다.
→ 선행사가 사람일 때는 who나 that을 쓴다.

I have a book **which[that]** is useful for children. 나는 아이들에게 유용한 책이 한 권 있다.
→ 선행사가 사물일 때는 which나 that을 쓴다.

Check-up

해설 p.156

STEP 1

1. I saw the man _____ stole the painting.
   (A) who   (B) which

2. I am wearing the ring _____ my mother left.
   (A) whom   (B) which

3. The boy _____ broke the window ran away.
   (A) that   (B) which

STEP 2

4. Our hotel guests _____ request a room service will receive their meals at around 7:00 A.M.
   (A) which   (B) they   (C) who   (D) we

5. You should pay customs duties on all electronic goods _____ are imported from other countries.
   (A) who   (B) they   (C) which   (D) whom

2 관계대명사의 격

관계대명사는 자신이 이끄는 절 안에서 주어, 목적어 또는 소유격의 역할을 한다. 때문에 구조적인 특징이 다음과 같이 나타난다.

1 주격 관계대명사 who, which

주격 관계대명사는 자신이 관계절에서 주어 역할을 해야 하므로 뒤에 주어가 없어야 하고, 곧바로 동사가 온다. 선행사가 사람이면 who, 사물이면 which를 쓰는데, 둘 다 that으로 바꿔 쓸 수 있다.

Individuals **who arrive** late should wait here. 늦게 도착하는 사람들은 여기서 기다려야 한다.
→ 주격 관계대명사 who 다음에 주어가 없이 곧바로 arrive라는 동사가 온다.

We sent a memo **which includes** the schedule. 우리는 일정이 담긴 메모를 보냈다.
→ 주격 관계대명사 which 다음에 주어가 없이 includes라는 동사가 온다.

2 목적격 관계대명사 whom, which

목적격 관계대명사는 자신이 관계절에서 목적어 역할을 해야 하므로 뒤에 주어와 동사는 있되, 목적어는 없는 불완전한 문장이 온다. 선행사가 사람이면 whom, 사물이면 which를 쓴다.

❶ 관계대명사절의 동사가 타동사일 때

목적격 관계대명사 whom/which는 모두 that으로 바꾸어 쓸 수 있다.

Ask a doctor **whom** you trust. (O) 당신이 신뢰하는 의사에게 물어보세요.
Ask a doctor **whom** you trust him. (X)

Here is a hotel **which** I mentioned. (O) 내가 언급했던 호텔이 여기 있네요.
Here is a hotel **which** I mentioned it. (X)
→ 목적격 관계대명사 다음에 반드시 목적어가 없는 불완전한 문장으로 끝나야 한다.

❷ 관계대명사절의 동사가 자동사일 때

관계절의 동사가 타동사가 아닌 자동사일 때는 동사 다음에 전치사까지 오고 나서 목적어가 없는 불완전한 문장이 와야 한다.

The man **whom I talked to** was very helpful. (O) 내가 얘기 나누었던 그 남자는 정말 도움이 많이 되었다.
The man **whom I talked to him** was very helpful. (X; 목적어 him이 있으므로 틀린 문장)
The man **whom I talked** was very helpful. (X; 전치사 to가 없으므로 틀린 문장)

The problem **which I deal with** is almost resolved. (O) 내가 다루는 문제점은 거의 해결이 되었습니다.
The problem **which I deal with it** is almost resolved. (X; 목적어 it이 있으므로 틀린 문장)
The problem **which I deal** is almost resolved. (X; 전치사 with가 없으므로 틀린 문장)

3 소유격 관계대명사 whose

소유격 관계대명사 whose는 선행사가 사람이든 사물이든 관계없이 사용하며 관계대명사 that으로 바꾸어 쓸 수 없다. 그리고 관계절에서 주어나 목적어 역할을 하지 않으므로 뒤에 완전한 문장이 온다.

I need a photographer **whose** portfolio would fit with our theme.
우리의 주제와 맞는 포트폴리오가 있는 사진사가 필요하다.

→ 소유격 whose 다음에 〈주어 + 동사〉가 있는 완전한 문장이다.

We prefer a hotel **whose** rooms have a seaside view. 우리는 바닷가 전망의 방이 있는 호텔을 선호한다.

→ 소유격 whose 다음에 〈주어 + 동사 + 목적어〉까지 있는 완전한 문장이다.

관계대명사 which의 격 구분법

관계대명사 which는 who/whom과 달리 주격과 목적격의 형태가 동일하므로 그 뒤의 구조를 봐야 격을 판단할 수 있다. 뒤에 동사가 나오면 주격이고, 〈주어 + 동사〉가 나오고 다음에 목적어가 없으면 목적격이다.

I just read a letter **which came** yesterday. 나는 어제 온 편지를 이제 막 읽었다.

→ 여기서 which는 뒤에 동사 came이 있으므로 주격 관계대명사이다.

This is the new policy **which everyone must follow**. 이것은 모든 사람이 따라야 하는 새로운 정책입니다.

→ 여기서 which는 뒤에 〈주어 + 동사〉가 있으므로 목적격 관계대명사이다.

Check-up

해설 p. 157

STEP 1

1. I have a brother _____ is a doctor.
   (A) who   (B) whom

2. Here are some techniques _____ they use.
   (A) who   (B) which

3. We need a system which we can _____.
   (A) rely   (B) rely on

STEP 2

4. The company usually recruits people _____ experience is over three years in the field.
   (A) who   (B) which   (C) whom   (D) whose

5. Due to increased security concerns, we should develop a new system which we can truly _____.
   (A) rely   (B) relied   (C) rely on   (D) relies

3 주의해야 할 관계대명사 특징

1 선행사와 관계대명사의 일치

관계대명사절은 명사를 뒤에서 수식하는 역할을 하기 때문에 형용사절이라 불리기도 한다. 그래서 보통은 선행사 바로 뒤에 관계대명사가 오지만, 때로는 그 거리가 멀어질 수도 있다.

❶ 선행사 + 관계대명사
대부분의 경우 관계대명사는 선행사 바로 다음에 위치한다.

Any member who is interested in the ski trip should fill out the form.
그 스키 여행에 관심 있는 회원은 누구든 그 양식을 작성해야 한다.

❷ 선행사 + 전치사구 + 관계대명사
선행사를 수식하는 전치사구가 뒤에 있을 경우 관계대명사와의 사이가 벌어질 수 있다. 이 경우 선행사를 잘 판단해야 한다.

Members of the sports club **who** are interested in the ski trip should fill out the form.
그 스키 여행에 관심 있는 스포츠클럽의 회원들은 그 양식을 작성해야 한다.
→ 여기서 선행사는 the sports club이 아니라 members이다. 따라서 사람을 지칭하는 who와 복수동사인 are를 썼다.

2 관계대명사의 생략

❶ 목적격 관계대명사 (단독 생략)

The book **which she bought** recently was stolen. = The book **she bought** recently was stolen.
그녀가 구입했던 그 책이 최근에 도난당했다.
→ which가 주격이라면 생략될 수 없지만, 목적격으로 사용되었으므로 생략이 가능하다.

❷ 주격 관계대명사 (be동사와 동시 생략)

We have a lot of books **which are useful** for children. = We have a lot of books **useful** for children.
우리는 아이들에게 유용한 책들이 많이 있습니다.
→ 주격 관계대명사 which와 be동사 are가 동시에 생략되면서 형용사 useful이 남게 된다.

3 관계대명사의 전치사

❶ 원래 접속사로 이어진 두 문장

This is **the house, and** he lives in **it**. 이것은 그 집이고 그는 그 안에 살고 있다.
→ 접속사 and로 두 개의 짧은 문장을 연결하여 효율적이지 못한 구조이다. (the house = it)

❷ 관계대명사로 이어진 문장 1 (전치사가 맨 뒤에 있는 구조)

This is **the house which** he lives in. 이것이 그가 살고 있는 집이다.
→ 접속사 and를 빼고, 대명사 it을 관계대명사 which로 바꾸어서 관계대명사절을 이끌도록 했다. 여기서 which는 전치사 in의 목적어가 되는 목적격 관계대명사이다.

❸ 관계대명사로 이어진 문장 2 (전치사가 관계대명사 앞에 있는 구조)

This is the house **in which** he lives. 이것이 그가 살고 있는 집이다.
→ 전치사 in은 관계대명사절 끝에 있어도 되고 관계대명사 앞으로 나가도 된다.

4 관계대명사 that

관계대명사 that은 선행사가 사람인지 사물인지 구분하기 귀찮아서 대신 쓰게 된 어휘이다. 때문에 구어체에서는 who, whom, which를 대신해서 that을 많이 사용한다. 하지만 다음의 두 가지 경우에는 사용할 수 없다.

❶ 콤마 다음 사용 불가

They have a new system **which[that]** is so convenient. (O) 그들은 매우 편리한 새로운 시스템을 가지고 있다.
They have a new system, **which** is so convenient. (O) 그들은 새로운 시스템을 가지고 있는데, 이는 매우 편리하다.
They have a new system, **that** is so convenient. (X)

→ 관계대명사 앞에 콤마가 있으면 이를 서술적 용법이라 하며 that으로 바꾸어 쓸 수 없다.

❷ 전치사 다음 사용 불가

We are finding a place **in which** we plan to live for over 5 years. (O) 우리는 5년 이상 살 곳을 찾고 있다.
We are finding a place **in that** we plan to live for over 5 years. (X)

Check-up

해설 p.157–158

STEP 1

1. The items you have requested _____ out of stock.
   (A) is   (B) are

2. The meeting _____ for this morning has been cancelled.
   (A) was scheduled   (B) scheduled

3. The company offers a service, _____ is very unique.
   (A) which   (B) that

STEP 2

4. The manager sent a memo to employees _____ is about the new vacation policy.
   (A) who   (B) whom   (C) which   (D) whose

5. Please send the requested document before the date on _____ your employment starts.
   (A) who   (B) which   (C) that   (D) whose

4 관계대명사 what / 관계부사

1 관계대명사 what

❶ 선행사가 없음

관계대명사 what은 the thing which의 개념으로 이미 선행사를 포함하고 있다.

What you need is a long vacation. 네가 필요한 것은 긴 휴가이다.
→ What 앞에는 어떤 선행사도 없음을 알 수 있다.

❷ 불완전한 문장을 수반

what도 일반 관계대명사처럼 주어나 목적어, 보어 역할을 하면서 뒤에 불완전한 문장이 나온다.

What is beautiful is not always good. 아름다운 것이 항상 좋은 것은 아니다.
→ what이 is beautiful의 주어 역할(주격 관계대명사)을 하면서 '아름다운 것'이라는 명사절을 만든다.

This is **what my son said**. 이것이 내 아들이 한 말이다.
→ what이 동사 said의 목적어 역할(목적격 관계대명사)을 하면서 '내 아들이 말했던 것'이라는 명사절을 만든다.

2 관계부사

선행사	관계부사	특징
the time (day, year 등)	when	〈접속사 + 부사〉의 개념
the place (house, town, city 등)	where	선행사는 생략 가능
the reason	why	관계대명사와 다르게 완전한 절이 수반됨
the way	how	〈전치사 + 관계대명사〉로 바꿀 수 있음

❶ 선행사가 시간 지칭 어휘일 때 사용하는 관계부사 when

I don't know **the date and** he ordered the supplies **on the date**. = I don't know (the date) **when** he ordered the supplies. 나는 그가 물품을 주문한 날짜를 모르겠다.
→ 선행사인 the date를 생략할 수도 있고 써도 된다.

❷ 선행사가 장소 지칭 어휘일 때 사용하는 관계부사 where

That is **the town and** I was born **there**. = That is (the town) **where** I was born. 저기가 내가 태어난 곳이다.
→ 선행사인 the town을 생략할 수도 있고 써도 된다. where같은 경우는 in which나 at which, on which 등으로 바꿀 수 있는데, 이 문장 같은 경우는 the town이 전치사 in과 어울리기 때문에 in which로 바꿀 수 있다.

❸ 선행사가 이유(the reason)일 때 사용하는 관계부사 why

This is **the reason and** I quit the job **for the reason**. = This is (the reason) **why** I quit the job.
이것이 내가 그 일을 관둔 이유이다.
→ 선행사인 the reason을 생략할 수도 있고 써도 된다.

❹ 선행사가 방법(the way)일 때 사용하는 관계부사 how

Tell me **the way** and you did it **in the way**. = Tell me (the way) **how** you did it.
어떻게 그렇게 했는지 내게 말해주세요.

→ 관용적으로 the way와 how는 나란히 쓰지 않는다.

잠깐!

관계부사와 관계대명사 문제 접근 방법

파트 5나 6에서 보기에 관계부사와 관계대명사가 동시에 있으면, 빈칸 다음의 문장이 완전한지 불완전한지를 첫 번째로 봐야 한다. 빈칸 앞에 전치사가 있으면 관계부사는 쓸 수 없다는 점도 알아야 한다.

I found a store **which** offers truly good services. (O) 나는 정말 좋은 서비스를 제공하는 상점 하나를 발견했다.
I found a store **where** offers truly good services. (X)

→ 관계부사 where 다음에는 완전한 문장이 있어야 하는데, 주어가 없는 불완전한 문장이 왔으므로 이 경우는 which가 맞다.

This is the building **in which** our office is located. (O) 이것은 우리 사무실이 있는 빌딩이다.
This is the building **where** our office is located. (O)
This is the building **in where** our office is located. (X)

→ 전치사 다음에는 관계부사를 사용할 수 없으므로 관계대명사 which가 in과 함께 쓰이거나 in which를 where로 표현한 문장이 맞다.

Check-up

STEP 1

1. _____ I want is a new computer.
   (A) Who   (B) What

2. This is the restaurant _____ we had dinner last night.
   (A) where   (B) when

3. There are several reasons _____ some people don't get enough sleep.
   (A) which   (B) why

STEP 2

4. December is the season _____ we are busiest, so our room rates are higher.
   (A) where   (B) why   (C) how   (D) when

5. _____ the two softwares have in common is their user-friendly graphic interfaces.
   (A) Which   (B) What   (C) Who   (D) Where

토익 필수 어휘 12_ 어구

1. be aware of
~을 알다, ~을 인지하다
be aware of the new engine specifications 새로운 엔진 설명서를 알고 있다
be not **aware of** the new legislation 새로운 법안을 알지 못하다

2. be supposed to
~하기로 되어있다, ~해야만 한다
be supposed to be a very useful book 매우 유용한 책이 될 것이다
be supposed to protect the company's intellectual property
회사 지적 재산권을 보호해야 한다

3. be essential to
~하는 데 필수적이다
be essential to the well-being of our staff 우리 직원의 복지에 필수적이다
be essential to setting future revenue goals
미래 수입 목표를 설정하는 데 필수적이다

4. be familiar with
~에 익숙하다, ~에 대해 잘 알다
be familiar with database management 데이터베이스 관리에 대해 잘 알고 있다
be familiar with the most important issues 가장 중요한 이슈를 잘 알고 있다

5. be equipped with
~을 갖추고 있다, ~을 장착하다
be equipped with built-in speakers 빌트인 스피커를 갖추고 있다
be equipped with a state-of-the-art monitor 최첨단 모니터를 장착하다

6. be similar to
~와 비슷하다, ~와 유사하다
be remarkably **similar to** the logo 그 로고와 현저하게 유사하다
be similar to his work style 그의 작업 스타일과 유사하다

7. be capable of
~할 수 있다
be capable of measuring radiation 방사능 측정을 할 수 있다
be capable of appreciating music 음악 감상을 할 수 있다

8. be involved in
~와 관련되다, ~에 참여하다, ~에 몰두하다
be involved in developing this new computer software
새로운 컴퓨터 소프트웨어 개발에 참여하다
be involved in manufacturing car engines 자동차 엔진 제조에 참여하다

9. be entitled to	~에 대한 자격이 있다, ~에 대한 권리가 있다	
	be entitled to receive paid holidays 유급휴가를 받을 자격이 있다	
	be entitled to a full refund 전액 환불을 받을 권리가 있다	
10. be concerned about	~을 걱정하다, ~에 관심을 가지다	
	be not **concerned about** the shipping delay 선적 지연에 대해 걱정하지 않다	
	be concerned about short-term profits 단기 이익에 대해 관심을 가지다	
11. be faced with	~에 직면하다	
	be faced with a large and complicated set of regulations 규모가 크고 복잡해진 규정에 직면하다	
	be faced with adverse economic conditions 불리한 경제 상황에 직면하다	
12. be consistent with	~와 일치하다, ~와 일관성을 보이다	
	be consistent with the findings 결과와 일치하다	
	be consistent with his views 그의 관점과 일치하다	
13. be dedicated to	~에 전념하다, ~에 열심이다	
	be dedicated to providing quality customer service 양질의 고객 서비스 제공에 전념하다	
	be dedicated to preserving the natural environment 자연 환경 보존에 전념하다	

Check-up

해설 p.158-159

1. You should be aware (with / of) the new policy.   당신은 새로운 정책에 대해서 알아야 한다.

2. The meeting was (suppose / supposed) to take place on Tuesday.   회의는 화요일에 열리기로 예정되어 있었다.

3. The new system is (similar / similarly) to the old one.   새로운 시스템은 예전 것과 유사하다.

4. The company was not (capability / capable) of handling all the orders.   회사는 그 모든 주문을 처리할 수 없었다.

5. All of them are (involve / involved) in the new project.   그들 모두가 새로운 프로젝트에 연관되어 있다.

PART 5&6_ 실전연습 12

1. Manhattan is _____ has been an ideal location for financial, cultural, and banking corporations.
   (A) what   (B) which
   (C) that   (D) where

2. Brianna is the only candidate _____ has outstanding communication and multitasking skills.
   (A) whom   (B) who
   (C) whose   (D) which

3. Ms. Clemons encountered clients _____ she provided with consulting services a few days ago.
   (A) whose   (B) which
   (C) whom   (D) what

4. Visitors at the museum should read the regulations, _____ are posted on the wall at the entrance.
   (A) that   (B) who
   (C) which   (D) whose

5. The firewall software program _____ Mr. Lucas developed prevents computer viruses from being entered.
   (A) whom   (B) that
   (C) who   (D) what

6. The conference hall _____ the job fair will be held is conveniently located near the train station.
   (A) what   (B) which
   (C) that   (D) where

7. November is _____ high school students are highly concerned about entrance examination.
   (A) which   (B) that
   (C) when   (D) what

8. Angela Jones, a musician _____ work received a good response became an international celebrity.
   (A) that   (B) who
   (C) which   (D) whose

9. All employees in the company are _____ of dealing with customer complaints politely and quickly.
   (A) able   (B) capable
   (C) ready   (D) eligible

10. The fitness center is _____ to close facility briefly because trainers will go on vacation soon.
    (A) aware   (B) accustomed
    (C) supposed (D) reluctant

11. Each computer is _____ with a graphic processor that could handle most advanced programs.
    (A) comparable (B) subject
    (C) reflective (D) equipped

12. Mr. Lucas _____ in creating the new products has finally received promotion opportunities.
    (A) involved   (B) involves
    (C) involving   (D) who involved

13. The department head submitted a recent report to CEO _____ is about the advertising strategy.
    (A) what
    (B) who
    (C) which
    (D) whom

14. Both full-time and part-time employees are _____ to receive health insurance.
    (A) similar
    (B) entitled
    (C) accustomed
    (D) equal

Questions 15-18 refer to the following e-mail.

To: Jakub Nadolski <chef@jakubkitchen.jp>
From: Sora Nishimura <soranishimura@mingroup.jp>
Date: September 3
Subject: Commercial Lease Renewal

Dear Mr. Nadolski,

Thank you for coming in today. Our meeting discussing the renewal of your commercial lease was very ------- . We value your business and look forward to continuing our successful relationship. I have attached a copy of the renewal form we examined this morning. It includes the revised section ------- reflects the new building codes. ------- . I would like to confirm that our next appointment will take place on Tuesday, September 8, at our office in Marunouchi. If you have any questions before ------- please contact me at 5322-3359.

King regards,

Sora Nishimura
Soramin Group
Enclosure

15. (A) product
    (B) productively
    (C) productive
    (D) productivity

16. (A) who
    (B) which
    (C) what
    (D) why

17. (A) Please review it at your earliest convenience.
    (B) Arrive at the meeting by three o'clock.
    (C) The lease is due to expire at the end of the month.
    (D) They are located on the second floor of the building.

18. (A) when
    (B) there
    (C) now
    (D) then

UNIT 12

PART 5&6 Review Test

1. Shareholders are allowed to cast --------- proxy votes via the Internet instead of regular mail.
   (A) they
   (B) them
   (C) their
   (D) themselves

2. Increasing prices for raw materials are likely to have an ------- effect on the entire industry.
   (A) affordable
   (B) adverse
   (C) adjacent
   (D) advised

3. The company is very active in --------- its image and maximizing exposure of the products to the potential customers.
   (A) promotion
   (B) promote
   (C) promoting
   (D) promoted

4. During the summer season, all employees must notify their department head of their vacation schedules at least 2 weeks --------- advance.
   (A) of
   (B) at
   (C) on
   (D) in

5. The local government should use the --------- cash to help people who really need it.
   (A) rechargeable
   (B) surplus
   (C) opportune
   (D) lasting

6. If you encounter any problems, please -------- all relevant information to one of our representatives.
   (A) forwards
   (B) forwarding
   (C) forward
   (D) forwarded

7. New -------- are being developed to make the assembly line operate more efficiently.
   (A) techniques
   (B) responses
   (C) combinations
   (D) goals

8. The hotel is -------- entirely booked for the weekend, but several rooms are on hold for wedding guests at $295 a night.
   (A) well
   (B) soon
   (C) ever
   (D) already

9. Savings banks throughout the country have begun to recover from the recent -------- downturn.
   (A) economic
   (B) economical
   (C) economically
   (D) economy

10. Shining your shoes on a regular basis is a process that you should perform in order to --------- the life of your shoes.
    (A) survive
    (B) endure
    (C) prolong
    (D) enlarge

11. The travel agent told us that the flight from Detroit to Houston would take ------- five hours.

    (A) primarily
    (B) originally
    (C) approximately
    (D) frequently

12. --------- the local sales representatives are still accepting the order, the production of the item will end in the near future.

    (A) Although
    (B) Until
    (C) Despite
    (D) During

13. The most important criteria for this position are emotional maturity and the ability -------- with troubled businessmen.

    (A) consult
    (B) consulting
    (C) consulted
    (D) to consult

14. If there are ------- in the office, they must be protected by placing them in the safe.

    (A) value
    (B) valued
    (C) valuable
    (D) valuables

15. The local electric company, along with several -------- energy providers, is lowering rates in response to consumer action.

    (A) another
    (B) other
    (C) others
    (D) the other

16. The new building is needed --------- the library's collection of books has grown so quickly in recent years.

    (A) moreover
    (B) therefore
    (C) because
    (D) however

17. We pride ourselves on -------- priced cars prepared to the highest standards with an emphasis on customer service.

    (A) virtually
    (B) gratefully
    (C) thoroughly
    (D) competitively

18. The Konak Hotel is -------- situated for all major airlines, travel agencies, international hotels, night clubs and shopping centers.

    (A) ideal
    (B) idealize
    (C) ideally
    (D) idealism

19. When you attempt to -------- the video graphic card with a new one, you will have to follow basic guidelines.

    (A) replace
    (B) remove
    (C) repair
    (D) reproduce

20. Since the ------- topics were not a priority, we decided to move them to next week's agenda.

    (A) remains
    (B) remaining
    (C) remain
    (D) remained

Questions 21 - 24 refer to the following advertisement.

FERNDALE — Renley Construction Group signed two contracts with the Ferndale Public Works Authority on Saturday. -------, the contracts are worth 20.7 million dollars. The larger of the two contracts is for rebuilding the Wilson Park Community Center from the ground up. The 25-year-old ------- is scheduled to be demolished in June. -------. The new building is expected be finished in slightly less than a year. Additionally, the construction firm will build a road ------- increased traffic from the new Shine Corporate Center.

21. (A) At last
    (B) Individually
    (C) All told
    (D) Instead

22. (A) facility
    (B) agreement
    (C) hotel
    (D) catalogue

23. (A) Ferndale has three new community centers.
    (B) Construction will begin immediately afterwards.
    (C) Renley has worked in Ferndale for two decades.
    (D) The other contract is for building new playgrounds.

24. (A) to accommodate
    (B) will accommodate
    (C) for accommodation
    (D) that accommodated

Questions 25 - 28 refer to the following letter.

Dear Mr. Amir,

Thank you for trusting Ronson Tech to _____ the technology needs of your company. Please find attached our proposal for a computer system that will help you meet your business goals. You may notice that we _____ more powerful computers than you requested. It is our professional opinion that the video editing work you plan on doing will require computers with the _____ indicated in the attachment. We would be happy to go over these suggestions in more detail, if you would like. _____. If you decide that you are not interested in making any purchases at this time, please send $199.99 to the address on this envelope to pay for the consultation.

Regards,

Wes Chamberlain
Ronson Tech Customer Consultant

25. (A) assess
    (B) decrease
    (C) broadcast
    (D) ingrain

26. (A) recommended
    (B) to recommend
    (C) recommending
    (D) will recommend

27. (A) specifies
    (B) specifying
    (C) specifically
    (D) specifications

28. (A) A consultation is a free service for Ronson Tech customers.
    (B) A Ronson Tech engineer will repair your computers on Friday.
    (C) The Ronson Tech warranty will expire at the end of the year.
    (D) Thank you for completing your payment to Ronson Tech.

PART 7

Unit 13	편지 / 이메일 / 광고
Unit 14	문자 메시지 및 온라인 채팅 / 기사 / 정보문 / 회람
Unit 15	이중지문 / 삼중지문

UNIT 13 편지 / 이메일 / 광고

★ 콕콕 찍어주는 출제 포인트
TOEIC은 기본적으로 비즈니스와 일상생활을 기반으로 만든 내용이므로 편지, 이메일, 광고 지문은 파트 7에서 가장 빈번하게 출제되는 독해 유형이다.

1 편지

1 편지의 질문 유형

| 발신인을 묻는 유형 | Who is writing the letter? 누가 편지를 쓰고 있는가?
Which organization sent the letter? 어떤 단체가 편지를 썼는가? |

→ 글의 상단이나 마지막에 발신인에 대한 정보(이름, 직책, 주소 등)가 나와 있다.

| 수신인을 묻는 유형 | For whom is the letter intended? 이 편지는 누구를 위한 것인가?
Who received this letter? 누가 이 편지를 받았는가? |

→ 편지 상단 발신인 정보 바로 밑에서 수신인 정보를 찾을 수 있다.

| 주제와 목적 | What is the purpose of the letter? 편지의 목적은 무엇인가?
Why was this letter written? 편지는 왜 쓰였는가? |

→ 편지의 목적은 주로 앞부분에 위치하는 경우가 많다. 특히 I'm writing to부정사 구문을 유심히 봐야 한다.

| 동봉물을 묻는 유형 | What is included[enclosed] with the letter? 편지와 함께 포함[동봉]된 것은?
What is attached to the letter? 무엇이 편지에 첨부되었는가? |

→ included/enclosed/attached/sent with라는 표현을 찾으면 무엇이 동봉되었는지 쉽게 알 수 있다.

2 가장 전형적인 편지 지문

2525 17th Ave.
Spring Hope, Virginia, 85455 ──▶ **발신인 이름과 주소**
여기서처럼 좌측에 위치하기도 하지만 중앙이나 우측 모두 가능하다.

Tuesday, July 12, 2016 ──▶ **서신의 작성 일자**
생략하거나 편지 가장 상단에 위치하는 경우도 종종 있다.

Nikki King
Erickson Publishing
1399 Moss Road ──▶ **수신인 이름과 주소**
Spring Hope, Virginia 208875

Dear Ms. King,

We are sorry to inform you that your request for a Masters Card with the Bank of Virginia is denied. We have reviewed your credit record and found inconsistency in your payments regarding your mortgage. We have thoroughly discussed your matter and have decided to do so. If you have any questions, please call me at above number at any time. ──▶ **편지 본문**

Sincerely,
Margaret Mayor ──▶ **발신인 서명**
Margaret Mayor

2525 17번가
스프링 호프, 버지니아 85455
2016년 7월 12일 화요일

니키 킹
에릭슨 출판사
1399 모스 가
스프링 호프, 버지니아 208875

친애하는 킹 씨
우리는 버지니아 은행에 당신의 마스터스 카드에 대한 신청이 거부되었음을 알려드리게 되어서 유감입니다. 우리는 당신의 신용 기록을 검토했고 당신의 융자에 관한 납부에 있어서 오류를 발견했습니다. 우리는 당신의 문제를 철저히 논의했고 그렇게 하기로(거부하기로) 결정했습니다. 어떠한 질문이라도 있으면 상기의 번호로 언제든지 연락주십시오.

마가렛 메이어

어휘   inform 알리다, 통보하다   inconsistency 오류, 불일치   regarding ~에 관해서   mortgage 융자   thoroughly 철저히

Check-up

해설 p. 166

다음 지문을 읽고 아래 질문에 우리말로 답하세요.

September 23

Evangeline Mehta
The Carmichael Arts Center
76 Wellington Avenue
Chicago, Illinois 60657

Dear Ms. Mehta,

My name is Tim Goslan and I am the music director of the Chicago Philharmonic. Every October, we hold a special performance to raise money to support the orchestra. Davis Hall, our regular venue, will be closed for renovations this October. Therefore, we are currently searching for an alternative venue to host the event. If you are interested, please contact me at (773) 975-0097. Thank you for your consideration and I look forward to hearing from you.

Sincerely,
Tim Goslan

1. Who is Mr. Goslan? _____
2. What is mentioned about Davis Hall? _____

2 이메일

1 이메일의 질문 유형

편지와 다르게 이메일에서는 발신인과 수신인이 명확하게 표시되고, 제목까지 붙어 있으므로 발신인과 수신인을 물어보는 것보다는 글의 내용을 파악해서 세부 내용을 물어보는 경우가 많다.

| 주제와 목적 | What is the purpose of the e-mail? 이메일의 목적은 무엇인가?
Why was the e-mail written? 왜 이 이메일이 쓰였는가?
Why did Teresa write this e-mail? 왜 테레사는 이메일을 썼는가? |

→ 편지와 달리 글의 제목을 나타내는 Subject 또는 Re에서 찾을 수도 있고, 편지와 같이 글의 앞부분에서 주로 찾을 수 있다.

| 인물이나 회사 | What kind of company is Global Corporation? 글로벌 사는 어떤 회사인가?
What did Grover do at the company? 그로버는 회사에서 무엇을 했는가?
Who is Angela Rathburn? 앤젤라 래쓰번은 누구인가? |

→ 질문에 나온 인물 이름을 본문에서 찾아서 그 앞뒤를 해석해서 풀어야 한다.

| 시간이나 날짜 | When will the event be held? 행사는 언제 열리는가?
When will the Internet service be unavailable? 언제 인터넷을 이용할 수 없는가?
What will happen on July 4th? 7월 4일에 무슨 일이 일어나는가? |

→ 본문에 제시된 시간이나 날짜 부분을 해석해서 풀어야 한다.

2 가장 전형적인 이메일 지문

From: Fontana Publications, Customer Service (fontana@mail.com) — 발신인
To: Gretchen Lopez (glopez@mail.com) — 수신인
Subject: Confirmation — 주제
Date: February 17, 3:23 P.M. — 날짜
Attachment: cards (xf.7714.docs) — 첨부

이메일의 필수 요소는 아님. 이외에도 부가적인 요소로서 CC(참조=carbon copy)가 있다.

Thank you for renewing your subscription to *World of Cars* magazine (confirmation #6776G) this morning. The first issue was mailed out today. To show our appreciation for your continued business, we have attached some printable greeting cards that you can use to celebrate special occasions such as friends' birthdays. We hope you will always be happy with our publication.

Regards,
The Customer Service Team — 발신인 정보

(이메일 본문)

발신: 폰타나 출판 고객서비스 담당
수신: 그레첸 로페즈 (glopez@mail.com)
제목: 확인
날짜: 2월 17일 오후 3시 23분
첨부: 카드 (xf.7714.docs)

〈자동차 세계〉 잡지에 대한 당신의 구독을 오늘 아침에 갱신해주셔서 감사합니다. (확인 번호 6776G) 첫 번째 호가 오늘 발송되었습니다. 계속되는 거래에 대한 감사를 표현하기 위해서 우리는 당신이 친구의 생일과 같은 특별한 날을 축하하는 데 사용할 수 있는 인쇄 가능한 축하 인사 카드를 첨부했습니다. 저희 잡지에 대해서 항상 만족하시길 바랍니다.

고객서비스 팀 배상

어휘 renew ~를 갱신하다   subscription 구독   confirmation 확인   issue 판, 호   be mailed out 발송되다
appreciation 감사   continued business 계속되는 거래   attach ~를 첨부하다   printable 인쇄할 수 있는
greeting cards 인사장   celebrate ~를 기념하다   special occasion 특별한 일[날]   such as ~와 같은
publication 잡지

Check-up

해설 p.166-167

다음 지문을 읽고 아래 질문에 우리말로 답하세요.

To: Karen@musictian.co.org
From: Rachel_Green@hillcomputer.co.uk
CC: Maclim@hillcomputer.co.uk
Date: 17 June
Subject: Special Promotion

Dear Customers:

Hillcomputer is offering a special promotion on our X-1000 optical mouse - 20% off for customers who order 10 or more before June 20. With the highly sensitive 1000DPI function, the X-1000 is ideal for both desktop users and laptop owners. For more information, please call us at 330-9999. Thank you.

Best regards,
Rachel Green
Customer Service Representative

1. What is the subject of the e-mail?
2. Who is Rachel Green?

UNIT 13 **305**

3 광고

1 광고의 질문 유형

일반 광고는 보통 상품의 특징 및 광고 대상이 앞부분에 나오고, 구체적 설명, 혜택, 예외 사항 등은 나중에 나오는 편이다.

| 광고의 목적 | What is being advertised? 무엇이 광고되고 있는가?
What is the purpose of the advertisement? 광고의 목적은 무엇인가? |

→ 제목이 있을 경우 제목에서 단서를 찾을 수 있으며, 제품의 특징을 설명한 부분을 읽으면 쉽게 파악할 수 있다.

| 혜택 제공 | Why is the chair on sale? 왜 의자가 할인되는가?
Why have prices been reduced? 왜 가격이 할인되었는가?
Why are they offering a free bag? 왜 무료로 가방을 제공하는가? |

→ 광고 지문 초반에 단서가 제시된다. 보통 사업 개업이나 판매량 돌파, 고객 성원에 대한 감사 등의 내용이 제시된다.

| 광고의 대상 | For whom is this advertisement intended? 이 광고는 누구를 위한 것인가?
Who would be interested in the advertisement? 누가 이 광고에 관심을 갖겠는가? |

→ 제품의 소개와 더불어 주로 지문 초반에 대상에 대한 언급을 하는 경우가 많다.

| 상품의 특징 | What feature is NOT mentioned in the advertisement? 이 광고에서 언급되지 않은 특징은?
What is an advertised feature of the product? 광고되고 있는 제품의 특징은 무엇인가? |

→ 초반에 상품 소개가 나온 후에 보통 중간 부분에 특징을 열거하는 경우가 많다.

2 가장 전형적인 광고 지문

Posted April 5 ── 광고를 게재한 날짜 종종 없는 경우도 있다.

APARTMENTS FOR RENT ── 제목 무엇을 광고하는지 압축적으로 보여준다.

We are proud to announce the grand opening of two apartments. ── 본문 첫 번째 문장
광고 품목을 알려준다.

Harwood Apartment
Fully renovated two-bedroom apartments. Conveniently located and cable TV available. Prices start at $650 a month. ── 첫 번째 광고 품목

Victoria Garden
Brand-new one-bedroom, one-bathroom apartments. Perfectly situated in the downtown. ── 두 번째 광고 품목

Interested?
Please visit www.franlinrealty.com for more information or call us at 818-555-2837. ── 광고 대상이 취할 행동 안내

4월 5일 게재

임대 아파트

우리는 두 개의 아파트의 개장을 발표하게 되어 자랑스럽습니다.

하우드 아파트
완전히 보수된 침실 두 개짜리 아파트. 편리한 위치에 있으며 케이블 TV도 이용가능함. 가격은 월 650달러에서 시작합니다.

빅토리아 가든
완전히 새로운 침실 한 개, 욕실 한 개가 구비된 아파트. 시내에 있는 더할 나위 없이 좋은 위치

관심 있나요?
더 많은 정보를 원하신다면 우리의 www.franlinrealty.com을 방문하거나 818-555-2837로 전화 주십시오.

어휘 posted 게재되다   for rent 임대를 위한   be proud to부정사 ~해서 자랑스럽다   announce 발표하다
grand opening 개점, 개장   fully 완전히   renovated 보수된   conveniently located 편리하게 위치된
available 이용 가능한   brand-new 완전히 새로운   perfectly situated 완벽하게 위치된   interested 관심 있는

Check-up

해설 p. 167

다음 지문을 읽고 아래 질문에 우리말로 답하세요.

South Africa Sale starting at £400

RealJet is having a sale on all flights to South Africa. Buy now, the sale lasts for only a limited time! Purchases must be made between July 1 and August 31 with departures from November 15 to January 15. Sale price excludes departures on January 1. For more information on this deal, including city guides and hotel deals, visit www.realjet.com.

1. What is being advertised? _____
2. How long does the sale last? _____

4 편지, 이메일, 광고에서 자주 나오는 표현

1 편지 빈출 표현

① 자기 소개	I'm sending this letter from ~ 나는 이 편지를 ~에서 보냅니다. I work for ~ 나는 ~에서 일합니다. On behalf of ~ ~를 대신하여
② 인사	How are you (doing)? 안녕하신지요? Best regards. 안부를 전합니다.
③ 감사	Thank you for ~ ~해서 감사합니다. We would appreciate it if ~ 만약 ~해주시면 감사하겠습니다. I am writing to thank you for ~ ~에 대해 감사드리기 위해 씁니다.

2 이메일 빈출 표현

① 목적	I'm writing to ~ 저는 ~하기 위해서 편지를 쓰고 있습니다. This is in response to ~ 이것은 ~에 답변 드리는 것입니다. In regard to your question, 귀하의 질문에 대하여
② 첨부파일 언급	Attached to this e-mail is ~ 이 이메일에 첨부된 것은 ~입니다. Included is ~ 포함된 것은 ~입니다.
③ 제안	Are you interested in ~ing? ~하는 데 관심 있으신가요? Why don't you ~? ~하는 게 어때요? Would you mind telling me ~? ~을 제게 말해주시겠어요?

3 광고 빈출 표현

① 지점이나 상품 소개	We have opened a new ~ 우리는 새로운 ~를 열었습니다. Let us ~! 우리가 ~하도록 해 주세요! We offer a full range of services. 저희는 다양한 서비스를 제공합니다.
② 상품 특징/설명	be suitable for all ages 모든 연령층에 적합합니다. In addition to basics ~ ~한 기본 사항 외에 Price ranges from A to B. 가격대는 A에서 B까지입니다.
③ 영업 시간 안내	We are open (from) A through B. 우리는 A부터 B시간까지 엽니다. Business hours 영업 시간
④ 광고 대상에게 취해야 할 행동 언급	Please bring/mention ~ ~를 가져와/언급해 주세요. Please note that ~ ~를 주의해 주세요. If you have any questions, call ~ 문의 사항이 있으면 ~에게 전화주세요.

5 패러프레이징 표현 모음

Part 7 독해 문제의 특징은 정답이 있는 지문의 어구나 문장이 정답과 같은 형태로 나오기보다는, 의미는 같으면서도 형태가 다른 표현으로 바뀌어 제시되는 경우가 많다는 점이다. 이를 패러프레이징(paraphrasing)이라고 한다.

1 시간 관련 표현 총정리

will end soon 곧 끝이 날 것이다	**will be finished in the near future** 가까운 미래에 끝이 날 것이다
hold the event annually 행사를 연례적으로 연다	**host the event once a year** 1년에 한 번 행사를 주최하다
The first Monday of each month 매달 첫째 월요일에	**every other Monday** 격주 월요일마다
quarterly 분기마다	**every three months** 3개월마다, 일 년에 4번
two day's notice 이틀 전 통지	**a short notice** 촉박한 통지

2 장소 관련 표현 총정리

is near the airport 공항 근처에 있다	**located close to the airport** 공항에 가까이 위치한
within walking distance of the hotel 호텔에서 걸어갈 수 있는 거리에	**beside the hotel** 호텔 옆에
far from downtown 도심에서 멀리 떨어진	**not close to the center of the city** 도심과 가깝지 않은
sell throughout the world 전세계적으로 팔리다	**sell internationally** 국제적으로 팔리다
domestically produced 국내에서 제작된	**locally made** 현지에서 만들어진

3 회사 관련 표현 총정리

get promoted 승진되다	**receive a promotion** 승진을 하다
managerial staff 관리, 경영 직원들	**people in positions of management** 운영진
go out of business 폐업하다	**close the door forever** 영원히 문을 닫다
established company 중견기업	**has been in business for a long time** 업계에 오랫동안 있어왔다
do a lot of work on-site 현장에서 많은 일을 하다	**visit clients often** 고객들을 자주 방문하다

UNIT 13

PART 7_ 실전연습 13

Questions 1-3 refer to the following letter.

February 2

Carrie Fenway
312 President Street
Baltimore, MD 21202

Dear Ms. Fenway,

Thank you for your information and sample request of Fair Coffee for the World. We are happy to send you a sample of Ethiopian Elite.

If you would like to join the Fair Coffee for the World Club, simply submit a request online at www.faircoffeeclub.com. You can also receive a 10 percent discount on your membership if you sign up online and enter code 8392-FEN.

Please remember that coffee farmers get a fair price with the purchase of all coffee from our club. By supporting fair trade coffees, you are supporting coffee farmers.

Sincerely,
Virginia Jackson
Customer Relations Manager
Fair Coffee for the World

---

1. What can be implied from this letter?

(A) Ms. Fenway enjoys coffee.
(B) Ms. Fenway requested information.
(C) Ms. Fenway has visited Ethiopia.
(D) Ms. Fenway recently joined a club.

2. What will Ms. Fenway receive?

(A) A coupon
(B) A gift set
(C) A free sample
(D) A free coffee mug

3. How can Ms. Fenway receive a discount?

(A) By introducing a friend
(B) By calling a phone number
(C) By returning a questionnaire
(D) By registering online

Questions 4-7 refer to the following advertisement.

LOWEST PROMOTION PRICE EVER!

For a limited time only, you can get an ElectroMart 320GB Desktop Hard Drive for $89.99. With this much storage, you can protect your entire computer, digital photos, music downloads, and videos. Plus, the hard drive is pre-formatted for an easy setup so you can just start using it.

Plus, you'll get 50 percent off the purchase of a service plan and free backup software. Hurry! Offer valid through January 14 while supplies last!

Other ElectroMart Products

External hard drives	Network storage	DVD & CD burners
Multimedia drive	Accessories	Software
Service plans	Data recovery	

Click on the above links to see what we offer!

---

4. What item is being advertised?

   (A) A DVD drive
   (B) A hard drive
   (C) A service plan
   (D) A laptop computer

5. What is the sale price?

   (A) $69.99
   (B) $79.99
   (C) $89.99
   (D) $99.99

6. When does the sale end?

   (A) In January
   (B) In February
   (C) In March
   (D) In April

7. What does ElectroMart NOT carry?

   (A) External hard drives
   (B) Data recovery
   (C) Network storage
   (D) Monitors

Questions 8-11 refer to the following e-mail.

From	henshaw@mayers.co.nz
To	stevens@mayers.co.nz
Date	August 3
Subject	Some notes on a great speech

Hi Mr. Stevens,

I want to tell you how much I enjoyed your presentation on maximizing brand recognition. — [1] —. Even though your career at Mayers, Inc., has just begun, I can already tell you will be a valuable asset to our company. You may know about the Mayers, Inc., Strong Chain program, in which senior employees are asked to give guidance to newer ones in the same department. To follow through on this initiative, I'd like to offer some simple tips that could make your future talks even stronger.

First, consider the pacing of your lecture. Our break was given near the end of the presentation, when about 15 minutes remained. If you move the break to the middle of the presentation, it will help the audience refresh so they can focus better for more of the lecture. — [2] —. It was clear that a portion of the audience struggled to pay attention toward the end of the talk. I've found that many audiences have difficulty in staying focused on lectures for more than 30 minutes – no matter how dynamic the presenter is. To keep the listeners engaged, try peppering your presentation with opportunities for audience interaction. For some ideas, I can point you to a useful video you can access on the Internet. You can watch it by clicking here. — [3] —. It is a helpful tutorial on how to make memorable slideshows that engage the audience. Even though your slide presentation was excellent, following the tutorial's advice will make your next one even more engaging.

These suggestions should help you deliver even better presentations in the future. Again, I want to thank you for the lecture you gave. Even though I've been in the wholesale industry for over two decades, I learned a lot from you. Should you have any questions about my feedback, don't hesitate to stop by my office for a chat. — [4] —. My door is always open.

Warm regards,
Sheila Henshaw, Distribution Manager
Mayers, Inc.

8. What is implied about Mr. Stevens?
   (A) He is Ms. Henshaw's supervisor.
   (B) He will not give any more presentations.
   (C) He is a longtime employee at Mayers, Inc.
   (D) He works in the area of wholesale.

9. What does Ms. Henshaw indicate about the presentation?
   (A) It was recorded and uploaded to the Internet.
   (B) Some audience members could not focus on it.
   (C) There was a technical malfunction during the talk.
   (D) She already knew the material that was presented.

10. What does Ms. Henshaw NOT suggest to improve presentations?
    (A) Increasing audience participation
    (B) Taking a break at a different time
    (C) Researching a topic more thoroughly
    (D) Making visual aids more interesting

11. In which of the positions marked [1], [2], [3], and [4] does the following sentence best belong?

    "I especially liked the personal story you told about viral marketing."

    (A) [1]
    (B) [2]
    (C) [3]
    (D) [4]

UNIT 14 문자메시지 및 온라인채팅 / 기사 / 정보문 / 회람

★ **콕콕 찍어주는 출제 포인트**

토익 독해에서 편지, 이메일, 광고 다음으로 많이 나오는 지문의 유형은 기사, 정보문, 회람 순이다. 이들의 특징은 특별하게 정형화된 형식이 따로 없다는 점과 일반적으로 핵심내용을 첫머리에 꺼내놓는 두괄식 구성이 많다는 점이다. 신토익에 새로 등장한 문자메시지와 온라인채팅에서는 의도 파악 문제가 반드시 출제되니, 앞뒤 문맥을 잘 파악하도록 한다.

1 문자메시지 및 온라인채팅

1 문자 메시지 및 온라인채팅의 질문 유형

문자메시지 및 온라인채팅은 신토익에서 처음 도입된 신유형 지문이다. 기존 토익과 같은 일반적인 문제와 더불어 구어체 표현의 대화 속에서 의도를 파악하는 문제가 나온다. 실제 원어민들이 일상 생활에서 많이 사용하는 표현을 알아두면 좋다.

| 장소와 상황 | For what type of company does Ms. Lo most likely work? 로우 씨는 어떤 종류의 회사를 위해 일을 하는가?
Where does Ms. Hovespian work? 호베스피안 씨는 어디에서 일하는가? |

→ 문자메시지 및 온라인채팅에서는 다른 독해지문과 달리 주제와 목적을 직접적으로 물어보지 않고 장소와 상황이 무엇인지 물어봄으로써 수험생의 주제 목적에 대한 이해를 판단한다.

| 의도 파악 | What does Ms. Park most likely mean when she writes "Okay, got it"? 박 씨가 "응 알았어."라고 쓸 때 의미하는 것은?
What does Ms. Davis most likely mean when she writes "I'm in"? 데이비스 씨가 "나도 합류할게."라고 쓸 때 의미하는 것은? |

→ 이런 말이 쓰인 앞뒤 문맥을 통해 말하고자 하는 의도를 파악하는 문제이다. 여러 사람이 등장하는 경우에는 사람들의 관계에도 주의하도록 한다.

| 세부정보 추론 | What is indicated about the presentation? 발표에 대해서 알 수 있는 것은?
What is suggested about Mr. Cooke? 쿡 씨에 대해서 알 수 있는 것은? |

→ 전체 대화 속에 그 키워드가 되는 명사(the presentation, Mr. Cooke)를 먼저 찾고 그 앞뒤의 흐름을 파악해서 추론하는 유형이다. 사람에 대한 추론문제의 경우 때로는 대화 전체를 읽어봐야 정답이 나오기도 한다.

| 향후 예측 | What will Ms. Wilson most likely tell Mr. Tran? 윌슨 씨는 트랜 씨에게 뭐라고 말할 것 같은가?
What does Mr. Takahashi indicate he will do? 타카하시 씨는 그가 무엇을 할 것이라고 암시하는가? |

→ 문자메시지 및 온라인채팅에서 가장 쉬운 유형의 질문이며, 대부분 지문의 마지막 부분에 키워드가 있고 질문 번호도 마지막 부분에 배치되는 편이다. 본문의 흐름파악만 된다면 쉬운 유형이지만 보통 수험생들이 틀리는 이유는 본문의 흐름파악보다 보기 문장들을 정확히 해석하지 않아서이다. 따라서 보기의 문장들을 확실히 해석하는 습관이 중요하다.

2 전형적인 문자메시지 및 온라인채팅 지문

David Goh — 제목: 제목 없이 곧바로 첫 번째 대화로 시작한다.   11:32 A.M. — 시간 표시: 분 단위로 시간이 표시된다.
Jennifer, where are you now?

Jennifer Morris   11:40 A.M. — 대화 인원: 문자메시지는 두 사람의 대화로 이루어지며, 온라인채팅은 최소한 세 명이 등장한다.
Mr. Goh. I'm in New York at the moment.

David Goh   11:42 A.M.
Oh, to meet with the clients from London, right?

Jennifer Morris   11:43 A.M.
Yes, how can I help you?

David Goh   11:57 A.M.
AL Service called this morning and said they will deliver our order that you should sign when we receive.

Jennifer Morris   11:58 A.M.
Oh, is it being delivered today?
I will call the warehouse department and <u>let them take care of it</u>. — 의도 파악 문제: 대화 중에서 어떤 의미로 하는 말인지 묻는 문제가 출제된다.

데이빗 고   11: 32 A.M.
제니퍼, 지금 어딨어요?

제니퍼 모리스   11: 40 A.M.
미스터 고, 저는 지금 뉴욕에 있습니다.

데이빗 고   11: 42 A.M.
오, 런던에서 오는 고객들을 만나기 위해서군요, 맞죠?

제니퍼 모리스   11: 43 A.M.
네, 무엇을 도와드릴까요?

데이빗 고   11: 57 A.M.
에이엘 서비스가 오늘 아침 전화해서 우리의 주문품을 오늘 배송하겠다고 하는데 우리가 받을 때 당신이 서명해야 한답니다.

제니퍼 모리스   11: 58 A.M.
아, 오늘 온다고 했나요? 제가 창고부에 연락해서 그들에게 그 일을 처리하라고 하겠습니다.

어휘   at the moment 지금 이 순간   clients 고객들   deliver 배송하다   warehouse department 물류부서
let + 명사 + 동사원형 ~가 ~하도록 하다   take care of ~를 돌보다, (일을) 처리하다

Check-up 1

다음 지문을 읽고 아래 질문에 우리말로 답하세요.

Joy Walker   11:12 A.M.
Hawk, I am wondering about the changes you asked for. I mean… the floor plan of the shopping center.

Hawk Lee   11:14 A.M.
Certainly. What's up?

Joy Walker   11:15 A.M.
Would I email you the whole thing or only page 5 with some revisions?

Hawk Lee   11:16 A.M.
I prefer a paper. I don't have my laptop with me.

Joy Walker   11:17 A.M.
Then, I think it takes a while.

Hawk Lee   11:18 A.M.
Why wait? Could you fax it to me?

Joy Walker   11:24 A.M.
Sure, no problem.

1. Who most likely is Mr. Walker? _____
2. At 11:18 A.M., what does Mr. Hawk most likely mean when he writes, "Why wait"?
   _____

Check-up 2

다음 지문을 읽고 아래 질문에 우리말로 답하세요.

Elsa Rocamora [02:12 P.M.]		Can anyone have some time to help me get ready for tomorrow?
Mai Chung [02:13 P.M.]		Are you talking about the clients from YBN company?
Elsa Rocamora [02:13 P.M.]		Yes, that's right.
Michael Riley [02:15 P.M.]		I have to finish a budget report this morning because it's due at noon, but I'm free anytime this afternoon. What do you need?
Elsa Rocamora [02:15 P.M.]		The conference room needs to be prepared. We'll need a projection screen, a projector, a laptop, and the portable sound system. Because the items have to be checked out from your department, Michael, do you think you can be in charge of that?
Michael Riley [02:16 P.M.]		Sure. I'll take care of it.

1. What is Ms. Rocamora preparing for? _____
2. At 02:16 P.M., what does Michael mean when he writes, "I'll take care of it"?
   _____

2 기사

1 기사의 질문 유형

| 주제와 목적 | What is the purpose of the article? 기사의 목적은 무엇인가?
What is this article about? 이 기사는 무엇에 관한 글인가? |

→ 일반적으로 글의 초반부에 주제나 목적에 대한 단서가 제시된다. 제목이 있는 경우 제목만으로도 풀릴 수 있는 문제가 많으니 꼭 확인하자.

| 인물 | What is stated about Ms. Wasow? 와소우 씨에 대해 무엇이 진술되는가?
Who is Jacques Cordet? 자크 코데는 누구인가?
What position does Mr. Hong hold? 홍 씨는 무슨 직책을 가지고 있나? |

→ 기사문에 등장하는 인물에 관련된 문제에서는 인물이 많이 등장해서 정보가 서로 혼동될 수 있으니 주의하도록 하자.

| 과거 사실 | What situation did Mac Publishing face ten years ago?
맥 출판사는 10년 전에 어떤 상황에 직면했었는가?
Where did Ms. Brown meet with Mr. Dickson? 브라운 씨는 어디서 딕슨 씨를 만났는가? |

→ 기사문에서 과거 사실에 대한 정보는 글의 초반부에 많이 등장한다. 일반적으로 기사문은 시간 순서대로 전개되기 때문이다.

| 세부 정보 | What is implied about the book? 이 책에 대해 암시되는 것은?
What is suggested about Belco? 벨코에 대해서 알 수 있는 것은?
What is indicated about the company? 이 회사에 대해서 알 수 있는 것은? |

→ 기사문에서 가장 수험생들이 어려워하는 문제 유형이다. 문제에서 키워드가 제시될 경우 키워드에 대한 정보를 찾아서 잘 이해해야 풀 수 있다. 키워드가 제시되지 않을 경우, 지문 전반을 꼼꼼히 읽고 이해한 다음 문제를 풀자.

2 가장 전형적인 기사 지문

Archway Starts Outsourcing ── 기사의 제목 기사의 제목 자체가 없는 경우도 있다.

Peoria, March 15 ── 지역, 날짜 기사에서 다루는 내용의 배경이 되는 지역 명칭과 날짜가 나오기도 한다.

Archway Mining Systems has announced it will outsource the machine operations at its Peoria plant. The outsourcing will begin immediately and will be completed by the end of 2017, the company said last Friday.

> 도입부
> 주로 제목을 뒷받침하는 주제에 대한 얘기를 한다.

Kevin Kocher, head of a union that represents 350 workers at the plant, said that the outsourcing could cause the loss of 100 jobs. Kevin Casey, vice president and general manager of the Peoria operations, said that the plant must reduce its cost structure.

> 세부사항이나 마무리
> 기사는 열린 결론으로 내용이 마무리되는 경우도 많다.

아치웨이 아웃소싱 시작

피오리아, 3월 15일

아치웨이 마이닝 시스템즈는 피오리아 공장의 기계 운영을 아웃소싱 할 것이라고 발표했다. 아웃소싱은 바로 시작하여 2017년 말까지 완료될 것이라고 지난 금요일 회사측은 말했다.

공장의 350명 근로자를 대표하는 노조위원장 케빈 코처 씨는 아웃소싱으로 공장의 100명의 일자리의 손실을 초래할 수 있을 것이라 말했다. 피오리아 공장의 부사장겸 총매니저인 케빈 케이시 씨는 공장은 비용구조를 반드시 줄여야 한다고 말했다.

어휘 announce ~를 발표하다   outsource ~를 아웃소싱하다, 외주를 주다   plant 공장   outsourcing 외주 작업
immediately 즉시, 바로   be completed 완료되다   union 노조   represent ~를 대표하다   cause ~를 초래하다
loss 손실   vice president 부사장   general manager 총매니저   reduce ~를 줄이다   cost structure 비용 구조

Check-up

다음 지문을 읽고 아래 질문에 우리말로 답하세요.

Washington Weather

Thursday, August 13
From Weather Center

Forecasters predicted severe thunderstorm in most of Washington City. Heavy rain is expected to begin on Friday morning and will continue throughout the weekend. Although it is unlikely that the storms will produce more than 10 centimeters of rain, some areas may experience minor flooding. The showers will end late next Monday morning, but clouds will continue until next Wednesday.

1. Where is the article from? _____
2. What did the weather forecasters predict? _____

3 정보문

1 정보문의 질문 유형

| 주제와 목적 | What is the information about? 이 정보문은 무엇에 관한 글인가?
What is the purpose of the information? 이 정보문의 목적은? |

→ 정보문은 말 그대로 정보를 제공하는 것이 목적이므로, 글의 제목이나 첫 문장에서 주제나 목적을 밝히는 경우가 많다.

| 정보의 대상 | For whom is the information intended? 이 정보는 누구를 위한 것인가?
Where would this information most likely appear? 이 정보는 어디에 나올 것 같은가?
Who would be interested in the information? 누가 이 정보에 관심을 갖겠는가? |

→ 보통 제품 설명서나 광고 지문에서 많이 등장하는 질문 유형이다. 정보문 유형으로 광고가 종종 출제된다.

| 시간과 날짜 | When will the event take place? 행사는 언제 열리는가?
When does the dinner start? 저녁식사는 언제 시작하는가?
What happened on July 2? 7월 2일에 무슨 일이 일어났는가? |

→ 시간과 날짜에 관련된 문제는 어렵지 않은 유형이다. 단, 여러 개의 시간, 날짜가 본문에 동시에 나올 경우에는 꼼꼼하게 따져봐야 한다.

| Not true형 | What is NOT stated about the bag? 가방에 대해서 진술되지 않은 것은?
What is NOT mentioned in the information? 정보에서 언급되지 않은 것은?
According to the information, what is NOT offered?
이 정보에 따르면, 무엇이 제공되지 않는가? |

→ 다른 지문에서도 종종 나오지만 정보 지문에서는 거의 꼭 나오는 유형으로 본문에서 언급된 내용과 부합되지 않은 한 가지를 가려내야 한다. 시간이 가장 많이 걸리는 문제 유형이기도 하다.

2 가장 전형적인 정보문 지문

Registration Information — 제목
글의 주제나 목적을 압축적으로 표현하여 보여주지만 없는 경우도 많다.

Thank you for your interest in the Millbourne Gaming Expo to be held at the STN conference center on the March 20 and 21. Register online between March 1 and March 16 and get a reduced registration fee.

On-site registration is available on the first day of the Expo.

도입부
제목을 뒷받침하는 주제 문장은 주로 앞쪽에 나오게 된다.

Online registration (credit card payment only)
Single: $135 Group: $ 125

세부 정보 1
숫자가 있는 부분은 문제로 나올 가능성이 크다.

On-site registration (credit card, cash or checks are accepted)
Single: $150 Group: $ 125

세부 정보 2

*Group rates are per person in groups consisting of at least four prople.

작은 별표(*)가 찍혀 있는 문장은 특이사항에 대한 설명이므로 반드시 문제화 된다.

등록 정보

3월 20일과 21일 사이에 STN 컨퍼런스 센터에서 열리게 될 밀버른 게임 박람회에 대한 여러분의 관심에 감사드립니다. 3월 1일에서 16일 사이에 인터넷으로 신청을 하시면 등록비를 할인해 드립니다.

현장 등록은 박람회 첫날에 이용 가능합니다.

인터넷 등록 (신용카드 결제만 가능)
개인 : 135달러   단체 : 125달러

현장 등록 (신용카드, 현금, 수표가 인정됩니다)
개인 : 150달러   단체 : 125달러

*단체 요금은 한 사람당 가격이며, 적어도 4명 이상이어야 합니다.

어휘 registration 등록 interest 관심 be held 열리다 register 등록하다 online 인터넷으로 reduced 감소된 fee 요금 on-site 현장의 available 이용 가능한 payment 지불, 납부 group rate 단체 요금

Check-up

다음 지문을 읽고 아래 질문에 우리말로 답하세요.

Clearex Hand Cleaner – Product Information

Clearex hand cleaner eliminates most common germs and bacteria while leaving your hands soft and smooth. It is the country's top seller.

Warnings
Clearex should only be used externally and should never be taken or used near the eyes. In case of accidental ingestion, please contact your nearest health care provider for assistance.

Directions
Place a small amount of Clearex Hand Cleaner in your hands and rub together with water. Rinse thoroughly.

Questions
For questions about Clearex Hand Cleaner, please call 777-9933 or visit www.clearex.com.

1. What is being advertised? _____
2. What does the information advise against? _____

4 회람

1 회람의 질문 유형

주제와 목적	What is the main topic of the memo? 이 회람의 주제는 무엇인가? What is the purpose of the memorandum? 이 회람의 목적은 무엇인가? What is the memorandum about? 무엇에 관한 회람인가?

→ 회람도 이메일처럼 Subject나 Re의 제목이 있다. 제목은 내용을 요약하고 있으므로 글의 주제나 목적을 찾는 데 도움이 된다.

날짜와 장소	When will the event be held? 행사는 언제 열릴 것인가? When will electric service be turned off? 언제 전기가 끊기는가? Where does Mr. Anderson work? 앤더슨 씨는 어디서 일하는가?

→ 시간이나 날짜, 장소를 물어보는 질문은 보통 두 개 이상의 정보가 제공되므로 혼동하지 않도록 한다.

요청 사항	What is Ms. Hobbs being asked to do? 홉스 씨는 무엇을 하도록 요청받았는가? What is the customer to do? 고객은 무엇을 해야 하는가? What should the employees do? 직원들은 무엇을 해야 하는가?

→ 요청 문제의 단서는 보통 후반부에 단서가 제시된다. 일반적으로 요구 사항을 언급하는 부분은 please로 시작하는 명령문으로 표현하거나 require, suggest, ask 등의 동사로 표현한다.

세부 사항	How many books have been sent? 몇 권의 책이 발송되었는가? What is NOT included in the membership? 멤버십에 포함되지 않는 것은 무엇인가? Where will the event take place? 행사는 어디서 열릴 것인가?

→ 회람에 대한 구체적인 사항에 대해 물어보는 문제는 육하원칙형이나 정오 판별형으로 출제된다. 문제에서 키워드가 제시되면 그 유사 단어가 지문에 등장하는지 찾고, 고유명사가 문제에 있으면 그 고유명사를 본문에서 찾는다.

2 가장 전형적인 회람 지문

Memorandum — 제목 Memorandum이나 Memo라고 나올수 있다.

To : All employees — 수신인
From : Kimberly Barrymore — 발신인 From을 줄여서 FR이라고 쓰기도 한다.
Date : Feb 25, 2016 — 작성 날짜 Date를 줄여서 DT라고 쓰기도 한다.
Re : March Computer Classes — 제목 Re(Regarding) 대신에 Subject, For를 쓰기도 한다.

Morris & Slater will be holding computer classes for all employees in Room 411. Beginners' classes will teach basic skills from using the Internet to basic word processing programs. Classes are Mondays and Wednesdays.

— 도입부 본문에서 알리고자 하는 주된 내용이 앞에서 언급된다.

Intermediate classes will focus on working with spreadsheets. Classes are Tuesdays and Thursdays. The deadline for registration is February 20. Class times will be from 6:30 to 8 P.M.

— 마무리 세부사항이나 어떻게 해야 하는지에 대한 안내의 내용으로 보통 마무리 된다.

회람

수신 : 모든 직원들
발신 : 킴벌리 베리모어
날짜 : 2016년 2월 25일
제목 : 3월 컴퓨터 강좌

모리스 & 슬레이터는 전 직원을 대상으로 411호에서 컴퓨터 강좌를 열 예정입니다. 초급자 과정에서는 인터넷 사용부터 워드 프로세싱 프로그램을 다루는 기본 스킬을 가르칠 예정입니다. 수업은 월요일과 수요일마다 있습니다.

중급 과정에서는 스프레드시트 작업에 포커스를 맞출 예정입니다. 수업은 화요일과 목요일마다 있습니다. 등록 마감일은 2월 20일입니다. 수업 시간은 오후 6시 30분부터 8시까지입니다.

어휘　hold (행사)를 열다　beginner 초급자　teach ~를 가르치다　basic 기본적인　from A to B A부터 B까지
intermediate 중급의　focus on ~에 집중하다　work with ~를 가지고 일하다　spreadsheet 스프레드시트, 전자계산서
deadline 마감시간　registration 등록

Check-up

다음 지문을 읽고 아래 질문에 우리말로 답하세요.

INTEROFFICE MEMO

To: All employees
From: Yuho Lim, Manager, Maintenance Department
Subject: Unused equipment

We know that many of you have unused computer and electronic equipment that you would like to move out of your work spaces. So, starting on July 1, we will collect the equipment that you want to dispose of. Please contact Paul Dickson of the Maintenance Department at extension 4338 by the end of this week to schedule a pick-up.

Thank you for your cooperation.

1. What is the memo about? _____
2. When will they start to collect unused equipment? _____

5 문자 메시지 및 온라인 채팅, 기사, 정보문, 회람에서 자주 나오는 표현

1 문자 메시지 및 온라인 채팅 빈출표현

① 도움 요청	appreciate it if you can help ~ 도와주실 수 있으면 감사하겠습니다 Is there anyone able to help ~? 누군가 도와줄 수 있는 사람 있나요?
② 우려 표명	I'm worried that ~ 나는 ~에 대해서 걱정합니다 I'm concerned about ~ 나는 ~에 대해서 우려합니다
③ 구어체 표현	Give me a minute. 잠깐만 기다려주세요. I've got to ~ ~해야 한다

2 기사 빈출 표현

① 계획	be planning to ~할 계획이다	be expected to ~할 것으로 예상되다
② 내용 전달	It is reported that ~ ~라고 보고되다	Recent research shows ~ 최근 조사는 ~을 보여준다.
③ 인용	saying that ~ ~라고 말하면서	according to ~ ~에 따르면

3 정보문 빈출 표현

① 소개	We would like to introduce ~ 우리는 ~를 소개하고 싶습니다. in celebration of ~ ~을 기념하여
② 위치 안내	located in/near ~ ~에/근처에 위치된 The meeting will be held at ~ 회의는 ~에서 개최될 것입니다.
③ 주의	Please note that ~ ~를 주의해주세요. Please follow ~ ~를 따라주십시오.

4 회람 빈출 표현

① 행사 안내	We are pleased to announce ~ ~을 발표하게 되어 기쁩니다. ~ will be held ~가 열릴 것이다 ~ will take place ~가 열릴 것이다, 있을 것이다
② 공지사항 안내	This is a reminder ~ 이것은 공지사항입니다. You are reminded ~ ~을 알아두십시오.
③ 연락 안내	If you have any questions, please ~ 만약 어떠한 질문 있으시면 ~해주세요. I can be reached ~ 나는 ~로 연락 받을 수 있습니다.

6 패러프레이징 표현 모음

파트 7에서는 패러프레이징을 통해 같은 의미를 다양한 표현으로 나타낸다. 다음 표현들을 익혀 두면 독해 속도가 빨라질 수 있다.

1 요금, 가격 표현 총정리

We offer a special price. 우리는 특별가를 제공합니다.	**You can get a discount.** 당신은 할인을 받을 수 있습니다.
Rates will increase. 요금이 올라갈 것이다.	**have to raise the price** 가격을 올려야 한다
at a fixed rate 고정가로	**price will not change** 가격은 변동 없을 겁니다
reasonably priced 적당하게 가격이 매겨진, 적당한 가격의	**The product is affordable.** 그 제품은 가격이 적당하다.
give a competitive salary 경쟁력 있는 급여를 제공하다	**You will receive a high salary.** 당신은 높은 봉급을 받을 것입니다.

2 구인, 구직 관련 표현 총정리

although your qualifications are impressive 비록 당신의 자격은 인상적이지만	**despite your excellent credentials** 당신의 훌륭한 자격에도 불구하고
We are seeking ~ 우리는 ~를 구하고 있습니다.	**Help wanted** 구인
Your responsibilities include ~ 당신의 책임은 ~를 포함합니다.	**Job description** 업무 내용[설명]
We have an immediate opening. 우리는 즉시 사람이 필요한 공석이 있습니다.	**The position has to be filled immediately.** 이 직책은 즉시 충원해야 합니다.
You will report to ~ 당신은 ~에게 보고할 것입니다.	**You will work under ~** 당신은 ~밑에서 일하게 될 것입니다.

3 호텔 관련 표현 총정리

Rooms are available. 빈 방 있습니다.	**You can reserve the room.** 당신은 방을 예약할 수 있습니다.
make a reservation two months in advance 두 달 전에 미리 예약을 하다	**book the room two months ahead** 두 달 앞서서 방을 예약하다
There is a cancellation fee. 취소 비용이 있습니다.	**will be charged for cancellation** 취소 비용이 부과될 것이다
Room service is available. 룸서비스가 이용 가능합니다.	**You can order a meal from the room.** 당신은 방에서 식사를 주문할 수 있습니다.
complimentary breakfast 무료 아침 식사	**offer a free meal in the morning** 무료 아침 식사를 제공하다

Questions 1-2 refer to the following text message chain.

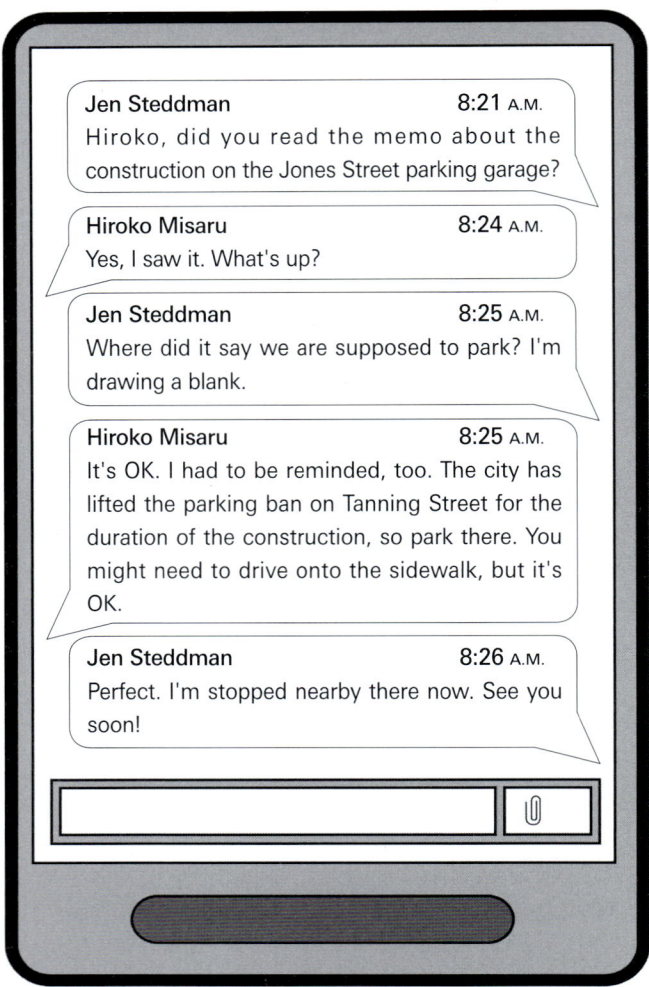

1. At 8:24 A.M., what does Ms. Misaru mean when she writes, "I saw it"?

   (A) She read a memo.
   (B) She found a missing item.
   (C) She did not receive a message.
   (D) She watched a television program.

2. Where most likely will Ms. Steddman park?

   (A) In a parking garage
   (B) On Jones Street
   (C) On Tanning Street
   (D) In an office parking lot

Questions 3-5 refer to the following information.

Convenience Air Flight Information

Ticketless Flight
Convenience Air does not issue paper tickets. Once you receive an e-mail confirmation after booking online, you do not need to contact us before flying.

Check-in Information
Convenience Air check-in counters will be open two hours before your flight's scheduled departure and will close 40 minutes before the flight is scheduled to leave. In order to check in, you need to present the confirmation details, passport and another piece of identification such as a driver's license.

Luggage Policy
Convenience Air allows passengers to fly with one free carry-on bag weighing up to 20 pounds. Larger bags and other check-in luggage are subject to additional fees.

3. What is true about the airline?
   (A) It makes only domestic flights.
   (B) It allows two free carry-on bags.
   (C) Boarding begins 1 hour before take-off.
   (D) Its ticket counters open two hours before a flight.

4. What is NOT needed to check in?
   (A) A passport
   (B) A flight ticket
   (C) A confirmation number
   (D) An identification card

5. What is the maximum weight for a carry-on bag?
   (A) 20 pounds
   (B) 30 pounds
   (C) 40 pounds
   (D) 50 pounds

Questions 6-8 refer to the following article.

A sheep's fur is soft, very warm, and especially attractive when made into a beautiful sweater. It is not always easy to take care of wool garments, though, and the tiny instructions printed on labels are not always clear. Follow these directions to keep your wool sweaters clean and looking good.

It is important to remember that wool is very sensitive to heat. — [1] —. This means it should never be washed with warm water, and certainly never put in a dryer. In fact, besides having a professional dry clean wool sweaters, the only way to clean them is to gently handwash them. — [2] —. Luckily, it's pretty simple to do that. First, put two tablespoons of a fabric detergent in a tub of room temperature water. Turn the garment inside out and swish it around the tub for a few minutes. — [3] —. Take the sweater out of the tub to dry it.

Wool stretches easily, so never wring out water or hang wool articles of clothing. — [4] —. Instead, take a dry towel, lay it flat, and then lay the wet sweater on top of it. Let it airdry for one or two nights. That's it! If you have a lot of cotton clothing in your wardrobe, make sure to read next month's issue to see our tips for dealing with those types of sweaters.

6. According to the article, what should wool sweaters be protected from?

    (A) Heat
    (B) Water
    (C) Dry cleaning
    (D) Insects

7. What does the article imply about wool sweaters?

    (A) They sometimes require a full day to dry.
    (B) They are easier to care for than cotton sweaters.
    (C) They are well suited for warm weather.
    (D) They must be cleaned professionally.

8. In which of the positions marked [1], [2], [3], and [4] does the following sentence best belong?

    "Doing so could easily ruin them."

    (A) [1]
    (B) [2]
    (C) [3]
    (D) [4]

Questions 9-12 refer to the following online chat discussion.

Sipho Ekene [3:13 P.M.]	Hi Ms. Asha. The accountants need some odds and ends, so I'm running to the store in a little bit. Does your department need anything?
Yewande Asha [3:14 P.M.]	Oh, thanks for asking. Do you know the brand of printer toner we use? Our machine's low ink warning light has been on for two days now.
Sipho Ekene [3:14 P.M.]	I'm sorry, I don't know. Let me check with the IT Support Department.
	Ian Juan has been added to the conversation
Sipho Ekene [3:17 P.M.]	Hey Ian, quick question for you. The Marketing Department needs replacement toner for their printer. What kind should I buy?
Ian Juan [3:18 P.M.]	The big poster printing machine? That requires special ink drums from the manufacturer. I'll have to call and place an order.
Yewande Asha [3:19 P.M.]	Sorry, Ian. The poster printer is fine. It's the smaller desk printer in my office that needs ink. It's Naoki brand, but I don't know the model number.
Ian Juan [3:20 P.M.]	Oh. All of our Naoki printers are the same. You can use any Naoki ink cartridges that start with the letters DX. Anything else I can do for you?
Yewande Asha [3:20 P.M.]	That's it. Thanks Ian.
Ian Juan [3:21 P.M.]	No problem. Bye.
	Ian Juan has left the conversation
Sipho Ekene [3:21 P.M.]	I'll head out now, then. You can send a text message to my phone if you think of anything else you need, Ms. Asha.

9. In what department does Ms. Asha most likely work?

    (A) Accounting
    (B) IT Support
    (C) Marketing
    (D) Human Resources

10. Why is Mr. Juan added to the conversation?

    (A) To order a printer
    (B) To provide information
    (C) To contact an ink seller
    (D) To authorize a purchase

11. At 3:19 P.M., why does Ms. Asha write, "Sorry, Ian"?

    (A) She broke a device.
    (B) She is making a correction.
    (C) She does not understand him.
    (D) She ordered the wrong product.

12. What most likely will Mr. Ekene do next?

    (A) Call a repairperson
    (B) Visit Mr. Juan
    (C) Send a text message
    (D) Go to a store

Questions 13-17 refer to the following memorandum.

Memorandum

From: Howard Fowler
To: Outcall Productions Employees
Re: Office Changes
Date: November 30

As always, with the coming of the new year, it is time for our office to make some changes. This time we're going to do things a little differently.

I'd like some feedback on what you would like to change about our office. Please make one reasonable suggestion on how we can adjust our working space. Everyone is required to make one anonymous suggestion.

You can find the forms on the intranet server. Simply open the file, fill it out with your suggestion, print it, and give it to Melissa. Don't forget, your name should not be added onto the file.

I'll look over the suggestions and see what I can do. To help me with this task, I will be gathering a group of you to go over the suggestions. If they are all great, then they will all be accepted.

Additionally, I'd like to share that my suggestion for improving the office is to reorganize our backup system. It's a large, but much needed task. You are also welcome to suggest how we can manage this.

Your feedback and cooperation is appreciated.

Regards,
Howard

13. What is implied in the memorandum?

    (A) The office is small.
    (B) Outcall is a new company.
    (C) Melissa is a company manager.
    (D) The office makes changes every year.

14. What is stated about the suggestion?

    (A) They should be anonymous.
    (B) They should be about company policy.
    (C) They should be given to Mr. Fowler.
    (D) They should not be corrected.

15. Who will judge the suggestions?

    (A) Mr. Fowler
    (B) Chief Executive Officer
    (C) A group of employees
    (D) The entire employees

16. What does Mr. Fowler want to do?

    (A) Hire more assistants
    (B) Move to another floor
    (C) Create a new department
    (D) Restructure a backup system

17. The word "manage" paragraph 5, line 3 is closest in meaning to

    (A) divide
    (B) exchange
    (C) distribute
    (D) handle

UNIT 15 이중지문/삼중지문

★ 콕콕 찍어주는 출제 포인트

토익 파트 7의 176번부터 200번까지는 이중지문과 삼중지문 문제이다. 이중지문이 2세트, 총 10문항이 출제되며, 삼중지문은 3세트, 총 15문항이 출제되어 삼중지문 비중이 더 높다. 이중·삼중지문은 지문 간의 연관된 요소를 파악하여 문제를 풀어야 하는 것이 관건이다.

1 이메일/편지 이중지문

인터넷의 발달과 더불어 현재 의사소통 수단으로 많이 활용되는 것은 편지보다도 이메일이다. 때문에 이중지문에서도 이메일의 전달과 이메일의 답변이 가장 많이 나오는 구성이라 할 수 있다.

Refer to the following e-mails. — 두 지문의 종류 파악
다음의 이중지문이 둘 다 이메일임을 확인할 수 있다.

From: Dylan Roberts <dylanrob@ovilmail.com> — 첫 번째 지문의 발신자와 수신자 파악
To: John Kimble <johnkimb@ovilmail.com>
Date: November 12
Subject: Lebanon Trip

Greetings Mr. Kimble,

Congratulations on your recent promotion to management. My name is Dylan Roberts, and I am taking over your old position in the Sales Department. I will be visiting your old client, Ms. Shalhoub, next Monday, but I've never been to Lebanon. I was wondering if you could answer some questions for me. — 첫 번째 지문의 목적 요청하거나 질문하는 문장 자체가 보통 편지/이메일의 목적이 된다.

Firstly, which hotel would you recommend for me while in Beirut? Secondly, what languages are most commonly spoken there? Thirdly, what is the current exchange rate for their currency? And finally, what dishes would you recommend? If you could answer some or all of these questions, I would really appreciate it. Thank you. — 첫 번째 지문의 세부 정보

Sincerely,
Dylan Roberts

From: John Kimble <johnkimb@ovilmail.com> — 두 번째 지문의 발신자와 수신자 파악
To: Dylan Roberts <dylanrob@ovilmail.com>
Date: November 12
Subject: Re: Lebanon Trip

Hello Mr. Roberts,

It's always nice to meet one's successor. Of course, I will gladly answer your questions.
I always stayed at the Grand Cypress Hotel. It's rather expensive, but the company will cover your accommodations, so stay in comfort. They officially speak Arabic and French, but English is also fairly common. I don't know the current exchange rate, but you should be able to locate that information on the Internet. I often ate Shawarma, which is a meat dish called "Arabian Taco". If you have any other questions, feel free to ask them. I'd like to meet you when you return. — 두 번째 지문의 목적

Sincerely,
John Kimble

발신: 딜런 로버츠 〈dylanrob@ovilmail.com〉
수신: 존 킴블 〈johnkimb@ovilmail.com〉
날짜: 11월 12일
제목: 레바논 여행

안부 인사 드려요, 킴블 씨.

최근 경영진으로의 승진에 대해서 축하드립니다. 제 이름은 딜런 로버츠입니다. 그리고 저는 영업부에서의 당신의 이전 직책을 맡을 것입니다. 저는 당신의 예전 고객인 샬홉 씨를 다음 월요일에 방문할 것입니다만, 저는 한 번도 레바논에 가본 적이 없습니다. 저는 당신이 몇 가지 질문에 답변해 주실 수 있는지 궁금합니다.

첫 번째로 베이루트에 있는 동안에 어떤 호텔을 추천해주시겠습니까? 두 번째로 그곳에서 가장 흔하게 사용되는 언어는 무엇인가요? 세 번째로 그들의 통화에 대한 현재의 환율은 어떤가요? 그리고 마지막으로 어떤 음식을 추천하시겠습니까? 당신이 이 중 몇 가지 또는 모든 질문에 답변해 주신다면, 정말 감사드리겠습니다. 고맙습니다.

딜런 로버츠

어휘 congratulations 축하 promotion 승진 management 경영진 take over ~를 맡다 wonder 궁금하다
exchange rate 환율 currency 통화 dish 음식 appreciate ~에 대해서 감사하다

발신: 존 킴블 〈johnkimb@ovilmail.com〉
수신: 딜런 로버츠 〈dylanrob@ovilmail.com〉
날짜: 11월 12일
제목: 답변: 레바논 여행

안녕하세요, 로버츠 씨.

후임자를 만나는 것은 항상 즐겁습니다. 물론 저는 당신의 질문에 기쁘게 답변을 드리겠습니다. 저는 항상 그랜드 싸이프레스 호텔에서 체류를 했었습니다. 그 호텔은 다소 비쌉니다만, 회사에서 당신의 숙박비용을 지불할 것입니다. 그러니 편안하게 체류하십시오. 그들은 아랍어와 프랑스어를 공식적으로 사용합니다만, 영어 또한 꽤 보편적인 편입니다. 저는 현재 환율을 알고 있지 못합니다. 그러나 당신은 인터넷에서 그 정보를 찾을 수 있을 것입니다. 저는 샤와마를 종종 먹었는데, 이는 아랍인들의 타코라 불리우는 고기 요리입니다. 어떤 다른 질문이라도 있다면 맘껏 물어보십시오. 당신이 돌아오면 만나고 싶군요.

존 킴블

어휘 successor 후임자 gladly 기쁘게 rather 약간, 다소 cover 비용을 지불하다 accommodation 숙박(업체)
in comfort 편안하게 officially 공식적으로 fairly 꽤, 상당히 common 흔한, 보편적인 locate ~를 찾다

PART 7_ 실전연습 15 이메일/편지 이중지문

Questions 1-5 refer to the following e-mails.

From: Martin Ferry (ferrymartin@frasier.com)
To: customer@harbin.com
Subject: Return Policy
Date: June 29

To Whom It May Concern:

I purchased a Smithson Wireless Mouse through your site a week ago (order#839870-28440). I just received it today, and it is not what I expected.

According to the pictures of the mouse, the connection is a small USB stick that plugs into a USB outlet. However, I received a connection that is almost the size of my regular mouse.

I didn't realize that there are two types of wireless connections that connect the computer to the mouse. I purchased this mouse for my notebook, and since the connection is the same size of my current mouse, I do not want it.

What do I need to make a return, and will I have to pay for shipping?

Thank you,
Martin Ferry

From: customer@harbin.com
To: Martin Ferry (ferrymartin@frasier.com)
Subject: Re: Return Policy
Date: June 30

Dear Mr. Ferry,

Thank you for your recent purchase. I'm sorry about the problem you have experienced, and I understand why you want to return the mouse. We can either refund money to your card in the full amount, or we can send you the mouse with the smaller connection.

In the meantime, please return the mouse. You do not have to pay for shipping, simply follow this link and print out the shipping label and attach it to the box.

www.harbin.com/returns/shipping/a8y3oi_ijhs

We apologize for any inconvenience this may have caused. Please respond to me or call 1-800-793-2849 to let us know if we should refund money or send you a new mouse.

Have a nice day.

Sincerely,

Pamela Johnson
Customer Service, Harbin Electronics

1. When did Mr. Ferry most likely make his purchase?

   (A) May 30
   (B) June 1
   (C) June 22
   (D) June 28

2. What did Mr. Ferry buy?

   (A) A mouse
   (B) A computer
   (C) A digital camera
   (D) A memory card

3. What is mentioned about Mr. Ferry?

   (A) He is a photographer.
   (B) He owns a laptop computer.
   (C) He is a small business owner.
   (D) He frequently purchases from Harbin.

4. What is the purpose of Ms. Johnson's e-mail?

   (A) To resolve Mr. Ferry's problem
   (B) To thank Mr. Ferry for his purchase
   (C) To get Mr. Ferry's credit card information
   (D) To accept Mr. Ferry's apology

5. Why would Mr. Ferry visit the given link?

   (A) To view his order
   (B) To view a similar item
   (C) To fill out information
   (D) To print a shipping label

2 광고/정보문 이중지문

첫 번째 지문에서는 광고를 비롯한 다양한 종류의 서식이 나오고, 두 번째 지문에서는 그에 대한 이메일이나 편지를 보내는 내용도 반드시 하나 이상 나오는 유형이다.

Refer to the following advertisement and e-mail. ······ 두 지문의 종류 파악
하나는 광고이고 또 하나는 이메일임을 알 수 있다.

Learn to Dance! ······ 첫 번째 지문의 제목
광고의 내용을 압축적으로 보여준다.

Gina's Dance Studio is offering new weekday classes for both children and adults.

Adults and Children :

	Tap	Jazz	Ballet
MWF	5:00	6:00	7:00
TTH	4:30	6:00	7:30

Adults :

	Ballroom	Salsa	Swing
MWF	4:00	5:00 & 6:00	7:00 & 8:00
TTH	4:30	5:30 & 6:30	7:30 & 8:30

······ 첫 번째 지문의 내용
광고의 세부 정보를 알 수 있다.

Classes will be divided according to skill level.
Adults and children will have different instructors.

For a schedule of weekend classes, visit our Web site at www.danceatginas.com or call 937-2840.

From: Shirley Rogers (shirley003@mymail.com)
To: info@danceatginas.com
Subject: Ballroom Dancing
Date: February 2

······ 두 번째 지문의 발신자와 수신자 파악

Hello,

I would like to know more about your ballroom dancing class. I used to take classes a few years ago, so I have some experience. However, I want to dance with my husband. He's never danced before and we would like to learn so that we can dance at our upcoming anniversary celebration. Can we be in the same class even though we are at different levels?

I also see that the classes are offered at two different times during the week. Will the classes be the same amount of hours per week?

······ 두 번째 지문의 목적
정보를 요청하는 문장이 편지나 이메일의 주된 목적이다.

Thank you for your help.

Sincerely,
Shirley Rogers

댄스를 배우자!

지나의 댄스 스튜디오가 어린이와 성인 모두를 위해서 새로운 평일 수업을 제공합니다.

성인/어린이 :

	탭 댄스	재즈	발레
월수금	5:00	6:00	7:00
화목	4:30	6:00	7:30

성인 :

	볼룸	살사	스윙
월수금	4:00	5:00 & 6:00	7:00 & 8:00
화목	4:00	5:30 & 6:30	7:30 & 8:30

수업은 난이도에 따라서 나누어 질 것입니다.
성인과 어린이는 각기 다른 강사들에게 지도를 받을 것입니다.

주말 수업의 일정을 원하시면, 우리의 웹사이트인 www.danceatginas.com으로 방문하시거나 937-2840으로 전화 주세요.

어휘 form ~를 구성, 형성하다   weekday class 주중 수업   both A and B A와 B 둘 다
MWF 월수금(Monday, Wednesday, and Friday의 축약형)   TTH 화목(Tuesday and Thursday의 축약형)
be divided 나누어지다   according to ~에 따르면   different 다른   instructor 강사

발신: 셜리 로져스 (shirley003@mymail.com)
수신: info@danceatginas.com
제목: 볼룸 댄스
날짜: 2월 2일

안녕하세요.

저는 당신의 볼룸 댄스 수업에 대해서 조금 더 알고 싶습니다. 저는 몇 년 전에 수업을 받았었습니다. 그래서 약간의 경험이 있습니다. 그러나 저는 제 남편과 함께 춤추고 싶거든요. 그는 이전에 한 번도 춤을 춰 본적이 없어요. 그리고 우리는 다가오는 기념일 파티에서 춤을 출 수 있도록 하기 위해서 배우고 싶습니다. 비록 우리가 다른 수준이지만 같은 클래스에 들어갈 수 있을까요?

저는 또한 주중에 두 개의 다른 수업이 제공된다는 점을 압니다. 이 수업들은 주당 수업 시간은 같은가요?

도움에 감사드립니다.

셜리 로져스

어휘 would like to부정사 ~하고 싶다   know more about ~에 대해서 더 알다   ballroom dancing 볼룸 댄스 (춤의 일종)
used to부정사 ~했었다 (지금은 아니다)   take classes 수업을 받다   however 그러나   anniversary party 기념일 파티
even though 비록 ~하지만   amount 양   per (하나) 당

PART 7_ 실전연습 15 광고/정보문 이중지문   해설 p.175-176

Questions 1-5 refer to the following information and e-mail.

The Orchid Regency Resort

	4/15 - 11/15	11/16 - 4/14
Standard single/double with breakfast	$49.99	$79.99
Full Bloom Queen* with breakfast, use of gym	$81.99	$99.99
Full Bloom King* with breakfast, use of gym	$89.99	$129.99
Full Bloom King Suite* with breakfast, use of gym and business center	$119.99	$159.99

*Extra bed available for $15 charge.

From: Roberta Olivier (r.olivier@easymail.com)
To: Indira Patel (ipatel@recordplace.com)
Subject: Hotel Options
Date: November 19

Hi Indira,

How are you today? At your request, I've been looking for hotels, and I think I found the perfect one. It overlooks a beach, has large rooms, and is much cheaper than the other places you saw earlier. The only problem is that it is rather isolated, so you would have to take a bus or taxi if you want to go into the city. You can view the hotel at www.orchidregencyresort.com.

I'm positive you will agree with this selection. It's within your $80 total per night price range. Call me tonight after you have a chance to look at the rooms. You should book soon before the hotel is fully booked for the holidays.

Roberta

1. What is included in the price of all rooms?

   (A) Breakfast
   (B) A spa day pass
   (C) Use of fitness center
   (D) Use of business center

2. How much would the suite cost on New Year's Day?

   (A) $89.99
   (B) $119.99
   (C) $129.99
   (D) $159.99

3. What is implied in the e-mail?

   (A) The hotel is on a private beach.
   (B) Indira and Roberta are old friends.
   (C) Indira requested information about hotels.
   (D) The hotel is located in a foreign country.

4. According to the e-mail, what is a disadvantage of the hotel?

   (A) Its waiting list
   (B) Its small room size
   (C) Its remote location
   (D) Its lack of a swimming pool

5. What room will most likely be chosen?

   (A) Standard Single
   (B) Full Bloom Queen
   (C) Full Bloom King
   (D) Full Bloom King Suite

3 회람/기타 이중지문

Refer to the following memo and form.

From: Matthew Everett
To: Department managers
Subject: Transportation reimbursement
Date: September 13

To encourage more energy efficiency, employees who take public transportation or carpool to and from work will be reimbursed for their travel expenses on a quarterly basis. In order to receive reimbursement, employees must file the appropriate paperwork for the following periods:

January 1 to March 31 April 1 to June 30
July 1 to September 31 October 1 to December 31

Reimbursement forms will be available in the accounting office beginning on September 25. In order to receive reimbursement, completed paperwork must be received by the accounting office no later than the 20th of the month. Please note that reimbursement will not be given for any public holidays.

Please discuss this change in policy with the employees in your department.
Thanks,
Matthew Everett

Darwin, Co. Transportation Reimbursement Form

Date: October 14
Name: Dawn Willis
Title: Resource Allocation manager
Department: Human Resources
Mode of transportation: Chopper Metropolitan Bus
Lafayette Station to Chopper Central Station
Dates of use: July 1 to September 30
Cost: $369
Additional Information: X
Signature: *Dawn Willis*

발신: 매튜 에버렛
수신: 부서장들
제목: 교통비 환급
날짜: 9월 13일

더 많은 에너지 절약을 장려하기 위해서, 직장으로 출퇴근 할 때 대중교통이나 카풀을 하는 직원들은 분기별로 교통비용에 대해서 환급을 받게될 것입니다. 환급을 받으려면 직원들은 반드시 다음의 기간 동안 적절한 서류를 제출해야 합니다.

        1월 1일부터 3월 31일까지   4월 1일부터 6월 30일까지
        7월 1일부터 9월 30일까지   10월 1일부터 12월 31일까지

환급 양식은 9월 25일부터 회계부서에서 구할 수 있을 것입니다. 환급을 받기 위해서는 작성된 서류가 반드시 해당 월 20일까지는 회계부서에 접수되어야 합니다. 모든 공휴일에는 환급이 이루어지지 않을 것이라는 점에 대해서 주의하십시오.
당신의 부서에 있는 직원들과 이러한 정책 변화에 대해서 얘기 나누시길 바랍니다.

감사합니다.
매튜 에버렛

어휘 encourage 장려하다 efficiency 효율성 take (탈 것) 타다 public transportation 대중교통
carpool 카풀, 자동차 함께 타기 be reimbursed 환급받다 travel expenses 교통비용 on a quarterly basis 분기별로
reimbursement 환급 file ~를 (서류로) 제출하다 appropriate 적절한 paperwork 서류 following 다음의
available 이용 가능한 accounting office 회계부서 completed 작성된 public holiday 공휴일 policy 정책

다윈 사 교통비 환급 양식

날짜:	10월 14일
이름:	돈 윌리스
직책:	자원 할당 부장
부서:	인사부
교통수단:	쵸퍼 메트로폴리탄 버스 (라파예트 정류장부터 쵸퍼 중앙역까지)
이용 날짜:	7월 1일부터 9월 30일까지
비용:	369 달러
추가 정보:	없음
서명:	*Dawn Willis*

PART 7_ 실전연습 15 회람/기타 이중지문

Questions 1-5 refer to the following memos.

To: Buildstruct Amercia Ltd Employees
From: Director of Human Resources
Re: Changes at the fitness center

Dear Coworkers,

We know the significance of maintaining a good exercise facility for our employees. In recent years, we have bought new exercise equipment, renovated locker rooms, and are offering a new safety-training course called "Safety First."

Just a month ago, we conducted a survey about our fitness facility. Based on your comments, we plan to make changes soon. These changes will take effect on November 22. Firstly, the fitness facility will extend its operating hours by three hours from Monday through Friday. Additionally, there will be new group exercise programs. Finally, long-term instructor Jacob Soares has been promoted to the manager of the facility.

Membership is still 30$ per month, but those who sign up before December 7 will pay 25$ per month for 6 months. For those who are interested, please contact Jacob Soares for the special offer.

To: Buildstruct Amercia Ltd Employees
From: Jacob Soares, Fitness Center
Re: Please follow the rules.

Attention:
- If other patrons are waiting, please limit equipment use to 30 minutes.
- One guest with a member is allowed for one time for free.
- Group classes are limited to 20 members so arrive early to ensure a place.
- Please leave belongings in lockers to maximize space in the classroom.
- Newcomers are required to take the "Safety First" class before using the facility.
- Please carry membership card at all times when in the facility.

1. What is the purpose of the memo?

   (A) To announce the opening of a new facility
   (B) To notify employees of the changes at the facility
   (C) To ask for recommendations to improve the facility
   (D) To address the problems about the facility

2. What can be inferred from the memo?

   (A) Jacob Soares is a new employee.
   (B) The company will build another fitness center.
   (C) Employees requested extended hours of operation.
   (D) Some employees use the facility for free.

3. What will happen from November 22?

   (A) New exercise classes will begin.
   (B) The new equipment will be shipped to the center.
   (C) Employees will attend the facility's new opening.
   (D) The fitness facility will not be in operation.

4. What is NOT asked to use this facility?

   (A) Carry membership card
   (B) Use the equipment for a limited time
   (C) Arrive early for classes
   (D) Bring belongings into classrooms

5. What must a new member do in order to use the facility?

   (A) Get a physical examination
   (B) Take the safety training course first
   (C) Fill out an application form
   (D) Come with an existing member

4 이메일/광고 삼중지문

Refer to the following advertisement and e-mails.

American Management Association
Sales Management Training Programs

Make your selling techniques work harder for you with AMA's sales training programs. AMA's sales training programs deliver practical and ready-to-use selling techniques.

Choose any one of the sales training programs below to keep your existing customer base intact as you continue to expand your client list.

1. Fundamentals of Sales Management for the Newly Appointed Sales Manager
2. Fundamental Selling Techniques for the New or Prospective Salesperson
3. Principles of Professional Selling

To: Steven Alvarez <Salvarez@mlindustries.com>
From: Melanie Davis <mdavis@mlindustries.com>
Subject: AMA
Date: July 10

Hi Steven,

I've just gotten back from the taking the course at AMA. It taught all the basics of sales in a way that was very easy to follow. In addition, the instructor was highly knowledgeable and credible. I think we should hire this company to train our staff.

Now, I realize we had originally planned to do just one course, but if I can negotiate a lower price for two, I'd like to add one more course. I spoke to the other participants and they gave positive feedback about this course. I'll update you further.

Melanie

To: Melanie Davis <mdavis@mlindustries.com>
From: Marcus Tan <mtan@AMA.com>
Date: July 23
Subject: Sales Management Training Programs

Dear Ms. Davis,

As agreed, we will hold a one-day seminar at your company's location on Wednesday, August 12. **"Fundamental Selling Techniques for the New or Prospective Salesperson"** will be held in the morning and **"Principles of Professional Selling"** in the afternoon. Please ensure that the participants are ready to begin on time. We require a deposit of 50 percent by August 1, with the balance due upon completion of the seminar.

Marcus Tan, AMA

아메리카 경영 연합
영업 관리 교육 프로그램

AMA의 영업 교육 프로그램으로 당신의 판매테크닉이 당신을 위해서 더 열심히 작동하도록 만들어 보십시오. AMA의 영업 교육 프로그램들은 실용적이고, 즉시 사용할 수 있는 판매 기술을 전달합니다.

당신의 고객 명단은 계속 확장 하면서 기존의 고객 기반을 헤치지 않도록 유지하기 위해서 하단에 영업 교육 프로그램들 중의 하나를 선택 하십시오.

1. 새롭게 지명된 영업부장을 위한 영업 관리의 근본
2. 신입 또는 미래의 영업사원들을 위한 근본적인 판매기술
3. 전문적 영업의 원리

어휘 deliver 전달하다 practical 실용적인 ready-to-use 즉시 사용할 수 있는 below 하단에 fundamental 근본
appointed 지명된 existing 기존의 intact 손상되지 않은 expand 확장하다 principle 원리

수신 : 스티븐 알바레즈 〈Salvarez@mlindustries.com〉
발신 : 멜라니 데이비스 〈mdavis@mlindustries.com〉
제목 : AMA
날짜 : 7월 10일

안녕하세요 스티븐,

저는 이제 막 AMA에서의 과정을 밟고 돌아왔습니다. 거기에서는 쉽게 따라갈 수 있는 방식으로 판매의 모든 기본기들을 가르쳐주었어요. 게다가 강사는 매우 박식했고 믿을 만 했습니다. 저는 우리 직원들 교육을 시키기 위해서 이 회사를 고용해야 한다고 생각합니다.

지금 저는 우리가 원래 딱 한 과정을 하기로 계획했었다고 깨달았는데, 만약 제가 두 개를 위해서 더 낮은 가격을 협상할 수 있다면 하나를 추가하고 싶습니다. 저는 다른 참가자들과도 얘기를 해 보았구요. 그들은 이 과정에 대해서 긍정적인 피드백을 주었습니다. 추가적으로 소식을 알려드리겠습니다.

멜라니

어휘 get back 돌아오다 take the course 과정을 밟다 in addition 게다가 instructor 강사 highly 매우
knowledgeable 박식한 credible 신뢰할 만한 train ~를 교육시키다 realize ~를 깨닫다 negotiate ~를 협상하다
add ~를 추가하다 positive feedback 긍정적인 피드백 update ~에게 (최신)소식을 알려주다 further 추가적으로

수신 : 멜라니 데이비스 〈mdavis@mlindustries.com〉
발신 : 마커스 탄 〈mtan@AMA.com〉
날짜 : 7월 23일
제목 : 영업 관리 교육 프로그램

친애하는 데이비스 씨,

동의된 대로 우리는 8월 12일 수요일에 귀하의 회사에서 1일간의 세미나를 주최할 것입니다. "**신입 또는 미래의 영업사원들을 위한 근본적인 판매기술**"이 오전에 열릴 것이고, "**전문적 영업의 원리**"가 오후에 있을 것입니다. 참가자들이 정시에 시작할 수 있도록 준비되도록 확실히 해 주십시오. 우리는 8월 1일까지 50퍼센트의 보증금을 요구하며 세미나가 종료되자마자 잔액이 납부되어야 합니다.

마커스 탄, AMA

어휘 as agreed 동의 된대로 hold ~를 주최하다 ensure ~를 확실히 하다, 보장하다 be ready to부정사 ~할 준비가 되다
on time 정시에 require ~를 요구하다 deposit 보증금 balance 잔액 due 만기가 된 upon ~하자마자
completion 완성, 완수

PART 7_ 실전연습 15 이메일/광고 삼중지문

Questions 1-5 refer to the following advertisement, review, and e-mail.

Upgrade to a Jensen X3 - Upgrade your life

The Jensen X3 is the next evolution in mobile computing. With software engineered by the brightest minds in Japan, exterior components crafted by Sweden's most elite design firm and a microprocessor built by industry pioneers in Germany, the X3 delivers the best performance and style on the planet. The 12-inch tablet computer provides a screen large enough to complete all computing tasks, but is small enough to fit easily in a backpack or briefcase. It is also remarkably light at 14 ounces, so you can hold it for hours without getting tired. All that use is sustained by a lithium ion battery that powers the device for 12 hours. And, thanks to the Crutcher Group's new ultra-durable screen, the screen is scratch-proof and can survive most drops and impacts. What really sets the X3 apart from its competitors, though, is the Jensen-branded assistant software, Best Friend. Best Friend automatically retrieves your appointments and other important scheduling information from e-mail and social media. Buy an X3 today and step into tomorrow with your new Best Friend.

The Jensen X3 is being promoted as the most incredible development in mobile computing technology in several years. Does it live up to the hype? In this humble reviewer's opinion, absolutely not.

While the tablet computer is undeniably attractive, it is simply too large to hold comfortably. The television advertisements that show a woman strolling down a grocery aisle, X3 in hand, are totally unrealistic. The only comfortable way I found to use the device was on my lap or in its docking station with an attached keyboard and mouse which essentially turns the device into a standard desktop computer. Many users have even reported dropping the tablet while trying to use it, which led to cracked screens and dead hard drives.

The one feature that lives up to all of its advertising promises is Jensen's new organization assistant. While using the X3, I was amazed at the accuracy with which the program filled in my calendar. Sadly, this one triumph is not enough to save the X3. The tablet is simply too large, too expensive, and too frustrating for it to be a smart purchase for anyone.

A silver lining to the disappointment surrounding the X3's release is Jensen's speedy and customer-friendly reaction to the numerous complaints they have received. To customers that can't comfortably use the tablet without putting it down, Jensen is giving free cases with a built-in handle. These cases, it is claimed, make the device much easier to use while walking around. For those that are too fed up with the X3 and just want to be done with it, Jensen is issuing full cash refunds.

My advice? Wait for the X4.

- Mark Hampton for *Tech Times*

```
┌─────────────────── E-Mail message ───────────────────┐
│ From:    │ hitch@broadworld.com                       │
│ To:      │ customersupport@jensen.com                 │
│ Subject: │ My X3 is being a pain …                    │
├──────────────────────────────────────────────────────┤
│ I recently purchased a Jensen X3 and I have a significant problem. I cannot use the
│ machine at my job. As a quality assurance consultant, most of my day is spent walking up
│ and down assembly lines at a production plant. I purchased the X3 to use during work,
│ but I have to find a table or some other surface to rest the X3 on each time I want to use it.
│ It is so disruptive that it essentially makes the device non-functional for me. I need to be
│ able to use the tablet while standing up, like the television commercials advertise. I do
│ like several of the X3's features, so I want to continue using it, but if you cannot propose a
│ solution I will need to return my X3 and buy a tablet from a different manufacturer.
│ Please advise.
│
│ Regards,
│
│ Stan Hitchens
└──────────────────────────────────────────────────────┘
```

1. According to the advertisement, what is mentioned about the Jensen X3?

    (A) Companies from different countries helped build it.
    (B) It is compact enough to fit in a user's pants pocket.
    (C) Word processing software is pre-installed on it.
    (D) It uses a Jensen brand social networking service.

2. What does the reviewer indicate about the Jensen X3?

    (A) The price is reasonable.
    (B) The device does not look good.
    (C) The Best Friend software works well.
    (D) The component from Crutcher Group is strong.

3. In the review, the word "hold" in paragraph 2, line 1, is closest in meaning to

    (A) reserve
    (B) carry
    (C) stop
    (D) conceal

4. Where does Mr. Hitchens work?

    (A) In a factory
    (B) In a grocery store
    (C) In an office building
    (D) In a computer store

5. What will Jensen most likely offer Mr. Hitchens?

    (A) A computer case
    (B) A replacement part
    (C) A docking station
    (D) A free consultation

5 기사/정보문 삼중지문

Refer to the following article, e-mail, and advertisement.

GLOBIZ REPORT

May 7, Hong Kong - Apex Corporation announced today that it plans to open two new branch offices, one in London and the other in Zurich, on September 15 and on December 1, respectively. Headquartered in Hong Kong, Apex already operates branch offices in Seoul, New York and Tokyo. This is in large part the work of Ronald Park, who has completely transformed the company since joining it ten years ago.

In recent weeks, there's been a lot of speculation about the company's future because Mr. Park, 68, informed his staff last March that he will be retiring at the end of the year.

To : Ronald Park <rpark@apextech.com.hk>
From : Anja Visser <avisser@apextech.com.hl>
Subject : Arrangements
Date : August 23

Dear Mr. Park,

Thank you for sending us your itinerary. I will certainly attend the opening ceremony on September 15. I would like to let you know that everything appears to be on schedule, though we're still in the process of hiring employees at all levels, and we will be placing job advertisements for the next several weeks.

Looking forward to seeing you soon.

Sincerely,
Anja Visser

Regional manager, European Division
Apex Technology Corporation

SALES OPPORTUNITY

Apex Technology Corporation is seeking an ambitious and motivated individual to fill a vacancy in our local office in London. This position requires a candidate with outstanding communication skills. Sales representatives receive competitive salaries as well as generous bonuses for big sales. Prior sales experience is a plus but not required. Qualified applicants should send their résumés to the Human Resources Manager, European Division of Apex Technology Corporation 3180 Yonge St. Suite 2120, Lodon.

글로비즈 보고서

5월 7일, 홍콩 – 에이팩스 회사는 두 개의 새로운 지점을 오픈할 계획이라고 오늘 발표했습니다. 하나는 런던이고 다른 하나는 취리히이며 날짜는 9월 15일과 12월 1일 각각입니다. 홍콩에 본사를 둔 에이팩스는 이미 서울, 뉴욕, 그리고 도쿄에 지점들을 운영하고 있습니다. 이것은 대부분 10년 전에 회사에 입사한 이래로 회사를 완전히 변신시켜온 로날드 박의 작품입니다.

최근 몇 주 동안 회사의 미래에 관한 많은 추측이 있었습니다. 68세인 박 씨가 지난 3월에 직원들에게 연말에 은퇴할 것이라고 통보했기 때문입니다.

어휘 deliver 전달하다 practical 실 announce ~를 발표하다 plan to부정사 ~할 계획이다 branch 지점 respectively 각각 headquartered in ~ ~에 본사가 있는 already 벌써, 이미 operate 운영하다 in large part 대부분 completely 완전히 transform ~를 변형, 변신시키다 since ~이래로 speculation 추측 retire 은퇴하다

수신 : 로날드 박 ⟨rpark@apextech.com.hk⟩
발신 : 안쟈 비제 ⟨avisser@apextech.com.hl⟩
제목 : 일정
날짜 : 8월 23일

친애하는 박 씨,

당신의 일정표를 보내주셔서 감사합니다. 저는 분명히 9월 15일에 있을 개점행사에 참석할 것입니다. 비록 우리는 여전히 모든 수준에서의 직원들을 채용하는 과정에 있습니다만, 저는 모든 것이 일정대로 나타나고 있음을 알려드리고 싶습니다. 우리는 다음 몇 주 동안 구인 광고를 게재할 것입니다.

당신을 곧 뵙기를 기대합니다.
안쟈 비제
에이팩스 유럽 지부장

어휘 itinerary 일정표 certainly 분명히 attend ~에 참석하다 opening ceremony 개점행사 let you know 당신에게 알려주다 appear to부정사 ~한 것으로 나타나다 be on schedule 일정대로 진행되다 though 비록 ~하지만 in the process of ~ing ~하는 과정 속에 있는 at all levels 모든 수준에서의 place (광고)를 게재하다

영업 기회

에이팩스 기술 회사는 런던에 있는 우리 지점의 공석을 채우기 위해서 야망차고 적극적인 사람을 구하고 있는 중입니다. 이 직책은 뛰어난 커뮤니케이션 기술을 가진 사람을 요구합니다. 영업직원들은 대량판매에 대한 후한 보너스뿐만 아니라 경쟁력 있는 급여를 받습니다. 이전 경력은 플러스이긴 하지만 요구되지는 않습니다. 자격 있는 지원자들은 이력서를 런던의 에이팩스 기술 회사의 유럽지점의 인사부장에게 보내주십시오.

어휘 seek ~를 찾다, 구하다 ambitious 야망 있는 motivated 적극적인 fill ~를 채우다 vacancy 공석 outstanding 뛰어난 prior 이전의 as well as ~뿐만 아니라 qualified 자격 있는 résumé 이력서

Questions 1-5 refer to the following article, e-mail, and notice.

What's Up, London?   February 3   Jen Schall

On Monday, the Faracom Group purchased the Sitwell Building on Chiswick Lane from Red Dutch Holdings. Chuck Grable, a Faracom spokesperson, believes the Sitwell Building can cater to a growing market of young professionals in surrounding neighborhoods, and businesses that want to tap into that market will be happy to rent space in the Sitwell Building. "The Sitwell building is perfectly located to attract residents from the nearby Bloomsbury neighborhood," said Mr. Grable.

The Sitwell building is currently abandoned after the closing of the Sitwell Lofts. Under the management of Red Dutch, the lofts struggled to retain residents for years before they were finally closed last year. The failure of the lofts has led some to question the viability of any businesses in the building. "Good luck to Faracom, but I think they might have made a mistake," said Graham Gordon of London Business Times magazine. "This part of town just doesn't pull in enough visitors to support restaurants."

Faracom apparently has more faith in the area. The real estate group has invested heavily in Chiswick Lane over the past five years, and the commercial district seems to be slowly responding to the investment. Property prices have increased, and Hector Anselmo, owner and chef of the popular Spanish restaurant Mi Casa Es Su Casa, has already announced he will be renting space to open a restaurant branch in the Sitwell Building.

The building is expected to open for business in June.

E-Mail message

From:	katmaella@creek.co.uk
To:	jschall@wul.co.uk
Date:	February 4
Subject:	Excited for Sitwell!

Dear Ms. Schall,

I wanted to respond to your article about the purchase of the Sitwell Building. As a resident of the Bloomsbury neighborhood, I need to respectfully disagree with Mr. Gordon. Myself and several friends love the idea of more restaurants opening close by. Now, if we want to eat something other than fast food, it involves a tiring drive across town to Chelsea for a good meal. Any exciting places to eat that open in the Sitwell Building will be well attended, I am sure. I believe that the issues the Sitwell Lofts faced had more to do with their management than with the area's desirability.

Thanks for reading,
Katella Maella

Mi Casa Es Su Casa is having its grand opening!

This June 29, join us on the ground floor of the Sitwell Building
to enjoy music, dancing, and good food.

All entrees are 'buy one, get one free,' so don't forget to bring a friend.

Live music will be played by the chef's band, the Salty Quay.

Call today to reserve a seat—they are expected to go quickly.

1. What does Mr. Grable say about the Sitwell Building?

   (A) Patrons will visit it from another neighborhood.
   (B) Faracom will purchase it after a price reduction.
   (C) It was recently photographed by a journalist.
   (D) Some restaurants will move out of it.

2. What company does Ms. Maella suggest caused the Sitwell Lofts to close?

   (A) London Business Times
   (B) Mi Casa Es Su Casa
   (C) Red Dutch Holdings
   (D) Faracom Group

3. What does Ms. Maella imply about her neighborhood?

   (A) It is rapidly growing.
   (B) It has many hotels.
   (C) It has limited dining options.
   (D) It is better than Chelsea.

4. In the e-mail, the word "drive" in paragraph 1, line 4, is closest in meaning to

   (A) trip
   (B) request
   (C) need
   (D) motivation

5. What is suggested about Mr. Anselmo?

   (A) He is a real estate investor.
   (B) He prepares French cuisine.
   (C) He performs in a musical band.
   (D) He is friends with a journalist.

6 양식/기타 삼중지문

Refer to the following summary, letter, and e-mail.

지문의 종류 파악
첫 번째 지문은 요약문, 나머지는 편지와 이메일이다.

Name	Description
Runner-up	Second prize winner of contest
Sebastian A	John Sebastian, First place winner playing his finale
Sebastian B	Sebastian receiving award
Sebastian C	Sebastian exchanging handshake with concert coordinator, Alex Walsh
Judges	Judges conferring after concert

May 15
Howard Johnson
Music and Arts Magazine
Timberland Drive 1502

Dear Mr. Johnson, ── 두 번째 지문의 수신자 파악

I was recently present at the World Piano Contest. While I was there, I took pictures that I believe would be well suited for your magazine.

The photographs are enclosed with this letter and are provided with a title and short summary. I hope that my photographs will appear in your upcoming editorial.

Sincerely,
Regina Carter
Independent photographer
RCphotos@photobank.com

두 번째 지문의 내용
내용 파악과 함께 첫 번째 지문과의 관계를 파악한다.

From : Howard Johnson <hjohnson@musicartmag.com>
To : Regina Carter <RCphotos@photobank.com>
Date : May 17

세 번째 지문의 발신자와 수신자 파악

Dear Ms. Carter

Thank you for submitting your pictures. The rest of the editors and I have reviewed your work and we would like to have "Sebastian C" as our cover page photograph. We also want to use "Sebastian A" and "Judges" for the upcoming article.

세 번째 지문의 내용 파악
내용 파악과 함께 앞 지문과의 관계를 파악한다.

Our standard rate per picture is $250. If there is any problem in the compensation, please let us know; otherwise, we will send you our photograph release agreement for your signature.

With regards,
Howard Johnson
Music and Arts Magazine
Timberland Drive 1502

이름	설명
2등 수상자	이 대회의 2등 우승자
세바스챤 A	존 세바스챤: 마지막 우승 곡을 연주하는 1등 수상자
세바스챤 B	상을 받고 있는 세바스챤
세바스챤 C	이 대회의 담당자인 알렉스 월시와 악수를 하고 있는 세바스챤
심사위원들	콘서트 후에 상을 주고 있는 심사위원들

어휘 description 설명　runner-up 2등, 차점자　first place winner 1등 수상자　exchange handshake 악수를 나누다　concert coordinator 콘서트 담당자　confer (상을) 주다, 수여하다

5월 15일
하워드 존슨
〈뮤직 앤 아트〉 매거진
팀버랜드 도로 1502

친애하는 존슨 씨

저는 최근에 '국제 피아노 경연대회'에 참석했습니다. 제가 그 곳에 있는 동안에 몇 가지 사진들을 찍었는데, 그것들이 귀사의 잡지에 잘 맞을 것이라고 믿습니다.

이 사진들은 이 편지에 첨부되어 있고, 약간의 간단한 요약문과 함께 제공됩니다. 저는 저의 사진들이 귀사의 다음 글에서 실리길 희망합니다.

레지나 카터
독립 사진작가
RCphotos@photobank.com

어휘 recently 최근에　be present 참석하다, 참여하다　take pictures 사진을 찍다　be suited for ~에 적합하다　be enclosed with ~와 동봉되다　be provided with ~를 제공받다　summary 요약(서)　appear 나타나다　upcoming 다가오는　editorial 글　independent 독립적인

발신 : 하워드 존슨 〈hjohnson@musicartmag.com〉
수신 : 레지나 카터 〈RCphotos@photobank.com〉
날짜 : 5월 17일

친애하는 카터 씨

당신의 사진을 제출해 주셔서 정말 감사합니다. 다른 편집자들과 나는 당신의 작품을 검토했고, 우리는 "세바스챤 C"를 우리의 표지사진으로 선택하고 싶습니다. 또한 "세바스챤 A"와 "심사위원들"을 다가오는 기사에 사용하고 싶습니다.

사진 당 우리의 기준비용은 250달러입니다. 만약에 이 금액에 어떤 문제가 있다면, 우리들에게 알려 주십시오. 그렇지 않다면, 우리는 당신의 서명을 받기 위해서 사진공개 동의서를 보내드리겠습니다.

하워드 존슨
〈뮤직 앤 아트〉 매거진
팀버랜드 도로 1502

어휘 submit ~를 제출하다　rest 나머지　editor 편집자　review ~를 검토하다　as ~로써　cover page 표지　also 또한　upcoming article 다가오는 기사　standard rate 표준 요금　compensation 보상금　release 공개　agreement 동의(서)　signature 서명

PART 7_ 실전연습 15 양식/기타 삼중지문

해설 p.181-182

Questions 1-5 refer to the following schedule, notice, and e-mail.

GALLATIN COUNTY REGULAR TRAIN SCHEDULE

Train Number	Butte	Whitehall	Three Forks	Bozeman
112*	6:10 A.M.	6:55 A.M.	7:50 A.M.	8:25 A.M.
120	6:43 A.M.	---	7:53 A.M.	8:35 A.M.
141	7:49 A.M.	8:36 A.M.	---	9:05 A.M.
194	8:11 A.M.	8:49 A.M.	9:32 A.M.	10:03 A.M.
300	9:15 A.M.	9:56 A.M.	---	10:30 A.M.
307	9:44 A.M.	10:17 A.M.	11:09 A.M.	---
310	10:00 A.M.	---	---	12:00 P.M.
315	10:48 A.M.	11:18 A.M.	12:10 P.M.	12:38 P.M.

*No service on Saturdays or Sundays

Attention Gallatin County Train Passengers

The train schedule will be altered throughout the month of June. Please take note of the following adjustments:

1. During the first week of June, all trains will be delayed by one hour so maintenance crews can do some routine, yearly maintenance to the tracks in the morning.

2. During the second week of June, the express train that stops only at Butte and Bozeman will be out of operation because the train's engine will be replaced with a more energy efficient model.

3. For the last two weeks of June, the Three Forks station will be closed while it undergoes a renovation. Passengers wishing to visit Three Forks are recommended to take the number 111 bus from Whitehall, or the 16 bus from Bozeman.

These changes are occurring to improve the performance and safety of the Gallatin County Rail System, so we appreciate your cooperation and understanding during this time.

Thank you,
Gallatin County Transit Authority

```
================= E-Mail message =================
From:    jonnyfie@jfenterprises.com
To:      maroney@equineinterests.com
Subject: Today's appointment
```

Dear Ms. Maroney,

I am very sorry for missing our meeting this morning. I did not realize it until it was too late, but all of the trains this week are delayed by one hour because of some work being done on the tracks. When I arrived at your office, you had left for lunch. I left a message with your receptionist, but I wanted to send you a personal message, too. I hope that we can reschedule our appointment to discuss my proposal for the article I would like to write about the wild horses of Patagonia for your magazine. Please let me know a convenient time for you and I can meet you then. Again, I apologize for the inconvenience this surely caused you.

All my best,
Jonathan Fie

1. How early can a passenger take a train from Whitehall to Three Forks on a Saturday?

   (A) At 6:55 A.M.
   (B) At 7:53 A.M.
   (C) At 8:36 A.M.
   (D) At 8:49 A.M.

2. Which train number will operate with new equipment in June?

   (A) 300
   (B) 307
   (C) 310
   (D) 315

3. What is suggested about Whitehall?

   (A) It is closed for the month of June.
   (B) Its train station will be renovated.
   (C) It is serviced by an express train.
   (D) It is connected to a bus service.

4. When did Mr. Fie have an appointment with Ms. Maroney?

   (A) In the first week of June
   (B) In the second week of June
   (C) In the third week of June
   (D) In the fourth week of June

5. What does Mr. Fie wish to discuss with Ms. Maroney?

   (A) A potential job
   (B) A documentary film
   (C) A transportation schedule
   (D) A construction project

FINAL TEST

Part 1
Part 2
Part 3
Part 4
Part 5&6
Part 7

LISTENING TEST

In the Listening test, you will be asked to demonstrate how well you understand spoken English. The entire Listening test will last approximately 45 minutes. There are four parts, and directions are given for each part. You must mark your answers on the separate answer sheet. Do not write your answers in your test book.

PART 1

Directions: For each question in this part, you will hear four statements about a picture in your test book. When you hear the statements, you must select the one statement that best describes what you see in the picture. Then find the number of the question on your answer sheet and mark your answer. The statements will not be printed in your test book and will be spoken only one time.

Statement (C), "They're sitting at a table," is the best description of the picture, so you should select answer (C) and mark it on your answer sheet.

1.

2.

3.

4.

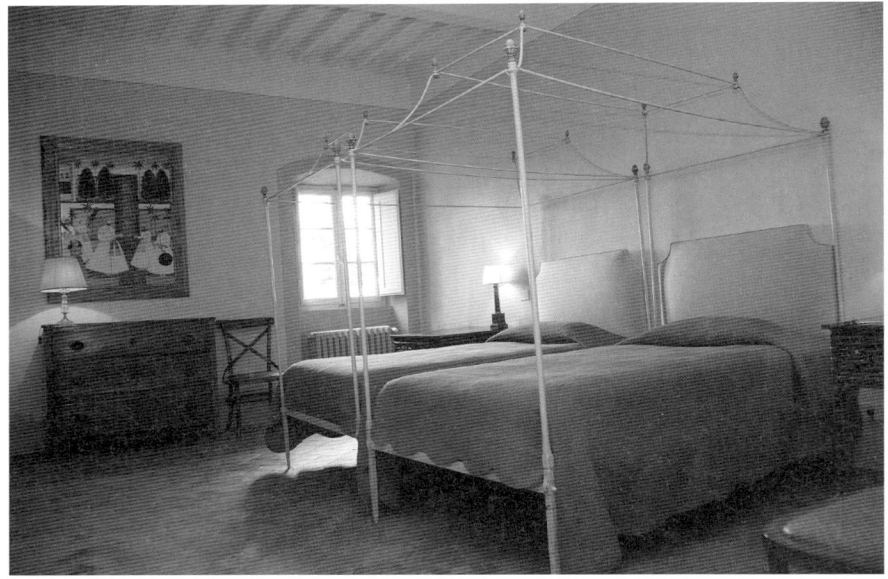

5.

6.

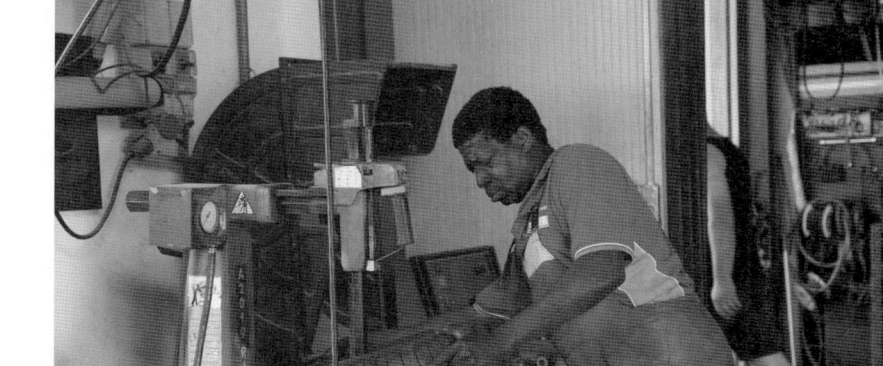

PART 2

Directions: You will hear a question or statement and three responses spoken in English. They will not be printed in your test book and will be spoken only one time. Select the best response to the question or statement and mark the letter (A), (B), or (C) on your answer sheet.

7. Mark your answer on your answer sheet.
8. Mark your answer on your answer sheet.
9. Mark your answer on your answer sheet.
10. Mark your answer on your answer sheet.
11. Mark your answer on your answer sheet.
12. Mark your answer on your answer sheet.
13. Mark your answer on your answer sheet.
14. Mark your answer on your answer sheet.
15. Mark your answer on your answer sheet.
16. Mark your answer on your answer sheet.
17. Mark your answer on your answer sheet.
18. Mark your answer on your answer sheet.
19. Mark your answer on your answer sheet.
20. Mark your answer on your answer sheet.
21. Mark your answer on your answer sheet.
22. Mark your answer on your answer sheet.
23. Mark your answer on your answer sheet.
24. Mark your answer on your answer sheet.
25. Mark your answer on your answer sheet.
26. Mark your answer on your answer sheet.
27. Mark your answer on your answer sheet.
28. Mark your answer on your answer sheet.
29. Mark your answer on your answer sheet.
30. Mark your answer on your answer sheet.
31. Mark your answer on your answer sheet.

PART 3

Directions: You will hear some conversations between two or more people. You will be asked to answer three questions about what the speakers say in each conversation. Select the best response to each question and mark the letter (A), (B), (C), or (D) on your answer sheet. The conversations will not be printed in your test book and will be spoken only one time.

32. What are the speakers discussing?
    (A) A software program
    (B) A merger proposal
    (C) A marketing project
    (D) A department's budget

33. What does the woman recommend?
    (A) Postponing a visit to a client
    (B) Buying a new computer system
    (C) Contacting the IT department
    (D) Holding a meeting

34. What will the woman probably do next?
    (A) Make a list
    (B) Write an e-mail
    (C) Reserve a meeting room
    (D) Take a lunch break

35. What does the woman want to do?
    (A) Work in a new location
    (B) Organize a special event
    (C) Request a promotion
    (D) Review a sales contest

36. Where do the speakers most likely work?
    (A) At a real estate firm
    (B) At an interior design firm
    (C) At a moving company
    (D) At a furniture store

37. What does the woman say about Gateway City?
    (A) Most of her family lives there.
    (B) She worked there in the past.
    (C) It has mostly small stores.
    (D) She has never visited it.

38. Why will Michael leave his position?
    (A) He will leave the company.
    (B) He will be promoted.
    (C) He will open his own business.
    (D) He will transfer to another office.

39. When will Michael leave his position?
    (A) At the end of the week
    (B) The following week
    (C) The following month
    (D) At the end of the year

40. What does the woman mention about Alicia?
    (A) She also works in Bangkok.
    (B) She should replace Michael.
    (C) She should hire someone soon.
    (D) She will also leave the company.

41. What are the speakers discussing?
    (A) Their recent vacation
    (B) The man's weekend plans
    (C) The weather in Hawaii
    (D) The woman's travel plans

42. How will the weather be this Saturday?
    (A) Sunny
    (B) Snowy
    (C) Rainy
    (D) Foggy

43. When is the woman expecting to leave?
    (A) Early Saturday morning
    (B) Saturday afternoon
    (C) Saturday evening
    (D) Late Saturday night

GO ON TO THE NEXT PAGE

44. According to the man, where is Dr. Jackson now?
    (A) In his office
    (B) At a nearby hospital
    (C) At a pharmacy
    (D) At a medical conference

45. Why does the woman want to speak to Dr. Jackson?
    (A) To reschedule an appointment
    (B) To get information about an exercise
    (C) To invite him to a seminar
    (D) To recommend a pharmacy

46. What will the man probably do next?
    (A) Make an announcement
    (B) Phone another doctor
    (C) Look up some information
    (D) Request a delivery

47. Who most likely is the woman?
    (A) A delivery person
    (B) A travel agent
    (C) A landlord
    (D) A painter

48. What problem does the man mention?
    (A) He missed a message.
    (B) His trip was canceled.
    (C) He cannot wait at home.
    (D) His apartment is empty.

49. What does the woman ask the man to do?
    (A) Submit a schedule
    (B) Move some furniture
    (C) Call her supervisor
    (D) Purchase supplies

50. What does the man mention about an article?
    (A) It said homegrown food is healthy.
    (B) He is writing it for a newspaper.
    (C) The photography in it was attractive.
    (D) Fertile Ground Nursery was reviewed in it.

51. Why is the man concerned?
    (A) His garden is small.
    (B) He has never gardened.
    (C) He does not have tomatoes.
    (D) His budget is limited.

52. What will the woman most likely give the man?
    (A) A garden shed key
    (B) A discount coupon
    (C) A box of tomatoes
    (D) A plant care guide

53. What does the man ask the woman about?
    (A) The temperature in a factory
    (B) A technician's availability
    (C) A production schedule
    (D) A piece of machinery

54. Why does the man say, "so there's nothing wrong with the belts"?
    (A) To inquire about a problem
    (B) To suggest a solution
    (C) To express gratitude
    (D) To report on a repair

55. What does the woman mention about air conditioners?
    (A) New ones were installed.
    (B) A technician repaired them.
    (C) They do not stay turned on.
    (D) They make the room too cold.

56. What does the woman want to change about her reservation?
    (A) The time of a meal
    (B) The number of guests
    (C) The date of the event
    (D) The dishes to be served

57. What does the man mention about the restaurant?
    (A) Many customers come on Fridays.
    (B) A new seating area just opened.
    (C) It does not accept walk-in guests.
    (D) The menu changes on the weekend.

58. What does the woman mean when she says, "I'll just have to start my search again"?
    (A) She will find another restaurant.
    (B) She will look for an alternative job.
    (C) She will choose a different activity.
    (D) She will order from a separate menu.

59. What is the conversation mainly about?
    (A) Creating a restaurant menu
    (B) Receiving identification badges
    (C) Using a company discount
    (D) Selling a new line of coffee

60. What type of products does Depp's Place sell?
    (A) Juice
    (B) Baked goods
    (C) Salads
    (D) Sandwiches

61. What does the woman mean when she says, "That sounds good"?
    (A) She enjoys listening to a song.
    (B) She thinks Jeremy speaks clearly.
    (C) She wants to apply for a job.
    (D) She will go with Jeremy.

KENNINGS LITHOGRAPHY	
Employee	**Extension**
Curtis Coe	1
Dave Mitkey	2
Alice Dedham	3
Lara Bezel	4

62. What is the woman decorating?
    (A) A restaurant
    (B) An office
    (C) A residence
    (D) A shop

63. What does the man say about a printer?
    (A) It malfunctions.
    (B) It ran out of ink.
    (C) It only makes black-and-white images.
    (D) It is newly purchased.

64. Look at the graphic. Who will the woman most likely call?
    (A) Curtis Coe
    (B) Dave Mitkey
    (C) Alice Dedham
    (D) Lara Bezel

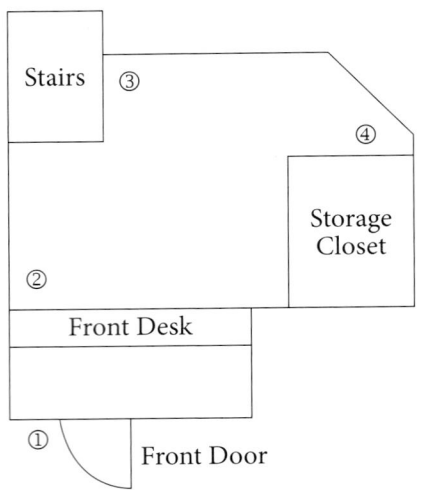

Class Block	Start Time
A	9 A.M.
B	10 A.M.
C	11 A.M.
D	12 noon

65. Why does the woman want to buy a refrigerator?

(A) To allow the staff to store food
(B) To offer snacks to customers
(C) To expand a kitchen's cooking capacity
(D) To replace an old one

66. Look at the graphic. In which position does the woman suggest putting the refrigerator?

(A) 1
(B) 2
(C) 3
(D) 4

67. What will the man most likely do next?

(A) Hire a builder
(B) Greet a customer
(C) Empty a space
(D) Draw a map

68. What does the man mention about his relatives?

(A) They are professional cooks.
(B) They live in another country.
(C) They gave him a present.
(D) They need a schedule.

69. Look at the graphic. When will the man's class start?

(A) At 9:00 A.M.
(B) At 10:00 A.M.
(C) At 11:00 A.M.
(D) At 12:00 noon

70. What payment method will the man use?

(A) Cash
(B) Credit card
(C) Bank transfer
(D) Gift certificate

PART 4

Directions: You will hear some talks given by a single speaker. You will be asked to answer three questions about what the speaker says in each talk. Select the best response to each question and mark the letter (A), (B), (C), or (D) on your answer sheet. The talks will not be printed in your test book and will be spoken only one time.

71. Where does the speaker probably work?
    (A) At an Internet service provider
    (B) At a telemarketing center
    (C) At an electronics store
    (D) At a retail store

72. What does the speaker recommend listeners do first?
    (A) Restart the computer
    (B) Call again later
    (C) Wait for an agent
    (D) Replace the wireless equipment

73. How can listeners arrange a return call?
    (A) By visiting the phone center
    (B) By leaving a message
    (C) By pressing the star key
    (D) By calling a different number

74. Who is the intended audience of the advertisement?
    (A) Gym owners
    (B) Experienced runners
    (C) Fitness instructors
    (D) People older than 60

75. What can users of the Fit-tech X600 do?
    (A) Run at high speeds
    (B) Watch television shows
    (C) Track their heart rate
    (D) Transport the treadmill easily

76. What is available with the Fit-tech X600?
    (A) Coupons
    (B) A rebate
    (C) A warranty
    (D) A gift certificate

77. What does the speaker recommend listeners do?
    (A) Get out of town
    (B) Avoid certain roads
    (C) Use public transportation
    (D) Schedule events well

78. What will happen in town?
    (A) Heavy traffic on Peterson Avenue
    (B) A live radio show with contests
    (C) A concert for the holiday
    (D) The closure of certain roads

79. What will listeners hear next?
    (A) A music show
    (B) A weather report
    (C) More traffic news
    (D) An interview with Joyce Lin

80. Who most likely is the speaker?
    (A) The team's new manager
    (B) A travel agent
    (C) A replacement team member
    (D) An outside consultant

81. What is the audience's company planning to do?
    (A) Close some domestic stores
    (B) Expand into an overseas market
    (C) Merge with another company
    (D) Open a new factory

82. How many other companies has the woman worked with?
    (A) 3
    (B) 4
    (C) 5
    (D) 6

GO ON TO THE NEXT PAGE

83. What record did Cheryl set?
    (A) Selling the most products
    (B) Gaining the most new clients
    (C) Having the most satisfied customers
    (D) Serving the longest period of time

84. What does the speaker mean when she says, "And if that's not enough, there's more"?
    (A) The meal has several dishes.
    (B) Extra seats are stored in a closet.
    (C) An employee had multiple achievements.
    (D) Many salespeople will be honored.

85. What is different about Willton Glass compared to last year?
    (A) Its speed of operation
    (B) The size of its sales staff
    (C) The types of products it sells
    (D) Its office location

86. Who is probably speaking?
    (A) A tour guide
    (B) A travel agent
    (C) A hotel employee
    (D) A fitness instructor

87. What does the speaker mention about swimming pools?
    (A) They are included in the package.
    (B) They are open to all hotel guests.
    (C) They are not as popular as the beaches.
    (D) They are located in the basement of the gym.

88. What will the speaker probably give listeners?
    (A) A receipt
    (B) A brochure
    (C) An application
    (D) A membership card

89. Where is the job fair being held?
    (A) At a hotel
    (B) At a university
    (C) At a convention center
    (D) At a company's headquarters

90. What are attendees advised to do?
    (A) Attend an introductory speech
    (B) Dress professionally
    (C) Bring résumés
    (D) Pay a fee

91. Who most likely is Steve Buckley?
    (A) The organizer of the fair
    (B) A recruiter at the fair
    (C) A university student
    (D) A radio host

92. What does the speaker imply when he says, "Please finish making your selections soon"?
    (A) A product will expire soon.
    (B) Shoppers should leave a store.
    (C) He needs to confirm information.
    (D) There is a limited number of goods.

93. Where most likely is the announcement taking place?
    (A) At an automotive shop
    (B) At a grocery store
    (C) At a restaurant
    (D) At a post office

94. What does the speaker say about a home delivery service?
    (A) It is only available in the morning.
    (B) Deliveries are made within one day.
    (C) Orders must be placed on the Internet.
    (D) Certain products cannot be shipped.

The Writer's Muse		Order # 917
Part #	Desc.	Qty.
L1	Ballpoint Pens	20
L3	Highlighters	4
P3	Colored Paper	10
P4	Large Envelope	10

Units Sold Internationally (In 1000s)

	Q3	Q4
France	12	15
Belgium	9	20
England	23	21
Germany	14	14

95. Look at the graphic. What item will be delivered separately?
    (A) Pens
    (B) Highlighters
    (C) Paper
    (D) Envelopes

96. What will the speaker give the listener?
    (A) Extra pens
    (B) Free shipping
    (C) A store coupon
    (D) Entry into a contest

97. Why does the speaker ask the listener to contact her?
    (A) To specify an order detail
    (B) To schedule a meeting
    (C) To pay for a purchase
    (D) To complete a survey

98. What type of company does the speaker most likely work for?
    (A) A phone accessory manufacturer
    (B) An international banking firm
    (C) A broadcast news network
    (D) An industry publication

99. What does the speaker say customers like about the product?
    (A) It looks unique.
    (B) It holds money.
    (C) It has a mirror.
    (D) It is durable.

100. Look at the graphic. What country is Richard in charge of sales for?
    (A) France
    (B) Belgium
    (C) England
    (D) Germany

This is the end of the Listening test. Turn to Part 5 in your test book.

GO ON TO THE NEXT PAGE

READING TEST

In the Reading test, you will read a variety of texts and answer several different types of reading comprehension questions. The entire Reading test will last 75 minutes. There are three parts, and directions are given for each part. You are encouraged to answer as many questions as possible within the time allowed.

You must mark your answers on the separate answer sheet. Do not write your answers in your test book.

PART 5

Directions: A word or phrase is missing in each of the sentences below. Four answer choices are given below each sentence. Select the best answer to complete the sentence. Then mark the letter (A), (B), (C), or (D) on your answer sheet.

101. We assured Mr. Nelson that ------- application must be accepted by the end of this month.

    (A) he
    (B) him
    (C) himself
    (D) his

102. ------- Ms. Chae or Ms. Nahm will give a speech at the Marcio Convention Center.

    (A) Both
    (B) Each
    (C) Either
    (D) Neither

103. Any employee who lack experience with programming must ------- a training session.

    (A) attendance
    (B) attend
    (C) attending
    (D) attendee

104. Various changes occurring ------- the airline industry reflect recent trends in air transportation.

    (A) into
    (B) during
    (C) throughout
    (D) as

105. Successful implementation of a strategy requires careful consideration and -------.

    (A) planner
    (B) plan
    (C) planned
    (D) planning

106. Coal production has ------- been an important part of local industrial growth.

    (A) history
    (B) historically
    (C) historian
    (D) historical

107. After reviewing your resume, we found your qualification for the position to be -------.

    (A) impressive
    (B) interested
    (C) grateful
    (D) absolute

108. According to the schedule, our visitors will have ------- half an hour to take the guided tour of the factory.

    (A) approximate
    (B) approximated
    (C) approximately
    (D) approximation

109. Customers can be refunded for defective products ------- a week of purchase.
    (A) by
    (B) within
    (C) during
    (D) until

110. Mr. Reed requested that the minutes ------- to the Bundang branch office.
    (A) were sent
    (B) be sent
    (C) to send
    (D) will send

111. I am confident that the seminar will provide ------- opportunities to interact with colleagues.
    (A) valuing
    (B) valuable
    (C) value
    (D) to value

112. Discount ------- for the movie are available at the box office.
    (A) tickets
    (B) ticket
    (C) ticketing
    (D) ticketed

113. It is highly recommended that passengers ------- all required documents in advance.
    (A) inform
    (B) promote
    (C) progress
    (D) obtain

114. SuperCleaner should be used only ------- cleaning computers and other peripherals.
    (A) for
    (B) to
    (C) over
    (D) on

115. For a more ------- description of our products, please read the instructions carefully before using them.
    (A) extensive
    (B) limited
    (C) qualified
    (D) impressed

116. ------- you would like to sell your property, be sure to consult a real estate agent with broad knowledge of the market.
    (A) Therefore
    (B) In order
    (C) Due to
    (D) If

117. Specialists from the Hollo Company have ------- new ideas for the smart device.
    (A) existed
    (B) thought
    (C) resulted
    (D) developed

118. We will schedule a meeting to determine whether we can use our resources more -------.
    (A) nearly
    (B) largely
    (C) efficiently
    (D) quite

119. Starting ------- Monday morning, new carpeting will be installed on the third floor of the building.
    (A) until
    (B) in
    (C) on
    (D) by

120. If you are not satisfied for any reason, simply send your order with the original receipt ------- to the department.
    (A) direction
    (B) directing
    (C) directly
    (D) directive

GO ON TO THE NEXT PAGE

121. I am writing this letter to ------- receipt of the document you sent a week ago.
    (A) comment
    (B) notify
    (C) acknowledge
    (D) suggest

122. To make the office more environmentally -------, employees are required to sort and recycle all office wastes.
    (A) friendly
    (B) unexpected
    (C) pleased
    (D) competent

123. There are several musical performances this month ------- highlight local musicians and artists.
    (A) which
    (B) when
    (C) where
    (D) who

124. Researchers at Knox Inc., gather diverse data to ------- downward trends in the sale of its products.
    (A) analyzing
    (B) analyze
    (C) analyzed
    (D) analysis

125. Initiating the new product line is the ------- project our division has ever undertaken.
    (A) most challenging
    (B) challenging
    (C) challenged
    (D) more challenged

126. The sales director will officially announce branches of ------- during the last month.
    (A) statement
    (B) rise
    (C) result
    (D) growth

127. We ask that you send the ------- contract back to our department by June 20.
    (A) corrected
    (B) correctly
    (C) correctness
    (D) corrects

128. ------- the restructuring of the company, Ms. Hernandez is in charge of shipping and packaging.
    (A) Within
    (B) Until
    (C) Due to
    (D) Since

129. Rosy Fresh Laundry has a ------- scent and it removes stains effectively.
    (A) pleases
    (B) pleased
    (C) please
    (D) pleasing

130. Any employee who reaches the sales goal is ------- to win a complimentary trip.
    (A) active
    (B) valued
    (C) eligible
    (D) estimated

PART 6

Directions: Read the texts that follow. A word, phrase, or sentence is missing in parts of each text. Four answer choices for each question are given below the text. Select the best answer to complete the text. Then mark the letter (A), (B), (C), or (D) on your answer sheet.

Questions 131-134 refer to the following notice.

ATTENTION!

After 34 years, Jim Cheekwood is moving on ------- Franklin Realty. He will retire on Friday to spend
                                             131.
more time with his family. Everyone is invited to attend his ------- dinner on Thursday evening.
                                                              132.
Everyone is also requested to contribute five dollars towards a retirement gift we will buy for him.

-------. Please give your ------- to the evening's organizer, Sylvia Herndon in the accounting
 133.   134.
department.

131. (A) to
     (B) for
     (C) with
     (D) from

132. (A) farewell
     (B) birthday
     (C) graduation
     (D) anniversary

133. (A) They will be available after the meal.
     (B) We will present it to him during the dinner.
     (C) Please prepare an individual gift to give him.
     (D) He will spend more time with his large family.

134. (A) donor
     (B) donate
     (C) donation
     (D) to donate

GO ON TO THE NEXT PAGE

Questions 135-138 refer to the following article.

TOWNSEND—The Construction Authority of Townsend (CAT) has been criticized for spending too much time on the planning phases of the Townsend Subway expansion. ------. On Monday, the exploratory committee ------ a two-month extension to answer questions raised by Townsend residents. CAT then voted to grant the extension that Thursday. The most significant question the committee wants to answer is whether or not the subway should extend to the Townsend Community College. CAT plans to ------ student representatives before making a decision. The extension will cost ------ £60,000.

135. (A) Consequently, CAT will begin the construction phase immediately.
(B) Supposedly, CAT will hear a proposal for a project extension.
(C) Finally, CAT committed to a much lengthier investigation.
(D) Regardless, CAT has again extended this phase of the project.

136. (A) will request
(B) requested
(C) to request
(D) requests

137. (A) enroll
(B) survey
(C) support
(D) mention

138. (A) approximate
(B) approximated
(C) approximately
(D) approximating

Questions 139-142 refer to the following e-mail.

FROM: cdrecker@clear-line.co.uk
TO: stafflist@clear-line.co.uk
DATE: December 1
SUBJECT: The end of year dinner

Hello Clear Line employees,

Thank you to ------- that has already confirmed that they can come to our end of year dinner. If you have not yet informed me about whether or not you -------, please do so as soon as possible. The Big Stirrup restaurant informed me that their parking area sometimes fills up, so carpooling is recommended. Please organize ride sharing with your friends. -------. I am driving a sedan with three extra seats and would be happy to share. I live in the Blue Dream subdivision on the west side of town. After dinner, anyone that lives close by can ride with me back to there, -------.

Kindly,

Carol Drecker

139. (A) one
(B) they
(C) those
(D) everyone

140. (A) attentive
(B) attended
(C) attendant
(D) can attend

141. (A) All contracts must be signed and delivered in person next week.
(B) She kindly acknowledged your gratitude.
(C) I sincerely appreciate your endorsement.
(D) I completed the project last week.

142. (A) too
(B) well
(C) away
(D) instead

Questions 143-146 refer to the following memo.

Memorandum

To: Carl-Tech Employees
From: Carl Pfadt
Date: September 27
Subject: Repairing some pipes

Many of you may have noticed problems with the water pressure on the third floor. This was caused by old water mains rusting. ------ . Interestingly, we have not noticed any water damage from the
                                        143.
pipe. It is ------ where this leaked water is going. If you see any dark ------ developing on the walls,
         144.   145.
please notify the maintenance staff immediately. A plumber will replace the pipe on the weekend of October 3. ------ that time, please refrain from using the restrooms or sinks on the third floor. The
              146.
facilities should be fully operational by the following Monday.

Carl

---

143. (A) The issue was quickly resolved.
(B) The low pressure is caused by them leaking.
(C) A stress reduction counselor is available to help them.
(D) The whole floor is off-limits to all employees until further notice.

144. (A) known
(B) unclear
(C) unstable
(D) abundant

145. (A) spotted
(B) spottily
(C) spotter
(D) spots

146. (A) Until
(B) After
(C) Prior
(D) Later

PART 7

Directions: In this part you will read a selection of texts, such as magazine and newspaper articles, e-mails, and instant messages. Each text or set of texts is followed by several questions. Select the best answer for each question and mark the letter (A), (B), (C), or (D) on your answer sheet.

Questions 147-148 refer to the following advertisement.

Fly for Under 99 Euros

If you're looking for a cheap weekend getaway, look no further. GoJet is offering a post-summer special until November 30.

Fly from London or Frankfurt to anywhere within the European Union for under 99 euros. Enjoy a romantic weekend in Paris or a trip to the islands of Greece for much less than any other travel agency.

Prices listed include tax. For more information and for a complete list of our destinations, visit www.gojet.com.

147. From what city can customers depart?
- (A) Paris
- (B) Athens
- (C) Greece
- (D) Frankfurt

148. What is true about the sale?
- (A) The price includes tax.
- (B) It starts on November 30.
- (C) All tickets are 99 euros.
- (D) Tickets must be purchased online.

GO ON TO THE NEXT PAGE

Questions 149-150 refer to the following text message chain.

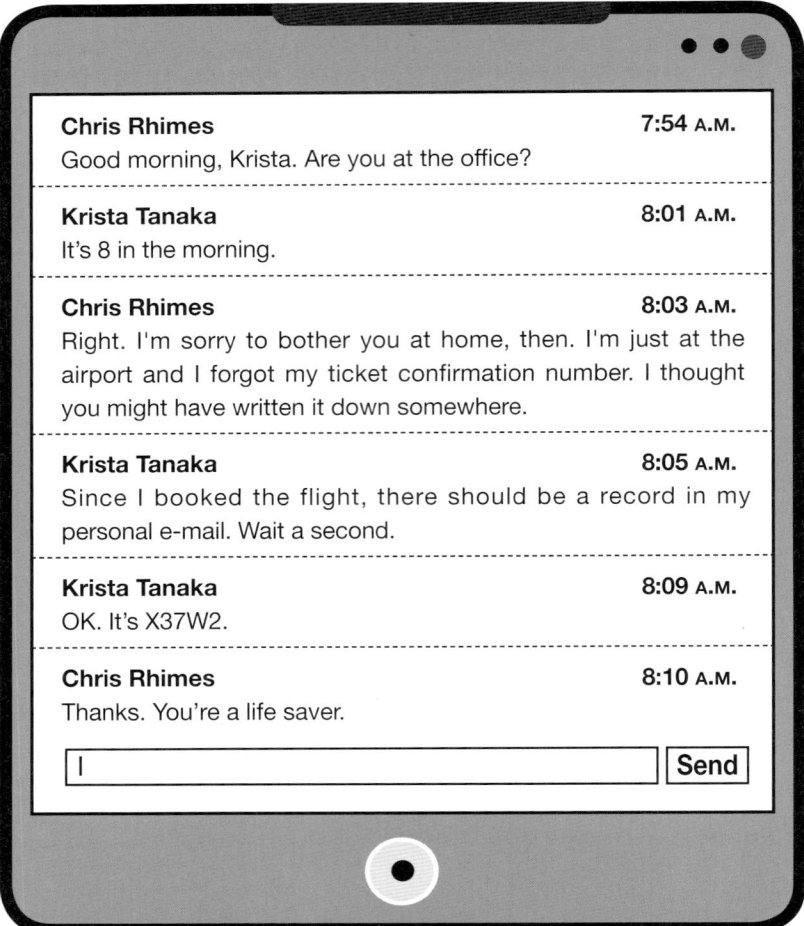

149. At 8:01 A.M., what does Ms. Tanaka mean when she writes, "It's 8 in the morning"?

(A) A meeting is at 8 A.M.
(B) Her office opened early.
(C) She has not left for work.
(D) Mr. Rhimes flight is delayed.

150. What was Ms. Tanaka most likely doing between 8:05 and 8:09 A.M.?

(A) Checking her e-mail
(B) Buying a ticket
(C) Calling an airline
(D) Driving to work

Questions 151-152 refer to the following e-mail.

From: Samantha Maxwell (sammaxwell@herrington.com)
To: ricky@askricky.com
Subject: Thank you
Date: March 18, 5:02 P.M.

Dear Ricky,

First, I'd like to thank you for all of the great advice you give. I was not very familiar with Ricky Realtor, but started reading your column after a friend recommended it to me since I'm interested in buying a home.

I've become an avid reader and have learned a lot about home improvements and financing, but I still have some basic questions that I find difficult to have answered.

I'm in the process of saving up for a down payment on a house, but once I have a substantial amount, which I hope will be at the end of the year, I don't know what to do. There are many real estate agents out there, but how do I know who is right for me? I'm new to this and somewhat worried, so I don't want to be naive and buy a house I'm not absolutely happy with.

If you would, please help! What are the basic rules to finding a good realtor and house?

Thank you very much.

Best regards,
Samantha Maxwell

151. What does Ms. Maxwell want to do?
(A) Open an account
(B) Renovate her house
(C) Invest in real estate
(D) Purchase her first home

152. What can be implied from this e-mail?
(A) Ms. Maxwell has money saved.
(B) Ms. Maxwell will move abroad.
(C) Ms. Maxwell is a subscriber to a magazine.
(D) Ms. Maxwell has spoken with a realtor.

GO ON TO THE NEXT PAGE

Questions 153-154 refer to the following notice.

International Association of Architects (IAA)

If you are going to attend the International Association of Architects (IAA) conference this year, you don't want to miss the chance to see a documentary film entitled *Simple but Chic*, which concentrates on the designs of world-renowned architect Jean Beaufort, who has designed private and public buildings across the world.

This noteworthy documentary film, with Steve Cassidy as director, highlights interviews with Beaufort. Moreover, the director wanted to provide moviegoers with an insider's view of Heavenly Sight, the residential structure on the outskirts of Paris which Beaufort created for his beloved family and where he spent fifteen years of his life. The film makers, therefore, asked for special consent from the Beaufort family to shoot the documentary film inside the house.

At 4:00 P.M. on June 25, the last day of the conference, *Simple but Chic* will be shown at the Conference Hall of the Parisian Hotel. Right after the film showing, you may participate in a discussion about the movie with Amanda Chua, former president of IAA. The film showing is free for all conference participants; however, to ensure that you have seats, registration is required. You may register at www.iaa.org/congress/simplebutchic.

153. Why is the notice posted?

(A) To advertise a film to be shown
(B) To inform the public of the sale of a house
(C) To invite people to a new building
(D) To attract movie makers

154. What will Amanda Chua do on June 25?

(A) Plan a design for a new project
(B) Give a speech at the opening
(C) Interview a famous architect
(D) Attend a discussion

Questions 155-157 refer to the following letter.

Arch Bay Studio
Kee Road, SIS Building, Singapore 158088
Tel: (453) 4545 2367

June 15

Avery Gardner
Bookland Publishers Inc.
241 Superior Street
Troy, Michigan, MI 7710
USA

Dear Mr. Gardner,

I'm writing this letter on behalf of Lea Ohara. I know that currently, she is being considered for a position in the marketing department of your company.

Ms. Ohara had worked here at Arch Bay Studio as a marketing assistant for five years. Subsequently, she was promoted to the position of the manager in the Department of International Marketing, which she has been occupying up to the present. She is in charge of the advertising and distribution to the worldwide market of animated movies. Also, she is responsible for marketing in other countries, and handles a group of sales representatives who do business with companies all over the world.

She has good communication skills both in English and Chinese and has the ability to exercise very careful attention to even the smallest details of any tasks given to her. She has consistently shown her dedication to selling our movies and has established excellent professional connections with various types of people in the movie making industry. I am certain that she will show the same commitment and dedication in whatever kind of job she has to do.

We are really sorry to see her leave us; however, we know that Ms. Ohara's family is in the United States, and we understand her wish to be with them. She has been an exemplary member of this company. You can contact me any time if you want to talk more about her competence and work.

Sincerely,

Mai Ling
President, Arch Bay Studio

---

155. What is the purpose of the letter?

(A) To ask about the performance of Ms. Ohara
(B) To let employees know about the promotion of Ms. Ohara
(C) To give Ms. Ohara a position
(D) To recommend Ms. Ohara for a job

156. What is NOT mentioned about Ms. Ohara?

(A) She can communicate excellently.
(B) She has good knowledge in publishing.
(C) She pays attention to various aspects.
(D) She has international business backgrounds.

157. What is Ms. Ohara's reason to stop working for Arch Bay Studio?

(A) She wants to relocate to another country.
(B) She likes to finish her master's degree.
(C) She wants to have bigger income.
(D) She seeks opportunities to travel frequently.

GO ON TO THE NEXT PAGE

Questions 158-160 refer to the following e-mail.

E-Mail message

From:	ashleythomas@asansol.ac.in
To:	damodarkumar@interiormind.in
Subject:	February 12
Date:	Looking for designer

Hello Mr. Kumar,

— [1] —. I was impressed by your booth at the Kolkata Symposium of Decorators, and I am interested in possibly employing your services. Asansol University is building a new student union, and we are looking for an interior designer that can make an environment that is attractive to our students. Our students are known for their academic diligence. They need a student union with quiet places for them to spend long hours preparing for classes or collaborating on group projects. — [2] —.

It is specifically the work you did for the Orissa Coffee Shop that makes me believe you would be appropriate for this job. The decor there is attractive but not overly obtrusive, and the lighting is bright but not distracting. You created a diner that visitors enjoy reading or working in.

— [3] —. It is this same atmosphere that I would like you to create for the student union.

I am sure that a designer of your standing currently has many assignments, so if you are unavailable, I of course understand. Otherwise, please let me know a convenient time and place for you to meet to discuss the details of this project. — [4] —. You can reach me at this e-mail or by calling my office at 0341-6788, 6688.

Kind regards,

Ashley Thomas

Asansol University Development Team

158. What does Ms. Thomas say about Asansol University students?

(A) They design buildings.
(B) They enjoy drinking coffee.
(C) They are committed to studying.
(D) They organize a yearly conference.

159. Why does Ms. Thomas want to hire Mr. Kumar?

(A) His TV ad was convincing.
(B) She likes a cafe he designed.
(C) A colleague recommended him.
(D) He won a contest at a university.

160. In which of the positions marked [1], [2], [3], and [4] does the following sentence best belong?

"In either case, a reply by the end of the week would be appreciated."

(A) [1]
(B) [2]
(C) [3]
(D) [4]

GO ON TO THE NEXT PAGE

Questions 161-163 refer to the following letter.

Dear Mr. Saunders,

Thank you for your recent purchase of the RoxPro Home Theater System. We are confident that you will be more than satisfied with your purchase.

Should you need help installing any part of your system, do not hesitate to call us at 1-800-389-8748 on weekdays from 8 A.M. to 8 P.M. and on Saturdays from 10 A.M. to 6 P.M. Our technicians will be happy to assist you with easy step-by-step directions, and if needed, we can send a technician to your home for a small fee.

Enclosed is our standard three-year limited warranty. Please keep this for your records. Also, enclosed is a gift certificate for five free movie rentals at your local RentFlix rental store.

Again, thank you for your purchase and enjoy your new home theater system.

Sincerely,

Eugene Smith
Customer Service Representative
RoxPro Home Theater System

161. What is the purpose of the letter?
 (A) To thank a customer
 (B) To schedule a service date
 (C) To request customer feedback
 (D) To notify a customer of an outstanding balance

162. What service is offered to RoxPro customers?
 (A) Free delivery
 (B) A special payment plan
 (C) Home installation service
 (D) 24-hour customer support

163. What is enclosed with the letter?
 (A) An assembly manual
 (B) A gift certificate
 (C) An upgraded warranty
 (D) An estimate

Questions 164-167 refer to the following letter.

To: Emma Powers
From: Min-Ho Choi

May 28

Dear Ms. Powers,

This is about our talk regarding your decision to move out of your apartment, Unit 13B in the City Land apartment complex by 4:00 P.M. on June 1.

Upon receiving all the keys to your apartment unit when you leave, I will check the unit immediately. A report describing in detail the condition of the apartment will be sent to you on or before June 3. You will have to sign this report and send it back to me at your earliest convenience. If the apartment is deemed clean and in good condition, your security deposit will be refunded to you in full, except for $10 from the amount of $1,000 which will be used to pay for the delivery of your check to you by express mail as you requested.

After I receive back the inspection report from you, I will send your refund check no later than June 18, which you said is the date of your departure to Zurich. Best wishes to you and with your new job in Zurich.

Regards,

Min-Ho Choi
Min-Ho Choi
Administrative Agent
City Land Apartments

164. What is the purpose of the letter?
    (A) To confirm the procedure for vacating the apartment
    (B) To notify the tenant of the increased fee
    (C) To promote a cleaning service
    (D) To announce a change in management

165. When will Mr. Choi conduct the inspection of the apartment unit?
    (A) On May 28
    (B) On June 1
    (C) On June 3
    (D) On June 15

166. Why will the tenant NOT receive the full refund?
    (A) She was late in returning the inspection report.
    (B) She refused to pay the cost of renovation.
    (C) She moved out without giving any advance notice.
    (D) She asked the agent for fast delivery.

167. What can be implied about Ms. Powers?
    (A) She will relocate to another apartment.
    (B) She has lived in Zurich for a long time.
    (C) She will use a moving company.
    (D) She will relocate owing to her new work.

GO ON TO THE NEXT PAGE

Questions 168-171 refer to the following online chat discussion.

Paora Tama [3:10 P.M.]		I want to remind everyone that because of the long weekend, we need to get this month's issue to the printer by Thursday evening instead of Friday. I'd like all team heads to give me a status update.
Anders Bertil [3:13 P.M.]		All of our photographers have submitted their work except for Aaron Rogers. He said he should be able to submit his work by Wednesday, which should give the Design team enough time to get it in the magazine.
Isabel Catarina [3:14 P.M.]		Yeah, as long as we get it by Wednesday, it won't be a problem.
Paora Tama [3:15 P.M.]		Good. I'll talk to Aaron and urge him to submit it quickly. What about you Melissa? Do you think the editorial team can finish by Thursday?
Melissa Alba [3:18 P.M.]		Oh no ... I forgot that we aren't coming in on Friday. I don't think we'll be able to finish during our normal work days. Can you authorize us to work overtime?
Paora Tama [3:19 P.M.]		I'll see what I can do. In the meantime, send the rough drafts of the articles to Isabel so her team can make some progress on the layout.
Isabel Catarina [3:20 P.M.]		That would be helpful. Thanks in advance.
Melissa Alba [3:20 P.M.]		Sure. I'll do that right now.
Paora Tama [3:22 P.M.]		All right, everyone. We have a lot of work to do, but let's make sure that we finish on time so we can have fun on our holiday weekend. Good luck, and feel free to message me if any problems come up.

SEND

168. For what team does Ms. Catarina most likely work?

(A) Design
(B) Editorial
(C) Photography
(D) Advertising

169. At 3:19 P.M., what does Mr. Tama mean when he writes, "I'll see what I can do"?

(A) He will try to edit a document quickly.
(B) He will try to let employees do extra work.
(C) He will try to organize some photos.
(D) He will try to repair a printer.

170. At 3:20 P.M., who does Ms. Catarina thank?

(A) Paora Tama
(B) Anders Bertil
(C) Aaron Rogers
(D) Melissa Alba

171. Why does Mr. Tama say staff should finish work on time?

(A) To please a client
(B) To earn a bonus
(C) To enjoy a break
(D) To get a promotion

Questions 172-175 refer to the following advertisement.

Taking a photo of yourself is difficult. — [1] —. You can go through the hassle of setting up a tripod, but who has the time? You can hold your camera out with your arm and point it at yourself, but it's too hard to aim accurately. Sure, you can find someone to take the photo for you, but what if there's no one around?

Now, thanks to Hadley Toys, you can get a handle on personal photography with The Handle. — [2] —. This three-foot (91-centimeter) pole lets you easily take pictures from a comfortable distance. Just attach your smartphone or camera to the end of the pole and connect the included cable into the port you use to charge your device. Then you can press a button on the end of the handle to take a picture. — [3] —. When you're done with The Handle, it collapses into the size of a whiteboard marker that you can easily fit in a purse or pocket.

Visit any authorized Hadley products retail store to receive an in-person demonstration. — [4] —. You'll be amazed at how quickly you'll be taking professional quality photos of yourself.

172. What is NOT mentioned as a difficulty of taking a photo of yourself?

(A) Finding a person to help
(B) Setting a countdown timer
(C) Holding a device in one hand
(D) Erecting a camera stand

173. What is indicated about The Handle?

(A) It operates wirelessly.
(B) It includes a warranty.
(C) It can be easily stored.
(D) It was built for children.

174. What can a visitor to a company store receive?

(A) A promotional discount
(B) A product demonstration
(C) A photography lesson
(D) A customized handgrip

175. In which of the positions marked [1], [2], [3], and [4] does the following sentence best belong?

"There are several mediocre solutions to the problem."

(A) [1]
(B) [2]
(C) [3]
(D) [4]

Questions 176-180 refer to the following e-mail and listing.

E-Mail message

From:	Paula Cruz <paula109@fastmail.com>
To:	Carmen Mendoza <c.mendoza@youmail.com>
Date:	May 2, 1:29 P.M.
Subject:	Thursday

Carmen,

I was wondering if you would like to join me on Thursday. I'm going to see new IMAX movie about the environmental problem. I have to see it for my biology class, and I remember you mentioned that you wanted to see it.

I'm free Thursday after 11:15 A.M. Let me know by Wednesday afternoon if you'd like to go. I'll talk to you soon.

Paula

Life at the Barrier
Oceanographer Andy James explores the unique marine life at the Great Barrier Reef.
Admission: $12 (Adult), $9 (Children & Students), $7 (Senior Citizens)
Showtimes: 11:00 A.M. | 1:45 P.M. | 3:05 P.M. | 6:45 P.M. | 8:00 P.M.

The Forest is Our Home
Anthropologist Robert Walker spends two weeks with the Kubus nomadic tribe in Indonesia.
Admission: $12 (Adult), $9 (Children & Students), $7 (Senior Citizens)
Showtimes: 11:25 A.M. | 2:10 P.M. | 5:45 P.M. | 7:25 P.M. | 9:40 P.M.

An Exhausted World
Overfishing and deforestation are rapidly changing the Earth's ecosystems.
Admission: $12 (Adult), $9 (Children & Students), $7 (Senior Citizens)
Showtimes: 11:45 A.M. | 2:30 P.M. | 5:05 P.M. | 7:45 P.M. | 10:00 P.M.

Space Oddities
Journey light years away into a realm of black holes, red giants, and new discoveries.
Admission: $12 (Adult), $9 (Children & Students), $7 (Senior Citizens)
Showtimes: 12:15 P.M. | 3:00 P.M. | 5:25 P.M. | 8:15 P.M. | 10:30 P.M.

176. Why does Ms. Cruz want to see the movie?
    (A) It is a school assignment.
    (B) Her friend wants to see it.
    (C) Her classmate invited her to go.
    (D) The theater has a special promotion.

177. In the e-mail, the word "free" in paragraph 2, line 1, is closest in meaning to
    (A) empty
    (B) available
    (C) complimentary
    (D) independent

178. What is an available time for Ms. Cruz to see the movie?
    (A) At 12:15 P.M.
    (B) At 2:10 P.M.
    (C) At 5:05 P.M.
    (D) At 8:00 P.M.

179. Who is Andy James?
    (A) A scientist
    (B) A film director
    (C) A professor
    (D) A student

180. What film focuses on people?
    (A) *Space Oddities*
    (B) *An Exhausted World*
    (C) *Life at the Barrier*
    (D) *The Forest is Our Home*

Questions 181-185 refer to the following memo and e-mail.

MEMO

To: All Members
From: Leonel Kim, Manager
Subject: Winter Break
Date: December 10

Since the first opening of BodyFlex Fitness Club, it has been customary to put off operations from December 31 through January 6. This period called 'Winter Break' has been a long tradition here. However, the management has found that not a few members feel this practice to be inconvenient.

After some discussion, the management has decided to remain open this year to meet the needs of our members. However, due to the shortage of staff, our service will be somewhat limited during this period. We expect to return to normal on January 7.

If you have any questions about this change, please e-mail me at leonel@bodyflex.com

Thank you for your support.

From: charles@gurubox.net
To: leonel@bodyflex.com
Subject: Fitness Classes
Date: December 12

Dear Mr. Kim,

As a member of the BodyFlex Fitness Club for over five years, I was happily surprised to read your memo of December 10. Changing a practice that has been in place for that long could not have been easy, but it speaks to your commitment to accommodating the needs of club members.

In consideration of this change, I would like to know how classes will be affected during the period. I am very interested in the Stretching class offered at 8 P.M. on Mondays and Wednesdays, which I have found quite helpful for me.

Thanks,

Charles White

181. What is the purpose of the memo?
(A) To advertise a new fitness class
(B) To promote job openings
(C) To commend some employees
(D) To announce a change

182. What is stated about the BodyFlex Fitness Club?
(A) It offers afternoon fitness classes.
(B) It will have fewer employees work for a week.
(C) It has a special offer for new members.
(D) It is preparing for new programs.

183. What is indicated about Winter Break?
(A) It was introduced at least five years ago.
(B) It customarily lasted for two weeks.
(C) It included regular renovations.
(D) It was welcome to all members.

184. In the e-mail, the phrase "speaks to" in paragraph 1, line 3, is closest in meaning to
(A) complains
(B) follows
(C) shows
(D) affects

185. What is mentioned about Ms. White?
(A) She finds the stretching class to be beneficial.
(B) She exercises daily.
(C) She discussed with Mr. Kim on December 10.
(D) She wants to introduce a class.

GO ON TO THE NEXT PAGE

Questions 186-190 refer to the following article, information and ticket.

BERLIN — On Friday evening the Berlin Zoo officially joined the Consortium of Wildlife Advocates, or the CWA. The CWA is a group of European zoos that exchange animals with each other in the name of conservation. This allows rare animals to be seen by people across the continent. The idea is that exposing visitors to these animals in the flesh will encourage them to preserve the natural habitats of all animals. "You can tell kids that we need to protect the environment, and they probably won't pay attention," said Berlin Zoo's Director of Operations Dieter Gerthfried. "But when you show them an endangered snow leopard and tell them this rare creature won't have a place to live unless we protect nature ... well, that really makes sense to them."

Of course, another beneficial aspect of bringing in guest animals from other zoos is its positive effect on attendance rates. Whenever the zoo gets a new animal, the facility reports a spike in ticket sales. The zoo's first guest from the CWA will be Pogo the elephant, which will be visible to the general public from September 1st. In December, visitors will be able to see flamingos for the first time in Germany when Madrid loans their flock for the year.

Welcome to the Berlin Zoo!

There is a lot to see, so plan your day wisely. The following are our four most popular exhibits. Please review the safety reminders on the back of this card for the well being of yourself, your family, and the animals.

African Safari
Go on a real safari! You'll travel in a jeep along dirt roads through our open-air "African wildlife" exhibit and you might see giraffes, rhinoceroses, water buffalo, or all three. Daily reservations taken – book early for this popular attraction! Gold ticket holders receive priority seating.

Oriental Exploration
See exotic wildlife from the far side of the globe. Pass giant salamander and komodo dragon enclosures on your way to our most popular attraction, Ming Ming the panda bear. Afterwards, try an exciting Japanese dish for lunch at Shiro's Sushi Bar before it closes at the end of August.

Creepy Crawlies
The lighting inside our arachnid and insect hall is kept dim so that our thousands of insect species will stay active in their natural environments. Silver and gold ticket holders can access the live insect petting zoo where they get to hold different species under staff supervision.

Under the Sea
Peek into a world that is usually invisible to us. See rays, tortoises, and sharks from under the waves in our new walkway that takes you under our 3 million liter tank through a glass tube. By reservation, professional divers (applicable licenses must be noted on all passes) can accompany our tank master on a guided tour of the tank from the inside.

Welcome to the **Berlin Zoo**!	
This pass grants the following ticket holder entry to the Berlin Zoo on the date indicated. Ticket holder is eligible for all benefits for their ticket level.	
Name	**Martina Kleid**
Date of Entry	**September 27**
Ticket Level	**Silver**
Relevant Licenses	**None**

186. What does the article imply about the CWA?

    (A) It encourages people to protect nature.
    (B) It operates from a headquarters in Berlin.
    (C) It discourages the relocation of animals.
    (D) It organizes educational events with schools.

187. In the article, the word "spike" in paragraph 2, line 4, is closest in meaning to

    (A) boost
    (B) spear
    (C) hose
    (D) belief

188. What will Ms. Kleid most likely be able to do at the zoo?

    (A) Receive special seating on a tour
    (B) Eat lunch at a Japanese restaurant
    (C) Handle some living creatures
    (D) Swim in an aquarium

189. What kind of zoo exhibit is NOT mentioned?

    (A) An exhibit with roads
    (B) An exhibit with low lighting
    (C) An exhibit with ice formations
    (D) An exhibit with a viewing tunnel

190. What animal will Ms. Kleid most likely be unable to see?

    (A) A rhinoceros
    (B) A panda bear
    (C) An elephant
    (D) A flamingo

GO ON TO THE NEXT PAGE

Questions 191-195 refer to the following advertisement, letter, and information.

Free your music with Maestro

We were told it was impossible to duplicate the success of our Rubin Design Blue Ribbon winning music player, the Legato. After two years of development at Pomegranate, Inc. Headquarters, though, we finally have a device that we think is up to the task.

Meet the Maestro. Maestro is the world's first totally wireless portable music player. You'll never be slowed down by tangled wires or knotted cords when you use the Maestro. You can load your music library onto Maestro's internal hard drive via a wireless network connection to your home computer. If you forget to add one of your favorite songs, don't worry, because you can play any music you have stored on the Internet in your Pomegranate account on the Maestro through a cellular data network. You can even connect Pomegranate headphones to the device wirelessly. And if all that music gets you excited for a real performance, then log into the Concert Now application directly from Maestro. Using its built-in GPS chip, Maestro and Concert Now will help you find live music close to your location. At the end of the night, when you need to recharge your battery with a good night's sleep, recharge Maestro, too—of course, without any wires. Just place it on the Maestro Mate recharging station, and an electric current will safely recharge the player through its metal body.

Buy a Maestro today and never be tied down again.

November 3

Pomegranate, Inc. Refurbishing Center
5910 North Prospect Road
Peoria, IL 61614

To whom it may concern:

Please find my broken Maestro music player and receipt of purchase attached. I purchased this music player about five months ago as indicated on the receipt. Lately, after playing one or two songs, the device shuts down and I have to restart it. Obviously, this is very frustrating. Please note that sometimes the issue only occurs after using the device for longer, like thirty minutes or so. So while investigating the defect, it might be necessary to let the device play for an extended period. Also, while it didn't bother me or affect my use of the device, the built-in GPS chip has never worked, so I could not use the related functions. Please fix that too, if possible.

Thank you,
Jisoo Park

Pomegranate, Inc. Return Policy

Pomegranate, Inc., offers a 100% satisfaction guaranteed return policy within the first seven days of your purchase. If for any reason your Pomegranate product does not live up to your expectations, simply return it to any Pomegranate store with all of its original packaging and a sales receipt, and we will issue a full cash refund.

After the first week and within thirty days of purchase, products defective from flaws in manufacturing may be returned or exchanged at the point of sale. Products that are functional and undamaged may be returned for store credit.

Thirty days after the original sale, the Pomegranate's limited warranty applies. Products with defects in manufacturing or craftsmanship may be mailed to an authorized Pomegranate, Inc. refurbishing center. Just include a copy of your receipt and an explanation of the problem. Pomegranate, Inc., will replace the faulty item with a used product in equal or better condition. The warranty does not apply to products that are affected by normal wear and tear, improper use, or accidents.

---

191. What is suggested about the Legato?
(A) It had a design flaw.
(B) It received an award.
(C) It is no longer available.
(D) It replaced the Maestro.

192. What wireless feature has Ms. Park NOT used on her Maestro?
(A) Maestro Mate
(B) Lost device location
(C) Concert Now
(D) Music streaming

193. In the information, the word "point" in paragraph 2, line 2, is closest in meaning to
(A) tip
(B) opinion
(C) location
(D) purpose

194. What is indicated about Pomegranate, Inc.'s return policy?
(A) It changed in the past year.
(B) A receipt is always required.
(C) Online purchases are excluded.
(D) All damaged goods can be returned.

195. What will Pomegranate Inc. probably do for Ms. Park?
(A) Repair an instrument
(B) Refund a payment
(C) Replace a device
(D) Recall a product

Questions 196-200 refer to the following Web page, form, and e-mail.

http://www.pwms.com/about.html

Pro Wear Mega Store

| **About** | Catalogue | Shop | Contact |

Pro Wear Mega Store is the oldest and most trusted store in Michigan to get the uniforms and gear your staff need to run an efficient kitchen. Restaurant owners across the state rely on Pro Wear Mega Store to outfit their servers with comfortable and safe shoes to navigate slippery kitchens or to look stylish on the serving floor. Anyone working on the cooking line will appreciate our easy-to-clean pants and shirts, or the professional look of our aprons and hats. Whatever you need, we've got it. Visit our store on Conner Street, or browse our online catalogue to take a look at what we can offer you. Order in the month of October to take advantage of our flat, low-rate shipping charge of $9.00 for standard delivery, or $29.00 for overnight delivery on purchases under $500.00.

Pro Wear Mega Store
Record Number: CB206
Customer: Adobo
Date: October 11
Shipping Address: 1219 East Adams Ave., Detroit, Michigan 48202

Item Number	Item Description	Quantity	Unit Price	Total Price
207	Collared shirts	12	$5.00	$60.00
319	Non-slip shoes	6	$15.00	$90.00
212	Hoodies	4	$19.00	$76.00
401	Slacks	8	$10.00	$80.00
11	Graphic design + logo printing	/	$150.00	$150.00
			Subtotal	$456.00
			Shipping	$29.00
			Total	$485.00

FROM: regina@adobo.com
TO: support@pwms.com
SUBJECT: A slight modification
DATE: October 11

Hi, this is Regina McIntosh from Adobo writing in regards to an order I placed this morning. The record locater number is CB206. I am starting to advertise Adobo through various methods, and one of my strategies will be to give out some of your company's clothing items that have been customized with our logo. Your products are so comfortable and look so good that we're sure our customers will love them. So I would like to increase the order size for item 212 to twenty units. It is not necessary to ship those with the rest of the items I purchased, but it would be appreciated if you do. Also, if possible, please charge the same credit card account that was used originally. Otherwise, send me an invoice and I will pay as quickly as possible.

Thank you,

Regina McIntosh

196. What is true about Pro Wear Mega Store?
   (A) It has a physical location for shoppers.
   (B) It is owned by the McIntosh family.
   (C) It is the second largest store of its kind in the region.
   (D) Its deliveries will be delayed because of a holiday.

197. What can be inferred from the form?
   (A) The items will be shipped via overnight delivery.
   (B) An image will not be printed on the clothes.
   (C) An item is unavailable.
   (D) The items are for the owner's personal use.

198. In the e-mail, paragraph 1, the word "order" in line 1 is closest in meaning to
   (A) sequence
   (B) group
   (C) request
   (D) inventory

199. What item does Ms. McIntosh want to purchase more of?
   (A) Collared shirts
   (B) Non-slip shoes
   (C) Hoodies
   (D) Slacks

200. According to Ms. McIntosh, what is true about Adobo?
   (A) It is beginning a marketing campaign.
   (B) It is hiring new employees.
   (C) It is changing its seasonal inventory.
   (D) It is moving to a new location.

Stop! This is the end of the test. If you finish before time is called, you may go back to Parts 5, 6, and 7 and check your work.

Jump Up TOEIC

DATA SHEET

응시일자 : 201   년   월   일

ANSWER SHEET

Jump Up TOEIC

수험번호
성 한글
명 한자
좌석번호

LISTENING (Part I ~ IV)

NO.	ANSWER	NO.	ANSWER	NO.	ANSWER	NO.	ANSWER	NO.	ANSWER
	A B C D		A B C D		A B C D		A B C D		A B C D
1	ⓐ ⓑ ⓒ ⓓ	21	ⓐ ⓑ ⓒ ⓓ	41	ⓐ ⓑ ⓒ ⓓ	61	ⓐ ⓑ ⓒ ⓓ	81	ⓐ ⓑ ⓒ ⓓ
2	ⓐ ⓑ ⓒ ⓓ	22	ⓐ ⓑ ⓒ ⓓ	42	ⓐ ⓑ ⓒ ⓓ	62	ⓐ ⓑ ⓒ ⓓ	82	ⓐ ⓑ ⓒ ⓓ
3	ⓐ ⓑ ⓒ ⓓ	23	ⓐ ⓑ ⓒ ⓓ	43	ⓐ ⓑ ⓒ ⓓ	63	ⓐ ⓑ ⓒ ⓓ	83	ⓐ ⓑ ⓒ ⓓ
4	ⓐ ⓑ ⓒ ⓓ	24	ⓐ ⓑ ⓒ ⓓ	44	ⓐ ⓑ ⓒ ⓓ	64	ⓐ ⓑ ⓒ ⓓ	84	ⓐ ⓑ ⓒ ⓓ
5	ⓐ ⓑ ⓒ ⓓ	25	ⓐ ⓑ ⓒ ⓓ	45	ⓐ ⓑ ⓒ ⓓ	65	ⓐ ⓑ ⓒ ⓓ	85	ⓐ ⓑ ⓒ ⓓ
6	ⓐ ⓑ ⓒ ⓓ	26	ⓐ ⓑ ⓒ ⓓ	46	ⓐ ⓑ ⓒ ⓓ	66	ⓐ ⓑ ⓒ ⓓ	86	ⓐ ⓑ ⓒ ⓓ
7	ⓐ ⓑ ⓒ ⓓ	27	ⓐ ⓑ ⓒ ⓓ	47	ⓐ ⓑ ⓒ ⓓ	67	ⓐ ⓑ ⓒ ⓓ	87	ⓐ ⓑ ⓒ ⓓ
8	ⓐ ⓑ ⓒ ⓓ	28	ⓐ ⓑ ⓒ ⓓ	48	ⓐ ⓑ ⓒ ⓓ	68	ⓐ ⓑ ⓒ ⓓ	88	ⓐ ⓑ ⓒ ⓓ
9	ⓐ ⓑ ⓒ ⓓ	29	ⓐ ⓑ ⓒ ⓓ	49	ⓐ ⓑ ⓒ ⓓ	69	ⓐ ⓑ ⓒ ⓓ	89	ⓐ ⓑ ⓒ ⓓ
10	ⓐ ⓑ ⓒ ⓓ	30	ⓐ ⓑ ⓒ ⓓ	50	ⓐ ⓑ ⓒ ⓓ	70	ⓐ ⓑ ⓒ ⓓ	90	ⓐ ⓑ ⓒ ⓓ
11	ⓐ ⓑ ⓒ ⓓ	31	ⓐ ⓑ ⓒ ⓓ	51	ⓐ ⓑ ⓒ ⓓ	71	ⓐ ⓑ ⓒ ⓓ	91	ⓐ ⓑ ⓒ ⓓ
12	ⓐ ⓑ ⓒ ⓓ	32	ⓐ ⓑ ⓒ ⓓ	52	ⓐ ⓑ ⓒ ⓓ	72	ⓐ ⓑ ⓒ ⓓ	92	ⓐ ⓑ ⓒ ⓓ
13	ⓐ ⓑ ⓒ ⓓ	33	ⓐ ⓑ ⓒ ⓓ	53	ⓐ ⓑ ⓒ ⓓ	73	ⓐ ⓑ ⓒ ⓓ	93	ⓐ ⓑ ⓒ ⓓ
14	ⓐ ⓑ ⓒ ⓓ	34	ⓐ ⓑ ⓒ ⓓ	54	ⓐ ⓑ ⓒ ⓓ	74	ⓐ ⓑ ⓒ ⓓ	94	ⓐ ⓑ ⓒ ⓓ
15	ⓐ ⓑ ⓒ ⓓ	35	ⓐ ⓑ ⓒ ⓓ	55	ⓐ ⓑ ⓒ ⓓ	75	ⓐ ⓑ ⓒ ⓓ	95	ⓐ ⓑ ⓒ ⓓ
16	ⓐ ⓑ ⓒ ⓓ	36	ⓐ ⓑ ⓒ ⓓ	56	ⓐ ⓑ ⓒ ⓓ	76	ⓐ ⓑ ⓒ ⓓ	96	ⓐ ⓑ ⓒ ⓓ
17	ⓐ ⓑ ⓒ ⓓ	37	ⓐ ⓑ ⓒ ⓓ	57	ⓐ ⓑ ⓒ ⓓ	77	ⓐ ⓑ ⓒ ⓓ	97	ⓐ ⓑ ⓒ ⓓ
18	ⓐ ⓑ ⓒ ⓓ	38	ⓐ ⓑ ⓒ ⓓ	58	ⓐ ⓑ ⓒ ⓓ	78	ⓐ ⓑ ⓒ ⓓ	98	ⓐ ⓑ ⓒ ⓓ
19	ⓐ ⓑ ⓒ ⓓ	39	ⓐ ⓑ ⓒ ⓓ	59	ⓐ ⓑ ⓒ ⓓ	79	ⓐ ⓑ ⓒ ⓓ	99	ⓐ ⓑ ⓒ ⓓ
20	ⓐ ⓑ ⓒ ⓓ	40	ⓐ ⓑ ⓒ ⓓ	60	ⓐ ⓑ ⓒ ⓓ	80	ⓐ ⓑ ⓒ ⓓ	100	ⓐ ⓑ ⓒ ⓓ

READING (Part V ~ VII)

NO.	ANSWER	NO.	ANSWER	NO.	ANSWER	NO.	ANSWER	NO.	ANSWER
	A B C D		A B C D		A B C D		A B C D		A B C D
101	ⓐ ⓑ ⓒ ⓓ	121	ⓐ ⓑ ⓒ ⓓ	141	ⓐ ⓑ ⓒ ⓓ	161	ⓐ ⓑ ⓒ ⓓ	181	ⓐ ⓑ ⓒ ⓓ
102	ⓐ ⓑ ⓒ ⓓ	122	ⓐ ⓑ ⓒ ⓓ	142	ⓐ ⓑ ⓒ ⓓ	162	ⓐ ⓑ ⓒ ⓓ	182	ⓐ ⓑ ⓒ ⓓ
103	ⓐ ⓑ ⓒ ⓓ	123	ⓐ ⓑ ⓒ ⓓ	143	ⓐ ⓑ ⓒ ⓓ	163	ⓐ ⓑ ⓒ ⓓ	183	ⓐ ⓑ ⓒ ⓓ
104	ⓐ ⓑ ⓒ ⓓ	124	ⓐ ⓑ ⓒ ⓓ	144	ⓐ ⓑ ⓒ ⓓ	164	ⓐ ⓑ ⓒ ⓓ	184	ⓐ ⓑ ⓒ ⓓ
105	ⓐ ⓑ ⓒ ⓓ	125	ⓐ ⓑ ⓒ ⓓ	145	ⓐ ⓑ ⓒ ⓓ	165	ⓐ ⓑ ⓒ ⓓ	185	ⓐ ⓑ ⓒ ⓓ
106	ⓐ ⓑ ⓒ ⓓ	126	ⓐ ⓑ ⓒ ⓓ	146	ⓐ ⓑ ⓒ ⓓ	166	ⓐ ⓑ ⓒ ⓓ	186	ⓐ ⓑ ⓒ ⓓ
107	ⓐ ⓑ ⓒ ⓓ	127	ⓐ ⓑ ⓒ ⓓ	147	ⓐ ⓑ ⓒ ⓓ	167	ⓐ ⓑ ⓒ ⓓ	187	ⓐ ⓑ ⓒ ⓓ
108	ⓐ ⓑ ⓒ ⓓ	128	ⓐ ⓑ ⓒ ⓓ	148	ⓐ ⓑ ⓒ ⓓ	168	ⓐ ⓑ ⓒ ⓓ	188	ⓐ ⓑ ⓒ ⓓ
109	ⓐ ⓑ ⓒ ⓓ	129	ⓐ ⓑ ⓒ ⓓ	149	ⓐ ⓑ ⓒ ⓓ	169	ⓐ ⓑ ⓒ ⓓ	189	ⓐ ⓑ ⓒ ⓓ
110	ⓐ ⓑ ⓒ ⓓ	130	ⓐ ⓑ ⓒ ⓓ	150	ⓐ ⓑ ⓒ ⓓ	170	ⓐ ⓑ ⓒ ⓓ	190	ⓐ ⓑ ⓒ ⓓ
111	ⓐ ⓑ ⓒ ⓓ	131	ⓐ ⓑ ⓒ ⓓ	151	ⓐ ⓑ ⓒ ⓓ	171	ⓐ ⓑ ⓒ ⓓ	191	ⓐ ⓑ ⓒ ⓓ
112	ⓐ ⓑ ⓒ ⓓ	132	ⓐ ⓑ ⓒ ⓓ	152	ⓐ ⓑ ⓒ ⓓ	172	ⓐ ⓑ ⓒ ⓓ	192	ⓐ ⓑ ⓒ ⓓ
113	ⓐ ⓑ ⓒ ⓓ	133	ⓐ ⓑ ⓒ ⓓ	153	ⓐ ⓑ ⓒ ⓓ	173	ⓐ ⓑ ⓒ ⓓ	193	ⓐ ⓑ ⓒ ⓓ
114	ⓐ ⓑ ⓒ ⓓ	134	ⓐ ⓑ ⓒ ⓓ	154	ⓐ ⓑ ⓒ ⓓ	174	ⓐ ⓑ ⓒ ⓓ	194	ⓐ ⓑ ⓒ ⓓ
115	ⓐ ⓑ ⓒ ⓓ	135	ⓐ ⓑ ⓒ ⓓ	155	ⓐ ⓑ ⓒ ⓓ	175	ⓐ ⓑ ⓒ ⓓ	195	ⓐ ⓑ ⓒ ⓓ
116	ⓐ ⓑ ⓒ ⓓ	136	ⓐ ⓑ ⓒ ⓓ	156	ⓐ ⓑ ⓒ ⓓ	176	ⓐ ⓑ ⓒ ⓓ	196	ⓐ ⓑ ⓒ ⓓ
117	ⓐ ⓑ ⓒ ⓓ	137	ⓐ ⓑ ⓒ ⓓ	157	ⓐ ⓑ ⓒ ⓓ	177	ⓐ ⓑ ⓒ ⓓ	197	ⓐ ⓑ ⓒ ⓓ
118	ⓐ ⓑ ⓒ ⓓ	138	ⓐ ⓑ ⓒ ⓓ	158	ⓐ ⓑ ⓒ ⓓ	178	ⓐ ⓑ ⓒ ⓓ	198	ⓐ ⓑ ⓒ ⓓ
119	ⓐ ⓑ ⓒ ⓓ	139	ⓐ ⓑ ⓒ ⓓ	159	ⓐ ⓑ ⓒ ⓓ	179	ⓐ ⓑ ⓒ ⓓ	199	ⓐ ⓑ ⓒ ⓓ
120	ⓐ ⓑ ⓒ ⓓ	140	ⓐ ⓑ ⓒ ⓓ	160	ⓐ ⓑ ⓒ ⓓ	180	ⓐ ⓑ ⓒ ⓓ	200	ⓐ ⓑ ⓒ ⓓ

한 권으로 끝내는

Jump Up
TOEIC

저자 임지완, 임정섭

Jump Up prep book for the TOEIC® Test

신토익
완벽반영

Intermediate LC+RC
해설집

TOEIC is a registered trademark of Educational Testing Service in the United States of America and other countries throughout the world.

한 권으로 끝내는

Jump Up TOEIC

저자 임지완, 임정섭

Jump Up prep book for the TOEIC® Test

신토익
완벽반영

Intermediate LC+RC
해설집

TOEIC is a registered trademark of Educational Testing Service in the United States of America and other countries throughout the world.

한 권으로 끝내는

Jump Up TOEIC

Intermediate LC+RC
해설집

LC 정답 및 해설

UNIT 1 1인 등장 사진

받아쓰기 연습 본책_p. 17

> 1. is painting 2. is repairing 3. is talking
> 4. is lying 5. are sitting

청취 집중 훈련 1 본책_p. 18

1.

(A) He's reading a pamphlet. (T)
그는 팸플릿을 읽고 있다.
(B) He's writing in a calendar. (F)
그는 달력에 글씨를 쓰고 있다.
(C) He's buying some postcards. (F)
그는 엽서 몇 장을 사고 있다.
(D) He's standing in front of a store. (T)
그는 가게 앞에 서 있다.

2.

(A) She's sending a fax. (F)
그녀는 팩스를 보내고 있다.
(B) She's greeting a customer. (F)
그녀는 고객을 맞이하고 있다.
(C) She's talking on the phone. (T)
그녀는 전화 통화를 하고 있다.
(D) She's working in an office. (T)
그녀는 사무실에서 일하고 있다.

3.

(A) He's going for a walk in the park. (F)
그는 공원으로 산책을 가고 있다.
(B) He's wearing a uniform. (T)
그는 유니폼을 입고 있다.
(C) He's pushing a cart down the sidewalk. (T)
그는 인도에서 카트를 밀고 있다.
(D) He's carrying some utensils. (F)
그는 몇 개의 주방도구를 나르고 있다.

4.

(A) He's sitting in the lobby. (T)
그는 로비에 앉아 있다.
(B) He's looking in the bag. (T)
그는 가방 안을 보고 있다.
(C) He's making a fire. (F)
그는 불을 지피고 있다.
(D) He's watering the plants. (F)
그는 화초에 물을 주고 있다.

청취 집중 훈련 2 본책_p. 19

> 1. (A)   2. (A)   3. (B)   4. (A)

1.

(A) She is adjusting her coat.
그녀는 코트를 단정히 하고 있다.
(B) She is checking the price.
그녀는 가격을 확인하고 있다.

2.

(A) He's loading the truck with furniture.
그는 트럭에 가구를 싣고 있다.

(B) He's moving the boxes into the apartment.
그는 아파트 안으로 상자를 옮기고 있다.

3.

(A) He's using a copier. 그는 복사기를 사용하고 있다.
(B) He's looking at the monitor. 그는 모니터를 보고 있다.

4.

(A) He's reaching for a brochure.
그는 소책자를 집어려 하고 있다.

(B) He's browsing in the store.
그는 상점 안을 둘러보고 있다.

실전 감각 익히기 _ 본책 _ p. 20–21

| 1. (D) | 2. (B) | 3. (C) | 4. (D) |
| 5. (B) | 6. (C) | 7. (D) | 8. (A) |

1.

(A) She is reaching for one of the boxes.
그녀는 상자 중 하나를 향해 손을 뻗고 있다.

(B) She is hanging her clothes on the rack.
그녀는 옷을 옷걸이에 걸고 있다.

(C) She is paying for some skates.
그녀는 스케이트에 대한 값을 지불하고 있다.

(D) She is placing some shoes on the shelf.
그녀는 선반 위에 신발을 올려놓고 있다.

해설 (A) 사진 속 인물이 손을 뻗고(reaching for) 있는 것은 맞지만 상자를 향해 손을 뻗고 있는 것은 아니다. 사진 속에 없는 단어가 등장하면 오답이 된다. (B) 사진 속에 옷걸이(rack)가 보이지 않으므로 오답이다. (C) pay for는 '값을 치르다'라는 의미이므로 계산대(counter) 장면에서 어울리는 표현이다.

어휘 reach for ~을 향해 손을 뻗다   rack 옷걸이, 선반
pay for ~에 대한 값을 지불하다   place 놓다, 두다   shelf 선반

2.

(A) He is setting up the ladder.
그는 사다리를 설치하고 있다.

(B) He is cleaning the windows.
그는 창문을 청소하고 있다.

(C) He is painting the store.
그는 가게에 페인트칠을 하고 있다.

(D) He is looking in the window.
그는 창문 안을 보고 있다.

해설 (A) 사다리(ladder)가 보이지만 남자가 설치하고 있는 것은 아니다. 사다리가 벽에 기대어 있으므로 A ladder is leaning against the wall.이라고 하면 정답이 될 수 있다. (C) 사진 속에서 페인트나 페인트 붓 등이 보이지 않으므로 오답이다. (D) 남자는 창문을 닦고 있는 것이지 창문 안을 들여다보는(looking in) 것은 아니므로 오답이다.

어휘 set up 설치하다   ladder 사다리   look in ~ 안을 들여다보다

3.

(A) The man is leaning against the wall.
남자는 벽에 기대고 있다.

(B) The man is operating the escalator.
남자는 에스컬레이터를 작동시키고 있다.

(C) The man is wearing a necktie.
남자는 넥타이를 매고 있다.

(D) The man is enjoying the exhibit.
남자는 전시회를 즐기고 있다.

해설 (A) 남자가 의자에 앉아 있는 중이지 벽에 기대고(lean against) 있지는 않다. (B) 에스컬레이터가 사진 속에 보이긴 하지만 남자가 그것을 작동하고(operating) 있지는 않다. (D) 남자는 의자에 앉아 있을 뿐 전시회(exhibit)를 즐기고 있는 것은 아니므로 오답이다.

어휘 lean against ~에 기대다   operate 작동시키다   wear 입다. 쓰다. 매다(착용의 상태를 나타냄)   exhibit 전시회; 전시하다

4.

(A) He is hanging up some pants.
그는 바지를 걸고 있다.

(B) He is trying on a jacket.
그는 재킷을 입어보고 있다.

(C) He is buying a new jacket online.
그는 온라인으로 새 재킷을 사고 있다.

(D) He is checking an item on the computer.
그는 한 물품을 컴퓨터로 확인하고 있다.

해설 (A) 남자가 바지를 걸고(hanging up) 있는 동작을 하고 있지는 않다. (B) try on은 '옷이나 신발이 잘 맞는지 입어보다'라는 뜻이다. 그러므로, 손님이 거울 앞에서 옷이나 신발을 착용해볼 때 쓸 수 있는 표현이다. (C) 남자가 컴퓨터로 확인을 하고 있는 모습이지 재킷을 구매하는 모습은 아니므로 오답이다.

어휘 hang up ~을 걸다   try on ~을 입어보다   check 확인하다   item 물품

5.

(A) He is eating in a restaurant.
그는 식당에서 식사 중이다.

(B) He is making some food.
그는 음식을 만들고 있다.

(C) He is looking at the menu.
그는 메뉴를 보고 있다.

(D) He is serving a customer.
그는 고객을 응대하고 있다.

해설 (A) 남자가 식사를 하고 있는 모습은 아니므로 오답이다. (C) 남자가 메뉴를 보고 있는 것이 아니라 음식을 만들고 있다. 참고로 '메뉴를 보다'를 'study the menu'라고 할 수도 있다는 것을 알아두자. (D) 현재 사진 속에는 고객(customer)이 보이지 않는다. 사진에 없는 단어를 썼으므로 오답이다.

어휘 look at ~을 보다   serve 고객을 응대하다   customer 고객

6.

(A) She is posting a notice on the board.
그녀는 게시판에 통지문을 붙이고 있다.

(B) She is reading a newspaper.
그녀는 신문을 읽고 있다.

(C) She is writing in a notebook.
그녀는 공책에 글씨를 쓰고 있다.

(D) She is looking at the monitor.
그녀는 모니터를 보고 있다.

해설 (A) 여자가 책상에 앉아 있는 모습이지 게시판에 통지문(notice)을 게시하고(posting) 있지는 않으므로 오답이다. (B) 현재 사진 속에 신문은 없으므로 오답이다. (D) 모니터가 있지만 여자가 보고 있는 것은 아니므로 오답이다. 참고로 '~을 보다'라는 표현으로 look at, stare at, gaze at이 있다는 것을 알아두자.

어휘 post 게시하다, 붙이다   notice 통지문   board 게시판   notebook 공책

7.

(A) He is preparing his meal.
그는 음식을 준비하고 있다.

(B) He is putting on an apron.
그는 앞치마를 입으려는 중이다.

(C) He is ordering some vegetables.
그는 몇몇 채소를 주문하고 있다.

(D) He is stocking the shelves.
그는 선반을 채우고 있다.

해설 (A) 남자는 현재 상점에서 일을 하고 있는 모습이지 음식(meal)을 준비하고 있지는 않다. (B) put on은 착용의 동작을 진행 중일 때 쓰는 표현이다. 착용의 상태를 나타내는 wear를 써서 He is wearing an apron.이라고 하면 정답이 될 수 있다. (C) 채소가 많이 보이지만 현재 주문을 하는(ordering) 모습은 아니라 오답이다. 물건을 채우거나 비축할 때는 stock이라는 동사가 적합하다.

어휘 prepare 준비하다   meal 음식   put on (옷 등을) 착용하다(동작)   vegetable 채소   stock ~에 물건을 재다, 비축하다

8.

(A) He is using some equipment.
그는 어떤 장비를 사용하고 있다.

(B) He is playing an instrument.
그는 악기를 연주하고 있다.

(C) He is manufacturing the engine parts.
그는 엔진 부품을 제조하고 있다.

(D) He is rowing a boat.
그는 노를 젓고 있다.

해설 (B) play an (musical) instrument는 '악기를 연주하다'라는 뜻이므로 오답이다. (C) 남자가 장비를 들고 있지만 무언가를 제조하는 동작이라고 볼 수는 없다. 또한 엔진 부품(engine parts)을 제조한다고 생각하는 것은 주관적인 판단인데 Part 1에서는 주관적인 판단을 배제한 채 객관적인 사실만을 묘사해야 한다는 점을 알아두자. (D) 남자가 노를 젓고(rowing) 있는 것은 아니므로 오답이다.

어휘 equipment 장비 play an instrument 악기를 연주하다 manufacture 제조하다 engine parts 엔진 부품 row 노를 젓다

UNIT 2 2인 이상 다수 등장 사진

받아쓰기 연습 본책_p. 25

1. is empty   2. are open   3. runs   4. overlook
5. is by the window   6. are on   7. along
8. over the river   9. have stopped   10. has arrived

청취 집중 훈련 1 본책_p. 26

1.

(A) They're holding a conference. (F)
그들은 회의를 열고 있다.

(B) They're waving to each other. (F)
그들은 서로에게 손을 흔들고 있다.

(C) They're shaking hands. (T)
그들은 악수를 하고 있다.

(D) They're facing each other. (T)
그들은 서로 마주보고 있다.

2.

(A) The floor in the lobby is carpeted. (T)
로비 바닥에 카펫이 깔려 있다.

(B) The bookshelf is empty. (F)
책장이 비어 있다.

(C) One woman is watching a movie. (F)
여자 한 명이 영화를 보고 있다.

(D) One of the women is using a computer. (T)
여자들 중 한 명은 컴퓨터를 쓰고 있다.

3.

(A) The people are crossing the intersection. (F)
사람들이 교차로를 건너고 있다.

(B) Some people have gathered on the corner of the street. (T)
몇몇 사람들이 길 모퉁이에 모여 있다.

(C) The equipment is placed in front of the building. (T)
장비가 건물 앞에 놓여 있다.

(D) The furniture is being loaded into a truck. (F)
가구가 트럭에 실리고 있다.

4.

(A) One woman is weighing the luggage. (T)
한 여자가 수화물의 무게를 재고 있다.

(B) There is a monitor on each counter. (T)
각각의 카운터에 모니터가 있다.

(C) The women are boarding the plane. (F)
여자들은 비행기에 탑승하고 있다.

(D) They are ordering their meals. (F)
그들은 식사를 주문하고 있다.

청취 집중 훈련 2 본책_p. 27

| 1. (A) | 2. (A) | 3. (B) | 4. (B) |

1.

(A) He is using a laptop computer.
그는 휴대용 컴퓨터를 사용하고 있다.

(B) A menu is on the table.
메뉴가 탁자 위에 있다.

2.

(A) They are wearing protective clothing.
그들은 보호복을 착용하고 있다.

(B) The vehicle has stopped at the traffic light.
차량이 교통 신호 앞에 멈췄다.

3.

(A) Skyscrapers overlook the water.
고층건물들이 물을 내려다보고 있다.

(B) The water is calm.
물이 잔잔하다.

4.

(A) Traffic is heavy at the intersection.
교차로에 교통이 혼잡하다.

(B) They are waiting at the intersection.
그들은 교차로에서 기다리고 있다.

실전 감각 익히기 본책_p. 28–29

| 1. (D) | 2. (A) | 3. (B) | 4. (D) |
| 5. (B) | 6. (D) | 7. (C) | 8. (A) |

1.

(A) The men are opening the boxes.
남자들이 상자를 열고 있다.

(B) Lampposts are along the road.
가로등이 도로를 따라 있다.

(C) The men are pushing a cart.
남자들이 손수레를 밀고 있다.

(D) The men are unloading the truck.
남자들이 트럭에서 짐을 내리고 있다.

> **해설** (A) 남자들이 상자를 내리고 있는(unloading) 중이지 상자를 열고 있는(opening) 모습은 아니므로 동작 묘사에 대한 오류이다. (B) 가로등이 사진에 보이진 않으므로 오답이다. (C) 사진에 손수레가 보이지만 손수레를 밀고 있는(pushing) 것은 아니므로 동작 묘사 오류에 해당된다.

> **어휘** open 열다 lamppost 가로등 기둥 push 밀다 cart 손수레 unload (짐을) 내리다 (cf. load 싣다)

2.

(A) The women are admiring the artwork.
여자들이 예술품을 감상하고 있다.

(B) The women are painting some pictures.
여자들이 그림을 그리고 있다.

(C) The women are looking in the opposite direction.
여자들이 (서로) 반대 방향을 보고 있다.

(D) There is a statue in the middle of a room.
방 가운데 조각상이 있다.

> **해설** (B) 여자들은 앉아서 예술품을 감상하고 있는(admiring) 중이지 그림을 그리고 있는 것은 아니므로 오답이다. (C) 두 여자의 시선은 모두 예술품을 향하고 있으므로 The women are looking in the same direction.(여자들이 같은 방향을 보고 있다.)라고 해야 한다. (D) 사진에는 조각상(a statue)이 없으므로 정답이 될 수 없다.

어휘 admire 감상하다   in the opposite direction 반대 방향으로
(cf. in the same direction 같은 방향으로)   statue 조각상
in the middle of ~의 가운데에

어휘 stairs 계단   lead up to ~로 나 있다   next to ~ 옆에
machine 기계   be seated 앉아 있다
form a line 줄을 서다(=stand in line)

3.

(A) Some people are standing on the train.
몇몇 사람들이 기차 안에 서 있다.

(B) The train is approaching the platform.
기차가 승강장에 접근하고 있다.

(C) The passengers are getting off the train.
승객들이 기차에서 내리고 있다.

(D) A railing runs along the platform.
난간이 승강장을 따라 나 있다.

해설 (A) 기차 안의 모습은 보이지 않으므로 사람들이 기차 안에 서 있는지 아닌지 판단할 수가 없다. (C) 승객들이 승강장에 서 있지 기차에서 내리고 있는 것이 아니므로 동작 묘사에 대한 오류이다. (D) 승강장 옆에 난간(railing)이 없으므로 상태 묘사에 대한 오류이다.

어휘 stand on the train 기차 안에 서 있다   approach 접근하다
platform 승강장   passenger 승객
get off 내리다 (cf. get on 타다)   railing 난간

4.

(A) The stairs lead up to the door.
계단이 문까지 나 있다.

(B) There is a chair next to the machine.
기계 옆에 의자가 있다.

(C) They are seated in the lobby.
그들은 로비에 앉아 있다.

(D) Some people have formed a line.
몇몇 사람들이 줄을 서 있다.

해설 (A) lead (up) to 길이나 계단이 '~로 이어지다, 나 있다'라는 뜻이다. 그런데 사진에는 계단(stairs)이 보이지 않으므로 정답이 될 수 없다. (B) 사진에 의자(chair)가 보이지 않으므로 오답이다. 참고로 남자가 이용하고 있는 기계는 현금인출기(automated teller machine)이다. (C) 〈사람 + be seated〉는 '사람이 앉아 있다'라는 뜻인데 사진 속의 사람들은 현재 줄을 서 있는 모습이므로 오답이다.

5.

(A) The computer is not in use.
컴퓨터를 사용하고 있지 않다.

(B) One woman is motioning with her hand.
한 여자가 손동작을 하고 있다.

(C) Both women are looking at the same document.
두 여자가 같은 서류를 보고 있다.

(D) A potted plant is on the shelf.
화분에 담은 식물이 선반 위에 있다.

해설 (A) 컴퓨터의 화면이 켜져 있으므로 컴퓨터를 사용하고 있다고 봐야 한다. (C) 서 있는 여자는 앉아 있는 여자를 보고 있는 것이지 서류(document)를 보고 있는 것이 아니므로 오답이다. (D) 화분에 담은 식물(potted plant)이 사진에 없으므로 상태 묘사에 대한 오류이다.

어휘 in use 사용 중인   motion 동작을 하다   document 서류
potted plant 화분에 담은 식물   shelf 선반

6.

(A) The waiter is serving some soup.
남자 종업원이 수프를 제공하고 있다.

(B) The men are ordering some food.
남자들이 음식을 주문하고 있다.

(C) Some of the men are washing the dishes.
남자들 중 일부는 접시를 닦고 있다.

(D) There are different sizes of pans in the kitchen.
주방에 서로 다른 크기의 냄비들이 있다.

해설 (A) 사진 속 남자들은 남자 종업원(waiter)이 아니라 요리사들이다. 또한 음식을 제공하고(serving) 있지도 않다. (B) 남자들은 지금 음식을 만들고 있는 것이지 주문을 하고 있는 것이 아니므로 동작 오류 묘사이다. (C) 사진에는 설거지를 하고 있는(washing the dishes) 사람이 없으므로 오답이다.

어휘 order 주문하다   wash[do] the dishes 설거지하다
different 다른   pan 냄비

7.

(A) The women are sitting at the table.
여자들은 탁자에 앉아 있다.
(B) The man is pointing at some flowers.
남자는 꽃을 가리키고 있다.
(C) The women are standing across from each other.
여자들은 서로 맞은편에 서 있다.
(D) There are some flowers under the table.
테이블 밑에 꽃 몇 송이가 있다.

해설 (A) 남자만 앉아 있고 여자들은 서 있으므로 상태 묘사 오류이다. (B) 탁자 위에 꽃이 있긴 하지만 남자가 가리키고 있는(pointing at) 것은 아니므로 동작 묘사 오류이다. (D) 꽃이 탁자 아래에 있는 것이 아니라 탁자 위에 있으므로 There are some flowers on the table.(테이블 위에 꽃이 있다.)이라고 해야 한다. 아울러 '꽃병에 꽃이 꽂혀 있다'라는 말은 Some flowers are put in the vase.라고 한다.

어휘 point at ~을 가리키다 stand[sit] across from each other 서로 맞은편에 서대[앉다] under ~ 밑에

8.

(A) They are riding their bicycles.
그들은 자전거를 타고 있다.
(B) A tree has fallen across the path.
나무 한 그루가 오솔길을 가로질러 쓰러졌다.
(C) A path winds through the garden.
정원에 오솔길이 굽어져 있다.
(D) They are running in the park.
그들은 공원에서 뛰고 있다.

해설 (B) 나무가 쓰러져 있는 모습이 보이지 않으므로 오답이다. (C) wind through는 '길이 굽어지다, 구불구불하다'라는 뜻인데 사진에는 오솔길이 구부러져 있다. 다만 이곳이 정원이 아니므로 정답이 될 수 없다. A path winds through the field.(오솔길이 들판에 굽어져 있다.)라고 할 수 있다. (D) 두 남자는 뛰고 있는 것이 아니라 자전거를 타고 있으므로 동작 묘사 오류이다.

어휘 ride 타다 fall 쓰러지다 path 오솔길
wind through (길이) 굽어지다 run 뛰다

UNIT 3 사물/배경 사진

받아쓰기 연습 본책_p.33

1. are displayed 2. is docked 3. are parked
4. has been completed 5. have been loaded
6. has been placed 7. is being painted
8. is being washed 9. is being built

청취 집중 훈련 1 본책_p.34

1.

(A) Papers are stacked on a table. (T)
서류들이 탁자 위에 쌓여 있다.
(B) The mailboxes are being carried. (F)
우편상자들이 운반되는 중이다.
(C) Copy machines are on the floor. (F)
복사기가 바닥 위에 있다.
(D) The shelf is empty. (T)
선반이 비어 있다.

2.

(A) Cars are being washed. (F)
차들이 세차되는 중이다.
(B) A parking garage is being built. (F)
주차장이 지어지고 있는 중이다.
(C) Cars are parked in a garage. (T)
차들이 주차장에 주차되어 있다.
(D) Pillars are lined up in the garage. (T)
기둥이 주차장에 일렬로 늘어서 있다.

3.

(A) The platform is filled with equipment. (F)
승강장이 장비로 가득 채워져 있다.

(B) The ship has many windows. (T)
배에 창문이 많다.

(C) The passengers are boarding the boat. (F)
승객들이 배에 탑승 중이다.

(D) The cruise ship is docked at the terminal. (T)
유람선이 터미널에 정박해 있다.

4.

(A) The road is covered with rocks. (F)
길이 바위로 덮여 있다.

(B) A road has been made at the work site. (T)
공사장에 길이 하나 만들어져 있다.

(C) The trail winds through the park. (F)
오솔길이 공원을 가로질러 굽어져 있다.

(D) There is heavy machinery on both sides of the road. (T) 길 양쪽에 중장비가 있다.

청취 집중 훈련 2 본책 _ p. 35

| 1. (A) | 2. (B) | 3. (B) | 4. (B) |

1.

(A) The car is parked at a gas station.
차가 주유소에 주차되어 있다.

(B) The car is being assembled.
차가 조립되고 있다.

2.

(A) The empty shelf is on the table.
빈 선반이 탁자 위에 있다.

(B) Some documents have been put in the shelves.
일부 서류들이 선반들 안에 놓여 있다.

3.

(A) The windows are being cleaned.
창문들이 청소되고 있는 중이다.

(B) The chairs have wheels.
의자에 바퀴가 달려 있다.

4.

(A) The plane is about to land on the runway.
비행기가 활주로에 막 착륙하려 한다.

(B) The plane is floating in the water.
비행기가 물에 떠 있다.

실전 감각 익히기 본책 _ p. 36

| 1. (A) | 2. (B) | 3. (C) | 4. (A) |
| 5. (B) | 6. (B) | 7. (B) | 8. (C) |

1.

(A) Some dishes are arranged on the counter.
몇몇 접시들이 카운터 위에 정리되어 있다.

(B) The sink has been filled with dishes.
싱크대에 접시들이 가득 차 있다.

(C) Some food has been served on the table.
약간의 음식이 탁자 위에 제공되었다.

(D) The dishes are stacked in the cupboard.
접시들이 찬장에 쌓여 있다.

해설 (B) 사진에 접시들은 보이지만 싱크대(sink)는 보이지 않으므로 오답으로 처리한다. (C) 음식이 보이지 않으므로 food라는 단어를 사용할 수 없다. 사진에 보이지 않는 단어가 언급되면 오답이다. (D) 접시들이 찬장(cupboard)에 쌓여 있는 것이 아니라 탁자 위에 쌓여 있으므로 The dishes are stacked on the table.(접시들이 탁자 위에 쌓여 있다.)이라고 해야 한다.

어휘 dish 접시 arrange 정리하다, 정돈하다 sink 싱크대
fill A with B A를 B로 채우다 serve (음식을) 제공하다
cupboard 찬장

2.

(A) The clothes are folded in the closet.
옷들이 옷장에 개어져 있다.
(B) There are various goods available.
다양한 상품들을 구할 수 있다.
(C) The clothes are being packed into a bag.
옷들이 가방에 챙겨 넣어지고 있다.
(D) The shoes are stored in boxes.
신발들이 상자들 안에 보관되어 있다.

해설 (A) 옷이 보이긴 하지만 옷장(closet) 안에 개어져(folded) 있는 것은 아니므로 사물의 상태 묘사에 대한 오류이다. (C) 〈is / are being + 과거분사〉는 사람이 사물에 특정 동작을 가할 때 쓰는 동사형인데 지금 옷을 챙겨 넣는 사람이 보이지 않으므로 오답이다. (D) 신발이 상자 안에 보관되어(stored) 있는 것이 아니라 선반에 진열되어 있으므로 The shoes are on display on the shelves.(신발이 선반에 진열되어 있다.)라고 해야 한다.

어휘 clothes 옷 fold 개다, 접다 closet 옷장 various 다양한
goods 상품 available 이용 가능한 pack 꾸리다, 챙겨 넣다
store 보관하다

3.

(A) The trees have fallen across the street.
나무들이 거리를 가로질러 쓰러졌다.
(B) The logs are stacked on the road.
통나무가 도로에 쌓여 있다.
(C) The logs have been loaded onto the trucks.
통나무가 트럭에 실려 있다.
(D) The vehicles are being towed.
차량들이 견인되고 있다.

해설 (A) 거리에 쓰러져 있는 나무가 없으므로 정답이 될 수 없다. (B) 통나무가 도로에 쌓여 있는(stacked) 것이 아니라 트럭에 쌓여 있으므로 오답이다. '~이 쌓여 있다'라고 할 때는 'be piled up' 또는 'be stacked up'을 쓴다. (D) 견인되는(towed) 차량의 모습은 보이지 않으므로 오답이다.

어휘 fall 쓰러지다 across ~을 가로질러 log 통나무 stack 쌓다
load 싣다 (cf. unload 내리다) vehicle 차량 tow 견인하다

4.

(A) The laundry has been separated.
세탁물이 분리되어 있다.
(B) The clothes are being ironed.
옷들이 다려지고 있다.
(C) The containers have been closed.
통들이 닫혀 있다.
(D) The towels are hung out on a line.
수건들이 줄에 널려 있다.

해설 (B) 누군가 옷을 다림질하고 있다면 정답이 될 수 있지만 사진에는 다림질하는 사람이 없으므로 오답이다. (C) 통(containers)들이 모두 열려 있으므로 The containers are open.(통들이 열려 있다.)이라고 해야 한다. (D) 수건들이 줄에 널려 있는(hung out) 것이 아니라 모두 통에 담겨 있으므로 오답이다.

어휘 laundry 세탁물 separate 분리하다 clothes 옷 iron 다림질하다
container 용기, 통 towel 수건 hang out 내다 걸다

5.

(A) The shelves are being stocked with the bottles.
선반에 병들이 채워지고 있다.
(B) A variety of goods are displayed.
다양한 상품들이 진열되어 있다.
(C) The store is crowded with shoppers.
상점이 쇼핑객들로 붐빈다.
(D) All the products are identical.
모든 상품들이 똑같이 생겼다.

해설 (A) 지금 선반에 병들이 채워지고 있는 것이 아니라 이미 상품들로 가득 채워져 있는 상태이므로 The shelves are filled with merchandise[products, goods].(선반은 상품들로 가득 채워져 있다.)라고 해야 한다. (C) 상점에 쇼핑객들이 한 명도 보이지 않으므로 붐빈다고 할 수 없다. (D) 상품들의 모양이 똑같은 것이 아니라 다양하므로 오답이다.

어휘 shelf 선반 (cf. 복수형은 shelves)　stock 쟁이다, 채우다
a variety of 다양한　goods 상품　be crowded with ~로 붐비다
shopper 쇼핑객　identical 모양이 똑같은

6.

(A) People are waiting in front of the elevator.
사람들이 엘리베이터 앞에서 기다리고 있다.

(B) There is a directory next to the elevator.
엘리베이터 옆에 안내판이 있다.

(C) There are some mailboxes on the floor.
바닥에 우편함 몇 개가 있다.

(D) The floor is being cleaned.
바닥이 청소되고 있다.

해설 (A) 사진에 사람이 없으므로 people이란 단어를 쓸 수 없다. (C) 바닥에는 우편함뿐만 아니라 아무 것도 없으므로 오답이다. (D) 사람이 현재 바닥을 청소하고 있어야만 The floor is being cleaned.라고 할 수 있는데 청소를 하고 있는 사람이 보이지 않으므로 오답이다.

어휘 wait 기다리다　in front of ~ 앞에서
directory (빌딩의) 입주자 안내판　next to ~ 옆에　floor 층, 바닥
clean 청소하다

7.

(A) Some of the flowers have been picked.
몇몇 꽃들이 꺾였다.

(B) The trees have been planted in rows.
나무들이 여러 줄로 심어졌다.

(C) Farmers are working in the orchard.
농부들이 과수원에서 일을 하고 있다.

(D) The plants are being watered.
식물에 물을 주고 있다.

해설 (A) 사진에 꽃이 보이지만 꺾인(picked) 상태가 아니므로 사물 묘사에 대한 오류이다. (C) 농부들(farmers)이 보이지 않으므로 오답이다. (D) 식물에 물을 주는 사람이 보이지 않으므로 오답이다. 〈is / are being + 과거분사〉는 사람이 사물에 해당 동작을 가하고 있을 때 사용해야 한다.

어휘 pick 꺾다　plant 심다; 식물　in rows 여러 줄로 (cf. in a row 한 줄로)　farmer 농부　orchard 과수원　water 물을 주다

8.

(A) A fence surrounds the garden.
울타리가 정원을 둘러싸고 있다.

(B) A sheet has been placed over the bicycle.
얇은 천이 자전거 위에 덮여 있다.

(C) The apartments have been covered.
아파트들이 덮여 있다.

(D) Work on the buildings has been completed.
건물 공사가 완료되었다.

해설 (A) 울타리(fence)는 보이지만 정원이 보이지 않으므로 오답이다. (B) 자전거는 보이지만 얇은 천으로 덮여 있는 것이 아니므로 오답이다. 참고로 '자전거가 기둥에 묶여 있다'라는 말은 The bicycle is chained[locked, secured, fastened] to a post.라고 한다. (D) 사진 속 아파트는 완공된 상태가 아니므로 공사가 완료되었다고 할 수 없다.

어휘 fence 울타리　surround 둘러싸다　sheet 얇은 천
place 놓다, 두다　cover 덮다　work 작업, 공사
complete 완료하다

Part 1 Review Test 본책_p.38-42

1. (B)	2. (B)	3. (A)	4. (C)	5. (B)
6. (D)	7. (C)	8. (C)	9. (D)	10. (A)

1.

(A) He is repairing a car.
(B) He is wearing a protective mask.
(C) He is putting out the fire.
(D) He is turning off the lights.

(A) 그는 자동차를 수리하고 있다.
(B) 그는 보호용 마스크를 착용하고 있다.
(C) 그는 불을 끄고 있다.
(D) 그는 전등을 끄고 있다.

해설 (A) 사진에 자동차(car)가 없으므로 오답이다. 사진에 없는 단어가 들리면 오답으로 처리한다. (B) 남자가 보호용 마스크(protective mask)를 착용하고 있는 상태이므로 정답이다. 그런데 He is putting on a protective mask.라고 하면 오답이 된다. 왜냐하면 wear는 착용의 상태를 나타내는 반면, put on은 착용의 동작을 나타내기 때문이다. (C) put out the fire는 '진화하다(= extinguish)'라는 뜻으로 사진과 관련이 없으므로 오답이다. (D) 남자가 전등을 끄고 있는(turning off the lights) 모습이 아니므로 오답이다.

어휘 repair 수리하다 wear 착용하다(착용의 상태를 나타냄) (cf. put on 착용하다(착용의 동작을 나타냄)) protective 보호용의 put out the fire 불을 끄다, 진화하다 turn off[on] (전기·가스·전자제품 등을) 끄다[켜다] light 전등

2.

(A) A man is reading a traffic sign.
(B) A man is working on the power lines.
(C) A man is directing traffic.
(D) A man is driving a truck.

(A) 한 남자가 교통 표지판을 읽고 있다.
(B) 한 남자가 송전선 작업을 하고 있다.
(C) 한 남자가 교통 정리를 하고 있다.
(D) 한 남자가 트럭을 운전하고 있다.

해설 (A) 사진에 교통 표지판(a traffic sign)이 없으므로 오답이다. 사진에 없는 단어가 들리면 오답으로 처리한다. 참고로 '신호등'은 a traffic light라고 한다. (B) 남자가 기계에 올라타 송전선(power lines) 작업을 하고 있으므로 정답이다. 참고로 '전신주'는 a utility pole이라고 한다. (C) 남자가 교통 정리를 하는(directing traffic) 모습이 아니므로 오답이다. (D) 남자가 송전선 작업을 하고 있는 것이지 트럭을 운전하고 있지는(driving a truck) 않으므로 오답이다.

어휘 read 읽다 traffic sign 교통 표지판 work on ~에 대해 작업하다 power line 송전선 direct traffic 교통 정리를 하다 drive 운전하다

3.

(A) There are some staff members in the office.
(B) One man is making a copy.
(C) They are moving some furniture.
(D) One staff member is hanging a picture on the wall.

(A) 사무실에 직원들이 몇 명 있다.
(B) 한 남자가 복사를 하고 있다.
(C) 그들은 가구를 옮기고 있다.
(D) 직원 한 명이 벽에 사진을 걸고 있다.

해설 (A) 사무실에 직원들이(some staff members) 몇 명 있는 모습이므로 정답이다. '직원들'은 workers, employees, staff members라고 할 수 있다. (B) 사진에 복사를 하고 있는(making a copy) 사람은 아무도 없으므로 오답이다. 관련해서 '복사기'는 a copy machine 또는 a copier라고 한다. (C) 사람들이 가구를 나르고 있는(moving some furniture) 모습이 아니므로 오답이다. (D) 사진을 걸고 있는(hanging a picture) 모습이 아니므로 오답이다. 현재 사진이 벽에 걸려 있으므로 There are some pictures hanging on the wall.(벽에 사진이 몇 개 걸려 있다.)이라고 할 수 있다.

어휘 There + be동사 + 주어 (주어)가 있다 a staff member 직원 make a copy 복사하다 move 옮기다 furniture 가구 hang 걸다

13

4.

(A) Some people are enjoying a movie.
(B) The photographers are facing each other.
(C) A man is sitting in a wheelchair.
(D) Some people are taking out their cameras.

(A) 몇몇 사람들이 즐겁게 영화를 보고 있다.
(B) 사진작가들이 서로 마주보고 있다.
(C) 한 남자가 휠체어에 앉아 있다.
(D) 몇몇 사람들이 카메라를 꺼내고 있다.

해설 (A) 사람들이 영화를 즐기고 있는(enjoying a movie) 모습이 아니므로 오답이다. (B) 사진작가들이 서로 마주보고 있는(facing each other) 모습이 아니므로 오답이다. 만약 The photographers are taking some pictures.(사진작가들이 사진을 찍고 있다.)라고 하면 정답이 될 수 있다. (C) 사진 오른쪽에 한 남자가 휠체어에 앉아 있는(sitting in a wheelchair) 모습이므로 정답이다. (D) 사진에 카메라를 꺼내고 있는(taking out their cameras) 사람이 없으므로 오답이다.

어휘 photographer 사진작가   face each other 마주보다
wheelchair 휠체어   take out 꺼내다

5.

(A) The man is walking down the stairs.
(B) The man is carrying some containers.
(C) The man is holding on to the railing.
(D) The man is loading some boxes in a cart.

(A) 남자가 계단을 내려가고 있다.
(B) 남자가 용기 몇 개를 나르고 있다.
(C) 남자가 난간을 꼭 잡고 있다.
(D) 남자가 카트에 상자를 싣고 있다.

해설 (A) 남자가 계단을 내려가고 있는(walking down the stairs) 모습이 아니므로 오답이다. 만약 The man is walking up the stairs.(남자가 계단을 올라가고 있다.)라고 하면 정답이 될 수 있다. (B) 남자가 용기를 나르고 있는(carrying some containers) 모습이므로 정답이다. (C) 사진 오른쪽에 난간(railing)이 보이지만 남자가 그것을 잡고 있는(holding on to) 모습이 아니므로 오답이다. (D) 사진에 카트(cart)가 보이지 않으므로 오답이다. 사진에 보이지 않는 단어가 들리면 오답으로 처리한다.

어휘 walk down[up] the stairs 계단을 내려가다[올라가다]
carry 나르다   container 용기, 통   hold on to ~을 꼭 잡다
load 싣다 (cf. unload 내리다)   cart 카트, 수레

6.

(A) He is taking an order.
(B) He is serving some food.
(C) He is eating in a restaurant.
(D) He is setting the table.

(A) 그는 주문을 받고 있다.
(B) 그는 음식을 제공하고 있다.
(C) 그는 식당에서 음식을 먹고 있다.
(D) 그는 식탁을 차리고 있다.

해설 (A) 남자가 손님에게 주문을 받고 있는(taking an order) 모습이 아니므로 오답이다. 손님 입장에서 '주문을 하고 있는'은 ordering some food라고 하고, '메뉴를 보고 있는'은 looking at[studying] the menu라고 한다. (B) 사진에 음식이 보이지 않으므로 오답이다. 사진에 없는 단어가 들리면 오답으로 처리한다. (C) 남자가 식당에서 일을 하고 있는 모습이지 식사를 하는(eating) 모습이 아니므로 오답이다. (D) 남자가 식탁을 차리고 있는(setting the table) 모습이므로 정답이다. 또한 남자가 식탁보를 펴고 있으므로 He is spreading a cloth on the table.(남자가 식탁보를 펴고 있다.)이라고 할 수도 있다.

어휘 take an order 주문을 받다   serve (음식 등을) 제공하다
set the table 식탁을 차리다

7.

(A) People are seated in groups.
(B) The guests are standing in a row.
(C) The lobby is crowded with guests.
(D) People are making some food.

(A) 사람들이 무리지어 앉아 있다.
(B) 손님들이 한 줄로 서 있다.
(C) 로비가 손님들로 붐빈다.
(D) 사람들이 음식을 만들고 있다.

해설 (A) 사람들이 앉아 있는(are seated) 모습이 아니므로 오답이다. 만약 사람들이 테이블 주변에 앉아 있으면 People are seated around the table.(사람들이 테이블 주변에 앉아 있다.)라고 할 수 있다. (B) 사람들이 한 줄로(in a row) 서 있는 모습이 아니므로 오답이다. 한 줄이 아닌 '여러 줄로'라는 말은 in rows라고 한다. (C) 로비가 많은 손님들로 붐비는(crowded with guests) 모습이므로 정답이다. (D) 사람들이 음식을 만들고 있는(making some food) 모습이 아니므로 오답이다.

어휘 be seated 앉아 있다   in groups (삼삼오오) 떼지어
stand around ~ 주변에 서다   be crowded with ~로 붐비다

8.

(A) The chairs have been stacked.
(B) The bottles are being arranged.
(C) The tables are not occupied.
(D) The windows are being cleaned.

(A) 의자들이 쌓여 있다.
(B) 병을 가지런히 놓고 있다.
(C) 탁자들이 비어 있다.
(D) 창문을 닦고 있다.

해설 (A) 의자들이 쌓여 있는(stacked) 모습이 아니므로 오답이다. '쌓다'는 stack (up) 또는 pile (up)이라고 한다. (B) ⟨be being+과거분사⟩는 사람이 사물에 해당 동작을 가할 때 쓸 수 있는 표현인데, 사진에 병을 가지런히 놓고 있는 사람이 없으므로 오답이다. (C) 테이블이 모두 비어 있는(not occupied) 상태이므로 정답이다. 같은 의미로 The tables are not taken.이라고 할 수 있다. (D) ⟨be being+과거분사⟩는 사람이 사물에 해당 동작을 가할 때 쓸 수 있는 표현인데, 사진에 창문을 닦고 있는 사람이 없으므로 오답이다.

어휘 stack 쌓다   bottle 병   arrange 가지런히 놓다
occupied (자리 등이) 차지된, 사용 중인   clean 청소하다, 닦다

9.

(A) People are walking in opposite directions.
(B) Some people are parking their cars.
(C) People are entering the building.
(D) People are crossing the street.

(A) 사람들이 반대 방향으로 걷고 있다.
(B) 몇몇 사람들이 주차를 하고 있다.
(C) 사람들이 건물로 들어가고 있다.
(D) 사람들이 길을 건너고 있다.

해설 (A) 사람들이 반대 방향으로(in opposite directions) 걷고 있는 모습이 아니므로 오답이다. 참고로 '같은 방향으로'는 in the same direction이라고 한다. (B) 사람들이 주차를 하는(parking their cars) 모습이 아니므로 오답이다. (C) 사진 오른쪽에 건물이 보이지만 사람들이 그 건물 안으로 들어가는(entering the building) 모습이 아니므로 오답이다. 만약 건물이 물가에 있을 경우 Some buildings overlook the water.(몇몇 건물에서 물이 내려다보인다.) 또는 Some buildings are reflected in the water.(몇몇 건물들이 물에 반사되어 있다.)라고 할 수 있다. (D) 사람들이 길을 건너고 있으므로 정답이다. 아울러 '보행자들'은 pedestrians라고 한다는 것을 알아두자.

어휘 in opposite directions 반대 방향으로   park one's car 주차하다
enter 들어가다   cross the street 길을 건너다

10.

(A) The shelf has been filled with meat.
(B) The meat is being weighed on the scale.
(C) The cook is using a machine.
(D) The meat is being cut into several pieces.

(A) 선반이 고기로 채워져 있다.
(B) 저울에 고기의 무게를 재고 있다.
(C) 요리사가 기계를 이용하고 있다.
(D) 고기를 여러 조각으로 썰고 있다.

해설 (A) 선반(shelf)이 고기로 채워져 있는(filled with meat) 모습이므로 정답이다. 아울러 '~으로 채워져 있다'라고 할 때 be stocked with라는 표현도 쓸 수 있다. (B) ⟨be being+과거분사⟩는 사람이 사물에 해당 동작을 가할 때 쓸 수 있는 표현인데, 저울에 고기의 무게를 재고 있는 사람이 없으므로 오답이다. (C) 사진에 기계를 사용하고 있는(using a machine) 요리사가 없으므로 오답이다. (D) ⟨be being+과거분사⟩는 사람이 사물에 해당 동작을 가할 때 쓸 수 있는 표현인데, 고기를 썰고 있는 사람이 없으므로 오답이다.

어휘 shelf 선반   be filled with ~로 채워지다
weigh 무게를 재다, 무게가 ~이다   scale 저울   machine 기계
cut 자르다   several 여러 개의   piece 조각

UNIT 4 Who / When / Where 의문문

받아쓰기 연습 본책 _ p. 47

1. Where / park / building / park
2. Who / copy / Call / coffee
3. When / due / Next Friday / do

청취 집중 훈련 1 본책 _ p. 48

| 1. (A) | 2. (A) | 3. (B) | 4. (C) |
| 5. (C) | 6. (B) | 7. (A) | 8. (C) |

1. When can we register for the seminar?
(A) Anytime before the 25th.
(B) The speaker was great.
(C) Thank you for registering.

우리는 언제 세미나에 등록할 수 있죠?
(A) 25일 전 언제라도요.
(B) 발표자는 훌륭했습니다.
(C) 등록해주셔서 감사합니다.

2. Who do I have to submit the report to?
(A) To the accounting department.
(B) The least expensive one available.
(C) By the end of every month.

제가 누구에게 보고서를 제출해야 하죠?
(A) 회계부서로요.
(B) 있는 것 중 가장 저렴한 것으로요.
(C) 매월 말까지입니다.

3. Where do you think you'll go for lunch?
(A) After the meeting.
(B) Maybe that new seafood place.
(C) It was delicious.

점심식사를 하러 어디로 가실 겁니까?
(A) 회의 끝난 후에요.
(B) 아마도 그 새로 생긴 해산물 식당으로요.
(C) 맛있었어요.

4. When will you conduct a customer survey?
(A) Participants have to complete the form.
(B) To our loyal customers.
(C) As soon as I get the manager's approval.

당신은 언제 고객 설문조사를 실시할 겁니까?
(A) 참가자들은 양식을 작성해야 합니다.
(B) 우리 단골 고객들에게요.
(C) 제가 관리자의 승인을 받자마자요.

5. Where did you go yesterday?
(A) I'm too busy today.
(B) I need to call a client.
(C) I had a doctor's appointment.

어제 어디에 갔었죠?
(A) 저는 오늘 너무 바쁩니다.
(B) 저는 고객을 방문해야 해요.
(C) 의사와 약속이 있었어요.

6. Who is attending the contest?
(A) Oh, is he going to attend?
(B) Everyone on the sales team.
(C) No, it was cancelled.

누가 대회에 참석하죠?
(A) 오, 그가 참석하나요?
(B) 영업팀 전원이요.
(C) 아니요, 그건 취소되었어요.

7. Who put the folders on my desk?
(A) Steve dropped them off for you.
(B) His desk is in the corner.
(C) Yes, they just need to be folded.

누가 서류철을 제 책상 위에 놓았죠?
(A) 스티브가 당신을 위해 두었습니다.
(B) 그의 책상은 모퉁이에 있습니다.
(C) 네, 그것을 접어야 합니다.

8. Where can I get my shoes repaired?
(A) They are very expensive.
(B) I buy all my clothes online.
(C) There's a good store on Main Street.

제가 어디에서 신발을 수선할 수 있죠?
(A) 그것은 매우 비쌉니다.
(B) 저는 온라인에서 모든 옷을 구입합니다.
(C) 메인 가에 좋은 곳이 있어요.

청취 집중 훈련 2 본책_p. 49

| 1. (C) | 2. (A) | 3. (B) | 4. (C) |
| 5. (B) | 6. (A) | 7. (A) | 8. (C) |

1. When do you need my proposal?
(A) No, I'd rather not.
　→ 의문사의문문에 yes/no 대답 불가
(B) I haven't finished it yet.
　→ 제안서와 연상작용을 일으키는 오답
(C) Before I leave the office.
　→ when에 대해 시간 접속사 before를 이용한 답변

저의 제안서가 언제 필요하십니까?
(A) 아니요, 차라리 하지 않겠습니다.
(B) 아직 그것을 끝내지 못했습니다.
(C) 제가 퇴근하기 전에요.

어휘 proposal 제안서
　would rather not + 동사원형 차라리 ~하지 않겠다

2. Where do we store our extra copy paper?
(A) In the supply cabinet.
　→ where의 질문에 어울리는 장소 답변
(B) The store is closed.
　→ 동일 단어(store)를 사용한 오답
(C) Five or six pages.
　→ paper와 연상작용을 일으키는 오답

여분의 복사용지를 어디에 보관하죠?
(A) 비품 캐비닛에요.
(B) 그 상점은 문을 닫았어요.
(C) 5~6 페이지요.

어휘 store 보관하다　supply 용품　closed 문을 닫은

3. When is the managers' meeting?
(A) In Room C.
　→ where에 대한 답변
(B) Tomorrow at 2 P.M.
　→ 정확한 시점 제시
(C) Everybody attended.
　→ who에 대한 답변

관리자 회의는 언제죠?
(A) C 회의실에서요.
(B) 내일 오후 2시요.
(C) 전원 참석했습니다.

어휘 attend 참석하다

4. Who is in charge of the Henderson account?
(A) Yes, we charged the batteries.
　→ 의문사의문문에 yes/no 대답 불가
(B) Just pay in cash this time.
　→ charge(청구하다)와 연상작용을 일으키는 오답
(C) Janet handles it, I think.
　→ who 질문에 대해 사람 이름으로 답변 가능

누가 핸더슨 계정을 담당하나요?
(A) 네, 우리가 건전지를 충전했습니다.
(B) 이번에는 현금으로 지불하세요.
(C) 제 생각에 재닛이 관리합니다.

어휘 be in charge of ~을 담당하다　charge 충전하다
　handle 처리하다, 관리하다

5. When is the meeting scheduled for?
(A) In the conference room.
　→ where에 대한 답변
(B) Thursday at 3, I think.
　→ 구체적인 시점 제시
(C) To discuss the sales figures.
　→ why의 질문에 대한 답변

회의가 언제로 예정되어 있습니까?
(A) 회의실에서요.
(B) 제 생각에 목요일 3시입니다.
(C) 매출액을 논의하기 위해서요.

어휘 be scheduled for ~로 예정되다　sales figures 매출액

6. Who is the manager of the Hampshire office?
(A) I have no idea.
　→ 회피성 표현으로 정답
(B) No, it's in the same location.
　→ 의문사의문문에 yes/no 대답 불가
(C) He stepped out a few minutes ago.
　→ where의 질문에 대한 답변

누가 햄프셔 사무실의 관리자입니까?
(A) 모르겠습니다.
(B) 아뇨, 그것은 같은 지점에 있습니다.
(C) 그는 몇 분 전에 나갔습니다.

어휘 location 지점, 장소　step out 나가다

7. Who's leading this week's staff meeting?
(A) I think Anna will.
→ who에 대한 답변으로 사람 이름 제시 가능
(B) It has been postponed until next week.
→ meeting과 연상작용을 일으키는 오답
(C) I really enjoy reading.
→ 유사발음 reading을 사용한 오답

누가 이번 주 직원회의를 주도합니까?
(A) 제 생각에는 애나입니다.
(B) 다음 주까지 연기되었습니다.
(C) 저는 독서를 매우 좋아합니다.

어휘 lead 이끌다, 주도하다 postpone 연기하다

8. Where is the Berkowitz file?
(A) About 250 pages long.
→ file의 분량에 대한 연상작용을 일으키는 오답
(B) I'll file it now.
→ 동일 발음(file)을 사용한 오답
(C) Ask the accounting manager.
→ 우회적 답변 가능

버코비츠 파일이 어디 있죠?
(A) 대략 250페이지 분량입니다.
(B) 제가 지금 정리해서 보관하겠습니다.
(C) 회계부장에게 물어보세요.

어휘 file 문서를 정리해서 보관하다 accounting 회계

청취 집중 훈련 3 본책 _ p. 50

| 1. (B) | 2. (B) | 3. (A) | 4. (A) |
| 5. (C) | 6. (A) | 7. (C) | 8. (B) |

1. When will the company announce staff promotions?
(A) You deserve it!
→ 승진과 연상작용을 일으키는 오답
(B) It hasn't been decided yet.
→ 회피성 답변 가능
(C) Lisa will be promoted to sales manager.
→ 유사발음 promoted를 사용한 오답

회사는 언제 직원 승진을 발표할까요?
(A) 당신은 그럴 자격이 있습니다!
(B) 아직 결정되지 않았습니다.
(C) 리사가 영업부장으로 승진할 거예요.

어휘 announce 발표하다 promotion 승진, 홍보
deserve ~을 받을 만하다, 자격이 있다
be promoted to ~로 승진하다 sales manager 영업부장

2. Who is the new desk for?
(A) It's made of wood.
→ desk와 연상작용을 일으키는 오답
(B) We hired a new employee.
→ who에 대한 답변으로 인물이나 직책 제시 가능
(C) His desk is next to the copier.
→ 동일 발음 desk를 사용한 오답

새 책상은 누가 쓸 겁니까?
(A) 그것은 나무로 만들어졌어요.
(B) 우리가 신입 직원을 고용했습니다.
(C) 그의 책상은 복사기 옆에 있어요.

어휘 be made of ~로 만들어지다 hire 고용하다 employee 직원
next to ~ 옆에 copier 복사기

3. Where's Ms. Finchley?
(A) She's in Toronto.
→ 질문과 어울리는 구체적인 장소 제시
(B) Our new accountant.
→ who에 대한 답변
(C) She's getting better.
→ how에 대한 답변

핀칠리 씨는 어디에 있죠?
(A) 그녀는 토론토에 있습니다.
(B) 우리의 신임 회계사입니다.
(C) 그녀는 점점 나아지고 있어요.

어휘 accountant 회계사 get better 나아지다, 좋아지다

4. When is your doctor's appointment?
(A) At 9 tomorrow morning.
→ 질문과 어울리는 구체적인 시점 제시
(B) I'm getting my eyes checked.
→ doctor와 연상작용을 일으키는 오답
(C) She has to leave early.
→ 의미상 she를 주어로 쓸 수 없으므로 인칭 오류로 인한 오답

당신의 진료 예약은 언제입니까?
(A) 내일 아침 9시입니다.
(B) 저는 안과 검진을 받을 겁니다.
(C) 그녀는 일찍 나가야 합니다.

어휘 doctor's appointment 진료 예약
get + A(목적어) + 과거분사 A가 ~되게 하다 check 검진하다
leave 나가다, 퇴근하다 early 일찍

5. Where can I exchange Japanese yen for U.S. dollars?
(A) You should transfer at Yakasa Station.
　→ exchange와 연상작용을 일으키는 오답
(B) Here is your change.
　→ 유사발음 change를 사용한 오답
(C) At Simmons Bank.
　→ 구체적인 장소 제시

어디에서 일본 엔화를 미 달러로 교환할 수 있습니까?
(A) 야카사 역에서 갈아타야 합니다.
(B) 여기 잔돈 있습니다.
(C) 시몬스 은행에서요.

어휘 exchange 교환하다 transfer 갈아타다 change 잔돈

6. Who's overseeing the Hamilton construction project?
(A) Mr. Jenson is managing the project.
　→ 사람 이름 제시로 정답
(B) They moved the headquarters overseas.
　→ 유사발음(overseas)을 사용한 오답
(C) It will be completed next month.
　→ construction project에 대한 연상작용을 일으키는 오답

누가 해밀튼 공사 프로젝트를 감독하고 있습니까?
(A) 젠슨 씨가 그 프로젝트를 관리하고 있습니다.
(B) 그들은 본사를 해외로 옮겼습니다.
(C) 그 공사 프로젝트는 다음 달에 완료될 것입니다.

어휘 oversee 감독하다 headquarters 본사 overseas 해외로
complete 완료하다

7. When is your job interview?
(A) In the meeting room.
　→ where의 질문에 대한 답변
(B) I am a little nervous.
　→ job interview에 대한 연상작용을 일으키는 오답
(C) I haven't been informed yet.
　→ 회피성 표현으로 정답

당신의 취업 면접은 언제입니까?
(A) 회의실에서요.
(B) 저는 약간 긴장됩니다.
(C) 저는 아직 통지 받지 못했습니다.

어휘 job interview 취업 면접 nervous 긴장되는, 불안한
inform 통지하다

8. Where is the nearest convenience store?
(A) It's very comfortable, too.
　→ 편의(convenience)와 연상작용을 일으키는 오답
(B) There's one on Mott Street.
　→ 구체적인 거리명 제시
(C) The store is still open.
　→ 동일 발음(store)을 쓴 오답

가장 가까운 편의점이 어디에 있습니까?
(A) 그것은 또한 아주 편안합니다.
(B) 모트 가에 하나 있습니다.
(C) 그 상점은 아직 열려 있습니다.

어휘 convenience store 편의점 comfortable 편안한
still 여전히, 아직도 open (상점이) 문을 연

실전 감각 익히기 본책_p. 51

| 1. (A) | 2. (C) | 3. (B) | 4. (A) | 5. (B) |
| 6. (A) | 7. (C) | 8. (B) | 9. (A) | 10. (B) |

1. When is Maria's first day of work?
(A) Next Monday, the 15th.
　→ 질문과 어울리는 시점 제시
(B) I had a wonderful time.
　→ how에 대한 답변
(C) In the customer service department.
　→ where에 대한 답변

마리아의 근무 첫날이 언제입니까?
(A) 다음 주 월요일 15일이요.
(B) 근사한 시간을 보냈습니다.
(C) 고객 서비스 부서에서요.

어휘 first day of work 근무 첫날 customer 고객
department 부서

2. Who's organizing the banquet this year?
(A) I'm going to the bank later.
　→ 유사발음(bank)을 사용한 오답
(B) Rachel organized the shelves yesterday.
　→ 유사발음(organized)을 사용한 오답
(C) Kent is in charge of that.
　→ 질문과 어울리는 사람 이름 제시

누가 올해 연회를 준비하고 있죠?
(A) 제가 나중에 은행에 갈 겁니다.
(B) 레이첼이 어제 선반을 정리했습니다.
(C) 켄트가 담당합니다.

어휘 banquet 연회 shelf 선반 be in charge of ~을 맡다

3. When do you think the copy machine will be repaired?
(A) I like coffee with cream and sugar.
→ 유사발음(coffee)을 사용한 오답
(B) We're not sure yet.
→ 회피성 답변으로 정답 제시
(C) He fixed supper last night.
→ repair와 연상작용을 일으키는 오답

복사기가 언제 수리될 거라고 생각하세요?
(A) 저는 크림과 설탕을 넣은 커피를 좋아합니다.
(B) 아직 확실하지 않습니다.
(C) 그는 어젯밤 저녁을 준비했습니다.

어휘 repair 수리하다 fix supper 저녁을 준비하다 (cf. fix 고치다, 준비하다)

4. Where is the best place to buy office furniture?
(A) Try Furniture Plus on Broad Street.
→ 질문과 어울리는 구체적인 장소 제시
(B) It looks great.
→ furniture와 연상작용을 일으키는 오답
(C) No, his office is on the first floor.
→ 의문사의문문에 yes/no 대답 불가

사무용 가구를 사기에 가장 좋은 곳은 어디죠?
(A) 브로드 가에 있는 퍼니쳐 플러스에 가보세요.
(B) 그것은 훌륭해 보입니다.
(C) 아니요, 그의 사무실은 1층에 있습니다.

어휘 office furniture 사무용 가구 look ~해 보이다 floor 층

5. Who should I see about upgrading our computers?
(A) I didn't buy that laptop.
→ computer와 연상작용을 일으키는 오답
(B) That would be Ken in the IT department.
→ 질문과 어울리는 사람 이름 제시
(C) The computer equipment is outdated.
→ 동일 발음(computer)을 사용한 오답

우리 컴퓨터 업그레이드에 관해서 제가 누구를 만나야 합니까?
(A) 아니요, 저는 그 휴대용 컴퓨터를 사지 않았습니다.
(B) IT 부서의 켄일 겁니다.
(C) 그 컴퓨터 장비는 구식입니다.

어휘 upgrade 개선하다, 향상시키다 outdated 낡은, 구식인

6. Where will we hold Mr. Park's retirement party?
(A) Mr. Kim has information about that.
→ 회피성 답변으로 정답 제시
(B) Congratulations on your retirement!
→ party에 대한 연상작용을 일으키는 오답
(C) Jill in Human Resources will retire soon.
→ 유사발음(retire)을 사용한 오답

우리 어디에서 박 씨의 은퇴 파티를 열까요?
(A) 김 씨가 그것에 대한 정보를 갖고 있습니다.
(B) 당신의 은퇴를 축하 드립니다!
(C) 인적자원부의 질은 곧 은퇴할 겁니다.

어휘 hold 열다, 개최하다 retirement 은퇴 Congratulations! 축하합니다!

7. Who was chosen as the employee of the year?
(A) You can choose from the items.
→ 유사발음(choose)을 사용한 오답
(B) No, they are not eligible.
→ 의문사의문문은 yes/no 대답 불가
(C) The board of directors are still considering.
→ 우회적 답변으로 정답 제시

누가 올해의 직원으로 선정되었죠?
(A) 그 물건들 중에서 고르시면 됩니다.
(B) 아니요, 그들은 자격이 없습니다.
(C) 이사진이 여전히 고려 중이에요.

어휘 the employee of the year 올해의 직원 eligible 자격이 있는 board of directors 이사회 consider 고려하다

8. When are the department expense reports due?
(A) It was very expensive.
→ 유사발음(expensive)을 사용한 오답
(B) I haven't heard about that.
→ 회피성 답으로 정답 제시
(C) I'm going to do it next week.
→ 유사발음(do)을 사용한 오답

부서 비용 보고서의 마감 기한이 언제죠?
(A) 그것은 매우 비쌌습니다.
(B) 그것에 대한 얘기를 못 들었습니다.
(C) 저는 그것을 다음 주에 할 예정입니다.

어휘 expense report 비용 보고서 due 마감 기한인

9. When are you leaving for the airport?
(A) Around five.
  → 질문과 어울리는 구체적인 시점 제시
(B) My flight arrives at nine.
  → 공항과의 연상작용을 이용한 오답
(C) That's Okay. I'm taking a shuttle bus.
  → 공항과 연상작용을 일으키는 오답

언제 공항으로 떠납니까?
(A) 대략 5시에요.
(B) 제 비행편이 9시에 도착합니다.
(C) 괜찮습니다. 저는 셔틀 버스를 탈 겁니다.

어휘 leave for ~로 떠나다 around 대략 take (교통수단을) 타다

10. Where do we keep our mailing envelopes?
(A) It took about three days.
  → 우편 발송과 연상작용을 일으키는 오답
(B) There are some in the top cabinet.
  → 질문과 어울리는 구체적인 장소 제시
(C) No, he already sent me a letter.
  → 의문사의문문에 yes/no 대답 불가

우리는 우편 봉투를 어디에 보관하죠?
(A) 대략 3일 걸렸습니다.
(B) 제일 위쪽 캐비닛에 조금 있습니다.
(C) 아니요, 그는 벌써 저에게 편지를 보냈습니다.

어휘 keep 보관하다 envelope 봉투 take + 기간 기간이 걸리다

UNIT 5 Why/How/What 의문문

받아쓰기 연습 본책 _ p. 55

1. calling / To / of our / cold
2. Why / noise / place
3. last / went hiking / lasts

청취 집중 훈련 1 본책 _ p. 56

| 1. (B) | 2. (A) | 3. (C) | 4. (C) |
| 5. (C) | 6. (A) | 7. (B) | 8. (B) |

1. Why was the training session cancelled?
(A) The train already left.
(B) The instructor had a scheduling conflict.
(C) I learned a lot.

교육이 왜 취소되었나요?
(A) 기차는 벌써 떠났습니다.
(B) 강사의 일정이 겹쳤습니다.
(C) 저는 많이 배웠습니다.

2. How often is the Web site updated?
(A) Usually every hour.
(B) Yes, it looks very new.
(C) It'll start on January 7.

웹사이트는 얼마나 자주 업데이트 되죠?
(A) 보통 매시간마다 됩니다.
(B) 네, 아주 새로워 보입니다.
(C) 1월 7일에 시작될 겁니다.

3. What type of software does the accounting team use?
(A) They have to wear formal clothing.
(B) By the time the shipment is arrived.
(C) Let me check for you.

회계팀은 어떤 종류의 소프트웨어를 씁니까?
(A) 그들은 정장을 입어야 합니다.
(B) 배송물이 도착할 때까지요.
(C) 제가 확인해 볼게요.

4. How were our sales during the holiday period?
(A) For two weeks.
(B) Ten percent off most items.
(C) Better than expected.

연휴 동안 우리 매출은 어땠나요?
(A) 2주간요.
(B) 대부분의 물품이 10% 할인됩니다.
(C) 예상보다 좋았습니다.

5. How long will it take to ship the items?
(A) For the client.
(B) By sea and air.
(C) About 3 to 5 days.

그 물품을 보내는 데 얼마나 걸릴까요?
(A) 고객을 위해서요.
(B) 배편과 항공편으로요.
(C) 대략 3일에서 5일입니다.

6. Why don't we go out for lunch now?
(A) I will try today's lunch special.
(B) The restaurant is too far.
(C) Sure, where do you want to go?

지금 점심 먹으러 나가는 게 어때요?
(A) 저는 오늘의 점심 특선메뉴를 먹어볼래요.
(B) 그 식당은 너무 멀어요.
(C) 좋아요, 어디로 가고 싶으세요?

7. How many people entered the competition?
(A) I won first place.
(B) There were about three hundred.
(C) The entrance is through those doors.

얼마나 많은 사람들이 시합에 참가했죠?
(A) 제가 1등을 했습니다.
(B) 대략 300명이 있었습니다.
(C) 입장은 저쪽 문으로 하십니다.

8. What are you going to do at the convention?
(A) No, I don't have the time.
(B) I'm giving a speech.
(C) Yes, they often host it.

회의 때 무엇을 할 예정입니까?
(A) 아니요, 저는 그럴 시간이 없습니다.
(B) 저는 연설을 할 겁니다.
(C) 네, 그들이 자주 그것을 주최합니다.

청취 집중 훈련 2 본책_p. 57

| 1. (A) | 2. (B) | 3. (C) | 4. (B) |
| 5. (A) | 6. (B) | 7. (C) | 8. (C) |

1. Why don't you join us after the meeting?
(A) Good idea, I think I will.
→ 제안의문문에 대한 긍정적인 답변으로 정답
(B) We met yesterday.
→ 질문과는 무관하게 meeting과의 연상작용으로 met를 쓴 오답
(C) No, it's before the meeting.
→ 동일 단어(meeting)를 사용했지만 의미상 부적절한 오답

회의 후에 저희와 함께 하시는 게 어때요?
(A) 좋은 생각이네요. 그렇게 할게요.
(B) 우리는 어제 만났습니다.
(C) 아니요, 그것은 회의 전입니다.

어휘 Why don't you ~? ~하는 게 어때요?   join 합류하다

2. How much is this jacket?
(A) It's the smallest size.
→ 가격을 묻는 질문에 크기로 답했으므로 오답
(B) It's $80.
→ 정확한 재킷 가격을 제시하고 있으므로 정답
(C) It's leather.
→ 가격을 묻는 질문에 재킷의 소재로 답변했으므로 오답

이 재킷은 얼마죠?
(A) 그것이 가장 작은 사이즈입니다.
(B) 80달러입니다.
(C) 그것은 가죽입니다.

어휘 How much+be+주어? ~이 얼마죠?   leather 가죽

3. What time are our reservations for?
(A) Four more people.
→ 예약 시간을 묻는 질문에 인원 수로 대답했으므로 오답
(B) They usually serve chicken.
→ 예약(reservations)에서 연상 가능한 오답
(C) They're for 6 o'clock.
→ 예약 시간을 정확히 언급하고 있으므로 정답

우리의 예약 시간이 언제죠?
(A) 네 명 더요.
(B) 그들은 보통 닭고기를 제공합니다.
(C) 6시로 예약되어 있습니다.

어휘 reservation 예약   serve (음식을) 내놓다

4. Why are so many people late this morning?
(A) About 9 A.M. at the latest.
→ 이유를 묻는 질문에 시점을 대답했으므로 오답
(B) Maybe the subway was delayed.
→ 사람들이 늦는 이유를 언급하고 있으므로 정답
(C) Sure, I'll call you if I'm late.
→ 질문과 무관한 내용으로 동일 단어(late)를 쓴 오답

오늘 아침 왜 이렇게 많은 사람들이 지각을 하죠?
(A) 늦어도 오전 9시쯤입니다.
(B) 아마도 지하철이 지연되었나봐요.
(C) 네, 제가 늦으면 전화 드릴게요.

어휘 at the latest 늦어도   delay 지연시키다

5. How did you like the conference?
(A) It was very informative.
  → 의견을 묻는 질문에 대한 적절한 답변이므로 정답
(B) No, I won't attend.
  → 제안의문문을 제외하고는 의문사의문문에 yes나 no로 대답할 수 없으므로 오답
(C) By shuttle bus.
  → How did you go to the conference?에 대한 답변이므로 오답

회의는 어땠나요?
(A) 매우 유익했습니다.
(B) 아니요, 저는 참석하지 않을 겁니다.
(C) 셔틀버스로요.

어휘 How do you like ~? ~은 어떻습니까? conference 회의 informative 유익한 attend 참석하다

6. What type of software do you develop?
(A) It's still under development.
  → 질문과 관계 없는 유사발음(development)을 사용한 오답
(B) Antivirus program.
  → 개발의 종류에 대한 구체적인 답변이므로 정답
(C) I need to type this report.
  → 질문의 type과 다른 의미로 type을 사용한 오답

어떤 종류의 소프트웨어를 개발하시죠?
(A) 여전히 개발 중입니다.
(B) 바이러스 방지 프로그램입니다.
(C) 저는 이 보고서를 타이핑해야 해요.

어휘 develop 개발하다 under development 개발 중 antivirus 바이러스 방지의

7. Why don't we try the restaurant on Fifth Street?
(A) No, dinner's at 6 o'clock.
  → 질문과 무관하게 시점을 제시했으므로 오답
(B) Right next to the dry cleaner's.
  → 제안의문문에 위치로 대답했으므로 오답
(C) Okay, I heard their food is good.
  → 제안의문문에 어울리는 적절한 답변이므로 정답

5번가에 있는 식당을 가보는 게 어때요?
(A) 아니요, 저녁식사는 6시입니다.
(B) 세탁소 바로 옆입니다.
(C) 좋아요, 그곳 음식이 맛있다고 들었어요.

어휘 try ~을 시도해보다 right 바로 next to ~ 옆에 dry cleaner's 세탁소

8. How many employees have signed up for the contest?
(A) It's very interesting.
  → 인원수에 대한 질문과 무관한 답변이므로 오답
(B) Your signature is required.
  → signed에 대한 연상작용을 일으키는 오답
(C) I will ask and let you know soon.
  → 질문에 대한 회피성 답변이므로 정답

얼마나 많은 직원들이 경연대회에 신청했죠?
(A) 매우 재미있습니다.
(B) 당신의 서명이 필요합니다.
(C) 제가 물어보고 곧 알려드릴게요.

어휘 sign up for 신청하다 signature 서명 require 필요로 하다

청취 집중 훈련 3 본책_ p. 58

| 1. (B) | 2. (A) | 3. (C) | 4. (B) |
| 5. (A) | 6. (C) | 7. (B) | 8. (C) |

1. Why don't you give me a hand with this box?
(A) Mr. Jennings sent it to me.
  → box에 대한 연상작용을 일으키는 오답
(B) Sure, where are we going to move it?
  → 제안의문문에 대한 긍정적인 답변이므로 정답
(C) I will hand it in tomorrow.
  → 동일 단어(hand)를 사용한 오답

이 상자를 옮기는 것 좀 도와주실래요?
(A) 제닝스 씨가 그것을 저에게 보냈어요.
(B) 물론이죠. 어디로 옮길 건가요?
(C) 저는 내일 그것을 제출할 겁니다.

어휘 give ~ a hand ~를 돕다 send 보내다 move 옮기다 hand[turn] in 제출하다

2. How do you usually come to work?
(A) I take the commuter train.
  → 이동 수단을 묻는 질문에 적합한 답변이므로 정답
(B) At the branch office.
  → Where do you work?에 어울리는 답변이므로 오답
(C) I usually arrive at 8.
  → What time do you come to work?에 어울리는 답변이므로 오답

보통 어떻게 출근하세요?
(A) 저는 통근 기차를 탑니다.
(B) 지점에서입니다.
(C) 저는 보통 8시에 도착합니다.

어휘 come[get] to work 출근하다　commuter 통근자
branch office 지점　arrive 도착하다

3. What does Andy do at his firm?
(A) The form should be filled out.
→ firm과 유사발음인 form을 사용한 오답
(B) He got a job offer.
→ firm에 대한 연상작용을 일으키는 오답
(C) He's the advertising director.
→ 회사에서 하는 일에 대한 질문에 직책으로 대답했으므로 정답

앤디는 회사에서 무엇을 합니까?
(A) 양식이 작성되어야 합니다.
(B) 그는 취업 제의를 받았습니다.
(C) 그는 홍보 이사입니다.

어휘 firm 회사(= company)　fill out 작성하다　job offer 취업[입사] 제의
advertising 홍보, 광고　director 이사

4. What time are you supposed to meet with your client?
(A) It's with Dr. Lansfield.
→ 시간을 묻는 질문에 약속 상대로 대답했으므로 오답
(B) It's at three.
→ 구체적인 약속 시간을 언급하고 있으므로 정답
(C) I talked to him on the phone this morning.
→ When did you contact your client?에 대한 대답이므로 오답

몇 시에 고객을 만나기로 했나요?
(A) 랜스필드 박사님과의 약속입니다.
(B) 3시입니다.
(C) 저는 오늘 아침에 그와 전화 통화를 했습니다.

어휘 be supposed to부정사 ~하기로 되어 있다
meet with ~를 만나다　client 고객
talk to ~ on the phone ~와 전화 통화를 하다

5. Why did Ms. Lee leave so suddenly?
(A) She's not feeling well.
→ 질문과 어울리는 퇴근의 이유를 언급했으므로 정답
(B) She lives near here.
→ leave와 유사발음인 lives를 사용한 오답
(C) Because she hasn't come yet.
→ because를 썼지만 의미상 질문과 무관하므로 오답

왜 이 씨가 그렇게 갑자기 나갔죠?
(A) 그녀는 몸이 좋지 않습니다.
(B) 그녀는 이 근처에 삽니다.
(C) 그녀가 아직 오지 않았기 때문이에요.

어휘 leave 나가다　suddenly 갑자기　feel well 건강 상태가 좋다
near ~ 근처에　yet 아직

6. How did you like the concert?
(A) Yes, I went last week.
→ 제안의문문을 제외하고는 의문사의문문에 yes나 no로 대답할 수 없으므로 오답
(B) I like playing the piano.
→ 동일 단어 like를 쓴 오답
(C) It was wonderful.
→ 의견을 묻는 질문에 대한 자연스러운 답변이므로 정답

콘서트는 어땠습니까?
(A) 네, 저는 지난주에 갔었습니다.
(B) 저는 피아노 치는 것을 좋아해요.
(C) 훌륭했습니다.

어휘 How do you like ~? ~은 어떻습니까?
play the piano 피아노를 치다

7. How much time should we allow to get to the airport?
(A) Flight 927 to Bangkok.
→ airport에 대한 연상작용을 일으키는 오답
(B) At least 2 hours.
→ 질문에 어울리는 시간을 제시했으므로 정답
(C) Four times a year.
→ 빈도를 나타내는 답변이므로 오답

공항에 가기 위해 얼마나 많은 시간적 여유를 두어야 합니까?
(A) 방콕행 927 비행편입니다.
(B) 적어도 2시간 입니다.
(C) 1년에 네 번이오.

어휘 allow+시간 (시간의 여유를 두다)　get to 도착하다　at least 적어도
four times 네 번　a year 1년에, 1년마다

8. Why did Jack postpone his presentation?
(A) It was hard to understand.
　→ presentation에 대한 연상작용을 일으키는 오답
(B) Next week.
　→ When will Jack give his presentation?에 대한 답변이므로 오답
(C) I haven't heard about that.
　→ 질문에 대한 정보를 갖고 있지 않을 때 쓰는 '모른다' 식의 답변이므로 정답

잭은 왜 발표를 연기했죠?
(A) 이해하기 어려웠어요.
(B) 다음 주요.
(C) 그것에 대해 들은 바가 없어요.

어휘　postpone 연기하다(= put off)　presentation 발표, 설명
(cf. give[make, deliver] a presentation 발표하다)
hard to부정사 ~하기 어려운　hear about ~에 관해 듣다

실전 감각 익히기　본책_p. 59

| 1. (A) | 2. (A) | 3. (C) | 4. (B) | 5. (C) |
| 6. (A) | 7. (B) | 8. (C) | 9. (A) | 10. (B) |

1. What's the fastest way to go to the city?
(A) I'd take Highway Five.
　→ 질문에 맞게 가장 빠른 길을 언급하고 있으므로 정답
(B) No, it is very slow.
　→ 제안의문문을 제외하고는 의문사의문문에 yes나 no로 대답할 수 없으므로 오답
(C) It takes around one hour.
　→ 질문과는 관계없이 소요 시간을 얘기하고 있으므로 오답

그 도시로 가는 가장 빠른 길은 무엇입니까?
(A) 저라면 5번 고속도로를 탈 겁니다.
(B) 아니요, 그건 아주 느립니다.
(C) 대략 1시간 정도 걸립니다.

어휘　fastest 가장 빠른　take (길을) 타다, ~로 가다
take+시간 (시간이) 걸리다　around 대략

2. How are sales going this month?
(A) So far they're steady.
　→ 매출 상황에 대한 적절한 답변이므로 정답
(B) I often go to the store.
　→ 질문의 going은 상황을 나타내는 반면 (B)의 go는 '가다'라는 뜻으로 의미상 차이가 있으므로 오답
(C) They are having a sale now.
　→ sales와 유사발음인 sale을 사용한 오답

이번 달 매출이 어떻습니까?
(A) 지금까지는 꾸준합니다.
(B) 저는 그 상점에 자주 갑니다.
(C) 그들은 지금 세일 중입니다.

어휘　How+be+주어+going? ~가 어떻게 진행되고 있죠?
so far 지금까지　steady 꾸준한　have a sale 염가로 팔다, 세일하다

3. Why did you buy the trees and flowers?
(A) Yes, they are beautiful.
　→ 의문사의문문에 yes나 no로 대답할 수 없으므로 오답
(B) Because I am busy.
　→ why 의문문에 이유의 접속사 because를 썼지만 의미상 질문과 연결되지 않으므로 오답
(C) I'm interested in gardening.
　→ 나무와 꽃을 구입한 이유를 나타내므로 정답

왜 그 나무와 꽃들을 사셨죠?
(A) 네, 그것들은 아름답군요.
(B) 제가 바쁘기 때문에요.
(C) 저는 원예에 관심이 있습니다.

어휘　be interested in ~에 관심이 있다　gardening 원예, 정원 가꾸기

4. How can I install this program?
(A) It's very convenient.
　→ 설치 방법을 묻는 질문과는 어울리지 않는 답변이므로 오답
(B) Refer to the manual.
　→ 설치 방법에 대한 우회적 답변이므로 정답
(C) On your computer.
　→ install 및 program과 연상작용을 일으키는 오답

이 프로그램 어떻게 설치하죠?
(A) 매우 편리합니다.
(B) 매뉴얼을 참고하세요.
(C) 당신의 컴퓨터에요.

어휘　install 설치하다　convenient 편리한　refer to 참고하다

5. Why don't you take the training course?
(A) That train doesn't stop here.
　→ training과 유사발음인 train을 사용한 오답
(B) It was a bit boring.
　→ 질문과는 무관하게 training course와의 연상작용에 의한 답변이며 과거시제를 썼으므로 오답
(C) Let me check my schedule first.
　→ 제안의문문에 대해 자신의 의견을 전달하고 있으므로 정답

그 교육과정을 들으시는 게 어때요?
(A) 그 기차는 여기에 서지 않습니다.
(B) 약간 지루했습니다.
(C) 먼저 제 일정을 확인해볼게요.

어휘 take (과목 등을) 듣다　training course 교육과정　stop 멈추다　a bit 약간　let me + 동사원형 제가 ~할게요.

6. What time is the managers' meeting?
(A) It's scheduled for 10 this morning.
→ 회의 시간을 묻는 질문에 구체적인 시점을 제시하고 있으므로 정답
(B) Yes, I met him yesterday.
→ 의문사의문문에는 yes나 no로 대답할 수 없으므로 오답
(C) That room is occupied now.
→ 시점에 대한 질문에 장소로 대답했으므로 오답

매니저 회의는 몇 시죠?
(A) 오늘 아침 10시로 예정되어 있습니다.
(B) 네, 저는 어제 그를 만났습니다.
(C) 그 방은 지금 쓰고 있습니다.

어휘 be scheduled for ~로 예정되어 있다
be occupied (방·의자 등이) 차지되어 있다

7. How much does the shop charge for delivery?
(A) I always pay by credit card.
→ 비용을 묻는 질문에 지불 방법으로 대답했으므로 오답
(B) It is free for online orders.
→ 배송료에 대한 질문에 어울리는 답변이므로 정답
(C) I am not in charge of delivery.
→ in charge of는 '~을 담당하다'라는 뜻인데 질문과는 어울리지 않는 답변이므로 오답

그 상점은 배달료로 얼마나 청구하나요?
(A) 저는 항상 신용카드로 계산합니다.
(B) 온라인 주문은 배송이 무료입니다.
(C) 저는 배달을 담당하지 않습니다.

어휘 charge 청구하다　pay by credit card 신용카드로 계산하다
free 무료인　be in charge of ~을 담당하다

8. Why don't we take a short break now?
(A) The technician already fixed it.
→ 질문에 쓰인 break를 '깨다, 고장나다'로 잘못 이해한 답변이므로 오답
(B) I don't drive so fast.
→ break를 brake(브레이크)로 잘못 알아들었을 때의 연상작용으로 생기는 오답
(C) Let me finish this first.
→ 제안의문문과 어울리는 답변이므로 정답

우리 지금 잠깐 쉬는 게 어때요?
(A) 기술자가 벌써 그것을 고쳤어요.
(B) 저는 그렇게 빨리 운전하지 않아요.
(C) 제가 이것을 먼저 끝낼게요.

어휘 take a break 쉬다　technician 기술자　fix 고치다　fast 빠르게

9. How do you like working at the headquarters?
(A) So far I'm enjoying it.
→ 의견을 묻는 질문에 긍정으로 대답하고 있으므로 정답
(B) It's a short train ride.
→ 질문과는 무관하게 이동 거리로 대답하고 있으므로 오답
(C) I'll check the map.
→ 본사 근무에 대한 의견을 묻는 질문에는 어울리지 않으므로 오답

본사에서 일하시는 게 어떤가요??
(A) 지금까지는 재미있습니다.
(B) 기차로 짧은 거리입니다.
(C) 제가 지도를 확인해보겠습니다.

어휘 How do you like ~? ~은 어떻습니까?　so far 지금까지
ride 타기; 탈것　map 지도

10. What should I bring to the interview?
(A) The vice president will interview you.
→ 면접 때 가져와야 할 것에 대한 질문과는 의미상 어울리지 않으므로 오답
(B) You have to have your ID.
→ 가져와야 할 것을 구체적으로 언급하고 있으므로 정답
(C) Please arrive 10 minutes early.
→ 질문과는 관련없이 도착 시점을 얘기하는 오답

제가 면접에 올 때 무엇을 가지고 와야 합니까?
(A) 부사장님이 당신을 인터뷰할 겁니다.
(B) 신분증이 있어야 합니다.
(C) 10분 일찍 도착해주세요.

어휘 bring 가져오다　vice president 부사장　arrive 도착하다
early 일찍

UNIT 6　일반의문문 / 선택의문문

받아쓰기 연습　본책 _ p. 63

1. collect / them / You
2. old / It was / just / all
3. Does / run / I think / learned

청취 집중 훈련 1　본책 _ p. 64

| 1. (A) | 2. (B) | 3. (A) | 4. (B) |
| 5. (C) | 6. (B) | 7. (A) | 8. (C) |

1. Do you know the extension for Mr. Ken's office?
(A) Yes, it's 902.
(B) His office is on the third floor.
(C) Go down the hall and to your left.

켄 씨 사무실의 내선번호를 아십니까?
(A) 네, 902입니다.
(B) 그의 사무실은 3층에 있습니다.
(C) 복도를 따라가시면 왼쪽에 있습니다.

2. Should I call a moving company?
(A) Actually, he's moving to a new city.
(B) No, my friends are going to help me.
(C) Call me at your earliest convenience.

제가 이삿짐 센터에 전화를 해야 하나요?
(A) 사실 그는 신도시로 이사를 갈 겁니다.
(B) 아니요, 제 친구들이 저를 도와줄 거예요.
(C) 가능한 한 빨리 시간 되실 때 제게 전화해주세요.

3. Would you like to sit in the center or on the side?
(A) I prefer the center.
(B) She's waiting inside.
(C) It has a great view.

가운데에 앉고 싶으세요, 아니면 측면에 앉고 싶으세요?
(A) 저는 가운데가 좋습니다.
(B) 그녀가 안에서 기다리고 있습니다.
(C) 그곳은 전망이 매우 좋습니다.

4. Have you heard that Carol is leaving next week?
(A) She lives in Westchester.
(B) No, I didn't know that.
(C) No, but I can see you.

캐롤이 다음 주에 퇴사한다는 얘기 들으셨어요?
(A) 그녀는 웨스트체스터에 삽니다.
(B) 아니요, 몰랐어요.
(C) 아니요, 하지만 당신이 보입니다.

5. Is there any salad left?
(A) It comes with soup.
(B) It's sweet.
(C) No, but more is being made.

남은 샐러드 있나요?
(A) 샐러드는 수프와 함께 나옵니다.
(B) 그것은 달콤해요.
(C) 아니요, 하지만 더 만드는 중입니다.

6. Would you mind helping me with these bags?
(A) Sure, I'll remind you later.
(B) No, not at all.
(C) Yes, I was looking for them.

이 가방들 옮기는 것 좀 도와주실래요?
(A) 네, 제가 나중에 다시 알려드릴게요.
(B) 네, 물론입니다.
(C) 네, 제가 그것을 찾고 있었습니다.

7. Do you have a brochure?
(A) To a coworker.
(B) It was revised.
(C) Sure, I'll get you one.

안내 책자를 가지고 있습니까?
(A) 직장동료에게요.
(B) 그것은 개정되었습니다.
(C) 네, 제가 한 부 갖다드릴게요.

8. Would you like to pay by cash or credit card?
(A) We accept major credit cards.
(B) Sure, here's my business card.
(C) I'll pay by cash.

현금으로 내시겠습니까, 카드로 내시겠습니까?
(A) 저희는 주요 신용카드를 받습니다.
(B) 네, 여기 제 명함입니다.
(C) 현금으로 지불하겠습니다.

청취 집중 훈련 2 본책 _ p. 65

1. (B)	2. (A)	3. (C)	4. (C)
5. (A)	6. (B)	7. (A)	8. (B)

1. Did you reserve a table for four?
(A) Please, put them on the table.
→ 동일 단어 table을 썼지만 질문과 무관한 내용의 오답
(B) Oh, I forgot to do it.
→ 일반의문문에 대해 yes나 no를 생략한 채 질문과 어울리는 답변을 하고 있으므로 정답
(C) I will treat you to dinner tonight.
→ reserve와 table에 대한 잘못된 연상작용으로 대답한 오답

4인용 테이블을 예약하셨어요?
(A) 그것을 테이블 위에 놓아주세요.
(B) 아, 제가 그 일을 잊었네요.
(C) 제가 오늘밤 당신에게 저녁을 대접할게요.

어휘 reserve 예약하다 a table for four 4인용 테이블 forget 잊다
treat A(사람) to + 식사 A에게 식사를 대접하다

2. Can I ask you a question, or are you busy right now?
(A) Sorry, I'm working on something urgent.
→ 급한 일을 하고 있어서 질문을 받을 수 없다는 함축적 의미를 갖고 있으므로 정답
(B) No, I don't have any.
→ 이것은 Do you have any questions?에 대한 대답이 되므로 오답
(C) They're usually busy on Saturdays.
→ 동일 단어인 busy를 썼지만 질문과 관련이 없는 답변이므로 오답

제가 질문을 해도 될까요, 아니면 지금 바쁘신가요?
(A) 죄송하지만 제가 급한 일을 하고 있습니다.
(B) 아니요, 아무것도 없습니다.
(C) 그들은 보통 토요일에 바쁩니다.

어휘 ask A(사람) a question A에게 질문을 하다
work on ~에 대해 작업하다 urgent 시급한

3. Is it easy to catch taxis in this area?
(A) I couldn't catch what he said.
→ 질문에서는 catch가 '잡다'라는 의미인데 답변에서는 '이해하다'라는 뜻으로 잘못 쓴 것이므로 오답
(B) The fare was less than $10.
→ 이것은 How much was the taxi fare?의 답변이 되는 것이므로 오답
(C) Yes, there's a cab stand up the street.
→ 긍정적 답변을 먼저 한 후에 관련된 추가 내용을 언급하고 있으므로 정답

이 지역에서 택시를 잡는 것이 쉽습니까?
(A) 그가 말한 것을 이해하지 못했습니다.
(B) 요금은 10달러 이하였습니다.
(C) 네, 길 위쪽에 택시 승차장이 있습니다.

어휘 catch 잡다; 이해하다 fare (교통 수단의) 요금
cab[taxi] stand 택시 승차장 up the street 길 위쪽에

4. Would you mind handing me some paper?
(A) It's five cents per copy.
→ 질문에 쓰인 paper를 복사 상황으로 잘못 연상하였으므로 오답
(B) I saw the advertisement in the paper.
→ 동음이의어(질문에서는 '종이', 여기서는 '신문') 오답
(C) How many pieces do you want?
→ 질문에 대해 오히려 보충 정보를 원하는 역질문으로 응답한 정답

저에게 종이 좀 건네주시겠습니까?
(A) 한 장당 5센트입니다.
(B) 저는 신문에서 그 광고를 봤습니다.
(C) 몇 장이나 필요하십니까?

어휘 Would you mind ~ing? ~해도 괜찮겠습니까? hand 건네주다
per copy 한 장당 advertisement 광고 piece (종이의) 한 장

5. Can we walk from here to the train station?
(A) No, it's too far to walk.
→ 걸어갈 수 있는지 묻는 질문에 어울리는 응답으로 정답
(B) The train departed on time.
→ 동일 단어 train을 썼지만 의미상 질문과 연관 없는 오답
(C) They will build a new station.
→ 새로운 역을 짓는다는 내용은 질문과 무관하므로 오답

여기에서 기차역까지 걸어갈 수 있을까요?
(A) 걸어가기에는 너무 멀어요.
(B) 기차가 정시에 출발했습니다.
(C) 그들은 새로운 역을 지을 겁니다.

어휘 train station 기차역 far 먼 depart 출발하다 on time 정시에
build 짓다

6. Is this sofa imported?
(A) It's very important.
→ imported와 유사발음인 important를 썼지만 의미상 연결되지 않으므로 오답
(B) Yes, it's from Italy.
→ 소파의 수입 여부에 대한 구체적인 언급을 하고 있으므로 정답
(C) No, I'm not going to purchase it.
→ 소파의 구매에 대한 언급은 질문과 어울리지 않으므로 오답

이 소파는 수입된 겁니까?
(A) 그것은 아주 중요합니다.
(B) 네, 이탈리아에서 수입된 것입니다.
(C) 아니요, 저는 그것을 구입하지 않을 겁니다.

어휘 import 수입하다   purchase 구입하다

7. May I look at the plan now, or later?
(A) Here you go.
  → 상대방에게 물건을 건넬 때 '여기 있습니다'라는 뜻으로 쓰이는 적절한 표현이므로 정답
(B) I plan to go later.
  → 질문에 쓰인 것과 동일 단어인 plan과 later를 썼지만 의미상 무관한 오답
(C) The plants are growing well.
  → 질문과 의미는 연결되지 않은 채 단지 plan과 유사발음인 plants를 사용한 오답

제가 그 계획을 지금 봐도 될까요, 아니면 나중에 볼까요?
(A) 여기 있습니다.
(B) 나는 나중에 갈 계획입니다.
(C) 그 식물들은 잘 자라고 있습니다.

어휘 later 나중에   plants 식물   grow 자라다

8. Should we invite our patrons to the awards ceremony?
(A) Thank you for the invitation.
  → invite에 대한 잘못된 연상작용으로 인한 반응이므로 오답
(B) I think that we should.
  → 조동사의문문에 대해 yes를 생략한 채 초대를 해야 한다는 의견을 말하고 있으므로 정답
(C) I am honored to receive this award.
  → the awards ceremony에 대한 잘못된 연상작용으로 생긴 응답이므로 오답

우리는 시상식에 단골 고객들을 초대해야 하나요?
(A) 초대해 주셔서 감사합니다.
(B) 그래야 한다고 생각해요.
(C) 제가 이 상을 받게 되어 영광입니다.

어휘 invite 초대하다   invitation 초대   patron 단골 고객
awards ceremony 시상식
be honored to부정사 ~하게 되어 영광이다   award 상

청취 집중 훈련 3   본책_p. 66

| 1. (B) | 2. (A) | 3. (A) | 4. (C) |
| 5. (C) | 6. (B) | 7. (A) | 8. (B) |

1. Are there any samples left?
(A) No, they're on the right side.
  → left를 '왼쪽'으로 잘못 이해하여 반의어인 right를 쓴 것이므로 오답
(B) There are just a few.
  → 견본의 존재 여부를 묻는 질문에 어울리는 답변이므로 정답
(C) The design is very attractive.
  → samples에 대한 연상작용을 일으키는 오답

남은 견본이 있나요?
(A) 아니요, 그것은 오른쪽에 있습니다.
(B) 몇 개 정도 있습니다.
(C) 디자인이 매우 매력적입니다.

어휘 there+be동사+주어 ~가 있다   명사+left 남은 ~
on the right[left] side 오른[왼]쪽에   a few 몇몇, 조금
attractive 매력적인

2. Would you rather walk to the office or take a subway?
(A) Well, I'll drive there.
  → 선택의문문에서 제시된 걷기와 지하철 타기가 아닌 운전이라는 제3의 선택 사항을 제시했으므로 정답
(B) I think I have to work late tonight.
  → walk의 유사발음 work를 사용한 오답
(C) It is on Urban Street.
  → Where is your office?에 대한 답변이므로 오답

사무실로 걸어가실 거예요, 아니면 지하철을 타고 가실 거예요?
(A) 음, 저는 운전해서 갈 겁니다.
(B) 저는 오늘밤 늦게까지 일해야 할 거예요.
(C) 사무실은 어번 가에 있어요.

어휘 Would you rather+동사원형? ~하실 겁니까?
take (교통 수단을) 타다   work late 늦게까지 일하다

3. Does the store have a delivery service?
(A) I think they do.
  → 일반의문문에 대해 yes를 생략한 채 적절히 응답했으므로 정답
(B) He sent it by express mail.
  → delivery에 대한 잘못된 연상작용으로 by express mail을 쓴 것이므로 오답
(C) No, we don't store our supplies there.
  → 여기서 동사 store는 '보관하다'라는 뜻으로 질문과 의미상 무관하므로 오답

29

그 상점은 배달 서비스가 있나요?
(A) 그렇다고 생각합니다.
(B) 그는 속달우편으로 그것을 보냈습니다.
(C) 아니요, 우리는 그곳에 사무용품을 보관하지 않습니다.

어휘 store 상점; 보관하다   delivery service 배달 서비스
by express mail 속달우편으로   supplies 비품, 용품

4. Did you hear taxi fares are going up?
(A) The accountant handles all the taxes.
→ taxi와 유사발음인 taxes를 썼으므로 오답
(B) The trade fair was well-attended.
→ fare와 동일 발음인 fair를 사용한 오답
(C) No. How much?
→ 부정으로 대답을 한 다음, 얼마나 많이 오르는지 역질문을 하고 있으므로 정답

택시 요금이 오를 것이라는 얘기를 들으셨어요?
(A) 회계사가 모든 세금을 처리합니다.
(B) 무역 박람회에 많은 사람들이 참석했어요.
(C) 아니요, 얼마나요?

어휘 fare (교통 수단의) 요금   go up 오르다   accountant 회계사
handle 처리하다   tax 세금   trade fair 무역 박람회
well-attended 참석자가 많은 (cf. poorly-attended 참석자가 적은)

5. Can you join us for a quick meeting?
(A) No, it is very slow.
→ quick의 반의어인 slow는 질문과 어울리지 않으므로 오답
(B) Yes, I'll meet them at two this afternoon.
→ 의미상 them을 쓸 수 없으므로 인칭 오류에 의한 오답
(C) Sure, I have some time.
→ '간단한 회의를 할 수 있다'는 긍정적 답변이므로 정답

저희와 간단하게 회의를 하실 수 있으세요?
(A) 아니요, 그것은 굉장히 느려요.
(B) 네, 저는 오늘 오후 2시에 그들을 만날 겁니다.
(C) 네, 저는 시간이 좀 있습니다.

어휘 join 합류하다   quick meeting 간단한 회의

6. Does this bus go to Central Plaza?
(A) It's very famous.
→ Central Plaza가 유명하다는 것은 버스 노선과는 관계없으므로 오답
(B) It stops near there.
→ 질문과 관련된 버스의 정차 위치를 언급하고 있으므로 정답
(C) I'm sorry, but I'm too busy to go there.
→ 동일 발음 go를 쓴 오답

이 버스가 센트럴 플라자로 가나요?
(A) 그곳은 매우 유명합니다.
(B) 버스가 그곳 근처에 정차합니다.
(C) 죄송하지만 저는 너무 바빠서 그곳에 갈 수가 없어요.

어휘 famous 유명한   stop 정차하다   near ~ 근처에
too + 형용사 + to부정사 너무 ~해서 ~할 수 없다

7. Should we have our office party this weekend or next?
(A) Any week would be okay with me.
→ 두 개의 선택 사항 중 어느 것도 상관없다는 답변이므로 정답
(B) There are five people in my party.
→ 여기서 party는 '일행'이란 뜻인데, 일행의 인원수를 묻는 질문이 아니므로 오답
(C) Let's have it at Luigi's Café.
→ Where should we have our office party?에 대한 답변이므로 오답

우리는 사무실 파티를 이번 주에 해야 합니까, 아니면 다음 주에 해야 합니까?
(A) 저에겐 어떤 주라도 좋습니다.
(B) 제 일행은 다섯 명입니다.
(C) 루이지 카페에서 합시다.

어휘 office 사무실   party 일행, 단체   have (파티를) 열다

8. Is there anything you want to find?
(A) Yes, I can help you.
→ 질문자에게 오히려 Yes, please help me.라고 대답해야 하므로 오답
(B) No, I'm just browsing.
→ '단지 구경을 하고 있다'는 말로 질문과 어울리므로 정답
(C) There are some unclaimed items here.
→ find에 대한 연상작용을 일으키는 오답

찾고 계신 것이 있으세요?
(A) 네, 제가 도와드릴게요.
(B) 아니요, 저는 그냥 둘러보는 중입니다.
(C) 여기 찾아가지 않은 물건들이 몇 개 있습니다.

어휘 find 찾다   browse (상점에서) 여유롭게 둘러보다
unclaimed 주인이 찾아가지 않은   item 물건, 물품

실전 감각 익히기 본책 _ p. 67

| 1. (C) | 2. (B) | 3. (B) | 4. (B) | 5. (C) |
| 6. (A) | 7. (C) | 8. (A) | 9. (C) | 10. (A) |

1. Did you decide to apply for the opening?
(A) No, I didn't open it.
　→ 의미상 질문과 관계없는 유사발음 오답(opening-open)
(B) You have to submit your resume.
　→ Did you ~로 물어본 질문에 You로 대답할 수 없으므로 인칭 오류에 의한 오답
(C) I'm not sure if I'd be qualified.
　→ 지원을 했는지에 대한 질문에 어울리는 답변

그 공석에 지원하기로 결정했습니까?
(A) 아니요, 제가 열지 않았습니다.
(B) 당신은 이력서를 제출해야 합니다.
(C) 제가 자격이 있을지 모르겠어요.

어휘 decide 결정하다　apply for ~에 지원하다　opening 공석
　　　submit 제출하다　resume 이력서　qualified 자격을 갖춘

2. Is there parking available near the building?
(A) No, I'm afraid the park is closed.
　→ 질문에 쓰인 parking(주차)과 유사발음인 park(공원)를 썼지만 의미상 전혀 관계없는 오답
(B) Sure, it has its own garage.
　→ 주차장 유무에 대한 질문에 '있다'는 답변을 한 것이므로 정답
(C) It is free for members only.
　→ 비용 관련 언급은 parking에 대한 잘못된 연상작용에서 나온 것이므로 오답

건물 근처에 이용할 수 있는 주차장이 있습니까?
(A) 아니요, 유감이지만 공원은 닫혔습니다.
(B) 네, 건물 자체 주차장이 있습니다.
(C) 회원들에게만 무료입니다.

어휘 parking 주차장　near ~ 근처에　afraid 유감인
　　　garage 주차장, 차고　free 무료인

3. Should we advertise the position online or in the newspaper?
(A) It hasn't been filled yet.
　→ It은 the position을 가리키는데, 질문과 관계없는 오답
(B) Why don't we use our Web site?
　→ 제시된 선택 사항이 아닌 제3의 선택 사항을 제안한 정답
(C) We stopped subscribing to it.
　→ 질문과 무관하게 newspaper에 대한 잘못된 연상작용으로 인한 대답이므로 오답

우리는 그 자리를 온라인에 광고해야 합니까, 아니면 신문에 광고해야 합니까?
(A) 그 자리는 아직 채워지지 않았습니다.
(B) 우리 웹사이트를 활용하는 게 어때요?
(C) 우리는 구독을 중단했습니다.

어휘 advertise 광고하다　fill 채우다　subscribe to ~을 구독하다

4. Did you look at our new brochures?
(A) I'm not sure, either.
　→ brochures와 유사발음인 sure를 사용한 오답
(B) They look very professional.
　→ They는 brochures를 가리키는 것으로, 안내 책자에 대한 의견을 말하고 있는 정답
(C) He took one home to study.
　→ Did you ~로 물어본 질문에 He로 응답한 인칭 오답

우리의 새 안내 책자를 보셨어요?
(A) 저도 잘 모르겠습니다.
(B) 매우 전문성 있게 보이더군요.
(C) 그가 살펴보려고 한 부 가져갔어요.

어휘 brochure 안내 책자　either (부정문에서) 또한
　　　professional 전문적인　take 가져가다　study 살펴보다

5. Have you finished your assignment?
(A) I didn't sign it.
　→ 질문과는 관계없이 assignment와 유사하게 발음되는 sign을 사용했으므로 오답
(B) No, you can't.
　→ 〈Have you + 과거분사 ~?〉에 대해서는 〈Yes, I have.〉 또는 〈No, I haven't.〉로 답변해야 하므로 오답
(C) Yes, I have.
　→ 완료시제 의문문에 대해 have를 사용해서 답변했으므로 정답

당신은 과제를 끝냈습니까?
(A) 저는 그것에 서명하지 않았어요.
(B) 아니요, 당신은 할 수 없습니다.
(C) 네, 끝마쳤습니다.

어휘 finish 끝마치다　assignment 과제　sign 서명하다

6. Should we hold the staff meeting in the morning, or the afternoon?
(A) Just before lunch would be best.
　→ 선택의문문에 주어진 선택 사항이 아닌 제3의 선택 사항을 적절하게 제시하고 있으므로 정답
(B) What did you do after that?
　→ 질문과는 관계없는 역질문이므로 오답
(C) It's good to see you, too.
　→ 질문과 무관하게 meeting에 대한 연상작용을 일으키는 것이므로 오답

우리는 아침에 직원 회의를 해야 합니까, 아니면 오후에 해야 합니까?
(A) 점심시간 바로 전이 가장 좋겠습니다.
(B) 그 이후에 무엇을 했습니까?
(C) 저도 당신을 봐서 좋습니다.

어휘 hold 열다, 개최하다　staff meeting 직원 회의
just before ~ 직전

7. May I use your computer now?
(A) You should check your computer for viruses.
→ computer라는 동일 단어를 사용했지만 질문과 의미상 전혀 연결되지 않는 오답
(B) I used to work here.
→ use와 유사발음인 used를 썼지만 질문과는 관계없는 답변이므로 오답
(C) Yes, just give me a minute.
→ 컴퓨터 사용의 가능 여부에 대해 긍정으로 답한 정답

제가 지금 당신의 컴퓨터를 써도 됩니까?
(A) 당신은 컴퓨터 바이러스 체크를 해야 합니다.
(B) 저는 이곳에서 근무를 했었죠.
(C) 네, 잠시만 기다려주세요.

어휘 check + A(대상) + for ~가 있는지 A를 검사하다
used to부정사 ~하곤 했다, 한때 ~했다

8. Would you prefer to eat indoors or outdoors?
(A) We'd like a table inside, please.
→ 두 가지 선택 사항 중에서 indoors를 inside로 바꿔 적절히 대답했으므로 정답
(B) No, we've never tried those.
→ 식사 장소에 대한 언급이 아니므로 오답
(C) Mine was delicious.
→ 질문은 음식의 맛에 대한 것이 아니므로 오답

실내에서 식사하시겠어요, 아니면 야외에서 하시겠어요?
(A) 저희는 안쪽 테이블로 부탁합니다.
(B) 아니요, 저희는 결코 그것을 먹어본 적이 없습니다.
(C) 제 것은 맛있었어요.

어휘 indoors 실내에서　outdoors 야외에서　inside 안쪽에
try 맛보다　delicious 맛있는

9. Were there any calls for me while I was out?
(A) I'll call later.
→ 질문에 쓰인 calls와 동일 단어인 call을 사용했지만 의미상 무관하므로 오답
(B) I tried, but the line was busy.
→ 전화를 걸어봤지만 통화 중이었다는 말은 질문과 의미상 관련성이 없으므로 오답
(C) I received some messages for you.
→ 메시지를 받았다는 말은 전화가 왔었다는 함축적 의미를 갖고 있으므로 정답

제가 나가 있는 동안 전화 온 거 있습니까?
(A) 제가 나중에 전화하겠습니다.
(B) 제가 시도를 했습니다만 통화 중이었습니다.
(C) 제가 당신에게 온 메시지 몇 개를 받았습니다.

어휘 while ~하는 동안　later 나중에　try 시도하다
The line is busy. 통화 중이다.

10. Are we still planning to open an office in Singapore?
(A) It hasn't been decided yet.
→ 질문에 대한 정보가 없을 때 쓸 수 있는 불확실성 표현이므로 정답
(B) They're open until 7 P.M.
→ 동일 단어인 open을 썼지만 질문과는 의미상 무관한 오답
(C) The trip was great.
→ Singapore를 여행지로 잘못 연상한 오답

우리는 여전히 싱가포르에 사무실을 열 계획인가요?
(A) 아직 결정되지 않았습니다.
(B) 그들은 오후 7시까지 문을 엽니다.
(C) 멋진 여행이었습니다.

어휘 office 사무실, 지사(= branch office)　decide 결정하다

UNIT 7 간접의문문 / 부정의문문 / 부가의문문

받아쓰기 연습 본책 _ p. 71

1. why / declined / Because / declined
2. Aren't / ready / placed / already
3. why / concert / equipment / concerned

청취 집중 훈련 1 본책 _ p. 72

| 1. (C) | 2. (A) | 3. (B) | 4. (C) |
| 5. (B) | 6. (A) | 7. (A) | 8. (C) |

1. Can you tell us when we reach the museum?
(A) It's out of my reach.
(B) No, you can't.
(C) Okay, don't worry.
우리가 박물관에 도착하면 말씀 좀 해주시겠습니까?
(A) 그것은 제 손에 닿지 않습니다.
(B) 아니요, 당신은 그렇게 할 수 없습니다.
(C) 좋아요, 걱정 마세요.

2. Aren't you going to the bank this afternoon?
(A) No, I went this morning.
(B) I deposited the check.
(C) No, I don't.
오늘 오후에 은행에 가지 않습니까?
(A) 아니요, 저는 오전에 갔었어요.
(B) 제가 수표를 입금했습니다.
(C) 아니요, 저는 안 합니다.

3. The deadline is on Friday, isn't it?
(A) We are behind schedule.
(B) Yes, at 4 o'clock sharp.
(C) Today is Wednesday.
마감일이 금요일이죠, 그렇죠?
(A) 우리는 일정보다 늦고 있습니다.
(B) 네, 정각 4시입니다.
(C) 오늘은 수요일입니다.

4. You bought tickets for the movie, didn't you?
(A) It's a comedy.
(B) I've never seen it before.
(C) Sorry, I haven't had a chance.
당신은 영화표를 구입하셨죠, 그렇죠?
(A) 그것은 코미디 영화입니다.
(B) 저는 결코 전에 그것을 본 적이 없습니다.
(C) 죄송하게도 제가 기회가 없었습니다.

5. Isn't this John's latest novel?
(A) He was 30 minutes early.
(B) Yes, it came out last Friday.
(C) He is a good writer.
이것이 존의 최신 소설 아닙니까?
(A) 그는 30분 일찍 왔어요.
(B) 네, 지난주 금요일에 나왔어요.
(C) 그는 훌륭한 작가입니다.

6. Do you know when the next train will arrive?
(A) Not for another 10 minutes.
(B) It'll leave tomorrow morning.
(C) The train to Centerville.
다음 기차가 언제 도착하는지 아십니까?
(A) 10분 더 있어야 합니다.
(B) 기차는 내일 아침에 떠납니다.
(C) 센터빌행 기차입니다.

7. Shouldn't we wait for Mr. Harrington?
(A) He's already there.
(B) He's the one in the brown suit.
(C) I can schedule you for 3 o'clock.
우리는 해링튼 씨를 기다려야 하지 않나요?
(A) 그는 벌써 그곳에 있습니다.
(B) 그는 갈색 정장을 입은 사람입니다.
(C) 제가 당신을 3시로 일정 잡아드릴 수 있습니다.

8. Smith is giving a speech in Oakland, isn't he?
(A) I haven't registered yet.
(B) No, he didn't.
(C) Yes, at the Devlin Center.

스미스가 오클랜드에서 연설을 하죠, 그렇죠?
(A) 저는 아직 등록하지 않았어요.
(B) 아니요, 그가 하지 않았습니다.
(C) 네, 데블린 센터에서 합니다.

청취 집중 훈련 2 본책_p.73

| 1. (B) | 2. (B) | 3. (A) | 4. (A) |
| 5. (C) | 6. (B) | 7. (C) | 8. (A) |

1. Didn't you see the show?
(A) It will be fun.
→ 과거에 공연을 봤는지 여부에 대한 답변이 없으므로 오답
(B) No, I didn't have time to.
→ 시간이 없어서 공연을 못 봤다는 의미이므로 정답
(C) Yes, I want to see it.
→ Yes는 공연을 봤다는 뜻인데 이어서 공연을 보고 싶다고 한 것이므로 의미상 모순이 되어 오답

그 공연을 못 보셨어요?
(A) 재미있을 겁니다.
(B) 못 봤어요, 시간이 없었거든요.
(C) 네, 보고 싶습니다.

어휘 fun 재미있는   don't have time to부정사 ~할 시간이 없다

2. Do you know when the game starts?
(A) It was exciting.
→ 의문문 중간에 있는 when에 대한 답변이 아니므로 오답
(B) Yes, at 6:30.
→ when에 대한 정확한 시점을 제시하고 있으므로 정답
(C) In the main stadium.
→ when이 아닌 경기가 열리는 장소에 대한 답변이므로 오답

경기가 언제 시작하는지 아십니까?
(A) 흥미진진했어요.
(B) 네, 6시 30분입니다.
(C) 주경기장에서 합니다.

어휘 exciting 흥미진진한   main stadium 주경기장

3. You edited the press release, didn't you?
(A) No, Francis did.
→ 부정으로 답한 뒤, 편집자를 언급하고 있으므로 정답
(B) I didn't realize that.
→ release와 유사발음인 realize를 썼지만 의미상 질문과 무관하므로 오답
(C) I pressed the button.
→ press와 유사발음인 pressed를 썼지만 질문과 관련없는 답변이므로 오답

당신이 보도자료를 편집하셨죠, 그렇죠?
(A) 아니요, 프랜시스가 했습니다.
(B) 저는 그걸 깨닫지 못했어요.
(C) 제가 그 단추를 눌렀습니다.

어휘 edit 편집하다   press release 보도자료   realize 깨닫다   press 누르다

4. Didn't you get the memo from Jack?
(A) No, when did he send it?
→ 부정으로 답한 뒤, 추가 정보를 요구하는 역질문을 한 것이므로 정답
(B) I'll send it before I leave for the day.
→ 메모를 받았는지에 대한 질문에 '내가 보낼 것이다'라고 답하는 것은 오답
(C) Mr. Jack is in his office.
→ 잭이 어디에 있는지는 질문과 관련이 없으므로 오답

잭한테 온 메모를 못 받았습니까?
(A) 네, 그가 언제 보냈죠?
(B) 제가 퇴근 전에 그것을 보내겠습니다.
(C) 잭 씨는 그의 사무실에 있습니다.

어휘 get 받다   leave for the day 퇴근하다

5. Aren't there any more pencils in the supply closet?
(A) That's not my pencil.
→ 동일 단어 pencil을 썼지만 질문과 무관하므로 오답
(B) Could you close it, please?
→ closet의 유사발음으로 close를 썼을 뿐, 질문과는 관련이 없는 답변이므로 오답
(C) No, we're all out.
→ 부정으로 답한 뒤, 연필이 다 떨어졌다는 의미를 전달한 것이므로 정답

물품 보관함에 연필이 더 없나요?
(A) 그건 제 연필이 아닙니다.
(B) 문을 좀 닫아주시겠습니까?
(C) 네, 다 떨어졌어요.

어휘 supply closet 물품 보관함   be all out 다 떨어지다

6. The elevator is out of service, isn't it?

(A) They always provide good service.
→ service라는 동일 단어만 썼을 뿐, 질문과 의미상 관련이 없으므로 오답

(B) Yes, it stopped working earlier.
→ 엘리베이터가 운행되지 않는다는 의미로 Yes라고 했으므로 정답

(C) Yes, you can take the elevator.
→ Yes는 엘리베이터가 운행되지 않는다는 뜻인데, 이어서 엘리베이터를 탈 수 있다고 한 것은 의미상 모순이므로 오답

엘리베이터가 운행되지 않죠, 그렇죠?
(A) 그들은 항상 좋은 서비스를 제공합니다.
(B) 네, 얼마 전에 작동을 멈췄어요.
(C) 네, 엘리베이터를 타실 수 있습니다.

어휘 out of service 운행되지 않는   work 작동되다   take 타다

7. Can you tell me where the storage room is?

(A) Yes, the store is open now.
→ 의문문 중간에 있는 where에 대한 답변이 아니므로 오답

(B) Yes, but there is no room.
→ 동일 단어 room을 썼지만 답변에서의 room은 '방'이 아니라 '공간'이라는 뜻으로 질문과는 관련이 없으므로 오답

(C) It's on the first floor.
→ where에 대한 정확한 위치를 말해주고 있으므로 정답

창고가 어디에 있는지 말씀해주실래요?
(A) 네, 상점은 지금 열려 있습니다.
(B) 네, 하지만 공간이 없습니다.
(C) 1층에 있습니다.

어휘 storage room 창고   open 열린   room 공간

8. The office supplies arrived this morning, didn't they?

(A) Yes, before lunch.
→ 긍정의 답변과 함께 사무용품의 도착 시점을 언급한 것이므로 정답

(B) No employee has come yet.
→ 직원의 도착 여부는 질문과 관련이 없으므로 오답

(C) No, he was five minutes late.
→ he라는 인칭을 언급할 필요가 없으므로 오답

사무용품이 오늘 아침에 도착했죠, 그렇죠?
(A) 네, 점심시간 전에요.
(B) 아직 아무 직원도 오지 않았어요.
(C) 아니요, 그는 5분 늦었어요.

어휘 office supplies 사무용품   employee 직원   yet 아직

청취 집중 훈련 3   본책 _ p. 74

| 1. (A) | 2. (B) | 3. (C) | 4. (A) |
| 5. (B) | 6. (A) | 7. (A) | 8. (C) |

1. Don't you want to try the new restaurant?

(A) Yes, let's go there for lunch.
→ Yes로 응답하고 점심을 먹으러 가자고 했으므로 정답

(B) No, I'll eat there.
→ No는 새로운 식당에 가고 싶지 않다는 뜻인데 이어서 그곳에서 식사를 하겠다고 했으니 의미상 모순이 되어 오답

(C) I ordered smoked salmon.
→ restaurant에 대한 연상작용을 일으키는 오답

새로운 식당에 가보고 싶지 않으세요?
(A) 네, 오늘 그곳으로 점심을 먹으러 가죠.
(B) 아니요, 저는 그곳에서 식사할 겁니다.
(C) 저는 훈제 연어를 주문했어요.

어휘 try + 장소 ~에 가보다   for lunch 점심을 먹으러   order 주문하다   smoked salmon 훈제 연어

2. May I ask why you work from home?

(A) Yes, I like my job.
→ work에 대한 연상작용을 일으키므로 오답

(B) Because my office is too far.
→ why에 대한 이유를 제시하고 있으므로 정답

(C) Approximately once a month.
→ How often do you work from home?에 대한 대답이므로 오답

왜 재택근무를 하는지 여쭤봐도 될까요?
(A) 네, 저는 저의 직업이 좋습니다.
(B) 제 사무실이 너무 멀기 때문에요.
(C) 대략 한 달에 한 번이오.

어휘 work from home 재택근무를 하다   far 먼   approximately 대략   once a month 한 달에 한 번

3. Do you know where the nearest convenience store is?

(A) The store remains open until 11 P.M.
→ store라는 동일 단어를 썼지만 where에 대한 답변이 아니므로 오답

(B) I am a part-timer.
→ convenience store에 대한 연상작용을 일으키는 오답

(C) There's one on the corner.
→ 편의점(convenience store)을 one으로 받아 위치에 대해 설명한 정답

가장 가까운 편의점이 어디에 있는지 아세요?
(A) 그 가게는 오후 11시까지 문을 엽니다.
(B) 저는 시간제 근무자입니다.
(C) 모퉁이에 하나 있습니다.

어휘 nearest 가장 가까운　convenience store 편의점
remain open 열어 놓다　until ~까지　part-timer 시간제 근무자

4. Aren't we supposed to finish this report today?
(A) Yes, it's almost done.
→ Yes는 보고서를 오늘 끝내야 한다는 의미이고 이어서 거의 다 했다는 말을 하고 있으므로 정답

(B) No, I didn't write it.
→ report에 대한 연상작용을 일으키는 오답

(C) Our manager talked to the reporter.
→ report와 유사발음 reporter를 사용한 오답

우리가 오늘 이 보고서를 끝내야 하지 않나요?
(A) 네, 거의 다 되었습니다.
(B) 아니요, 제가 보고서를 쓰지 않았습니다.
(C) 우리 매니저가 기자에게 얘기했습니다.

어휘 be supposed to부정사 ~하기로 되어 있다　finish 끝내다　almost 거의　done (일을) 끝낸, 마친　reporter 기자

5. The new interns start working today, don't they?
(A) Welcome to the company.
→ new interns에 대한 연상작용을 일으키는 오답

(B) Yes, the whole group is here now.
→ 전체 인턴사원들이 여기에 와 있다고 말한 것이므로 정답

(C) No, it's an older model.
→ new에 대한 반의어로 older를 썼지만 의미상 무관하므로 오답

새 인턴사원들이 오늘 일을 시작하죠, 그렇죠?
(A) 입사를 환영합니다.
(B) 네, 인턴 전체가 지금 와 있습니다.
(C) 아니요, 그것은 구형입니다.

어휘 intern 인턴사원　whole 전체의　old 오래된
model (상품의) 모델, 모형, 본보기

6. We can reserve train tickets by phone, can't we?
(A) No, we have to book them online.
→ 부정으로 응답한 뒤 online으로 예약해야 한다는 관련 내용을 추가한 것이므로 정답

(B) No, they got there by bus.
→ 전화 예약이 가능한지에 대한 답변이 아니라 이동 수단을 말한 것이므로 오답

(C) The express train is much faster.
→ 동일 단어 train을 사용한 오답

우리는 전화로 기차표를 예약할 수 있죠, 그렇죠?
(A) 아니요, 우리는 온라인으로 예약해야 합니다.
(B) 아니요, 그들은 버스로 그곳에 갔어요.
(C) 고속 열차가 훨씬 더 빠릅니다.

어휘 reserve 예약하다(= book)　by phone 전화로　by bus 버스 타고　express train 고속 열차　fast 빠른

7. The discussion ends at 3, doesn't it?
(A) Yes, so there's just 30 minutes left.
→ 긍정으로 대답한 뒤, 단지 30분이 남았다는 추가 정보를 제시한 것이므로 정답

(B) They dealt with energy conservation.
→ discussion에 대한 연상작용을 일으키는 오답

(C) It'll be held this Saturday.
→ When will the discussion be held?에 대한 답변이므로 오답

토론이 3시에 끝나요, 그렇죠?
(A) 네, 그래서 단지 30분 남았습니다.
(B) 그들은 에너지 절약에 대해 다루었습니다.
(C) 그것은 이번 주 토요일에 열릴 겁니다.

어휘 discussion 토론　end 끝나다　기간+left (기간)이 남은
deal with ~을 다루다　energy conservation 에너지 절약
hold 열다, 개최하다

8. Do you know where the staff lounge is?
(A) Every employee can take a break at the lounge.
→ 동일 단어 lounge를 사용한 오답

(B) It's currently under renovation.
→ Do you know why the staff lounge is closed?에 대한 답변이므로 오답

(C) Sure, right this way.
→ 의문문 중간에 있는 where에 대한 답변이므로 정답

직원 휴게실이 어디에 있는지 아세요?
(A) 모든 직원들이 휴게실에서 쉴 수 있습니다.
(B) 그곳은 현재 보수공사 중입니다.
(C) 물론이죠, 바로 이쪽입니다.

어휘 staff lounge 직원 휴게실　take a break 쉬다　currently 현재
under renovation 보수공사 중

실전 감각 익히기 본책_p. 75

| 1. (B) | 2. (C) | 3. (A) | 4. (C) | 5. (B) |
| 6. (C) | 7. (A) | 8. (A) | 9. (B) | 10. (B) |

1. Can't we use the air conditioner now?
(A) No, they can't.
→ Can't we use ~로 물어본 질문에 they로 답할 수 없으므로 오답
(B) Let's turn on the fans instead.
→ 부정어 No를 생략한 채, 대신 선풍기를 켜자는 의미이므로 정답
(C) Weather conditions are good.
→ 질문과 무관하게 conditioner와 유사발음인 conditions를 사용했으므로 오답

우리가 지금 에어컨을 사용할 수 없나요?
(A) 아니요, 사용할 수 없습니다.
(B) 대신 선풍기를 켭시다.
(C) 날씨 상황이 좋군요.

어휘 air conditioner 에어컨 turn on 켜다 fan 선풍기
instead 대신에 weather conditions 날씨 상황

2. Do you know how far the convention center is from the airport?
(A) By shuttle bus.
→ 의문문 중간에 있는 how far(얼마나 먼)에 대한 답변이 아니므로 오답
(B) It will be held next week.
→ convention이 열리는 시점에 대한 답변이므로 오답
(C) It's just across the road.
→ how far에 대한 답변으로 회의장의 위치를 나타내고 있으므로 정답

회의장이 공항에서 얼마나 먼지 아세요?
(A) 셔틀버스로요.
(B) 다음주에 열릴 겁니다.
(C) 바로 길 건너편에 있습니다.

어휘 how far 얼마나 먼 hold 열다, 개최하다 across ~ 건너편에

3. Aren't you ready to go?
(A) No, not quite yet.
→ No, I'm not quite yet.을 줄여 응답한 것이므로 정답
(B) You can go anytime.
→ Aren't you ~에 대한 답변으로 you를 쓸 수 없으므로 오답
(C) For here, thanks.
→ to go를 듣고 음식 주문 상황에서 종업원이 말하는 For here or to go?(여기서 드시겠어요, 아니면 가지고 가겠습니까?)를 연상한 것이므로 오답

나갈 준비가 되지 않았나요?
(A) 아니요, 아직 안 됐습니다.
(B) 당신은 언제라도 갈 수 있습니다.
(C) 여기서 먹겠습니다. 고맙습니다.

어휘 not quite yet 아직 끝나지 않은 for here 여기서 먹는

4. Can you tell me why you need to close the store early?
(A) It opens at 10 every morning.
→ Can you tell me 뒤에 있는 이유의 의문사 why와 관련이 없으므로 오답
(B) No, the store is open 24 hours a day.
→ close에 대한 연상작용으로 반의어 open을 썼지만 질문과 무관하므로 오답
(C) We need to do inventory.
→ why에 대한 이유를 제시하고 있으므로 정답

왜 상점을 일찍 닫아야 하는지 말씀해주실 수 있습니까?
(A) 매일 아침 10시에 문을 엽니다.
(B) 아니요, 가게는 24시간 영업을 합니다.
(C) 우리는 재고 정리를 해야 합니다.

어휘 close 닫다 a day 하루에 do inventory 재고 정리를 하다

5. This computer is connected to the printer, isn't it?
(A) No, I didn't correct anything.
→ connected와 유사발음인 correct를 썼을 뿐 질문과는 의미상 무관하므로 오답
(B) Yes, it is.
→ Yes, it is connected to the printer.를 줄여 응답한 것이므로 정답
(C) The printer is working well.
→ 동일 단어 printer를 썼지만 질문과 무관한 내용이므로 오답

이 컴퓨터는 프린터에 연결되어 있죠, 그렇죠?
(A) 아니요, 저는 어떤 것도 수정하지 않았어요.
(B) 네, 맞습니다.
(C) 프린터는 잘 작동되고 있습니다.

어휘 connect 연결하다 correct 바로잡다 work 작동되다

6. Do you know where the finance department is?
(A) Thank you for your financial advice.
→ finance와 유사발음의 financial을 썼지만 질문과 관련없는 답변이므로 오답
(B) Yes, I will.
→ 재무부서의 위치에 대한 답변은 아니므로 오답
(C) It's just down this hallway.
→ 의문문 중간에 있는 where에 대한 답변이므로 정답

재무부서가 어디에 있는지 아세요?
(A) 당신의 재정 조언에 감사 드립니다.
(B) 네, 제가 하겠습니다.
(C) 이 복도 아래쪽에 있습니다.

어휘 financial 재정의   hallway 복도

7. Didn't you receive any phone calls?
(A) Not that I'm aware of.
→ 전화를 받은 것이 없다는 뜻이므로 정답
(B) I didn't call you.
→ 전화를 받았는지에 대한 질문과 관련이 없으므로 오답
(C) No, you didn't.
→ Didn't you ~에 대한 답변으로 다시 you를 쓸 수는 없으므로 오답

당신은 어떠한 전화도 못 받았나요?
(A) 제가 알기론 없습니다.
(B) 저는 당신에게 전화를 걸지 않았어요.
(C) 아니요, 당신은 하지 않았어요.

어휘 Not that I'm aware of. 제가 알기론 아닙니다.

8. Our new Web site looks great, doesn't it?
(A) Yes, it's easy to use, too.
→ 웹사이트에 대해 긍정 응답을 한 후, 추가 장점을 말하고 있으므로 정답
(B) Through the Internet.
→ 질문과 관계없이 Web site와의 연상작용으로 Internet을 쓴 것이므로 오답
(C) Please, visit our Web site.
→ Web site를 반복해서 썼지만 질문과 무관하므로 오답

우리 웹사이트가 좋아보이지 않나요?
(A) 네, 이용하기도 쉽고요.
(B) 인터넷을 통해서요.
(C) 우리 웹사이트를 방문해 주세요.

어휘 look + 형용사 ~해보이다   through ~을 통해

9. Haven't you reviewed the proposal?
(A) Yes, I will.
→ have동사로 물어본 의문문에는 will이 아니라 have로 답변해야 하므로 오답
(B) No, not yet.
→ No, I haven't reviewed it yet.을 줄여 말한 것이므로 정답
(C) No, it has good reviews.
→ Haven't you ~로 물어본 질문에 it으로 대답할 수 없으므로 오답

그 제안서를 검토하지 않았나요?

(A) 네, 제가 할 겁니다.
(B) 아니요, 아직 아닙니다.
(C) 아니요, 그것은 좋은 평가를 받고 있습니다.

어휘 review 검토하다; 평가   proposal 제안서

10. You have quite a busy schedule today, don't you?
(A) No, it's not noisy.
→ quite를 quiet로 잘못 들었을 때의 답변이므로 오답
(B) That's because of all the meetings.
→ 바쁜 일정의 이유를 제시하고 있으므로 정답
(C) Yes, I'm available.
→ Yes라고 하면 일정이 바쁘다는 뜻인데 그 뒤에는 시간이 된다고 했으므로 의미상 모순이 되어 오답

당신은 오늘 일정이 아주 바쁘죠, 그렇죠?
(A) 아니요, 시끄럽지 않습니다.
(B) 모든 회의 때문입니다.
(C) 네, 저는 시간이 됩니다.

어휘 quite 꽤, 상당히   noisy 시끄러운   because of ~ 때문에

UNIT 8 평서문

받아쓰기 연습 본책 _ p. 77

1. return / date / will / read / day
2. deliver / address / good / delivered / address
3. review / already / view / online

청취 집중 훈련 1 본책 _ p. 78

| 1. (B) | 2. (A) | 3. (B) | 4. (B) |
| 5. (C) | 6. (C) | 7. (A) | 8. (C) |

1. I need to find a new assistant.
(A) I haven't seen him.
(B) I'll put out an advertisement.
(C) You assist me a lot.

저는 새 비서를 찾아봐야 합니다.
(A) 저는 그를 못 봤습니다.
(B) 제가 광고를 낼게요.
(C) 당신은 저를 많이 도와줍니다.

2. Let's go jogging.
(A) Sure, at what time?
(B) No, it stopped.
(C) No, I haven't been there yet.

조깅하러 가죠.
(A) 좋아요, 몇 시에요?
(B) 아니요, 그것이 멈추었어요.
(C) 아니요, 저는 아직 그곳에 가본 적이 없습니다.

3. I'm not feeling very good.
(A) She said she enjoyed it.
(B) Why don't you go home early?
(C) No, it was better.

저는 컨디션이 썩 좋지 않아요.
(A) 그녀는 좋았다고 했어요.
(B) 일찍 집에 들어가는 게 어때요?
(C) 아니요, 그게 더 나았어요.

4. I'd like to confirm my flight.
(A) I've come for the seminar.
(B) All right, your ticket number, please.
(C) I'll be leaving tomorrow at two.

제 비행편을 확인하고 싶습니다.
(A) 저는 세미나를 위해 왔습니다.
(B) 좋습니다. 티켓 번호 좀 말씀해 주세요.
(C) 저는 내일 2시에 떠날 겁니다.

5. These documents need to be filed.
(A) I received the files by e-mail.
(B) No, where are they?
(C) Sure, I'll take care of that.

이 서류들을 철해야 해요.
(A) 제가 이메일로 그 파일들을 받았어요.
(B) 아니요, 그것이 어디에 있죠?
(C) 네, 제가 처리할게요.

6. I'm thinking of painting the wall.
(A) He thought he would.
(B) Where do you want to hang it?
(C) That's a good idea.

저는 벽에 페인트 칠을 할까 생각 중입니다.
(A) 그는 그럴 거라고 생각했어요.
(B) 어디에 그것을 걸고 싶으세요?
(C) 좋은 생각입니다.

7. I need a box to send some things.
(A) What size do you need?
(B) There's tape in the drawer.
(C) You can buy tickets at the box office.

저는 몇 가지 물건을 보낼 상자가 필요합니다.
(A) 어떤 크기가 필요하세요?
(B) 서랍 안에 테이프가 있습니다.
(C) 매표소에서 표를 사실 수 있습니다.

8. I wish this rain would stop.
(A) It's the next stop.
(B) Just let me know when.
(C) It's supposed to continue the entire week.

이 비가 멈췄으면 좋겠네요.
(A) 다음 정거장입니다.
(B) 언제인지 제게 알려주세요.
(C) 한 주 내내 계속 내릴 겁니다.

청취 집중 훈련 2 본책_p. 79

| 1. (B) | 2. (C) | 3. (A) | 4. (C) |
| 5. (A) | 6. (A) | 7. (B) | 8. (C) |

1. I'm here to see Mr. Wiggins.
(A) Yes, he saw it yesterday.
　→ it이 가리키는 대상을 알 수 없으므로 오답
(B) Okay, I'll let him know.
　→ him은 Mr. Wiggins를 가리키며, 그에게 알려주겠다고 응답한 것이므로 정답
(C) We didn't hear the news.
　→ 동음 이의어 here-hear를 함정으로 사용한 오답 보기

위긴스 씨를 만나기 위해 여기 왔습니다.
(A) 네, 그는 어제 그것을 봤습니다.
(B) 좋아요, 제가 그에게 알려줄게요.
(C) 우리는 그 소식을 듣지 못했어요.

어휘 be here to see ~을 만나러 여기 왔다
　　　let A(사람) know A에게 알려주다

2. Let's visit the science museum this weekend.
(A) Admission for children under 12 is free.
→ museum에 대한 잘못된 연상작용으로 어린이의 입장료를 언급한 것이므로 오답
(B) You can visit me anytime.
→ 박물관에 가자는 제안에는 적합하지 않은 응답이므로 오답
(C) Sure, let's go on Saturday.
→ Sure로 긍정적인 반응을 하고 있으므로 정답

이번 주말에 과학 박물관에 갑시다.
(A) 12세 미만 어린이는 무료입니다.
(B) 언제든지 저를 찾아오셔도 좋습니다.
(C) 네, 토요일에 가요.

어휘 visit 방문하다 museum 박물관 admission 입장(료)
under 12 12세 미만의 anytime 언제라도

3. I want to pay by credit card.
(A) I'm sorry, we only take cash.
→ I'm sorry로 부정적인 반응을 보인 후 다른 지불 수단을 언급한 것이므로 정답
(B) You will be paid by the hour.
→ pay와 유사발음인 paid를 썼지만 의미상 관련이 없으므로 오답
(C) It only takes a minute to apply.
→ 주어진 평서문은 신용 카드 신청에 대한 내용이 아니므로 오답

저는 신용카드로 지불하고 싶습니다.
(A) 죄송합니다만 저희는 현금만 받습니다.
(B) 당신은 시급으로 받게 됩니다.
(C) 신청하는 데 단지 1분이면 됩니다.

어휘 pay by credit card 신용카드로 지불하다 by the hour 시간당으로
apply 신청하다

4. I'm looking for a new computer.
(A) I looked at it on the Web site.
→ look for는 '찾다'라는 뜻이고 look at은 '보다'라는 뜻으로 의미상 서로 관련이 없으므로 오답
(B) I lost them.
→ a new computer를 them으로 바꿔 쓸 수 없으며 맥락상 올바른 응답도 아니므로 오답
(C) Is there a particular one you'd like?
→ 신형 컴퓨터를 찾고 있다는 말에 역질문으로 응답한 것이므로 정답

저는 신형 컴퓨터를 찾고 있습니다.
(A) 제가 그것을 웹사이트에서 봤어요.
(B) 저는 그것을 잃어버렸어요.
(C) 특별히 마음에 드는 게 있나요?

어휘 look for 찾다 look at 보다 lose 잃다 particular 특별한

5. The paper order will be delayed.
(A) Oh no, please find out how long.
→ Oh, no로 부정적인 반응을 보인 후 소요 시간을 알아보라는 응답이므로 정답
(B) No, she put them on the table.
→ 대명사 she가 가리키는 대상을 알 수 없으므로 오답
(C) Please make double-sided copies.
→ 현재 복사를 하고 있는 상황이 아니므로 오답

종이 주문이 지연될 겁니다.
(A) 오, 이런, 얼마나 오래 걸리는지 알아봐주세요.
(B) 아니요, 그녀는 그것을 탁자 위에 두었어요.
(C) 양면 복사를 해 주세요.

어휘 delay 지연시키다 find out 알아보다
make a double-sided copy 양면복사를 하다

6. I'd like to leave a message.
(A) Okay, let me get a pen.
→ 메시지를 적기 위해 펜을 가져오겠다는 의미이므로 정답
(B) I'll give you a massage.
→ message와 비슷한 발음인 massage를 쓴 것이므로 오답
(C) Tom called you this morning.
→ message와의 연상작용으로 called를 쓴 것이지만 의미상 무관한 응답이므로 오답

제가 메시지를 남기고 싶습니다.
(A) 좋아요, 제가 펜을 가지고 올게요.
(B) 제가 당신에게 마사지를 해줄게요.
(C) 톰이 오늘 아침에 당신에게 전화를 했어요.

어휘 leave a message 메시지를 남기다 get 가져오다
give ~ a massage ~에게 마사지를 해주다

7. Don't forget to pack some warm clothes.
(A) No, I remember to close them.
→ clothes와 유사발음인 close를 썼지만 의미 무관하므로 오답
(B) Thank you for reminding me.
→ 따뜻한 옷을 챙기라는 말에 '고맙다'고 응답한 것이므로 정답
(C) I still need to pack for the trip.
→ 동일 단어인 pack을 썼지만 의미상 적합하지 않은 응답이므로 오답

따뜻한 옷을 좀 챙기는 거 잊지 마세요.
(A) 아니요, 저는 그것을 닫아야 한다는 것을 기억합니다.
(B) 상기시켜 주셔서 감사합니다.
(C) 저는 아직도 여행 준비를 위해 짐을 꾸려야 합니다.

어휘 pack (짐을) 챙기다 warm clothes 따뜻한 옷 remind 상기시키다

8. They've agreed to sign the contract.
(A) Where should I sign it?
→ 추가 정보를 요구할 때 역질문을 할 수 있으나 이 역질문은 의미상 관련성이 없으므로 오답
(B) No, I haven't contacted them yet.
→ contract와 유사발음인 contacted를 쓴 것이며, No라고 대답할 수도 없으므로 오답
(C) Congratulations.
→ 계약 체결에 대해 축하한다는 응답을 한 것이므로 정답

그들은 계약에 서명하기로 동의했어요.
(A) 제가 어디에 서명해야 합니까?
(B) 아니요, 저는 아직 그들에게 연락하지 않았어요.
(C) 축하합니다.

어휘 agree 동의하다 sign 서명하다 contract 계약
Congratulations. 축하합니다.

청취 집중 훈련 3 본책_p. 80

| 1. (B) | 2. (A) | 3. (B) | 4. (A) |
| 5. (C) | 6. (C) | 7. (A) | 8. (C) |

1. I'll pick you up at seven sharp this evening.
(A) Sorry, but I only have six.
→ 숫자 seven과 six가 연상작용을 일으키지만 내용상 서로 관련이 없으므로 오답
(B) Well, can you come a little earlier?
→ 역질문으로 요청사항을 전달하고 있으므로 정답
(C) Please pick up the phone.
→ 동일 표현 pick up을 사용한 오답

제가 오늘 저녁 정각 7시에 데리러 가겠습니다.
(A) 미안하지만 저는 6개밖에 없습니다.
(B) 음, 좀 더 일찍 와주실 수 있나요?
(C) 전화 좀 받아주세요.

어휘 pick ~ up ~를 데리러 가다 sharp 정각에
a little earlier 좀 더 일찍 pick up the phone 전화를 받다

2. The bathroom sink is leaking.
(A) I'll call a plumber.
→ 세면대가 새고 있다는 말에 대한 우회적 답변이므로 정답
(B) No, but it has two bedrooms.
→ bathroom과 유사발음인 bedrooms를 쓴 오답
(C) I think it's a little expensive.
→ sink와 유사발음인 think를 쓴 오답

욕실 세면대가 샙니다.
(A) 제가 배관공에게 전화할게요.
(B) 아니요, 하지만 침실이 두 개 있습니다.
(C) 그것은 좀 비싸다고 생각해요.

어휘 bathroom 욕실 plumber 배관공 bedroom 침실
expensive 비싼

3. I'm going to be late for work tomorrow.
(A) It starts at 9 o'clock.
→ work에 대한 연상작용을 일으키는 오답
(B) OK, what time will you be here?
→ 역질문으로 추가 정보를 요구하는 것이므로 정답
(C) The interest rate has increased slightly.
→ late의 유사발음 rate를 쓴 오답

제가 내일 늦게 출근할 겁니다.
(A) 그것은 9시에 시작됩니다.
(B) 좋아요, 몇 시에 여기 올 거죠?
(C) 이자율이 약간 상승했어요.

어휘 be late for ~에 늦다 work 직장 interest rate 이자율
increase 오르다 slightly 약간

4. If the radio is too loud, I can turn it down.
(A) No, it's fine for me.
→ No를 써서 볼륨을 줄일 필요가 없다는 반응을 보인 것이므로 정답
(B) It's better to turn the job down.
→ 제시문의 turn down은 '볼륨을 줄이다'라는 뜻인 반면, 보기에서는 '거절하다'라는 뜻이므로 오답
(C) I like listening to the radio, too.
→ 동일 단어 radio를 쓴 오답

만약 라디오가 너무 시끄러우면 제가 볼륨을 줄일게요.
(A) 아니요, 제겐 괜찮아요.
(B) 그 일을 거절하는 게 더 낫습니다.
(C) 저도 라디오 듣는 것을 좋아해요.

어휘 loud 시끄러운 turn down (볼륨을) 줄이다; 거절하다
listen to the radio 라디오를 듣다

5. I think I'm catching a cold.
(A) You won't miss your train.
→ catch의 반의어로 miss를 쓴 것이지만 의미상 관련이 없으므로 오답
(B) OK, I will call you after the meeting.
→ cold의 유사발음 call을 쓴 오답
(C) Let me get you some tea.
→ 차를 갖다 주겠다는 것은 의미상 제시문과 어울리므로 정답

제가 감기에 걸렸나 봐요.
(A) 당신은 기차를 놓치지 않을 겁니다.
(B) 좋아요, 회사 끝나고 제가 전화 드릴게요.
(C) 제가 차를 좀 갖다 드릴게요.

어휘 catch a cold 감기에 걸리다   miss 놓치다   call 전화하다

---

6. I have ten copies of the report for the presentation.
(A) Your presentation was very good.
　→ 동일 단어 presentation을 사용한 오답
(B) It will take place in about five minutes.
　→ When will the presentation start?에 대한 대답이므로 오답
(C) Well, I don't think that's enough.
　→ I don't think로 부정적 반응을 보인 것이므로 정답

발표용으로 보고서 사본 10부를 갖고 있습니다.
(A) 당신의 발표는 매우 좋았어요.
(B) 대략 5분 후에 열릴 겁니다.
(C) 음, 충분하지 않은 거 같은데요.

어휘 copy 사본   presentation 발표   take place 열리다, 개최되다
in + 시간 ~ 후에

---

7. Let's invite George to our grand opening.
(A) Great, I'll contact him.
　→ 제안에 대한 긍정적 반응이므로 정답
(B) He will apply for the vacancy.
　→ opening을 '공석'으로 잘못 이해한 응답이므로 오답
(C) The event will be a great success.
　→ grand opening에 대한 연상작용을 일으키는 오답

조지를 우리 개장 행사에 초대합시다.
(A) 좋아요, 제가 그에게 연락할게요.
(B) 그가 그 공석에 지원할 겁니다.
(C) 그 행사는 대성공일 겁니다.

어휘 grand opening 개장(일)   apply for ~에 지원하다   vacancy 공석
event 행사   a great success 대성공

---

8. It's raining really hard outside.
(A) I can hardly wait to see you.
　→ hard의 유사발음인 hardly를 쓴 것이므로 오답
(B) My training session was easy.
　→ raining과의 유사발음인 training을 쓴 것이므로 오답
(C) Do you have an umbrella?
　→ 맥락상 주어진 평서문에 어울리는 역질문이므로 정답

밖에 비가 아주 세차게 오네요.
(A) 저는 빨리 당신을 보고 싶어요.
(B) 제 교육과정은 쉬웠어요.
(C) 우산 갖고 있으세요?

어휘 hard 세차게   can hardly wait to 부정사 빨리 ~하고 싶다
training session 교육과정

실전 감각 익히기   본책 _ p. 81

| 1. (A) | 2. (B) | 3. (C) | 4. (A) | 5. (C) |
| 6. (B) | 7. (A) | 8. (C) | 9. (B) | 10. (B) |

1. I can't make it to dinner this evening.
(A) Oh, are you not feeling good?
　→ 역질문으로 저녁 식사에 참석할 수 없는 이유를 묻고 있으므로 정답
(B) Thank you for inviting me.
　→ dinner에 대한 잘못된 연상작용으로 응답한 것이므로 오답
(C) Yes, I made steak.
　→ make it to는 '~에 가다'라는 뜻이지만 여기의 made는 '만들었다'라는 뜻이므로 오답

오늘 저녁 식사에 갈 수가 없어요.
(A) 오, 몸이 안 좋은가요?
(B) 초대해 주셔서 감사합니다.
(C) 네, 제가 스테이크를 만들었어요.

어휘 make it to ~에 가다   feel good 기분이 좋다, 몸 상태가 좋다

---

2. I'd like to open a new savings account.
(A) Here is my account number.
　→ 동일 단어인 account를 썼을 뿐, 의미상 관련이 없으므로 오답
(B) No problem, just fill this out.
　→ 긍정의 반응을 보인 후, 요구 사항을 전달하고 있으므로 정답
(C) Yes, I will save some money.
　→ savings account에 대한 잘못된 연상작용으로 응답한 것이므로 오답

새로운 보통예금을 개설하고 싶어요.
(A) 여기 제 계좌번호가 있습니다.
(B) 좋습니다. 이것을 작성해주세요.
(C) 네, 제가 돈을 좀 모으겠습니다.

어휘 open a savings account 보통예금을 개설하다
account number 계좌번호   fill out 작성하다

3. Vacation requests must be turned in by Friday.
(A) No, she gets back on Monday.
　→ she가 누구를 가리키는지 알 수 없으므로 오답
(B) To the sales department.
　→ 휴가 요청서의 제출 장소에 대한 답변이므로 오답
(C) OK, I'll give it to you tomorrow.
　→ 긍정의 응답과 함께 turn in을 give로 바꿔 쓴 것이므로 정답

휴가 요청서는 금요일까지 제출해야 합니다.
(A) 아니요, 그녀는 월요일에 돌아옵니다.
(B) 영업부로요.
(C) 좋아요, 제가 내일 당신에게 드릴게요.

어휘 request 요청(서)　turn in 제출하다　get back 돌아오다

4. We're having a barbeque this Saturday.
(A) That sounds like fun.
　→ 바비큐 파티에 대한 긍정적인 반응을 보인 것이므로 정답
(B) I don't know.
　→ '모른다' 식 응답이지만 주어진 평서문에는 부적합한 반응이므로 오답
(C) Did you go?
　→ 역질문이지만 제시문과는 시제 측면에서 어울리지 않으므로 오답

이번 주 토요일 우리는 바비큐 파티를 합니다.
(A) 재미있겠네요.
(B) 몰라요.
(C) 당신은 갔었나요?

어휘 barbeque 바비큐 파티　sound like ~처럼 들리다

5. I heard you're opening a restaurant.
(A) Let's go for lunch.
　→ restaurant에 대한 연상작용으로 lunch를 쓴 것이므로 오답
(B) I think it serves Indian food.
　→ 식당 개업을 한 것이 아니므로 인도 음식의 제공은 내용과 관련이 없는 오답
(C) No, actually, my sister is planning to.
　→ 부정의 반응으로 No라고 한 후, 식당 개업을 계획하고 있는 실제 인물을 언급하고 있으므로 정답

당신이 식당을 개업한다고 들었어요.
(A) 점심 먹으러 가요.
(B) 인도 음식을 제공한다고 생각해요.
(C) 아니요, 사실 제 언니가 계획 중이에요.

어휘 open 개업하다　serve (음식을) 내다　actually 사실

6. We have to be there at three.
(A) They're my colleagues.
　→ there와 비슷한 발음인 They're를 이용한 유사발음 오답
(B) No, it was changed to five.
　→ No로 부정적 반응을 보인 후 5시라는 수정된 정보를 제시하고 있으므로 정답
(C) Yes, there were three of us.
　→ 평서문에서의 three는 시각, 응답에서의 three는 인원수를 말하므로 오답

우리는 3시까지 그곳에 가야 해요.
(A) 그들은 제 직장동료입니다.
(B) 아니요, 5시로 변경되었어요.
(C) 네, 우리 3명이 있었습니다.

어휘 colleague 직장동료　change 변경하다

7. The door to the warehouse is locked.
(A) Janet should have the key.
　→ 문이 잠겼다는 말에 대한 우회적 답변이므로 정답
(B) I'll close the door.
　→ locked에 대한 연상작용으로 close를 썼을 뿐, 의미상 무관한 내용이므로 오답
(C) I don't know where the house is.
　→ 빠르게 발음될 경우 warehouse와 유사발음인 where the house를 쓴 것이므로 오답

창고 문이 잠겨 있어요.
(A) 재닛이 열쇠를 갖고 있을 겁니다.
(B) 제가 문을 닫을게요.
(C) 저는 그 집이 어디에 있는지 모릅니다.

어휘 warehouse 창고　lock 잠그다　should ~일 것이다　close 닫다

8. Let's discuss Mr. Planter's proposal.
(A) The supervisor approved it.
　→ proposal에 대한 연상작용으로 approved를 쓴 것이지만 내용상 무관하므로 오답
(B) It was right before lunch.
　→ 주어진 평서문에 과거시제로 응답할 수 없으므로 오답
(C) O.K., when should we meet?
　→ 긍정의 반응을 보인 후, 역질문으로 추가 정보를 요구하고 있는 것이므로 정답

플랜터 씨의 제안에 대해 논의해봅시다.
(A) 감독관이 그것을 승인했습니다.
(B) 점심시간 직전이었어요.
(C) 좋아요, 언제 만나야 할까요?

어휘 proposal 제안　supervisor 감독관　approve 승인하다
　　　right before ~ 직전에

9. We could hold the meeting in the office.
(A) You can fold it in half.
　→ 의미상 무관하게 hold와 유사발음인 fold를 썼으므로 오답
(B) Don't you think it's too small?
　→ 부정 역질문으로 부정적 의견을 나타내고 있으므로 정답
(C) Where do you want to hold it?
　→ 역질문이긴 하지만 내용상 주어진 평서문에는 적절하지 않으므로 오답

우리는 회의를 사무실에서 열 수도 있겠어요.
(A) 그것을 반으로 접어도 됩니다.
(B) 사무실이 너무 작다고 생각하지 않으세요?
(C) 어디에서 회의를 열고 싶으세요?

어휘 hold 열다, 개최하다　fold 접다　in half 반으로

10. You have some mail from your bank.
(A) I have to deposit it.
　→ bank와의 연상작용으로 deposit을 썼지만 의미상 무관하므로 오답
(B) Thanks, please put it on my desk.
　→ 주어진 평서문과 어울리는 응답이므로 정답
(C) No, I didn't send it yet.
　→ 문맥상 No로 응답할 수 없으므로 오답

은행에서 온 우편물이 좀 있습니다.
(A) 저는 그것을 입금해야 합니다.
(B) 고마워요. 제 책상 위에 놓아주세요.
(C) 아니요, 아직 그것을 보내지 않았습니다.

어휘 deposit 입금하다　put 놓다　yet 아직

Part 2　Review Test　본책 _ p. 82

1. (B)	2. (A)	3. (B)	4. (A)	5. (A)
6. (C)	7. (C)	8. (B)	9. (A)	10. (B)
11. (A)	12. (C)	13. (A)	14. (A)	15. (C)
16. (B)	17. (A)	18. (C)	19. (B)	20. (A)
21. (C)	22. (B)	23. (C)	24. (B)	25. (C)
26. (C)	27. (C)	28. (B)	29. (C)	30. (A)

1. What day is it today?
(A) On the twenty fourth.
(B) It's Monday.
(C) Almost noon.

오늘은 무슨 요일입니까?
(A) 24일이에요.
(B) 월요일입니다.
(C) 거의 정오쯤 됐어요.

해설 (A) 요일을 묻는 질문에 날짜로 대답했으므로 오답이다. 만약 What date is it today?(오늘 며칠이에요?)라고 물어보면 It's October ninth.(10월 9일입니다.)와 같이 대답할 수 있다. (B) 요일을 말하고 있으므로 정답이다. (C) What time is it now?에 대한 답변이므로 오답이다.

어휘 What day is it today? 오늘이 무슨 요일입니까?　almost 거의　noon 정오

2. Where was Mr. Chiang this afternoon?
(A) At the museum.
(B) He often visits.
(C) Yes, he already left.

오늘 오후 치앙 씨는 어디에 있었죠?
(A) 박물관에요.
(B) 그는 종종 방문합니다.
(C) 네, 그는 벌써 퇴근했어요.

해설 (A) 장소를 묻는 Where 의문문에 맞게 장소의 전치사구 At the museum으로 대답하고 있으므로 정답이다. (B) 치앙 씨가 있었던 장소에 대한 답변이 아니므로 오답이다. (C) 의문사의문문에는 yes나 no로 대답할 수 없으므로 오답이다.

어휘 museum 박물관　often 자주　visit 방문하다　already 벌써　leave 퇴근하다, 나가다, 떠나다

3. Why is the restaurant closed today?
(A) It's not far from here.
(B) They don't open every Sunday.
(C) They have a great new menu.

왜 오늘 그 식당이 문을 닫았죠?
(A) 여기에서 멀리 않아요.
(B) 그들은 매주 일요일에는 문을 열지 않아요.
(C) 그들은 새로운 좋은 메뉴가 있어요.

해설 (A) closed(문을 닫은)를 close(가까운)로 잘못 듣고 이와 연관해서 not far를 쓴 것이므로 오답이다. (B) 이유를 묻는 why 의문문에 because를 생략한 채 이유를 제시하고 있으므로 정답이다. (C) 질문과는 의미상 무관하게 restaurant에 대한 연상작용으로 a great new menu를 쓴 것이므로 오답이다.

어휘 closed 문을 닫은　far from here 여기에서 먼　open 문을 열다; 열린　great 좋은, 훌륭한

4. How was the customer feedback on our new Web site?
(A) It was very positive.
(B) No, he forgot his password.
(C) Just click here and you can order one.

우리의 새 웹사이트에 대한 고객의 반응은 어땠나요?
(A) 매우 긍정적이었어요.
(B) 아니요, 그는 비밀번호를 잊어버렸어요.
(C) 여기만 클릭하면 주문하실 수 있어요.

> **해설** (A) 웹사이트에 대한 고객의 반응이 매우 긍정적(very positive)이었다는 뜻이므로 정답이다. (B) 의문사의문문에는 yes나 no로 대답할 수 없으므로 오답이다. (C) 질문은 고객의 반응에 관한 것인데 웹사이트에서의 주문 방법을 말하고 있으므로 오답이다.

> **어휘** customer feedback 고객 반응 positive 긍정적인 forget 잊다 order 주문하다

5. Where are the questionnaires?
(A) Sorry, we have run out.
(B) I don't have any questions.
(C) You should fill out the form.

설문지는 어디에 있습니까?
(A) 미안하지만 다 떨어졌어요.
(B) 저는 질문이 없습니다.
(C) 양식을 작성하셔야 합니다.

> **해설** (A) run out은 '다 떨어졌다'는 의미로 설문지가 없다는 뜻을 전달한 것이므로 정답이다. (B) 질문과는 의미상 무관하게 questionnaires에 대한 유사발음으로 questions를 쓴 것이므로 오답이다. (C) questionnaires에 대한 연상작용으로 fill out the form을 썼을 뿐, 설문지가 어디에 있는지에 대한 답변은 아니므로 오답이다.

> **어휘** questionnaire 설문지 run out 다 떨어지다 fill out[complete] a form 양식을 작성하다

6. What did the doctor say about your headache?
(A) He will take an aspirin.
(B) Let's take a coffee break.
(C) He said not to worry.

두통에 대해 의사가 뭐라고 하던가요?
(A) 그는 아스피린을 복용할 겁니다.
(B) 커피를 마시며 좀 쉽시다.
(C) 걱정하지 말라고 했어요.

> **해설** (A) He는 의문문의 the doctor를 가리키므로 결국 The doctor will take an aspirin.이 되어 의미상 부적절하므로 오답이다. (B) headache에 대한 연상작용으로 커피를 마시며 휴식을 취하자는 뜻의 coffee break를 쓴 것일 뿐, 두통에 대한 의사의 의견이 아니므로 오답이다. (C) 두통에 대한 의사의 의견을 말하고 있으므로 정답이다.

> **어휘** headache 두통 take (약을) 복용하다 take a coffee break 커피를 마시며 쉬다 say not to부정사 ~하지 말라고 말하다

7. Do you want to join us for lunch?
(A) I'm glad you enjoyed it.
(B) He's a member already.
(C) Sure, that would be great.

저희와 같이 점심 드실래요?
(A) 맛있었다니 다행이네요.
(B) 그는 벌써 회원입니다.
(C) 물론이죠, 그거 좋겠네요.

> **해설** (A) lunch에 대한 연상작용으로 enjoyed it을 썼지만 질문과는 관련없는 답변이므로 오답이다. (B) 질문과는 의미상 무관하게 join us에 대한 연상작용으로 member를 쓴 것이므로 오답이다. (C) 질문과 어울리는 긍정적인 반응이므로 정답이다.

> **어휘** join 함께 하다 glad 기쁜 enjoy 즐기다 member 회원 already 이미, 벌써 great 좋은, 훌륭한

8. You should take a night class at the college.
(A) They registered for the wrong day.
(B) Yes, I'd like to do that.
(C) I'm not busy tonight.

당신은 그 대학에서 야간 수업을 들어야 해요.
(A) 그들은 엉뚱한 날짜에 등록했어요.
(B) 네, 그렇게 하고 싶어요.
(C) 저는 오늘밤 바쁘지 않아요.

> **해설** (A) They가 가리키는 대상을 알 수 없으므로 인칭 오류에 의한 오답이다. (B) 제시된 평서문에 어울리는 긍정적인 반응을 보이고 있으므로 정답이다. (C) take a night class에 대한 연상작용으로 tonight을 썼지만 의미상 무관한 답변이므로 오답이다.

> **어휘** take a class 수업을 듣다 register for 등록하다(= enroll in, sign up for) wrong 잘못된, 틀린 would like to부정사 ~하고 싶다 busy 바쁜

9. Do the sales and marketing teams meet together or separately?
(A) It depends on the agenda.
(B) I bought mine as a set.
(C) Let's go together after the meeting.

영업팀과 마케팅팀이 회의를 같이 하나요, 따로 하나요?
(A) 그건 안건에 달려 있습니다.
(B) 저는 그것을 세트로 샀어요.
(C) 회의 끝난 후 같이 갑시다.

해설 (A) 두 개의 선택 사항을 제시하는 선택의문문에 대해 '안건에 달려 있다'는 불확실성 답변을 하고 있으므로 정답이다. (B) separately 에 대한 반대 의미로 set를 썼을 뿐, 질문과 의미상 관련이 없으므로 오답이다. (C) 의미상 무관하게 meet와의 유사발음으로 meeting 을 썼으므로 오답이다.

어휘 sales team 영업팀 marketing team 마케팅팀
separately 따로 depend on ~에 달려 있다 agenda 안건
buy 사다 go together 함께 가다

10. You've finished writing the contracts, haven't you?
(A) She's an excellent business contact.
(B) I think I'll be done this afternoon.
(C) Oh, where should I sign it?

계약서 작성을 끝내셨죠, 네?
(A) 그녀는 좋은 거래처 사람입니다.
(B) 오늘 오후면 다 끝날 겁니다.
(C) 오, 제가 어디에 사인해야 하죠?

해설 (A) contracts와 유사발음으로 contact을 쓴 것을 뿐, 의미상 무관 하므로 오답이다. (B) 계약서 작성의 완료 여부를 묻는 질문에 this afternoon이라는 완료 시점을 언급하고 있으므로 정답이다. (C) 의 미상 관련없이 contracts에 대한 연상작용으로 sign이란 단어를 쓴 것이므로 오답이다.

어휘 finish 끝내다 contract 계약서
business contact 업무상 연락을 취하는 사람, 거래처 사람
be done 끝나다, 다 하다 sign 서명하다

11. Don't you want to bring a camera to the awards ceremony?
(A) I'll just use my cell phone's camera.
(B) No, I'm not in that picture.
(C) You deserved the award.

시상식에 카메라를 가져가고 싶지 않으세요?
(A) 저는 제 휴대폰 카메라를 쓸 겁니다.
(B) 아니요, 저는 그 사진에 없어요.
(C) 당신은 상을 받을 자격이 있었어요.

해설 (A) 부정어 No를 생략한 채, 시상식에서 휴대폰의 카메라를 쓰겠다고 한 것이므로 정답이다. 질문에 쓰인 발음과 동일 발음 또는 유사발음을 쓴 보기는 대개 오답인 경우가 많다. 하지만 지금처럼 동일 발음 (camera)이 쓰였지만 정답인 경우가 간혹 있으므로 조심해야 한다. (B) camera와의 연상작용으로 picture를 쓴 것일 뿐, 의미상 관련이 없으므로 오답이다. (C) 유사발음 award를 썼지만 의미상 질문과 관련이 없는 답변이므로 오답이다.

어휘 bring 가져오다, 가져가다 awards ceremony 시상식
cell phone's camera 휴대폰 카메라 picture 사진, 그림
deserve an award 상을 받을 자격이 있다

12. Would you mind if I borrowed one of your pens?
(A) Thanks, but I have one, too.
(B) Please lend me some.
(C) No, help yourself to anything you need.

제가 펜 하나를 빌려도 될까요?
(A) 고맙습니다만 저도 하나 있어요.
(B) 저에게 좀 빌려주세요.
(C) 물론이죠, 어떤 거라도 마음껏 쓰세요.

해설 (A) You can borrow one of my pens.(제 펜 하나를 빌리셔도 됩니다.)에 대한 답변이므로 오답이다. (B) lend는 '빌려주다'라는 뜻으로 borrow의 반대말인데, 여기서는 질문과 어울리지 않는 단어이므로 오답이다. (C) 〈Would[Do] you mind if ~?〉는 '~라면 꺼리시겠습니까?'라는 뜻이므로 부정으로 대답하는 것이 결국 질문자의 의향에 따르는 것이 된다. 여기서도 No라고 대답해서 '꺼리지 않는다'는 뜻을 전달한 후, 마음껏 쓰라는 내용을 추가하고 있다.

어휘 Would[Do] you mind if ~? ~해도 될까요? borrow 빌리다
lend 빌려주다 Help yourself to ~. ~을 마음껏 쓰세요[드세요]

13. Did you get a chance to see my e-mail?
(A) No, I've been away from my desk.
(B) Please read my resume attached to this e-mail.
(C) The post office is open until 6 P.M.

제가 보낸 이메일을 볼 기회가 있었나요?
(A) 아니요, 제가 자리에 없었어요.
(B) 이 이메일에 첨부된 제 이력서를 읽어주세요.
(C) 우체국은 6시까지 문을 엽니다.

해설 (A) No로 부정의 대답을 한 후, 이메일을 읽지 못한 이유를 말하고 있으므로 정답이다. (B) 동일 발음으로 e-mail을 썼지만 질문과 관련이 없으므로 오답이다. (C) e-mail을 mail로 잘못 들었을 경우, mail 에 대한 연상작용으로 post office를 떠올리게 만든 것이므로 오답이다.

어휘 get a chance to 부정사 ~할 기회가 있다
be away from one's desk 자리에 없다 resume 이력서
attach A to B A를 B에 첨부하다 post office 우체국
open until + 시점 (시점)까지 문을 여는

14. Can you tell me where I have to put this projector?
(A) Please set it up in the meeting room.
(B) No, I know how to use it.
(C) They made sales projections.

제가 이 프로젝터를 어디에 놓아야 하는지 말씀해주실래요?
(A) 회의실에 설치해주세요.
(B) 아니요, 저는 그것의 사용법을 압니다.
(C) 그들은 영업에 대한 예측을 했습니다.

해설 (A) 의문사 where에 맞게 장소의 전치사구 in the meeting room을 써서 답변하고 있으므로 정답이다. 〈Can you tell me [Do you know, May I ask]+의문사+주어+동사 ~?〉의 간접의 문문에서는 문장 중간에 있는 의문사를 잘 듣고 그에 맞는 답변을 선택해야 한다. (B) 프로젝트트를 놓아야 할 장소에 대한 답변이 아니므로 오답이다. (C) projector와 유사발음인 projections를 썼지만 질문과 의미상 무관하므로 오답이다.

어휘 put 놓다, 두다   projector 영사기, 프로젝터   set up 설치하다
how to부정사 ~하는 법   use 사용하다
make a projection 예측하다

15. Was the seminar successful last week?
(A) You will do a good job.
(B) Our entire department will participate in it.
(C) Don't you know it has been postponed until next weekend?

지난주 세미나는 성공적이었나요?
(A) 당신은 잘 해내실 겁니다.
(B) 우리 부서는 모두 참석할 겁니다.
(C) 다음 주말로 연기된 거 모르세요?

해설 (A) 세미나가 주어인 질문에 You를 주어로 잘못 답변했으므로 인칭 오류에 의한 오답이다. (B) 과거시제의 의문문에 미래 동사로 답변했으므로 시제 오류에 의한 오답이다. (C) 세미나가 연기되었다는 것을 역질문으로 알려주고 있으므로 정답이다.

어휘 successful 성공적인   do a good job 잘 해내다   entire 전체의
participate in ~에 참석하다   postpone 연기하다

16. When did the package arrive?
(A) It was shipped to the warehouse.
(B) I have no idea.
(C) Yes, it will be broadcast live.

언제 이 소포가 도착했나요?
(A) 그것은 창고로 배달되었습니다.
(B) 잘 모르겠습니다.
(C) 네, 그것은 생방송될 겁니다.

해설 (A) Where was the package delivered?에 대한 답변이므로 오답이다. (B) 질문의 내용과 관계없이 I don't know, I'm not sure, I have no idea와 같은 '모른다' 류의 응답이 가능하므로 정답이다. (C) 의문사의문문에 yes나 no로 대답할 수 없으므로 오답이다.

어휘 package 소포   arrive 도착하다   ship 배달하다(= deliver)
warehouse 창고   be broadcast live 생방송되다

17. What do you think about our new office?
(A) It certainly has a lot more space.
(B) They are going to open a branch office soon.
(C) You always have to get official approval.

우리 새 사무실에 대해 어떻게 생각하세요?
(A) 분명히 공간이 더 넓네요.
(B) 그들은 곧 새 지점을 열 예정입니다.
(C) 당신은 항상 공식적인 승인을 받아야 합니다.

해설 (A) 새 사무실에 대한 의견을 제시하고 있으므로 정답이다. (B) office라는 동일 발음을 썼지만 질문과 내용상 무관하므로 오답이다. (C) What do you think about ~?(~에 대해 어떻게 생각하세요?)에 대해 You를 주어로 대답할 수 없으므로 인칭 오류에 의한 오답이다.

어휘 What do you think about ~? ~에 대해 어떻게 생각하세요?
certainly 분명히   space 공간   branch office 지점
official 공식적인   approval 승인

18. Who will lead the meeting this morning?
(A) Probably in Meeting Room 2.
(B) Every employee should read the notice.
(C) I will be in charge.

누가 오늘 아침 회의를 주도할 겁니까?
(A) 아마도 2번 회의실에서요.
(B) 모든 직원들이 통지문을 읽어야 합니다.
(C) 제가 맡을 겁니다.

해설 (A) Where will the meeting take place?(어디에서 회의가 열립니까?)에 대한 답변이므로 오답이다. (B) lead와 유사발음인 read를 썼지만 질문과 관련없는 답변이므로 오답이다. (C) 사람에 대해 묻는 Who 의문문에 맞게 인칭대명사 I로 대답하고 있으므로 정답이다.

어휘 lead 이끌다, 주도하다   meeting room 회의실   read 읽다
notice 통지문   be in charge (of) (~을) 맡다, 담당하다

19. How long is the trade show in Paris?
(A) It's less than 10 kilometers.
(B) It runs for three days.
(C) It was wonderful.

무역 박람회는 파리에서 얼마나 오랫동안 진행됩니까?
(A) 10킬로미터 미만입니다.
(B) 3일 동안 진행됩니다.
(C) 훌륭했습니다.

해설 (A) 무역 박람회가 열리는 기간에 대한 답변이 아니라 거리를 나타내고 있으므로 오답이다. (B) How long ~?에 대해 for three days라는 기간으로 답변하고 있으므로 정답이다. (C) How was the trade show?(무역 박람회는 어땠습니까?)에 대한 답변이므로 오답이다.

어휘 How long ~? 얼마나 오랫동안 ~입니까? trade show 무역 박람회
less than ~ 미만 (cf. more than ~ 초과) run 진행되다

20. Didn't you get your tickets for the employee banquet?
(A) Yes, but I have a scheduling conflict.
(B) It's held annually.
(C) At the Midtown Hotel.

직원 연회 티켓을 못 받았어요?
(A) 받았습니다만 저는 일정이 겹쳐요.
(B) 연회는 해마다 열립니다.
(C) 미드타운 호텔에서 합니다.

해설 (A) Yes로 티켓을 받았다는 대답을 먼저 한 후, 일정이 겹친다(a scheduling conflict)는 말을 덧붙이고 있다. (B) How often is the employee banquet held?(직원 연회는 얼마나 자주 열립니까?)에 대한 답변이므로 오답이다. (C) Where is the employee banquet held?(직원 연회가 어디에서 열립니까?)에 대한 답변이므로 오답이다.

어휘 get 받다 banquet 연회 have a scheduling conflict 일정이 겹치다 hold 열다, 개최하다 (cf. take place 열리다, 개최되다) annually 해마다

21. Who will take you to the airport?
(A) It will take approximately two hours.
(B) I have to pick up my client.
(C) A friend is driving me there.

누가 당신을 공항으로 데려가죠?
(A) 대략 두 시간이 걸릴 겁니다.
(B) 제가 고객을 태우러 가야 합니다.
(C) 친구가 저를 거기까지 태워줄 겁니다.

해설 (A) How long will it take to get to the airport?(공항까지 얼마나 걸리나요?)에 대한 답변이므로 오답이다. (B) 의미상 무관하게 airport와의 연상작용으로 pick up my client를 쓴 것이므로 오답이다. (C) 의문사 Who에 대한 답변으로 A friend라는 사람을 언급하고 있으므로 정답이다.

어휘 take+사람+to+장소 (사람)을 ~로 데려가다 take+시간 (시간)이 걸리다 approximately 대략 drive+사람 (사람)을 태우다

22. How about booking a later flight?
(A) The due date was the 19th.
(B) I'll see what's available.
(C) It departed on time.

더 늦은 항공편을 예약하는 게 어때요?
(A) 마감날짜는 19일이었어요.
(B) 이용 가능한 게 있는지 볼게요.
(C) 정시에 출발했어요.

해설 (A) booking에 대한 연상작용으로 due date를 쓴 것이지만 의미상 질문과 관련이 없으므로 오답이다. (B) 예약 가능한 항공편이 있는지 알아보겠다고 했으므로 정답이다. (C) later에 대한 연상작용으로 on time을 쓴 것이지만 항공편 예약에 관한 답변이 아니므로 오답이다.

어휘 How[What] about ~? 하는 게 어때요? book 예약하다 a later flight 더 늦은 항공편 due date 마감날짜 see 알아보다 available 이용 가능한 depart 출발하다 on time 정시에

23. I heard Mr. Sato works for a consulting firm now.
(A) The construction is ahead of schedule.
(B) No, we haven't decided yet.
(C) Yes, it's a good career move for him.

사토 씨가 지금 컨설팅 회사에서 일한다는 얘기를 들었어요.
(A) 공사가 일정보다 빠릅니다.
(B) 아니요, 우리는 아직 결정을 못했어요.
(C) 네, 그는 직업을 잘 바꾼 겁니다.

해설 (A) works와 관련해서 construction을 썼지만 내용상 서로 관련이 없으므로 오답이다. (B) 사토 씨에 대한 질문에 we를 주어로 써서 부적절한 답변이 되었으므로 인칭 오류에 의한 오답이다. (C) 사토 씨가 컨설팅 회사에 근무한다는 것에 대한 긍정적인 반응이므로 정답이다.

어휘 work for+회사 ~에서 일하다 construction 공사 ahead of schedule 일정보다 빠른 (cf. behind schedule 일정보다 늦은/on schedule 일정대로) decide 결정하다 career move 직업 전환

24. I'm excited that a new fitness center opened nearby.
(A) I work out regularly to keep in shape.
(B) I heard it's quite good, too.
(C) I'll shut the door for you.

근처에 새로운 헬스클럽이 생겨서 아주 좋아요.
(A) 저는 건강을 위해 규칙적으로 운동을 해요.
(B) 저도 아주 좋다는 얘기를 들었어요.
(C) 제가 대신 문을 닫아드릴게요.

해설 (A) 의미상 관련없이 fitness center에 대한 연상작용으로 work out을 쓴 것이므로 오답이다. (B) 헬스클럽에 대해 본인이 들은 얘기를 말해주고 있으므로 정답이다. (C) opened에 대한 반의어로 shut을 썼지만 내용상 관련이 없으므로 오답이다.

어휘 I'm excited that ~ ~라서 아주 좋다
fitness center 헬스클럽   nearby 근처에, 근처의
work out 운동하다(= exercise)
regularly 규칙적으로(= on a regular basis)
keep in shape 건강을 유지하다   quite 아주   too 또한
shut the door 문을 닫다

25. We don't have any workshops this month, do we?
(A) We have a lot of work to do.
(B) We will focus on time management.
(C) No, but we have one in early April.

이번 달에는 워크숍이 없죠, 그렇죠?
(A) 우리는 할 일이 많아요.
(B) 우리는 시간관리에 초점을 맞출 겁니다.
(C) 네, 하지만 4월 초에 있어요.

해설 (A) workshops와의 유사발음으로 work를 썼을 뿐, 의미상 관련이 없으므로 오답이다. (B) 워크숍 개최 여부와 관계없이 workshops에 대한 연상작용으로 time management를 쓴 것이므로 오답이다. (C) 질문에 맞게 워크숍이 열리는 시점을 말하고 있으므로 정답이다. 부가의문문은 평서문의 〈주어 + 동사(not)〉를 긍정·부정을 반대로 전환해 문장 끝에 〈동사(not)+주어?〉를 덧붙이는 의문문인데, 이에 대한 응답은 평서문 앞부분의 〈주어+동사〉만 잘 듣고 대답하면 된다.

어휘 workshop 워크숍, 연수회   focus on ~에 초점을 맞추다
time management 시간 관리   in early April 4월 초에

26. Shouldn't we complete all the interviews by the end of the week?
(A) Some applicants were late for the interviews.
(B) How was it?
(C) No, we don't have to.

주말까지 모든 면접을 끝내야 하지 않나요?
(A) 몇몇 지원자들은 면접에 늦었어요.
(B) 어땠어요?
(C) 아니요, 그럴 필요 없습니다.

해설 (A) 동일 발음 interviews를 썼지만 의미상 질문과 관련이 없으므로 오답이다. (B) 인터뷰를 끝내야 하는 시점에 대한 답변이 아니라 interviews에 대한 연상작용으로 How was it?을 쓴 것이므로 오답이다. (C) 먼저 부정으로 No라고 대답한 후, 주말까지 인터뷰를 완료할 필요가 없다(we don't have to)는 뜻을 전달한 것이므로 정답이다.

어휘 complete 완료하다   applicant 지원자   be late for ~에 늦다
don't have to 부정사 ~할 필요가 없다

27. Would you like some ice cream or cake for dessert?
(A) That's my favorite dessert.
(B) I've never tried the new flavor.
(C) Neither. Thanks.

후식으로 아이스크림과 케이크 중 어떤 걸 드시겠어요?
(A) 그건 제가 제일 좋아하는 후식이에요.
(B) 저는 그 새로운 맛을 먹어본 적이 없어요.
(C) 둘 다 안 먹을래요. 고마워요.

해설 (A) 동일 발음으로 dessert를 썼을 뿐, 질문에서 제시한 두 가지 선택 사항(ice cream, cake)에 대한 답변이 아니므로 오답이다. (B) ice cream과의 연상작용으로 flavor를 썼을 뿐, 후식 선택에 대한 답변이 아니므로 오답이다. (C) 선택의문문에서 제시한 두 가지 선택 사항 모두 원하지 않을 경우 neither를 쓸 수 있으므로 정답이다. 선택의문문에 대한 답변으로는 either(둘 중 하나), neither(둘 다 아닌), both(둘 다), any(어떤 것이라도)와 같은 단어를 흔히 쓴다.

어휘 Would you like + 명사? ~을 원하세요?, ~을 드실래요?
dessert 후식   favorite 가장 좋아하는   try 먹어보다   flavor 맛
neither 둘 다 아닌

28. Did everyone turn in their expense reports?
(A) They turned down our offer.
(B) I'm still waiting on a few, actually.
(C) They are very expensive.

모든 사람들이 비용 보고서를 제출했나요?
(A) 그들은 우리의 제안을 거절했어요.
(B) 사실 저는 여전히 몇몇 보고서를 기다리고 있어요.
(C) 그것은 매우 비쌉니다.

해설 (A) turn과 유사발음인 turned를 썼지만 turn in은 '제출하다'이고, turn down은 '거절하다'라는 뜻으로 의미상 서로 관련이 없으므로 오답이다. (B) 아직 몇 개의 보고서를 기다리고 있다는 의미이므로 정답이다. (C) 의미상 무관하게 expense와 유사발음인 expensive를 쓴 것이므로 오답이다.

어휘 turn in 제출하다(= hand in, submit)   expense report 비용 보고서
turn down 거절하다   offer 제안(하다)   wait on ~을 기다리다
expensive 비싼

29. Why don't we buy some new plants for the reception room?
(A) It's one of their largest factories.
(B) No, he's not coming.
(C) That's a good idea.

응접실에 둘 새로운 화초를 사는 게 어때요?
(A) 그곳이 가장 큰 공장 중 하나입니다.
(B) 아니요, 그는 오지 않아요.
(C) 좋은 생각이네요.

해설 (A) 질문에서의 plants는 '식물, 화초'란 뜻인 반면, 여기에서는 '공장'이란 뜻으로 이해하고 대답한 것이므로 오답이다. (B) reception (응접, 환영)에 대한 연상작용으로 he's not coming을 썼을 뿐, 의미상 관련이 없으므로 오답이다. (C) Why don't we ~?(같이 ~하는 게 어때요?)로 시작하는 제안의문문에 어울리는 긍정적 답변을 하고 있으므로 정답이다.

어휘 Why don't we ~? 같이 ~하는 게 어때요? plant 식물, 화초; 공장 reception room 응접실 large 큰 factory 공장

30. When does the next bus leave for Pittsburgh?
(A) In half an hour, I think.
(B) She's been living there since last year.
(C) The round-trip tickets cost less.

다음 피츠버그행 버스는 언제 출발합니까?
(A) 제 생각에 30분 후입니다.
(B) 그녀는 작년부터 그곳에서 살고 있어요.
(C) 왕복표가 더 저렴해요.

해설 (A) 시간 의문사 When에 맞게 In half an hour라는 시간 답변을 하고 있으므로 정답이다. (B) leave와 유사발음인 living을 썼지만 내용상 질문과 어울리지 않으므로 오답이다. (C) 다음 버스의 출발 시점에 대한 언급 없이 단지 bus와의 연상작용으로 round-trip tickets를 쓴 것이므로 오답이다.

어휘 leave for + 장소 ~로 떠나다 in half an hour 30분 후에 since + 과거 시점 (과거 시점)부터 round-trip ticket 왕복표 cost less[more] 비용이 덜[더] 들다

UNIT 9 업무

어휘 및 표현 점검 본책 _ p. 86

1. deadline 2. look over 3. take a day off
4. applicants 5. take a business trip

청취 집중 훈련 1 본책 _ p. 87

1. think / meeting / don't / food / eating / somewhere / healthy / selection / other / quiet
2. have a meeting / requested an interview / familiar with / interview you / product launch / schedule a meeting

청취 집중 훈련 2 본책 _ p. 88

1. (B) 2. (A) 3. (B) 4. (A) 5. (B) 6. (A)

1-2

1. 남자는 여자에게 무엇에 대해 물어보는가?
(A) 견적서   (B) 손님 명단

2. 무엇이 문제인가?
(A) 숫자가 명확하지 않다.   (B) 가격이 인상되었다.

M: Pamela, did you print out the guest list for the upcoming banquet?
W: No, I didn't. Not everyone has confirmed attendance yet.
M: OK, let me know the exact number of participants as soon as possible.

남: 파멜라, 다가오는 연회의 손님 명단을 출력했어요?
여: 아니요, 못했습니다. 모든 사람들이 다 참석을 확인해준 것이 아니라서요.
남: 좋아요, 가능한 한 빨리 저에게 정확한 참석자 수를 알려주세요.

어휘 price quote 견적서 guest list 손님 명단 raise 올리다, 인상하다 print out 출력하다 upcoming 다가오는 banquet 연회 confirm 확인하다 attendance 참석 participant 참석자 as soon as possible 가능한 한 빨리

3-4

3. 여자는 무엇을 하고 있는가?
(A) 복사   (B) 정산표 만들기

4. 다음 주에 어떤 행사가 열리는가?
(A) 회의   (B) 시상식

M: Olivia, are you busy or do you have time to help me now?
W: Well, I have to finish these spreadsheets first, but I should be free after that.
M: Can you book a hotel for the conference on organic farming next weekend?

남: 올리비아, 바쁘신가요, 아니면 지금 저를 도울 시간이 있나요?
여: 음. 제가 먼저 이 정산표를 끝내야 합니다만 그 다음에는 시간이 될 거예요.
남: 다음 주말 유기 농법 회의를 위한 호텔을 예약해 주실래요?

어휘 **make a copy (of)** (~을) 복사하다　**spreadsheet** 정산표
　　hold 열다, 개최하다　**awards ceremony** 시상식　**busy** 바쁜
　　finish 끝내다　**free** 시간이 되는　**book** 예약하다
　　organic farming 유기 농법

5-6

5. 남자는 왜 전화를 하고 있는가?
(A) 약속을 연기하기 위해　　(B) 약속을 잡기 위해

6. 로렌스 씨는 무엇을 검토하고 싶어하는가?
(A) 청사진　　　　　　　　(B) 공사 비용

> M: Hello, Ms. West. I'm calling to <u>set up an appointment</u> with you for some time next week.
> W: Sure, Mr. Lawrence. What is the appointment about?
> M: It's about the <u>construction project</u>. I just want to <u>go over the blue prints</u> with you.

남: 안녕하세요, 웨스트 씨. 다음 주쯤에 당신과 약속을 잡기 위해 전화 드립니다.
여: 물론입니다, 로렌스 씨. 약속은 무엇에 관한 것입니까?
남: 공사 프로젝트에 관한 것입니다. 당신과 청사진을 검토해보고 싶습니다.

어휘 **postpone** 연기하다　**make an appointment** 약속을 잡다
　　blue print 청사진　**construction cost** 공사비　**go over** 검토하다

청취 집중 훈련 3　본책 _ p. 89

| 1. (A) | 2. (C) | 3. (B) | 4. (B) | 5. (C) | 6. (D) |

1-2

1. 남자 컴퓨터의 문제점은 무엇인가?
(A) 매우 느리다.
(B) 켜지지 않는다.
(C) 늦게 도착할 것이다.
(D) 프린터에 연결되어 있지 않다.

해설 남자 컴퓨터의 문제점에 대한 질문이므로 남자의 말에 집중해야 한다. 첫 번째 문장에 나온 Is your computer slow today? Mine is so slow.를 통해 남자의 컴퓨터가 매우 느리다는 것을 알 수 있으므로 정답은 (A)이다.

2. 여자는 남자에게 무엇을 하라고 제안하는가?
(A) 새로운 컴퓨터 요청
(B) 여자의 컴퓨터 사용
(C) 남자의 컴퓨터에 대한 바이러스 검사
(D) 프린터용 소프트웨어 빌리기

해설 질문은 여자의 제안 사항을 묻고 있다. 따라서 이번에는 여자의 말에 집중을 해야 한다. 제안을 할 때는 '~하는 게 어때요?'라는 뜻으로 Why don't you ~? What[How] about ~?을 흔히 쓴다. 대화 하단에서 why don't you use your security software to scan for viruses?라고 제안을 하고 있으므로 (C)가 정답이다.

> M: Susan, Is your computer slow today? **Mine is so slow.**[1] I've been waiting five minutes for this application to open.
> W: No, my computer is fine, and I haven't heard anything about the server being slow today.
> M: I hope I don't have a virus or something. I think I'll restart my computer and see what happens.
> W: Good idea. If it's still not working normally after that, **why don't you use your security software to scan for viruses?**[2]

남: 수잔, 오늘 당신의 컴퓨터가 느린가요? 제 것은 너무 느리군요. 이 응용 프로그램이 뜨는 데 5분을 기다리고 있는 중입니다.
여: 아뇨, 제 컴퓨터는 괜찮습니다. 그리고 오늘 서버가 느리다는 얘기는 전혀 못 들었는데요.
남: 바이러스 같은 것에 걸리지 않으면 좋겠네요. 컴퓨터를 다시 시작해서 어떻게 되나 봐야겠어요.
여: 좋은 생각입니다. 그래도 정상적으로 작동되지 않으면 보안 소프트웨어로 바이러스가 있는지 스캔을 해보는 것이 어떨까요?

어휘 **wait** 기다리다　**application** 응용 프로그램　**open** 열리다, 뜨다
　　restart 다시 시작하다　**normally** 정상적으로
　　scan (바이러스가 있는지) 검사하다

3-4

3. 여자는 남자에게 무엇에 관해 물어보는가?
(A) 남자의 출장　　　　　(B) 남자의 구직
(C) 남자의 주말 계획　　　(D) 남자의 발표

해설 여자가 남자에 관해 물어보는 것에 대한 문제이므로 여자의 말에 집중해야 한다. 첫 문장에 나온 Did you ever send in the application for the position을 통해 여자는 남자의 구직에 대해 물어보고 있음을 알 수 있으므로 정답은 (B)이다.

4. 남자는 왜 걱정이 된다고 말하는가?
(A) 그는 영수증을 못 찾고 있다.
(B) 그는 마케팅 경험이 없다.
(C) 그는 표를 예약하지 않았다.
(D) 그는 일자리에 지원하지 않았다.

해설 이 문제에서의 키워드는 why, he, worried이다. 즉, 남자가 걱정을 하는 이유를 찾아야 한다. I'm a little worried about it since I don't have marketing experience.에서 동일 단어 worried가 등장하므로 이 문장에서 정답이 (B)라는 것을 알 수 있다.

51

W: **Did you ever send in the application for the position**[3] at Lincoln's Department Store?
M: Yes, I submitted it last week. I have to go back on Tuesday for an interview with the manager.
W: That's great. Why didn't you mention it sooner?
M: I wanted to wait to see how the interview went before I said anything. I'm a little worried about it **since I don't have marketing experience.**[4]

여: 링컨 백화점에서의 일자리에 지원서를 제출했나요?
남: 네, 지난주에 제출했어요. 저는 매니저와의 인터뷰를 위해 화요일에 다시 가야 합니다.
여: 잘됐네요. 왜 좀 더 일찍 말하지 않았어요?
남: 저는 무슨 말 하기 전에 인터뷰가 어떻게 진행될지 기다리면서 보고 싶었거든요. 제가 마케팅 경험이 없어서 인터뷰가 약간 걱정돼요.

어휘 send[hand, turn] in 제출하다(=submit)   application 지원(서)
department store 백화점   mention 언급하다
go (상황이) 진행되다   since ~이기 때문에

5-6
5. 쉴즈 씨는 왜 퇴사를 할 것인가?
(A) 그는 은퇴를 할 것이다.
(B) 그는 학교로 돌아갈 것이다.
(C) 그는 새로운 경력을 시작할 것이다.
(D) 그는 자신의 상점을 열 것이다.

해설 쉴즈 씨가 퇴사를 하는 이유로 여자가 he's just switching careers라고 했는데 he는 앞 문장의 Mr. Shields를 가리키므로 정답은 (C)이다. 사람 이름이 처음 언급된 다음에는 지금처럼 he나 she와 같은 인칭대명사로 바꾸어 언급되므로 명사와 대명사의 관계를 잘 이해하면서 들어야 한다.

6. 남자는 아담스 씨에 대해 뭐라고 말하는가?
(A) 그녀는 무역 박람회에 참석해야 한다.
(B) 그녀는 추가 직원을 고용할 것이다.
(C) 그녀는 다른 사무실로 전근을 갈 것이다.
(D) 그녀가 쉴즈 씨를 대신해야 한다.

해설 남자가 아담스에 대해 무슨 말을 했는지에 대한 문제이므로 남자의 말에서 정답의 단서를 찾아야 한다. 대화 후반부에 남자가 I think Ms. Adams in the planning department should take over Mr. Shield's position.이라고 했으므로 정답은 (D)이다.

M: Becky, I heard that Mr. Shields is leaving the company next month. Is he going to retire? Or perhaps transfer to the Singapore office?
W: Oh, **he's just switching careers,**[5] and will start working as a freelance photographer. I've heard he really enjoys photography. We will have to look for someone who will replace him soon.
M: I see. Well, **I think Ms. Adams in the planning department should take over Mr. Shield's position.**[6] She knows a lot about the company's upcoming projects.

남: 베키, 다음 달에 쉴즈 씨가 퇴사한다는 얘기를 들었어요. 그가 은퇴를 하는 건가요? 아니면 싱가포르 사무소로 전근을 가나요?
여: 아, 그는 직업을 바꿔서 프리랜서 사진작가로 일할 거예요. 쉴즈 씨는 사진 찍는 것을 정말로 좋아한다고 들었어요. 우리는 그의 후임자를 곧 찾아야 할 겁니다.
남: 그렇군요. 음, 저는 기획부서의 아담스 씨가 쉴즈 씨의 자리를 맡아야 한다고 생각해요. 그녀는 회사의 향후 프로젝트에 대해 많이 알잖아요.

어휘 leave the company 퇴사하다   retire 은퇴하다
transfer to ~로 전근가다   switch careers 직업을 바꾸다
freelance 자유 계약의   photographer 사진작가
photography 사진 촬영   replace 대신하다, 교체하다
planning department 기획부서   take over 넘겨받다
upcoming 다가오는

실전 감각 익히기 본책 _ p. 90~91

1. (D) 2. (B) 3. (B) 4. (A) 5. (D) 6. (B)
7. (C) 8. (D) 9. (D) 10. (B) 11. (B) 12. (D)

1-3

M: We have to **design a new energy-efficient table lamp.**[1]
W: As you know, we will market the lamp as an environmentally-friendly product.
M: Right. I've already scheduled a **department meeting for Thursday afternoon**[2] so we can discuss the project.
W: OK. **I will go downstairs**[3] to see if the sales department has some samples of the lamps.

남: 우리는 에너지 효율성이 뛰어난 탁상용 램프를 디자인해야 합니다.
여: 당신도 아시듯, 우리는 그 램프를 친환경적인 상품이라고 마케팅을 할 겁니다.
남: 맞습니다. 저는 이번 프로젝트에 대해 논의하기 위해 이미 목요일 오후로 부서 회의 일정을 잡았습니다.
여: 좋아요. 영업부에 램프 견본이 있는지 아래층에 내려가볼게요.

어휘 design 설계하다   energy-efficient 에너지 효율성이 좋은
market 마케팅하다, 광고하다

environmentally-friendly 친환경적인
schedule ~의 일정을 잡다   discuss 논의하다
go downstairs 아래층으로 내려가다   see if ~인지 알아보다
sales department 영업부서

1. 화자들은 무엇을 해야 하는가?
(A) 에너지 절약 계획 세우기   (B) 고객에게 시설 견학 시켜주기
(C) 사무용품 구입   **(D) 제품 디자인**

해설 대화 첫 문장의 design a new energy-efficient table lamp를 통해 화자들이 해야 할 일이 무엇인지 알 수 있다. 정답은 순차적으로 제시되는 경우가 많으므로 대화의 첫 부분을 잘 듣는 것이 아주 중요하다.

2. 부서 회의는 언제 열리는가?
(A) 수요일   **(B) 목요일**   (C) 금요일   (D) 월요일

해설 문제를 통해 부서 회의가 열린다(take place)는 것을 알 수 있다. 그러므로 대화에서 department meeting이 언급되는 문장 내에 있는 시점을 잘 들어야 한다. 남자가 department meeting for Thursday afternoon이라고 말하는 부분이 바로 정답의 단서이다.

3. 여자는 아마도 다음에 무엇을 하겠는가?
(A) 고객에게 상품 보내기   **(B) 다른 층으로 가기**
(C) 몇 가지 물건 풀기   (D) 제안서 제출

해설 미래의 행동 계획에 대한 정답 단서는 일반적으로 대화의 하단에 제시되는 경우가 많다. 대화 마지막에 나온 I will go downstairs를 통해 여자가 다른 층으로 갈 것이라는 것을 알 수 있다.

4-6

W: Have you **finished writing our Help-Wanted ad**?[4] **We need to submit it before 6:00**[5] this evening.

M: Yes, could you check it to make sure that I didn't miss anything?

W: Let me see. You included a minimum of **3 years of relevant experience**.[6] Do we want to include the salary as well?

M: Well, the salary for the position varies with experience. Let's just say that the salary is "negotiable."

여: 당신은 구인 광고 작성을 다 마쳤나요? 우리는 오늘 저녁 6시 이전에 제출해야 합니다.

남: 네, 제가 빠뜨린 것이 없는지 확인을 해주시겠어요?

여: 봅시다. 최소 3년의 관련 경험을 포함시켰군요. 급여도 포함시키는 게 좋을까요?

남: 음.. 이 직책에 대한 급여는 경험에 따라 다양합니다. 그냥 급여는 "협상 가능"이라고 하죠.

어휘 help-wanted ad 구인광고   submit 제출하다
make sure that ~ ~을 분명히 하다   include 포함시키다
a minimum of 최소한의 ~   relevant 관련된   vary with experience 경험에 따라 다양하다   negotiable 협상 가능한

4. 남자는 무엇을 하고 있는가?
(A) 광고 준비   (B) 일자리 지원
(C) 인터뷰 실시   (D) 신입 직원 만나기

해설 이번에는 여자의 질문을 통해 남자가 무엇을 하고 있는지 알 수 있다. 여자가 남자에게 finished writing our Help-Wanted ad에 대해 물어보고 있으므로 남자는 현재 광고를 준비하고 있다.

5. 남자의 마감시간은 언제인가?
(A) 오후 3시   (B) 오후 4시
(C) 오후 5시   **(D) 오후 6시**

해설 먼저 문제 또는 보기에 시점이 제시되어 있을 경우 대화 속에도 그 점이 언급될 것이라는 점을 유의해야 한다. 이 문제의 키워드는 deadline인데 deadline을 나타낼 때 잘 어울리는 표현으로는 before(~ 전에), by(~까지), no later than(~까지)이 있다는 것을 알아두자. 대화 속에서는 before를 사용해 We need to submit it before 6:00이라고 하면서 마감시간을 언급하고 있다.

6. 직책에 대해 언급된 내용은 무엇인가?
(A) 급여는 고정액이다.
(B) 3년의 경험이 필요하다.
(C) 시간제 직책이다.
(D) 다음 날까지 채워져야 한다.

해설 '~에 관해 언급된 내용'을 찾는 문제는 대화 전체를 잘 들어야 하는 난이도 높은 문제에 해당한다. 본문에서 언급된 3 years of relevant experience라는 말이 직책과 관련 언급이라는 것을 이해할 수 있어야 정답을 찾을 수 있다.

7-9

M: Well, I think we're ready for our grand opening on Saturday. **As the newest coffee shop**[7] in the University City, we'll have to work hard to succeed.

W: Right. I hope a lot of people will come to the grand opening.

M: It should be a great event. Don't forget that **Jeff, our pastry chef**,[8] will be doing cooking demonstrations all day.

W: Oh, also, **I'll bring two extra boxes of coffee cups**[9] to give away on Saturday.

남: 음, 저는 토요일 대규모 개점에 준비가 되었다고 생각합니다. 유니버시티 시에서 가장 최근에 생긴 커피숍으로서 우리는 성공을 위해 열심히 일해야 합니다.

여: 맞아요. 저는 많은 사람들이 대규모 개점에 오길 바라고 있어요.

남: 훌륭한 행사일 겁니다. 우리 제빵사 제프가 하루 종일 요리 시범을 보인다는 걸 잊지 마세요.

여: 오, 또한 토요일에 무료로 나눠줄 커피 컵 추가 두 상자를 제가 가져올게요.

어휘 grand opening 대규모 개점[개장] succeed 성공하다
pastry chef 제빵사 cooking demonstration 요리 시범
extra 추가의 give away 거저 주다

7. 어떤 종류의 업체가 토요일에 문을 여는가?
(A) 컴퓨터 가게 (B) 옷 가게
(C) 커피숍 (D) 가구점

해설 문제를 통해 토요일에 어떤 가게가 개점을 한다는 것을 미리 알 수 있다. 그러므로 On Saturday 주변에 언급된 단어에 집중해야 한다. 남자의 말에서 on Saturday 뒤에 바로 언급된 As the newest coffee shop이라는 말을 통해 토요일에 커피숍이 개점을 한다는 것을 알 수 있다.

8. 제프는 누구인가?
(A) 의류 디자이너 (B) 가게 주인
(C) 음악가 (D) 요리사

해설 영어는 사람 이름 뒤에 동격의 표현으로 직책이나 소속 기관을 언급하는 경우가 많다는 것을 알아두자. 대화 속에서도 Jeff, our pastry chef라고 하면서 동격 관계인 Jeff와 our pastry chef를 연속으로 말하고 있다.

9. 여자는 토요일에 무엇을 가져올 것인가?
(A) 티셔츠 (B) 음료수
(C) 전단지 (D) 컵

해설 먼저 미래의 행동에 대한 정답의 단서는 대화의 후반부에 있는 경우가 많다는 것을 알아두자. 이번 대화에서도 여자가 마지막에 I'll bring two extra boxes of coffee cups라고 하고 있다.

10-12

M: Shelly, **we need to make 500 T-shirts**[10] for Brentwood, our biggest client.

W: I know. We'll have to work overtime on Wednesday, and then **we'll have the shirts shipped out Thursday morning.**[11] Does Brentwood have any special designs in mind?

M: Yes. Later today, **they'll send me an e-mail with a scanned image of their logo.**[12] I'll pass that on to you as soon as I get it.

W: Great. Once I have that, I'll set up the printing equipment right away.

남: 쉘리, 우리는 우리의 가장 큰 고객사인 브렌트우드를 위해 500장의 티셔츠를 만들어야 해요.

여: 알고 있습니다. 우리는 수요일 초과근무를 해야 목요일 아침에 셔츠를 발송하게 될 겁니다. 브렌트우드가 어떤 특별한 디자인을 염두에 두고 있나요?

남: 네, 오늘 늦게 그들이 그들의 로고를 스캔한 이미지를 이메일로 보낼 겁니다. 제가 그것을 받자마자 당신에게 전달할게요.

여: 좋습니다. 제가 일단 그것을 받으면 바로 인쇄 장비를 설치하죠.

어휘 work overtime 초과근무를 하다 ship out 배송하다
have ~ in mind ~을 염두에 두다 later today 오늘 늦게
pass ~ on to +사람 ~을 ~에게 전달하다
printing equipment 인쇄 장비 right away 당장

10. 화자들의 회사는 무엇을 만들어야 하는가?
(A) 모자
(B) 티셔츠
(C) 소풍용 바구니
(D) 교육용 매뉴얼

해설 문제의 키워드는 '무엇을 만들어야 하는가'이다. 대화 도입부에 남자가 we need to make 500 T-shirts라고 했으므로 그들이 만들어야 하는 것이 티셔츠임을 쉽게 알 수 있다.

11. 화자들의 회사는 언제 물품을 배송할 계획인가?
(A) 수요일
(B) 목요일
(C) 금요일
(D) 월요일

해설 보기에 시간과 관련된 단어가 들어 있는 경우에 그 시점 중 하나가 대화에서도 언급될 것이다. 먼저 보기에 나온 시점을 잘 읽어둔 후 질문의 키워드와 연결시켜야 한다. 질문의 키워드는 ship the items인데 대화에서 언급된 we'll have the shirts shipped out Thursday morning에서 시점과 키워드를 연결시킬 수 있다.

12. 고객은 화자에게 무엇을 보낼 것인가?
(A) 몇 장의 셔츠 견본
(B) 몇몇 디자인 소프트웨어
(C) 대금
(D) 로고

해설 문제의 키워드는 what, the client, send이다 즉, 고객이 무엇을 보낼지에 초점을 맞추어야 한다. 남자가 한 말인 they'll send me an e-mail with a scanned image of their logo에서 logo를 보낼 것이라는 것을 알 수 있다. 이처럼 문제의 키워드와 대화에 나온 정답 단서를 연결시킬 수 있어야 한다.

UNIT 10 사무기기/주문/구매/계약

어휘 및 표현 점검 본책_p. 94

1. delivery   2. get a refund   3. exchange, for
4. expires   5. office supplies

청취 집중 훈련 1 본책_p. 95

1. visited / How / signed / clean / leave / belongings / floor / wet
2. How may I / using my laptop / stopped working / sounds like / over the phone / get the message / Thanks so much

청취 집중 훈련 2 본책_p. 96

1. (A)   2. (A)   3. (B)   4. (B)   5. (B)   6. (A)

1-2

1. 남자는 무엇을 빌리고 싶어하는가?
(A) 자동차   (B) 펜

2. 남자는 무엇을 요청하는가?
(A) 계약서   (B) 영수증

> M: Hi, I'd like to rent a car for July and August. Do you have any available?
> W: Yes, this car is one of our most popular rentals and available for the two months.
> M: OK, it looks good. Could you show me a contract that I have to sign?

남: 안녕하세요, 저는 7월과 8월에 쓸 자동차를 예약하고 싶습니다. 이용할 만한 게 있습니까?
여: 네, 이 차가 가장 인기 있는 임대차량 중 하나이며 2개월간 이용하실 수 있습니다.
남: 좋아요, 멋있어 보이네요. 제가 서명해야 할 계약서를 보여주시겠습니까?

어휘 receipt 영수증   rent 빌리다, 임대하다   available 이용할 수 있는
popular 인기 있는   rental 임대(차량)   contract 계약서

3-4

3. 남자는 왜 여자의 사무실에 왔는가?
(A) 회의를 하기 위해   (B) 소포를 배달하기 위해

4. 여자는 어떤 요청을 받았는가?
(A) 동료에게 전화하기   (B) 이름 서명하기

> M: Good afternoon, I have a delivery here for Ms. Green.
> W: She just stepped out of the office. Could I receive the package for her?
> M: Sure. Would you sign here, please?

남: 안녕하세요, 저는 여기 그린 씨를 위한 배달물을 갖고 있습니다.
여: 그녀는 잠시 사무실을 비웠는데요. 제가 그녀 대신 소포를 받아도 될까요?
남: 물론이죠. 여기 서명을 해주시겠어요?

어휘 sign 서명하다   delivery 배달(물)   step out of ~에서 나가다
receive 받다   package 소포

5-6

5. 여자는 무엇을 구매하고 싶어하는가?
(A) 책   (B) 캐비닛

6. 그녀는 어떻게 지불하겠는가?
(A) 현금으로   (B) 신용카드로

> W: Excuse me, I want to buy filing cabinets. How much are they?
> M: Each one is 30 dollars. You can pay for them with your store bonus credit.
> W: I know but I'll pay in cash this time. I'm going to use it for my next purchase.

남: 실례합니다만 제가 이 서류 캐비닛을 사고 싶습니다. 얼마죠?
여: 한 개당 30달러입니다. 고객님께서는 매장 보너스 적립금으로 지불하셔도 됩니다.
남: 저도 압니다만 이번에는 현금으로 낼게요. 매장 적립금은 다음 번 구매 때 쓸게요.

어휘 purchase 구매하다; 구매(품)   buy 사다
how much is[are] ~? ~이 얼마입니까?   each 각각의
pay for ~에 대한 값을 치르다   store credit 매장 적립금
pay in cash 현금으로 내다

청취 집중 훈련 3 본책_p. 97

| 1. (B) | 2. (A) | 3. (B) | 4. (A) | 5. (D) | 6. (C) |

1-2

1. 여자의 문제점은 무엇인가?
(A) 문서가 없어졌다.
(B) 기계 사용법을 모른다.
(C) 기사가 늦게 제출될 것이다.
(D) 고객의 전화번호를 찾을 수 없다.

해설 여자의 문제점에 대한 질문이므로 여자의 말에 초점을 맞추어야 한다. 여자가 I don't know how to use our fax machine이라고 말했으므로 정답은 (B)이다.

2. 미정은 언제 계약서를 검토할 것인가?
(A) 주말 동안
(B) 다음 주 월요일
(C) 다음 주 화요일
(D) 다음 주 수요일

해설 고유명사인 사람 이름이 문제에 언급될 경우, 그 이름이 대화에서도 분명히 나올 것을 예상할 수 있다. 여기서는 여자가 She's going to look it over during the weekend라고 했는데 She가 앞에 있는 Mi-Jung을 가리키므로 정답은 (A)가 된다.

> W: Frank, can you help me? I want to fax a contract to Mi-Jung, our freelance writer, but **I don't know how to use our fax machine.**[1]
> M: Oh, you could just e-mail her an electronic copy of the contract. She usually e-mails us her articles, doesn't she?
> W: Yes, but she prefers that we fax a paper contract so she can stamp it. **She's going to look it over during the weekend**[2] and fax it back to us next Monday.

여: 프랭크, 저 좀 도와줄래요? 제가 우리 자유기고가인 미정 씨에게 계약서를 보내고 싶은데 팩스기 사용법을 모르겠어요.

남: 음, 그녀에게 이메일로 계약서 전자 사본을 보내실 수 있잖아요. 그녀도 보통 우리에게 이메일로 기사를 보내거든요, 그렇죠?

여: 네, 하지만 그녀는 계약서에 도장을 찍을 수 있도록 종이 계약서를 팩스로 보내주길 원해요. 그녀는 주말에 그것을 검토하고 다음 주 월요일에 우리에게 다시 팩스로 보내줄 겁니다.

어휘 fax ~을 팩스로 보내다; 팩스기 contract 계약서
freelance 자유 계약자로 일하는 how to부정사 ~하는 법
electronic copy 전자 사본 article 기사 stamp ~에 도장을 찍다
look over 검토하다

3-4

3. 남자는 무엇을 하고 싶어하는가?
(A) 세미나를 여는 것
(B) 컴퓨터를 사용하는 것
(C) 책을 빌리는 것
(D) 수업에 참석하는 것

해설 질문이 남자가 하고 싶은 일에 관한 것이므로 남자의 말에 초점을 맞추어야 한다. 남자가 I just want to use a computer라고 말했으므로 정답은 (B)이다.

4. 여자는 남자에게 무엇을 줄 것인가?
(A) 비밀번호
(B) 웹사이트 주소
(C) 이메일 주소
(D) 주차 허가증

해설 여자가 남자에게 줄 것에 관한 질문이므로 여자의 말에 집중해야 한다. 여자가 I'll let you know a temporary password라고 말하고 있으므로 정답은 (A)이다.

> M: Hi, Ms. Winfrey. **I just want to use a computer**[3] here in the seminar room because all the computers in my department are being checked for viruses now. Would that be possible?
> W: Sure. The technicians are inspecting all the office equipment throughout this week. However, in order to use a computer here, you need to fill out this form.
> M: OK, I'll complete it first.
> W: When you are done, **I'll let you know a temporary password**[4] that you should enter into the computer.

남: 안녕하세요, 윈프리 씨. 제 부서에 있는 모든 컴퓨터가 지금 바이러스 점검 중이어서 이곳 세미나실에 있는 컴퓨터를 썼으면 합니다. 가능할까요?

여: 물론이죠. 기술자들이 이번 주 내내 모든 사무장비를 점검하고 있잖아요. 그런데 이곳에서 컴퓨터를 사용하려면 이 양식을 작성해주셔야 합니다.

남: 좋아요, 제가 이 양식부터 작성할게요.

여: 작성을 마치시면 제가 컴퓨터에 입력해야 할 임시 비밀번호를 알려드릴게요.

어휘 check + A(목적어) + for ~이 있는지 A를 점검하다 technician 기술자 inspect 점검하다 office equipment 사무용 장비
throughout ~ 내내 in order to부정사 ~하기 위해
fill out 작성하다 complete 완성하다
사람 + be done ~가 (일·업무 등을) 끝마치다
let A(목적어) know A에게 알려주다 temporary 임시의
enter into ~에 입력하다

5-6

5. 남자는 여자에게 무엇을 요청하는가?
(A) 교육 일정
(B) 몇몇 송장
(C) 재무 보고서
(D) 몇몇 사무용품

해설 남자의 요청 사항에 대한 문제이므로 남자의 말에서 정답의 단서를 찾아야 한다. 남자가 I need a few more file folders and pens. Do you have any extras?라고 했는데 file folders와 pens가 사무용품이므로 정답은 (D)이다.

6. 여자가 '제가 그의 휴대폰으로 문자 메시지를 보내볼게요'라고 말할 때 의미하는 바는 무엇인가?
(A) 매니저가 지금 통화를 할 수 없다.
(B) 매니저가 메시지를 기다리고 있다.
(C) 여자가 주문과 관련해 매니저와 확인해 보겠다.
(D) 여자가 오늘 일찍 퇴근하길 원한다.

해설 매니저는 보통 목요일에 사무용품을 주문하는데 남자는 그 전에 사무용품이 필요하다(he usually orders office supplies on Thursdays. I need them before that.)고 했다. 이에 대해 여자가 지금 매니저가 복사 가게에 있을 거라면서 휴대폰으로 문자 메시지를 보내보겠다(Actually, he's probably at the copy shop now. I'll send a text message to his mobile phone.)고 했다. 즉, 여자는 매니저에게 메시지를 보내서 사무용품을 주문할 수 있는지 알아보겠다는 말을 한 것이므로 정답은 (C)이다.

M: Rachel, I'm putting together training materials for the new salespeople. But **I need a few more file folders and pens.**[5] Do you have any extras?
W: No, I don't. All of my colleagues here in accounting used them all up. You can see if Greg, our office manager, can order some more.
M: Well, he usually orders office supplies on Thursdays. I need them before that.
W: Actually, **he's probably at the copy shop now. I'll send a text message to his mobile phone**[6].

남: 레이첼, 제가 신입 영업직원들을 위한 교육 자료를 준비하고 있어요. 그런데 제가 서류철과 펜이 좀 더 필요합니다. 여분이 좀 있나요?
여: 아니요, 없습니다. 여기 회계부서의 모든 동료들이 다 써버렸어요. 사무실 매니저인 그렉한테 좀 더 주문할 수 있는지 확인해보세요.
남: 음, 매니저는 보통 목요일에 사무용품을 주문해요. 저는 그 전에 필요하고요.
여: 사실 매니저가 지금 복사가게에 있을 거예요. 제가 그의 휴대폰으로 문자 메시지를 보내볼게요.

어휘 put together 준비하다, 조립하다 material 자료
salespeople 영업직원들 extra 여분 colleague 동료
accounting 회계(부서) use up 다 쓰다 see if ~인지 확인하다
order 주문하다 office supplies 사무용품 copy shop 복사가게
text message 문자 메시지

실전 감각 익히기 본책 _ p. 98~99

| 1. (B) | 2. (D) | 3. (B) | 4. (A) | 5. (C) | 6. (D) |
| 7. (C) | 8. (B) | 9. (C) | 10. (A) | 11. (B) | 12. (D) |

1-3

M: Hi, this is Ron Tuttle calling. **I just want to check on a repair order.**[1] I brought in a desktop computer for upgrades and servicing two days ago.
W: Hi, Mr. Tuttle. Your machine is up on the repair table now. **Mr. Farmer, our technician, is giving the insides a cleaning.**[2] Then he'll install an antivirus program and update the software. He should be done by around 4.
M: That's great. I'll come by after I finish work this afternoon. **I should be there at about 5 or so.**[3]

남: 안녕하세요, 저는 론 터틀입니다. 저는 수리 주문에 대해 확인하고 싶습니다. 제가 이틀 전에 성능 향상과 점검을 위해 탁상용 컴퓨터 한 대를 맡겼습니다.
여: 안녕하세요, 터틀 씨. 당신의 컴퓨터는 지금 수리용 탁자 위에 올려져 있습니다. 우리 기술자인 파머 씨가 내부를 청소하고 있어요. 그리고 나서 바이러스 방지 프로그램을 설치하고 소프트웨어를 업데이트할 겁니다. 그는 대략 4시쯤 작업을 끝낼 거예요.
남: 좋아요. 제가 오늘 오후 퇴근하고 나서 들를게요. 5시쯤 그곳에 갈 겁니다.

어휘 check on ~에 대해 확인하다 repair order 수리 주문
bring in ~을 맡기다 service 점검(하다) be up on
~에 올려져 있다 give the insides a cleaning 내부 청소를 하다
install 설치하다 antivirus program 바이러스 방지 프로그램
done 일을 마친 around 대략 come by 들르다
should ~일 것이다 숫자+or so (숫자)쯤

1. 남자는 왜 전화를 하고 있는가?
(A) 수리 비용을 확인하기 위해
(B) 언제 수리가 완료될지를 알기 위해
(C) 장비 몇 점을 주문하기 위해
(D) 주문을 취소하기 위해

해설 남자가 전화를 하고 있는 이유를 물어보고 있으므로 남자의 말에 집중해야 한다. 대화 초반에 남자가 I just want to check on a repair order.라고 했으므로 수리 주문에 대해 문의하고 있는 것이다. 그리고 그 뒤에 수리 완료 시점(by around 4)이 언급되어 있으므로 정답은 (B)이다.

2. 파머 씨는 지금 무엇을 하고 있는가?
(A) 인터넷 접속 확인
(B) 소프트웨어 프로그램 설치
(C) 자동차 수리
(D) 기기 청소

해설 질문에 사람 이름이 있을 경우, 그 이름이 대화 중에도 언급될 것이라는 것을 예상할 수 있다. 그러므로 대화 중에 Farmer가 언급되는 부분에서 정답의 단서를 찾아야 한다. 여자가 Mr. Farmer, our technician, is giving the insides a cleaning.이라고 말을 하고 있으므로 정답은 (D)이다.

3. 남자는 상점에 언제 도착할 것 같은가?
(A) 오후 4시
(B) 오후 5시
(C) 오후 6시
(D) 오후 7시

해설 남자의 도착 시간에 대한 질문이므로 남자의 말을 잘 들어야 한다. 남자가 I should be there at about 5 or so.라고 했으므로 정답은 (B)이다. 먼저 언급된 He should be done by around 4.는 남자의 도착 시점이 아니라 기술자의 작업 완료 시점임을 주의해야 한다. 이렇게 대화 중에 두 개 이상의 시점이 나올 때는 질문에 쓰인 핵심어가 들어 있는 문장에서 정답을 찾아야 한다.

4-6

M: Excuse me, **I have an air purifier for Ms. Neilson,**[4] the office manager, but I can't find her office.
W: She did work here on the second floor, but her team has moved four floors up. **She's on the sixth floor in Room 601 now.**[5]
M: Thank you. I'll go up there. If you happen to be interested, I can show you our new air purifier.
W: OK, I'd like one for my work area. **Just come back down to this floor**[6] when you're finished visiting Ms. Neilson.

남: 실례합니다만 제가 사무실 매니저인 닐슨 씨께 드릴 공기 청정기를 가지고 있는데 사무실을 못 찾겠습니다.
여: 매니저님이 이곳 2층에서 근무를 했었지만 팀 전체가 네 층 위로 옮겼어요. 지금은 6층 601호실에 계십니다.
남: 고맙습니다. 제가 그곳으로 올라갈게요. 혹시 관심 있으시면 제가 우리의 신형 공기 청정기를 보여드릴 수 있겠는데요.
여: 좋아요, 제 작업장에 한 대 두고 싶군요. 닐슨 매니저님을 방문하고 나서 이쪽 층으로 다시 내려오세요.

어휘 air purifier 공기 청정기 move four floors up 네 층 위로 옮기다
happen to 부정사 혹시 ~이다 interested 관심이 있는
I'd like + 명사 저는 ~을 원합니다
주어 + be finished ~ing 주어가 ~하는 것을 마치다

4. 남자는 지금 무엇을 가지고 있는가?
(A) 공기 청정기
(B) 노트북
(C) 카메라
(D) 선풍기

해설 특정 물건에 대한 질문은 먼저 보기를 빠르게 읽어야 한다. 왜냐하면 대화 중에 보기에서 나온 단어 중 하나가 언급될 경우 그것이 정답일 가능성이 매우 높기 때문이다. 여기서도 남자가 한 말인 I have an air purifier for Ms. Nielson을 듣고 보기에서 언급된 air purifier가 반복되어 나온 것을 알면 정답을 쉽게 찾을 수 있다.

5. 닐슨 씨의 사무실은 어디에 있는가?
(A) 2층
(B) 4층
(C) 6층
(D) 10층

해설 여자가 She's on the sixth floor in Room 601 now.라고 했는데 여기서 She가 닐슨을 가리키므로 정답은 (C)이다. 지금처럼 사람 이름이나 사물이 대명사로 바뀐 문장에 정답의 단서가 들어 있을 수 있으므로 주의해야 한다.

6. 남자는 어떤 요청을 받는가?
(A) 1시간 후에 전화하기
(B) 보고서 검토하기
(C) 연장 근무하기
(D) 2층으로 다시 오기

해설 이 문제는 남자가 요청 받은 사항에 대한 질문이므로 남자의 말이 아닌 여자의 말에 초점을 맞추어야 한다는 점을 주의해야 한다. 여자가 Just come back down to this floor라고 했으므로 정답은 (D) 이다.

7-9

M: Hello, my name is Gerard Mason, and I work for Acres Accounting. **We'd like to rent a beverage machine**[7] from your company. **Can we choose items for the vending machine?**[8]
W: Yes, you can choose from a list we have prepared. You can view this list on our Web site. Would you like to arrange an appointment with one of our representatives? He will let you know how to use the machine.
M: Yes, please. **Could your representative come by our office tomorrow morning at 10:30?**[9]

남: 안녕하세요. 저는 제라드 매이슨이고 에이커스 어카운팅에서 근무합니다. 저희는 당신 회사로부터 음료수 자판기를 임대하고 싶습니다. 우리가 자판기에 들어갈 품목을 선택할 수 있나요?
여: 네, 저희가 준비한 목록에서 고르실 수 있습니다. 고객님께서는 저희 웹사이트에서 이 목록을 보실 수 있습니다. 우리 직원 한 명과 약속을 잡고 싶으신가요? 그 직원이 자판기 사용법을 알려줄 겁니다.
남: 네, 부탁합니다. 당신의 직원이 내일 아침 10시 30분에 저희 사무실에 들를 수 있을까요?

어휘 work for + 회사명 ~에서 근무하다 rent 임대하다
beverage 음료수 item 품목 vending machine 자판기
choose from ~에서 고르다 prepare 준비하다
arrange an appointment 약속을 잡다 representative 직원
how to 부정사 ~하는 방법 come by 들르다

7. 전화 통화의 목적은 무엇인가?
(A) 서비스에 대해 불평하기 위해
(B) 환불을 요청하기 위해
(C) 임대를 준비하기 위해
(D) 공석에 관해 문의하기 위해

> 해설 전화 통화의 목적은 대화의 초반부에 언급된다. 여기서도 남자의 We'd like to rent a beverage machine이라는 말을 통해 자판기 임대와 관련하여 전화를 했다는 것을 알 수 있다.

8. 화자들은 어떤 상품에 대해 얘기하고 있는가?
(A) 커피 제조기   (B) 자판기
(C) 복사기   (D) 컴퓨터 소프트웨어

> 해설 특정 상품이나 대상에 관한 질문이 나오면 먼저 보기를 빠르게 읽어 둔다. 왜냐하면 대화 중에서 보기와 같은 단어가 반복되어 언급되면 그 단어가 정답일 가능성이 매우 높기 때문이다. 여기서도 자판기라는 말이 beverage machine, vending machine, machine 등으로 반복해서 나오고 있다는 것을 알 수 있다.

9. 남자는 언제 회의를 하고 싶어하는가?
(A) 오늘 오후   (B) 오늘 저녁
(C) 내일 아침   (D) 내일 오후

> 해설 남자가 원하는 회의 시점에 대한 질문이므로 남자의 말에서 정답 단서를 찾아야 한다. 대화 마지막에 남자가 Could your representative come by our office tomorrow morning at 10:30?라고 했으므로 정답은 (C)이다.

10-12

W: Holy Oaks Foodstuffs. Can I help you?
M: Hi, I received a shipment Tuesday...
W: Uh-huh.
M: **And when I opened the box, all of the jars of spaghetti sauce were broken.**[10] I apologize for reporting this late, but a different person originally placed the order.
W: I see. They must not have been packaged properly. I'm very sorry. **I'll get some replacement jars delivered to you overnight.**[11]
M: Well, I ordered that sauce for a dinner party that was on Wednesday...
W: Oh, then let me apologize again for the inconvenience. **I can give you a voucher to use on your next order.**[12] Will that work?
M: Definitely. Thank you very much. The original order number was W-5-Z-2.

여: 홀리 오크스 식품입니다. 도와 드릴까요?
남: 안녕하세요, 제가 화요일에 물건을 받았는데요…
여: 네, 그런데요.
남: 상자를 열었더니, 스파게티 소스 병들이 모두 깨져 있더라고요. 이렇게 늦게 알려 드려서 죄송합니다만, 원래는 다른 사람이 주문을 했던 거라서요.
여: 알겠습니다. 적절하게 포장이 안 되었던 것 같습니다. 정말 죄송합니다. 내일 도착하도록 다른 병으로 보내 드리겠습니다.
남: 아, 전 그 소스를 수요일에 있었던 저녁 파티에 쓰려고 주문했던 겁니다.
여: 아, 불편을 끼쳐 드린 데 대해 다시 한 번 사과의 말씀을 드립니다. 고객님께는 다음에 주문하실 때 쓸 수 있는 할인권을 제가 드릴 수 있습니다. 그렇게 하면 될까요?
남: 물론입니다. 정말 고맙습니다. 최초 주문 번호는 W-5-Z-2입니다.

> 어휘 foodstuff 식품, 식량   shipment 수송품, 화물   jar 병, 단지   place an order 주문하다   replacement 대체, 교체   overnight 밤사이에, 하룻밤 동안   inconvenience 불편   voucher 할인권, 쿠폰, 상품 교환권

10. 남자가 어떤 문제를 언급하고 있는가?
(A) 깨진 물건을 받았다.
(B) 주문 번호를 찾을 수 없다.
(C) 배송 주소를 잘못 알려줬다.
(D) 제품에 대해 과잉 청구를 받았다.

> 해설 화요일에 받은 물건의 상자를 열었더니 스파게티 소스 병들이 모두 깨져 있었다고(And when I opened the box, all of the jars of spaghetti sauce were broken.) 남자는 말하고 있다. 따라서 정답은 (A)이다.

11. 남자가 "전 그 소스를 수요일에 있었던 저녁 파티에 쓰려고 주문했던 것이거든요"라고 말할 때 의미하는 바는 무엇인가?
(A) 특정 소스 브랜드의 품질이 최고라고 생각한다.
(B) 더 이상 소스가 필요하지 않다.
(C) 엉뚱한 물건을 받았다.
(D) 더 많은 소스를 주문하고 싶다.

> 해설 남자는 여자가 다른 병으로 소스를 보내 주겠다(I'll get some replacement jars delivered to you overnight)고 했을 때 이렇게 응답했다. 즉, 파티에 쓰기 위해 주문했던 소스인데 파티는 이미 끝나 버렸으므로 이젠 소스를 보내 줘도 소용이 없다는 말을 남자는 하고 있는 것이므로 정답은 (B)이다.

12. 여자는 남자에게 무엇을 줄 것 같은가?
(A) 대체품
(B) 발송 할인권
(C) 현금 환불
(D) 상점 포인트

해설 다음에 주문할 때 쓸 수 있는 할인권을 줄 수 있다면서(I can give you a voucher to use on your next order.), 그러면 되겠냐고 여자가 묻자, 남자는 고맙다면서 그 제의를 받아들이고 있다. 보기 중 주문 시 받는 할인과 관련이 있는 것은 (D)의 포인트 점수(credit) 이다. 물품 발송 할인에 대해서는 언급된 적이 없으므로 (B)는 답이 될 수 없음에 주의한다.

UNIT 11 여행/여가/교통/쇼핑

어휘 및 표현 점검   본책 _ p. 102

1. in stock   2. sold out   3. aisle seat
4. destination   5. proof of purchase

청취 집중 훈련 1   본책 _ p. 103

1. use / vacation / request / submit / taking / planning / been / beaches
2. Could you recommend / on sale / great photos / detailed maps / let me show / that feature

청취 집중 훈련 2   본책 _ p. 104

1. (B)   2. (A)   3. (A)   4. (B)   5. (A)   6. (B)

1-2

1. 여자는 무엇을 하고 싶은가?
(A) 주차   (B) 쇼핑

2. 남자는 건물의 지하에 무엇이 있다고 말하는가?
(A) 슈퍼마켓   (B) 선물 가게

> W: Excuse me, where can I do some grocery shopping?
> M: There is a supermarket in the basement of the building.
> W: Thank you. I will be back at least 30 minutes prior to departure.

여: 실례합니다만 어디에서 식료품 쇼핑을 할 수 있죠?
남: 건물 지하에 슈퍼마켓이 있습니다.
여: 고맙습니다. 제가 적어도 출발 30분 전에는 돌아올게요.

어휘 do shopping 쇼핑을 하다   grocery 식료품   basement 지하
at least 적어도   prior to ~전에   departure 출발

3-4

3. 화자들은 아마도 어디에 있는가?
(A) 기차에   (B) 식당에

4. 화자들은 언제 도착할 예정인가?
(A) 8시에   (B) 10시에

> M: Helen, we left the station at 4, and it's 8 now. How much longer do we have to go?
> W: Well, we're scheduled to arrive at 10, so about two more hours. Aren't you hungry?
> M: Yes, I haven't eaten anything since lunch. I think this train has a dining car.

남: 헬렌, 우리가 4시에 역에서 출발했는데 지금이 8시예요. 우리가 얼마나 더 가야죠?
여: 음, 우리는 10시에 도착할 예정이니까 대략 두 시간 더요. 배 안 고프세요?
남: 고프네요. 점심 먹고 나서 아무것도 안 먹었거든요. 이 기차에 식당 칸이 있을 걸요.

어휘 leave 떠나다, 출발하다   how much longer 얼마나 더 오래
be scheduled to부정사 ~할 예정이다
since + 과거시점 ~ 이래로   dining car (기차에서) 식당 칸

5-6

5. 여자는 무엇을 사고 싶은가?
(A) 자전거   (B) 드레스

6. 그 물품에 대해 무엇이 언급되었는가?
(A) 현대적인 디자인이다.   (B) 3년간 보증이 된다.

> W: Hello, I'm looking for a bicycle for my 10-year-old daughter.
> M: OK, this BX-10 bike is designed for children and comes with a three-year warranty.
> W: It looks like it's too big. Is this easy to ride?

여: 안녕하세요, 저는 10살 난 제 딸을 위한 자전거를 찾고 있어요.
남: 그렇군요, 이 BX-10 자전거는 어린이용으로 설계되었으며 3년간 보증이 됩니다.
여: 너무 커 보이네요. 타기가 쉬운가요?

어휘 look for ~을 찾다   daughter 딸   design 설계하다
come with ~와 함께 나오다   warranty 보증
look like ~처럼 보이다   ride 타다

청취 집중 훈련 3   본책 _ p. 105

1. (B)   2. (C)   3. (A)   4. (B)   5. (C)   6. (D)

1-2

애플비 공원 국제 음식 축제	
6월 1일(목요일)	프랑스 음식
6월 2일(금요일)	이탈리아 음식
6월 3일(토요일)	한국 음식
6월 4일(일요일)	일본 음식

1. 무엇이 여자가 행사에 가지 못하게 했는가?
(A) 출장   (B) 바쁜 근무 일정
(C) 교통 체증   (D) 악천후

해설 남자가 여자에게 국제 음식 축제에 가봤는지 물었을 때 여자가 연장 근무를 하느라 바빴다(I've been busy doing some overtime work.)고 했으므로 정답은 (B)이다.

2. 도표를 보세요. 화자들은 어떤 음식을 먹어볼 것 같은가?
(A) 프랑스 음식   (B) 이탈리아 음식
(C) 한국 음식   (D) 일본 음식

해설 대화 후반부에 여자가 이번 주 토요일에 갈 수 있겠다(we can go sometime this Saturday.)고 했다. 도표를 보면 토요일에는 한국 음식(Korean Food) 축제가 열리므로 정답은 (C)이다.

M: Fiona, have you been to Applebee Park? They're having an international food festival until this Sunday.
W: No, I haven't had a chance to. **I've been busy doing some overtime work.**¹
M: That's too bad. If you have some time when you finish your work, we should go together. I heard the food is great.
W: Sure, I'd love to. I should be finished with everything this Friday, **so maybe we can go sometime on Saturday.**²

남: 피오나, 애플비 공원에 가본 적 있으세요? 그곳에서 이번 주 일요일까지 국제 음식 축제를 하더라고요.
여: 아니요, 기회가 없었어요. 저는 연장근무를 좀 하느라 바빴거든요.
남: 안됐네요. 일을 끝내고 나서 시간이 있으면 같이 가봐야죠. 음식이 훌륭하다는 얘기를 들었어요.
여: 물론 그러고 싶어요. 이번 주 금요일에 모든 게 다 끝나니까 아마도 토요일에 갈 수 있겠어요.

어휘 have been to+장소 ~에 가본 적 있다   international 국제적인
have a chance to부정사 ~할 기회가 있다
do overtime work 연장근무를 하다

3-4

3. 여자는 무엇을 찾고 있는가?
(A) 버스
(B) 일정표
(C) 기차역
(D) 매표소

해설 여자가 찾고 있는 대상에 대한 질문이므로 여자의 말에 초점을 맞추어야 한다. 여자가 Excuse me, is this the bus to Berkeley?라고 물어보고 있으므로 여자는 버클리행 버스를 찾고 있는 것이다.

4. 남자는 고속버스에 대해 뭐라고 말하는가?
(A) 10분 후에 떠난다.
(B) 버클리에 정차하지 않는다.
(C) 남은 좌석이 없다.
(D) 지역 버스보다 더 비싸다.

해설 〈What does the man[woman] mention about + 명사?〉가 남자[여자]의 의견을 묻는 문제임을 알고 빠르게 about 뒤의 명사를 본다. 이 문제에서는 about 뒤에 the express bus가 있으므로 대화에서 이 단어가 쓰인 부분에서 정답을 찾아야 한다. 남자가 The express bus will go straight to Simon Station without stopping.이라고 했으므로 결국 정답은 (B)이다.

W: Excuse me, **is this the bus to Berkeley?**³
M: Yes, this is the local bus to Simon Station. It stops at both Humphries Road and Peterson Street in Berkeley. Do you have a ticket?
W: No, I didn't buy one yet.
M: Well, you'd better hurry. The next bus is leaving in ten minutes. Make sure you buy a ticket for the local bus. **The express bus will go straight to Simon Station without stopping.**⁴

여: 실례합니다만 이 버스가 버클리로 가나요?
남: 네, 시몬 역으로 가는 지역 버스입니다. 이 버스는 버클리에 있는 험프리스 로와 피터슨 가에 정차합니다. 티켓 있으세요?
여: 아니요, 아직 구입하지 않았어요.
남: 음, 서둘러야겠어요. 다음 버스가 10분 후에 출발하거든요. 꼭 지역 버스용 티켓을 구입하세요. 고속버스는 정차 없이 시몬 역까지 바로 갑니다.

어휘 the bus to+장소 (장소)행 버스   local bus 지역 버스
both A and B A와 B 둘 다   you'd better ~하는 게 낫다
leave 출발하다   in+시간 ~ 후에   go straight 직행하다
stop 정차하다

5-6

5. 화자들은 어디에 있겠는가?
(A) 대학에 (B) 식당에
(C) 상점에 (D) 회사 오리엔테이션에

해설 화자들의 대화 장소는 대화의 초반부에 나온 단어들을 통해 알 수 있다. 여자가 I'm trying to locate an item I saw in this store's advertisement라고 말한 부분에 this store가 있으므로 정답은 (C)이다.

6. 광고 상품에 대해 무엇이 언급되었는가?
(A) 매우 비싸다.
(B) 단지 한 가지 색깔로 나온다.
(C) 현재 다 팔렸다.
(D) 매우 인기가 좋다.

해설 광고 상품에 대해 언급된 내용을 찾는 문제인데, 5번 문제를 통해 광고 상품이 briefcase라는 것을 알았다. 그러므로 남자가 briefcase에 대해 언급하는 부분에서 정답의 단서를 찾아야 한다. 남자가 상품에 대해 설명하면서 it's very popular with people in their 20s and 30s lately.라고 했으므로 정답은 (D)이다.

W: Excuse me, **I'm trying to locate an item I saw in this store's advertisement**[5] yesterday. It's a briefcase. My nephew will graduate from university next week, and I want to buy one for him.
M: Oh, this is the briefcase you are looking for. It has a modern design and is also very high quality, so **it's very popular with people in their 20s and 30s lately.**[6]
W: It looks good. I hope he can keep it for a long time.
M: Absolutely.

여: 실례합니다만 저는 어제 이 상점 광고에서 본 물건을 찾고 있습니다. 그건 서류 가방이에요. 제 조카가 다음 주에 대학을 졸업해서 하나 사주려고요.
남: 오, 이게 바로 찾고 계시는 서류 가방입니다. 현대적인 디자인이고 품질도 아주 좋아서 최근에 2, 30대들에게 매우 인기가 좋습니다.
여: 좋아 보이네요. 제 조카가 오랫동안 간직했으면 좋겠네요.
남: 물론이죠.

어휘 locate 찾다 item 물품, 물건 advertisement 광고 briefcase 서류 가방 graduate from+학교 ~를 졸업하다 high quality 품질이 좋은 be popular with ~에게 인기가 있다 people in their 20s and 30s 2, 30대 사람들 keep 간직하다 absolutely 물론, 틀림없이

실전 감각 익히기 본책 _ p. 106-107

1. (C) 2. (A) 3. (D) 4. (B) 5. (B) 6. (C)
7. (D) 8. (A) 9. (A) 10. (C) 11. (B) 12. (D)

1-3

M: Did you check your e-mail? **I forwarded you the discount ticket information you wanted for Asia.**[1]
W: Yes, thanks. I've been going through it. **I think I am going to visit Tokyo at the end of the month.**[2]
M: Wow, that sounds interesting. Why do you want to go to Tokyo?
W: My cousin moved there from Melbourne about six months ago, and she's been asking me to visit. **I'm looking forward to meeting her**[3] and it's also the perfect opportunity to see a new place.

남: 이메일을 확인하셨어요? 제가 당신이 원하시던 아시아에 대한 할인 티켓 정보를 보냈거든요.
여: 네, 고마워요. 지금 훑어보는 중입니다. 전 월말에 도쿄를 방문할 생각이에요.
남: 와, 재미있겠네요. 왜 도쿄를 가고 싶으세요?
여: 제 사촌이 6개월 전에 멜버른에서 그곳으로 이사를 갔는데 계속 저한테 오라고 해요. 사촌을 아주 만나고 싶기도 하고, 또 새로운 장소를 볼 수 있는 정말 좋은 기회잖아요.

어휘 check 확인하다 forward 전송하다 discount ticket 할인 티켓 go through ~을 훑어보다, 살펴보다 sound+형용사 ~하게 들리다 cousin 사촌 ask+A(사람)+to부정사 A에게 ~하길 부탁하다 look forward to ~ing ~하기를 고대하다 opportunity 기회

1. 남자는 여자에게 무엇을 보냈는가?
(A) 여행 일정표 (B) 이메일 주소
(C) 티켓 정보 (D) 예약 확인서

해설 남자가 여자에게 보낸 것을 물어보고 있으므로 남자의 말에 초점을 맞춰야 한다. 남자가 대화 초반부에 I forwarded you the discount ticket information you wanted for Asia.라고 했으므로 정답은 (C)이다. 질문에 있는 send와 유사 의미로 대화에서는 forward가 쓰였다. 이렇게 질문이나 보기에 있는 단어가 유사 의미의 다른 단어로 바꿔 사용되는 패러프레이징(paraphrasing)에 유의해야 한다.

2. 여자는 어디에 가고 싶어하는가?
(A) 아시아 (B) 아프리카
(C) 호주 (D) 남미

해설 보기가 모두 지역을 나타내는 고유명사인데, 그 중 특정 보기가 정답으로 대화에서 나올 때 친숙하게 잘 들리도록 속으로 미리 발음해 두어야 한다. 남자의 말에서 Asia가 언급되었고 여자도 I think I am going to visit Tokyo at the end of the month.라고 했으므로 정답은 (A)이다.

3. 여자의 여행에 대해 무엇이 언급되어 있는가?
(A) 그녀는 그 지역을 자주 방문한다.
(B) 그녀는 6개월간 여행을 할 것이다.
(C) 그녀의 첫 번째 해외 여행이 될 것이다.
(D) 그녀는 사촌을 방문할 것이다.

해설 여자의 여행에 대한 질문인데, 여자가 I'm looking forward to meeting her라고 했으므로 정답은 (D)이다. 지금처럼 보기가 문장으로 제시되는 경우에는 보기 네 개를 미리 읽어두는 것이 결코 쉽지 않다. 하지만 실제 시험에서는 단어나 구가 아닌 문장으로 보기를 제시하는 문제가 매회 출제되므로 짧은 시간 내에 보기를 빨리 읽는 연습을 할 필요가 있다.

4-6

W: **Hi, I'm hoping to buy a chair for my office.**[4] The chair catching my eye is on the display stand.

M: Oh, the chair on display has recently been released. **It will provide you with enough support to keep you comfortable**[5] throughout your sitting duration.

W: That would be great since I spend much of my day sitting in my desk.

M: It can also be adjusted for height, and **comes in five different colors**,[6] so it will match almost any desk.

여: 안녕하세요, 저는 제 사무실에서 쓸 의자를 하나 사고 싶습니다. 제 눈에 들어온 의자는 진열대에 있는 겁니다.

남: 오, 진열된 그 의자는 최근에 출시된 겁니다. 고객님께서 앉아계시는 내내 편안함을 유지시켜줄 겁니다.

여: 제가 하루 중 많은 시간을 책상에 앉아서 보내니까 아주 좋겠는데요.

남: 이 의자는 또한 높이 조절이 가능하며, 다섯 가지 색상으로 나와서 거의 모든 책상과 어울릴 겁니다.

어휘 catch one's eye ~의 눈에 띄다. 눈을 사로잡다
display stand 진열대   recently 최근에   release 출시하다
provide A with B A에게 B를 제공하다   support 지탱, 지지(하다)
keep+A(사람)+형용사 A를 ~하게 하다   throughout ~ 내내
duration 지속 기간   since ~이니까
spend+시간+~ing ~하는 데 시간을 쓰다   adjust 조절하다
height 높이   come in+색깔 (색깔로) 나오다   match 어울리다

4. 여자는 무엇을 사고 싶어하는가?
(A) 책상   (B) 의자
(C) 신발 한 켤레   (D) 책꽂이

해설 여자가 사고 싶은 물건에 대한 질문이므로 여자의 말에 집중해야 한다. 여자가 Hi, I'm hoping to buy a chair for my office.라고 했으므로 정답은 (B)이다. 쇼핑 상황에서는 사고 싶은 물건이 대화 초반에 언급되는 경우가 많으므로 특히 첫 화자의 말을 잘 들어야 한다.

5. 남자는 상품에 대해서 뭐라고 말하는가?
(A) 비싸다.   (B) 안락하다.
(C) 튼튼하다.   (D) 인기가 있다.

해설 〈What does the man[woman] say about + 명사?〉는 명사에 대한 남자[여자]의 의견을 물어보는 문제이다. 그런데 여기서는 명사가 the item인데, 이것은 대화에 나오는 chair를 미리 노출시키고 싶지 않아 the item으로 바꿔 쓴 것이다. 즉, 상품에 대해 언급되는 부분에서 정답을 찾아야 한다. 남자가 It will provide you with enough support to keep you comfortable이라고 했으므로 정답은 (B)이다.

6. 구입할 수 있는 색상은 몇 가지인가?
(A) 세 가지   (B) 네 가지
(C) 다섯 가지   (D) 여섯 가지

해설 How many로 시작하는 질문에는 대개 숫자로 대답을 하기 때문에 대화 중에 숫자가 언급되는 부분을 잘 들어야 한다. 대화 후반부에 색깔과 관련해서 숫자가 들어간 comes in five different colors라는 말이 나오므로 정답은 (C)이다.

7-9

W: I'd like to check the status of a flight. I looked online but **the Web site seems to be down right now**.[7]

M: Oh, really? OK, I could help you. What is the airline and flight number?

W: Flight 287, Mideastern Airlines. **It had a 3:00 A.M. departure time from Dubai.**[8]

M: Thank you. Hold on a moment. Well, **there was a delay in the London layover**,[9] and it left 20 minutes past its 8:20 departure time. It's now expected to arrive at 11:25. Is there anything else I can help you with?

여: 저는 비행편 상황을 확인하고 싶어요. 제가 온라인으로 봤는데 지금은 웹사이트가 다운된 것 같아요.

남: 오, 정말요? 좋아요, 제가 도와드릴게요. 항공사와 항공편 번호가 어떻게 되죠?

여: 미드이스턴 항공 287편입니다. 두바이에서 오전 3시 출발로 되어 있어요.

남: 고맙습니다. 잠깐만 기다려주세요. 음, 런던 경유에서 지연되어 출발 시간인 8시 20분에서 20분이 지나 출발했군요. 지금은 11시 25분에 도착할 예정입니다. 또 다른 도움이 필요하세요?

어휘 would like to부정사 ~을 하고 싶다 status 상황, 지위
flight 비행편, 항공편 seem to부정사 ~인 것 같다
down 다운된 airline 항공사 departure time 출발 시간
hold on a moment 잠깐만 기다리다 layover 경유, 도중 하차
past ~을 지나

7. 여자는 어떤 문제점을 언급하는가?
(A) 그녀는 티켓을 가져오지 않았다.
(B) 그녀는 수화물을 찾지 못했다.
(C) 셔틀버스가 늦게 도착했다.
(D) 웹사이트가 제대로 작동되지 않는다.

해설 여자가 언급한 문제점에 대한 질문이므로 여자의 말에서 정답을 찾아야 한다. 여자가 the Web site seems to be down right now 라고 했으므로 정답은 (D)이다. 이 문제도 보기가 문장으로 제시되어 미리 읽어두기가 쉽지 않다. 따라서 평상시 문장으로 된 보기 읽는 연습을 많이 해야 한다.

8. 비행편은 어디에서 출발했는가?
(A) 두바이   (B) 런던
(C) 덴버   (D) 리스본

해설 보기가 모두 도시를 나타내는 고유명사이므로 각 단어를 미리 읽어 둔 다음, 대화 속에서 반복되는 단어를 찾아야 한다. 여자가 It had a 3:00 A.M. departure time from Dubai.라고 한 부분에 Dubai가 언급되었으므로 정답은 (A)이다. 간혹 보기 중에서 언급되는 단어가 두 개 이상일 경우에는 질문의 핵심어가 쓰인 부분에서 정답의 단서를 찾아야 한다.

9. 비행편에 대해 무엇이 언급되었는가?
(A) 지연되었다.
(B) 예약이 완전히 찼다.
(C) 지금 승객들이 탑승 중이다.
(D) 대기 승객들을 받을 수 있다.

해설 지금처럼 질문에 the man이나 the woman이 없는 경우에는 어떤 화자가 정답의 단서를 얘기할지 모르므로 화자와 관계없이 질문의 핵심어가 언급되는 부분에 주목해야 한다. 이 질문의 핵심어는 the flight인데, 남자가 there was a delay in the London layover라고 했으므로 정답은 (A)이다.

10-12

M: Welcome to the Rexton Information Center. **Take a look at our brochures on the shelf here if you're interested in exploring one of our several popular tourist attractions.**¹⁰ If you have any questions, just let me know.

W: Thanks. Actually, my family and I are in town for the Jazz Festival on Saturday, and we're looking for a quick place to eat lunch. Do you have any recommendations?

M: Sure. Take a look at this map on the wall. **This restaurant between Prairie Road and Flat Street is one of my favorites.**¹¹ Here, I even have a 20 percent off coupon you can use.¹²

W: Nice. We'll go check it out now, than. Thanks a lot.

남: 렉스턴 관광 안내소에 오신 것을 환영합니다. 저희 여러 관광 명소 중 한 곳에 가 보실 생각이시라면, 여기 책장에 있는 책자를 살펴보시기 바랍니다. 질문이 있으면 알려 주시고요.

여: 고맙습니다. 사실 제 가족들하고 저는 토요일에 열리는 재즈 축제에 참가하기 위해 시내에 와 있는 중인데요. 간단하게 점심 식사를 할 수 있는 장소를 찾고 있습니다. 추천해 주실 만한 곳이 있나요?

남: 그럼요. 벽에 있는 이 지도를 보세요. 프레어리 로와 플랫 가 사이에 있는 이 레스토랑은 제가 가장 좋아하는 곳 중 하나입니다. 사용하실 수 있는 20 퍼센트 할인 쿠폰도 여기 이렇게 있습니다.

여: 좋은데요. 그럼 이제 가서 한 번 확인해 봐야겠습니다. 정말 감사합니다.

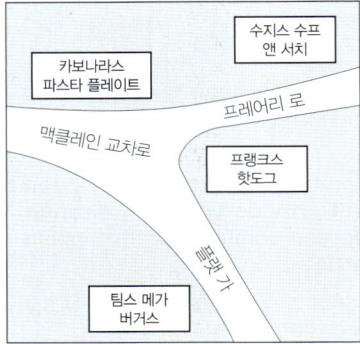

어휘 brochure 브로셔, 소책자 explore 답사하다, 탐험하다
several 몇몇의, 여럿의 tourist attraction 관광 명소, 관광지
recommendation 추천, 권고 junction (도로·선로의) 교차로

10. 남자는 렉스턴에 대해 뭐라고 말을 하는가?
(A) 주말이 되면 바빠진다.
(B) 그곳에서의 축제가 연기되었다.
(C) 많은 관광 명소가 있다.
(D) 그곳에 있는 식당들을 좋아하지 않는다.

해설 관광 안내원으로 추정되는 남자는 렉스턴의 여러 관광 명소 중 한 곳에 가 볼 생각이 있다면 책장에 있는 책자를 살펴보라(Take a look at our brochures on the shelf here if you're interested in exploring one of our several popular tourist attractions.)고 여자에게 말하고 있다. 대화에 나온 several을 many로 바꾸어 표현한 (C)가 정답이 된다.

11. 도표를 보세요. 여자는 어디에서 점심을 먹을 것 같은가?
(A) 수지스   (B) 프랭크스
(C) 팀스   (D) 카보나라스

해설 남자가 프레어리 로와 플랫 가 사이에 있는 레스토랑이 자신이 가장 좋아하는 곳 중 하나(This restaurant between Prairie Road and Flat Street is one of my favorites.)라고 소개해 주자, 여자가 그곳에 가봐야겠다고 했으므로 정답은 (B)이다.

12. 남자가 여자에게 주는 것은?
(A) 축제 지도
(B) 시 안내 책자
(C) 관광지 티켓
(D) 식당 쿠폰

해설 남자는 자신이 소개해 주는 레스토랑에서 사용할 수 있는 20 퍼센트 할인 쿠폰을 여자에게 건네주고 있다(Here, I even have a 20 percent off coupon you can use.). 따라서 정답은 (D)이다.

UNIT 12 부동산/은행/병원/호텔/식당(기타 일상생활)

어휘 및 표현 점검 본책_ p. 110

1. bank account 2. realtor 3. landlord
4. regular checkup 5. server

청취 집중 훈련 1 본책_ p. 111

1. reservation / need / won't / hold / let / wait / order / get
2. wanted to remind / regular checkup / may not finish / Would it be / closes at / the side doors

청취 집중 훈련 2 본책_ p. 112

1. (A) 2. (B) 3. (B) 4. (A) 5. (B) 6. (A)

1-2

1. 이 대화는 아마도 어디에서 일어나겠는가?
(A) 호텔에서
(B) 식당에서

2. 남자는 무엇을 주문하는가?
(A) 피자
(B) 치킨

> M: Hello, I'd like to order room service for room 1309.
> W: Of course, what would you like to order?
> M: I'd like the honey-glazed chicken with green beans. When will it be delivered?

남: 안녕하세요, 저는 1309호로 룸서비스를 주문하고 싶습니다.
여: 좋습니다. 무엇을 주문하고 싶으세요?
남: 껍질콩을 곁들인 꿀 바른 치킨을 주세요. 언제 배달이 될까요?

어휘 order room service 호텔 방으로 식사를 주문하다 honey 꿀 glaze (꿀 등을) 바르다 deliver 배달하다

3-4

3. 여자는 무엇을 맞추고 싶어하는가?
(A) 정장
(B) 드레스

4. 여자는 어떤 종류의 직물을 원하는가?
(A) 모직
(B) 실크

> W: I'm interested in getting a custom-tailored dress made. What are your rates?
> M: It depends on the fabric and some other factors.
> W: I would like a wool dress appropriate for winter.

여: 저는 드레스를 맞추는 데 관심이 있습니다. 가격이 어떻게 되죠?
남: 그건 직물과 다른 요인들에 따라 다릅니다.
여: 저는 겨울에 적합한 모직 드레스를 원합니다.

어휘 be interested in ~에 관심이 있다 custom-tailored 맞춤식의 rate 가격, 요금 depend on ~에 달려 있다 fabric 직물 factor 요인 wool 모직 appropriate 적합한

5-6

5. 화자들은 어디에 있는가?
(A) 은행에
(B) 부동산 중개소에

6. 여자는 어디에 살고 싶은가?
(A) 사무실 근처
(B) 지하철역 근처

> W: Excuse me, I'd like to lease a house. My company is transferring me here next fall.
> M: OK, let me help you. What kind of house do you have in mind?
> W: Well, I'd just prefer an apartment within walking distance of my office.

여: 실례합니다만 저는 집을 임차하고 싶습니다. 다음 가을에 회사에서 저를 이곳으로 전근을 보내거든요.

남: 좋아요, 제가 도와드릴게요. 어떤 종류의 집을 염두에 두고 계시죠?

여: 음, 저는 제 사무실에서 걸어갈 수 있는 범위 내의 아파트면 좋겠어요.

어휘 lease 임대[임차]하다　transfer 전근을 보내다　have A(목적어) in mind A를 염두에 두다　I'd prefer ~이면 좋겠어요　within walking distance of ~에서 걸어갈 수 있는 범위 내에

청취 집중 훈련 3 본책_ p. 113

1. (A)　2. (B)　3. (B)　4. (A)　5. (D)　6. (C)

1-2

1. 이 대화를 어디에서 들을 수 있겠는가?
(A) 우체국에서
(B) 세탁소에서
(C) 호텔에서
(D) 공항에서

해설 대화 장소는 대화 초반부에 화자들이 쓰는 단어에서 정답의 단서를 찾을 수 있다. 남자가 I need this package shipped overnight to Sydney.라고 했는데 package, shipped 그리고 overnight은 일반적으로 우체국에서 소포를 보낼 때 쓰는 단어들이므로 정답은 (A)이다.

2. 소포는 언제 도착할 예정인가?
(A) 이번 주 토요일
(B) 다음 주 월요일
(C) 다음 주 화요일
(D) 다음 주 수요일

해설 시점에 대한 질문은 보기에 있는 시점이 대화에서도 그대로 나온다는 것을 예상할 수 있다. 만약 대화 중에 두 개 이상의 시점이 언급되면 질문의 핵심어가 쓰인 문장에서 정답을 찾아야 한다. 질문의 핵심어인 arrive가 여자의 말인 your package will arrive on next Monday에서 언급되므로 정답은 (B)이다.

> M: **I need this package shipped**[1] overnight to Sydney. How much will it cost?
>
> W: For international express mail, it's 105 pounds. Since it's a Thursday evening, the guaranteed delivery date is on Monday.
>
> M: Oh, I need the package to get there tomorrow, on Saturday. Is that possible?
>
> W: Well, since it's going so far away, and it's afternoon, we can only guarantee that **your package will arrive on next Monday.**[2]

남: 저는 이 소포를 하루 만에 시드니로 보내야 해요. 비용이 얼마죠?

여: 국제 속달 우편의 경우에는 105파운드입니다. 목요일 저녁이니까 배달 보장일은 월요일입니다.

남: 오, 저는 이 소포를 내일 토요일에 그곳에 도착하도록 보내야 합니다. 가능할까요?

여: 음, 아주 멀리 배송하는 것이고 지금이 오후이기 때문에, 고객님 소포는 다음 주 월요일에 도착할 겁니다.

어휘 package 소포　ship 배송하다　overnight 하루 만에　cost 비용이 들다　express mail 속달 우편　guaranteed 보장되는　delivery date 배달일　get there 그곳에 도착하다　since ~이니까　so far away 아주 멀리　arrive 도착하다

3-4

3. 남자는 왜 전화를 걸고 있는가?
(A) 예약을 취소하기 위해
(B) 행사 장소를 변경하기 위해
(C) 예약 시간을 변경하기 위해
(D) 식당 메뉴 품목에 대해 문의하기 위해

해설 남자가 전화를 걸고 있는 목적은 남자의 말에서 정답의 단서를 찾아야 한다. 남자가 Could I possibly move the event to an indoor room?이라고 물어보고 있으므로 정답은 (B)이다.

4. 팸은 남자에게 무엇을 보낼 것인가?
(A) 새로운 메뉴
(B) 신용카드 신청서
(C) 새로운 예약 번호
(D) 서비스 송장

해설 팸(W1)의 말에 집중해야 한다. 팸이 I will e-mail our latest menu라고 했으므로 정답은 (A)이다. 이메일로 보내는 자료에 대한 말은 대화를 마무리하는 부분에서 언급되는 경우가 많으므로 대화의 후반부를 잘 들어야 한다.

> W1: Lakeside Grill, this is Pam speaking.
>
> M: Hi, this is Curtis. I've booked your outdoor patio for a family gathering this Friday, but I heard it's going to rain. **Could I possibly move the event to an indoor room?**[3]
>
> W1: Well, wait a second. Let me check with our booking clerk. Clara, do we have any indoor rooms left for this Friday?
>
> W2: Yes, there is only one private room left. The rates for the outdoor patio and indoor rooms are different, though.
>
> W1: I know, thanks Clara. Mr. Curtis, we can make that switch. The room rental is less expensive, so we'll credit your account. Also, **I will e-mail our latest menu**[4] with some new salad choices on it.
>
> M: That's great. Thank you.

여1: 레이크사이드 그릴의 팸입니다.

남: 안녕하세요, 저는 커티스입니다. 제가 이번 주 금요일 가족 모임을 위해 야외 뜰을 예약했는데 비가 올 거라는 말을 들었습니다. 행사를 실내로 옮길 수 있을까요?

여1: 음, 잠깐만요, 제가 저희 예약 담당자와 확인해 볼게요. 클라라, 이번 주 금요일에 쓸 실내 공간이 남은 게 있나요?

여2: 네, 전용실이 딱 하나 남았어요. 하지만 야외 뜰과 실내 공간의 요금이 달라요.

여1: 알고 있어요. 고마워요, 클라라. 커티스 씨, 저희가 변경해 놓을게요. 실내 대여비가 더 저렴하므로 저희가 고객님 계정에 입금해 드리겠습니다. 또 제가 몇 가지 새로운 샐러드 선택사항이 있는 최신 메뉴를 이메일로 보내드릴게요.

남: 좋습니다. 고마워요.

어휘 this is + 이름 + speaking (전화 상에서) 저는 ~입니다 book 예약하다 outdoor patio 야외 뜰 family gathering 가족 모임 possibly 아마도 move 옮기다 event 행사 indoor 실내의 check with ~와 확인하다 booking clerk 예약 담당 직원 rate 요금 though (문미에서) 그렇지만 make a switch 변경하다 rental 대여 less 덜 credit one's account ~의 계좌에 입금하다 latest 최근의

5-6

5. 남자는 왜 사무실을 방문하고 있는 것인가?
(A) 임대 보증금을 지불하기 위해
(B) 아파트를 보기 위해
(C) 임대 계약을 협상하기 위해
(D) 교육 프로그램에 대해 문의하기 위해

해설 남자의 사무실 방문 목적을 묻는 질문이므로 남자의 말에서 정답의 단서를 찾아야 한다. 남자가 I'm interested in enrolling in her training courses라고 했으므로 정답은 (D)이다. 대화의 주제나 목적은 일반적으로 대화의 초반부에 언급되므로 대화의 맥락을 파악할 수 있도록 처음 시작하는 부분을 잘 들어야 한다.

6. 여자는 남자가 무엇을 하기를 제안하는가?
(A) 다른 시간에 그녀를 만나는 것
(B) 다른 아파트를 보는 것
(C) 연락처를 제공하는 것
(D) 다른 부동산 사무실을 방문하는 것

해설 여자의 제안 사항에 대한 질문이므로 여자의 말에 집중해야 한다. 여자가 대화 마지막에 Why don't you give me your cell phone number and e-mail address?라고 했으므로 정답은 (C)이다. 제안 사항은 Why don't you ~?, I suggest ~, I recommend ~, I ask ~, 또는 I'd like you to + 동사원형의 형태를 취하는 경우가 많다는 것을 알아두자.

M: Hi, I'm Kay. I'm hoping I can talk to Ms. Lopez. **I'm interested in enrolling in her training courses**[5] for becoming an apartment rental agent.

W: Oh, hi. Well, she can't see you here now because she made a transfer to our Webster branch office. Do you want her office number?

M: No, that's OK. I'd like to train to get rental agent certification here in the city.

W: **Why don't you give me your cell phone number and e-mail address?**[6] Then, my manager Marino will contact you about the class.

남: 안녕하세요, 저는 케이입니다. 저는 로페즈 씨와 얘기를 하고 싶은데요. 제가 로페즈 씨의 아파트 임대 중개인 교육 과정에 관심이 있거든요.

여: 오, 안녕하세요. 음, 그녀는 저희 웹스터 지점으로 전근을 갔기 때문에 지금 이곳에서는 만날 수가 없습니다. 로페즈 씨의 사무실 번호를 드릴까요?

남: 아니요, 괜찮습니다. 저는 이 도시에서 임대 중개인 자격증을 위한 교육을 받고 싶거든요.

여: 휴대폰 번호와 이메일 주소를 알려주시겠어요? 그럼 제 매니저인 마리노가 수업에 대해 연락을 드릴 겁니다.

어휘 be interested in ~에 관심이 있다 enroll in ~에 등록하다 training course 교육 과정 rental agent 임대 중개인 make a transfer to + 장소 ~로 전근을 가다 branch office 지점 train 교육을 받다 certification 자격(증), 증명(서)

실전 감각 익히기 본책 _ p. 114-115

1. (C) 2. (A) 3. (B) 4. (C) 5. (A) 6. (A)
7. (B) 8. (D) 9. (D) 10. (B) 11. (C) 12. (D)

1-3

M: **The landlord wants us to build the fence**[1] around the garden pond. I have the drills and spare batteries here. We have the paint and brushes too, so we can start work right away.

W: Oh, wait. **I don't see the wood pieces**[2] and screws for the fence.

M: Ah, right. They're in the truck. I'll run and get them. If we put up the fence by the end of the morning, we'll have plenty of time to do the painting.

W: Right. **We'll be done with the whole job by 4 or 5 this afternoon.**[3]

남: 집주인이 정원 연못 주변으로 울타리를 치라고 합니다. 제가 여기 드릴과 여분의 건전지를 갖고 있어요. 페인트와 붓도 있으니까 바로 작업을 시작할 수 있겠어요.

여: 아, 잠깐만요. 울타리에 쓸 나무토막과 나사가 없어요.

남: 아, 그렇군요. 그건 트럭에 있어요. 제가 얼른 가서 가져올게요. 오전까지 울타리를 세우면 페인트 작업을 할 시간은 충분할 겁니다.

여: 맞아요. 오늘 오후 4시나 5시에 모든 작업이 끝날 겁니다.

어휘 landlord 집주인 build 짓다 fence 울타리 pond 연못
drill 드릴, 송곳 spare 여분의 brush 붓 right away 당장
wood piece 나무토막 screw 나사 get 가져오다 put up 세우다
by the end of the morning 오전까지 plenty of 많은
do painting 페인트 작업을 하다 be done 끝나다
whole 전체의

1. 화자들은 무엇을 하고 있는가?
(A) 트럭 수리
(B) 수영장 청소
(C) 울타리 작업
(D) 정원에 나무 심기

해설 화자들이 하고 있는 일은 대화 초반부에 쓰인 단어들로 알 수 있다. 남자가 The landlord wants us to build the fence라고 했으므로 정답은 (C)이다. 대화의 초반부를 잘 들으면 대화의 주제를 알 수 있으므로 항상 첫 화자의 말에 최대한 집중해야 한다.

2. 여자는 무엇이 없다고 하는가?
(A) 나무토막
(B) 트럭 부품
(C) 건전지
(D) 페인트

해설 여자가 말한 내용에 대한 질문으로 여자의 말에서 정답의 단서를 찾아야 한다. 여자가 I don't see the wood pieces라고 했으므로 정답은 (A)이다. 이 문제처럼 대화의 모든 세부 내용을 잘 들으려고 하기보다는 문제와 보기를 미리 읽어서 필요한 정보만을 정확하게 들을 수 있는 연습을 많이 해야 한다.

3. 여자는 언제 작업이 완료될 것이라고 하는가?
(A) 오늘 아침
(B) 오늘 오후
(C) 내일 아침
(D) 내일 오후

해설 시점에 대한 문제는 보기의 시점 중 하나가 대화 중에도 언급될 것임을 예상할 수 있다. 보기에 있는 this afternoon이 여자가 We'll be done with the whole job by 4 or 5 this afternoon.이라고 말한 부분에서 그대로 나오므로 정답은 (B)이다. 만약 대화 중에 시점이 두 개 이상 언급되면 문제의 핵심어가 들어 있는 부분에서 정답을 찾아야 한다.

4-6

W: **I saw the listings for the apartments**[4] in the Westaville Tower. Would it be possible to schedule an appointment today or tomorrow?

M: Yes, of course. Right now, however, **we only have a few studios available.**[5]

W: Oh, that's fine. I'm interested in looking at some studios. When is the earliest that I could come and take a look?

M: Well, **I could give you a tour of the place this afternoon**[6] if you'd like. If you could come around 2:30, that would be perfect. Is that time O.K. for you?

여: 제가 웨스터빌 타워에 있는 아파트 목록을 봤어요. 오늘이나 내일 약속을 잡을 수 있을까요?

남: 네, 물론입니다. 그런데 지금 당장은 몇몇 원룸만 이용 가능합니다.

여: 오, 괜찮습니다. 제가 원룸에 관심이 있거든요. 제가 가서 둘러볼 수 있는 제일 빠른 시간은 언제인가요?

남: 음, 괜찮으시면 제가 오늘 오후에 그곳을 구경시켜 드릴게요. 2시 30분까지 오시면 아주 좋겠습니다. 그 시간이 괜찮으십니까?

어휘 listing 목록 would it be possible to 부정사? ~하는 것이 가능할까요? schedule an appointment 약속을 잡다
studio 원룸 available 이용 가능한
be interested in ~에 관심이 있다
take a look 둘러보다
give + A(사람) + a tour of A에게 ~을 구경[견학]시켜주다

4. 여자는 무엇을 하고 싶은가?
(A) 호텔 방 예약   (B) 회의 참석
(C) 몇몇 아파트 보기   (D) 일자리 지원

해설 여자가 하고 싶은 일에 대한 질문이므로 여자의 말에서 정답의 단서를 찾을 수 있다. 여자가 I saw the listings for the apartments라고 한 부분에서 여자가 아파트를 구하고 있다는 것을 알 수 있으므로 정답은 (C)이다.

5. 어떤 종류의 집이 제시되고 있는가?
(A) 원룸   (B) 방 2개 주택
(C) 방 3개 주택   (D) 방 4개 주택

해설 housing option이라는 생소한 단어가 나오지만, 보기를 보고 집의 종류에 대한 질문이라는 것을 알 수 있다. 남자가 we only have a few studios available이라고 했으므로 정답은 (A)이다.

6. 화자들은 아마도 언제 만날 것인가?
(A) 오후에   (B) 저녁에
(C) 다음날 아침   (D) 다음날 저녁

해설 시점에 대한 문제는 보기를 먼저 읽은 후, 보기의 시점 중 어떤 것이 대화에서 언급되는지를 확인함으로써 정답을 찾을 수 있다. 남자가 I could give you a tour of the place this afternoon이라고 한 부분에서 afternoon이 언급되므로 정답은 (A)이다.

7-9

> M: Welcome to Rose's Café and Restaurant. Will anyone be joining you today?
> W: Yes, two of my coworkers are on their way. So **there will be three of us.**[7] But we didn't make a reservation. Will there be a long wait for tables?
> M: Actually, I'm afraid yes. We're quite busy for lunch today. **You could have your meal at the counter.**[8] It's not busy there.
> W: Sure, that would work. Oh, I heard you have the Discount Dining Club. **Could you give me a sign-up form**[9] for it? I can fill that out while I'm waiting.

남: 로즈 카페 식당에 오신 걸 환영합니다. 오늘 다른 일행이 있으신가요?
여: 네, 제 직장 동료 두 명이 오고 있는 중이에요. 그래서 3명이 될 거예요. 그런데 저희가 예약을 하지 않았거든요. 테이블이 나는 데 오래 걸릴까요?
남: 실은 그렇습니다. 오늘은 점심 시간에 아주 바쁘네요. 손님께서 카운터에서 드실 수도 있습니다. 그곳은 안 바쁘거든요.
여: 네, 괜찮아요. 오, 제가 할인 식사 클럽이 있다는 얘기를 들었어요. 그것에 대한 신청 양식 좀 주실래요? 제가 기다리는 동안 작성하려고요.

어휘 join 합류하다 coworker 직장 동료
be on one's way 오고 있는 중이다
make a reservation 예약하다 a long wait 오랜 기다림
I'm afraid ~ 유감이지만 ~이다 meal 식사 work 괜찮다, 좋다
dining 식사 sign-up form 등록 양식, 신청 양식 fill out 작성하다
while ~하는 동안

7. 여자의 일행은 몇 명인가?
(A) 두 명   (B) 세 명
(C) 네 명   (D) 다섯 명

해설 여자의 일행이 몇 명인지에 대한 질문이므로 대화 중에서 질문의 핵심 어인 the woman's group이 언급되는 부분에서 숫자를 들을 수 있어야 한다. 여자가 there will be three of us라고 했는데 us가 the woman's group이므로 결국 정답은 (B)이다.

8. 남자는 여자의 일행에게 무엇을 제안하는가?
(A) 식당의 다른 지점에 가는 것
(B) 온라인으로 예약할 것
(C) 나중에 다시 올 것
(D) 카운터에서 식사할 것

해설 여자에 대한 남자의 제안 사항에 대한 질문이다. 제안 사항은 why don't you ~, how[what] about ~, you can[could] ~, you should ~, I suggest ~, I recommend ~ 등으로 나타낼 수 있다. 여기서는 남자가 you could를 써서 You could have your meal at the counter.라고 했으므로 정답은 (D)이다.

9. 여자는 남자에게 무엇을 요청하는가?
(A) 다른 구역에 있는 좌석   (B) 저녁 식사 예약
(C) 점심 메뉴   (D) 클럽 등록 양식

해설 여자의 요청 사항에 대한 질문으로 여자의 말에 초점을 맞추어야 한다. 여자가 남자에게 Could you give me a sign-up form for it?이라고 물어보고 있는데 여기서 sign-up form이 registration form과 같은 것이므로 정답은 (D)이다.

10-12

> M: Hello, I'm calling from Albany Bank. Can I speak to Ms. Jackson?
> W1: Who shall I say is calling?
> M: My name is Matthew Hendricks.
> W1: Okay, please hold while I transfer your call.
> W2: Hello, this is Jackson.
> M: Hi, this is Matthew Hendricks. **I'm replacing Mr. Garbutt as Small Business Accounts manager,**[10] so I'll be taking care of all your banking needs from now on.
> W2: Oh, hi. Right, Mr. Garbutt told me he would be leaving this week. **He helped me open an online account with the bank.**[11]
> M: For now, we've just prepared an information sheet about new tax rules for small businesses. **I can send an electronic copy**[12] of that to your e-mail account today for you.
> W2: I'd appreciate that.

남: 안녕하세요, 알바니 은행에서 전화드립니다. 잭슨 씨와 통화할 수 있을까요?
여1: 누구시라고 전해드릴까요?
남: 제 이름은 매튜 헨드릭스입니다.
여1: 네, 전화를 돌려드릴 테니 잠시만 기다려 주세요.
여2: 안녕하세요. 제가 잭슨입니다.
남: 안녕하세요. 저는 매튜 헨드릭스입니다. 제가 소기업 계정 관리자로서 가벗 씨를 대신해 지금부터 고객님의 모든 은행 거래를 관리해드릴 겁니다.
여2: 오, 안녕하세요. 맞아요, 가벗 씨가 제게 이번 주에 떠난다는 얘기를 하더군요. 가벗 씨는 제가 온라인 계정을 만들 수 있게 도와줬어요.
남: 지금은 저희가 소기업을 위한 새로운 세금 규정 안내서를 준비했습니다. 제가 오늘 고객님께 이메일 계정으로 그것의 전자 사본을 보내드릴 수 있습니다.
여2: 그렇게 해주시면 고맙겠습니다.

어휘 hold 기다리다 transfer (전화를) 돌리다 replace 대신하다, 대체하다 small business 소기업 take care of ~을 관리하다, 처리하다 banking 은행 거래 needs 요구사항 from now on 지금부터 leave 떠나다, 사직하다
help+사람+(to)+동사원형 ~가 ~하는 것을 도와주다
open an account 계정을 만들다 for now 지금은
prepare 준비하다 information sheet 안내서, 도표
tax rules 세금 규정 electronic copy 전자 사본

10. 남자는 잭슨 씨에게 왜 전화를 하고 있는가?
(A) 은행 거래 오류에 대해 사과하기 위해
(B) 직원 변경에 대해 알리려고
(C) 새로운 계정 개설을 제안하기 위해
(D) 다가오는 출장에 대해 논의하기 위해

해설 여자가 전화를 걸고 있는 이유는 여자의 말에서 정답의 단서를 찾을 수 있다. 여자가 I'm replacing Mr. Garbutt as Small Business Accounts manager라고 했으므로 여자는 직원 변경에 대해 알리고 있는 것이다. 따라서 정답은 (B)이다. 이 문제처럼 보기가 길게 제시되는 문제에 대비하기 위해 평상시에 보기를 빨리 읽는 연습을 할 필요가 있다.

11. 잭슨 씨가 알바니 은행에 대해 언급한 내용은 무엇인가?
(A) 그녀는 그곳에 매주 간다.
(B) 그녀는 그곳에서 근무를 했었다.
(C) 그녀는 그곳에 온라인 계정을 갖고 있다.
(D) 그녀는 그들의 재무 관리자를 고용했다.

해설 잭슨 씨가 알바니 은행과 관련해서 언급한 내용을 찾는 문제이므로 두 번째 여자의 말에서 정답의 단서를 찾아야 한다. 여자가 He helped me open an online account with the bank.라고 했으므로 정답은 (C)이다. Albany Bank와 같은 고유명사의 발음은 듣기가 어려우므로, 문제나 보기에 고유명사가 있을 경우에는 미리 속으로 읽어두어서 그 발음에 친숙하게 만들어둘 필요가 있다.

12. 남자는 잭슨 씨에게 무엇을 해주겠다고 제안하는가?
(A) 추가 직원을 고용하는 것
(B) 복사를 하는 것
(C) 새로운 신용카드를 발급하는 것
(D) 서류를 이메일로 보내는 것

해설 남자의 제안 사항을 묻는 질문이므로 남자의 말에서 정답의 단서를 찾아야 한다. 대화 마지막에 남자가 I can send an electronic copy라고 했으므로 정답은 (D)이다.

Part 3 Review Test 본책 _ p. 116–117

1. (A)	2. (D)	3. (B)	4. (B)	5. (D)
6. (C)	7. (B)	8. (D)	9. (C)	10. (A)
11. (C)	12. (A)	13. (D)	14. (C)	15. (A)
16. (A)	17. (C)	18. (B)	19. (B)	20. (A)
21. (C)				

1-3

W: **How should we advertise for our film festival?**[1] Last year we took out ads in the newspaper, but not many people came.

M: I think that **we should promote the event online.**[2] It would be cheaper than buying radio or print media ads, and we can potentially reach far more people.

W: Okay, you have me convinced. Do you know of any sites in particular where we can purchase ad space?

M: Well, **Dan, my friend from the photography club, runs a bulletin board site. I'm sure he can help us.**[3]

여: 우리 영화 축제를 어떻게 광고해야 할까요? 작년에 신문 광고를 냈지만 사람들이 많이 오지 않았잖아요.

남: 이번 행사는 온라인으로 홍보해야 한다고 생각해요. 라디오나 인쇄 매체 광고를 사는 것보다 더 저렴할 것이고 아마도 우리가 훨씬 더 많은 사람들에게 알릴 수 있거든요.

여: 좋아요, 설득력 있네요. 우리가 광고란을 살 수 있는 어떤 특별한 사이트를 아세요?

남: 음, 사진 클럽에서 아는 제 친구 댄이 게시판 사이트를 운영하고 있어요. 그가 분명히 우리를 도와줄 겁니다.

어휘 advertise for (행사·일자리 등을) 광고하다
take out an ad 광고를 내다 promote 홍보하다
print media 인쇄 매체 potentially 아마도, 잠재적으로
reach 이르다, 닿다 far more 훨씬 더 많은
convince 설득시키다, 확신을 주다 in particular 특별히
purchase 구입하다 ad space 광고란
photography club 사진 클럽 run 운영하다
bulletin board site 게시판 사이트

1. 화자들은 어떤 종류의 행사를 준비하고 있는가?
(A) 영화 축제
(B) 세미나
(C) 기자회견
(D) 인터뷰

해설 대화를 시작하면서 여자가 How should we advertise for our film festival?이라고 했으므로 정답은 (A)이다. 먼저 문제와 보기를 읽고 나서 대화를 들으면 정답을 쉽게 찾을 수 있으므로 대화가 나오기 전에 문제와 보기를 빠르게 읽어두어야 한다. 또한 정답은 대개 순차적으로 제시된다는 것도 알아두자.

2. 화자들은 행사를 어떻게 광고할 계획인가?
(A) 라디오로
(B) 신문에
(C) TV에
(D) 인터넷으로

해설 행사를 홍보하는 방법을 묻는 질문인데 남자가 we should promote the event online이라고 했으므로 정답은 (D)이다. 대화문에서의 promote는 질문에서 advertise로, online은 보기에서 Internet으로 패러프레이징(바꿔 말하기)되었다.

3. 남자는 누구에게 도움을 청할 것인가?
(A) 그의 동료
(B) 그의 친구
(C) 그의 형
(D) 그의 매니저

해설 대화 마지막에 남자가 Dan, my friend from the photography club, runs a bulletin board site. I'm sure he can help us.라고 했으므로 정답은 (B)이다.

4-6

W: It's hard to believe it's almost spring already. **We need to clear out our winter clothing to make room for a huge shipment of summer clothing we just received.**[4]

M: I think we should have a special sale this weekend. **It's still winter**,[5] and it's pretty cold these days, so people will be willing to buy winter clothing if it's at a discount.

W: Yes, that's a good idea, but today is already Wednesday. We should hurry.

M: Don't worry. **I'll send an e-mail to all of our store members**[6] and post an ad on our Web site today.

여: 이제 곧 봄이라니 믿기지가 않네요. 우리가 지금 받은 많은 양의 여름 옷을 둘 공간을 마련하기 위해 겨울 옷을 처분해야 해요.
남: 이번 주말에 특별 세일을 해야겠어요. 아직도 겨울이고 요즘 꽤 추우니까 할인을 해주면 사람들이 겨울 옷을 살 거예요.
여: 네, 좋은 생각이지만 오늘이 벌써 수요일이잖아요. 서둘러야겠어요.
남: 걱정하지 마세요. 제가 오늘 모든 우리 가게 회원들에게 메일을 보내고 웹사이트에 광고를 올릴게요.

어휘 hard to believe 믿기지 않는 almost 거의 already 벌써
clear out 처분하다, 없애다   make room for ~을 위한 공간을 마련하다
shipment 선적물, 배송물   have a special sale 특별 세일을 하다
pretty 꽤   be willing to부정사 ~할 의향이 있다
at a discount 할인되는   hurry 서두르다
post an ad 광고를 게재하다

4. 화자들은 왜 세일을 하고 싶어하는가?
(A) 상점의 기념일을 홍보하기 위해
(B) 새로운 재고품을 위한 공간을 마련하기 위해
(C) 새로운 상점의 개업을 축하하기 위해
(D) 새로운 상품을 광고하기 위해

해설 여자가 대화를 시작하면서 We need to clear out our winter clothing to make room for a huge shipment of summer clothing we just received.라고 했는데 a huge shipment of summer clothing we just received가 보기에서는 new inventory로 패러프레이징된 것이므로 정답은 (B)이다.

5. 아마도 지금은 어떤 계절인가?
(A) 봄
(B) 여름
(C) 가을
(D) 겨울

해설 남자가 It's still winter라고 했으므로 정답은 (D)이다. 주의해야 할 점은 대화 초반부에 여자가 it's almost spring already라고 했는데 이것을 듣고 spring을 골라선 안 된다는 것이다. 여자의 말은 '거의 봄이 되었다'라는 뜻이지 지금이 완전히 봄이라는 뜻은 아니다.

6. 세일에 대해 언급된 내용은 무엇인가?
(A) 1주일간 지속될 것이다.
(B) 수요일에 시작될 것이다.
(C) 상점 회원들이 세일에 대한 이메일을 받을 것이다.
(D) 최대 50% 할인될 것이다.

해설 남자가 대화 후반부에 I'll send an e-mail to all of our store members라고 했으므로 정답은 (C)이다. 여자가 today is already Wednesday라고 했는데 Wednesday를 듣고 (B)를 답으로 고르지 않도록 주의해야 한다.

7-9

M: Hi, I've got an appointment for a teeth cleaning in about fifteen minutes, but I'm afraid I'm going to be late. There's so much traffic that I think it will be, oh, at least thirty minutes before I arrive.

W: You must be stuck in traffic from the May Day Festival. **They had to shut down a few roads for the parade**,[7] so patients have been coming in late all day. The dentist is running behind schedule, too.

M: **Oh, that's a relief.**[8] I was nervous that I would have to rush. **I'll call you back when I'm about ten minutes away.**[9] That should make it easier to rearrange the schedule.

남: 안녕하세요, 제가 15분쯤 후로 스케일링 예약이 되어 있습니다만, 늦을 것 같아서요. 차량이 너무 막혀서, 제가 도착하려면 최소한 30분은 걸릴 것 같습니다.

여: 메이 데이 축제 때문에 막히는 모양이군요. 퍼레이드를 하느라 도로 몇 곳을 폐쇄해 놓는 바람에 환자분들이 하루 종일 늦게 도착하고 있는 상황입니다. 의사 선생님도 일정보다 늦어지고 있습니다.

남: 아, 그것 참 다행이군요. 서둘러야 해서 신경이 쓰였거든요. 한 10분 정도 남았을 때 다시 전화드리겠습니다. 그럼 일정을 다시 잡기가 보다 수월할 테니까요.

어휘 appointment (특히 업무 관련) 약속
stuck in traffic 교통이 막힌[정체된]
May Day 메이 데이: 서양에서 봄맞이 축제가 열리는 5월 1일
run behind schedule 일정보다 늦어지다   relief 안도, 안심
rush 서두르다   rearrange (일정 등을) 재조정하다

7. 여자는 교통 상황에 대해 뭐라고 말하고 있는가?
(A) 피할 수 있다.
(B) 축하 행사 때문에 나타난 현상이다.
(C) 지체를 유발하지는 않을 것이다.
(D) 곧 상황이 종료될 것이다.

해설 도로가 혼잡해 도착하려면 시간이 더 걸릴 것 같다고 남자가 말하자, 여자는 메이데이 축제(the May Day Festival)를 언급한 후, 퍼레이드 때문에 도로 몇 곳이 폐쇄되어(They had to shut down a few roads for the parade,) 환자들이 늦어지고 있다고 설명하고 있다. festival과 parade를 celebration으로 바꾸어 표현한 (B)가 정답이다.

8. 여자가 "의사 선생님도 일정보다 늦어지고 있습니다"라고 말할 때 의미하는 바는 무엇인가?
(A) 치과 의사가 예약된 진료 시간을 지키지 않았다.
(B) 남자가 다른 치과 의사에게 가봐야 한다.
(C) 사무실에 몇 가지 문제가 발생했다.
(D) 늦게 도착하는 남자 때문에 문제가 발생하지는 않을 것이다.

해설 도착이 늦어지는 것을 염려하는 남자에게 여자가 해 주고 있는 이 말은, 의사 역시 원래 예정보다 진료를 보는 속도가 늦어지고 있으니 좀 늦는 것에 대해 걱정을 할 필요가 없다는 의미를 담고 있다. 따라서 정답은 (D)가 된다.

9. 남자는 무엇을 하겠다고 말하는가?
(A) 지름길로 간다.
(B) 퍼레이드에 참가한다.
(C) 나중에 다시 전화를 한다.
(D) 치과 의사와 통화를 한다.

해설 대화 후반부에 남자는 병원으로부터 10분 정도 떨어진 거리에 도착하는 대로 다시 전화를 걸겠다(I'll call you back when I'm about ten minutes away,)고 말하고 있다. 따라서 정답은 (C)이다.

10-12

W: Hi, **I'm taking the local train bound for City Hall**,¹⁰ but I'm not sure which track number it's leaving from. The information isn't posted on the departure board or any of the monitors.

M: Let me see your ticket. You're departing at 8:30, and the track information usually isn't posted until one hour prior to departure. **The computer says that it'll board on track 11**,¹¹ but you'll still want to double-check the monitors.

W: Track 11? Oh, that's over there by the food court. I guess **I'll head over there and sit in the waiting room**.¹² Thank you so much for the information.

여: 안녕하세요, 제가 시청행 지역 열차를 타는데요, 기차가 몇 번 선로에서 출발하는지 잘 모르겠습니다. 안내 정보가 출발 게시판이나 다른 어떤 모니터에도 나와 있지 않아서요.

남: 제가 티켓을 좀 볼게요. 고객님께서는 8시 30분에 출발하는데요, 선로 정보는 보통 출발 1시간 전까지는 게시되지 않습니다. 컴퓨터 상으로는 11번 선로에서 탑승하는 것으로 되어 있습니다만 모니터를 다시 한 번 확인하시는 게 좋겠습니다.

여: 11번 선로요? 오, 저쪽 식당가 옆이군요. 저쪽으로 가서 대기실에 앉아 있어야겠습니다. 알려주셔서 정말 감사합니다.

어휘 take (기차・버스 등을) 타다   local 지역의   bound for ~행의
track 선로   leave from ~에서 출발하다   post 게시하다, 게재하다
departure board 출발 게시판
시간+prior to departure 출발 ~ 전   board 탑승하다
double-check 다시 한 번 확인하다   food court 푸드 코트, 식당가
head 가다, 향하다   waiting room 대기실

10. 대화 장소는 어디이겠는가?
(A) 기차역
(B) 버스 정류장
(C) 공항
(D) 회의장

해설 대화를 처음 시작하면서 여자가 I'm taking the local train bound for City Hall이라고 했으므로 정답은 (A)이다. 대화가 일어나는 장소나 대화의 주제에 대한 질문은 대화의 초반부에 언급되므로 항상 대화 앞부분을 잘 들어야 한다.

11. 남자는 여자를 위해 무엇을 하는가?
(A) 식사 쿠폰을 제공한다.
(B) 새 컴퓨터를 보여준다.
(C) 정보를 준다.
(D) 환불해 준다.

해설 남자가 여자를 위해 하는 일을 묻는 문제이므로 남자의 말에서 정답의 단서를 찾아야 한다. 남자가 The computer says that it'll board on track 11이라고 하면서 기차의 출발 선로를 알려주고 있으므로 정답은 (C)이다.

12. 여자는 다음에 무엇을 하겠는가?
(A) 대합실로 간다.   (B) 티켓을 구입한다.
(C) 식사값을 지불한다.   (D) 차량에 탑승한다.

해설 미래의 행동에 대한 질문은 대개 대화의 후반부에서 정답의 단서를 찾을 수 있다. 여자가 대화 마지막에 I'll head over there and sit in the waiting room이라고 했으므로 정답은 (A)이다.

13-15

W1: Excuse me, have you seen this morning's paper?
M: Hi, Ms. Jones. No, I haven't looked at it yet. Is there a problem?
W1: I'll say. Look at the article on page A7 about Rinkley Security.
M: Uh-oh.
W1: Right. **That photo is, um, the wrong person.**[14]
M: Caroline, **this is your article**[13], isn't it? What happened?
W2: Oh no. That photo was supposed to be printed with my story on a local farmer in tomorrow's newspaper.
W1: So the photos got mixed up?
W2: The photo editors must have swapped the pictures …
W1: Talk to them and find out what happened. In the meantime, **I'll start working on an apology to print in tomorrow's paper.**[15]

여1: 실례합니다. 오늘 아침 신문 보셨나요?
남: 안녕하세요, 존스 씨. 아뇨, 아직 안 봤습니다. 무슨 문제라도 있나요?
여1: 그렇습니다. 페이지 A7에 실린 린클리 보안 사에 대한 기사를 보세요.
남: 오, 이런.
여1: 그래요. 그 사진, 엉뚱한 사람이에요.
남: 캐롤라인, 이거 당신 기사 맞죠? 어찌 된 일입니까?
여2: 오, 이런. 그 사진은 내일 신문의 지역 농부에 관한 제 기사에 들어갈 것이었는데요.
여1: 그럼 사진이 뒤바뀌었다는 말인가요?
여2: 사진 담당 편집자들이 사진을 바꾼 게 분명해요…
여1: 그들에게 말해서 무슨 일이 일어난 건지 알아보도록 하세요. 나는 내일 신문에 실을 사과문을 작성할게요.

어휘 I'll say. 정말 그렇다.   article 기사
security 경비, 보안 cf. securities 증권
be supposed to부정사 ~하기로 되어 있다, ~할 예정이다
local 현지의, 그 지방의   get mixed up 뒤섞이다
swap 바꾸다, 교대로 하다   in the meantime 그러는 동안에
work on ~에 대해 작업하다   apology 사과 cf. apologize 사과하다

13. 화자들이 일하는 곳은 어디이겠는가?
(A) TV 방송국
(B) 포토 스튜디오
(C) 보안 회사
(D) 신문사

해설 페이지 A7에 실린 기사(the article on page A7), 당신 기사(this is your article.), 내일 신문에 실릴 지역 농부에 관한 제 기사(my story on a local farmer in tomorrow's newspaper), 내일 신문에 실을 사과문(an apology to print in tomorrow's paper) 등 대화 곳곳에서 신문 기사에 대한 내용이 등장하고 있다. 따라서 화자들이 일하는 곳이 신문사임을 알 수 있으므로 정답은 (D)이다.

14. 어떤 문제가 논의되고 있는가?
(A) 경비원에게 연락을 할 수가 없다.
(B) 신문이 배달되지 않았다.
(C) 이미지가 잘못 사용되었다.
(D) 농장이 문을 안 열었다.

해설 사진이 뒤바뀌는 바람에 기사에 엉뚱한 사진이 들어가는 사건이 발생한 상황이다. 대화에 등장하는 photo 대신 image를 사용해 표현한 (C)가 정답이다.

15. 내일은 어떤 일이 일어날 것인가?
(A) 한 회사에서 사과를 할 것이다.
(B) 고객들이 환불을 받게 될 것이다.
(C) 약속 시간이 지켜지지 않을 것이다.
(D) 제품들이 회수될 것이다.

해설 맨 마지막에 여자가 내일 신문에 실을 사과문 작성 작업을 시작하겠다 (I'll start working on an apology to print in tomorrow's paper.)고 말하고 있다. 즉 내일은 화자들이 일하는 신문사에서 사과문을 실을 것이 예상되므로 정답은 (A)이다.

16-18

M: Hi, **I'm wondering if you have a Lost and Found office here in the hotel.**[16] I was reading a tour guide in the lounge while charging my cell phone, and now **I can't find the charger for the batteries.**[17]

W: No one has brought any lost items up here to the front desk, but you might want to double check your guest room or ask the concierge by the coatroom.

M: OK, I'll try that.

W: I'll do my best to help you locate it. **Well, let me call the staff in the cafeteria.**[18] Maybe they found something.

남: 안녕하세요, 여기 호텔에 분실물 보관실이 있는지 궁금합니다. 제가 휴대폰을 충전하는 동안 휴게실에서 관광 안내책자를 읽고 있었는데 지금 제 충전기를 못 찾겠어요.

여: 아무도 여기 안내 데스크로 분실물을 가져오지 않았는데, 고객님 객실을 다시 한 번 확인하시거나 휴대품 보관소 옆에 있는 안내원에게 물어보시죠.

남: 네, 그렇게 해볼게요.

여: 저도 고객님께서 충전기를 찾으실 수 있도록 최선을 다해 도와드리겠습니다. 음, 제가 구내 식당에 있는 직원에게 전화를 해볼게요. 아마도 그들이 뭔가 찾았을 지도 몰라요.

어휘 lost and found office 분실물 보관실   lounge 휴게실
while ~ing ~하는 동안   charge 충전하다   charger 충전기
bring 가져오다   lost item 분실물
double check 다시 한 번 확인하다   concierge 안내원
coatroom 휴대품 보관소   do one's best 최선을 다하다
locate 발견하다, 찾다

16. 대화는 아마도 어디에서 일어나고 있는가?
(A) 호텔   (B) 도서관   (C) 출판사   (D) 의류점

해설 대화 장소는 대화 초반부에 언급되므로 시작 부분을 잘 들어야 한다. 남자가 I'm wondering if you have a Lost and Found office here in the hotel.이라고 했으므로 정답은 (A)이다.

17. 남자는 무엇을 잃어버렸는가?
(A) 휴대폰   (B) 지갑   (C) 충전기   (D) 지도

해설 남자가 잃어버린 물건에 대한 질문이므로 남자의 말에 초점을 맞추어야 한다. 남자가 I can't find the charger for the batteries라고 했으므로 정답은 (C)이다.

18. 여자는 아마도 다음에 무엇을 하겠는가?
(A) 남자에게 지도를 보여준다.
(B) 전화를 건다.
(C) 구내식당에 간다.
(D) 컴퓨터에 정보를 입력한다.

해설 여자가 다음에 할 일에 대한 질문인데, 향후 행동에 대한 언급은 후반부에 제시되는 경우가 많다. 여자가 대화 마지막에 Well, let me call the staff in the cafeteria.라고 했으므로 정답은 (B)이다.

19-21

M: Are you OK, Sheila? I heard you're feeling sick today.

W: Oh, thanks for asking, Rick. I'm fine, I just have allergies.

M: You should visit a clinic I go to on the other side of town. The doctor there helped me get over my allergies with just some changes to my diet.

W: Really? You've got to give me that doctor's name, then.

M: Sure, **I'll e-mail you his name and phone number.**[19] **His clinic closes right at five**[20], though, so you'll probably have to leave work early.

W: OK. Do you know who I should talk to about leaving early?

M: **Try Beth Parrent in Human Resources.**[21]

W: Thanks. I owe you one.

남: 괜찮아요, 쉴라? 오늘 몸이 안 좋다고 들었는데.

여: 오, 물어봐 줘서 고마워요, 릭. 괜찮아요, 알레르기가 좀 있을 뿐이에요.

남: 시내 반대쪽에 제가 다니는 병원에 꼭 가 보세요. 거기 의사가 내가 먹는 음식에 약간의 변화를 줬을 뿐인데 내가 알레르기를 이겨내는 데 도움이 되었거든요.

여: 정말요? 그럼 그 의사 이름을 좀 알려 주세요.

남: 물론이죠. 의사 이름과 전화번호를 이메일로 보내 드릴게요. 그런데 그 병원은 정각 5시에 문을 닫으니까 퇴근을 일찍 해야 할 겁니다.

여: 알겠어요. 일찍 퇴근하려면 누구에게 말을 해야 하는지 아세요?

남: 인사부의 베스 패런트에게 말해 보세요.

여: 고마워요. 이번에 신세 한 번 졌네요.

직원 전화번호	
에블린 피어스	+521
척 휘틀리	+522
베스 패런트	+523
타일러 웡	+524

어휘 allergy 알레르기   get over (질병 등에서) 회복하다, 극복하다
diet (어떤 사람이 일상적으로 취하는) 음식, 식습관
right (시간·위치 등을 나타내어) 정확히   Human Resources 인사부
owe A one A에게 한 차례 신세를 지다
directory 명부, 인명록, 전화번호부

19. 남자는 여자에게 무엇을 보내 주겠는가?
(A) 건강에 좋은 요리법
(B) 의사 이름
(C) 병원 주소
(D) 알레르기 약

해설 남자는 식이요법을 통해 자신의 알레르기를 치료해 준 의사의 이름과 전화번호를 여자에게 이메일로 보내 주겠다(I'll e-mail you his name and phone number.)고 했으므로 정답은 (B)이다.

20. 의사의 진료소에 대해 남자는 뭐라고 말하는가?
(A) 5시에 문을 닫는다.
(B) 그의 사무실 옆에 위치해 있다.
(C) 다음 주에 문을 연다.
(D) 비용이 저렴하다.

해설 병원이 정확히 5시에 문을 닫으므로(His clinic closes right at five,) 일찍 퇴근할 필요가 있다고 남자가 여자에게 말해 주고 있다. 따라서 정답은 (A)이다.

21. 도표를 보세요. 여자는 어떤 번호로 전화를 걸겠는가?
(A) 521   (B) 522   (C) 523   (D) 524

해설 여자가 조퇴를 하려면 누구에게 말해야 하냐고 남자에게 묻자, 남자는 인사부의 베스 패런트에게 말해 보라고(Try Beth Parrent in Human Resources.) 대답하고 있다. 도표에서 Beth Parrent의 내선 번호는 +523이므로 정답은 (C)이다.

UNIT 13 광고/방송

어휘 및 표현 점검 본책_p. 122

1. inconvenience   2. don't forget that
3. special offer   4. discount   5. stay tuned

청취 집중 훈련 1 본책_p. 123

1. blowout / 60 / popular / Whether / replacement / save / accessories / located / open / weekend
2. weather update / current temperature / light winds / high temperatures / No snow / outdoor plants / cover them up / Coming up / update for / Stay tuned

청취 집중 훈련 2 본책_p. 124

1. (A) 2. (B) 3. (A) 4. (B) 5. (B) 6. (A)

1-2

1. 누가 선프로텍트를 사용할 수 있는가?
(A) 모든 사람   (B) 성인들만

2. 선프로텍트는 어디에서 구입할 수 있는가?
(A) 온라인으로   (B) 대부분의 슈퍼마켓에서

It's important that you protect your skin every day. SunProtect sun lotions can be used for people of all ages from young children to adults. SunProtect sun lotions are set at $10.99, so you don't have to shop around for cheaper lotions. SunProtect is available at most supermarkets.

매일 피부를 보호하는 것이 중요합니다. 선프로텍트 햇빛 차단 로션은 어린이부터 성인까지 모든 연령이 이용할 수 있습니다. 선프로텍트 햇빛 차단 로션은 10달러 99센트이라서 더 싼 로션을 찾기 위해 주변을 돌아다닐 필요가 없습니다. 선프로텍트는 대부분의 슈퍼마켓에서 구입하실 수 있습니다.

어휘 protect 보호하다   use 사용하다   adult 성인
be set at+금액 (금액)으로 정해져 있다   shop 쇼핑하다   cheap 싼
available 이용 가능한, 구입할 수 있는   most 대부분의

3-4

3. 어떤 프로그램을 알리고 있는가?
(A) 여행 쇼   (B) 요리 쇼

4. 프로그램은 언제 방송될 것인가?
(A) 목요일   (B) 금요일

This week on PLN Travel, we will cover Bulgaria. We'll show you all that Bulgaria has to offer. Boasting nine UNESCO heritage sites, Bulgaria is becoming a popular tourist destination these days. To find out more about this beautiful country, join us on Friday at 7 P.M. only on PLN.

저희는 이번 주 PLN 트래블에서 불가리아를 다룹니다. 저희는 불가리아가 제공할 수 있는 모든 것을 보여드리겠습니다. 아홉 곳의 유네스코 문화유산을 자랑하는 불가리아는 요즘 인기 있는 관광지가 되고 있습니다. 이 아름다운 나라에 대해 더 많이 알고 싶으시면 오직 PLN에서 금요일 저녁 7시에 저희와 함께해 주세요.

어휘 travel 여행(하다)   cover 다루다, 보도하다   boast 자랑하다
UNESCO 유네스코   heritage site 문화유산
tourist destination 관광지   find out 알아보다

5-6

5. 매튜스 씨는 토요일에 사람들에게 무엇을 하라고 제안하는가?
(A) 우산 가져오기   (B) 야외에서 즐기기

6. 일요일 밤에 무슨 일이 있겠는가?
(A) 비가 내릴 것이다.   (B) 더욱 따뜻해질 것이다.

> I'm Sarah Matthews with the weather report for this weekend. Saturday is the perfect day to plan outdoor activities. However, there's an 80 percent chance of rain on Sunday. The rain will continue into Monday morning and start to clear up Monday afternoon.

저는 이번 주말 일기예보를 전하는 사라 매튜스입니다. 토요일은 야외 활동을 계획할 수 있는 최적의 날입니다. 그러나 일요일에는 비 올 확률이 80%입니다. 비는 월요일 아침까지 계속되다가 월요일 오후부터 개기 시작하겠습니다.

어휘 weather report 일기예보   plan 계획하다
outdoor activities 야외 활동
a ~ percent chance of rain[snow] ~ 퍼센트의 비[눈] 올 확률
continue into ~까지 계속되다   clear up 개다

청취 집중 훈련 3   본책 _ p. 125

```
1. (B)   2. (C)   3. (B)   4. (A)   5. (A)   6. (D)
```

1. 어떤 보험이 광고되고 있는가?
(A) 자동차   (B) 주택
(C) 생명   (D) 여행

해설 키워드인 insurance(보험)를 보고 보험 광고라는 것을 알 수 있다. 이야기 내용이 광고일 경우 광고 상품이나 서비스를 이야기의 초반부에 제시하므로 앞부분을 잘 들어야 한다. 첫 문장인 It's important that you have good insurance for your home.을 통해 (B)가 정답이라는 것을 알 수 있다.

2. 라이트 보험에 대해 언급된 내용은 무엇인가?
(A) 신입 직원을 채용 중이다.
(B) 무료 견적서를 제공한다.
(C) 전국적으로 지점을 보유하고 있다.
(D) 최근에 유럽에 새 사무실을 열었다.

해설 질문에 회사명(Wright Insurance)이 등장했으므로 마음속으로 미리 회사명을 읽어두어야 한다. 회사는 회사명(Wright Insurance)이나 the company 또는 we로 나타내므로 이런 단어가 쓰인 문장에 회사에 관한 내용이 들어 있게 된다. 여기서는 회사를 we로 나타내어 We have 100 locations across the nation이라고 했다.

1-2

> It's important that **you have good insurance for your home.**[1] Whether you live alone or with a large family, at Wright Insurance, we have the plan that's right for you. Just call one of our employees at 212-4555 and we will find the best policy to protect your home. Wright Insurance offers the best protection at prices you can afford. So what are you waiting for? Pick up the phone and make your appointment today. **We have 100 locations across the nation.**[2]

고객님 집을 위한 좋은 보험을 갖고 있는 것이 중요합니다. 고객님께서 혼자 사시든, 대가족과 함께 사시든, 라이트 보험에서는 고객님께 딱 맞게 설계해 드립니다. 212-4555로 저희 직원 중 한 명에게 전화 주시면 고객님 집을 보호할 수 있는 최상의 보험 증권을 찾아드리겠습니다. 라이트 보험은 부담 없는 가격으로 최상의 보호를 제공해드립니다. 그러므로 무엇을 망설이십니까? 오늘 수화기를 들고 약속을 잡으세요. 저희는 전국에 걸쳐 100개 지점을 갖추고 있습니다.

어휘 insurance 보험   whether A or B A이든 B이든 간에   alone 혼자
a large family 대가족   employee 직원   policy 보험 증권
protection 보호   make an appointment 만날 약속을 하다
location 지점   across the nation 전국에 걸쳐

3. 교통부는 무엇을 할 것인가?
(A) 도로 포장
(B) 가드레일 보수
(C) 인도 만들기
(D) 신호등 설치

해설 질문에 나온 transportation department는 본문에서 분명히 언급될 것이기 때문에 문제를 볼 때 미리 속으로 읽어두면 발음으로 듣기가 훨씬 수월해진다. 첫 번째 문장에서 교통부가 가드레일을 수리할 것(will be repairing guardrails)이라고 언급하고 있으므로 정답은 (B)가 된다.

4. 화자는 통근자들에게 어떤 조언을 하는가?
(A) 평상시보다 일찍 나서기
(B) 오른쪽 차선 유지
(C) 대체 도로 이용
(D) 대중교통 이용

해설 조언이나 권유를 할 때는 〈주어 + may[might] want to + 동사원형〉, 〈주어 + should + 동사원형〉, 〈주어 + recommend〉, 또는 〈주어 + be encouraged[asked, required] to + 동사원형〉의 구조를 흔히 사용한다. 여기서는 should를 써서 Commuters ~ should leave for work earlier than usual.이라고 하고 있으므로 정답은 (A)이다.

3-4

The Clinton Department of Transportation will be repairing guardrails³ along Route 86. Work on the guardrails is scheduled to take place between 6 A.M. and 2 P.M. during the week beginning on Monday March 3. **Commuters planning to take Route 86 should leave for work earlier than usual.**⁴ There may be temporary traffic delays, as the right lane will be closed throughout the morning and afternoon. The Department of Transportation hopes to complete the guardrail repairs by late March if the weather remains favorable.

클린턴 교통부는 86번 도로변의 가드레일을 수리할 것입니다. 가드레일에 대한 작업은 3월 3일 월요일에 시작해 주중에 오전 6시와 오후 2시 사이에 있을 예정입니다. 86번 도로를 이용할 통근자들은 평상시보다 일찍 직장으로 나서야 합니다. 오른쪽 차선이 아침과 오후 내내 폐쇄될 것이기 때문에 일시적인 교통 체증이 있을 겁니다. 교통부는 날씨가 계속 좋다면 3월 말까지 가드레일 수리를 완료하고자 합니다.

어휘 department of transportation 교통부 repair 수리하다
guardrail (도로의) 가드레일 route 도로, 노선
take place 열리다, 일어나다 take (길을) 이용하다, (어떤 길로) 가다
leave 나서다, 떠나다 than usual 평상시보다
temporary 일시적인 throughout ~ 내내, 줄곧
complete 완료하다 favorable (날씨가) 좋은

5. 비는 언제 그칠 것으로 예상되는가?
(A) 아침
(B) 저녁
(C) 내일 아침
(D) 내일 저녁

해설 일기예보는 일반적으로 〈방송사 언급 → 현재의 날씨 → 날씨와 관련된 조언 → 다음 프로그램 소개〉의 순서대로 진행된다. 따라서 방송의 앞부분을 잘 들으면 날씨에 대한 정보를 알 수 있다. 여기서도 방송 앞부분에서 all the rain we've been having recently will finally stop this morning이라고 했으므로 정답은 (A)이다.

6. 다음으로 무엇을 듣겠는가?
(A) 건강 뉴스
(B) 요리 조언
(C) 교통 최신 정보
(D) 비즈니스 조언

해설 방송 마지막에 the area's number one program giving tips for small businesses라고 했으므로 정답은 (D)이다. 날씨나 교통 방송의 경우, 방송의 끝부분에 다음 프로그램에 대한 간략한 소개를 하는 경우가 많다.

5-6

This is a WMQ radio morning weather update. Well, **all the rain we've been having recently will finally stop this morning.**⁵ That's good news for people planning to do gardening work or outdoor activities. However, be careful if you're hiking, as the ground will be soft and many walking paths will be slippery from fallen leaves. Those who are flying should anticipate some delays due to fog and poor visibility around the airport. **Coming up, we'll have "You, the Entrepreneur," the area's number one program giving tips for small businesses.**⁶ Stay tuned.

WMQ 라디오 오전 날씨 정보입니다. 음, 최근에 계속 내리던 비가 드디어 오늘 아침에 그치겠습니다. 정원일이나 야외 활동을 계획하시는 분들에게는 좋은 소식입니다. 그렇지만 땅이 무르고 많은 산책로가 낙엽들로 인해 미끄럽기 때문에 하이킹을 하시려면 조심하셔야겠습니다. 비행기를 이용하시는 분들은 공항 주변의 안개와 짧은 가시거리 때문에 어느 정도 지연을 예상하시는 게 좋겠습니다. 다음은 소기업체를 위한 조언을 제공해 드리는 지역 최고의 프로그램 '당신, 사업가'가 이어집니다. 채널 고정해 주세요.

어휘 weather update 날씨 정보 gardening work 정원일
outdoor activities 야외 활동 soft 무른 walking path 산책로
slippery 미끄러운 fallen leaves 낙엽 anticipate 예상하다
delay 지연 due to ~ 때문에 fog 안개
poor visibility 짧은 가시거리 come up 이어지다, 나오다
entrepreneur 기업가 tip 조언 stay tuned 채널을 고정하다

실전 감각 익히기 본책 _ p. 126–127

1. (B) 2. (C) 3. (D) 4. (B) 5. (D) 6. (C)
7. (A) 8. (C) 9. (A) 10. (D) 11. (C) 12. (A)

1-3

Attention customers. Did you know you could save this weekend on **ABC Books' annual clearance sale?**¹ **On Friday, Saturday, and Sunday,**² **you can save as much as 75 percent off**³ all regularly priced new and used books. ABC Books has to clear our shelves for inventory, so we're marking down books anywhere from 35 to 75 percent off. The clearance sale will be at both south and downtown locations, so take advantage of the savings. And don't forget, we'll be closed on Monday for inventory. Thank you for shopping and have a nice day.

고객 여러분 주목해주세요. 이번 주말에 ABC 북스의 연례 재고 정리 할인으로 돈을 아끼실 수 있다는 것을 아셨습니까? 금요일, 토요일, 그리고 일요일에 여러분들은 모든 정상 가격의 신간과 중고 서적에 대해 최대 75% 할인을 받을 수 있습니다. ABC 북스는 재고 정리를 위해 선반을 비워야 해서 35%에서 75%까지 도서 가격을 인하 중입니다. 재고 정리 할인은 남부와 시내 지점 모두에서 진행되니 할인을 이용하시기 바랍니다. 그리고 재고 정리를 위해 월요일에는 문을 닫는다는 것을 잊지 마세요. 쇼핑 감사 드리고요 좋은 하루 되세요.

어휘 attention + 사람 ~ 여러분 주목해주세요 save 절약하다, 아끼다
annual 연례의   clearance sale 재고 정리 할인
as much as (양으로) ~ 만큼이나   regularly priced 정상 가격의
clear ~를 비우다, 치우다   shelf 선반   inventory 재고(품)
mark down 인하하다   anywhere from A to B
A와 B 사이 어느 정도로   location 지점
take advantage of ~을 이용하다   saving 절약

1. 어디에서 이 광고를 들을 수 있겠는가?
(A) 신발 가게
(B) 서점
(C) 전자제품 가게
(D) 백화점

해설 광고의 경우 서두에 광고 상품이나 광고 회사명이 언급된다. 지문 초반부에 나온 ABC Books' annual clearance sale을 통해 광고하는 회사가 ABC Books라는 것을 알 수 있다. 회사명에 Books라는 말이 있으므로 이 광고는 서점에서 들을 수 있다.

2. 할인은 언제 끝나는가?
(A) 금요일
(B) 토요일
(C) 일요일
(D) 월요일

해설 할인 기간으로는 날짜나 요일을 언급하므로 지문 중에 날짜나 요일이 등장하는 부분에 정답의 단서가 있게 마련이다. 광고에서 On Friday, Saturday, and Sunday라고 했으므로 할인 마지막 날은 (C) 일요일이라는 것을 알 수 있다.

3. 고객들은 최대 얼마나 절약할 수 있는가?
(A) 15퍼센트
(B) 35퍼센트
(C) 55퍼센트
(D) 75퍼센트

해설 할인율은 대개 금액이나 퍼센트로 나오므로 〈숫자 + dollars〉 또는 〈숫자 + 퍼센트〉로 언급되는 부분에 초점을 맞추어야 한다. 광고에서 you can save as much as 75 percent off라고 했으므로 정답은 (D) 75퍼센트이다. 또한 뒤쪽에서 anywhere from 35 to 75 percent off라는 말로 최대 할인율이 75퍼센트라는 것을 다시 한 번 언급해주고 있다.

4-6

Hello, listeners, this is **Michelle Kim with your weather forecast**.[4] Today has already been the coldest day so far this year, and it may become one of the coldest on record. The high today was -10 degrees, and temperatures are expected to keep dropping after sunset. They could drop **as low as -25 degrees Celsius**[5] by morning. If you have pets, bring them indoors tonight, and keep your heaters on to avoid broken pipes. The roads will probably be more crowded than usual tomorrow with many commuters opting to drive instead of using public transportation. So, **leave a little early**[6] if you want to drive.

청취자 여러분 안녕하세요. 저는 일기예보를 전해드리는 미쉘 김입니다. 오늘은 올해 중 벌써 가장 추운 날이었는데 아마도 기록상 제일 추운 날이 될 것 같습니다. 오늘 최고 기온은 영하 10도이고 기온은 일몰 후 계속 떨어질 전망입니다. 아침에는 영하 25도까지 떨어질 가능성이 있습니다. 애완동물이 있으시면 오늘 밤 실내로 데려가시고 파이프 파열을 피하기 위해 난방기를 켜놓으십시오. 도로는 아마 대중교통 이용보다는 차를 몰고 출근하려는 많은 통근자들로 인해 내일 평상시보다 더 혼잡할 것 같습니다. 그러니 운전을 하시려면 조금 일찍 나서시기 바랍니다.

어휘 weather forecast 일기예보   on record 기록상   high 최고 기온
degree 도   temperature 기온   drop 떨어지다   sunset 일몰
Celsius 섭씨   pet 애완동물   keep ~ on ~을 켜놓다
avoid 피하다   crowded 혼잡한   commuter 통근자
opt to 부정사 ~할 것을 선택하다
public transportation 대중교통

4. 김 씨는 아마도 어디에서 근무하겠는가?
(A) 교통 시스템   (B) 라디오 뉴스 프로그램
(C) 지역 신문   (D) 도시 지하철

해설 김 씨가 키워드이므로 내용 중 김 씨가 언급되는 부분에 주목해야 한다. 첫 문장인 Hello, listeners, this is Michelle Kim with your weather forecast.에서 김 씨는 라디오의 날씨 방송을 하는 사람인 것을 알 수 있으므로 정답은 (B)이다. 영어에서는 사람 이름이 처음 언급될 경우 이름 뒤에 직책이나 소속 기관 등을 언급하는 것이 일반적이다.

5. 기온은 얼마나 낮게 떨어질 것으로 예상되는가?
(A) 영하 10도   (B) 영하 15도
(C) 영하 20도   (D) 영하 25도

해설 보기에 숫자가 있으므로 청취를 할 때 숫자가 언급되는 부분에 주목해야 한다. 중간쯤에 as low as -25 degrees Celsius라고 나오므로 정답이 (D)인 것을 알 수 있다. 문제나 보기에 숫자가 있는데 10이상의 숫자라면 속으로 미리 발음을 해놓는 것이 좋다. 10 이하인 경우는 발음이 짧아서 잘 들리지만 10 이상이 되면 발음이 길어져서 다소 복잡하게 들리기 때문이다.

6. 청취자들에게 어떤 조언을 하고 있는가?
(A) 애완동물을 밖에 내놓기
(B) 난방기 끄기
(C) 직장으로 일찍 나서기
(D) 차에 스노우 타이어 달기

해설 요청 사항이나 조언은 이야기의 후반부에 나오는 경우가 많다. 즉, 문제에 be advised, be asked, 또는 be required라는 말이 있으면 정답의 단서가 이야기의 후반부에 들어 있을 확률이 높다. 여기서도 제일 마지막에 나온 So, leave a little early if you want to drive.라는 말을 통해 정답이 (C)라는 것을 알 수 있다.

8. 도시에서 나가려는 사람들에게 무엇을 조언하고 있는가?
(A) 파크웨이로 가기   (B) 대중교통 이용하기
(C) 대체 도로로 가기   (D) 아침에 일찍 나서기

해설 일반적으로 조언이나 권유 등은 〈주어 + may[might] want to + 동사원형〉, 〈주어 + should + 동사원형〉, 〈주어 + recommend〉, 또는 〈주어 + be encouraged[asked, required] to + 동사원형〉의 구조를 많이 쓰게 된다. 여기서는 recommend를 써서 we recommend an alternative route라고 권하고 있으므로 (C)가 정답이다.

9. 몇 시간 후에 무슨 일이 생길 것으로 예상할 수 있는가?
(A) 지체가 훨씬 더 길어질 것이다.
(B) 교통이 풀릴 것이다.
(C) 도로로 들어가는 데 시간이 오래 걸릴 것이다.
(D) 행사가 열릴 것이다.

해설 문제에 나온 expect라는 동사를 먼저 보고 이야기에서 똑같은 단어나 유사 의미의 단어가 언급될 때 그 부분에 초점을 맞춰 들으면 정답을 쉽게 찾을 수 있다. 지문에서는 똑같은 단어인 expect를 써서 We expect this to just get worse~ 라고 했다. 즉, 교통 혼잡 시간대(rush hour)에 다가가면서 지체가 심해질 것이라고 예상하고 있으므로 (A)가 정답이다.

7-9

Here's the traffic for this afternoon. We've got massive delays on the Parkway heading out of the city. Two southbound lanes have been closed **because of a car accident**,[7] but the northbound side is running smoothly. For those of you planning to get out of the city, **we recommend an alternative route**[8] on Austin Street. It looks like it will be taking everyone quite a while to get anywhere outside of the city tonight. **We expect this to just get worse as we come up on rush hour**,[9] and we'll be keeping you posted on developments.

이제 오늘 오후의 교통 상황입니다. 도시 밖으로 향하는 파크웨이에서 지체가 심합니다. 교통사고로 인해 두 개의 남쪽행 차선이 폐쇄되었습니다만, 북쪽행은 흐름이 순조롭습니다. 도시를 벗어나려는 사람들은 오스틴 가에서 대체 도로를 이용해주시길 권해드립니다. 오늘 밤은 어딘든 도시 밖으로 나가는 데에는 시간이 꽤 걸릴 것 같습니다. 이런 상황은 교통 혼잡 시간이 다가오면서 더욱 더 심해질 전망이며, 계속 여러분께 진행 상황을 알려드리겠습니다.

어휘 massive 대대적인, 심한   head out of ~ 밖으로 향하다
southbound 남쪽행   lane 차선
get out of the city 도시에서 벗어나다
alternative route 대체 도로   quite a while 꽤 오랫동안
get worse 더 나빠지다
come up on rush hour 교통 혼잡 시간에 다가가다
keep + 사람 + posted[updated, informed] ~에게 계속 정보를 주다
development 진행 상황

7. 지연이 되는 이유는 무엇인가?
(A) 자동차 사고   (B) 마라톤 경주
(C) 도로 공사   (D) 악천후

해설 이유를 묻는 질문은 '~ 때문에'를 뜻하는 접속사(because, since, as)나 전치사(because of, owing to, due to) 뒤에 정답의 단서가 있을 가능성이 아주 높다. 여기서도 Two southbound lanes ~ because of a car accident라는 말 속에 정답이 제시되었다.

10-12

In celebration of the start of spring, **Paul's Sporting Goods is having a sale**[10] on all hiking goods and equipment. **From now until March 31**,[12] you can save 25 to 50 percent off. Backpacks are on sale from $4.99 to $69.99, hiking boots start at $49.99, and you can save up to 50 percent off **selected sunglasses**.[11] The spring sale is good at all Paul's Sporting Goods locations. For more information, visit our Web site at www.paulssports.com.

봄맞이를 기념하여 폴 스포츠 용품은 모든 하이킹 용품과 장비에 대해 할인 판매를 하고 있습니다. 지금부터 3월 31일까지 25%에서 50%까지 할인을 받으실 수 있습니다. 배낭은 4.99달러에서 69.99달러에 판매 중이고 하이킹 부츠는 49.99달러부터 있으며 일부 선별된 선글라스는 최대 50% 할인을 해드립니다. 봄맞이 할인은 모든 폴 스포츠 용품점에서 유효합니다. 더 많은 정보를 원하시면 저희 웹사이트 www.paulssports.com을 방문해주세요.

어휘 in celebration of ~을 기념하여
have a sale on ~에 대해 할인 판매하다   goods 물품, 상품
save 절약하다   backpack 배낭   up to 최대 ~까지
selected 선택된, 정해진   good 유효한   location 지점

10. 무엇이 할인되는가?
(A) 신발   (B) 액세서리
(C) 전자제품   (D) 스포츠 용품

해설 광고 상품이나 광고 회사명은 소비자를 주목시키기 위해 광고 초반에 언급되는 경우가 많다. 여기서도 도입부에 Paul's Sporting Goods is having a sale이라고 했으므로 (D) 스포츠 용품이 할인된다는 것을 알 수 있다.

11. 화자는 어떤 품목을 언급하고 있는가?
(A) 재킷   (B) 공책
(C) 선글라스   (D) 정장 구두

해설 보기에 네 가지 품목이 제시되어 있을 경우 적어도 한 번이라도 미리 읽어두어야 한다. 어떤 단어가 지문에 언급될지는 모르지만 한 번이라도 눈으로 보면서 읽어둔 단어는 친숙해져서 좀 더 또렷하게 들린다. 여기서는 본문에 selected sunglasses라고 했으므로 정답은 (C)이다.

12. 할인은 언제 끝나는가?
(A) 3월   (B) 4월
(C) 5월   (D) 6월

해설 할인 기간은 요일, 날짜, 또는 〈from ~ to[until] ~〉 또는 〈until + 시점〉으로 제시되는 경우가 많다. 여기서도 할인 기간을 From now until March 31라고 했으므로 정답은 (A) 3월이다.

UNIT 14 안내 방송 / 소개

어휘 및 표현 점검   본책_p. 130

1. held   2. prohibited   3. sign up for
4. a great honor   5. introduce

청취 집중 훈련 1   본책_p. 131

1. Attention / present / seminar / new / attendance / encouraged / Following / necessary / recommended / sign up
2. our guest speaker / well known as / innovative changes / travels around the country / in the workplace / recently wrote / published a book / business bestseller's / give us a speech / warm welcome

청취 집중 훈련 2   본책_p. 132

1. (A)   2. (A)   3. (B)   4. (A)   5. (B)   6. (A)

1-2

1. 축제에 대해 무엇이 언급되었는가?
(A) 매년 열린다.   (B) 한 주간 열린다.

2. 넬슨 씨는 누구겠는가?
(A) 영화 제작자   (B) 행사 기획자

Welcome to the annual Andover Culture Festival. We have lots of great events planned over the next three weekends, including this week's independent film festival. Our first film screening tonight is the documentary film *A Photographer's Life*, produced by local resident Ray Nelson.

연례 앤도버 문화 축제에 오신 걸 환영합니다. 이번 주의 독립 영화 축제를 포함해 앞으로 3주간에 걸쳐 많은 훌륭한 행사들이 준비되어 있습니다. 오늘밤 첫 번째 상영 영화는 지역 주민인 레이 넬슨이 제작한 다큐멘터리 영화 〈어느 사진작가의 인생〉입니다.

어휘 annual 연례의   lots of 많은   plan 계획하다
over ~ 동안, ~에 걸쳐   including ~을 포함해
independent film 독립 영화   screening 상영
photographer 사진작가   produce 제작하다   local 지역의
resident 주민

3-4

3. 무엇을 알리고 있는가?
(A) 두 회사가 합병될 것이다.   (B) 회사 CEO가 은퇴할 것이다.

4. 프라임 솔루션스는 어떤 종류의 회사인가?
(A) 컨설팅 회사   (B) 보험 회사

I have an announcement to make. Our founder and CEO of Prime Solutions Justin Yoon will formally retire in December. Mr. Yoon founded the company 28 years ago. Under Mr. Yoon's leadership, Prime Solutions became the leading consultation firm. Vice president Dale Montvale will replace Mr. Yoon.

안내 말씀이 있습니다. 저희 프라임 솔루션스의 설립자이자 CEO인 저스틴 윤이 12월에 공식적으로 은퇴를 하십니다. 윤 사장님은 28년 전에 회사를 설립하셨습니다. 윤 사장님의 지도력 하에서 프라임 솔루션스는 선도적인 컨설팅 회사가 되었습니다. 데일 몬트베일 부사장이 윤 사장님의 후임자가 될 것입니다.

어휘 have an announcement to make 안내 사항이 있다
founder 설립자 (*cf*. found 설립하다)   formally 공식적으로
retire 은퇴하다   under one's leadership ~의 지도력 하에서
leading 선도적인   consultation firm 컨설팅 회사
vice president 부사장   replace 대신하다

5-6

5. 이 안내 방송을 어디에서 들을 수 있겠는가?
(A) 전시관에서   (B) 개관식에서

6. 존 달시는 누구인가?
(A) 시장   (B) 기업가

> Welcome to the grand reopening of the Buckley Center. First, I'd like to take the time to thank Pitney and Sommers for their donations to the center. The City of Greenville was also instrumental in remodeling the center. With that in mind, please give a warm welcome to our Mayor, John Darcy.

버클리 센터의 재개관에 오신 것을 환영합니다. 먼저 저는 이 시간을 빌어 본 센터에 기부를 해주신 피트니와 소머스에게 감사의 말씀을 전하고 싶습니다. 그린빌 시 또한 센터를 리모델링 하는 데 도움을 주셨습니다. 이 점을 염두에 두고 우리의 존 달시 시장님을 반갑게 맞아주시길 바랍니다.

어휘
grand reopening 재개관
take the time to부정사 시간을 내서 ~하다   donation 기부(금)
instrumental in ~하는 데 도움이 되는
with ~ in mind ~을 염두에 둔 채
give a warm welcome to ~를 반갑게 맞이하다

청취 집중 훈련 3   본책_p. 133

| 1. (A)   2. (B)   3. (D)   4. (B)   5. (C)   6. (C) |

1-2

1. 안내 방송의 목적은 무엇인가?
(A) 다가오는 행사를 검토하기 위해
(B) 일정 변경을 알리기 위해
(C) 초청 연사를 소개하기 위해
(D) 박물관 개관을 알리기 위해

해설 안내 방송의 목적은 이야기의 초반에 등장하므로 앞부분을 잘 들어야 한다. 여기서도 안내 방송을 시작하면서 Everyone, please listen while I review a couple of important events라고 했으므로 정답은 (A)이다.

2. 화자가 "엄격하게 초대자 명단을 관리해야 합니다"라고 말할 때 의미하는 바는 무엇인가?
(A) 우리는 제때 초대자 명단을 제출해야 한다.
(B) 초대장을 가진 사람만이 미술관에 들어와야 한다.
(C) 우리는 새로운 회원을 받아들여야 한다.
(D) 초대자 명단이 6월 8일 전에 작성되어야 한다.

해설 제시문 바로 앞에서 이 특별 행사는 초대장이 있어야 한다(This particular function is by invitation only)고 했고 이어서 we must be sure to maintain a strict guest list라고 했다. 그러므로 문맥상 제시문은 초대장이 있는 사람만 미술관에 받아들여야 한다는 의미이므로 정답은 (B)이다.

> Everyone, please listen **while I review a couple of important events**[1] for the upcoming month. On Friday, June 8, the Toby Erickson exhibit will begin. Mr. Erickson will come to the gallery two days prior to the exhibit debut to set up the display. On the following weekend, the McGilligan Society will host their annual art social here at the Windmere Museum. **This particular function is by invitation only**,[2] so we must be sure to maintain a strict guest list. As the dates draw near, I will review more specific procedures. Thank you for listening.

여러분, 제가 다음 달에 있을 두 가지 중요한 행사를 검토하는 동안 경청해 주시기 바랍니다. 6월 8일 금요일에 토비 에릭슨 전시회가 시작됩니다. 에릭슨 씨는 전시물을 설치하기 위해 전시 개시일 이틀 전에 미술관에 오실 겁니다. 그 다음 주말에는 맥길리건 학회가 이곳 윈드미어 박물관에서 연례 미술 친목회를 열 것입니다. 이 특별 행사는 단지 초대장이 있는 사람만이 입장이 가능하므로 엄격하게 초대자 명단을 관리해야 합니다. 날짜가 가까워지면 제가 더욱 구체적인 절차를 검토하도록 하겠습니다. 경청해 주셔서 감사합니다.

어휘
review 검토하다   a couple of 두 가지의
upcoming 다가오는, 다음의   exhibit 전시회; 전시하다
gallery 미술관   prior to ~에 앞서   debut 첫 출연, 첫 등장
set up 설치하다   following 다음의   society 학회
host 주최하다, 개최하다   annual 연례의   social 친목회
particular 특정한   function 행사
by invitation only 초대장이 있는 사람만을 위한
maintain 유지하다, 관리하다   strict 엄격한   guest list 초대자 명단
draw near 가까워지다, 다가오다   specific 구체적인
procedure 절차

3-4

3. 로건 씨는 최근에 무엇을 했는가?
(A) 상을 받았다.
(B) 책을 썼다.
(C) 새로운 제품을 디자인했다.
(D) 라디오 토크쇼를 시작했다.

해설 질문에 Ms. Logan이라는 고유명사가 있으므로 속으로 미리 발음해둔 다음, 이 말이 나오는 부분을 집중해서 들어야 한다. 지문에서 She recently started her own radio talk show라고 했는데 she가 Ms. Logan을 가리키므로 정답은 (D)이다. 이 경우처럼 앞에 나온 사람 이름이나 사물이 대명사로 처리된 문장에서 정답의 단서가 언급될 수도 있음을 유의해야 한다.

4. 청자들에게 강의 후 무엇을 하라고 권장하는가?
(A) 온라인 상점에서 쇼핑
(B) 워크숍 참석
(C) 회사 CEO 만나기
(D) 양식 작성

해설 당부나 요청 사항은 대개 이야기의 후반부에 등장하는 경우가 많다. 여기서도 Please stay after the speech, as we plan to break up into small groups and participate in workshops.이라고 하면서 워크숍 참석을 권장하고 있다.

> Good evening. Tonight's closing speech will be delivered by Donna Logan, an international authority on marketing and innovation. Ms. Logan helps companies create new products and services. **She recently started her own radio talk show**[3] in which she discusses innovation issues with top CEOs. In just a moment she'll speak to us on the entire process of bringing products to the market. **Please stay after the speech, as we plan to break up into small groups and participate in workshops.**[4] OK, now, let's welcome Ms. Logan to the podium.

안녕하세요. 오늘 밤 마무리 연설은 마케팅과 혁신의 국제적 권위자인 도나 로건이 할 것입니다. 로건 씨는 회사들이 새로운 제품과 서비스를 만들어 내는 데 도움을 줍니다. 그녀는 최근에 최고의 CEO들과 혁신 문제를 논의하는 자신의 라디오 토크쇼를 시작했습니다. 잠시 후 그녀는 상품을 시장에 출시하는 전체 과정에 대해 말씀해 주실 겁니다. 저희는 작은 그룹으로 나눠서 워크숍에 참여할 것이기 때문에 연설이 끝난 후 남아주시기 바랍니다. 좋습니다. 이제 로건 씨를 연단으로 모시겠습니다.

어휘 deliver a closing speech 마무리 연설을 하다
authority 대가, 권위자 innovation 혁신
help+A(목적어)+(to)+동사원형 A가 ~하는 것을 돕다
recently 최근에 in just a moment 잠시 후에
entire 전체의 bring A(목적어) to the market A를 시장에 내놓다
break up into ~로 나누다 participate in ~에 참여하다
podium 연단

5-6

5. 연설의 목적은 무엇인가?
(A) 새로운 영업 콘테스트를 설명하기 위해
(B) 연간 매출액에 대해 논의하기 위해
(C) 한 직원의 공로를 인정하기 위해
(D) 새로운 공석을 언급하기 위해

해설 연설의 목적은 연설의 초반부에 언급되므로 항상 처음 시작하는 부분을 잘 들어야 한다. 연설의 첫 문장에서 Every year, Hanford Industries recognizes one employee라고 했으므로 정답은 (C)이다.

6. 쳉 씨는 얼마나 오랫동안 근무했는가?
(A) 2년간
(B) 5년간
(C) 10년간
(D) 20년간

해설 보기에 숫자가 있을 경우, 그 숫자들 중에서 어떤 것이 본문에서 언급되는지를 확인해야 한다. 보기 (C)의 숫자 10이 Ms. Cheng started work here 10 years ago에서 나오므로 정답은 (C)이다. 근무연수를 말할 때 〈사람+joined[started work]+기간+ago〉 또는 〈사람+has been with us for+기간〉으로 나타낸다는 것을 알아두자.

> Every year, **Hanford Industries recognizes one employee**[5] who consistently goes above and beyond the call of duty. While everyone gives a great effort at their job, there is always someone who gives just a little bit more. This year, I'm proud to announce that our Employee of the Year is Lucy Cheng. **Ms. Cheng started work here 10 years ago**[6] as a sales associate, and she was named Salesperson of the Month five times in her career. Recently, she has been promoted to marketing manager. Now, please help me in honoring Ms. Cheng.

매년 핸포드 인더스트리스는 지속적으로 직무 범위를 넘어서는 한 직원에게 표창을 하고 있습니다. 모두가 각자의 일에 있어 많은 노력을 하지만 언제나 좀 더 많은 노력을 기울이는 사람이 있습니다. 올해 저는 올해의 직원이 루시 쳉이라는 것을 발표하게 되어 기쁩니다. 쳉 씨는 10년 전 이곳에서 영업 직원으로 근무를 시작했으며 그의 경력 동안 다섯 번이나 이달의 영업 직원으로 임명되었습니다. 최근에는 마케팅 부장으로 승진을 하기도 했습니다. 이제 저희는 쳉 씨에게 영광을 안겨드립니다.

어휘 recognize 공로를 인정하다, 표창하다 consistently 지속적으로
go above and beyond the call of duty 직무의 범위를 넘어서다
give[make] an effort 노력하다
be proud[pleased] to announce ~ ~을 발표하게 되어 기쁘다
sales associate 영업 직원 name 임명하다
career 경력, 직업 be promoted to+직책 ~로 승진되다
honor 영예를 주다, 영광을 안기다

실전 감각 익히기 본책 _ p. 134-135

| 1. (D) | 2. (B) | 3. (B) | 4. (D) | 5. (A) | 6. (D) |
| 7. (A) | 8. (A) | 9. (B) | 10. (A) | 11. (B) | 12. (A) |

1-3

> Good morning, everyone. As vice president, **I just wanted to remind all of our sales managers**[2] that **Thursday is the release date for our new photo editing software.**[1] Our programmers have done a fantastic job in creating this powerful, well-designed product, and now it's time to promote it. Please make sure your sales staff is thoroughly familiarized with the product so that they are ready to demonstrate it effectively at upcoming trade shows. For today, **I'm asking that all of you meet up with your entire sales teams**[3] and review the product's features. Thanks again, and have a great day.

여러분, 안녕하세요. 부사장으로서 제가 모든 우리 영업 부장님들께 목요일이 새로운 사진 편집 소프트웨어의 출시일이라는 것을 상기시켜 드리고자 합니다. 우리 프로그래머들이 성능 좋고 잘 설계된 이 상품을 훌륭하게 만들어냈으니 이제 홍보를 할 때입니다. 여러분의 영업 직원들이 본 상품에 대해 철저하게 익혀서 다가오는 무역 박람회에서 효과적으로 시연할 수 있도록 준비시켜 주십시오. 오늘은 여러분 모두가 여러분의 전체 팀을 만나서 제품의 기능을 검토해주시기 바랍니다. 다시 한번 감사 드리며 좋은 하루 보내십시오.

어휘 remind+A(사람)+that ~ A에게 ~을 상기시키다
release date 출시일   editing 편집
do a fantastic job 일을 훌륭히 해내다   well-designed 잘 설계된
it is time to부정사 ~할 때이다   make sure ~ 분명히 ~하다
thoroughly 철저히   be familiarized with ~을 잘 알다
demonstrate 시연하다   effectively 효과적으로
upcoming 다가오는   review 검토하다   feature (제품의) 기능

1. 담화의 목적은 무엇인가?
(A) 최고의 영업 직원 칭찬
(B) 설문조사 결과 논의
(C) 직원 사교 행사 일정 잡기
(D) 소프트웨어 출시 준비

해설 안내 방송의 목적은 이야기의 초반부에 언급되므로 초반부를 잘 들어야 한다. 부사장이 Thursday is the release date for our new photo editing software라고 말한 것을 통해 소프트웨어 출시에 대한 준비 사항을 언급하고 있는 것을 알 수 있으므로 정답은 (D)이다.

2. 청자들은 누구겠는가?
(A) 사진작가들
(B) 영업 부장들
(C) 제품 설계자들
(D) 컴퓨터 프로그래머들

해설 안내 방송의 청자들이 누구인지는 처음 시작하는 부분을 잘 들으면 알 수 있다. 이야기의 초반부에서 I just wanted to remind all of our sales managers라고 했으므로 정답은 (B)이다. 안내 방송에서 자주 쓰이는 구문인 〈주어+remind+사람+that ~〉은 '~가 ~에게 ~을 상기시키다'라는 뜻이므로 remind 뒤에 청취자가 나온다는 것을 알아두자.

3. 청자들은 어떤 요청을 받았는가?
(A) 웹사이트 설계
(B) 그들의 팀 만나기
(C) 교육 세미나 참석
(D) 일찍 업무 끝내기

해설 당부나 요청 사항은 안내 방송의 후반부에 언급된다. 여기서도 후반부에 I'm asking that all of you meet up with your entire sales teams라고 했으므로 정답은 (B)이다. 당부나 요청을 할 때는 주로 encourage, ask, require, suggest, 또는 recommend 등의 동사들이 쓰이게 된다.

4-6

> **Attention Barney's Bookshelf customers.**[4] In just a few minutes, **acclaimed children's book author Stephanie Cohen**[5] will read her latest best seller, *Winnie Goes to the Market*. Seating is limited, so please head towards the children's book corner now for the best seating. Copies of *Winnie Goes to the Market* are available at the monthly feature display near the entrance. Please join award-winning author Stephanie Cohen for an entertaining tale of mischief **in just 10 minutes at 2 P.M.**[6] at the children's book corner. Thank you for shopping at Barney's Bookshelf.

바니 북셀프 고객 여러분들께 알려드립니다. 몇 분 후에 호평을 받고 있는 아동서적 작가인 스테파니 코헨이 그녀의 최신 베스트셀러 〈위니가 시장에 가다〉에 대한 낭독회를 가집니다. 좌석이 제한되어 있으니 좋은 자리에 앉을 수 있도록 지금 아동서적 코너로 가주시기 바랍니다. 〈위니가 시장에 가다〉는 출입문 근처 월간 특별 전시 구역에서 구입하실 수 있습니다. 아동서적 코너에서 10분 후인 2시에 재미 있는 장난 이야기를 듣고 싶으시면 수상 경력이 있는 스테파니 코헨 작가와 함께 해 주십시오. 바니 북셀프를 찾아주신 점 감사 드립니다.

어휘 attention+사람 ~에게 알려 드립니다, ~ 여러분 주목해 주십시오
bookshelf 책꽂이   acclaimed 호평을 받는
children's book 아동서적   author 작가   latest 최신의
seating 좌석   limited 제한된   head towards ~로 향하다
available 이용 가능한, 손에 넣을 수 있는   monthly 월간의
feature 특집   near ~ 근처에   award-winning 수상 경력이 있는
entertaining 재미있는   tale 이야기   mischief 장난

4. 이 안내 방송은 어디에서 들을 수 있겠는가?
(A) 사무실에서
(B) 학교에서
(C) 도서관에서
(D) 서점에서

해설 안내 방송의 장소는 이야기를 하는 사람이 처음에 〈welcome to ~〉 또는 〈attention ~〉이라고 말하는 부분에서 알 수 있다. 여기서도 첫 부분에 나온 Attention Barney's Bookshelf customers.라는 말에서 정답이 (D)인 것을 알 수 있다.

5. 코헨 씨는 누구인가?
(A) 작가
(B) 고객
(C) 도서관 사서
(D) 교사

해설 Ms. Cohen이 누구인지를 묻는 질문이므로 Cohen이 언급되는 부분에서 정답의 단서를 찾아야 한다. 안내 방송 초반부에 acclaimed children's book author Stephanie Cohen이라고 했으므로 정답은 (A)이다. 사람을 소개할 때는 〈직책+사람 이름〉 또는 〈사람 이름+직책〉의 구조를 많이 쓴다는 것을 알아두자.

6. 행사는 언제 시작되는가?
(A) 오전 10시
(B) 오전 11시
(C) 오후 1시
(D) 오후 2시

해설 보기에 시간이 언급되어 있을 경우 빠르게 그 시간들을 먼저 훑어본 다음, 그 중 어떤 것이 본문에서 언급되는지를 포착해야 한다. 안내 방송 후반부에 in just 10 minutes at 2 P.M.이라는 말이 나오므로 정답은 (D)이다. 여기에 나온 10 minutes를 듣고 성급히 (A)를 고르지 않도록 조심해야 한다.

7-9

You're listening to the Golden Pasture, Newberry's radio hour for agricultural news. Today I'll be speaking with Kenneth Ray. **Mr. Ray's unique approach to watering his crops is so effective that almost every farm in the region has copied his method.**[7] He was not always so popular, though. For years **banks turned him down when he asked for loans because his farming ideas were new and unfamiliar**[8]. But today he is spreading his innovative approach to farming through national media appearances. You might have seen him last night on The Graham Report on CBT. In case you missed it, **I'll play a brief excerpt from the interview**[9] before speaking with him in person. Let's listen now.

여러분은 뉴베리 지역의 라디오 농업 뉴스 시간인 '황금 목장'을 청취하고 계십니다. 오늘 저는 케네스 레이 씨와 이야기를 나누어보겠습니다. 레이 씨가 자신의 농작물에 물을 대는 독특한 방법은 워낙 효율이 좋아 이 지역의 거의 모든 농장들이 그의 방법을 따라 하고 있습니다. 하지만 그가 항상 인기가 좋았던 것은 아닙니다. 농사에 대한 그의 아이디어는 새롭고도 낯선 것이었기 때문에 수년간 그가 융자를 신청했을 때 은행들은 그에게 퇴짜를 놓았습니다. 하지만 오늘날 그는 농사에 대한 자신의 혁신적인 접근 방법을 국내 미디어에 출연하면서 확산시켜 나가고 있죠. 어젯밤에 CBT의 '그레이엄 리포트'에 출연한 그를 보셨을 겁니다. 못 보신 경우를 위해, 그와 직접 이야기를 나누어보기에 앞서 간략한 인터뷰 내용 일부를 여러분에게 들려 드리겠습니다. 지금 들어보시죠.

어휘 pasture 초원, 목초지 agricultural 농업의 approach to ~에의 접근 crop (농)작물 turn down 거절하다, 거부하다 unfamiliar 익숙지 않은, 낯선 innovative 혁신적인 in case ~의 경우에 excerpt 발췌[인용] (부분)

7. 화자는 지역 농민들에 대해 뭐라고 말을 하는가?
(A) 레이 씨의 농사 기술을 이용하고 있다.
(B) 지속 가능한 농업의 선구자들이다.
(C) 함께 일하며 농작물을 수확한다.
(D) 최근에 TV에 나왔다.

해설 이 지역의 거의 모든 농장들이 레이 씨가 농작물에 물을 대는 독특한 방법을 따라 하고 있다(Mr. Ray's unique approach to watering his crops is so effective that almost every farm in the region has copied his method.)고 했다. 지문의 has copied his method를 use Mr. Ray's farming technique로 바꾸어 표현한 (A)가 정답이다.

8. 화자가 "은행들은 그에게 퇴짜를 놓았습니다"라고 말할 때 의미하는 바는 무엇인가?
(A) 은행들이 레이 씨의 요청을 거절했다.
(B) 은행들이 레이 씨를 헷갈리게 했다.
(C) 은행들이 레이 씨에게 다른 곳을 소개해 줬다.
(D) 은행들이 레이 씨를 지원해 줬다.

해설 이 표현에 나온 turn down은 '(요청 등을) 거절하다'라는 뜻으로 decline과 의미가 같은 숙어이다. 따라서 정답은 (A)이다.

9. 화자는 다음에 무엇을 하겠는가?
(A) 농장을 방문한다.
(B) 인터뷰 일부를 들려준다.
(C) 대학생과 얘기한다.
(D) 일기 예보를 한다.

해설 어젯밤 Graham Report에서 Mr. Ray를 못 본 사람들을 위해 녹취한 그 프로의 일부 인터뷰 내용을 들려 주겠다고 말하고 있다. 지문의 play a brief excerpt from the interview를 Play an interview clip으로 바꾸어 표현한 (B)가 정답이다.

10-12

> Attention visitors of the Trenton Museum of Fine Arts. **The museum will be closing in approximately 30 minutes at 9 P.M.**[10] We hope that you have enjoyed your visit today, and we will open again tomorrow at 10 A.M. Remember that memberships are half-priced this week, and that **children can visit free for the entire month.**[11] Next month we will be featuring the impressionist paintings of local artist Diego Montoya[12] in our Hessen Gallery. At this time, please begin making your way to the main entrance so that we may close in a punctual fashion. Thank you, and please visit us again soon.

트렌튼 미술 박물관 방문자 여러분께 알려드립니다. 박물관이 대략 30분 후인 9시에 문을 닫습니다. 오늘 방문이 즐거우셨기를 바라며 저희는 내일 오전 10시에 다시 문을 엽니다. 이번 주에는 회원권이 반값이며, 어린이들은 한 달 내내 무료 입장이라는 것을 말씀드립니다. 다음 달에 저희는 헤센 미술관에서 지역 예술가인 디에고 몬토야의 인상주의 그림에 대한 특별 전시회를 엽니다. 지금 저희가 시간 맞춰 문을 닫을 수 있도록 정문으로 가주십시오. 감사 드리며 곧 다시 찾아주시길 바랍니다.

어휘 attention + 사람 ~에게 알려드립니다. ~ 여러분 주목해주십시오
approximately 대략   membership 회원 자격, 회원 수
half-priced 반값인   entire 전체의
feature (미술품 등을) 특별 전시하다   impressionist 인상파 화가
local 지역의   make one's way to ~로 가다
so that ~ ~할 수 있도록
in a punctual fashion 시간 맞춰 (cf. punctual 시간을 지키는)

10. 박물관은 언제 문을 닫는가?
(A) 오후 9시
(B) 오후 9시 30분
(C) 오후 10시
(D) 오후 10시 30분

해설 보기 중에 시간이 제시되어 있을 경우, 지문에서도 분명히 시간이 언급될 것임을 예상할 수 있다. 따라서 시간이 언급되는 부분에서 보기와 일치하는 시간을 정답으로 선택하면 된다. The museum will be closing in approximately 30 minutes at 9 P.M.이라고 했으므로 정답은 (A)이다.

11. 박물관에 대해 무엇이 언급되었는가?
(A) 내일 문을 닫을 것이다.
(B) 이번 달 어린이 입장료는 무료이다.
(C) 회원들은 무료 입장이 가능하다.
(D) 이번 달 새로운 지점으로 옮길 것이다.

해설 이 문제는 박물관에 대해 언급된 내용을 찾는 종합적인 문제이므로 다소 어려울 수 있다. 즉, 전체 내용을 잘 들어야만 정답을 찾을 수 있는 문제이다. 하지만 문제와 보기를 먼저 읽어두었다가 지문과 일치하는 것을 찾으면 비교적 쉽게 문제를 풀 수 있다. 보기 (B)가 본문에서 children can visit free for the entire month라고 언급되었으므로 정답은 (B)이다.

12. 다음 달에 무엇이 전시되는가?
(A) 그림
(B) 도자기
(C) 조각
(D) 사진

해설 문제에 시점으로 next month가 있으므로 지문에서 next month가 언급된 부분에서 정답의 단서를 찾아야 한다. 지문에서 Next month we will be featuring the impressionist paintings of local artist Diego Montoya라고 했으므로 정답은 (A)이다.

UNIT 15 녹음 메시지/설명문

어휘 및 표현 점검 본책 _ p. 138

> 1. immediately   2. wondering if   3. extension
> 4. as soon as possible   5. cancel

청취 집중 훈련 1 본책 _ p. 139

> 1. responsibilities / according / guidelines / meeting / requires / chosen / position / background / experience / description
> 2. message is for / make sure / procedure for / shuttle bus service / booked with us / coming in / turn on / scheduled to / you'll see / safe flight

청취 집중 훈련 2 본책 _ p. 140

> 1. (B)   2. (B)   3. (A)   4. (A)   5. (B)   6. (A)

1-2

1. 화자는 어떤 종류의 회사에 전화를 걸고 있는가?
(A) 이사 회사
(B) 아파트 임대 중개업체

2. 화자는 넬슨 씨에게 무엇을 요청하는가?
(A) 약속을 취소하기
(B) 좀 더 빠른 시간에 만나기

> Hello, this is Henry Dodson calling. This message is for one of your rental agents, Liz Nelson. I have a 3 o'clock appointment with her to view an apartment on Irving Street. I'm actually in the Irving Street area now and am wondering if I can see her at 2 if possible. Please give me a call back on my mobile as soon as possible. Thank you.

안녕하세요, 저는 헨리 도슨입니다. 이 메시지는 임대 중개인 중 한 명인 리즈 넬슨 씨를 위한 것입니다. 저는 어빙 가에 있는 아파트를 보기 위해 그녀와 3시에 약속이 되어 있습니다. 저는 사실 지금 어빙 가 지역에 있어서 가능하면 2시에 그녀를 볼 수 있을지 궁금합니다. 가능한 한 빨리 제 휴대폰으로 전화 주시기 바랍니다. 감사합니다.

어휘 This is + 사람 이름 + calling. (전화를 걸 때) 저는 ~입니다.
rental agent 임대 중개인 have an appointment with + A(사람) + to부정사 A와 ~하기 위한 약속이 있다
actually 사실 wonder if ~인지 궁금하다 if possible 가능하면
give A(사람) a call back A에게 다시 전화하다

3-4

3. 이 이야기는 어디에서 일어나고 있는가?
(A) 무역 박람회에서   (B) 사진관에서

4. 프로그램에 대해 무엇이 언급되었는가?
(A) 사용하기 쉽다.   (B) 매우 저렴하다.

> Greetings, everyone. I hope you're all enjoying our trade fair today. Now, I'll show the features of the Photo-Maker software program. It's been a big success since it hit store shelves last month. While it's not the cheapest editing software on the market, it has the simplest features. Even beginners can use it.

여러분, 안녕하세요. 오늘 여러분 모두 저희 무역 박람회에서 좋은 시간을 보내고 계시길 바랍니다. 제가 지금 포토메이커 소프트웨어 프로그램의 기능을 보여 드릴 겁니다. 이 프로그램은 지난 달 매장에 출시된 이래로 큰 성공을 거두고 있습니다. 이 제품이 시장에서 가장 저렴한 편집 소프트웨어는 아니지만 제일 간단한 기능을 갖추고 있습니다. 심지어 초보자들도 사용할 수 있습니다.

어휘 trade fair 무역 박람회 feature 기능, 특징
a big success 큰 성공을 거둔 것
hit store shelves 시장에 출시되다 (cf. shelf 선반)
while ~이지만, ~인 반면 cheap 저렴한 even 심지어
beginner 초보자

5-6

5. 화자는 언제 건물 설계를 시작했는가?
(A) 5년 전   **(B) 7년 전**

6. 화자는 누구에게 고마워하는가?
(A) 건물 소유주들   (B) 디자인 직원

> When I started the design for the Lincoln Building seven years ago, I had no idea it would be successful. I'd like to thank the owners of the Lincoln Building for approaching me to work on the project and for collaborating with me in designing something that was both artistic and practical.

제가 7년 전 링컨 건물에 대한 설계를 시작했을 때 저는 성공하리라고는 생각하지 못했습니다. 저는 이번 프로젝트에 참여할 수 있도록 저를 찾아와주시고, 또한 예술적이면서도 실용적인 것을 설계하고자 저와 협력해 주신 링컨 건물의 소유주들께 감사 드리고 싶습니다.

어휘 have no idea ~을 모르다 successful 성공적인 owner 소유주
approach 접근하다 work on ~에 대해 작업하다
collaborate with ~와 협력하다 both A and B A와 B 모두
artistic 예술적인 practical 실용적인

청취 집중 훈련 3   본책 _ p. 141

1. (D)   2. (A)   3. (C)   4. (A)   5. (B)   6. (B)

1-2

이번 주 베스트셀러 (3/10–3/16)

제목	저자	출판사
1. 자연의 신비	미첼 소로	센트리 서클
2. 요리의 즐거움	에밀리 리베라	오리온 퍼블리싱
3. 달라지는 법	라이언 하워드	휴먼 알파
4. 최종 선택	엘런 타일러	그린러브

1. 누가 말하고 있겠는가?
(A) 저자   (B) 고객
(C) 미술 교수   **(D) 서점 주인**

해설 전화 메시지에서는 메시지의 첫 부분에 인사말과 함께 메시지를 남기는 사람의 이름과 회사명이 나오게 된다. This is Jose Grenier calling from Grenier's Rare Books.에서 Rare Books를 듣고 서점 주인의 메시지라는 것을 알 수 있다. Rare라는 단어를 모른다 해도 그 뒤에 나오는 out of print(절판된), one of those books(그 책들 중 한 권), 또는 the book you requested(요청하신 책)와 같은 표현이 나오므로 정답은 (D)이다.

2. 도표를 보세요. 화자는 어떤 책을 추천할 것 같은가?

(A) 자연의 신비
(B) 요리의 즐거움
(C) 달라지는 법
(D) 최종 선택

> **해설** 화자가 고객이 관심이 있을지도 모를 미쳄 소로의 몇몇 다른 책들을 보유하고 있다(we have a few other titles from Mitchem Thoreau you might be interested in)고 하면서 더 많은 정보를 원하시면 전화를 달라고 했다. 도표를 보면 미쳄 소로의 책이 자연의 신비(A Final Choice)이므로 정답은 (A)이다.

> Good afternoon. This message is for Elaine O'Riley. This is Jose Grenier calling from Grenier's **Rare Books**.[1] Unfortunately, we were not able to find *The Mona Lisa Chronicles* by Mitchem Thoreau because it's out of print. **If you'd like, we have a few other titles from Mitchem Thoreau you might be interested in.**[2] If you'd like more information on one of those books instead, please call me back. Again, I'm sorry we were unable to locate the book you requested.

안녕하세요. 이 메시지는 일레인 오릴리를 위한 것입니다. 저는 그레니어 희귀 도서의 호세 그레니어입니다. 아쉽게도 미쳄 소로의 〈모나리자 연대기〉는 절판되었기 때문에 그 책을 찾을 수가 없었습니다. 괜찮으시다면 저희는 고객님께서 관심이 있을지도 모를 미쳄 소로의 몇몇 다른 책들을 보유하고 있습니다. 대신 그 책들 중 한 권에 대한 더 많은 정보를 원하시면 저에게 다시 전화를 주십시오. 다시 한 번 고객님께서 요청하신 책을 찾을 수 없어 죄송하다는 말씀을 드립니다.

> **어휘** rare 희귀한 unfortunately 불행히도, 아쉽게도
> chronicle 연대기 out of print 절판된 title 책, 출판물
> be interested in ~에 관심이 있다 instead 대신 locate 찾다
> request 요청하다

3-4

3. 이 이야기의 청자는 누구겠는가?

(A) 신입 직원들
(B) 방문한 학생들
(C) 인턴 지망자들
(D) 고위 중역들

> **해설** 메시지의 대상은 메시지의 앞부분에 언급되므로 첫 도입 부분을 잘 들어야 한다. 여기서도 메시지 초반부에 나온 for summer intern marketing positions라는 말을 통해 말을 듣고 있는 사람은 인턴 지망자들이라는 것을 알 수 있다.

4. 소개 시간 후에 무엇이 있겠는가?

(A) 개별 면접
(B) 제품 시연회
(C) 질의 응답 시간
(D) 다른 부서 견학

> **해설** 질문에 introduction session이라는 말이 있으므로 이 말이 언급된 부분에서 정답의 단서를 찾아야 한다. 메시지에서 After the session, you will meet individually for an interview라고 했는데 the session이 질문에 나온 introduction session을 말하므로 결국 정답은 (A)이다.

> Hello everyone, good afternoon. Welcome to the Taylor Electronics group interview for summer **intern marketing positions**.[3] First, I'll hand out surveys concerning work habits and styles. There are no right or wrong answers, so please answer honestly. Then, after the paperwork, there will be a short introduction session where we will meet a few of the department managers. **After the session, you will meet individually for an interview with**[4] one of our senior managers. This is a daylong process, so there will be an hour-long lunch break at twelve.

여러분 모두 안녕하세요. 하계 마케팅 인턴직을 위해 테일러 전자의 단체 면접에 오신 걸 환영합니다. 먼저 저는 근무 습관과 방식에 대한 설문지를 나눠드리겠습니다. 정답이나 오답이 있는 것은 아니니 솔직하게 답변해주세요. 서류 작성 이후에 짧은 소개 시간이 있는데 그때 저희 회사 부서 매니저 몇 분을 만나게 될 겁니다. 소개 시간 후에 여러분들은 개별적으로 저희 선임 매니저 한 분과 면접을 하게 될 것입니다. 이 과정은 종일 계속되므로 12시에 1시간의 점심 시간이 있습니다.

> **어휘** hand out 나누어 주다 survey 설문조사 concerning ~에 관한
> work habit 근무 습관 right[wrong] answer 정답[오답]
> paperwork 서류 업무[작업] introduction session 소개 시간
> individually 개별적으로 daylong 종일의 lunch break 점심 시간

5-6

5. 어디에서 이 담화를 들을 수 있겠는가?

(A) 버스 정거장
(B) 관광 버스에서
(C) 식당에서
(D) 해변에서

> **해설** 이야기의 장소는 화자가 쓰는 단어를 통해 알 수 있다. 처음 시작하는 부분에서 Attention passengers.라고 했으므로 청자들은 승객들이다. 그리고 다음 문장에서 At approximately 11:30 we will be stopping for lunch.라고 했으므로 청자들이 지금 차 안에 있다는 것을 알 수 있다. 그러므로 이야기의 장소는 관광 버스 안이 되는 것이다. 만약 이야기의 초반부를 놓쳤더라도 마지막 부분에 나온 the bus will return you to your hotel을 듣고 정답을 찾을 수 있다.

6. 화자는 청자들에게 무엇을 하지 말라고 요청하는가?

(A) 낚시
(B) 수영
(C) 사진 촬영
(D) 버스에서 내리기

> **해설** 메시지나 설명문에서 청자들에게 전달하는 요청 사항은 대개 이야기의 후반부에 나온다. 또한 〈We ask[suggest, recommend] that ~〉, 〈You should ~〉, 또는 〈Please ~〉를 써서 요청 사항을 전달하는 경우가 많다는 것을 알아두자. 여기서도 We ask를 써서 We ask that you do not try to go swimming이라고 했으므로 정답은 (B)이다.

Attention passengers.[5] At approximately 11:30 we will be stopping for lunch. We will be dining at a restaurant that has been serving the surrounding village for over 100 years. They offer many local dishes and beverages, so you are guaranteed an authentic meal. After lunch, we will continue our tour by driving down to the coast. **We ask that you do not try to go swimming**[6] as the water is still far too cold at this time of year. After two hours at the beach, the bus will return you to your hotel. Thank you.

승객 여러분 주목해주세요. 대략 11시 30분에 점심 식사를 위해 멈출 것입니다. 저희는 100년이 넘게 주변 마을을 상대로 운영 중인 한 식당에서 식사를 할 것입니다. 그 식당에는 많은 지역 음식과 음료수가 있어서 여러분께 정통 식사를 보장해 드립니다. 점심 식사 후 저희는 관광을 계속하며 해변까지 달려갈 것입니다. 연중 이맘때는 물이 아직도 많이 차갑기 때문에 수영은 하지 마시길 부탁 드립니다. 해변에서 두 시간을 보낸 후, 버스는 여러분을 호텔로 다시 모셔 드릴 겁니다. 감사합니다.

어휘 Attention + 사람. ~ 여러분 주목해 주세요. approximately 대략 dine 식사하다 serve 음식을 제공하다 surrounding 주변의 dish 음식, 요리 beverage 음료수 guarantee 보장하다 authentic 진품의 meal 식사 drive down to ~까지 운전해 가다 go ~ing ~하러 가다 far too 지나치게, 너무 at this time of year 연중 이맘때에

실전 감각 익히기 본책 _ p. 142–143

1. (A) 2. (C) 3. (C) 4. (A) 5. (B) 6. (D)
7. (B) 8. (D) 9. (C) 10. (A) 11. (D) 12. (C)

1-3

Hi, this message is for Jason Yu. It's Sandra calling from Seasons Food Products. We just finished reviewing all the Web site design proposals and **your sample Web site was chosen**[1] by our management. Congratulations! We were especially impressed with your sample site's graphics and ease of use. If you decide to work with us on designing our new Web site, **we will give you a short-term contract**[2] with partial staff benefits. I'd like to meet up with you after our lunch hour this Friday to discuss this more. **How about 2 o'clock?**[3] Give me a call back if this is convenient for you, and, again, congratulations!

안녕하세요. 이 메시지는 제이슨 유를 위한 것입니다. 저는 시즌스 식품의 산드라입니다. 저희가 모든 웹사이트 디자인 제안에 대한 검토를 마쳤는데 제이슨 유님의 웹사이트 견본이 우리 경영진에 의해 채택되었습니다. 축하합니다! 저희는 특히 이 샘플 사이트의 그래픽과 이용의 용이함에 좋은 인상을 받았습니다. 만약 저희 새 웹사이트를 디자인하는 데 함께 작업하시기로 결정하시면 저희와 일부 직원 혜택이 따르는 단기 계약을 맺게 됩니다. 이 문제를 더 논의하기 위해 이번 주 금요일 점심 시간 이후에 만나고 싶습니다. 2시가 어떻겠습니까? 이 시간이 괜찮으시면 제게 다시 전화를 주시고요. 다시 한 번 축하드립니다!

어휘 this message is for+사람 이 메시지는 ~를 위한 것이다
review 검토하다 proposal 제안 choose 고르다
be impressed with ~에 좋은 인상을 받다
ease of use 이용의 용이함 short-term contract 단기 계약
partial 부분적인 benefit 혜택 meet up with ~를 만나다
How about ~? ~가 어때요? convenient 편리한

1. 유 씨는 누구겠는가?
(A) 웹사이트 개발자   (B) 식당 요리사
(C) 부동산 관리자   (D) 의상 디자이너

해설 질문에 사람 이름으로 Yu가 있으므로 이 사람이 언급되는 문장에서 정답의 단서를 찾아야 한다. 메시지에서 your sample Web site was chosen이라고 했는데 your는 메시지의 수신자인 Yu를 가리키는 것이므로 정답은 (A)이다.

2. 유 씨는 무엇을 제안 받고 있는가?
(A) 사진 촬영 강좌
(B) 최신 소프트웨어 상품
(C) 고용 계약
(D) 예술 작품 한 점

해설 이 문제는 메시지의 대상이나 목적을 묻는 질문이 아니라 세부 사항을 묻는 질문이므로 메시지 중간 부분에 정답의 단서가 있게 된다. 메시지 중간에 we will give you a short-term contract라고 했으므로 Yu에게 고용 계약을 제안하고 있는 것이다. 그러므로 정답은 (C)이다.

3. 전화를 건 사람은 금요일 몇 시에 만날 것을 제안하는가?
(A) 오후 12시   (B) 오후 1시
(C) 오후 2시   (D) 오후 3시

해설 보기에 시간이 제시되어 있을 경우 미리 그 시간을 읽어둔 다음, 어떤 시간이 본문에서 언급되는지를 확인하면 쉽게 정답을 찾을 수 있다. 메시지 후반부에 How about 2 o'clock?이라고 했으므로 정답은 (C)이다. 일반적으로 제안이나 요청 사항은 메시지의 후반부에 언급된다는 것을 알아두자.

4-6

> Thank you for calling the Profex Computer technical support center.⁴ All of our technicians are currently busy helping other customers. Please remain on the line and the next available technician will assist you. In order to expedite your call, please have the following information available: the model number of your computer, **the serial number on your computer's hard drive**,⁵ and any warranty information you were provided with by your computer retailer. If you are calling from a location outside of the United States, please hang up and **call our international number at 289-7773**.⁶ Thank you for your patience.

프로펙스 컴퓨터 기술 지원 센터에 전화주셔서 감사합니다. 현재 모든 저희 기술자들이 바쁘게 다른 고객들을 돕고 있는 중입니다. 끊지 않고 대기해주시면 준비가 되는 다음 기술자가 고객님을 도와드릴 것입니다. 통화를 신속히 하기 위해 다음 정보를 준비해주시기 바랍니다. 컴퓨터 모델 번호, 컴퓨터 하드 드라이브 일련번호, 컴퓨터 소매업체에게서 받은 모든 보증 정보입니다. 만약 미국이 아닌 곳에서 전화를 걸고 계시다면 전화를 끊고 저희 국제 번호 289-7773으로 전화해 주십시오. 기다려주셔서 감사합니다.

어휘 technical support 기술 지원 technician 기술자
currently 현재 be busy ~ing ~하느라 바쁘다
remain on the line (전화를) 끊지 않고 대기하다
available 시간이 되는 assist 돕다
in order to 부정사 ~하기 위해서 expedite 신속히 처리하다
following 다음의 serial number 일련번호 warranty 보증
retailer 소매업체 location 위치, 지점 outside of ~ 밖에
hang up 전화를 끊다 patience 인내

4. 프로펙스는 무엇을 팔 것 같은가?
(A) 컴퓨터   (B) 인쇄기
(C) TV   (D) 복사기

해설 질문에 고유명사 Profex가 있으므로 미리 이 단어를 읽어두어서 발음에 친숙하게 만들어 놓아야 한다. 회사 ARS 메시지의 경우 그 회사가 어떤 회사인지는 메시지의 초반부에 나오는 첫 한두 문장을 잘 들으면 알 수 있다. Thank you for calling the Profex Computer technical support center.라고 했으므로 정답은 (A)이다.

5. 전화를 건 사람들은 무엇을 준비해야 하는가?
(A) 전화번호   (B) 일련번호
(C) 영수증 번호   (D) 신용카드 번호

해설 요청 사항은 〈We ask[suggest, recommend] that ~〉, 〈You should ~〉, 또는 〈Please ~〉와 같은 표현을 써서 전달하는 경우가 많다. 여기서도 please have the following information available이라고 한 다음 이어서 the serial number on your computer's hard drive라고 했으므로 정답은 (B)이다.

6. 화자는 해외에서 전화를 건 사람들에게 무엇을 요청하는가?
(A) 소프트웨어 구입   (B) 웹사이트 방문
(C) 주소 제공   (D) 다른 번호로 전화하기

해설 질문에 international callers라는 말이 있으므로 메시지에서 이와 똑같은 말이나 관련된 표현이 언급되는 부분에 초점을 맞추어야 한다. 메시지 후반부의 If you are calling from a location outside of the United States, please hang up and call our international number at 289-7773.에서 다른 international number를 알려주고 있으므로 정답은 (D)이다.

7-9

> OK, now, briefly, I just want to review the procedure for reserving a conference room. The first thing **you need to do is check the conference room schedule in the employee e-mail system**.⁷ After you log in to your e-mail account, click "updates" and you'll see the schedule. You can then choose one of **our four conference rooms to reserve**.⁸ After that, simply phone or e-mail Annie, the office manager, to request a reservation. When you talk to her, **please tell her the reason for your meeting**⁹ so she can list it on the schedule. All the rooms have the same types of audio-visual equipment. That's about it, thanks.

좋습니다. 이제 간략하게 제가 회의실 예약 절차를 검토해 드리겠습니다. 여러분이 제일 먼저 할 일은 직원 이메일 시스템에서 회의실 일정을 확인하는 겁니다. 여러분의 이메일 계정에 들어간 다음 '최신 정보'를 클릭하면 일정을 보게 될 겁니다. 그런 다음 네 개의 회의실 중에서 예약할 곳 하나를 선택해주세요. 그 다음에 사무실 부장인 애니에게 전화나 이메일로 예약을 요청하시기 바랍니다. 애니와 얘기할 때는 회의 목적을 말해야 일정을 잡아줄 겁니다. 모든 회의실에는 똑같은 종류의 시청각 장비가 있습니다. 대략 이 정도이고요, 고맙습니다.

어휘 briefly 간략히 review 검토하다 procedure 절차
reserve 예약하다 conference room 회의실
e-mail account 이메일 계정 choose 고르다 simply 간단히
request 요청하다 list 기재하다
audio-visual equipment 시청각 장비

7. 청자들은 회의실을 예약하기 전에 무엇을 해야 하는가?
(A) 회의실 크기 확인   (B) 이메일 프로그램에 접속
(C) 참석자 명단 작성   (D) 회의 안건 검토

해설 청자들이 회의실 예약 전에 해야 할 일을 묻는 질문이다. 메시지 초반부에 해야 할 의무나 필요성을 나타내는 표현인 〈need to + 동사원형〉을 써서 The first thing you need to do is check the conference room schedule in the employee e-mail system.이라고 했으므로 정답은 (B)이다. 지문에서의 e-mail system이 보기에서는 e-mail program으로 패러프레이징(바꿔 쓰기) 된 것에 유의해야 한다.

8. 회사는 얼마나 많은 회의실을 보유하고 있는가?
(A) 한 개   (B) 두 개
(C) 세 개   (D) 네 개

해설 회의실의 개수를 묻는 질문이다. 그러므로 숫자가 언급되는 부분에 초점을 맞춰 들어야 한다. 본문에서 You can then choose one of our four conference rooms to reserve.라고 했으므로 정답은 (D)이다.

9. 청자들은 예약 요청서에 무엇을 포함시켜야 하는가?
(A) 회의 때 제공되는 다과의 종류
(B) 회의 참가자 수
(C) 회의 목적
(D) 회의에 필요한 장비

해설 메시지나 설명문에서 앞으로 해야 할 요청 사항이나 당부는 이야기 후반부에 나오는 경우가 많다. 여기서도 이야기 후반부에 please tell her the reason for your meeting이라고 했으므로 정답은 (C)이다. 아울러 지금처럼 질문과 보기가 긴 문제는 제한 시간 8초 만에 정답을 찾기가 쉽지 않다. 그러므로 이야기가 나오기 전에 미리 빠르게 읽어두는 문제 풀이 접근법을 취해야 한다.

10-12

> So far we've heard lots of good ideas about how to increase our product sales. Carl, I particularly liked your idea for **sponsoring sports teams so the public can see athletes drinking our product during their events**.¹⁰ It will help sell the idea that, um, our beverages help athletes perform at their best. Now, let's talk about what's not working. Take a look at this graph. Clearly, TV advertisements aren't very effective. I propose canceling all of our television advertising and **putting it into the medium where we're reaching the most customers**¹¹. Redirecting funds like this will help us increase our brand recognition **before we release our new series of nutritional supplements next year.**¹²

지금까지 우리는 제품 매출을 늘리는 방법에 대한 좋은 아이디어를 많이 들어봤습니다. 칼, 저는 스포츠 팀을 후원해 운동 선수들이 경기를 하는 동안 우리 제품을 마시는 모습을 볼 수 있게 하자는 당신의 아이디어가 정말 마음에 들었습니다. 그렇게 하면 사람들로 하여금 운동 선수들이 최고의 성적을 내는 데 있어 우리 음료가 도움을 준다는 생각을 갖도록 하는 데 도움이 될 수 있을 것입니다. 자, 이제 뭐가 효과가 없는지 이야기해 봅시다. 이 도표를 보세요. 확실히, TV 광고는 그다지 효과가 없군요. 저는 우리의 모든 TV 광고를 취소하고, 그것을 가장 많은 고객들에게 다가갈 수 있는 미디어에 집중시킬 것을 제안합니다. 이렇게 자금 투자를 조정하면 내년에 새로운 영양 보조제 제품을 출시하기에 앞서 브랜드 인지도를 높이는 데 도움이 될 것입니다.

어휘 athlete 운동 선수   sell (생각 등을) 받아들이게 하다, 납득시키다
beverage 음료   perform 행하다, 수행하다
at one's best 최고의 상태로   work 효과가 있다, (어떤 결과를) 가져오다
redirect (돈 같은 것을 다른 용도로) 전용하다, 돌려쓰다
brand recognition 브랜드 인지도
release (신제품을) 출시하다, 공개하다
nutritional supplement 영양 보조제
billboard (옥외의 커다란) 광고판

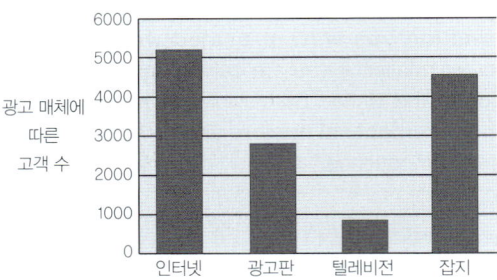

10. 화자는 어떤 종류의 제품에 대해 말하고 있는가
(A) 스포츠 음료
(B) 컴퓨터 프로그램
(C) 금융 서비스
(D) 텔레비전 모델

해설 스포츠 팀을 후원해 운동 선수들이 경기를 하는 동안 자사의 제품을 마시는 모습을 일반 사람들이 볼 수 있게 한다(sponsoring sports teams so the public can see athletes drinking our product during their events.)고 했다. 이를 통해 화자가 말하고 있는 제품은 스포츠 음료임을 유추할 수 있으므로 정답은 (A)이다.

11. 도표를 보세요. 화자는 어떤 종류의 광고에 더 많이 투자하고 싶어하는가?
(A) 텔레비전
(B) 잡지
(C) 광고판
(D) 인터넷

해설 화자는 가장 효과가 없는 TV 광고를 모두 취소하고 그 돈을 가장 많은 고객들에게 다가갈 수 있는 미디어에 집중할 것(putting it into the medium where we're reaching the most customers)을 제안하고 있다. 도표에서 가장 많은 고객들에게 전달이 되고 있는 광고는 인터넷이므로 정답은 (D)이다.

12. 화자에 따르면 내년에는 어떤 일이 있을 것인가?
(A) 광고가 기록될 것이다.
(B) 스포츠 대회가 시작될 것이다.
(C) 신제품 라인이 출시될 것이다.
(D) 로고가 새로 디자인될 것이다.

해설 담화 마지막 부분에서 내년에 새로운 영양 보조제 제품군을 출시하기에 앞서(before we release our new series of nutritional supplements next year) 브랜드 인지도를 높인다는 말이 있었다. 지문의 release our new series of nutritional supplements를 보기에서 A new product line will launch. 로 바꾸어 표현한 (C)가 정답이다.

Part 4 Review Test
본책 _ p. 144–145

1. (A) 2. (B) 3. (D) 4. (A) 5. (D)
6. (A) 7. (D) 8. (A) 9. (A) 10. (A)
11. (C) 12. (C) 13. (B) 14. (D) 15. (D)
16. (B) 17. (C) 18. (C) 19. (D) 20. (C)
21. (B)

1-3

Hello, everyone. I'm Max Cohen from Woodson's Furniture. **Please visit the Woodson's Furniture showroom**[1] to view the best office furniture in the area this weekend. With over 200 pieces to choose from, and **prices 30 to 60 percent lower than those in competing stores**,[2] you're sure to find the exact piece of furniture you're looking for at an affordable price. We have everything from office desks and chairs to filing cabinets. **We even offer free delivery and installation services**[3] when you purchase furniture from our showroom or catalog. Come and see our great selection for yourself. Visit Woodson's Furniture this Saturday and Sunday.

여러분, 안녕하세요. 저는 우드슨 가구의 맥스 코헨입니다. 이번 주말 우드슨 가구의 전시실에 오셔서 지역 내 최상의 사무용 가구를 구경하시기 바랍니다. 200점 이상의 선택 품목과 경쟁사보다 30%에서 60%까지 저렴한 가구를 보유하고 있어서 고객님께서 저렴한 가격에 원하시는 가구를 바로 찾으실 수 있습니다. 저희는 사무용 책상과 의자에서부터 서류 정리용 캐비닛에 이르기까지 모든 것을 갖추고 있습니다. 저희 전시실이나 카탈로그에서 가구를 구입하시면 무료 배달 및 설치 서비스도 제공해드립니다. 직접 오셔서 저희의 엄선된 다양한 상품을 보시기 바랍니다. 이번 주 토요일과 일요일에 우드슨 가구를 방문해주십시오.

어휘 사람 이름 + from + 회사명 (회사)의 (사람 이름) showroom 전시실
office furniture 사무용 가구 piece (가구 등의) 한 점[개]
choose from ~에서 고르다 competing 경쟁하는
exact 바로 그 at an affordable price 저렴한 가격에
free delivery 무료 배달 installation 설치
great selection 엄선된 다양한 상품 for oneself 직접, 스스로

1. 무엇이 광고되고 있는가?
(A) 가구점 (B) 백화점
(C) 저장 시설 (D) 실내 디자인 서비스

해설 광고의 대상은 이야기 초반부에 등장한다. 여기서도 광고 초반부에 Please visit the Woodson's Furniture showroom이라고 했으므로 정답은 (A)이다.

2. 가격에 대해 무엇이 언급되었는가?
(A) 단지 상점 회원들에게만 더 저렴하다.
(B) 다른 상점보다 더 저렴하다.
(C) 원가에서 최대 30% 할인된다.
(D) 단지 2주 동안만 가격이 할인된다.

해설 질문에 prices라는 단어가 있으므로 지문에서 prices가 언급되는 부분에서 정답의 단서를 찾아야 한다. 광고에서 prices 30 to 60 percent lower than those in competing stores라고 했으므로 정답은 (B)이다.

3. 광고에서 어떤 서비스가 소개되고 있는가?
(A) 3년 보증 (B) 정기적인 이메일 최신 정보
(C) 24시간 보안 관찰 (D) 무료 배달 및 설치

해설 질문의 핵심어가 service이므로 내용을 들을 때 service라는 단어가 나오는 부분에 집중해야 한다. 광고 후반부에 We even offer free delivery and installation services라고 했으므로 정답은 (D)이다.

4-6

Good afternoon. I'm Sarah Matthews with the WPT Radio weather report for this weekend. **Going into tonight, skies will be clear with temperatures around 58 degrees Fahrenheit.**[4] Then on Saturday, afternoon temperatures will reach into the seventies. **Saturday is the perfect day to plan outdoor activities**[5] because Sunday will be cloudy and temperatures will drop down to 62 degrees Fahrenheit. **There's also an 80 percent chance of rain on Sunday,**[6] with at least an inch of rain expected to accumulate by midnight. The rain will continue into Monday morning and start to clear up Monday afternoon. Coming up next on WPT, Isabelle Jameson has the local traffic report.

안녕하세요. 저는 이번 주말 일기 예보를 전하는 WPT 라디오의 사라 매튜스입니다. 밤으로 접어들면서 기온은 화씨 58도 정도에 하늘은 맑겠습니다. 그러다가 토요일 오후 기온은 70도 대에 이르겠습니다. 일요일은 구름이 끼고 기온이 화씨 62도까지 떨어질 전망이어서 토요일이 야외 활동을 계획하시기에는 가장 좋은 날이 되겠습니다. 일요일에 비 올 확률은 80%이며 자정까지 1인치 정도의 강수량이 예상됩니다. 비는 월요일 아침까지 계속되다가 월요일 오후에 개기 시작할 전망입니다. WPT에서 바로 이어서 이사벨 제임슨이 지역 교통 정보를 말씀드립니다.

어휘 weather report 일기 예보　go into ~로 들어가다
clear 맑은　temperature 기온　around 대략
degree (온도 단위의) 도　Fahrenheit 화씨 (cf. centigrade 섭씨)
a ~ percent chance of rain[snow] ~퍼센트의 비[눈] 올 확률
at least 적어도　accumulate 누적되다　continue 계속되다
clear up 개다　local traffic report 지역 교통 정보

4. 오늘밤 기온은 몇 도이겠는가?
(A) 화씨 58도
(B) 화씨 62도
(C) 화씨 70도
(D) 화씨 80도

해설 보기에 지금처럼 숫자가 있을 경우에는 미리 그 숫자를 읽어둔 다음, 이 숫자들 중에서 어떤 것이 본문에 언급되는지를 포착해야 한다. 또한 질문이 오늘밤(tonight)의 기온을 말하므로 tonight이란 단어가 나오는 부분에서 정답의 단서를 찾는다. 이야기 초반부에 Going into tonight, skies will be clear with temperatures around 58 degrees Fahrenheit.라고 했으므로 정답은 (A)이다.

5. 매튜스는 사람들이 토요일에 무엇을 하길 제안하는가?
(A) 재킷을 입는 것
(B) 실내에 머무르는 것
(C) 우산을 가져오는 것
(D) 야외 활동을 즐기는 것

해설 질문에 Saturday가 있으므로 본문을 들을 때 Saturday가 나오는 부분에서 정답의 단서를 찾아야 한다. Saturday is the perfect day to plan outdoor activities라고 했으므로 정답은 (D)이다.

6. 일요일에는 무슨 일이 있겠는가?
(A) 비가 올 것이다.
(B) 더 따뜻해질 것이다.
(C) 강풍이 불 것이다.
(D) 기온이 높을 것이다.

해설 일기 예보에서는 특정 요일의 날씨를 언급하기 때문에 질문에 나온 요일을 미리 보고 그 요일에 해당하는 부분만 잘 들으면 된다. 질문에서 Sunday에 관해 물었는데 지문에서 There's also an 80 percent chance of rain on Sunday라고 했으므로 정답은 (A)이다.

7-9

Good morning, everyone. **I'm Marsha Colfax, and on behalf of everyone of us in the market research department**,⁷ I'd like to welcome you to the company. This morning, I'll review the information contained in your new employee orientation packets you got from the human resources department. Then, after we take our lunch break in the cafeteria, we'll discuss company benefits as well as employee development programs. In your packet, you'll see some sample pay forms like the ones the accounting department uses to process your paychecks. **Let's fill those out now**,⁸ and **in 20 minutes, I'll be back to talk about how to fill out your time sheets**.⁹

여러분, 안녕하세요. 저는 마샤 콜팩스이며 시장 조사 부서의 모든 직원들을 대신해 여러분의 입사를 환영합니다. 오늘 아침, 저는 여러분께서 인적 자원 부서에서 받은 신입 직원 오리엔테이션 자료집에 담긴 안내 사항을 검토해드리겠습니다. 그런 다음 구내 식당에서 점심 식사를 한 후, 직원 개발 프로그램뿐만 아니라 회사 복리후생에 대해서도 함께 얘기할 것입니다. 회계 부서에서 여러분의 급여를 처리하는 데 사용하는 것과 같은 급여 양식 견본이 여러분의 자료집에 있을 겁니다. 지금 그것을 작성하시고, 20분 후에 제가 다시 여러분의 근무 시간 기록표의 작성 방법에 대해 말씀드리겠습니다.

어휘 on behalf of ~을 대신해, ~을 대표해
welcome ~ to the company ~의 입사를 환영하다
review 검토하다　contain 담다, 포함시키다　packet 자료집
take a lunch break 점심 시간을 갖다
company benefits 회사 복리후생
A as well as B B뿐만 아니라 A도　development 개발
pay form 급여 양식　process 처리하다　paycheck 급여
fill out 작성하다　time sheet 근무 시간 기록표

7. 화자는 어떤 부서에서 근무할 것 같은가?
(A) 회계
(B) 고객 서비스
(C) 인적 자원
(D) 시장 조사

해설 화자가 자신을 소개하면서 I'm Marsha Colfax, and on behalf of every one of us in the Market Research department라고 했으므로 정답은 (D)이다.

8. 청자들에게 무엇을 지시하는가?
(A) 서류 작성하기
(B) 급여 받기
(C) 구내 식당으로 가기
(D) 워크숍에 등록하기

해설 지시 사항이나 당부 등은 대개 이야기 후반부에 언급되는 경우가 많다. 여기서도 이야기 후반부에 Let's fill those out now라고 했는데 those가 앞에 나온 sample pay forms를 가리키므로 정답은 (A)이다.

9. 20분 후에 무슨 일이 있겠는가?
(A) 절차가 설명된다.
(B) 식사 시간이 시작된다.
(C) 조사 연구가 시작된다.
(D) 워크숍이 끝난다.

해설 질문에 in 20 minutes가 있으므로 이 표현이 나오는 부분에서 정답의 단서를 찾아야 한다. 이야기 제일 마지막에 in 20 minutes, I'll be back to talk about how to fill out your time sheets라고 했는데 근무시간 기록표를 작성하는 방법이 양식 작성의 절차이므로 결국 (A)가 정답이다.

10-12

Welcome to the Smarter Lighting Expo. There is no charge for admission, but **all attendees must register at the front desk to view the exhibits**.[10] Please have a photo ID ready. You will then receive a badge and be allowed to enter the exhibit room. **The Smarter Lighting Expo is the only trade show of its kind in this region**,[11] and we hope you enjoy it. The show runs today only, from 10 A.M. to 8 P.M., and **product demonstrations kick off at 11 A.M.**[12] Please line up to register now, as we don't want you to miss the show. Thank you.

스마터 조명 박람회에 오신 걸 환영합니다. 입장료는 무료이지만 모든 참석자들은 안내 데스크에서 등록을 하셔야 전시품을 보실 수 있습니다. 사진이 붙은 신분증을 준비해 주십시오. 그런 다음 배지를 받고 전시실로 입장을 하시게 됩니다. 스마터 조명 박람회는 지역 내의 유일한 무역 박람회이며, 여러분 모두 즐거운 시간을 보내시기 바랍니다. 이번 전시회는 오전 10시부터 오후 8시까지 오늘 하루 동안만 진행되며 제품 시연회는 오전 11시에 시작됩니다. 전시회를 놓치지 않도록 지금 줄을 서서 등록해주십시오. 감사합니다.

어휘 lighting 조명 expo 박람회(exposition의 줄임말)
no charge for admission 무료 입장 attendee 참석자
register 등록하다 front desk 안내 데스크 view 보다
exhibit 전시품; 전시하다 photo ID 사진이 붙은 신분증
exhibit room 전시실 trade show 무역 박람회
run (행사 등이) 진행되다 product demonstration 제품 시연회
kick off 시작되다 line up 줄 서다 miss 놓치다

10. 안내 방송의 주목적은 무엇인가?
(A) 등록 과정을 설명하는 것
(B) 시작 시간 지연을 알리는 것
(C) 신상품의 이점을 홍보하는 것
(D) 전시장으로 오는 길을 알려주는 것

해설 안내 방송의 목적은 이야기의 앞부분에 제시된다. 화자가 이야기 초반부에 all attendees must register at the front desk to view the exhibits라고 말하면서 박람회 등록을 요청하고 있으므로 정답은 (A)이다.

11. 스마터 조명 박람회에 대해 언급된 내용은 무엇인가?
(A) 사진작가들을 위해 준비되었다.
(B) 입장료가 필요하다.
(C) 지역에서 유일한 것이다.
(D) 이틀 동안 열린다.

해설 질문에 Smarter Lighting Expo라는 말이 있으므로 이 표현이 언급된 부분에서 정답의 단서를 찾아야 한다. The Smarter Lighting Expo is the only trade show of its kind in this region이라고 했으므로 정답은 (C)이다. 문제나 보기에 지명, 인명, 행사명 또는 제품명과 같은 고유명사가 있으면 그 단어를 미리 읽어두어서 발음에 친숙해져야 지문을 들을 때 쉽게 알아들을 수 있다.

12. 언제 제품 시연회가 시작되는가?
(A) 오전 8시   (B) 오전 10시
(C) 오전 11시   (D) 오후 12시

해설 문제의 핵심어로 product demonstration이라는 말이 있고 보기에 시간이 제시되어 있다. 그러므로 지문에서 product demonstration이라는 말이 나오는 부분에서 언급되는 시간을 포착해야 한다. 안내 방송 후반부에 product demonstrations kick off at 11 A.M.이라고 했으므로 정답은 (C)이다.

13-15

Thank you for calling Rapid Reserve. Unfortunately, all of our operators are busy at the moment. **If you wish to find out about flight schedules, please use our online booking service at www.rapidreserve.com.**[13] If this is a personal call, and you know the extension of the person you wish to speak to, please press pound and enter their extension now. For other inquiries, **please hold for the next available customer service representative**.[14] Calls will be answered in the order they are received, so please do not hang up to try again. Please note that our customer service hours have been extended. To serve you better, **we are now taking calls on Saturdays from 9 A.M. to 5 P.M.**[15]

래피드 리저브에 전화 주셔서 감사합니다. 죄송하지만 지금은 우리 교환원 모두가 통화 중입니다. 만약 비행 일정에 대해 알고 싶으시면 www.rapidreserve.com에서 온라인 예약 서비스를 이용해 주십시오. 만약 개인적인 용무이고 통화하고 싶은 사람의 내선번호를 알고 계시면 지금 우물 정자 키를 눌러주시고 내선번호를 입력해주세요. 다른 문의 사항이 있으시면 다음 고객 서비스 직원을 기다려주십시오. 전화는 걸려 온 순서대로 받게 되니 끊었다 다시 걸지 마시기 바랍니다. 저희 고객 서비스 시간이 연장되었다는 말씀을 드립니다. 고객 여러분을 더 잘 모시기 위해 저희는 이제부터 토요일 오전 9시에서 오후 5시까지 전화를 받고 있습니다.

어휘 unfortunately 아쉽게도, 죄송하게도 busy 바쁜, 통화 중인
at the moment 현재, 지금 find out about ~에 대해 알아보다
booking service 예약 서비스 personal call 사적인 용무의 전화
extension 내선번호 press pound 우물 정자 키를 누르다
inquiry 문의 hold 기다리다, 대기하다
available 이용 가능한, 시간이 되는
customer service representative 고객 서비스 직원
answer[take] a call 전화를 받다
in the order + 주어 + 동사 ~한 순서대로 hang up 끊다
note 주목하다 extend 연장하다

13. 화자에 따르면 누가 회사 웹사이트를 방문해야 하는가?
(A) 래피드 리저브 직원들
(B) 비행 시간을 알고 싶은 고객들
(C) 직원을 찾는 사람들
(D) 특별 예약이 필요한 고객들

해설 질문에 Web site라는 말이 있으므로 지문에서 Web site 또는 online이라는 단어가 언급되는 부분에서 정답의 단서를 찾아야 한다. 메시지 초반부에 If you wish to find out about flight schedules, please use our online booking service at www.rapidreserve.com이라고 했으므로 정답은 (B)이다.

14. 화자가 "다음 고객 서비스 직원을 기다려주십시오"라고 말할 때 의미하는 바는 무엇인가?
(A) 끊고 다시 전화하기
(B) 다른 시간에 전화하기
(C) 회신 번호 남기기
(D) 다음 교환원을 기다리기

해설 지문에서 please hold for the next available customer service representative라고 했는데 hold for가 wait for를 의미하므로 정답은 (D)이다. hold for ~는 주로 전화상에서 '끊지 말고 ~를 기다리다'는 의미를 전달할 때 자주 쓰인다. 아울러 stay on the line도 '끊지 않고 기다리다'라는 뜻이라는 것을 알아 두자.

15. 화자는 전화를 건 사람들에게 무엇을 상기시켜 주는가?
(A) 할인 티켓
(B) 취소 정책
(C) 비행 시간 변경
(D) 주말 서비스

해설 청자들에게 상기시키거나 강조하고 싶은 내용이 있을 경우 〈Please note that ~〉이라는 말을 흔히 쓴다. 이 메시지 후반부에 Please note that이라고 한 다음 그 뒤로 we are now taking calls on Saturdays from 9 A.M. to 5 P.M.이라고 했으므로 정답은 (D)이다.

16-18

> OK, everyone. I would now like to introduce the latest addition to our staff, Ms. Donna Medford. Ms. Medford comes to us from All-Events Ltd., an event planning organization, where she worked as the marketing manager. **She started work yesterday here as human resources manager,**[16] and she is also overseeing our Employee Life Committee. As you know, our staff's well-being is important. To help Ms. Medford as a new committee head, **I will pass out our monthly "workplace satisfaction" surveys this afternoon**[17] and have you fill them out. Also, **please give Ms. Medford your newest e-mail addresses and mobile phone numbers.**[18] Alright, now I'll turn the podium over to Ms. Medford.

좋습니다. 여러분. 저는 이제 가장 최근에 입사한 도나 메드포드 씨를 소개해드리겠습니다. 메드포드 씨는 그녀가 마케팅 매니저로 일했던 이벤트 기획사인 올 이벤트 사에서 저희 회사로 오셨습니다. 그녀는 인적 자원 매니저로서 어제부터 이곳에서 근무를 시작했고, 또한 직원 생활 위원회를 맡고 있습니다. 여러분도 아시듯 우리 직원들의 복지는 중요합니다. 신임 위원회장인 메드포드 씨를 돕기 위해 저는 오늘 오후에 월례 '직장 만족도' 설문지를 나눠드릴 테니 작성해주시기 바랍니다. 또한 메드포드 씨에게 여러분의 최신 이메일 주소와 휴대폰 번호를 알려주시기 바랍니다. 좋습니다. 이제 연단으로 메드포드 씨를 모시겠습니다.

어휘 latest 최신의 addition 추가된 직원 planning 기획
oversee 감독하다 committee 위원회 well-being 복지, 행복
head 책임자, 장 pass out 나눠주다 workplace 직장
satisfaction 만족(도) fill out 작성하다 newest 최신의
turn ~ over to ~을 ~에게 넘기다 podium 연단

16. 메드포드 씨의 새 직책은 무엇인가?
(A) 마케팅 매니저
(B) 인적 자원 매니저
(C) 영업 이사
(D) 부사장

해설 본문에서 She started work yesterday here as human resources manager라고 했는데 She가 Medford를 말하므로 정답은 (B)이다. 이야기 초반에 marketing manager라는 직책이 먼저 언급되었는데 이것은 Medford의 이전 직장에서의 직책이므로 혼동하지 않도록 조심해야 한다.

17. 오후에 무슨 일이 있겠는가?
(A) 새로운 절차가 시연될 것이다.
(B) 교육 프로그램이 시작될 것이다.
(C) 직원 설문지가 배부될 것이다.
(D) 시상식이 열릴 것이다.

해설 문제에 시점으로 in the afternoon이라는 말이 있으므로 이 표현이 언급되는 부분에서 정답의 단서를 찾아야 한다. I will pass out our monthly "workplace satisfaction" surveys this afternoon이라고 했으므로 정답은 (C)이다.

18. 화자는 청자에게 무엇을 요청하는가?
(A) 새로운 직원 ID 카드 받기
(B) 상 받을 동료 추천하기
(C) 최신 연락처 제공하기
(D) 소그룹 회의 개최

해설 청자들에게 하는 요청이나 당부는 이야기의 후반부에 제시되는 경우가 많다. 여기서도 please give Ms. Medford your newest e-mail addresses and mobile phone numbers라고 했는데 이메일 주소와 휴대폰 번호가 contact information에 해당하므로 정답은 (C)이다.

19-21

Thank you everyone for coming in to work on time today. Because of the bad weather, we don't expect many customers to come here to dine at the restaurant today. **Unfortunately, though, one of our suppliers couldn't deliver some tomatoes and other vegetables**[19] to us this morning. So, for our lunch servings, some soup and pasta items won't be available. **Please suggest that our diners try an item from our "daily snack specials" menu**[20] instead. I'll run to the food store to pick up tomatoes once they open. For now, **I'll pass out a list of menu items**[21] we may run out of. Please look it over now. Thanks, all.

여러분 모두 오늘 정시에 출근해주신 점 감사드립니다. 날씨가 좋지 않기 때문에 오늘은 식당에 손님들이 많이 올 것 같지는 않습니다. 그렇지만 아쉽게도 오늘 아침에 우리 납품업자 한 명이 토마토와 몇 가지 채소들을 배달해주지 못했습니다. 그래서 점심 식사로 일부 수프와 파스타 품목은 준비가 안 될 겁니다. 대신 손님들에게 우리 '일일 특별 간식' 메뉴에 있는 것을 드셔보라고 제안해주세요. 제가 식품점이 열자마자 얼른 가서 토마토를 사오겠습니다. 제가 지금 다 떨어질 수도 있는 메뉴 품목의 목록을 나눠드리겠습니다. 지금 검토해주십시오. 여러분 모두 감사합니다.

어휘 come in to work 출근하다   on time 정시에
because of ~ 때문에(= due to)
expect + A(목적어) + to부정사 A가 ~할 것으로 예상하다
dine 식사하다 (cf. diner 식사 손님)   though 그렇지만
supplier 납품업자, 공급업자   deliver 배달하다   vegetable 채소
serving 손님 접대; 음식의 1인분   available 이용 가능한   try 먹어보다
snack 간식, 간단한 식사   food store 식품 가게   pick up 사다
once ~하자마자   for now 지금은   pass out 나눠주다
run out of ~가 다 떨어지다   look over 검토하다

납품업체 목록	
납품업체	물품
탑스 실버웨어 사	식사 도구와 접시
클린올 스토어	냅킨과 물수건
데일리데어리 팜	버터와 치즈
홀뉴트리 스토어	과일과 채소

19. 도표를 보세요. 어느 납품업체가 물건을 가져오지 못했는가?
(A) 탑스 실버웨어 사
(B) 클린올 스토어
(C) 데일리데어리 팜
(D) 홀뉴트리 스토어

해설 담화 초반부에 아쉽게도 오늘 아침에 우리 납품업자 한 명이 토마토와 몇 가지 채소들을 배달해주지 못했다(one of our suppliers couldn't deliver some tomatoes and other vegetables)고 했다. 도표를 보면 과일과 채소를 납품하는 업체는 Wholnutri Store이므로 정답은 (D)이다.

20. 화자는 점심 시간에 청자들에게 무엇을 하라고 말하는가?
(A) 휴식을 취하기
(B) 지역 상점에서 용품을 받기
(C) 특별 메뉴에 있는 항목 권하기
(D) 온라인 주문 시스템 홍보하기

해설 화자가 직원들에게 Please suggest that our diners try an item from our "daily snack specials" menu라고 요구했는데 suggest가 recommend로 패러프레이징(바꿔 쓰기) 된 것이므로 정답은 (C)이다.

21. 화자는 다음에 무엇을 하겠는가?
(A) 식당 주방에 간다.
(B) 목록을 배부한다.
(C) 창고에 간다.
(D) 배달 시간을 확인한다.

해설 화자의 향후 일정 등은 대개 이야기의 후반부에 제시된다. 여기서도 마지막 부분에 I'll pass out a list of menu items라고 했으므로 정답은 (B)이다.

RC 정답 및 해설

UNIT 1 명사와 대명사

Check-up Step 1 본책 _ p. 153

1.
- 해설: 빈칸 앞에 every(모든)가 있으므로, 빈칸에는 무조건 가산 단수명사만 가능하다. 따라서 단수명사인 (A) member가 정답이다.
- 해석: 모든 구성원들은 세미나에 등록해야 한다.
- 어휘: every 모든   register ~를 기록하다, 나타내다, 등록되다, ~를 등록하다   seminar 세미나, 모임   member 구성원, 회원
- 정답: (A)

2.
- 해설: 빈칸 앞에 a few(약간의)가 있으므로, 빈칸에는 무조건 가산 복수명사만 가능하다. 따라서 복수명사인 (B) problems가 정답이다.
- 해석: 우리는 최근에 새로운 시스템에 약간의 문제가 있었다.
- 어휘: recently 최근에   a few 약간의   system 조직, 체제, 제도   problem 문제, 걱정거리
- 정답: (B)

3.
- 해설: 빈칸에는 명사 information(정보)을 앞에서 수식할 수 있는 어휘를 선택해야 한다. information은 불가산명사이므로 (B) much가 정답이다.
- 해석: 우리는 문제를 찾아서 해결하기 위해 많은 정보가 필요하다.
- 어휘: need 요구, 요구사항, 필요성; ~이 필요하다   information 정보   fix 해결책; ~를 고치다, ~를 해결하다, ~를 고정시키다
- 정답: (B)

Check-up Step 2 본책 _ p. 153

4.
- 해설: each 다음에 오는 알맞은 어휘를 고르는 문제이다. 일단, 동사는 더 이상 올 수 없으므로 (A) apply는 탈락된다. 동명사인 (D) applying 역시 오답이다. each 다음에는 가산 단수명사만 오므로 (B) applicant가 정답이다.
- 해석: 우리의 새로운 인사 관리자는 면접 일정을 잡기 위해 각각의 지원자들에게 연락할 것이다.
- 어휘: personnel 직원들, 인사부서   manager 관리자, 매니저   contact 접촉, 연락; ~에 연락하다   schedule 일정표, 스케줄; ~의 일정을 잡다   apply 신청하다, 적용되다, ~를 적용하다, ~를 사용하다, ~를 바르다   applicant 신청자, 지원자
- 정답: (B)

5.
- 해설: 복수명사 considerations를 수식할 수 있는 알맞은 형용사를 고르는 문제이다. 보기 중 유일하게 복수명사를 수식 가능한 (C) a few(약간의, 몇몇의)가 정답이 된다. 나머지 보기 어휘들은 불가산명사를 수식할 경우에 사용된다.
- 해석: 우리는 회의 전에 당신과 함께 몇몇 기본적 고려사항들을 공유하길 원합니다.
- 어휘: share ~을 공유하다   a few 약간의, 몇몇의   basic consideration 기본 고려사항   meeting 회의   little 거의 없는   much 많은   less 더 적은
- 정답: (C)

Check-up Step 1 본책 _ p. 155

1.
- 해설: 빈칸은 문장의 주어가 되는 명사의 자리인데, 보기 둘 다 명사이다. 일단, (B) Competitor는 가산명사로 a competitor 또는 competitors로 사용되므로 탈락된다. 또한 (B) Competitor는 동사 will increase와 의미적으로 어울리지 않는다. 따라서 불가산명사인 (A) Competition이 정답이 된다.
- 해석: 자동차 산업의 경쟁이 증가할 것이다.
- 어휘: competition 경쟁, 경합, 대회   competitor 경쟁자   increase 증강, 상승; ~를 증가시키다, 증가하다
- 정답: (A)

2.
- 해설: 명사 health와 빈칸이 결합하여 복합명사를 만들어야 한다. 복합명사의 수는 뒤의 명사가 결정하는데, (A) professional은 가산명사로 수일치에서 제외된다. 따라서 health professionals(건강 전문가들, 의사들)이라는 올바른 표현을 만든 (B) professionals가 정답이다.
- 해석: 그 위원회는 건강 전문가들로 구성되어 있다.
- 어휘: board 이사회, 위원회; 탑승하다   consist of ~로 구성되다   professional 전문가; 전문적인
- 정답: (B)

96

3.

해설 빈칸 앞에 부정관사 a가 있으므로 빈칸은 명사의 자리이다. 또한 형용사 dramatic의 수식을 받아야 하는데, 보기 중에서 명사는 (A) rise(상승, 증가)이다.

해석 연료비의 급격한 상승이 많은 사람들을 놀라게 했다.

어휘 dramatic 급격한, 인상적인 cost 비용; 비용이 들다, ~가 들게 하다
surprise ~를 놀라게 하다 rise 인상, 증가; 상승하다

정답 (A)

Check-up Step 2 본책 _ p. 155

4.

해설 빈칸에는 명사 salary와 함께 쓰여 주어를 이루면서, 동사 are decided와도 어울려야 한다. 일단, 형용사 (B) increasing과 (D) increased는 오더라도, 주어와 동사의 수일치가 틀리다. 복합명사를 이루는 (A) increase는 수일치에서 탈락된다. 따라서 복수명사 (C) increases가 정답이다.

해석 대부분의 회사에서, 급여 인상은 실적평가에 의해 결정된다.

어휘 increase 상승, 증가; ~를 증가시키다, 증가하다 salary 급여, 월급
decide 결심하다, ~를 결정하다 performance 실적, 성능, 공연
review 평가, 검토; ~를 검토하다

정답 (C)

5.

해설 정관사 the 뒤에서 문장의 주어로 사용될 명사를 고르는 문제다. 보기의 단어들은 형용사를 지칭하는 접미사 -tive 형태이지만 보기 중 유일하게 (C) objective는 '목적, 목표'라는 의미의 명사로도 사용되므로 정답이 된다.

해석 그 프로그램의 목적은 참가자들에게 새로운 정보를 제공해주는 것이다.

어휘 objective 목적, 목표; 객관적인
provide A with B A에게 B를 제공하다 participant 참가자
effective 효과적인 creative 창조적인 protective 보호하는, 보호용의

정답 (C)

Check-up Step 1 본책 _ p. 157

1.

해설 빈칸 앞뒤로 전치사 during과 명사 vacation이 있으므로, 주어 자리에만 사용하는 주격 대명사 (A) he는 바로 탈락된다. 따라서 vacation을 앞에서 수식하는 소유격 대명사 (B) his가 정답이다.

해석 그의 휴가동안에, 페도르는 프랑스와 이탈리아를 여행했다.

정답 (B)

2.

해설 알맞은 대명사의 격을 선택하는 문제로, 빈칸 앞의 contact가 중요한 힌트가 된다. 이 문장에서 contact는 명령문을 이끄는 타동사이므로, 뒤에는 목적어 역할을 하는 (B) us가 와야 한다.

해석 만약 당신이 질문이 있다면, 우리에게 연락하세요.

어휘 question 질문, 쟁점, 문제; ~에게 질문하다
contact 접촉, 연락; ~에 연락하다

정답 (B)

3.

해설 알맞은 대명사 어휘를 선택하는 문제이다. 문맥상 '자신을 소개한 후에, 몇몇 주제에 대해 이야기했다'라는 의미가 어울리므로 (B) herself가 와야 한다. 여기서 (B) herself는 주어와 목적어가 동일할 때 사용하며, 문장의 목적어로 생략이 불가능하다.

해석 그녀는 자신을 소개한 후에, 몇몇 주제에 대해 이야기했다.

어휘 introduce ~를 소개하다, ~를 도입하다, ~를 선보이다
several 몇몇의 topic 화제, 주제

정답 (B)

Check-up Step 2 본책 _ p. 157

4.

해설 전치사 by 다음에 올 수 있는 대명사를 고르는 문제인데, (A) your는 전치사 다음에 올 수 없다. 전치사 on과 쓰여 on one's own(스스로)이라는 표현을 만드는 (B) your own도 역시 제외된다. 나머지 보기 중에서 by yourself(스스로)라는 표현을 이루는 (C) yourself가 정답이다.

해석 만약 그 상품이 적절하게 작동하지 않아도, 당신은 그것을 혼자 수리할 수 있습니다.

어휘 item 상품, 항목 operate 운영되다, ~를 운영하다, ~를 수술하다
properly 적절하게 repair 수리; ~를 고치다
by oneself 홀로, 스스로

정답 (C)

5.

해설 인칭대명사의 적절한 격을 선택해야 하는 문제이다. 빈칸은 주어인 the director와 과거동사 decided 사이의 부사 자리이며, 보기의 대명사들 중 부사로 사용가능한 재귀대명사 (C) himself가 정답이 된다. 재귀대명사(oneself)는 문장 내 주어와 동일할 경우 목적어(재귀용법)와 부사 자리(강조용법)에서 사용이 가능하다.

해석 전문가를 초빙하는 것 대신에, 담당자는 직접 직원들을 교육시키기로 결심했다.

어휘 instead of -ing/명사 ~을 대신하여
invite ~을 초대하다, ~에게 권하다 specialist 전문가
decide 결심하다, ~을 결정하다 train ~을 교육시키다

정답 (C)

Check-up Step 1 본책_p. 159

1.
해설 빈칸은 전치사 to의 목적어인 동시에, 지시형용사 this의 수식을 받는 자리이다. this는 뒤에는 단수명사가 오기 때문에 (A) message가 정답이다.

해석 이 메시지에 응답하세요.

어휘 respond 응답하다, 반응하다   message 메시지, 교훈

정답 (A)

2.
해설 빈칸은 전치사 of 이하의 수식을 받으면서, 앞의 명사를 지칭하는 지시대명사의 자리이다. 여기서 지칭하는 명사는 products(제품들)이므로, 복수를 지칭하는 (B) those가 정답이 된다.

해석 우리 제품들은 경쟁사의 제품보다 더 내구성이 있다.

어휘 product 상품, 제품   durable 내구성 있는, 오래가는
competitor 경쟁자, 경쟁업체

정답 (B)

3.
해설 첫 문장에서 주어는 one of the two plans(두 개의 계획들 중 하나)이고, 동사는 is이다. but으로 연결된 뒤 문장은 '나머지 그 하나'의 의미가 되어야 하므로, 부정대명사 (B) the other가 정답이다.

해석 두 개의 계획들 중 하나는 실행이 가능하지만, 나머지 하나는 그렇지 않다.

어휘 plan 계획; ~을 계획하다   possible 가능한
implement ~을 실행하다; 연장, 도구

정답 (B)

Check-up Step 2 본책_p. 159

4.
해설 '스캐너가 고장이 난다'는 해석으로 보아, 빈칸에 들어갈 명사는 the scanner를 지칭함이 틀림없다. 하지만 빈칸 앞의 대명사 it이 그 역할을 하고 있으며, 문맥상 '다른 것으로 교체해 준다'는 의미가 필요하다. 따라서 '또 다른 하나'를 의미하는 (C) another가 정답이다.

해석 만약 스캐너가 고장 난다면, 우리는 그것을 다른 것으로 교체해 주거나, 당신의 돈을 환불해 줄 것입니다.

어휘 scanner 스캐너   out of order 고장 난
replace ~를 대신하다, ~를 교체하다
refund 환불, 환불금; ~를 환불해 주다

정답 (C)

5.
해설 빈칸은 전치사구 'on the daytime'의 수식을 받으며, 앞의 명사를 지칭하는 대명사의 자리이다. 해석상 지칭하는 명사를 wages(임금)로 확인할 수 있으므로, 복수명사를 지칭하는 지시대명사 (D) those가 정답이 된다.

해석 야간 근무자들의 임금은 주간 임금보다 꾸준히 더 높아 왔다.

어휘 wage 임금   consistently 지속적으로, 꾸준히
nighttime worker 야간근무자   daytime 주간

정답 (D)

Check-up 본책_p. 161

1. 정답 **employees**
어휘 employment 직장, 채용 / employee 직원

2. 정답 **attendants**
어휘 attend 참석하다 / attendant 승무원

3. 정답 **strategy**
어휘 strategy 전략 / appearance 외모

4. 정답 **choice**
어휘 choose 선택하다 / choice 선택

5. 정답 **development**
어휘 develop 개발하다 / development 개발

Part 5&6_ 실전연습 1 본책_p. 162-163

1.
해설 타동사 hire의 목적어를 고르는 문제로, 동사 (D) employ는 올 수 없다. (A) employers(고용주)와 (B) employment(채용)는 의미상 동사 hire의 목적어가 될 수 없다. 따라서 명사 (C) employees(직원들)가 정답이 된다.

해석 LKH 화학회사는 다음 주부터 조립라인에서 일하기 원하는 직원을 우선적으로 채용할 것입니다.

어휘 several 몇몇의   company 회사   hire ~를 고용하다, ~를 채용하다
employer 고용주   employment 채용, 고용, 취업
employee 직원   employ ~를 채용하다, ~를 고용하다
assembly 조립, 의회, 모임

정답 (C)

2.
해설 동사 instruct의 목적어로 가능한 대명사를 고르는 문제이다. (D) ours는 '우리의 것'이라는 의미로 instruct의 목적어가 될 수 없다. 따라서 목적격 대명사 (B) us가 정답이다.

해석 오늘 고객들이 사무실을 방문할 것으로 예상되기 때문에, 관리자는 우리들에게 책상을 정리하도록 지시했다.

어휘 manager 관리자, 경영자
instruct ~를 지시하다, ~를 가르치다, (정보 따위를) 알려주다
organize 정리하다, 준비하다, 조직하다   possible 가능한, 잠재적인
be expected to부정사 ~할 것으로 예상되다
visit 방문; ~를 방문하다   office 사무실, 공직

정답 (B)

3.
해설 빈칸은 of the nation's currency(국가의 통화, 화폐)의 수식을 받는 명사의 자리이다. 문맥상 '통화가치가 급격히 하락했다'는 의미가 필요하므로 (C) value(가치)가 정답이다.

해석 보고서에 따르면, 불경기 동안에 국가의 통화가치가 급격히 떨어졌습니다.

어휘 currency 통화   fall 추락, 감소; 넘어지다, 떨어지다
recession 불경기, 불황, 후퇴
cost 비용, 비용이 들다, ~에게 ~를 부과하다   expense 비용
value 가치, 중요성; 가치 있는; (가치, 가격을) 평가하다   fare (교통) 요금

정답 (C)

4.
해설 동사 thank는 사람을 목적어로 수반하므로 (B) attendance(참석, 참석률)는 빈칸에 올 수 없다. 문맥상 '참석자'가 아니라, '수행원, 시중드는 승무원'을 의미하는 (A) attendant가 정답이다.

해석 우리 부부의 반복된 요청에도 불구하고, 비행기 내에서 대단한 보살핌을 보여준 그 승무원에게 감사한다.

어휘 thank ~에게 감사하다   care 돌봄, 관리, 관심; 돌보다
attendant 수행원, 간병인   attendance 출석, 출석률, 참석률
attendee 참석자   attend ~에 참석하다
in spite of ~에도 불구하고
request 요청; ~를 요청하다, ~를 요구하다

정답 (A)

5.
해설 전치사 by 다음에 오는 대명사의 격을 고르는 문제이다. 목적격인 (C) them이 오게 되면, '그들에 의해'라는 이상한 의미가 된다. 따라서 by themselves(그들 스스로)라는 관용표현을 만드는 (D) themselves가 정답이다.

해석 소비자들은 상점을 떠나기 전에, 만족도 설문조사를 작성하도록 요청받았다.

어휘 customer 소비자   be asked to부정사 ~하도록 요청받다
complete 완성된; ~를 마무리하다, 완성하다, 작성하다
satisfaction 만족(도)   survey 설문조사; ~를 조사하다
leave 휴가; 떠나다, ~을 남기다   by oneself 홀로, 스스로

정답 (D)

6.
해설 명사구 innovative promotion(혁신적인 홍보)과 결합하여 주어를 완성하는 문제이다. '고객의 관심을 끌다'라는 의미로 미루어 볼 때, '홍보전략(promotion strategy)'이라는 표현이 적합하다. 따라서 (B) strategy가 정답이다.

해석 마케팅 부서에 의해 제안된 혁신적인 홍보 전략은 소비자의 관심을 끌 것이다.

어휘 innovative 혁신적인   proposed 제안된
propose ~를 제안하다, ~를 (공식적으로) 요청하다
draw ~를 도출하다, ~를 그리다, ~를 끌어들이다, ~를 획득하다, ~를 뽑다
goal 목표 (= purpose, aim)   strategy 전략, 계획
department 부서, 국, 백화점   responsibility 책임, 책무, 책임감

정답 (B)

7.
해설 빈칸 앞에 manager's라는 일반명사의 소유격이 있으므로, 그 뒤에는 명사가 와야 한다. 따라서 보기의 유일한 명사 (B) approval이 정답이다.

해석 직원들이 부서장의 승인을 얻는다는 전제 하에, 우리는 직원들로 하여금 그들의 근무 시간을 스스로 정하도록 허용하고 있습니다.

어휘 allow A to부정사 A가 ~하도록 허락하다
schedule 일정표, 스케줄; ~의 일정을 잡다
working hours 근무 시간   as long as ~하기만 하면, ~하는 한
receive ~를 받다   approve ~을 승인하다, 찬성하다

정답 (B)

8.
해설 문맥상 동사 indicate의 목적어가 되는 대상은 앞 문장의 the workshop이다. 즉, '워크샵 중에서 마음에 드는 것, 참가하기로 선택한 워크샵'을 가리키는 (C) choice(선택)가 가장 적절하다.

해석 다음 달에 예정된 워크숍에 참가하고자 하신다면, 공란에 원하시는 워크샵을 표시해 주십시오.

어휘 attend ~에 참석하다 (= participate in)   workshop 모임, 워크숍
schedule 일정, 일정을 잡다   indicate ~를 나타내다, 표시하다
option 선택, 선택과목   suggestion 제안, 의견, 추정
choice 선택, 선택권, 선택한 것, 선택 범위, 선택된 사람

정답 (C)

9.
해설 빈칸은 동사 provide의 목적어가 되는 명사의 자리로, 형용사 financial의 수식을 받아야 한다. 따라서 보기의 유일한 명사인 (D) support(지지, 지원)가 정답이다.

해석 시 위원회는 진귀한 책들을 소장한 도서관을 짓는 데 재정적인 지원을 제공하기로 결정했다.

어휘 committee 위원회   decide to부정사 ~하기로 결정하다, 결심하다
financial 재정적인   be equipped with ~를 장착하다, 갖추다
rare 드문, 진귀한   artwork 예술품, 삽화
supportive 지원하는, 도와주는   support 지지, 지원; ~를 지원하다

정답 (D)

10.
해설 전치사와 전치사 사이에 올 수 있는 것은 명사뿐이다. 따라서 보기의 유일한 명사 (C) comparison(비교)이 정답이다.

해석 타사와 비교하면, 우리 회사 제품의 성능이 훨씬 더 우수합니다.

어휘 performance 실적, 성능   compare A with B A를 B와 비교하다
in comparison with ~와 비교하면   comparison 비교, 유사성
comparable 비슷한, 필적할만한

정답 (C)

11.
해설 빈칸은 형용사 used(사용되는)의 수식을 받으며, 문장의 주어인 brick(벽돌)의 보어가 되는 명사 자리이다. 보기의 단어들 모두 '요소, 성분'의 의미이지만, 문맥상 가장 적합한 것은 (C) materials이다.

해석 최근 조사에 따르면, 벽돌은 오늘날 건축에 가장 널리 사용되는 자재 중 하나입니다.

어휘 according to ~에 따르면, ~에 의하면
survey (설문)조사, 투표; ~를 조사하다   ingredient 성분, 요소, 원료
parts 기계 부품   material 물질, 재료, 자료   portion 일부, 부분

정답 (C)

12.
해설 빈칸 앞에 부정관사 a가 있으므로 빈칸은 명사의 자리이다. receive a promotion(승진하다)이라는 표현을 이루는 명사 (A) promotion(승진)이 정답이다.

해석 브루노 씨는 지난 분기의 월등한 공적으로 인하여 승진할 것이다.

어휘 promotion 승진, 촉진, 홍보
promote ~를 승진시키다, ~를 홍보하다, ~를 촉진시키다
receive ~를 받다   outstanding 뛰어난, 훌륭한

정답 (A)

13.
해설 빈칸은 명사 housing, project와 함께 쓰여 하나의 복합명사를 만드는 자리이다. 문맥상 '주택 개발 계획'이라는 의미가 필요하므로, (A) development가 정답이다.

해석 이제 겨울이 다 지나갔으니 주택 개발 계획의 최종 단계 공사가 재개될 것이다.

어휘 now that ~이니까   resume ~을 재개하다, 재개되다
phase 단계, 국면 (= stage)
housing development 주택 개발, 주택 건설
refreshment 휴식, 다과   supplement 추가, 보충, 제공
requirement 필수 요건

정답 (A)

14.
해설 빈칸 앞의 명사 hotel(호텔)과 어울리는 형태를 고르는 문제로, 일단 동사 (C) reserves, (D) reserve 모두 탈락된다. 결국 a hotel reservation(호텔 예약)이라는 복합명사를 이루는 (A) reservation이 정답이다.

해석 예기치 못한 문제들이 발생하는 것에 대비하여, 출발 전에 호텔 예약을 반드시 확인하세요.

어휘 confirm ~를 확인하다   in case ~하면, ~할 경우에 대비해서
unexpected 예기치 못한, 예상치 못한   problem 문제, 걱정거리
occur (문제점, 병 따위가) 발생하다   departure 출발
reservation 의심, 예약   reserve ~를 예약하다, ~를 보관하다

정답 (A)

15-18

발신: samnorth@kmobile.net
수신: rachelk@bradley.nz.edu
제목: 광고에 나온 아파트에 관한 질문
날짜: 6월 1일

쿤츠 씨께,

로프티 골즈 웹 사이트에 올린 귀하의 아파트에 대해 질문이 있어 글을 씁니다. 그 아파트를 임차하고 싶습니다. 임대차 계약서에 서명하기에 앞서 몇 가지 질문에 대해 명확히 설명해 주셨으면 합니다. 목록을 보면 아파트에 가구가 완전히 갖추어져 있다고 나와 있는데요. 좀 더 상세히 설명해 주실 수 있나요? 정확히 어떤 것들이 포함되어 있는 것인지요? 또한, 그 건물에서는 어떤 종류의 편의 시설을 제공하고 있나요? 당신이 요구하는 가격대의 아파트에서는 운동 시설과 차고를 이용할 수 있는 경우가 보통입니다. 미리 감사드립니다.

새뮤얼 노스

어휘 inquire about ~에 관해 묻다   lofty 아주 높은, 우뚝한
lease 임대차 계약   clear up (쟁점·불확실성 등을) 명확히 하다
furnish (가구를) 비치하다   specific 구체적인, 명확한
include 포함하다   offer (이용할 수 있도록) 내놓다, 제공하다
in advance 미리, 사전에

15.

(A) 그 아파트를 임차하고 싶습니다.
(B) 제 아파트를 추천하고 싶습니다.
(C) 저는 최근에 옆집의 방 하나를 임차했습니다.
(D) 더 이상 목록을 구할 수 없다고 들었습니다.

해설 임대차 계약서에 서명하기 전에 몇 가지 질문이 있다는 말이 빈칸 뒤에 나오고 있다. 즉, Samuel North는 Ms. Koontz가 웹 사이트에 올린 아파트 임대 광고에 관심이 있음을 알 수 있으며, 따라서 아파트를 빌리고 싶다는 내용의 (A)가 답으로 적절하다.

정답 (A)

16.

해설 동사 is와 형용사 보어인 과거분사 furnished(가구가 설비된) 사이에 올 수 있는 것은, 형용사를 수식해 줄 수 있는 부사 (B) fully이다.

정답 (B)

17.

해설 적절한 의문사를 고르는 문제이다. 모든 가구가 설치되어 있다고 하는데, 그것에 포함되는 것이 '무엇'이냐는 문맥이 가장 자연스러우므로 (A) What이 정답이다.

정답 (A)

18.

해설 '어떤 종류의 ~을 그 건물에서 제공하느냐'는 이 문장 뒤의 내용을 보면, 운동 시설과 차고(fitness centers and parking garage)가 빈칸에 들어갈 어휘의 예로 언급되고 있다. 운동 시설과 차고를 나타낼 수 있는 어휘는 '편의 시설'을 뜻하는 (A) amenities이다.

정답 (A)

UNIT 2 형용사와 부사

Check-up Step 1 본책 _ p. 165

1.

해설 빈칸 앞에 정관사 the가 있고, 그 다음에 명사 report(보고서)가 있다. 즉, 빈칸은 명사를 앞에서 수식하는 형용사의 자리이므로, 형용사 (A) annual(연례의, 1년의)이 정답이 된다.

해석 우리는 연례 보고서를 업데이트해야 한다.

어휘 update ~를 최신의 것으로 하다, ~를 업데이트시키다
report 보고서, 공식문서; ~에게 알리다, 보도하다   annual 연례의, 1년의
annually 매년마다

정답 (A)

2.

해설 빈칸 앞에 be동사 was가 있고, 그 다음에 형용사 보어 helpful (유용한)이 있다. 형용사를 앞에서 꾸며주는 품사는 부사이므로 (B) really(정말로)가 정답이다.

해석 그녀의 조언은 정말로 유용했다.

어휘 advice 충고, 조언   helpful 유용한, 기꺼이 돕는
real 진짜의, 실제의   really 실제로, 정말로

정답 (B)

3.

해설 빈칸 다음의 new companies는 '형용사+명사'로 이루어져 있으므로, 그 앞에 명사 (A) innovation이 올 수 없다. 하지만 형용사는 두 개 이상이 명사 앞에 있어도 괜찮기 때문에, (B) innovative가 정답이다.

해석 우리는 혁신적인 새로운 회사들과 함께 일하기를 원한다.

어휘 would like to부정사 ~하고 싶다   work 일, 작업; 일하다
innovation 혁신   innovative 혁신적인

정답 (B)

Check-up Step 2 본책 _ p. 165

4.

해설 빈칸 앞의 동사 become은 뒤에 명사나 형용사 보어를 수반하는 불완전 자동사이다. 하지만 명사 (B) operator(운영자)는 주어 the factory(공장)와 동격이 될 수 없어 탈락된다. 따라서 형용사 (D) operational(가동되는, 작동이 되는)이 정답이다.

해석 그 공장은 모든 안전 장비가 검사받을 때까지 가동되지 않을 것이다.

어휘 factory 공장   safety equipment 안전 장비
test 시험, 검사, 실험; ~를 시험하다, ~를 검사하다
operate ~를 운영하다, 가동되다
operator 전화교환원, 기계 작동하는 사람, 운영자
operational 가동되는, 작동이 되는

정답 (D)

5.

해설 수동태(be p.p.) 사이에 들어갈 수 있는 알맞은 품사를 고르는 문제다. 빈칸에 들어갈 수 있는 품사는 부사이므로 정답은 (C) conveniently이다. 또한 'conveniently located(편리하게 위치된)'이라는 덩어리 표현으로 자주 사용되니 꼭 알아두도록 하자.

해석 그 호텔은 국제공항과 쇼핑지역 사이 편리한 곳에 위치하고 있다.

어휘 conveniently located 편리하게 위치된   between ~중에, ~사이에
international airport 국제공항   district (특정 목적의) 지구, 구역

정답 (C)

Check-up Step 1 본책 _ p. 167

1.
- 해설: 빈칸은 부정관사 a와 전치사 of 사이의 자리로 명사의 자리이다. 따라서 명사 (A) variety(다양성)가 정답이 된다. 여기서 a variety of는 '다양한'이라는 의미의 형용사구로 복수명사 salads를 꾸며준다.
- 해석: 그들은 다양한 샐러드를 제공합니다.
- 어휘: offer 제안, 제공; ~를 제공하다   a variety of 다양한 (= various)
- 정답: (A)

2.
- 해설: 빈칸 앞의 형용사 reluctant(꺼려하는, 주저하는)와 어울리는 표현을 고르는 문제이다. (A) talk가 동사로 쓰이든 명사로 쓰이든 모두 문법상 올 수 없다. 결국, be reluctant to talk의 표현을 이루는 (B) to talk가 정답이다.
- 해석: 많은 사람들은 그들의 개인적인 정보에 관해 말하는 것을 꺼려한다.
- 어휘: be reluctant to부정사 ~하는 데 주저하다   about ~에 관하여, 대략   personal 개인적인   talk 이야기, 회담, 대화; 이야기하다, 말하다
- 정답: (B)

3.
- 해설: 알맞은 형용사 어휘를 선택하여 문맥을 완성하는 문제로, 빈칸 다음의 전치사 with가 힌트가 된다. 전치사 with와 쓰여 be familiar with(~에 정통하다)라는 표현을 이루는 (A) familiar가 정답이다.
- 해석: 관리자는 모든 회사의 정책들에 정통해야 합니다.
- 어휘: manager 관리자, 매니저   policy 정책, 방침   be familiar with ~에 정통하다   be accustomed to ~에 익숙하다
- 정답: (A)

Check-up Step 2 본책 _ p. 167

4.
- 해설: 빈칸은 be동사 다음에 오면서, 전치사 for 이하와 어울리는 형용사의 자리이다. (A) entitled와 (D) able은 to부정사를 수반하기 때문에 탈락된다. (C) capable은 전치사 of를 수반하므로 역시 제외된다. 결국, be eligible for the position(자리에 자격이 있다)라는 표현을 이루는 (B) eligible이 정답이다.
- 해석: 그 직위에 자격이 있으려면, 후보자들은 경제학 학위가 있어야 한다.
- 어휘: position 직위, 위치; ~를 배치하다   candidate 후보자, 지원자   university degree 대학학위   economics 경제학   entitled 자격 있는   be eligible for ~에 자격이 있다 (= be eligible to부정사)   be able to부정사 ~할 수 있다 (= be capable of)
- 정답: (B)

5.
- 해설: 동사 is 뒤에 보어로 위치하며, 동시에 전치사 on을 수반하는 형용사 어휘를 고르는 문제이다. (D) dependent가 dependent on(~에 의존하는, ~에 달린)의 형태로 사용되므로 정답이다. 또한, be dependent on(~에 의존하다)을 하나의 표현으로 기억해두자. (A) aware는 aware of / that 주어 + 동사(~을 인지하는), (B)는 able to부정사(~할 수 있는), (C) ready는 ready for / to부정사(~할 준비가 된)의 형태로 각각 사용된다.
- 해석: 우리 회사의 성공은 헌신적인 직원들을 유지하는 데 달려 있다.
- 어휘: success 성공   dependent on ~에 의존하는, ~에 달린   maintain ~을 유지하다   dedicated 헌신적인
- 정답: (D)

Check-up Step 1 본책 _ p. 169

1.
- 해설: 구조를 살펴보면 빈칸 앞에 조동사 will이 있고, 그 다음에 동사원형 be가 있다. 조동사와 동사원형 사이는 부사 자리이므로, 부사 (B) not이 정답이 된다.
- 해석: 그들은 우리와 함께 할 수 없을 것이다.
- 어휘: be able to부정사 ~할 수 있다   join ~의 구성원이 되다, ~에 입사하다, (행동 따위를) 함께하다
- 정답: (B)

2.
- 해설: 알맞은 의미의 부사 어휘를 선택하는 문제이다. (B) yet(아직)은 긍정문, 평서문에서는 사용하지 않으므로 바로 탈락된다. 문맥상 '도착했을 때, ~시작했다'는 의미가 필요하므로 (A) already(이미, 벌써)가 정답이다.
- 해석: 우리가 도착했을 때, 공연은 이미 시작되었다.
- 어휘: performance 연주, 공연   start 시작하다   arrive 도착하다   already 이미, 벌써   yet 하지만, 아직
- 정답: (A)

3.
- 해설: 올바른 부사 어휘를 선택하는 문제로, 빈칸 뒤의 부사 not이 중요한 힌트가 된다. 부사 still은 not 앞에 쓰고, yet은 not 뒤에 사용하는 특징이 있으므로 (A) still이 정답이다.
- 해석: 나는 아직 결정을 내리지 않았다.
- 어휘: still 여전히, 그런데도, 그럼에도 불구하고, (비교급 강조부사) 훨씬   make a decision 결정하다   have still not p.p. 아직 ~ 하지 않았다 (= have not yet p.p.)
- 정답: (A)

Check-up Step 2   본책 _ p. 169

4.
- 해설: 빈칸 다음의 명사 notices(공지들, 통지들)를 앞에서 꾸며주는 어휘를 고르는 문제이다. 명사 수식은 형용사이기 때문에, (A) No가 정답이다.
- 해석: 관리인의 승인 없이는, 어떠한 공지도 문에 게재되어서는 안 된다.
- 어휘: notice 통지, 공지; ~를 알아채다
  post 우편물, 우편; ~를 게재하다, ~를 발송하다
  approval 승인, 찬성   custodian 관리인
- 정답: (A)

5.
- 해설: 부정부사 not과 현재완료 동사(have p.p) 사이에 어울리는 부사 어휘를 고르는 문제이다. 보기 중 (C) yet(아직)은 부정문에서 사용되며, not ~ yet의 형태로 부정부사 not 뒤에서 사용될 수 있으므로 정답은 (C) yet이다. (A) still(여전히)은 긍정문과 부정문에서 모두 사용되지만 부정문에서는 yet과는 반대로 still ~ not의 형태로 not보다 앞에 위치해야 한다. (B) already(이미, 벌써)는 긍정문에서 사용되는 부사이며, (D) never(결코 ~하지 않다)는 not과 부정의 의미가 중복되므로 어울리지 않는다.
- 해석: 몇 달간의 연구에도 불구하고, 그렌빌 박사는 아직도 그 프로젝트를 끝내지 못했다.
- 어휘: despite ~임에 불구하고   several 몇몇의   study 연구
- 정답: (C)

Check-up Step 1   본책 _ p. 171

1.
- 해설: 부사 어휘를 선택하는 문제로, 빈칸 앞의 hardly가 힌트가 된다. hardly ever(거의 ~아니다)라는 올바른 표현을 만들면서, '설거지를 거의 하지 않는다'는 문맥을 완성하는 (B) ever가 정답이 된다.
- 해석: 그는 설거지를 거의 하지 않는다.
- 어휘: hardly 거의 ~아니다, 않다   wash the dises 설거지하다
- 정답: (B)

2.
- 해설: 빈칸 다음의 1,000 people을 앞에서 꾸미는 어휘를 선택하는 문제이다. 1,000 people에서 1,000은 숫자인데, 숫자를 앞에서 수식하는 품사는 부사이다. 따라서 부사 (B) Nearly(거의)가 정답이다.
- 해석: 거의 1,000명의 사람들이 행사에 참여할 것 같다.
- 어휘: near ~의 근처에, ~옆에; 가까운; 가까이   nearly 거의
  be likely to부정사 ~할 것 같다   attend ~에 참여하다, ~에 참석하다
- 정답: (B)

3.
- 해설: 빈칸 앞의 동사구 have increased(증가했다)를 수식하는 어휘가 필요하다. (A) extremely(대단히, 극도로)는 의미적으로 가능하지만, 동사를 수식하지 못하는 부사로 탈락된다. 따라서 정답은 (B) dramatically(급격하게)가 된다.
- 해석: 새로운 스마트폰 판매가 급격하게 증가했다.
- 어휘: sale 판매   increase 증가; ~를 증가시키다, 증가하다
  extremely 극도로, 대단히   dramatically 급격하게, 극적으로, 엄청나게
- 정답: (B)

Check-up Step 2   본책 _ p. 171

4.
- 해설: 알맞은 부사 어휘를 선택하여 문맥을 완성하는 문제인데, 여기서 결정적인 힌트는 that절에 있다. 보기 중에서 결과의 의미를 나타내는 that절을 수반하는 부사는 (D) so(매우)가 유일하다.
- 해석: 보고서가 매우 기밀이라서 오직 3명의 사람들만 그것에 접근 권한을 가지고 있다.
- 어휘: report 보고서, 공식문서; ~에게 알리다, 보도하다
  confidential 기밀의, 은밀한
  access 접근, 접속, 접속권; ~에 접근하다, 접속하다
- 정답: (D)

5.
- 해설: 20,000을 수식할 수 있는 알맞은 부사를 고르는 문제로 보기 중 유일하게 숫자를 수식할 수 있는 부사 (C) Over(~이상)가 정답이 된다. 나머지 보기의 어휘들 중 (A) More는 more than(~이상)으로, (B) Approximate는 approximately(대략)로, (D) Near는 nearly(거의)와 같이 부사의 형태가 되면 숫자를 수식할 수 있다.
- 해석: 2만 명 이상의 통근자들은 2개의 새로운 지하철 노선의 추가로 혜택을 받게 될 것이다.
- 어휘: benefit from ~로부터 혜택을 받다   addition 추가
  approximate 근사치의, 거의 근접한
- 정답: (C)

Check-up   본책 _ p. 173

1. 정답 **care**
  어휘 care 조심 / careful 조심스러운

2. 정답 **response**
  어휘 respond 응답하다 / response 응답

3. 정답 **exception**
  어휘 except ~를 제외하고 / exception 예외

4. 정답 **addition**
   어휘 addition 추가 / additional 추가적인

5. 정답 **request**
   어휘 request 요청 / request 요청하다

Part 5&6_ 실전연습 2   본책 _ p. 174-175

1.
해설 빈칸 앞에서 이미 문장이 완성되었으므로, 문장에서 있어도 되고 없어도 되는 수식어 부사의 자리이다. 즉, 빈칸은 동사 review를 뒤에서 수식하는 부사 (B) carefully의 자리이다.

해석 편지에 민감한 정보가 포함되었으므로, 편지를 부치기 전에 신중하게 검토하세요.

어휘 review 평가, 검토; ~를 검토하다   letter 편지
carefully 신중하게, 주의하여   care 돌봄, 관리, 관심; 돌보다
careless 부주의한, 조심성 없는
contain ~를 포함하다   sensitive 민감한

정답 (B)

2.
해설 be동사 뒤에는 형용사나 명사가 보어로 올 수 있으므로 부사 (B) responsibly는 탈락한다. 주어와 동격관계가 성립하지 않는 명사 (A)와 (D) 역시 오답이다. 따라서 전치사 for와 함께 사용되어 의미를 완성하는 형용사 (C) responsible(책임 있는)이 정답이다.

해석 마르코는 리오 건설 사의 직원들에 의해 지켜져야 할 안전절차를 확실히 할 책임이 있습니다.

어휘 ensure ~를 보장하다, ~를 확실히 하다   procedure 절차
follow ~가 뒤이어 발생하다, 뒤따르다, (뒤이어) ~을 하다
employee 직원   response 응답, 반응
responsible 책임이 있는, 원인이 되는
be responsible for ~에 책임 있다 (= be liable for)
responsibility 책임, 책무; 책임감

정답 (C)

3.
해설 동사 dress를 꾸며주는 알맞은 부사를 고르는 문제이다. 일단, (B) extremely와 (D) very(바로 그; 매우)는 동사를 수식하지 못하는 부사로 탈락된다. (A) approximately(대략)는 형용사를 수식하는 부사로 역시 제외된다. 따라서 '적절하게'라는 의미의 부사 (C) appropriately가 정답이다.

해석 구직자들은 면접에서 적절하게 옷을 입도록 충고 받는다.

어휘 candidate 지원자 (= applicant)   interview 면접; ~를 인터뷰하다
advise ~에게 권고하다, ~에게 충고하다   approximately 대략
extremely 대단히, 극도로   appropriately 적절하게

정답 (C)

4.
해설 빈칸 앞의 동사 leave는 leave A with B의 형태로 'A를 B에 남기다'라는 의미로 사용되었다. 즉, 사무실에 있지 않은 상황이라면, 누군가에게 남기라는 의미이므로 문맥상 가장 적합한 (A) secretary(비서)가 정답이다.

해석 아마드 씨가 사무실에 계시지 않으면, 메시지를 그녀의 비서에게 항상 남겨주세요.

어휘 out of the office 사무실에 있지 않은   leave ~를 남기다, 떠나다
all the time 항상   secretary 비서   attendant 수행원, 간병인
professional 전문가; 전문적인

정답 (A)

5.
해설 동명사 being 뒤에 오면서 전치사 of와 어울리는 어휘를 고르는 문제이다. 가산명사인 (B) critic은 수일치로 먼저 탈락되며, 뒤에 목적어가 필요한 (D) criticizing 역시 올 수 없다. 따라서 be critical of(~을 비난하다)라는 표현을 이루는 (C) critical이 정답이다.

해석 그 이사는 자신의 기준을 충족하지 못하는 근무 실적에 비난하는 것으로 정평이 나있다.

어휘 be well-known for ~로 유명하다 (= be famous for)
work 근무, 일, 작품, 연구; 일하다   performance 성능, 실적
meet one's standards ~의 기준에 부합되다
standard 규범, 표준; 표준의, 일반적인   critic 비평가, 평론가
be critical of ~을 비판[비난]하다
criticize A for B B의 이유로 A를 비난하다

정답 (C)

6.
해설 빈칸 앞의 pay와 함께 하나의 표현을 이루는 명사를 고르는 문제이다. 직원들이 '올해의 목표를 초과달성했다'는 앞 문장에 미루어 보면, '봉급인상(pay raises)'이라는 표현이 필요하다. 따라서 정답은 (D) raises이다.

해석 올해의 판매목표를 초과달성한 몇몇의 직원들은 내년부터 상당히 오른 임금을 받을 것이다.

어휘 employee 직원   exceed ~를 초과하다, (법, 규제) 한도를 넘어서다
sales 영업, 판매   goal 목표   substantial 상당한   cost 비용; 비용이 들다, ~가 들게 하다   freeze 동결, 금지; 한파   budget 예산, 예산안; 저렴한, 저가의; 예산을 세우다
raise 상승, 증가; ~을 증가시키다

정답 (D)

7.
해설 명사 fees(요금, 수수료)를 수식할 수 있는 품사를 고르는 문제이다. 형용사와 명사를 따져 봐야 하는데, 명사 (B) addition은 fees와 복합명사를 만들 수 없다. 따라서 형용사 (A) additional이 정답이다.

해설 승객들은 20kg 제한규정을 초과하는 짐은 추가요금을 부가 받을 수 있다는 점을 유념해야 한다.

어휘 passenger 승객　note ~를 주의하다, 유념하다
luggage 짐 (= baggage)　exceed ~를 초과하다, (법, 규제) 한도를 넘어서다　limit 제한, 제약; ~를 제한하다
be subject to 명사 ~을 부과 받다, ~을 받기 쉽다, ~를 당할 것이다
fee 수수료, 요금　additional 추가적인
addition : 덧셈, 추가, 추가된 것　additionally 추가적으로

정답 (A)

8.
해설 빈칸은 형용사 important를 수식하는 부사 자리이므로, 부사 (C) extremely(매우, 대단히)가 정답이다.

해석 근무하는 동안, 동료들과 좋은 관계를 유지하는 것은 매우 중요하다.

어휘 relationship 관계　colleague 동료　while 동안에, 반면에
on duty 근무 중인　extreme 극도의, 지나친
extremely 매우, 극도로, 대단히

정답 (C)

9.
해설 형용사 full(완전한)의 수식을 받는 동시에, 문맥에 적합한 명사를 찾는 문제이다. 고객들(customers)이 영수증(receipt)을 보여주어야 한다는 말이 있고, 뒤에 purchase(구매한 것)라는 말이 나온 것으로 보아 (B) refund(환불)가 가장 적합하다.

해석 고객들은 구매한 것에 대하여 완전한 환불을 받기 위해서는 영수증을 제시해야 한다.

어휘 present 보여주다, 제시하다　receipt 영수증
in order to부정사 ~하기 위하여　purchase 구매, 구매한 것

정답 (B)

10.
해설 빈칸은 명사 manner를 수식할 수 있는 형용사 또는 명사의 자리이다. 보기 중에 manner를 수식하는 것은 '적시에, 시기에 알맞은'이라는 뜻을 가진 형용사 (C) timely가 유일하다. in a timely manner(제때에, 시기적절하게)라는 표현을 이루는 (C) timely가 정답이다.

해석 내용을 빠짐없이 정확하게 작성하여 제때에 제출하지 않으면, 가입 신청이 취소될 수 있습니다.

어휘 submit ~를 제출하다, ~를 제안하다
result in ~의 결과를 낳다, ~을 초래하다 (= cause)
cancellation 취소　application 지원서, 신청, 신청서
association 협회, 연계, 유대, 유대감　timed 시한의, 정기의
in a timely manner 제때에, 시간을 엄수하여, 시기적절하게

정답 (C)

11.
해설 빈칸 뒤의 내용을 보면 다음달에 개인적인 행사에 음식을 조달해달라는 무엇을 거절했다는 의미가 되므로, 문맥상 '고객의 요청'이라는 말이 가장 적합하다. 따라서 정답은 (B) request이다.

해석 주인은 다음달에 있을 개인적인 행사에 음식을 조달해달라는 고객의 요청을 정중히 거절했다.

어휘 owner 주인　politely 정중히　refuse 거절하다, 거부하다
customer 고객, 소비자　cater 음식·서비스 등을 제공하다
private 사적인, 개인적인

정답 (B)

12.
해설 명사 charges를 앞에서 수식하는 알맞은 형용사를 고르는 문제이다. (D) every 다음에는 가산단수명사가 오므로 탈락된다. 문맥상 '어떠한 요금 또는 거래수수료'라는 의미가 필요하므로 (A) any가 정답이 된다.

해석 우리 회사의 소비자들은 언제나 어떠한 요금 또는 거래수수료 없이 온라인으로 돈을 지불할 수 있다.

어휘 pay 임금; ~를 납부하다, ~를 지불하다　online 온라인으로
charge 요금, 책임, 기소; ~를 책임지다, ~를 부과하다, ~를 기소하다
transaction 거래, 매매, 처리과정　at all times 항상, 언제나

정답 (A)

13.
해설 빈칸 다음에 있는 'half of the 명사(~ 의 반)'를 앞에서 꾸며줄 수 있는 부사를 선택하는 문제이다. half는 '반'을 의미하는 '대명사'이자 '수사'이다. 따라서 '수사나 숫자'를 앞에서 꾸며줄 수 있는 어휘로 (B) Roughly(대략)가 가능하다.

해석 HNC의 대략 반 정도의 직원들이 근처 극장의 자선공연에 참여하기를 지원하고 있다.

어휘 roughly 대략 (= about, around, approximately)
volunteer to부정사 ~ 에 자원하다
benefit 복리후생, 이점; ~에게 혜택을 주다, 혜택을 받다
nearby 근처의　rarely 드물게
considerably 상당히 (= substantially)　urgently 긴급하게

정답 (B)

14.
해설 빈칸은 동사 fill out(~를 작성하다)의 목적어 documents를 앞에서 수식하는 자리이다. 명사를 수식할 수 없는 부사 (B) officially(공식적으로)는 바로 탈락되며, 나머지 보기 중에서 적합한 것은 형용사 (C) official(공식적인)이다.

해석 공식적인 문서들을 파란색 또는 검은색 잉크로 작성하는 것을 명심하시고 그것들을 동봉된 봉투 안에 넣어서 부치세요.

어휘 fill out ~를 작성하다 (= fill in, complete)
document 문서, 서류; ~을 문서로 기록하다
mail 메일, 우편; ~를 우편으로 보내다　enclosed 동봉된
office 사무실　official 공식적인　officially 공식적으로
officialdom 관료집단

정답 (C)

15-18

풀먼 인쇄 & 문구용품 주식회사는 주문제작용 연하장 인쇄와 디자인 분야에서 선두적인 기업입니다. 우리는 달력, 노트, 다이어리, 봉투를 포함한 폭넓은 인쇄된 물품들을 제조하기 위해 필요한 노하우를 가지고 있습니다. 우리의 전문적인 직원들은 그래픽디자인부터 종이 선택까지 인쇄업무의 모든 측면에서 당신을 도와드릴 수 있습니다. 프로젝트에 필요한 것이 무엇이든간에, 우리는 프린팅 솔루션을 제공해 드릴 수 있습니다. 우리 회사는 저렴한 가격에 양질의 결과물을 보장합니다. 당신의 다음 프로젝트를 논의하길 원하시면 오늘 연락주세요.

어휘 manufacture 제조하다, 생산하다　expert 전문가　staff 직원
requirement 필요한 것, 필요조건　offer 제안하다, 제공하다
guarantee 보장하다　affordable price 저렴한 가격
discuss 상의하다, 논의하다

15.
해설 빈칸은 명사 name을 수식할 수 있는 형용사 또는 명사의 자리이다. 보기 중에 name을 수식하는 것은 '선두의, 중요한'이라는 뜻을 가진 형용사 (B) leading이 유일하다. 명사 (C) leader는 문맥상 어울리지 않아 탈락된다.

정답 (B)

16.
해설 빈칸은 명사 range를 수식할 수 있는 형용사 또는 명사의 자리이다. 일단, 구조적으로 부사 (B) fully와 동사 (C) fulfill은 올 수 없다. 형용사 (D) fulfilling은 '만족감을 주는'이라는 의미로 명사 range를 꾸밀 수 없다. 따라서 a full range of(폭넓은)라는 표현을 만드는 형용사 (A) full이 정답이다.

정답 (A)

17.
해설 형용사 every의 수식을 받는 동시에, 뒤의 전치사구 of your next printing job 이하와의 연결을 고려해야 한다. '그래픽디자인부터 종이 선택에 이르기까지' 도와준다는 의미이므로 '모든 측면'이라는 의미를 완성시키는 명사 (D) aspect가 적합하다.

정답 (D)

18.
(A) 제공되는 프린터는 무료로 반송될 수 있습니다.
(B) 프로젝트를 예정대로 마무리해야 합니다.
(C) 우리 회사는 저렴한 가격에 양질의 결과물을 보장합니다.
(D) 선택한 일부 종이가 재고가 없습니다.

해설 문맥에 맞는 문장을 고르는 문제이다. 빈칸 앞 문장에서 프로젝트에 필요한 것이 무엇이든지간에 프린팅 솔루션을 제공할 수 있다고 언급했고 우리 회사는 양질의 결과물을 보장합니다라는 표현으로 이어지는 것이 자연스러우므로 (C)가 정답이다.

정답 (C)

UNIT 3　부정사와 동명사

Check-up Step 1　본책 _ p. 177

1.
해설 문장의 구조를 살펴보고 알맞은 품사를 고르는 문제이다. 이 문장에 동사가 없으므로, 빈칸에는 과거시제 동사 (B) met이 들어가야 한다.
해석 우리는 지난주 회의에서 만났다.
어휘 meet ~를 충족시키다, ~를 만나다, 모이다　meeting 회의, 모임
정답 (B)

2.
해설 빈칸 앞에 조동사 will이 있으므로, 빈칸의 자리는 동사의 원형이 들어갈 자리이다. 따라서 정답은 (A) increase(~를 증가시키다)이다.
해석 깨끗한 업무환경이 생산성을 증가시킬 것입니다.
어휘 clean 청소; 깨끗한; ~를 깨끗이 하다　work 일, 업무, 작품; 일하다
increase 인상, 증가; ~를 증가시키다, 증가하다　productivity 생산성
정답 (A)

3.
해설 알맞은 어휘의 형태를 결정해야 하는데, 빈칸 앞에 전치사 by가 힌트가 된다. 전치사는 그 다음 목적어로 명사나 동명사를 취하게 되므로, 동명사인 (B) working이 정답이다.
해석 우리는 지역 판매상들과 일함으로써 가치를 만들어 낸다.
어휘 create ~를 만들다　value 가치, 중요성; ~를 귀중히 여기다
local 현지의, 국소의; 현지인　vendor 행상인, 판매상
정답 (B)

Check-up Step 2 본책 _ p. 177

4.

해설 주어와 동사가 있는 완전한 문장으로, 더 이상 동사는 올 수 없어 (A) speak와 (B) spoke 모두 탈락된다. 전치사 because of(~ 때문에) 다음에 목적어로 명사나 동명사를 취하게 되므로 (D) speaking이 정답이다.

해석 3개 국어를 말할 수 있기 때문에, 그는 국제적인 회사에 반드시 고용될 것이다.

어휘 because of ~때문에 language 언어 definitely 분명히, 절대로
hire 임대; ~를 빌리다, ~를 고용하다 international 국제적인
speak 말하다, 이야기하다

정답 (D)

5.

해설 전치사 without 뒤에서 full information을 목적어로 수반할 수 있는 명사구를 고르는 문제이다. 우선 동사인 (A) receive와 (B) receives는 정답에서 제외되며, 부정사인 (B) to receive 또한 전치사 뒤에 사용할 수 없으므로 정답이 될 수 없다. 보기 중 유일하게 전치사 뒤에서 명사 형태로 사용될 수 있는 동명사 (C) receiving이 정답이다.

해석 우리는 더 많은 정보를 수령하지 못하면 그 프로젝트를 계속 진행할 수가 없다.

어휘 continue 계속하다, 계속되다 proceed with ~을 진행하다

정답 (C)

Check-up Step 1 본책 _ p. 179

1.

해설 빈칸 앞에 주어와 동사가 모두 존재하므로, 빈칸에는 더 이상 동사 (B) meet는 올 수 없다. 결국 want A to부정사(A가 ~하기를 원하다)라는 표현을 이루는 to부정사 (A) to meet이 정답이다.

해석 나는 당신이 내일 신입사원들과 만나기를 원한다.

어휘 meet ~를 만나다, ~을 충족시키다, ~를 달성하다

정답 (A)

2.

해설 빈칸 앞에 부정관사 a가 있으므로, 빈칸에는 명사가 필요하다. 동명사 역시 품사적으로는 명사이지만, 명사 앞에는 관사가 붙고, 동명사 앞에는 붙지 않는다. 따라서 정답은 (A) investigation이다.

해석 우리는 최근에 조사를 시행했다.

어휘 recently 최근에 conduct ~를 실시하다, 실행하다
investigation 조사

정답 (A)

3.

해설 빈칸 다음에 considering은 전치사 after 다음에 오는 동명사라는 점이 힌트이다. 동명사를 앞에서 수식하는 것은 형용사가 아니라 부사이므로 정답은 (B) carefully이다.

해석 그녀의 업무 경험을 신중하게 생각한 후에, 그들은 그녀를 고용했다.

어휘 consider ~를 고려하다, ~를 배려하다, ~를 숙고하다 work 일; 일하다
experience 경험, 체험; ~를 경험하다, ~를 겪다
hire 임대; ~를 빌리다, ~를 고용하다

정답 (B)

Check-up Step 2 본책 _ p. 179

4.

해설 문장 전체의 주어가 deleted files라면, 그 다음에 이어지는 동사가 is가 아니라 are가 되어야 한다. 때문에 deleted files는 주어가 될 수 없고, 빈칸에는 주어의 역할을 할 수 있는 동명사 (D) Recovering이 정답이 된다.

해석 많은 효과적인 도구들을 인터넷 상에서 구할 수 있기 때문에 삭제된 파일들을 복구하는 것이 아주 어렵지는 않다.

어휘 recover 회복하다, ~를 되찾다 deleted files 삭제된 파일
difficult 어려운 because 때문에, 왜냐하면 powerful 강력한
available 이용 가능한

정답 (D)

5.

해설 빈칸에는 in order to(~하기 위해서) 뒤에 사용될 동사원형이 들어가야 한다. 보기 중 유일한 동사원형 형태인 (A) concentrate가 정답이다. 참고로 concentrate는 자동사로 사용될 경우 전치사 on과 함께 'concentrate on(~에 전념하다, ~에 집중하다)'의 형태로 사용된다.

해석 책을 집필하는 데 전념하기 위해서, 플로레스 씨는 그녀의 직책에서 물러났습니다.

어휘 in order to부정사 ~하기 위해서
concentrate on ~에 전념하다, ~에 집중하다
resign from ~에서 사임하다

정답 (A)

Check-up Step 1 본책 _ p. 181

1.

해설 빈칸 앞에 동사 hope와 더불어 알맞은 동사의 형태를 완성시키는 문제이다. 동사 hope는 뒤에 명사 목적어나 부정사 목적어를 사용하는 동사이므로, (A) to join이 정답이다.

해석 우리는 당신의 그룹이 곧 함께하기를 희망한다.

어휘 hope ~를 바라다, 희망하다
join ~의 구성원이 되다, ~에 입사하다, (행동 따위를) 함께하다

정답 (A)

2.
해설 빈칸 앞의 동사 discontinue 다음에 오는 알맞은 형태를 고르는 문제이다. discontinue는 뒤에 명사나 동명사를 목적어로 취하는 동사이므로, (B) producing이 정답이다.

해석 그 회사는 이 카메라 모델 생산하는 것을 중단할 것이다.

어휘 discontinue ~을 중단하다 produce ~를 생산하다, ~를 만들어내다

정답 (B)

3.
해설 빈칸 앞의 동사 mind 다음에 오는 알맞은 형태를 고르는 문제이다. mind는 뒤에 명사나 동명사를 목적어로 취하는 동사이므로, (B) driving이 정답이다.

해석 나는 오랫동안 운전하는 것을 꺼려하지 않는다.

어휘 mind ~ing ~하기를 꺼려하다 drive 운전하다, ~를 태워주다

정답 (B)

Check-up Step 2 본책_p. 181

4.
해설 문장의 동사가 would like이기 때문에, 동사 (A) confirm, (D) confirms는 빈칸에 올 수 없다. would like는 뒤에 to부정사를 목적어로 수반하므로 (B) to confirm이 정답이다.

해석 저희는 당신의 호텔 예약에 대한 취소를 확인하고 싶습니다.

어휘 cancellation 취소 would like to부정사 ~하고 싶다
reservation 예약 confirm ~를 확인하다

정답 (B)

5.
해설 타동사 recommend 뒤에 목적어 역할을 하면서 동시에 some additional office equipment를 자체 목적어로 수반할 수 있는 형태를 고르는 문제. 이미 동사가 있기 때문에 동사로 사용할 수 있는 (A) purchase와 (D) purchases는 탈락되며, 명사로 고려한다 하더라도 이미 목적어가 있으므로 오답이다. recommend는 동명사를 목적어로 수반하는 대표적인 동사이므로 (C) purchasing이 정답이다.

해석 우리는 다음번 세미나들을 위한 몇몇 추가 사무 장비를 구매하는 것을 추천한다.

어휘 recommend ~을 추천하다 purchase 구매, 구매품; ~을 구매하다
additional 추가적인 equipment 장비

정답 (C)

Check-up Step 1 본책_p. 183

1.
해설 접속사 how는 뒤에 완전한 문장을 수반하거나, to부정사가 올 수 있다. 하지만 how 다음에 주어가 없어서 동사인 (A) operate는 빈칸에 올 수 없다. '의문사+부정사'로 하나의 명사구 역할을 하는 (B) to operate가 정답이다.

해석 당신은 복사기를 어떻게 작동하는지 알아야 한다.

어휘 photocopier 복사기 operate 작동하다, ~를 운영하다

정답 (B)

2.
해설 be dedicated to는 뒤에 명사나 동명사가 오는 표현이다. 따라서 전치사 to의 목적어 역할을 하면서 동시에 또 다른 목적어를 취할 수 있는 (B) providing이 정답이다.

해석 그 상점은 좋은 상품들을 제공하는 데 헌신한다.

어휘 store 상점, 창고 be dedicated to 명사 ~에 전념하다, 헌신하다
provide ~를 제공하다, 주다

정답 (B)

3.
해설 문장의 구조를 보면 주어는 the teacher이고, 동사는 will let이다. 동사 let은 목적어 다음에 목적격 보어로 동사원형(원형부정사)을 수반하기 때문에, (A) know가 정답이다.

해석 선생님은 학생들이 그들의 점수를 알게 할 것이다.

어휘 score 득점, 점수

정답 (A)

Check-up Step 2 본책_p. 183

4.
해설 형용사 subject는 뒤에 전치사 to를 수반하여 be subject to 명사 (~에 영향받다, ~의 대상이다)라는 표현을 이루고 있다. 따라서 보기의 유일한 명사 형태인 (C) cancellation(취소)이 정답이다.

해석 승객들은 몇몇의 항공편이 나쁜 날씨 때문에 취소될 수 있다는 점을 주의해야 한다.

어휘 passenger 승객 note 주의하다, 주목하다 flight 비행기, 항공편
bad weather 나쁜 날씨 cancel ~를 취소하다, 무효화시키다

정답 (C)

5.

해설 동사 determine의 적절한 형태를 선택하는 문제이다. 하지만, 이미 문장 속의 동사 help가 존재하기 때문에 determine은 동사의 역할을 할 수 없다. 문제의 포인트는 동사 help가 준사역동사로서 원형부정사(동사원형)와 to부정사를 목적격 보어로 수반할 수 있다는 점이다. 따라서 정답은 원형부정사인 (A) determine이다. 또한 to determine도 정답으로 가능하다.

해석 인사부는 우리가 가장 효과적인 교대 스케줄을 결정하는 데 도움을 줄 것입니다.

어휘 personnel department 인사부   determine 결정하다
help A(사람)+(to) 동사원형 A가 ~하도록 돕다   effective 효과적인
rotation schedule 교대 스케줄

정답 (A)

Check-up 본책 _ p. 185

1. 정답 charge
어휘 charge 담당 / responsible 책임 있는

2. 정답 schedule
어휘 scheduled 예정된 / schedule 예정

3. 정답 transaction
어휘 transact 거래하다 / transaction 거래

4. 정답 discussion
어휘 discuss 논의하다 / discussion 논의

5. 정답 reimbursement
어휘 reimburse 보상하다 / reimbursement 보상

Part 5&6_ 실전연습 3 본책 _ p. 186-187

1.

해설 빈칸 앞의 to의 성격을 규명하고, 알맞은 어휘의 형태를 고르는 문제이다. fail은 뒤에 to부정사가 올 수 있는 동사이므로 빈칸에는 동사 원형이 필요하다. 따라서 comply with(~를 따르다, 준수하다)라는 표현을 이루는 (A) comply가 정답이다.

해석 건축 규정을 지키지 않는 도급업자는 면허 정지 처분을 받을 수 있다.

어휘 contractor 계약자, 도급업자
fail to부정사 ~하는 데 실패하다, ~하지 못하다
building regulations 건축 규정
be subject to ~을 받기 쉽다, ~의 대상이다
license 허가증, 면허증; ~를 허가하다
suspension (징계로서) 정지, 중지, 정직
comply with ~에 따르다, ~을 준수하다 (= abide by)

정답 (A)

2.

해설 빈칸은 '고객을 만족시키다'라는 to부정사 이하의 수식을 받는 명사의 자리이다. '완성된 자동차를 검사하다'는 문맥으로 미루어 볼 때, '노력'이라는 의미가 필요하다. 따라서 (B) effort가 정답이다.

해석 노던 자동차는 고객들을 만족시키기 위한 노력으로 모든 완성된 자동차를 검사하기로 결정했다.

어휘 inspect ~를 검사하다   satisfy ~를 만족시키다   client 고객, 소비자
influence 영향, 영향력; ~에 영향을 끼치다
in an effort to부정사 ~하려는 노력으로   strength 강점

정답 (B)

3.

해설 접속사 that 앞뒤로 is와 works라는 동사가 있으므로, 빈칸은 동사의 자리가 아니다. 따라서 보기 중에서 유일하게 문장의 주어 역할을 할 수 있는 동명사 (B) Keeping이 정답이 된다. 동명사가 문장의 주어일 경우 단수 취급을 한다는 점도 주의하자.

해석 고객들을 계속 만족시키는 것이 이 가게에서 일하는 모든 사람의 일이다.

어휘 duty 의무, 업무, 근무

정답 (B)

4.

해설 빈칸은 extra의 수식을 받는 알맞은 명사를 선택하는 문제이다. '클럽의 시설들을 자유롭게 사용하다'는 내용으로 볼 때, '무료로(at no extra charge)'라는 의미가 필요하다. 따라서 (D) charge가 정답이다.

해석 멤버들과 그들의 가족들은 추가적인 비용 없이 클럽의 시설들을 자유롭게 이용할 수 있다.

어휘 be free to부정사 자유로이 ~하다   use 이용, 사용; ~를 이용하다
facility 기관, 시설   concern 걱정, 관심사, 관심   right 권리
guideline 지침, 지침서   charge 요금, 책임

정답 (D)

5.

해설 어휘의 형태를 결정하여 문맥을 완성시키는 문제로, 타동사 want가 힌트가 된다. want는 뒤에 명사나 to부정사를 목적어로 수반하는 동사이므로, to부정사 (C) to succeed가 정답이다.

해석 만약 빠르게 성공하고 싶다면, 당신에게 발생하는 예측하지 못하는 많은 어려움을 견뎌야만 한다.

어휘 endure ~를 견디다, ~를 인내하다   a lot of 많은
unexpected 예상 밖의, 예기치 않은   trouble 어려움, 문제, 곤경
succeed 성공하다, (자리, 지위 등) 뒤를 잇다, ~를 승계하다

정답 (C)

6.
해설 '현재 새로운 백신 소프트웨어를 설치하는 과정이다'라는 문맥이 자연스러우므로 be in the process of(~하는 과정이다)가 적합한 표현이다. 따라서 정답은 (A) process(과정)가 된다.

해석 애틀랜틱 인더스트리즈 사는 보안을 강화하기 위해서, 현재 새로운 바이러스 백신 소프트웨어를 설치하는 중이다.

어휘 presently 현재   strengthen ~를 강화하다   security 보안, 경비
process 과정; ~를 처리하다; ~를 가공처리하다
resource (인적, 물적) 자원, 재원; (자원 등을) 제공하다
reflection 반사, 반영, 심사숙고   assembly 조립, 의회, 모임

정답 (A)

7.
해설 전치사 upon(~하자마자) 다음에는 동명사와 명사가 올 수 있다. 명사 (D) receipt는 related documents와 복합명사를 이룰 수 없다. 결국, related documents를 목적어로 받는 동명사 (B) receiving이 정답이다.

해석 관련 필수 서류를 우리가 수령하자마자 소비자들은 변제를 받을 수 있다.

어휘 customer 소비자   reimbursement 변제, 배상, 환불
document 문서, 서류; ~을 문서로 기록하다
required 필요로 하는, 요구되는   upon ~하자마자
invoice 송장, 청구서

정답 (B)

8.
해설 빈칸은 동사 held의 목적어가 되는 동시에 to부정사구 in order to reduce risks of heart surgery와 연결이 가능한 명사의 자리이다. 따라서 hold a discussion(논의를 하다)라는 표현을 이루는 (C) discussion(논의, 토론)이 정답이다.

해석 파텔 박사는 심장 수술의 위험을 줄이기 위해서 몇몇의 의사들과 함께 논의를 했습니다.

어휘 reduce ~를 줄이다 (= lessen)   surgery 수술, 진료
along with ~와 함께   physician 내과 의사
contribution 공헌, 기부, 기여, 기부금
survey 조사, 투표; ~를 조사하다   agreement 합의, 약속, 동의

정답 (C)

9.
해설 어휘의 형태를 결정하여 문맥을 완성시키는 문제로, 타동사 considered가 힌트가 된다. consider는 뒤에 명사나 동명사를 목적어로 수반하는 동사이므로, 동명사 (B) reducing이 정답이다.

해석 떨어지는 수익 때문에, 애틀랜틱 항공사는 내년부터 광고 예산을 줄이는 것을 고려했다.

어휘 consider ~로 간주하다, 여기다, ~를 고려하다
advertising 광고, 광고업   budget 예산, 예산안; 저렴한; 예산을 세우다
due to ~ 때문에   falling 떨어지는   profit 이익, 이익금
reduce ~를 줄이다, ~를 삭감시키다

정답 (B)

10.
해설 빈칸은 형용사 tight(빡빡한)의 수식을 받으며, 문장을 완성하는 명사가 필요하다. '빡빡한 일정(a tight schedule)에도 불구하고, 마침내 그 책을 완성해냈다'는 내용이 문맥에 적합하기 때문에 (C) schedule(일정)이 정답이다.

해석 브라이언은 빡빡한 일정에도 불구하고, 마침내 그 책을 완성해냈다.

어휘 even though ~에도 불구하고   tight 빡빡한, 꽉 조인   finally 마침내
manage to부정사 결국 ~해내다   position 직위; ~를 배치하다
appointment 약속, 임무, 임명, 직위, 직책
schedule 일정표, 스케줄; ~의 일정을 잡다
consideration 고려, 이해

정답 (C)

11.
해설 알맞은 동사 표현을 선택하여 문맥을 완성하는 문제로, 동사 helped가 중요한 힌트가 된다. help는 목적어 다음에 목적격보어로 원형부정사(동사원형) 또는 to부정사를 수반하므로, executives 다음에 (A) understand라는 동사원형이 정답이 된다.

해석 앤젤라의 설명은 내년에 효력을 발휘하는 새로운 세법을 중역들이 이해하는 것을 도왔다.

어휘 explanation 설명, 설명서   help 도움, 일손; ~를 돕다
executive 중역, 이사; 중역의, 고급의   tax 세금; ~에 세금을 부과하다
effect 결과, 효과, 영향   take effect 효력을 발휘하다 (= go into effect)

정답 (A)

12.
해설 빈칸에는 shown by the players in the field(운동장에서 선수들이 보여주는)의 수식을 받는 명사의 자리이다. 또한 명사 the energy(에너지)와 병치를 이루어야 하는데, 의미적으로 적합한 명사는 (C) commitment(열정, 전념)이다.

해석 관중들은 경기장에서 선수들이 보여주는 에너지와 열정에 감명을 받았다.

어휘 spectator 관중, 관객, 응원하는 사람
impress ~에 인상을 주다, ~에 감명을 주다
show 경치, 경관, 공연, TV 프로그램; ~을 나타내다, ~을 보여주다
warranty 품질 보증서   extension 연장, 확대
commitment 전념, 헌신, 약속   reference 참조, 참고, 언급, 추천서

정답 (C)

13.
해설 문장 전체를 앞에서 꾸며줄 수 있는 수식구가 필요한데, (A) By achieving와 (B) To achieve가 가능하다. 문맥상 '8백만 달러의 영업목표를 달성하기 위해서'라는 의미가 자연스럽기 때문에, to부정사의 부사적 용법으로 사용된 (B) To achieve가 정답이다.

해석 8백만 달러의 영업목표를 달성하기 위해서, 우리는 소비자의 요구를 충족시키는 데 전념해야 한다.

어휘 be dedicated to ~하는 데 전념하다, 헌신하다
achieve ~를 달성하다, ~를 해내다
achievement 성취, 업적, 성취한 것

정답 (B)

14.
해설 빈칸은 전치사구 of business(사업의) 이하의 수식을 받는 명사의 자리이다. 문두의 '고객의 신뢰를 얻기 위해서'라는 to부정사 표현과 의미적으로 어울리는 명사는 (C) transactions(거래, 매매)가 유일하다.

해석 고객의 믿음을 얻기 위해서, 사업의 모든 거래내역은 대중에게 공개되어야 한다.

어휘 faith 믿음, 신뢰 be open to ~에 공개되다
public 대중, 대중의, 공공의 alternative 대안, 대안적인
transaction 거래, 매매, 처리내역 measurement 치수, 측정

정답 (C)

15-18

상금 청구 센터
9302 프라이머리 로
알링턴, 텍사스 76013

르네 톰슨 씨에게,

귀하께서 우리의 신차 홍보 행사의 공식적인 수상자임을 알려드립니다. 저희는 새로운 페르세데스, VMW, 아우디스 또는 40,000달러의 상금을 고를 수 있는 선택권을 드립니다. 다른 상품으로는 하와이 왕복표 두 장, 럭셔리 4박 캐리비언 크루즈, 2,000달러 상당의 쇼핑권이 포함됩니다. 수상자로서 자격이 박탈되는 것을 피하기 위해 당신은 7월 1일 전까지 저희 사무실로 연락주셔야만 합니다. 평일 오전 8시부터 오후 6시까지 무료전화 1-800-392-9583 그리고 토요일에는 오전 9시부터 오후 4시까지 연락할 수 있습니다. 구매할 의무는 없습니다. 귀하는 상품을 받을 수 있도록 보장됩니다.

마이클 에반스

어휘 official 정식의, 공식의 prizewinner 수상자
round-trip ticket 왕복표 (cf. one-way ticket 편도표)
forfeit 몰수당하다, 박탈당하다 status 신분, 자격, 지위

15.
해설 빈칸 앞의 to는 to부정사이므로, 빈칸에는 동사원형이 필요하다. 보기 중에서 유일한 동사원형은 (A) notify(~에게 알리다, 통보하다)이다.

정답 (A)

16.
해설 어휘의 형태를 결정하여 문맥을 완성시키는 문제로, 타동사 avoid(~를 피하다)가 힌트가 된다. avoid는 뒤에 명사나 동명사를 목적어로 수반하는 동사이므로, 동명사 (C) forfeiting이 정답이다.

정답 (C)

17.
(A) 예를 들어, 직접 사무실장과 만나실 수 있습니다.
(B) 그러나 마감일자가 빠르게 오고 있다.
(C) 구매할 의무는 없습니다.
(D) 모든 직원들이 토요일에는 비번입니다.

해설 문맥에 맞는 문장을 고르는 문제이다. 빈칸 앞 문장에서 연락을 취할 수 있는 시간대를 알렸고 뒷 문장에서는 상을 받을 수 있다고 언급했는데 사이에 적절한 내용으로는 상금으로 주어지는 상품은 따로 구매할 필요가 없다가 의미상 자연스러우므로 (C)가 정답이다.

정답 (C)

18.
해설 동사어휘를 선택하는 문제이다. 〈be p.p to부정사〉 형태로 어울리는 동사는 be guaranteed to do (~하는 것이 보장되다)가 어울리므로 (A)가 정답이다.

정답 (A)

UNIT 4 분사

Check-up Step 1 본책 _ p. 189

1.
해설 동사 was 다음에 동사가 다시 올 수 없으므로 (A) find는 바로 탈락된다. 따라서 was finding이라는 과거진행시제를 이루는 현재분사 (B) finding이 정답이다.

해석 나는 그 당시에 음식점을 찾는 중이었다.

어휘 find ~를 찾다, ~를 알아내다   at that time 그 때, 그 당시에

정답 (B)

2.

해설 have와 더불어 알맞은 동사의 형태를 완성하는 문제이다. 일단, have와 현재분사 (A) increasing은 나란히 올 수 없다. 결국, have increased라는 현재완료시제를 이루는 (B) increased가 정답이다.

해석 자동차의 판매가 최근에 증가했다.

어휘 recently 최근에 increase 증강, 상승; ~를 증가시키다, 증가하다

정답 (B)

3.

해설 접속사 that 앞뒤로 '주어 + 동사'로 이루어진 두개의 문장이 있다. 즉, 빈칸은 동사 (A) build의 자리가 아니다. be동사와 결합하여 수동태 표현을 이루는 과거분사 (B) built가 정답이다.

해석 모든 사람들은 시청이 1880년에 지어졌다는 것을 알고 깜짝 놀랐다.

어휘 surprise ~를 놀라게 하다   city hall 시청
build ~를 건설하다, ~를 짓다

정답 (B)

Check-up Step 2 본책 _ p. 189

4.

해설 문장에 동사 will be repaired가 있으므로, 빈칸에 동사 (B), (C), (D)는 올 수 없다. (C) purchase는 '구매품, 구매'라는 명사로도 쓰이지만, 빈칸 앞에 부사 recently의 수식을 받을 수 없다. 결국, recently의 수식을 받는 동시에, vehicles 앞에서 형용사 역할을 하는 과거분사 (A) purchased가 정답이다.

해석 SM 자동차에서 최근에 구매된 자동차들은 처음 20,000km 동안은 무료로 수리를 받을 것이다.

어휘 purchase 구매, 구매품; ~를 구매하다   vehicle 차량, 자동차, 탈 것
repair 수리; ~를 고치다   free of charge 무료로, 공짜로

정답 (A)

5.

해설 빈칸 앞 have는 타동사로 '~을 가지다'라는 의미로 사용되거나, 현재완료시제(have p.p.)를 만드는 조동사 역할을 한다. 보기 중 have의 목적어로 사용될 수 있는 명사가 없으므로 타동사로는 볼 수 없으며, 현재완료형으로 동사를 이룰 수 있는 (C) obtained가 정답이 된다.

해석 총회 조직위원들은 메리온 호텔로부터 특별 단체할인 비용을 얻어냈다.

어휘 convention organizer 총회 조직위원
obtain A from B B로부터 A를 획득하다   rate 비율, 비용, 등급

정답 (C)

Check-up Step 1 본책 _ p. 191

1.

해설 빈칸은 명사 speech를 앞에서 수식하는 형용사를 고르는 문제이다. 과거분사 (B) bored(따분해진)는 사람의 감정을 나타낼 때 사용하므로 탈락된다. 따라서 사물을 수식할 때 사용하는 현재분사 (A) boring(따분한)이 정답이다.

해석 그것은 따분한 연설이었다.

어휘 boring 따분한   bored 따분해진   speech 연설

정답 (A)

2.

해설 빈칸은 동사 was의 보어인 동시에 부사 so의 수식을 받는 형용사의 자리이다. 보기 중에서 주어 Last night's performance(지난 밤 공연)의 묘사가 가능한 것은 현재분사 (A) exciting(흥미진진한)이다.

해석 지난 밤 공연은 매우 흥미진진했다.

어휘 performance 수행, 공연, 실적, 성능   exciting 흥미진진한
excited 신이 난, 흥분한

정답 (A)

3.

해설 빈칸은 명사 water(물)를 앞에서 수식하는 형용사 자리이다. water는 '오염을 시키는' 주체가 아니라 '오염이 된' 대상이므로 (B) polluted(오염된)가 정답이다.

해석 여행자들은 오염된 물을 마시지 않도록 주의해야 한다.

어휘 traveller 여행자, 여행객   careful 주의 깊은, 신중한
drink 마시다; 음료, 마실 것   water 물; ~에 물을 주다
pollute ~를 오염시키다, ~를 망치다   polluting 오염시키는
polluted 오염된

정답 (B)

Check-up Step 2 본책 _ p. 191

4.

해설 명사 customers(고객들)를 꾸며주는 어휘를 선택해야 하는데, 동사인 (A) exist, (D) exists는 불가능하다. 동사 exist(존재하다)는 자동사이므로 수동의 의미를 갖는 과거분사의 형태로 사용하지 않고 현재분사만 사용한다. 따라서 정답은 현재분사 (B) existing이다.

해석 AFI 크리에이티브 디자인의 특별한 서비스는 모든 기존의 고객들도 이용 가능하다.

어휘 available 이용 가능한   exist 존재하다, 살아가다   customer 고객

정답 (B)

5.

해설 빈칸 앞뒤에 과거동사 made와 목적어인 impression이 나와 있다. 따라서 빈칸은 명사를 앞에서 꾸며주는 형용사 자리가 된다. 보기 중 형용사로 가능한 것은 현재분사인 (B) lasting(지속되는) 밖에 없다. 동사 last(지속하다)는 자동사로서 과거분사의 형태로 사용되지 않고 현재분사만 사용하므로, (A) lasted는 정답이 될 수 없다.

해석 라모스 씨는 너무나 친절하고 온화했기에 모든 그의 고객들에게 지속적인 깊은 인상을 남겼다.

어휘 gentle 온화한   make impression on ~에게 인상을 주다
lasting 지속되는   last 지난, 마지막의, 최후의; 지속하다
lastly 최후에, 마지막으로

정답 (B)

Check-up Step 1 본책_ p. 193

1.

해설 빈칸은 a letter를 뒤에서 꾸며주는 동시에 the proof of residence를 목적어로 수반하는 자리이다. show는 '~를 보여주다'라는 타동사로, 타동사의 현재분사는 뒤에 목적어를 수반하기 때문에 (B) showing이 정답이다.

해석 나는 당신에게 거주의 증거를 보여주는 편지 한 통을 보낼 것입니다.

어휘 show 경치, 경관, 공연, TV프로그램; ~을 나타내다, ~을 보여주다
proof 증거   residence 주택, 거주지, 체류 허가

정답 (B)

2.

해설 빈칸에는 명사 the meeting을 뒤에서 꾸며주는 어휘가 들어가야 한다. meeting(회의, 모임)은 의미적으로 '예정하는' 주체가 아니라 '예정된' 대상에 들어가므로 과거분사 (B) scheduled가 정답이 된다.

해석 오늘로 예정된 그 회의는 취소되었다.

어휘 meeting 모임, 회의   schedule 일정, 스케줄; ~의 일정을 잡다
cancel ~를 취소하다, 무효화시키다

정답 (B)

3.

해설 명사 people을 뒤에서 꾸미는 알맞은 분사를 고르는 문제이다. wait는 '기다리다'라는 의미의 자동사인데, 자동사의 분사는 현재분사만 사용하기 때문에 (A) waiting이 정답이다.

해석 인터뷰를 기다리는 사람들은 곧 전화를 받을 것입니다.

어휘 interview 인터뷰; ~를 인터뷰하다
call 전화통화; ~에게 전화하다, ~라고 부르다

정답 (A)

Check-up Step 2 본책_ p. 193

4.

해설 문장의 구조를 보면 주어는 the engineers이고, 동사는 must wear이다. 더 이상 동사는 올 수 없기 때문에 (C)와 (D) 모두 탈락된다. work는 '일하다'라는 자동사인데, 자동사의 분사는 현재분사만 사용하기 때문에 (A) working이 정답이다.

해석 조립구역에서 일하는 기술자들은 항상 안전 장치를 착용해야 한다.

어휘 work 일, 작품, 연구; 일하다   assembly 조립, 의회, 모임
safety gear 안전 장치

정답 (A)

5.

해설 문장의 주어는 anyone이고 동사는 must attend이다. 이미 문장에 동사가 있으므로 (A) involve와 (D) involves는 정답에서 제외되며 나머지 보기인 현재분사 (B) involving과 과거분사 (C) involved 중에서 정답을 골라야 한다. 주어 anyone을 후치수식하며, 동시에 목적어를 수반하지 않는 수동의미의 과거분사 (C) involved가 정답이 된다.

해석 공지에 따르면, 프로젝트에 관련한 누구라도 반드시 내일 회의에 참석해야만 합니다.

어휘 according to ~에 따르면   involved in ~에 관련한, ~에 연관된
attend 주의하다, 집중하다, ~에 참석하다

정답 (C)

Check-up Step 1 본책_ p. 195

1.

해설 접속사 if 다음에 오는 알맞은 분사의 형태를 고르는 문제이다. 주절의 주어 the products는 '~를 손상시키는' 주체가 아니라, '손상을 당하는' 대상이므로 과거분사 (B) damaged가 알맞다.

해석 상품들이 운송 중에 손상이 된다면 교환될 수 있다.

어휘 in transit 운송 중에   product 상품, 제품
exchange 교환; ~을 교환하다, ~을 맞바꾸다
damage 손상, 피해, 훼손; ~를 훼손시키다

정답 (B)

2.

해설 접속사 while(~동안에) 다음에 올 수 있는 형태는 주어와 동사로 이루어진 문장이나 분사구문이다. 주어 없이 동사 (B) made만 올 수 없다. 따라서 a speech를 목적어로 수반하는 현재분사 (A) making이 정답이다.

해석 연설하는 동안에는 분명하고 큰 소리로 말하세요.

어휘 while ~동안에, 반면에, 비록 ~하지만   make a speech 연설하다
loudly 큰 소리로, 사치스럽게

정답 (A)

3.

해설 접속사 although 다음에 오는 알맞은 분사의 형태를 고르는 문제이다. 주절의 주어 the computer는 '~를 구매하는' 주체가 아니라, '구매를 당하는' 대상이므로 과거분사 (B) bought가 필요하다.

해석 컴퓨터가 월요일에 구매되었음에도 불구하고, 금요일까지 배달되지 않았다.

어휘 ship 선박, 배; ~를 운송하다, ~를 실어 나르다

정답 (B)

Check-up Step 2 본책 _ p. 195

4.

해설 접속사 when 다음에는 주어와 동사로 이루어진 문장이나 분사가 올 수 있는데, 보기에 '주어+동사'의 형태가 없으므로 분사가 필요하다. 따라서 cars를 목적어로 수반하는 현재분사 (C) renting이 정답이다.

해석 여행자들은 자동차를 빌릴 때, 모든 서비스 계약 사항을 신중하게 읽어보아야 한다.

어휘 contract 계약(서); 줄어들다, 병에 걸리다, ~와 계약하다
carefully 신중하게, 주의 깊게   rent 임차료, 방세, 사용료; ~를 빌리다

정답 (C)

5.

해설 접속사 unless 뒤에는 주어와 동사를 갖춘 문장이나 분사구문 형태가 이어질 수 있다. 위 문제에서는 unless 뒤에 주어가 없으므로 동사는 자연히 탈락되며, 분사인 (B) accompanied와 (C) accompanying 중에서 선택해야 한다. 뿌리가 되는 동사인 accompany(동반하다)는 타동사이므로 현재분사일 경우 목적어를 수반하고, 과거분사는 목적어를 수반하지 않는다. 빈칸 뒤에는 목적어 없이 전치사구 by an adult가 있으므로 정답은 (B) accompanied가 된다.

해석 14세 이하의 어린이들은 성인 한명을 동반하지 않으면 이 구역에 입장할 수 없습니다.

어휘 allow 허락하다   enter 입장하다, 입력하다   unless ~하지 않으면
be accompanied by ~을 동반하다, ~와 동행하다

정답 (B)

Check-up 본책 _ p. 197

1. 정답 **procedure**
어휘 procedure 절차 / proceed 진행하다

2. 정답 **remainder**
어휘 remain 남다 / remainder 나머지

3. 정답 **morale**
어휘 moral 도덕(적인) / morale 사기

4. 정답 **concerns**
어휘 concern 우려, 걱정 / concerned 우려되는

5. 정답 **agreement**
어휘 agree 합의하다 / agreement 합의

Part 5&6_ 실전연습 4   본책 _ p. 198–199

1.

해설 문장의 구조상 접속사 없이는 동사 (A) create, (B) creates는 올 수 없다. 과거분사 (D) created는 뒤에 목적어를 수반할 수 없어 탈락된다. 따라서 a factory를 뒤에서 수식하는 동시에 more than a thousand jobs를 자체 목적어로 수반하는 현재분사 (C) creating이 정답이다.

해석 해니 케미컬스 사는 천 개 이상의 일자리를 만들어 낼 공장 하나를 개업할 것이라고 발표했다.

어휘 announce ~을 발표하다, 공표하다
open 열려 있는, 개방하는, 영업 중인; ~를 열다, 열리다   factory 공장
more than ~이상 (= over)   create ~를 만들다

정답 (C)

2.

해설 government's와 어울리는 명사를 고르는 문제로, 빈칸 앞의 전치사 against가 힌트가 된다. '인터넷 공급업자들과 함께 ATT가 가격을 인상할 것이다'라는 문맥으로 미루어 볼 때, against 이하에는 가격을 제한할 수 있는 명사인 (D) procedure(규제)가 와야 한다.

해석 전국의 인터넷 공급업자들과 함께 ATT는 정부의 규제에 맞서 요금을 인상할 것이다.

어휘 along with ~와 함께   national 전국적인
Internet provider 인터넷 공급업자
increase 인상, 증가; ~를 증가시키다, 증가하다   rate 요금, 속도, 비율
against ~에 반대하여, ~에 맞서   government 정부
quality 품질, 자질, 특징; 질 좋은   quantity 양, 수량
development 개발, 성장, 사건   procedure 절차, 규제

정답 (D)

3.

해설 문장의 구조상 접속사 없이는 동사 (C) fills, (D) fill은 올 수 없다. 이제 a large shopping mall을 뒤에서 수식할 수 있는 형태를 골라야 한다. fill은 '~를 가득 채우다'라는 타동사이므로 현재분사 (A) filling이 오면 뒤에 목적어가 필요하다. 빈칸 뒤에 목적어가 없으므로, 과거분사 (B) filled가 정답이다.

해석 패션 스퀘어는 값싼 의류와 액세서리 상점들로 가득 찬 거대한 쇼핑몰이다.

어휘 shopping mall 쇼핑몰　be filled with ~로 가득 차다, 채워지다
inexpensive 값싼

정답 (B)

4.
해설 빈칸 앞의 접속사 while(~동안에)은 뒤에 완전한 문장이나 분사구문이 가능하다. while 다음에 주어가 없으므로, 분사인 (B) studied와 (C) studying 중에서 선택해야 한다. 빈칸 뒤에 목적어 economics(경제학)를 수반할 수 있는 것은 능동의 의미를 가진 현재분사 (C) studying만 가능하다.

해석 제인은 중국에서 경제학을 공부하는 동안, 어학 강좌에 등록했다.

어휘 while ~동안에, 반면에, ~에도 불구하고　economics 경제학
course 강좌, 과목, 수업, 방향, 전개
enroll in ~에 등록하다, 신청하다 (= apply for)
study 조사, 연구, 학업; 공부하다, ~를 조사하다

정답 (C)

5.
해설 문장의 주어는 products이고, 동사는 will be distributed이다. 즉, 빈칸에는 동사 (A) remain과 (B) remains 모두 들어갈 수 없다. 복합명사가 불가능한 (D) remainder(나머지) 역시 탈락되며, 뒤에서 명사 products를 수식하는 현재분사 (C) remaining이 정답이다.

해석 브랜드 인지도를 상승시키기 위해서, 창고에 남아있는 상품들이 행인들에게 무료로 배포될 것입니다.

어휘 increase 증강, 상승; ~를 증가시키다, 증가하다
presence 인지도, 위상, 존재, 참석　warehouse 창고
distribute ~을 배포하다, ~을 나누어 퍼트리다　passers-by 행인
for free 무료로 (= free of charge)　remain ~한 상태로 남다, 유지하다
remaining 남아있는　remainder 나머지 (= rest)

정답 (C)

6.
해설 빈칸은 동사 boost의 목적어가 되는 동시에 빈칸 뒤의 전치사구 among employees와 연결 가능한 명사를 고르는 문제이다. boost morale among employees(직원들의 사기를 올리다)라는 표현을 이루는 (A) morale(사기, 의욕)이 정답이다.

해석 부서장은 직원들의 사기를 고무하는 효과적인 방법을 생각해냈습니다.

어휘 head 부서장, 마음, 머리, 앞면; ~를 담당하다, 향하다
come up with ~를 생각해내다　effective 효과적인
boost 상승, 증가; ~를 증가시키다　morale 사기, 의욕
behavior 행위, 행동　workplace 근무지, 직장, 작업현장

정답 (A)

7.
해설 주어는 anyone이고, 동사는 should contact이다. 접속사가 없이는 동사 (A) interest, (D) interests는 올 수 없다. interest는 '~에게 관심을 주다'라는 타동사이므로, 뒤에 목적어가 와야 하는 현재분사 (C) interesting은 제외된다. 결국 '관심 있는'이라는 과거분사 (B) interested가 정답이 된다.

해석 올해의 시상식에 관심 있는 사람은 누구든지 목요일까지 내선번호 523으로 모니카에게 연락하세요.

어휘 interest 관심, 흥미; ~에 관심을 보이다　awards ceremony 시상식
contact 접촉, 연락; ~에 연락하다　extension 연장, 확장, 증축, 내선번호

정답 (B)

8.
해설 people's와 어울리는 명사를 고르는 문제로, 빈칸 뒤의 전치사 이하가 힌트가 된다. '일자리 부족에 대한'이라는 문맥으로 미루어 볼 때, 동사 address의 목적어로 가능한 명사는 (D) concern(걱정, 우려)밖에 없다.

해석 정부는 일자리 부족에 대한 국민들의 걱정을 고심할 계획이다.

어휘 government 정부　address 주소; 주소를 써서 보내다, 다루다, 연설하다
shortage 부족 (= lack)　job opportunities 일자리, 고용기회
effort 노력, 작품, 행사　caution 조심, 주의, 경고; ~에게 주의를 주다
agreement 합의, 약속, 동의, 협정서
concern 걱정, 관심사, 관심, 책임, 회사; ~를 걱정시키다, ~에 영향을 미치다

정답 (D)

9.
해설 빈칸은 be동사의 보어가 되는 형용사나 명사의 자리이다. 주어 Novartis와 명사 (B) commitment(전념, 헌신)는 동격관계가 될 수 없다. be동사와 함께 be committed to(~에 헌신하다, 전념하다)라는 표현을 이루는 (A) committed가 정답이다.

해석 노바르티스는 직원들의 안전에 신경 쓰고 있으며, 전 직원의 안전을 보장하기 위해 모든 기준들을 정기적으로 검사하고 있다.

어휘 be committed to ~에 전념하다, 신경 쓰다　security 보안, 경비, 안전
measure 기준, 방편, 조치, 척도; ~를 측정하다, ~를 평가하다
regularly 규칙적으로　review 평가; ~를 검토하다
ensure ~를 보장하다, ~를 확실히 하다
commit ~를 범하다, ~를 저지르다, ~에 헌신하다, ~을 충당하다
commitment 전념, 헌신, 약속, 신념

정답 (A)

10.
해설 빈칸 다음의 전치사 in 이하와 연결이 가능한 명사 어휘를 고르는 문제이다. '화학기술의 ~가 경제적인 위상을 드높였다'는 문맥으로 미루어 볼 때, (D) Advances가 어울린다. 전치사 in과 함께 쓰여 문장을 완성하는 어휘 또한 (D) Advances(진보, 발전)가 유일하다.

해설 화학기술의 발전은 전 세계에서 우리 회사의 경제적 위상을 드높이는 것을 가능하게 했다.

어휘 chemical technology 화학기술
enable A to부정사 A가 ~하는 것을 가능하게 하다
increase 증가; ~를 증가시키다, 증가하다
presence 존재, 참석, 위상, 면모   approach 접근; ~에 접근하다
advantage 유리한 점, 이점   opening 공석, 시작, 개막식
advance 진보, 발전; ~를 증진시키다, 진격하다

정답 (D)

11.

해설 빈칸은 has 다음에 위치하면서, 부사 not yet의 수식을 받는 자리이다. has 뒤에는 동사원형과 현재분사는 올 수 없다. 명사 (D) announcement 역시 부사 not yet의 수식을 받지 못한다. 따라서 현재완료(have p.p.)를 이루는 과거분사 (C) announced가 정답이다.

해설 이사회는 제조 공정에 관한 문제 때문에, 아직 신제품을 공표하지 않았다.

어휘 the board of directors 이사회
have not yet p.p. 아직 ~하지 않다 (= have yet to부정사)
announce ~를 발표하다, 공표하다   manufacturing 제조
operation (생산적·공업적) 공정, 운영, 작업, 사업

정답 (C)

12.

해설 문미의 in order to take steps against government's rules가 결정적인 힌트가 된다. '정부의 규제에 반하는 대책을 세우기 위해서'라는 내용과 어울리며, 빈칸 뒤의 of every dairy(모든 유제품 회사의)의 수식을 받을 수 있는 명사는 (D) representatives (대표, 대표자)가 유일하다.

해설 모든 유제품 회사의 대표자들이 정부의 규제에 반하는 대책을 세우기 위해서 모였다.

어휘 dairy 유제품 회사, 유제품, 유제품 제조농장
gather 모이다, ~를 모으다   take steps 조치를 취하다, 대책을 세우다
rule 규제, 규칙, 법   opponent 상대, 반대자
presenter 진행자, 발표자   announcer 방송 진행자, 아나운서
representative 대표자, 직원; 대표하는, 전형적인

정답 (D)

13.

해설 관계대명사 who 뒤에 동사 may register, 그 뒤에 문장의 본동사 should take가 오는 구조이다. 즉, 더 이상 동사는 올 수 없으므로 (A) begin와 (B) begins 모두 탈락된다. 따라서 빈칸 뒤의 next Monday와 연결하여 올바른 표현을 이루는 분사표현인 (D) beginning(~부터)이 정답이다.

해설 다음 주 월요일 8월 26일에 시작하는 가을학기 수업을 등록한 학생들은 역사 수업을 먼저 이수해야 한다.

어휘 register for ~에 등록하다   fall 추락, 감소, 가을; 넘어지다, 떨어지다
course 강좌, 과목, 수업   beginning 처음, 시작, ~부터 (= as of)

정답 (D)

14.

해설 빈칸 앞의 comes into의 목적어를 고르는 문제로, 문두의 the law (법)가 중요한 힌트이다. 빈칸 다음에 '소비자의 피해가 줄어들 것이다'라는 문맥과의 연결을 고려하면, '법이 효력을 발휘하다'는 의미가 어울린다. 따라서 comes into effect(효력을 발휘하다)라는 표현을 이루는 (C) effect가 정답이다.

해설 소비자들을 보호하는 법이 효력을 발휘하기만 하면, 그 법은 소비자의 심각한 피해를 감소시킬 것이다.

어휘 once 일단 ~하기만 하면 (= as soon as)
protect 보호하다, 보장하다   customer 소비자
come into effect 효력을 발휘하다
reduce ~를 줄이다, ~를 삭감시키다
damage 손상, 피해; ~를 훼손시키다   progress 진전, 진행; 나아가다
result 결과, 성과   effect 결과, 효과, 영향; ~을 야기하다
order 주문, 명령, 순서; ~를 주문하다, ~에 명령하다

정답 (C)

15-18

발신: 잭 피어스[jackpierce@solisco.com]
수신: 헤일리 브라운[haleybrown@solisco.com]
제목: 이동 준비
날짜: 11월 7일

헤일리,

이 메시지는 12월 2일 수요일 오후 3시 댄버리와 다빌라에서 온 고객과 그들의 사무실에서 만날 예정임을 다시 한 번 상기시켜드리기 위한 것입니다. 운전기사가 2시 15분에 우리 회사 빌딩 앞에 있을 것입니다. 그는 당신을 태워 회의 장소로 모셔갈 것입니다. 회의가 끝나고나서, 회사 차량과 운전기사가 당신의 집으로 다시 모셔다 드릴 것입니다. 당신은 또한 회의 동안 고객과 점심을 먹기 위해 회사 차량을 이용할 수 있는 사전 허가를 받았습니다. 회의와 오고 가는 교통편에 관하여 질문이 있으시면, 내선번호 1172로 저에게 연락주시기 바랍니다.

잭

어휘 pick somebody up ~를 (차에) 태우러 가다
upon ~하자마자 곧   available 이용할 수 있는   prior 사전의, 이전의
authorization 허가, 인가   extension 확대, 연장, 내선전화

15.

해설 빈칸은 be동사의 보어가 되는 형용사나 명사의 자리이다. 동사는 들어갈 수 없으므로 (A) meet와 (D) meets는 바로 탈락된다. 과거분사 (B) met는 be동사와 결합하여 뒤에 목적어를 수반하지 않는 수

동태를 만들기 때문에 제외된다. 따라서 뒤에 자체 목적어를 수반하는 현재분사 (C) meeting이 정답이다.

정답 (C)

16.
(A) 회사 운전사가 2시 15분에 건물 앞에 있을 것입니다.
(B) 그러나 귀하는 가이드와 함께 사무실을 둘러 볼 것입니다.
(C) 제출해야 할 문서작업이 귀하에게 배정되었습니다.
(D) 다른 말로 표현하자면 그 고객은 자신의 실수에 사죄할 것입니다.

해설 문맥에 맞는 문장을 고르는 문제이다. 빈칸 앞 문장에서 미팅건에 대한 사항을 전달했고, 빈칸 뒷 문장에는 그 운전사가 모시고 회의장까지 갈 것이라고 언급되어 있다. 따라서 (A)가 정답이다.

정답 (A)

17.
해설 빈칸은 be동사의 보어가 되는 형용사나 명사의 자리이다. 동사는 들어갈 수 없으므로 (C) make는 바로 탈락된다. make는 타동사로 뒤에 목적어가 오기 때문에, (A) making과 (D) to make는 올 수 없다. 따라서 〈make + 목적어 + 형용사〉 형태가 수동태로 사용된 (B) made가 정답이 된다.

정답 (B)

18.
해설 빈칸 앞뒤의 명사를 연결하는 전치사를 고르는 문제이다. 빈칸 다음이 '당신의 회의와 교통편'에 대한 내용이므로 (D) concerning(~에 관하여)이라는 분사형 전치사가 문맥상 어울린다.

정답 (D)

UNIT 5 동사의 종류

Check-up Step 1 본책 _ p. 201

1.
해설 동사 comply는 자동사로 뒤에 전치사 with와 함께 써야 한다. 때문에 (B) comply with를 택해야 '~를 준수하다'라는 올바른 표현이 완성된다.

해석 당신은 그 규정을 준수해야 합니다.

어휘 comply with ~를 준수하다   rule 규정

정답 (B)

2.
해설 동사 apologize는 자동사로 뒤에 전치사 to와 for를 모두 수반할 수 있다. apologize to는 '~에게 사과하다'의 뜻이지만 apologize for는 '~에 대해서 사과하다'라는 의미이다. 이 문제에서는 뒤에 사과하는 이유에 해당되는 the inconvenience(불편함)이 있으므로 (B) for가 적절하다.

해석 우리는 그 불편함에 대해서 사과드리고 싶습니다.

어휘 would like to부정사 ~하고 싶다   apologize 사과하다
inconvenience 불편함

정답 (B)

3.
해설 동사 attend와 participate는 둘 다 '참석/참가하다'라는 의미가 있다. 하지만 attend는 타동사이고, participate는 자동사이므로 뒤에 전치사 in과 같이 사용하는 것은 (B) participate이다.

해석 그는 배구 경기에 참가하는 것에 대해서 기뻐하고 있다.

어휘 be excited to부정사 ~하는 것에 대해서 흥분하다, 기뻐하다
participate in ~에 참가하다   volleyball 배구

정답 (B)

Check-up Step 2 본책 _ p. 201

4.
해설 보기가 다 다른 동사어휘들로 구성된 어휘 문제이다. 빈칸 다음에 목적어인 the finest goods(가장 훌륭한 제품들)가 있으므로 빈칸은 타동사의 자리이다. (A) deal(다루다)은 뒤에 전치사 with가 필요하며 (B) speak(말하다)도 뒤에 전치사 to나 with 등이 수반되는 자동사이다. (D) respond(응답/대답하다)도 뒤에 전치사 to가 필요한 자동사이다. (C) handle(~를 다루다, 취급하다)은 유일한 타동사이므로 정답이 된다.

해석 우리는 사우샘프턴 하우스가 시장에서 가장 훌륭한 제품들을 취급한다는 점을 보장합니다.

어휘 guarantee ~를 보장하다   handle ~를 다루다, 취급하다
fine 품질이 좋은, 훌륭한   goods 제품(들)   on the market 시장에서

정답 (C)

5.
해설 부정사 뒤에 동사원형으로서 쓰이는 동시에 목적어로 tourists를 수반할 수 있는 어휘를 선택하는 문제이다. 보기 중 목적어를 수반할 수 있는 타동사는 (D) attract 뿐이다. 나머지는 모두 자동사이므로 정답이 될 수 없다. 참고로 동사 attract는 'attract + 사람(~을 매혹하다)', 'attract attention to(~로 주의를 이끌다)'와 같은 표현으로 자주 사용되니 기억해두자.

해석 많은 특징들 때문에, 새로운 박물관은 그 도시로 관광객들을 유치할 것이라고 기대됩니다.

어휘 feature 특징; ~을 특징으로 하다
be expected to부정사 ~할 것으로 예상되다   tourist 관광객

정답 (D)

Check-up Step 1   본책 _ p. 203

1.
해설 동사 live는 완전 자동사이므로 곧바로 명사 목적어가 뒤에 나올 수 없다. 따라서 전치사 in을 수반한 (B)가 정답이 된다.

해석 그들은 지금 디트로이트에 산다.

정답 (B)

2.
해설 be동사 뒤에 오는 보어를 선택하는 문제인데, 명사 (A) importance (중요)가 들어가면 주어인 Mr. Kim과 동격관계를 형성할 수 없으므로 탈락이고, 형용사 (B) important(중요한)가 들어가야 주어의 상태를 설명하는 올바른 표현이 완성된다.

해석 김 씨는 우리들에게 매우 중요하다.

정답 (B)

3.
해설 빈칸 앞의 동사 seem은 '~인 듯 보이다'라는 의미의 불완전 자동사이다. 때문에 뒤에 형용사나 명사 보어를 수반해야 한다. 따라서 (A) high(높은)가 들어가야 seem high(높은 듯 보인다)라는 올바른 표현이 된다.

해석 그 제안된 로열티 요금은 높은 듯 보인다.

어휘 proposed 제안된   royalty 로열티   rate 요금
seem ~처럼 보이다, ~인 듯 보이다   high 높은
highly 크게, 높이, 대단히

정답 (A)

Check-up Step 2   본책 _ p. 203

4.
해설 빈칸 앞의 동사 became(~해졌다)는 불완전 자동사이므로 뒤에 명사나 형용사 보어를 수반한다. 때문에 부사인 (C) popularly를 제외하고 명사 (B), (D)와 형용사 (A) 중에서 선택을 해야 하는데, 명사 (B) popularity(인기)와 복수형인 (D) popularities는 주어인 Chinese tea(중국차)와 동격관계가 될 수 없으므로 형용사 (A) popular(인기 있는)가 주어의 상태를 설명하는 올바른 보어로 정답이다.

해석 중국차는 유럽으로 수출되었고, 곧 많은 서양 국가들에서 인기가 많아졌다.

어휘 tea 차   be exported to ~로 수출되다   soon 곧

정답 (A)

5.
해설 동사 뒤에 알맞은 품사를 선택하는 문제인데, seem(~인 듯 보이다)의 특징을 파악하는 것이 중요 포인트다. seem은 대표적인 불완전 자동사로서 뒤에 형용사나 부사를 보어로 수반할 수 있다. 따라서 보기 중 유일한 형용사인 (C) knowledgeable(많이 알고 있는, 박식한)이 정답이 된다.

해석 모든 후보자들이 박식해 보이기에, 그 직책을 맡길 한 사람을 선택하는 일은 쉽지 않다.

어휘 candidate 후보자   seem ~인 듯 보이다   select 고르다, 선택하다
fill 채우다, 보충하다   position 직책

정답 (C)

Check-up Step 1   본책 _ p. 205

1.
해설 동사 lend는 '빌려주다', share는 '공유하다'의 의미인데, 뒤에 A with B 구문을 수반하는 것은 (B) share이다.

해석 우리는 정보를 다른 팀들과 공유하지 않습니다.

어휘 share A with B A를 B와 공유하다   other 다른

정답 (B)

2.
해설 동사 notify는 뒤에 A of B를 수반하는 타동사로, 'A에게 B에 대해 통보하다'는 의미로 사용하는 어휘이다.

해석 그 회사는 최종 결정에 대해서 우리에게 통보할 것이다.

어휘 notify A of B A에게 B에 대해서 통보하다   final 최종(의)
decision 결정

정답 (B)

3.
해설 빈칸 다음을 보면 목적어인 customers(고객들)와 better service (더 좋은 서비스)가 나란히 있는 구조이다. 즉, 목적어 두 개를 수반하는 수여동사가 필요하므로 (B) offer가 정답이 된다.

해석 우리 회사는 고객들에게 더 좋은 서비스를 제공할 수 있을 것이다.

어휘 be able to부정사 ~할 수 있다   offer A B A에게 B를 제공하다
customer 고객   better 더 좋은

정답 (B)

Check-up Step 2 본책 _ p. 205

4.
해설 빈칸 다음을 보면 목적어 you와 a bike 두 개가 나란히 있는 구조이다. 즉, 목적어 두 개를 수반할 수 있는 수여동사가 필요하므로 보기 중에서 유일한 수여동사인 (D) lend(빌려주다)가 정답이 된다.
해석 만약 당신의 자전거가 도난당하면, 상점은 당신에게 일주일 동안 무료로 자전거를 빌려줄 것이다.
어휘 bike 자전거   steal 훔치다, 도둑질하다   for free 무료로
정답 (D)

5.
해설 보기는 모두 동사어휘로 구성되어 있다. 동사문제는 해석으로 접근할 수 있고, 동사의 용례로도 접근 가능하다. 위 문제에서는 전치사 to와 함께 사용 가능한 동사를 선택하는 게 포인트이며 (C) attributed는 attribute A to B(A를 B의 탓으로 돌리다)의 용례로 사용되므로 정답이 된다. 보기에 나온 동사어휘들의 용례를 살펴보면 share A with B(A를 B와 공유하다), obtain A from B(A를 B로부터 얻다), replace A with B(A를 B로 대신하다)로 각각 사용되니 기억해두자.
해석 담당자들은 회사의 높은 수준의 생산성을 헌신적인 직원들 덕으로 돌렸다.
어휘 director 책임자, 담당자   attribute A to B A를 B의 탓으로 돌리다   high level of productivity 높은 수준의 생산성   devoted 헌신적인   share 공유하다, 나누다   obtain 획득하다   replace 대신하다
정답 (C)

Check-up Step 1 본책 _ p. 207

1.
해설 본동사 have가 사역동사이므로 사람 목적어인 my children 다음에 목적격 보어로 동사원형이 사용되어야 한다. 때문에 (A) study가 정답이 된다.
해석 나는 다가오는 시험에 대비하여 아이들에게 열심히 공부하도록 시킬 것이다.
정답 (A)

2.
해설 본동사 saw가 지각동사이므로 목적어 him 다음에 동사원형이 목적격 보어로 들어가야 한다. 때문에 (A) leave가 정답이 된다.
해석 나는 그가 몇 분 전에 떠나는 것을 보았습니다.
정답 (A)

3.
해설 본동사 requested(요청했다)는 목적어 다음에 to부정사를 목적격 보어로 수반하는 동사이다. 따라서 (B) to work가 정답이 된다.
해석 부장은 직원들이 주말 동안에 일을 하도록 요청했다.
어휘 manager 매니저, 부장   request 요청하다   staff member 직원
정답 (B)

Check-up Step 2 본책 _ p. 207

4.
해설 빈칸 다음에 있는 목적어 customers(고객들) 뒤에 부정사 to get이 힌트이다. 목적격 보어로 부정사를 수반하는 동사가 필요하므로 정답은 (A) allows(허용하다)가 된다.
해석 이 쿠폰은 고객들에게 첫 주문 총액의 20% 할인을 받도록 허용해 준다.
어휘 coupon 쿠폰   allow 허용하다   get a discount 할인을 받다   total amount 총액   order 주문
정답 (A)

5.
해설 알맞은 동사의 형태를 고르는 문제이며, 본동사로 let이 정답의 핵심 포인트이다. let(~하도록 시키다)은 원형부정사(동사원형)를 목적보어로 사용하는 사역동사이다. 따라서 정답은 (A) know가 된다. 사역동사는 〈let/make/have+목적어+원형부정사〉로 쓰이고, help는 〈help+목적어+to부정사/원형부정사〉와 〈help+to부정사/원형부정사〉로 사용되는 준사역동사이다.
해석 새로운 장비를 어떻게 운영하는지에 관한 문의사항이 있으시면 완다에게 알려주십시오.
어휘 operate ~을 운영하다   machine 기계, 장비
정답 (A)

Check-up 본책 _ p. 209

1. **정답** hold
어휘 make 만들다 / hold 주최하다, 열다

2. **정답** prohibit
어휘 prohibit 금지하다 / allow 허락하다

3. **정답** enroll
어휘 enroll 등록하다 / apply 신청하다

4. **정답** raise
어휘 rise 상승하다 / raise ~를 올리다

5. **정답** depends
어휘 depend 의존하다 / participate 참가하다

Part 5&6_ 실전연습 5 본책 _ p. 210–211

1.

해설 빈칸 뒤에 heavy fines(중한 벌금)를 목적어로 취하는 동사를 선택하는 문제이다. 일단, 자동사 (A) look은 올 수 없으며, (C) feature와 (D) express는 heavy fines와 어울리지 않는다. 따라서 face heavy fines(중한 벌금에 직면하다)라는 표현을 만드는 (B) face가 정답이다.

해석 그 법은 회사들이 탄소 배출을 줄이도록 하거나 중한 벌금에 직면하도록 할 것입니다.

어휘 force 힘, 세력; ~를 강요하다, ~에게 ~하게하다 reduce ~를 줄이다
emission 배출 fine 벌금; 좋은, 건강한; ~에게 벌금을 부과하다
face 얼굴, 표정, 사람; (어려운 상황) ~에 직면하다
feature 특징, 특집기사; ~를 특징으로 하다, ~를 특집으로 다루다
express 급행의, 속달로; 표현하다, 보여주다

정답 (B)

2.

해설 알맞은 동사의 형태를 선택하는 문제로, 빈칸 뒤의 its annual dinner concert가 힌트가 된다. 일단, 목적어를 수반할 수 없는 (B) will be held가 먼저 탈락된다. 빈칸 다음의 부사 tonight(오늘 밤)과 시간적으로 함께 올 수 있는 동사는 (C) is holding이 유일하다.

해석 오토모빌 사는 가난한 사람들을 위한 자선모금을 하기 위하여, 오늘 밤 연례 디너 콘서트를 개최할 것입니다.

어휘 annual 연례의, 매년
raise 상승, 증가; ~을 증가시키다, (돈을) 모금하다
hold ~을 수용하다, ~을 열다, ~를 개최하다 the poor 가난한 사람들

정답 (C)

3.

해설 to부정사 다음에 오는 동사를 고르는 문제로, 빈칸 뒤의 전치사 from 이하가 힌트가 된다. 문맥상 '비회원들이 주차장을 이용하는 것을 금지하기로 결정했다'는 의미가 필요하므로 전치사 from과 함께 '~하는 것을 금지하다'의 표현을 완성하는 (A) prohibit이 정답이 된다.

해석 회원 수의 급속한 증가로 본 협회에서는 비회원들이 주차장을 이용하는 것을 금지하기로 결정했습니다.

어휘 decide to부정사 ~하기로 결정하다 non-member 비회원
prohibit A from ~ing A가 ~하는 것을 금지하다
parking garage 주차장 because of ~ 때문에
refuse ~를 거절하다, ~를 거부하다 (= turn down)
check 수표; ~를 검토하다, 확인하다 shield 보호자; ~를 보호하다

정답 (A)

4.

해설 문장의 구조를 살펴보면 주어는 Honey Entertainment이고, 빈칸은 동사 자리이다. 일단, 동사가 아닌 (B) planning이 먼저 탈락된다. (A) plan과 (D) have been planned는 주어와의 수일치에서 탈락된다. 따라서 단수동사인 (C) is planning이 정답이다.

해석 허니 엔터테인먼트는 생산성을 향상시키기 위해서 최신식 운영시스템을 설치할 계획이다.

어휘 state-of-the-art 최신식의 operation 수술, 운영, 작업, 사업
system 제도, 체계, 시스템 improve 나아지다, ~를 개선시키다
productivity 생산성 plan 계획; ~을 계획하다

정답 (C)

5.

해설 to 다음에 알맞은 품사의 어휘를 고르는 문제인데, 여기서 to는 '~하기 위해서'라는 to부정사이므로 전치사 (B) except는 탈락된다. 문맥상 '추가적인 요금을 피하기 위해, 미리 취소되어야 한다'는 의미로 (A) avoid가 정답이 된다.

해석 추가적인 요금을 피하기 위해서, 비행기 예약은 최소한 24시간 전에 취소되어야 한다.

어휘 reservation 예약, 지정, 확보 cancel ~를 취소하다
at least 최소한 in advance 미리, 먼저 fee 요금, 수수료
avoid ~를 피하다 except ~를 제외하고
permit 허가증; ~를 허가하다, ~를 가능하게 하다
withdraw ~를 인출하다, ~를 철수시키다

정답 (A)

6.

해설 빈칸 앞의 조동사 must 다음에 올 수 있는 올바른 어휘의 형태를 고르는 문제이다. 조동사 다음에는 동사원형을 수반하기 때문에 (A) be prepared가 정답이다.

해설 회의장의 모든 장비는 행사 시작 최소 20분 전에는 준비가 되어야 한다.

어휘 equipment 장비, 기계 conference hall 회의장
prepare ~을 준비하다

정답 (A)

7.

해설 알맞은 동사를 고르는 문제로 전치사 with와의 연결을 고려해야 한다. 즉, 목적어를 수반하는 타동사 (B) tell, (D) express 모두 탈락된다. (A) say는 뒤에 전치사 to와 함께 사람명사가 오지만, (C) speak는 전치사 with가 쓰이므로 정답이다.

어휘 duty 의무, 직무 rule 규칙, 법, 자 regulation 규제, 규칙, 통제
express 급행의, 속달로; ~를 표현하다, ~를 보여주다
speak 말하다, ~를 말하다

해석 신입 사원들 각자에게 회사의 규칙과 규제를 주지시키는 것은 인사부장의 직무이다.

정답 (C)

8.

해설 빈칸은 조동사 will 다음에 오는 자리로, 동사원형이 와야 한다. 일단, 동사가 아닌 (C) offering이 먼저 탈락되며, 단수동사 (A) offers와 (D) has offered 역시 올 수 없다. 결국 '제공될 것이다'라는 의미로 수동태를 이루는 (B) be offered가 정답이다.

해석 모든 새로운 전자제품들이 우리의 겨울 판매행사 동안에 40%까지 할인된 가격에 제공될 것입니다.

어휘 electronics 전자제품, 전자공학, 전자기술
discount 할인; ~을 할인하다   up to ~까지   sales 판매
offer 제안, 제공; ~을 제공하다, (기꺼이) ~해주겠다고 하다

정답 (B)

9.

해설 빈칸 다음의 money를 목적어로 수반하는 타동사를 고르는 문제이다. (A) happen, (B) take place, (D) arise 모두 자동사로 빈칸에 올 수 없다. money와 함께 쓰여 raise money(모금하다)라는 표현을 만드는 타동사 (C) raise가 정답이다.

해석 그 기구는 가난한 사람들을 위해 기금을 마련하고, 그리하여 그들 스스로 자립하도록 돕는다.

어휘 stand on one's own feet 자립하다
happen 발생하다 (= take place)
raise 증가, 상승; ~을 증가시키다, ~를 모금하다
arise (문제점, 어려움 따위가) 발생하다

정답 (C)

10.

해설 주어 Reports 다음의 in *Autos Today Magazine*은 〈전치사+명사〉로 이루어진 수식어구이다. 따라서 빈칸에는 문장 전체의 동사가 들어가야 한다. 주어가 Reports라는 복수명사이므로 보기의 유일한 복수동사인 (D) help가 정답이 된다.

해석 〈오토스 투데이 매거진〉의 보고서는 소비자들이 정확하게 원하는 자동차를 고르는 데 도움을 준다.

어휘 report 보고서; ~에게 보고하다   help A 동사원형 A가 ~하는 것을 돕다
consumer 고객 (= client)   choose 선정하다, ~를 선택하다
exactly 정확하게

정답 (D)

11.

해설 알맞은 동사어휘를 선택하여 문맥을 완성하는 문제이다. 보기 중에서 빈칸 뒤의 명사 a sales representative를 목적어로 수반하는 타동사는 (B) contact(~에게 연락하다)가 유일하다. 나머지 (A) speak, (C) depend, (D) talk 모두 자동사로 탈락된다.

해석 제품에 관한 질문이 있으시면, 안내창구에 있는 판매 직원에게 연락하세요.

어휘 question 질문, 쟁점, 문제, 의심; ~에게 질문하다
representative 대표자, 직원, 대표하는   speak 말하다, 이야기하다
contact 접촉; ~에 연락하다
depend on ~에 의존하다 (= be reliant on)
talk 이야기, 회담, 논의, 연설; 이야기하다, 말하다

정답 (B)

12.

해설 불완전 자동사 is의 보어로 사용하는 품사를 고르는 문제이다. 동사 (B) depends와 (C) depend가 먼저 제외된다. 전치사 on을 수반하면서 의미가 통하는 품사는 형용사 (A) dependent(의존하는, 달려있는)가 유일하다.

해석 당신도 아시다시피, 자동차의 속도는 엔진의 크기와 규칙적인 유지관리에 달려있어요.

어휘 as you know 당신도 아시다시피
be dependent on ~에 의존하다, 달려있다 (= depend on)
dependence 의존, 의지   maintenance 유지, 보수, 유지관리

정답 (A)

13.

해설 명사 a presentation을 목적어로 취할 수 있는 동사를 고르는 문제이다. make a presentation(발표하다)이라는 올바른 표현을 이루는 (C) make가 정답이다.

해석 에어 트래블 사는 마케팅 이사에게 회사의 최근 업무에 관하여 고객들에게 발표하도록 지시를 내렸다.

어휘 instruct ~를 지시하다, ~를 가르치다, (정보 따위를) 알려주다
director 이사, 중역, 임원   division 부서, 분열, 분배
make a presentation 발표하다 (= give a presentation)
concerning ~에 관해   demonstrate 증명하다   elect 선출하다

정답 (C)

14.

해설 알맞은 동사어휘를 선택하여 문장을 완성하는 문제이다. 빈칸 뒤에 all employees와 permanent jobs라는 목적어가 2개 있다는 사실이 결정적인 힌트이다. 따라서 정답은 목적어 2개를 수반하는 수여동사 (D) offers가 된다.

해석 브로스 영화사는 5년 이상 일해온 모든 직원들에게 정규직 일자리를 제공합니다.

어휘 film company 영화사   employee 직원
permanent job 정규직   reward 상; ~에게 보답하다, 상을 주다
provide ~를 제공하다   offer 제공, 제안; ~를 제공하다

정답 (D)

15-18

식물들을 살리기 위해 분투하는 아마추어 정원사들을 위해, A-포트는 꽃과 허브, 그리고 야채 재배를 관리가 가능한 일로 만듭니다. 다양한 센서를 채용한 A-포트는 토양이 너무 건조하다든지, 현재의 위치가 빛을 충분히 받지 못하는 곳이라는 것과 같은 사실을 감지해냅니다. 그러면 내장된 디스플레이를 통해 포트가 사용자에게 그 사실을 통보해 줍니다. 뿐만 아니라, A-포트는 인터넷에 무선으로 연결이 가능하므로 원격으로 모니터링을 할 수도 있습니다. 이 경우 사용자들은 다양한 종류의 식물을 키우는 데 요구되는 환경 정보를 다운받는 것도 가능합니다. 어디에서 정원용 물품을 구입하시든 A-포트를 찾아 주십시오.

어휘 gardener 취미로 정원을 가꾸는 사람, 정원사
struggle to부정사 ~하기 위해 분투하다   pot 화분
an array of ~의 대집합[집결], 죽 늘어선 ~   detect 탐지하다
soil 흙, 토양   current 현재의   remotely 멀리서, 원격으로
permit A to부정사 A가 ~하는 것을 허용하다[가능케 하다]
setting 환경, 설정   gardening supplies 정원용 물품

15.
해설 관사와 명사 사이는 형용사 자리이다. 빈칸에는 형용사인 (C) manageable(관리할 수 있는)을 넣어 명사 task를 수식하게 해 주면 된다.

정답 (C)

16.
해설 적절한 대명사를 고르는 문제이다. A-Pot가 '자신의 현재 위치'가 적합한지를 감지한다는 문맥이므로, 단수 명사 A-Pot를 받는 소유격 대명사 (B) its가 정답이다.

정답 (B)

17.
(A) 그러면 내장된 디스플레이를 통해 포트가 사용자에게 그 사실을 통보해 줍니다.
(B) 좋은 비료는 건강한 식물에 필수적입니다.
(C) 전문가들만이 이런 종류의 기술을 이용하고 있습니다.
(D) 오토 포트는 내년 여름 일찍 구입할 수 있습니다.

해설 토양이 너무 건조하거나 빛이 충분치 않은 경우에 A-Pot가 그런 사실을 감지하며, 인터넷에 무선으로 연결이 가능해 원격으로 모니터링도 할 수 있다는 등, A-Pot의 다양한 기능을 설명하고 있는 내용의 중간에 빈칸이 위치하고 있다. 따라서 역시 A-Pot의 기능 설명에 해당되는 내용인 (A)가 정답으로 적절하다.

정답 (A)

18.
해설 인터넷에 무선으로 연결이 될 경우 '다양한 식물을 키우는 데 필요한 환경 정보를 ~할 수 있다'는 문맥이다. 빈칸에는 (B) download를 넣어 '다운받을 수 있다'는 뜻이 될 때 문장의 의미가 가장 자연스럽다.

정답 (B)

UNIT 6 시제

Check-up Step 1   본책_p. 213

1.
해설 문장의 구조상 빈칸은 동사의 자리이므로, 동사 (A) read가 정답이다.

해석 나는 어제 그 보고서를 읽었다.

어휘 read ~를 읽다

정답 (A)

2.
해설 빈칸 앞에 were라는 동사가 있으므로, 동사 (A) have는 바로 탈락된다. 따라서 be동사 were와 함께 진행형을 이루는 현재분사 (B) having이 정답이다.

해석 그들은 영업에 관하여 대화를 하는 중이었다.

어휘 have a conversation 대화하다   sales 판매, 영업, 매출(량), 할인판매

정답 (B)

3.
해설 빈칸 앞에 조동사 has와 함께 올바른 동사의 형태를 완성시키는 문제이다. has 다음에 현재분사 (A) conducting은 올 수 없다. 따라서 완료시제(have/has+p.p.) 형태를 형성하는 과거분사 (B) conducted가 정답이다.

해석 그녀는 전국에서 설문조사를 실시했다.

어휘 conduct 행동, 규칙; ~를 실시하다, 실행하다
survey 조사, 투표; ~를 조사하다, ~를 검토하다

정답 (B)

Check-up Step 2   본책_p. 213

4.
해설 수일치, 태 모두 적합하기 때문에 시제를 고려해야 한다. 문장 마지막에 last week라는 과거시제를 나타내는 어휘가 있으므로 (B) showed가 정답이다.

해석 본 차이나 어플라이언스는 지난주 무역 박람회에서 최신 주방용품들을 선보였다.

어휘 show 경치, 경관, 공연; ~을 보여주다   product 상품, 제품
trade 거래, 무역; 매매하다, ~를 거래하다, ~를 교환하다

정답 (B)

5.

해설 명사절인 that절 내에 알맞은 동사의 형태를 고르는 문제다. 빈칸 앞에 have는 '~을 가지다'라는 타동사가 아닌 현재완료동사(have p.p.)를 이끄는 조동사이므로 빈칸에는 과거분사가 와야 한다. 동사 become은 'become(원형) - became(과거) - become(과거분사)'으로 사용되며 동사원형과 과거분사의 형태가 동일한 특징이 있다. 따라서 정답은 (A) become이 된다.

해석 탑승객들은 밴쿠버 공항에서의 지연이 잦아졌다고 불평합니다.

어휘 passenger 탑승객   complain 불평하다
delay 지연; ~을 지연시키다   frequent 잦은, 빈번한

정답 (A)

Check-up Step 1   본책 _ p. 215

1.

해설 빈칸은 동사 자리로 올바른 시제를 선택해야 하는데, 빈칸 앞의 usually(보통, 주로)가 중요한 힌트가 된다. usually는 반복적인 일을 나타내는 부사로 현재시제와 잘 어울린다. 따라서 현재시제 (A) reads가 정답이다.

해석 그는 보통 아침에 신문을 읽는다.

어휘 usually 보통, 대개   in the morning 아침에

정답 (A)

2.

해설 문장의 마지막에 next week(다음 주)라는 미래를 나타내는 부사표현이 있다. 일단, 과거시제 (A) opened가 먼저 탈락되고, 가까운 미래를 의미하는 현재진행 (B) are opening이 정답이다.

해석 그들은 다음 주에 새로운 지점을 열 것이다.

어휘 open 열려있는, 개방하는, 영업 중인; ~를 열다, 열리다
branch 지점, 지사, 가지

정답 (B)

3.

해설 문장의 마지막에 since 2009(2009년 이후로)이 중요한 힌트가 된다. since는 '과거 이래로 지금까지'라는 의미의 어휘로 현재완료(have p.p.)와 어울리므로 (B) has worked가 정답이 된다.

해석 그는 2009년 이후로 그 회사에서 일해 왔다.

어휘 work 작업, 작품, 업무; 일하다, 작동하다   since ~이후로, ~때문에

정답 (B)

Check-up Step 2   본책 _ p. 215

4.

해설 알맞은 동사의 시제를 고르는 문제이다. 문장의 마지막에 over the past two quarters라는 현재완료와 어울리는 부사표현이 있으므로, 빈칸에는 현재완료 (C) has exceeded가 정답이 된다.

해석 지난 2분기 동안의 회사의 성장은 주주들의 기대치를 넘어섰다.

어휘 growth 성장   quarter 4분의 1, 15분, 분기   shareholder 주주
expectation 예상, 기대
exceed ~를 초과하다, (범위·한도)를 넘어서다

정답 (C)

5.

해설 빈칸 앞뒤에 나와 있는 동사 is held(개최되다) 사이에서 이를 수식하는 알맞은 부사어휘를 고르는 문제이다. 시제가 현재시제라는 것이 정답의 근거가 되는데, 보기 중 유일하게 현재시제와 쓰일 수 있는 (B) usually(보통)가 답이 된다. 현재시제는 '반복적인 일, 습관, 일반적 사실' 등을 나타내는 시제이다. usually 또한 반복적인 일을 나타내는 표현이므로 주로 현재시제와 잘 어울린다. 참고로 (A) recently(최근에는) 과거시제, 현재완료시제와 사용되며 (C) lately(최근에)는 현재완료시제와, (D) yesterday는 과거시제와 사용된다.

해석 집행위원회의는 보통 매월 첫째 주 월요일에 열립니다.

어휘 executive committee meeting 집행위원회   be held 개최되다
usually 보통, 일반적으로   recently 최근에   lately 최근에

정답 (B)

Check-up Step 1   본책 _ p. 217

1.

해설 문장의 끝에 과거시간을 말해주는 two months ago(두 달 전)가 있으므로 과거동사 (B) went가 정답이다.

해석 그들은 두 달 전에 일본으로 갔다.

어휘 ago ~ 전에

정답 (B)

2.

해설 문장의 끝에 과거시간을 말해주는 last night(지난 밤)가 있으므로 과거동사 (B) worked가 정답이다. 확실한 과거시간 표현이 나오면 절대 현재완료시제와 사용할 수 없다.

해석 직원들은 지난 밤 판매 보고서에 관한 업무를 했다.

어휘 employee 직원   report 보고서; ~을 보고하다
sales report 판매 보고서

정답 (B)

123

3.
해설 문장의 끝에 과거시간을 말해주는 last year(작년에)가 있으므로 과거동사 (A) revised가 정답이다.

해석 지방 정부는 작년에 세제 계획을 개정했다.

어휘 local 현지인; 현지의, 지역의   government 정부
tax 세금, 세제; ~에 세금을 부과하다   plan 계획; ~을 계획하다
revise ~를 개정하다, ~를 수정하다

정답 (A)

Check-up Step 2   본책 _ p. 217

4.
해설 동사 had는 타동사로 '~를 가지고 있다'는 의미이거나, 현재완료 (have p.p.)를 만드는 조동사이다. 동사 had가 있으므로 (A) leave와 (D) leaves는 올 수 없다. (C) leaving 역시 had 다음에 올 수 없다. 따라서 had left라는 과거완료를 이루는 (B) left가 정답이다.

해석 그 여행 단체는 완성된 일정표를 받기 전에 파리로 떠났다.

어휘 tour 여행, 견학   before ~전에
receive ~를 받다, ~에 반응하다, ~를 수신하다
complete 완성된; ~를 마무리하다, 완성하다
itinerary 여행일정, 일정표   leave 휴가; 떠나다, ~을 남기다

정답 (B)

5.
해설 Although는 접속사로서 뒤에 주어와 동사가 있는 완전한 문장을 수반한다. 빈칸 앞에 주어 they가 있으므로 보기 중 알맞은 동사를 선택해야 하는데, 우선 (B) investing과 (C) to invest는 동사가 아니므로 탈락된다. 다음으로 주어와의 수일치 관계를 고려해보면 현재완료동사인 (A) has invested는 단수형이므로 복수주어인 they와는 어울리지 않는다. 따라서 수일치에 관계없이 사용가능한 과거완료 (D) had invested가 정답이 된다.

해석 그들이 프로젝트에 많은 돈을 투자했음에도 불구하고, 그것은 성공하지 못했다.

어휘 although 비록 ~일지라도, ~에도 불구하고   invest 투자하다
a lot of 많은   successful 성공적인

정답 (D)

Check-up Step 1   본책 _ p. 219

1.
해설 조동사 will 다음에는 동사의 원형이나 be + p.p. 형태만 가능하므로, 일단 3인칭 단수 형태인 (B) brings는 바로 탈락된다. 따라서 동사원형 (A) bring이 정답이다.

해석 그녀는 회의를 위해 보고서를 가져올 것이다.

어휘 report 보고서; ~에게 보고하다   meeting 모임, 회의
bring ~을 가져오다, ~를 데려오다

정답 (A)

2.
해설 be동사 다음에 동사는 더 이상 나올 수 없으므로 (A) install은 바로 제외된다. 따라서 뒤에 나오는 미래표현 tomorrow(내일)와 어울려 미래진행시제를 완성하는 현재분사 (B) installing이 정답이다.

해석 우리는 내일 새 복사기를 설치할 것이다.

어휘 copy machine 복사기   install ~를 설치하다

정답 (B)

3.
해설 빈칸 뒤에 when we get to the theater(우리가 극장에 도착할 때)는 미래를 나타내는 시제이므로, 문맥상 앞 문장에도 미래시제가 필요하다. 따라서 미래시제 (B) will have started가 정답이다.

해석 나는 우리가 극장에 도착할 때 그 영화가 시작할 것이라고 생각한다.

어휘 think ~를 생각하다   get to ~로 가다, ~에 도달하다
theater 극장, 영화관   start ~를 시작하다

정답 (B)

Check-up Step 2   본책 _ p. 219

4.
해설 조동사 will 다음에는 동사의 원형이나 be + p.p. 형태만 가능하다. 따라서 동사원형 (A) reveal이 정답이다. 여기서 will reveal은 tomorrow(내일)라는 시간표현과 어울리는 미래시제이다.

해석 내일 기자 회견에서, 세키자키 씨는 회사의 신계획을 드러낼 것이다.

어휘 press conference 기자 회견   plan 계획; ~를 계획하다
reveal ~를 밝히다, ~를 드러내다

정답 (A)

5.
해설 접속사 that 뒤의 절 안에 들어갈 알맞은 동사의 형태를 고르는 문제로 우선 주어인 the company와 수일치가 맞지 않는 (A) merge는 제외된다. 정답의 근거는 by the end of next year(내년 연말까지)이며, 미래를 나타내는 부사표현이다. 따라서 미래완료 (C) will have merged가 정답이다. 미래완료는 미래에 어떤 일이 완료된다는 의미로, '내년 말까지는 합병이 완료될 것이다'라는 적절한 의미가 완성된다.

해석 그 회사는 내년 말까지는 얀센 프로덕션 사와 합병하게 될 것으로 알려져 있다.

어휘 report 기록, 보고서; 알리다, 보도하다   merge with ~와 합병하다

정답 (C)

Check-up 본책 _ p. 221

1. 정답 **accommodate**
   어휘 accommodate 수용하다 / accommodation 수용, 숙박

2. 정답 **affect**
   어휘 affect ~에 영향을 끼치다 / effect 효과

3. 정답 **complain**
   어휘 complain 불평을 하다 / complaint 불평, 불만

4. 정답 **recommended**
   어휘 recommend 추천하다 / recommendation 추천

5. 정답 **compare**
   어휘 comparison 비교 / compare 비교하다

Part 5&6_ 실전연습 6 본책 _ p. 222-223

1.
해설 빈칸은 문장의 시제를 고르는 문제로, that절의 마지막에 있는 next month(다음 달)가 힌트가 된다. next month는 미래시제를 나타내는 표현이므로 (D) will acquire가 정답이다.
해석 이사회는 우리 회사가 다음 달에 다른 경쟁사들을 인수할 것이라고 발표했습니다.
어휘 the board of directors 이사회
announce ~를 발표하다, 공표하다   competing 경쟁하는
firm 회사; 딱딱한, 변치 않을; ~를 단단하게 하다
acquire ~를 인수하다, ~를 획득하다

정답 (D)

2.
해설 빈칸 뒤의 명사 you를 목적어로 수반하면서, 동사 relax and sleep도 함께 취하는 동사가 필요하다. 동사 help는 목적어 다음에 목적보어로 'to부정사' 또는 '동사원형(원형부정사)'을 동반할 수 있다. 즉, help + A + 원형부정사(A가 ~하도록 돕다)의 형태로 사용되는 (A) help가 정답이다.
해석 바이오 테크놀로지가 새롭게 출시한 허브 제품들은 당신이 휴식을 취하고 수면을 취하는 것을 돕는다.
어휘 herbal 허브의, 허브로 만든   product 제품   newly 새롭게, 최근에
release 발간, 출시; ~를 풀어주다, ~를 공개하다
relax 휴식을 취하다, 긴장이 풀리다   sleep 자다; 수면, 잠
enable ~를 가능하게 하다   allow 허락하다
raise ~를 기르다, ~를 증가시키다

정답 (A)

3.
해설 to부정사의 to 다음에 오는 알맞은 동사를 고르는 문제로, 빈칸 뒤의 명사 approximately 30,000 people이 힌트가 된다. 일단, 목적어가 올 수 없는 자동사 (D) talk가 먼저 탈락된다. 문맥상 '대략 30,000명의 사람들을 수용하다'는 의미가 필요하므로 (C) accommodate(~를 수용하다)가 정답이 된다.
해석 시 외곽에 위치한 그 경기장은 대략 30,000명의 사람들을 수용하도록 고안되었다.
어휘 locate ~를 위치시키다, ~를 찾다   stadium 경기장
be designed to ~하도록 고안되다
approximately 대략 (= around, about)
prohibit ~를 금지하다, ~를 하지 못하게 하다
face 얼굴, 표정; ~에 직면하다, ~와 대면하다
accommodate ~를 숙박시키다, ~를 수용하다

정답 (C)

4.
해설 빈칸은 동사의 시제를 고르는 문제로, that절의 마지막에 있는 in the near future(가까운 미래에, 머지않아)가 힌트가 된다. in the near future는 미래시제를 나타내는 표현이므로 (D) will be fired가 정답이다.
해석 파업이 있은 후에, 많은 직원들이 머지않아 해고를 당할 것이라고 보도되었다.
어휘 after ~후에   strike 파업, 공격   report 보고서; ~을 보고하다
employees 직원들   in the near future 곧, 머지않아 (= soon)
fire 화재, 불, 발사, 분노; ~를 해고하다, 발사되다, ~를 굽다

정답 (D)

5.
해설 명사 the contents of luggage(가방의 내용물)를 목적어로 수반하는 알맞은 동사를 고르는 문제이다. 접속사 before 이하에 '불법적인 상품들이 공항 밖으로 나오다'는 내용으로 볼 때, '검사하다'라는 의미의 동사가 필요하다. 따라서 (A) inspect(~를 검사하다)가 정답이다.
해석 불법적인 상품들이 공항 밖으로 나오기 전에, 세관 직원들은 가방의 내용물을 신중하게 검사할 것입니다.
어휘 customs officer 세관 공무원   contents 내용물
luggage 가방 (= baggage)   carefully 신중하게   before ~전에
illegal 불법적인   goods 상품   out of ~밖에, ~밖으로, 중에서
airport 공항   inspect ~를 검사하다, ~를 시찰하다
affect ~에게 영향을 끼치다   plan 계획; ~을 계획하다
conduct ~를 실시하다, 실행하다

정답 (A)

6.
해설 알맞은 동사의 시제를 고르는 문제이다. 문장의 처음에 In the last five years라는 현재완료와 어울리는 부사표현이 있으므로, 빈칸에는 현재완료 (A) has increased가 정답이 된다.

해석 지난 5년 동안, 주거비용은 연 평균 5퍼센트 상승해 왔다.

어휘 last 지난, 마지막의; 지속되다, ~을 견디다 housing expense 주거비
average 평균   per 각, 매, ~당
increase 증가; ~를 증가시키다, 증가하다

정답 (A)

7.
해설 빈칸 뒤의 명사 all used cellphones를 목적어로 취하는 동사를 고르는 문제이다. 일단, 목적어가 올 수 없는 자동사 (D) appear는 탈락된다. and 이하는 '재판매를 위해서 그것들을 수리하다'는 내용이므로, '중고 휴대폰을 받다'를 의미하는 동사가 필요하다. 따라서 (B) accept가 정답이다.

해석 그 재활용 회사는 모든 중고 휴대폰을 받을 것이고 재판매를 위해서 그것들을 수리할 것이다.

어휘 recycling 재활용   used 중고의   cellphone 휴대폰
repair 수리; ~를 고치다   resale 재판매   enable ~를 가능하게 하다
accept ~을 수용하다, ~를 수락하다, ~을 받아들이다
access 접근, 접속; ~에 접속하다, 접근하다   appear 나타나다

정답 (B)

8.
해설 알맞은 동사의 시제를 고르는 문제이다. 문장의 끝에 과거시간을 말해주는 eight years ago(8년 전)가 있으므로 과거동사 (A) joined가 정답이다.

해석 다니엘은 8년 전에 스포츠 마케팅을 전문으로 하는 한 광고회사에 입사했다.

어휘 corporation 기업, 법인단체
specialize in ~에 전문이다, ~을 전문으로 하다
sports marketing 스포츠 마케팅
join ~의 구성원이 되다, ~에 입사하다, (행동 따위를) 함께하다

정답 (A)

9.
해설 명사절 접속사 that을 목적어로 취하는 동사의 자리이다. (A) notify, (C) satisfy, (D) tell은 바로 뒤에 접속사 that이 올 수 없다. 따라서 complain that 주어 + 동사(~하는 것을 불평하다)의 표현을 이루는 (B) complain이 정답이다.

해석 새 공항을 이용하는 관광객들은 불편한 편의시설과 형편없는 서비스가 있다는 점에 불평한다.

어휘 tourist 여행객   uncomfortable 불편한
facility 기관, 시설, 재능, 특징   poor 가난한, 빈곤한, 형편없는
notify ~에게 통보하다 (= inform)   complain 불평하다
satisfy ~를 만족시키다, ~를 확신시키다   tell ~에게 말하다

정답 (B)

10.
해설 빈칸 다음의 for nearly 25 years(거의 25년 동안)만 보고, 현재완료 (C) has worked를 선택하면 틀리는 문제이다. 종속절 by the time he retires가 미래시간을 나타내므로, 주절인 앞 문장 역시 미래시제가 필요하다. 따라서 미래완료 (D) will have worked가 정답이다.

해석 더글라스 씨가 은퇴할 때까지, 그는 리지우드 항공사에서 거의 25년 동안을 일하게 될 것이다.

어휘 nearly 거의 (= almost)   by the time ~할 때까지   retire 은퇴하다
work 일, 작품, 연구; 일하다

정답 (D)

11.
해설 알맞은 동사의 시제를 고르는 문제로, 빈칸 앞의 빈도부사 usually (보통, 대개)가 힌트가 된다. 빈도부사 'usually, sometimes, often, normally'나 'every + 시간명사' 또는 'each + 시간명사' 다음에는 현재동사를 사용한다. 따라서 현재동사 (C) delivers가 정답이 된다.

해석 우리 배송회사는 고객의 장소에 관계없이 보통 3일 이내에 모든 상품을 배송합니다.

어휘 shipping company 배송회사   usually 보통, 대개
product 제품, 상품   within ~ 이내에
regardless of ~에 상관없이   location 장소, 위치
deliver ~을 배달하다, ~를 인계하다

정답 (C)

12.
해설 전치사 from을 동반하여 문맥을 완성하는 동사를 고르는 문제이다. (A) receive, (B) provide, (D) offer 모두 목적어를 수반하는 타동사이므로 탈락된다. 따라서 benefit from(~로부터 혜택을 받다)이라는 표현을 이루는 (C) benefit이 정답이다.

해석 소비자들은 인터넷 공급업체들의 치열해지는 경쟁에서 혜택을 볼 것입니다.

어휘 customer 소비자   growing 증가하는
competition 경쟁, 경쟁자, 경연대회   among ~중에서
Internet provider 인터넷 사업자, 인터넷 공급업자
receive ~를 받다   provide ~를 제공하다, 주다, ~를 규정하다
benefit 혜택; ~에게 혜택을 주다   offer ~를 제공하다

정답 (C)

13.

해설 접속사 when 이하의 동사 arrived(도착했다)가 과거시제이므로 주절에 알맞은 동사시제는 과거완료인 (D) had started(시작했다)이다. 그 이유는 일의 선후관계상 '제레미와 그의 여자친구가 공연장에 도착했을 때, 뮤지컬 공연은 (이미) 시작했다'는 말이 문맥상 적합하기 때문이다.

해석 제레미와 그의 여자친구가 공연장에 도착했을 때, 뮤지컬 공연은 시작했다.

어휘 performance 실적, 공연, 성능 arrive at ~에 도착하다
theater 극장, 공연장 start 시작하다

정답 (D)

14.

해설 명사절 접속사 that을 목적어로 취하는 동사의 자리이다. 일단, 자동사인 (A) specialize는 바로 탈락된다. (B) consider, (C) compare 모두 바로 뒤에 접속사 that이 올 수 없다. 따라서 recommend that 주어+동사(~하는 것을 추천하다)의 표현을 이루는 (D) recommend가 정답이다.

해석 우리는 당신이 떠나기 전에, 미리 호텔을 예약하는 것을 추천합니다.

어휘 make a reservation 예약하다 in advance 미리, 앞서서, 사전에
before ~전에 (= prior to) leave 떠나다, ~을 남기다; 허가, 휴가
specialize 전공하다, 전문적으로 다루다
consider ~를 고려하다, ~에 숙고하다 compare ~를 비교하다
recommend ~를 추천하다, 권고하다

정답 (D)

15-18

5월 31일

일본 대사관
비자 분야
299 파크 애비뉴 18층
뉴욕, 뉴욕 10171

글랙스톤 제너 사는 특허 및 계약 담당 부장인 페이 시 씨를 소개하려고 합니다. 그녀는 제조 인가를 받아내기 위해서 6월 13일부터 22일까지 도쿄로 떠날 예정입니다.

시 씨는 도쿄에 있는 동안에, 컴퓨터 부품들과 액세서리를 포함하는 전자제품의 생산승인계약에 대해 논의하고 협상하기 위해, 마츠모토 사의 중역을 만날 것입니다.

글랙스톤 제너 사는 시 씨에게 일본을 방문하는 동안에 지낼 수 있도록 체재비를 제공할 것입니다. 또한 그녀에게 뉴욕행 표를 제공할 것입니다.

우리는 글랙스톤 제너 사를 대표하여 시 씨의 비자 발급에 도움을 주시는 것에 대해서 대단히 감사드립니다.

진리 장
관리자, 글랙스톤 제너 사

어휘 introduce ~를 소개하다, ~를 도입하다, ~를 선보이다
head 부서장, 머리, 앞면; ~를 담당하다, 향하다
licensing 허가, 라이센싱 contract 계약; ~와 계약하다
obtain ~를 얻다, 획득하다
return 귀환, 반납, 되돌아오다, ~를 되돌려주다, ~에게 답변하다
ticket 표, 승차권; 표를 팔다, ~에게 딱지를 발부하다
mean 수단, 방법, 재산 sustain ~를 지지하다, (생계를) 꾸리다
on behalf of ~를 대신하여, ~를 대표하여
issue 문제, 쟁점, 판, 호, 발급; ~를 다루다, 발급하다

15.

해설 접속사 who 이하에 오는 동사의 시제를 고르는 문제이다. '제조 인가를 받아내기 위해서 6월 13일부터 22일까지 떠날 것이다'라는 의미가 오는 것이 문맥에 적합하다. 따라서 미래시제 (A) will be traveling이 정답이다.

정답 (A)

16.

해설 명사 a manufacturing license agreement를 목적어로 취하는 동사를 선택해야 한다. 일단, 목적어가 올 수 없는 자동사 (A) depend와 (B) proceed 둘 다 탈락된다. 빈칸에 올 동사는 discuss와 의미적으로 병치구조를 이루어야 하는데, (D) negotiate(~를 협상하다)가 가장 어울린다.

정답 (D)

17.

(A) 새로운 전자제품은 출시될 예정입니다.
(B) 면허를 취득하는 것은 뉴욕에서는 상당히 어렵습니다.
(C) 또한, 그녀에게 뉴욕행 표를 제공할 것입니다.
(D) 도쿄 방문이 그녀의 요청에 따라 일정이 재조정될 것입니다.

해설 문맥에 맞는 문장을 고르는 문제이다. 빈칸 앞 문장에서 일본 체류시 지낼 수 있는 재정적인 수단을 제공해준다고 언급하고 있으므로 이어지는 자연스러운 내용은 '복귀하기 위한 표를 제공해줄 것이다'가 어울리므로 (C)가 정답이다.

정답 (C)

18.

해설 주어와 수일치가 틀린 (C) was appreciated가 먼저 탈락된다. (A) appreciated는 '당신의 도움에 감사했다'는 과거의 의미로, '현재'와의 연관성이 없다. 따라서 '편지를 쓰는 지금 이 순간에 감사하다' 의미를 나타내는 현재시제 (B) appreciate가 정답이다.

정답 (B)

UNIT 7 수동태

Check-up Step 1 본책_p. 225

1.

해설 stay(머무르다, 유지하다)는 형용사를 보어로 수반하거나, 뒤에 아무 것도 오지 않는 자동사이다. 자동사는 기본적으로 수동태로 전환이 불가능하므로, (B) are stayed는 빈칸에 들어갈 수 없다. 따라서 stay in the designated hotel(지정된 호텔에서 머무르다)이라는 표현을 이루는 (A) stay가 정답이다.

해석 회의 참가자들은 지정된 호텔에서 머무른다.

어휘 conference 회담, 회의   participant 참석자, 참가자 (= attendee)
designated 지정된

정답 (A)

2.

해설 빈칸 앞의 have been과 함께 쓰여 올바른 동사구를 만드는 문제이다. review는 타동사로 뒤에 목적어를 반드시 수반하므로, 수동태를 이루는 (A) reviewed는 빈칸에 올 수 없다. 따라서 현재완료진행시제 have been reviewing을 이루는 현재분사 (B) reviewing이 정답이다.

해석 나는 대략 3시간 동안 세금 서류를 검토하는 중이다.

어휘 tax 세금, 세제; ~에 세금을 부과하다
document 문서, 서류; ~을 문서로 기록하다, ~을 증거서류로 입증하다
about 대략 (= around, roughly)   review 평가, 검토; ~를 검토하다

정답 (B)

3.

해설 문장 구조를 살펴본 후 알맞은 동사 형태를 결정하는 문제이다. 주어 The economic researchers(경제 연구원들)는 '~를 강조하는' 주체이므로 능동태 동사가 필요하다. 따라서 〈emphasize that 주어 + 동사〉라는 표현을 이루는 (A) emphasized가 정답이다. 여기서 that the data must be interpreted accurately는 동사 emphasized의 목적어인 명사절이다.

해석 경제 연구원들은 데이터가 정확하게 분석되어야 한다는 것을 강조했다.

어휘 economic 경제의, 채산성이 있는   researcher 조사자, 연구원
interpret 통역하다, 설명하다, 이해하다, 분석하다
accurately 정확하게 (= exactly)
emphasize ~을 강조하다, 힘주어 말하다, ~을 두드러지게 하다

정답 (A)

Check-up Step 2 본책_p. 225

4.

해설 알맞은 동사의 형태를 결정하여 문맥을 완성하는 문제로, 빈칸 앞의 조동사 can이 힌트가 된다. 조동사 다음에는 동사의 원형이나 be + p.p. 형태만 가능하므로 (B) are seemed, (C) seems, (D) to seem 모두 올 수 없다. 따라서 보기에서 유일한 동사원형의 형태인 (A) seem이 정답이다.

해석 도시의 교통 표지는 때때로 그 지역에 익숙하지 않은 사람들에게 혼란스러워 보일 수 있다.

어휘 traffic 차량, 교통량, 밀거래, 수송   sign 징후, 상징, 표지; ~에 서명하다
seem ~인 듯하다, ~처럼 보이다   confusing 혼동을 주는, 혼란시키는
unfamiliar with ~에 익숙하지 않은

정답 (A)

5.

해설 알맞은 동사의 형태를 선택하는 문제인데, 빈칸 앞에 조동사 will이 나와 있으므로 동사원형인 (A) remain과 (D) be remained 중에서 답을 선택해야 한다. remain(~상태로 남아있다)은 형용사를 보어로 취하는 불완전자동사로서 기본적으로 자동사는 수동태가 불가능하므로 (D) be remained는 답이 될 수 없다. 따라서 정답은 (A) remain이 된다.

해석 그 회사는 내일 전기 시스템을 보수하더라도, 모든 사무실들은 문을 열어 둘 것이다.

어휘 even though ~에도 불구하고   electrical 전기의
remain ~인 상태로 남아있다

정답 (A)

Check-up Step 1 본책_p. 227

1.

해설 has been과 함께 쓰여 문맥을 완성시키는 동사의 형태를 고르는 문제이다. encourage는 타동사로 뒤에 목적어를 수반해야 한다. 빈칸 다음에 명사 its employees가 있으므로, 능동태 동사구를 이루는 (A) encouraging이 정답이다.

해석 그 회사는 주말동안 직원들이 일하도록 권장해오고 있는 중이다.

어휘 company 회사   employee 직원
work 작업, 작품, 업무; 일하다, 작동하다
over the weekend 주말동안, 주말 내내
encouraging 고무적인, 격려하는, 힘을 북돋아 주는
encouraged 고무된, 권고 받는, 장려되는

정답 (A)

2.
해설 알맞은 동사의 형태를 선택하여 문장을 완성시키는 문제이다. 빈칸 다음에 its divisions(그것의 부서들)라는 명사 목적어가 존재하므로, 수동태 (A) was restructured는 탈락된다. 따라서 was restructuring its divisions(부서들을 구조조정하고 있었다)라는 표현을 이루는 (B) was restructuring이 정답이다.

해석 회사가 부서들 구조조정을 하고 있었을 때, 몇몇의 관리자들이 해고되었다.

어휘 firm 회사; 딱딱한, 단호한; ~를 단단하게 하다   division 부서, 분배
manager 관리자   lay off ~를 해고하다
restructure 조직개편하다, ~를 구조조정하다

정답 (B)

3.
해설 invest는 자동사와 타동사가 모두 가능한데, invest만 본다면 보기 (A), (B) 모두 빈칸에 올 수 있다. 하지만 문장의 주어 a great deal of money(아주 많은 돈)는 '~를 투자하는' 주체가 아닌 '투자가 되는' 대상이므로, 의미적으로 수동태 (B) had been invested가 정답이 된다. 즉, invest가 자동사나 타동사 어느 경우든, 문장의 주어에는 '행위의 주체'가 온다는 점이다.

해석 아주 많은 돈이 그 프로젝트에 투자되었음에도 불구하고, 그것은 실패했다.

어휘 although ~에도 불구하고
a great deal of 아주 많은, 상당한 양의   project 프로젝트, 과제
failure 실패, 불이행, 태만   invest ~를 투자하다, ~를 부여하다

정답 (B)

Check-up Step 2   본책 _ p. 227

4.
해설 알맞은 동사의 형태를 결정하는 문제로 가장 먼저 수일치를 고려해야 한다. many items는 복수주어이므로 단수동사 (B) is offered는 탈락된다. 주어 many items는 '~를 제공하는' 주체가 아니라, '제공되는' 대상이므로, 보기의 유일한 수동태인 (D) are being offered가 정답이다. 또한 동사 offer(~를 제공하다)는 뒤에 목적어를 동반하는 타동사인데, 뒤에 목적어가 없으므로 수동태가 필요하다.

해석 상점의 많은 상품들이 웹사이트에서는 할인된 가격으로 제공되는 중이다.

어휘 at a discounted price 할인된 가격으로
offer 제안, 제의; ~를 제공하다

정답 (D)

5.
해설 조동사 can 뒤에는 동사원형이 와야 하므로 (A) buy와 (C) be bought 중에 답을 선택해야 한다. buy는 '~을 구매하다'라는 타동사인데 빈칸 뒤에 at the main box office라는 전치사구가 있으므로 정답은 수동태인 (C) be bought(구매되다)가 된다.

해석 티켓은 영화제가 시작하기 전에 본관 매표소에서 구매할 수 있습니다.

정답 (C)

Check-up Step 1   본책 _ p. 229

1.
해설 빈칸 앞의 분사형 형용사 composed(구성된) 다음에 올 수 있는 전치사를 선택하는 문제이다. be composed of(~로 구성되다)라는 표현을 이루는 (B) of가 정답이다.

해석 그 팀은 7명의 사람들로 구성되어 있다.

어휘 be composed of ~로 구성되다 (= consist of)

정답 (B)

2.
해설 빈칸 앞의 분사형 형용사 interested(관심 있는) 다음에 올 수 있는 전치사를 선택하는 문제이다. be interested in(~에 관심 있다)이라는 표현을 알고 있다면, 쉽게 (B) in을 정답으로 선택할 수 있다.

해석 만약 당신이 그 직위에 관심이 있다면, 내일까지 신청서를 제출하세요.

어휘 position 직위, 위치, 태도; ~를 배치하다
submit ~를 제출하다 (= send in, hand in, turn in)
application 적용, 신청, 신청서

정답 (B)

3.
해설 빈칸 앞의 are encouraged라는 동사구와 함께 쓰여 하나의 표현을 이루는 보기를 고르는 문제이다. 동사 encourage는 encourage A to부정사(A가 ~하도록 권장하다)의 형태로, 목적보어에 to부정사를 수반한다. 즉, encourage A to부정사의 형태가 수동태 be encouraged로 바뀌더라도 to부정사는 그대로 남아있어야 하는 것이다. 따라서 정답은 (B) to arrive가 된다.

해석 회의 참석자들은 오전 9시 전에 도착하는 것이 권장된다.

어휘 conference 회담, 회의   participant 참석자, 참가자
be encouraged to부정사 ~하도록 권장되다, ~하도록 장려되다
arrive 도착하다

정답 (B)

Check-up Step 2 본책_p.229

4.

해설 일단 주어 Motorists와 수일치가 틀린 (A) is advised가 가장 먼저 탈락된다. 구조적으로 advise는 advise A to부정사의 형태이므로, 수동태로 전환되어도 to부정사는 그대로 남아있어야 한다. 의미적으로 주어 motorists는 '~하도록 충고 받는' 대상이므로 (C) are advised가 정답이 된다.

해석 운전자들은 다리를 건너갈 때, 매우 조심스럽게 운전하도록 충고 받는다.

어휘 motorist 운전자   drive 드라이브, 진입로; 운전하다, ~를 태워주다
carefully 신중하게, 주의 깊게   cross 건너다
be advised to부정사 ~하도록 충고되다

정답 (C)

5.

해설 빈칸 앞 동사 are prohibited와 빈칸 뒤 동명사 taking photographs를 연결하는 알맞은 전치사를 선택하는 문제다. be prohibited from ~ing(~이 금지되다), prohibit A from ~ing(A가 ~하는 것을 금지시키다)라는 표현을 알고 있으면 쉽게 답이 (C)라는 것을 알 수 있는 문제이니 알아두도록 하자. 같은 표현으로는 'prevent A from ~ing = stop A from ~ing = discourage A from ~ing(A가 ~하는 것을 못하게 하다)' 등이 있으니 또한 참고해두자.

해석 박물관에 오시는 방문객들은 모든 전시물의 촬영을 하는 것이 금지되어 있습니다.

어휘 visitor 방문객   take a photograph 사진촬영하다
exhibit 전시물, 전시회; ~을 전시하다

정답 (C)

Check-up Step 1 본책_p.231

1.

해설 be동사 was와 함께 올바른 동사의 형태를 완성시키는 문제이다. 일단, be동사 다음에 일반동사의 형태가 들어갈 수 없으므로, 3인칭 단수동사 (B) offers가 바로 탈락된다. 따라서 was offered a job(일자리를 제안 받았다)이라는 수여동사의 수동태 표현을 이루는 (A) offered가 정답이다.

해석 그는 어제 일자리를 제안 받았다.

어휘 offer 제안, 제의; ~를 제공하다, ~를 제의하다   job 직업, 일자리

정답 (A)

2.

해설 문장 전체의 구조를 살펴보고 알맞은 동사의 형태를 선택하는 문제이다. 조동사 다음에 오는 빈칸에는 동사의 원형이 필요하므로 (A) given은 무조건 올 수 없다. 따라서 will be given an option(선택권을 받을 것이다)이라는 표현을 이루는 (B) be given이 정답이다. 여기서 〈be given+명사〉는 수여동사의 수동태 표현이다.

해석 승객들은 업그레이드된 큰 좌석을 예약할 수 있는 선택권을 받을 것이다.

어휘 passenger 승객   option 선택, 선택과목   book 책; ~을 예약하다
seat 좌석, 의석, 자리; ~에 앉히다, ~를 수용하다

정답 (B)

3.

해설 알맞은 동사를 선택하여 문장을 완성하는 문제이다. 일단, 문장의 주어 Mr. Chen과 수일치가 틀린 (A) consider가 제외된다. 따라서 (B) is considered가 정답이 되어 is considered the expert(전문가로 고려된다)라는 올바른 수동태 표현을 완성한다.

해석 Mr. Chen은 고객들을 다루는 데 있어서는 전문가로 간주된다.

어휘 expert 전문가   when it comes to ~에 있어서는
deal with 다루다, 처리하다
consider ~를 고려하다, ~를 배려하다, ~를 숙고하다

정답 (B)

Check-up Step 2 본책_p.231

4.

해설 알맞은 동사의 형태를 선택하는 문제이다. 일단, 주어 The workshop presenters와 수일치가 틀린 (B) was sending이 가장 먼저 탈락된다. 빈칸 다음에 있는 last week(지난주)이 결정적인 힌트가 되어 과거시제의 동사가 필요한 것을 알 수 있는데 보기 중 수동태 과거시제인 (A) were sent가 적절하다.

해석 워크샵 발표자들은 지난주 일정을 받았고, 모든 일정을 따라야 한다.

어휘 presenter 발표자   schedule 일정표, 스케줄; ~의 일정을 잡다
follow ~를 따르다, ~를 지키다   item 상품, 항목

정답 (A)

5.

해설 be동사와 전치사 of를 연결해줄 수 있는 알맞은 어휘를 고르는 문제이다. 'be critical of(~을 비판하다)'라는 표현을 덩어리로 외우면 쉽게 해결할 수 있는 문제이다. 과거분사인 (D) criticized를 선택할 수도 있지만 이는 전치사 of와 함께 사용되지 않으며, 대신 for와 함께 사용되어 '~ 때문에 비판받다'의 의미로 쓰인다.

해석 고객 서비스 직원들은 불만사항 때문에 전화하는 고객들을 비판해서는 안 된다.

어휘 personnel 직원, 인사부   be critical of ~을 비판하다, 비평하다
complaint 불만사항

정답 (B)

Check-up 본책 _ p. 233

1. 정답 costly
어휘 costly 비싼 / price 가격

2. 정답 valid
어휘 valid 유효한 / validate 유효하게 하다

3. 정답 affordable
어휘 affordable 적당한, 저렴한 / afford ~할 여유가 있다

4. 정답 frequent
어휘 frequent 자주 오는, 빈번한 / frequently 자주

5. 정답 eager
어휘 eagerness 열망 / eager 열망하는

Part 5&6_ 실전연습 7 본책 _ p. 234-235

1.
해설 빈칸 앞의 조동사 will과 함께 올바른 동사구를 만드는 문제이다. postpone은 타동사로 뒤에 목적어를 반드시 수반하므로, 능동태 (A) be postponing, (B) postpone, (D) have postponed 모두 탈락된다. 따라서 목적어가 뒤에 올 수 없는 수동태 (C) be postponed가 정답이다.

해석 폭우 때문에 오늘 야구경기는 다음 월요일까지 연기될 것입니다.

어휘 baseball game 야구경기 until ~까지
because of ~ 때문에 (= due to, on top of) heavy rain 호우, 폭우
postpone ~을 연기하다 (= delay, put off)

정답 (C)

2.
해설 명사 delivery(배달)를 수식하는 알맞은 형용사를 고르는 문제이다. (C) aware(알고 있는)와 (D) limited(제한된)는 의미적으로 어울리지 않아 탈락된다. 문맥상 '빠른 배달을 보장하기 위해서'라는 의미가 필요하기 때문에 (B) timely(빠른, 시기적절한)가 정답이다.

해석 빠른 배달을 보장하기 위해서, 당신은 주소와 전화번호를 명확하게 써야 합니다.

어휘 in order to부정사 ~하기 위해서 (= so as to부정사)
ensure ~를 보장하다, ~를 확실히 하다 delivery 배달, 배송
address 주소; 주소를 써서 보내다, 다루다, 발표하다 clearly 명확하게
tentative 임시의, 일시적인, 잠정적인 timely 빠른, 시기적절한
aware 알고 있는 limited 제한된

정답 (B)

3.
해설 빈칸 앞의 to는 are expected to부정사(~로 예상되다)에 오는 부정사이므로, 빈칸에는 동사원형이 필요하다. 일단, (B) delivering은 바로 탈락된다. 동사 deliver는 '~를 배달하다, 발표하다'는 의미의 타동사로 뒤에 목적어가 필요한데, 빈칸 뒤에 목적어가 없으므로 수동태 (C) be delivered가 정답이다.

해석 건축 자재들은 오후 늦게 배달될 것으로 예상됩니다.

어휘 construction 건축 material 재료, 자재
be expected to부정사 ~로 예상되다 late 늦은, 늦게, 지각한
deliver ~를 인계하다, 넘겨주다, ~을 배달하다

정답 (C)

4.
해설 문장에 어울리는 비교급 형용사를 고르는 문제이다. 일단, (A) wealthy(부유한, 재산이 많은)의 비교급은 wealthier이므로, 비교급을 만드는 less와 충돌한다. 문맥상 '브랜드 이미지를 확립하는 것보다 덜 비싸다'라는 의미가 필요하기 때문에 (C) costly(값비싼)가 정답이다.

해석 시장 점유율과 이윤을 증가시키는 것이 브랜드 이미지를 확립하는 것보다 덜 비싸다.

어휘 increase 증가하다, ~를 증가시키다 market share 시장 점유율
profits 이윤금, 수익금 less 더 적은, 더 적게
establish 설립하다, 구축하다 wealthy 부유한
friendly 친절한, 친숙한 costly 비싼 doubtful 의심하는

정답 (C)

5.
해설 복수주어 they와 수일치가 틀린 단수동사 (D) has been using이 먼저 탈락된다. use는 뒤에 목적어를 수반하는 타동사인데, 빈칸 뒤에 목적어가 없으므로 수동태 동사 (C) are used가 정답이다. 나무 책상과 의자들은 '사용하는 주체'가 아니라 '사용되는 대상'이므로 의미적으로도 수동태가 필요하다.

해석 이 나무 책상과 의자들은 거실에서 사용되기 전에 특별한 관리가 필요하다.

어휘 treatment 치료, 대우, 처리, 관리 living room 거실

정답 (C)

6.
해설 빈칸은 be동사의 보어가 되는 동시에 to부정사와 어울리는 형용사를 고르는 문제이다. be likely to develop new drugs(신약을 개발할 것 같다)라는 의미를 이루는 (A) likely가 정답이다.

해석 노바르티스는 미세먼지에 의해 발생되는 폐암에 관한 신약을 개발할 것 같다.

어휘 develop ~를 개발하다, ~를 발전시키다　new drug 신약
regarding ~에 관해서 (= as for, as to)　lung cancer 폐암
result from ~이 원인이다　fine dust 미세먼지
likely ~할 것 같은, 그럴듯한　potential 잠재적인, 잠재력
appropriate 적절한　skillful 능숙한 (= adept)

정답 (A)

7.

해설 빈칸 앞의 to는 be asked to부정사(~하도록 요청받다)에 오는 부정사이므로, 빈칸에는 동사원형이 필요하다. 일단, (A) completing은 바로 탈락된다. 빈칸 뒤에 목적어 a survey가 있으므로 능동태 (C) complete(~를 작성하다, 끝내다)가 정답이다.

해석 모든 학생들은 강사들을 평가하기 위해서 강의가 끝나고 설문지를 작성하도록 요구받는다.

어휘 be asked to부정사 ~하도록 요청받다
survey 조사, 투표; ~를 조사하다　lecture 강의, 강연
in order to부정사 ~하기 위해서 (= so as to부정사)
evaluate ~를 평가하다 (= appraise, assess)　professor 교수
complete 완성된; ~를 끝마치다, ~을 완료하다, ~를 작성하다

정답 (C)

8.

해설 명사 photo identification을 앞에서 꾸며주는 형용사를 고르는 문제이다. (A) costly(값비싼), (B) frequent(빈번한), (C) poor(형편없는)는 의미상 적절하지 않다. 따라서 have a valid photo identification(유효한 신분증을 가지다)라는 표현을 이루는 (D) valid가 정답이다.

해석 신용카드를 신청하기 위해서는 사진이 부착된 유효한 신분증을 갖고 있어야 한다.

어휘 photo identification 사진이 부착된 신분증
in order to부정사 ~하기 위해서 (= so as to부정사)
apply for ~를 신청하다　credit card 신용카드　costly 비싼
frequent 빈번한, 자주 있는　poor 가난한, 형편없는
valid 유효한, 효력 있는

정답 (D)

9.

해설 빈칸 앞에 접속사 who가 있으므로 빈칸은 동사의 자리이다. 기본적으로 자동사는 수동태로 전환하는 것이 불가능하므로, (B) are stayed, (D) have been stayed는 빈칸에 들어갈 수 없다. 따라서 능동태 (C) stay가 정답이다.

해석 웨스커 호텔에 머무르는 여행객들은 지하철로 사노이 국제공항에 갈 수 있다.

어휘 traveler 여행객　by subway 지하철로　stay 머무르다, 유지하다

정답 (C)

10.

해설 명사 performances(성과, 실적)를 수식하는 알맞은 형용사를 고르는 문제이다. (A) timely(시기적절한, 빠른)와 (B) eager(열정적인)는 의미적으로 적합하지 않다. 앞뒤 문맥을 보아 '꾸준한 실적 때문에 승진하지 못할 것이다'는 부적합하므로 (D) steady 역시 제외된다. 따라서 (C) poor(형편없는)가 정답이다.

해석 형편없는 실적 때문에, 도나는 올해 말에 승진하지 못할 것입니다.

어휘 due to ~ 때문에　performance 실적, 공연, 성능
promote ~를 승진시키다, ~를 홍보하다, ~를 촉진시키다
timely 빠른, 시기적절한　eager 열렬한, 간절히 바라는, 열심인
poor 가난한, 형편없는　steady 한결 같은, 꾸준한

정답 (C)

11.

해설 주어 Mr. Stevens와 수일치가 틀린 (D) have been considering이 답에서 제외된다. (A) considered와 (C) is considering이 오게 되면, '스티븐스 씨는 마케팅 이사를 생각하다'는 의미로 적합하지 않다. 따라서 '마케팅 이사로 고려되다, 생각되다'라는 수동태를 이루는 (B) is considered가 정답이다.

해석 지난 10년간 일해 왔던 스티븐스 씨는 마케팅 이사로 고려되었다.

어휘 work 일, 작품, 연구; 일하다　director 임원, 중역, 이사
department 부서, 국　consider ~를 고려하다, ~를 배려하다

정답 (B)

12.

해설 빈칸은 동사의 자리이므로 동사가 아닌 (A) closing이 먼저 탈락된다. 주어 our store(우리 상점)와 수일치가 틀린 (C) have closed 역시 제외된다. 나머지 보기 중에서, '우리 상점은 일요일마다 닫는다'라는 문맥을 이루는 수동태 (B) is closed가 정답이다.

해석 우리 상점은 월요일부터 토요일, 아침 10시에서 저녁 7시에 문을 열고 일요일마다 문을 닫습니다.

어휘 close 가까운; 가까이에; ~을 닫다

정답 (B)

13.

해설 빈칸 앞에 있는 is의 보어가 되면서 전치사 to와도 같이 어울리는 형용사를 고르는 문제이다. 따라서 be comparable to 명사(~와 비슷하다, ~와 필적할 만하다)라는 표현을 이루는 (D) comparable(비슷한, 필적할 만한)이 정답이다.

해석 HMK 사는 더 이상 이용할 수 없는 그 브랜드와 질적으로 비슷한 대체가능한 타일을 구하고 있다.

어휘 seek ~을 찾다, ~를 구하다   alternative 대안, 대책; 대안적인
be comparable to ~와 비슷하다, ~와 필적할 만하다
in quality 질적으로   no longer 더 이상 ~이 아니다
available 이용할 수 있는, 이용 가능한   balanced 균형 잡힌, 안정된
affordable 이용할 수 있는, 구입 가능한, 저렴한 (= reasonable)
common 공통 관심사; 흔한, 공통의, 평범한

정답 (D)

14.

해설 주어 people과 수일치가 틀린 (C) is giving이 가장 먼저 탈락된다. (A) have given과 (B) will be giving이 오게 되면, '~를 주었다, ~를 줄 것이다'라는 의미가 되어, 문맥과 어울리지 않는다. 따라서 수여동사의 수동태로 목적어를 수반하는 (D) will be given이 정답이다.

해석 콘서트를 가기만 하면, 사람들은 새로운 음악을 들을 기회를 얻을 것이다.

어휘 once 한때, 한번; ~하자마자, ~하면   visit 방문; ~를 방문하다
give an opportunity to부정사 ~할 기회를 주다
listen to ~를 듣다

정답 (D)

15-18

발신: 알란 모스버그
수신: 모든 부서 직원들
제목: 새로운 컴퓨터들

친애하는 직원 여러분,

시장조사 부서의 새 컴퓨터들이 6월 9일 금요일, 오후 4시와 6시 사이에 설치될 것입니다. 이 시간 동안에 IT 직원들은 당신이 현재 사용하는 컴퓨터를 치우고, 그것들을 사무실 밖으로 옮길 것입니다. 회사는 오래된 컴퓨터 장비들을 필요로 하는 학교들과 다른 단체들에 기부할 계획입니다. 새 컴퓨터들은 메모리와 더 빠른 프로세서로 확장했으며, 그것들은 당신의 컴퓨팅 요구를 처리할 수 있습니다. 그러나 만약 컴퓨터가 점점 느려지는 것을 알게 되면, IT 부서(내선번호 1582)에 연락하세요, 그러면 직원들이 손보고, 시스템을 업그레이드 할 것입니다. 교체 과정에 관해 다른 질문이 있으시면, 저에게 알려주세요.

알란 모스버그,
사무실 관리자

어휘 market 시장, 구매층; ~을 팔다
research 조사, 연구; ~를 조사하다, 연구하다
department 부서, 국
remove ~를 제거하다, ~를 해고하다, ~를 치우다
plan 계획; ~을 계획하다   donate ~에 기부하다, ~를 기증하다
organization 조직, 단체, 기관   need 요구, 필요성; ~을 필요로 하다
handle ~를 다루다, ~를 취급하다   notice 통지, 공지; ~를 알아채다
service 서비스, 점검; ~를 제공하다, ~를 고치다
upgrade ~를 향상시키다   replacement 교체, 교체품, 후임자

process 과정; ~을 가공하다, ~를 처리하다

15.

해설 주어와 수일치가 틀린 단수동사 (A) has been installed가 먼저 탈락된다. 보기의 동사 install은 '~를 설치하다'는 의미의 타동사로 뒤에 목적어가 필요한데 빈칸 뒤에 목적어가 없으므로 (D) will install은 올 수 없다. 문맥상 '새로운 컴퓨터가 설치될 것이다'라는 의미가 필요하므로, 미래시제 수동태인 (B) will be installed가 정답이다.

정답 (B)

16.

해설 주어와 수일치가 틀린 단수동사 (D) has expanded가 먼저 탈락된다. 목적어가 있으므로, 수동태 (A) have been expanded는 올 수 없다. 현재시제인 (B) expand는 '규칙적, 반복적 습관'에 사용하므로 적합하지 않다. 따라서 현재완료시제 (C) have expanded가 정답이다.

정답 (C)

17.

해설 빈칸은 be동사의 보어가 되는 동시에 to부정사와 어울리는 형용사를 고르는 문제이다. (C) capable(할 수 있는)은 전치사 of를, (D) responsible(책임 있는)은 전치사 for를 수반하므로 탈락된다. (A) able과 (B) unlikely 둘 다 뒤에 to부정사가 오지만, 의미적으로 적합한 것은 (A) able이다.

정답 (A)

18.

(A) 그러나 시스템은 훨씬 더 악화될 수 있습니다.
(B) 추후에 귀하는 새 컴퓨터가 과거보다 덜 안정적인 것을 확인할 수 있습니다.
(C) 연구부서가 새로운 시스템을 구동할 것입니다.
(D) 그러면 직원들이 시스템을 손보고, 업그레이드할 것입니다.

해설 문맥에 맞는 문장을 고르는 문제이다. 빈칸 앞 문장에서 컴퓨터가 점차 느려지는 것을 확인하게 되면 IT부서에 연락하라고 했고 이어지는 내용으로 IT 직원이 컴퓨터를 손볼 것이라는 의미가 어울리므로 (D)가 정답이다.

정답 (D)

UNIT 8 전치사 (1)

Check-up Step 1   본책 _ p. 237

1.
해설 빈칸은 전치사 with 다음에 오는 명사의 자리로 (A) care가 정답이다. with care(조심스럽게)는 carefully라는 한 단어의 부사로 바꿀 수 있다.

해석 당신은 그것을 신중하게 다루어야 한다.

어휘 handle ~를 다루다, ~를 취급하다   care 돌봄, 관리, 관심; 관리하다
carefully 신중하게, 조심히   with care 조심스럽게

정답 (A)

2.
해설 전치사 before 다음에 동사는 올 수 없으므로 (A) write는 탈락된다. 따라서 명사 an official proposal을 수반하는 동시에, 전치사 before 뒤에 올 수 있는 동명사 (B) writing이 정답이다.

해석 공식적인 제안서를 작성하기 전에, 그것을 여러 차례 검토해야 한다.

어휘 before ~전에, ~앞에서   official 공식적인   proposal 제안, 제안서
review 평가, 검토; ~를 검토하다   several times 여러 번, 여러 차례
write ~를 쓰다, 작성하다

정답 (B)

3.
해설 빈칸 앞뒤의 구조를 살펴보고 품사를 고르는 문제이다. 빈칸 다음에 명사 the rain만 있으므로 전치사 (B) in spite of(~에도 불구하고)가 정답이다.

해석 우리는 비가 왔음에도 불구하고 밖에 나갔다.

어휘 go out 나가다, 외출하다   although 비록 ~하지만, ~에도 불구하고
in spite of ~에도 불구하고

정답 (B)

Check-up Step 2   본책 _ p. 237

4.
해설 빈칸 다음에 있는 명사 peak hours가 중요한 힌트가 된다. 따라서 그 앞에는 접속사가 아니라 전치사 (B) during(~동안에)이 맞는 표현이다.

해석 새로운 도로 프로젝트는 가장 바쁜 시간 동안의 도시 교통 흐름을 개선할 것 같다.

어휘 project 프로젝트, 과제   be likely to부정사 ~할 것 같다
improve 나아지다, 개선되다; ~를 개선시키다
traffic flow 교통 흐름, 교통량   peak 정점, 절정, 최고조; 정점에 달하다

while ~동안에, 반면에   during ~동안에   when ~할 때
as soon as ~하자마자

정답 (B)

5.
해설 전체적인 구조를 보면 한 문장 내에 동사가 2개 있고 전치사 on 뒤에는 완벽한 문장이 나와 있는 것을 확인할 수 있다. 전치사 뒤에는 명사뿐 아니라 명사절 또한 나올 수 있다. 빈칸 다음에는 문장이 사용되었으므로 명사절접속사인 (C) whether(~인지)가 정답이 된다. 나머지 보기들은 전치사로서 문장을 수반할 수 없다. 명사절접속사 whether(~인지)는 주어, 목적어, 보어 자리에 사용되며 whether or not(~인지 아닌지) / whether to부정사(~할지 안할지)로도 표현되니 꼭 기억해두자.

해석 회사의 최종 결정은 그 제안이 예산이 있는지 없는지에 달려있다.

어휘 final decision 최종 결정   depend on ~에 달려 있다
whether or not ~인지 아닌지   budget 예산

정답 (C)

Check-up Step 1   본책 _ p. 239

1.
해설 알맞은 전치사를 선택하여 문맥을 완성하는 문제이다. 빈칸 다음에 명사 9 P.M.은 '시각'을 나타내는 표현으로 전치사 (A) at과 어울린다.

해석 그 가게는 저녁 9시에 닫을 것이다.

어휘 store 가게, 상점   close ~을 닫다, 닫히다

정답 (A)

2.
해설 빈칸 뒤의 명사 tomorrow만 보고 전치사 (A) by와 (B) until을 구분하긴 어렵다. 앞에 있는 동사로 구분할 수 있는데, complete(~끝마치다)는 동작이 완료되는 의미이므로 (A) by와 같이 사용한다.

해석 그들은 내일까지 그 업무를 끝마쳐야 한다.

어휘 complete 완성된; ~를 마무리하다, 완성하다, 작성하다
task 업무, 과제; ~에게 업무를 주다

정답 (A)

3.
해설 전치사 since 다음에 오는 명사를 고르는 문제이다. since는 원래 '~ 이래로 지금까지'라는 의미로 뒤에 과거시점이나 사건만 수반할 수 있으므로 (A) last year가 정답이다.

해석 몇몇의 직원들은 작년부터 회사에서 일해 왔다.

정답 (A)

Check-up Step 2 본책_p. 239

4.
- 해설: 빈칸 다음의 8 o'clock(8시 정각)은 시점명사이므로, (A) until과 (B) by 중에서 선택해야 한다. 앞에 있는 동사로 구분할 수 있는데, remain open(열려있다)은 동작의 지속을 의미이므로 (A) until과 같이 사용한다.
- 해석: 지방 전역에 있는 몇몇의 공공 의료기관은 토요일마다 8시까지 문을 열고 있습니다.
- 어휘: a few 약간의, 몇몇의 public 대중의, 공공의 hospital 병원, 의료기관 throughout ~내내, ~에 걸쳐서 province 지방, 분야
- 정답: (A)

5.
- 해설: 명사 last April을 수반하는 전치사를 고르는 문제로 접속사인 (D) when은 제일 먼저 탈락된다. 빈칸 뒤 과거시점을 가리키는 명사 last April(지난 4월)과 문장의 시제 현재완료 have increased에서 정답의 힌트를 찾을 수 있다. (C) since(~이후로)는 전치사일 경우 '과거의 특정시점 이후로 지금까지 그 상황이 유지된다'는 의미이며 주절의 시제는 현재완료(have p.p.)가 사용된다. 따라서 정답은 (C) since가 된다. since는 접속사와 부사로도 활용되는데, 접속사일 경우 since절에는 과거시제, 주절의 시제가 현재완료(have p.p.)가 사용되면 '~이후로'로 해석되며, 다른 시제로 사용되면 '~ 때문에'로 이유를 나타내는 접속사로 활용된다. 부사일 경우에는 'have since p.p. (~한 이후로 쭉 ~하다)'의 형태로 현재완료시제 사이에서 나올 수 있으니 암기해두자.
- 해석: 지난 4월 이후로 신형 소프트웨어의 판매량이 6퍼센트까지 증가했다.
- 어휘: sales 판매 increase 증가, 증가시키다, 증가하다 since ~이후로, ~ 때문에
- 정답: (C)

Check-up Step 1 본책_p. 241

1.
- 해설: six years(6년)라는 기간 명사를 수반하는 전치사를 고르는 문제이다. (A) since(과거이래로 지금까지)는 뒤에 과거시점이나 사건만 오므로 탈락된다. 따라서 for six years(6년 동안)라는 표현을 이루는 (B) for가 정답이다.
- 해석: 그녀는 6년 동안 여기서 살고 있다.
- 정답: (B)

2.
- 해설: 빈칸에는 two weeks(2주)라는 기간 명사를 수반하는 전치사의 자리이다. (A) until은 뒤에 시점 명사가 오므로 올 수 없으며, 결국 기간명사를 취하여 in two weeks라는 표현을 이루는 (B) in이 정답이다.
- 해석: 결과들은 2주 후에 공표될 것이다.
- 어휘: results (선거, 스포츠, 연구) 결과, 시험성적, 성과 announce ~를 발표하다, 공표하다, 알리다
- 정답: (B)

3.
- 해설: three hours(3시간)라는 기간 명사를 수반하는 전치사를 고르는 문제이다. before 다음에는 시점 명사가 수반되므로 탈락된다. 따라서 within three hours(3시간 안에)라는 표현을 이루는 (B) within이 정답이다.
- 해석: 그들은 3시간 안에 공항에 도착할 것으로 예상된다.
- 어휘: be expected to부정사 ~하기로 예상되다, ~할 것으로 예상되다
- 정답: (B)

Check-up Step 2 본책_p. 241

4.
- 해설: 명사 the year와 함께 사용되는 전치사를 고르는 문제이다. (A) among(~사이에서)과 (C) between(~사이에서)은 뒤에 복수 명사가 오므로 탈락된다. '처음부터 끝까지'라는 개념으로 그 다음에 기간 명사를 수반하는 (B) throughout이 정답이다.
- 해석: 더 많은 소비자들을 끌어들이기 위해서, 몇몇 상점들은 일 년 내내 주말마다 문을 연다.
- 어휘: attract ~를 끌어들이다, ~를 매혹시키다 customer 소비자 every weekend 주말마다 throughout the year 일 년 내내
- 정답: (B)

5.
- 해설: 빈칸 다음에 명사 the past six months를 수반하는 알맞은 전치사를 선택하는 문제이다. the past six months는 기간 표현이므로 (B) between, (C) by, (D) until 모두 탈락된다. 특히 by와 until은 뒤에 시점 표현만 수반할 수 있다. 따라서 정답은 (A) over(~에 걸쳐서)가 되며 over 뒤에 〈the last / the past + 기간〉이 사용되면 문장의 시제는 현재완료(have p.p.)가 사용된다. 이 경우 over를 대신하여 전치사 in, for, during, within을 사용해도 무관하다.
- 해석: 새로운 직원들은 지난 6개월에 걸쳐 본사에서 교육을 받았다.
- 어휘: employee 직원 train 교육시키다 headquarter 본사 past 지난, 이전의
- 정답: (A)

Check-up Step 1 본책 _ p. 243

1.
- 해설: 명사 the third floor와 함께 사용되는 전치사를 고르는 문제이다. 일단, 셋 이상을 나타내는 복수명사 앞에서 사용하는 (A) among은 탈락된다. 따라서 on the third floor(3층에)라는 표현을 이루는 (B) on(~위에)이 정답이다.
- 해석: 회의실은 3층에 있다.
- 어휘: meeting 회의, 모임 room 방, 공간 on the third floor 3층에서
- 정답: (B)

2.
- 해설: 빈칸 다음의 명사 service와 함께 쓰이는 전치사를 고르는 문제이다. '서비스가 중단된, 고장 난'이라는 의미를 이루는 표현은 out of service이다. 따라서 전치사 (B) out of가 정답이다.
- 해석: 엘리베이터가 고장이 난 상태이다.
- 어휘: service 서비스, 이용 out of service 서비스 중지의, 고장 난
- 정답: (B)

3.
- 해설: 빈칸 뒤의 명사 the company(회사)를 수반하는 전치사를 고르는 문제이다. 일단, 뒤에 복수명사가 오는 (A) between은 바로 탈락된다. 따라서 기간 명사 또는 범위를 지칭하는 명사를 수반하는 (B) within이 정답이다.
- 해석: 우리는 회사 내에 새로운 관리자를 고용할 것이다.
- 어휘: hire ~를 고용하다 within the company 회사 내에
- 정답: (B)

Check-up Step 2 본책 _ p. 243

4.
- 해설: 문맥상 '철도 근로자들 중에서 2천명'이라는 의미가 필요하다. 따라서 '~속에서'라는 의미로 쓰이며, 뒤에 복수명사를 수반하는 (A) among(~속에서)이 정답이다.
- 해석: 산업의 새로운 변화가 철도 근로자 중 2천명의 실직을 초래할 것이다.
- 어휘: change 변화, 기분전환, 교체 industry 산업, 업계 result in ~를 초래하다 (= cause, lead to) loss 손실, 죽음, 상실 railway worker 철도 근로자
- 정답: (A)

5.
- 해설: 빈칸에 들어갈 알맞은 전치사를 선택하는 문제이다. 우선 정답은 (D) into이며 'come into effect(효력을 발휘하다)'라는 덩어리 표현을 알고 있으면 쉽게 해결할 수 있는 문제다. go into effect도 동의어로 사용되니 기억해두자.
- 해석: 허위 광고로부터 고객들을 보호할 새로운 법은 내년에 효력을 발휘할 것이다.
- 어휘: protect ~을 보호하다 consumer 소비자 against ~에 반대하여 false advertising 허위 광고 come into effect 효력을 발휘하다
- 정답: (D)

Check-up 본책 _ p. 245

1. 정답 considerable
- 어휘: consider 고려하다 / considerable 상당한

2. 정답 common
- 어휘: common 공통의, 흔한 / differ 다르다

3. 정답 useful
- 어휘: usefully 유용하게 / useful 유용한

4. 정답 informative
- 어휘: inform 통보하다 / informative 유익한 정보를 주는

5. 정답 partial
- 어휘: partial 부분적인 / partially 부분적으로

Part 5&6_ 실전연습 8 본책 _ p. 246-247

1.
- 해설: 빈칸 다음의 4 A.M.(새벽 4시)은 시점 명사이므로, 이와 어울리는 전치사를 선택해야 한다. 하지만 (B) during, (C) for, (D) within은 뒤에 기간 명사가 오기 때문에 탈락된다. 따라서 (A) until(~까지)이 정답이다.
- 해석: 우리의 직원들은 프로젝트를 예상보다 더 빨리 끝내기 위해 새벽 4시까지 일했다.
- 어휘: faster than expected 예상보다 빨리 until ~까지 during ~동안에 for ~를 위한, ~에 대해, ~동안 within ~이내에
- 정답: (A)

2.
- 해설: 명사 brochures(소책자들)를 수식하는 알맞은 형용사를 고르는 문제이다. (A) experienced, (C) comparable, (D) positive 모두 의미적으로 적합하지 않다. 따라서 'will be given informative brochures(정보를 주는 소책자를 받을 것이다)'라는 자연스러운 표현을 이루는 (B) informative가 정답이다.
- 해석: 모든 신입직원들은 회사의 규칙과 절차에 관한 정보를 주는 책자를 받을 것입니다.
- 어휘: new employee 신입직원 be given ~을 받다(사람 주어), ~이 주어지다(사물 주어) brochure 책자 rules and procedures 규칙과 절차들

experienced 경험이 많은, 능숙한 (= skilled, informed)
informative 정보를 주는, 유익한 (= enlightening)
comparable 비슷한, 필적할만한   positive 긍정적인

정답 (B)

3.
해설 빈칸 다음의 May 23rd(5월 23일)은 시점 명사이므로, (B) until과 (C) by 중에서 선택해야 한다. 앞에 있는 동사로 구분할 수 있는데, call(연락하다)은 동작의 완료를 의미하므로 (C) by와 같이 사용한다.

해석 우리는 회의에 참석하는 사람들의 정확한 수를 계산해야 하기 때문에, 5월 23일까지는 저희에게 연락을 주시기 바랍니다.

어휘 call 전화통화; ~에게 전화하다   since ~때문에, ~이후로
calculate ~를 계산하다   exact 정확한   attend ~에 참석하다
meeting 모임, 회의   for ~를 위한, ~에 대해, ~동안   until ~까지
by ~까지, ~옆에   during ~동안에

정답 (C)

4.
해설 명사 professionals(전문가들)를 수식하는 알맞은 형용사를 고르는 문제이다. (A) considerable, (B) competitive, (D) valid 모두 의미적으로 적합하지 않다. 따라서 (C) experienced(경험 많은)가 정답이다.

해석 우리는 친절하게 고객 불평을 해결하는 경험 많은 전문가들을 찾고 있습니다.

어휘 seek ~을 찾다, ~를 구하다   professional 전문가
deal with ~를 다루다   complaint 불평사항
in a friendly manner 친절한 태도로
considerable 상당한 (= significant, substantial)
competitive 경쟁력 있는
experienced 경험이 많은, 능숙한 (= skilled, informed)
valid 유효한, 효력 있는

정답 (C)

5.
해설 'nearly 25 years(거의 25년)'라는 기간 명사를 수반하는 전치사를 고르는 문제이다. (A) until, (B) by는 뒤에 과거시점이나 사건만 오므로 탈락된다. 특히 (D) since는 뒤에 '과거시점 명사' 또는 '주어 + 과거동사'와 함께 쓰여 현재완료가 오지만, 기간 명사는 올 수 없다. 따라서 (C) for가 정답이다.

해석 새뮤얼은 그 회사에서 거의 25년 간 근무해 왔는데, 이달 말에 퇴직할 것이다.

어휘 company 회사   nearly 거의 (= almost)   retire 은퇴하다
until ~까지   by ~까지, ~옆에   for ~를 위한, ~에 대해, ~동안
since ~때문에, ~이후로

정답 (C)

6.
해설 명사 version(판, 버전)을 수식하는 알맞은 형용사를 고르는 문제이다. (A) responsible, (B) common, (C) creative 모두 의미적으로 적합하지 않다. 따라서 'has developed an expanded version(확장판을 개발했다)'이라는 자연스러운 표현을 이루는 (D) expanded가 정답이다.

해석 딜루와트 사는 사소한 문제들을 해결하기 위해서 회계 소프트웨어의 확장판을 개발했다.

어휘 develop ~를 개발하다   accounting 회계, 회계학
software 소프트웨어   resolve ~를 해결하다   trivial 사소한, 하찮은
error 오류, 실수   responsible 책임 있는
common 흔한, 공통의, 평범한   creative 창조적인, 독창적인
expanded 넓어진, 확대된, 확장된, 열린

정답 (D)

7.
해설 명사 the year와 함께 사용되는 전치사를 고르는 문제이다. (A) among과 (D) between은 뒤에 복수명사가 오므로 탈락된다. (C) by는 뒤에 시점 명사를 수반하므로 역시 제외된다. '처음부터 끝까지'라는 개념으로 그 다음에 기간 명사를 수반하는 (B) throughout이 정답이다.

해석 블루 컨설팅 사는 서비스 정신이 부족한 직원들에게 일 년 내내 훈련 프로그램을 제공합니다.

어휘 the lack of ~의 부족   service mind 서비스 마인드, 봉사정신
training program 훈련 프로그램   among ~중에서
throughout ~에 걸쳐서, ~내내   by ~까지, ~옆에
between ~사이에서

정답 (B)

8.
해설 명사 way(방법)를 수식하는 알맞은 형용사를 고르는 문제이다. '상품을 구매하는 유용한 방법'이라는 의미가 적절하므로 (A) useful(유용한)이 정답이다.

해석 온라인 쇼핑은 소비자들이 어디에 있든지 간에 상품을 구매하는 유용한 방법이다.

어휘 online shopping 온라인 쇼핑, 인터넷 쇼핑
way to buy ~을 사는 방법   products 제품, 물건 (= goods)
wherever 어디든지   customer 고객   useful 유용한
leading 가장 중요한, 선두적인   temporary 임시적인
existing 존재하는, 현존하는

정답 (A)

9.
해설 two months(2달)라는 기간 명사를 수반하는 전치사를 고르는 문제이다. (A) by, (B) until, (C) before 다음에는 시점 명사가 수반되므로 탈락된다. 따라서 'within two months(2달 안에)'라는 표현을 이루는 (D) within이 정답이다.

해석 높은 임대료를 줄이기 위해서, 우리는 결산일로부터 2달 내에 새 사무실로 이전할 예정입니다.

어휘 reduce ~를 줄이다, ~를 삭감시키다 (= curtail)   rent 집세, 임대료
be scheduled to부정사 ~할 예정이다
move ~로 이사하다, 이직하다, 나아가다   by ~까지, ~옆에
until ~까지   before ~전에 (= prior to 명사)   within ~이내에

정답 (D)

10.
해설 명사 amount(양)를 수식하는 알맞은 형용사를 고르는 문제이다. '상당한 양의 시간을 쓰다'라는 의미가 적절하므로 (B) considerable(상당한)이 정답이다.

해석 대학교들은 뛰어난 학생들을 모집하기 위한 마케팅 전략을 개발하는 데 상당한 양의 시간을 쓰고 있다.

어휘 spend ~를 쓰다   develop 개발하다   strategy 계획, 전략
attract ~를 끌어들이다 (= appeal to, draw, be attractive to, entice)
outstanding 뛰어난, 미결제의, 미해결의
available 이용 가능한, 사용할 수 있는
considerable 상당한 (= significant, substantial)
detailed 상세한   understanding 이해심 많은

정답 (B)

11.
해설 시점 명사를 수반하는 (C) by와 (D) until은 '10:00 and 12:00(10시와 12시 사이)'라는 명사구와 올 수 없다. (A) between과 (B) among 중에서 선택해야 하는데, '10:00 and 12:00'라는 범위와 어울리는 것은 (A) between이다.

해석 발표자는 오늘 아침 10시와 12시 사이에 발표할 것으로 예상됩니다.

어휘 speaker 연설가, 발표자   be expected to부정사 ~할 것으로 예상되다
deliver a presentation 연설하다 (= give a speech, make a speech, address)   between ~사이에서   among ~중에서
by ~까지, ~옆에   until ~까지

정답 (A)

12.
해설 빈칸 앞의 is located와 빈칸 뒤의 to Pine Creek Stadium을 연결해 볼 때 위치나 거리를 표현할 때 많이 사용하는 close to (~가까이에)라는 표현이 쓰였음을 알 수 있다. 따라서 정답은 (C) close이다.

해석 컨퍼런스가 열리는 로얄 한센 호텔은 파인 크릭 경기장 가까이에 위치해 있다.

어휘 conference 회담, 회의   be held 열리다, 개최되다
be located 위치되어 있다   permanent 영구적인
proper 적절한, 제대로 된   close 면밀한, 가까운
timely 때맞춘, 시기적절한

정답 (C)

13.
해설 알맞은 전치사 어휘를 선택하여 문맥을 완성하는 문제이다. '재정적인 성과금과 의료보험 이외에도 유급휴가를 받을 수 있다'는 문맥이 필요하다. 따라서 '~이외에도'라는 전치사 (D) In addition to가 정답이다.

해석 재정적인 장려금과 의료보험 이외에, 모든 직원들은 유급휴가도 받게 될 것이다.

어휘 financial 재정적인   incentive 동기부여, 혜택, 장려책
health benefits 의료보험   paid vacation 유급휴가
due to ~때문에   because of ~때문에   despite ~에도 불구하고
in addition to ~이외에도

정답 (D)

14.
해설 빈칸에 오는 형용사는 some workers를 뒤에서 꾸미면서, enthusiastic(열정적인)과 의미상 병치를 이루어야 한다. '앞으로 이 프로젝트를 이끌어야 한다'는 의미로 볼 때, 형용사 (D) creative(창의적인)가 가장 적합하다.

해석 우리는 앞으로 이 프로젝트를 맡을 창의적이고 열정적인 몇몇의 직원들이 필요합니다.

어휘 need ~를 필요로 하다   enthusiastic 열렬한, 열정적인
take on ~를 맡다 (= assume)   forward 앞으로, 앞에
poor 가난한, 형편없는   partial 부분적인, 불완전한
current 현재의, 통용되는   creative 창의적인, 창조적인

정답 (D)

15-18

오사카 — 당신이 언제든 소시스 파이를 방문한다면 메뉴를 찾으려고 애쓰지 마십시오. 그곳에서는 매일 점포 내에서 굽는 한 가지 메뉴인 레몬 파이만 제공합니다. 소시 하라다는 손님들에게 이 특별한 디저트를 15년 넘게 내놓고 있습니다. 하루에 그는 500개나 되는 파이를 판매합니다. 그러나 그가 자신의 메뉴를 늘릴 것을 고려할까요? 하라다는 여러 해 동안 사람들이 이 질문을 하고 있다고 말합니다. 그리고 그의 답변은 언제나 같았습니다. "어쩌면"이라고 그는 눈을 찡긋하며 말합니다. 소시스 파이는 매일 오전 11시에서 오후 8시까지 영업합니다.

어휘 ever 언제든, 한 번이라도   visit 방문하다   bother 신경 쓰다, 애를 쓰다
look for 찾다   menu 메뉴   offer 제공하다   item 품목
bake 굽다   on premises 점포 내에서   daily 매일, 날마다
serve 내놓다, 대접하다   customer 고객   dessert 디저트, 후식
consider 고려하다   for years 여러 해 동안
with a wink 눈을 찡긋하며   be open 문을 열다, 영업하다

15.
해설 전치사를 선택하는 문제이다. 빈칸 앞에 동사 시제로 have p.p 현재완료 시제가 있고 빈칸 뒤에 over fifteen years 15년 이상이라는 기간표현이 나왔기 때문에 기간과 어울리는 전치사 (C) for가 정답이다. (A) since 뒤에는 시점이 나와야하므로 시간명사가 복수형태가 될 수 없다.

정답 (C)

16.
(A) 그 제빵업자는 다음 달에 이 장소로 이사할 계획입니다.
(B) 하루에 그는 500개나 되는 파이를 판매합니다.
(C) 그것은 딸기, 바닐라, 초콜릿을 포함합니다.
(D) 그리고 나서 그 제빵류는 전국으로 배송됩니다.

해설 문맥에 맞는 문장을 고르는 문제이다. 두 번째 문장 It only offers one item that is baked on premises daily—lemon pie.에서 그곳에서는 매일 점포에서 굽는 한 가지 메뉴인 레몬 파이만 제공한다고 했으므로 (C)와 (D)부터 제외한다. 문맥상 이사에 대한 단서도 없으므로 (A)도 어색하다. 따라서 (B)가 정답이다.

정답 (B)

17.
해설 적절한 어형을 고르는 문제이다. 빈칸은 앞의 동사 consider의 목적어인 명사의 역할과 뒤의 his menu를 목적어로 취하는 동사의 역할을 동시에 할 수 있는 동명사가 들어갈 자리이다. 따라서 (B) expanding이 정답이다.

정답 (B)

18.
해설 문맥에 맞는 명사를 고르는 문제이다. 빈칸에는 형용사 his의 수식을 받아 가장 자연스럽게 의미가 통하는 명사가 와야 한다. 앞 문장의 동사 question이 문제 해결의 단서가 된다. 따라서 '답변'이라는 의미의 (D) answer가 정답이다.

정답 (D)

UNIT 9 전치사 (2)

Check-up Step 1 본책 _ p. 249

1.
해설 알맞은 전치사를 선택하는 문제로, 명사 the request와의 관계보다는 동사 respond가 힌트가 된다. respond는 뒤에 전치사 to를 동반하여 '~에 반응하다, 응답하다'라는 표현으로 쓰이므로 (A) to가 정답이다.

해석 그들은 곧 요청에 응답할 것이다.

어휘 respond 응답하다, 반응하다   soon 곧, 즉시, 머지않아
request 요청, 신청

정답 (A)

2.
해설 명사 the library와 어울리는 전치사를 고르는 문제로 동사 borrow가 힌트가 된다. borrow는 목적어 다음에 전치사 from을 수반하여, borrow A from B(A를 B로부터 빌리다)라는 표현을 만든다.

해석 이용객들은 도서관에서 3일 동안 책들을 빌릴 수 있습니다.

어휘 patron 이용자, 후원자, 단골고객   borrow ~을 빌려오다
borrow A from B A를 B로부터 빌리다   library 도서관

정답 (B)

3.
해설 명사 development와 함께 쓰여 문장을 완성하는 전치사 문제이다. 문맥상 '신제품이 개발 중이다'라는 의미가 필요한데, under development가 바로 그 표현이다. 따라서 정답은 (B) under이다.

해석 몇몇 새로운 제품들이 지금 개발 중이다.

어휘 several 몇몇의   product 제품, 상품
development 개발, 발전, 성장, 신제품, 행사
under development 개발 중인

정답 (B)

Check-up Step 2 본책 _ p. 249

4.
해설 알맞은 전치사를 선택하는 문제로 동사 benefit가 중요한 힌트가 된다. benefit는 뒤에 전치사 from을 동반하여 '~로부터 혜택을 얻다'라는 표현으로 쓰이므로 (C) from이 정답이다.

해석 우리는 도시의 많은 거주민들이 더 좋은 교통체계로부터 혜택을 받을 것이라고 생각한다.

어휘 believe ~를 믿는다, ~를 생각하다   resident 거주자, 거주민
benefit 혜택, 이점; 혜택을 받다
transportation 운송체계, 교통체계, 운송, 수송

정답 (C)

5.

해설 동사 are 뒤에서 명사와 함께 보어로 사용될 알맞은 전치사를 선택하는 문제이다. consideration(고려)에서 정답의 키워드를 잡을 수 있는데 consideration은 전치사 under와 함께 '고려 중인'이라는 의미의 표현으로 사용된다. 따라서 정답은 (C) under가 된다. 전치사 under은 '~아래에, ~하는 중에, ~하에'라는 의미로 사용되며 under consideration(고려 중), under construction(공사 중인), under development(개발 중인)등과 같은 표현들도 잘 사용되니 꼭 기억해두자.

해석 두 회사 간의 합병에 대한 약관은 고려 중에 있다.

어휘 terms and conditions 조건, 약관   merger 합병
under consideration 고려 중인

정답 (C)

Check-up Step 1 본책 _ p. 251

1.

해설 빈칸에는 명사 bad weather(나쁜 날씨)를 수반하는 품사를 고르는 문제이다. 일단, 뒤에 '주어 + 동사'가 오는 접속사 (A) Because는 탈락된다. 따라서 뒤에 명사를 동반하는 전치사 (B) Due to(~ 때문에)가 정답이다.

해석 나쁜 날씨 때문에, 야외 콘서트는 취소되었다.

어휘 bad weather 나쁜 날씨   outdoor 야외에, 옥외에
concert 콘서트, 연주회, 음악회   cancel ~를 취소하다, 무효화시키다
because ~ 때문에   due to ~ 때문에 (= because of)

정답 (B)

2.

해설 적절한 전치사를 고르는 문제로 빈칸 앞의 형용사 responsible(책임 있는)이 힌트가 된다. responsible은 전치사 for와 함께 쓰여 be responsible for(~에 책임 있다)라는 표현을 완성한다.

해석 그녀는 사무용 비품을 주문하는 데 책임이 있다.

어휘 be responsible for ~에 책임 있다 (= be in charge of)
order 주문; ~를 주문하다   office equipment 사무용 비품

정답 (B)

3.

해설 적절한 전치사를 고르는 문제로 빈칸 앞의 형용사 appreciative(감사하는)가 힌트가 된다. appreciative는 전치사 of와 함께 쓰여 be appreciative of(~에 대해 감사하다)라는 표현을 완성한다.

해석 저희 상품에 관심 가져주셔서 감사합니다.

어휘 be appreciative of ~에 대해 감사하다 (= appreciate)
interest 관심, 흥미; ~에게 관심을 끌다   product 상품, 제품

정답 (B)

Check-up Step 2 본책 _ p. 251

4.

해설 명사 convenience(편리함)는 앞에 전치사 for 또는 at을 붙여서 관용구를 만든다. for your convenience(편의를 위해서), at your convenience(당신이 편할 때)의 표현이 만들어지는데, 이 문제에서는 (C) For가 정답이다.

해석 당신의 편의를 위해서, 우리는 국경일을 포함해서 24시간 영업을 합니다.

어휘 for your convenience 당신의 편의를 위해서
open 열려있는, 개방하는, 영업 중인; ~를 열다, 열리다
open 24 hours a day 24시간 영업 중인   including ~를 포함하여
national holidays 국경일, 공식적인 휴일

정답 (C)

5.

해설 문장의 동사는 자동사인 dispose이며 동사와 함께 사용될 알맞은 전치사를 고르는 문제이다. dispose는 항상 전치사 of를 수반하는 '자동사+전치사' 구조로 정답은 (C) of가 된다. '(쓰레기 따위를) ~을 처리하다, 폐기하다'로 해석되며 비슷한 의미로는 get rid of(~을 버리다)가 있으니 알아두도록 하자.

해석 전 직원들은 모든 기밀문서들을 적절한 방법으로 폐기해야 한다.

어휘 dispose of ~를 처리하다, 폐기하다   confidential 기밀의
in a proper manner 적절한 방법으로

정답 (C)

Check-up Step 1 본책 _ p. 253

1.

해설 알맞은 전치사 어휘를 선택하여 문맥을 완성하는 문제이다. '높은 봉급 이외에도, 많은 상여금을 받을 수 있다'는 문맥이 필요하기 때문에, '~이외에도'라는 전치사 (B) In addition to가 정답이다.

해석 높은 봉급 이외에도, 당신은 많은 상여금을 받을 수 있다.

어휘 salary 봉급, 급여   a lot of 많은   bonus 상여금, 보너스
due to ~ 때문에 (= because of)   in addition to ~이외에도

정답 (B)

2.

해설 문장을 완성하는 품사를 고르는 문제이다. 명사 (A) exception이 오게 되면 the seminar exception for me라는 불가능한 표현이 만들어진다. 따라서 except for me(나를 제외하고)라는 표현을 이루는 전치사 (B) except가 정답이다.

해석 나를 제외하고 모두가 그 세미나에 참석할 것이다.

어휘 attend ~에 참석하다 (= participate in)   seminar 세미나, 회의
exception 예외, 제외   except (for) ~를 제외하고 (= excluding)

정답 (B)

3.

해설 문장을 완성하는 품사를 고르는 문제이다. (A) concern은 명사 또는 동사로 사용되는데, 문장구조상 빈칸에 올 수 없다. 따라서 명사 special discounts를 앞에서 수반할 수 있는 전치사 (B) concerning(~에 관하여)이 정답이다.

해석 상점은 특별한 할인에 관하여 소비자들에게 편지를 자주 보냅니다.

어휘 discount 할인; ~을 할인하다   concern 걱정, 관심사, 관심
concerning ~에 관하여 (= about)

정답 (B)

Check-up Step 2   본책 _ p. 253

4.

해설 문장의 구조상 동사는 들어갈 수 없으므로 (A) regard와 (D) regards 모두 탈락된다. 전치사 (A) regarding(~관하여)은 전치사 of와 충돌된다. 따라서 regardless of(~에 상관없이)라는 전치사구를 만드는 (C) regardless(상관없이)가 정답이다.

해석 우리는 나이와 국적에 상관없이 자격을 갖춘 구직 신청자 모두에게 통보할 것임에 주목하세요.

어휘 note 주목, 주의; ~를 주의하다, 유념하다
note that 주어 + 동사 ~를 통보하다, 주목하다, 알아차리다
consider ~를 고려하다, ~를 배려하다, ~를 숙고하다
qualified 능력 있는, 자격 있는   applicant 지원자, 신청자
nationality 국적, 민족   regard ~를 고려하다, 여기다, ~를 보다
regarding ~에 관하여   regardless of ~에 상관없이

정답 (C)

5.

해설 전체적인 문장의 구조를 볼 때 명사 local sales taxes를 수반하여 the total amount를 수식하는 알맞은 전치사를 고르는 문제이다. 보기 중에 전치사는 (B) excluding(~을 제외하고) 밖에 없으므로 정답은 (B)가 된다. 오답인 (A) included는 과거분사로서 뒤에 목적어를 수반하지 못하고, 부사 (C) regardless(개의치 않고)와 (D) unless(~하지 않다면)는 접속사로 구조상 어색하다. excluding은 대표적인 현재분사형 전치사이며, 'including(~을 포함하여), considering(~을 고려해볼 때), regarding / concerning (~에 관해서), barring(~만 없다면)' 등과 같이 숙지해 두는 것이 좋다.

해석 중개인들은 지역 판매세를 제외한 총 금액의 5% 수수료를 번다.

어휘 agent 중개인, 에이전트   commission on ~에 대한 수수료
total amount 총액   excluding ~을 제외하고

정답 (B)

Check-up Step 1   본책 _ p. 255

1.

해설 빈칸에는 명사 severe competition을 수반하는 전치사의 자리이다. 일단, 전치사가 아닌 (A) In spite는 바로 탈락된다. 따라서 '~에도 불구하고'라는 의미의 전치사 (B) Despite가 정답이다.

해석 극심한 경쟁에도 불구하고, 그 회사는 매우 성공했다.

어휘 severe 극심한, 가혹한   competition 경쟁, 경쟁자, 경연대회
successful 성공적인   in spite of ~에도 불구하고 (= despite)

정답 (B)

2.

해설 빈칸 뒤의 명사 phone(전화)을 수반하는 전치사를 선택하는 문제이다. phone은 셀 수 있는 명사인데, 관사도 없으며 복수형태도 아니라는 점이 힌트이다. 즉, 전치사 by 다음에 교통, 통신수단이 오면 관사 없이 사용하기 때문에 (B) by가 정답이다.

해석 당신은 승차권을 전화로 예약할 수 있습니다.

어휘 reserve ~를 예약하다   ticket 표, 승차권
by phone 전화로 (= on the phone, over the telephone)

정답 (B)

3.

해설 명사 a sales manager(영업 관리자)를 수반하는 전치사를 고르는 문제이다. 문맥상 a sales manager와 he는 의미상 동격이 되어야 하므로, '~로서'라는 자격을 나타내는 전치사 (B) As가 정답이다.

해석 영업 관리자로서, 그는 많은 책임들을 가지고 있다.

어휘 manager 관리자, 매니저   responsibility 책임, 업무

정답 (B)

Check-up Step 2   본책 _ p. 255

4.

해설 알맞은 품사를 결정하고 의미를 고려하는 문제이다. 빈칸 뒤에 '주어 + 동사'의 형태가 아니라 명사이므로, 빈칸에는 전치사가 들어가야 한다. 보기의 유일한 전치사 (B) without(~없이)이 정답이다.

해석 회사들은 고객의 동의 없이는 그들의 개인적인 정보를 공개하지 말아야 한다.

어휘 company 회사   disclose ~를 밝히다, ~를 공개하다 (= reveal)
customer 고객, 손님   personal 개인적인
consent 동의, 허락; 동의하다, 허락하다
unless 만약 ~하지 않으면, ~가 아니라면   without ~없이
although ~에도 불구하고, 비록 ~하지만

정답 (B)

141

5.

해설 빈칸을 중심으로 앞에는 완전한 문장이 있고 뒤에는 등위접속사 and가 명사인 benefits와 company safety procedures를 연결하고 있다. 따라서 빈칸은 뒤에 명사를 수반하며 목적어인 topics를 수식해줄 전치사가 올 자리임을 확인할 수 있는데 보기 중에 전치사는 (A) such as 밖에 없으므로 정답은 (A)이다. (B) same은 the same의 형태로서 '형용사(똑같은), 대명사(똑같은 것), 부사(똑같이)'의 품사로 사용된다. (C) so는 접속사(그래서)와 부사(매우)로 사용되며, (D) when은 문장을 수반하는 접속사다.

해석 그 오리엔테이션은 복지혜택과 회사의 안전 절차 같은 주제들을 다룰 것입니다.

어휘 include ~을 포함하다 such as 예를 들어, ~와 같이
benefit 복지혜택, 이익 safety procedure 안전절차

정답 (A)

Check-up 본책 _ p. 257

1. **정답** finally
어휘 final 마지막의 / finally 마침내

2. **정답** significantly
어휘 significant 상당한 / significantly 상당히

3. **정답** specially
어휘 specify 명시하다 / specially 특별히

4. **정답** increasingly
어휘 increase 증가하다 / increasingly 점점, 더욱 더

5. **정답** strongly
어휘 strong 강한 / strongly 강력하게

Part 5&6_ 실전연습 9 본책 _ p. 258-259

1.

해설 알맞은 전치사를 선택하는 문제로, 명사 consumers' complaints와의 관계보다는 동사 react가 힌트가 된다. react는 뒤에 전치사 to를 동반하여 '~에 반응하다, 응답하다'라는 표현으로 쓰이므로 (B) to가 정답이다.

해석 기업들은 직원들에 의해 초래된 소비자들의 불만사항에 즉시 반응해야만 한다.

어휘 react 반응하다 immediately 곧, 즉시 (= soon)
consumer 소비자 complaint 불평, 불평거리
cause ~를 초래하다 (= lead to 명사, result in) employee 직원
despite ~에도 불구하고

정답 (B)

2.

해설 명사 the city center와 어울리는 전치사를 고르는 문제로, 빈칸 뒤의 to the airport가 힌트가 된다. 즉, from A to B(A부터 B까지)라는 표현을 이루는 (C) from이 정답이다.

해석 몬데일 호텔에서는 셔틀 서비스가 도시 중심지부터 공항까지 무료로 운행됩니다.

어휘 shuttle service 셔틀 서비스 operate ~를 작동하다, 운영하다
city center 도시 중심부 airport 공항
at no extra cost 추가비용을 들이지 않고, 무료로

정답 (C)

3.

해설 명사 consideration(고려, 숙고, 생각)을 수반하는 알맞은 전치사를 고르는 문제이다. under consideration(고려 중인, 숙고 중인)이라는 표현을 만드는 (D) under가 정답이다.

해석 근무지에 보육 시설을 건설하려는 계획이 현재 고려 중이다.

어휘 plan to부정사 ~할 계획 construct 건설하다, 구성하다
child-care facilities 보육시설 workstation 근무지, 작업장소
currently 현재 consideration 고려, 이해, 배려
along ~를 따라서 among ~중에서 toward ~를 향해서
under consideration 고려 중인, 심사숙고 중인

정답 (D)

4.

해설 빈칸 다음의 the inclement weather만 보고 전치사를 선택하는 문제가 아니다. '일시적으로 연기가 되었다'는 내용으로 미루어 볼 때, '악천후 때문에'라는 원인의 의미가 필요하다. 따라서 '~ 때문에'라는 전치사 (C) because of가 정답이다.

해석 악천후의 날씨 때문에 주택 건축이 일시적으로 연기되었습니다.

어휘 construction 건축, 건축물 temporarily 일시적으로
housing construction 주택건설
temporarily 잠정적으로, 일시적으로 postpone 연기하다, 미루다
inclement weather 나쁜 날씨 in spite of ~에도 불구하고
as to ~에 관해서 (= as for, about) because of ~때문에 (= due to)
besides ~이외에도 (= on top of)

정답 (C)

5.

해설 알맞은 전치사를 고르는 문제로, 동사 dispose가 힌트가 된다. dispose는 전치사 of와 함께 쓰여 dispose of(~를 없애다, ~를 치우다)라는 표현으로 쓰이므로 (B) of가 정답이다.

해석 설문조사 결과를 분석한 후에, 개인 정보를 포함한 서류들을 폐기하세요.

어휘 survey 설문조사; ~를 조사하다　result 연구 결과물 (= findings)
analyze ~을 분석하다　dispose 처리하다, 버리다
document 문서, 서류; ~을 문서로 기록하다　contain ~를 포함하다
personal information 개인정보

정답 (B)

6.

해설 구조적으로 빈칸은 명사를 수반하는 전치사의 자리이므로, 접속사 (B) Although는 올 수 없다. (C) In spite 역시 of 없이 단독으로 사용하지 않는다. '뛰어난 성능이지만, 소비자들이 구매하지 않는다'는 문맥에 어울리는 (A) Despite(~에도 불구하고)가 정답이다.

해석 자동차 MD-300의 뛰어난 성능에도 불구하고, 소비자들 대다수는 그것을 구매하기를 주저했다.

어휘 extraordinary 놀라운, 비범한, 대단한
performance 실적, 성과, 성능　vehicle 차량, 자동차
be reluctant to 부정사 ~하기를 주저하다
despite ~에도 불구하고 (= in spite of)　thanks to ~덕분에, ~때문에

정답 (A)

7.

해설 알맞은 전치사를 고르는 문제로, 동사 work만 보고 답을 고르면 틀리는 문제이다. 동사 work는 보기의 전치사가 모두 올 수 있으므로, 그 뒤의 an intern과 문맥을 고려해야 한다. 'Miami Airline에서 인턴으로서 일하다'는 의미가 필요하므로, 자격을 나타내는 전치사 (C) as가 정답이다.

해석 지난 달 인사 위원회에 의해 뽑힌 에밀리는 마이애미 항공사에서 인턴으로 일하게 될 것입니다.

어휘 select 엄선된, 고급의; ~를 선택하다
personnel committee 인사위원회　toward ~향하여

정답 (C)

8.

해설 명사 prior permission(사전 허가)과의 관계와 문맥을 모두 따져보아야 하는 전치사 문제이다. '사전 허가 없이 퇴근할 수 없다'는 문맥이 필요하므로 (D) without(~없이)이 정답이다.

해석 직원들은 부서장의 사전 허가 없이는 일찍 퇴근할 수 없다.

어휘 allow to ~를 허락하다, ~를 하게 하다　leave for work 퇴근하다
prior 이전의, 사전의　permission 허락, 허가
department head 부서장　beyond ~를 초월하여, ~을 넘어서
besides ~이외에도

정답 (D)

9.

해설 동사 joined를 수식하는 부사를 선택하는 문제이다. 일단, '퇴직과 입사'라는 시간의 전후 관계를 고려했을 때, (D) previously(이전에)는 부적절하다. (A) nearly(거의)와 (B) significantly(상당히)는 의미상 어울리지 않는다. 따라서 '곧바로 경쟁회사에 입사했다'는 내용을 이루는 (C) shortly가 정답이다.

해석 마리오는 회사에서 퇴직한 후에, 그는 곧바로 다른 경쟁회사 한 곳에 입사했다.

어휘 after ~후에　retire 은퇴하다　company 회사
join ~의 구성원이 되다, ~에 입사하다
another (세 개 이상의 범위에서) 또 다른 하나
competing 서로 경합하는, 경쟁하는　nearly 거의, 가까이
significantly 상당히, 중요하게　shortly 곧
previously 이전에, 미리

정답 (C)

10.

해설 동사 contributed를 수식하는 알맞은 부사를 선택하는 문제이다. '회사의 성장에 기여했다'는 문맥으로 미루어 볼 때, '상당히'라는 의미의 (B) significantly가 적합하다.

해석 혁신적인 마케팅 전략을 만드는 직원들이 회사의 성장에 상당히 기여했습니다.

어휘 employee 직원　creating 창출하는　innovative 혁신적인
marketing strategy 마케팅 전략　contribute to ~에 기여하다
growth 성장　currently 현재　significantly 상당히, 현저하게
easily 쉽게　immediately 곧, 즉시 (= soon)

정답 (B)

11.

해설 동사 consider를 수식하는 알맞은 부사를 선택하는 문제이다. '계획이 수익성이 있는지를 고려해야만 한다'는 문맥으로 미루어 볼 때, '먼저, 처음에'라는 의미의 (A) initially가 적합하다. 나머지 보기 모두 의미상 부적합하다.

해석 경영진은 또 다른 공장을 짓는 계획을 실행하기 전에, 그 계획이 수익성이 있는지를 처음에 고려해야만 한다.

어휘 before ~전에 (= ahead of, in advance of)
management 경영진, 관리
implement ~를 실시하다, ~조치를 취하다
plan to 부정사 ~할 계획이다　build ~를 건설하다, ~를 짓다
another (세 개 이상의 범위에서) 또 다른 하나　plant 공장
consider ~를 고려하다, ~를 배려하다, ~를 숙고하다
profitable 수익성이 있는
initially 초기에, 처음에 (= at first, at the beginning)　easily 쉽게
already 이미, 벌써　dramatically 급격하게, 극적으로, 엄청나게

정답 (A)

12.
해설 동사 have p.p. 사이에 오는 알맞은 부사를 고르는 문제이다. 일단, (D) extremely는 동사를 수식할 수 없다. (A) severely(심각하게), (C) closely(밀접하게)는 둘 다 의미상 부적절하다. 따라서 '최근에서야 밝혀냈다'는 문맥을 완성하는 (B) lately가 정답이다.

해석 조사관들은 장비가 적절하게 작동하지 않은 문제점을 최근에서야 밝혀냈다.

어휘 inspector 조사관, 검사관 find out ~를 알아내다, 밝혀내다
problem 문제, 걱정거리 equipment 장비, 기계
properly 적절하게 severely 심하게, 엄하게, 엄격하게, 혹독하게
lately 최근에 (= recently) closely 면밀하게, 밀접하게
extremely 대단히, 극도로

정답 (B)

13.
해설 동사 rose(올랐다, 증가했다)를 수식하는 부사를 고르는 문제이다. 일단, (A) willingly(기꺼이), (B) efficiently(효율적으로), (D) productively(생산적으로)는 의미상 모두 부적합하여 빈칸에 올 수 없다. 따라서 rose dramatically(급격히 올랐다)라는 올바른 표현을 이루는 (C) dramatically가 정답이다.

해석 아파트 가격이 급격하게 올랐기 때문에, 잠재적인 고객들이 그것을 구매하기를 주저합니다.

어휘 price 가격, 시세; ~에 값을 매기다, ~에 가격을 붙이다
apartment 아파트 rise 상승하다 potential 잠재적인; 잠재력
client 고객, 의뢰인 be reluctant to부정사 ~하기를 주저하다
buy ~을 사다, ~을 구매하다 willingly 기꺼이, 자진해서
efficiently 효율적으로, 유효하게 dramatically 급격하게, 극적으로
productively 생산적으로

정답 (C)

14.
해설 동사 will revise를 뒤에서 수식하는 동사를 고르는 문제이다. 일단, 미래시제에 올 수 없는 (A) initially와 (B) lately(최근에)는 바로 탈락된다. '~는 정보를 수정하고, 그에 따라서 ~를 수정하다'는 의미가 적합하므로 (D) accordingly(그에 따라서)가 정답이다.

해석 인사 위원회는 관련 정보를 수집하고 나서, 그리고 그에 따라서 채용 기준을 수정할 것입니다.

어휘 personnel committee 인사위원회 gather ~를 모으다, 수집하다
related 관련된 (= relevant) revise 변경하다, 수정하다, 개정하다
employment 직장, 고용 standard 규범, 표준
initially 초기에, 처음에 (= at first, at the beginning)
lately 최근에 (= recently) easily 쉽게
accordingly 따라서, 그러므로

정답 (D)

15-18

> **멜버른 아파트 주민들께 드리는 공지**
>
> 10월 23일부터 12월 7일까지, 아파트 주차장이 폐쇄될 것이고, 새로운 주차시스템을 설치하기 위하여 공사가 진행될 것입니다.
>
> 새 주차장은 공간절약형이면서 수동으로 작동될 수 있는 조절 가능한 2층 시스템이 될 것입니다. 이 새로운 시설로, 우리는 250대의 차량을 수용할 수 있는 충분한 공간을 가지게 되는 것입니다.
>
> 그래서 공사가 시작되는 10월 23일부터, 아파트 앞에 있는 임시 주차공간을 이용하시기 바랍니다.
>
> 불편을 드려서 죄송합니다. 새로운 주차 시스템이 여러분들에게 이전보다 더 편리함을 줄 것이라고 생각합니다.
>
> 여러분들의 협조에 감사드립니다.
>
> 감사합니다.
>
> 테리 존
> 멜버른 아파트 관리인

어휘 apartment parking area 아파트 주차장 close ~을 닫다, 닫히다
under construction 건설 중인 in order to부정사 ~하기 위하여
install ~를 설치하다 discussion 토론, 논의
control 통제, ~을 통제하다 starting 처음, 시작, ~부터
work 일, 작업 start 시작, 시초, ~를 시작하다, 시작하다
be sure to부정사 ~하는 것을 확신하다
temporary 임시적인, 임시의 (= provisional) in front of ~앞에
be appreciative of ~에 감사하다 (= appreciate)
appreciate ~를 감사히 여기다 appreciative 감탄하는, 감사하는

15.
해설 명사 construction(건설, 건축)을 수반하는 전치사를 고르는 문제이다. '아파트 주차장이 폐쇄될 것이며, 건설 중이다'라는 내용으로 미루어 볼 수 있다. 따라서 '공사 중인(under consideration)'이라는 표현을 이루는 (C) under가 정답이다.

정답 (C)

16.
해설 동사구 be operated(작동되다) 사이에 오는 부사를 고르는 문제이다. which 이하가 명사 adjustable two-level system(조절이 가능한 2층 시스템)을 꾸며주는 형태로, '수동으로 작동되다'라는 의미가 어울린다. 따라서 (D) manually(수동으로)가 정답이다.

정답 (D)

17.
해설 명사 our apartments(우리 아파트)를 수반하는 전치사를 선택하여 문맥을 완성하는 문제이다. '아파트 앞의 임시주차장을 이용하다'는 문맥이 적절하므로 (B) in front of(~앞에)가 정답이다.

정답 (B)

18.
(A) 불편을 드려서 죄송합니다.
(B) 그러므로, 그 지역은 주민들로 붐빌 것입니다.
(C) 멜버른에서 당신이 우리와 함께 하길 바랍니다.
(D) 당신과 함께 일하게 되기를 기대합니다.

해설 공사기간 동안 임시 주차장을 이용하라는 말이 바로 앞에 나오므로, 불편에 대해 사과하는 말이 문맥상 어울린다. 따라서 정답은 (A)이다.

정답 (A)

UNIT 10 접속사 (1)

Check-up Step 1 본책_p. 261

1.
해설 알맞은 접속사를 결정하는 문제로, 빈칸 앞의 not only가 힌트가 된다. not only는 뒤에 보통 but also를 동반하여 '~뿐만 아니라 ~도'라는 의미로 상관접속사를 이룬다. 따라서 정답은 (B) but also가 된다.

해석 그들의 음식은 값이 저렴할 뿐만 아니라 아주 맛있기도 하다.

어휘 cheap 값싼   not only A but also B A뿐만 아니라 B 또한
delicious 맛있는

정답 (B)

2.
해설 빈칸은 동사 remember의 목적어 역할을 하는 명사절을 이끄는 접속사의 자리이다. 빈칸 다음에 완전한 문장이 오기 때문에 명사절 접속사 (B) that이 정답이다. (A) what은 뒤에 불완전한 문장이 오기 때문에 탈락된다.

해석 당신은 내일까지 그것을 끝마쳐야 한다는 것을 명심하세요.

어휘 remember ~를 기억하다, ~를 명심하다   finish 끝나다, ~를 끝마치다

정답 (B)

3.
해설 구조적으로 보면 '--------- we have a chance to meet him'까지가 문장의 주어이다. 즉, 빈칸에는 문장을 주어로 만드는 명사절 접속사의 자리인데, 보기 중에서는 (A) Whether가 가능하다. 주어 역할을 하는 명사절의 경우 whether를 if로 바꿀 수 없다.

해석 우리가 그를 만날 기회를 가질지는 확실하지 않다.

어휘 chance 가능성, 기회   meet ~를 충족시키다, ~를 만나다, 모이다

정답 (A)

Check-up Step 2 본책_p. 261

4.
해설 빈칸은 동사 know의 목적어 역할을 하는 명사절을 이끄는 접속사의 자리이다. 또한 빈칸 다음에 동사 are doing의 목적어가 없는 불완전한 문장이 오기 때문에 접속사 (A) what이 정답이다.

해석 선두 타이어 제조업체로서, 우리는 경쟁사들이 무엇을 하는지 알려고 항상 노력한다.

어휘 leading 가장 중요한, 선두의   manufacturer 생산자, 제조업자
try to부정사 ~를 노력하다 (= strive to부정사)
competitor 경쟁자, 경쟁사   regarding ~에 관하여

정답 (A)

5.
해설 빈칸은 전치사 뒤에 명사로서 to부정사와 함께 이용 가능한 형태를 선택해야 한다. 우선 (B) both와 (C) either는 각각 both A and B(A와 B 둘 다), either A or B(A 또는 B)의 형태가 돼야 하므로 정답에서 제외된다. 접속사 (A) if는 명사절(~인지 아닌지)로 사용되지만 타동사의 목적어 자리로만 나올 수 있으므로 답이 될 수 없다. 따라서 정답은 (C) whether가 된다. 명사절 whether는 완벽한 문장을 수반하고, 또한 whether to부정사(~할지 안 할지)의 형태로도 사용이 가능하다.

해석 이 브로슈어는 당신이 새로운 소프트웨어를 구매할지 안할지에 관해 결정하도록 도와줄 것입니다.

어휘 help 목적어 to부정사 (목적어)가 ~하도록 돕다
whether to부정사 ~할지 안할지
purchase 구매, 구매품; ~을 구매하다

정답 (C)

Check-up Step 1 본책_p. 263

1.
해설 구조적으로 명사절 접속사 (A) That이 오려면, '--------- he was young'이라는 문장이 주어 역할을 해야 한다. 따라서 문장에서 떨어져 나가도 영향을 주지 않는 부사절을 이끄는 접속사 (B) Because가 정답이다.

해석 그는 어리기 때문에, 허락받지 못했다.

어휘 young 어린, 젊은   admit ~를 인정하다, (입장을) 허락하다

정답 (B)

2.
해설 빈칸 다음에 두 개의 문장이 있다. 일단, 뒤에 명사 또는 동명사를 수반하는 전치사 (B) Despite는 탈락된다. 두 문장을 이어주는 부사절 접속사 (A) Although가 정답이다.

해석 그것의 값이 비싸지만, 우리는 그것을 구매하기로 결정했다.

어휘 expensive 비싼, 돈이 많이 드는 (= costly)
decide 결심하다, ~를 결정하다
although 비록 ~이지만, ~에도 불구하고
despite ~에도 불구하고

정답 (A)

3.

해설 전치사 (B) In case of가 빈칸에 오려면, 뒤에 명사 또는 동명사가 와야 한다. 하지만 빈칸 다음에 〈주어＋동사〉로 이루어진 두 문장이 있으므로, 빈칸에는 부사절 접속사 (A) In case가 와야 한다.

해석 비가 올 경우를 대비해서, 당신은 우산을 가져가야만 한다.

어휘 rain 비, 빗물; 비가 오다 take an umbrella 우산을 가져가다

정답 (A)

Check-up Step 2 본책 _ p. 263

4.

해설 빈칸 앞뒤의 문장 구조를 살펴보면, 〈주어＋동사〉로 이루어진 두 개의 문장이 있다. 즉, 빈칸은 문장을 연결하는 접속사의 자리이므로, 보기의 유일한 접속사인 (C) unless가 정답이 된다. 나머지 보기 모두 전치사이므로 탈락된다.

해석 관리자의 서면 허가 없이는, 모든 직원들은 회의에 참석해야 한다.

어휘 employee 직원 attend ~에 참석하다 meeting 모임, 회의
written 서면의, 쓰여진 permission 허락, 허가, 승인
unless 만약 ~이 아니라면, ~하지 않는다면

정답 (C)

5.

해설 전체적인 구조를 볼 때 두 문장이 사용되었으므로 빈칸에는 알맞은 접속사를 선택해야 한다. 우선 보기 중 전치사인 (D) Despite(~에도 불구하고)는 제일 먼저 탈락되며 등위접속사인 (A) But(그러나)과 (B) and는 문장 맨 앞자리에 위치할 수 없어 정답이 될 수 없다. 따라서 정답은 (C) Although(~임에 불구하고)가 된다. Although는 '상반된 양보의 의미'로 해석되며 (D) Despite 역시 '~에도 불구하고'라는 같은 의미를 갖지만 전치사이므로 답이 될 수 없다.

해석 그 건물이 몇 년 전에 지어졌음에도 불구하고, 여전히 몇몇 사무실은 비어 있다.

어휘 although ~임에 불구하고 complete 완전한, 완료된; ~을 완료하다
several 몇몇의 vacant 빈, 사람이 없는

정답 (C)

Check-up Step 1 본책 _ p. 265

1.

해설 문두의 Before(~전에)는 시간 부사절을 만드는 부사절 접속사이다. 시간 부사절에서는 현재시제가 미래를 대신하므로, will을 쓰지 않으므로 (B) will leave는 틀리다. 주절이 문맥상 가까운 미래를 의미하는 명령문이기 때문에, 빈칸에는 현재시제 (A) leave가 와야 한다.

해석 당신은 사무실을 떠나기 전에, 전등을 끄세요.

어휘 before ~전에, ~앞에서 office 사무실 turn off ~를 끄다
light 전등, 빛, 불빛 leave ~를 떠나다, ~을 남기다

정답 (A)

2.

해설 시간 접속사 (A) when이 오면 '회사에 입사했다'는 과거시제와 '승진 되었다'는 주절의 시제와 의미가 충돌된다. 따라서 '주어＋have(has)＋p.p.＋since＋주어＋과거동사'의 구조를 이루며, 동시에 문맥을 완성하는 접속사 (B) since가 정답이다.

해석 그는 회사에 입사한 이후로 세 번 승진했다.

어휘 promote ~를 승진시키다, ~를 홍보하다, ~를 증진시키다
join ~의 구성원이 되다, ~에 입사하다 since ~이후로, ~ 때문에

정답 (B)

3.

해설 빈칸 앞뒤의 문장 구조를 살펴보면, 〈주어＋동사〉로 이루어진 두 개의 문장이 있다. 즉, 빈칸은 문장을 연결하는 접속사의 자리이므로, 전치사인 (B) by는 바로 탈락된다. 따라서 접속사 (A) until이 정답이 된다.

해석 그는 그녀가 말하는 것을 끝마칠 때까지 기다렸다.

어휘 wait 기다리다 finish 끝나다, ~를 끝마치다 speak 말하다, 이야기하다

정답 (A)

Check-up Step 2 본책 _ p. 265

4.

해설 동사의 시제를 결정하는 문제로 두 문장의 시간 전후를 판단해야 한다. 시간 접속사 by the time 이하의 문장이 과거시제이므로, 주절의 동사는 과거완료시제 (C) had left로 표현해야 두 문장의 시간관계가 맞게 된다.

해석 우리가 단체사진을 찍을 때쯤, 로베르토 리오넬로 박사는 공항을 향해 떠난 상태였다.

어휘 airport 공항 by the time ~했을 때쯤 take a photo 사진을 찍다
leave for ~를 향해 떠나다

정답 (C)

5.

해설 알맞은 의미의 접속사를 고르는 문제이다. 전체적인 문장의 구조를 보면 두 문장으로 이루어져 있으며 각 문장의 시제를 판단해서 두 문장의 의미를 결합시켜야 한다. 주절의 문장에서는 have been productive로 현재완료시제가, 빈칸이 수반하는 종속절 문장은 was installed로 과거시제가 각각 사용되었다. 보기 중 이러한 두 문장의 시제를 연결해 줄 수 있는 접속사는 (A) since(~이후로)이다. '이후로'로 해석될 때 since가 이끄는 절은 '과거에 사건이 발생한 특정시점'을 나타내는 과거시제가 사용되며, 주절의 시제는 '그 후로 지금까지 지속성이 계속됨'을 의미하는 현재완료(have p.p.)가 사용된다.

해석 새로운 소프트웨어가 설치된 이후로, 전 직원들의 생산성은 더 높아졌다.

어휘 employee 직원 productive 생산적인 install ~을 설치하다

정답 (A)

Check-up Step 1 본책 _ p. 267

1.

해설 빈칸 앞뒤의 문장 구조를 살펴보면, 〈주어 + 동사〉로 이루어진 두 개의 문장이 있다. 즉, 빈칸은 문장을 연결하는 접속사의 자리이므로, 전치사인 (A) For는 바로 탈락된다. 따라서 접속사 (B) Because가 정답이 된다.

해석 날씨가 매우 안 좋았기 때문에, 우리는 소풍을 즐길 수 없었다.

어휘 weather 날씨 enjoy ~를 즐기다 picnic 소풍

정답 (B)

2.

해설 빈칸에는 접속사 that과 함께 쓰이는 어휘를 선택하는 문제이다. 일단, 전치사 (B) Due to(~ 때문에)는 문법적으로도 접속사 that 앞에 올 수 없다. 따라서 now와 that이 합쳐져서 하나의 접속사구인 now that(~이니까)을 만드는 (A) Now가 정답이 된다.

해석 그녀는 승진했으므로 그녀는 더 많은 책임이 있다.

어휘 promote ~를 승진시키다, ~를 홍보하다, ~를 촉진시키다
responsibility 책임, 의무, 임무 now that 지금은 ~이니까
due to ~때문에

정답 (A)

3.

해설 빈칸 앞뒤의 문장 구조를 살펴보면, 〈주어 + 동사〉로 이루어진 두 개의 절이 있다. 즉, 빈칸은 문장을 연결하는 접속사의 자리이므로, 전치사인 (A) except(~를 제외하고)는 바로 탈락된다. 따라서 접속사 (B) as if(마치 ~인 것처럼)가 정답이 된다.

해석 그 건물은 오래 동안 비어있는 것처럼 보인다.

어휘 look 보다, 관망 building 건물 vacant 비어있는, 공석의
for a long time 오래 동안 except ~를 제외하고 (= excluding)

정답 (B)

Check-up Step 2 본책 _ p. 267

4.

해설 빈칸 앞뒤의 문장 구조를 살펴보면, 〈주어 + 동사〉로 이루어진 두 개의 절이 있다. 즉, 빈칸은 문장을 연결하는 접속사의 자리이므로, 전치사인 (B) In spite of(~에도 불구하고)와 (C) According to(~따르면)는 바로 탈락된다. 나머지 중에서 문맥상 적합한 접속사는 (D) Even though가 정답이 된다.

해석 비록 작업자들이 내일 정기적인 유지보수 업무를 수행할 것이지만, 모든 사무실은 문을 열 것이다.

어휘 perform 공연하다, ~를 수행하다
regular 정기적인, 규칙적인, 정규의 maintenance 유지보수, 관리
as though ~인 것처럼, 마치 ~인양, 마치 ~처럼 (= as if)
in spite of ~에도 불구하고 (= despite) according to ~에 따르면
even though 그럼에도 불구하고 (= although)

정답 (D)

5.

해설 빈칸 다음에 있는 문장을 수반할 알맞은 접속사를 선택하는 문제이다. 보기 중 접속사는 (A) whereas밖에 없으므로 정답은 (A)가 된다. 나머지 보기들은 모두 전치사로서 문장을 수반할 수 없다. 접속사 whereas(~인 반면에)는 '주절과 상반된 양보의 의미'로 사용되며 while과 바꾸어도 무방하다.

해석 구형 프로그램이 많은 시간을 필요로 했던 반면에, 우리의 신형 소프트웨어는 매우 신속하게 데이터를 처리합니다.

어휘 process 처리, 절차; ~을 처리하다 take time 시간이 걸리다
whereas 반면에 through ~을 통해 such as ~와 같은, 예를 들어

정답 (A)

Check-up 본책 _ p. 269

1. 정답 **nearly**
어휘 near 근처의, 옆의 / nearly 거의

2. 정답 **immediately**
어휘 immediate 즉각적인 / immediately 즉시

3. 정답 **carefully**
어휘 care 주의, 관리 / carefully 주의 깊게

4. 정답 **clearly**
어휘 clear 명확한 / clearly 명확하게

5. 정답 **frequently**
어휘 frequent 빈번한 / frequently 자주, 빈번하게

Part 5&6_ 실전연습 10 본책 _ p. 270–271

1.

해설 알맞은 접속사를 결정하는 문제로, 빈칸 앞뒤 문장을 고려해 보아야 한다. 일단, 등위접속사 (B) nor(또한 ~아니다)는 앞 문장에 부정문이 와야 한다. (A) as(~ 때문에, ~할 때, 하면서)와 (D) because(때문에)는 의미상 어울리지 않는다. 따라서 '역접'의 의미를 지니고 있는 (C) but이 정답이다.

해설 저스틴은 시설을 확장하고는 싶지만 비용에 대해 걱정하고 있다.

어휘 would like to부정사 ~하고 싶다   expand ~을 확장하다
facility 기관, 시설   be concerned about ~에 대해서 걱정하다
cost 비용; 비용이 들다, ~가 들게 하다

정답 (C)

2.

해설 알맞은 상관접속사를 고르는 문제이다. 빈칸 뒤의 a raincoat or umbrella와 구조적으로 어울리는 것은 (D) either이다. either A or B(A 또는 B)의 구조를 취하는 (D) either가 정답이다.

해설 관광 가이드는 비가 올 경우를 대비해서, 우리가 비옷 또는 우산을 가져오기를 권장합니다.

어휘 tour guide 관광 가이드   guide 관광 안내책자, 안내인
recommend ~를 추천하다, 권고하다   bring ~를 가져오다
raincoat 비옷   umbrella 우산   in case of ~의 경우에 대비해서
neither A nor B A와 B 둘 다 아니다
between A and B A와 B 사이에   both A and B A와 B 둘 다
either A or B A 또는 B

정답 (D)

3.

해설 알맞은 접속사를 고르는 문제로, 일단 문두에 올 수 없는 (A) But이 먼저 탈락된다. (C) That은 관계대명사 또는 명사절을 이끄는 접속사로 역시 제외된다. '회사는 작지만, 급여는 높다'라는 '양보'의 의미이므로 (B) While(~인 반면에)이 정답이다.

해설 그 회사의 규모는 비교적 작은 반면에, 평균 급여는 꽤 높은 편이다.

어휘 company 회사   relatively 상대적으로
average 평균, 보통; 평균의, 보통의   salary 급여, 봉급
tend to부정사 ~하는 경향이 있다   fairly 꽤, 아주
while ~동안에, 반면에, ~에도 불구하고
so that 주어 + 동사 ~하기 위해서

정답 (B)

4.

해설 〈주어 + 동사〉로 이루어진 두 개의 문장이 있으므로, 전치사 (C) due to(~ 때문에)는 올 수 없다. 문두에 올 수 없는 접속사 (D) yet(그러나) 역시 탈락된다. 나머지 보기 중에서, (B) Unless(~하지 않으면)는 의미상 not이 포함되어 있기 때문에 빈칸 뒤의 not과 충돌된다. 따라서 (A) In case(~할 경우에)가 정답이다.

해설 네트워크가 적절하게 작동하지 않는 경우에, 서비스 센터로 바로 연락하세요.

어휘 network 네트워크, 망   function 기능, 행사; 작동하다
properly 적절하게   contact 접촉; ~에 연락하다
promptly 즉시, 정확하게
in case (that) 주어 + 동사 ~할 경우에 대비해서
unless ~가 아니라면, ~하지 않으면
due to ~때문에 (= because of, owing to)   yet 그러나, 아직

정답 (A)

5.

해설 알맞은 접속사를 선택하여 문장을 완성시키는 문제이다. '당신이 클럽에 들어오면, 카드가 발급되다'는 의미가 문맥상 적절하므로, 시간 접속사 (B) as soon as(~하자마자)가 정답이다.

해설 클럽에 들어오자마자, 새로운 회원카드가 당신에게 즉시 발급될 것입니다.

어휘 be issued to ~에게 발급되다   immediately 즉시, 바로
join ~에 가입하다, ~에 구성원이 되다, ~에 참여하다
as soon as ~하자마자, ~하는 한
unless 주어 + 동사 만약 ~이 아니라면, ~하지 않는다면
whereas 반면에

정답 (B)

6.

해설 〈주어 + 동사〉로 이루어진 두 개의 문장이 있으므로, 일단 전치사 (D) In spite of(~에도 불구하고)가 먼저 탈락한다. (A) That은 관계대명사 또는 명사절을 이끄는 접속사로 역시 구조적으로 올 수 없다. '상반된 양보의 의미'의 해석이 필요하므로 (C) Even though(비록 ~에도 불구하고)가 정답이다.

해설 이자율이 매우 낮은데도 불구하고, 주택 융자를 신청하는 사람들은 더 적다.

어휘 interest rates 이자율   highly 매우, 상당히
low 낮은, 부족한   fewer 더 적은
apply for ~를 신청하다, ~에 지원하다   loan 대출; ~에게 돈을 빌려주다
whether 주어 + 동사 or not ~인지 아닌지, ~할지 말지

정답 (C)

7.

해설 구조적으로 '-------- the price is fully refunded'가 문장의 주어 역할을 해야 한다. 빈칸은 문장을 명사로 만드는 명사절 접속사의 자리이므로 부사절 접속사 (C) Once, (D) Although는 올 수 없다. 따라서 뒤에 완전한 문장을 수반하여 명사절을 이끄는 (A) That이 정답이다.

해설 소비자들이 상품에 만족하지 않으면, 완전히 환불을 해주는 것이 우리의 정책이다.

어휘 price 가격, 시세; ~에 값을 매기다, ~에 가격을 붙이다 fully 완전히
refund 환불, 환불금; ~를 환불하다 policy 정책, 증권
be satisfied with ~에 만족하다 goods 상품 once 한때, 한번

정답 (A)

8.
해설 동사 determine의 목적어 역할을 하면서, to부정사와 연결이 되어야 한다. 일단, (A) While(~동안에), (C) That(~것) 모두 to부정사를 연결할 수 없다. (D) What은 to부정사는 올 수 있지만, or not과 연결이 불가능하다. 따라서 (B) Whether가 정답이다.

해석 에리카는 고속도로를 건설하는 프로젝트를 맡을지 아닐지 결정해야만 한다.

어휘 determine ~를 결정하다 assume ~를 떠맡다, ~를 가정하다
project 프로젝트, 과제 highway 고속도로

정답 (B)

9.
해설 동사 describes의 목적어 역할을 하는 명사절 접속사를 고르는 문제이다. 빈칸 다음은 동사 know의 목적어가 없는 불완전한 문장이므로, 완전한 문장을 이끄는 (C) that과 (D) whether 모두 탈락된다. 따라서 불완전한 문장을 이끄는 (B) what이 정답이다.

해석 오리엔테이션 책자는 신입생들이 학교 정책과 규정에 관하여 알아야 할 필요가 있는 것을 설명합니다.

어휘 orientation 오리엔테이션, 예비교육 handbook 안내서
describe ~를 설명하다 freshman 신입생
need to부정사 ~할 필요가 있다 regarding ~에 관하여
regulation 규정

정답 (B)

10.
해설 동사 withdraw(~를 인출하다)를 뒤에서 꾸며주는 부사를 고르는 문제이다. (A) especially, (C) recently, (D) easily 모두 의미적으로 어울리지 않는다. 따라서 'withdraw all deposits immediately(모든 예금을 즉시 인출하다)'라는 표현을 만드는 (B) immediately가 정답이다.

해석 만약 30,000명 이상의 사람들이 모든 예금을 즉시 인출한다면, 그 금융사는 곧 파산할 것이다.

어휘 over ~이상 withdraw ~를 인출하다, ~를 철회하다
deposit 보증금, 공탁금 financial 재정적인 company 회사
go bankrupt 파산하다 soon 곧, 머지않아 (= in the near future)
especially 특히 immediately 즉시, 곧
recently 최근에 (= lately) easily 쉽게

정답 (B)

11.
해설 부사 ever를 앞에서 꾸며주는 알맞은 부사를 고르는 문제이다. '폴라로이드 사진은 지금은 거의 사용되지 않는다'는 문맥이 와야 앞뒤 문장의 연결이 가능하다. 따라서 부정어(hardly, seldom, rarely 등) + ever(거의, 전혀 ~ 않다)의 표현을 이루는 (C) hardly가 정답이다.

해설 폴라로이드 사진은 지금 거의 사용되지 않으며, 그것을 사용할 수 있는 카메라는 우리 상점에는 없습니다.

어휘 within ~이내에 mainly 주로 (= largely) hardly 거의 ~아니다
closely 면밀하게, 밀접하게

정답 (C)

12.
해설 빈칸은 be동사와 p.p. 사이에 들어가는 알맞은 부사를 고르는 문제이다. 문맥상 '노력과 전문기술과 밀접하게 연결되어 있다'라는 표현이 와야 앞뒤 문장의 연결이 가능하다. 따라서 (D) closely가 정답이다.

해설 성공한 기업가로서의 그의 성취는 노력과 전문기술과 밀접하게 연결되어 있다.

어휘 development 개발, 성장 as ~처럼, ~로서
successful 성공적인 entrepreneur 사업가
connect with ~과 연결되다, ~와 관련되다 efforts 노력, 수고
expertise 전문지식, 전문기술 softly 부드럽게 properly 적절하게
soon 곧, 머지않아 (= in the near future) closely 면밀하게, 밀접하게

정답 (D)

13.
해설 빈칸 뒤의 형용사 effective(효과적인)를 꾸며주는 부사를 고르는 문제이다. '실적을 향상시키는 데 효과적이다'라는 의미가 적합하므로, (A) extremely(대단히)가 정답이다.

해설 서비스 훈련은 직원들이 자신의 실적을 향상하는 것을 보장하는 데 대단히 효과적이다.

어휘 service training 서비스 교육 effective in ~에 있어 효과적인
ensure ~를 보장하다 improve 나아지다, 개선되다, ~를 개선시키다
performance 실적, 공연, 성능 extremely 극도로, 대단히
carefully 주의 깊게, 신중하게 previously 이전에
approximately 대략 (= about, roughly, around)

정답 (A)

14.
해설 동사구 should be examined(검토되어야 한다)를 뒤에서 수식하는 부사를 고르는 문제이다. '신중하게'라는 의미가 문맥상 가장 적합하므로, (B) carefully가 정답이다.

해설 신제품 광고는 전국적으로 방송되기 전에 신중하게 검토되어야 한다.

어휘 advertisement 광고 new product 신제품
examine 검토하다 before ~전에 (= ahead of, in advance of)
broadcast 방송; 방송하다 nationally 전국적으로
lately 최근에 (= recently) carefully 신중하게
possibly 어쩌면, 아마 extremely 대단히, 극도로

정답 (B)

15-18

〈자전거를 타는 사람들〉 잡지 – 매달 전문적인 자전거 주행 조언 제공

친애하는 독자 여러분.

저희는 독자들에게 더 나은 서비스를 제공하기 위해서, 잡지의 내용과 배치에 관한 간단한 설문을 실시하는 중입니다. 〈자전거를 타는 사람들〉은 설문조사의 독자정보를 외부 회사와 공유하지 않기 때문에, 설문을 작성한 독자들은 어떠한 우편 목록에도 있지 않을 것입니다.

설문에 참여하려면, www.bicycle-rider.com/survey로 가세요, 그리고 8가지 질문에 답변하세요. 모든 작성된 설문지는 자동적으로 투표에 적용될 것입니다. 당첨자는 연례 특별판 잡지 〈위대한 자전거 여행〉과 함께 〈자전거를 타는 사람들〉 잡지 1년 무료 구독권을 받을 것입니다.

어휘 serve ~을 제공하다, 접대하다, 일하다
conduct 행동, 규칙; ~를 실시하다, 실행하다
complete 완전한, 완성된; ~를 끝마치다, ~을 완료하다
brief 잠시 동안의, 간략한
survey 조사, 투표; ~를 조사하다, ~를 검토하다
place ~를 두다, ~를 배치하다 content 내용, 내용물
share ~을 공유하다 participate in ~에 참석하다 (= attend)
answer 응답하다 drawing 추첨 receive ~를 받다
subscription 구독, 구독료 along with ~를 가진, ~와 함께
issue 호, 판

15.
해설 빈칸 다음에 명사가 있으므로, 접속사 (B) that(~것)과 (D) as though(마치 ~인 것처럼)는 올 수 없다. 보기의 전치사 중에서 선택해야 하는데, '잡지의 내용과 배치에 관하여'라는 의미가 필요하므로 (A) regarding(~에 관하여)이 정답이 된다.

정답 (A)

16.
해설 알맞은 접속사를 선택하여 문맥을 고르는 문제이다. 일단, (C) nor(또한 ~아니다)는 not의 의미를 포함하고 있으므로, 그 뒤의 문장에 부정어가 올 수 없다. '독자정보를 외부회사와 공유하지 않아서, ~는 우편목록에 없다'는 내용으로 미루어 보면, '이유'를 뜻하는 (B) as (~ 때문에)가 정답이다.

정답 (B)

17.
(A) 우리는 자전거를 모든 자전거타는 사람에게 무료로 배송할 것입니다.
(B) 점차, 해외 회사들이 리스트에 관심을 가지고 있습니다.
(C) 모든 작성된 설문지는 자동적으로 투표에 적용될 것입니다.
(D) 다른 한편으로는 귀하는 설문지에서 어떠한 실수도 찾아볼 수 없습니다.

해설 문맥에 맞는 문장을 고르는 문제이다. 빈칸 앞의 문장에서 사이트에 들어가서 설문에 응해달라고 요청을 하고 있으므로 이후 자연스러운 표현은 설문에 대한 내용이 언급된 (C)가 정답이 된다.

정답 (C)

18.
해설 문맥에 맞는 명사를 고르는 문제이다. 해석상 '잡지 일년 구독을 받을 것이다'가 자연스러우므로 (C)가 정답이다.

정답 (C)

UNIT 11 접속사 (2)

Check-up Step 1 본책 _ p. 273

1.
해설 빈칸은 문장을 연결하는 접속사의 자리이다. 하지만 등위접속사는 문두에 사용되지 않기 때문에 (A) And는 바로 탈락된다. 따라서 '만약 ~라면'이라는 의미의 부사절 접속사 (B) If가 정답이다.

해석 만약 질문이 있다면, 나에게 즉시 말하세요.

어휘 question 문제, 질문 immediately 곧, 즉시 (= soon)

정답 (B)

2.
해설 빈칸 뒤에 〈주어 + 동사〉로 이루어진 두 개의 문장이 있다. 즉, 빈칸은 접속사의 자리이므로, 전치사인 (B) In the event of는 바로 탈락된다. 따라서 접속사 (A) In case that(~할 경우에)가 정답이 된다.

해석 그것이 적절하게 작동하지 않는 경우에, 당신은 그것을 우리에게 가져와야 한다.

어휘 work 일하다, 작동하다 properly 적절하게
bring ~을 가져오다, ~를 데려오다 in case that ~할 경우에
in the event of ~할 경우에

정답 (A)

3.

해설 빈칸 앞뒤에 〈주어+동사〉로 이루어진 두 개의 문장이 있다. 즉, 빈칸은 접속사의 자리이므로, 전치사인 (A) without(~없이)은 바로 탈락된다. 따라서 접속사 (B) unless(~하지 않으면)가 정답이 된다.

해석 비용보고서를 제출하지 않으면, 직원들은 변제를 받을 수 없다.

어휘 employee 직원 reimbursement 변제, 상환
submit ~를 제출하다, ~를 제안하다 expense 비용, 지출
report 보고서; ~에게 알리다, 보도하다 without ~없이
unless ~하지 않으면 (= if ~ not)

정답 (B)

Check-up Step 2 본책 _ p. 273

4.

해설 빈칸 앞뒤에 〈주어+동사〉로 이루어진 두 개의 문장이 있다. 즉, 빈칸은 접속사의 자리이므로, 전치사인 (A) due to와 to부정사를 수반하는 (C) in order to 모두 탈락된다. 나머지 보기 중에서 '~하기만 하면'이라는 조건의 부사절 접속사 (D) provided that이 정답이다.

해석 지역 관리자들은 판매목표를 달성한다면, 상당량의 상여금을 받을 수 있다.

해석 regional 지역의 manager 관리자, 매니저
receive ~를 받다, (치료, 대우 따위)를 받다 considerable 상당한
bonus 상여금 reach ~에 도달하다 sales 영업, 판매 goal 목표
due to ~때문에 as if 마치 ~인양 in order to ~하기 위해서
provided that ~하기만 하면

정답 (D)

5.

해설 빈칸 다음에는 〈주어+동사〉로 이루어진 완벽한 절이 사용되고 있다. 따라서 접속사를 선택해야 하는 문제인데 보기 중 유일한 접속사인 (D) only if(오직 ~일 경우에만)가 정답이다. (A) except는 전치사로 '~를 제외하고'라는 뜻으로 except for의 형태로도 가능하다. in case of(~일 경우에 대비하여)는 전치사이며, of대신 that절이 사용되면 접속사로서 〈in case that 주어+동사〉로도 활용 가능하다.

해석 저희는 오직 30일 내로 반환될 경우에만 손상된 컴퓨터 소프트웨어에 대한 환불을 해드릴 것입니다.

해석 issue ~을 발행하다 within (시간·장소) 내에서 except ~을 제외하고 in case of ~일 경우에 대비하여
despite ~에도 불구하고

정답 (D)

Check-up Step 1 본책 _ p. 275

1.

해설 빈칸 앞뒤에 〈주어+동사〉로 이루어진 두 개의 문장이 있다. 즉, 빈칸은 접속사의 자리이므로, to부정사인 (B) in order to는 바로 탈락된다. 따라서 접속사 (A) so that(~하기 위해서)이 정답이 된다.

해석 그는 마감시간을 맞추기 위해서, 초과근무를 했다.

어휘 work 일; 일하다 overtime 초과근무 meet ~를 충족시키다
deadline 기한, 마감시간

정답 (A)

2.

해설 빈칸 앞뒤에 〈주어+동사〉로 이루어진 두 개의 문장이 있다. 즉, 빈칸은 접속사의 자리이므로, 전치사인 (B) because of는 바로 탈락된다. 따라서 '그래서'라는 의미의 접속사 (A) so가 정답이 된다.

해석 우리는 충분한 자금을 얻을 수 없어서, 그 프로젝트를 포기해야만 했다.

어휘 be unable to부정사 ~할 수 없다 funding 자금, 자금지원
give up ~를 포기하다 project 프로젝트, 과제

정답 (A)

3.

해설 빈칸은 부사 much를 수식하는 동시에, 그 뒤의 접속사 that과 어울리는 어휘의 자리이다. 일단, 뒤에 명사를 동반하는 (A) such는 탈락된다. 따라서 부사 much를 수식하면서, 결과의 의미를 나타내는 that절을 수반하는 (B) so가 정답이다.

해석 당신에게 너무 많이 감사해서, 나는 당신에게 뭔가를 드리고 싶습니다.

어휘 would like to ~하고 싶다

정답 (B)

Check-up Step 2 본책 _ p. 275

4.

해설 빈칸은 〈관사+형용사+명사〉로 이루어진 명사구 a big car를 꾸미는 어휘의 자리이다. 정답은 (C) such이며, 〈such+명사+that+주어+동사(그처럼 ~해서 ~하다)〉라는 접속사 구문을 이끌고 있다.

해석 이것은 8명의 성인들을 상당히 편안하게 수용할 수 있는 그런 대형차입니다.

어휘 accommodate ~를 수용하다, ~에 편의를 주다 adult 성인
comfortably 편안하게 so 그래서, 그러므로; 매우
such 그처럼, 그러한 such ~ that 주어+동사 그처럼 ~해서 ~하다

정답 (C)

5.

해설 전체적인 구조를 볼 때 두 문장이 사용되었고, 문장을 서로 연결해줄 접속사가 없으므로 빈칸에 알맞은 형태의 접속사를 선택해야한다. 보기에서 접속사 기능을 하는 것은 (A) that밖에 없으므로 정답은 (A)가 된다. 빈칸 앞에 있는 in order 때문에 (B) to로 오답을 고르는 학생들이 많은데 in order to(~하기 위해서)는 to부정사 뒤에 꼭 동사원형이 나와야 한다. 또한 in order that(~하기 위해서)은 접속사 표현으로 암기해두자.

해석 우리가 가장 최근의 문제점들을 논의할 수 있도록 우리는 곧 회의를 개최할 것이다.

어휘 hold ~을 개최하다   soon 곧   in order that ~하기 위해서
discuss ~을 논의하다   recent 최근의

정답 (A)

Check-up Step 1   본책 _ p. 277

1.

해설 문장을 매끄럽게 연결하는 접속부사를 고르는 문제이다. 앞 문장은 '일자리를 제안받았다'는 의미이고, 빈칸 뒤의 문장은 '거절했다'는 내용이다. 문맥상 '그러나'를 의미하는 (A) However가 정답이다.

해석 그 회사는 나에게 일자리를 제안했다. 그러나 나는 그것을 받아들이지 않았다.

어휘 offer ~를 제안하다   position 직위, 위치, 일자리
accept ~를 받아들이다   however 그러나
moreover 더욱이, 게다가

정답 (A)

2.

해설 빈칸 앞뒤로 〈주어 + 동사〉로 이루어진 두 개의 문장만 보고, 접속사 (B) so that을 선택하면 틀리게 된다. 빈칸 앞에 세미콜론(;)이 있으므로 접속사가 들어갈 자리가 아니다. 따라서 부사인 (A) therefore가 정답이다.

해석 그 제품은 손상이 되었다. 그러므로 나는 바로 환불을 원한다.

어휘 damaged 손상된   refund 환불; ~를 환불해 주다
therefore 그러므로

정답 (A)

3.

해설 빈칸 앞에 마침표(.)가 있으므로, 빈칸은 접속사 (A) Before가 들어갈 자리가 아니다. 따라서 접속부사 (B) Otherwise(그렇지 않으면)가 정답이다.

해석 당신은 흡연하는 것을 그만두어야 한다. 그렇지 않으면, 당신의 건강을 잃게 될 것이다.

어휘 quit ~를 그만두다   smoking 흡연   lose ~를 잃다   health 건강
before ~전에   otherwise 그렇지 않으면

정답 (B)

Check-up Step 2   본책 _ p. 277

4.

해설 알맞은 접속부사를 고르는 문제이다. '좋은 조건의 급여를 주다'는 앞 문장과 '폭넓은 복리후생을 제공한다'는 뒤 문장을 의미적으로 고려해야 한다. 문맥을 매끄럽게 연결하는 (C) in addition(게다가)이 정답이다.

해석 매그너코어 사는 매우 좋은 조건의 급여를 준다. 게다가 그 회사는 폭넓은 복리후생도 제공한다.

어휘 competitive 경쟁력 있는   salary 월급, 급여
offer 제공; ~를 제공하다   comprehensive 종합적인, 폭넓은
benefit 혜택, 복리후생

정답 (C)

5.

해설 빈칸 앞뒤 문장을 연결할 알맞은 어휘를 고르는 문제인데 빈칸 앞에 세미콜론(;)이 이미 접속사 역할을 하므로 보기 중 접속사인 (A) but과 (B) although는 정답에서 제외된다. 세미콜론(;)은 접속사의 기능은 없지만 두 문장을 문맥의 흐름상 매끄럽게 연결해주는 접속부사와 주로 사용된다. 따라서 보기 중 유일한 접속부사인 (C) therefore (그러므로)가 정답이 된다. therefore는 '결과'를 의미하는 접속부사이며 (D) according은 accordingly(따라서)로 바뀔 경우 therefore와 동의어가 된다.

해석 지금까지 진행이 매우 잘되고 있습니다. 그러므로 저희는 그 업무가 제시간에 완료되길 바랍니다.

어휘 progress 진전, 진척; 진행하다   so far 지금까지
complete 완전한; ~을 완료하다   on time 정시에, 정각에

정답 (C)

Check-up Step 1   본책 _ p. 279

1.

해설 빈칸 앞뒤로 as ~ as 원급 비교구문이 형성되어 있으므로, 문장의 동사만 확인하면 된다. 따라서 빈칸에는 be동사 is의 보어인 형용사 (A) reliable(믿을만한)이 들어가야 한다.

해석 그 새로운 시스템은 오래된 것만큼이나 믿을만하다.

어휘 system 시스템, 체계   reliable 믿을만한   reliably 믿을만하게

정답 (A)

2.

해설 (B) that은 지시대명사로 a higher salary와 복합명사를 만들 수 없다. 따라서 비교급 형용사 higher와 하나의 표현을 이루는 전치사 (A) than(~보다)이 정답이다.

해석 그는 지금보다 더 높은 급여를 받을 것이다.

정답 (A)

3.

해설 빈칸 뒤의 형용사 qualified와 어울리는 표현을 골라야 한다. 문두의 of all the applicants(모든 신청자들 중에서는)는 최상급의 힌트이므로, 최상급에 사용되는 (B) the most가 정답이다.

해석 모든 지원자들 중에서, 그가 최고의 자격을 갖추었다.

어휘 applicant 신청자, 지원자 qualified 자격을 갖춘

정답 (B)

Check-up Step 2   본책 _ p. 279

4.

해설 알맞은 부사 어휘를 선택하는 문제이다. 보기 중에서, 빈칸 앞에 the most efficient model이라는 최상급 표현을 수식하는 부사는 (C) ever(여태껏)만 가능하다.

해석 우리의 새로운 히터가 여태껏 나온 것 중에 가장 효율적인 모델이라는 것을 우리는 보장합니다.

어휘 guarantee 보증; ~을 보장하다   efficient 효율적인

정답 (C)

5.

해설 문맥상 알맞은 부사 어휘를 고르는 문제이며 빈칸 뒤에 수식을 받는 형용사 more(더 많은)가 결정적 힌트가 된다. more는 비교를 나타내는 형용사 / 부사로 사용되는데 보기 중 비교급 표현과 어울리는 것은 (C) even밖에 없다. even은 'much, far, a lot, far'와 같이 형용사나 부사의 비교급을 강조해주는 표현으로 사용되며 이 경우 모두 '훨씬'이라고 해석된다. (A) very와 (B) so 역시 '매우'라는 의미의 강조부사이지만 비교급을 수식하지는 못한다.

해설 그 프로젝트를 제때에 끝내기 위해서, 우리는 훨씬 더 많은 행정적 지원이 필요할 것이다.

어휘 complete ~을 완료하다   on time 정시에, 정각에
administrative 관리상의, 행정상의   support 지원; ~을 지원하다

정답 (C)

Check-up   본책 _ p. 281

1. 정답 behalf
어휘 half 반 / behalf 대신 / on behalf of ~대신에

2. 정답 observance
어휘 observe 준수하다 / observance 준수 / in observance of ~를 준수해서

3. 정답 consideration
어휘 consider 고려하다 / consideration 고려 / take A into consideration A를 고려하다

4. 정답 consistent
어휘 consistent 일치하는 / consistently 연속적으로, 계속적으로

5. 정답 dedicated
어휘 dedication 전념 / dedicated 전념하는 / be dedicated to ~에 전념하다

Part 5&6_ 실전연습 11   본책 _ p. 282-283

1.

해설 빈칸 뒤에 〈주어+동사〉로 이루어진 두 개의 문장이 있다. 즉, 빈칸은 접속사의 자리이므로, 전치사인 (D) In the event of는 탈락한다. 등위접속사 (C) But은 문두에 사용할 수 없다. 나머지 보기 중에서, (B) In case(~인 경우를 대비하여)가 의미적으로 적합하므로 정답이다.

해석 예상치 못한 사건이 발생하는 것을 대비하여, 적어도 의료보험 중 하나는 가입하세요.

어휘 unexpected 예상치 못한   accident 사고
occur (문제점 따위가) 발생하다   obtain ~를 얻다, ~를 획득하다
at least 최소한, 적어도   medical insurance 의료 보험
unless 만약 ~이 아니라면, ~하지 않는다면   in case ~할 경우에
in the event of ~할 경우에

정답 (B)

2.

해설 빈칸 뒤의 명사 apartments(아파트들)를 수식하는 형용사 표현을 골라야 한다. 빈칸 앞에 정관사 the가 있고, 문장의 끝에 in the construction industry(건설업계에서)라는 최상급의 힌트가 있으므로, 최상급에 사용되는 (C) strongest가 정답이다.

해설 카라 사는 혁신적인 공법을 사용하여 건설업계에서 가장 튼튼한 아파트를 만듭니다.

어휘 corporation 기업, 법인   innovative 혁신적인   technology 기술
construction 건축, 건설   industry 산업, 업계   strong 강한
strongly 강하게

정답 (C)

3.

해설 명사 all employees(모든 직원들)와의 관계와 문맥을 모두 따져보아야 하는 전치사 문제이다. 일단, 문장의 처음에 사용하지 않는 (B) Except(~를 제외하여)는 탈락된다. 따라서 '모든 직원들을 대신해서'라는 문맥을 이루는 (D) On behalf of가 정답이다.

해설 우리 직원을 대신해서, 저는 당신이 지난 달 우리에게 베푼 특별한 서비스에 대해 진심으로 감사드립니다.

어휘 sincerely 진심으로   appreciate ~를 감사히 여기다
service 서비스   extend ~를 제공하다, ~를 베풀다
despite ~에도 불구하고   except ~를 제외하여
in addition to ~이외에도   on behalf of ~를 대신하여

정답 (D)

4.
해설 빈칸 앞에 세미콜론(;)이 있으므로 접속사 (B) so that은 들어갈 수 없다. 나머지 접속부사 중에서 선택해야 하는데, 의미적으로 적합한 것은 (D) therefore이다. 왜냐하면 앞 문장은 '수익이 떨어졌다'는 내용이고, 그 뒤의 문장은 '운영비용을 줄이기로 결정했다'는 내용이기 때문이다.

해석 1분기 수익이 떨어졌다. 그래서 이사회는 운영비용을 줄이기로 결정했다.

어휘 quarter 분기   profits 이익금, 수익금
the board of directors 이사회   decide 결심하다
reduce ~를 줄이다, ~를 삭감시키다 (= curtail)
operational costs 유지비, 운영비   in addition 더욱이, 게다가
so that ~하기 위해서   however 그러나   therefore 그러므로

정답 (D)

5.
해설 앞뒤 문장을 연결하는 접속사의 자리이므로, 전치사 (B) in case of와 (D) pending은 일단 탈락한다. (A) what은 앞에 선행사가 없으며, 뒤에 불완전한 문장이 온다. '다르게 통보받지 않았다면, 추가비용이 있다'는 의미이므로, (C) provided that(만약 ~라면)이 정답이다.

해석 우리의 보험에 관하여 다르게 통보받지 않았다면, 추가비용이 있을 겁니다.

어휘 additional 추가적인   fee 요금   be notified ~에게 통보받다
otherwise 그렇지 않다면   about ~에 관해서   insurance 보험
whatever 어떤 ~이든지   in case of ~하면, ~할 경우에 대비해서
provided that ~하기만 하면   pending ~에 따라

정답 (C)

6.
해설 전치사 into와 함께 문맥을 완성하는 명사를 고르는 문제이다. 의미적으로 '최종 결정을 하기 전에 ~를 고려하라'는 내용이 필요하다. 따라서 take A into consideration(A를 고려하다)라는 표현을 완성하는 (B) consideration이 정답이다.

해석 최종 결정을 하기 전에, 우리는 다양한 상품들의 품질과 가격을 고려해야만 합니다.

어휘 make a decision 결정하다   quality 품질   price 가격
various 다양한   care 돌봄, 관리, 관심
take A into care A를 맡기다
take A into consideration A를 고려하다
take A into custody A를 수감하다
take A into one's confidence A에게 ~의 비밀을 털어놓다

정답 (B)

7.
해설 빈칸 뒤의 형용사 important(중요한)와 어울리는 표현을 골라야 한다. 형용사 important 뒤에 than(~보다)은 비교급의 힌트이므로, 비교급에 사용되는 (D) more가 정답이다.

해석 모든 사람들은 제품을 구매하는 데 있어서 가격보다 품질이 더 중요하다는 것을 알고 있다.

어휘 everyone 모든 사람들   know ~를 알다   quality 품질
important 중요한   price 가격   buy ~을 사다, ~을 구매하다
product 제품 (= goods)

정답 (D)

8.
해설 문장을 의미적으로 연결하는 접속부사를 고르는 문제이다. 앞 문장은 '회의에 참석하지 않았다'는 의미이고, 빈칸 뒤의 문장은 '인상적인 발표를 했다'는 내용이다. 문맥상 '그러나, 하지만'을 의미하는 (B) however가 정답이다.

해석 브랜든은 회의에 참석하지 않았지만, 그는 인상적인 발표를 했다.

어휘 participate in 참석하다 (= attend)   conference 회의, 회담
deliver a presentation 발표를 하다   impressive 인상적인
moreover 더욱이, 게다가   however 그러나
additionally 덧붙여, 게다가, 부가적으로   accordingly 그러므로

정답 (B)

9.
해설 be동사의 보어를 고르는 문제로, 전치사 to가 힌트가 된다. (B) about과 (D) willing은 뒤에 to부정사를 수반하므로 답이 될 수 없다. (A) used는 be used to ~ing(~하는 데 익숙하다)라는 표현으로 부적절하다. 따라서 be dedicated to ~ing(~하는 데 전념하다)라는 표현을 이루는 (C) dedicated가 정답이다.

해석 고객 서비스 부서는 신속하고 친절한 서비스를 제공할 것을 약속합니다.

어휘 customer service department 고객 서비스 부서
be used to ~ing ~하는 데 익숙하다
be used to부정사 ~하는 데 사용되다
be about to부정사 지금 막 ~하려고 하다
be dedicated to ~ing ~하는 데 전념하다
be willing to부정사 기꺼이 ~하려고 하다   prompt 신속한, 즉각적인
friendly 친절한

정답 (C)

10.
해설 빈칸은 앞뒤 문장을 연결하는 접속사 자리이므로, 전치사 (A) except는 일단 탈락한다. '퇴근할 때를 제외하고, 단단히 잠가라'라는 의미가 된다. (B) while과 (D) unless가 오게 되면 문맥적으로 부적합하다. 따라서 '~할 때'의 의미로 쓰이는 (C) when이 정답이다.

해석 보석상점에서 퇴근할 때, 직원들은 그곳을 단단히 잠가야 한다.

어휘 keep ~를 유지하다 (= retain) tightly 단단히
keep A locked A를 잠궈 두다 except ~를 제외하고
while ~동안에, 반면에 when ~할 때

정답 (C)

11.
해설 빈칸 앞뒤로 as ~ as 원급 비교구문이 형성되어 있다. 동사 has worked를 뒤에서 수식할 수 있는 부사의 원급이 필요하기 때문에 (A) hardest와 (D) harder는 탈락된다. (C) more hard는 사용할 수 없는 표현이다. 따라서 as hard as(~만큼 열심히 ~한) 표현을 이루는 부사 (B) hard(열심히)가 정답이다.

해석 로널드는 우리 회계부서의 다른 어떤 팀원만큼이나 열심히 일했다.

어휘 work 일하다 any 어떤 other 다른 member 일원, 단원
accounting 회계, 회계학 division 부서

정답 (B)

12.
해설 be동사의 보어를 고르는 문제로, 전치사 with가 힌트가 된다. (B) conscious는 전치사 of, (C) accessible은 전치사 to, (D) different는 전치사 from을 수반한다. 따라서 be consistent with(~와 일치하다, 유사하다)라는 표현을 만드는 (A) consistent가 정답이다.

해석 모든 건축물은 건축법의 세부규정과 품질기준에 일치해야 한다.

어휘 be consistent with ~에 유사하다, 일치하다
be conscious of ~를 인식하다, 깨닫다
be accessible to ~에게 이용될 수 있다
be different from ~와 다르다 specification 세부규정
quality 품질, 자질 standard 규범, 표준

정답 (A)

13.
해설 빈칸은 명사 many people을 꾸며주면서, 그 뒤의 접속사 that과 어울리는 어휘의 자리이다. (B) very와 (D) too는 부사로 many를 수식하지만, 뒤에 접속사를 동반하지 않는다. 따라서 <such+명사+that+주어+동사>의 형태를 만드는 (A) such가 정답이다.

해석 락 콘서트에 많은 사람들이 몰려서, 우리는 그들의 안전에 특히 집중을 했다.

어휘 concert 콘서트, 연주회, 음악회 attract ~를 끌어들이다
focus on ~에 집중하다 (= concentrate on) safety 안전, 안정성
particularly 특히, 특별하게

정답 (A)

14.
해설 빈칸은 접속사의 자리이므로, to부정사인 (A) in order to는 바로 탈락된다. '~를 준비해주면, 탑승절차를 빠르게 진행할 수 있다'는 내용으로 미루어 볼 때, (B) so that(~하기 위해서)이 가장 적합하다.

해석 당신의 여권과 티켓을 항상 준비해주세요, 그러면 우리는 탑승절차를 빠르게 진행할 수 있습니다.

어휘 passport 여권 ticket 표, 승차권 ready 준비된, 미리
at all times 항상, 언제나 speed up 속도를 더 내다
boarding procedures 탑승절차
in order to부정사 ~를 위해서 (= so as to부정사)
so that ~하기 위해서 (= in other that) if 만약 ~하면
provided that ~하기만 하면

정답 (B)

15-18

엑설런트 운송회사

거의 모든 공항과 기차역으로 이동합니다. 또한 편리하고 편안한 운송 서비스를 아침부터 저녁까지 24시간 내내 제공합니다. 결혼식, 은퇴식, 송별회, 리셉션 행사 등 다양한 서비스를 위한 고급차량이 구비되어 있습니다.

전 차량은 냉방장치와 최신의 서라운딩 음향 시스템이 장착되어 있습니다. 24시간 전에 예약하십시오, 예약 시 본 광고를 언급하시면 공항까지 15달러 할인된 가격으로 이동하실 수 있습니다.

지금 바로 342-5885로 전화 주시거나 팩스(342-5886) 또는 이메일(reservevation@etc.com)로 문의하세요.

어휘 offer ~를 제공하다 convenient 편리한 comfortable 편안한
service 서비스 in addition to ~이외에도 (= besides)
beside ~옆에 be equipped with ~을 갖추다
consist of ~로 구성되다 (= be made up of) in advance 미리
mention ~을 언급하다 ride 타고가다, ~를 몰다
discount 할인; ~을 할인하다

15.
해설 주어인 we는 인칭대명사로 의미가 분명하고, 독자성이 강하다. 수식어(분사, 형용사, 전치사)가 올 수 없으므로 전치사 (A) In addition to(~이외에도), 형용사 (C) Additional(추가적인), 전치사 (D) Beside(~옆에) 모두 빈칸에 들어갈 수 없다. 결국, 문장을 완성하는 부사 (B) Also가 정답이다.

정답 (B)

16.
해설 be동사의 보어를 고르는 문제로, 빈칸 뒤의 전치사 with가 힌트가 된다. 일단, (D) consisted는 자동사로 수동태가 불가능하다. (A) capable과 (C) composed는 뒤에 전치사 of를 수반하며, 의미상 어울리지 않는다. 따라서 be equipped with(~로 장착되다)라는 표현을 이루는 (B) equipped가 정답이다.

정답 (B)

17.
(A) 때때로, 시스템이 오래되었다고 말합니다.
(B) 아마도 차량은 심한 교통체증을 일으킬 것입니다.
(C) 모든 차를 완전 무료로 이용할 수 있습니다.
(D) 24시간 전에 예약하십시오.

해설 빈칸 앞의 문장에서 모든 차량이 에어컨과 최신 음향시스템을 갖추고 있다고 언급하고 있고 이어서 차량 예약을 하라고 말하는 것이 자연스러우므로 (D)가 정답이다. (C)가 정답이 아닌 이유는 빈칸 뒤에 할인받을 수 있다고 언급하고 있기 때문에 완전 무료로 차량이용은 할 수가 없다.

정답 (D)

18.
해설 빈칸 다음에 2개의 문장이 있으므로 접속사의 자리이다. 일단, 전치사 (C) Except와 (D) During은 바로 탈락된다. 나머지 보기 중에서 '당신이 이 광고를 언급하면, ~할 수 있다'의 의미이므로 (A) If(만약 ~하면)가 정답이다.

정답 (A)

UNIT 12 관계사

Check-up Step 1 본책 _ p. 285

1.
해설 알맞은 관계사를 선택하여 문장을 완성하는 문제이다. 선행사 the man(그 남자)이 사람을 지칭하므로 (B) which가 바로 탈락된다. 따라서 주격 관계대명사 (A) who가 정답이다.

해석 나는 그림을 훔치는 그 남자를 보았다.

어휘 see ~를 보다 ~를 알아내다   painting 그림   steal ~를 훔치다

정답 (A)

2.
해설 알맞은 관계사를 선택하여 문장을 완성하는 문제이다. 선행사 the ring(그 반지)이 사물을 지칭하므로 (A) whom이 바로 탈락된다. 따라서 목적격 관계대명사 (B) which가 정답이다.

해설 나는 나의 어머니가 남긴 반지를 끼고 있다.

어휘 wear ~를 착용하다   leave ~을 남기다

정답 (B)

3.
해설 알맞은 관계사를 선택하여 문장을 완성하는 문제이다. 선행사 the boy(그 소년)가 사람을 지칭하므로 (B) which가 바로 탈락된다. 따라서 사람, 사물, 동물 선행사 모두 지칭할 수 있는 주격 관계대명사 (A) that이 정답이다.

해설 창문을 깨뜨린 그 소년은 도망쳤다.

어휘 break 깨뜨리다, 고장나다   run away 도망가다

정답 (A)

Check-up Step 2 본책 _ p. 285

4.
해설 빈칸 뒤에 동사 두 개가 있으므로, 빈칸은 접속사의 자리이다. 일단, 대명사 (B) they와 (D) we가 먼저 탈락된다. 선행사는 사람을 지칭하는 our hotel guests(호텔 손님들)이며, 빈칸 뒤에 동사가 바로 있으므로, 주격 관계대명사 (C) who가 정답이다.

해설 룸서비스를 요청한 우리 호텔 손님들은 대략 아침 7시에 그들의 식사를 받을 것이다.

어휘 hotel guest 호텔 손님   request 요청; ~를 요청하다
service 서비스   meal 식사, 음식   around 대략

정답 (C)

5.
해설 알맞은 관계대명사의 격을 선택하는 문제이다. 접속사 기능이 없는 대명사 (B) they가 가장 먼저 제외되며, 빈칸 다음에 주어가 없는 문장이 있으므로 목적격 관계대명사 (D) whom 또한 제외된다. (A) who와 (C) which 중에 정답을 선택해야 하는데 선행사 all electronic goods(모든 전자 제품들)가 사물을 지칭하므로 정답은 (C) which가 된다. 관계대명사는 선행사가 누구냐에 따라 그 형태가 결정되는데 선행사가 사람이면 who나 whom, 사물이나 상태면 which, 둘 다 사용가능한 that이 있다. 꼭 알아두도록 하자.

해설 당신은 해외에서 수입해온 모든 전자제품들에 대한 관세를 지불해야 한다.

어휘 customs duties 관세   electronic goods 전자제품

정답 (C)

Check-up Step 1 본책_ p. 287

1.
- 해설 보기의 관계사 둘 다 사람을 선행사로 받으므로, 관계사의 격만 선택하면 된다. 빈칸 다음에 동사 is가 바로 오므로, 주격 관계대명사 (A) who가 정답이다.
- 해석 나는 의사인 동생이 한 명 있다.
- 정답 (A)

2.
- 해설 선행사가 사물을 지칭하는 some techniques(몇 가지의 기술들)이므로 (A) who가 바로 탈락된다. 따라서 빈칸 뒤의 동사 use의 목적어 역할을 하는 목적격 관계대명사 (B) which가 정답이다.
- 해석 여기에 그들이 사용하는 몇 가지 기술들이 있다.
- 어휘 some 몇몇의, 몇 가지의 technique 기술, 기법 use ~를 이용하다
- 정답 (B)

3.
- 해설 동사를 선택하여 문장을 완성하는 문제인데, 빈칸 앞에 which라는 목적격 관계대명사가 있다. 즉, 빈칸에는 a system을 목적어로 받는 동사가 필요한데, (B) rely on이 가능하다. 원래 rely는 자동사로 뒤에 목적어를 수반할 수 없지만, 전치사 on이 있으면 타동사의 역할을 할 수 있다.
- 해석 우리가 의존할 수 있는 시스템이 필요하다.
- 어휘 rely on ~에 의존하다 (= depend on)
- 정답 (B)

Check-up Step 2 본책_ p. 287

4.
- 해설 빈칸 앞뒤 문장이 완전하기 때문에, 불완전한 문장을 이끄는 (A) who, (B) which, (C) whom 모두 탈락된다. 즉, 주격, 목적격 관계대명사는 주어, 목적어 자리가 비어있어야 한다는 의미이다. 결국 선행사와 어울리고 빈칸 뒤의 명사와 소유관계를 이루는 소유격 관계대명사 (D) whose가 정답이다.
- 해석 회사는 그 분야에서 3년 이상의 경험을 한 사람들을 주로 모집합니다.
- 어휘 usually 보통, 대개 recruit 모집하다 experience 경험, 체험 in the field 그 분야에
- 정답 (D)

5.
- 해설 관계대명사 which의 상황을 고려하여 알맞은 동사 형태를 선택하는 문제다. which는 주어나 목적어가 없는 불완전한 문장을 수반하는데 이미 주어인 we가 있으니 목적어가 없는 불완전한 문장으로 끝이 나야한다. 또한 보기에서 사용된 동사 rely는 자동사로서 반드시 전치사 on과 함께 끝이 나야 올바른 문장이 된다. 위 문제에서는 전치사 뒤에 명사가 없는 불완전한 형태여야 하므로 정답은 (C) rely on(~에 의존하다)이 된다.
- 해석 증가된 보안문제 때문에, 우리는 진심으로 의존할 수 있는 새로운 시스템을 개발해야 한다.
- 어휘 due to ~때문에 concern 걱정, 우려 truly 진심으로
- 정답 (C)

Check-up Step 1 본책_ p. 289

1.
- 해설 빈칸 앞에 have requested라는 동사구가 있고, 그 다음에 동사가 와야 한다면 문장이 삽입되어 있다는 근거이다. 즉, 명사 the items 를 you have requested라는 문장이 뒤에서 꾸며주고 있는 것이다. 따라서 빈칸에는 주어 the items와 어울리는 복수동사 (B) are가 와야 한다.
- 해석 당신이 요청했던 그 상품들은 재고가 없습니다.
- 어휘 item 상품, 항목 request 요청; ~를 요청하다 out of stock 재고가 없는
- 정답 (B)

2.
- 해설 문장의 구조를 보면 주어가 the meeting이고, has been cancelled가 동사이다. 즉, 접속사 없이는 동사 (A) was scheduled는 올 수 없다. 따라서 주격 관계대명사 which와 be동사 was가 동시에 생략되면서 남은 과거분사 (B) scheduled(예정된)가 정답이다.
- 해석 오늘 아침으로 예정된 그 회의는 취소되었다.
- 어휘 meeting 모임, 회의 cancel ~를 취소하다 schedule ~의 일정을 잡다
- 정답 (B)

3.
- 해설 선행사 a service(서비스)가 사물을 지칭하므로, 주격 관계대명사 (A) which와 (B) that 모두 빈칸에 올 수 있다. 하지만 that은 콤마(,) 다음에 사용할 수 없기 때문에 (A) which가 정답이다.
- 해석 그 회사는 매우 독특한 서비스를 제공합니다.
- 어휘 offer 제공; ~를 제공하다 service 서비스 unique 독특한, 유별난
- 정답 (A)

Check-up Step 2 본책 _ p. 289

4.
해설 일단, 빈칸 다음에 동사가 있으므로 (B) whom과 (D) whose는 올 수 없다. 선행사를 employees(직원들)로 보게 되면, 빈칸 뒤의 동사 is와 수일치가 되지 않는다. 결국 이 문제의 선행사는 a memo (메모)가 되므로 사물을 지칭하는 주격 관계대명사 (C) which가 정답이다.

해석 관리자는 새로운 휴가 정책에 관한 메모를 직원들에게 보냈다.

어휘 manager 관리자   vacation 휴가   policy 정책

정답 (C)

5.
해설 전치사 뒤에 있는 빈칸이 문제풀이를 위한 힌트가 되는데 우선 '전치사 + 관계대명사'는 관계대명사의 목적격을 사용한다는 점을 알아야한다. 따라서 주격관계대명사인 (A) who와 소유격 관계대명사인 (D) whose는 정답에서 탈락된다. 정답은 남은 관계대명사인 (B) which와 (C) that 중에 하나인데 기본적으로 that은 전치사 뒤에 쓰여 문장을 수반하는 것이 불가능하므로 정답은 (B) which가 된다. '전치사의 관계대명사'에서 전치사는 관계사 앞에 있어도, 맨 끝에 있어도 상관없지만. 관계사로 that이 사용될 경우 전치사는 항상 맨 끝에 사용되어야 한다.

해석 요청된 서류를 당신의 채용 개시일 전에 보내시기 바랍니다.

어휘 send ~을 보내다   requested 요청된   document 문서, 서류   employment 고용

정답 (B)

Check-up Step 1 본책 _ p. 291

1.
해설 빈칸 뒤의 I want는 동사 want의 목적어가 없는 불완전한 문장이다. 따라서 주격에 사용되는 (A) Who는 탈락된다. 따라서 선행사가 필요없이 명사절을 만들어내는 관계대명사 (B) What(~인 것, ~하는 것)이 정답이다.

해석 내가 원하는 것은 새로운 컴퓨터이다.

정답 (B)

2.
해설 알맞은 관계부사를 고르는 문제이다. 빈칸 앞에 장소를 언급하는 선행사 the restaurant(식당, 음식점)이 있으므로 관계부사 (A) where가 정답이다.

해석 이곳은 우리가 어젯밤에 저녁을 먹었던 식당이다.

어휘 restaurant 식당, 음식점   have dinner 저녁을 먹다

정답 (A)

3.
해설 빈칸 뒤에 완전한 문장이 있으므로, 관계대명사 (A) which는 올 수 없다. 따라서 이유를 언급하는 선행사 several reasons와 함께 사용하는 관계부사 (B) why가 정답이다.

해석 일부 사람들이 충분한 수면을 취하지 못하는 몇 가지 이유들이 있다.

어휘 reason 이유, 근거, 이성

정답 (B)

Check-up Step 2 본책 _ p. 291

4.
해설 적절한 관계부사를 선택하는 문제이다. 빈칸 앞에 the season(계절)이라는 시간을 지칭하는 선행사가 있으므로, 빈칸에는 (D) when이 와야 한다.

해설 12월은 우리가 가장 바쁜 계절입니다. 그래서 우리의 객실 요금이 더 높습니다.

어휘 season 계절   room rate 객실 요금

정답 (D)

5.
해설 빈칸 앞에는 선행사가 없으며 have 동사 뒤에는 목적어가 없으므로 불완전한 문장을 수반하는 관계대명사가 필요하다. 따라서 이런 두가지 특징을 모두 갖는 (B) What이 정답이 된다. 위 문장의 구조를 살펴보면 빈칸에서 in common까지의 문장이 본동사 is의 주어 역할을 하고 있는데, 관계대명사 what은 선행사가 없고 불완전한 문장을 이끄는 명사절을 만든다는 것을 정확히 기억해두자.

해석 두 소프트웨어가 공통으로 갖고 있는 것은 그들이 사용하기 쉬운 그래픽 인터페이스이다.

어휘 in common 공통으로   user-friendly 사용하기 쉬운

정답 (B)

Check-up 본책 _ p. 293

1. 정답 **of**
어휘 be aware of ~을 알다, 인지하다

2. 정답 **supposed**
어휘 suppose 예정하다, 가정하다 / be supposed to부정사 ~하기로 되어 있다

3. 정답 **similar**
어휘 similar 유사한 / be similar to ~와 유사하다 / similarly 유사하게

4. 정답 **capable**
   어휘 capability 능력 / capable 할 수 있는 / be capable of ~을 할 수 있다

5. 정답 **involved**
   어휘 involve 연관시키다 / involved 연관된 / be involved in ~에 연루되다

Part 5&6_ 실전연습 12 본책 _ p. 294-295

1.
해설 빈칸 앞에 선행사가 없다는 점이 가장 큰 힌트가 된다. 즉, 선행사가 필요한 (B) which와 (C) that 모두 탈락된다. 관계부사 (D) where는 장소를 지칭하는 선행사의 생략이 가능하지만, 뒤에 완전한 문장을 수반하므로 올 수 없다. 따라서 이미 선행사를 포함하고 있는 (A) what이 정답이다.

해석 맨하탄은 재무, 문화, 금융회사들을 위해 이상적인 입지를 갖춘 도시이다.

어휘 ideal 이상적인 (= perfect)   location 위치, 장소
financial 금융의, 재정적인   cultural 문화의
banking corporation 금융회사

정답 **(A)**

2.
해설 선행사 the only candidate(유일한 지원자)가 사람을 지칭하므로, (D) which는 올 수 없다. 일단, 빈칸 다음에 동사가 있으므로, 소유격 관계대명사 (C) whose와 목적어의 역할을 하는 (A) whom 모두 탈락된다. 따라서 주격 관계대명사 (B) who가 정답이다.

해석 브리에나는 뛰어난 의사소통 그리고 멀티태스킹 능력을 가진 유일한 지원자이다.

어휘 candidate 후보자   outstanding 뛰어난
communication 의사소통   multitasking 다중 작업
skill 기술, 능력

정답 **(B)**

3.
해설 선행사가 사람을 지칭하는 clients(고객들)이므로 (B) which가 바로 탈락된다. (D) what은 이미 선행사를 포함하고 있으므로 역시 제외된다. 따라서 빈칸에는 provided의 목적어 역할을 하는 목적격 관계대명사 (C) whom이 정답이다.

해석 클레몬스 씨는 며칠 전에 컨설팅 서비스를 제공했던 고객을 우연히 만났다.

어휘 encounter (뜻밖에) 누구와 마주치다, ~에 직면하다   client 고객
provide A with B A에게 B를 주다, 제공하다   consulting 상담의

정답 **(C)**

4.
해설 선행사 regulations(규제들)가 사물을 지칭하므로, (B) who는 바로 탈락된다. 뒤에 완전한 문장을 수반하는 (D) whose 역시 제외된다. 나머지 보기 중에서 (A) that은 콤마(,) 다음에 사용할 수 없기 때문에 (C) which가 정답이다.

해석 박물관의 방문객들은 출입구 벽면에 붙여놓은 규정들을 읽어야 한다.

어휘 museum 박물관   regulations 규제, 규정   post 게시하다
entrance 입구

정답 **(C)**

5.
해설 선행사 The firewall software program(방화벽 소프트웨어 프로그램)이 사물을 지칭하므로, (A) whom과 (C) who 모두 탈락된다. 나머지 보기 중에서, (D) what은 이미 선행사를 포함하고 있으므로 역시 제외된다. 따라서 사람과 사물을 모두 선행사로 취하는 (B) that이 정답이다.

해석 루카스 씨가 개발한 방화벽 소프트웨어 프로그램은 컴퓨터 바이러스가 침범하는 것을 예방한다.

어휘 developed 개발한   prevent 막다, 방지하다   enter ~로 들어가다

정답 **(B)**

6.
해설 (A) what은 이미 선행사를 포함하고 있으므로 바로 탈락된다. 빈칸 다음에 완전한 문장이 오기 때문에, 불완전한 문장을 수반하는 (B) which와 (C) that 모두 제외된다. 따라서 완전한 문장을 수반하며, 장소를 나타내는 관계부사 (D) where가 가장 적절하다.

해석 채용박람회가 개최될 회의장은 기차역 근처 편리한 곳에 위치해 있다.

어휘 conference hall 회의장   job fair 채용박람회
be held 개최되다, 열리다   conveniently 편리하게
be located ~에 위치하다 (= be situated)

정답 **(D)**

7.
해설 빈칸 앞에 선행사가 없고, 뒤에 완전한 문장이 오기 때문에 (A) which, (B) that, (D) what 모두 올 수 없다. 따라서 관계부사 (C) when이 정답이 된다. 참고로 빈칸 앞에는 the time 또는 the season이라는 선행사가 생략되었다고 볼 수 있다.

해석 11월은 고등학생들이 입학시험에 대해 대단히 걱정하는 달이다.

어휘 highly 매우, 대단히   be concerned about ~에 대해서 걱정하다, 염려하다   entrance examination 입학시험

정답 **(C)**

8.

해설 선행사 a musician(음악가)이 사람을 지칭하므로, (C) which는 바로 탈락된다. 빈칸 다음에 〈주어＋동사＋목적어〉의 완전한 문장이 수반되므로, (A) that, (B) who 둘 다 제외된다. 따라서 소유격 관계대명사 (D) whose가 정답이다.

해석 음악으로 좋은 반응을 얻은 뮤지션인 앤젤라 존스는 국제적인 유명인사가 되었다.

어휘 musician 음악가, 뮤지션   work 일, 작품   receive ~를 받다
a good response 좋은 반응   international 국제적인
celebrity 명성

정답 (D)

9.

해설 be동사의 보어를 고르는 문제로, 전치사 of가 힌트가 된다. (A) able, (C) ready는 to부정사, (D) eligible은 전치사 for를 수반하므로 탈락된다. 따라서 전치사 of를 수반하여, be capable of(~을 할 수 있다)라는 표현을 이루는 (B) capable이 정답이다.

해석 회사 내의 모든 직원들은 고객 불만을 공손하면서 빠르게 처리할 수 있습니다.

어휘 be capable of ~을 할 수 있다 (= be able to부정사)
be ready to부정사 ~할 준비가 되어 있다
be eligible for ~할 자격이 있다
deal with ~를 다루다 (= issue, address)   complaint 불평

정답 (B)

10.

해설 be동사의 보어를 고르는 문제로, 부정사 to가 힌트가 된다. (A) aware는 전치사 of, (B) accustomed는 전치사 to를 수반하므로 탈락된다. (D) reluctant(주저하는)도 to부정사를 수반하지만, 의미상 부적합하다. 따라서 be supposed to부정사(~하기로 되어 있다)를 이루는 (C) supposed가 정답이다.

해석 그 피트니스 센터는 트레이너들이 곧 휴가를 가기 때문에 잠시 동안 문을 닫기로 했습니다.

어휘 close 가까운; 가까이에; ~을 닫다, 닫히다   facility 시설
briefly 잠시, 간단히   be aware of ~을 잘 알고 있다
be accustomed to ~하는 데 익숙하다
be supposed to ~하기로 되어 있다
be reluctant to ~하기를 꺼려하다
vacation 방학, 휴가; 휴가를 보내다

정답 (C)

11.

해설 be동사의 보어를 고르는 문제로, 전치사 with가 힌트가 된다. (B) subject는 전치사 to, (C) reflective는 전치사 of를 수반하므로 탈락된다. (A) comparable(필적할 만한)은 의미상 부적절하다. 따라서 be equipped with(~을 장착하다)라는 올바른 표현을 만드는 (D) equipped가 정답이다.

해석 각각의 컴퓨터는 최고급 프로그램들을 다룰 수 있는 그래픽 프로세서를 갖추고 있다.

어휘 be comparable with ~와 필적할만하다, 비슷하다
be subject to ~를 받기 쉽다   be reflective of ~를 반영하다
be equipped with ~을 장착하다

정답 (D)

12.

해설 루카스 씨가 주어이며, has finally received가 동사이므로, 동사 (B) involves는 올 수 없다. involve는 목적어를 취하는 타동사이므로 (B) involves, (D) who involved 둘 다 탈락된다. Mr. Lucas와 in 사이에 '주격관계대명사＋be동사(who was)'가 생략되고, 남은 과거분사 (A) involved가 정답이다.

해석 신제품을 만드는데 참여했던 루카스 씨는 마침내 승진 기회를 얻었다.

어휘 involve ~를 연루시키다, ~를 수반하다   be involved in ~와 관련되다
receive ~를 받다. (치료, 대우 따위를) 받다   promotion 승진
opportunity 기회, 가능성

정답 (A)

13.

해설 (A) what은 이미 선행사를 포함하고 있으므로 제외된다. 빈칸 앞의 선행사 CEO만 보고 (B) who를 선택하면 바로 틀리게 된다. 여기서 선행사는 CEO가 아니라, a recent report(최근의 보고서)이다. 따라서 주격 관계대명사 (C) which가 정답이 된다.

해석 부서장은 CEO에게 광고 전략에 대한 최신 보고서를 제출했습니다.

어휘 department 부서, 국   head 부서장
submit ~를 제출하다, ~를 제안하다
advertising strategy 광고 전략

정답 (C)

14.

해설 be동사의 보어를 고르는 문제로, 부정사 to가 힌트가 된다. (A) similar, (C) accustomed, (D) equal은 전치사 to를 수반한다. 따라서 be entitled to부정사(~에 대한 자격이 있다)라는 알맞은 표현을 만드는 (B) entitled가 정답이다.

해석 정규직원과 비정규직원들 모두 건강보험을 받는 것에 대한 자격이 있다.

어휘 be entitled to부정사 ~에 대한 자격이 있다 (= be eligible for)
be equal to ~와 똑같다, ~와 동등하다
health insurance 건강보험

정답 (B)

15-18

수신: 자쿠브 나돌스키 <chef@jakubkitchen.jp>
발신: 소라 니시무라 <soranishimura@mingroup.jp>
날짜: 9월 3일
제목: 상업용 임대차 계약 갱신

나돌스키 씨께,

오늘 와 주셔서 감사합니다. 당신의 상업용 임대차 계약의 갱신을 논의하는 우리 회의는 매우 생산적이었습니다. 저희는 당신의 사업을 가치 있게 생각하며 우리의 성공적인 관계를 지속하기를 고대합니다. 오늘 오전에 우리가 검토한 갱신 양식 한 부를 첨부했습니다. 여기에는 새 건축 법규를 반영하는 개정된 조항이 포함되어 있습니다. <u>가능한 한 빨리 그것을 재검토해 주시기 바랍니다.</u>

우리의 다음 약속이 9월 8일 화요일에 마루노우치에 있는 저희 사무실에서 있을 예정임을 확인하고자 합니다. 그때 이전에 질문이 있으시면 5322-3359번으로 제게 연락 주시기 바랍니다.

소라 니시무라
소라민 그룹
동봉 서류

어휘 commercial 상업용의   lease 임대차 계약   renewal 갱신
discuss 논의하다   value 가치 있게[소중하게] 생각하다
business 사업   look forward to 고대하다   successful 성공적인
relationship 관계   attach 첨부하다   copy 사본, (서류의) 한 부
form 양식   examine 조사하다, 검토하다   revised 개정된
section 조항, 항목   reflect 반영하다   building codes 건축 법규
confirm 확인하다   appointment 약속   take place 일어나다
enclosure (편지에) 동봉한 것

15.
해설 적절한 어형을 고르는 문제이다. 빈칸 앞에 be동사와 부사 very가 있으므로 빈칸은 be동사의 보어로 부사의 수식을 받는 형용사가 들어갈 자리이다. 따라서 (C) productive가 정답이다.

정답 (C)

16.
해설 관계사를 묻는 문제이다. 빈칸 앞의 section이 선행사이고 사물이기 때문에 빈칸 뒤의 동사 reflects와 연결할 수 있는 관계사로서 (B) which가 가장 어울린다.

정답 (B)

17.
(A) 가능한 한 빨리 그것을 재검토해 주시기 바랍니다.
(B) 3시까지 회의에 도착하십시오.
(C) 임대차 계약은 월말에 만료될 예정입니다.
(D) 그들은 그 건물의 2층에 위치해 있습니다.

해설 문맥에 맞는 문장을 고르는 문제이다. 빈칸 앞 문장 I have attached a copy of the renewal form에서 갱신 양식을 첨부했다고 했으므로 (A)가 정답이다.

정답 (A)

18.
해설 문맥에 맞는 부사를 고르는 문제이다. 빈칸 앞 문장에서 미래의 특정한 시점인 Tuesday, September 8을 언급했으므로 '그때'라는 의미의 (D) then이 정답이다.

정답 (D)

Part 5&6   Review Test   본책_ p. 296-299

1. (C)	2. (B)	3. (C)	4. (D)	5. (B)
6. (C)	7. (A)	8. (D)	9. (A)	10. (C)
11. (C)	12. (A)	13. (D)	14. (D)	15. (B)
16. (C)	17. (D)	18. (C)	19. (A)	20. (B)
21. (C)	22. (A)	23. (B)	24. (A)	25. (A)
26. (A)	27. (D)	28. (A)		

1.
해설 알맞은 대명사의 격을 선택하는 문제로 매 회 두 문제 가량 출제되는 유형이다. 빈칸 다음에 proxy votes(대리로 하는 투표)는 '형용사+명사'의 구조이므로 빈칸에는 궁극적으로 명사를 꾸며줄 수 있는 대명사가 들어가야 한다. 명사를 앞에서 수식하는 대명사는 소유격밖에 없으므로 정답은 (C) their가 된다. 그리고 cast a vote(투표를 하다)라는 기본표현을 꼭 기억해 두도록 하자.

해석 주주들은 일반우편 대신에 인터넷을 통해서 그들의 대리투표(위임투표)를 하도록 허락받는다.

어휘 shareholder 주주   be allowed to부정사 ~하도록 허락받다
cast a vote 투표를 하다   a proxy vote 대리 투표
via ~을 통해서   instead of ~ 대신에   regular mail 일반우편

정답 (C)

2.
해설 빈칸 다음에 있는 effect(영향)를 꾸밀 수 있는 알맞은 형용사를 선택하는 문제이다. (A) affordable(저렴한, 가격이 적당한), (C) adjacent(인접한, 근접한), (D) advised(권유 받은)는 모두다 effect와는 상관없는 어휘들이다. 때문에 (B) adverse(부정적인, 불리한, 나쁜)가 유일하게 effect를 꾸미는 어휘로 정답이 된다.

해석 상승하는 원자재 가격이 전체 산업에 부정적인 영향을 끼칠 것이다.

어휘 increasing 상승하는   price 가격   raw material 원자재
be likely to부정사 ~할 것 같다, ~할 가능성이 있다
have an effect on ~에 대한 영향을 끼치다, 갖다
adverse effect 부정적인 영향   entire 전체의   industry 산업

정답 (B)

3.
해설 어휘의 올바른 형태를 결정하는 문제이며, 빈칸 앞에 있는 전치사 in이 커다란 힌트가 된다. 전치사 다음에는 목적어로 명사나 동명사가 수반되기 때문에 보기 중에서 일단 명사인 (A) promotion(촉진, 승진)과 동명사인 (C) promoting(~를 촉진시키는 것)이 후보가 된다. 명사와 동명사 중에서 선택의 기준이 되는 것 중의 하나가 바로 뒤에 또 다른 명사 목적어의 유무이다. 뒤에 명사를 목적어로 수반할 수 있는 것은 명사가 아니라 동사의 성격을 유지하는 동명사이므로, 이 문제에서는 its image를 수반할 수 있는 동명사 (C) promoting이 정답이다. 그리고 and 다음에 있는 동명사 maximizing과 병치를 이루고 있다는 것도 구조적인 힌트가 된다.

해석 그 회사는 자신의 이미지를 홍보하는 것과 잠재 고객들에게 제품 노출을 극대화시키는 것에도 매우 적극적이다.

어휘 be active in ~ing ~하는 데 적극적이다
maximize exposure of ~의 노출을 극대화시키다
potential customer 잠재 고객

정답 (C)

4.
해설 알맞은 전치사 어휘를 선택하여 빈칸 다음에 있는 명사 advance와 더불어 하나의 관용구를 만들어내는 문제이다. 보기 중에서 가능한 것은 (D)밖에 없으며, in advance는 '미리, 전에'라는 하나의 부사구를 형성한다. 이는 부사 ahead(미리, 앞서서)와 동일한 표현이며, 뒤에 of를 수반할 경우 하나의 전치사 덩어리 표현 in advance of 명사(= ahead of 명사 = before 명사 = prior to 명사:~전에)가 된다는 것도 알아두자.

해석 여름 시즌 동안에 모든 직원들은 반드시 적어도 2주 전에 그들의 휴가 스케줄을 부서장에게 통보해야 한다.

어휘 notify A of B A에게 B를 통보하다   department head 부서장
at least 적어도, 최소한   in advance 미리, 앞서서 (= ahead)

정답 (D)

5.
해설 빈칸 다음에 있는 명사 cash(돈, 현찰)를 앞에서 꾸며줄 수 있는 알맞은 형용사 어휘를 선택하는 문제이다. 문장 전체적인 의미와 상관없이 단순히 cash를 꾸밀 수 있는 어휘가 (B) surplus(남는, 잉여의)밖에 없으므로 정답이 된다. surplus는 이 문제에서는 형용사이지만, 명사로 '남는 것, 흑자'라는 의미 또한 알아두어야 한다. 참고로 복합명사 trade surplus(무역 흑자)라는 표현을 기억해두자.

해석 지방정부는 정말로 필요한 사람들을 돕기 위해서 남는 돈을 사용해야 한다.

어휘 the local government 지방정부   surplus cash 남는 돈
people who really need it 그것을 정말로 필요로 하는 사람들

정답 (B)

6.
해설 알맞은 동사의 형태를 결정하는 문제인데, 문장 전체의 구조를 보고 쉽게 판단할 수 있다. 전체적으로는 if라는 접속사로 시작을 했으므로 〈주어+동사〉의 성분을 갖춘 문장이 두 번 나와야 하는데, 한 문장이 완성된 후에 두 번째 문장의 주어가 없다. 게다가 please라는 어휘는 명령문을 공손한 표현으로 만들 때 문두에 잘 사용되기 때문에 뒷 문장 자체가 명령문임을 알 수가 있다. 명령문은 동사의 원형으로 시작하기 때문에 정답은 (C) forward(~를 발송하다, 보내다)가 되며, 〈if 주어+동사, please+동사(만약 ~한다면, ~해주십시오)〉라는 조건문의 구조가 보여야 한다.

해석 만약에 당신이 어떤 문제점들을 직면하게 되면, 우리의 직원들 중 한 명에게 모든 관련 정보를 발송해주십시오.

어휘 encounter problems 문제점들에 직면하다
forward A to B A를 B에게 발송하다
relevant information 관련된 정보

정답 (C)

7.
해설 빈칸 앞에 있는 형용사 new의 수식을 받으면서 문장 전체적인 의미에 부합하는 명사 어휘를 선택하는 문제이다. 여기서 정답을 결정할 수 있는 힌트는 new라는 형용사라기보다는 are being developed(개발되고 있는 중이다)라는 동사의 의미와 그 뒤쪽에 있는 to 이하의 내용이다. '조립라인을 좀더 효율적으로 운영하도록 하기 위해서'라는 의미와 맞는 것은 new techniques(새로운 기술들)이며, develop a technique(기술을 개발하다)이라는 능동태 표현에도 부합한다. 따라서 정답은 (A) techniques가 되는데, 나머지 보기들 또한 동사 'are being developed'와는 결합이 가능하긴 하지만 뒤쪽의 문맥과 맞지 않아서 탈락이 된다.

해석 새로운 기술들이 조립라인을 더욱 효율적으로 운영하도록 하기 위해서 개발되고 있는 중이다.

어휘 make the assembly line operate efficiently 조립라인을 효율적으로 운영하도록 하다

정답 (A)

8.
해설 빈칸 앞뒤로 형성된 is entirely booked(완전히 예약되다)를 사이에서 꾸며주면서 문맥 전체에 맞는 부사어휘를 선택해야 한다. 일단 (A) well(잘, 훨씬)은 booked를 꾸며줄 수는 있지만 의미적으로 entirely(완전히)와 나란히 사용하기가 어려우므로 탈락이 되고, (B) soon(곧)은 이 문장에 쓰인 현재시제가 아니라 미래시제와 어울린다. 즉, will soon be entirely booked(곧 완전히 예약될 것이다)가 되면 가능하다. 하지만 그렇게 고치더라도 but 이하의 뒷 문장과 어울릴 수 없으므로 탈락이 된다. (C) ever(여태껏)는 일반 평서문에 사용되는 어휘가 아니라, 최상급이나 부정어 강조, 현재완료 의문문 등에서 사용되는 어휘이므로 역시 제거된다. 따라서 정답은 (D) already(벌써, 이미)가 된다.

162

해석 그 호텔은 주말 동안에 이미 완전히 예약되었지만, 몇 개의 방들은 하룻밤에 295달러로 신혼부부 손님들을 위해서 유보되어 있다.

어휘 be already entirely booked 이미 완전히 예약되다
on hold 유보된, 멈춘 상태로   wedding guest 신혼부부

정답 (D)

9.

해설 빈칸 다음에 있는 명사 downturn(불황)을 앞에서 꾸며줄 수 있는 올바른 어휘 형태를 결정하는 문제인데, 명사는 형용사가 꾸며줄 수 있으므로 (A) economic(경제의)과 (B) economical(절약적인)이 후보가 될 수 있다. 그리고 복합명사가 가능하다면 (D) economy(경제) 또한 가능하다. 이 중에서 일단 (B) economical은 '돈을 아끼는, 절약적인'이라는 뜻이므로 downturn과 그 의미가 가장 멀다. 그리고 '경제 불황'이라는 복합명사가 존재하지 않으므로 정답은 일반 형용사인 (A) economic이 된다. '복합명사'인가 '형용사 + 명사'인가를 결정하는 것은 문법적인 개념이 아니라 표현적인 문제일 뿐이므로, 수험생의 입장에서는 암기가 최선책일 수밖에 없다.

해석 전국적으로 저축은행들이 최근의 경제 불황으로부터 회복되기 시작했다.

어휘 savings bank 저축은행   throughout the country 전국적으로
recover from ~로부터 회복하다   economic downturn 경제 불황

정답 (A)

10.

해설 알맞은 동사 어휘를 선택하여 문맥을 완성시키는 문제이다. 하지만 문장 전체의 의미를 보지 않아도 빈칸 다음에 있는 목적어 the life of 명사(~의 수명, 생명)와의 관계로 찾을 수 있다. (A) survive는 기본적으로 '생존하다'라는 자동사이고 타동사일 경우 '~를 극복해내다'라는 의미로 survive the plane crash(비행기 사고에서 살아남다)라는 식으로 사용되고, (B) endure(~를 견뎌내다)도 endure pain(고통을 견디다)의 형태로 사용되므로 탈락이 된다. (D) enlarge는 '~를 확장하다'라는 의미이므로 the life와는 어울리지 않는다. 결국 정답은 (C) prolong(~를 연장하다)인데, 거의 the life를 목적어로 수반하여 사용되므로 하나의 덩어리 표현으로 prolong the life of 명사(~의 수명을 연장시키다)를 암기해두는 편이 좋다.

해석 규칙적으로 당신의 신발을 닦는 것은 신발의 수명을 연장시키기 위해서 당신이 해야 하는 하나의 과정이다.

어휘 shine one's shoes ~의 신발을 닦다
on a regular basis 규칙적으로
perform a process 과정을 수행하다   in order to부정사 ~하기 위해서   prolong the life of 명사 ~의 수명을 연장하다

정답 (C)

11.

해설 빈칸 다음에 있는 five hours(5시간)를 앞에서 수식해 줄 수 있는 부사 어휘를 선택하는 문제이다. five hours에서 five를 구체적으로 따지면 '숫자 수사'가 된다. '수사'는 '수량 형용사'도 되고 '수량 명사'도 되는데 여기서는 hours라는 명사를 앞에서 꾸미고 있으므로 형용사적인 개념이 된다. 이러한 '수사'를 앞에서 꾸미는 부사들은 특정 어휘들로 정해져 있다. '대략'이라는 의미의 어휘들이 거기에 포함되는데 보기 중에서는 바로 (C) approximately(대략)가 대표적인 어휘이다. approximately의 동의어인 around = about = roughly(대략)가 모두 다 '숫자 수사'를 앞에서 꾸밀 수 있고, 이 밖에도 정도를 나타내는 almost = nearly(거의) 또한 숫자를 앞에서 잘 꾸민다.

해석 여행사 직원이 우리들에게 말하기를 디트로이트부터 휴스턴까지의 비행 시간이 대략 5시간 걸린다고 했다.

어휘 tell A that 주어 + 동사 A에게 ~를 말하다
the flight from A to B A부터 B까지 가는 비행기
take + 시간 ~시간만큼 걸리다
approximately 대략 (= around, about, roughly)

정답 (C)

12.

해설 알맞은 품사를 결정하고나서 의미를 따져보는 문제이다. 문장 전체적으로 〈주어 + 동사〉가 두 번 연결되는 구조이므로 빈칸에는 일단 접속사가 필요하다. 따라서 전치사인 (C) Despite와 (D) During이 가장 먼저 탈락이 되고, (A) Although와 (B) Until 중에서 선택을 해야 한다. (B) Until은 전치사와 접속사가 동시에 가능한 어휘이므로 후보가 될 수 있다. 하지만 두 문장의 의미를 비교해 보면 빈칸에 시간적인 개념의 어휘가 필요한 것이 아니라 상반되는 의미가 필요하므로 양보의 접속사 (A) Although가 정답이 된다.

해석 현지의 영업사원들이 여전히 그 주문을 받고 있긴 하지만, 그 물건의 생산은 가까운 미래에 중단될 것이다.

어휘 although 비록 ~하지만
the local sales representatives 현지의 영업사원들
accept the order 주문을 받다   production 생산   item 제품
end 중단되다   in the near future 가까운 미래에

정답 (A)

13.

해설 알맞은 형태의 어휘를 선택해서 문장을 완성하는 문제인데, 기본적으로 문장의 뼈대가 되는 동사가 이미 are라는 be동사로 존재하고 있기 때문에 빈칸에는 더 이상의 동사가 들어갈 수 없다. 따라서 동사의 원형인 (A) consult(상담하다)는 무조건 탈락이 된다. 따라서 명사 the ability(능력)를 뒤에서 꾸며줄 수 있는 어휘의 형태가 필요한데, ability라는 명사의 특징은 뒤에 분사의 수식을 받지 않고 to부정사의 수식을 받는다. an ability to부정사(~할 수 있는 능력)라는 형태로 굳어져서 사용되는 것이 이 어휘의 특징이므로 정답은 (D) to consult가 된다.

해설 이 직책의 가장 중요한 판단의 기준은 감정적인 성숙함과 난처해진 사업가들을 상담할 수 있는 능력이다.

어휘 important criteria 중요한 판단의 기준
emotional maturity 감정적인 성숙함 consult with ~와 상담하다
troubled businessman 난처해진 사업가

정답 (D)

14.
해설 알맞은 품사를 결정하는 문제인데, 단순히 빈칸 앞에 있는 be동사 are를 보고 형용사 보어나 분사 보어를 선택해서는 안되는 문제이다. 기본적인 뼈대가 존재를 나타내는 유도부사 there로 시작하고 있으므로 〈there+주어+동사〉가 아닌 〈there+동사+주어〉라는 점을 알아야 한다. 따라서 빈칸에 들어갈 구성요소는 주어가 되는 것이고, 주어가 될 수 있는 품사는 명사이므로 보기 중에서 명사를 찾는 문제이다. (A) value는 '가치'라는 불가산 명사이고 (D) valuables(귀중품)는 복수 형태의 명사인데 동사가 are라는 복수 형태이므로 주어 또한 복수 명사인 (D) valuables가 되야 정답이 된다.

해석 사무실에 귀중품들이 있다면 금고 안에 넣어 보호되도록 해야 한다.

어휘 valuable 귀중품   must be protected 반드시 보호되도록 하다
by ~ing ~함으로써   place A in the safe A를 금고 안에 두다

정답 (D)

15.
해설 보기들이 전부 부정대명사와 형용사이므로 먼저 빈칸에 들어갈 품사를 결정해야 한다. 빈칸 다음에 복합명사인 energy providers(에너지 공급업자들)가 존재하므로, 명사를 꾸밀 수 없는 대명사 (C) others(다른 것들, 다른 사람들)가 가장 먼저 탈락이 된다. 나머지 보기들 중에서 (A) another(또 다른 하나의)는 뒤에 단수명사만을 수반하므로 역시 제거될 수 있다. 따라서 (B) other(다른)와 (D) the other(나머지의) 중에서 선택을 해야 하는데, 문장 속에서 '정해진 범위'가 있는지 없는지에 따라 결정된다. 이 문장에서는 정해진 '범위 안에 있는 나머지 에너지 공급업자들'이 아니라 '일반적인 다른 회사들'을 뜻하는 것이므로 정답은 (B) other가 된다.

해석 몇몇 다른 에너지 공급업자들과 함께 그 지역 전기회사는 소비자 조치에 응답하여 가격을 내리고 있다.

어휘 the local electric company 그 지역 전기회사
along with 명사 ~와 함께, 더불어
several other+복수명사 몇몇 다른 ~들
lower rates 요금을 내리다   in response to 명사 ~에 응답하여
consumer action 소비자 조치

정답 (B)

16.
해설 문장의 구조에 맞는 품사를 먼저 결정을 해야 하는데, 보기에 나온 어휘들을 살펴보면 (A) moreover(일반 부사), (B) therefore(접속부사), (C) because(접속사), (D) however(접속부사)로 이루어져 있다. 빈칸 앞뒤에는 각기 〈주어+동사〉로 구성된 문장이 있으므로 (A) moreover(더욱이)는 그 의미를 떠나서 무조건 탈락이 된다. (B), (C), (D) 중에서 '원인과 이유'를 의미하는 접속사 (C) because가 의미적으로나 용법적으로 가장 적절한 정답이 된다. 참고로 (B) therefore(그러므로)와 (D) however(하지만)는 일반 접속사가 아니라 접속부사이므로 그 앞에 세미콜론(;)이나 콤마(,)의 도움을 받아서 두 문장을 연결시키는 게 기본적인 용법이므로 의미를 떠나서 용법적으로도 적합하지 않다.

해석 새로운 빌딩이 필요하다. 왜냐하면 그 도서관의 장서들이 최근 몇 년 동안 매우 빠르게 증가했기 때문이다.

어휘 be needed 요구되다
the library's collection of books 도서관의 장서
grow 증가하다, 성장하다   in recent years 최근 몇 년 안에

정답 (C)

17.
해설 알맞은 부사 어휘를 선택하여 빈칸 뒤에 있는 분사형 형용사 priced를 꾸며주는 문제이다. priced는 일반형용사가 아니라 분사형 형용사이므로 동사 price의 해석에 맞추어야 하는데, price가 명사일 경우 '가격'이지만, 동사일 경우는 '~에 가격을 매기다, 가격을 설정하다'라는 의미이므로 priced는 '가격이 매겨진, 가격이 설정된'이라는 뜻이다. 따라서 보기 중에서 의미상 어울릴 수 있는 어휘는 (D) competitively(경쟁력있게, 경쟁적으로)밖에 없다. competitively priced(경쟁력있게 가격이 매겨진)를 통째로 기억해야 하며, 또한 reasonably priced(합리적으로 가격이 매겨진, 저렴한)라는 표현도 이전에 출제된 바 있으니 알아두자. (A) virtually(실질적으로, 거의), (B) gratefully(감사히), (C) thoroughly(철저히)는 의미상 priced를 꾸며주지 못한다.

해석 우리는 고객서비스를 강조하는 높은 기준에 맞춰 경쟁력 있게 가격이 매겨진 자동차들에 대해서 자랑스러워한다.

어휘 pride oneself on ~에 대해 자랑스러워하다
prepared to the highest standard 가장 높은 기준에 맞추어 준비된   an emphasis on ~에 대한 강조
customer service 고객 서비스

정답 (D)

18.
해설 알맞은 품사를 결정하여 문맥을 완성하는 문제로 간단한 유형에 속하는 문제이다. 빈칸 앞에 be동사 is가 있고 빈칸 다음에 과거분사 situated(위치된)가 있으니 수동태 동사구를 꾸밀 수 있는 품사는 부사밖에 없다. 보기 중에 부사 어휘는 (C) ideally(이상적으로)밖에 없으므로 정답이 되며, perfectly(완벽하게)로 바꾸어도 정답으로 가능하다. 또는 conveniently(편리하게)가 정답으로 출제될 수도 있고, situated 대신에 located를 써도 된다는 점을 알아두자.

해석 코낙 호텔은 모든 주요 항공사들, 여행사들, 국제 호텔들, 나이트클럽들, 그리고 쇼핑센터들을 위해서 이상적으로 위치해 있다.

어휘 be ideally situated 이상적으로 위치해 있다 (= be perfectly situated, be ideally located) major airline 주요 항공사
travel agency 여행사 international hotel 국제 호텔

정답 (C)

19.

해설 알맞은 동사 어휘를 선택해서 문맥을 완성하는 문제이다. 단순히 빈칸 다음에 있는 목적어 the video graphic card만 보고서는 해결하기가 어렵고 그 다음에 있는 전치사 with까지 같이 보아야 한다. 목적어 다음에 전치사 with를 수반하는 동사는 바로 (A) replace이다. 동사 replace는 replace A with B(A를 B와 교체하다)라는 식으로 사용되므로 이 구문을 하나의 덩어리로 기억해 두어야 한다.

해설 당신이 비디오 그래픽 카드를 새 것으로 교체하려고 시도할 때, 기본적인 가이드라인을 따라야만 할 것이다.

어휘 attempt to부정사 ~하려고 시도하다
replace A with B A를 B와 교체하다
follow basic guideline 기본적인 가이드라인을 따르다

정답 (A)

20.

해설 빈칸 다음에 있는 topics(주제들) 앞에서 수식할 수 있는 형태의 어휘를 결정하는 문제이다. 명사 수식은 형용사가 하므로 보기 중에서 현재분사인 (B) remaining과 과거분사인 (D) remained 중에서 선택을 해야 한다. 보통 현재분사와 과거분사 중에서 선택을 해야 하는 경우 그 다음에 있는 명사와의 의미를 고려하여 결정을 하는데, remain(남다)은 자동사이므로 수동의 의미가 없고 따라서 과거분사 형태로 명사를 수식하지 못한다는 점을 알면 쉽게 결정할 수 있다. 따라서 능동의 의미를 가진 현재분사 (B) remaining(남아 있는)이 정답이 된다.

해설 남아 있는 주제들은 우선 중요한 문제가 아니므로, 우리는 그 사안들을 다음주 의제로 옮기기로 결정했다.

어휘 remaining topic 남아 있는 주제 a priority 중요한 문제, 우선 사항
decide to부정사 ~하기로 결정하다 move A to B A를 B로 옮기다
next week's agenda 다음주 의제

정답 (B)

21-24

펀데일-렌리 건설 그룹이 토요일 펀데일 공공 사업국과 두 개의 계약에 서명했다. 모두 합해, 계약액은 2천 70만 달러에 달한다. 두 계약 중 액수가 더 큰 것은 윌슨 파크 커뮤니티 센터를 처음부터 끝까지 책임지고 새로 짓는 것이다. 25년 된 이 시설은 6월에 철거될 예정이다. 공사는 이후 즉시 시작될 예정이다. 새 건물은 1년이 약간 안 되는 시간 안에 완공될 것으로 예상된다. 게다가, 이 건설 회사는 샤인 코퍼릿 센터에서 유발된 늘어난 교통량을 수용할 도로를 건설할 계획이다.

어휘 construction 건설, 공사 public work 공공 사업[공사]
authority (특정 분야의 권한을 가진) 관청, 국(局)
worth (금전 등의 면에서) ~의 가치가 되는
rebuild 재건하다, 다시 세우다
from the ground up 밑바닥부터 끝까지, 처음부터 다시 시작하여
demolish 파괴하다, 헐다 additionally 게다가, 덧붙여

21.

해설 계약의 총액을 말하고 있는데, 바로 앞 문장에서 두 건의 계약에 서명을 했다고 언급했으므로, '모두 합해서'를 뜻하는 (C) All told가 빈칸에 적합하다. At last는 '마침내', Individually는 '개인적으로', Instead는 '대신에'를 뜻한다.

정답 (C)

22.

해설 철거될 예정인 것은 윌슨 파크 커뮤니티 센터(the Wilson Park Community Center)이므로, 이 센터를 대신해 받을 수 있는 명사를 보기에서 고르면 된다. '시설'을 뜻하는 (A) facility가 정답이다.

정답 (A)

23.

(A) 펀데일은 세 군데의 새 커뮤니티 센터를 보유하고 있다.
(B) 공사는 이후 즉시 시작될 예정이다.
(C) 렌리는 펀데일에서 20년 동안 일해 왔다.
(D) 다른 하나는 새로운 놀이터를 몇 곳에 만드는 내용을 담고 있는 계약이다.

해설 빈칸 앞에서는 기존 건물의 '철거 예정 시간'을 언급했고, 뒤에서는 새로 지어질 건물의 '예상되는 완공 시간'을 언급하고 있음에 주목한다. 철거와 완공의 두 개념 사이에는 '공사가 곧 시작될 것'이라는 (B)의 내용이 들어가는 것이 가장 자연스럽다.

정답 (B)

24.

해설 빈칸에는 to부정사 형태인 (A) to accommodate을 넣어, to accommodate 이하 이 문장 끝까지의 내용이 빈칸 앞의 명사 a road를 형용사적으로 꾸며 주게 하면 된다. 그러면 '~할 도로'라는 문맥이 되면서 문장의 의미가 자연스럽게 통한다. (B) will accommodate은 문장에 동사 will build가 이미 있으므로 접속사 없이는 사용할 수 없다.

정답 (A)

25-28

아미르 씨에게,

론슨 테크를 신뢰해 주시고, 귀사에 요구되는 기술적 니즈를 평가하도록 해 주셔서 감사합니다. 귀사에서 사업상의 목표를 달성하는 데 도움이 될 컴퓨터 시스템에 대한 저희의 제안 내용을 첨부했으니 확인하시기 바랍니다. 귀하께서 요청했던 것보다 강력한 컴퓨터를 저희가 추천했다는 사실을 알 수 있을 것입니다. 귀하께서 계획하고 있는 비디오 편집 작업에는 첨부물에 나와 있는 사양을 갖춘 컴퓨터가 필요하리라는 것이 저희 전문가들의 의견입니다. 원하신다면, 기꺼이 이러한 권고 내용들을 보다 상세히 검토해 드릴 수 있습니다. 론슨 테크의 고객님들께는 컨설팅 서비스를 무료로 해 드립니다. 이번에는 아무것도 구입할 생각이 없으시다면, 컨설팅비로 199달러 99센트를 이 봉투에 있는 주소로 보내 주시기 바랍니다.

웨스 챔버레인
론슨 테크 고객 담당 컨설턴트

어휘 trust 신뢰하다, 믿다
attached 첨부된 (cf. attachment 첨부물, 부속물)
request 요청하다 go over ~을 검토하다, 점검하다
in detail 상세히 make a purchase 구입하다 envelope 봉투

25.
해설 to부정사를 완성할 적절한 동사 원형을 고르는 문제이다. assess는 '평가하다', '재다', decrease는 '감소시키다', broadcast는 '방송하다', ingrain은 '(생각 등을) 배어들게 하다'라는 뜻으로, 빈칸에는 (A) assess를 넣어 '론슨 테크가 평가하게 하다'라는 의미가 되는 것이 문맥에 가장 자연스럽다.

정답 (A)

26.
해설 빈칸에 필요한 것은 이 문장의 목적어 역할을 하고 있는 that절을 완성시켜 줄 동사이다. Mr. Amir의 사무실에 적합하다고 생각되는 컴퓨터 사양을 Wes Chamberlain이 첨부 편지를 통해 이미 추천한 상황이므로 과거 시제인 (A) recommended가 적절하다.

정답 (A)

27.
해설 정관사 the의 뒤에 위치한 빈칸은 명사 자리로, 이 명사는 형용사 역할을 하는 분사구 indicated in the attachment의 수식도 받게 된다. '첨부물에 나와 있는 사양'이라는 자연스러운 의미를 완성하는 (D) specifications가 정답이다.

정답 (D)

28.
(A) 론슨 테크의 고객님들께는 컨설팅 서비스를 무료로 해 드립니다.
(B) 론슨 테크의 기술자들이 금요일 귀사의 컴퓨터를 수리할 것입니다.
(C) 론슨 테크의 보증 기간은 연말에 종료됩니다.
(D) 론슨 테크에 대금 지불을 완료해 주셔서 감사합니다.

해설 '만일 아무것도 구입하지 않는다면 컨설팅 비를 내라'는 말이 빈칸 뒤에 나오고 있음에 주목한다. 만일 구매를 한다면, 즉 '론슨 테크의 고객이 된다면 컨설팅 서비스를 무료로 해 준다'는 (A)의 내용이 빈칸에 들어가는 것이 적절하다.

정답 (A)

UNIT 13 편지 / 이메일 / 광고

Check-up 본책 _ p. 303

9월 23일
에반젤린 메타
카미켈 아트센터
76 웰링턴 에비뉴
시카고, 일리노이 60657

친애하는 메타 씨

저의 이름은 팀 고슬랜이며, 저는 시카고 필하모닉의 음악 감독입니다.[1] 매 10월마다 우리는 우리 오케스트라를 지원하기 위한 돈을 모금하기 위한 특별 공연을 엽니다. 우리가 늘 이용하던 **데이비스 홀이 이번 10월에 보수 공사 때문에 문을 닫을 것입니다.[2]** 그러므로 우리는 현재 이 행사를 주최할 다른 장소를 찾고 있는 중입니다. 관심이 있으시면 (773) 975-0097로 부디 전화 주십시오. 고려해주셔서 감사드리며, 소식 듣기를 기대하고 있겠습니다.

팀 고슬랜

어휘 raise money 모금하다 customary 관례적인, 전통적인
renovation 보수공사 therefore 그러므로
search for ~를 찾다, 구하다 consideration 고려

1. 고슬랜 씨는 누구인가? 음악 감독
2. 데이비스 홀에 대해 언급된 것은? 보수 공사 때문에 10월에 문을 닫는다.

Check-up 본책 _ p. 305

수신 : Karen@musictian.co.org
발신 : Rachel_Green@hillcomputer.co.uk
참조 : Maclim@hillcomputer.co.uk
날짜 : 6월 17일
제목 : **특별 판촉 할인[1]**

친애하는 고객님들
힐리 컴퓨터는 지금 X-1000 광마우스에 대한 특별 판촉 할인을 제공하고 있습니다. 6월 20일 전에 10개 이상을 주문하시는 고객에게는 20% 할인해드립니다. 매우 민감한 1000DPI 기능을 가진 X-1000은 데스크톱 사용자와 랩톱 사용자들 모두에게 이상적입니다. 더 많은 정보를 원하시면 330-9999로 전화 주십시오. 감사합니다.

레이첼 그린
고객서비스 직원[2]

어휘 offer ~를 제공하다　special promotion 특별 판촉 (할인)
optical mouse 광마우스　20% off 20% 할인　order ~를 주문하다
10 or more 10개나 그 이상　highly 매우　sensitive 민감한
function 기능　be ideal for ~에 이상적이다, 적합하다
both A and B A와 B 둘 다　best regards (관용구) 안부를 전합니다

1. 이메일의 주제는 무엇인가? **특별 판촉 할인**
2. 레이첼 그린은 누구인가? **고객서비스 직원**

Check-up　본책 _ p. 307

남아프리카 할인 400파운드부터 시작

리얼제트는 **남아프리카로 가는 모든 비행편에 대한 할인**¹을 진행 중입니다. 지금 구매하세요. 할인은 단지 제한된 시간 동안에만 지속됩니다. **구매는 반드시 7월 1일과 8월 31일 사이에 이루어져야 하며**², 출발은 11월 15일과 1월 15일 사이에 이루어져야 합니다. 1월 1일에 출발하는 경우는 가격 할인에서 제외됩니다. 시내 가이드와 호텔 할인을 포함하여 이번 거래에 대한 더 많은 정보를 원하시면 www.realjet.com을 방문해보세요.

어휘 have a sale 할인을 하다　last 지속되다　limited 제한된
purchases must be made 구매가 이루어져야 한다
between A and B A와 B 사이에　exclude ~를 제외하다
deal (할인) 거래　including ~를 포함하여　guide 가이드, 안내
visit ~를 방문하다

1. 무엇이 광고되고 있는가? **남아프리카로 가는 비행편**
2. 할인 판매는 얼마나 오랫동안 지속되는가? **두 달**

Part 7_ 실전연습 13　본책 _ p. 310–313

1-3

2월 2일
캐리 펜웨이
312 프레지던트 가
볼티모어, 메사추세츠 21202

펜웨이 씨에게,

페어 커피 포 더 월드에 대한 정보 및 샘플을 요청하신 데 감사드립니다.¹ 우리는 당신에게 에티오피안 엘리트의 샘플을 보내드리게 되어 기쁩니다.²

만약 당신이 페어 커피 포 더 월드 클럽에 가입하고 싶으시면, 간단히 온라인으로 www.faircoffeeclub.com에 요청서를 제출하십시오. 만약 온라인으로 등록하고 8392-FEN 코드번호를 입력하시면 회원권에 대한 10퍼센트 할인 또한 받으실 겁니다.³

저희 클럽에서 커피를 구매하시면 커피 농부들은 정당한 가격을 받을 수 있다는 점을 기억하십시오. 공정한 커피 거래를 지원함으로써, 당신은 커피 농부들을 지원하고 있는 셈입니다.

버지니아 잭슨
고객 관리 매니저
페어 커피 포 더 월드

어휘 sample request 샘플(에 대한) 요청
be happy to부정사 ~해서 기쁘다　send A B A에게 B를 보내다
would like to부정사 ~하고 싶다　join ~에 가입하다
simply 간단히　submit ~를 제출하다　membership 회원자격
enter ~를 입력하다　farmer 농부　fair price 적절한 가격

1. 이 편지로부터 무엇을 유추할 수 있는가?
(A) 펜웨이 씨는 커피를 즐긴다.
(B) 펜웨이 씨가 정보를 요청했다.
(C) 펜웨이 씨는 에티오피아를 방문했었다.
(D) 펜웨이 씨는 최근에 클럽에 가입했다.

해설 본문 첫 줄에 Thank you for your information and sample request.(정보와 샘플에 대한 당신의 요청에 대해 감사합니다)에서 단서를 찾을 수 있다.

정답 (B)

2. 펜웨이 씨는 무엇을 받을 것인가?
(A) 쿠폰　　　　　　　(B) 선물 세트
(C) 무료 샘플　　　　(D) 무료 커피 머그잔

해설 본문 첫 문단에 We are happy to send you a sample.(우리는 샘플을 보내게 되어서 기쁩니다)에서 단서를 찾을 수 있다.

정답 (C)

3. 펜웨이 씨는 어떻게 할인을 받을 수 있는가?
(A) 친구를 소개함으로써　(B) 전화를 걸어서
(C) 설문지를 반송함으로써　(D) 온라인으로 등록함으로써

해설 본문 두 번째 문단 마지막에 if you sign up online(당신이 온라인으로 등록하면)에서 단서를 찾을 수 있다. 본문의 sign up(등록하다)이 정답 보기에서 register(등록하다)로 변형되었다.

정답 (D)

4-7

지금껏 가장 낮은 판촉가!

오직 제한된 시간 동안에만 당신은 일렉트로마트 320GB 데스크톱 하드 드라이브⁴를 89.99달러⁵에 사실 수 있습니다. 이렇게 많은 용량과 더불어 당신은 컴퓨터 전체와 디지털 사진들, 다운로드 받은 음악들, 그리고 영상물을 보호할 수 있습니다. 게다가 이 하드 드라이브는 쉬운 셋업을 위해서 미리 포맷되어 있으므로 바로 사용하실 수 있습니다.

게다가 당신은 서비스 계획의 구매에 대한 50퍼센트 할인과 무료 백업 소프트웨어를 받으실 것입니다.

서두르세요! 재고가 있을 경우 1월 14일까지⁶ 이 할인이 유효합니다.

다른 일렉트로마트 제품들
외장 하드 드라이브⁷⁻ᴬ　네트워크 저장(장비)⁷⁻ᶜ　DVD & CD버너
멀티미디어 드라이브　액세서리들　소프트웨어
서비스 계획　데이터 복구⁷⁻ᴮ

상기의 링크들에 클릭하셔서 우리가 제공하는 것을 보십시오!

어휘 lowest 가장 낮은 promotion price 판촉[할인] 가격
  limited 제한된 storage 저장[용량] entire 전체의 plus 게다가
  be pre-formatted 미리 포맷되어 있다 easy setup 쉬운 설치
  valid 유효한 supplies 물품 last 지속되다

4. 어떤 제품이 광고되고 있는가?
(A) DVD 드라이브 (B) 하드 드라이브
(C) 서비스 계획 (D) 노트북 컴퓨터

해설 본문 첫 줄에 ElectroMart 320GB Desktop Hard Drive(일렉트로마트 320GB 데스크톱 하드 드라이브)에서 단서를 찾을 수 있다.

정답 (B)

5. 할인 가격은 얼마인가?
(A) 69달러 99센트 (B) 79달러 99센트
(C) 89달러 99센트 (D) 99달러 99센트

해설 본문 첫 줄 마지막에 for $89.99(89.99 달러에)에 명시되어 있다.

정답 (C)

6. 할인은 언제 끝이 나는가?
(A) 1월 (B) 2월
(C) 3월 (D) 4월

해설 본문 중간에 offer valid through January 14 while supplies last(물품이 지속되는 동안 1월 14일까지 이 할인이 유효합니다)에서 단서를 찾을 수 있다. 할인은 1월 14일에 끝이 난다는 의미이다.

정답 (A)

7. 일렉트로마트가 취급하지 않는 상품은 무엇인가?
(A) 외장 하드 드라이브 (B) 데이터 복구
(C) 네트워크 저장 (D) 모니터

해설 본문 마지막에 (A) External hard drives(외장 하드 드라이브), (B) Data recovery(데이터 복구), (C) Network storage(네트워크 저장)는 언급되어 있지만 (D) Monitors(모니터)는 언급된 바가 없다.

정답 (D)

8-11

발신: henshaw@mayers.co.nz
수신: stevens@mayers.co.nz
날짜: 8월 3일
제목: 멋진 발표에 대한 몇 말씀

안녕하세요 스티븐스 씨,

브랜드 인지도를 높이는 방안에 대해 당신이 발표했던 내용을 감명 깊게 들었음을 알려 드리고 싶습니다.[11] 바이럴 마케팅에 대해 말씀하신 개인적인 이야기가 특히 좋았습니다. 메이어스 사에서 일을 시작하신 지 얼마 되지 않지만, 저는 당신이 우리 회사의 소중한 자산이 될 것이라고, 미리 말씀 드릴 수 있습니다. 선배 직원들이 신입 직원들을 이끌어 주도록 요구되는 메이어스 사의 튼튼 체인 프로그램에 대해 알고 계시리라 믿습니다. 이러한 안을 따르는 의미에서, 저는 앞으로 당신의 연설이 한층 더 강력해질 수 있도록 해줄 몇 가지 간략한 조언을 드리고자 합니다.

첫째로, 연설 속도에 신경을 쓰십시오. 우리에게 휴식 시간이 주어졌던 것은 발표가 끝나 갈 무렵이었는데, 그때 한 15분 정도가 남아 있었습니다. 휴식 시간을 발표 시간 중간으로 옮긴다면, 청중이 정신을 가다듬고 강연 내용에 보다 집중할 수 있도록 도움을 줄 것입니다.[10-B] 연설이 끝나갈 때, 청중 중 일부는 집중을 위해 고투하고 있는 모습이 역력했습니다.[9] 많은 청중들이 30분 이상은 강연에 집중하기 힘들어한다는 사실을 저는 알게 되었습니다. 발표자가 아무리 활기에 넘치는 사람이라 할지라도 말입니다. 청중의 주의를 집중시키려면, 발표를 할 때 청중이 반응을 보일 수 있는 기회를 그들에게 수시로 제공해 줘야 합니다.[10-C] 아이디어에 도움이 될 수 있도록 인터넷에서 볼 수 있는 유용한 비디오를 하나 소개해 드리겠습니다. 여기를 클릭하면 그것을 볼 수 있습니다. 이 비디오는 청중의 관심을 집중시키는, 기억에 남을 슬라이드쇼를 진행하는 방법에 대해 유용한 가르침을 주고 있습니다. 당신이 했던 슬라이드 발표도 훌륭했지만, 여기서 가르치는 내용을 따라 하면 다음에는 훨씬 더 멋진 발표를 할 수 있게 될 것입니다.[10-D]

이러한 제안들은 당신이 앞으로 보다 나은 발표를 할 수 있도록 하는 데 도움이 될 것입니다. 당신이 했던 강연에 대해 감사의 마음을 전합니다. 저는 20년 이상을 도매 업계에 몸담아 왔지만, 당신으로부터 많은 것을 배웠습니다.[8] 제 의견에 대해 질문이 있으시면 주저하지 말고 제 사무실에 들러 이야기해 주십시오. 제 사무실의 문은 항상 열려 있습니다.

쉴라 헨쇼, 유통 매니저
메이어스 사

어휘 maximize 극대화하다 brand recognition 브랜드 인지도
  valuable 소중한, 귀중한 asset 자산, 재산
  follow through on ~을 실천하다, ~을 완수하다
  initiative (특정 목적 달성을 위한 새로운) 계획, 방안, 구상
  consider ~을 고려하다 pacing 이야기 전개 속도 break 휴식 시간
  refresh 생기를 되찾다 portion 부분, 일부
  dynamic 역동적인, 활발한
  engage (주의·관심을) 사로잡다 cf. engaging 호감이 가는, 매력적인
  pepper 후추를 치다, ~의 공세를 퍼붓다

8. 스티븐스 씨에 대해 시사하고 있는 것은?
(A) 헨쇼 씨의 상사이다.
(B) 더 이상 발표를 하지 않을 것이다.
(C) 메이어스 사에서 오랫동안 일해 온 직원이다.
(D) 도매 업계에서 일하고 있다.

해설 이메일을 쓴 Sheila Henshaw는 20년 이상을 도매 업계에 몸담아 왔다고 세 번째 단락에서 밝히고 있다. 그런데 그녀는 Mr. Stevens의 선배 직원이므로 Mr. Stevens가 일하고 있는 분야 역시 도매 업계임을 알 수 있다. 따라서 정답은 (D)이다.

정답 (D)

9. 헨쇼 씨가 발표 내용에 대해 언급하고 있는 것은?
(A) 녹화 후 인터넷에 업로드되었다.
(B) 일부 청중들은 발표 내용에 집중할 수 없었다.
(C) 말하는 동안 기술적인 문제가 발생했었다.
(D) 발표가 된 내용을 그녀는 이미 알고 있었다.

해설 두 번째 단락 중간 부분을 보면, 연설이 끝나갈 때, 청중 중 일부는 집중을 위해 고투하고 있는 모습이 역력했다고(It was clear that a portion of the audience struggled to pay attention toward the end of the talk.) 언급했다. 따라서 이러한 의미의 내용을 담고 있는 (B)가 정답이 된다.

어휘 malfunction (기기의) 오작동

정답 (B)

10. 발표 개선을 위해 헨쇼 씨가 제의하고 있지 않은 것은?
(A) 청중들의 참여도 높이기
(B) 다른 시간에 휴식 취하기
(C) 주제에 대해 보다 철저히 조사하기
(D) 보다 흥미로운 시각 자료 준비하기

해설 (A)는 두 번째 단락의 To keep the listeners engaged, try peppering your presentation with opportunities for audience interaction. 부분, (B)는 If you move the break to the middle of the presentation, ~ 부분, 그리고 (D)는 It is a helpful tutorial on how to make memorable slideshows ~ make your next one even more engaging. 부분에 해당한다. (C)에 대해서는 언급되지 않았다.

어휘 improve 개선하다, 향상시키다

정답 (C)

11. [1], [2], [3], [4] 중 다음 문장이 들어가기에 가장 적합한 곳은?

"바이럴 마케팅에 대해 말씀하신 개인적인 이야기가 특히 좋았습니다."

(A) [1]
(B) [2]
(C) [3]
(D) [4]

해설 주어진 문장은 필자가 들었던 발표 내용에서 범위를 좁혀 '특히' 즐겁게 들었던 부분에 대해 언급하고 있다. 따라서 발표 내용을 그냥 잘 들었다고 처음에 뭉뚱그려 말한 바로 뒤인 [1]에 이 문장이 들어가는 것이 자연스럽다.

어휘 viral marketing 바이럴 마케팅: 네티즌들이 이메일 교환 등을 통해 자발적으로 입소문을 내 제품 등을 홍보하게 하는 마케팅 기법

정답 (A)

UNIT 14 문자 메시지 및 온라인 채팅/기사/정보문/회람

Check-up 1   본책 _ p. 316

조이 워커 [11:12 A.M]
호크, 당신이 요청했던 변경사항에 대해서 궁금합니다. 음... 쇼핑센터의 평면도 말이에요.

호크 리 [11:14 A.M]
물론이죠. 무슨 일이세요?

조이 워커 [11:15 A.M]
제가 이메일로 전체를 보내드릴까요, 아니면 약간의 수정사항이 있는 5페이지만 보내드릴까요?¹

호크 리 [11:16 A.M]
저는 종이로 보는 것이 좋겠는데, 지금 노트북 컴퓨터가 저한테 없네요.

조이 워커 [11:17 A.M]
그러면 제 생각에는 조금 시간이 걸릴 것 같은데요.

호크 리 [11:18 A.M]
왜 기다려요? 저한테 팩스로 보내주실 수 있나요?²

조이 워커 [11:19 A.M]
물론이죠. 문제없습니다!

어휘 wonder about ~에 대해서 궁금해하다   ask for ~를 요청하다   floor plan 평면도   the whole thing 전체, 모든 것   revision 수정   prefer ~를 선호하다

1. 워커 씨는 어떤 사람일 것 같은가? 건축가
2. 오전 11시 18분에 호크 씨가 "왜 기다려요?"라고 쓸 때, 그 의도는 무엇인가?
그는 그것을 지금 보기를 원한다.

Check-up 2   본책 _ p. 317

엘사 로카모라 [02:12 P.M.]   내가 내일을 위해 준비하는데 도와 줄 시간이 있는 사람 있나요?

메이 청 [02:13 P.M.]   지금 YBN 회사로부터 오는 고객들에 대해서 말하고 있는 건가요?¹

엘사 로카모라 [02:13 P.M.]   네, 맞습니다.

마이클 라일리 [02:15 P.M.]   저는 오늘 아침에 예산 보고서를 끝내야 해요. 점심까지 마감이거든요. 하지만 오늘 오후에는 언제든 자유시간이에요. 무엇이 필요하나요?

엘사 로카모라 [02:15 P.M.]   회의실이 준비되어야 합니다. 우리는 프로젝션 스크린, 프로젝터, 랩탑, 그리고 포터블 사운드 시스템이 필요할 겁니다. 이것들은 당신의 부서로부터 체크아웃 되어야 하므로, 마이클, 당신이 책임질 수 있다고 생각하나요?²

마이클 라일리 [02:16 P.M.]   물론이죠. 제가 처리할게요.

1. 로카모라 씨는 무엇에 대해 준비하고 있는가? 몇몇 고객들의 방문

2. 오후 2시 16분에 마이클이 "제가 처리할게요."라고 쓸 때 무엇을 의미하는가?
그는 몇몇 장비를 빌릴 것이고, 설치할 것이다.

Check-up 본책 _ p. 319

> **워싱턴 날씨**
>
> 8월 13일, 목요일
> **기상센터로부터**[1]
>
> 일기예보관들은 워싱턴 시의 대부분 지역에서 **혹독한 폭풍우**[2]를 예상했습니다. 폭우가 금요일 아침에 시작될 것으로 예상되고, 주말 내내 계속 될 것입니다.
> 비록 이 폭풍우는 10센티미터 이상의 비를 뿌릴 가능성은 희박하지만, 몇몇 지역들은 약간의 침수를 겪을 수도 있습니다. 이번 비는 다음 주 월요일 아침 늦게 끝날 것이지만, 다음 주 수요일까지는 흐린 날씨가 계속될 것입니다.

어휘 forecaster 일기예보관 predict ~를 예상하다 severe 혹독한
thunderstorm 폭풍우 most of ~의 대부분
heavy rain 폭우 be expected to ~할 것으로 예상되다
continue 계속되다 throughout ~내내
unlikely ~할 가능성이 없는 produce ~를 생산하다, 초래하다
flooding 범람, 침수 until ~까지

1. 이 기사는 어디에서 나온 것인가? 기상센터
2. 일기예보관들은 무엇을 예상했는가? 혹독한 폭풍우

Check-up 본책 _ p. 321

> **클리어렉스 손 세정제**[1] **– 제품 정보**
>
> 클리어렉스 **손 세정제**[1]는 당신의 손을 부드럽게 유지하면서 대부분의 병균과 박테리아를 제거합니다. 이것은 전국에서 가장 잘 팔리는 상품이죠.
>
> **주의**
> 클리어렉스는 외용제로만 사용되어야 하고 결코 복용해서는 안 되며 **눈가에 사용해서도 안 됩니다.**[2] 모르고 먹었을 경우 도움을 받으려면 가장 가까운 병원으로 연락 주십시오.
>
> **사용법**
> 클리어렉스 손 세정제 소량을 손에 묻히고, 물과 함께 문지르십시오. 깨끗하게 행구셔야 합니다.
>
> **문의**
> 클리어렉스 손 세정제에 대한 질문을 하시려면 777–9933으로 전화 주시거나 www.clearex.com으로 방문해 주십시오.

어휘 hand cleaner 손 세정제 product information 제품 정보
eliminate ~를 제거하다 common 보편적인 germ 병균
leave + A + 형용사 A를 ~하게 두다
top seller 가장 잘 팔리는 상품 externally 외부적으로
be taken 섭취되다 in case of ~의 경우에 accidental 우발적인
ingestion 섭취 nearest 가장 가까운
health care provider 병원 assistance 도움

a small amount of 소량의 rub 문지르다 rinse 행구다
thoroughly 철저히

1. 무엇이 광고되고 있는가? 손 세정제
2. 이 정보는 무엇을 하지 말라고 충고하는가? 눈가에 사용하는 것

Check-up 본책 _ p. 323

> **사내 회람**
>
> 수신 : 모든 직원들
> 발신 : 유호 임, 관리부장
> 제목 : **사용하지 않는 장비**[1]
>
> 우리는 많은 분들이 사무 공간 밖으로 옮기고 싶어하는 사용하지 않는 컴퓨터와 전자 장비를 가지고 있다는 것을 알고 있습니다. 그래서 **7월 1일**[2]부터 우리는 여러분이 버리길 원하는 장비를 수거할 것입니다. 수거 일정을 잡기 위해 이번 주말까지 내선번호 4338번으로 관리부의 폴 딕슨에게 연락해 주십시오.
>
> 협조에 감사드립니다.

어휘 unused 사용하지 않는 electronic equipment 전자 장비
would like to 부정사 ~하고 싶다
move A out of B B로부터 A를 빼내다
starting on ~에 시작하여 collect ~를 수거하다
dispose of ~를 버리다 contact ~에게 연락하다
maintenance department 관리부 schedule 날짜를 잡다
pick-up 수거

1. 회람은 무엇에 대한 것인가? 사용하지 않는 장비
2. 사용하지 않는 장비를 언제 수거하기 시작하는가? 7월 1일

Part 7_ 실전연습 14 본책 _ p. 326–331

1-2

> **젠 스테드먼**   오전 8시 21분
> 히로코, 존스 가의 주차장 공사에 관한 회람 읽었어요?
>
> **히로코 미사루**   오전 8시 24분
> 네, 봤어요.[1] 그런데 왜요?
>
> **젠 스테드먼**   오전 8시 25분
> 우리보고 어디에 주차를 하라고 그러던가요? 주차할 자리를 못 찾겠어요.
>
> **히로코 미사루**   오전 8시 25분
> 걱정하지 말아요. 나도 누가 말해 줘서 알았거든요. 태닝 가에 내려져 있던 주차 금지 조치를 시에서 공사 기간 동안 해제했어요. 그러니까 거기 주차하면 돼요.[2] 인도 위로 차를 몰고 들어가야 하는데, 문제될 것 없습니다.
>
> **젠 스테드먼**   오전 8시 26분
> 완벽합니다. 지금 그 근처에 멈추어 있거든요. 잠시 후에 봐요!

어휘 parking garage (실내) 주차장
draw a blank 원하는 것을 찾지 못하다
remind 상기시키다, 다시 한 번 알려 주다   ban 금지
duration 지속되는 기간   sidewalk 보도, 인도

1. 오전 8시 24분에 미사루 씨가 "봤어요"라고 쓸 때 그녀가 의미하는 것은?
(A) 회람을 읽었다.
(B) 잃어버린 물건을 찾았다.
(C) 메시지를 받지 못했다.
(D) 텔레비전 프로그램을 봤다.

해설 바로 위에서 존스 가의 주차장 공사에 관한 회람을 읽었냐고(did you read the memo about ~) Jen Steddman이 질문한 데 대해 이렇게 답한 것이므로, 회람을 읽었다는 (A)가 정답이 된다.

정답 (A)

2. 스테드먼 씨는 어디에 주차를 하겠는가?
(A) 실내 주차장에
(B) 존스 가에
(C) 태닝 가에
(D) 회사 주차장에

해설 Tanning Street에 내려져 있던 주차 금지 조치가 해제되었으므로 그곳에 주차하면 된다고 Hiroko Misaru가 언급하자, Ms. Steddman은 지금 그 근처에 멈추어 있다고 설명하고 있다. 따라서 그녀는 (C)의 Tanning Street에 주차를 할 것이다.

정답 (C)

3-5

컨비니언스 항공사 정보

표 없는 비행
컨비니언스 항공은 종이로 된 비행기 표를 발행하지 않습니다. 일단 온라인으로 예약한 후에 이메일 확인을 받으면 비행기를 타기 전에 우리에게 연락하실 필요가 없습니다.

체크인 정보
컨비니언스 항공 체크인 카운터는 예정된 비행기 이륙 두 시간 전에 오픈을 하고³ 비행기가 떠나기 40분 전에 닫을 것입니다. 체크인하시려면 확인 세부사항, 여권, 그리고 운전면허증과 같은 다른 종류의 신분증 하나를 제시해야 합니다.⁴

수하물 정책
컨비니언스 항공은 가방 무게가 20파운드를 넘지 않는 선에서⁵ 하나를 가지고 무료 탑승하도록 허용합니다. 더 큰 가방들이나 다른 체크인 수하물은 추가 요금이 부과될 수 있습니다.

어휘 ticketless 표가 없는   paper ticket 종이 표   once 일단 ~하면
confirmation 확인   booking 예약   scheduled 예정된
departure 출발   passport 여권
another piece of 다른 한 가지 종류의   identification (card) 신분증   carry-on bag 기내 휴대 가능 수하물

3. 항공사에 대해서 사실인 점은?
(A) 국내선만 운영한다.
(B) 2개의 무료 탑승 수하물을 허용한다.
(C) 이륙하기 1시간 전에 탑승을 시작한다.
(D) 비행 2시간 전에 티켓 카운터를 오픈한다.

해설 본문 두 번째 문단의 check-in counters will be open two hours before flight's scheduled departure(체크인 카운터는 비행기의 예정된 출발 두 시간 전에 오픈한다)에서 단서를 찾을 수 있다.

정답 (D)

4. 체크인하기 위해서 무엇이 필요없는가?
(A) 여권   (B) 비행기 표
(C) 확인 번호   (D) 신분증

해설 본문 첫 번째 문단의 타이틀 Ticketless Flight(표 없는 비행)에서도 알 수 있고, Convenience Air does not issue paper tickets.(컨비니언스 항공은 종이로 된 비행기 표를 발행하지 않습니다)에서도 단서를 찾을 수 있다.

정답 (B)

5. 탑승 수하물의 최대 무게는 얼마인가?
(A) 20파운드   (B) 30파운드
(C) 40파운드   (D) 50파운드

해설 본문 마지막 문단 weighing up to 20 pounds(20파운드까지 무게가 나가는)에서 단서를 찾을 수 있다.

정답 (A)

6-8

양털은 부드럽고 매우 따스하며, 아름다운 스웨터로 만들어졌을 때 특히 아주 매력적입니다. 하지만 울로 된 옷을 관리하기가 늘 쉽기만 한 것은 아니며, 라벨에 인쇄된 깨알같은 글씨 또한 항상 읽기가 쉬운 것도 아닙니다. 당신의 울 스웨터를 깨끗하고 보기 좋게 관리하려면 다음 설명 내용을 따르시기 바랍니다.

울은 열에 매우 민감하다는 사실을⁶ 기억하는 것이 중요한데요. 이는 울을 온수로 빨아서는 안 되며, 드라이기의 바람을 쐬어서도 안 된다는 것을 의미합니다. 사실, 전문가에게 맡겨 드라이 클리닝을 하는 것 외에 울 스웨터를 세탁하는 유일한 방법은 부드럽게 손빨래를 해 주는 것입니다. 다행히도 손빨래 방법은 아주 간단합니다. 먼저 상온의 물이 담긴 욕조에 섬유 세제를 큰 스푼으로 두 개 넣습니다. 옷의 겉과 속을 뒤집어 욕조 안에서 몇 분간 이리저리 흔들어 줍니다. 스웨터를 욕조에서 꺼내 말려 줍니다.

울은 쉽게 늘어나므로 손으로 물을 짜내거나 울로 된 옷을 옷걸이에 걸면 안 됩니다.⁸ 그렇게 하면 옷이 쉽게 망가집니다. 대신, 마른 수건을 평평하게 깔고, 젖은 스웨터를 그 위에 올려 줍니다. 하루나 이틀 밤 동안 공기 중에서 건조시켜 줍니다.⁷ 그러면 끝입니다! 옷장에 면으로 된 옷을 많이 갖고 계시다면, 다음달 호에서 그런 종류의 스웨터를 취급하는 방법에 대한 저희 팁을 꼭 찾아 읽어 보시기 바랍니다.

어휘 fur (양·토끼 등의) 털 attractive 매력적인, 멋진
     garment 의복, 옷 tiny 아주 작은 sensitive to ~에 예민한[민감한]
     handwash 손빨래하다 tablespoon 테이블 스푼, 큰 스푼
     fabric detergent 섬유 세제 tub 목욕통, 욕조(= bathtub)
     swish 휙[쌩] 소리를 내며 움직이다 stretch 늘어나다
     wring out ~을 짜내다 article 물품, 품목 cotton 목화, 면직물
     wardrobe 옷장 issue (잡지 같은 정기 간행물의) 호

6. 기사에 따르면 울 스웨터는 무엇으로부터 보호해 줘야 하는가?
(A) 열
(B) 물
(C) 드라이 클리닝
(D) 곤충

해설 울은 열에 매우 민감하므로(wool is very sensitive to heat.) 온수로 빨아서도 안 되고, 드라이기의 바람을 쐬어서도 안 된다고(This means it should never be washed with warm water, and certainly never put in a dryer.) 했다. 따라서 정답은 (A)이다.

정답 (A)

7. 기사에서 울 스웨터에 대해 시사하는 것은?
(A) 말릴 때 하루 종일 시간이 걸리는 경우가 종종 있다.
(B) 면 스웨터보다 관리하기가 쉽다.
(C) 온화한 날씨에 잘 맞는다.
(D) 전문가에게 맡겨 세탁해야 한다.

해설 손빨래를 한 울 스웨터는 마른 수건 위에서 하루나 이틀 밤 동안 말려 준다고(Let it airdry for one or two nights.) 했으며, 이 내용에 해당하는 (A)가 정답이다. 울 스웨터 세탁은 드라이 클리닝을 맡기거나 직접 손빨래를 하는 두 가지 방법이 있으므로 (D)는 틀린 설명이다.

정답 (A)

8. [1], [2], [3], [4] 중 다음 문장이 들어가기에 가장 적합한 곳은?
"그렇게 하면 옷이 쉽게 망가집니다."
(A) [1]
(B) [2]
(C) [3]
(D) [4]

해설 울로 된 옷을 망가뜨리는 잘못된 취급 방법 뒤에 이 내용이 들어가면 된다. 울은 쉽게 늘어나므로 손으로 짜거나 옷걸이에 걸면 안 된다는 내용(Wool stretches easily, so never wring out water or hang wool articles of clothing.) 바로 뒤인 [4]가 정답이다.

정답 (D)

9-12

시포 에킨 [오후 3시 13분]:
안녕하세요 아샤 씨. 회계과 분들이 이것저것 필요로 하는 게 있어서, 제가 잠시 후에 급히 상점으로 가볼까 하는데요. 당신 부서에서도 뭐 필요한 게 있나요?

예완데 아샤 [오후 3시 14분]:
오, 물어봐 줘서 고맙습니다. 저희가 사용하는 프린터 토너의 브랜드가 뭔지 아세요? 기계의 잉크 교체 경고등이 며칠째 켜져 있어서요.

시포 에킨 [오후 3시 14분]:
미안합니다, 모르겠는데요. IT 지원과에 확인해 볼게요.

이안 후안 씨가 대화에 참가하셨습니다

시포 에킨 [오후 3시 17분]:
안녕하세요 이안, 잠깐 뭣 좀 물어볼게요.¹⁰ 마케팅과에서 프린터에 쓸 교체용 토너를 필요로 하고 있습니다.⁹ 어떤 종류로 사야 하나요?

이안 후안 [오후 3시 18분]:
포스터를 인쇄하는 그 커다란 기계요? 그 기계는 제조업체에서 특별 제작한 드럼을 필요로 합니다. 제가 전화해서 주문해야 해요.

예완데 아샤 [오후 3시 19분]:
실례합니다, 이안. 포스터용 프린터는 괜찮아요. 잉크가 필요한 건 제 사무실에 있는 작은 데스크용 프린터입니다.¹¹ 나오키 브랜드인데, 모델 번호는 모르겠고요.

이안 후안 [오후 3시 20분]:
아, 우리가 쓰는 나오키 브랜드는 다 같습니다. DX로 시작하는 나오키 카트리지로 아무거나 쓰면 돼요. 제가 도와 드릴 수 있는 게 뭐 또 있나요?

예완데 아샤 [오후 3시 20분]:
됐습니다. 고마워요 이안.

이안 후안 [오후 3시 21분]:
천만에요. 그럼 이만.

이안 후안 씨가 퇴장하셨습니다

시포 에킨 [오후 3시 21분]:
그럼 저는 이제 나갑니다.¹² 다른 것 필요한 게 혹시 생각 나시면 제 전화로 문자 메시지 보내 주세요, 아샤 씨.

어휘 accountant 회계부 직원, 회계사
     odds and ends 잡동사니, 자질구레한 것 in a little bit 잠시 후에
     replacement 교체, 대체 place an order 주문하다
     head out 밖으로 나가다

9. 아샤 씨는 어느 부서에서 일하고 있겠는가?
(A) 회계과
(B) IT 지원과
(C) 마케팅과
(D) 인사과

해설 Yewande Asha [오후 3시 14분]의 내용을 보면 프린터의 토너를 교체해야 하는 곳은 Asha가 일하는 부서임을 알 수 있다. 그런데 Ian Juan이 대화에 참여한 바로 뒤인 [오후 3시 17분]에 Sipho Ekene이 '마케팅과에서 프린터에 쓸 교체용 토너를 필요로 하고 있다'고 Ian Juan에게 언급하고 있는 것으로 보아 Asha가 일하는 곳은 (C)의 Marketing임을 알 수 있다.

정답 (C)

10. 후안 씨가 대화에 동참하게 된 이유는?
(A) 프린터를 주문하기 위해
(B) 정보를 제공하기 위해
(C) 잉크 판매업체와 접촉하기 위해
(D) 구매를 승인하기 위해

해설 Yewande Asha가 자신의 사무실에서 쓰는 토너의 브랜드가 뭔지 아냐고 Sipho Ekene에게 묻자, Sipho Ekene은 모른다면서 IT 지원과의 Ian Juan을 대화에 끌어들여 그 정보를 알아내고 있다. 따라서 정답은 (B)이다.

정답 (B)

11. 오후 3시 19분에 아샤 씨가 "실례합니다, 이안"이라고 쓴 이유는?
(A) 그녀가 기계를 망가뜨렸다.
(B) 그녀가 정정을 하고 있다.
(C) 그녀가 그의 말을 이해하지 못한다.
(D) 그녀가 엉뚱한 제품을 주문했다.

해설 Yewande Asha가 일하는 사무실에서 토너 교체가 필요한 프린터는 탁상용인데 Ian Huan은 포스터 인쇄용 프린터의 토너를 교체해야 하는 것으로 잘못 알고 있다. 이에 Asha가 실례한다면서 그 잘못된 정보를 정정해 주고 있으므로 (B)가 정답이 된다.

정답 (B)

12. 에킨 씨는 다음에 무엇을 하겠는가?
(A) 수리 기사에게 전화를 건다.
(B) 후안 씨를 방문한다.
(C) 문자 메시지를 보낸다.
(D) 상점으로 간다.

해설 대화 마지막에서 Sipho Ekene은 '이제 나갈 것'이라고 적고 있다. Sipho Ekene은 애초에 회계과 사람들이 필요로 하는 물건을 사러 상점에 가려고 했었으므로(so I'm running to the store in a little bit.) (D)가 정답이다.

정답 (D)

13-17

회람

발신: 하워드 파울러
수신: 아웃콜 프로덕션 직원들
제목: 사무실 변화
날짜: 11월 30일

늘 그렇듯이 다가오는 새해와 더불어, 우리 사무실이 약간의 변화를 해야 할 시간이 된 것 같습니다.[13] 이번에는 약간 다르게 일을 할 것입니다.

나는 우리 사무실에 대해서 여러분이 변화시키고 싶어 하는 것에 대한 피드백을 원합니다. 우리가 근무 공간을 어떻게 조정할지에 대한 합리적인 제안을 하나씩 해 주십시오. 모든 사람은 하나의 익명의 제안을 해주셔야만 합니다.[14]

당신은 인트라넷 서버에서 양식을 찾을 수 있습니다. 그냥 파일을 열어서 당신의 제안을 작성하고, 출력한 다음 멜리사에게 주십시오. 잊지 마세요. 당신의 이름은 파일에 추가되어서는 안 됩니다.

나는 제안들을 검토할 것이고 무엇을 할 수 있을지 볼 것입니다. 이번 일을 돕기 위해서 나는 여러분들 중에서 한 그룹을 소집해서 제안을 검토하겠습니다.[15] 만약 모두 다 좋으면, 모두 다 인정될 것입니다.

게다가 나는 사무실을 개선하고자 하는 나의 제안은 우리의 백업시스템을 재구성하는 것이라는 점[16]을 공유하고 싶습니다. 이것은 큰 일이지만 매우 필요한 일이기도 합니다. 우리가 이것을 어떻게 다룰 수 있을지 제안하는 것 또한 환영합니다.[17]

여러분의 피드백과 협조에 감사합니다.

하워드

어휘 it is time for A to부정사 A가 ~할 시간이 되었다　a little 약간
differently 다르게　feedback 반응　reasonable 합리적인
suggestion 제안　adjust 조정하다　working space 근무 공간
be required to부정사 ~하도록 요구되다　anonymous 익명의
fill out ~를 작성하다　be added 추가되다　onto ~위에
look over ~를 검토하다　gather ~를 모으다
go over ~를 검토하다　additionally 추가적으로
reorganize 재구성하다　appreciate 감사하다

13. 회람에서 암시되는 바는?
(A) 사무실이 작다.　(B) 아웃콜은 새로운 회사이다.
(C) 멜리사는 회사의 매니저이다.　(D) 사무실은 매년 변화를 한다.

해설 본문 첫 문단에 As always, with the coming of the new year, it is time for our office to make some changes.(늘 그렇듯이 다가오는 새해와 더불어, 우리 사무실에 약간의 변화를 주어야 할 시간이 된 것 같습니다)에서 단서를 찾을 수 있다. as always(늘 그렇듯이)라고 했으므로 정기적으로 무엇인가를 한다는 것과 the coming of the new year(다가오는 새해와 더불어)이라고 했으므로 매년 한다는 의미로 이해할 수 있다.

정답 (D)

14. 제안에 대해서 암시되는 바는?
(A) 익명이어야 한다.
(B) 회사 정책에 관한 것이어야 한다.
(C) 파울러 씨에게 전달되어야 한다.
(D) 수정될 수 없다.

해설 본문 두 번째 문단의 Everyone is required to make one anonymous suggestion.(모든 사람은 하나의 익명의 제안을 하도록 요구받는다)에서 단서를 찾을 수 있다.

정답 (A)

15. 누가 제안을 판단할 것인가?
(A) 파울러 씨
(B) 최고 경영자
(C) 한 무리의 직원들
(D) 전체 직원들

해설 본문 네 번째 문단의 I will be gathering a group of you to go over the suggestions.(나는 이 제안들을 검토하도록 여러분들 중의 한 그룹을 모을 것입니다)에서 단서를 찾을 수 있다.

정답 (C)

16. 파울러 씨는 무엇을 하기를 원하는가?
(A) 더 많은 직원들을 뽑는 것
(B) 다른 층으로 이전하는 것
(C) 새로운 부서를 만드는 것
(D) 백업 시스템을 재편하는 것

해설 본문 다섯 번째 문단의 my suggestion for improving the office is to reorganize our backup system(사무실을 개선하고자 하는 나의 제안은 우리의 백업 시스템을 재구성하는 것)에서 단서를 찾을 수 있다.

정답 (D)

17. 다섯 번째 단락 3행의 manage와 의미가 가장 가까운 것은?
(A) 나누다
(B) 교환하다
(C) 배포하다
(D) 다루다

해설 동사 manage는 '관리, 감독하다, 다루다'는 의미가 있다. 여기서 manage는 '다루다'는 의미이며 따라서 동의어는 deal with나 handle이 된다.

정답 (D)

UNIT 15 이중지문/삼중지문

Part 7_ 실전연습 15 본책_p. 334-335

1-5

발신 마틴 페리 (ferrymartin@frasier.com)
수신 customer@harbin.com
제목 반품 정책
날짜 6월 29일[1]

관계자 분께

나는 스밋슨 무선 마우스[2]를 일주일 전에 귀사의 사이트를 통해서 구매했습니다.[1] (주문 번호 839870-28440) 저는 그것을 오늘 막 받았는데, 이것은 내가 예상했던 것이 아닙니다.

마우스의 사진에 따르면, 연결 부분은 USB 콘센트에 끼울 수 있는 작은 USB 막대입니다. 그러나 나는 보통의 마우스 사이즈에 가까운 연결 장치를 받았습니다.

나는 컴퓨터와 마우스를 연결하는 두 가지 종류의 무선 연결 장치가 있다는 것을 몰랐습니다. 나는 내 노트북을 위해 이 마우스를 구매했고,[3] 이 연결 장치는 현재 나의 마우스의 크기와 동일하므로 나는 원하지 않습니다.

반품을 하려면 어떻게 해야 하나요? 그리고, 배송 비용을 지불해야 하나요?

감사합니다.
마틴 페리

어휘 concern ~에 관계하다 purchase ~를 구매하다 wireless 무선의 through ~를 통해서 according to ~에 따르면 connection 연결 stick 스틱, 막대 plug into ~안에 끼워 넣다 outlet (전기) 콘센트 however 그러나 regular 보통의 realize 깨닫다 since 때문에 make a return 반품하다 shipping 배송

발신 customer@harbin.com
수신 마틴 페리 (ferrymartin@frasier.com)
제목 답변: 반품 정책
날짜 6월 30일

친애하는 페리 씨,

당신의 최근의 구매에 대해 감사합니다. 당신이 겪은 문제에 대해서 유감스럽네요. 그리고 저는 당신이 왜 그 마우스를 반품하시길 원하는지 이해합니다. 우리는 당신의 신용카드로 전액을 환불해 드리거나 또는 더 작은 연결 장치가 있는 마우스를 보내드릴 수 있습니다.[4]

그 동안 그 마우스를 반납해 주십시오. 당신은 배송비를 지불하실 필요가 없습니다. 그저 이 링크를 따라가서 배송 라벨을 출력해서 상자에 붙여주십시오.[5]

www.harbin.com/returns/shipping/a8y3oi_ijhs

우리는 이것으로 인한 모든 불편에 대해서도 사과드립니다. 저에게 응답을 해 주시거나 1-800-793-2849로 연락해서 우리가 환불을 해드릴지 새로운 마우스를 보내드려야 하는지 알려주십시오.

기분 좋은 하루 보내십시오.

파멜라 존슨
고객 서비스, 하빈 전자

어휘 purchase 구매(품) be sorry about ~에 대해서 유감이다
return ~를 반품하다 refund 환불하다 full amount 전액
smaller connection 더 작은 연결 장치
in the meantime 그 사이에, 한편으로 have to ~해야 한다
pay for ~에 대해 지불하다 simply 그저, 간단히
print out ~를 출력하다 attach ~를 부착하다
apologize for ~에 대해 사과하다 inconvenience 불편

1. 페리 씨는 언제 구매를 했겠는가?
(A) 5월 30일   (B) 6월 1일
(C) 6월 22일   (D) 6월 28일

해설 첫 번째 이메일의 발신 날짜를 보면 6월 29일로 되어 있고, 본문 앞부분에서 I purchased ~ a week ago.(나는 일주일 전에 ~를 구매했습니다)라고 했으므로 6월 22일이 정답이다.

정답 (C)

2. 페리 씨는 무엇을 구매했는가?
(A) 마우스   (B) 컴퓨터
(C) 디지털 컴퓨터 (D) 메모리 카드

해설 첫 번째 지문 앞부분 I purchased a Smithson Wireless Mouse(나는 스밋슨 무선 마우스를 구매했습니다)에 명확하게 '마우스'라고 나와 있다.

정답 (A)

3. 페리 씨에 대해서 무엇이 언급되었는가?
(A) 그는 사진사이다.
(B) 그는 노트북 컴퓨터를 가지고 있다.
(C) 그는 중소기업 사장이다.
(D) 그는 하빈으로부터 자주 구매한다.

해설 첫 번째 지문 세 번째 문단에서 I purchased this mouse for my notebook(나는 내 노트북 컴퓨터를 위해서 이 마우스를 구매했다)에서 단서를 찾을 수 있다. notebook(노트북 컴퓨터)는 laptop computer(랩탑 컴퓨터)와 같은 말이다.

정답 (B)

4. 존슨 씨의 이메일의 목적은?
(A) 페리 씨의 문제를 해결하려고
(B) 페리 씨의 구매에 대해서 감사하려고
(C) 페리 씨의 신용카드 정보를 얻으려고
(D) 페리 씨의 사과를 받으려고

해설 두 번째 지문의 첫 번째 문단에 We can either refund money or we can send you ~.(우리가 돈을 환불해 드리거나 또는 ~를 보내드리겠습니다)에서 단서를 찾을 수 있다. 페리 씨가 제기한 문제를 해결하려고 이 이메일을 썼다는 점을 알 수 있다.

정답 (A)

5. 페리 씨는 주어진 링크를 왜 방문할 것인가?
(A) 그의 주문을 보려고   (B) 유사한 물건을 보려고
(C) 정보를 작성하려고   (D) 배송 라벨을 출력하려고

해설 두 번째 지문 두 번째 문단에 You will not have to pay for shipping, simply follow this link and print out the shipping label(당신은 배송비를 지불할 필요가 없습니다. 그저 이 링크를 따라가서 배송 라벨을 출력하십시오)에서 단서를 찾을 수 있다.

정답 (D)

Part 7_ 실전연습 15   본책 _ p. 338-339

1-5

오키드 리젠시 리조트

	4월 15일 - 11월 15일	11월 16일 - 4월 14일
표준 싱글 / 더블 조식 포함[1]	49달러 99센트	79달러 99센트[5]
풀 불룸 퀸* 조식 포함, 체육관 사용	81달러 99센트	99달러 99센트
풀 불룸 킹* 조식 포함, 체육관 사용	89달러 99센트	129달러 99센트
풀 불룸 킹 스위트* 조식 포함, 체육관, 비즈니스 센터 사용	119달러 99센트	159달러 99센트[2]

*침대 추가는 15달러로 이용 가능

발신 로베르타 올리비에 (r.olivier@easymail.com)
수신 인디라 파텔 (ipatel@recordplace.com)
제목 호텔 옵션
날짜 11월 19일

안녕, 인디라

오늘 기분은 어때요? 당신의 요청대로 나는 호텔들을 살펴보았는데요.[3] 완벽한 것을 찾은 것 같습니다. 해변을 내려다 보고 있고, 큰 방들도 있고 당신이 이전에 보았던 다른 곳들보다 훨씬 쌉니다. 유일한 문제점은 이곳이 약간 외지다는 점인데,[4] 그래서 당신이 시내로 가고 싶다면 버스나 택시를 타야 한다는 것입니다. 당신은 www.orchidregencyresort.com에서 이 호텔을 볼 수 있습니다.

나는 당신이 이 선택에 대해서 동의할 것이라 확신합니다. 이것은 하루 밤에 총 80달러를 넘지 않으니까요.[5] 당신이 방을 볼 수 있는 기회를 가진 후에 오늘 밤에 전화 주십시오. 휴가 때문에 호텔 예약이 꽉 차기 전에 빨리 예약하셔야 하니까요.

로베르타

어휘 at one's request ~의 요청대로   look for ~를 찾다, 구하다
perfect 완벽한   beach 해변   rather 다소, 약간
isolated 고립된, 멀리 떨어진   so 그래서
would have to ~해야만 할 것이다   positive 확신하는
price range 가격 범위   book 예약하다   be taken 예약되다

1. 모든 방들의 가격에 포함된 것은 무엇인가?
(A) 아침식사   (B) 스파 일일 이용권
(C) 피트니스 센터 이용   (D) 비즈니스 센터 이용

해설 첫 번째 지문에서 소개된 모든 방들에 대한 설명에 with breakfast(아침식사 포함)가 있으므로 정답은 (A)이다.

정답 (A)

2. 새해 첫 날에 스위트룸은 얼마의 비용이 들 것인가?
(A) 89달러 99센트   (B) 119달러 99센트
(C) 129달러 99센트   (D) 159달러 99센트

해설 the suite(스위트 룸)은 호텔에서 가장 큰 방을 일컫는 표현이고, 본문에서 가장 마지막에 소개된 방 Full Bloom King Suite(풀 불룸 킹 스위트)의 가격을 봐야 한다. 새해 첫 날은 11 / 16 - 4 / 14(11월 16일부터 4월 14일까지)안의 기간에 포함되므로 정답은 (D)이다.

정답 (D)

3. 이메일에서 암시되는 것은 무엇인가?
(A) 호텔은 개인 해변에 있다.
(B) 인디라와 로베르타는 오래된 친구이다.
(C) 인디라가 호텔에 대한 정보를 요청했었다.
(D) 호텔은 외국에 있다.

해설 두 번째 지문 첫 번째 단락 첫 줄에 At your request(당신의 요청대로), I've been looking for hotels.(나는 호텔들을 찾아보았다)에서 단서를 찾을 수 있다. 인디라가 먼저 호텔에 대한 정보를 요청했다는 점을 알 수 있다.

정답 (C)

4. 이메일에 따르면, 호텔의 단점은 무엇인가?
(A) 대기자 명단   (B) 작은 방 사이즈
(C) 외딴 장소   (D) 수영장의 부족

해설 두 번째 지문 첫 번째 단락의 the only problem is that it is rather isolated(유일한 문제점은 이곳이 약간 외지다는 것이다)에서 단서를 찾을 수 있다. isolated(고립된, 떨어진)가 정답 보기에서 remote(외딴)로 패러프레이징되었다.

정답 (C)

5. 어떤 방이 선택될 것 같은가?
(A) 표준 싱글   (B) 풀 불룸 퀸
(C) 풀 불룸 킹   (D) 풀 불룸 킹 스위트

해설 두 번째 지문 두 번째 단락의 첫줄에서 It's within your $80 total per night price range.(이것은 하루 밤에 총 80달러의 가격 범주 안에 있습니다)에서 첫 번째 단서를 찾고, 첫 번째 지문에서 방 가격을 살펴보면 80달러 미만의 가격을 충족하는 방은 standard single / double(표준 싱글/더블)밖에 없다. 이 기간이 '4월 15일 - 11월 15일'이든 또는 '11월 16일 - 4월 14일'이든지 상관없이 둘 다 하루 밤에 80달러 미만이므로 정답은 (A)이다.

정답 (A)

Part 7_ 실전연습 15   본책 _ p. 342-343

1-5

수신 : 빌드스트럭트 아메리카 회사 직원들
발신 : 인사부장
제목 : 헬스장에서의 변화[1]

친애하는 동료직원들,

우리는 우리 직원들을 위해서 뛰어난 운동시설을 유지해야 하는 것의 중요성을 알고 있습니다. 최근 몇 년 동안 우리는 새로운 운동 장비를 구매했고, 라커룸을 보수해왔으며, '안전 제일'이라고 불리는 새로운 교육 과정을 제공하고 있습니다.

딱 한 달 전에 우리는 운동시설에 대한 설문조사를 실시했습니다. 여러분의 언급에 기초해서 우리는 곧 변화를 주려고 계획하고 있습니다.[2] 이러한 변경사항들은 11월 22일에 효력을 발휘합니다.[3] 우선, 체육관은 운영시간을 3시간 연장합니다.[2] 월요일부터 금요일까지 말이죠.

게다가 새로운 단체 운동 프로그램들이 생길 것입니다.[3] 마지막으로 오랜 기간 동안 강사였던 제이콥 소레스가 체육관의 매니저로 승진되었습니다.

회원권은 여전히 한 달에 30달러입니다. 하지만 12월 7일 전에 등록하는 분들은 6개월 동안 한 달에 15달러를 내게 될 것입니다. 관심있는 분들은 특별 할인을 위해서 제이콥 소레스에게 연락하십시오.

어휘 significance 중요함   maintain 유지하다
facility 시설물 (여기서는 헬스장을 지칭하는 표현)   equipment 장비
safety-training 안전교육   called ~라고 불리는
renovated 보수된   conduct 실시하다   based on ~에 기초하여
make changes 변화를 주다   encourage 장려하다
utilize ~를 활용하다   special offer 특별 제안 (할인 가격)

수신 : 빌드스트럭트 아메리카 회사 직원들
발신 : 제이콥 소레스, 헬스장 매니저
제목 : 규정을 따라 주십시오.

주의사항
• 다른 손님이 기다리고 있다면 장비 사용시간을 30분으로 제한해주세요.
• 회원과 함께 오는 한 명의 손님은 1회 무료 이용 가능합니다.
• 단체 수업은 20명으로 제한되므로 자리를 확보하기 위해 일찍 오세요.
• 교실 공간을 극대화하기 위해 소지품은 라커룸에 보관하세요.[4]
• 신입 회원들은 시설물을 이용하기 전 '안전 제일' 수업을 들어야 합니다.[5]
• 헬스장에서는 회원카드를 항상 소지해주세요.

어휘 patron 손님   registration 등록   ensure 확보하다
belongings 소지품   at all times 항상

1. 회람의 목적은?
(A) 새로운 시설의 개장을 발표하려고
(B) 직원들에게 체육시설의 변화에 대해서 통보하려고
(C) 체육시설을 개선하기 위한 추천 사항을 요청하려고
(D) 체육시설에 대한 문제점을 다루려고

해설 첫 번째 지문 상단 Re(~에 관해서, 제목)에서 Changes at the fitness center(헬스장에서의 변화)에서도 단서를 찾을 수 있고, 두 번째 단락의 we plan to make changes soon(우리는 곧 변화를 줄 것이다)에서도 단서를 찾을 수 있다.

정답 (B)

2. 회람에서 추론될 수 있는 점은 무엇인가?
(A) 제이콥 소레스는 새로운 직원이다.
(B) 회사는 또 다른 헬스장을 만들 것이다.
(C) 직원들은 시설물의 운영시간 연장을 요청했다.
(D) 직원들은 시설을 무료로 이용할 수 있다.

해설 첫 번째 지문 두 번째 단락의 Based on your comments, we plan to make changes soon.(여러분의 언급에 기초해서 우리는 곧 변화를 주려고 계획하고 있습니다)에서 먼저 단서를 찾고 그 뒤에 이어지는 문장에서 the fitness facility will extend its daily hours(헬스장은 주간 운영시간을 연장할 것입니다)에서 또 하나의 단서를 찾는다. 즉, 직원들이 운영시간 연장을 요청했다는 점을 알 수 있다.

정답 (C)

3. 11월 22일에 어떤 일이 일어날 것인가?
(A) 새로운 운동 강좌가 시작될 것이다.
(B) 새로운 장비들이 센터로 배달될 것이다.
(C) 직원들이 시설물의 개장에 참석할 것이다.
(D) 헬스장이 운영되지 않을 것이다.

해설 첫 번째 지문 두 번째 단락 중간에 changes will take effect on November 22(변화는 11월 22일에 효력을 발휘할 것입니다)에서 첫 번째 단서를 찾고, 밑에 이어지는 문장 there will be new group exercise programs(새로운 단체 운동 프로그램들이 생길 것이다)에서 두 번째 단서를 찾을 수 있다.

정답 (A)

4. 이 시설물을 이용하기 위해 요청되지 않는 것은?
(A) 회원카드를 소지할 것
(B) 장비를 제한된 시간 동안 이용할 것
(C) 수업에 일찍 도착할 것
(D) 교실로 소지품을 가져올 것

해설 두 번째 지문 '주의사항'에서 네 번째 항목 Please leave belongings in lockers to maximize space in the classroom.(교실에서 공간을 극대화하기 위해 소지품은 라커룸에 보관하세요)에서 단서를 찾을 수 있다. '소지품을 라커룸에 두고 오라'고 했으므로 교실로 가져가는 것은 하지 말아야 한다.

정답 (D)

5. 시설을 이용하기 위해 신규 회원들은 무엇을 해야 하는가?
(A) 신체검사를 받는 것
(B) 안전 훈련 수업을 먼저 들을 것
(C) 신청서를 작성할 것
(D) 기존의 회원 한 명과 같이 올 것

해설 두 번째 지문 '주의사항'에서 다섯 번째 항목 New comers are required to take the "Safety First" class before using the facility.(신입 회원들은 시설물을 이용하기 전 '안전 제일' 수업을 들어야 합니다)에서 단서를 찾을 수 있다.

정답 (B)

Part 7_ 실전연습 15   본책 _ p. 346–347

1-5

젠센 X3로 업그레이드하세요 – 당신의 생활도 업그레이드하세요

젠센 X3는 모바일 컴퓨팅 분야에서 차세대 진화의 산물입니다. 일본 최고의 두뇌들에 의해 제작된 소프트웨어, 스웨덴 최고의 엘리트 디자인 회사에 의해 만들어진 외부 부품, 그리고 독일의 업계 선도자들에 의해 제작된 마이크로프로세서를 갖춘 X3는 세계 최고의 성능과 스타일을 선사합니다.[1] 이 12인치 태블릿 컴퓨터는 모든 컴퓨팅 업무를 끝내기에 충분한 크기의 스크린을 제공하지만, 백팩이나 서류 가방 안에 들어가기에 충분할 정도로 작기도 합니다. 또한 14온스로 놀라울 정도로 가볍기 때문에 피곤해지는 일 없이 몇 시간 동안이라도 휴대하고 있을 수 있습니다. 그러한 모든 사용 능력은 12시간 동안 컴퓨터에 전기를 제공해 주는 리튬 전지에 의해 지속됩니다. 그리고 크러셔 그룹에서 새로 내놓은 내구성이 매우 뛰어난 스크린 덕분에 스크린은 흠집이 나지 않으며 대부분의 낙하나 충격시 상처가 나지 않습니다. 하지만 X3를 대부분의 경쟁 상품들과 구분해 주는 것은 뭐니뭐니해도 젠센 브랜드의 지원 소프트웨어인 베스트 프렌드입니다.[2] 베스트 프렌드는 이메일과 소셜 미디어에서 약속과 그 밖의 중요한 일정 등을 자동으로 불러옵니다. 오늘 X3를 구입하시고 당신의 새로운 베스트 프렌드와 함께 내일을 향해 걸어가십시오.

어휘 evolution 발달(의 산물), 진화(의 산물)   mind (지성이 뛰어난) 사람
craft 공들여 만들다   deliver 배달하다, (사람들의 기대대로 결과를) 내놓다
fit in ~에 잘 맞다   remarkably 두드러지게, 현저하게
sustain (필요한 것을 제공하여) 지탱하게 하다, 지속시키다
device 장치, 기구   ultra-durable 내구성이 매우 강한, 아주 오래가는
scratch-proof 흠집이 나지 않는
retrieve (메모리에서 데이터 · 정보 등을) 불러오다

젠센 X3는 모바일 컴퓨팅 분야에서 최근 몇 년 동안 등장한 제품들 중 가장 믿기지 않는 개발 제품이라고 광고되고 있다. 과연 그런 광고만큼 기대에 미치고 있을까? 이 평범한 비평가의 의견에 따르면 절대 그렇지 않다는 것이다.

이 태블릿 컴퓨터가 매력적이라는 사실은 부인할 수 없으나, 편안하게 손으로 잡기에는 한마디로 너무나도 크다. 한 여성이 손에 X3를 든 채 식료품점 통로를 따라 거니는 모습을 보여주는 텔레비전 광고는 너무도 비현실적이다. 내가 발견한 바로는 이 기기를 편리하게 사용하는 유일한 방법은 내 무릎 위에 올려 놓거나, 키보드와 마우스가 부착되어 있어 이 기기를 표준적인 데스크톱 컴퓨터로 변환시켜 주는 도킹 스테이션에 연결해 주는 것이다. 많은 유저들이 이 태블릿을 사용하려다 떨어뜨렸다는 신고를 해 왔는데, 스크린이 깨지고 하드 드라이브가 망가졌다고 했다.

광고에서 약속하는 모든 내용을 만족시키는 것 한 가지는 젠센의 새로운 조직 지원 기능이다. X3를 사용하는 도중에 나는 그 프로그램이 나의 일정에 채워 가는 정확성에 놀라움을 금치 못했다. 슬프게도 이 한 가지 환희는 X3를 구해 주기에는 역부족이다. 이 태블릿은 너무 크고 너무 비싸며, 현명하게 구매한 상품이 되기에는 그 누가 생각해도 불만스러운 점이 너무 많다.

X3의 발매를 둘러싼 실망에 대해 한 가지 희망은, 접수된 수많은 불만 사항에 대해 젠센이 보여주고 있는 신속하고 고객 친화적인 대응이다. 내려놓지 않고는 이 태블릿을 편안하게 사용하지 못하는 고객들에게, 젠센은 손잡이가 달린 케이스를 무료로 주고 있다. 이 케이스는 걸어 다닐 때 이 장치를 훨씬 사용하기 편안하게 해 준다는 것이 그들의 주장이다. X3에 너무 진절머리가 나서 더 이상 손대고 싶어하지 않는 사람들의 경우, 젠센은 전액 현금으로 환불을 해 준다.

나의 조언이 뭐냐고? X4를 기다리시라.

〈테크 타임즈〉의 마크 햄프턴

어휘 incredible (너무 좋아서) 믿어지지 않을 정도의, 믿을 수 없는
live up to (기대 등) ~에 부응하다 hype 광고, 선전
humble 변변찮은, 초라한 undeniably 명백하게, 틀림없이
stroll down 거닐다, (느긋하게) 걷다 grocery aisle 식료품점의 통로
docking station 도킹 스테이션: 노트북 컴퓨터를 데스크톱처럼 쓸 수 있게 연결시키는 장치 attached 부착된, 첨부된
lead to ~로 이어지다, ~을 초래하다 accuracy 정확(도)
triumph 승리감, 환희 frustrating 불만스러운, 좌절감을 주는
purchase 구입(품) silver lining 밝은 희망[전망], 구름의 흰 가장자리
-friendly ~에 적합한, ~에 친화적인 built-in 붙박이의, 내장된
be fed up with ~에 진저리가 나다 be done with ~을 끝장내다
issue 지급하다, 발부하다

발신: hitch@broadworld.com
수신: customersupport@jensen.com
제목: X3를 사용하기 힘들어서…

저는 최근에 젠센 X3를 구입했는데 심각한 문제가 있습니다. 업무 중에 이 기기를 사용할 수가 없어요. 저는 품질 보증 컨설턴트라, 하루 중 대부분을 생산 공장의 조립 라인에서 이리저리 걸어 다니며 시간을 보냅니다. 일하는 중에 사용하려고 X3를 구입했습니다만, 그것을 사용할 때마다 테이블이나 다른 올려놓을 곳을 찾아야 하는 실정입니다. 지장이 너무 큰지라 제게 있어 이 기기는 근본적으로 제 기능을 하지 못하고 있습니다. TV 광고에 나오는 것처럼 서 있는 동안에도 이 태블릿을 사용하고 싶습니다. X3의 몇 가지 기능이 마음에 들기 때문에 저는 이

것을 계속 사용하고 싶지만, 해결책을 제시해 주시지 못한다면 X3를 반품하고 다른 제조업체에서 나온 태블릿을 구입해야 할 것 같습니다. 조언을 주시기 바랍니다.

스텐 히친스

어휘 quality assurance 품질 보증 assembly line (공장의) 조립 라인
disruptive 지장을 주는
non-functional 기능적이지 못한, 실용적이지 못한

1. 광고에 따르면, 젠센 X3에 대해 언급되고 있는 것은?
(A) 다양한 나라의 회사들이 협조해 만들었다.
(B) 유저의 바지 주머니에 들어갈 정도로 콤팩트하다.
(C) 워드 프로세싱 소프트웨어가 이미 들어 있다.
(D) 젠센 브랜드의 소셜 네트워킹 서비스를 사용한다.

해설 광고문을 보면 소프트웨어는 일본에서, 외부 부품은 스웨덴의 디자인 회사에서, 그리고 마이크로프로세서는 독일 업계에서 만들었다고 (With software engineered by the brightest minds in Japan, ~ by industry pioneers in Germany,) 설명하고 있다. 따라서 정답은 (A)이다.

정답 (A)

2. 평론가는 젠센 X3에 대해 뭐라고 말하는가?
(A) 가격이 적당하다.
(B) 기기의 겉모습이 좋지 않다.
(C) 베스트 프렌드 소프트웨어는 잘 작동한다.
(D) 크리처 그룹의 부품은 튼튼하다.

해설 평론가는 젠센 X3에 대해 전반적으로 혹평을 하고 있지만, 딱 한 가지 젠센의 새로운 조직 지원 기능에 대해서는 칭찬을 아끼지 않고 있으며 그 프로그램의 정확성에 놀랐다는 의견도 내놓고 있다. 그런데 광고문의 What really sets the X3 apart from its competitors, though, is the Jensen-branded assistant software, Best Friend. 부분을 보면 그 지원 프로그램의 이름이 Best Friend임을 알 수 있으므로 (C)가 정답이 된다.

정답 (C)

3. 논평 두 번째 단락 1행의 hold와 의미가 가장 가까운 것은?
(A) 예약하다
(B) 휴대하다
(C) 중단하다
(D) 숨기다

해설 여기에서 hold는 '(물건 등을) 쥐다'라는 뜻으로 쓰이고 있다. 보기를 살펴보면 reserve는 '예약하다', carry는 '휴대하다', '가지고 다니다', stop은 '중단하다', conceal은 '감추다'라는 뜻이므로 (B)가 정답이다.

정답 (B)

4. 히친스 씨는 어디에서 일을 하는가?
(A) 공장에서
(B) 식료품점에서
(C) 사무실 빌딩에서
(D) 컴퓨터 상점에서

해설 Mr. Hitchens는 세 번째 지문인 이메일을 쓴 사람이다. 이메일을 보면 자신은 품질 보증 컨설턴트이며, 하루의 대부분을 생산 공장의 조립 라인에서 보내고 있다고(As a quality assurance consultant, ~ assembly lines at a production plant.) 언급하고 있다. 따라서 정답은 (A)이다.

정답 (A)

5. 젠센은 히친스 씨에게 무엇을 제공할 것 같은가?
(A) 컴퓨터 케이스
(B) 대체 부품
(C) 도킹 스테이션
(D) 무료 컨설팅

해설 이메일을 보면 Mr. Hitchens는 X3를 사용할 때마다 테이블이나 다른 올려놓을 곳을 찾아야 한다며 문제를 해결해 줄 것을 요청하고 있다. 그런데 논평의 네 번째 단락을 보면 내려놓지 않고는 X3를 편안하게 사용하지 못하는 고객들을 위해 젠센에서 손잡이가 달린 케이스를 무료로 주고 있다고(To customers that can't comfortably use the tablet without putting it down, Jensen is giving free cases with a built-in handle.) 설명하고 있다. 따라서 정답은 (A)이다.

정답 (A)

Part 7_ 실전연습 15 본책 _ p. 350-351

1-5

안녕, 런던   2월 3일   젠 샬

월요일에 파라콤 그룹은 레드 더치 홀딩스에서 치직 레인에 있는 시트웰 빌딩을 매입했다. 파라콤 대변인인 척 그레이블은 시트웰 빌딩이 주변 지역의 젊은 전문가들로 이루어진 성장하는 시장의 수요를 충족시키고 그 시장에 진입하고자 하는 기업들이 기꺼이 시트웰 빌딩에 공간을 임대할 것으로 생각한다.[1] "시트웰 빌딩은 인근 블룸즈버리 지역에서 주민들을 유치하기에 완벽한 위치에 있습니다."라고 그레이블 씨가 말했다.

시트웰 빌딩은 시트웰 로프트가 문을 닫은 후 현재 방치되어 있다. 레드 더치의 관리 하에 그 아파트는 작년에 마지막으로 문을 닫기 전 몇 년간 힘겹게 주민을 유지했다.[2] 아파트가 실패하자 몇몇 사람은 그 건물 업체들의 생존 능력에 의문을 갖게 되었다. "파라콤에 행운을 빌지만, 그들이 실수했을지도 모른다고 생각합니다. 시의 이 지역은 식당을 유지할 만큼 충분한 방문객을 끌어들이지 못합니다."라고 〈런던 비즈니스 타임즈〉 지(誌)의 그레이엄 고든이 말했다.

파라콤은 그 지역에 더 많은 믿음이 있다. 그 부동산 그룹은 치직 레인에 지난 5년간 상당한 투자를 해 왔고 그 상업 지구는 천천히 투자 효과가 나타나고 있는 것으로 보인다. 부동산 가격이 상승했고 유명 스페인 식당인 Mi Casa Es Su Casa의 소유주 겸 주방장인 헥토르 안셀모[5]는 이미 시트웰 빌딩에 식당 지점을 개점할 공간을 임대할 것이라고 발표했다.

그 건물은 6월에 영업을 시작할 것으로 기대된다.

어휘 What's up? 무슨 일이야?, 요즘 어때? purchase 구매하다
lane 도로, 길, 거리 holding 보유 주식 수, 지주(持株), 자회사
cater to ~의 구미에 맞추다, ~을 충족시키다
professional 전문직 종사자, 전문가 surrounding 인근의, 주위의
neighborhood 지역, 동네, 이웃, 주민 business 사업체
tap into ~에 다가가다, ~와 친구가 되다, ~을 활용[이용]하다
attract 끌어들이다 resident 주민 nearby 인근의, 가까운
currently 현재 abandon 버리다, 떠나다, 포기하다
departure 떠남, 퇴사, 출발
loft 고미다락, 로프트(예전의 공장 등을 개조한 아파트)
management 경영[운영] struggle to 부정사 ~하기 위해 애쓰다
retain 유지하다, 보유하다 failure 실패, 고장 lead 유도하다
question 의심하다, 이의를 제기하다
viability 생존 능력, (계획 등의) 실행 가능성 pull in (손님을) 끌다
apparently 분명히, 외관상으로 have faith in ~을 믿고 있다
real estate 부동산 invest in ~에 투자하다
commercial district 상업 지구
respond to 반응하다, 효과를 나타내다 investment 투자
property 부동산, 토지 branch 지점, 지사

발신: katmaella@creek.co.uk
수신: jschall@wul.co.uk
날짜: 2월 4일
제목: 시트웰에 대한 흥분

샬 씨께,

시트웰 빌딩의 구매에 관한 귀하의 기사에 응답하고 싶었습니다. 블룸즈버리 지역의 주민으로서 고든 씨의 의견에 정중하게 반대합니다. 저와 몇몇 친구는 가까이에 더 많은 식당이 개업하는 아이디어가 마음에 듭니다. 현재 우리는 패스트푸드가 아닌 뭔가를 먹고 싶다면, 맛있는 식사를 위해 시내를 가로질러 첼시까지 피곤하게 운전해서 가야 합니다.[3, 4] 시트웰 빌딩에 개업하는 어떤 멋진 식당이라도 손님이 많이 들 것이라고 확신합니다. 시트웰 로프트가 직면했던 문제는 그 지역의 가치보다는 그들의 경영진과 관련이 있습니다.

읽어 주셔서 감사합니다.
카텔라 마엘라

어휘 respectfully 공손하게 disagree with ~에 동의하지 않다
close by (~의) 인근[가까이]에 fare 요금 complicated 복잡한
fish and chips 피시 앤 칩스(생선살에 튀김옷을 입혀 튀긴 것과 감자튀김을 함께 먹는 음식) involve 포함하다, 수반하다
tiring 피곤하게 만드는, 피곤한 drive 드라이브, 자동차 여행[주행]
well attended 많은 사람이 참석한
have to do with ~와 관련이 있다
management 관리진, 경영진 desirability 바람직함

Mi Casa Es Su Casa가 대개장할 예정입니다.

오는 6월 29일에 시트웰 빌딩 1층으로 오셔서 우리와 함께 음악과 춤과 맛있는 음식을 즐기세요.

모든 주요리는 '하나를 사시면 하나를 더 드리는 행사'를 하오니 친구를 동반하는 것을 잊지 마세요.

주방장의 밴드인 더 솔티 키가 실황 음악을 연주할 것입니다.⁵

오늘 전화하셔서 자리를 예약하세요 — 자리는 금방 매진될 것으로 예상됩니다.

어휘 ground floor 1층 entree 앙트레(식당이나 만찬에서 주요리)
live (공연이) 라이브의, 실황인 salty 짠, 짭짤한, 재미있는
quay 부두, 선창

1. 그레이블 씨가 시트웰 빌딩에 관해 이야기한 것은?
(A) 고객들은 다른 지역에서 그곳을 방문할 것이다.
(B) 파라콤은 가격 인하 후에 그곳을 구매할 것이다.
(C) 최근에 기자가 사진을 찍었다.
(D) 몇몇 식당이 그곳에서 철수했다.

해설 기사 첫 번째 단락의 두 번째 문장을 보면 척 그레이블은 시트웰 빌딩이 주변 지역의 늘어나는 시장의 수요를 충족시킬 수 있다(the Sitwell Building can cater to a growing market of young professionals in surrounding neighborhoods)고 했다. 따라서 (A)가 정답이다.

정답 (A)

2. 마엘라 씨는 어느 회사가 시트웰 로프트가 문을 닫도록 했다고 암시했나?
(A) 런던 비즈니스 타임스
(B) Mi Casa Es Su Casa
(C) 레드 더치 홀딩스
(D) 파라콤 그룹

해설 기사 두 번째 단락의 두 번째 문장에서, 시트웰 빌딩이 레드 더치 관리 하에서 시트웰 로프트가 힘겹게 거주민들을 유지하려고 애썼으나 결국 문을 닫았다(Under the management of Red Dutch, the lofts struggled to retain residents for years before they were finally closed last year.)는 말이 나온다. 따라서 시트웰 로프트가 문을 닫은 것은 레드 더치 때문이라는 것을 알 수 있으므로 정답은 (C)이다.

정답 (C)

3. 마엘라 씨가 자기 이웃에 관해 암시하는 것은?
(A) 빠르게 성장하고 있다.
(B) 호텔이 많다.
(C) 식사 선택권이 제한되어 있다.
(D) 첼시보다 낫다.

해설 이메일의 Now, if we want any fare more complicated than fish and chips, it involves a tiring drive across town to Chelsea for a good meal.에서 마엘라 씨 주변에 좋은 식당이 많이 없음을 알 수 있으므로 이를 바꿔 표현한 (C)가 정답이다.

정답 (C)

4. 이메일 첫 번째 단락 4행의 drive와 의미가 가장 가까운 것은?
(A) 여행
(B) 요청
(C) 필요
(D) 동기 부여

해설 drive는 '드라이브, 자동차 여행[주행]'이라는 뜻이다. 따라서 '여행'이라는 뜻의 (A) trip이 정답이다.

정답 (A)

5. 안셀모 씨에 관해 언급된 것은?
(A) 부동산 투자자이다.
(B) 프랑스 요리를 준비한다.
(C) 음악 밴드에서 연주한다.
(D) 기자와 친구 사이이다.

해설 안셀모라는 이름을 찾아보면, 기사 하단에 Hector Anselmo, owner and chef of the popular Spanish restaurant Mi Casa Es Su Casa라는 말이 나오는 것을 볼 수 있다. 즉 안셀모는 이 레스토랑의 사장이자 주방장인데, 세 번째 지문인 Mi Casa Es Su Casa의 광고 하단을 보면, 주방장 밴드의 공연(Live music will be played by the chef's band)이 있다고 나온다. 따라서 정답은 (C)이다.

정답 (C)

Part 7_ 실전연습 15 본책 _ p. 354-355

1-5

갤러틴 카운티 정규 열차 운행 시간표

열차 번호	뷰트	화이트홀	쓰리 포크스	보즈먼
112*	오전 6:10	오전 6:55	오전 7:50	오전 8:25
120	오전 6:43	—	오전 7:53	오전 8:35
141	오전 7:49	오전 8:36	—	오전 9:05
194	오전 8:11	오전 8:49[1]	오전 9:32	오전 10:03
300	오전 9:15	오전 9:56	—	오전 10:30
307	오전 9:44	오전 10:17	오전 11:09	—
310[2]	오전 10:00	—	—	오후 12:00
315	오전 10:48	오전 11:18	오후 12:10	오후 12:38

*토요일과 일요일에는 운행하지 않음

어휘 regular 정규의, 정기적인 schedule 일정, 시간표 service (열차·버스 등의) 운행편

갤러틴 카운티 열차 승객 여러분께 알려 드립니다.

열차 운행 일정이 6월 내내 변경될 예정입니다. 다음 조정 사항들에 유의하시기 바랍니다.

1. 6월 첫 주 동안 모든 열차가 1시간씩 지연되어 오전에 정비팀들이 정기 연례 선로 정비를 할 수 있도록 할 것입니다.[4]
2. 6월 둘째 주 동안 뷰트와 보즈먼에만 정차하는 급행열차가 연료 효율이 더 좋은 모델로 열차 엔진을 교체할 것이기 때문에 운행을 중단할 것입니다.[2]
3. 6월의 마지막 2주 동안 쓰리 포크스 역이 개조 작업을 하는 동안 문을 닫을 것입니다. 쓰리 포크스를 방문하기 원하시는 승객들께서는 화이트홀에서 111번 버스를 타시거나 보즈먼에서 16번 버스를 탈 것을 권해 드립니다.[3]

갤러틴 카운티 철도 시스템의 성능과 안전을 개선하려고 이러한 변화들이 생기는 것이므로 이 기간 동안 여러분의 협조와 이해에 감사드리겠습니다.

감사합니다.
갤러틴 카운티 교통 공단

어휘 alter 변경하다 throughout ~ 내내 take note of ~에 유의하다 following 다음의 adjustment 조정, 수정 maintenance 유지 (관리), 정비 crew 팀, 반, 조 routine 일상적인, 정례적인 yearly 매년 하는, 연례의 track 선로 express 급행의, 직행의 be out of operation 운행하지 않는 replace 교체하다 energy-efficient 연료 효율이 좋은 renovation 개조 (작업) occur 일어나다, 생기다 improve 개선하다, 향상하다 performance 성능 safety 안전 cooperation 협조, 협력 understanding 이해 transit 수송, 교통 체계 authority 당국, 공공 기관

발신: jonnyfie@jfenterprises.com
수신: maroney@equineinterests.com
제목: 오늘 약속

매로니 씨께,

오늘 오전 미팅에 가지 못해 정말 죄송합니다. 너무 늦게서야 알아챘지만 이번 주에 모든 열차들이 선로에 진행되는 작업 때문에 한 시간 지연되고 있습니다.[4] 제가 당신의 사무실에 도착했을 때는 점심 식사를 하러 나가셨더군요. 접수 직원에게 메시지를 남겨 놓았지만 개인적으로도 메시지를 보내고 싶었습니다. 약속 시간을 다시 잡아서 당신의 잡지에 파타고니아의 야생마에 관한 기사를 쓰고자 하는 저의 제안을 논의할 수 있기를 희망합니다.[5] 편리하신 시간을 알려 주시면 그때 만나 뵐 수 있습니다. 다시 한 번 이번 일로 겪으셨을 불편에 대해 사과드립니다.

조너선 파이

어휘 appointment 약속, 예약 miss 놓치다, ~에 가지 못하다 realize 깨닫다, 알아차리다 receptionist 접수 직원 reschedule 일정을 다시 잡다 proposal 제안 article 기사 wild horse 야생마 magazine 잡지 convenient 편리한 apologize 사과하다 inconvenience 불편, 폐 surely 확실히, 틀림없이 cause ~에게 (폐를) 끼치다

---

1. 토요일에 승객이 화이트홀에서 쓰리 포크스까지 가는 열차를 가장 일찍 탈 수 있는 시각은?

(A) 오전 6:55   (B) 오전 7:53
(C) 오전 8:36   (D) 오전 8:49

해설 운행 시간표를 보면 Whitehall에서 Three Forks로 가는 첫 열차 시각은 6:55 A.M.이지만 해당 열차 번호 112*에 딸린 맨 아래쪽의 참고 사항 *No service on Saturdays or Sundays에서 토요일과 일요일에는 운행하지 않는다고 되어 있다. 따라서 토요일에 Three Forks로 가는 첫 열차 시각은 8:49 A.M.이므로 (D)가 정답이다.

정답 (D)

2. 6월에 새 장치를 갖추고 운행할 열차 번호는?

(A) 300   (B) 307
(C) 310   (D) 315

해설 공고문과 운행 시간표를 연계해 풀어야 하는 추론 문제이다. 공고문의 2. During the second week of June, the express train that stops only at Butte and Bozeman will be out of operation because the train's engine will be replaced with a more energy efficient model.에서 6월 둘째 주 동안 뷰트와 보즈먼에만 정차하는 급행열차가 엔진을 교체하기 위해 운행을 중단한다고 했으므로 셋째 주부터 새 엔진으로 운행한다는 것을 알 수 있다. 운행 시간표를 보면 Butte와 Bozeman에만 정차하는 열차 번호는 310번이므로 (C)가 정답이다.

정답 (C)

3. 화이트홀에 관해 시사되는 것은?
(A) 6월 내내 문을 닫는다.
(B) 기차역이 개조될 것이다.
(C) 급행열차 서비스가 제공될 것이다.
(D) 버스 서비스와 연계되어 있다.

해설 공고문 후반부의 to take the number 111 bus from Whitehall에서 화이트홀에서 버스 편이 연계되어 있음을 알 수 있으므로 (D)가 정답이다.

정답 (D)

4. 파이 씨가 매로니 씨와 약속을 잡은 때는?
(A) 6월 첫 주   (B) 6월 둘째 주
(C) 6월 셋째 주   (D) 6월 넷째 주

해설 이메일과 공고문을 연계해 풀어야 하는 추론 문제이다. 이메일 두 번째 문장의 all of the trains this week are delayed by one hour에서 이번 주에 모든 열차들이 한 시간 지연되고 있다고 했다. 공고문의 1. During the first week of June, all trains will be delayed by one hour에서 6월 첫 주 동안에 모든 열차가 1시간씩 지연된다고 했으므로 (A)가 정답이다.

정답 (A)

5. 파이 씨가 매로니 씨와 논의하고 싶어 하는 것은?
(A) 잠재적인 일거리   (B) 기록 영화
(C) 교통편 운행 일정   (D) 건설 프로젝트

해설 이메일 후반부의 to discuss my proposal for the article I would like to write about the wild horses of Patagonia for your magazine에 파이 씨가 매로니 씨의 잡지에 기사를 싣는 건을 논의하려고 한다고 했으므로 (A)가 정답이다.

정답 (A)

Part 1　Final Test　본책 _ p. 358-361

| 1. (D) | 2. (A) | 3. (B) | 4. (B) | 5. (A) |
| 6. (C) | | | | |

1.

(A) One man is paying for a laptop computer.
(B) One man is crossing his arms.
(C) The men are sitting across from each other.
(D) Most of the seats are not occupied.

(A) 한 남자가 휴대용 컴퓨터의 값을 지불하고 있다.
(B) 한 남자가 팔짱을 끼고 있다.
(C) 남자들이 서로 마주 보고 앉아 있다.
(D) 대부분의 자리가 비어 있다.

해설 (A) 남자가 지불하고 있는(paying for) 모습이 아니므로 오답이다. 만약 One man is using a laptop computer.(한 남자가 휴대용 컴퓨터를 사용하고 있다.)라고 하면 정답이 될 수 있다. (B) 남자가 팔짱을 끼고 있는(crossing his arms) 모습이 아니므로 오답이다. 참고로 '다리를 꼬다'는 cross one's legs라고 한다. (C) 남자들이 서로 마주 보고 앉아 있는(sitting across from each other) 모습이 아니므로 오답이다. 남자들이 나란히 앉아 있는 모습은 The men are sitting next to each other.(남자들이 나란히 앉아 있다.)라고 한다. (D) 의자들이 대부분 비어 있으므로 정답이다. 의자나 탁자가 비어 있는 상태면 be not taken, be not occupied 또는 be empty라고 하고, 사람이 앉아 있으면 be taken 또는 be occupied라고 한다.

어휘 pay for ~의 값을 지불하다　cross one's arms 팔짱을 끼고 있다　sit across from each other 서로 마주 보고 앉다　seat 자리, 좌석　occupied (자리가) 차지된

2.

(A) There are various kinds of magazines on the racks.
(B) He is writing some articles.
(C) The newsstand is closed.
(D) Some newspapers are being put into a backpack.

(A) 받침대에 다양한 잡지들이 있다.
(B) 그가 몇 가지 기사를 쓰고 있다.
(C) 신문 가판대가 문을 닫았다.
(D) 몇몇 신문들을 배낭에 집어 넣고 있다.

해설 (A) 받침대(the racks)에 다양한 종류의 잡지(various kinds of magazines)가 보이므로 정답이다. (B) 남자가 기사를 쓰는(writing articles) 동작을 하고 있지 않으므로 오답이다. (C) 현재 신문 가판대(newsstand)는 닫혀 있는(closed) 것이 아니라 열려 있는(open) 상태이므로 오답이다. (D) ⟨be being + 과거분사⟩는 사람이 사물에 해당 동작을 가할 때 쓸 수 있는 표현이다. 즉, 남자가 신문을 배낭에 집어 넣고 있는(are being put into a backpack) 모습이라면 정답이 될 수 있지만 그렇지 않으므로 오답이다.

어휘 various 다양한 kind 종류 magazine 잡지 rack 걸이, 받침대
article 기사 newsstand 신문 가판대
put A into B A를 B에 넣다 backpack 배낭

3.

(A) The passengers are getting off the train.
(B) One woman is about to board the train.
(C) The platform is empty.
(D) The train is approaching the station.

(A) 승객들이 기차에서 내리고 있다.
(B) 한 여성이 막 기차를 타려고 한다.
(C) 승강장이 비어 있다.
(D) 기차가 역에 접근하고 있다.

해설 (A) 승객들이 기차에서 내리고 있는(getting off the train) 모습이 아니므로 오답이다. 만약 Some passengers are getting on the train.(몇몇 승객들이 기차에 타고 있다.)이라고 하면 정답이 될 수 있다. (B) <be about to + 동사원형>은 '막 ~하려 하다'라는 뜻인데 여자가 기차에 막 타려는 모습이므로 정답이다. (C) 승강장(platform)이 비어(empty) 있지 않고 승객들이 보이므로 오답이다. (D) 기차가 역에 접근하고 있는(approaching the train) 것이 아니라 벌써 도착한 상태이므로 오답이다. 만약 The train is at the platform.(기차가 승강장에 있다.)이라고 하면 정답이 될 수 있다.

어휘 passenger 승객   get off 내리다
be about to 부사 막 ~하려 하다   board (기차·버스 등에) 타다
platform 승강장   empty 빈   approach 접근하다

4.

(A) The maid is cleaning the desk.
(B) There is a painting hanging on the wall.
(C) The walls are being painted.
(D) There is a window above the bed.

(A) 가정부가 책상을 청소하고 있다.
(B) 벽에 그림이 걸려 있다.
(C) 벽에 페인트 칠을 하고 있다.
(D) 침대 위에 창문이 있다.

해설 (A) 사진에 가정부(maid)가 보이지 않으므로 오답이다. 사진에 보이지 않는 단어가 들리면 오답으로 처리한다. (B) 벽에 사진이 걸려 있으므로(a painting hanging on the wall) 정답이다. (C) <be being + 과거분사>는 사람이 사물에 해당 동작을 가할 때 쓸 수 있는 표현이다. 그런데 사진에는 페인트를 칠하는 사람이 없으므로 오답이다. 누군가 벽에 페인트를 칠하는 모습이라면 He[She] is applying paint to a wall.(그[그녀]가 벽에 페인트를 칠하고 있다.)이라고 할 수 있다. (D) 창문이 침대 위에 있는 것이 아니므로 오답이다. 만약 There is a window on the wall.(벽에 창문이 있다.) 또는 There is a window in the corner of a room.(방 구석에 창문이 있다.)이라고 하면 정답이 될 수 있다.

어휘 maid 가정부   painting 그림   hang 걸리다, 걸다
paint 페인트를 칠하다   above ~ 위에

5.

(A) The workers are loading the luggage on the container.
(B) They are transferring to another flight.
(C) The passengers are packing their suitcases for a trip.
(D) The workers are adjusting the equipment.

(A) 직원들이 컨테이너에 수화물을 싣고 있다.
(B) 그들은 다른 항공편으로 갈아타고 있다.
(C) 승객들이 여행을 위해 가방을 싸고 있다.
(D) 직원들이 장비를 조정하고 있다.

해설 (A) 직원들이 컨테이너에 수화물을 싣고 있는(loading the luggage) 모습이므로 정답이다. The luggage를 주어로 하면 The luggage are being loaded on the container.(수화물이 컨테이너에 실리고 있다.)가 된다. (B) 직원들이 일을 하는 모습이지 다른 항공편으로 갈아타고 있는(transferring to another flight) 모습이 아니므로 오답이다. (C) 사진에 승객들이 보이지 않으므로 오답이다. 사진에 보이지 않는 단어가 들리면 오답으로 처리한다. (D) 직원들이 장비를 조정하고 있는(adjusting the equipment) 모습이 아니므로 오답이다.

어휘 worker 근로자, 직원   load 싣다   luggage 수화물
container (화물 수송용) 컨테이너, 통   transfer to ~로 갈아타다
flight 항공편   pack 싸다, 꾸리다   suitcase 여행 가방
adjust 조정하다   equipment 장비

6.

(A) He is stepping into the vehicle.
(B) He is leaning against the pillar.
(C) He is working in a repair shop.
(D) He is replacing his tools.

(A) 그는 차에 타고 있다.
(B) 그는 기둥에 기대고 있다.
(C) 그는 정비소에서 일하고 있다.
(D) 그는 그의 도구를 교체하고 있다.

해설 (A) 사진에는 차량(vehicle)이 보이지 않으므로 오답이다. 사진에 보이지 않는 단어가 들리면 오답으로 처리한다. (B) 남자가 기둥에 기대고 있는(leaning against the pillar) 모습이 아니므로 오답이다. 만약 남자가 허리를 숙이고 있는 모습이라면 He is bending over.(그는 허리를 숙이고 있다.)라고 할 수 있다. (C) 남자가 정비소에서(in a repair shop) 일하고 있으므로 정답이다. (D) 남자가 타이어에 대한 작업을 하는 것이지 도구를 교체하는(replacing his tools) 모습이 아니므로 오답이다. 지금 남자가 입고 있는 '멜빵바지'는 overalls라고 하므로 He is wearing overalls.(남자는 멜빵바지를 입고 있다.)라고 할 수 있다. 관련해서 '작업복'은 work clothes 라고 한다.

어휘 step into ~ 안으로 들어가다   lean against ~에 기대다 (cf. bend over 허리를 숙이다)   pillar (다리·건물 지붕 등을 받치는) 기둥
repair shop 정비소   replace 교체하다   tool 도구

Part 2 Final Test   본책 _ p. 362

7. (A)	8. (B)	9. (A)	10. (B)	11. (A)
12. (B)	13. (C)	14. (B)	15. (B)	16. (A)
17. (C)	18. (C)	19. (C)	20. (C)	21. (B)
22. (A)	23. (A)	24. (C)	25. (B)	26. (A)
27. (A)	28. (B)	29. (C)	30. (C)	31. (A)

7. Where did you have breakfast?
(A) We ate in the hotel restaurant.
(B) I have already eaten.
(C) I usually prefer eggs in the morning.

어디서 아침을 드셨어요?
(A) 저희는 호텔 식당에서 먹었어요.
(B) 저는 벌써 먹었어요.
(C) 저는 보통 아침에 달걀을 좋아합니다.

해설 (A) 장소 의문사 Where에 맞게 in the hotel restaurant이라는 구체적인 장소를 언급하고 있으므로 정답이다. (B) breakfast 와의 연상작용으로 eaten을 썼지만 식사 장소에 대한 답변이 아니므로 오답이다. 이것은 Why don't we eat breakfast?(같이 아침식사를 하는 게 어때요?)에 대한 답변이 될 수 있다. (C) 식사 장소에 대한 답변이 아니므로 오답이다. 이것은 What do you eat for breakfast?(아침 식사로 뭘 드세요?)에 대한 답변이 될 수 있다.

어휘 have breakfast[lunch, dinner] 아침[점심, 저녁]을 먹다
already 벌써   prefer ~을 좋아하다, 선호하다

8. What do you think of transferring to another branch?
(A) No, I will not meet with him.
(B) I am definitely ready for a change.
(C) You don't have to change trains.

다른 지점으로 전근 가는 것에 대해 어떻게 생각하세요?
(A) 아니요, 저는 그를 만나지 않을 겁니다.
(B) 저는 변화에 대한 준비가 확실히 되었어요.
(C) 기차를 갈아탈 필요가 없어요.

해설 (A) 의문사의문문에 Yes나 No로 대답할 수 없으므로 오답이다. (B) 다른 지점으로 전근을 가는 것(transferring to another branch)을 하나의 변화(a change)로 여겨 답변한 것이므로 정답이다. (C) '전근 가다'라는 뜻의 transfer를 '갈아타다'로 잘못 이해했을 때의 연상작용으로 trains를 쓴 것이므로 오답이다.

어휘 transfer to ~로 전근을 가다   branch 지점
definitely 확실히, 분명히   be ready for ~에 준비가 되다
don't have to 부정사 ~할 필요가 없다
change trains 기차를 갈아타다

9. What did the supervisor say about revising the work schedule?
(A) She said she'll have it done by Friday.
(B) I made some minor revisions to the report.
(C) Early morning shifts suit me the best.

관리자가 작업 일정의 수정에 관하여 뭐라고 말했나요?
(A) 금요일까지 수정을 완료할 거라고 했어요.
(B) 제가 그 보고서에서 사소한 몇 가지 사항을 수정했어요.
(C) 조조 근무가 제게 가장 잘 맞아요.

해설 (A) 의견을 묻는 What 의문문에 맞게 she'll have it done by Friday(금요일까지 수정을 완료할 것이다)라는 구체적인 내용을 언급하고 있으므로 정답이다. (B) 질문과는 의미상 무관하게 revising과의 유사발음으로 revisions를 언급한 것이므로 오답이다. (C) work schedule과의 연상작용으로 early morning shifts를 언급한 것일 뿐, 질문과는 내용상 관련이 없으므로 오답이다.

어휘 supervisor 관리자   revise 수정하다 (cf. revision 수정)
early morning shift 조조 근무   suit ~에 맞다, 어울리다
the best 가장

10. When does the office close?
(A) Mr. Jones will open it tomorrow.
(B) Usually at nine.
(C) Monday is a national holiday.

사무실 문을 언제 닫죠?
(A) 존스 씨가 내일 열 겁니다.
(B) 보통 9시입니다.
(C) 월요일은 국경일입니다.

해설 (A) close의 반의어로 open을 써서 연상작용을 유도한 것일 뿐, 질문과는 의미상 관련이 없으므로 오답이다. (B) 시간에 대한 의문사 When에 맞게 at nine이라는 구체적인 시점을 제시하고 있으므로 정답이다. (C) 시점으로 Monday를 썼지만 사무실이 문을 닫는 시점에 대한 답변이 아니므로 오답이다.

어휘 close 닫다 (cf. closed 닫힌)   open 열다; 열린
national holiday 국경일

11. Didn't you correct the errors in your article?
(A) Yes, I checked to make sure.
(B) Well, I don't want to collect them.
(C) She made a mistake.

당신이 쓴 기사의 오류를 수정하지 않았나요?
(A) 네, 제가 분명히 확인했어요.
(B) 음, 저는 그런 건 수집하고 싶지 않아요.
(C) 그녀가 실수를 했습니다.

해설 (A) 부정의문문에 Yes라고 대답했으므로 '오류를 수정했다'는 의미이고 이어서 '확인도 했다'라고 했으므로 정답이다. (B) correct와 유사발음으로 collect를 썼을 뿐, 기사의 오류 수정 여부에 대한 질문과는 관련이 없는 답변이므로 오답이다. (C) Didn't you ~?로 시작하는 의문문에 대해 누군지 알 수 없는 she를 주어로 쓸 수 없으므로 인칭 오류에 의한 오답이다.

어휘 correct 수정하다; 옳은   error 오류   article 기사
check to make sure 분명히 하기 위해 확인하다   collect 수집하다

12. You have to wear your safety glasses in the laboratory.
(A) May I have a glass of water?
(B) I won't forget to do that.
(C) The class is next week, I think.

실험실에서는 보호용 안경을 착용하셔야 합니다.
(A) 제게 물 한 컵 주실래요?
(B) 잊지 않고 착용할게요.
(C) 제 생각에 그 수업은 다음 주입니다.

해설 (A) glasses와의 유사발음으로 glass를 썼을 뿐, 의미상 제시된 평서문과는 관련이 없으므로 오답이다. (B) '보호용 안경(safety glasses)을 착용해야 한다'는 말에 어울리게 '잊지 않고 착용하겠다.(I won't forget to do that.)'라고 적절히 대답했으므로 정답이다. (C) 보호용 안경의 착용과는 의미상 관계없이 단지 glasses와의 유사발음으로 class를 쓴 것이므로 오답이다.

어휘 wear 입다, 착용하다   safety glasses 보호용 안경
laboratory 실험실   a glass of water 물 한 잔   forget 잊다

13. How about giving them a brochure before they leave?
(A) They've been invoiced.
(B) They used to live here.
(C) Right, I will do that.

그들이 나가기 전에 홍보 책자를 주는 게 어떨까요?
(A) 그들은 청구서를 받았어요.
(B) 그들은 이곳에 살았었죠.
(C) 좋아요, 제가 그렇게 할게요.

해설 (A) 동일 발음 they를 썼을 뿐, '그들에게 홍보 책자(brochure)를 주자'는 제안과는 의미상 관련이 없는 답변이므로 오답이다. (B) leave와 유사발음으로 live를 썼지만 질문과는 의미상 무관하므로 오답이다. (C) How about ~?(~하는 게 어때요?)으로 시작하는 제안의문문에 긍정적 반응을 하고 있으므로 정답이다. 의문사의문문에는 Yes나 No로 대답할 수 없지만 예외적으로 제안의문문(Why don't you ~?, Why don't we ~?, How[What] about ~?)에는 Yes, Sure, OK, Right 또는 No로 대답할 수 있다는 것에 유의해야 한다.

어휘 How[What] about ~? ~하는 게 어때요?   brochure 홍보 책자
invoice 송장(을 보내다)   used to부정사 ~하곤 했다, ~했었다

14. Does this machine do color copying?
(A) No, that's not the same color.
(B) Yes, but it takes a long time.
(C) There is a vending machine in the lobby.

이 기계는 칼라 복사가 되나요?
(A) 아니요, 그건 똑같은 색깔이 아니에요.
(B) 네, 그렇지만 시간이 많이 걸립니다.
(C) 로비에 자판기가 있습니다.

해설 (A) 질문에 쓰인 color와 동일 발음으로 color를 썼지만 질문과는 의미상 무관한 답변이므로 오답이다. (B) 칼라 복사(color copying)의 가능 여부에 대해 긍정으로 답하고 그와 관련된 내용을 추가한 것이므로 정답이다. (C) 동일 발음으로 machine을 썼지만 vending machine은 '자판기'라는 뜻으로 칼라 복사와는 관련이 없는 단어이므로 오답이다.

어휘 do color copying 칼라 복사를 하다   take (시간이) 걸리다
vending machine 자판기

15. Can you ask Maria to call me when she has a chance?
(A) I think she is called Susan.
(B) OK, I will leave her a message.
(C) I will speak to you tomorrow then.

마리아가 기회가 될 때 제게 전화하라고 해주시겠어요?
(A) 제 생각에 그녀는 수잔으로 불립니다.
(B) 네, 제가 그녀에게 메시지를 남겨놓을게요.
(C) 그럼 제가 내일 말씀드릴게요.

해설 (A) call과의 유사발음으로 called를 썼지만 질문에서의 call은 '전화하다'라는 뜻이고 보기에서는 '부르다'라는 의미로 쓰인 것으로 서로 내용상 관련성이 없으므로 오답이다. (B) 상대방에게 부탁을 하는 Can you ask ~? 의문문과 어울리는 긍정적인 반응을 하고 있으므로 정답이다. (C) 부탁을 하는 의문문에 Yes나 No와 같은 긍[부]정의 답변이 없으며 내용상 질문과도 어울리지 않는 반응이므로 오답이다.

어휘 when ~ have a chance ~가 기회가 될 때
be called + 이름 ~로 불리다   leave 남기다
speak to ~와 얘기하다   then 그럼, 그때

16. Why don't you take a seat over there?
(A) Will it be a long wait?
(B) The doctor will see you now.
(C) It took about 30 minutes to get there.

저쪽에 앉는 게 어때요?
(A) 오래 기다려야 하나요?
(B) 의사 선생님이 이제 당신을 볼 겁니다.
(C) 그곳에 가는데 30분 정도 걸렸어요.

해설 (A) Why don't you ~?(~하는 게 어때요?)로 시작하는 제안의문문에 역질문으로 추가 정보를 요청하고 있으므로 정답이다. (B) seat와의 유사발음으로 see를 썼을 뿐, 제시된 제안의문문과는 의미상 무관한 답변이므로 오답이다. (C) take와의 유사발음으로 took을 썼지만 질문에서는 '자리에 앉다'라는 의미로 'take a seat'을 쓴 것이고, 보기에서는 '시간이 걸렸다'라는 의미로 took을 쓴 것으로 두 단어가 의미상 관련이 없으므로 오답이다.

어휘 Why don't you + 동사원형 ~? ~하는 게 어때요?
a long wait 오랜 기다림
It takes + 시간 + to부정사 ~하는 데 (시간이) 걸리다

17. Do you want me to contact you by e-mail or fax?
(A) I already faxed you the memo.
(B) That would be great, thanks.
(C) Please just call me.

제가 당신에게 이메일로 연락할까요, 아니면 팩스로 연락할까요?
(A) 제가 벌써 당신에게 팩스로 회람을 보냈어요.
(B) 그게 좋겠네요, 고마워요.
(C) 그냥 저에게 전화 주세요.

해설 (A) fax와의 유사발음으로 faxed를 썼을 뿐, 선택의문문과는 의미상 관련이 없는 응답이므로 오답이다. (B) 선택 사항에 대한 답변이 아니라 의미상 무관하게 '고맙다(thanks)'고 한 것이므로 오답이다. (C) 선택의문문에서 주어진 두 가지 선택 사항(e-mail, fax)이 아닌 전화를 해달라는(just call me) 제3의 선택 사항을 제시하고 있으므로 정답이다.

어휘 contact 연락하다   by e-mail[fax] 이메일[팩스]로
fax 팩스(를 보내다)   already 이미, 벌써

18. Do you know when the conference is next year?
(A) Please come prepared.
(B) It will be held at the Crown Hotel.
(C) It will be the same time as this year.

내년에는 회의가 언제 있는지 아세요?
(A) 준비를 해서 오시기 바랍니다.
(B) 크라운 호텔에서 열릴 겁니다.
(C) 올해와 똑같은 때일 겁니다.

해설 (A) conference와의 연상작용으로 come prepared를 쓴 것일 뿐, 회의가 열리는 시점에 대한 답변이 아니므로 오답이다. (B) 회의가 열리는 시점이 아니라 장소로 답변한 것이므로 오답이다. 이것은 Where will the conference be held next year?(내년에는 회의가 어디에서 열립니까?)에 대한 답변이 될 수 있다. (C) Do you know 뒤에 있는 의문사 when에 맞게 the same time as this year라는 시점을 제시하고 있으므로 정답이다. May I ask + 의문사 ~?, Can you tell me + 의문사 ~?, 또는 Do you know + 의문사 ~? 등으로 시작하는 간접의문문에서는 문장 중간에 있는 의문사를 잘 듣고 그 의문사에 어울리는 답변을 찾아야 한다.

어휘 Do you know when + 주어 + 동사 ~? 언제 ~인지 아세요?
prepared 준비가 된   the same + 명사 + as ~와 똑같은 (명사)

19. How did you like last night's orchestra performance?
(A) No, he works in the morning.
(B) You can order them online.
(C) It was great.

어젯밤 오케스트라 공연 어땠어요?
(A) 아니요, 그는 아침에 근무합니다.
(B) 온라인으로 그것들을 주문할 수 있어요.
(C) 훌륭했어요.

해설 (A) How did you like ~?라는 질문에 누군지 알 수 없는 he를 주어로 쓸 수 없으므로 인칭 오류에 의한 오답이다. (B) 온라인 주문 (order them online)은 어젯밤 공연에 대한 질문과는 관계없는 답변이므로 오답이다. (C) 의견을 묻는 질문인 How did you like ~?(~은 어땠어요?)와 어울리는 긍정적인 반응으로 응답하고 있으므로 정답이다.

어휘 How do you like ~? ~가 어떻습니까? performance 공연 order 주문(하다)

20. Should I tell the manager about the changes we made?
(A) During yesterday's meeting.
(B) OK, let's change the subject.
(C) No, please wait until tomorrow.

제가 매니저에게 우리가 변경한 사항에 대해 얘기해야 할까요?
(A) 어제 회의 동안에요.
(B) 좋아요, 주제를 바꿉시다.
(C) 아니요, 내일까지 기다려주세요.

해설 (A) 매니저에게 변경 사항을 말해야 하는지에 대한 답변이 아니므로 오답이다. 이것은 When did you make the changes?(언제 변경을 하셨나요?)에 대한 답변이 될 수 있다. (B) changes와의 유사 발음으로 change를 썼을 뿐, 질문과는 의미상 관련이 없으므로 오답이다. (C) 부정적인 응답으로 No라고 한 다음, 내일까지 기다려보자는 의미이므로 정답이다.

어휘 make a change 변경하다 change 바꾸다; 변경 subject 주제

21. Why didn't you answer my e-mail?
(A) I'll mail it to you right now.
(B) My computer locked up.
(C) Let me answer the phone.

왜 제 이메일에 답장을 안 하셨죠?
(A) 제가 당장 그것을 당신에게 부칠게요.
(B) 제 컴퓨터가 먹통이 되었어요.
(C) 제가 전화를 받을게요.

해설 (A) e-mail에 답장을 하지 않은 이유에 대한 언급 없이 단지 e-mail과의 유사발음으로 mail을 쓴 것이므로 오답이다. (B) 이유를 물어보는 Why 의문문에 '컴퓨터가 먹통이 되었다'라는 이유를 제시하고 있으므로 정답이다. (C) 동일 발음으로 answer를 썼지만 이메일에 답장을 하지 않은 이유에 대한 언급은 없으므로 오답이다.

어휘 answer 대답하다, 답장하다 mail 우편(으로 부치다) right now 당장 lock up (기계 등이) 움직이지 않다(= freeze up)

22. The marketing department is upstairs, isn't it?
(A) No, it's on this floor.
(B) I like the street market.
(C) We'll discuss our new marketing campaign.

마케팅 부서는 위층이죠, 그렇죠?
(A) 아니요, 이 층에 있습니다.
(B) 저는 거리 시장을 좋아합니다.
(C) 우리는 새로운 마케팅 캠페인을 논의할 겁니다.

해설 (A) 먼저 No로 부정적인 응답을 한 다음, 마케팅 부서의 정확한 위치를 알려주고 있으므로 정답이다. 부가의문문의 경우, 평서문 문두에 나오는 주어, 동사를 잘 듣고 그것에 대한 적절한 응답을 선택하면 된다. (B) marketing과의 유사발음으로 market을 썼지만 마케팅 부서의 위치에 대한 응답이 아니므로 오답이다. (C) 동일 단어 marketing을 썼지만 위치에 대한 응답이 아니므로 오답이다.

어휘 upstairs 위층의, 위층에 (cf. downstairs 아래층의, 아래층에) street market 거리 시장

23. When will this product be on the market?
(A) They say it will be a month or so.
(B) Our market competition is weak.
(C) Pricing strategy is very important.

이 상품은 언제 시장에 나옵니까?
(A) 그들은 한 달 정도 있어야 할 거라고 하더군요.
(B) 우리는 시장 경쟁력이 약합니다.
(C) 가격 책정 전략은 매우 중요합니다.

해설 (A) 시간 의문사 When에 맞게 a month or so라는 구체적인 기간을 제시하고 있으므로 정답이다. (B) 동일 발음으로 market을 썼지만 제품의 출시 시점에 대한 답변이 아니므로 오답이다. (C) market과의 연상작용으로 pricing strategy를 쓴 것이지만 의미상 제품의 출시 시점과는 관련이 없으므로 오답이다.

어휘 on the market 시장에 나와 있는 it will be + 기간 (기간)이 걸리다 or so ~쯤, 정도 competition 경쟁(력) weak 약한 pricing 가격 책정 strategy 전략

24. Hasn't Judy found a park for the picnic?
(A) You can bring dessert.
(B) Two weeks from now.
(C) She's still looking.

주디가 소풍 갈 공원을 못 찾았나요?
(A) 후식을 가져오셔도 됩니다.
(B) 지금부터 2주 후예요.
(C) 그녀가 여전히 찾고 있는 중입니다.

해설 (A) picnic과의 연상작용으로 dessert를 언급한 것이지만 소풍 갈 장소에 대한 답변이 아니므로 오답이다. (B) 소풍 갈 장소에 대한 답변이 아니므로 오답이다. 이것은 When will you go on a picnic?(언제 소풍을 갈 거예요?)에 대한 답변이 될 수 있다. (C) 부정적 응답인 No를 생략한 채 '여전히(still) 소풍 갈 장소를 찾고 있다'고 응답한 것이므로 정답이다.

어휘 park 공원 bring 가져오다 dessert 후식
기간+from now 지금부터 (기간) 후에 still 여전히

25. Who do I talk to about printer toner?
(A) They are being printed at this moment.
(B) Mary, the office manager, orders supplies.
(C) Yes, they spoke last week.

프린터 토너에 대해서 누구에게 얘기하죠?
(A) 그것은 현재 인쇄되는 중입니다.
(B) 사무실 매니저인 메리가 물품을 주문합니다.
(C) 네, 그들이 지난주에 얘기했어요.

해설 (A) printer와의 유사발음으로 printed를 썼을 뿐, 프린터 토너에 대해 누구와 얘기를 해야 하는지에 대한 언급이 없으므로 오답이다. (B) 사람에 대해 묻는 Who 의문문에 맞게 사람 이름 Mary로 응답하고 있으므로 정답이다. (C) 의문사의문문에 Yes나 No로 대답할 수 없으므로 오답이다.

어휘 at this moment 바로 지금 (office) supplies (사무) 용품

26. Were you at the concert yesterday?
(A) Regrettably, I had to work overtime.
(B) I love music.
(C) Forty minutes from here.

어제 콘서트에 가셨나요?
(A) 아쉽게도 저는 연장 근무를 해야 했어요.
(B) 저는 음악을 좋아해요.
(C) 여기에서 40분 걸려요.

해설 (A) No를 생략하고 콘서트에 가지 못한 이유를 언급하고 있으므로 정답이다. (B) concert와의 연상작용으로 music을 썼을 뿐, 콘서트에 갔는지에 대한 답변이 아니므로 오답이다. (C) 콘서트에 갔는지에 대한 응답 없이 시간에 대한 답변을 하고 있으므로 오답이다.

어휘 regrettably 유감스럽게도, 아쉽게도
work overtime 연장 근무하다 (= work extended hours)

27. Mr. Gladstone didn't say when he was getting here, did he?
(A) Yes, he should arrive at seven o'clock.
(B) He's coming from Rome.
(C) No, he didn't send it.

글래드스톤 씨는 언제 여기에 도착할지 얘기 안 했죠, 그렇죠?
(A) 네, 그는 7시에 도착할 겁니다.
(B) 그는 로마에서 오고 있어요.
(C) 아니요, 그는 그것을 보내지 않았습니다.

해설 (A) Yes라고 대답했으므로 글래드스톤이 그가 언제 도착할 것인지에 대해 말을 했다는 의미이다. 그리고 at seven o'clock이라는 구체적인 도착 시점을 제시하고 있으므로 정답이다. (B) 글래드스톤의 도착 시점에 대한 언급이 아니므로 오답이다. 이것은 Where is Mr. Gladstone coming from?(글래드스톤 씨가 어디에서 오고 있나요?)에 대한 답변이 될 수 있다. (C) say에 대한 유사발음으로 send를 쓴 것일 뿐, 글래드스톤의 도착 시점과는 관련없는 답변이므로 오답이다.

어휘 get here 이곳에 도착하다 should ~일 것 같다(추측)
come from ~에서 오다 Rome 로마 send 보내다

28. Ms. Taylor gave an excellent presentation.
(A) Thank you for that gift.
(B) Yes, she's a very talented presenter.
(C) I'll take notes if she'll be absent.

테일러 씨의 발표는 훌륭했어요.
(A) 그 선물에 감사 드립니다.
(B) 네, 그녀는 매우 재능 있는 발표자입니다.
(C) 만약 그녀가 못 오면 제가 필기를 할게요.

해설 (A) '선물을 주셔서 감사하다'라는 말은 테일러 씨의 훌륭한 발표와는 의미상 관련이 없는 답변이므로 오답이다. (B) '테일러 씨가 훌륭한 발표를 했다'는 말에 Yes로 긍정 동의를 한 후, 그녀와 관련된 언급을 하고 있으므로 정답이다. (C) presentation에 대한 연상작용으로 take notes를 썼을 뿐, 테일러 씨의 발표와는 관련없는 언급이므로 오답이다.

어휘 give a presentation 발표하다 talented 재능 있는
take notes 기록하다, 필기하다 absent 빠진, 불참한

29. Would you like to rent a mid-size car or an SUV?
(A) They're a mid-sized company.
(B) No, I prefer to make reservations online.
(C) It doesn't matter. Whatever is available.

중형차와 SUV 중 어떤 것을 빌리시겠습니까?
(A) 그들은 중간 규모의 회사입니다.
(B) 아니요, 저는 온라인 예약을 선호합니다.
(C) 상관없어요. 이용 가능한 건 어떤 것도 좋습니다.

해설 (A) mid-size와의 유사발음으로 mid-sized를 썼지만 차량 대여와는 관련이 없는 답변이므로 오답이다. (B) 선택의문문에는 Yes나 No로 대답할 수 없으므로 오답이다. (C) 선택의문문에서 제시된 두 가지 선택 사항(a mid-size car, an SUV) 중 하나를 바로 선택하지 않고 '이용 가능한 것은 어떠한 것이라도(whatever is available) 좋다'고 했으므로 정답이다.

어휘 rent 빌리다   mid-sized 중간 크기의
prefer to부정사 ~하는 것을 선호하다
make a reservation 예약하다   matter 중요하다
available 이용 가능한

30. Aren't you friends with Betty?
(A) From a friend of mine.
(B) She will join us, too.
(C) Yes, since we were kids.

당신은 베티와 친구 아닙니까?
(A) 제 친구 중 한 명으로부터요.
(B) 그녀도 우리와 함께 할 거예요.
(C) 네, 어렸을 때부터요.

해설 (A) friends와 유사발음 friend를 썼지만 베티와 친구 관계인지에 대한 답변이 아니므로 오답이다. (B) she가 Betty를 가리키는 것으로 볼 수 있지만 베티와 친구 관계인지를 묻는 질문과는 관련이 없으므로 오답이다. (C) Yes라고 했으므로 Betty와 친구인 것이며 그녀를 언제부터 알게 되었는지를 언급하고 있으므로 정답이다.

어휘 be friends with ~와 친구이다   join 합류하다   too 또한
since ~ 이래로   kid 아이

31. Have we renewed our subscription to the magazine?
(A) I'll have to check our records.
(B) It also covers business updates.
(C) No, I bought an older model.

우리가 잡지 구독을 연장했나요?
(A) 제가 기록을 확인해봐야겠어요.
(B) 그것은 최신 비즈니스 정보도 다루고 있어요.
(C) 아니요, 저는 구형 모델을 구입했어요.

해설 (A) 잡지 구독을 연장했는지에 대한 즉답을 피한 채, 구독에 관한 기록을 확인해보겠다는 의미이므로 정답이다. (B) magazine과의 연상 작용으로 business updates를 쓴 것이지만 잡지 구독의 연장 여부에 대한 답변은 아니므로 오답이다. (C) renewed와의 연상작용으로 older model을 썼지만 잡지 구독의 연장에 대한 답변이 아니므로 오답이다.

어휘 renew 갱신하다, 연장하다   subscription to ~의 구독
cover 다루다

Part 3   Final Test   본책 _ p. 363-366

32. (C)	33. (D)	34. (B)	35. (A)	36. (D)
37. (A)	38. (A)	39. (C)	40. (B)	41. (D)
42. (B)	43. (A)	44. (D)	45. (B)	46. (C)
47. (D)	48. (A)	49. (B)	50. (A)	51. (B)
52. (D)	53. (D)	54. (A)	55. (C)	56. (B)
57. (A)	58. (A)	59. (C)	60. (B)	61. (D)
62. (A)	63. (A)	64. (D)	65. (A)	66. (C)
67. (C)	68. (B)	69. (D)	70. (D)	

32-34

M: Judy, I guess you heard **our client, Joy Computing, Inc., wants us to come up with a complete marketing plan**[32] for their new line of laptop computers.

W: Right. The client hopes to focus on how these devices are inexpensive and easy to use. **Our whole team should meet**[33] and discuss new marketing strategies.

M: Sounds good. I think everyone is free after lunch. Why don't we meet then? We can use the small conference room.

W: Terrific. **I'll write a group e-mail**[34] to our team about the meeting.

남: 주디, 우리 고객사인 조이 컴퓨팅 사가 우리에게 그들의 새 노트북을 위한 완성된 마케팅 안을 제시해달라는 얘기를 들었을 겁니다.

여: 네. 그 회사는 이 장치들이 얼마나 저렴하고 사용하기 쉬운지에 초점을 맞추고 싶어합니다. 우리 팀 전체가 만나서 새로운 마케팅 전략들에 대해 논의를 해야겠어요.

남: 맞아요. 점심 식사 이후에 모두 시간이 될 겁니다. 그때 만나는 게 어때요? 우리는 소회의실을 쓸 수 있거든요.

여: 아주 잘됐네요. 제가 회의에 대해 우리 팀에게 단체 이메일을 쓸게요.

어휘 client 고객, 고객사   come up with ~을 제시하다, 내다
complete 완전한   marketing plan 마케팅 안   line (상품의) 종류
focus on ~에 초점을 맞추다   device 장치   inexpensive 저렴한
easy to use 사용하기 쉬운   whole 전체의   strategy 전략
free 시간이 있는   conference room 회의실   terrific 아주 좋은

32. 화자들은 무엇에 대해 얘기하고 있는가?
(A) 소프트웨어 프로그램   (B) 합병 제안
(C) 마케팅 프로젝트   (D) 부서의 예산

해설 대화 주제는 대화의 초반부에 언급되므로 처음 시작하는 부분을 잘 들어야 한다. 남자가 our client, Joy Computing, Inc., wants us to come up with a complete marketing plan이라고 했으므로 정답은 (C)이다.

33. 여자는 무엇을 권하는가?
(A) 고객 방문을 연기하는 것
(B) 새로운 컴퓨터 시스템 구입
(C) IT 부서에 연락하는 것
(D) 회의를 하는 것

해설 질문이 여자의 제안 사항에 대한 것이므로 여자의 말에서 정답의 단서를 찾아야 한다. 여자가 Our whole team should meet라고 했으므로 정답은 (D)이다.

34. 여자는 아마도 다음에 무엇을 하겠는가?
(A) 목록 작성   (B) 이메일 쓰기
(C) 회의실 예약   (D) 점심 시간 갖기

해설 여자의 다음 행동에 대한 질문이므로 여자의 말에서 정답의 단서를 찾아야 한다. 대화 마지막에 여자가 I'll write a group e-mail이라고 했으므로 정답은 (B)이다. 화자의 향후 계획이나 행동에 대한 언급은 주로 대화 후반부에 제시된다는 것을 알아두자.

35-37

> W: Tony, I heard the big news. We're opening a new store in Gateway City. **I was wondering if I could possibly get transferred to that location.**³⁵
> M: Oh, it could be a good opportunity. I guess **it's going to be the biggest furniture store**³⁶ in our region, even bigger than this one. But, I'm curious. Why are you interested in making the move to Gateway City?
> W: Well, as you know, I like it here a lot. But **most of my family lives and works in Gateway City,**³⁷ so it would be a chance for me to see them more often.

여: 토니, 제가 굉장한 소식을 들었어요. 우리가 게이트웨이 시에 새로운 상점을 열 거예요. 제가 아마도 그 지점으로 전근을 갈 수 있을지 모르겠네요.
남: 오, 좋은 기회 같은데요. 이곳보다도 훨씬 크고 우리 지역에서도 가장 큰 가구점일 겁니다. 그런데, 궁금한 게 있어요. 왜 게이트웨이 시로 가는 데 관심이 있는 거죠?
여: 음, 아시는 것처럼 저는 여기가 아주 좋아요. 하지만 저의 가족 대부분이 게이트웨이 시에서 살면서 일하고 있어서, 제가 더 자주 가족들을 볼 수 있는 기회가 될 거예요.

어휘 wonder if + 주어 + 동사 ~인지 궁금하다   possibly 아마도
get transferred to + 장소 ~로 발령받다, 전근되다   location 지점
opportunity 기회   furniture store 가구점   curious 궁금한
be interested in ~에 관심이 있다
make a move to + 장소 ~로 가다, 이동하다
most of + the[소유격] + 명사 ~의 대부분

35. 여자가 하고 싶은 것은 무엇인가?
(A) 새 지점에서의 근무   (B) 특별 행사 준비
(C) 승진 요청   (D) 영업 콘테스트 평가

해설 여자가 원하는 것에 대한 질문이므로 여자의 말에서 정답의 단서를 찾아야 한다. 여자가 I was wondering if I could possibly get transferred to that location이라고 했으므로 정답은 (A)이다. 일반적으로 정답의 단서는 질문의 순서대로 제시되는 경우가 많으므로 문제와 보기를 미리 읽어둔 다음 순차적으로 정답을 찾는 연습을 해야 한다.

36. 화자들은 아마도 어디에서 근무하겠는가?
(A) 부동산 회사   (B) 실내 디자인 회사
(C) 이삿짐 운송 회사   (D) 가구점

해설 화자들의 근무지는 대화에 등장하는 단어에서 정답의 단서를 찾을 수 있다. 남자가 it's going to be the biggest furniture store라고 했으므로 정답은 (D)이다.

37. 여자는 게이트웨이 시에 대해 뭐라고 말하는가?
(A) 그녀의 가족 대부분이 그곳에 산다.
(B) 그녀가 과거에 그곳에서 근무했다.
(C) 그곳의 상점들은 대체로 작다.
(D) 그녀는 그곳을 방문해본 적이 없다.

해설 여자가 Gateway City에 대해 언급한 내용을 찾는 문제이므로 여자가 Gateway City라는 말을 언급하는 부분에서 정답의 단서를 찾아야 한다. 대화 마지막에 most of my family lives and works in Gateway City라고 했으므로 정답은 (A)이다.

38-40

> M: Did you hear that **Michael is going to turn in his resignation**?³⁸
> W: No, I hadn't heard. Have they found anyone to replace him?
> M: No, not yet, but **he won't leave us until next month**.³⁹ They're having trouble finding a qualified candidate to replace him though.
> W: Well, there's still plenty of time to find someone. **I think they should consider asking Alicia.**⁴⁰ She's filled in for Michael on a few projects, so she's already familiar with his job responsibilities.

남: 마이클이 사표를 낼 거라는 얘기 들었어요?

여: 아니요, 못 들었어요. 회사에서 그의 후임자를 구했나요?

남: 아니요, 아직이요. 하지만 그는 다음 달에나 퇴사할 거예요. 그렇긴 해도 회사에서 그를 대신할 적임자를 찾는 데 어려움을 겪고 있어요.

여: 음, 그래도 누군가를 구하기에는 시간이 충분하네요. 제 생각에 회사는 앨리샤에게 물어보는 것도 고려해봐야 해요. 앨리샤가 몇 가지 프로젝트에서 마이클을 대신했기 때문에 마이클의 직무에 대해 이미 잘 알고 있거든요.

어휘 turn in[hand in, submit] one's resignation 사표를 내다
replace 대신하다   not ~ until+시점 (시점)에야 ~하다
have trouble+~ing ~하는 데 어려움을 겪다
qualified candidate 적임자   though 그렇지만, 그래도
plenty of 많은   consider 고려하다
fill in for+사람 (사람)을 대신하다
be familiar with ~에 대해 잘 알다   job responsibility 책무

38. 마이클은 왜 그의 자리에서 물러나는가?
(A) 그는 퇴사를 한다.
(B) 그는 승진한다.
(C) 그는 자신의 사업을 개업한다.
(D) 그는 다른 사무실로 전근을 간다.

해설 남자가 대화를 시작하면서 Michael is going to turn in his resignation이라고 했는데 turn in his resignation이란 말이 '사직서를 내다'라는 의미이므로 정답은 (A)이다. 즉, turn in his resignation이 leave the company라는 말로 패러프레이징(바꿔 말하기) 된 것이다.

39. 마이클은 언제 그의 자리에서 물러나는가?
(A) 주말
(B) 다음 주
(C) 다음 달
(D) 연말

해설 남자가 he won't leave us until next month라고 했으므로 정답은 (C)이다. <not ~ until+시점>은 '(시점)에야 ~하다'라는 뜻이라는 것을 알아두자.

40. 여자가 앨리샤에 대해 언급한 내용은 무엇인가?
(A) 그녀 또한 방콕에서 근무한다.
(B) 그녀가 마이클을 대신해야 한다.
(C) 그녀가 곧 누군가를 고용해야 한다.
(D) 그녀도 곧 퇴사를 할 것이다.

해설 여자가 Alicia에 대해 언급한 내용을 찾는 문제이므로 여자의 말 중에서 Alicia가 나오는 부분에 집중해야 한다. 대화 후반부에 여자가 I think they should consider asking Alicia.라고 했는데 이 말 속에는 결국 앨리샤가 마이크를 대신해야 한다는 의미가 들어 있으므로 정답은 (B)이다.

41-43

M: **I hear you're going to Hawaii**,[41] Adel. How wonderful. I wish I was going somewhere warm to escape all this snow. It's been a long winter. When are you leaving?

W: I'm so excited. But **my flight leaves this Saturday and they're predicting a big snowstorm**.[42]

M: Uh-oh. I hope your flight doesn't get delayed because of it.

W: Well, **it leaves at six o'clock in the morning**.[43] I'm just hoping the snowstorm won't hit until later in the day. Cross your fingers!

남: 아델, 하와이에 갈 거라고 들었어요. 얼마나 좋을까. 저도 이런 눈 좀 피해 어디 따뜻한 곳에 가면 좋겠어요. 겨울이 참 기네요. 언제 가세요?

여: 저는 아주 신나요. 그런데 제 항공편이 이번 토요일에 떠나는데 폭설이 올 거라는 예보가 있어요.

남: 이런. 폭설로 항공편이 지연되지 않았으면 좋겠어요.

여: 음, 비행기가 아침 6시에 출발해요. 그날 늦게까지 폭설이 몰아치지 않길 바랄 뿐이에요. 행운을 빌어주세요.

어휘 somewhere 어딘가   escape 탈출하다, 벗어나다   leave 떠나다
excited 들뜬, 신이 난   flight 항공편   predict 예상하다
snowstorm 폭설   get delayed 지연되다   hit 강타하다
later in the day 그날 늦게   cross one's fingers 행운을 빌다

41. 화자들은 어떤 얘기를 하고 있는가?
(A) 그들의 최근 휴가
(B) 남자의 주말 계획
(C) 하와이의 날씨
(D) 여자의 여행 계획

해설 대화의 주제는 대화의 초반부에 언급되므로 항상 처음 시작하는 부분을 잘 들어야 한다. 남자가 대화를 시작하면서 여자에게 I hear you're going to Hawaii라고 했는데 이것은 여자의 여행에 대해 언급한 것이므로 정답은 (D)이다.

42. 이번 주 토요일 날씨는 어떻겠는가?
(A) 화창하다.
(B) 눈이 내린다.
(C) 비가 온다.
(D) 안개가 낀다.

해설 문제에 시점으로 this Saturday가 있으므로 대화에서 Saturday가 언급되는 부분을 잘 들어야 한다. 여자가 my flight leaves this Saturday and they're predicting a big snowstorm이라고 했으므로 정답은 (B)이다.

43. 여자는 언제 떠나길 기대하는가?
(A) 토요일 아침 일찍
(B) 토요일 오후
(C) 토요일 저녁
(D) 토요일 늦은 밤

해설 여자가 출발을 기대하는 시점에 대한 질문이므로 여자의 말에서 정답의 단서를 찾아야 한다. 여자가 it leaves at six o'clock in the morning이라고 했고 앞에서 항공편이 토요일에 출발한다고 했으므로 결국 정답은 (A)이다.

44-46

W: Hi, I'm a regular patient of Dr. Jackson's. Would he be available to answer a quick question over the phone?
M: I'm afraid Dr. Jackson is not in the office. **Right now he's lecturing at a medical conference.**⁴⁴ Can I leave a message with him?
W: Oh, that's OK. **I just wanted to talk to him about a stretching exercise he showed me.**⁴⁵ I can't seem to find the instruction booklet he gave me for the exercise.
M: Well, I have images of all our clinic's exercise booklets here in my computer. **Let me bring them up and see if we can find yours.**⁴⁶ Hold for one moment.

여: 안녕하세요. 저는 잭슨 선생님의 정기 진료 환자입니다. 선생님께서 전화로 간단한 질문에 대답해주실 수 있을까요?
남: 죄송하지만 잭슨 선생님은 진료실에 안 계세요. 지금 의학 회의에서 강의를 하고 계십니다. 제가 선생님께 메시지를 남겨드릴까요?
여: 오, 좋아요. 저는 선생님께서 제게 보여주신 스트레칭 운동에 대해 얘기하고 싶었습니다. 그 운동용으로 선생님께서 주신 설명서를 못 찾겠거든요.
남: 음. 제 컴퓨터에 우리 병원의 모든 운동 안내서에 대한 사진이 있거든요. 제가 그걸 띄워서 환자분의 것을 찾을 수 있는지 볼게요. 잠깐만 기다려주세요.

어휘 regular patient 정규 진료 환자 available 시간이 있는
quick question 간단한 질문 over the phone 전화로
I'm afraid ~ 죄송하지만[유감이지만] ~이다 lecture 강의(하다)
medical conference 의학 회의
leave a message with 메시지를 ~에게 남기다
instruction 설명, 지시 booklet 소책자
bring up 꺼내다. (컴퓨터 화면에) 띄우다 see if ~인지 알아보다
hold for one moment 잠깐 기다리다

44. 남자에 따르면 잭슨 선생님은 지금 어디에 있는가?
(A) 진료실 (B) 근처 병원
(C) 약국 (D) 의학 회의

해설 질문에 사람 이름인 Dr. Jackson이 있으므로 대화 중에 Jackson이 언급되는 부분에서 정답의 단서를 찾아야 한다. 남자가 Right now he's lecturing at a medical conference.라고 했는데 he가 Jackson을 말하므로 정답은 (D)이다. 이처럼 앞에 언급된 사람 이름은 대명사로 바뀌어 제시되므로 그 흐름을 잘 따라갈 수 있어야 정답을 찾을 수 있다.

45. 여자는 왜 잭슨 선생님과 통화를 하고 싶어하는가?
(A) 진료 시간을 조정하기 위해
(B) 운동에 대한 정보를 얻기 위해
(C) 그를 세미나에 초대하기 위해
(D) 약국을 추천하기 위해

해설 여자가 Dr. Jackson과 통화하고 싶은 이유에 대한 질문이므로 여자의 말에 초점을 맞춰야 한다. 여자가 I just wanted to talk to him about a stretching exercise he showed me.라고 했으므로 정답은 (B)이다.

46. 남자는 다음에 무엇을 할 것 같은가?
(A) 발표를 한다.
(B) 다른 의사에게 전화한다.
(C) 몇 가지 정보를 찾아본다.
(D) 배달을 요청한다.

해설 남자의 다음 행동에 대한 질문이므로 남자의 말에 집중해야 한다. 대화 마지막에 남자가 Let me bring them up and see if we can find yours.라고 했는데 이것은 여자가 원하는 정보를 찾아보겠다는 의미이므로 정답은 (C)이다. 화자의 향후 계획이나 동작은 대개 대화의 후반부에 언급된다는 것을 알아두자.

47-49

W: Hi, Mr. Lemont? **I'm here to do your walls.**⁴⁷
M: My walls? There must be a mistake. I never called a painter.
W: Didn't you get a message from your landlord? He hired me to paint all the units in the building this week.
M: **I must not have gotten it. I just got back from a trip this morning.**⁴⁸
W: No problem. **Just push your bed and everything else away from the walls to the center of the room.**⁴⁹ I'll come back this afternoon after I finish the other units.

여: 안녕하세요, 레몽 씨? 벽 작업하러 여기 왔습니다.
남: 벽이라고요? 착오가 있는 게 틀림없어요. 페인트공에게 전화한 적이 전혀 없어요.
여: 집주인에게서 메시지를 받지 않으셨나요? 그분이 저를 고용해서 이번 주에 이 건물의 모든 집에 페인트칠 하라고 했어요.
남: 분명히 메시지를 못 받은 것 같아요. 오늘 아침에 막 여행에서 돌아왔어요.
여: 괜찮아요. 침대와 다른 모든 것을 벽에서 방 가운데로 밀어놓기만 하세요. 다른 집들 작업을 마치고 나서 오늘 오후에 다시 올게요.

어휘 must be ~임이 틀림없다 mistake 실수 painter 페인트공, 칠장이
landlord 집주인(cf. tenant 세입자) hire 고용하다
unit (아파트 같은 공동 주택 내의) 가구
must have p.p. ~했어야 했다 get back (특히 자기 집에) 돌아오다
trip 여행 come back 돌아오다

47. 여자는 누구일 것 같은가?
(A) 배달원 (B) 여행사 직원
(C) 집주인 **(D) 페인트공**

해설 여자는 첫째 대화문의 I'm here to do your walls.에서 벽 작업을 하러 왔다고 했다. 이에 남자가 I never called a painter.라며 페인트공을 부른 적이 없다고 했다. 이어서 여자는 He hired me to paint all the units in the building this week.에서 페인트칠이라는 구체적인 작업 내용을 밝혔으므로 정답은 (D)이다.

48. 남자는 어떤 문제점을 언급하는가?
(A) 그가 메시지를 놓쳤다.
(B) 그의 여행이 취소되었다.
(C) 그는 집에서 기다릴 수 없다.
(D) 그의 아파트는 비어 있다.

해설 벽 페인트칠 작업을 하러 온 여자가 첫째 대화문의 Didn't you get a message from your landlord?에서 집주인한테서 메시지 못 받았느냐고 하자 남자는 I must not have gotten it. I just got back from a trip this morning.에서 여행에서 막 돌아와서 메시지를 못 받았다고 했다. 따라서 정답은 (A)이다.

49. 여자가 남자에게 해 달라고 요청하는 것은?
(A) 일정표 제출하기
(B) 가구 옮기기
(C) 여자의 상사에게 전화하기
(D) 비품 구매하기

해설 여자는 마지막 대화문의 Just push your bed and everything else away from the walls to the center of the room.에서 침대 등을 방 가운데로 밀어 놓으라고 요청했다. 따라서 정답은 (B)이다.

50-52

W: Welcome to Fertile Ground Nursery. Can I help you with anything today?
M: Yes, please. **I read an article about how growing your own food is very healthy, so I want to start a tomato garden.**[50] But ...
W: Yes?
M: **Actually, I've never grown any plants before.**[51]
W: Well, it's pretty simple. You just need the right soil and seeds, and you can buy both of those here.
M: What about watering and sunlight?
W: That's easy, too. **I can give you a booklet that explains how to raise healthy plants, including how much light and water they need.**[52]
M: OK. Can you also show me what soil I should buy?
W: Sure. Follow me.

여: 퍼틀 그라운드 너서리에 오신 것을 환영합니다. 오늘 뭐 도와드릴 일이 있을까요?
남: 네, 도와주세요. 자기가 먹을 음식을 재배하는 것이 얼마나 건강에 좋은지에 관한 기사를 읽고서 토마토밭을 시작하고 싶습니다. 하지만…
여: 네?
남: 실은 전에 식물을 키워 본 적이 전혀 없어요.
여: 음, 매우 간단해요. 좋은 흙과 씨앗만 있으면 되고 여기에서 둘 다 사실 수 있습니다.
남: 물 주기와 햇빛은요?
여: 그것도 쉽습니다. 얼마나 많은 햇빛과 물이 필요한지를 포함해 건강한 식물을 키우는 방법을 설명한 소책자를 드릴 수 있습니다.
남: 좋아요. 어떤 흙을 사야 하는지도 알려 주시겠어요?
여: 물론입니다. 저를 따라오세요.

어휘 fertile 비옥한, 기름진 ground 땅, 토양 nursery 묘목장
article 기사 healthy 건강한, 건강에 좋은
garden 뜰, 정원, 채소밭, 과수원; 정원 가꾸다, 재배하다
plant 식물, 초목 pretty 꽤, 상당히
simple 간단한(복잡하지 않고 이해하기 쉬운), 단순한 soil 토양, 흙
seed 씨앗, 종자 water 물; (화초 등에) 물을 주다
sunlight 햇빛, 햇살, 일광 booklet 소책자, 팸플릿 explain 설명하다
raise (작물을) 재배하다 including ~을 포함하여
follow (~의 뒤를) 따라가다[오다]

50. 남자가 기사에 관해 언급한 것은?
(A) 집에서 재배한 음식이 건강에 좋다고 했다.
(B) 남자는 신문에 실을 기사를 쓰고 있다.
(C) 기사의 사진이 매력적이었다.
(D) 기사에서 퍼틀 그라운드 너서리에 대해 다루었다.

193

해설 남자는 첫째 대화문의 I read an article about how growing your own food is very healthy, so I want to start a tomato garden.에서 자기가 먹을 음식을 기르는 것이 얼마나 건강에 좋은지에 관한 기사를 읽었다고 했다. 따라서 정답은 (A)이다.

51. 남자는 왜 걱정하는가?
(A) 정원이 작다.
(B) 전혀 재배해 본 적이 없다.
(C) 토마토가 없다.
(D) 예산이 제한되어 있다.

해설 남자는 둘째 대화문의 Actually, I've never grown any plants before.에서 식물을 길러 본 적이 없다고 했으므로 정답은 (B)이다.

52. 여자가 남자에게 무엇을 줄 것 같은가?
(A) 정원 창고 열쇠   (B) 할인 쿠폰
(C) 토마토 한 상자   (D) 식물 관리 안내서

해설 여자의 넷째 대화문인 I can give you a booklet that explains how to raise healthy plants, including how much light and water they need.에서 건강한 식물을 키우는 방법을 설명한 소책자를 줄 수 있다고 했다. 따라서 정답은 (D)이다.

53-55

W: Mason, this is Jill on the assembly floor.
M: Hi, Jill. **Are the assembly lines OK?**[53]
W: Yes, but ...
M: We finished repairing them late last night.
W: Right, but there's a problem ...
M: You're kidding. The head technician promised me those belts would be working.
W: Mason, hold on. The belts are fine.
M: OK, so there's nothing wrong with the belts ...
W: **The problem is, when we turn the belts on, the air conditioners turn off.**[54, 55] It's too hot to work in the production room without them, so we need to fix this quickly.
M: I see ... Hmm ... I'll send the head technician back down there to check it out.
W: Thanks, Mason.

여: 메이슨, 조립 작업장의 질이에요.
남: 안녕하세요, 질. 조립 설비는 괜찮은가요?
여: 네, 하지만…
남: 지난밤 늦게 조립 설비 수리를 마쳤는데요.
여: 그래요, 하지만 한 가지 문제가 있어요…
남: 농담이시죠. 수석 기사가 제게 벨트가 작동할 거라고 약속했어요.
여: 메이슨, 잠시만요. 벨트는 괜찮아요.
남: 네, 그럼 벨트에 아무 문제가 없다는 거죠…
여: 문제는 우리가 벨트를 켜면 에어컨이 꺼진다는 점이에요. 너무 더워서 에어컨이 없이는 생산실에서 작업할 수 없으니 바로 이 문제를 해결해야 해요.
남: 알겠어요… 음… 수석 기사를 거기로 다시 보내서 확인해 보라고 할게요.
여: 고마워요, 메이슨.

어휘 assembly (차량·가구 등의) 조립
floor (건물 내에서 특정한 활동이 벌어지는) 작업장
assembly line (대량 생산의) 일관 작업(열), 조립 설비[라인]
finish (완성하여) 끝내다[마치다/마무리 짓다]   repair 수리(하다)
problem (다루거나 이해하기 힘든) 문제   kid 농담하다
head 수석의, 책임자의   technician 기술자, 기사
hold on (전화상으로 상대방에게 하는 말) 기다려라
turn on (전기·가스·수도 등을) 켜다(↔ turn off (전기·가스·수도 등을) 끄다)   air conditioner 에어컨
production (식품·상품·자재의, 특히 대량) 생산   fix 수리하다, 바로잡다
check out 조사하다, 확인하다

53. 남자는 여자에게 무엇에 대해 물었는가?
(A) 공장 온도   (B) 기사 이용 가능 여부
(C) 생산 일정   (D) 하나의 기계

해설 남자는 첫째 대화문의 Are the assembly lines OK?에서 조립 설비가 이상 없는지 물었다. 따라서 assembly lines을 바꿔 표현한 (D)가 정답이다.

54. 남자는 왜 "그럼 벨트에 아무 문제가 없다는 거죠"라고 했는가?
(A) 문제점에 관해 문의하려고
(B) 해결책을 제안하려고
(C) 감사를 표현하려고
(D) 수리에 관해 보고하려고

해설 여자의 세 번째 대사인 Right, but there's a problem에서 문제가 있음을 밝힌 후, 네 번째 대사 The belts are fine.에서 벨트는 이상이 없다고 했다. 이에 남자는 so there's nothing wrong with the belts …의 줄임표(ellipsis) 부분에서 벨트에 문제가 없다면 어떤 문제가 있는지 궁금해하고 있음을 짐작할 수 있다. 이어서 여자가 The problem is, when we turn the belts on, the air conditioners turn off.에서 어떤 문제가 있는지 밝혔으므로 정답은 (A)이다.

55. 여자가 에어컨에 관해 언급한 것은 무엇인가?
(A) 새 에어컨이 설치되었다.
(B) 기사가 에어컨을 수리했다.
(C) 에어컨이 계속 켜져 있지 않다.
(D) 에어컨 때문에 방이 너무 춥다.

해설 여자의 다섯 번째 대사인 The problem is, when we turn the belts on, the air conditioners turn off.에서 벨트를 켜면 에어컨이 꺼진다고 했으므로 정답은 (C)이다.

56-58

> W: Hi, I made a reservation for this Friday on behalf of Riley Capital. I need to make a change, though. **Originally the reservation was just for my department, which is twelve people. But now our supervisor wants to invite the entire company to dinner—sixty people in total.**[56]
>
> M: I see. **We're very busy on Fridays, so I doubt we'll have room.**[57] I'm checking the bookings now … **Yes, I'm sorry but almost all of our tables are already full.**[58]
>
> W: I totally understand. I apologize for giving you such last-minute notice. Please cancel the reservation then. I'll just have to start my search again.

여: 안녕하세요, 라일리 캐피털을 대표해서 이번 주 금요일에 예약했습니다. 하지만 변경해야 합니다. 원래 예약은 12명이 있는 우리 부서만을 위한 것이었습니다. 하지만 지금 저희 상사가 회사 전 직원 60명을 초대하고 싶어 하십니다.

남: 알겠습니다. 금요일에는 매우 바빠서 공간이 날지 모르겠네요. 지금 예약을 확인해 볼게요… 네, 죄송하지만, 거의 모든 테이블이 이미 찼습니다.

여: 전적으로 이해합니다. 마지막 순간에 알려 드린 데 대해 사과드립니다. 그럼 예약을 취소해 주세요. 다시 물색을 시작해야겠네요.

어휘 make a reservation 예약하다
on behalf of ~을 대신하여[대표하여] capital 자본금, 자금, 자본가
make a change 변경하다 originally 원래
supervisor 상사, 감독관 invite 초대[초청]하다 entire 전체의
in total 전체로, 통틀어
doubt 확신하지 못하다, 의심하다, 의문[의혹]을 갖다
room (특정 목적을 위한) 자리[공간]
check (무엇의 진위ㆍ사실 여부를) 알아보다[확인하다]
booking 예약(cf. book 예약하다) full (~이) 가득한, 공간이 없는
totally 완전히, 전적으로
understand (남의 말ㆍ단어의 의미ㆍ언어 등을) 이해하다, 알아듣다, 알다
apologize for ~에 대해 사과하다
last-minute 마지막 순간의, 막바지의
notice (앞으로 있을 일을 미리) 알림, 통지, 예고, 경고 cancel 취소하다
search 찾기, 수색

56. 여자는 예약에 관해 무엇을 변경하고자 하는가?
(A) 식사 시간
(B) 손님 수
(C) 행사 날짜
(D) 제공되는 음식

해설 대화 맨 처음 여자는 Originally the reservation was just for my department, which is twelve people. But now our supervisor wants to invite the entire company to dinner—sixty people in total.에서 참석자 수가 늘어나서 예약을 변경해야 한다고 했으므로 정답은 (B)이다.

57. 남자가 식당에 관해 언급하는 것은 무엇인가?
(A) 금요일에는 손님이 많이 온다.
(B) 새 좌석 구역이 막 열렸다.
(C) 예약하지 않고 오는 손님을 받지 않는다.
(D) 메뉴는 주말에 변경된다.

해설 남자는 We're very busy on Fridays, so I doubt we'll have room.에서 금요일에는 매우 바빠서 자리가 없을 거라고 했으므로 정답은 (A)이다.

58. 여자가 "다시 물색을 시작해야겠네요."라고 말했을 때 의미하는 바는 무엇인가?
(A) 다른 식당을 찾을 것이다.
(B) 대체 일자리를 찾을 것이다.
(C) 다른 활동을 선택할 것이다.
(D) 별도 메뉴에서 주문할 것이다.

해설 남자의 첫 대사 중 Yes, I'm sorry but almost all of our tables are already full.에서 테이블이 이미 찼다고 했다. 그러므로 인용문은 예약을 취소하고 다른 식당을 찾아야겠다는 의미이므로 정답은 (A)이다.

59-61

> W: What are you drinking? It looks delicious.
>
> M1: It's a new coffee drink called Hazelnut Whirls. I bought it at Depp's Place.
>
> M2: **That's the coffee shop where we can get a company discount, right?**[59] Was it ten … fifteen percent off?
>
> M1: That's correct, Jeremy. I showed the cashier my identification badge and received a fifteen percent discount.
>
> W: Hmm … do they sell food too?
>
> M1: **They mainly sell coffee, but they do offer a few cakes and cookies.**[60] The discount applies to those pastries, too.
>
> M2: Maybe I should try going there tomorrow. **Do you want to go with me, Linh?**[61] And you too, Sergio, if you don't mind going again.
>
> W: That sounds good!
>
> M1: Sure!

여: 뭘 마시고 있나요? 맛있어 보여요.
남1: 헤이즐넛 휠스라는 새 커피 음료예요. 뎁스 플레이스에서 샀어요.
남2: 회사 할인을 받을 수 있는 커피숍이지요? 10%였나… 15%였나?
남1: 맞아요, 제러미. 계산대 직원에게 신분 확인 명찰을 보여 주고 15% 할인을 받았어요.
여: 음… 음식도 파나요?
남1: 주로 커피를 팔지만, 몇 가지 케이크도 쿠키도 팔아요. 할인이 페이스트리에도 적용돼요.
남2: 내일 거기 가 봐야겠네요. 저랑 같이 가실래요, 린? 다시 가는 게 괜찮으시다면 세르지오, 당신도요.
여: 그거 좋겠군요!
남1: 물론이에요!

어휘 drink (음료를) 마시다; 음료, 마실 것　delicious 맛있는
hazelnut 헤이즐넛, 개암　whirl 빙빙 돌기, 선회하기　discount 할인
cashier 계산대 직원　identification badge 신분 확인 명찰
mainly 주로　apply to ~에 적용되다
pastry 페이스트리(페이스트리 반죽으로 만든 작은 케이크)
mind -ing ~하기를 꺼리다

59. 대화는 주로 무엇에 관한 것인가?
(A) 식당 메뉴 만들기
(B) 신분 확인 명찰 받기
(C) 회사 할인 이용하기
(D) 새 커피 제품군 판매하기

해설 한 남자가 It's a new coffee drink called Hazelnut Whirls. I bought it at Depp's Place.라며 Depp's Place에서 파는 Hazelnut Whirls라는 커피 음료를 언급하자 다른 남자가 That's the coffee shop where we can get a company discount, right?라며 Depp's Place가 회사 할인이 적용되는 커피숍인지 물었다. 이어 회사 할인 적용받는 방법과 적용되는 상품 등에 관한 대화가 이어지고 있으므로 정답은 (C)이다.

60. 뎁 플레이스에서 파는 제품의 종류는?
(A) 주스　(B) 오븐에 구운 상품
(C) 샐러드　(D) 샌드위치

해설 They mainly sell coffee, but they do offer a few cakes and cookies.에서 커피, 빵, 과자 등을 파는 곳임을 알 수 있으므로 정답은 (B)이다.

61. 여자가 "그거 좋겠군요"라고 말했을 때 의미하는 것은?
(A) 노래 듣기를 즐긴다.
(B) 제러미가 분명하게 말한다고 생각한다.
(C) 일자리에 지원하고 싶어 한다.
(D) 제러미와 함께 갈 것이다.

해설 인용문은 Do you want to go with me, Linh?에 대한 긍정적 응답이므로 정답은 (D)이다.

62-64

W: Hi, **I'm doing the interior design for a new Italian lunch café downtown**,⁶² and I just received a large order of prints from your company. After I hung them up on the walls, though, I realized some of the colors were printed incorrectly. Who should I talk to about getting them fixed?

M: You know, **we discovered one of our printers has a problem aligning correctly**,⁶³ so that must have caused your problem. The person that can help you has unfortunately gone home for the day. **Call back tomorrow after 9 A.M. and dial extension four.**⁶⁴

W: Extension 4? OK, I'll do that. Thanks for your help.

여: 안녕하세요. 저는 시내에 있는 새 이탈리아 런치 카페의 실내 장식 디자인을 하고 있는데 귀사에 주문했던 대량 인쇄물을 막 받았어요. 하지만 인쇄물을 벽에 걸고 나서 일부 색상이 잘못 인쇄된 것을 알았어요. 색상을 수정하려면 누구와 이야기해야 하죠?

남: 음, 저희 프린터 중 하나가 제대로 수평을 맞추는 데 문제가 있다는 것을 발견했는데 그게 문제를 일으킨 게 틀림없어요. 도움을 드릴 직원이 아쉽게도 퇴근했습니다. 내일 오전 9시 이후에 다시 전화하셔서 내선 번호 4번을 누르세요.

여: 내선 번호 4번이요? 알겠습니다. 그렇게 하죠. 도와주셔서 감사합니다.

케닝스 석판 인쇄	
직원	내선 번호
커티스 코	1
데이브 미트키	2
앨리스 데드햄	3
라라 베젤	4

어휘 interior 인테리어, 실내 장식　café 카페(음료수를 마시거나 간단한 식사를 할 수 있는 곳. 영국이나 미국의 카페에서는 보통 술을 팔지 않음)
downtown 시내의　order 주문(하다)
print 인쇄물(printed matter), (신문·잡지 따위의) 간행물; 인쇄하다
hang up ~을 걸다, 내걸다, 매달다(-hung-hung)
though (문장 끝에 와서) 그렇지만[하지만]
realize 깨닫다, 알아차리다, 인식[자각]하다
incorrectly 부정확하게(↔ correctly 정확하게)　fix 수리하다, 바로잡다
discover 발견하다　align 나란히[가지런히] 만들다, 일직선으로 하다
must have p.p. ~했음이 틀림없다　cause ~을 야기하다[초래하다]
problem 문제　unfortunately 불행하게도
go home for the day 퇴근하다　dial 다이얼을 돌리다, 전화를 걸다
extension 내선, 구내전화　lithography 석판 인쇄 (과정)

62. 여자는 무엇을 장식하고 있는가?
(A) 식당
(B) 사무실
(C) 주택
(D) 상점

> 해설 여자의 첫 번째 대사인 Hi, I'm doing the interior design for a new Italian lunch café downtown에서 lunch café의 실내 장식을 하고 있다고 했으므로 정답은 (A)이다.

63. 남자가 프린터에 관해 말하는 것은?
(A) 제대로 작동하지 않는다.
(B) 잉크가 떨어졌다.
(C) 흑백으로만 이미지가 출력된다.
(D) 새로 구매했다.

> 해설 남자는 we discovered one of our printers has a problem aligning correctly라며 프린터의 수평을 제대로 맞추는 데 문제가 있다고 했으므로 정답은 (A)이다.

64. 표를 보세요. 여자가 누구에게 전화할 것 같은가?
(A) 커티스 코
(B) 데이브 미트키
(C) 앨리스 데드햄
(D) 라라 베젤

> 해설 남자는 도와줄 사람이 퇴근했으니 Call back tomorrow after 9 A.M. and dial extension four.라면서 내일 오전 9시 이후에 다시 전화해서 내선 번호 4번을 누르라고 했다. 표를 보면 Lara Bezel의 내선 번호가 4번이므로 정답은 (D)이다.

65-67

W: Phil, I've been thinking about buying a refrigerator for employees. **I know that some people like to bring their own lunches, and I think it would be convenient for them.**⁶⁵

M: That's thoughtful of you. Where would we put it, though? There's not enough room in the front of the store.

W: **What about next to the stairwell?**⁶⁶ We can move the shelves a little bit and that should make enough room.

M: That could work. Let's move the shelves before we buy the fridge so we can imagine what the room will look like with it by the stairs. **I'll start clearing the shelves now so it will be easier to move them.**⁶⁷

여: 필, 직원들을 위해 냉장고 구매를 고려해 왔어요. 제가 알기론 일부 직원이 점심 싸오는 걸 좋아하는데 냉장고가 있으면 편리할 것 같아요.

남: 사려가 깊으시네요. 하지만 냉장고를 어디에 놓죠? 가게 앞에는 공간이 충분하지 않아요.

여: 계단 통로 옆은 어떨까요? 진열대를 약간 이동하면 충분한 공간이 나올 거 같은데요.

남: 그러면 되겠네요. 계단 옆에 냉장고를 두면 어떤 모습일까 상상해 볼 수 있도록 냉장고를 사기 전에 진열대를 옮기죠. 제가 지금 진열대를 비우면 옮기기가 더 쉬워질 거예요.

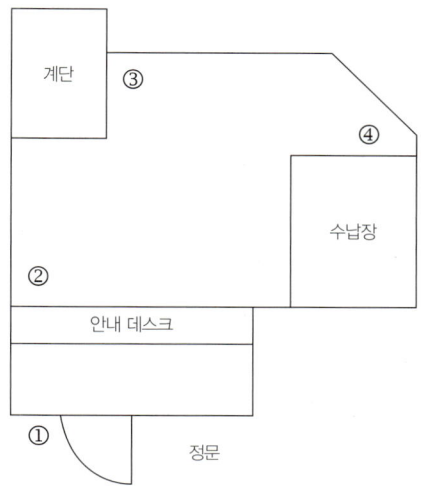

> 어휘 refrigerator 냉장고(= fridge) convenient 편리한
> thoughtful 배려심 있는, 친절한, 사려 깊은
> though (문장 끝에 와서) 그렇지만[하지만] front (사물의) 앞면[앞부분]
> stairwell (건물 내부의) 계단 통로 shelf 선반, 진열대(*pl.* shelves)
> work (원하는) 효과가 나다[있다] imagine 상상하다 stairs 계단
> clear 치우다, 깨끗하게 하다 front desk 프런트, 안내 데스크
> storage closet 물건을 간단하게 저장할 수 있는 벽장

65. 여자는 왜 냉장고를 사고 싶어 하는가?
(A) 직원들이 음식을 보관할 수 있게 하려고
(B) 고객들에게 간식을 제공하려고
(C) 주방의 요리 가능 용량을 확장하려고
(D) 낡은 냉장고를 교체하려고

> 해설 여자의 첫 번째 대사인 I know that some people like to bring their own lunches, and I think it would be convenient for them.에서 점심을 싸오는 직원들에게 냉장고가 있으면 편리하겠다고 했다. 따라서 정답은 (A)이다.

66. 표를 보세요. 여자가 냉장고를 놓자고 제안하는 자리는 어디인가?
(A) 1 (B) 2
(C) 3 (D) 4

해설 여자의 두 번째 대사인 What about next to the stairwell?에서 계단 통로 옆에 냉장고를 둘 것을 제안했으므로 정답은 (C)이다.

67. 남자가 이어서 무엇을 할 것 같은가?
(A) 건축업자 고용하기
(B) 고객 맞이하기
(C) 공간 비우기
(D) 지도 그리기

해설 남자의 마지막 대사인 I'll start clearing the shelves now so it will be easier to move them.에서 진열대를 비우기 시작할 거라고 했다. 따라서 clear the shelves를 바꿔 표현한 (C)가 정답이다.

68-70

W: Hi. Are you interested in registering for a class?
M: Yes. **My relatives are visiting this summer from Guatemala, and I wanted to cook them something they're familiar with.**⁶⁸ Do you have a class that teaches how to prepare Latin dishes?
W: Sure, it's our most popular class. The A block classes have already filled up, but the others are still open. Look at this schedule and tell me which time is convenient for you.
M: Thanks. **Please sign me up for the D block time slot.**⁶⁹
W: Great. How would you like to pay for that?
M: **I received a voucher for a free class as a gift. Here. Will this work?**⁷⁰
W: Certainly. OK, now you're all set.

여: 안녕하세요. 강좌 등록에 관심이 있으신가요?
남: 네, 제 친척들이 올여름에 과테말라에서 방문하는데 그들에게 익숙한 음식을 요리해 주고 싶습니다. 라틴 요리 만드는 법을 가르치는 강좌가 있나요?
여: 물론이죠. 그것은 가장 인기 있는 강좌예요. A 단위 강좌는 이미 정원이 찼지만, 다른 강좌들은 아직 자리가 있어요. 이 시간표를 보시고 어느 시간이 편하신지 제게 말씀해 주세요.
남: 고맙습니다. 저를 D 단위 시간대에 등록해 주세요.
여: 좋습니다. 어떻게 지급하시겠습니까?
남: 무료 강좌 쿠폰을 선물로 받았어요. 여기요. 이 쿠폰이 유효할까요?
여: 물론입니다. 좋아요. 이제 준비가 되었습니다.

강좌 단위	시작 시각
A	오전 9시
B	오전 10시
C	오전 11시
D	12시 정오

어휘 be interested in ~에 관심이 있다 register for ~에 등록하다 class (한 주제에 대한 연속적인) 수업[강좌] relative 친척, 동류, 부류 cook 요리하다 be familiar with ~을 잘 안다, ~에 정통하다 prepare 준비하다 Latin 라틴의 dish 요리, 음식 popular 인기 있는 fill up 채워지다, 가득 차다, 만원이 되다 schedule 시각표 convenient 편리한 sign up for (강좌에) 등록하다 block (양적인) 덩어리, 뭉치, 단위 time slot 시간대 pay for ~에 대해 지급하다 voucher 쿠폰, 상품권 gift 선물 work (원하는) 효과가 나다[있다] certainly 그럼요, 물론이지요 be all set 준비가 되어 있다

68. 남자는 자신의 친척들에 관해 무엇을 언급하는가?
(A) 그들은 전문 요리사이다.
(B) 그들은 다른 나라에 산다.
(C) 그들은 그에게 선물을 주었다.
(D) 그들은 시간표가 필요하다.

해설 남자의 첫 번째 대사인 My relatives are visiting this summer from Guatemala, and I wanted to cook them something they're familiar with.에서 친척들이 과테말라에서 온다고 했으므로 정답은 (B)가 정답이다.

69. 표를 보세요. 남자의 강좌는 언제 시작할 것인가?
(A) 오전 9시
(B) 오전 10시
(C) 오전 11시
(D) 12시 정오

해설 남자의 두 번째 대사인 Please, sign me up for the D block time slot.에서 D 단위에 등록해 달라고 했다. 표에서 D block에 해당하는 시각은 12:00 noon이므로 정답은 (D)이다.

70. 남자는 어떤 결제 방법을 사용할 것인가?
(A) 현금
(B) 신용 카드
(C) 은행 이체
(D) 상품권

해설 남자의 세 번째 대사인 I received a voucher for a free class as a gift. Here. Will this work?에서 voucher를 받았다고 한 후 Here.라며 그것을 건넸다. 따라서 voucher를 바꿔 표현한 (D)가 정답이다.

Part 4 Final Test

본책 _ p. 367–369

71. (A)	72. (A)	73. (B)	74. (B)	75. (B)
76. (C)	77. (B)	78. (D)	79. (A)	80. (D)
81. (B)	82. (C)	83. (A)	84. (C)	85. (A)
86. (B)	87. (A)	88. (B)	89. (B)	90. (C)
91. (A)	92. (B)	93. (B)	94. (B)	95. (C)
96. (B)	97. (A)	98. (A)	99. (B)	100. (B)

71-73

Thank you for calling Communex. All of our technicians are busy at the moment. **Are you having trouble with your Internet connection?**[71] Before troubleshooting with our staff, **please turn your device off and on**[72] to see if that resolves the problem. **If you'd like to speak with a technical support agent, please press 7 and leave a message.**[73] A member of our staff will return your call as soon as possible. For other options, press the star key on your keypad. Thank you.

커뮤넥스에 전화 주셔서 감사합니다. 현재 모든 저희 기술자들이 통화 중입니다. 인터넷 접속에 문제가 있으십니까? 우리 직원과 문제 해결을 하시기 전에 고객님의 컴퓨터를 껐다가 켜서 문제가 해결되는지 보십시오. 만약 기술 지원 직원과 통화를 하고 싶으시면 7번을 누르시고 메시지를 남겨주시기 바랍니다. 저희 직원이 가능한 한 빨리 회신 전화를 드릴 겁니다. 다른 선택 사항을 원하시면 키패드의 별표를 눌러주시기 바랍니다. 감사합니다.

어휘 technician 기술자 at the moment 바로 지금
have trouble[difficulty] with ~에 어려움을 겪다
troubleshoot 문제를 해결하다 turn on[off] 켜다[끄다]
see if ~ ~인지 알아보다 resolve 해결하다
speak with ~와 통화하다 return one's call 회신 전화를 하다
star key 별표 keypad (숫자 등이 적힌) 번호판, 키패드

71. 화자는 아마도 어디에서 근무하겠는가?
(A) 인터넷 서비스 제공 업체
(B) 전화 광고 센터
(C) 전자제품 가게
(D) 소매점

해설 전화 메시지 초반부에 Are you having trouble with your Internet connection?이라고 물어보고 있으므로 정답은 (A)이다. 전화 메시지에서 화자의 소속 부서나 근무지 등은 메시지의 초반부에 언급된다.

72. 화자는 청자들에게 먼저 무엇을 권하는가?
(A) 컴퓨터를 다시 시작하기
(B) 나중에 다시 전화하기
(C) 중개인 기다리기
(D) 무선 장비 교체하기

해설 화자가 please turn your computer off and on to see if that resolves the problem이라고 했으므로 정답은 (A)이다. turn your device off and on이 restart the computer로 패러프레이징(바꿔 말하기) 된 것이다.

73. 청자들은 어떻게 하면 회신 전화를 받을 수 있는가?
(A) 전화 센터를 방문함으로써
(B) 메시지를 남김으로써
(C) 별표를 누름으로써
(D) 다른 번호로 전화를 함으로써

해설 메시지 중간 부분에 If you'd like to speak with a technical support agent, please press 7 and leave a message.라고 했으므로 정답은 (B)이다.

74-76

If you're an experienced runner in search of a new treadmill,[74] stop into Sporting World to get the latest model. The Fit-tech X600 provides users with a smooth and stable running surface for indoor training. **You can even watch your favorite television shows,**[75] listen to MP3s, or play video games while you exercise with the X600's advanced audio and visual equipment. **The X600 even comes with both a store and manufacturers warranty**[76] to ensure years of excellent performance. Visit Sporting World on Route 211 in Westbrook to get your Fit-tech X600 treadmill today.

고객님께서 달리기에 경험이 많은 분으로서 새로운 러닝머신을 찾고 계시다면 스포팅 월드에 오셔서 최신 모델을 구입하시기 바랍니다. 핏테크 X600은 사용자들에게 실내 운동을 위한 부드럽고 안정적으로 뛸 수 있는 표면을 제공해 드립니다. 심지어 X600의 첨단 시청각 장비로 운동을 하시면서 여러분이 가장 좋아하는 TV 프로그램을 보시거나 MP3를 들으시거나 비디오 게임을 하실 수도 있습니다. X600은 다년간의 훌륭한 성능을 보장해드리고자 상점 및 제조업체 보증서도 제공합니다. 오늘 웨스트부룩 211로에 있는 스포팅 월드에 오셔서 핏테크 X600을 구입하시기 바랍니다.

어휘 experienced 경험이 많은 treadmill 러닝머신
stop into ~로 들어오다 get 구입하다 latest 최신의
provide A with B A에게 B를 제공하다 stable 안정적인
surface 표면 indoor 실내의 exercise 운동하다 (= work out)
advanced 첨단의 audio and visual 시청각의
come with ~와 함께 나오다 warranty 보증
ensure ~을 분명히 하다, 보장하다 performance 성능

199

74. 광고의 대상은 누구겠는가?
(A) 체육관 주인들
(B) 달리기에 경험 많은 사람들
(C) 헬스 강사들
(D) 60세 이상인 사람들

해설 광고를 시작하면서 If you're an experienced runner in search of a new treadmill이라고 했으므로 정답은 (B)이다. 광고의 대상은 광고가 시작되는 초반부에 언급되므로 처음 시작하는 부분을 잘 들어야 한다.

75. 핏테크 X600의 사용자들은 무엇을 할 수 있는가?
(A) 고속으로 달리기
(B) TV 프로그램 보기
(C) 심장 박동 수 재기
(D) 쉽게 러닝머신 나르기

해설 질문에 제품명으로 Fit-tech X600이 있으므로 이 단어를 미리 읽어서 발음을 친숙하게 만들어 놓아야 본문을 들을 때 쉽게 알아 들을 수 있다. 광고에서 You can even watch your favorite television shows라고 했으므로 정답은 (B)이다.

76. 핏테크 X600과 함께 제공하는 것은 무엇인가?
(A) 쿠폰   (B) 리베이트(환급금)
(C) 보증서   (D) 상품권

해설 광고 후반부에 The X600 even comes with both a store and manufacturers warranty라고 했으므로 정답은 (C)이다. 정답은 대부분 순차적으로 제시되므로 두 번째 정답의 단서가 제시된 이후부터 세 번째 정답의 단서를 찾도록 한다.

77-79

This is Omar Haynes at PQR with your traffic report. The holiday weekend is finally here, and everyone is getting ready for it. **People heading out for the weekend will want to avoid the 400 and 401**[77] because traffic is expected to be backed up and moving slow. If there's another route, you might want to take it. For those of you staying in town, **remember that Peterson Avenue and Lilac Lane will both be blocked off**[78] for events. We'll be back every hour with the latest traffic reports. **Stay tuned for Joyce Lin's "Heart Uncovered" for the greatest love songs.**[79]

교통 정보를 전하는 PQR의 오마르 헤인즈입니다. 마침내 주말 연휴가 왔고 모든 사람들이 주말 연휴에 대한 준비를 하고 있습니다. 주말을 위해 외부로 나가는 분들은 차량이 정체되어 서행할 것으로 예상되므로 400번과 401번 도로는 피해주시기 바랍니다. 만약 다른 길이 있다면 그 길을 이용하시는 것이 좋겠습니다. 시내에 머무르시는 분들은 피터슨 가와 라일락 도로가 모두 행사 때문에 차단될 것이라는 것을 기억해주세요. 매 시간마다 최신 교통 정보를 전해드리겠습니다. 최고의 사랑 노래를 들으시려면 조이스 린의 '하트 언커버드'에 채널을 고정시켜주세요.

어휘 traffic report 교통 정보 방송
holiday weekend 주말 연휴(공휴일이 낀 주말)
get ready for ~을 준비하다, ~에 대비하다   head out 떠나다, 나가다
avoid 피하다   be backed up 밀리다, 정체되다   route 길, 노선
take (길을) 이용하다, 타다
lane (양쪽으로 건물이 늘어서 있는 좁은) 도로, 길   block off 차단하다
stay tuned 채널을 고정하다

77. 화자는 청자들에게 무엇을 권하는가?
(A) 시외로 나가기
(B) 특정 도로 피하기
(C) 대중 교통 이용하기
(D) 행사 일정을 잘 짜기

해설 라디오 교통 방송 초반에 People heading out for the weekend will want to avoid the 400 and 401이라고 했으므로 정답은 (B)이다. 교통 방송에서는 대체로 도로 공사나 교통 정체 등에 대해 다룬다는 것을 알아두자.

78. 시내에서 무슨 일이 있겠는가?
(A) 피터슨 가에서의 교통 체증
(B) 생방송 라디오 콘테스트 쇼
(C) 휴일 콘서트
(D) 특정 도로 폐쇄

해설 방송 중간 부분에서 remember that Peterson Avenue and Lilac Lane will both be blocked off라고 했는데 be blocked off가 보기에서 closure로 바뀌어 제시된 것이므로 정답은 (D)이다.

79. 청자들은 다음으로 무엇을 듣겠는가?
(A) 음악 쇼
(B) 날씨 보도
(C) 더 많은 교통 소식
(D) 조이스 린과의 인터뷰

해설 방송 후반부에 Stay tuned for Joyce Lin's "Heart Uncovered" for the greatest love songs라고 했으므로 정답은 (A)이다. 날씨나 교통 방송에서 다음에 이어질 프로그램에 대해서는 방송의 후반부에 언급된다는 것을 알아두자.

80-82

Good morning everyone, it's a pleasure to meet all of you. My name is Kim Yoon-joo, and I will be working with your team on your next project. **Your company is preparing to expand into South Korea in six months,**[81] and my company has been hired to help you make that transition go as smoothly as possible. **I will be acting as a consultant for your marketing team**[80] in matters of Korean culture and commerce. **I have worked with five other companies**[82] on similar projects, and I feel confident that we can make your expansion into the Korean economy a success. If you have any questions for me, please feel free to ask.

여러분, 안녕하세요. 여러분 모두를 뵙게 되어 기쁩니다. 제 이름은 김윤주이며 다음 프로젝트에 대해 여러분 팀과 함께 작업을 할 것입니다. 여러분 회사는 6개월 후 한국으로의 사업 확장을 준비 중인 가운데, 저희 회사가 가능한 순조롭게 그러한 전환이 이루어질 수 있도록 돕기 위해 고용되었습니다. 저는 한국적인 문화와 상업의 문제에 있어서 여러분 마케팅 팀의 컨설턴트 역할을 할 것입니다. 저는 유사한 프로젝트와 관련해 다섯 곳의 다른 회사와 함께 일을 했으며 여러분의 한국 경제로의 확장을 성공으로 이끌 수 있다고 자신합니다. 제게 궁금한 점이 있으시면 편하게 질문하시기 바랍니다.

어휘 It is a pleasure to부정사. ~하게 되어 기쁘다.
prepare to부정사 ~할 준비를 하다
expand into ~로 사업을 확장하다 hire 고용하다 transition 전환
go as smoothly as possible 가능한 한 순조롭게 진행되다
act as ~의 역할을 하다 commerce 상업
feel confident 자신감이 있다 expansion 확장
feel free to부정사 편하게 ~하다

80. 화자는 누구이겠는가?
(A) 팀의 새로운 매니저
(B) 여행사 직원
(C) 후임 팀원
(D) **외부 컨설턴트**

해설 화자가 자신을 소개하며 I will be acting as a consultant for your marketing team이라고 했으므로 정답은 (D)이다. 일반적으로 화자의 신분이나 직업은 이야기 초반부에 언급되는데 이 경우는 이야기 중간 부분에 나와서 조금 어려운 문제에 속한다.

81. 청자들의 회사는 무엇을 계획하고 있는가?
(A) 몇몇 국내 상점 닫기
(B) **해외 시장으로의 확장**
(C) 다른 회사와의 합병
(D) 새로운 공장 열기

해설 화자가 Your company is preparing to expand into South Korea in six months라고 했으므로 정답은 (B)이다. Part 3, 4에서 대부분의 정답이 순차적으로 제시되지만 80번과 81번의 정답 단서는 서로 순서가 바뀌어 제시되었다. 최근에는 실제 시험에서도 정답의 단서가 순차적으로 제시되지 않는 경우가 있다는 것을 알아두자.

82. 여자는 얼마나 많은 회사들과 함께 일했는가?
(A) 세 곳   (B) 네 곳
(C) **다섯 곳**   (D) 여섯 곳

해설 질문의 핵심어가 How many other companies이고 보기에 숫자가 제시되어 있으므로 회사의 수가 언급되는 부분에서 정답의 단서를 찾아야 한다. 화자가 I have worked with five other companies라고 했으므로 정답은 (C)이다.

83-85

It is an honor to introduce Cheryl Beattie, my old friend and Willton Glass's salesperson of the year. As usual, Cheryl surpassed all of her sales goals by our third quarter. **She even set the record for selling more units of "Never-Break" glass than any other salesperson.**[83, 84] And if that's not enough, there's more. Cheryl completely redesigned the work flow for our sales team. **Thanks to her innovations, this year we operate more quickly, and customers are more satisfied.**[85] As a result, customer retention has improved by fifteen percent. Please help me give Cheryl a warm round of applause.

제 오랜 친구이자 윌턴 글래스 올해의 영업 사원인 셰릴 비티를 소개하게 되어 영광입니다. 언제나처럼 셰릴은 3분기까지 자신의 모든 영업 목표를 초과 달성했습니다. 그녀는 "네버-브레이크" 유리를 다른 어느 영업 사원보다 더 많이 판매해서 기록을 세우기도 했습니다. 그리고 그걸로 충분하지 않다면, 더 많은 업적이 있습니다. 셰릴은 우리 영업팀의 작업 흐름을 완전히 다시 설계했습니다. 그녀가 이룬 혁신 덕분에 올해 우리는 더 신속하게 업무를 진행해서 고객을 더욱 만족시켰습니다. 결과적으로 고객 유지율이 15% 정도 향상되었습니다. 저와 함께 셰릴에게 따뜻한 박수를 한 차례 보내 주시기 바랍니다.

어휘 honor 영광, 영예   introduce 소개하다
salesperson 판매원, 점원, 영업 사원
as usual 늘 그렇듯이, 평상시와 같이   surpass 능가하다, 초과하다
set (모범·수준 등을) 만들다[세우다]   record 기록
completely 완전히(cf. complete 완벽한, 필요한 모든 것이 갖춰진)
redesign 다시 디자인하다, 재설계하다
work flow (각 사업 부서 또는 종업원 간의) 작업[일]의 흐름
innovation 혁신, 쇄신   operate 영업하다, 작업하다
customer 고객   satisfied 만족하는, 만족스러운
as a result 결과적으로
retention (어떤 것을 잃지 않는) 보유[유지], 기억(력)   improve 개선하다
a round of applause 한 차례의 박수

83. 셰릴은 어떤 기록을 세웠는가?
(A) 제품을 가장 많이 판매한 것
(B) 신규 고객을 가장 많이 확보한 것
(C) 만족도가 높은 고객들을 가장 많이 보유한 것
(D) 최장기간 근무한 것

해설 소개 세 번째 문장인 She even set the record for selling more units of "Never-Break" glass than any other salesperson.에서 판매 기록을 세웠음을 알 수 있으므로 정답은 (A)이다.

84. 화자가 "그리고 그걸로 충분하지 않다면, 더 많은 업적이 있습니다."라고 말했을 때 의미하는 바는 무엇인가?
(A) 식사에는 몇 가지 요리가 있다.
(B) 여분의 의자가 벽장에 보관되어 있다.
(C) 한 직원이 여러 가지 업적을 이뤘다.
(D) 많은 영업 사원에게 영예가 주어질 것이다.

해설 앞 문장인 She even set the record for selling more units of "Never-Break" glass than any other salesperson.에서 Cheryl Beattie가 판매 기록을 세웠다고 했다. 그리고 다음 문장에서 작업 흐름에 대한 혁신으로 인해 고객 만족도와 유지율이 향상되었다는 셰릴의 추가 업적을 나열하고 있다. 따라서 정답은 (C)이다.

85. 월턴 글래스가 작년과 비교해서 다른 점은 무엇인가?
(A) 업무 진행 속도
(B) 영업 사원 규모
(C) 판매하는 제품의 종류
(D) 사무실 위치

해설 소개 후반의 Thanks to her innovations, this year we operate more quickly, and customers are more satisfied.에서 Cheryl Beattie의 작업 흐름 재설계로 인한 혁신 덕분에 올해 영업이 더욱 신속해졌다고 했으므로 정답은 (A)이다.

86-88

If you're interested in taking a cruise this vacation, **we have some great Caribbean cruise packages**[86] from Sea Breeze Cruises. For less than $700, you can take a round-trip, six-day cruise on one of Sea Breeze Cruises five-star ships to locations in Southern Florida, coastal Mexico, the Bahamas, or the Cayman Islands. **All of our cruise packages include three meals a day as well as free access to passenger services including fitness facilities, swimming pools,**[87] and private lounges. If you'd like to see some of the packages we offer through Sea Breeze Cruises, **I can give you this brochure.**[88]

이번 휴가 때 유람선 여행에 관심이 있으시면 저희에게 씨 브리즈 크루즈에서 나온 멋진 카리브해 유람선 패키지 상품이 몇 가지 있습니다. 700달러도 안 되는 금액에 플로리다 남부, 멕시코 해안, 바하마 또는 케이맨 제도에 있는 여러 곳으로 씨 브리즈 크루즈의 5성급 유람선을 타고 왕복 6일간의 여행을 하실 수 있습니다. 모든 유람선 패키지에는 체육관, 수영장, 그리고 개인 휴게실을 포함한 무료 승객 서비스에 대한 이용 뿐만 아니라 1일 3식이 포함되어 있습니다. 씨 브리즈 크루즈를 통해 저희가 제공하는 몇 가지 패키지를 보고 싶으시면 제가 여러분들에게 이 홍보 책자를 드리겠습니다.

어휘 be interested in ~에 관심이 있다
take a cruise 유람선 여행을 하다   sea breeze 해풍
less than ~ 미만(의)   take a round-trip 왕복 여행을 하다
location 장소   coastal 해안의
include 포함하다 (cf. including ~을 포함해)   meal 식사
A as well as B B뿐만 아니라 A도
free access to ~로의 무료 이용[접근]   fitness facilities 운동 시설
private lounge 개인 휴게실   brochure 홍보 책자

86. 말하는 사람은 누구겠는가?
(A) 여행 가이드
(B) 여행사 직원
(C) 호텔 직원
(D) 헬스 강사

해설 화자가 누구인지는 이야기의 초반부에 나오는 단어들로 알 수 있다. 화자가 we have some great Caribbean cruise packages from Sea Breeze Cruises라고 하면서 패키지 여행 상품을 소개하고 있으므로 정답은 (B)이다.

87. 화자가 수영장에 대해 언급한 내용은 무엇인가?
(A) 패키지에 포함되어 있다.
(B) 모든 호텔 손님들에게 개방되어 있다.
(C) 해변만큼 인기가 있지는 않다.
(D) 체육관 지하에 있다.

해설 질문의 핵심어가 swimming pools이므로 이 단어가 언급되는 부분에서 정답의 단서를 찾아야 한다. 광고 후반부에 All of our cruise packages include three meals a day as well as free access to passenger services including fitness facilities, swimming pools라고 했으므로 정답은 (A)이다.

88. 화자는 청자들에게 아마도 무엇을 주겠는가?
(A) 영수증
(B) 홍보 책자
(C) 신청서
(D) 회원 카드

해설 질문을 통해 화자가 청자들에게 무엇인가를 준다는 것을 알 수 있다. 보기 네 개를 빠르게 읽어둔 다음, 그 중 어떤 단어가 광고 속에 언급되는지를 포착해야 한다. 광고 마지막에 I can give you this brochure라고 했으므로 정답은 (B)이다.

89-91

The Jefferson County Association of Career Counselors will hold its annual job fair from 10 A.M. to 7 P.M. this Saturday and Sunday, and the event is free for everyone to attend. **It will be held in the Grisby Reception Room in Laramie University's Student Center building.**[89] More than 40 local companies will be coming to look for new employees, and **everyone attending should bring a résumé.**[90] **Steve Buckley, the career counselor who puts the fair together every year,**[91] said that this year's event will be bigger than ever.

제퍼슨 카운티 직원 상담 전문가 협회는 이번 주 토요일과 일요일 오전 10시에서 오후 7시까지 연례 취업 박람회를 개최하며 이 행사는 모든 사람들이 무료로 참석하실 수 있습니다. 이번 행사는 라라미 대학 학생회관 건물에 있는 그리스비 환영 회장에서 열립니다. 40개 이상의 지역 업체들이 신입 직원들을 찾으오 올 것이기 때문에 참석하시는 모든 분들은 이력서를 가지고 오시기 바랍니다. 매년 박람회를 주최하는 직업 상담가인 스티브 버클리에 따르면 올해의 행사는 그 어느 때보다도 규모가 클 것입니다.

어휘 association 협회 career counselor 직업 상담 전문가
hold 열다, 개최하다 annual 연례의 job fair 취업 박람회
more than ~보다 많은 local 지역의 attend 참석하다
bring 가져오다 résumé 이력서 put together 마련하다, 만들다

89. 취업 박람회는 어디에서 열리는가?
(A) 호텔
(B) 대학교
(C) 컨벤션 센터
(D) 회사의 본사

해설 방송에서 It will be held in the Grisby Reception Room in Laramie University's Student Center building.이라고 했으므로 정답은 (B)이다. 행사나 회의 등을 개최할 때 가장 흔히 쓰이는 동사가 hold(개최하다)와 take place(개최되다)이다. 주어로 행사(회의)가 올 경우 〈행사(회의)+be held+시간(장소)〉 또는 〈행사(회의)+take place+시간(장소)〉의 구조가 된다는 것을 알아두자.

90. 참석자들에게 어떤 조언을 하는가?
(A) 소개 연설에 참석하기
(B) 전문가답게 차려 입기
(C) 이력서 가져오기
(D) 입장료 내기

해설 참석자들에게 everyone attending should bring a résumé 라고 했으므로 정답은 (C)이다. 일반적으로 청자에 대한 요청 사항이나 당부의 말은 이야기의 후반부에 등장하는 경우가 많다.

91. 스티브 버클리는 누구이겠는가?
(A) 박람회 주최자
(B) 박람회에서의 채용 담당자
(C) 대학생
(D) 라디오 진행자

해설 질문에 사람 이름으로 Steve Buckley가 있으므로 속으로 이 단어를 미리 읽어두어서 발음에 친숙하게 만든 다음, 본문에서 Steve Buckley가 언급되는 부분에서 정답의 단서를 찾아야 한다. 이야기 후반부에 Steve Buckley, the career counselor who puts the fair together every year라고 했는데 puts the fair together라는 말이 organize the fair의 의미이므로 정답은 (A)이다.

92-94

Attention, Fresh Lane shoppers. **We are closing in thirty minutes.**[92] Please finish making your selections soon. **If you're purchasing more than fifty dollars of groceries, don't forget to take advantage of our new delivery program.**[93] Just bring your cart and receipt to the customer service desk and **we will deliver everything to your home the following morning,**[94] or at a convenient time for you. We'll store your goods in a refrigerated holding center, so your milk, eggs, and frozen goods won't spoil while we hold them. Again, please begin making your way to the checkout lane, and have a safe drive home.

프레시 레인 쇼핑객 여러분께 알려 드립니다. 저희는 30분 후에 문을 닫을 예정입니다. 바로 선택을 마치시기 바랍니다. 50달러 이상의 식료품을 구매하셨다면 저희의 새로운 배송 프로그램을 이용하는 것을 잊지 마시기 바랍니다. 카트와 영수증을 고객 서비스 데스크로 가져오시기만 하면 저희가 모든 상품을 다음 날 아침이나 여러분께서 편하신 시간에 집으로 배달해 드릴 것입니다. 저희는 냉장 보관 센터에 고객님의 상품을 보관하오니 우유, 달걀, 냉동 상품은 보관 중에 상하지 않을 것입니다. 다시 한 번 말씀드립니다. 계산대 줄로 가기 시작하시고 댁까지 안전 운전하시기 바랍니다.

어휘 attention (안내 방송에서) 알려 드립니다 shopper 쇼핑객
make a selection 선택하다 purchase 구매하다
grocery 식료품 forget to부정사 (미래에) ~할 것을 잊다
take advantage of ~을 이용하다
delivery (물품・편지 등의) 배달 (cf. deliver (물건・편지 등을) 배달하다)
cart 손수레, 카트 receipt 영수증
customer service desk 고객 서비스 데스크 convenient 편리한
store 저장하다, 보관하다 goods 상품, 제품 refrigerated 냉장한
frozen 냉동의 spoil (음식이) 상하다
make one's (own) way 나아가다, 가다
checkout (슈퍼마켓의) 계산대
lane (경주・수영 대회 등의) 레인, 도로, 길, 차선 safe 안전한
drive 드라이브, 자동차 여행(주행)

92. 화자가 "바로 선택을 마치시기 바랍니다."라고 말했을 때 의미하는 바는 무엇인가?
(A) 제품 유효 기간이 곧 만료될 것이다.
(B) 쇼핑객들은 상점을 떠나야 한다.
(C) 그는 정보를 확인해야 한다.
(D) 한정 판매 상품이 있다.

[해설] 앞 문장인 We are closing in thirty minutes.에서 상점이 곧 문을 닫는다는 것을 알 수 있다. 즉, 상품을 빨리 고르고 계산한 다음 상점을 나가라는 의미이므로 정답은 (B)이다.

93. 안내 방송이 어디에서 나오는 것 같은가?
(A) 자동차 수리점   (B) 식료품점
(C) 식당   (D) 우체국

[해설] 안내 방송 첫 문장인 Attention, Fresh Lane shoppers.와 If you're purchasing more than fifty dollars of groceries, don't forget to take advantage of our new delivery program.에 나온 groceries라는 단어를 통해 안내 방송의 장소가 식료품점인 것을 알 수 있으므로 정답은 (B)이다.

94. 화자가 택배 서비스에 관해 어떤 말을 하는가?
(A) 아침에만 이용할 수 있다.
(B) 배달이 하루 내에 이뤄진다.
(C) 인터넷으로 주문해야 한다.
(D) 어떤 상품은 배송할 수 없다.

[해설] 안내 방송 중반의 we will deliver everything to your home the following morning에서 다음 날 아침에 집으로 배달해 준다고 했으므로 정답은 (B)이다.

95-97

Hi, this is Susan calling from The Writer's Muse in regards to order nine-one-seven. I just wanted to let you know that part number P3 is currently out of stock. We should get more by the end of the week, but we'll ship that to you by itself, so it will arrive a little late.⁹⁵ To make up for the inconvenience we'll waive the shipping charge for the whole order.⁹⁶ Also, you didn't mention the colors you wanted for part L1. Please call us back before the end of the workday with that information so we can get everything else ready to ship right away.⁹⁷ Thank you.

안녕하세요, 주문 번호 917과 관련하여 전화한 라이터 뮤즈의 수잔입니다. 부품 번호 P3가 현재 재고가 없다는 것을 알려 드리고 싶었습니다. 우리는 금요일까지 더 많이 받아 놓겠지만, 그것을 귀하에게 따로 배송할 것이라서 다소 늦게 도착할 것입니다. 불편을 드린 점에 대한 보상으로 전체 주문의 배송료를 면제해 드리겠습니다. 또한, 부품 L1의 원하시는 색상을 언급하지 않으셨습니다. 업무 마감일 전에 회신 전화하셔서 그 정보를 알려 주시면 바로 배송할 수 있도록 다른 모든 것도 준비할 수 있습니다. 감사합니다.

라이터 뮤즈		주문 번호 917
부품 번호	명세	수량
L1	볼펜	20
L3	형광펜	4
P3	색종이	10
P4	대봉투	10

[어휘] in regards to ~와 관련하여   order 주문(하다)   currently 현재
out of stock 재고가 없는, 품절의   the end of the week 금요일
ship 운송하다(cf. shipment 배송되는 물건)   by oneself 혼자
a little 약간, 조금   make up for ~을 보상하다
inconvenience 불편   waive 포기하다, 철회하다
shipping charge 배송료   whole 전체의   mention 언급하다
call back (전화해 왔던 사람에게) 다시 전화하다   workday 근무일, 평일
right away 즉시, 곧바로   ballpoint pen 볼펜
highlighter 형광펜   colored 색깔이 있는   envelope 봉투

95. 표를 보세요. 어떤 품목이 따로 배달될 것인가?
(A) 펜   (B) 형광펜
(C) 종이   (D) 봉투

[해설] 메시지 초반의 I just wanted to let you know that part number P3 is currently out of stock. We should get more by the end of the week, but we'll ship that to you by itself, so it will arrive a little late.에서 부품 번호 P3가 현재 재고가 없어서 따로 배송할 것(we'll ship that to you by itself)이라고 했다. 양식을 보면 부품 번호 P3에 해당하는 품목은 Colored Paper이므로 정답은 (C)이다.

96. 화자는 청자에게 무엇을 줄 것인가?
(A) 추가 펜
(B) 무료 배송
(C) 상점 쿠폰
(D) 대회 참가권

[해설] 메시지 중반의 To make up for the inconvenience we'll waive the shipping charge for the whole order.에서 불편에 대한 보상으로 전체 주문의 배송료를 면제해 주겠다고 했으므로 정답은 (B)이다.

97. 화자는 청자에게 왜 자신에게 연락해 달라고 하는가?
(A) 주문 세부 사항을 명시하려고
(B) 회의 일정을 잡으려고
(C) 구매품의 값을 치르려고
(D) 설문 조사를 완료하려고

해설 메시지 후반의 Also, you didn't mention the colors you wanted for part L1. Please call us back before the end of the workday with that information so we can get everything else ready to ship right away.에서 part L1의 색상을 지정하지 않았으니 다시 전화해서 알려 달라고 했다. 따라서 정답은 (A)이다.

98-100

I want to congratulate everyone on the success of our newest cell phone case.⁹⁸ It is selling well, and trade magazines are praising it. Stanley, your team did a great job designing the case. Customers are very happy with it, especially with its special pocket for storing money.⁹⁹ Linda, the marketing was clearly effective because sales of the case have increased in almost every market. And Richard, fourth quarter sales in the country where you are head of sales improved more than anywhere else.¹⁰⁰ Well done. Everyone, please give yourselves a round of applause. I'm confident that when we release our line of headsets for smart phones next year, they will be just as successful.

최신형 휴대 전화 케이스의 성공에 대해 여러분 모두를 축하하고 싶습니다. 그것은 잘 팔리고 있으며 업계지(業界紙)들이 칭찬하고 있습니다. 스탠리, 귀하의 팀이 그 케이스를 훌륭하게 디자인했습니다. 고객들은 그 케이스에 매우 만족하고 있는데, 특히 돈을 수납할 수 있는 특수 주머니에 만족하고 있습니다. 린다, 케이스의 판매가 거의 모든 시장에서 증가했으므로 마케팅은 확실히 효과적이었습니다. 그리고 리처드, 당신이 판매 책임자로 있는 나라의 4분기 판매가 다른 어느 곳보다 증가했습니다. 훌륭합니다. 여러분, 스스로에게 한 차례의 박수를 보내시기 바랍니다. 내년에 스마트폰용 헤드셋 상품군을 출시하면 마찬가지로 성공적이리라 확신합니다.

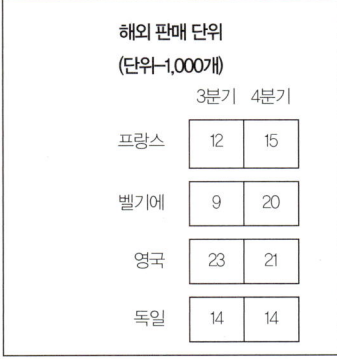

해외 판매 단위 (단위-1,000개)		
	3분기	4분기
프랑스	12	15
벨기에	9	20
영국	23	21
독일	14	14

어휘 congratulate A on B B에 대해 A에게 축하하다
success 성공(cf. successful 성공적인) cell phone 휴대 전화
trade magazine 업계지(특정 업계나 전문 직업인 상대의 잡지)
praise 칭찬하다 design 디자인하다, 설계하다 customer 고객
especially 특히 special 특수한, 특별한 pocket (호)주머니, 포켓
store 저장하다, 보관하다 marketing 마케팅
clearly 분명히, 뚜렷하게 effective 효과적인 increase 증가하다
market 시장 head (단체·조직의) 책임자 improve 개선하다
Well done. 잘했어, 훌륭했어.
a round of applause 한 차례의 박수 confident 확신하는
release 공개하다, 발표하다 line (상품의) 종류
headset (특히 마이크가 붙은) 헤드폰
smart phone 스마트폰 unit (상품의) 한 개[단위]
internationally 국제적으로(cf. international 국제적인)

98. 화자는 어떤 종류의 회사에서 일하는 것 같은가?
(A) 전화기 액세서리 제조사
(B) 국제 금융 회사
(C) 보도 전문 방송사
(D) 업계지 발행사

해설 회의록 첫째 문장인 I want to congratulate everyone on the success of our newest cell phone case.에서 최신형 휴대 전화 케이스의 성공을 축하한다고 했고, 마지막 문장인 I'm confident that when we release our line of headsets for smart phones next year, they will be just as successful.에서 내년에 스마트폰용 헤드셋을 출시할 것이라고 했으므로 정답은 (A)이다.

99. 화자는 고객들이 제품의 어떤 점을 좋아한다고 하는가?
(A) 독특해 보인다.
(B) 돈을 수납한다.
(C) 거울이 있다.
(D) 내구성이 좋다.

해설 회의록 중반의 Customers are very happy with it, especially with its special pocket for storing money.에서 고객들이 돈을 수납할 수 있는 특수 주머니를 특히 좋아한다고 했으므로 store를 hold로 바꿔 표현한 (B)가 정답이다.

100. 표를 보세요. 리처드가 판매 책임을 맡은 나라는 어디인가?
(A) 프랑스   (B) 벨기에
(C) 영국   (D) 독일

해설 회의록 후반의 And Richard, fourth quarter sales in the country where you are head of sales improved more than anywhere else.에서 리처드가 판매 책임자로 있는 나라의 4분기 판매가 다른 어느 곳보다 증가했다고 했다. 표를 보면 3분기에 비해 4분기에 판매량이 가장 많이 증가(9에서 20으로)한 나라는 벨기에이므로 정답은 (B)이다.

Part 5 Final Test   본책 _ p. 370–372

101. (D) 102. (C) 103. (B) 104. (C) 105. (D)
106. (B) 107. (A) 108. (C) 109. (B) 110. (B)
111. (B) 112. (A) 113. (D) 114. (A) 115. (A)
116. (D) 117. (D) 118. (C) 119. (C) 120. (C)
121. (C) 122. (A) 123. (A) 124. (B) 125. (A)
126. (D) 127. (A) 128. (C) 129. (D) 130. (C)

101.

해설 대명사 문제 가운데 가장 출제 빈도가 높은 대명사 격 문제이다. 빈칸 뒤에 명사가 주어 자리로 이어지므로 주어 자리 명사를 수식하는 대명사 소유격이 와야 한다. 따라서 (D) his가 정답이다.

해석 우리는 넬슨 씨에게 지원서는 이달 말까지 접수해야 한다는 것을 확인시켰다.

어휘 assure 확인시키다 application 지원서, 신청서
accept 수락하다, 받아들이다

정답 (D)

102.

해설 매월 거의 빠지지 않고 출제되는 상관접속사 문제이다. 빈칸 뒤에 or가 보이므로 either A or B (A나 B 둘 중에 하나) 표현으로 정답이 (C)이다.

해석 채 씨나 남 씨가 마르시오 컨벤션 센터에서 발표를 할 것이다.

어휘 give a speech 연설하다, 발표하다 convention 회의

정답 (C)

103.

해설 동사 어법 문제이다. 빈칸 앞에 must가 조동사이므로 그 뒤에는 동사의 원형이 와야 한다. 원형동사 자리로 (B)가 정답이 된다.

해석 프로그래밍에 대한 경험이 부족한 직원은 누구나 연수에 참석해야 한다.

어휘 lack 부족하다 experience with ~에 대한 경험

정답 (B)

104.

해설 출제 빈도가 가장 높은 전치사 문제이다. 해석상 '항공산업 전반에 걸쳐 일어나는'이 어울리므로 '전반에 걸쳐'의 의미로 가장 적합한 (C) throughout이 정답이 된다. (A) into(~ 안으로), (B) during(~ 동안에), (D) as(~로서)

해석 항공산업 전반에 걸쳐 일어나는 다양한 변화가 항공 교통의 최근 추세를 반영하고 있다.

어휘 various 다양한 occur 일어나다 airline industry 항공산업
reflect 반영하다 recent 최신의 trend 경향, 추세
transportation 운송, 교통

정답 (C)

105.

해설 빈칸에 들어갈 말은 앞에 and 접속사를 기준으로 앞뒤 같은 품사로 맞추는 것이 어울린다. 앞의 타동사 requires의 목적어 형태로 명사가 와야 하고, careful 형용사 앞에 관사 a / an / the 없이 바로 단수명사가 이어지므로 consideration을 불가산명사로 판단하면 빈칸에도 같은 짝의 불가산명사가 온다는 것을 파악할 수 있다. 보기 (A), (B), (D) 중 불가산명사는 (D)밖에 없다.

해석 성공적인 전략 실행은 주의 깊은 고려와 기획을 요구하고 있다.

어휘 successful 성공적인 implementation 이행, 실행
strategy 전략 require 요구하다 careful 주의 깊은
consideration 고려 planning 기획

정답 (D)

106.

해설 구조상 어울리는 품사를 선택하는 문제이다. 앞에 완료동사 has와 뒤에 과거분사 been 사이에는 부사가 와야 한다. 선택 보기 중 ly로 끝나는 형태의 부사는 (B)이다.

해석 석탄 생산은 역사적으로 지역 산업 성장에 중요한 부분이었다.

어휘 coal 석탄 production 생산 historically 역사적으로
local 현지의, 지역의 industrial 산업의 growth 성장

정답 (B)

107.

해설 해석상 '자격이 인상적이다'라는 의미이므로 (A) impressive가 정답이다. (B) interested(관심이 있는)는 자격(qualification)이 '관심을 가지는' 것이 아니므로, 정답이 되려면 interesting (흥미로운)으로 변경해야 한다. (C) grateful(감사히 여기는) 역시 qualification을 설명할 수 없다. (D) absolute(절대적인)는 be동사 뒤에 보어 자리로 올 수 없는 형용사이다. 항상 명사 앞에서 수식하는 형용사이다.

해석 귀하의 이력서를 검토한 후 우리는 그 직책에 대한 자격이 인상적이라고 생각했습니다.

어휘 review 검토하다 resume 이력서 qualification 자격, 자격 요건
impressive 인상적인, 훌륭한

정답 (A)

108.

해설 빈칸 뒤에 시간 표현 half an hour(30분)가 이어지며 해석상 '대략 30분'이 자연스럽기 때문에 '대략'의 의미로 부사가 와야 한다. 따라서 (C)가 정답이다.

해석 일정에 따르면 방문객은 가이드가 딸린 공장 견학을 하는 데 대략 30분 정도 시간을 가질 것이다.

어휘 according to ~에 따르면 schedule 일정
approximately 대략, 약 guided tour 가이드가 딸린 견학[관광]

206

정답 (C)

109.
해설 해석상 '일주일 이내'가 어울리며 그런 의미의 전치사는 (B) within 이다. 〈within+기간+of+동작〉 구조로 '~로부터 (기간) 이내에' 표현이다. (A) by나 (D) until 뒤에는 기간이 아닌 (완료) 시점이 와야 한다. (C) during 다음에는 시간 단위 명사(hour, week, month, year)가 이어질 때 부정관사가 아닌 정관사 the를 사용한다.

해석 고객은 구매로부터 일주일 이내에 하자가 있는 제품에 대한 환불을 받을 수 있다.

어휘 refund 환불하다 defective 결함이 있는 product 제품
purchase 구매

정답 (B)

110.
해설 적절한 동사 형태를 묻는 문제이다. 주절의 동사인 requested가 '요청'의 의미이므로 that 절 내에 원형동사가 들어가야 한다. 선택 보기에서 원형동사는 (B)밖에 없다.

해석 리드 씨는 회의록을 분당 지사로 보내달라고 요청했습니다.

어휘 request 요청하다 minutes 회의록 send 보내다
branch (office) 지사

정답 (B)

111.
해설 적절한 품사를 선택하는 문제이다. '가치 있는 기회를 제공하다'라는 의미로, 빈칸의 말은 명사 opportunities(기회)를 수식하는 형태가 되어야 한다. 보기 중 형용사 품사인 (B)가 정답이다.

해석 나는 그 세미나가 동료들과 소통할 가치 있는 기회를 줄 것이라는 점에 자신하고 있다.

어휘 be confident that ~에 대해 자신하다[확신하다] seminar 세미나
provide 제공하다 valuable 가치 있는 opportunity 기회
interact with ~와 교류하다, 협업하다

정답 (B)

112.
해설 주어 자리 명사를 선택하는 문제이다. 명사 형태로는 (A)와 (B) 두 개가 있지만 동사 are가 복수동사이기 때문에 주어 자리에는 복수명사가 와야 한다. 복수명사로는 (A)가 적절하다.

해석 영화 할인 티켓은 매표소에서 구입 가능하다.

어휘 discount ticket 할인 티켓 available 이용 가능한
box office 매표소

정답 (A)

113.
해설 해석으로 정답을 고르는 동사 어휘 문제이다. 빈칸 뒤의 documents (문서)와 어울리는 동사는 (D) obtain(얻다, 소유하다)이다. (A) inform(알리다)은 사람 따위를 목적어로 취하는 동사이다. (B) promote(개선시키다, 승진시키다)는 의미상 어울리지 않는다. (예: promote efficiency (효율성을 향상시키다)) (C) progress (발전하다)는 자동사로 목적어를 취하지 않는다. 이런 자동사가 타동사를 선택해야 하는 문제에서 자주 나오는 편이다. (예: proceed(나아가다), exist(존재하다), remain(남아 있다))

해석 승객들이 미리 모든 필요한 문서를 갖출 것을 적극 권장합니다.

어휘 highly 매우 recommend 추천하다, 권장하다 passenger 승객
obtain 얻다 required 필요한, 필수의 document 문서
in advance 사전에, 미리

정답 (D)

114.
해설 출제빈도가 가장 높은 전치사 문제이다. 해석상 '컴퓨터와 기타 주변기기 청소를 위해서만 사용되어야 한다'가 자연스러우므로 '~를 위해서'를 뜻하는 (A) for가 가장 적합하다. 전치사 문제로 for가 가장 많이 출제된다.

해석 수퍼클리너는 컴퓨터와 기타 주변기기를 청소하는 용도로만 사용되어야 한다.

어휘 be used 사용되다 for ~을 위해 clean 청소하다
peripheral 주변기기

정답 (A)

115.
해설 의미상 빈칸 뒤의 description(설명, 묘사)과 어울리는 형용사를 고르는 문제이다. '제품에 대한 더욱 (폭넓은) 설명을 얻기 위해'가 자연스럽기 때문에 '폭넓은'의 의미로 (A) extensive를 선택한다. 다른 표현으로 comprehensive가 있다. (B) limited(제한된), (C) qualified(자격을 갖춘) – 사람 따위를 수식하는 형용사, (D) impressed(인상을 받은) – 사람 따위를 수식하는 형용사.

해석 제품에 대한 보다 폭넓은 설명을 얻고자 하신다면 사용 전에 안내서를 주의깊게 읽으세요.

어휘 extensive 폭넓은 description 설명
instruction(s) 사용 설명서, 지시사항 carefully 주의 깊게

정답 (A)

116.
해설 문장 구조상 종속접속사를 선택하는 문제이다. 구조를 보았을 때, 〈(접속사)+주어+동사 ~, 명령문〉 구조로 접속사가 들어가야 할 자리이다. 선택 보기를 보았을 때, (A) Therefore(그러므로)는 부사이므로 〈Therefore, 주어+동사〉 구조 형태로 가야 하며, (B) In order는 '~하기 위해서, ~한 일이 일어날 수 있도록'이라는 뜻의 '목적'을 의미한다. (C) Due to(~ 때문에)는 전치사이므로 뒤에 〈주어+동사〉 구조가 아닌 명사구 형태가 와야 한다.

해설 만약 부동산을 팔고자 한다면, 반드시 시장에 대한 광범위한 지식을 갖추고 있는 부동산 중개인과 상담하십시오.

어휘 property 부동산   be sure to부정사 반드시 ~하다
consult ~와 상담하다   real estate agent 부동산 중개업자
broad 폭넓은   knowledge 지식   market 시장

정답 (D)

117.

해설 빈칸 뒤의 ideas(생각, 아이디어)와 어울리는 타동사를 선택하는 문제이다. 적절한 동사는 (D) developed(개발하다, 발전시키다)이다. (A) existed(존재하다)는 자동사이므로 뒤에 목적어 형태가 올 수 없다. (B) thought(생각하다)는 뒤에 목적어 형태가 올 경우 think of, think about, think over처럼 뒤에 전치사가 와야 한다. (C) resulted(결과로 발생하다)는 자동사로 result from (~로 비롯되다), result in (~의 결과로 끝나다) 등의 형태로 사용된다.

해설 홀로 사의 전문가들이 스마트 기기를 위한 새로운 아이디어를 발전시켰다.

어휘 specialist 전문가   develop 발전시키다
smart 똑똑한, 컴퓨터로 조정되는   device 장치, 기기

정답 (D)

118.

해설 의미상 어울리는 부사 어휘를 선택하는 문제이다. 빈칸 앞의 동사 use(사용하다)와 어울리는 부사는 (C) efficiently(효율적으로)이다. (A) nearly(거의), (B) largely(대개), (D) quite(꽤, 매우) – 동사를 수식할 수 없는 부사이다.

해설 우리는 재원을 더욱 효율적으로 활용할 수 있는지 여부를 결정하고자 회의 일정을 잡을 것이다.

어휘 schedule 일정을 잡다   determine 결정하다
resource 자원, 재원, 자료   efficiently 효율적으로

정답 (C)

119.

해설 해석상 '월요일 오전부터'가 어울리며 '월요일 오전' 앞에는 시간 전치사로서 on을 사용한다. 〈on + 하루 일자〉라는 것을 알아두자. (예: on Monday (월요일에), on May 13th (5월 13일에)), 전치사 in 다음에는 월 단위 이상의 표현이 온다. (예: in May (5월에), in the summer (여름에), in the 2nd quarter (2사분기에), in 2013 (2013년에))

해설 월요일 아침부터 새로운 카펫이 건물 3층에 설치될 것이다.

어휘 carpeting 카펫   install 설치하다

정답 (C)

120.

해설 구조상 적절한 품사를 선택하는 문제이다. '부서로 (바로) 주문품을 보내주시면 됩니다'로 해석되는 게 자연스러우므로 (C) directly(바로)가 정답이다.

해설 어떠한 이유로든 만족하지 못한다면 주문품을 부서에 바로 원본 영수증과 함께 보내시면 됩니다.

어휘 be satisfied 만족하다   for any reason 어떠한 이유에서든
order 주문품   original 원본의   receipt 영수증   directly 바로

정답 (C)

121.

해설 빈칸 뒤의 receipt(수신, 수령, 받음)와 어울리는 타동사를 선택하는 문제이다. acknowledge receipt of(~을 받았음을 알리다)라는 표현을 알아두자. 따라서 정답은 (C)이다. (A) comment(논평하다)는 'comment on + 명사' 형태로 사용된다. (B) notify(통보하다)는 '사람'을 목적어로 취하는 동사이다. (D) suggest(제안하다)는 해석상 자연스럽지 않다.

해설 일주일 전에 보내신 문서를 받았다는 말씀드리고자 편지를 씁니다.

어휘 acknowledge (편지 · 소포 등을) 받았음을 알리다
receipt 수령, 수신, 받음   document 문서   send 보내다

정답 (C)

122.

해설 해석상 어울리는 형용사 어휘를 선택하는 문제이다. '사무실을 더욱 더 환경 친화적으로 만들고자'라는 해석이 자연스럽다. 따라서 (A)가 정답이다. (B) unexpected(예상치 못한), (C) pleased(즐거워 하는)의 경우 정답이 되도록 하려면 pleasing(즐거움을 주는)이나 pleasant(즐거운)로 고쳐야 한다. (D) competent(유능한, 능력 있는)는 사람을 수식하는 형용사이다.

해설 사무실을 보다 환경 친화적으로 만들기 위해 직원들은 모든 사무실 쓰레기를 분류하고 재활용해야 한다.

어휘 environmentally friendly 환경 친화적인

정답 (A)

123.

해설 관계대명사 문제이다. 보통은 정답으로 who나 which를 묻는 문제가 가장 많이 출제된다. 빈칸 앞의 선행사인 concert series(콘서트 시리즈)가 사물이므로 (A)가 정답이 된다. 관계부사 (B)나 (C)가 정답이 되려면 빈칸 뒤에 구조가 완전한 문장이 와야 한다. 하지만 빈칸 뒤에 바로 동사 highlight가 이어지기 때문에 불완전한 문장이다. (D)는 빈칸 앞의 선행사가 사람일 때 가능하다.

해설 현지 음악가와 예술가를 부각시키는 몇몇 음악 공연이 이번 달에 있다.

어휘 several 몇몇   highlight 강조하다 (= emphasize)

정답 (A)

124.
해설 빈칸 앞의 to가 '~하기 위해서'라는 목적의 의미로 사용되는 to부정사이다. 따라서 다음에 원형동사가 와야 하므로 정답은 (B)이다.

해석 크녹스 사의 연구원들은 제품 판매의 하락세를 분석하고자 다양한 정보를 수집하고 있다.

어휘 researcher 연구원 gather 모으다 diverse 다양한
data 자료 analyze 분석하다 downward 하향의
trend 경향, 추세

정답 (B)

125.
해설 적절한 형태를 넣는 문제이다. 선택 보기에 비교급, 최상급이 함께 올 때, 빈칸 앞에 정관사 the가 있으면 보통은 최상급이 정답이 된다. 이 문제도 마찬가지로 빈칸 앞의 정관사 the와 함께 최상급 형용사가 빈칸 뒤의 project 명사를 수식하는 형태가 어울린다. 따라서 정답은 (A)이다. challenging은 '힘든, 까다로운'의 의미로 사용된다.

해석 새로운 제품군을 시작하는 것은 우리 부서가 지금까지 맡은 가장 도전적인 프로젝트이다.

어휘 initiate 시작하다 challenging 힘든, 어려운 division 부서
undertake 떠맡다

정답 (A)

126.
해설 까다로운 문제이다. 토익에서 난이도 상에 해당되는 문제로, 단순히 해석뿐만 아니라 명사가 가산인지 불가산인지를 따져서 풀어야 하는 문제이다. 빈칸 앞에 전치사 of 다음에 바로 명사가 관사 없이 연결된다는 것은 명사가 불가산명사라는 것이다. 불가산명사이면서 해석이 가장 자연스러운 명사는 (D) growth(성장)이다. (B) rise(증가)는 가산명사로 앞에 관사가 와야 한다. (A) statement(성명서), (C) result(결과).

해석 영업 이사가 지난 달 성장한 지사를 공식적으로 발표할 것이다.

어휘 sales director 영업이사 officially 공식적으로
announce 발표하다 branch 지사 growth 성장

정답 (D)

127.
해설 명사(contract)를 수식하는 형용사 자리이다. 복합명사로 명사가 올 수 있지만 (C)의 correctness(정확함)는 자연스럽지 않다. '수정된'이라는 의미로 (A)가 정답이 된다.

해석 귀하에게 6월 20일까지 수정된 계약서를 부서로 다시 보내시길 요청합니다.

어휘 corrected 수정된 contract 계약(서) department 부서

정답 (A)

128.
해설 구조상 뒤에 명사구가 이어지므로 전치사가 와야 한다. 선택 보기 모두가 전치사가 될 수 있는데 해석상 '구조조정으로 인해서, 책임지고 있다'가 어울리므로 (C) Due to (~ 때문에)가 정답이 된다. (A) Within(~ 이내에), (B) Until(~까지), (D) Since(~ 이래로) – 정답이 되려면 주절의 동사 시제가 is가 아닌 has been 형태의 현재완료시제가 와야 한다.

해석 회사 구조조정으로 인하여, 헤르난데스 씨는 배송과 포장에 책임을 지고 있다.

어휘 due to ~ 때문에 restructuring 구조조정, 기업 혁신 전략
in charge of ~을 책임지는 shipping 배송 packaging 포장

정답 (C)

129.
해설 분사 문제이다. 빈칸이 뒤의 명사 scent(향기)를 수식하고 있고 '향기로운'이란 의미로 (D)가 정답이 된다. (B) pleased는 '기쁜, 기쁨을 느끼는'의 뜻으로 수식 받는 명사로 감정을 느끼는 사람 명사 따위가 와야 한다.

해석 로지 프레시 런드리는 좋은 향기를 가지고 있으며 효율적으로 얼룩을 제거합니다.

어휘 laundry 세탁소 pleasing 기분 좋은 scent 향기
remove 제거하다 stain 얼룩, 때 effectively 효율적으로

정답 (D)

130.
해설 형용사 어휘 문제인데, 보통 to부정사와 어울리는 형용사를 선택하는 문제이다. 〈be + 형용사 + to부정사〉 구조로 자주 사용되는 표현으로 be eligible to부정사 (~할 자격이 있다)가 있다. (A) active(활동적인), (B) valued(가치 있는), (D) estimated(평가된, 추정된)

해석 영업 목표를 달성하는 직원은 누구나 무료 여행권을 받을 자격이 있다.

어휘 reach ~에 이르다 sales goal 영업 목표
be eligible to부정사 ~할 자격이 있다 win 얻다
complimentary 무료의

정답 (C)

Part 6 Final Test
본책 _ p. 373–376

131. (D) 132. (A) 133. (B) 134. (C) 135. (D)
136. (B) 137. (B) 138. (C) 139. (D) 140. (D)
141. (C) 142. (A) 143. (B) 144. (B) 145. (D)
146. (A)

131-133

> 알려 드립니다!
>
> 34년 근무한 후에 짐 칙우드가 프랭클린 부동산에서 물러날 예정입니다. 그는 자기 가족과 더 많은 시간을 보내기 위해 금요일에 퇴직할 것입니다. 모두 목요일 저녁 그의 송별 만찬에 참석해주십시오. 또한 그의 은퇴 기념 선물을 마련하기 위해 5달러씩을 기부해 주십시오. <u>우리는 만찬 중에 은퇴 선물을 그에게 증정할 것입니다.</u> 만찬 준비자인 경리부의 실비아 헌든에게 기부금을 전달해 주시기 바랍니다.

어휘 Attention! 주목하세요!, 알려 드립니다! move on 물러나다
realty 부동산(= real estate) retire 은퇴하다, 퇴직하다
(cf. retirement 은퇴) invite 초대[초청]하다 attend 참석하다
dinner 만찬 (행사) request 요청, 간청; 요청하다
contribute 기부하다 organizer 조직자, 준비자
accounting department 경리부

131.
해설 문맥에 어울리는 전치사를 고르는 문제이다. move on은 '(현재 하는 일에서) 물러나다'는 의미로 현재 직장인 Franklin Realty에서 물러난다는 문장이므로 '~에서, ~으로부터'라는 뜻의 (D) from이 정답이다.

정답 (D)

132.
해설 문맥에 어울리는 명사를 고르는 문제이다. 공지된 행사는 Jim Cheekwood의 은퇴 기념 만찬이므로 '작별, 송별회'라는 뜻의 (A) farewell이 정답이다.

정답 (A)

133.
(A) 그들은 식사 후에 시간이 될 것입니다.
(B) 우리는 만찬 중에 그것을 그에게 증정할 것입니다.
(C) 그에게 줄 개인 선물을 준비하시기 바랍니다.
(D) 그는 자기 대가족과 더 많은 시간을 보낼 것입니다.

해설 문맥에 어울리는 문장을 고르는 문제이다. 앞 문장인 Everyone is also requested to contribute five dollars towards a retirement gift we will buy for him.에서 은퇴 선물을 언급했으므로 (B)가 만찬 중에 은퇴 선물을 전달해 주겠다고 한 (B)가 문맥에 가장 잘 어울린다.

정답 (B)

134.
해설 알맞은 품사와 의미의 어휘를 고르는 문제이다. 대명사 you의 소유격인 your 뒤이므로 명사가 와야 하는 자리인데 앞에서 언급한 five dollars를 Sylvia Herndon에게 전해 주라는 문맥이므로 '기부, 기부금'이라는 뜻의 (C) donation이 정답이다.

정답 (C)

135-138

> 타운센드—타운센드 건설국(CAT)은 타운센드 지하철 확장 계획 단계에 너무 많은 시간을 소비한 것 때문에 비난받아 왔습니다. 이에 <u>개의치 않고 CAT는 다시 프로젝트의 이 단계를 연장했습니다.</u> 월요일에 탐구 위원회는 타운센드 주민들에 의해 제기된 질문에 답하기 위해 두 달 연장을 요청했습니다. 그러고 나서 CAT는 그 주 목요일에 연장 허가에 투표했습니다. 위원회가 답변하려고 하는 가장 중요한 질문은 지하철이 타운센드 지역 전문 대학까지 연장할 것인지 아닌지였습니다. CAT는 결정하기 전에 학생 대표들에게 설문 조사할 계획입니다. 연장에는 약 6만 파운드가 들 것입니다.

어휘 construction 건설, 공사 authority 당국, 권위자
criticize 비난하다, 비판하다 planning phase 계획 단계
expansion 확장, 확대 exploratory 탐사의, 탐구의
committee 위원회 extension 연장, 확장
(cf. extend 연장하다, 확장하다) raise (문제를) 제기하다
resident 주민 vote 투표하다 grant 주다, 수여하다
significant 중요한, 상당한 community college 지역 전문 대학
representative 대표자, 대리 make a decision 결정하다
cost (값·비용이) ~들다

135.
(A) 따라서 CAT는 즉시 건설 단계를 시작할 것입니다.
(B) 아마 CAT는 프로젝트 연장에 대한 제안을 들을 것입니다.
(C) 마침내 CAT는 훨씬 더 오랜 기간 조사를 약속했습니다.
(D) 개의치 않고 CAT는 다시 프로젝트의 이 단계를 연장했습니다.

해설 문맥에 어울리는 문장을 고르는 문제이다. 앞 문장인 The Construction Authority of Townsend (CAT) has been criticized for spending too much time on the planning phases of the Townsend Subway expansion.에서 타운센드 지하철 확장 계획 단계에 너무 많은 시간을 소비한 것 때문에 비난받아 왔다고 했고 다음 문장인 On Monday, the exploratory committee requested a two-month extension to answer questions raised by Townsend residents.에서 두 달 연장을 요청했다고 했으므로 그에 따라 단계를 연장했다고 한 (D)가 문맥에 가장 잘 어울린다.

정답 (D)

136.
해설 동사의 알맞은 형태를 고르는 문제이다. 빈칸은 전체 문장의 동사 자리이므로 to부정사형인 (C)는 답에서 제외한다. 이 문장에서 the exploratory committee가 월요일에 연장을 요청했고 다음 문장에서 CAT가 목요일에 연장 허가에 투표했다는 문맥이므로 과거 시제인 (B)가 정답이다.

정답 (B)

137.
해설 문맥에 어울리는 동사를 고르는 문제이다 student representatives를 목적어로 취해 문맥에 가장 자연스러운 것은 '(설문) 조사하다'라는 뜻의 (B) survey이다.

정답 (B)

138.
해설 알맞은 품사의 어휘를 고르는 문제이다. 주어, 동사, 목적어를 갖춘 빠진 문장 성분이 없는 문장이므로 동사 cost를 수식하는 부사인 (C) approximately가 정답이다.

정답 (C)

139-142

발신: cdrecker@clear-line.co.uk
수신: stafflist@clear-line.co.uk
날짜: 12월 1일
제목: 송년 만찬

클리어 라인 직원 여러분께,

우리 회사 송년 만찬에 오실 수 있다고 이미 확인해 주신 여러분 모두에게 감사드립니다. 아직 저에게 참석하실지 아닐지 알려 주지 않으셨다면 가능한 한 빨리 알려 주시기 바랍니다. 빅 스터럽 식당에서 주차장이 때로 만차가 되니 카풀을 추천한다고 알려 왔습니다. 귀하의 친구분들과 카풀을 준비하시기 바랍니다. 저에게 카풀 요청을 위해 연락하셔도 됩니다. 제가 세 자리의 여유가 있는 승용차를 몰고 있으니 카풀하게 된다면 기쁘겠습니다. 저는 시 서부에 있는 블루 드림 구역에 삽니다. 만찬 후에 근처에 사시는 분은 누구라도 제 차를 타고 집으로 가실 수도 있습니다.

감사합니다.

캐롤 드레커

어휘 confirm 확인하다   inform 알리다, 통지하다
as soon as possible 가능한 한 빨리
stirrup (말 안장 양쪽에 달린) 등자   parking area 주차 구역, 주차장
fill up 채워지다, 가득 차다   carpool 카풀[승용차 함께 타기]을 하다
recommend 추천하다   organize 준비하다, 조직하다
ride 탑승, 승차   sharing 공유(cf. share 공유하다)
sedan 세단형 자동차   extra 추가의, 별도의
subdivision (세분된) 한 부분, (대지의) 구획

139.
해설 문맥에 어울리는 대명사를 고르는 문제이다. 전치사의 목적어 자리이므로 주격 대명사인 (B)는 답에서 제외한다. 관계대명사절인 that has already confirmed의 선행사 자리이므로 단수 동사와 호응하지 않는 (C)는 답이 될 수 없다. 이미 확인해 준 모든 직원에게 감사한다는 문맥으로 if they can come to our end of year dinner의 they가 받은 대명사이므로 (D) everyone이 정답이다.

정답 (D)

140.
해설 알맞은 품사의 어휘를 고르는 문제이다. whether는 접속사로 주어와 동사를 갖춘 절이 와야 하므로 (D) can attend가 정답이다.

정답 (D)

141.
(A) 선택한 메뉴를 저에게 이메일로 보내십시오.
(B) 직원들은 셔틀버스를 이용할 수 있습니다.
(C) 저에게 카풀 요청을 위해 연락하셔도 됩니다.
(D) 만찬은 일주일 연기되었습니다.

해설 앞 두 문장인 The Big Stirrup restaurant informed me that their parking area sometimes fills up, so carpooling is recommended. Please, organize ride sharing with your friends.에서 카풀에 관한 논의를 하고 있으므로 (C)가 문맥에 가장 잘 어울린다.

정답 (C)

142.
해설 문맥에 어울리는 부사를 고르는 문제이다. 앞 두 문장인 I am driving a sedan with three extra seats and would be happy to share. I live in the Blue Dream subdivision on the west side of town.에서 카풀 의사를 밝히고 사는 지역을 말했으므로 카풀 요청 연락해도 된다는 의미의 문장 끝에는 (A) too가 가장 잘 어울린다.

정답 (A)

143-146

회람

수신: 칼-테크 직원들
발신: 칼 파트
날짜: 9월 27일
제목: 일부 파이프 수리

많은 분께서 3층의 수압 문제를 알아차리셨을 것입니다. 이것은 낡은 수도 본관이 부식해서 발생했습니다. 낮은 수압은 새는 수도 본관 때문에 발생했습니다. 흥미롭게도 우리는 파이프에서 물로 인한 어떤 손상도 발견하지 못했습니다. 새는 물이 어디에서 온 것인지 명확하지 않습니다. 벽에 발달한 검은 점이 보이면 유지 보수 직원에게 즉시 알려 주십시오. 배관공이 10월 3일 주말에 파이프를 교체할 것입니다. 그때까지 3층의 화장실이나 싱크대 사용을 삼가시기 바랍니다. 다음 주 월요일까지 시설은 완전히 사용 준비가 될 것입니다.

칼

211

어휘 memorandum 메모, 회람(= memo) notice 주의하다, 알아차리다
water main 급수[수도] 본관   rust 녹슬다, 부식하다
interestingly 흥미롭게도   damage 손상, 피해
develop 성장[발달]하다[시키다]   notify 알리다, 통보하다
maintenance 유지 보수   immediately 즉시
plumber 배관공   replace 교체하다   refrain from ~을 삼가다
facility 시설   fully 완전히, 충분히
operational 가동되는, 운전 가능한, 사용할 준비가 된

143.
(A) 문제는 신속히 해결되었다.
(B) 낮은 수압은 새는 수도 본관 때문에 발생했습니다.
(C) 스트레스 감소 상담사가 그를 도울 수 있다.
(D) 추가 공지가 있을 때까지 층 전체에 모든 직원의 출입을 금한다.

해설 문맥에 어울리는 문장을 고르는 문제이다. 앞 두 문장인 Many of you may have noticed problems with the water pressure on the third floor. This was caused by old water mains rusting.에서 3층의 수압 문제와 낡은 수도 본관 부식을 언급했으므로 수도 본관 누수가 낮은 수압의 원인이라고 한 (B)가 문맥에 가장 잘 어울린다.

정답 (B)

144.
해설 문맥에 어울리는 형용사를 고르는 문제이다. 앞 문장인 Interestingly, we have not noticed any water damage from the pipe.에서 파이프에서 물로 인한 손상을 발견하지 못했다고 했으므로 새는 물이 어디에서 온 것인지 명확하지 않다고 하는 것이 자연스럽다. 따라서 '불확실한, 분명하지 않은'이라는 뜻의 (B) unclear가 문맥에 가장 잘 어울린다.

정답 (B)

145.
해설 알맞은 품사의 어휘를 고르는 문제이다. 빈칸은 형용사 dark와 분사구인 developing on the walls의 수식을 받는 명사가 와야 하는 자리이므로 (D) spots가 정답이다.

정답 (D)

146.
해설 알맞은 품사와 의미의 어휘를 고르는 문제이다. that time은 the weekend of October 3를 가리키며 배관공이 파이프를 수리하는 시점까지 3층 화장실과 싱크대 사용을 삼가 달라는 문맥이므로 '~까지'라는 뜻의 (A) Until이 문맥에 가장 잘 어울린다.

정답 (A)

Part 7 Final Test
본책 _ p. 377-399

147. (D) 148. (A) 149. (C) 150. (A) 151. (D)
152. (A) 153. (A) 154. (D) 155. (D) 156. (B)
157. (A) 158. (C) 159. (B) 160. (D) 161. (A)
162. (C) 163. (B) 164. (A) 165. (B) 166. (D)
167. (D) 168. (A) 169. (C) 170. (D) 171. (C)
172. (B) 173. (C) 174. (B) 175. (A) 176. (A)
177. (B) 178. (C) 179. (A) 180. (D) 181. (D)
182. (B) 183. (A) 184. (C) 185. (A) 186. (A)
187. (A) 188. (C) 189. (C) 190. (D) 191. (B)
192. (C) 193. (C) 194. (B) 195. (C) 196. (A)
197. (A) 198. (C) 199. (C) 200. (A)

147-148

99유로 미만의 비용으로 해외여행을 하세요

저렴한 주말 휴가지를 찾고 있다면, 더 이상 보지 마세요. 고제트 사는 11월 30일까지 여름 이후 시즌 혜택을 제공할 것입니다.

99유로 미만으로 런던이나 프랑크푸르트[147]에서 출발하여 유럽 내 어느 곳이든 비행기를 타고 가세요. 파리에서의 로맨틱한 주말이나 그리스 섬 여행을 다른 여행사보다 훨씬 더 저렴한 비용으로 즐기세요.

나열된 가격에는 세금이 포함되어[148] 있습니다. 더 많은 정보와 전체 여행지에 대한 목록이 필요하다면 www.gojet.com을 방문하십시오.

어휘 euro 유로: EU의 화폐 단위   look for ~을 찾다   cheap 저렴한
getaway 휴가, 휴가지   post-summer 여름이 지난 후 시즌
special 혜택   anywhere 어디든지   romantic 낭만적인
for much less 훨씬 적은 비용으로   travel agency 여행사
listed 목록으로 기재된   tax 세금   complete 완성된, 완전한
destination 여행지, 목적지

147. 어떤 도시로부터 고객이 출발할 수 있는가?
(A) 파리
(B) 아테네
(C) 그리스
(D) 프랑크푸르트

해설 두 번째 단락에 런던이나 프랑크푸르트에서 출발한다는 내용이 나와 있기 때문에 정답은 (D)이다. (A) 파리나 (C) 그리스는 언급되어 있지만 출발지는 아니다.

148. 판매에 대해 올바른 것은?
(A) 가격에는 세금이 포함되어 있다.
(B) 판매가 11월 30일에 시작한다.
(C) 모든 표는 99유로이다.
(D) 표는 온라인으로 구입해야 한다.

해설 세 번째 단락에 include tax 부분에서 세금(tax)이 포함되어 있다는 것을 알 수 있다.

149-150

크리스 라임스	오전 7시 54분
안녕하세요, 크리스타. 사무실에 계세요?	
크리스타 다나카	오전 8시 01분
오전 8시예요.	
크리스 라임스	오전 8시 03분
그러네요. 집에 계시는데 번거롭게 해 드려서 죄송합니다.¹⁴⁹ 막 공항에 도착했는데 티켓 확인 번호를 깜빡했어요. 당신이 어디에 적어 두셨을 것 같아서요.	
크리스타 다나카	오전 8시 05분
제가 항공편을 예약했으니 제 개인 이메일에 기록이 있을 텐데요. 잠시 기다려 주세요.¹⁵⁰	
크리스타 다나카	오전 8시 09분
있네요. X37W2입니다.	
크리스 라임스	오전 8시 10분
고마워요. 생명의 은인이세요.	

어휘 bother 괴롭히다, 귀찮게 굴다 confirmation 확인
book 예약하다(= reserve) flight 항공편 record 기록
personal 개인적인 (cf. personally 직접, 친히)
second (시간 단위인) 초, (아주) 잠깐
life saver 인명 구조원, 생명의 은인

149. 오전 8시 1분에 다나카 씨가 "오전 8시예요."라고 쓸 때 그녀가 의미하는 것은?
(A) 회의가 오전 8시이다.
(B) 자기 사무실이 일찍 문을 열었다.
(C) 그녀는 아직 출근하러 가지 않았다.
(D) 라임스 씨의 비행편이 연기되었다.

해설 Chris Rhimes가 앞 메시지인 Are you at the office?라고 출근했는지 물었고 다음 메시지인 I'm sorry to bother you at home, then.에서 집에 있는데 번거롭게 해서 미안하다고 했으므로 Krista Tanaka는 아직 출근 전이라는 것을 알 수 있다. 따라서 (C)가 정답이다.

150. 다나카 씨가 오전 8시 5분과 8시 9분 사이에 무슨 일을 했을 것 같은가?
(A) 자신의 이메일 확인
(B) 표 구매
(C) 항공사에 전화
(D) 운전해서 출근

해설 Chris Rhimes가 앞 메시지의 I'm just at the airport and I forgot my ticket confirmation number. I thought you might have written it down somewhere.에서 티켓 확인 번

호를 알려 달라고 요청하자 Krista Tanaka는 Since I booked the flight, there should be a record in my personal e-mail. Wait a second.라며 자기 이메일을 확인해서 알려줄 것을 암시했다. 따라서 (A)가 정답이다.

151-152

발신: 사만다 맥스웰 〈sammaxwell@herrington.com〉
수신: ricky@askricky.com
제목: 감사합니다
날짜: 3월 18일 오후 5시 2분

리키에게

먼저 귀하가 해주신 모든 조언에 감사를 드립니다. 리키 부동산은 그다지 잘 알지 못하지만 집을 구매하는 데 관심을 가지고 있었기에¹⁵¹ 친구 추천으로 귀하의 칼럼을 읽기 시작했습니다.

열혈 독자가 되었고 주택 개조와 융자에 대해 많이 배웠습니다. 하지만 여전히 답을 찾기 어려운 기본적인 질문이 있습니다.

현재 주택 계약금 마련을 위해 저축을 하고 있습니다.¹⁵² 하지만 연말쯤 이루어질 것이라고 기대하는 상당한 금액이 마련되면, 무엇을 해야 할지 모르겠습니다. 많은 부동산 중개업자가 있지만 저에게 적합한 사람을 어떻게 알 수 있을까요? 이런 쪽은 처음이라¹⁵¹ 다소 걱정이 됩니다. 그래서 순진하게 원하지 않는 집을 구입하기는 싫습니다.

괜찮으시다면 도와주십시오. 좋은 부동산 중개업자와 집을 찾는 기본적인 법칙이 무엇인가요?

정말 감사합니다.

사만다 맥스웰

어휘 advice 조언 be familiar with ~을 잘 알다, ~에 익숙하다
realtor 부동산 업자 recommend 추천하다
home improvement 주택 개조 financing 융자
be in the process of ~의 과정에 있다
down payment 계약금, 보증금 substantial 상당한
real estate agent 부동산 중개업자 right 적합한
be new to ~에 새롭다, ~이 처음이다 absolutely 절대적으로

151. 맥스웰 씨가 하고자 하는 것은?
(A) 계좌 개설
(B) 집 보수
(C) 부동산 투자
(D) 첫 주택 구입

해설 편지의 발신자인 맥스웰 씨는 첫 번째 단락, 마지막 줄에서 주택 구입에 관심이 있다는 의사를 보이고 있고, 세 번째 단락, 네 번째 줄의 I'm new to this 부분에서 주택 구입이 처음인 것을 알 수 있다.

152. 이메일에서 알 수 있는 내용은?
(A) 맥스웰 씨는 저축을 하고 있다.
(B) 맥스웰 씨는 해외로 이사할 것이다.
(C) 맥스웰 씨는 잡지 구독자이다.
(D) 맥스웰 씨는 부동산 중개업자와 상담을 했다.

해설 세 번째 단락 첫 번째 문장의 I'm in the process of saving up for a down payment on a house 부분에서 주택 구입을 위해 down payment(계약금)를 saving up(저축하다)한다고 언급하고 있다.

153-154

국제 건축가 협회 (IAA)

올해 국제 건축가 협회(IAA) 회의에 참석할 계획이라면, 〈단순하지만 세련된〉이란 제목의 기록영화 시청을 놓치지 마십시오.¹⁵³ 그 영화는 세계적으로 유명한 건축가인 장 보퍼트의 디자인에 초점을 두고 있는데, 장 보퍼트는 전 세계적으로 사설 및 공공 건물을 디자인했습니다.

감독으로 스티브 캐시디가 참여한 이 주목할 만한 기록영화는 보퍼트와의 인터뷰를 부각하고 있습니다. 더욱이 감독은 영화팬들에게 보퍼트가 사랑하는 가족을 위해 만들었으며 본인이 15년 동안 살았던 파리 외곽에 있는 거주용 건물인 '천국의 풍경'에 대한 전문가 견해를 전달하고 싶어했습니다. 따라서 영화 제작자들은 그 집 내부에서 기록영화를 찍기 위해 보퍼트 가족에게 특별 승인을 요청했습니다.

회의 마지막 날인 6월 25일 오후 4시에, 〈단순하지만 세련된〉은 파리지엔 호텔 회의장에서 상영될 것입니다. 영화 상영이 끝난 후 바로, IAA 전 협회장인 아만다 추아 씨와 영화에 대해 토론을 할 수도 있습니다.¹⁵⁴ 영화는 모든 참석자에게 무료입니다. 하지만 자리를 위해 등록은 필수 사항입니다. www.iaa.org/congress/simplebutchic에서 등록할 수도 있습니다.

어휘 attend 참석하다 conference 회의 miss 놓치다
documentary film 기록영화 simple 단순한 chic 세련된
concentrate on ~에 집중하다
world-renowned 세계적으로 유명한 architect 건축가
private 개인의 public 공공의 noteworthy 주목할 만한
highlight 부각하다 interview 인터뷰 moreover 더욱이
moviegoer 영화팬 insider 전문가, 내부자 residential 주거(용)의
outskirts 교외 film maker 영화 제작자[회사]
consent 동의, 승인 shoot 영화를 찍다 showing 상영
free 공짜인 participant 참가자 ensure 확인하다
registration 등록 (cf. register 등록하다)

153. 공지가 왜 게시되는가?
(A) 영화 상영을 홍보하기 위하여
(B) 대중에게 주택 판매를 알리기 위하여
(C) 사람들을 새로운 건물에 초대하기 위하여
(D) 영화 제작사를 유치하기 위하여

해설 글의 목적을 묻는 문제로 내용의 앞부분에서 파악할 수 있다. 첫 번째 문장의 you don't want to miss the chance to see a documentary film entitled Simple but Chic에서 기록영화를 보라는 내용이 언급되어 있다.

154. 아만다 추아 씨는 6월 25일에 무엇을 할 것인가?
(A) 새 프로젝트에 대한 설계를 계획할 것이다.
(B) 오프닝 행사에서 연설을 할 것이다.
(C) 유명한 건축가와 인터뷰할 것이다.
(D) 토론에 참석할 것이다.

해설 마지막 단락에 아만다 추아 씨에 대한 언급이 나와 있다. Right after the film showing, you may participate in a discussion about the movie with Amanda Chua에 영화가 끝난 후 아만다 추아 씨와의 토론에 참가하라고 언급되어 있다.

155-157

아치 베이 스튜디오
키 도로, SIS 빌딩, 싱가포르 158088
전화: (453) 4545 2367

6월 15일

에이버리 가드너
북랜드 출판사
241 슈피리어 가
트로이, 미시간, 미시간 7710
미국

가드너 씨에게

저는 레아 오하라 씨를 대신하여 편지를 씁니다. 현재 레아 오하라 씨가 귀사의 마케팅부 직에 고려 대상이 되고 있다고 알고 있습니다.¹⁵⁵

오하라 씨는 5년 동안 마케팅 비서로 이곳 아치 베이 스튜디오에서 근무했습니다. 그 후, 그녀는 현재까지 재직 중인 국제 마케팅부의 관리자 직으로 승진이 되었습니다. 그녀는 전 세계적인¹⁵⁶⁻ᴰ 애니메이션 영화 시장 대상 광고와 유통을 책임지고 있습니다. 또한 다른 나라에서의 마케팅을 책임지고 있으며 전 세계 곳곳의 회사들과 사업을 하는 영업사원들을 관리하고 있습니다.

오하라 씨는 영어와 중국어 모두 능통한 의사소통 능력을 가지고 있으며,¹⁵⁶⁻ᴬ 자신에게 주어진 일은 어떤 것이든 세부 사항까지 매우 세심하게 신경 쓰는¹⁵⁶⁻ᶜ 능력을 갖추고 있습니다. 오하라 씨는 지속적으로 우리의 영화를 판매하려는 헌신을 보여주었고 영화 제작업계의 다양한 사람들과 뛰어난 업무 관계를 형성했습니다. 저는 오하라 씨가 맡은 어떠한 종류의 일이라도 같은 노력과 헌신을 보여줄 것이라 확신합니다.

우리는 오하라 씨가 떠나 정말로 유감스럽지만 오하라 씨의 가족이 미국에 있기 때문에 함께 하고자 하는 마음을 이해합니다.¹⁵⁷ 오하라 씨는 회사의 모범적인 사원이었습니다. 그녀의 능력과 과업에 대하여 이야기를 원한다면 언제라도 저에게 연락 주십시오.

감사합니다

마이 링
아치 베이 스튜디오 사장

어휘 on behalf of ~을 대신[대표]하여 currently 현재
consider 고려하다 position 직책, 직급, 지위
assistant 비서, 조수 subsequently 그 후에, 이어
be promoted 승진하다 occupy (직책을) 맡다
up to the present 현재까지 distribution 분배, 유통
in charge of ~을 맡고 있는, ~을 책임지고 있는
worldwide 세계적인 animated movie 애니메이션 영화
be responsible for ~을 책임지다 handle 처리하다
sales representative 영업사원
do business with ~와 거래하다
all over the world 전 세계 곳곳에
communication skill 의사소통 능력
exercise attention 신경 쓰다 task 일, 직무
consistently 지속적으로 dedication 헌신
establish 체계를 갖추다, 확립하다 professional 직업[업무] 상의
connection 관계 industry 업계
be certain that ~에 대해 확신하다 commitment 노력
whatever 무엇이든 exemplary 모범적인, 본보기가 되는
contact 연락하다 competence 능력

155. 편지의 목적은 무엇인가?
(A) 오하라 씨의 성과에 대해 문의하기 위해
(B) 직원들에게 오하라 씨의 승진을 알리기 위해
(C) 오하라 씨에게 직책을 주기 위해
(D) 오하라 씨에게 일자리를 추천하기 위해

해설 첫 번째 단락에서 오하라 씨가 다니고 있는 아치 베이 사의 사장인 마이 링 씨가 브랜드 출판사에 지원한 오하라 씨를 언급하고 있으며, 다음 단락에서 오하라 씨의 현재 다니고 있는 회사에서의 활약 상황을 언급하고 있다.

156. 오하라 씨에 대해 언급되지 않은 것은 무엇인가?
(A) 의사소통 능력이 좋다.
(B) 출판 분야에 관한 좋은 지식을 갖추고 있다.
(C) 다양한 면에 신경을 쓴다.
(D) 국제 비즈니스 배경을 가지고 있다.

해설 오하라 씨가 출판 분야에 좋은 지식을 가지고 있다고 언급한 내용은 없다. (A)는 세 번째 단락 첫 번째 문장의 has good communication skills에서 찾을 수 있고, (C)는 같은 문장의 ability to exercise very careful attention to even the smallest details 부분에서 알 수 있으며, (D)는 두 번째 단락 네 번째 줄의 worldwide market (해외시장)에서 해외 사업에 경험을 가지고 있음을 알 수 있다.

157. 오하라 씨가 아치 베이 스튜디오를 그만두는 이유는 무엇인가?
(A) 타국으로 이주하고 싶어서
(B) 석사 학위를 마무리하고 싶어서
(C) 더 많은 소득을 얻고 싶어서
(D) 자주 여행할 수 있는 기회를 찾고 싶어서

해설 마지막 단락을 보면 오하라 씨 가족이 미국에 있으며 함께 살기를 원한다는 내용이 있다.

158-160

발신: ashleythomas@asansol.ac.in
수신: damodarkumar@interiormind.in
날짜: 2월 12일
제목: 디자이너 구인

안녕하세요, 쿠마르 씨,

저는 콜카타 실내 장식가 심포지엄에서 귀하의 부스에 깊은 인상을 받았고 귀하의 서비스를 이용하는 데 관심이 생겼습니다. 아산솔 대학은 새 학생 회관을 지을 예정인데 우리 학생들에게 매력적인 환경을 만들 수 있는 실내 장식가를 찾고 있습니다. 우리 학생들은 학문적인 근면함으로 잘 알려져 있습니다.**158** 그들은 수업을 준비하거나 그룹 프로젝트 공동 작업을 하면서 오랜 시간을 보낼 조용한 장소를 갖춘 학생 회관이 필요합니다.

귀하가 이 일에 적합하리라고 생각하게 된 것은 특히 귀하가 오리사 커피숍에 한 작업입니다.**159** 그곳의 실내 장식은 매력적이지만 과도하게 현란하지 않고 조명은 밝지만, 시선을 분산시키지 않습니다. 귀하는 방문객들이 그 안에서 읽거나 일하는 것을 즐길 수 있는 식당으로 만들었습니다. 이와 같은 분위기야말로 제가 귀하가 학생 회관을 위해 만들어 주셨으면 하는 것입니다.

귀하의 현재 디자이너 평판으로 많은 업무가 있으리라 확신하므로 귀하가 할 수 없더라도 물론 이해합니다. 그렇지 않다면, 귀하를 만나서 이 프로젝트의 세부 사항을 논의하기 편하신 시간과 장소를 알려 주시기 바랍니다.**160** 어떤 경우라도, 금요일까지 답신해 주시면 감사하겠습니다. 이 이메일이나 제 사무실 번호인 0341-6788, 6688로 연락하실 수 있습니다.

애슐리 토머스
아산솔 대학 개발팀

어휘 impress 깊은 인상을 주다 decorator 장식자, 실내 장식가
be interested in ~에 관심이 있다 possibly 아마
employ (기술·방법 등을) 쓰다[이용하다] build (건물을) 짓다, 건설하다
student union 학생 자치회, 학생 회관 (= students' union)
environment (자연)환경 attractive 매력적인
be known for ~으로 잘 알려져 있다 academic 학업의, 학문의
diligence 근면함 prepare for ~을 준비하다
collaborate 협력하다, 공동으로 작업하다
specifically 특히, 구체적으로
be appropriate for ~에 어울리다, 적합하다
decor (건물의 실내) 장식 overly 과도하게, 지나치게
obtrusive (보기 싫게) 눈에 띄는, 현란한 lighting 조명
distracting 마음을 산란케 하는 diner (보통 음식값이 싼) 작은 식당
atmosphere 분위기 standing (단체·조직 내에서의) 지위[평판]
assignment 업무, 과제 unavailable 손에 넣을 수 없는
otherwise 그렇지 않으면 detail 세부 사항 reach 연락하다
development 개발

215

158. 토마스 씨가 아산솔 대학 학생들에 관해 말하는 것은?
(A) 건물들을 설계한다.
(B) 커피 마시기를 즐긴다.
(C) 학업에 전념한다.
(D) 연례 컨퍼런스를 준비한다.

> **해설** 이메일 첫째 단락 후반의 Our students are known for their academic diligence.에서 Asansol University 학생들이 학문적인 근면함으로 알려졌다고 했으므로 이를 바꿔 표현한 (C)가 정답이다.

159. 토마스 씨가 쿠마르 씨를 고용하고 싶어 하는 이유는?
(A) 쿠마르 씨의 TV 광고가 설득력이 있었다.
(B) 쿠마르 씨가 설계한 카페가 마음에 든다.
(C) 동료 하나가 그를 추천했다.
(D) 쿠마르 씨가 한 대학의 경연에서 우승했다.

> **해설** 이메일 둘째 단락 첫째 문장인 It is specifically the work you did for the Orissa Coffee Shop that makes me believe you would be appropriate for this job.에서 쿠마르 씨가 이 일에 적합하리라고 생각하게 한 것은 오리사 커피숍에 한 작업 때문이라고 했으므로 (B)가 정답이다.

160. [1], [2], [3], [4] 중 다음 문장이 들어가기에 가장 알맞은 곳은?

"어떤 경우라도, 금요일까지 답신해 주시면 감사하겠습니다."

(A) [1]
(B) [2]
(C) [3]
(D) [4]

> **해설** 이메일 마지막 단락의 I am sure that a designer of your standing currently has many assignments, so if you are unavailable, I of course understand. Otherwise, please let me know a convenient time and place for you to meet to discuss the details of this project.에서 쿠마르 씨가 일을 맡을 수 있는 경우와 맡을 수 없는 경우를 가정해서 말했으므로 [4]에 제시 문장이 오면 문맥이 자연스럽게 연결된다.

161-163

손더스 씨에게

록스프로 홈 시어터 시스템을 최근 구매해주셔서 감사 드립니다.[161] 우리는 귀하가 구입한 제품에 대해 매우 만족하리라 확신합니다.

귀하가 시스템 일부를 설치하는 데 도움이 필요하다면[162] 주저하지 말고 1-800-389-8748번으로 주중에는 오전 8시부터 오후 8시까지, 토요일에는 오전 10시부터 오후 6시까지 전화해주십시오. 기술자가 기꺼이 쉬운 단계별 안내로 도움을 줄 것입니다. 그리고 필요하다면, 약간의 비용으로 자택으로 기술자를 보내드릴 수 있습니다.[162]

기본 3년 보증서가 동봉되어 있습니다. 기록을 위해 보관하시기 바랍니다. 또한 지역 렌트플릭스 대여점에서 5편의 무료 영화를 빌릴 수 있는 상품권이 동봉되어[163] 있습니다.

다시 한 번 구매해주셔서 감사 드리며 새로운 홈 시어터 시스템을 즐기시길 바랍니다.

유진 스미스
고객 서비스 담당자
록스프로 홈 시어터 시스템

> **어휘** recent 최신의   purchase 구매   be confident that ~을 자신하다
> install 설치하다   hesitate to부정사 ~하는 것을 주저하다
> assist 돕다, 지원하다   step-by-step 단계별의
> directions 안내, 지시사항   enclosed 동봉된
> standard 표준의, 기본의   limited warranty 한정 보증
> gift certificate 상품권   rental store 대여점

161. 편지의 목적은 무엇인가?
(A) 고객에게 감사하기 위하여
(B) 서비스 날짜를 잡기 위하여
(C) 고객의 피드백을 요청하기 위하여
(D) 고객에게 잔금을 알리기 위하여

> **해설** 첫 번째 단락의 Thank you for your recent purchase 부분에서 제품 구매자에게 감사의 편지를 보내고 있음을 알 수 있다.

162. 록스프로 사의 고객들에게 제공되는 서비스는?
(A) 무료 배송
(B) 특별 지불 방법
(C) 가정방문 설치
(D) 24시간 고객 지원

> **해설** 두 번째 단락 첫 번째 문장의 Should you need help installing any part of your system(설치에 도움이 필요하다면)을 보고 설치를 해준다는 것을 알 수 있으며, 해당 단락의 마지막 부분 if needed, we can send a technician to your home for a small fee에 필요하다면 기술자를 보내줄 수 있다는 내용이 언급되어 있다.

163. 편지에 동봉된 것은?
(A) 조립 설명서
(B) 상품권
(C) 개선된 보증서
(D) 견적서

> **해설** 세 번째 단락 마지막 문장에서 Also, enclosed is a gift certificate 이 부분을 보고 동봉된 것은 gift certificate(상품권)이라는 것을 알 수 있다.

164-167

수신: 엠마 파워즈
발신: 민호 최

5월 28일

파워즈 씨에게

이 편지는 앞서 얘기한 6월 1일[165] 오후 4시, 씨티랜드 아파트의 13B호 퇴거 결정에 관한 내용입니다.[164]

퇴거 시 아파트 키를 받게 되면, 바로 아파트를 점검할 것입니다.[165] 아파트 상태를 상세하게 기술한 보고서가 6월 3일까지 발송될 것입니다. 보고서에 서명을 해서 가능한 한 빨리 보내주시면 되겠습니다. 아파트 상태가 깨끗하고 좋다면 보증금을 총 1000달러 중 10달러를 제외하고 전액 환불 받게 될 것입니다.[164] 10달러는 요청하신 대로 빠른 우편으로 수표를 보내는 비용으로 사용될 것입니다.[166]

검사 보고서를 다시 받은 후에, 늦어도 취리히로 출발하는 6월 18일까지 환불 수표를 보내드리겠습니다. 행운을 빌고 취리히에서 새로운 일 잘 하십시오.[167]

감사합니다.

민호 최

관리인
씨티랜드 아파트

어휘
talk 대화 regarding ~에 관하여
move out of ~에서 이사해 나가다, 퇴거하다 complex 단지, 건물
upon receiving 받자마자 check 점검하다, 확인하다
immediately 즉시, 바로 describe 설명하다, 묘사하다
in detail 상세히 condition 상태
at one's earliest convenience 편한 시간에 가능한 빨리 (= as soon as possible) deem 생각하다, 여기다
in good condition 좋은 상태인 security deposit 임대 보증금
refund 반환하다 except for ~을 제외하고
pay for ~ 댓가로 지불하다 delivery 배송
express mail 빠른 우편 request 요청하다
inspection report 검사 보고서

164. 편지의 목적은 무엇인가?
(A) 아파트를 비우는 절차를 확인시키기 위하여
(B) 입주자에게 인상된 금액을 통보하기 위하여
(C) 청소 서비스를 홍보하기 위하여
(D) 관리 변경을 알리기 위하여

해설 아파트 관리자가 입주자에게 보내는 편지이다. 첫 번째 단락의 This is about our talk regarding your decision to move out of your apartment.에서 입주자가 move out(퇴거하다, 나가다)할 예정이라는 것을 알 수 있다. 두 번째 단락부터는 구체적인 절차를 언급하고 있다.

165. 최 씨는 아파트 검사를 언제 할 것인가?
(A) 5월 28일
(B) 6월 1일
(C) 6월 3일
(D) 6월 15일

해설 첫 번째 단락에서 퇴거일로 June 1(6월 1일)가 언급되었고, 두 번째 단락, 첫 번째 문장 Upon receiving all the keys to your apartment unit when you leave, I will check the unit immediately.에서 퇴거 시점에 키를 받고 바로 아파트를 점검한다는 내용이 언급되었다.

166. 입주자가 전액 환불을 받지 못하는 이유는?
(A) 검사 보고서를 늦게 보냈기 때문에
(B) 보수 비용 지불을 거절했기 때문에
(C) 사전 통보 없이 퇴거했기 때문에
(D) 관리인에게 빠른 배송을 요청했기 때문에

해설 전액 환불을 받지 못한 이유는 두 번째 단락 마지막 문장 If the apartment is deemed clean and in good condition, your security deposit will be refunded to you in full, expect for $10 from the amount of $1,000 which will be used to pay for the delivery of your check to you by express mail as you requested.에 나와 있다. 1000달러에서 10달러가 빠지는 이유는 1000달러의 보증금을 수표로 받는 데 빠른 우편(express mail)을 이용해 비용이 10달러가 들기 때문이다.

167. 파워즈 씨에 대해서 알 수 있는 것은?
(A) 다른 아파트로 이사할 것이다.
(B) 오랫동안 취리히에 살았다.
(C) 이사 업체를 이용할 것이다.
(D) 새로운 직장 때문에 이사할 것이다.

해설 마지막 단락에서 편지 발신인이 수신인인 파워즈 씨에게 Best wishes to you and with your new job in Zurich.라고 전한 내용에서 파워즈가 취리히로 가는 이유가 새로운 일자리 때문이라는 것을 알 수 있다.

168-171

파오라 타마 [오후 3시 10분]:
긴 주말 때문에 이번 달 호를 금요일이 아닌 목요일 저녁까지 인쇄소에 넘겨야 한다는 것을 모두에게 상기시켜 드리고자 합니다. 모든 팀장은 저에게 상황 업데이트를 해 주시기 바랍니다.

앤더스 베르틸 [오후 3시 13분]:
애런 로저스를 제외한 모든 사진작가는 작품을 제출했습니다. 그는 자기 작품을 수요일까지 제출할 수 있을 거라고 했는데 디자인 팀에 잡지에 사진을 싣기에 충분한 시간을 주어야 하기 때문입니다.

이사벨 카타리나 [오후 3시 14분]:
네, 수요일까지만 사진을 받는다면, 문제 될 게 없습니다.¹⁶⁸

파오라 타마 [오후 3시 15분]:
좋아요. 애런에게 얘기해서 사진을 빨리 제출하라고 재촉할게요. 멜리사, 당신은 어떤가요? 편집팀이 목요일까지 끝낼 수 있을 것 같나요?

멜리사 알바 [오후 3시 18분]:
아, 아니요… 금요일에 출근하지 않는다는 걸 잊었어요. 평상시 업무일에 끝낼 수 없을 것 같아요. 시간 외 근무 허가를 받을 수 있을까요?¹⁶⁹

파오라 타마 [오후 3시 19분]:
무엇을 할 수 있는지 알아볼게요. 그동안에 대강의 기사 초고를 이사벨에게 보내서 그녀의 팀이 레이아웃을 진전시킬 수 있도록 하세요.

이사벨 카타리나 [오후 3시 20분]:
그러면 도움이 되겠네요. 미리 감사드려요.

멜리사 알바 [오후 3시 20분]:
물론이에요. 바로 일을 처리할게요.¹⁷⁰

파오라 타마 [3시 22분]:
좋습니다, 여러분. 우리 할 일이 많지만, 주말 연휴에 즐겁게 지낼 수 있도록 확실히 제시간에 일을 끝내도록 합시다.¹⁷¹ 힘내시고 문제가 발생하면 제게 주저하지 말고 메시지를 보내세요.

어휘 remind 상기시키다 issue (잡지·신문 같은 정기 간행물의) 호 head 책임자 status 상태, 신분, 자격 submit 제출하다 except for ~을 제외하고 as long as ~하는 한 urge A to부정사 A가 ~하도록 강력히 권고하다 editorial 편집의, 편집과 관련된(cf. edit 편집하다) normal 평범한, 정상적인 authorize 권한을 주다, 허가하다 in the meantime 그사이[동안]에, 한편 rough 대강의, 대충의 draft 초고(草稿), 초안, 밑그림 article 기사 progress 진행, 진척 layout (책·정원·건물 등의) 레이아웃[배치] in advance 미리, 사전에 on time 정시에, 제때 feel free to부정사 마음 편히 ~하다 message 메시지[문자/메일]를 보내다 come up 생기다, 발생하다

168. 카타리나 씨는 어디 팀에서 일하는 것 같은가?
(A) 디자인
(B) 편집
(C) 사진 촬영
(D) 광고

해설 Anders Bertil의 오후 3시 13분 메시지인 All of our photographers have submitted their work except for Aaron Rogers. He said he should be able to submit his work by Wednesday, which should give the Design team enough time to get it in the magazine.에서 Aaron Rogers가 디자인 팀에 사진을 제출할 일정을 언급하자 Isabel Catarina가 Yeah, as long as we get it by Wednesday, it won't be a problem.라며 수요일까지 사진을 받으면 문제가 없다고 했다. 따라서 Ms. Catarina는 디자인팀장이라는 것을 알 수 있으므로 (A)가 정답이다.

169. 오후 3시 19분에 타마 씨가 "무엇을 할 수 있는지 알아볼게요."라고 쓸 때 그가 의미하는 것은?
(A) 빨리 문서를 편집할 것이다.
(B) 직원들이 시간 외 근무를 할 수 있도록 할 것이다.
(C) 사진 몇 장을 준비할 것이다.
(D) 프린터를 수리할 것이다.

해설 Melisa Alba의 메시지인 Can you authorize us to do overtime work?에 대한 답변이므로 시간 외 근무 허가를 받기 위해 자기가 무엇을 할 수 있는지 알아본다는 의미이므로 (B)가 정답이다.

170. 오후 3시 20분에 카타리나 씨는 누구에게 감사를 표했나?
(A) 파오라 타마
(B) 앤더스 베르틸
(C) 애런 로저스
(D) 멜리사 알바

해설 Paora Tama는 In the meantime, send the rough drafts of the articles to Isabel so her team can make some progress on the layout.에서 편집팀장인 Melisa Alba에게 디자인팀장인 Isabel Catarina에게 대강의 기사 초고를 미리 보내서 레이아웃을 진전시키도록 지시했다. 따라서 디자인 팀장이 편집팀에서 기사 초고를 미리 보내줄 것에 대한 감사의 표시를 하는 것이므로 (D)가 정답이다.

171. 타마 씨가 직원들이 제시간에 일을 끝내야 한다고 말하는 이유는?
(A) 고객을 만족시키려고
(B) 상여금을 받으려고
(C) 휴식을 즐기려고
(D) 승진하려고

해설 Paora Tama는 We have a lot of work to do, but let's make sure that we finish on time so we can have fun on our holiday weekend.에서 주말 연휴에 즐겁게 지낼 수 있도록 확실히 제시간에 일을 끝내자고 했다. 따라서 have fun on our holiday weekend를 enjoy a break로 바꿔 표현한 (C)가 정답이다.

172-175

자가 촬영은 어렵습니다. 그 문제를 해결할 만한 몇 가지 그저 그런 방안이 있습니다. 삼각대를 설치하는 소동을 거치면 되지만, 누가 시간이 있겠습니까?[172-D] 팔로 카메라를 내밀어 자신을 겨눌 수 있지만, 정확하게 겨누기는 너무 힘듭니다.[172-C] 물론 당신 사진을 찍어 줄 누군가를 찾을 수 있지만, 주위에 아무도 없으면 어떻게 하실 건가요?[172-A, 175]

이제 해들리 토이즈 덕분에 The Handle로 개인 사진 촬영을 조작할 수 있습니다. 이 3피트(91cm)짜리 막대기를 이용하면 편안한 거리에서 쉽게 사진을 찍을 수 있습니다. 스마트폰이나 카메라를 막대기 끝에 부착하고 포함된 케이블을 기기를 충전하는 데 사용하는 포트에 연결하면 됩니다. 그리고 나서 핸들 끝에 있는 단추를 눌러서 사진을 찍을 수 있습니다. The Handle로 작업을 마치고 나면 화이트보드 마커 펜 크기로 접어서 쉽게 지갑이나 호주머니에 끼워 넣을 수 있습니다.[173]

직접 시연을 받아 보시려면 공인 해들리 제품 소매점 아무 곳이든 방문하세요.[174] 전문가가 품질의 자가 촬영 사진을 얼마나 빨리 찍을 수 있는지에 깜짝 놀라실 겁니다.

어휘 go through (절차를) 거치다 hassle 혼란, 소동 set up 설치하다
tripod 삼각대 hold out (손 등을) 내밀다
point A at B A를 B에 겨누다 aim 겨누다 accurately 정확하게
what if ~? ~면 어쩌지[~라면 어떻게 될까?](What would you do if ~?)
thanks to ~ 덕분에 get[have] a handle on ~을 조작하다
photography 사진술, 사진 촬영 pole 막대기, 장대, 기둥
connect 연결하다 port 포트(컴퓨터의 주변 기기 접속 단자)
charge 충전하다 device 장치, 기구 press 누르다
be done with ~을 다 하다
collapse (공간을 덜 차지하도록) 접다[접히다] fit in 끼워 넣다
authorized 권한이 부여된, 위임된 retail store 소매점
in-person 본인이 직접 출연하는, 직접의
demonstration (실물) 설명, 실연 be amazed at ~에 깜짝 놀라다

172. 자가 촬영의 어려움으로 언급되지 않은 것은?
(A) 도울 사람을 찾기
(B) 초읽기 타이머를 설치하기
(C) 한 손으로 기기 잡고 있기
(D) 카메라용 삼각대 세우기

해설 광고 첫째 단락에서 (A)는 Sure, you can find someone to take the photo for you, but what if there's no one around?에, (C)는 You can hold your camera out with your arm and point it at yourself, but it's too hard to aim accurately.에 (D)는 You can go through the hassle of setting up a tripod, but who has the time?에 해당한다. 초읽기 타이머에 관한 언급은 없으므로 (B)가 정답이다.

173. The Handle에 관해 언급된 것은?
(A) 무선으로 작동한다.
(B) 품질 보증서를 포함한다.
(C) 쉽게 보관할 수 있다.
(D) 어린이용으로 만들어졌다.

해설 광고 둘째 단락 마지막 문장인 When you're done with The Handle, it collapses into the size of a whiteboard marker that you can easily fit in a purse or pocket.에서 화이트보드 마커 펜 크기로 접어서 쉽게 지갑이나 호주머니에 끼워 넣을 수 있다고 했다. 이는 보관이 편리하다는 의미이므로 (C)가 정답이다.

174. 방문객이 회사 상점에서 받을 수 있는 것은?
(A) 판촉 할인
(B) 제품 시연
(C) 사진 촬영 교육
(D) 개인 맞춤 손잡이

해설 광고 셋째 단락 첫째 문장인 Visit any authorized Hadley products retail store to receive an in-person demonstration.에서 공인 해들리 제품 소매점을 방문해서 직접 시연을 받아 보라고 했다. 따라서 an in-person demonstration을 바꿔 표현한 (B)가 정답이다.

175. [1], [2], [3], [4] 중 다음 문장이 들어가기에 가장 알맞은 곳은?

"그 문제를 해결할 만한 몇 가지 그저 그런 방안이 있습니다."

(A) [1]
(B) [2]
(C) [3]
(D) [4]

해설 광고 첫째 단락의 [1] 앞 문장인 Taking a photo of yourself is difficult.에서 자가 촬영이 어렵다고 한 후 [1] 뒤의 You can go through the hassle of setting up a tripod, but who has the time? You can hold your camera out with your arm and point it at yourself, but it's too hard to aim accurately. Sure, you can find someone to take the photo for you, but what if there's no one around?에서 몇 가지 해결책을 제시하고 있다. 따라서 [1]에 제시 문장이 오면 문맥이 자연스럽게 연결된다.

176-180

발신: 폴라 크루즈 〈paula109@fastmail.com〉
수신: 카르멘 멘도사 〈c.mendoza@youmail.com〉
날짜: 5월 2일 오후 1시 29분
제목: 목요일

카르멘에게

목요일 날 같이 갈 생각이 있는지 궁금해. 환경 문제에 관한 새로운 아이맥스 영화를 볼 거야. 생물학 수업을 위해서 영화를 봐야 하고[176] 내 기억으로는 너도 보기를 원했던 것 같아.

나는 목요일 오전 11시 15분 후에[178] 시간 가능해.[177] 가길 원하면 수요일 오후까지 알려줘. 곧 얘기 나누자.

폴라

⟨산호초 생물⟩
해양학자 앤디 제임스가[179] 그레이트 배리어 리프에서 독특한 해양 생물을 탐구한다.
입장료: $12 (성인), $9 (아동/학생), $7 (노인)
상영 시간: 오전 11:00 | 오후 1:45 | 오후 3:05 | 오후 6:45 | 오후 8:00

⟨숲은 우리의 집⟩
인류학자 로버트 워커는 인도네시아에 사는 커버스 유목민족과[180] 2주를 보낸다.
입장료: $12 (성인), $9 (아동/학생), $7 (노인)
상영 시간: 오전 11:25 | 오후 2:10 | 오후 5:45 | 오후 7:25 | 오후 9:40

⟨고갈되는 세계⟩
남획과 삼림 파괴가 빠르게 지구의 생태계를 변화시키고 있다.
입장료: $12 (성인), $9 (아동/학생), $7 (노인)
상영 시간: 오전 11:45 | 오후 2:30 | 오후 5:05 | 오후 7:45 | 오후 10:00[178]

⟨신기한 우주⟩
블랙홀, 적색 거성, 새로운 발견의 영역으로의 광년 여행.
입장료: $12 (성인), $9 (아동/학생), $7 (노인)
상영 시간: 오후 12:15 | 오후 3:00 | 오후 5:25 | 오후 8:15 | 오후 10:30

어휘 wonder 궁금하다 join 합류하다, 참여하다 environmental 환경의 biology 생물학 free 한가한

oceanographer 해양학자 explore 탐험하다 marine 해양의, 바다의 barrier reef 산호초 admission 입장 senior citizen 노인 showtime 상영 시간 forest 숲 anthropologist 인류학자 nomadic 유목민의 exhausted 고갈된, 소모된, 지친 overfishing 남획 deforestation 산림 벌채, 산림 파괴 ecosystem 생태계 oddity 기이한 것 light year 광년 realm 영역 discovery 발견한 것

176. 크루즈 씨가 영화를 보고 싶어하는 이유는?
(A) 그것은 학교 과제이다.
(B) 그녀의 친구가 그것을 보고 싶어한다.
(C) 그녀의 동급생이 가자고 했다.
(D) 극장에서 특별한 판촉 행사가 있다.

해설 첫 번째 이메일에서 발신인이 폴라 크루즈임을 알 수 있고 첫 번째 단락에서 I have to see it for my biology class(생물학 수업 때문에 영화를 봐야 한다)라고 언급하고 있다.

177. 이메일 두 번째 단락 1행의 free와 의미가 가장 가까운 것은?
(A) 비어 있는
(B) 여유가 있는
(C) 무료의
(D) 독립하는

해설 첫 번째 이메일, 두 번째 단락의 I'm free Thursday after 11:15 A.M.에서 free는 '시간 여유가 있다'는 의미이다. available 형용사는 '이용 가능한'이라는 의미 외에 '시간 여유가 있는'의 의미로도 사용된다.

178. 크루즈 씨가 영화를 볼 수 있는 시간은?
(A) 오후 12시 15분
(B) 오후 2시 10분
(C) 오후 5시 5분
(D) 오후 8시

해설 첫 번째 지문의 I'm free Thursday after 11:15 A.M.에서 폴라 크루즈가 11시 15분 이후에 시간이 된다고 했다. 두 번째 지문인 영화 리스트에서 11시 15분 이후에 상영되고, 환경 문제와 관련 있는 영화는 세 번째 영화인 An Exhausted World이다. Earth's ecosystems (지구의 생태계)와 관련 있는 영화이므로 폴라가 생물학 수업과 관련해서 볼만한 영화라는 것을 알 수 있다. 상영시간 정보로 11시 15분 이후로 보기에 나와 있는 시간은 오후 5시 5분이다.

179. 앤디 제임스는 누구인가?
(A) 과학자
(B) 영화 감독
(C) 교수
(D) 학생

해설 앤디 제임스가 언급된 부분은 두 번째 지문 listing에서 첫 번째 영화인 Life at the Barrier를 설명한 Oceanographer Andy James explores the unique marine life이다. oceanographer(해양학자)는 과학자라고 할 수 있다.

180. 어떤 영화가 사람에 초점을 맞추고 있는가?
(A) ⟨신기한 우주⟩
(B) ⟨고갈되는 세계⟩
(C) ⟨산호초 생물⟩
(D) ⟨숲은 우리의 집⟩

해설 사람과 관련된 내용으로 두 번째 지문 영화 리스트에서 두 번째 영화인 The Forest is Our Home의 설명을 보면 Anthropologist Robert Walker spends two weeks with the Kubus nomadic tribe in Indonesia. 부분에서 유목민의 생활을 보여준다는 것을 알 수 있다.

181-185

회람

수신: 모든 회원
발신: 레오넬 김, 관리자
제목: 겨울 휴무
날짜: 12월 10일

바디플렉스 피트니스 클럽이 오픈한 이래, 12월 31일부터 1월 6일까지 운영을 연기하는 것이 관행이었습니다.[181] '겨울 휴무'로 불리는 이 기간은 이곳의 오랜 전통이었습니다. 하지만, 경영진은 적지 않은 회원들이 이러한 관행을 불편하게 느끼고 있다고 판단했습니다.

회의를 거친 후, 경영진은 올해에는 회원의 요구 사항을 충족시키고자 문을 열기로 결정했습니다. 하지만, 직원의 부족으로 이 기간 동안 서비스가 다소 제한적일 것입니다.[182] 1월 7일에 다시 정상 영업할 예정입니다.

이러한 변경 사항에 관해[181] 질문이 있다면 leonel@bodyflex.com으로 이메일 보내주십시오.

귀하의 후원에 감사 드립니다.

발신: charles@gurubox.net
수신: leonel@bodyflex.com
제목: 헬스 수업
날짜: 12월 12일

김 씨에게

5년 이상 바디플렉스 피트니스 클럽 회원으로서**¹⁸³** 12월 10일자 회람을 읽고 기쁨 반 놀라움 반이었습니다. 오랫동안 자리잡은 관행을**¹⁸³** 변경하는 것이 쉬운 일은 아니었을 것입니다. 그러나 그러한 조치는 클럽 회원의 요구 사항을 수용하려는 노력을 보여주는**¹⁸⁴** 일입니다.

이러한 변화를 고려하여 그 기간 동안 수업이 어떻게 영향을 받을지 알고 싶습니다. 월요일과 수요일 오후 8시에 제공되는 스트레칭 수업에 관심이 많습니다. 그 수업은 저에게 상당히 도움을 주었습니다.**¹⁸⁵**

감사합니다.

찰스 화이트

어휘 opening 개장 customary 관행적인 put off 연기하다
operation 운영 period 기간 tradition 전통
management 경영진 practice 관행 inconvenient 불편한
meet the needs 요구 사항을 충족하다 shortage 부족
somewhat 다소 limited 제한된
return to normal 정상으로 복귀하다

happily 행복하게 be in place 자리 잡다
commitment 헌신, 노력 accommodate 수용하다
in consideration of ~을 고려하여 affect 영향을 미치다
helpful 도움이 되는

181. 회람의 목적은 무엇인가?
(A) 새로운 운동 수업을 홍보하기 위하여
(B) 일자리를 홍보하기 위하여
(C) 직원들을 칭찬하기 위하여
(D) 변경 사항을 발표하기 위하여

해설 첫 번째 지문인 회람의 전반적인 내용을 보면, 관행상 연말에서 연초까지 쉬는데 고객의 불편으로 인해서 올해에는 적은 인력으로 그 기간 동안 헬스장을 운영한다는 내용이다.

182. 바디플렉스 피트니스 클럽에 대해 명시된 것은?
(A) 오후 운동 수업을 제공한다.
(B) 한 주간 적은 수의 직원이 근무를 할 것이다.
(C) 신규 회원을 위한 특별 혜택이 있다.
(D) 새로운 프로그램을 준비하고 있다.

해설 첫 번째 지문 두 번째 단락을 보면 due to the shortage of staff, our service will be somewhat limited during this period에서 적은 인원으로 제한적인 서비스를 하게 될 것이라고 언급하고 있다.

183. 겨울 휴무에 대해 올바른 것은?
(A) 적어도 5년 전부터 도입되었다.
(B) 관행상 2주 동안 지속되었다.
(C) 정기적인 보수가 이루어졌다.
(D) 모든 회원이 환영했다.

해설 두 번째 지문 첫 번째 단락에서 화이트 씨가 회원으로 5년 이상 되었다고 언급했고, 첫 번째 지문 첫 번째 문장에서 헬스장이 오픈한 이래로 매년 겨울 일주일 간 헬스장을 열지 않는다(Since the first opening of BodyFlex Fitness Club, it has been customary to put off operations from December 31 through January 6)고 했으므로 최소한 5년이 되었다는 것을 파악할 수 있다.

184. 이메일 첫 번째 단락 3행의 speaks to와 의미가 가장 가까운 것은?
(A) 불만이다
(B) 따르다
(C) 보여주다
(D) 영향을 미치다

해설 speak to는 '~에게 말하다'라는 의미뿐만 아니라 '~을 전달하다, ~을 보여주다'의 의미로 사용될 수 있다. 본문에서 speaks to your commitment는 '귀하의 노력을 보여준다'로 해석하는 것이 가장 어울린다.

185. 화이트 씨에 대해서 언급된 것은?
(A) 스트레칭 수업이 도움이 된다고 느끼고 있다.
(B) 매일 운동한다.
(C) 12월 10일에 김 씨와 토의했다.
(D) 수업을 소개하고 싶어한다.

해설 두 번째 지문 이메일의 마지막 부분 I am very interested in the Stretching class offered at 8 P.M. on Mondays and Wednesdays, which I have found quite helpful for me.에서 스트레칭 수업에 관심이 있으며 도움이 된다(helpful)고 언급하고 있다.

186-190

베를린 - 금요일 저녁에 베를린 동물원이 야생동물 보호단체 컨소시엄, 즉 CWA에 가입했다. CWA는 자연 환경 보호라는 이름으로 상호 간에 동물을 교환하는 유럽의 동물원 단체이다.[186] 이렇게 함으로써 진기한 동물들이 유럽 대륙 각곳에서 사람들에게 보여지는 것이 가능해진다. 관람객들을 이런 동물에 직접 노출시키면 그들이 모든 동물의 자연 서식지를 보호하기 위해 나서도록 분위기를 조성시켜 준다는 발상에서 나온 것이다. "아이들에게 환경을 보호할 필요가 있다고 말해 줄 수는 있습니다. 그런데 아이들이 관심을 갖지는 않을 것입니다."라고 베를린 동물원의 운영 책임자 디터 거스프리드 씨가 말했다. "하지만 멸종 위기에 처한 눈표범을 아이들에게 보여주면서 우리가 자연을 보호하지 않으면 이 희귀한 동물이 살 곳이 없어질 것이라고 말해 주면… 그러면 아이들에게 정말로 의미가 전달되는 것이죠."

물론 다른 동물원에서 손님 동물들을 데려오는 것의 또 다른 장점은 동물원 이용률에 긍정적인 영향을 미친다는 점이다. 동물원에서 새로운 동물을 받으면 티켓 판매가 급증한다고 동물원 측은 보고하고 있다.[187] 포코라는 이름의 코끼리가 CWA에서 이 동물원으로 오는 최초의 손님이 될 예정인데, 이 코끼리는 9월 1일에 일반 대중에게 공개될 것이다. 마드리드에서 1년간 홍학 무리들을 임대해주면, 12월에 독일에서는 최초로 홍학들을 구경할 수 있을 것이다.[190]

베를린 동물원에 오신 것을 환영합니다!

구경할 것이 많으니 현명하게 하루의 계획을 짜십시오. 다음은 저희 동물원에서 가장 인기 있는 네 가지 관람 상품입니다. 당신과 당신 가족, 그리고 동물을 위해 이 카드 뒤에 나와 있는 사파리 안전 지침을 잘 읽어 주시기 바랍니다.

아프리카 사파리
진짜 사파리를 구경하세요! 여러분은 지프를 타고 흙길을 따라 저희의 개방된 '아프리카 야생 동물' 관람 공간을 가로질러 가게 되며,[189-A] 기린이나 코뿔소, 물소, 또는 세 가지 모두를 구경하시게 됩니다. 매일 예약을 받고 있습니다. 인기 있는 이 구경거리를 관람하시려면 일찍 예약하십시오! 골드 티켓을 구입하신 분들은 좌석 선택에 우선권이 있습니다.

동양 탐험
지구 먼 곳에서 온 이국적인 야생 동물을 구경하십시오. 장수 도룡뇽과 코모도 왕도마뱀 우리를 지나 가장 인기가 좋은 팬다 곰 밍밍이 있는 곳으로 나아가십시오. 그 다음에는 시로의 스시 바에서 멋진 일본 요리를 점심으로 드셔 보시기 바랍니다. 8월 말에 문을 닫기 전에요.

곤충류
저희의 거미 및 곤충관은 수천 마리에 달하는 곤충의 종들이 자연스러운 환경 속에서 활동적으로 지낼 수 있도록 하기 위해, 내부 조명이 어둡게 유지되고 있습니다.[189-B] 실버 및 골드 티켓을 구입하신 분들은 직원의 감독 아래 다양한 종들을 만져 볼 수 있는 라이브 곤충 체험관을 이용하실 수 있습니다.[188]

바닷속
평소에 구경하기 힘든 세상 속을 들여다보시기 바랍니다. 가오리와 거북이, 그리고 상어를 바다 아래, 3백만 리터 수조 아래로 당신을 안내해 주는 새로운 도보 통로에서 유리 튜브를 통해 구경하시기 바랍니다.[189-D] 예약하시면 전문 다이버들이(모든 패스에 관련 자격증이 기록되어 있음) 수조 안에서 저희 수족관 가이드와 함께 안내해 드릴 것입니다.

베를린 동물원에 오신 것을 환영합니다!

이 패스는 다음과 같은 티켓 보유자가 표시된 날짜에 베를린 동물원에 입장하는 것을 허락합니다. 티켓 보유자는 티켓의 레벨에 해당하는 모든 특전을 누리실 수 있습니다.

이름	마티나 클레이드
입장 일자	9월 27일[190]
티켓 레벨	실버[188]
관련 자격증	없음

어휘
consortium 컨소시엄; 특정 사업 수행 목적의 공동 연합체
wildlife 야생 생물 advocate 옹호자, 지지자
conservation 보존, 보호 rare 드문, 진기한 expose 노출시키다
in the flesh 실물로, 직접 preserve 지키다, 보존하다
habitat 서식지 endangered 위험[위기]에 처한
creature 생물, 생명이 있는 존재
beneficial aspect 유익한[이로운] 면
attendance rate 참석률, 참가율 spike 급증, 급등
flamingo 플라밍고, 홍학 flock 떼, 무리

exhibit 전시품, 전시물
safety reminder 안전 수칙 (cf. reminder 상기시키는 것)
rhinoceros 코뿔소(= rhino) attraction (사람을 끄는) 명물
priority 우선, 우선권 exploration 탐험, 탐사
exotic 외국의, 이국적인 giant salamander 장수 도룡뇽
komodo dragon 코모도 왕도마뱀 enclosure 울타리[담]를 친 장소
creepy crawly (섬뜩해서 싫은) 곤충[벌레] arachnid 거미류
dim 어두운, 침침한 species pl. 종(種) pet 쓰다듬다
peek into ~안을 들여다보다 ray 가오리 tortoise 거북
the waves pl. 바다 applicable 해당되는, 적용되는
accompany 동행[동반]하다

grant A to부정사 A가 ~하는 것을 허락하다
eligible for ~에 자격이 있는 benefit 혜택, 특전 relevant 관련된

---

186. 기사에서 CWA에 관해 시사하는 것은?
(A) 사람들이 자연을 보호할 것을 권장한다.
(B) 베를린에 있는 본사에서 관리한다.
(C) 가급적이면 동물을 이동시키지 않으려고 한다.
(D) 학교와 함께 교육 행사를 조직한다.

해설 CWA는 자연 환경 보호(in the name of conservation)라는 이름으로 동물원들이 상호간에 동물을 교환하는 단체라고 했다. 또한 이 단체는 관람객들을 희귀한 동물에 노출시킴으로써 사람들이 동물의 자연 서식지 보호에 힘쓰게 할 수 있을 것으로 믿고 있다고 했으므로 (A)가 정답이다.

187. 기사 두 번째 단락 4행의 spike와 의미가 가장 가까운 것은?

(A) 증가
(B) 창
(C) 호스
(D) 믿음

해설 spike는 '급등', '급증'을 뜻하는 단어이다. 보기를 살펴보면 boost는 '증가', spear는 '창', '작살', hose는 '호스', belief는 '믿음'이라는 뜻으로, 정답은 (A)이다.

188. 클레이드 씨는 동물원에서 무엇을 할 수 있겠는가?

(A) 관람 시 특별한 자리를 배정받는다.
(B) 일식 레스토랑에서 점심을 먹는다.
(C) 살아 있는 동물들을 만진다.
(D) 수족관에서 수영을 한다.

해설 세 번째 지문인 Ms. Kleid의 티켓에서 Ticket Level을 보면 Silver이다. 그런데 두 번째 지문의 Creepy Crawlies의 내용을 보면 실버 및 골드 티켓을 구입한 사람들은 다양한 종들을 만져 볼 수 있는 라이브 곤충 체험관을 이용할 수 있다고(Silver and gold ticket holders can access the live insect petting zoo where they get to hold different species ~) 했다. 따라서 정답은 (C)이다.

189. 언급되지 않은 동물원의 관람 상품은?

(A) 도로가 있는 관람
(B) 어두운 조명 속의 관람
(C) 얼음이 만들어지는 곳에서의 관람
(D) 바라볼 수 있는 터널이 있는 관람

해설 Berlin Zoo에서 볼 수 있는 exhibits(관람 상품)는 두 번째 지문에 나와 있다. (A)는 African Safari의 You'll travel in a jeep along dirt roads 부분, (B)는 Creepy Crawlies의 The lighting inside our arachnid and insect hall is kept dim 부분, (D)는 Under the Sea의 our new walkway that takes you under our 3 million liter tank through a glass tube. 부분에 해당한다. (C)의 얼음 형성에 대한 내용은 지문에 나와 있지 않다.

190. 클레이드 씨는 어떤 종류의 동물을 볼 수 없을 것인가?

(A) 코뿔소
(B) 팬다 곰
(C) 코끼리
(D) 홍학

해설 첫 번째 지문인 기사의 마지막 부분을 보면, 마드리드의 동물원에서 새를 임대해 주면, 방문객들이 독일에서는 최초로 12월에 홍학을 구경할 수 있을 것이라고(In December, visitors will be able to see flamingos for the first time in Germany when Madrid loans their flock for the year.) 했다. 그런데 Ms. Kleid의 티켓에 찍혀 있는 날짜는 9월 27일이므로 아직 홍학을 볼 수 없으리라는 것을 알 수 있다. 따라서 정답은 (D)이다.

191-195

마에스트로로 음악을 자유롭게

우리는 루빈 디자인 블루 리본 상을 받은 음악 재생기인 레가토의 성공을 반복하는 것이 불가능하다고 들었습니다.[191] 하지만 포머그래너트 사 본사에서 2년에 걸친 개발 끝에 우리는 마침내 과제를 달성했다고 생각되는 기기를 갖게 되었습니다.

마에스트로를 이용해 보세요. 마에스트로는 세계 최초의 완전 무선 휴대용 음악 재생기입니다. 마에스트로를 사용하면 꼬인 선과 얽힌 코드 때문에 지체되는 일이 절대 없을 것입니다. 여러분의 음악 라이브러리를 여러분 집 컴퓨터의 무선 네트워크 연결을 통해 마에스트로의 내장 하드 드라이브에 로딩해 놓을 수 있습니다. 좋아하는 한 곡의 노래를 추가하는 것을 깜빡했다면, 걱정하지 마세요. 무선 전화 데이터 네트워크를 통해 여러분의 마에스트로 포머그래너트 계정으로 인터넷에 여러분이 저장해 놓은 어떤 음악이라도 재생할 수 있으니까요. 포머그래너트 헤드폰을 무선으로 기기에 연결할 수도 있습니다. 그리고 여러분을 흥분시키는 모든 음악의 실제 연주를 들으려면 마에스트로에서 직접 콘서트 나우 앱에 로그인하세요. 내장 위성 위치 확인 시스템 칩을 이용해서 마에스트로와 콘서트 나우가 여러분이 있는 지역에서 가까운 실황 음악을 찾아 줄 것입니다.[192] 밤이 끝나고 숙면으로 여러분의 활력을 충전할 때 마에스트로도 물론 무선으로 충전하세요. 마에스트로 메이트 충전 스테이션에 놓아두기만 하면 전류가 안전하게 금속 기체를 통해 재생기를 충전할 것입니다.

오늘 마에스트로를 구매하셔서 다시는 선에 얽매이지 마세요.

11월 3일

포머그래너트 사(社) 수리 센터
노스 프로스펙트 로(路) 5910번지
피오리아 일리노이 61614

관계자분께:

고장 난 마에스트로 음악 재생기와 첨부한 구매 영수증을 봐 주세요. 영수증에 표시된 대로 이 음악 재생기를 약 5달 전에 구매했습니다.[195] 최근에 한두 곡을 재생하고 나면 기기 작동이 중단되어 다시 시작해야 합니다. 확실히 이런 상황은 매우 실망스럽습니다. 때때로 이 문제가 30분 이상 장시간 기기를 사용한 후에만 발생한다는 점에 주목해 주세요. 따라서 결함을 조사하실 때 기기를 장시간 재생하셔야 할지도 모릅니다. 또한, 저를 성가시게 하거나 기기 사용에 영향을 미치지 않지만, 내장 위성 위치 확인 시스템 칩이 전혀 작동하지 않아서 관련 기능을 사용할 수 없었습니다.[192] 가능하면 그 기능도 수리해 주시기 바랍니다.

감사합니다.
지수 박

포머그래너트 사 반품 규정

포머그래너트 사는 구매 후 최초 7일 이내에 100% 만족을 보장하는 반품 규정을 제공합니다. 어떤 이유에서건 포머그래너트 제품이 귀하의 기대에 부응하지 않을 때는 구입시 포장 그대로 구입 영수증과 함께 어느 포머그래너트 지점에라도 돌려주기만 하신다면 전액 현금으로 환급해 드릴 것입니다.[194]

첫 주가 지나고 구매 후 30일 이내에 제조 과정에서 발생한 결함이 있는 제품은 판매점에서 반품이나 교환받으실 수 있습니다.[193] 작동이 잘 되고 손상되지 않은 제품은 상점에서 제공하는 상품권으로 돌려받으실 수 있습니다.

원 구매 후 30일이 지나면, 포머그래너트에서는 품질 보증이 제한적으로 적용됩니다. 제조나 가공 과정 결함이 있는 제품은 공인 포머그래너트 사 수리 센터에 우편으로 보내 주세요. 영수증 사본과 문제에 관한 설명을 포함하셔야만 합니다. 포머그래너트 사는 결함 제품을 동일하거나 더 나은 상태의 중고 제품으로 교환해 드립니다.[195] 일상적인 사용에 의한 마모, 부적절한 사용이나 사고로 영향받은 제품에는 품질 보증이 적용되지 않습니다.

어휘 duplicate 복사[복제]하다, 사본을 만들다 development 개발
headquarters 본사 device 장치, 기구 up to ~할 수
totally 완전히 wireless 무선의 slow down (속도를) 늦추다
tangled 복잡한, 뒤얽힌 knotted 매듭[장식]이 있는, 얽힌
internal 내부의 connection 연결(cf. connect 연결하다)
forget to부정사 (미래) ~할 것을 잊다 store 저장하다, 보관하다
cellular 무선[휴대] 전화의 performance 연기, 연주
log into ~에 접속하다 application 응용 프로그램(= app)
built-in (기계 등이) 내장된, 붙박이의
GPS 위성 위치 확인 시스템(= global positioning system)
chip 칩, 반도체 소자(素子)(= microchip)
recharge (전지를[가]) 충전하다[되다] place 놓다, 두다
station 스테이션, 국(局) electric current 전류 metal 금속의
tie down (일어서지 못하도록) ~을 묶어 놓다

refurbish 새로 꾸미다[재단장하다]
To whom it may concern (불특정 상대에 대한 편지·증명서 따위의 첫머리에 써서) 관계자 제위[각위] broken 고장 난 receipt 영수증
purchase 구매(하다) attach 첨부하다 indicate 표시하다, 시사하다
lately 최근에 shut down 작동이 중단되다
obviously 확실히, 분명히 frustrating 불만스러운, 좌절감을 주는
note 주목하다, 특별히 언급하다 issue 문제
occur 일어나다, 발생하다(= happen)
investigate 조사하다(cf. investigation 조사) defect 결함
extended 길어진, 늘어난 bother 괴롭다, 성가시게 하다
affect 영향을 미치다 work 작동되다 related 관련된
function 기능, 직무 fix 수리하다, 고치다

return policy 반품 규정, 환급 정책 satisfaction 만족
guaranteed 확실한, 보장된 live up to ~(기대)에 부응하다
expectation 기대, 예상 packaging 포장, 포장재
issue 배급(지급)하다, 넘겨주다 refund 환급 defective 결함이 있는
flaw 결함 manufacture 제조하다 exchange 교환하다
point 지점, 장소 functional 작동하는, 기능을 다 하는

undamaged 손상[훼손]되지 않은 limited 한정된, 제한된
warranty (제품의) 품질 보증서 apply 적용되다, 해당되다
craftsmanship (장인의) 기능, 숙련, 솜씨 authorized 공인된
refurbish 새로 꾸미다[재단장하다] include 포함하다
explanation 설명 replace 교체하다 faulty 결함이 있는
wear and tear (일상적인 사용에 의한) 마모[마손]
improper 부적절한

191. 레가토에 관해 언급된 것은?
(A) 디자인 결함이 있다.
(B) 상을 받았다.
(C) 더는 구할 수 없다.
(D) 마에스트로를 대체했다.

해설 광고 첫째 단락 첫 문장인 We were told it was impossible to duplicate the success of our Rubin Design Blue Ribbon winning music player, the Legato.에서 Legato가 Rubin Design Blue Ribbon 상을 받았음을 알 수 있으므로 (B)가 정답이다.

192. 박 씨는 자기 마에스트로에서 어떤 무선 기능을 사용하지 않는가?
(A) 마에스트로 메이트
(B) 분실 기기 위치
(C) 콘서트 나우
(D) 음악 스트리밍

해설 편지 후반의 Also, while it didn't bother me or affect my use of the device, the built-in GPS chip has never worked, so I could not use the related functions.에서 내장 위성 위치 확인 시스템 칩을 사용하는 관련 기능을 이용하지 않는다는 것을 알 수 있는데 광고 둘째 단락의 And if all that music gets you excited for a real performance, then log into the Concert Now application directly from Maestro. Using its built-in GPS chip, Maestro and Concert Now will help you find live music close to your location.에서 Concert Now가 내장 위성 위치 확인 시스템 칩을 이용한다는 것을 알 수 있다. 따라서 (C)가 정답이다.

193. 정보문 두 번째 단락 2행의 point와 의미가 가장 가까운 것은?
(A) 정보
(B) 의견
(C) 위치
(D) 목적

해설 point는 '시점'과 '장소'라는 의미가 모두 있는 단어인데 After the first week and within thirty days of purchase, products defective from flaws in manufacturing may be returned or exchanged at the point of sale.에서 the point of sale은 Pomegranate store를 말한다. 따라서 (C)가 정답이다.

194. 포머그래너트 사의 반품 규정에 관해 언급된 것은?
(A) 작년에 변경되었다.
(B) 항상 영수증이 필요하다.
(C) 온라인 구매는 제외된다.
(D) 모든 손상된 제품은 반품할 수 있다.

해설 정보문 첫째 단락의 If for any reason your Pomegranate product does not live up to your expectations, simply return it to any Pomegranate store with all of its original packaging and a sales receipt, and we will issue a full cash refund.에서 반품 시 구입시 포장 그대로 구입 영수증과 함께 보내라고 했다. 따라서 (B)가 정답이다.

195. 포머그래너트 사는 박 씨를 위해 무엇을 할 것 같은가?
(A) 기계 수리
(B) 지급금 환급
(C) 기기 교체
(D) 제품 회수

해설 편지의 I purchased this music player about five months ago as indicated on the receipt.에서 구매 후 5달이 지났음을 알 수 있는데 반품 규정 마지막 단락의 Thirty days after the original sale, the Pomegranate's limited warranty applies. ~ Pomegranate, Inc., will replace the faulty item with a used product in equal or better condition.에서 판매 30일이 지난 제품은 중고 제품으로 교환해 준다고 했으므로 (C)가 정답이다.

196-200

http://www.pwms.com/about.html

프로 웨어 메가 스토어

회사 소개   카탈로그   매장   연락처

프로 웨어 메가 스토어는 미시건 주에서 가장 오래되고 가장 신뢰받는 상점으로 귀사 직원들이 효율적인 주방을 운영하는 데 필요한 유니폼과 장비를 구하실 수 있습니다. 주 전역의 식당 주인들은 서빙 직원들이 미끄러운 주방을 돌아다닐 때나 서빙 구역에서 맵시 있게 보일 수 있도록 편안하고 안전한 신발을 갖추어 주는 일을 프로 웨어 메가 스토어에 의존하고 있습니다. 조리업 분야에서 일하는 분은 누구나 저희 세탁하기 쉬운 바지와 셔츠 또는 저희 앞치마와 모자의 전문가다운 모습의 진가를 아실 것입니다. 여러분이 무엇을 필요로 하시든 저희에게 그것이 있습니다. 코너 가의 저희 매장을 방문하시거나[196] 온라인 카탈로그를 검색하셔서 저희가 여러분에게 제공할 수 있는 것을 살펴보십시오. 10월에 주문하셔서 저희 표준 배송을 저렴한 균일가 9달러에 이용하시거나 500달러 이하 구입 시의 익일 배송 서비스 요금을 29달러에 이용하십시오.[197]

프로 웨어 메가 스토어
기록 번호: CB206
고객: 어도보
날짜: 10월 11일
배송 주소: 1219 이스트 애덤스 애비뉴, 디트로이트, 미시건 48202

품목 번호	품목명	수량	단위 가격	합산 가격
207	칼라 셔츠	12	5달러	60달러
319	미끄러짐 방지용 신발	6	15달러	90달러
212	후드티	4[199]	19달러	76달러
401	슬랙스	8	10달러	80달러
11	그래픽 디자인 + 로고 인쇄	/	150달러	150달러
	소계			456달러
	배송료			29달러[197]
	총계			485달러

발신: regina@adobo.com
수신: support@pwms.com
제목: 약간의 수정
날짜: 10월 11일

안녕하세요, 저는 어도보의 레지나 매킨토시이며 제가 오늘 아침에 넣은 주문에 관해 메일을 보냅니다.[198] 기록 검색 번호는 CB206입니다. 저는 다양한 방식으로 어도보를 광고하기 시작할 것이며,[200] 제 전략들 중의 하나는 우리 업체 로고를 넣어 주문 제작한 귀사의 의류 품목 일부를 나누어 주는 것입니다. 귀사의 제품들은 무척 편안하고 아주 보기 좋아서 우리는 고객들이 그것들을 무척 좋아할 것이라고 확신합니다. 그래서 저는 212번 품목에 대한 주문 수량을 20개로 늘리고 싶습니다.[199] 그것들을 제가 구입한 나머지 품목들과 함께 발송할 필요는 없지만 그렇게 해 주신다면 감사하겠습니다. 그리고 가능하면 원래 사용한 것과 동일한 신용 카드 계좌로 청구해 주십시오. 그렇지 않으면 제게 청구서를 보내 주시면 가능한 한 빨리 결제하겠습니다.

감사합니다.
레지나 매킨토시

어휘 contact 연락처   trusted 신뢰받는   gear 장비   run 운영하다
efficient 효율적인   rely on ~에 의존하다
outfit (복장·장비를) 갖추어 주다   server 서빙 직원
navigate 돌아다니다   slippery 미끄러운
stylish 유행에 맞는, 맵시 있는
serving 서빙용의, 식사 시중을 들기 위한   floor 작업장, 매장
line 방면, 분야   appreciate ~의 진가를 알다
easy-to-clean 세탁하기 쉬운   professional 전문가다운
apron 앞치마   browse 검색하다
take advantage of ~을 이용하다   flat 균일한   low-rate 저렴한
charge 요금   standard 표준의   overnight 하룻밤 사이의
record 기록   locater 검색 코드   shipping 발송, 배송
description 설명, 묘사   quantity 수량   unit (상품의) 단위, 한 개
total 전체의, 합산한; 총계   collared 칼라가 달린
non-slip 미끄러짐을 방지하는   hoodie 후드티
slacks 슬랙스 (헐렁한 바지)   subtotal 소계

slight 약간의   modification 변경, 수정
in regards to ~에 관해서   advertise 광고하다   various 다양한
method 방식   strategy 전략   give out 나누어 주다
customized 주문 제작한   increase 늘리다
ship 발송하다, 배송하다   rest 나머지   appreciate 감사하다
charge 청구하다   account 계좌   originally 원래, 처음에
otherwise 그렇지 않으면   invoice 송장, 청구서

196. 프로 웨어 메가 스토어에 관해 사실인 것은?
(A) 쇼핑객들을 위한 물리적인 장소가 있다.
(B) 매킨토시 가문이 소유하고 있다.
(C) 지역의 동종 업계에서 두 번째로 큰 매장이다.
(D) 공휴일 때문에 배송이 지연될 것이다.

해설 웹페이지 후반부의 Visit our store on Conner Street에서 코너 가에 있는 매장을 방문하라고 했으므로 (A)가 정답이다.

197. 양식에서 추론할 수 있는 것은?
(A) 물품들이 익일 배송을 통해 배송될 것이다.
(B) 옷에 이미지가 인쇄되지 않을 것이다.
(C) 한 품목은 입수할 수 없다.
(D) 물품들은 소유자 개인용이다.

해설 양식과 웹페이지를 연계해 풀어야 하는 추론 문제이다. 양식 하단의 Shipping 금액이 $29.00로 되어 있는데, 웹페이지 끝 부분의 $29.00 for overnight delivery on purchases under $500.00에서 500달러 이하 구입 시의 익일 배송 서비스 요금을 29달러에 이용하라고 했으므로 (A)가 정답이다.

198. 이메일 첫 번째 단락 1행의 단어 order와 의미가 가장 가까운 것은?
(A) 순서
(B) 단체
(C) 요청
(D) 재고

해설 an order I placed this morning에서 order는 '주문'이라는 의미로 쓰였으므로 '요청, 신청'이라는 의미의 (C)가 정답이다.

199. 매킨토시 씨가 더 많이 구입하기 원하는 품목은?
(A) 칼라 셔츠
(B) 미끄러짐 방지용 신발
(C) 후드티
(D) 슬랙스

해설 이메일과 양식을 연계해 풀어야 하는 추론 문제이다. 이메일 후반부의 I would like to increase the order size for item 212 to twenty units에서 212번 품목에 대한 주문 수량을 20개로 늘리고 싶다고 했다. 양식을 보면 Item Number 212는 Hoodies이므로 (C)가 정답이다.

200. 매킨토시 씨에 의하면 어도보에 관해 사실인 것은?
(A) 마케팅 캠페인을 시작할 것이다.
(B) 새 직원들을 채용할 것이다.
(C) 계절 물품 목록을 바꿀 것이다.
(D) 새 장소로 이전할 것이다.

해설 이메일 세 번째 문장의 I am starting to advertise Adobo through various methods에서 다양한 방식으로 어도보를 광고하기 시작할 것이라고 했다. 따라서 starting to advertise를 beginning a marketing campaign으로 바꾸어 표현한 (A)가 정답이다.

YBM 신토익 베스트 1위

토익 출제기관 ETS® 공식문제 독점 공개!

신토익의 진실 진짜실력 YBM

신토익 입문자를 위한
ETS® 공식입문서

교보문고 5월 월간 종합베스트 토익토플부문 1위

토익 중·고급으로 도약하는
ETS® 공식종합서

교보문고 7월 월간 종합베스트 토익토플부문 1위

출제기관 실전 문항 100%
ETS® 공식실전서

교보문고 토익토플부문(8월 2주), 인터파크 외국어부문(6월 4주)
YES24, 알라딘, 반디앤루니스 외국어부문(7월 3주) 1위

YBM 02.2000.0515 | www.ybmbooks.com | ETS 공식카페 www.etstoeicbook.com

 무료동영상   무료 MP3   학습어플

토익스피킹 출제기관 공식기본서

스피킹 초급부터 중급까지 2주 완성

ETS TOEIC® Speaking 공식기본서

- 정기시험과 100% 동일한 퀄리티와 난이도
- **온라인 실전테스트와 스마트폰 MP3 학습 지원**
- ETS 예제풀이 핵심전략 동영상 무료 제공(총6강)
- 최신경향 & 신유형 반영한 실전 문제 최다 수록

ETS 저 / 본책 + 해설집 + 온라인 실전테스트 + MP3 파일 / 20,000원

온라인 & 모바일 학습 지원!
Actual Test, Final Test 수록

스마트폰 MP3 듣기

02.2000.0515 | www.ybmbooks.com | ETS 토익스피킹 학습 지원 www.etstoeicbook.com

Jump Up
TOEIC

목표점수를 뛰어넘는
토익 완전정복 프로젝트!!

Jump Up TOEIC Basic :
토익 500점 뛰어넘기 프로젝트

주절주절 복잡하고 어려운 설명은 NO!
토익 입문자들에게 꼭 필요한 토익의 핵심 기본 사항만 콕콕 찍어준다.
이 한 권으로 토익 LC와 RC를 부담 없이 정리한다.

Jump Up TOEIC Intermediate :
토익 700점 뛰어넘기 프로젝트

입문 단계를 벗어나 중급 달성을 위한 토익 기본기를 탄탄히 쌓는다!
보다 심화된 핵심 사항을 학습한 후 다양한 훈련과 문제풀이로
토익 점수를 업그레이드 한다.